WINFIELD AND JOLOWICZ ON TORT

TWENTIETH EDITION

JAMES GOUDKAMP

*Professor of the Law of Obligations, University of Oxford
and Fellow of Keble College, Oxford*

DONAL NOLAN

*Professor of Private Law, University of Oxford
and Fellow of Worcester College, Oxford*

SWEET & MAXWELL

THOMSON REUTERS

Published in 2020 by Thomson Reuters, trading as Sweet & Maxwell.
Thomson Reuters is registered in England & Wales, Company No. 1679046.
Registered office and address for service:
5 Canada Square, Canary Wharf, London E14 5AQ.

For further information on our products and services,
visit *http://www.sweetandmaxwell.co.uk.*

Computerset by Thomson Reuters
Printed and bound by CPI Group (UK) Ltd, Croydon, CR0 4YY
A CIP catalogue record of this book is available from the British Library.

ISBN (print): 978-0-414-06621-2

ISBN (e-book): 978-0-414-06623-6

ISBN (proview): 978-0-414-06624-3

ISBN (print and proview): 978-0-414-06625-0

TITLE HISTORY

First Edition	(1937)	The Author
Second Edition	(1943)	The Author
Third Edition	(1946)	The Author
Fourth Edition	(1948)	The Author
Fifth Edition	(1950)	The Author
Sixth Edition	(1954)	T. Ellis Lewis
Seventh Edition	(1963)	J.A. Jolowicz and T. Ellis Lewis
Eighth Edition	(1967)	J.A. Jolowicz with T. Ellis Lewis
Ninth Edition	(1971)	J.A. Jolowicz with T. Ellis Lewis and D.M. Harris
Tenth Edition	(1975)	W.V.H. Rogers
Eleventh Edition	(1979)	W.V.H. Rogers
Twelfth Edition	(1984)	W.V.H. Rogers
Thirteenth Edition	(1989)	W.V.H. Rogers
Fourteenth Edition	(1994)	W.V.H. Rogers
Fifteenth Edition	(1998)	W.V.H. Rogers
Sixteenth Edition	(2002)	W.V.H. Rogers
Seventeenth Edition	(2006)	W.V.H. Rogers
Eighteenth Edition	(2010)	W.V.H. Rogers
Nineteenth Edition	(2014)	Edwin Peel and James Goudkamp

ACKNOWLEDGMENTS

Grateful acknowledgment is made to the following authors and publishers for permission to quote from their works:

American Law Institute:

> *Restatement (Second) of the Law of Torts* (American Law Institute, 1977).

The Incorporated Council of Law Reporting for England and Wales:

> *Alcock v Chief Constable of South Yorkshire* [1992] 1 A.C. 310.
> *Baker v Willoughby* [1970] A.C. 467.
> *Barrett v Enfield LBC* [2001] 2 A.C. 550.
> *Barrett v Ministry of Defence* [1995] 1 W.L.R. 1217.
> *Boyle v Kodak Ltd* [1969] 1 W.L.R. 661.
> *Bradford Corp v Pickles* [1895] A.C. 587.
> *Caparo Industries Plc v Dickman* [1990] 2 A.C. 605.
> *Collins v Wilcock* [1984] 1 W.L.R. 1172.
> *Crofter Hand-Woven Harris Tweed Co Ltd v Veitch* [1942] A.C. 435.
> *Donoghue v Stevenson* [1932] A.C. 562.
> *Emerald Construction Co Ltd v Lowthian* [1966] 1 W.L.R. 691.
> *Goldman v Hargrave* [1967] 1 A.C. 645.
> *Hotson v East Berkshire HA* [1987] A.C. 750.
> *Hunter v Canary Wharf Ltd* [1997] A.C. 655.
> *Jobling v Associated Dairies* [1982] A.C. 794.
> *Joyce v Sengupta* [1993] 1 W.L.R. 337.
> *London Passenger Transport Board v Upson* [1949] A.C. 155.
> *Martin v Watson* [1996] A.C. 74.
> *Morrison SS Co Ltd v Greystoke Castle* [1947] A.C. 265.
> *O'Rourke v Camden LBC* [1998] A.C. 188.
> *Parker v British Airways Board* [1982] Q.B. 1004.
> *R. v Ireland* [1998] A.C. 147.
> *Robinson v Balmain Ferry Co Ltd* [1910] A.C. 295.
> *Roe v Minister of Health* [1954] 2 Q.B. 66.
> *Roles v Nathan (t/a Manchester Assembly Rooms)* [1963] 1 W.L.R. 1117.
> *Rouse v Squires* [1973] Q.B. 889.
> *Slater v Clay Cross Co Ltd* [1956] 2 Q.B. 264.
> *Smith v Baker* [1891] A.C. 325.
> *Smith v Littlewoods Organisation Ltd* [1987] A.C. 241.
> *Speed v Thomas Swift & Co* [1943] K.B. 557.
> *Stovin v Wise* [1996] A.C. 923.
> *The Wagon Mound* [1961] A.C. 388.
> *Weld-Blundell v Stephens* [1920] A.C. 956.
> *White v Jones* [1995] 2 A.C. 207.
> *Wilkinson v Downton* [1897] 2 Q.B. 57.
> *Wilsons and Clyde Coal v English* [1938] A.C. 57.

Withers v Perry Chain Co [1961] 1 W.L.R. 1314.

Reed Elsevier (UK) Limited, trading as LexisNexis:

Daborn Bath Tramways [1946] 2 All E.R. 333.
Ginty v Belmont Building Supplies Ltd [1959] 1 All E.R. 414.
M v Newham LBC [1994] 4 All E.R. 602.
McKew v Holland & Hannen & Cubitts (Scotland) Ltd [1969] 3 All E.R. 1621.
Meering v Grahame-White Aviation Co Ltd [1918-19] All ER Rep Ext 1490.
Morriss v Marsden [1952] 1 All E.R. 925.

We have also quoted from the following sources:

Published by the Scottish Council of Law Reporting:

Stevenson v Glasgow Corp 1908 SC 1034.

While every care has been taken to establish and acknowledge copyright, and contact the copyright owners, the publishers tend their apologies for any accidental infringement. They would be pleased to come to a suitable arrangement with the rightful owners in each case.

PREFACE

Over 80 years have passed since the first edition of this textbook was published in 1937, and it now runs to 20 editions. Although certain aspects of the law of torts have remained largely static throughout this period, some of its features have been transformed almost beyond recognition, and much has also changed since the 19th edition was published in 2014.

Some of the more significant recent developments of which account is taken in this edition include the Supreme Court's decisions in: (1) *Robinson v Chief Constable of West Yorkshire Police* [2018] UKSC 4; [2018] A.C. 73, which makes it clear that the experiment with the so-called *Caparo* "test" for the existence of a duty of care has failed; (2) *Michael v Chief Constable of South Wales* [2015] UKSC 2; [2015] 1 A.C. 1732 and *Poole BC v GN* [2019] UKSC 25; [2019] 2 W.L.R. 1478, which confirm that the general no-liability rule for omissions applies with equal force to public authority defendants; (3) *Patel v Mirza* [2016] UKSC 42; [2017] A.C. 467, which raises formidable issues regarding the illegality doctrine as it applies in the law of torts; (4) *Willers v Joyce* [2016] UKSC 43; [2018] A.C. 779, which extends the tort of malicious prosecution to civil proceedings (a development advocated by Winfield in the early editions of this work); and (5) no fewer than five major decisions on vicarious liability and non-delegable duties, including most recently *WM Morrison Supermarkets Plc v Various Claimants* [2020] UKSC 12; [2020] 2 W.L.R. 941 and *Barclays Bank Plc v Various Claimants* [2020] UKSC 13; [2020] 2 W.L.R. 960, which judgments call at least a temporary halt to the offensive on which the Supreme Court had previously embarked to expand the boundaries of vicarious liability.

Other noteworthy decisions of the Supreme Court and Privy Council of which account is taken include *O v Rhodes* [2015] UKSC 32; [2016] A.C. 219 (intentional infliction of physical or emotional harm); *Dryden v Johnson Matthey Plc* [2018] UKSC 18; [2019] A.C. 403 (damage); *Williams v Bermuda Hospitals Board* [2016] UKPC 4; [2016] A.C. 888 (factual causation); *Campbell v Peter Gordon Joiners Ltd* [2016] UKSC 38; [2016] A.C. 1513 (breach of statutory duty); *Lachaux v Independent Print Ltd* [2019] UKSC 27; [2020] A.C. 612 (defamation); *JSC BTA Bank v Ablyazov (No.14)* [2018] UKSC 19; [2018] 2 W.L.R. 1125 (conspiracy); and *Fish & Fish Ltd v Sea Shepherd UK* [2015] UKSC 10; [2015] A.C. 1229 (joint tortfeasance).

Of the countless judgments of other courts delivered since 2014 in the law of torts, we would draw particular attention to *Dunnage v Randall* [2015] EWCA Civ 673; [2016] Q.B. 639 (objective standard of care); *Wilkes v DePuy International* [2016] EWHC 3096 (QB); [2018] Q.B. 627 (product liability); and *Williams v Network Rail Infrastructure Ltd* [2018] EWCA Civ 1514; [2019] Q.B. 601 (private nuisance). As for legislation, it has been a relatively quiet period, although the Social Action, Responsibility and Heroism Act 2015 is discussed in relation to breach of duty, while the treatment of exclusion of liability has been updated to take account of the Consumer Rights Act 2015.

These and many other legal developments since the last edition, as well as additions to the academic literature, have necessitated rewriting on a significant scale. Other rewriting has been driven not so much by developments in the law as by our desire to bring the text more into line with our (doubtless at times idiosyncratic) understanding of the field. For example, readers will notice that a new section on damage has been added to Chapter 7, which concept we consider to be fundamentally distinct from other concepts with which it is often conflated, such as the duty of care, causation and remoteness. Likewise, because the earlier focus of the economic torts on disputes involving trade unions has been largely replaced by the role that these torts discharge today in relation to civil fraud, Chapter 19 has been reoriented as a result. Readers will also notice that Chapters 5, 7, 11, 15–16 and 19 have been extensively rewritten, and the treatment of misfeasance in public office in Chapter 8 expanded. Rewriting of this kind is necessarily incomplete in a work of this scale. Further changes will need to await future editions.

James Goudkamp is sorry to have lost Edwin Peel as a co-author, but is delighted to be joined by Donal Nolan, with whom he has collaborated on several other projects. The burden of the work was roughly evenly divided between us, with James taking primary responsibility for Chapters 1–6, 13, 19, 23–24 and 26, and Donal assuming charge of Chapters 7–12, 14–18, 20–22 and 25. Both of us were, however, heavily involved in the preparation of all of the chapters regardless of who took the initial lead in relation to them.

Eleni Katsampouka provided invaluable research assistance in connection with the preparation of this edition, as well as offering many helpful comments on certain sections of the text, and we are indebted to her for her contributions. We are also grateful to the publishers for their support and patience, and in particular to Nicola Thurlow and Sarita Lewis.

We have sought to state the law as of 24 May 2020, although in some instances it was possible to make minor revisions to accommodate developments after that date.

James Goudkamp

Donal Nolan

12 July 2020

TABLE OF CONTENTS

TABLE OF CASES

TABLE OF STATUTES

TABLE OF STATUTORY INSTRUMENTS

TABLE OF CONVENTIONS AND EUROPEAN LEGISLATION

CHAPTER 1

INTRODUCTION

1. THE AIMS, DEFINITION AND DOMAIN OF THE LAW OF TORT

A. Aims of the Law of Tort

Numerous attempts have been made to define a "tort" with varying degrees of **1-001** lack of success. We will begin, therefore, with a general description rather than with a definition and must be content for the moment to sacrifice accuracy and completeness for the sake of simplicity. Having given a very broad description of the functions of the law of tort we can then turn to the problem of formal definition, and finally look at the relationship of the tort system with certain other legal and social institutions pursuing similar ends.

1-002   It is not possible plausibly to assign any one aim to the law of tort, which is not surprising when one considers that the subject comprehends situations as disparate as: A carelessly running B down in the street; C calling D a thief; E giving bad investment advice to F; G failing to diagnose H's dyslexia at school; and I selling J's car when he has no authority to do so. However, it is obvious that in any society of people living together numerous conflicts of interest will arise and the actions of one person or group of persons will periodically cause or threaten damage to others. This damage may take many forms—injury to the person, damage to physical property, damage to financial interests, injury to reputation and so on—and whenever a person suffers damage at the hands of another person, especially if it is serious, he may be inclined to look to the law for redress.

The redress granted by the law may take various forms. In the great majority of tort actions, it will involve monetary compensation (damages) for the injury the claimant has suffered, and this fact strongly emphasises the function of tort in allocating or redistributing loss. In many cases, however, the claimant is seeking an injunction to prevent the occurrence or recurrence of harm in the future and in this area the direct "preventive" function of tort predominates.[1] An injunction is usually sought, for example, in cases of private nuisance (wrongful interference with the use and enjoyment of land). This is not because damages are unavailable (they clearly are) but because the defendant may otherwise be prone to continue to commit the tortious conduct. Less commonly, tort law may require the defendant to disgorge profits he has made from his wrongdoing, whether or not the claimant has suffered any loss. And in a few situations, where punitive damages are awarded, the idea of compensation is dropped in favour of overt punishment; but much more frequently there are substantial awards of (nominally compensatory) damages for matters like injury to reputation and interference with liberty, which one cannot even begin to quantify in mathematical terms. A couple of nights of wrongful detention in the police station may attract more damages than a broken arm, and a libel in a national newspaper more than the loss of that arm. In these cases, the law is performing a complex function incorporating vindication, deterrence and appeasement.

Some tort actions (for example, some claims for trespass to land) may be brought mainly as a method of obtaining a declaration of rights, notwithstanding the availability under modern procedure of a specific remedy of that nature. Associated with this is what Linden has called the "Ombudsman" function of tort,[2] under which those responsible for losses (typically corporations whose activities cause major disasters) may be called upon to answer in public for their conduct. Although it is clear that it is not a function of tort law to provide an alternative route to a public inquiry, there are certainly cases which come close to that. In *Ashley v Chief Constable of Sussex*[3] A had been shot dead by a police officer in a drugs raid. The officer was acquitted on a charge of murder and the Chief Constable conceded liability for negligence in a civil claim by A's family and estate. The majority of the House of Lords rejected an application to strike out as an abuse of process the

---

[1]   An award of damages against A may also have an indirect "preventive" function in deterring B from behaving in the same way, but how far this works is controversial: see paras 1-034—1-036.

[2]   Linden (1973) 51 Can. B. Rev. 155.

[3]   [2008] UKHL 25; [2008] 1 A.C. 962.

alternative cause of action based upon trespass to the person even though it was accepted that in the circumstances no greater damages could be obtained under this action than under that on which the Chief Constable was prepared to concede liability. It was a fair inference that the family's purpose was to obtain a finding that A had not merely been the victim of organisational negligence in the planning of the raid but that he had been unlawfully killed, but they had pleaded a valid cause of action and the fact that they would recover no more damages for it did not mean that they had no legitimate interest in pressing it. As Lord Rodger observed[4]:

> "the very fact that the chief constable remains understandably concerned to defend the claim of [trespass] tends to confirm that the claimants may remain, equally understandably, concerned to pursue that claim".

There have also been cases in which a civil claim has been brought in order to provoke the prosecuting authorities into acting.[5] It is perhaps unkind to call tort the dustbin of the law of obligations, but it is certainly the great residuary category. No one theory explains the whole of the law.

B. Definition of Tortious Liability

Winfield's definition of tort was as follows[6]:   1-003

> "Tortious liability arises from the breach of a duty primarily fixed by law; this duty is towards persons generally and its breach is redressable by an action for unliquidated damages."

In framing this definition Winfield was not seeking to indicate what conduct is and what is not sufficient to involve a person in tortious liability, but merely to distinguish tort from certain other branches of law.[7] As we shall see, it cannot be accepted as entirely accurate but it has the merit of brevity and contains elements which deserve continuing emphasis. The third element of Winfield's definition (which is convenient to mention first) is that the breach of duty is redressable by an action for unliquidated damages. A claim is said to be "liquidated" when it is for a fixed, inelastic sum[8] or one which is calculable by the mere process of arithmetic.[9] It is not, of course, a sufficient test of tort liability that the remedy is unliquidated damages—for these are also the primary remedy for breach of contract—but it seems to be a necessary one. If the claimant cannot recover unliquidated damages then whatever claim he may have, it is not for tort.

Winfield would now be forced to retreat from the claim (the second element of

---

4   [2008] UKHL 25; [2008] 1 A.C. 962 at [69].
5   See *Halford v Brookes* [1991] 1 W.L.R. 428 (successful civil action arising from murder; defendant subsequently prosecuted and convicted: The Times, 1 August 1996).
6   See, further, Mitchell, *A History of Tort Law* (2015), Ch.2.
7   Many lawyers have endeavoured, like Winfield, to define a "tort" by distinguishing it from related concepts. This approach to definition led Wigmore to remark: "Never did a Name so obstruct a true understanding of the Thing. To such a plight has it brought us that a favorite mode of defining a Tort is to declare merely that it is not a Contract. As if a man were to define Chemistry by pointing out that it is not Physics nor Mathematics!": Wigmore, *Select Cases on the Law of Torts* (1912), p.vii. But see *R. v Secretary of State, Ex p. Factortame Ltd (No.7)* [2001] 1 W.L.R. 942 at 965.
8   But the fact that the claimant claims a specific sum in his pleadings (e.g., £5,000 as the value of a wrecked car) does not make it liquidated.
9   e.g., the price of goods sold and delivered at so much a unit or wages at so much a week.

his definition) that if a duty is towards a specific person or specific persons it cannot arise from tort,[10] but there is probably still some substance in his contention that the element of generality was an important factor in the definition. It is arguable that everything depends upon the level of abstraction at which the duty is expressed. It is true that D is under a tortious duty not to convert another person's goods to his own use, while D's contractual duty to deliver goods which D has sold is owed only to the person to whom D has sold them but this is to compare two statements at different levels. Just as D has a general duty not to commit the tort of conversion, D also has a general duty not to commit breaches of contract. If, on the other hand, we descend to the particular, then just as D's duty to deliver certain goods is owed only to their buyer, so also is D's duty not to convert certain goods to D's own use owed only to the person in possession, or having the immediate right to possession, of them.

Finally, with regard to the first element of Winfield's definition, there is considerable force in the claim that tortious duties are fixed primarily by law. It is the law rather than, for example, D's consent or agreement that generally determines when D will come under a duty in tort, and what the content of that duty is. There are, however, important exceptions to this proposition. For instance, we will see the fact that D has assumed responsibility for some interest of C can determine both whether he will owe an obligation in the law of tort to C and some of the content of that obligation (although even then it is the law that determines when D will have assumed responsibility).

C. Tort and Contract

1-004 **Overlap between tort and contract** There may be a considerable overlap in any factual situation between the law of contract and the law of tort. For example, a claim for damages arising from a defective product may involve a complex web of issues under the Sale of Goods Act 1979, the law of misrepresentation and collateral warranty, the tort of negligence, the Consumer Protection Act 1987 and a chain of contractual indemnities among retailer, middleman and manufacturer.[11] It is unlikely that any legal system can ever cut loose from general conceptual classifications such as "contract" and "tort" (at any rate they seem to be found everywhere) but the student will quickly come to recognise that the boundary must sometimes be crossed in the solution of a problem. It has long been trite law that a defendant may be liable on the same facts in contract to A and in tort to B (notwithstanding privity of contract);[12] it is now, after a period of uncertainty, also clearly established that there may be concurrent contractual and tortious liability to the same claimant, though he may not, of course, recover damages twice over. However, before we examine these propositions further, we must make some attempt at formally distinguishing the two heads of liability.

1-005 **Source of the duty** Winfield considered that tortious duties exist by virtue of the law itself and are not dependent upon the agreement or consent of the persons subjected to them. D is under a duty not to assault C, not to slander C and not to

---

10 Stevens, *Torts and Rights* (2007).

11 See, e.g., *Lexmead (Basingstoke) v Lewis* [1982] A.C. 225.

12 Modified by the Contracts (Rights of Third Parties) Act 1999, but it is still the basic rule that only a party to a contract may sue or be sued on it.

trespass on C's land because the law says that D is under such a duty and not because D has agreed with C to undertake such a duty. Winfield therefore considered that tortious liability could for this reason be distinguished from contractual liability and from liability on bailment, neither of which can exist independently of the parties' agreement or consent, or at least that of the defendant. However, and as observed in the discussion of Winfield's definition of a tort, there are several instances of liability in tort the existence of which depends on some prior consent or assumption of responsibility on the part of the defendant. Thus, and to deepen what was said earlier in this connection, the liability of the occupier of premises to his visitor, for example, which is now governed by the Occupiers' Liability Act 1957, is based upon breach of a duty of care owed by the occupier to persons whom he has permitted to enter upon his premises. The duty owed to trespassers, i.e., persons who enter without his consent, is not the same.[13] Again, the duty of care owed by a person who gives gratuitous advice upon a serious occasion is, doubtless, a tortious one,[14] but its existence is dependent upon the adviser's agreement to give the advice, if not necessarily upon his agreement to accept legal responsibility for it. Still more difficult is the fact that in some situations an undertaking (whether or not by contract) by A to B to perform a service, the object of which is to confer a benefit upon C, may give rise to liability in tort to C.[15] Not only do duties in tort sometimes depend upon the will of the defendant, but it is an oversimplification to say simply that contractual duties are always dependent on that will. For example, whether or not there is a contract normally depends upon the outward manifestations of agreement by the parties, not on their subjective states of mind.[16]

Content of the duty   Another mode of differentiation between tortious and   **1-006** contractual liability lies in the proposition that in tort the content of the duties is fixed by the law whereas the content of contractual duties is fixed by the contract itself. If D consents to C's entry upon his premises then the duty that D owes to C is the duty fixed by the Occupiers' Liability Act 1957, i.e., by the law itself, but whether, for example, D's duty is to deliver to C 10 or 20 tons of coal can only be discovered from the contract between C and D. Even this distinction, however, is by no means always valid, for today in many cases the content of contractual duties is also fixed by the law. Statute provides, for example, that certain quite specific obligations shall be contained in contracts for the sale or hire-purchase of goods and cannot be excluded;[17] and it is now no longer true, as perhaps it once was, that implied terms in a contract, in the absence of a statutory rule, are always based upon the presumed intention of the parties.[18] Conversely, there are tortious duties which are subject to variation by agreement, whether or not that agreement amounts in law to a contract between the parties.[19]

---

[13]   See para.10-034.
[14]   But a close relationship between adviser and advisee is required and for this purpose the relationship has been described as "equivalent to contract": *Hedley Byrne & Co Ltd v Heller & Partners Ltd* [1964] A.C. 465 at 530.
[15]   See para.5-040.
[16]   See, e.g., *Smith v Hughes* (1871) L.R. 6 Q.B. 597 at 607.
[17]   Sale of Goods Act 1979; Unfair Contract Terms Act 1977; Consumer Rights Act 2015.
[18]   *Marks & Spencer Plc v BNP Paribas Securities Services Trust Co (Jersey) Ltd* [2015] UKSC 72; [2016] A.C. 742 at [21].
[19]   See, e.g., Occupiers' Liability Act 1957 s.2(1); *Ashdown v Samuel Williams & Sons Ltd* [1957] 1 Q.B.

1-007 **Aims of contract and tort** Another basis for distinguishing between contract and tort may be sought in the aims of the two heads of liability. Arguably, the "core" of contract is the idea of enforcing promises, whereas tort aims principally to prevent or compensate harms, and this difference of function has two principal consequences. First, that a mere failure to act will not usually be actionable in tort, for that would render otiose the rule that even a positive promise will not give rise to legal liability unless it is intended as legally binding and supported by consideration or the formality of a deed. The second consequence is that damages cannot be claimed in tort for a "loss of expectation". Although damages for breach of contract and for tort have the same aim (i.e., to put the claimant in the position he would have been in had the wrong not been committed), in contract that involves a more forward-looking enquiry, since had the contract not been breached, it would have been performed, and contractual performance involves the defendant conferring a benefit on the claimant. However, these twin points are not universal truths. Thus, liability sometimes arises in tort for failing to confer a benefit on others in the sense of failing to protect their safety. Some of these are of very long standing, for example, the duty of an occupier to take steps to ensure that his visitors are not harmed by dangers on his land, even if those are not of his making. As to the second point regarding damages, the law of contract puts the claimant in the position he would have been entitled to occupy (subject to exceptions) as a result of the transaction agreed between the parties. While it is clear that (assuming the claim in tort to arise from some transaction between the parties) tort does not do the same, the distinction is less fundamental than might appear. If a surgeon operates negligently on a curable condition and leaves the condition incurable, the patient recovers damages on the basis that with careful surgery he would have been cured; if a solicitor negligently fails to carry out X's instructions to make a will in favour of an intended beneficiary, the latter can recover as damages the value of the lost legacy;[20] and if a trader enters into transactions due to the defendant's fraudulent misrepresentations,[21] although the trader cannot recover as damages the profits he would have made if the representation had been true, he may be able to recover the profits he would have earned by laying out his money elsewhere.[22]

D. Concurrent Liability in Tort and Contract

1-008 **Three-party situations** We now return to the point that contractual and tortious duties may co-exist on the same facts. The proposition that D may incur liability in tort to C from a matter or transaction in respect of which D had a contract with B was clearly established in *Donoghue v Stevenson*,[23] which is the basis of the manufacturer's common law liability in tort to the ultimate consumer.[24] It is noteworthy that the action in negligence rests upon the existence of a duty of care owed by the defendant to the claimant and the contractual context in which the events take place will often be relevant to that issue. For example, it has been held

---

409. This case would be decided differently since the Unfair Contract Terms Act 1977 but is still illustrative of the general principle of law.

[20] *White v Jones* [1995] 2 A.C. 207, see para.5-047.

[21] Fraud (deceit) is a tort and subject to the tort measure of damages: see para.12-021.

[22] *East v Maurer* [1991] 1 W.L.R. 461; *Parabola Investments Ltd v Browallia Cal Ltd* [2010] EWCA Civ 486; [2011] Q.B. 477 at [43].

[23] [1932] A.C. 562.

[24] See Ch.11.

that a building sub-contractor was not liable in negligence for damage to the works when the main contract provided that they were to be at the risk of and insurable by the building owner,[25] and an agent answering inquiries on behalf of his principal is not personally liable in negligence in respect of their accuracy unless he has assumed some direct responsibility.[26] Similarly, too great a readiness to hold that a director owes a personal duty of care to persons with whom his company has dealings risks setting at naught the protection of limited liability.[27]

Two-party situations   Where it is alleged that the defendant owes concurrent duties in contract and tort to the *same* person, some legal systems have a doctrine (known in French law as *non cumul des obligations*) that this is not possible.[28] Although there were signs of this in England in earlier days,[29] the "concurrence" approach was decisively affirmed by the House of Lords in *Henderson v Merrett Syndicates Ltd*.[30] In that case, it was held that Names at Lloyd's might sue members' agents (with whom they had a contract) in the tort of negligence as well as for breach of contract in the management of underwriting business so as to gain the advantage of the longer time limit that applied to the former cause of action pursuant to the Latent Damage Act 1986.[31] As Lord Goff put it[32]:

> "the result may be untidy; but, given that the tortious duty is imposed by the general law, and the contractual duty is attributable to the will of the parties, I do not find it objectionable that the claimant may be entitled to take advantage of the remedy which is most advantageous to him."

Thus, for example, concurrent liability arises between carrier and passenger, doctor and (private) patient, solicitor and client, and employer and employee. There are, however, limits to the extent to which concurrent liability allows claimants to avail themselves of more favourable rules in tort. For example, where the tortious conduct involves breach of a concurrent contractual obligation, the more demanding contractual remoteness rule may apply to the tort claim in place of the more relaxed tort remoteness test.[33]

Effect of allocation of responsibility by contract   Concurrent liability will not usually affect the substantive duty that the defendant owes: the duty will be the same in tort and contract. For example, a doctor's duty in tort is to exercise proper professional care and skill and the implied terms in his contract are the same[34]: he does

1-009

1-010

---

25 *Norwich CC v Harvey* [1989] 1 W.L.R. 828.
26 *Gran Gelato Ltd v Richcliff (Group) Ltd* [1992] Ch. 560 (the principal will be responsible to the claimant for the acts of the agent and may recover an indemnity under his contract with the agent. The point is significant for the claimant where the principal is insolvent). See para.12-035.
27 See para.25-034.
28 See generally *Weir in International Encyclopaedia of Comparative Law* (1983), Vol.XI, Ch.12.
29 See, e.g., *Groom v Crocker* [1939] 1 K.B. 194; *Bagot v Stevens Scanlan & Co Ltd* [1966] 1 Q.B. 197.
30 [1995] 2 A.C. 145.
31 See para.26-098.
32 [1995] 2 A.C. 145 at 194.
33 See para.7-076.
34 The implied term in a contract for the supply of a service where the supplier acts in the course of a business (which includes a profession) is found in the Supply of Goods and Services Act 1982 s.13, restating the common law.

not impliedly warrant that he will effect a cure,[35] though theoretically he may do so by an express promise to that effect.[36] However, there have been several cases in which attempts have been made to use the duty in tort to override the allocation of responsibility between the parties by contract. If the contract were to provide expressly that the defendant was not liable for "risk X" then (subject to the effect of the Unfair Contract Terms Act 1977 and Consumer Rights Act 2015 upon that term) it would be absurd to allow a tort duty to intrude and contradict that allocation.[37] The same must be true where there is an implied term in the contract that the defendant is not to be liable for "X" (or, as it would be more likely to be expressed, there is no implied term that he should be liable for that risk).[38]

E. Tort and Unjust Enrichment

1-011   The law of unjust enrichment is concerned with situations where one person has been unjustly enriched at the expense of another. The paradigm example of liability arising in this branch of the law is that to repay money which has been paid under a mistake of fact. Suppose that C mistakenly deposits £100 in D's bank account thinking that he was depositing the money in X's account. D is under a duty to return the money to C. The liability is distinct from liability in tort because the liability does not depend on any breach of duty. D does not owe C any duty not to accept money from C.[39] The law of unjust enrichment also stands apart from tort in relation to how it responds to liability. The remedy in unjust enrichment is always measured by reference to the gain that the defendant unjustly made. Although damages measured in this way are also available in tort,[40] they are just one of many different types of relief that may be ordered.

F. Tort and Equitable Wrongs

1-012   Wrongs that are redressable in equity include breach of trust and breach of fiduciary duty. A breach of trust occurs, for example, where a trustee misapplies trust property. A breach of fiduciary duty is committed, for instance, where a solicitor who is acting for a client in respect of a commercial opportunity seizes that opportunity for himself. Liability for equitable wrongs can arise concurrently with liability in tort, as where, for example, a fiduciary commits a fraud on his principal, which may give rise to liability for both breach of fiduciary duty and the tort of deceit.

Equitable wrongs are distinct, at least historically, from torts. In earlier times, equitable wrongs were actionable only in the chancery courts whereas proceedings in tort were commenced in the common law courts. However, the fact that equitable wrongs depend upon a breach of duty owed to the claimant has led some

---

[35]   "The surgeon does not guarantee the aspired outcome": *Wilkes v Depuy International Ltd* [2016] EWHC 3096 (QB); [2018] Q.B. 627 at [70] per Hickinbottom J.
[36]   *Thake v Maurice* [1986] Q.B. 644 shows that a court will require very clear evidence to establish such a warranty against a doctor.
[37]   *Robinson v P E Jones (Contractors) Ltd* [2011] EWCA Civ 9; [2012] Q.B. 44 at [84].
[38]   *National Bank of Greece S.A. v Pinios Shipping Co No.1* [1989] 3 W.L.R. 185 (on appeal, but not on this point: [1990] 1 A.C. 637); *Bank of Nova Scotia v Hellenic Mutual War Risks Association (Bermuda) Ltd* [1990] 1 Q.B. 818 (reversed on the construction of the contract: [1992] 1 A.C. 233)
[39]   See Birks in Owen (ed), *Philosophical Foundations of Tort Law* (1995).
[40]   See para.23-033.

authors to argue that they should be regarded as torts.[41] This view may now be dominant among theorists, although it certainly does not command universal support. It has been argued, for example, that torts and equitable wrongs are distinct on the ground that the former are concerned with the correction of losses whereas the latter are aimed at the diversion of wrongful gains.[42]

Perhaps the time is approaching to assimilate equitable wrongdoing with the law of tort but the force of history is powerful in English law and for the moment it is probably safer to say that the streams run in different channels even though the patterns they produce may have similarities. Even now, although law and equity have long been fused and questions relating to equitable wrongs may incidentally arise in tort cases, actions for equitable wrongs are allocated to the Chancery Division of the High Court whereas actions in respect of torts are issued in the Queen's Bench Division. The distinctiveness of equity (at least at a theoretical level) has been affirmed in situations which might have been absorbed into the tort of negligence. Thus, a mortgagee of property exercising a power of sale may have to take care to obtain a proper price and a receiver who carries on a debtor's business for the creditor may have to run it properly, but these duties are owed in equity and not in negligence on the basis of "neighbourhood".[43]

G. Tort and Bailment

A bailment involves one person taking custody of another person's goods. The person who delivers the goods is called a "bailor". The person to whom they are delivered is the "bailee". Common examples of bailment are hire of goods (such as hiring a car from a garage); gratuitous loan of goods (such as lending this book to a friend); and pawn or pledge. In very many cases, the delivery is on a condition, express or implied, that the goods shall be restored to the bailor as soon as the purpose for which they are bailed is completed, but it seems that this is not a necessary condition. For example, a standard hire-purchase agreement involves a bailment followed by an option to purchase and if the hire charges and option fee are paid the purpose of the exercise is that the bailee should become the owner. If the bailee misuses or damages the goods he is, of course, liable to the bailor in a civil action. Is this liability to be distinguished from liability in tort? Many bailments arise out of a contract, but it is undoubtedly possible for bailment to exist without a contract and, where this is the case, as in the gratuitous loan of something for the use of the borrower, what is the nature of the liability? Winfield's opinion was that the bailee's liability is not tortious because, he said, the duty arises from a relation, that of bailor and bailee, which is created by the parties. No one need be a

1-013

---

41 Birks in Owen (ed), *Philosophical Foundations of Tort Law* (1995); Edelman (2002) 10 T.L.J. 64.
42 Gardner (2012) 39 F. St. U.L. Rev. 43.
43 *Downsview Nominees Ltd v First City Corp Ltd* [1993] A.C. 295; *Medforth v Blake* [2000] Ch. 86. But see the remark of Scott VC at [2000] Ch. 86 at 102: "I do not accept that there is any difference between the answer that would be given by the common law to the question what duties are owed by a receiver managing a mortgaged property to those interested in the equity of redemption and the answer that would be given by equity to that question. I do not, for my part, think it matters one jot whether the duty is expressed as a common law duty or as a duty in equity. The result is the same. The origin of the receiver's duty, like the mortgagee's duty, lies, however, in equity and we might as well continue to refer to it as a duty in equity." A liquidator or administrator owes no duty to individual creditors: *Hague v Nam Tai Electronics* [2008] UKPC 13; [2008] B.C.C. 295; *Kyrris v Oldham* [2003] EWCA Civ 1506; [2004] 1 B.C.L.C. 305.

bailee if he does not wish to be one and no one can have liability for the safe custody of goods thrust upon him against his will.[44] It is certainly true that a person cannot be subjected to the duties of a bailee without his consent but, as we have already seen, there are duties which are undoubtedly tortious and which can only exist if there has been some prior agreement between the parties, so there is arguably no good reason for distinguishing the common law duties of a bailee from duties of this kind. Assumption of responsibility has been an important idea in the expansion of the modern law of negligence[45] but a little before this occurred it was said on high authority that the obligation of the bailee "arises because the taking of possession in the circumstances involves an assumption of responsibility for the safe keeping of the goods".[46] Furthermore, while it is a requirement of a bailment that the bailee voluntarily takes custody of the goods, it seems that it is not necessary that the bailor should consent to their custody.[47] If the bailor's claim is necessarily founded upon some specific provision in a contract, then, no doubt, the bailee's liability is not tortious but contractual; but if the bailor's claim rests upon a breach by the bailee of one of the bailee's common law duties, then might one not contend that his liability is as much attributable to the law of tort as is the claim of a visitor against the occupier of premises under the Occupiers' Liability Act 1957?[48] However, the Court of Appeal has held that a gratuitous bailment may create a legal obligation independent of that in tort, though on the facts there was also a parallel liability under that head.[49] Sometimes the legislature lays down rules by reference to the contract/tort distinction and no other. For example, the legislation on limitation of actions contains elaborate provisions on contract and tort but says nothing about bailment. The courts have nevertheless managed to accommodate bailment cases within this structure.[50] All this is typical of the common law's willingness to be pragmatic about "classification" and to admit parallel causes of action.

H. Tort and Crime

1-014   Crime and tort overlap.[51] Many torts are also crimes, sometimes with the same names and with similar elements (for example, assault and battery) and sometimes a civil action in tort is deduced from the existence of a statute creating a criminal

---

[44] See para.18-016. Winfield's view is set out in full in *The Province of the Law of Tort*, 2nd edn (1968), Ch.5, where he claims that bailment is more fittingly regarded as a distinct branch of the law of property under the title "Possession" than as appropriate to either the law of contract or the law of tort.

[45] See para.5-040.

[46] *Gilchrist Watt & Sanderson Pty Ltd v York Products Pty Ltd* [1970] 1 W.L.R. 1262 at 1268.

[47] *KH Enterprise v Pioneer Container* [1994] 2 A.C. 324.

[48] *Turner v Stallibrass* [1898] 1 Q.B. 56 at 59; *Morris v C.W. Martin & Sons Ltd* [1966] 1 Q.B. 716; *Chesworth v Farrar* [1967] 1 Q.B. 407; *Gilchrist, Watt and Sanderson Pty Ltd v York Products Pty Ltd* [1970] 1 W.L.R. 1262.

[49] *Yearworth v North Bristol NHS Trust* [2009] EWCA Civ 37; [2010] Q.B. 1. Where the bailment involves specific undertakings by the bailee the measure of damages may be more akin to that in contract than tort: at [50].

[50] See, e.g., *Chesworth v Farrar* [1967] 1 Q.B. 407. See also *American Express Co v British Airways Board* [1983] 1 W.L.R. 701 (protection from action in tort under Post Office Act 1969 extended to bailment or the legislation would be ineffective).

[51] Dyson (ed), *Unravelling Tort and Crime* (2014); Dyson (ed), *Comparing Tort and Crime* (2015).

offence.[52] The more serious, "traditional" criminal offences are likely to amount to torts[53] provided there is a victim.[54] However, there is no real difficulty in distinguishing criminal prosecutions from action in tort, if only because they are tried in different courts by different procedures. Generally speaking, criminal proceedings are brought by the Crown Prosecution Service or some authorised body and, although a private prosecution is still possible, the object of the proceedings in any case is the imposition of some sanction in the nature of punishment, for example, imprisonment or a pecuniary fine, even though the sanction imposed may have a reformative rather than a strictly punitive purpose.

Nevertheless, there are functional overlaps between the two categories. At least some of tort law, like crime, has the purpose of deterrence and in a very limited class of cases tort overtly punishes defendants in the shape of punitive damages.[55] On the other side, criminal proceedings may lead to a compensation order in favour of the victim. In this respect the distinction between crime and tort has become more blurred, though since tort originated in trespass, which to our eyes was in medieval times quasi-criminal, the law may only be returning to its roots. Furthermore, the compensatory sums awarded under these provisions are, until the court specifies their exact amount, quite uncertain and are therefore just as "unliquidated" as are damages in tort. There is, however, one peculiarity which marks them off from damages in tort. In every case they are obtainable only as a result of a process the primary purpose of which, when it is initiated, is the imposition of punishment, or something in the nature of punishment. In crime, the award of compensation is ancillary to the criminal process, whereas in tort it is normally its very object.

2. Tort Law or a Law of Torts?

Law of tort or law of torts?   Winfield's definition of tortious liability has been   **1-015** criticised on the ground that it is formal, not material, and does nothing to indicate the lawfulness or otherwise of a given act. However, Winfield did devote several pages of early editions of this work to discussion of a familiar controversy concerning the foundation of tortious liability which has some bearing on the problem of a material definition. Salmond had asked[56]:

"Does the law of torts consist of a fundamental general principle that it is wrongful to cause harm to other persons in the absence of some specific ground of justification or excuse, or does it consist of a number of specific rules prohibiting certain kinds of harmful activity, and leaving all the residue outside the sphere of legal responsibility?"

Put differently, the question is whether we have a law of tort, or a law of torts. Winfield chose the first alternative.[57] However, from the point of view of the practi-

---

52 See Ch.8.
53 But not always, e.g., perjury: para.20-028.
54 There is no law of "attempted tort". For discussion, see Goldberg and Zipursky (2002) 88 Va. L. Rev. 1625.
55 See para.23-012.
56 Salmond, *Law of Torts*, 2nd edn (1910), pp.8–9.
57 To take two examples, in *Furniss v Fitchett* [1958] N.Z.L.R. 396 at 401, Barrowclough CJ said: "The well-known torts do not have their origin in any all-embracing principle of tortious liability." In *Bollinger v Costa Brava Wine Co Ltd* [1960] Ch. 262 at 283, Danckwerts J said: "The substance of [the argument for the defendants] was that, before a person can recover for loss which he suffered from another person's act, it must be shown that his case falls within the class of actionable wrongs. But

cal lawyer concerned with the law at a particular moment there can be no doubt that the second view is correct. For example, a recording company was held to have no civil action in respect of "bootlegging" of its artists' performances where it was unable to establish any of the economic torts or the tort of breach of statutory duty,[58] even though the defendants' conduct was criminal and no justification for it could be offered. Despite occasional judicial canvassing of the idea,[59] English law has not adopted what in the United States is known as the "prima facie tort theory", whereby[60]: "the intentional infliction of temporal damages is a cause of action, which, as a matter of substantive law, whatever may be the form of pleading, requires a justification if the defendant is to escape". Nevertheless, it should be noted that we have for a good many years had something very close to a generalised principle of liability in situations where the defendant intends to inflict physical or psychological harm[61] on the claimant[62] and, despite the caution which characterises the courts' attitude to the duty of care in negligence,[63] it will be an unusual case in which the defendant is not liable where his negligent act has caused foreseeable physical damage to the claimant or his property.

1-016　**A general principle underpinning tortious liability?**　Despite the difficulties with the "law of tort" view as a practical, day-to-day matter, Winfield contended that from a broader perspective there was validity in the theory of a fundamental general principle of liability. He appears to have adopted this position on the basis that as the law of tort has grown for centuries, and is still growing, some such principle must be at the back of it. It is the difference between treating a tree as inanimate for the practical purposes of the moment (for example, for the purpose of avoiding collision with it, it is as lifeless as a block of marble) and realising that it is animate because we know that it has grown and is still growing. The caution and slowness which usually mark the creation of new rules by the judges tend to mask the fact that they have been created, for they have often come into existence only by a series of analogical extensions spread over a long period of time. To vary the metaphor, the process has resembled the sluggish movement of a glacier rather than the catastrophic charge of an avalanche but when once a new tort has come into being, it might fairly seem to have been recognised, if the whole history of its development is taken into account, in virtue of the principle that unjustifiably causing harm is tortious.[64]

---

the law may be thought to have failed if it can offer no remedy for the deliberate act of one person which causes damage to the property of another."

[58]　*RCA Corp v Pollard* [1983] Ch. 135. See also *Dunlop v Woollahra MC* [1982] A.C. 158; *Lonrho Ltd v Shell Petroleum Co Ltd (No.2)* [1982] A.C. 173.

[59]　e.g., The *Mogul Steamship Co Ltd v McGregor Gow & Co* (1889) 23 Q.B.D. 598 at 663. The High Court of Australia's flirtation in *Beaudesert SC v Smith* (1966) 120 C.L.R. 145 with the principle that independently of the "nominate" torts "a person who suffers harm or loss as the inevitable consequence of the unlawful, intentional and positive acts of another is entitled to recover damages from the other" was later abandoned: *Northern Territory of Australia v Mengel* (1995) 185 C.L.R. 307.

[60]　*Aikens v State of Wisconsin* 195 U.S. 194 at 204 (1904) per Holmes J. But see Dobbs (1980) 34 Ark. L. Rev. 335.

[61]　The American doctrine was primarily focused on interference with economic interests. We have had similar problems in attempting to generalise the economic torts.

[62]　*Wilkinson v Downton* [1897] 2 Q.B. 57. See para.4-031.

[63]　See para.5-028.

[64]　Damage for which compensation is not recoverable is known as *damnum sine injuria*; where a tort

An attempt to find some middle ground   Since the supporters of the second view   **1-017**
do not deny that the law of tort is capable of development, or even that new heads
of liability can come into existence, and since the supporters of the first view admit
that no action will lie if the conduct which caused the harm was justifiable, the difference between them is perhaps less than is sometimes supposed. Summing up his
investigation into the controversy, Professor Glanville Williams said this[65]:

> "The first school has shown that the rules of liability are very wide. The second school
> has shown that some rules of absence of liability are also very wide. Neither school has
> shown that there is any general rule, whether of liability or of non-liability, to cover novel
> cases that have not yet received the attention of the Courts. In a case of first impression—
> that is, a case that falls under no established rule or that falls equally under two conflict-
> ing rules—there is no ultimate principle directing the Court to find for one party or the
> other ... Why should we not settle the argument by saying simply that there are some
> general rules creating liability ... and some equally general rules exempting from li-
> ability ... Between the two is a stretch of disputed territory, with the Courts as an unbiased
> boundary commission. If, in an unprovided case, the decision passes for the claimant, it
> will be not because of a general theory of liability but because the court feels that here is
> a case in which existing principles of liability may properly be extended."

3. TORT AND OTHER SOURCES OF COMPENSATION

As will be seen, much of the law of tort in practice is concerned with the problem   **1-018**
of accidental injury to the person or damage to property, and the general approach
of the law to these problems rests on two broad principles. Both are subject to many
exceptions and qualifications but by and large it is the case that: (1) the victim of
accidental injury or damage is entitled to redress through the law of tort if, and only
if, his loss was caused by the fault of the defendant or those for whose fault the
defendant must answer; and (2) the redress due from the defendant whose liability
is established should be "full" or should, in other words, be as nearly equivalent as
money can be to the claimant's loss. Nevertheless, even in those accidents which
can be attributed to another's fault, the role played by the law of tort should not be
exaggerated. A century or so ago the law of tort was probably the primary vehicle
of compensation, but poverty, ignorance or economic pressure deprived many
injured persons of access to the law and threw them back on the Poor Law, charity
or the assistance of a trade union or friendly society. In more recent times the
development of insurance and social security has tended to relegate tort law to a
more secondary role. We must, therefore, address some of these other sources of
compensation and their relationship with the law of tort and in doing so consider
further some of the assumptions which underpin the tort system.

A.   Damage to Property

Types of insurance   There is little in the way of state provision for loss of or dam-   **1-019**
age to property,[66] which obviously occupies a much lower position of priority than

---

is actionable per se (without proof of loss, e.g., trespass) there is said to be *injuria sine damno*.
65   Williams (1939) 7 C.L.J. 131.
66   However, the Riot Compensation Act 2016 makes the police authority liable for property damage
caused by a riot within its area, presumably on the basis that it has failed to uphold order. In *Yarl's
Wood Immigration Ltd v Bedfordshire Police Authority* [2009] EWCA Civ 1110; [2010] Q.B. 698
it was held that a company carrying out public functions on a "contracted out" basis could rely on

personal injury.[67] Private insurance is, however, of very great significance in relation to property damage. Such insurance takes two basic forms: "loss" or "first party" insurance and "liability" or "third party" insurance. Under the former, the owner of property has cover against loss of or damage to specified property from the risks described in the policy, such as fire, flood and theft, whether or not the loss or damage occurs through the fault of any other person.[68] Under the latter, the insured himself is covered against legal liability which he may incur to a third party, and the establishment of such liability by the third party is an essential prerequisite to a claim on the policy. The two types of insurance can be combined in a single policy. A good example of this is a motor "comprehensive" policy,[69] which will: (1) cover the insured against legal liability to other road users and passengers; and (2) entitle the insured to claim from his insurer the cost of repairs should his vehicle be damaged, or the value of the vehicle if it becomes a "write-off".[70]

1-020 **Subrogation** A fundamental principle of the law on loss insurance is that it is irrelevant to tort liability.[71] Accordingly, if D wrongfully damages C's property and C fully recovers the cost of repair from a loss insurance policy, that in no way precludes C suing D for the same loss in tort.[72] Having said that, unless the policy provided cover worth less than the cost of the damage, it is unlikely that C would sue D because, property loss policies generally being contracts of indemnity, he would then have to reimburse the insurer with the damages recovered. A more likely outcome is that the insurer, after paying C under the policy will exercise its entitlement to be subrogated to C's rights against D, and sue D (in reality probably D's liability insurers) in C's name.

The opportunities for an effective exercise of the insurer's rights of subrogation may vary considerably from one type of case to another. In marine cases the right is probably commonly exercised because the size of the individual claim makes it worthwhile to do so; in home and contents insurance subrogation is much less likely since if the loss is the fault of a third party, such as a burglar, it is unlikely that that person will be worth pursuing. In the case of road accidents, repairing or replacing vehicles probably represents insurers' largest single cost. For many years nearly

---

the previous version of the legislation.

[67] In an emergency such as flood or fire the social security authorities would assist with clothing, bedding and other immediate needs. Provision may sometimes be made on an ad hoc basis for widespread disasters. For various mechanisms, see Faure and Hartlief, *Financial Compensation for Victims of Catastrophes* (2006).

[68] Indeed, the insured could normally claim on the policy even if the property was damaged through his own negligence (but not his own deliberate act) though the policy may restrict cover in certain circumstances, for example, where the key is left in the car and it is then stolen.

[69] The majority of motor policies are comprehensive, though all that is required by law is cover against liability to third parties for personal injury and property damage. A standard householder's policy will also combine both loss and liability insurance.

[70] The fact that the accident is the insured's own fault will not prevent a claim under (2), though there will normally be conditions as to the use of the vehicle and its maintenance in a roadworthy condition, breach of which will entitle the insurer to repudiate liability. In no circumstances can the insured claim under (1) in respect of his own injuries, though many policies contain a limited element of "no-fault" loss insurance for injury to driver and passengers.

[71] See para.23-123. And in relation to "collateral benefits" in personal injury cases (a similar issue), see para.23-091.

[72] *Bee v Jenson* [2007] EWCA Civ 923; [2007] 4 All E.R. 791 (hire charges). Informal settlements of minor motor claims without calling on the insurance are probably quite common because of the concern of both parties to maintain their no-claims bonuses.

all motor insurers operated a "knock for knock" agreement. This meant that if there was a collision between car A, comprehensively insured by Company X, and car B, comprehensively insured by Company Y, and the accident was caused by the fault of the driver of car A and led to damage to both vehicles, each insurer would bear its own loss in respect of the vehicle it insured and Company Y would not pursue subrogation rights against Company X in Company's X's capacity as liability insurer. There has been no such general agreement since 1994, though that does not mean that subrogation rights will be regularly pursued in this context.

It is arguable that allowing tort claims in respect of property damage when loss insurance is widely held or easily available is wasteful and that this is compounded by subrogation litigation, which only shifts money from one insurer to another. But it would require a major change in our intuitive ideas of justice to take away C's right to claim against D when D's fault has damaged C's property, and there would still remain the problem of uninsured losses, whether by total absence of cover,[73] inadequate cover or "excess" thresholds.[74] If, as is likely, the subrogation system is of limited application in smaller cases, it may be thought that the continued operation of tort law in large claims is not a serious social problem.

Impact of insurance and insurability   No one has yet gone so far as to suggest that the fact that the claimant is insured is in itself enough to defeat his claim but the presence (or likely presence) of loss insurance has sometimes, rightly or wrongly, been used in combination with other factors to reach that conclusion.[75] We may note, on the other side of the equation, that the fact that the defendant has (or is likely to have) liability cover is equally not generally thought to be a good reason for making him liable but that, too, has sometimes been a strong influence in favour of liability.[76]

1-021

B.   Personal Injury and Death

Generally   Personal injury and death are caused in myriad ways. Illness is a major factor in this regard but so too are accidents. Intentionally caused harm is another contributor but, in the scheme of things, a relatively minor one. The losses that flow from personal injury and death are sometimes left with the victim and their family to manage as best they can, but redress and other forms of support are often available from a wide array of sources,[77] and it is important to recognise at the outset that tort is just one of those sources. How important is tort law in this regard? The Royal Commission under Lord Pearson[78] reported in 1978, that tort law accounted for no more than one-quarter of the total amount of money which was then paid in

1-022

---

[73]   Compulsion to insure one's property could hardly be justified.

[74]   In motor cases the loss of no-claims bonus is also a significant factor.

[75]   See, e.g., Lord Denning MR in *Lamb v Camden LBC* [1981] Q.B. 625 at 637–638, though his Lordship was probably wrong on the facts to assume that there was cover. In *Norwich CC v Harvey* [1989] 1 W.L.R. 828, the fact that D was in a chain of building contracts, one of which, between C and X, required C to maintain insurance on the works, was held to be a good reason for holding D not liable to C.

[76]   See, again, most notably, Lord Denning MR in *Nettleship v Weston* [1971] 2 Q.B. 691 (discussed in para.6-007).

[77]   As to how the law deals with losses resulting from personal injury and death, see Cane and Goudkamp, *Atiyah's Accidents, Compensation and the Law*, 9th edn (2018).

[78]   *Royal Commission on Civil Liability and Compensation for Personal Injury* (1978), Cmnd.7054.

respect of compensation for personal injury. Although there is a striking lack of relevant data since the Pearson Report, there is no reason to believe that tort has advanced from the second rank in the intervening years. Loss insurance is an important source of compensation for personal injury and death, too, but the major player is social security. However, what is true of the whole system is not necessarily true of part of it. For example, tort damages play a very small role with regard to accidents in the home (an important source of disability) simply because there is rarely anyone on whom to pin liability; conversely, quite a high proportion of road accident victims recover under the tort system (such accidents are rarely no one's fault[79] and liability insurance is compulsory).

1-023   **Private Insurance, Occupational Pensions, etc.**   Three main types of insurance give protection against death or injury regardless of fault: life insurance, personal accident insurance and health insurance. The first is without doubt the most important: personal accident and health insurance are a good deal less common, with the Pearson Commission finding that such cover contributed only about six per cent to accident compensation. The main sources of short-term income replacement are probably occupational sick pay schemes. Individual schemes vary in detail but such schemes replace all or part of lost income for a maximum period which may be related to length of service but rarely exceeds six months. In cases of death or long-term injury leading to premature retirement a payment may be made under an occupational pension scheme. The chance of receipt of any one or more of the above benefits is heavily influenced by the social class of the victim and the nature of his employment, but it will readily be appreciated that some accident victims or their dependants stand to receive very large sums from such sources and it may be asked to what extent such receipts are taken into account in assessing tort damages for loss of earnings.[80] The question is complex and will be considered in more detail later,[81] but the broad answer is that the courts will ignore all charitable and comparable payments, all proceeds of private insurance and all occupational pension scheme payments, but will make a deduction in respect of sick pay. Quite apart, therefore, from social security benefits, there is a strong possibility that some accident victims who are successful in a tort claim will receive more than they have lost in income.

1-024   **Social Security**   The social security system is highly complex and it would be impossible to summarise it satisfactorily here. It is not even easy to define what "the system" is. The Criminal Injuries Compensation Scheme, for example, is a major provider of state assistance to a group of victims of misfortune, but it has never been within the legal framework of benefits and nor has it been administered by the Department for Work and Pensions. As for the benefits which are usually regarded as falling within the purview of the social security system, it is useful to draw a distinction between non-industrial and industrial injuries.

---

[79]   It may of course be entirely the victim's fault, which bars any claim.
[80]   The question usually arises in this way because the payment of such benefits nearly always precedes the recovery of tort damages. If the issue arose of whether tort damages were to be taken into account in assessing payments under the insurance policy or the pension scheme, everything would depend upon the construction of the contract. Tort damages, however, would almost invariably have no effect on payments from life or personal accident policies.
[81]   See para.23-091.

As to non-industrial injuries, some benefits (for example, income support, hous-   **1-025**
ing benefit and universal credit) are simply based on the fact that the recipient's
means are below a certain level and they have no connection with injury—though
an accident victim may receive them if the relevant conditions are satisfied.
Otherwise, non-industrial injury cases are dealt with in the same way as sickness
and the primary short-term benefit is in fact now paid by employers in the form of
"statutory sick pay" for up to 28 weeks. When the statutory sick pay entitlement
has been exhausted it is replaced by employment and support allowance. In addition, a claimant who needs constant care or assistance may receive personal
independence payments or attendance allowance.

As to industrial injuries, the Workmen's Compensation Act 1897 introduced into   **1-026**
English law the first important type of accident compensation not based on the law
of tort. Under that Act, workers injured in various types of employment could
recover compensation for personal injury "arising out of and in the course of
employment". This compensation was payable by the employer and was recoverable by action in the courts. However, the implementation of the Beveridge Report's
recommendations[82] resulted in the Workmen's Compensation Scheme being
abolished and replaced by a system of benefits payable by the state for such accidents and diseases.[83] This system, which is known as the Industrial Injuries
Scheme, covers industrial injuries (including certain prescribed diseases) and
provides for payment of "disablement benefit" to the injured worker. The basic
condition of award is that the injury was caused by an accident "arising out of and
in the course of employment". Injuries with short-term effects are excluded by the
rule that disablement benefit is not payable for the first 15 weeks after the accident.
It is important to note that disablement benefit is not necessarily looked upon as a
method of replacement of lost earnings (indeed, an employee may be entitled to the
benefit even though his earnings have been unaffected) but is based upon an objective assessment of disablement, fixed on a percentage basis either by regulations or
by a medical board. The system employs thresholds, which has the effect of making tort claims more important in smaller cases. Disablement benefit takes the form
of a pension.

The question of offsetting social security payments against damages where a tort   **1-027**
claim succeeds is governed by statute and is dealt with later.[84] Briefly, in the case
of personal injuries social security payments paid in the initial five-year period after
the accident are deducted by the defendant, who must reimburse the Secretary of
State. The reimbursement system also extends to the cost of providing medical and
social care services.[85] The cost of providing these services to the victims of accidental death, injury and industrial disease is probably much higher than the social
security payments made to such persons.

---

[82] *Beveridge Report* (1942), Cmd.6404.
[83] National Insurance (Industrial Injuries) Act 1946 subsequently replaced by other legislation (see, in
      particular, the Social Security Contributions and Benefits Act 1992). There may of course be further
      provision in particular employments, e.g., the Police (Injury Benefit) Regulations 2006 (SI 2006/
      932).
[84] See para.23-097.
[85] See para.23-097.

4. PAYING FOR THE TORT SYSTEM

1-028   **Who pays damages?**   Who pays damages awards (and settlement monies in the case of claims that are not resolved by the courts)? In the case of personal injuries, the great majority of claims are brought against defendants who are insured against liability. This means that the bill for damages awards is largely met by the premium-paying population rather than by the wrongdoer. It follows that the tort system, at least in the personal injury context, is overwhelmingly financed by the public.[86] These basic facts about the cost of the tort system have profound implications in relation to its rationales, as will be seen later.[87] Relatively little is known about who pays damages outside the personal injury context. However, it is probable that an insurer stands behind many defendants in property damage claims, whereas in relation to claims in, say, defamation and the economic torts the presence of an insurer is much less likely.

1-029   **Conditional fee agreements**   As observed in the previous paragraph, it is the public which largely foots the bill for damages awards, at least in relation to personal injury claims. However, who pays for the legal costs and disbursements that are incurred in pursuing a claim? A full answer to this question would be very lengthy, and it is impractical to go into the details here. What follows is a highly compact description of the relevant law and practice. Typically, claimants seeking compensation for personal injuries enter into a "conditional fee agreement" (CFA) with their lawyer, pursuant to which the lawyer agrees to charge the claimant for the cost of the legal services and disbursements only in the event that the claim is successful (success is defined as obtaining damages in any amount, however small).[88] CFAs are also known as "no-win no-fee" agreements. In return for taking the risk that the claim will fail and he will not be paid, the lawyer is entitled to a success fee if the claimant succeeds. The maximum success fee that can be charged depends on various factors including the type of proceedings and the issues that are in dispute.

1-030   **Damages-based agreements**   Provision has recently been made for claimants to enter into damages-based agreements (DBAs) with their lawyers.[89] DBAs are also no-win no-fee agreements, so that the lawyer carries the risk of pursuing the claim. However, instead of taking their normal hourly fee plus a success fee if the case is won, which is what occurs where a CFA is used, under a DBA the lawyer will charge the claimant a proportion of the damages up to a maximum of 25 per cent.[90] DBAs are sometimes referred to as "contingency fee agreements". They are likely to be offered by lawyers only in high-value claims.

1-031   **Costs shifting**   If the claim is successful, the defendant (or, more often, the defendant's insurer) will usually be ordered to pay the claimant's costs. An

---

[86] The Automated and Electric Vehicles Act 2018 bypasses the wrongdoer entirely in the case of accidents caused by automated vehicles. Section 2 of that statute places liability directly on the vehicle's insurer and thereby dispenses with the pretence that it is the defendant who pays.

[87] See paras 1-035, 1-037.

[88] Courts and Legal Services Act 1990 s.58.

[89] Courts and Legal Services Act 1990 s.58AA; Damages-Based Agreements Regulations 2013 (SI 2013/609).

[90] Damages-Based Agreements Regulations 2013 (SI 2013/609) reg.4(2).

important qualification to this rule is that the success fee charged by the claimant's lawyer under a CFA is not recoverable as costs.[91] Generally speaking, in the personal injury context claimants are not required to pay the defendant's costs if the claim is unsuccessful. Thus, in this setting the costs-shifting rule works only in one direction (it is hence known as "one-way costs shifting"). Where, exceptionally, claimants are required to pay the defendant's costs, their costs liability only extends to the value of any damages award made in favour of the claimant.[92] Outside the personal injury context, in order to guard against the risk of having to pay the defendant's costs in the event that the claim is unsuccessful, claimants may take out an insurance policy to cover this risk. The premium for this, which is normally paid after the claim has been concluded, is not recoverable as costs.[93]

5.   CRITICISMS OF THE TORT SYSTEM IN THE CONTEXT OF PERSONAL INJURY AND DEATH

A.   The "Fault Principle"

The privileged position of tort claimants   Although, overall, the law of tort is   **1-032** by no means the most important vehicle for accident compensation, an accident victim who can make out a tort claim stands to recover very substantially more than one who cannot. This is due in large part to the fact that the tort system, unlike other compensation systems, is committed to the principle that the claimant should recover compensation in respect of the full amount of his loss.[94] Accordingly, if, for example, the claimant is a high-income earner and is rendered unable to work due to the defendant's negligence, the claimant will prima facie be entitled to recover compensation in respect of the entirety of the income thereby lost. That is so even if this is many times greater than most people would earn over the same period and regardless of whether the claimant's injuries create a need for compensation at that level. No other compensation system is nearly as generous.

The fault principle[95]   However, the benefits of the tort system are generally only   **1-033** available to those claimants who can establish that their injuries were caused by the defendant's fault, and this principle (which is known as the "fault principle") excludes a very large percentage of those who suffer injury and disability from recovering tort damages. For example, persons who hurt themselves cannot access tort damages, nor can those who, due simply to bad luck, fall ill or are born disabled. These people need to fall back on one of the other systems of compensation, all of which are far less generous than the tort system. What justification is there for the fault principle, and what objections lie in respect of it?

---

91 Courts and Legal Services Act 1990 s.58(6).
92 CPR Pt.44.14(1).
93 Courts and Legal Services Act 1990 s.58C.
94 See para.23-010.
95 See, further, Cane and Goudkamp, *Atiyah's Accidents, Compensation and the Law*, 9th edn (2018) Ch.7.

B. Deterrence

1-034 **How precise is the guidance given by tort law?** It is arguable that the fault principle deters unwanted conduct. According to this line of reasoning, faulty conduct is undesirable and, if defendants are made to pay for the consequences of it, they and other similarly situated persons will be less likely to engage in it in the future. However, the extent to which tort law deters is controversial, especially in the context of negligently caused accidents. There are two main reasons for this. First, a generalised instruction to people to take reasonable care, which, for the most part, is all that tort law gives, is arguably of little practical use in guiding their behaviour in a given situation. Certain driving practices, for example driving at 60mph down a crowded shopping street, could be recognised as negligent by ordinary people without any judicial assistance, but the majority of cases do not present such clear-cut issues and the number of variable factors is so great that each case will turn on its own facts. The force of this criticism probably depends on the context. It is particularly strong in the case of road accidents, where the activity is, in the case of an experienced driver, largely instinctive and where a momentary lapse of attention can lead to catastrophic results with few realistic possibilities of taking other precautions to minimise or avoid the risk. Where, however, the accident arises from an alleged defect in a system of work or the organisation of a business, it is possible that a tort judgment may play a part in exposing the risk and leading others to take measures to prevent recurrence, whether voluntarily or at the insistence of their insurers.

1-035 **The impact of insurance** The second main reason why the deterrence argument is of limited force relates to the sources from which damages are paid. If it were the case that damages were paid out of the tortfeasor's own resources it could hardly be denied that the threat of legal liability would deter.[96] But in practice damages are, far more often than not, paid by an insurer[97] rather than by the tortfeasor himself,[98] and this undoubtedly blunts the deterrent edge of tort law very considerably. Liability insurance in respect of personal injuries is compulsory so far as concerns road accidents affecting third parties[99] and most work accidents,[100] and to meet the problem of the uninsured driver[101] there is an agreement under which the Motor

---

[96] "If it were not for insurance, the common law would operate with intolerable harshness in its application to driving": *Imbree v McNeilly* [2008] HCA 40; (2008) 236 C.L.R. 510 at [23] per Gleeson CJ. Damages may be much larger than any fine likely to be imposed by a criminal court for comparable conduct.

[97] The general position is that the claim is against the insured tortfeasor in person, though of course in practice his insurer will handle the claim. However, in the case of motor claims there is, without prejudice to the claim against the tortfeasor, a direct right of action against the insurer: European Communities (Rights Against Insurers) Regulations 2002 (SI 2002/3061), implementing Directive 2000/26.

[98] See Lewis [2005] J.P.I.L. 1. However, some large organisations, public and private, act as self-insurers. The National Health Service Litigation Authority administers a risk-pooling scheme for NHS trusts.

[99] Road Traffic Act 1988 s.143, which also extends to property damage. Cover must be unlimited in respect of personal injury but is generally only up to £20 million in respect of property damage.

[100] Employers' Liability (Compulsory Insurance) Act 1969 s.1.

[101] i.e., where there is no policy at all. Where there is a policy and the car is driven by a person not entitled to drive it (even if he has unlawfully taken the car) the insurer must pay: see, e.g., *Miller v Hales* [2006] EWHC 1529 (QB); [2007] Lloyd's Rep. I.R. 54.

Insurers' Bureau (i.e., the road traffic insurers acting collectively) satisfies claims.[102] Of course, the presence of insurance does not necessarily take away the deterrent effect completely because the premium may be related not only to the general risk presented by the activity or the actor (the nature of the employer's trade or the age of the driver) but also to the record of the particular insured. However, the setting of insurance premiums may depend on many factors and while, say, motor premiums are quite strongly "experience-related", this appears to be less so in relation to employers' liability. Where the defendant is in the business of supplying goods or services to the public, the cost of obtaining insurance cover (or of paying damages if he carries his own risk) will be reflected in the price charged to the public or in a reduced profit margin so that those who actually pay it are either the consumers or the shareholders or both. Nevertheless, the overall cost of the harmful conduct is still (in theory) reduced because if others can provide similar goods and services without this additional cost, they will gain an increased share of the market.

Deterrence is not only produced of course by the threat of direct imposition of a financial penalty. It is perfectly possible that a person may be induced to take greater care by, among other things, the harm to his reputation which may be caused by a successful tort suit against him.[103] Again, this effect is probably limited to certain fields of liability, such as professional negligence, product liability and employers' liability. While experience shows that a powerful public reaction can be triggered where, for example, a drug company is alleged to have produced a drug harmful to children, it is very unlikely that people would take much interest in a road accident caused by one of its delivery vans. In any event, a large corporate defendant is capable of avoiding much adverse publicity by an out-of-court settlement (the details of which will almost always be confidential), and the speed with which substantial compensation has been offered in the wake of some mass disasters suggests that in practice the victim's chances of recovery are in direct proportion to the scale of the accident and, hence, the amount of public attention it receives.

Conclusions   We may conclude, therefore, that the prospect of tort liability will have some influence on conduct but that this influence is variable and limited. Further, even if tort law under the fault principle deters undesirable behaviour, that fact would not necessarily justify the fault principle since a strict liability system (i.e., a regime in which liability is imposed irrespective of whether the defendant was at fault) may have just as great an effect. Our ambivalence on this issue is also observable in judicial decisions. Thus, in one case Staughton LJ said that[104]:   **1-036**

---

[102] There is a supplementary agreement covering claims by unidentified drivers (for discussion, see *Cameron v Liverpool Victoria Insurance Co Ltd* [2019] UKSC 6; [2019] 1 W.L.R. 1471 at [4]–[5]). The agreements are not strictly enforceable by the claimant, but the Bureau will never take the point. The Bureau may require the claimant to pursue any claims at law that he may have or to assign claims to it, but the existence of the Bureau means that we are far less likely than some countries to have tort claims against third parties who are in some way involved in the events leading up to an accident with an uninsured driver (see, e.g., *Childs v Desormeaux* [2006] SCC 18; [2006] 1 S.C.R. 643). By virtue of Directive 84/5 the agreements must provide protection equivalent to that which would be available against an insured and identified driver: *Byrne v MIB* [2008] EWCA Civ 574; [2009] Q.B. 66 (shorter time limit under unidentified drivers' agreement).

[103] See Linden (1973) 51 Can. Bar Rev. 155.

[104] *M v Newham LBC* [1994] 4 All E.R. 602 at 631 (on appeal sub nom. *X v Bedfordshire CC* [1995] 2 A.C. 633).

"One advantage that is claimed for imposing a duty of care is that it encourages people not to be negligent. I very much doubt if that is the case. The great expansion of tortious liability over the last hundred and fifty years has had the remarkable feature that the direct financial consequences almost invariably fall on someone whose purse is assumed to be bottomless, such as an insurance company or a large commercial concern or an organ of central or local government."

However, in the same case Sir Thomas Bingham MR said that he could not[105]:

"accept, as a general proposition, that the imposition of a duty of care makes no contribution to the maintenance of high standards. The common belief that the imposition of such a duty may lead to overkill [i.e., over-deterrence] is not easily reconciled with the suggestion that it has no effect".

C. Responsibility

1-037   **Calling wrongdoers to account**[106]   Another argument in favour of a tort system based on fault (or at least of a tort system, as opposed to other mechanisms of compensation) is still more difficult to assess but cannot be dismissed out of hand on that basis. It is that the notion of responsibility is a powerful, intuitive factor in people's attitudes to accidents and that there is a deep-seated idea that those who have negligently caused damage to others should pay.[107] "Corrective justice" requires that tortfeasors repair the damage that they have done and, in most cases, the payment of money is the only practical correction available.[108] This argument is not necessarily rebutted by the fact that the money may come from an insurer; indeed, since few awards of damages would otherwise be paid, it might be regarded as buttressing it. Of course, there is no logical reason why such a duty to correct harm should arise only where the defendant is at fault (although it seems inevitable that there should be a minimum requirement that he has caused the harm). However, even if it is only the product of a long-standing system dominated by fault, one may confidently say that the call for the duty to correct harm is stronger where fault is present.

One objection to the foregoing is that the tort system is a crude mechanism for apportioning blame. For example, it ignores massive disproportions that can occur between the defendant's negligence and the consequences for which he is obliged to pay.[109] Suppose two drivers career off a motorway onto a railway track and cause a train wreck in which there are dozens of casualties. The first has had no sleep the night before and knows full well that he is unfit to drive; the second is guilty only of a moment's inattention. As far as tort law is concerned the outcome of both cases is the same: the driver (in reality his insurer) pays all the resulting damages in full. The example can be extended. Suppose that the first driver's car slides off the railway track with the result that the train wreck does not occur. He

---

[105] [1994] 4 All E.R. 602 at 619.

[106] As to the significance of tort law providing victims with "civil recourse" against persons who have wronged them, see Goldberg and Zipursky, *Recognizing Wrongs* (2020).

[107] For exploration of this idea, see Goudkamp (2004) 28 M.U.L.R. 343.

[108] There are many varied accounts of the concept of "corrective justice". Influential treatments include Weinrib, *The Idea of Private Law* (1995) and Gardner (2011) 30 Law & Phil. 1.

[109] A classic discussion of this point is Waldron in Owen (ed), *Philosophical Foundations of Tort Law* (1995).

will incur no liability in tort whatsoever despite the fact that he is more culpable than the second driver and it was only due to luck that he caused no harm.

Other ways of holding wrongdoers responsible There may be more effective **1-038** means of requiring wrongdoers to account for what they did than tort liability. The most obvious is the criminal law. However, the criminal law's response to harm negligently caused is more partial than that of the civil law: while there are fairly comprehensive sanctions on careless conduct on the road and (as far as employers are concerned) at work, there are other areas of activity (medical treatment, for example) where the criminal law generally only operates if the fault is very grave and death ensues. A surgeon who kills his patient by gross negligence commits manslaughter; one who by the same means renders him quadriplegic commits no offence at all. That, of course, is not the whole story, for the surgeon is exposed to disciplinary proceedings and, since the outcome of these may be exclusion from the profession (whereas any tort damages will be paid by the hospital trust or insurer), they are a far more potent sanction. Again, however, the system operates in a random way: there is no equivalent of the General Medical Council for plumbers or electricians. In other cases, where there is a major disaster, there will commonly be a public inquiry and that may "point the finger" more effectively than a civil suit.

D. Expense and Inefficiency

The tort system is expensive to administer A tort law system based upon the **1-039** fault principle is undoubtedly exceptionally expensive to administer when compared with, say, social security, and this might be thought to be a serious defect in it. a large proportion of the money expended goes not to the compensation of persons who have suffered injury and disability but to the operation of the system. The Pearson Commission estimated that in personal injury claims the cost of operating the tort system was about 85 per cent of the value of the compensation paid, whereas the corresponding figure for social security was about 11 per cent.[110]

The reasons for the disparity are myriad but the expense incurred in establishing fault in a tort claim is undoubtedly a major contributing factor. Up-to-date, comprehensive figures are hard to come by and there is of course likely to be a very substantial difference between a claim which settles early and one which goes to trial. Most claims are for comparatively small amounts of money and then even fairly minimal legal input will loom quite large in the equation; the amount of costs incurred in a motor claim that is settled for £2,000 is likely to be proportionately a good deal more than in one that is settled for £200,000. In considering these points, however, one must bear in mind that in the majority of cases liability will not be contested at all and the cost will be generated by, for example, the issue of the quantum of damages, which would also arise if liability were imposed regardless

---

[110] The figures, however, favour social security because the cost of collection of national insurance contributions falls outside the account, i.e., on employers. The estimate by the *Civil Justice Review* (Cm. 394, 1988) was that the cost of the tort system was between 50 and 70 per cent of personal injury damages awarded. According to the Association of British Insurers (*Delivering a Fair and Efficient Compensation System*, 2005) claimants' costs (which are usually higher than defendants') average 38 per cent of sums recovered in motor vehicle accident claims.

of fault. Therefore, to some extent, the criticism on efficiency grounds is directed not so much at the fault principle as at the *tort* system.

1-040   **Delays in the tort system**   A second issue is the problem of delay. Although there is a paucity of hard evidence in this regard, it is likely that many tort claims take between two and four years to resolve and, in some cases involving catastrophic injuries to young children, much longer (since in such cases it may take several years for the full extent of the injuries and their impact on the claimant and his future to be determined). It is likely delay disproportionately affects claimants. Serious injured claimants may be well be very short of funds and may, consequently, be placed under significant pressure to settle their claims prematurely and at a sizable discount. Recent procedural changes may well have aggravated problems in this regard. Litigants are now obliged to go through extensive pre-action investigations and correspondence before litigating, with the court empowered to sanction non-compliance through adverse costs orders. It is arguable that such "frontloading" significantly delays the resolution of many claims or, at least, those claims that proceed to a full trial. However, it is also possible that, since the need to comply with pre-action protocols may facilitate the early settlement of claims, it reduces the backlog in the courts and thus allows those claims that end up in the courts to be processed more quickly than would otherwise be the case. The fault principle is probably responsible for causing some of the delay, since where fault is contested the parties will often undertake significant investigations into the circumstances that led to the claimant being injured.

E.   Unpredictability of Outcomes

1-041   The fault principle makes it difficult to predict the outcome of many claims (where the defendant denies fault, it may be hard for both parties to estimate the prospects that the claim will succeed). There are reasons to suspect that this factor impinges more significantly on claimants than on defendants.[111] Although this element of risk, leading to pressure to settle, is of course present in virtually all litigation, it is particularly powerful in the case of personal injuries because a very large part of the claimant's future wealth may be at stake. The problem is exacerbated by the fact that even if the claimant wins at the trial there may be a large element of irrecoverable costs if the defendant's insurers have made an accurately calculated offer of settlement (the basic rule here being that if the claimant fails to obtain an award at trial that exceeds the value of the defendant's offer he will need to bear his own costs from the date of the offer). Conversely, a claimant may make a settlement offer, with penal consequences to the defendant on interest and costs if a higher award is made at trial. The claimant is also entitled in such cases to an uplift of 10 per cent in his damages (up to a maximum of £75,000).[112]

F.   Compensation Based on Luck rather than Need

1-042   It is arguable that any rational compensation system must look to the need of those seeking support and deliver compensation accordingly. Tort law under the

---

[111] See Genn, *Hard Bargaining* (1987); Phillips and Hawkins (1976) 39 M.L.R. 497.
[112] CPR Pt.36.14(3)(d). This 10 per cent uplift applies where the damages recovered are up to £500,000. The uplift is reduced to five per cent to the extent that damages exceed this figure.

fault principle proceeds very differently. The mere fact that a claimant is in need, however desperate, of financial support, does not unlock any entitlement to damages. Such damages are available only where the claimant can prove that the defendant caused his injuries through fault and, from the claimant's perspective, it is often a matter of luck whether this can be done. For example, a claimant pedestrian who is run down by a motorist because the motorist unforeseeably suffered a cardiac arrest will be unable to establish fault and will recover nothing from the tort system, whereas a similarly situated pedestrian who is "fortunate" enough to be run down by an intoxicated driver will be able to access the benefits that tort law provides. However, neither pedestrian had any control over the circumstances in which they were injured. From their viewpoint, the way in which they were hurt is simply a matter of luck. Further, it makes no difference that the first pedestrian is catastrophically injured and the second only slightly. Although the second pedestrian may be able to get by without assistance, tort damages will be made available to him but not to the first.

6. ALTERNATIVES

Any reform of the law governing compensation for personal injuries might adopt one of two basic forms. First, the provision that the tort system currently makes for strict liability could be extended or, secondly, a compensation system could be created either in place of, or in addition to, the tort system. These solutions, both of which have many possible permutations, will be discussed in turn.[113] **1-043**

A. Strict Liability

Existing provision for strict liability   Despite the dominance of fault liability, tort law contains many pockets of strict liability, including with regard to personal injuries. Some of these are of common law origin and of respectable antiquity, while others were created by modern statutes[114] and have either been limited in their practical importance[115] or of rather haphazard application.[116] No consistent policy has been followed in the creation of these areas of strict liability, though it is perhaps possible to discern behind some of them a very hazy idea of unusual or increased risk. The strictness of the liability varies considerably along a spectrum from near absolute liability to little more than a reversed burden of proof, and almost always the defendant may plead the contributory fault of the claimant as a defence.[117] **1-044**

Although there are important exceptions, areas of strict liability are generally narrowly confined. Consider in this regard the Montreal Convention, which makes an air carrier liable regardless of fault for bodily injury suffered by a passenger caused by accident.[118] "Bodily injury" does not, in this context, include psychiatric

---

[113] See, further, Cane and Goudkamp, *Atiyah's Accidents, Compensation and the Law*, 9th edn (2018), Ch.18.

[114] A recent illustration is the Automated and Electric Vehicles Act 2018, which imposes strict liability on insurers for damages resulting from accidents involving automated vehicles: s.2(1).

[115] The liability under the Nuclear Installations Act 1965 is probably the strictest known to English law.

[116] See, e.g., the many statutory duties arising under industrial safety legislation, some of which are considered in Ch.9.

[117] e.g., the strict liability regime created by the Automated and Electric Vehicles Act 2018 provides for a defence of contributory negligence: s.3.

[118] For some unusual situations, see *Disley v Levine* [2001] EWCA Civ 1087; [2002] 1 W.L.R. 785 and

trauma[119] and an "accident" requires some unexpected event external to the passenger (deep vein thrombosis caused by cramped but normal seating is not an accident in this sense, nor is a fall by a passenger when the aircraft is in its normal state).[120] Nor, in this setting (though not necessarily in others), can the claimant fall back on a common law duty based on failure to warn or instruct, because the Convention is the exclusive basis for the carrier's liability.[121]

Because existing provision for strict liability often applies only in carefully prescribed circumstances involving unusual risks, it contributes relatively modestly to accident compensation and does not threaten the dominance of the fault principle. However, there are some instances in which a more significant contribution is made. One is the statutory strict liability regime that applies for damage caused by defective products.[122] This strict liability scheme stands apart from most others in that it is concerned with a risk that is commonplace. The other is the law of vicarious liability, which is of very great importance.[123] In outline, the vicarious liability doctrine holds employers strictly liable for torts committed by their employees.

1-045 **An extension of strict liability?**   One way of breaking free from the fault principle would be dramatically to extend the existing provision for strict liability. For example, Parliament could provide that in, say, the road accident context, it would henceforward no longer be necessary for claimants to prove that the defendant was at fault in order to establish an entitlement to redress. Compared with the fault principle, strict liability would minimise uncertainty in the outcomes of litigation and would, by reducing the number of issues that are in play, expedite proceedings, all other things being equal. Strict liability would also increase the number of accident victims entitled to compensation, since victims would no longer need to establish fault on the part of the defendant in order to recover. Possible objections to strict liability are that it would diminish tort law's potential to deter harmful behaviour (although this is hotly contested) and result in an undesirable disconnect between liability and culpability (although many defendants held strictly liable may in fact be at fault because strict liability is liability imposed regardless of whether or not the defendant is at fault). It is also worth highlighting another advantage of the fault principle, which is that it carries within itself the identification of the party who is to bear the liability. By contrast, if fault is not determinative of liability, other determinants must be identified instead. If, for example, two cars collide on a motorway, then in a system of fault liability, it is the driver who is to blame for the accident (assuming one is) who must pay damages, subject to any argument from contributory negligence. By contrast, under a strict liability regime other rules will be needed to determine who is liable and to what extent, and it may be difficult to avoid these rules becoming complex and their effects arbitrary.

Laroche v Spirit of Adventure (UK) Ltd [2009] EWCA Civ 12; [2009] Q.B. 778.
[119] *Morris v KLM Royal Dutch Airlines* [2002] UKHL 7; [2002] 2 A.C. 628.
[120] *Deep Vein Thrombosis and Air Travel Group Litigation, Re* [2005] UKHL 72; [2006] 1 A.C. 495; *Povey v Qantas Airways Ltd* [2005] HCA 33; (2005) 223 C.L.R. 189; *Barclay v British Airways Plc* [2008] EWCA Civ 1419; [2010] Q.B. 187.
[121] *Sidhu v British Airways Plc* [1997] A.C. 430.
[122] See Ch.11.
[123] See Ch.21.

B.   Compensation Schemes

Compensation schemes distinguished from the tort system   Tort law could be   **1-046**
replaced, in whole or in part, with a compensation scheme. Compensation schemes
are a type of social security. They provide benefits for injuries irrespective of
whether the injuries were caused by someone's fault and very often irrespective of
how the injuries were caused, with the result that they may not only do away with
the need to prove fault but also tort law's requirement to establish a causal connection between the defendant's conduct and the damage. Compensation schemes,
consequently, are capable of providing far broader coverage than the tort system,
which usually only awards compensation to the "lucky" victims who are able to
establish that their injuries were caused by the fault of an (insured) defendant. Unlike tort proceedings (whether based on fault or strict liability), compensation
systems do not involve litigation against the injurer. Instead, the claimant applies
for payments from a government administered fund. However, because of the large
number of people who can generally call on them for assistance, compensation
schemes tend to provide financial support at a far lower level than the tort system.

Ad hoc compensation schemes   Some compensation schemes are ad hoc in the   **1-047**
sense that they apply only in a particular context. Probably the most common type
of ad hoc compensation scheme is that which operates in the setting of criminal
injuries. Ad hoc compensation schemes that apply to motor vehicle accidents and
workplace injuries exist in many countries, including Australia and the United
States. These schemes vary greatly in the amount and range of benefits that they
offer and in the extent to which they limit the right to claim tort damages. Generally speaking, they do not provide compensation in respect of non-pecuniary losses
such as pain and suffering, and the entitlement to redress in respect of other types
of loss, such as a loss of earnings, is subject to both thresholds and caps. It is
questionable whether it makes sense to single out for special treatment the fields
of criminal injuries and (as is the case in relation to some other jurisdictions) road
accidents. From the claimant's perspective, why should the context in which they
were injured matter?

Comprehensive compensation schemes   Much more far-reaching than the ad hoc   **1-048**
schemes mentioned in the previous paragraph is the accident compensation scheme
that operates in New Zealand. The origin of this scheme is the Report of the
Woodhouse Commission, which had been appointed to deal only with compensation for work injuries but felt unable to limit itself to its terms of reference and
proposed an all-embracing compensation system based on the five guiding
principles of community responsibility, comprehensive entitlement, "real"
compensation (including non-pecuniary loss), the promotion of rehabilitation, and
administrative efficiency. Most of the proposals were implemented by the Accident Compensation Act 1972.[124] The law that underpins the scheme is now to be
found mainly in the Injury Prevention, Rehabilitation and Compensation Act 2001.
Claims are handled administratively, with the courts being relegated to the role of
reviewing administrative decisions said to be infected by an error of law.

---

[124] For a full account of the current scheme, see Todd (ed), *Todd on Torts*, 8th edn (2019). In Australia,
a National Committee of Inquiry in 1974 proposed a scheme that would cover all incapacity, whether
caused by accident or illness, but the proposal was lost with a change of government in 1975.

Broadly speaking, the scheme provides compensation for personal injury caused by accidents, occupational diseases and medical "treatment injuries". Cover for mental injury (other than that related to physical injury) is confined to cases involving certain sexual offences and to a single work-related event which the injured person experiences directly. As injury arising from an intentional act is "accidental" as far as the victim is concerned, there is no need for a separate criminal injuries compensation scheme in New Zealand. Although the original plan envisaged the extension of the scheme to disease in general and to disability, there now seems to be no prospect of this happening.

Where the compensation scheme applies the right of action in tort is abolished, although it remains possible to claim punitive damages,[125] and proceedings in tort can be brought for cases that fall outside the scheme.[126] In the case of total incapacity for work, compensation is at the rate of 80 per cent of earnings, subject to a statutory maximum. The scheme provides for fairly modest lump sum payments for non-pecuniary loss. According a low priority to non-pecuniary loss is a feature of most compensation schemes. It is no doubt true that "loss" of this description is very different from the loss of something having an obvious monetary value and that, at common law, damages for non-pecuniary loss are awarded more by way of "solace for unpleasantness and misfortune" than by way of replacement of something of which a person has been deprived. It is also true that it is difficult to find a basis for the assessment of some types of non-pecuniary damage.[127] Conversely, there is no a priori reason for saying that those who suffer pain or loss of amenity are undeserving of such solace as the payment of money can bring them. The reply to the last point is that compensation of this kind should be given to none until such time as the basic income losses of all can be restored through the chosen compensation system on the ground that loss of income has a particularly profound impact.

1-049   **Obstacles to reform**   As has been discussed, compensation schemes provide far greater coverage than the tort system, but the payments under them are generally significantly lower. It might be thought that a decent meal for all is preferable to a banquet for some. However, the complaint is often made that the level of benefits paid by compensation systems is too low. The difficulty is that public debate over medical negligence and some mass-disaster cases suggests that expectations of the "proper" level of compensation are at a level well beyond that which could be financed without significant additional taxation. This cannot be ignored if any reform is to be achieved.

A related difficulty concerns the scope of compensation schemes. It is widely felt among reformers that a rational compensation system cannot confine its coverage to accident victims, since the needs of a person under disability are not mitigated by the fact that it has arisen from illness or congenital cause rather than by accident.[128] On this view, even the "comprehensive" New Zealand scheme suffers from the vice of cause-related compensation. However, if we bring in illness, we enter a wholly different statistical dimension, since it is generally thought that the

---

[125]   See, e.g., *A v Bottrill* [2002] UKPC 44; [2003] 1 A.C. 449.
[126]   Hence, there is still common law litigation in New Zealand in, for example, "nervous shock" cases.
[127]   See paras 23-074—23-076.
[128]   See Stapleton, *Disease and the Compensation Debate* (1986).

contribution of accidents to all forms of disability is not more than about 10 per cent.[129] The implications of this in terms of cost are obvious.

Reform in this area is as much about politics as principle and there are major obstacles to change including stakeholders who benefit from the status quo being maintained and deep-seated commitments to ideas such as the fault principle. If there were no social security system and all persons suffering disability not attributable to another's fault were condemned to utter destitution, it might be possible to raise a sufficient head of steam for a new and comprehensive approach. But the basic social security system does exist and reform may well be perceived by the public as "fine tuning" brought about at the price of taking away existing rights— and there are no votes in that. Even the present social security system is proving difficult to sustain and the prospect of the additional funding necessary to support general disability compensation at more than subsistence level appears remote. There is perhaps more chance of the introduction of limited, ad hoc no-fault schemes, but these are likely to make comprehensive change even more difficult by creating further enclaves of preferential treatment.

C. First-Party Insurance

Although debates about reform for the most part centre on proposals to extend   **1-050** the existing provision for strict liability or to create a compensation scheme that would run alongside or in replacement of the tort system, it should be briefly mentioned that these are not the only ways in which the current arrangements could be changed. Professor Patrick Atiyah controversially argued in favour of abandoning tort compensation for personal injury (in most situations) and putting nothing in its place, thereby leaving it to the market (in the form of first-party insurance) to solve the problem of compensating accident victims.[130] Expressing his views crudely, Atiyah saw little of value in the tort system. For example, it was not, in his eyes, a personal responsibility system given that wrongdoers almost never pay personally for the losses that they cause (it is insurers and, hence, the premium-paying public that pays). And he rated it very poorly on its ability to deliver redress to people who had been injured in accidents since it awards redress not on the basis of need but based on whether the claimant happened to have been injured by the fault of an insured defendant.

However, in Atiyah's view the creation of a comprehensive compensation system was not the way forward given that there had been a profound and world-wide reaction to bureaucratic welfare schemes. Thus, his preference was to put nothing in the void left by the suggested abolition of tort liability for personal injury and to leave it up to people to buy first-party insurance cover for themselves and their families. He contended that this would ensure vastly increased coverage (since first-party insurance is not dependent upon fault). He also stressed that this solution would not be regressive since people would only buy the cover that they felt that they needed in the light of their income. Tort law, in contrast, is a highly regressive system since wealthier people tend to stand to gain the most from it, since tort law damages are designed fully to replace lost income.

---

[129] Pearson Report, Vol.2, p.12. Of course, tort liability applies to the wrongful causing of disease and is of importance in this respect in the employment context but, despite sporadic litigation about matters like smoking, hepatitis and CJD, its impact in disease cases outside that context is minimal.

[130] Atiyah, *The Damages Lottery* (1997).

7. TORT AND THE COMPENSATION CULTURE

1-051   **Introduction**   It is widely agreed that tort law is not a very efficient means of compensating misfortune, but one might reply that it never set out to do that, but rather to right wrongs. The question nevertheless arises whether, even in that more modest frame, it has not become somewhat out of control. We have all been brought up to believe (rightly or wrongly) that the United States has long been the home of rampant tort law, of multi-million dollar recoveries involving cars which did not prove crash-proof or cups of coffee which scalded the buyer. In 1991, an American writer asserted that "the American links adversity with recompense whereas the Englishman or woman accepts adversity as a routine part of life",[131] but recent events cast some doubt on the second proposition.

1-052   **"Tort reform" in other jurisdictions**   "Tort reform" has long been a matter of heated debate in the United States and this has led to various forms of legislative action, most commonly in the form of capping damages, especially for non-pecuniary loss and punitive damages, and abolishing or modifying the traditional common law rule that each of a number of tortfeasors causing indivisible harm is liable for the whole loss. More recently there has been large-scale legislative action in most Australian jurisdictions, driven by an "insurance crisis".[132] The New South Wales Civil Liability Act 2002 goes the furthest in most respects and contains provisions of three main types. First, some basic principles of the common law have been "restated" in a way that is presumably intended to render them immune from judicial tampering (however unlikely such tampering may have been).[133] So, for example, under s.5I(2) a person is not liable for the materialisation of a risk which cannot be avoided by the exercise of reasonable care and skill (except in so far as it is appropriate to require him to warn of such a risk). In this way, at least part of the common law in this area has been "codified". Secondly, extensive provision has been made for defences,[134] including potent illegality defences[135] and claimant-intoxication defences.[136] Thirdly, restrictions have been placed on the damages that are available for personal injury. Damages for loss of earnings are capped at three times average earnings.[137] Furthermore, the discount rate[138] (a concept that has a dramatic effect on the size of awards) is set at five per cent,[139] whereas the figure in England is -0.25 per cent. An index-linked cap was put on compensation for non-pecuniary loss, and there is now no payment at all for non-pecuniary loss unless there is long-term impairment of at least 15 per cent, which cuts out many cases of the "slip and fall" or "whiplash injury" variety. If the impairment is more than 15 per cent but less than 33 per cent damages are not based on a percentage of the

---

[131] Kritzer [1991] J. Law & Soc. 400 at 422.

[132] Overviews of the Australian reforms are offered in Cane (2003) 27 M.U.L.R. 649; Luntz (2004) 35 V.U.W.L.R. 879; McDonald (2005) 27 Syd. L. Rev. 443; McDonald (2006) 14 T.L.J. 268; Underwood (2004) 12 T.L.J. 39; Goudkamp (2012) 28 J.P.N. 4.

[133] The High Court of Australia may fairly be said to have shown a pro-plaintiff inclination until the mid-90s, but that was rather reversed before the legislation: see Luntz (2001) 1 O.U.C.L.J. 95.

[134] See Goudkamp in Arvind and Steele (eds), *Tort Law and the Legislature* (2013).

[135] Civil Liability Act 2002 (NSW) ss.54-54A. See Goudkamp (2007) 29 Syd. L. Rev. 445.

[136] Civil Liability Act 2002 (NSW) s.50.

[137] Civil Liability Act 2002 (NSW) s.12.

[138] See para.23-090.

[139] Civil Liability Act 2002 (NSW) s.14.

maximum, but on a reduced sliding scale, so someone with a 25 per cent impairment gets 6.5 per cent of the maximum.

The situation in England Since around the turn of the century, there has been **1-053** much discussion in England of a supposed compensation culture and an insurance crisis.[140] Much of the debate has been conducted at a rather superficial level and exploited for political ends.[141] Following various statements in the early 2000s by politicians and media reports that England was suffering a dramatic rise in the number of claims, an important independent study reported that the rate of claiming had remained relatively stable in the period from 1997 until 2005.[142] Substantial increases in liability insurance premiums are an undeniable fact but it does not follow that they are caused by the increased cost of liability, there being many influences on the level of premiums that have nothing to do with the tort system, such as the returns that insurers earn by investing the premiums. There is also no doubt that there is a social cost in the *perception* of a litigation-conscious society in the form of restrictions on activities which would formerly have been perceived as harmless[143]—safety overkill—something which the House of Lords strove to counter in a 2003 decision.[144] The Compensation Act 2006 also contains a rather pale imitation of the New South Wales legislation in the form of s.1:

"Deterrent effect of potential liability

   1. A court considering a claim in negligence or breach of statutory duty may, in determining whether the defendant should have taken particular steps to meet a standard of care (whether by taking precautions against a risk or othe rwise), have regard to whether a requirement to take those steps might—

     (a)   prevent a desirable activity from being undertaken at all, to a particular extent or in a particular way, or

     (b)   discourage persons from undertaking functions in connection with a desirable activity."

Some may consider this to be a rather futile exercise in the sense that not only is it implicit or explicit in the current approach taken by the courts[145] but it is hardly of such strength as to discourage a court determined to go in the opposite direction (unlikely as that may be).[146]

---

[140] See Williams (2005) 25 L.S. 499; Mullender (2006) 22 J.P.N. 2; Morris (2007) 70 M.L.R. 349; Hand (2010) 37 J.L.S. 569; Goudkamp (2012) 28 J.P.N. 4; Quill and Friel (eds), *Damages and Compensation Culture* (2016).

[141] See, e.g., David Davis, Shadow Home Secretary, in *The Spectator*, 20 August 2004, confusing the personal injury problem with the Human Rights Act 1998. Some estimates of the annual cost of clinical negligence to the NHS simply take the total value of all unsettled claims in the pipeline and assume that they will all succeed at 100 per cent.

[142] Lewis, Morris and Oliphant (2006) 14 T.L.J. 158.

[143] See, e.g., *Hampstead Heath Winter Swimming Club v Corporation of London* [2005] EWHC 713 (Admin); [2005] 1 W.L.R. 2930.

[144] *Tomlinson v Congleton BC* [2003] UKHL 47; [2004] 1 A.C. 46, see paras 6-023, 10-006, 10-021.

[145] Section 1 has been mentioned in passing in a handful of cases: see, e.g., *Uren v Corporate Leisure (UK) Ltd* [2011] EWCA Civ 66 at [13]; *Sutton v Syston Rugby Football Club Ltd* [2011] EWCA Civ 1182 at [13]. The view that emerges from these decisions is that s.1 adds nothing to the common law.

[146] Fulbrook, *Outdoor Activities, Negligence and the Law* (2005) is an interesting and detailed examination of the "law in action" in the context of outdoor activities, one of the contexts in which the charge of restriction of worthwhile activities by tort law has been most prominent.

Undeterred by such arguments, Parliament has more recently enacted an even more fatuous statute, the Social Action, Responsibility and Heroism Act 2015, which is designed to deal with the compensation culture and the asserted (but entirely undocumented) effect that it was having on volunteering rates and the willingness of rescuers to come to the assistance of those in danger.[147] To a certain extent, the 2015 Act simply replicates s.1 of the Compensation Act 2006 and hence the position at common law. The statute was widely ridiculed during its passage through Parliament, and predictions that it would be ignored by the courts seem to have been borne out.

Most recently, the legislature has enacted the Civil Liability Act 2018 due to concern about whiplash claims and the inflationary effect they were having on car insurance premiums. The Act, which for the most part is not yet in force, is convoluted and cannot be examined in detail here. In brief, however, the Act caps payments in respect of whiplash injuries the effects of which do not last for more than two years, and prohibits the settlement of claims in respect of such injuries unless they are substantiated by medical evidence. The Act represents part of an ongoing drive to reduce the number of low-value claims. Although the sense of the precise way in which the Act seeks to achieve this aim is open to serious doubt, a certain amount can be said in favour of the objective itself. For example, small claims are disproportionately costly to process, and victims of relatively minor injuries are generally better able to cope with the consequences thereof than persons who suffer catastrophic harm.

---

[147] See Goudkamp (2017) 37 L.S. 577.

INFLUENCES ON TORT LAW

1.   HISTORICAL INFLUENCES

The forms of action   The law of torts did not evolve around a broad central   **2-001**
principle of liability. Rather, it grew up, like other branches of our law, behind a
screen of legal procedure.[1] Until the mid 19th century, the question which arose
when a claimant sued a defendant for some alleged injury was not "Have the
claimant's rights been infringed by the defendant?" or even "Has the defendant
broken some duty which he owed to the claimant?" but "Has the claimant any form
of action against the defendant, and, if so, what form?" If the claimant could not
fit his claim into one of the recognised forms of action, he had no legal grievance.
An action was usually commenced by a royal writ issued from the Chancery, which
in this sense signified not a court of law but a government department, one of whose
functions was the creation and issue of these writs. It was known also as the *of-
ficina brevium* which has been conveniently translated as "the writ-shop", for a
claimant could not get a writ without paying for it. For a very considerable period
of our legal history the shape of the law was no more than a classification of writs.

The distinction between trespass and case   The writs that remedied the injuries   **2-002**
which in modern times are called torts were principally the writ of trespass and the
writ of trespass on the case or "case". Trespass in common parlance now signifies
unauthorised entry on another person's land, but in law it has a wider signification.
The writ of trespass lay for injuries to land or to goods, or to the person, though
"injuries" must be read in an extended sense[2] because the tort was actionable per
se, meaning that the claimant could sue even if there had been no damage. However,

---

[1]   Regarding historical influences on the law of torts, see Baker (ed), *The Oxford History of the Laws
      of England*; Ibbetson, *A Historical Introduction to the Law of Obligations* (1999); Mitchell, *A His-
      tory of Tort Law: 1900–1950* (2015).
[2]   The sense is the Latin *iniuria*, "wrong".

trespass was limited to injuries which were direct and immediate: so it was trespass if D threw a brick at C and hit C but not if D left an unilluminated pile of bricks in the alley at the side of C house's and C stumbled over them. However, indirect and consequential injuries came to be remediable through the action on the case, though this, unlike trespass, required proof of damage. These two classes of action, "trespass" and "case", existed side by side for centuries and to them we owe most of our law of tort. There were, however, definite distinctions between these two forms of action and until the 19th century it was vital for a claimant to choose correctly between them.[3] Only after the reforms of that century had broken up the cast-iron moulds of procedure did it cease to be necessary "to canvass the niceties of the old forms of action. Remedies now depend on the substance of the right, not on whether they can be fitted into a particular framework".[4]

2-003 **The continuing significance of the forms of action** Despite the foregoing, a basic knowledge of the forms of action is still necessary not only to understand the old authorities but also to comprehend the classification of much of the modern law.[5] As Maitland famously observed: "The forms of action we have buried, but they still rule us from their graves."[6] In the course of time certain types of claim acquired more specific names, such as assault, battery, libel, slander, private nuisance, negligence and so on, but they still have their roots in the ancient categories, so that even now (although trespass and case are long gone) a lawyer might explain that the reason why a claim for negligence requires proof of damage, whereas a claim for battery does not, is that the former is (or was) an action on the case, while the latter is trespass.

2-004 **Negligence as an organising principle for tort law generally?** It was noted at the outset of this chapter that tort law did not evolve around a single comprehensive concept of wrongdoing. Can tort law as it currently stands be reduced to a central organising principle? One might get the impression from studying the modern case law that the concept of "negligence", which dominates tort law (and which dominates tort courses even more than textbooks), is such a principle. However, the reality is that the notion that the whole of the law of torts orbits the star of negligence is an over-simplification. The negligence concept does not feature, or does not feature centrally, in a range of torts, such as battery and deceit, which came into existence long before any general conception of liability for negligence, and they continue to carry some of their history with them.

There is, therefore, no doubt that we have a collection of torts rather than a single principle of liability but this does not prevent the courts creating new heads of liability to meet changing circumstances or changing perceptions of the need for protection from harm. Sometimes this may occur very suddenly, as happened in the middle of the 19th century, when the tort of inducing breach of contract was

---

3   See Prichard [1964] C.L.J. 234.
4   *Nelson v Larholt* [1948] 1 K.B. 339 at 343 per Denning J.
5   See, e.g., *Watkins v Secretary of State for the Home Department* [2006] UKHL 17; [2006] 2 A.C. 395 (misfeasance in a public office), discussed at para.8-024.
6   Maitland, *Equity* (1936), p.296. Thus the distinction between trespass to land and private nuisance still turns upon the old distinction between trespass and case. See, e.g., *Esso Petroleum Co Ltd v Southport Corp* [1956] A.C. 218.

spontaneously established;[7] on other occasions the process may involve more of a synthesis of existing principles, the culmination of an evolution rather than a revolution, as happened when the foundation of the general law of negligence was laid in 1932.[8] The modern law has seen a marked development of the law of confidence and, propelled by the Human Rights Act 1998, this has now cut loose from any strict requirement that the information should have been *imparted* in confidence by the person to whom it relates. There is a growing tendency to refer to it as "misuse of private information", though it seems not quite to have become a general basis for the protection of privacy against wrongful intrusion.[9] The predominant view has been that the law of confidence rests upon equitable principles rather than upon tort but in practical terms this is perhaps a distinction without a difference, as witness the occasional judicial reference to the "tort of breach of confidence" or the "tort of misuse of private information".[10] The traffic is, of course, not all one way: a head of tortious liability may be born, acquire a name and be cut off by other developments before it reaches its prime.[11]

The need to establish a cause of action The forms of action have long gone: for   **2-005** a century and a half there has been a more or less uniform process for starting all civil claims for damages. But it has not been in accordance with the tradition of the common law to analyse rights as something separate from the remedy given to the claimant. Accordingly, although the procedural restrictions of the forms of action have been abolished, it is still necessary for the claimant to establish a cause of action. It is not therefore correct to say that a person has a basic right not to have, for example, untruths told about himself, for he is only able to restrain the publication of such untruths if the circumstances in which they are disseminated fall within a specific tort such as passing off, malicious falsehood or defamation.[12] To some extent this basic approach has changed under the Human Rights Act 1998, pursuant to which the court must give effect to the rights and freedoms guaranteed by the European Convention on Human Rights.[13] This guarantees, for example, the rights to life, to liberty and to the enjoyment of property but the courts have relied on these to modify existing rules of tort law where necessary rather than to rewrite the whole rule book in terms of rights[14] rather than liabilities.

Pleading a cause of action It is important to realise that the various torts are not   **2-006** exclusive of one another and that there is no reason why a given set of facts should not contain the elements of several of them. The claim form which initiates a civil case must contain "a concise statement of the nature of the claim"[15] and this is later supplemented by particulars of claim which contain "a concise statement of the

---

7 *Lumley v Gye* (1853) 2 El. & Bl. 216; 118 E.R. 1083. See para.19-006.
8 *Donoghue v Stevenson* [1932] A.C. 562. See para.5-017. Of course, judges are always reluctant to admit that a completely new departure has been made.
9 See para.13-136.
10 See para.13-136.
11 This seems, for example, to have been the effect of the Protection from Harassment Act 1997 (see para.4-034) on the common law tort of harassment rather tentatively advanced in *Khorasandjian v Bush* [1993] Q.B. 727.
12 *Kingdom of Spain v Christie, Manson & Woods Ltd* [1986] 1 W.L.R. 1120 at 1129.
13 See para.2-011.
14 In *Watkins v Secretary of State for the Home Department* [2006] UKHL 17; [2006] 2 A.C. 395 the court rejected an attempt to fashion an extension of tort liability based on "constitutional rights".
15 CPR Pt.16.2(1)(a).

facts on which the claimant relies".[16] The main purpose of the exercise is to enable the opposing party to know what case is being made in sufficient detail to enable him properly to answer it.[17] The claimant does not necessarily have to specify the particular tort on which he wishes to rely, for the issue is whether the matters that he alleges "disclose a cause of action", i.e., a set of facts for which there is a legal remedy.[18] Thus, it is open to the claimant to assert that the factual situation gives rise to a basis of liability which has never before been expressly recognised. In practice, however, it is prudent, and may be essential, for the claimant to identify by name the cause of action on which he relies: judges are presumed to know the law, but they are entitled to and should receive the assistance of counsel. Furthermore, subject to the court's power to allow amendment of pleadings (probably now to be exercised less generously than in the past) no one is allowed to lead evidence of facts which he has not pleaded. If the facts alleged in the claim do not show a sustainable legal basis for the claim even if they are all proven, the defendant may apply to have the claim struck out[19] or apply for summary judgment on the ground that the claim has no reasonable prospect of success.[20] So, what is necessary to get to trial is that the facts alleged should include those essential to liability under at least one tort, without at the same time including any which are fatal to that liability. For this purpose the court is not concerned with evidence, i.e., with whether the facts alleged can be proven, but with whether the facts if proven can realistically be regarded[21] as being the possible basis of a claim.[22] However, the whole sequence of events leading up to the claimant's damage may include the essentials of more than one tort, and where this is so the position is simply that there is more than one reason why the claimant should succeed.

Put simply, therefore, it is necessary for counsel for the claimant, in settling the particulars of claim, to plead all the facts which are essential to the particular tort or torts on which he intends to rely. One is therefore bound to select from the whole complex of facts those which are relevant to the claim in point of law and this, of course, one cannot do save by reference to particular torts which are recognised (or at least which one hopes to convince the court should be recognised). Suppose that the defendant has orally stated of the claimant, a shopkeeper, that the claimant habitually sells goods which he knows to have been stolen. Here the defendant's

---

[16] CPR Pt.16.4(1)(a).

[17] *British Airways Pension Trustees Ltd v Sir Robert McAlpine & Sons Ltd* (1994) 45 Con. L.R. 1 at 4.

[18] *Letang v Cooper* [1965] 1 Q.B. 232 at 242–244, where Diplock LJ states that a "cause of action" is simply a factual situation the existence of which entitles one person to obtain from the court a remedy against another person. An alternative definition is "every fact [though not every piece of evidence] which it would be necessary for the plaintiff to prove, if traversed, in order to support his right to the judgment of the court": *Read v Brown* (1888) 22 Q.B.D. 128 at 131. See also *Black v Yates* [1992] Q.B. 526.

[19] CPR Pt.3.4.2(a). This is the successor of what in former times was known as the demurrer procedure.

[20] CPR Pt.24.2(a)(i).

[21] It is not necessary for the court to be satisfied that the claim *will* succeed as a matter of law and it is undesirable to decide complex issues of law on hypothetical facts: *Farah v British Airways Plc, The Times,* 26 January 2000.

[22] However, under CPR Pt.24, where the issue is simply whether the claimant has a real prospect of success, the defendant may seek summary judgment on the ground that the evidence available to the claimant is too weak. See *Three Rivers DC v Bank of England (No.3)* [2001] UKHL 16; [2003] 2 A.C. 1, especially the speech of Lord Hutton at [120], where the distinction is drawn between the "attack on the pleadings" point and the "no real prospects of success" point.

words prima facie fall under the tort known as "slander of title" or "malicious false-hood"[23] and also within the tort of defamation.[24] Now it is not normally an essential element of the tort of defamation that the defendant should have used the words maliciously, but this is an essential element of malicious falsehood. If, therefore, the claimant wishes to make use in argument of that tort he must allege in his pleading that the defendant acted with malice. Otherwise, even though the defendant was in fact malicious, the claimant will be precluded from proving this at the trial and so will fail to bring his case within malicious falsehood. He will thus lose the advantage of an alternative line of argument which, on the facts as they actually occurred, should have been open to him.[25] The claimant may, of course, have practical reasons for not pursuing all the causes of action available. For example, a claimant who makes claims based on two torts but loses in one of those claims may be ordered to bear the costs that the defendant incurred in connection with the unsuccessful claim. This possibility may deter a claimant who has a good claim from bringing additional claims that are borderline. In *Joyce v Sengupta*[26] a statement published about the claimant was clearly defamatory on its face but the claimant sued only for the tort of malicious falsehood because legal aid was then available for that tort but not for defamation.[27] An argument that this was an abuse of the process of the court was rejected, for[28]:

"When more than one cause of action is available to him, a plaintiff may choose which he will pursue. Usually, he pursues all available causes of action, but he is not obliged to do so. He may pursue one to the exclusion of another ... I have never heard it suggested before that a plaintiff is not entitled to proceed in this way ... [or] that he must pursue the most appropriate remedy."

2.   NEWER INFLUENCES ON ENGLISH TORT LAW

A.   The European Convention on Human Rights and the Human Rights Act

The European Convention on Human Rights   The United Kingdom was the first state to ratify the European Convention on Human Rights and Fundamental Freedoms, signed in Rome in 1950. The Convention binds its signatories to secure to citizens the rights and freedoms defined in it but does not require that a state incorporate the Convention in domestic law. A person who claims to be a victim of a violation of the Convention might, however, petition the European Court of Human Rights in Strasbourg and if the Court finds that there has been a violation of the Convention it can award the applicant monetary compensation as "just satisfaction".[29] It has no power to undo what has been done on the domestic plane

2-007

---

23   See para.13-124.
24   See para.13-001.
25   But compare *Cornwall Gardens Pte Ltd v RO Garrard & Co Ltd* [2001] EWCA Civ 699; *The Times*, 19 June 2001, where the court refused to allow the claimant to dress up what was in substance a claim for malicious falsehood as one for interference with rights by unlawful means, in order to escape the limitation period.
26   [1993] 1 W.L.R. 337.
27   See also *Spring v Guardian Assurance Plc* [1995] 2 A.C. 296 (claim for negligence as a way of sidestepping privilege blocking defamation claim) which is discussed in para.12-050.
28   *Joyce v Sengupta* [1993] 1 W.L.R. 337 at 342–343 per Nicholls VC.
29   Article 41.

(e.g., a criminal conviction or dismissal from employment) but if the state of the domestic law led to the violation or prevented any local remedy for it, the Government will generally feel obliged to correct that situation.

2-008   **The Human Rights Act generally**   The Human Rights Act 1998 was enacted to guarantee in domestic law the rights provided for in the Convention. The Act has spawned a vast literature, and it is well beyond the scope of this book to engage with that body of learning, much of which has little relevance to tort law.[30] However, it is convenient to offer some general observations regarding the Act. It should be kept in mind throughout this discussion that, strictly speaking, the Act does not "incorporate" the Convention into English law,[31] and that the rights created by the Act are domestic ones.

2-009   **The interpretation of legislation**   Under s.3 of the Act the court is required to read primary and subordinate legislation in a way compatible with Convention rights *so far as it is possible to do so*. To avoid the effect of s.3 there must be a clear indication of an intention to legislate incompatibly with the Convention.[32] In that event, the court has no power to strike down primary legislation but may (at the level of the High Court or above) make a declaration of incompatibility under s.4.[33] This has no effect on the outcome of the suit in which the issue is raised, nor does it require the Government to take remedial action, though a fast-track legislative procedure is available if it chooses to do so.[34]

2-010   **The duty of public authorities to act compatibly with Convention rights**   Perhaps of greater relevance to tort law are the provisions of the Act concerned with the acts of "public authorities". There is no comprehensive definition of a public authority in the Act. But a public authority is said to include a court or tribunal or "any person certain of whose functions are functions of a public nature".[35] The mere fact that a body has functions some of which are of a public nature is not sufficient to make it a public authority in respect of its acts that are of a private nature.[36] The basic principle is that it is unlawful for a public authority to act in a way which is incompatible with a Convention right.[37] The victim of such an unlawful act may bring proceedings in which a court "may grant such relief or remedy, or make such order, within its powers as it considers just and appropriate".[38] The relief may

---

[30]   Although see Hoffman (ed), *The Impact of the UK Human Rights Act on Private Law* (2011).

[31]   *Re McKerr* [2004] UKHL 12; [2004] 1 W.L.R. 807 at [65] per Lord Hoffmann.

[32]   See *R v A (No.2)* [2001] UKHL 25; [2002] 1 A.C. 45 at [44].

[33]   As to subordinate legislation, see Human Rights Act 1998 s.4(4).

[34]   Human Rights Act 1998 s.10 and Sch.2.

[35]   Human Rights Act 1998 s.6(3). But not Parliament.

[36]   Human Rights Act 1998 s.6(5). For discussion see *Aston Cantlow PCC v Wallbank* [2003] UKHL 37; [2004] 1 A.C. 546. Regarding the difference between the public and private acts of a body consider, e.g., a security firm which: (1) operates a prison under contract with the state; and (2) guards private premises: *Quaquah v Group 4 Securities Ltd (No.2)* [2003] EWHC 1504 (QB); *The Times,* 27 June 2001.

[37]   Convention rights are those set out in arts.2-12 and 14 of the Convention and certain rights governed by the First and Sixth Protocols. A fundamental distinction is drawn between rights that are absolute (such as art.3, which secures the right not to be subjected to torture or degrading treatment or punishment) and qualified rights (such as art.8, which recognises a right to privacy but which permits interference with that right in certain circumstances).

[38]   Human Rights Act 1998 s.8(1).

include an award of damages but only if, taking account of all the circumstances of the case (including any other relief granted), such an award "is necessary to afford just satisfaction to the person in whose favour it is made".[39] The court is directed, on the issue of damages, to have regard to the principles applied by the European Court of Human Rights, and that body has quite frequently considered the vindication of the right as sufficient satisfaction.[40]

The position of courts Although a court is a public authority for the purposes of the Act, a claim in respect of a judicial act is only to be brought by way of appeal (or in some cases judicial review) and damages may not be awarded in respect of judicial acts done in good faith except with regard to wrongful detention under art.5(5) of the Convention.[41] However, that takes us to the central area of difficulty in mapping the relationship of the Act, the Convention and the common law of tort. Although the act of a court may not be subject to an award of damages except as set out above, because a court is a public authority it must not act in a way that is incompatible with the Convention. Does that mean that the courts, in declaring and applying the common law, are required to proceed in a way which is compatible with the rights that are recognised by the Convention?[42] Or, is it enough that they simply give effect to those rights by means of the mechanisms created by the Act? The first approach would have very significant implications: it would make the common law a subsidiary regime shaped by the Convention; and, since it is plain that the international obligations under the Convention may extend to creating and implementing a legal regime which protects the right in question against acts in the private sphere,[43] it would have the potential to create new causes of action against private persons, even though the Act applies only to public authorities. The broad approach would arguably be inconsistent with the doctrine of precedent, since it would give a trial judge a "trump card" (at least where the matter in question had not been considered by a higher court in the context of the Convention) which would enable him to escape otherwise binding decisions. The courts have been reluctant to supply clear guidance on the precise effect of the Act on the development of the common law. **2-011**

Overlap between Convention rights and common law rights There is a considerable overlap between the rights guaranteed by the Convention and the rights recognised by the common law. To a large extent, therefore, the existing common law fulfils the Convention requirements without more—the Convention, after all, is primarily an international instrument designed to ensure compliance by states with basic standards of protection and it would be surprising if none of them had achieved that in any area before the Convention. For example, art.5.2 provides: "Everyone who is arrested shall be informed promptly, in a language which he understands, of the reason for his arrest and of any charge against him." At com- **2-012**

---

39 Human Rights Act 1998 s.8(3).
40 *R. (on the application of Greenfield) v Secretary of State for the Home Dept* [2005] UKHL 14; [2005] 1 W.L.R. 673; *Gillan v United Kingdom* [2010] ECHR 4158/05; (2010) 50 E.H.R.R. 1105. See, generally, *Damages under the Human Rights Act 1998* Law Com. No.266 (2000).
41 Human Rights Act 1998 s.9.
42 On this point see Young in Hoffman (ed), *The Impact of the UK Human Rights Act on Private Law* (2011), p.16.
43 *Airey v Ireland* (1979) 2 E.H.R.R. 305; *X v Netherlands* (1985) 8 E.H.R.R. 235; *Johnston v Ireland* (1986) 9 E.H.R.R. 203.

mon law (and under the Police and Criminal Evidence Act 1984) a person arrested has a similar right to be informed of the reason for his arrest[44] and, if he is not, he has a claim for the tort of false imprisonment, which may lead to the award of substantial damages. However, some infringements of the Convention rights by a public body would not be a tort under the common law. For example, under art.8.1 everyone has the "right to respect for his private and family life, his home and his correspondence".[45] Now although the English common law of torts has always protected privacy in various indirect ways[46] and the law of confidence has been developed into a wrong of misuse of private information, which covers much of the ground, there is no general tort of infringement of privacy under that name. However, where the defendant is a public authority there is, as has just been discussed, the possibility of liability in damages under the Act. It would be impracticable in this book to provide a full account of the various Convention rights but it will be necessary to refer to them when they overlap with or qualify the common law.

2-013 **Restriction of common law rights by the Convention** Sometimes a Convention right does not so much create a cause of action as militate against an existing liability at common law—for example, the right of freedom of expression under art.10 has at least the potential to restrict the ability of the law to impose liability for defamation. In such a situation the court really has no choice but to alter the common law to make it compatible with the Convention. In one case a judge declined, as a result of art.10, to apply the common law rule of strict liability in "mistaken identity" libel cases even though that rule was supported by decisions of the House of Lords before the Act (and indeed before the Convention).[47]

2-014 **Parallel regimes** Where the Convention protects a right which is not protected by the common law of tort the general tendency since the Human Rights Act 1998 has been to take the line that there may be two parallel regimes governing the situation and the court's duty not to act inconsistently with the Convention is fulfilled by its giving a remedy, via the Act, for the infringement of the Convention right itself, even if one is denied under the common law. In *Wainwright v Home Office*,[48] where the events took place before the Act, the House of Lords declined to create a "high level" general tort of invasion of privacy, despite art.8, which provides for a right to private and family life. Lord Hoffmann remarked that a[49]:

> "finding that there was a breach of article 8 will only demonstrate that there was a gap in the English remedies for invasion of privacy which has since been filled by sections 6 and 7 of the 1998 Act. It does not require that the courts should provide an alternative remedy which distorts the principles of the common law."

---

44 See para.26-056.
45 Subject to art.8.2, which allows lawful interference which is necessary in a democratic society for national security, the prevention of crime, etc.
46 See para.13-136.
47 *O'Shea v MGN Ltd* [2001] E.M.L.R. 40, see para.13-016.
48 [2003] UKHL 53; [2004] 2 A.C. 406.
49 [2003] UKHL 53; [2004] 2 A.C. 406 at [52].

Actions available under the Human Rights Act do not necessarily mirror com- 2-015
mon law rights In *Smith v Chief Constable of Sussex Police*[50] the House of Lords
held that the common law rule that the police owed no duty of care to protect
individuals from crime[51] remained intact notwithstanding the positive duty in art.2
of the Convention to protect life. This reveals that the duties created by art.2 are
not simply a mirror image of the duties created by the tort of negligence. The
primary focus of art.2 is upon the need for public authorities to have suitable
systems in place to protect citizens—the provision of a criminal law and police
services, the assessment of detained persons for suicide risk and so on.[52] Even if
these requirements are fulfilled there may be an "operational" duty to take further
steps to protect an individual but then the Strasbourg jurisprudence on art.2 requires
the public authority to have reason to know of a "real and immediate risk" to life
and while this cannot be equated with "gross negligence" it is nonetheless a
stringent test and it should not be assumed that it is satisfied in every case where,
a duty of care being established, there would be negligence at common law.[53] Thus,
a public hospital is a "public authority" for the purposes of the Act and it must take
steps to secure competent staff and adequate equipment and safety systems, but
there is no liability under art.2 for every negligent treatment error which would lead
to liability at common law.[54]

B. A European Tort Law?

The search for Europe-wide principles Private law is generally outside the 2-016
competence of the European Union, though certain of its functions, most notably
that of consumer protection, have produced pockets of "European tort law" on matters like product liability[55] and unfair contract terms. However, in the last 20 years
there has been a remarkable amount of academic activity directed towards framing Europe-wide principles of private law. A "European Group on Tort Law"
produced a series of surveys of particular aspects of tort law which culminated in
a volume of *Principles of European Tort Law*.[56] A study group on a European Civil
Code was active on a broader front in preparing principles of private law and
combined with a number of other groups to produce in 2008 *Principles, Definitions and Model Rules of European Private Law*, the "Draft Common Frame of
Reference" (DCFR). The DCFR is an "enigmatic concept".[57] It declares itself to be
"an academic, not a politically authorised text"[58] but the European Parliament has
spoken in favour of a European Civil Code[59] and the Commission has envisaged a
common frame of reference being used as a "legislator's toolbox", at least in the
area of consumer law (though in that case it is difficult to see why it contains mate-

---

50   [2008] UKHL 50; [2009] A.C. 225.
51   See further *Michael v Chief Constable of South Wales* [2015] UKSC 2; [2015] A.C. 1732 at [127]–
     [128].
52   *Mitchell v Glasgow CC* [2009] UKHL 11; [2009] A.C. 874 at [66].
53   *Van Colle v Chief Constable of Hertfordshire Police* [2008] UKHL 50; [2009] A.C. 225; *Savage v
     South Essex Partnership NHS Foundation Trust* [2008] UKHL 74; [2009] A.C. 681.
54   *Savage v South Essex Partnership NHS Foundation Trust* [2008] UKHL 74; [2009] 1 A.C. 681.
55   See Ch.11.
56   European Group on Tort Law, *Principles of European Tort Law* (2005).
57   Eidenmüller, Faust, Grigoleit, Jansen, Wagner and Zimmermann (2008) 28 O.J.L.S. 659 at 661.
58   Introduction, para.4.
59   Resolution of May 1989.

rial on general tort law, commercial agency and unjust enrichment). People have also spoken of an "optional civil code" but, while that idea has real content in relation to contracts, the option idea would seem rather unsuitable to tort.

2-017 **Obstacles to unification** It is a truism of comparative law that the results in different systems are often rather similar although the routes by which they are reached may be different. Let us take the provisions from the DCFR and the *Principles of European Tort Law* which deal with a broadly similar issue.

> "DCFR:
> VI.–2:101 Meaning of legally relevant damage
>
> (1) Loss, whether economic or non-economic, or injury is legally relevant damage if:
> (a) one of the following rules of this Chapter so provides;
> (b) the loss or injury results from a violation of a right otherwise conferred by the law; or
> (c) the loss or injury results from a violation of an interest worthy of legal protection.
> (2) In any case covered only by sub-paragraphs (b) or (c) of paragraph (1) loss or injury constitutes legally relevant damage only if it would be fair and reasonable for there to be a right to reparation …
> (3) In considering whether it would be fair and reasonable for there to be a right to reparation … regard is to be had to the ground of accountability, to the nature and proximity of the damage …, to the reasonable expectations of the person who suffers … the damage, and to considerations of public policy."

> "*Principles of European Tort Law*:
> Art. 2:102. Protected interests
>
> (1) The scope of protection of an interest depends on its nature; the higher its value, the precision of its definition and its obviousness, the more extensive is its protection.
> (2) Life, bodily or mental integrity, human dignity and liberty enjoy the most extensive protection.
> (3) Extensive protection is granted to property rights, including those in intangible property.
> (4) Protection of pure economic interests or contractual relationships may be more limited in scope. In such cases, due regard must be had especially to the proximity between the actor and the endangered person, or to the fact that the actor is aware of the fact that he will cause damage even though his interests are necessarily valued lower than those of the victim.
> (5) The scope of protection may also be affected by the nature of liability, so that an interest may receive more extensive protection against intentional harm than in other cases.
> (6) In determining the scope of protection, the interests of the actor, especially in liberty of action and in exercising his rights, as well as public interests also have to be taken into consideration."

Those who progress through this book will be able to recognise, even if "through a glass darkly", a good deal of this in current English tort law, in particular the approach to the duty of care and the differing extent of protection of certain interests according to whether we are dealing with negligent or intentional conduct. And, while there are of course provisions in both drafts which are simply incompatible with current English law, some of those incompatibilities (most obviously the absence in England of strict liability for motor accidents) are really political rather than issues of legal doctrine. Nor are the incompatibilities a case of "English law v the Rest". The idea that "the civil law" is some monolithic unity is far from the truth: thus acceptance of either set of proposals would, for example, require German law to take a fundamentally different approach from that which it does at present to liability for the conduct of employees and neither draft contains anything resembling the distinctive French doctrine of liability for damage done by things. A more important question is whether, even if such substantive problems could be overcome, any "unification" of tort law in Europe is at all feasible. The legal cultures are very different even if they all embrace much the same principles at the highest level of abstraction. For example, in English civil cases the standard of proof is on a balance of probabilities: if something is shown to be just more likely than not it is treated as having been conclusively established for most purposes. In some continental systems on the other hand the damage must be proved with "certainty".[60] While it would be wrong to equate this with the "beyond a reasonable doubt" test of English criminal law, it does seem more onerous than the balance of probability standard. That has obvious implications for the approach the particular system will take to the issue of claims based on "loss of a chance". One must also not forget the considerable uncertainty which would result from unification, and the massive burden of re-education, not to mention the natural human fondness for the familiar. Perhaps most important of all is the fact that even if everyone adopted the same text, how would one prevent the system simply breaking up very quickly by divergences in local interpretation? In a few very narrow areas of private law (principally matters of jurisdiction) the European Court of Justice acts as the ultimate appellate court for an "autonomous" European law, but it is inconceivable that we could have a Supreme Court of Private Law for the whole of Europe or that we could expect local courts to keep up with legal developments in all the other countries.

The prospect of unification It seems most unlikely that there will be wholesale   **2-018**
unification or harmonisation of private law in the foreseeable future (even of the law of contract, which might appear more desirable and which would probably be a good deal easier to achieve than in the case of tort). However, it must also be borne in mind that for a century the English courts have been "comparativists" in the sense that they have been willing to look at developments in other common law countries and in the last 20 years at the highest level they have shown an increasing inclination to look at civil law systems.[61] So it is not inconceivable that the English courts might make "voluntary" use of things like the DCFR. There is, however, little evidence to date to suggest that they will do so, and the UK's departure from the EU means that the influence of European developments on our law is more likely to decrease, rather than increase, in the future.

---

[60] Thus, art.2:105 of the *Principles of European Tort Law* provides that damage "must be proved according to normal [national] procedural standards".
[61] Three well-known examples are *Henderson v Merrett Syndicates Ltd* [1995] 2 A.C. 145, *White v Jones* [1995] 2 A.C. 207 and *Fairchild v Glenhaven Funeral Services Ltd* [2002] UKHL 22; [2003] 1 A.C. 32.

3. STRUCTURE OF THE BOOK

2-019   Tort theorists have long debated how torts should be categorised. By and large, two schemas vie for acceptance. One arranges torts according to the different forms of liability. This arrangement, which was famously suggested by Oliver Wendell Holmes,[62] yields the following threefold classification: torts that require proof of a state of mind (generally intention), torts that are susceptible to commission by negligence and torts that impose liability regardless of whether or not the defendant is at fault. The other schema organises torts in terms of the interests that they protect.[63] So systematised, torts are herded together according to whether they protect interests in bodily integrity, real and personal property, reputation, economic relations and so on.[64] The order followed in the succeeding chapters of this book adheres strictly to neither course but has as its principal aim no more than the avoidance, so far as reasonably possible, of repetition and of references forward to later chapters. The object is comprehensibility and the convenience of the reader who wants to begin at the beginning and go on to the end. The result is not, therefore, "scientific". If it is convenient, that is enough.

4. TORTS NOT TREATED IN THIS BOOK

2-020   There are some wrongs which are certainly torts but which are outside the scope of a textbook on tort law. First, there are those matters which are commonly treated as specialised legal subjects in their own right. Actions for infringement of the intellectual property rights of copyright, patents, and trademarks are actions in tort (albeit statutory) but these matters are too specialised and complex for inclusion in a book of this kind and the statutory causes of action for wrongful discrimination are best looked at in the context of employment law, where they most commonly arise.[65] Then there is a range of minor tort causes of action based on the common law.[66] For example, there is a group of wrongs concerned with interference with a franchise—a royal privilege, or branch of the Queen's prerogative, subsisting in the hands of a subject.[67] The forms of it are various, but examples are the franchise of a number of persons to be incorporated and subsist as a body politic; franchises to have waifs, wrecks, strays, royal fish; and franchises to hold markets or fairs, and to take tolls for bridges and ferries.[68] Sometimes Parliament may sweep away whole areas of tort law, as happened with the group of torts which related to interference

---

[62]   This schema was proposed in an anonymous article ((1873) 7 Am. L. Rev. 652). Holmes is generally credited as the author.

[63]   This approach is usually associated with Pollock: see Pollock, *The Law of Torts* (1887), pp.6–12. It is endorsed in Stevens, *Torts and Rights* (2007), Ch.13. See also Descheemaeker, *The Division of Wrongs* (2009).

[64]   For analysis of these and other ways of classifying torts, see Keeton, Dobbs, Keeton and Owen (eds), *Prosser and Keeton on Torts*, 5th edn (1984), pp.31–33. Several commentators have expressed doubts about the usefulness of categorising torts: see, e.g., Friedman, *The Law of Torts in Canada*, 2nd edn (2002), p.26.

[65]   But note that these may overlap on the facts with common law claims: see *Farah v MPC* [1998] Q.B. 65 at 69.

[66]   See Rudden (1991–92) 6–7 Tulane Civ. L.F. 105.

[67]   Blackstone, Comm, ii, p.37.

[68]   Some of this is by no means obsolete, see, e.g., *Iveagh v Martin* [1961] 1 Q.B. 232; *Wyld v Silver* [1963] 1 Q.B. 169; *Sevenoaks DC v Patullo & Vinson Ltd* [1984] Ch. 211.

with family relationships.[69] Others may be preserved like legal fossils, the social circumstances which underlay them having passed away, for the time being at least. An example is usurpation of a public office.

---

[69] Law Reform (Miscellaneous Provisions) Act 1970 ss.4–15; Administration of Justice Act 1982 s.2.

CHAPTER 3

FOUNDATIONAL CONCEPTS

Introduction Some torts require proof of fault, which means acting with a   **3-001**
particular state of mind (usually with an intention to bring about a particular result)
or failing to take as much care as the reasonable person would have taken
(negligence). Other torts impose strict liability. In the case of strict liability torts,
proof of fault on the part of the defendant is not required. These three concepts—
intention, negligence and strict liability—are regularly encountered throughout this
book. They are foundational ideas in the law of torts and are regularly used, in
conjunction with certain other concepts, as "building blocks" of torts.[1] Accordingly, it is useful to explore them alongside each other before progressing further.
To understand properly these concepts, it is necessary to distinguish them from the
notions of motive and malice, and so a few words will also be said about those
ideas. We begin, however, by considering what is arguably the most basic requirement of liability in tort, i.e., voluntariness.

1. VOLITION

Volition Criminal law scholars generally agree that liability in that domain   **3-002**
requires, separately from any type of fault element that may form part of an offence in question, that the defendant has engaged in volitional conduct (this requirement is often referred to as a "voluntariness" requirement, or a requirement that
there be a "voluntary act").[2] Although the matter has not enjoyed the attention that
it deserves in the tort setting, it appears that liability in tort also depends upon
volition. The basic idea here is that unless the defendant acted, the defendant's
agency is not implicated with the result that there is nothing on which liability can
properly be affixed. Thus, the necessary volition will be absent, and a defendant will
not incur liability in tort if, for example, he injures the claimant as a result of a reflex

---

[1] For further analysis, see Cane, *The Anatomy of Tort Law* (1997), Ch.2.
[2] It is debatable whether need for a "voluntary act" is one requirement or two. For discussion, see Hart,
   Punishment and Responsibility, 2nd edn (2008), p.109.

action, or because a third party grabs the defendant's arm and uses it to strike the claimant, or another person or a gust of wind pushes the defendant onto the claimant's land,[3] or the defendant injured the claimant while thrashing about as a result of being attacked by a swarm of bees.[4] Where volition is absent, the claimant will often be unable to prove that the defendant was at fault, and that fact will prevent liability from arising if the claimant sues in a tort that requires proof of fault. However, it is important to appreciate that there is a fundamental difference between denying that the defendant was at fault and denying volition on the part of the defendant, and the fact that a lack of volition can undermine both a fault requirement and the requirement of volition should not be permitted to obscure that distinction.

3-003   **Exceptions**   A defendant's conduct will not be treated as lacking in volition simply because the defendant's mental functioning was impaired in some way (that is so even where the mental deficit concerned constitutes insanity since any other rule would be difficult to square with the fact that insanity is not a defence to liability in tort).[5] Nor will a defendant be regarded as lacking in volition if he knew or ought to have realised that there was a risk that he would be incapacitated and lose control over his behaviour. Thus, a defendant who is rendered unconscious while driving a car and who collides with the claimant pedestrian as a result will not be able to avoid liability if he was aware or should have known that he might fall unconscious but decided to drive anyway.[6] In one sense, of course, this is not truly an exception to the requirement of volition as the defendant's agency is implicated on account of the volitional conduct that is involved in driving in the first place.

2. INTENTION

3-004   **Intention is inferred from conduct**   Some torts require proof that the defendant acted with a particular intention. It is, of course, impossible for the law to do more than to infer a person's intention, or indeed any other mental state, from his conduct. Intention is simply not amenable to direct proof. Centuries ago, Brian CJ said "[i]t is common knowledge that the thought of man shall not be tried, for the Devil himself knoweth not the thought of man".[7] It is true that Bowen LJ in 1885 said that "the state of a man's mind is as much a fact as the state of his digestion".[8] However, there is no contradiction in these dicta. Brian CJ's point was merely that no one can know for sure what passes in the mind of another person. Brian CJ would certainly not have dissented from the proposition that what a person thinks is a question fact which must be deduced from what he says and does, and that is all that Bowen LJ meant.

3-005   **Intention in general terms**   It is generally accepted that a person intends to bring about a given consequence if it is his goal to cause it, but beyond that it is prob-

---

3   *Network Rail Infrastructure Ltd v Conarken Group Ltd* [2010] EWHC 1852 (TCC) at [65]. The third party may be liable for trespass to land: *Smith v Stone* (1647) Style 65; 82 E.R. 533.

4   *Kay v Butterworth* (1945) 61 T.L.R. 452 at 453.

5   See para.25-038.

6   e.g., *C (a child) v Burcombe* [2003] C.L.Y. 3030 (driver who ignored doctor's advice and suffered heart attack held liable).

7   *Year Book Pasch.* 17 Edw. 4, fol. 2, pl. 2.

8   *Edgington v Fitzmaurice* (1885) 29 Ch. D. 459 at 483.

ably not possible to lay down any universal definition of intention for the purposes of tort law. In crime, the law is that the trier of fact is entitled (but not, it seems, required) to infer intention where the defendant was aware that the harm was "virtually certain" to result from his act.[9] It is unclear whether tort law adopts a similar rule. It is, however, plain that the mere fact that a defendant foresees a given result does not mean that he intends it. Although the concepts of foreseeability and intention are related to each other, there is a wide gulf between foreseeing the risk that a given outcome may materialise and intending to bring about that outcome.[10]

Intention is an under-analysed concept in tort law   Whereas scholars have spent   **3-006**
much time exploring the concept of intention in the context of the criminal law,[11] there has been much less discussion of intention in the tort setting.[12] There are probably several reasons for this. First, actions in tort against persons who intend to cause harm are far less common than claims that are based on negligence. This is partly because it is often not worth suing intentional wrongdoers, who will usually be without relevant insurance cover. Secondly, even where a defendant has intentionally caused harm, the claimant may sometimes be able to establish liability in the tort of negligence.[13] This reduces the need for the courts to grapple with the concept of intention. Thirdly, intention is not an element of many torts and, even when intention is needed, tort law often only requires that the initial interference with the claimant's rights be intended and does not insist that the defendant intend the consequences of that interference. For instance, if A strikes B he will be liable for all of the consequences of that act regardless of whether those consequences were intended.[14] As Hart and Honoré put it, "[i]t is generally agreed that when a defendant is liable because he has intentionally done harm, his liability is not restricted to the harm intended".[15] Indeed, the defendant is liable for the greater harm even if it is the result of some unusual susceptibility of the claimant, a principle developed primarily in the context of negligence[16] but applying with even more force to intentional wrongdoers.[17]

The concept of intention to relation to specific torts   The concept of intention   **3-007**
has been given a specific definition in relation to particular causes of action. In one tort, conspiracy to injure, intention has the very narrow meaning of single-minded purpose to do harm, so that the defendant does not "intend" even what he foresees as inevitable if his purpose is to advance his own interests.[18] Other torts in the area

---

9   *R. v Woollin* [1999] 1 A.C. 82.
10   "The mere fact that X can foresee that an event might happen in the future does not mean that X intended that possibility to eventuate": *Kalma v African Minerals Ltd* [2020] EWCA Civ 144 at [85] per Coulson LJ.
11   See, e.g., Duff, *Intention, Agency and Criminal Liability* (1990).
12   But see Finnis in Owen (ed), *Philosophical Foundations of Tort Law* (1995); Cane (2000) 20 O.J.L.S. 533; Hylton (2010) 44 Val. U.L. Rev. 1217.
13   See para.3-012.
14   *Bettel v Yim* (1978) 20 O.R. (2d) 617; *Wainwright v Home Office* [2001] EWCA Civ 2081; [2002] Q.B. 1334 at [69] (on appeal [2003] UKHL 53; [2004] 2 A.C. 406).
15   Hart and Honoré, *Causation in the Law* (1959), p.235.
16   See para.7-066.
17   *Allan v New Mount Sinai Hospital* (1980) 109 D.L.R. (3d) 634; *Restatement (Third) of Torts: Liability for Physical and Emotional Harm*, §33(a) ("An actor who intentionally causes harm is subject to liability for that harm even if it was unlikely to occur").
18   See para.19-036.

of unlawful interference with economic interests require either that very narrow "purpose" intention or that the defendant acts so as to cause harm to the claimant as the means to some other end which it is his purpose to achieve: the claimant must therefore be the "target" of the defendant's actions.[19] In the context of trespass to land it has been said that indifference to a risk that trespass will occur by animals in the defendant's charge amounts to intention[20] and it is thought that the same approach should be taken in all the trespass torts: if D throws his coffee dregs out of the window of his office, knowing that others may be passing, that should be trespass if anyone is hit, whether the street is so crowded that it is a virtual certainty or is comparatively unfrequented.[21] To take another example, consider the case of someone who places a bomb for political reasons; he may give a warning on the basis of which the emergency services may be expected to act and he may not "intend" personal injury in the sense of desiring it; but he can hardly deny that he appreciates the real risk of something going wrong, and that will be enough for him to be held liable in the tort of trespass to the person if the risk materialises.[22]

3-008 **Intention and volition**   Certain torts are often referred to as being "intentional torts", such as trespass to land. It is important that this terminology does not lead one into error. Torts such as trespass to land are torts of strict liability. They do not require proof that the defendant intended (for example) to cause the claimant to suffer damage. The reason why torts such as trespass to land are sometimes referred to as "intentional torts" is simply to underscore that the defendant must have deliberately engaged in the physical movements that are involved in their commission. Thus, and to continue our illustration involving trespass to land, the defendant must have consciously placed himself onto the claimant's land[23] (although, being a strict liability tort, there is no requirement for the defendant to have known or ought to have known that the land was the claimant's).[24] Accordingly, the "intention" requirement in torts such as trespass to land adds nothing to the volition requirement that has been discussed above.

3-009 **Recklessness**   The example given in the previous paragraph of a person who places a bomb involves what criminal lawyers would refer to as "recklessness",[25] that is to say, the wrongdoer is subjectively aware of the risk he is taking. Whereas criminal lawyers distinguish between intention and recklessness (a person who is merely reckless with respect to the risk of death or grievous bodily harm is not, for example, liable for murder if death results), tort lawyers generally do not,[26] and so in tort the concept of intention is usually regarded as encompassing recklessness.[27] Further, where recklessness as to consequences suffices to give rise to liability in

---

19   See para.19-025.
20   *League Against Cruel Sports v Scott* [1986] Q.B. 240 at 252.
21   *Bici v Ministry of Defence* [2004] EWHC 786 (QB).
22   *Breslin v McKenna* [2009] NIQB 50.
23   See para.14-001.
24   See para.14-001.
25   The leading case is *R v G* [2003] UKHL 50; [2004] 1 A.C. 1034.
26   For discussion, see Cane (2000) 20 O.J.L.S. 533. An exception concerns the tort in *Wilkinson v Downton*: see para.4-031.
27   Though using "intention" to embrace recklessness may be convenient it is open to criticism as being wider than the ordinary usage. As Finnis points out, lecturers know that what they say will inevitably confuse some of their audience, but it would be strange to say that they intend to do so: Finnis in Owen (ed), *Philosophical Foundations of Tort Law* (1995), p.229.

tort, so too will recklessness as to circumstances. Thus, the tort of misfeasance in a public office is committed when a public officer acts knowingly outside the scope of his powers with the intention that the claimant will thereby be injured or if he is recklessly indifferent to the legality of his acts and the damage he may inflict on the claimant.[28] Although recklessness is sometimes described as a state of mind and as subjective form of fault, this is a half-truth. In reality, there is an important objective dimension to the concept of recklessness, since a defendant will be reckless only where the risk of damage was one that was unjustifiable for the defendant to take. Thus, while a cardiologist may foresee that a given procedure may involve the risk of death, that bare mental state does not mean that he was reckless in relation to that risk.

3. NEGLIGENCE

Negligence is both a tort and a type of fault The word "negligence" has two meanings in the law of torts and significant confusion has sometimes resulted from a failure to distinguish between the two senses in which the term is used. First, "negligence" is an independent tort. Secondly, "negligence" is a type of fault. The difference between these two senses in which the term "negligence" is used is made more difficult to understand than it may otherwise be on account of the fact that the tort of negligence has as one of its elements negligence in the sense of fault. In this chapter, the concern is with negligence in the second sense, and the focus will be on distinguishing it from intention.

3-010

Negligence as a form of fault is a type of conduct Negligence in the sense of a species of fault refers to a failure to take as much care as the hypothetical reasonable person in the defendant's position would have taken in the circumstances. It is, in other words, a falling short of the standard of care set by the reasonable person. The process of determining whether the defendant was negligent involves, therefore, comparing the defendant's conduct with that of the reasonable person. It is important to note that this means that negligence is a type of conduct rather than a state of mind.[29] Further, it is not required that a defendant be inadvertent (i.e., have a blank mind) with respect to a particular risk of injury in order to be negligent in relation to that risk. On the contrary, people who consciously run risks will often be negligent with respect to those risks. An illustration of advertent risk-taking constituting negligence can be found in the foundational case of *Vaughan v Menlove*,[30] where the defendant had been warned that his haystack was likely to overheat and catch fire, and that the fire might then spread to his neighbour's land. The defendant said that he would "chance it" and he was found to have been negligent when the haystack did indeed ignite and the fire spread.

3-011

---

[28] *Three Rivers DC v Bank of England (No.3)* [2001] UKHL 16; [2003] 2 A.C. 1. See also *White v White* [2001] UKHL 9; [2001] 1 W.L.R. 481. A requirement that a person "know" something will generally be satisfied if he suspects that it is so but takes the attitude that he will not ask further because he would rather not know: *Digicel (St Lucia) Ltd v Cable & Wireless Plc* [2010] EWHC 774 (Ch) Annex 1 at [88] per Morgan J ("knowledge includes "shut-eye" knowledge or wilful blindness").

[29] Mental and conduct theories of negligence are compared in Goudkamp (2004) 28 M.U.L.R 343, 349–351.

[30] (1837) 3 Bing N.C. 468; 132 E.R. 490.

3-012 **Overlap between negligence and intention** The concept of negligence overlaps with that of intention since it is perfectly possible for a defendant who acts intentionally also to be negligent. Provided that the defendant behaves with less care than the reasonable person would have exercised, the defendant will be negligent, and that is so irrespective of whether the defendant intended to cause a particular result. For example, if C entrusts D to care for C's property and D intentionally destroys it, D will also be regarded as negligent, since by destroying the property he will have acted with less care with respect to it than the reasonable person in his position would have exercised.[31]

3-013 **"Reasonable" and the "reasonable person"** It is convenient to provide an explanation of the terms "reasonable" and "reasonable person". They recur so frequently in the law of tort, and indeed in every branch of the law, that their meaning must be grasped at the outset. Negligence as a species of fault is synonymous with acting unreasonably, and the question of whether a person has acted unreasonably is determined by reference to the concept of the reasonable person. Acting unreasonably means acting other than as the reasonable person would have acted. The reasonable person is, of course, an abstraction. Lord Bowen visualised the reasonable person as "the man on the Clapham omnibus".[32] An American writer said that the reasonable person is "the man who takes the magazines home, and in the evening pushes the lawn-mower in his shirt sleeves".[33] It will be noticed that the two passages that have just been quoted refer to the "reasonable man". Until relatively recently, the tendency of the courts and writers was to speak of the "reasonable man" rather than the "reasonable person". Although unfortunate, these labelling practices were of no importance as a matter of legal principle. The norm today is to speak of the "reasonable person".

3-014 **Degrees of negligence** For the purposes of determining whether the defendant is guilty of negligence, it is irrelevant whether the defendant fell well below the standard of the reasonable person or just short of it[34]: the defendant has either reached a single required standard or he has not.[35] However, the gravity of the defendant's negligence can be relevant in various other ways. For example, it can be material where contributory negligence or contribution is in issue. This is because, in these instances, responsibility for an outcome must be apportioned between two actors (either claimant and wrongdoer, or two wrongdoers), and one consideration to be taken into account in that apportionment is their relative blameworthiness.

---

[31] A prominent illustration of intentional conduct constituting (contributory) negligence is found in *Reeves v Commissioner of Police of the Metropolis* [2000] 1 A.C. 360 (suicide by prisoner).

[32] Attributed to Lord Bowen in *McQuire v Western Morning News Co Ltd* [1903] 2 K.B. 100 at 109.

[33] Cited by Greer LJ in *Hall v Brooklands Auto Racing Club* [1933] 1 K.B. 205 at 224.

[34] See Nolan (2013) 72 C.L.J. 651, 672–687.

[35] "Generally speaking in civil cases 'gross' negligence has no more effect that [sic] negligence without an opprobrious epithet": *Caswell v Powell Duffryn Associated Collieries Ltd* [1940] A.C. 152 at 175 per Lord Wright. To similar effect, see *Wilson v Brett* (1843) 11 M. & W. 113 at 116; 152 E.R. 737 at 739.

4. STRICT LIABILITY

Strict liability is liability regardless of fault Some torts lack a fault element, **3-015**
such as intention or negligence, and, accordingly, a defendant may incur liability
for these torts irrespective of whether he was at fault.[36] Such torts impose strict
liability. It is important to note that strict liability simply means liability regardless of whether the defendant is at fault where the idea of fault is understood in a
technical legal sense as referring to concepts such as intention or negligence. Strict
liability torts do not require proof that the defendant was not at fault and, hence, it
is technically incorrect to say that strict liability is liability without fault. No tort
requires proof that the defendant was not at fault. Very often, a defendant who is
held strictly liable will in fact be at fault, but the claimant is not required to establish
fault on the part of the defendant in order to make out his cause of action. Nor can
a defendant prevent the elements of a strict liability tort from being satisfied by
establishing that he was not at fault. Put simply, in the case of strict liability torts,
the issue of fault is simply irrelevant.

Overlap between fault liability and strict liability Judges and tort scholars often **3-016**
refer to any given tort as being one of fault liability or one of strict liability.
However, it is not possible sharply to distinguish between torts in this way since it
is perfectly possible and, indeed, common for a given tort to be based on both fault
liability and strict liability.[37] A good example is defamation. Defamation, as we will
see below,[38] requires, relevantly, that D publish a defamatory statement that refers
to C. The need for the statement to refer to C, exceptions aside, is not paired with
a fault requirement. Accordingly, if the reference element of the tort is satisfied, it
is irrelevant for the purposes of liability whether D intended to refer to C or was
negligent with respect to the risk that the statement referred to C. In this (and other
ways that will be discussed later) defamation imposes strict liability. However, in
other respects defamation is concerned with whether the defendant was at fault, for
example, in connection with the publication requirement. For instance, if D's
notebook in which he had written remarks defamatory of C is taken and read by a
third party, D will not be liable unless he intended the third party to take his
notebook, or was negligent as to the risk that this would happen. Attempts to draw
a bright line between torts of fault liability and strict liability can be misleading for
other reasons. For example, torts whose elements are insensitive or largely insensitive to questions of fault often have a wide array of defences that are very much
concerned with whether the defendant was at fault. Accordingly, in some cases the
only difference between fault liability and strict liability relates to the party who carries the burden of proving or disproving fault.

---

[36] For discussion of the justifiability of strict liability in the tort context, see Honoré (1998) 104 L.Q.R.
530; Gardner in Austin and Klimchuk (eds), *Private Law and the Rule of Law* (2014).
[37] For reservations regarding the distinction between fault liability and strict liability, see Goldberg and
Zipursky (2016) 85 Fordham L. Rev. 743. For a critical response, see Keating (2017) 87 Fordham
L. Rev. 24.
[38] See Ch.13.

5. MOTIVE AND MALICE

3-017   **The general irrelevance of motive**   Motive signifies a person's reasons for committing a particular act. Motive is generally irrelevant in tort law, although there are, as always, exceptions. The mere fact that a defendant was virtuously motivated is, in principle, insufficient to exonerate him from liability if all of the elements of a tort are present. Similarly, if conduct is lawful apart from motive, a bad motive will not make the defendant liable. The general irrelevancy of motive to tort law was affirmed by the House of Lords in *Bradford Corp v Pickles*.[39] Pickles was annoyed by the refusal of the claimant corporation to purchase his land in connection with a scheme to supply water to the inhabitants of a town. In revenge, he sank a shaft on his land. The water which percolated through Pickles's land in unknown and undefined channels from the land of the corporation was consequently discoloured and diminished when it passed again to other land owned by the corporation. Pickles was held not liable for causing this loss. "It is the act", said Lord Macnaghten[40]:

> "not the motive for the act, that must be regarded. If the act, apart from motive, gives rise merely to damage without legal injury, the motive, however reprehensible it may be, will not supply that element".

Three years later this was again emphasised by the House of Lords in *Allen v Flood*[41] and, for better or worse, it remains the general rule today. As we shall see, however, there are certain exceptional cases in which the motive of the defendant, if established, will tip the scales of liability against him.[42]

3-018   **Mixed motives**   It is often the case that a person has more than one reason for doing a particular act. In other words, motives are often mixed. When this is the case, the law generally regards a person's dominant purpose as his motive[43] when, exceptionally, motive is relevant.

3-019   **Malice**[44]   The term "malice" is used in several different senses in the law of torts and, as such, has the significant potential to confuse. It may refer to that which the layperson usually takes it to mean, which is to say, the *purpose* of causing harm to someone. Alternatively, it may simply signify doing an act wilfully without justification or excuse. Understood in the latter way, "malice" really has nothing to do with motive but refers to intention, a term which ought to be confined to advertence to conduct and its consequences, and which is quite colourless as to the actor's motive. The meaning of malice has to be considered in the context of each tort where it is said to be relevant—for example, defamation,[45] malicious prosecution[46] and misfeasance in a public office.[47]

---

[39]   [1895] A.C. 587.
[40]   [1895] A.C. 587 at 601. See further as to this case, para.15-025.
[41]   [1898] A.C. 1.
[42]   The principal exceptions are misfeasance in a public office (see *Three Rivers* [2003] 2 A.C. 1 at 191 and Ch.8) and malicious prosecution (see Ch.20).
[43]   *Hayes v Willoughby* [2013] UKSC 17; [2013] 1 W.L.R. 935 at [17].
[44]   Murphy (2019) 78 C.L.J. 355.
[45]   See para.13-066.
[46]   See para.20-017.
[47]   See para.8-029.

CHAPTER 4

INTENTIONAL INTERFERENCE WITH THE PERSON

1. INTRODUCTION

The law of torts recognises several actions in trespass. This chapter deals with **4-001** the action in trespass to the person. The other actions in trespass—trespass to land and trespass to chattels—are addressed later.[1] There are three main forms of trespass to the person, namely, assault, battery and false imprisonment.[2] These forms of trespass are torts in their own right. However, it is clear that they exist under the umbrella of trespass to the person, and so references to trespass to the person encompass assault, battery and false imprisonment. After exploring the forms of trespass to the person, two further related actions will be dealt with. These are the action in *Wilkinson v Downton*, which deals with intentionally caused harm that does not constitute a trespass to the person because of the indirect way in which it was inflicted, and the statutory cause of action for harassment provided for in the Protection from Harassment Act 1997.

2. GENERAL PRINCIPLES OF TRESPASS TO THE PERSON

Trespass to the person requires direct interference with a person's body or **4-002**
liberty Trespass to the person involves direct interference with another person's body or freedom of movement. It is difficult precisely to define the concept of "directness". The classic example involves throwing a log into a highway. The requisite directness is present if the log hits a passer-by, but absent if the passer-by were to stumble on it. The broad idea of the notion is relatively straightforward to

---

[1] See Ch.14 and Ch.18.
[2] Trespass to the person was also the parent of some torts, now abolished, which protected family and service relationships: see para.2-020.

understand in the case of battery, where it seems to mean something in the nature of a blow (though even that may be hard to define with precision).[3] It is more difficult to give directness a clear meaning in relation to assault and false imprisonment: assault requires no physical contact and may (for example) be committed by making threats over the telephone,[4] and while the obvious form of false imprisonment is physical seizure of the claimant by a police officer, it is clear that false imprisonment is equally committed if the claimant submits to a legal authority asserted by the officer.[5]

4-003   **The requirement of intention**   Historically, the claimant did not need to prove fault on the part of the defendant to succeed in an action in trespass. The law in this regard underwent a significant change in the 20th century principally as a result of two decisions. The first of these decisions is *Fowler v Lanning*.[6] In this case Diplock J held that where the contact with the claimant was unintentional the claimant was required to plead and prove that the defendant had acted negligently. Accordingly, the statement of claim, which recorded laconically that "the defendant shot the plaintiff", was struck out as disclosing no cause of action since it lacked an allegation of intention or negligence. *Fowler* was concerned only with the burden of proof as reflected in the principles of pleading: it did not hold that there could not be a negligent trespass. The second important decision is *Letang v Cooper*.[7] The defendant in this case drove his car over the legs of the claimant who was sunbathing on a strip of grass outside a hotel where cars were parked. The claimant did not commence proceedings until more than three years had passed, which meant that a claim for negligence was time-barred,[8] but she argued that she had an alternative claim in trespass, which was not time-barred, the general tort limitation period being six years. This argument was rejected by the Court of Appeal for two reasons. One was that the three-year period prescribed by statute applied to all claims for personal injuries no matter what the cause of action.[9] However, the other reason is not a mere matter of statutory interpretation and concerns the structure of the law in this area. Lord Denning MR (with whom Danckwerts LJ agreed) expressed his agreement with *Fowler* but added: "I would go this one step further: when the injury is not inflicted intentionally, but negligently, I would say the only cause of action is negligence and not trespass."[10] It seems, therefore, that trespass to the person is a tort only of intention (including within that term "subjective recklessness"), although it is important to bear in mind that all that must be intended is the contact rather than any particular consequence.[11] Diplock LJ (as he had become) would not have gone quite so far. He considered that trespass could be committed negligently but that in such cases the claimant would need to plead and prove negligence and also that the contact with his body caused damage. In other words, Diplock LJ thought that it was possible to commit trespass negligently but that the victim of a

---

3   See para.4-009.
4   See para.4-019.
5   See para.4-023.
6   [1959] 1 Q.B. 426.
7   [1965] 1 Q.B. 232.
8   Nowadays the court might simply "disapply" the limitation period: see para.26-101.
9   This view was subsequently declared to be wrong but has now been restored to favour. See para.26-101.
10   [1965] 1 Q.B. 232 at 240.
11   As to this, see para.3-007.

negligent trespass would gain no advantage from framing his claim in trespass. Trespass liability becomes merely an alternative label for some cases of negligence. Although the matter has not been fully explored in England since *Letang*,[12] the net result appears to be that the action for unintentional trespass to the person has disappeared in practice (for Diplock LJ) or even in name (for Lord Denning MR).[13]

Trespass to the person is actionable per se   Damage is not an element of trespass to the person: the torts under this umbrella are actionable per se. It is therefore irrelevant to liability whether the claimant suffered any damage as a result of the defendant's actions. Because there is no damage element, it is unnecessary to consider any issues of causation in determining whether liability arises.[14]   **4-004**

Intersection with the criminal law   Conduct that amounts to trespass to the person will frequently be a crime as well as a tort. Consequently, judges deciding proceedings in tort based on trespass to the person often refer to criminal law cases and vice versa. To a great extent, the relevant principles are the same in both contexts, but it should not be assumed that this is universally the case.[15] The criminal justice system may provide compensation in respect of acts of trespass,[16] although discussion of such relief is beyond the scope of this book. In comparison with the volume of offences against the person handled by the criminal courts or the number of civil actions for negligence, civil actions for trespass to the person are not common. No doubt this has always been so, for in trivial cases the claimant is likely to hesitate at the risks of civil litigation once tempers have cooled, and in serious cases the defendant may well not be worth pursuing. However, as we have seen, civil suits are sometimes brought for rather indirect motives, for example, to make a "point of principle" or to encourage an investigation or to provoke the prosecution authorities into acting.[17] In other cases there may be the prospect of recovering large damages because, from a civil point of view, someone is vicariously liable for the act of the wrongdoer, even though it amounts to a crime. The best example is the large number of actions that have been brought in respect of abuse of children in institutional settings, sometimes many years after the event.[18]   **4-005**

3.   BATTERY

Elements of battery   The elements of battery are as follows: (1) an act; (2) by which contact is intentionally made with the claimant's body; (3) the contact must   **4-006**

---

[12]   In *Wilson v Pringle* [1987] Q.B. 237, the Court of Appeal referred to the necessity for the touching in trespass to be "deliberate" and that is really the only view reconcilable with the requirement of hostility (see para.4-011) emphasised in that case.

[13]   See *Bici v MoD* [2004] EWHC 786 (QB), where Elias J held that intention or subjective recklessness was required.

[14]   *R. (on the application of Lumba) v Secretary of State for the Home Department* [2011] UKSC 12; [2012] 1 A.C. 245 at [64]–[65]; *R. (on the application of Kambadzi) v Secretary of State for the Home Department* [2011] UKSC 23; [2011] 1 W.L.R. 1299.

[15]   There is perhaps a certain ambivalence in *R. v Barnes* [2004] EWCA Crim 3246; [2005] 1 W.L.R. 910 on whether the court is simply giving advice on prosecutorial policy or stating substantive differences between tort and crime.

[16]   For example, criminal courts in sentencing an offender may order the offender to pay compensation.

[17]   See para.1-002.

[18]   The limitation difficulties in these cases were ameliorated by *A v Hoare* [2008] UKHL 6; [2008] 1 A.C. 844, see para.26-101.

be direct; (4) the contact must be hostile; and (5) the claimant did not consent to the contact. Since battery is actionable per se, its lacks a damage element. Accordingly, it is irrelevant to liability whether the claimant suffered any injury.

4-007 **Terminology** Both inside and outside of the law, the word "assault" is frequently used to refer both to assaults and to batteries. Technically, an assault, as will be explained later, involves causing someone to apprehend that they will suffer a battery.[19] Accordingly, to throw water at a person may be an assault but if any drops fall upon him it is battery.[20] In this chapter the word "assault" will be used in its strict sense.

4-008 **The act element** For a battery to be committed there must be an act by the defendant that involves contact with the claimant. Hence, D does not commit battery against C if X seizes D's arm and uses it like a club to hit C, since there is no act by D in this instance (X and X alone is liable in this scenario). The act need be intentional or reckless only as to the contact, and neither an intention to cause harm nor recklessness with respect to the risk of harm is required.[21] Thus, if D pushes C into a swimming pool and injury occurs, then, assuming D's act to be "hostile", D is liable regardless of whether the injury was desired or foreseen by D.[22]

4-009 **The contact element** Any contact with the body of the claimant (or his clothing) is sufficient to amount to a battery. As Lord Holt CJ said in *Cole v Turner*, "the least touching of another in anger is a battery".[23] The contact does not have to involve the defendant's body literally coming into contact with the claimant's body. There is a battery when the defendant shoots the claimant from a distance just as much as when he strikes him with his fist, and the same is probably true when the defendant deliberately collides with the car in which the claimant is sitting, shaking him up.[24] It is unclear whether the infliction of such things as heat, light[25] or smoke on a person constitutes a battery, although they probably do not. Mere passive obstruction has been said not to be a battery,[26] although in a criminal case there was held to be a battery where the defendant innocently drove his car on to the victim's foot and declined to move it.[27]

4-010 **The contact must be direct** As has already been mentioned, for a battery to be committed the defendant must come into direct contact with the claimant.[28] Depending on the view one takes of this requirement it may not be battery if D smears dirt on a towel hoping that C will use it to wipe his face. The tendency in the criminal law seems to be to give a broad meaning to the word "directly". Hence, putting acid in a dryer so that it injured the next person to use it was held to amount to a criminal

---

19 See para.4-017.
20 *Pursell v Horne* (1838) 8 Ad. & El. 602; 112 E.R. 966.
21 *McCarthy v Chief Constable of Merseyside Police* [2016] EWCA Civ 1257 at [6].
22 *Wilson v Pringle* [1987] Q.B. 237 at 249; *Williams v Humphrey, The Times,* 20 February 1975.
23 (1704) 6 Mod. 149 at 149; 87 E.R. 907 at 907.
24 *Clark v State* 746 So. 2d 1237 (Fla. 1999).
25 Photographing a person is not a battery: *Murray v Ministry of Defence* [1985] 12 N.I.J.B. 12; *Kaye v Robertson* [1991] F.S.R. 62.
26 *Innes v Wylie* (1844) 1 C. & K. 257 at 263; 174 E.R. 800 at 803.
27 *Fagan v MPC* [1969] 1 Q.B. 439.
28 See para.4-009.

battery.[29] In *Haystead v Chief Constable of Derbyshire*[30] the defendant struck a woman in the face, with the result that the baby she was holding fell to the floor. The defendant was charged with an offence of assault (which in this context includes battery) on the baby and his conviction was upheld by the Divisional Court on the basis that[31]:

"[T]he movement of [the woman] whereby she lost hold of the child was entirely and immediately the result of the [defendant's] action in punching her. There is no difference in logic or good sense between the facts of this case and one where the defendant might have used a weapon to fell the child to the floor, save only that this is a case of reckless and not intentional battery."

Of course in private law, if the baby had been injured, there would have been the plainest possible case of negligence even if the defendant had never given any thought to the likely effect on the baby.

The contact must be hostile   Life would be too difficult if the law did not place limits on the types of bodily contact that were actionable. However, the courts have struggled to identify appropriate limits. In *Collins v Wilcock*[32] Robert Goff LJ said that bodily contact was not actionable if it was generally acceptable in the ordinary conduct of everyday life.[33] This is more satisfactory than the somewhat artificial approach whereby a person is deemed to consent to the multitude of minor contacts which take place in, for example, a crowded bus. Of course, the absence of consent is often relevant in the sense that it is open to a person to make it plain that he objects to contact that most people find trivial and thereby render actionable what would not be so if done to others, but there must be limits on this: the passenger on the crowded bus can hardly be allowed to appropriate to himself a disproportionate share of the space available because he objects to being jostled by others. In *Wilson v Pringle*,[34] however, the Court of Appeal, while not rejecting what was said in *Collins*, laid down the rule that a battery involves a "hostile" touching. The actual decision was that the trial judge had fallen into error in granting summary judgment to the claimant where the defendant, a schoolboy, had on his own admission pulled the claimant's bag from his shoulder and thereby caused him to fall to the ground and injure himself. Such horseplay, it seems, may or may not be battery, according to whether the tribunal of fact can discern the ingredient of "hostility". However, since the court expressly said that hostility did not require ill will or malevolence, the requirement seems hardly to mean any more than that the defendant has interfered in a way to which the claimant might object. Perhaps the closest we can get to the central idea is to say that the interference must be "offensive" in the sense that it infringes the claimant's right to be physically inviolate, to be "let alone". To say, however, that there must be something offensive to dignity seems

4-011

---

[29]   *DPP v K* [1990] 1 W.L.R. 1067 (offence of "assault" under s.47 of the Offences Against the Person Act 1861). In *Breslin v McKenna* [2009] N.I.Q.B. 50 (a civil action) planting a bomb set to go off later was held to be trespass.

[30]   [2000] 2 Cr. App. R. 339.

[31]   [2000] 2 Cr. App. R. 339 at [30]. The court did not consider an alternative approach based on "transferred malice" but was dubious about its success.

[32]   [1984] 1 W.L.R. 1172.

[33]   See also the same judge in *F v West Berkshire HA* [1990] 2 A.C. 1. *Collins* was applied in *McMillan v CPS* [2008] EWHC 1457 (Admin).

[34]   [1987] Q.B. 237.

to be going too far, at least if *Nash v Sheen*[35] is correctly decided. In that case it was held to be battery where the claimant went to a hairdresser for a permanent wave and the defendant, without her consent, applied a tone rinse which produced a skin reaction. Even this rather vague formulation may not cover every case: for example, indecent touching of a small child is clearly a battery even though the child may have insufficient understanding to "take offence". Whatever the theoretical basis of liability, we can say that touching another in the ordinary course of conversation or to gain his attention[36] is not a battery. Even some persistence may be justifiable, for[37]:

> "[T]he lost or distressed may surely be permitted a second touch, or possibly even more, on a reluctant or impervious sleeve or shoulder, as may a person who is acting reasonably in the exercise of a duty. In each case, the test must be whether the physical contact so persisted in has in the circumstances gone beyond generally accepted standards of conduct."

Into the assessment of this must enter not only any limitations laid down by the claimant but also the relationship (or lack of it) between the parties. An embrace of a complete stranger may be a battery; an embrace in an attempt to settle a lovers' quarrel may not be.

4-012 **The contact must be non-consensual** Where the claimant consents to the contact there is no battery.[38] The enquiry in this regard is objective, that is to say, the issue of whether the claimant consented is determined according to what the reasonable person would conclude given the claimant's behaviour. For example, if a claimant in a vaccination line presents his arm to a surgeon, the law will regard the claimant as having consented,[39] and the same is true of a boxer who enters the ring even though subjectively he does not wish to be struck. However, if the claimant has not consented in this objective sense, a mistaken belief in the fact of consent will not exempt the defendant from liability.[40]

4-013 **The right to bodily integrity is absolute** Subject to any defences, an adult with full capacity has an absolute right to the inviolability of his body and therefore has an absolute right to choose whether or not to consent to medical treatment, even if the treatment is necessary to save his life,[41] or, in the case of a pregnant woman, the life of her unborn child.[42] Similarly, an adult of full capacity has the right to choose whether to eat or not: "Even if the refusal is tantamount to suicide, as in the

---

35 *The Times*, 13 March 1953.
36 *Wiffin v Kincard* (1807) 2 Bos. & Pul. 471; 127 E.R. 713; *Coward v Baddeley* (1859) 4 H. & N. 478; 157 E.R. 927.
37 *Collins v Wilcock* [1984] 1 W.L.R. 1172 at 1178 per Robert Goff LJ.
38 It seems that the claimant has to prove absence of consent: see para.26-007. Regarding the relationship between consent and "offensiveness", see *Non-Marine Underwriters at Lloyd's v Scalera* [2000] SCC 24; [2000] 1 S.C.R. 551.
39 *O'Brien v Cunard SS Co* 28 N.E. 266 (Mass. 1891).
40 The concept of consent is considered in more detail in paras 26-007—26-016.
41 *An NHS Trust v Y* [2018] UKSC 46; [2019] A.C. 978 at [21].
42 *St George's Healthcare NHS Trust v S* [1999] Fam. 26; *Winnipeg Child and Family Services v G* [1997] 3 S.C.R. 925 (mentally competent woman addicted to glue sniffing). It is not possible to sidestep the problem via the wardship procedure for that does not arise until the child is born: *Re F (in utero)* [1988] Fam. 122.

case of a hunger strike, he cannot be compelled to eat or forcibly fed."[43] The same seems to be true even if the would-be suicide is a prisoner in lawful custody and the practice of forcible feeding, which was followed when suicide and attempted suicide were crimes,[44] has ceased: imprisonment limits a person's autonomy but does not deprive him of the power to choose to end his life.[45] Nor can the defendant justifiably contend that his well-meaning life-saving acts should attract only nominal damages since that would be to make the principle of autonomy no more than symbolic. Thus, in Canada damages of C$20,000 were awarded where the defendants ignored the claimant's known religious objections to a blood transfusion.[46]

Consent and capacity   These principles apply if the claimant has full capacity[47]   **4-014** to make decisions regarding his wellbeing. The issue of capacity usually arises in the context of medical care and treatment and the law is mostly found in the Mental Capacity Act 2005, though the position under the Act is generally similar to that at common law. A detailed analysis of the 2005 Act is beyond the scope of this book, and readers are advised to consult specialised works in the area. However, it is convenient to make some general observations. The 2005 Act does not confer any right to impose treatment unless the person lacks capacity (or, in certain cases, is reasonably believed to lack it) and it is presumed that a person has capacity unless the contrary is shown. A person is not to be treated as lacking capacity merely because the decision that he makes is an unwise one.[48] A person lacks capacity in relation to any matter[49]:

"if at the material time he is unable to make a decision for himself in relation to the matter because of an impairment of, or a disturbance in the functioning of, the mind or brain".[50]

---

[43]   *B v Croydon HA* [1995] Fam. 133 at 137.

[44]   See *Leigh v Gladstone* (1909) 26 T.L.R. 139.

[45]   In *Secretary of State for the Home Dept v Robb* [1995] Fam. 127, a declaration was granted that prison authorities might lawfully abide by the prisoner's refusal to take food. However, despite the negative form of the declaration the tenor of the judgment is plainly that the prison authorities would have been behaving unlawfully if they had chosen *not* to abide by the prisoner's decision.

[46]   *Malette v Shulman* (1990) 67 D.L.R. (4th) 321. cf. *B v An NHS Hospital Trust* [2002] EWHC 429 (Fam); [2002] 2 All E.R. 449 where the claimant sought only nominal damages and £100 was awarded.

[47]   Even where the claimant has the mental capacity to give a valid consent, any consent must be given freely and not as a result of threats, improper pressure or undue influence. See *T (Adult, Refusal of Treatment), Re* [1993] Fam. 95 (mother's religious influence). It seems likely that nowadays a case like *Latter v Braddell* (1881) 50 L.J.Q.B. 448 (housemaid compelled to submit to medical examination on suspicion of pregnancy) would go the other way and that threats of violence would not be required. In *Wainwright v Home Office* [2003] UKHL 53; [2004] 2 A.C. 406 this issue was not pursued because the limits on the strip-search procedure to which the claimant was said to have consented were exceeded by the defendants.

[48]   Mental Capacity Act 2005 s.1. The mere fact that a person is mentally ill does not necessarily mean that he lacks capacity.

[49]   Mental Capacity Act 2005 s.2(1). Clearly, there will be many cases in which a person has full capacity to decide matters relating to issue A but not issue B.

[50]   This may be permanent or temporary. The definition is amplified by s.3 by reference to understanding, retaining and using information and communication decisions.

If this requirement is fulfilled then any act done for (or decision made for or on behalf of) the incapable person must be in his "best interests",[51] though provided the person doing the act or making the decision complies with the requirements of s.4 (which enumerates factors that the defendant must consider) it is sufficient if he reasonably believes that it is in the best interests of the person concerned.[52] The 2005 Act is not confined to acts of medical care or treatment but this is specifically dealt with by s.5. If the person doing the act reasonably concludes, after making proper inquiries, that the person concerned lacks capacity and reasonably believes that the act will be in the latter's best interests, the former will not incur any liability in relation to the act that he would not have incurred if the person treated had enjoyed capacity and had consented.[53] So if C is brought into hospital in a coma and life-saving treatment, which cannot be postponed until he regains consciousness,[54] is administered to him by D, D will have a defence to any action for battery. If a person is not unconscious but, for example, suffering from mental disorder, it may be necessary to "restrain" him, that is to say, to use or threaten force or restrict his liberty of movement.[55] If that is the case then the person doing the act must also comply with two further conditions set out in s.6: (1) that he reasonably believes it is necessary to do the act to prevent harm to the person subjected to it; and (2) that the act is a proportionate response to the likelihood of harm and its potential seriousness.[56]

4-015   **Advance decisions to refuse treatment**   Sections 24–26 of the Mental Capacity Act 2005 govern "advance decisions to refuse treatment", that is to say, decisions made by a person with capacity that, if he becomes incapable at some time in the future, treatments specified by him may not be carried out or continued. Such a decision is only applicable to life-sustaining treatment if: (1) it is in writing, signed by the person and witnessed; and (2) contains an express statement that it is to apply even if there is a risk to life.[57] While going against an advance decision complying with requirements that are set forth in s.25 automatically makes the treatment wrongful,[58] where there is no such decision the wishes of the patient are a factor to be considered,[59] although the ultimate question is whether the doctor reasonably believes that he is acting in the patient's best interests.[60]

---

[51]   Mental Capacity Act 2005 s.1(5).
[52]   Mental Capacity Act 2005 s.4(9).
[53]   Mental Capacity Act 2005 s.5(2).
[54]   If it can be, the person administering the treatment is likely to fall foul of Mental Capacity Act 2005 s.4(3).
[55]   Mental Capacity Act 2005 s.6(4). This section does not cover "deprivation of liberty" under art.5 of the European Convention on Human Rights. Restraint amounting to this is governed ss.4A, 4B and 16A and by Sch.A1. For discussion of the concept of "deprivation of liberty" in this context see *Surrey CC v P* [2014] UKSC 19; [2014] A.C. 896.
[56]   For discussion, see *H v Commissioner of Police of the Metropolis* [2013] EWCA Civ 69; [2013] 1 W.L.R. 3021.
[57]   Mental Capacity Act 2005 s.25(5)–(6).
[58]   This is the effect of Mental Capacity Act 2005 s.26(1).
[59]   Mental Capacity Act 2005 s.4(6)(a).
[60]   This is the approach taken to s.4 in the context of making a will for an incapable person in *Re P (Statutory Will)* [2009] EWHC 163 (Ch); [2010] Ch. 33 at [42] per Lewison J: "[A]lthough the fact that P makes an unwise decision does not on its own give rise to any inference of incapacity ... once the decision-making power shifts to a third party (whether a carer, deputy or the court) I cannot see that it would be a proper exercise for the third party decision-maker consciously to make an unwise decision merely because P would have done so."

Consent and children   A minor who has reached the age of 16 may validly   **4-016**
consent to medical treatment under s.8 of the Family Law Reform Act 1969 and he
may do so at common law below that age provided that he is capable of a full
understanding of the consequences.[61] In these cases the child's power to consent to
treatment is concurrent with that of the parents[62] and a parental consent may render
lawful treatment to which the child objects,[63] though no doctor can be compelled
to administer treatment and in deciding whether or not to do so the doctor will be
influenced by the child's wishes. When the child has the capacity to validly consent
and does so, the parents' objection to the treatment will not invalidate the child's
consent.[64] In all cases involving a minor the court has an inherent jurisdiction to
override both the child's objection to treatment and the child's consent to
treatment.[65] In the case of young children the consent of the parents or guardian to
medical treatment which is reasonably necessary or to procedures which, though
not therapeutic, are generally acceptable,[66] constitutes a valid consent on behalf of
the child.

4. ASSAULT

Definition of assault and relationship to battery   Assault requires no contact   **4-017**
because its essence is conduct carried out intentionally or recklessly that leads the
claimant to apprehend the application of unlawful force. As with the other species
of trespass to the person, it is unnecessary for the defendant to have intended that
the claimant suffer any particular consequences, such as a psychological injury.[67]
In the majority of cases an assault precedes a battery,[68] perhaps by only a very brief
interval, but there are examples of battery in which the claimant has no opportunity of experiencing any apprehension before the force is applied, for example,
a blow from behind inflicted by an unseen assailant.[69] Just as there can be a battery without an assault, so also there can be an assault without a battery, as where
the defendant does not carry out his threat or even has no intention of doing so but
knows that the claimant is unaware of this.[70] There is similarly an assault without

---

61   *Gillick v West Norfolk AHA* [1986] A.C. 112.
62   *Re R* [1992] Fam. 11.
63   This is the effect of s.8(3) of the 1969 Act: *Re W* [1993] Fam. 64.
64   *Re W* [1993] Fam. 64.
65   Where the child has no capacity to consent the doctor should respect the parents' refusal to consent,
     but may apply to the court, which has the power to override the parents' decision: *A (Children)
     (Conjoined Twins: Surgical Separation), Re* [2001] Fam. 147. The Mental Capacity Act 2005 has
     no relevance in such cases because although the child lacks capacity it is not because of "an impair-
     ment of, or a disturbance in the functioning of, the mind or brain" (s.2(1)).
66   e.g., testing of blood to determine paternity (*S v McC* [1972] A.C. 24); ritual circumcision or ear-
     piercing (*R. v Brown* [1994] 1 A.C. 212 at 231) but not tattooing (Tattooing of Minors Act 1969). A
     parent clearly could not give a valid consent to the sterilisation of a minor (as opposed to a neces-
     sary therapeutic procedure of which sterility was a by-product). Where it is thought that sterilisa-
     tion would be in the best interests of a minor because of mental incapacity the leave of the court
     should be sought, as in the case of a mentally incompetent adult.
67   *GB v Stoke City Football Club Ltd* [2015] EWHC 2862 (QB) at [22].
68   "[A]ssault without battery appears to be relatively rare": *Kimathi v Foreign and Commonwealth Of-
     fice* [2017] EWHC 203 (QB) at [26] per Stewart J.
69   A biblical instance in point is the slaying of Sisera by Jael, the wife of Heber the Kenite. She drove
     a tent-peg through his head while he was asleep. A modern example can be found in *Bici v MoD*
     [2004] EWHC 786 (QB), in which one of the deceased was shot in the back.
70   e.g., *Herbert v Misuga* (1994) 111 D.L.R. (4th) 193.

a battery if the blow is intercepted or prevented by some third person. In *Stephens v Myers*[71] the defendant, advancing with clenched fist upon the claimant at a parish meeting, was stopped by the churchwarden, who was sitting near the claimant. The defendant was held to be liable for assault.

4-018 **The claimant must apprehend the application of force** It is irrelevant that the claimant is courageous and is not frightened by the threat or that he could easily defeat the defendant's attack: "apprehend" is used in the sense of "expect". The claimant must, however, have reason to apprehend that the defendant has the capacity to carry out the threat immediately.[72] It would not be an assault for the defendant to wave his fist (as opposed to pointing a gun) at the claimant on a passing train, nor where the claimant was under the effective protection of the police.[73] Pointing a loaded pistol at someone is of course an assault, unless his distance from the weapon is so great that any reasonable person would have realised he was out of range.[74] The same is true even if the pistol is unloaded,[75] unless the claimant knows this.

4-019 **An assault may be committed by threatening words** According to the House of Lords in *R. v Ireland*,[76] threatening words alone may constitute an assault. *Ireland* was a criminal case but there is no reason to doubt that the reasoning also applies to tort. Hence, threats made via telephone may be an assault provided the claimant has reason to believe that they may be carried out in the sufficiently near future to qualify as "immediate".[77] In fact, the House in *Ireland* went further and held that an assault could be committed by malicious silent telephone calls. The defendant's purpose was to convey a message to the victim just as surely as if he had spoken to her. In Lord Steyn's words[78]:

> "The victim is assailed by uncertainty about his intentions. Fear may dominate her emotions, and it may be the fear that the caller's arrival at her door may be imminent. She may fear the *possibility* of immediate personal violence."

4-020 **Conditional threats** While words alone may constitute an assault, they may also negate the threatening nature of a gesture which would otherwise be an assault. In *Tubervell v Savage*[79] D laid his hand on his sword and said to C: "If it were not as-size time, I would not take such language from you." This was a conditional threat. D's words made clear that, as it was assize time, he did not intend to make good

---

[71] (1840) 4 Car. & P. 349; 172 E.R. 735.

[72] See, e.g., *Mbasogo v Logo Ltd* [2006] EWCA Civ 1370; [2007] Q.B. 846 (presence of coup plotters in city insufficient); *Darwish v Egyptair Ltd* [2006] EWHC 1399 (QB). Holding out a baton in such a way as to show an intention to prevent the claimant's exit was an assault in *Hepburn v Chief Constable of Thames Valley* [2002] EWCA Civ 1841.

[73] What is sufficiently "immediate" is a question of fact. In *Thomas v NUM (South Wales Area)* [1986] Ch. 20 it was held that the immediacy requirement was not satisfied where pickets who were held back by a police cordon made violent threats and gestures at persons going into work in vehicles.

[74] *Restatement (Second) of the Law of Torts*, §29.

[75] cf. *Blake v Barnard* (1840) 9 Car. & P. 626 at 628; 173 E.R. 985 at 986.

[76] [1998] A.C. 147.

[77] See [1998] A.C. 147 at 162, where Lord Steyn refers to a threat which is to be carried out "in a minute or two". No doubt that should not be taken as the outer limit of "immediate" but, for example, a threat in a call which the claimant, who is in Cornwall, knows is from London is not an assault.

[78] [1998] A.C. 147 at 162 (emphasis in original).

[79] (1669) 1 Mod. 3; 86 E.R. 684.

on the threat.[80] Similarly, it would not be an assault if a landowner were to insist that a trespasser leave his land under threat of reasonable force in the event of a refusal; but a highwayman could not defend an action for assault by showing that he offered the claimant the opportunity to escape violence by handing over his money.

Alternative relief where the threat is not immediate Where the threat lacks the quality of immediacy necessary for an assault, it does not follow that there is no remedy. First, if the claimant suffers actual damage (for example, psychiatric illness) as a result of a threat of unlawful action, he may have a claim on the basis exemplified in *Wilkinson v Downton*[81] or, perhaps, intimidation.[82] In the case of repeated threats, the Protection from Harassment Act 1997 may also provide a remedy.[83]

4-021

5.   FALSE IMPRISONMENT

Definition of false imprisonment A defendant commits false imprisonment where he directly and intentionally imprisons the claimant.[84] Both "false" and "imprisonment" are somewhat misleading terms. "False" here does not necessarily signify "mendacious" or "fallacious"; rather, it means "erroneous", "wrong" or "unlawful". It is also quite possible to commit the tort without "imprisonment" of a person in the common acceptance of that term. In fact, neither physical contact nor anything resembling a prison is necessary. It is false imprisonment for a lecturer to lock his class in the lecture room after the usual time for dismissal has arrived; so, too, if a person be restrained from leaving his own house[85] or any part of it,[86] or be forcibly detained in the public streets.[87]

4-022

False imprisonment requires the absence of consent There is no false imprisonment where the claimant consents, but consent is not to be inferred simply from the absence of forcible resistance.[88] A difficult line must be drawn between consent on the one hand and peaceful but unwilling submission to express or implied threats of force or asserted legal authority (whether valid or not) on the other.[89]

4-023

---

[80] cf. *R. v Light* (1857) Dears & B. 332; 169 E.R. 1029.

[81] See para.4-031.

[82] See para.19-028.

[83] See para.4-034.

[84] *R. (on the application of Lumba) v Secretary of State for the Home Department* [2011] UKSC 12; [2012] 1 A.C. 245 at [65].

[85] *R. (on the application of Jalloh) v Secretary of State for the Home Department* [2020] UKSC 4; [2020] 2 W.L.R. 418 (claimant held to be imprisoned in his home by virtue of a curfew to which he was subject).

[86] *Warner v Riddiford* (1858) 4 C.B. (N.S.) 180; 140 E.R. 1052.

[87] Blackstone, Comm., iii, p.127.

[88] He is entitled to resist by using reasonable force (*Hepburn v Chief Constable of Thames Valley* [2002] EWCA Civ 1841) but resistance to arrest is generally unwise, because the arrest may turn out to be lawful.

[89] Thus, there is no false imprisonment when the claimant complies with a police request to accompany them to the police station, but the tort is committed if the "request" is made in such a manner as to lead the claimant to believe he has no choice in the matter: *Myer Stores Ltd v Soo* [1991] 2 V.R. 597. The position is otherwise where the claimant was subject to a curfew, fixed with an electronic ankle tag and warned of the consequences of non-compliance with the conditions of the curfew: *R. (on the application of Jalloh) v Secretary of State for the Home Department* [2020] UKSC

4-024   **State of mind of the defendant**   The law regarding the required state of mind on the part of the defendant is not especially clear. Historically, negligence may have sufficed (for example, locking a room without checking whether there is anyone inside) but false imprisonment is a species of trespass to the person and intention (or at least recklessness) is probably now required for all forms of this wrong. There is no requirement that the defendant have acted in bad faith.[90] Nor is there any necessity that the defendant intend to bring about any particular consequences as a result of the imprisonment.

4-025   **Relevance of the claimant's knowledge of his imprisonment**   In *Grainger v Hill*[91] it was held that imprisonment is possible even if the claimant is so ill that he could not have moved anyway. In *Meering v Grahame-White Aviation Co Ltd*[92] the court went much further by holding that the tort is committed even if the claimant did not know that he was being detained. The claimant in this case was suspected of stealing a keg of varnish from the defendants, his employers. He was asked by two of their policemen to go with them to the company's office. He agreed to do so. On arrival the claimant was taken or invited to go to the waiting room, and the two policemen remained nearby. In an action for false imprisonment the defendants pleaded that the claimant was to his knowledge perfectly free to go where he liked and that he did not desire to leave. However, a majority of the Court of Appeal held that the defendants were liable because the claimant from the moment that he came under the influence of the police was no longer a free man. Atkin LJ said[93]:

> "It appears to me that a person could be imprisoned without his knowing it. I think a person can be imprisoned while he is asleep, while he is in a state of drunkenness, while he is unconscious, and while he is a lunatic. Those are cases where it seems to me that the person might properly complain if he were imprisoned, though the imprisonment began and ceased while he was in that state. Of course, the damages might be diminished and would be affected by the question whether he was conscious of it or not."

Atkin LJ's ground for this opinion was that, although a person might not know he was imprisoned, his captors might be boasting elsewhere that he was.[94] This point might be regarded as more relevant to defamation than to false imprisonment, but Atkin LJ's view has been approved by the House of Lords in an appeal from Northern Ireland, *Murray v Ministry of Defence*,[95] although with the rider that a person who is unaware that he has been falsely imprisoned and has suffered no harm can normally[96] expect to recover no more than nominal damages. The basis of the law as stated in *Meering* and *Murray* is no doubt that personal liberty is so supremely important that interference with it must be deterred even where there is neither consciousness nor harm. There must, however, be a detention. A patient who

---

4; [2020] 2 W.L.R. 418.

[90]   See, e.g., *R. v Governor of Brockhill Prison, Ex p. Evans (No.2)* [2001] 2 A.C. 19; para.26-061.

[91]   (1838) 4 Bing. N.C. 212; 132 E.R. 769.

[92]   (1920) 122 L.T. 44.

[93]   *Meering v Grahame-White Aviation Co Ltd* [1918-19] All ER Rep Ext 1490 at 1507; (1920) 122 L.T. 44 at 53.

[94]   (1920) 122 L.T. 44 at 53–54.

[95]   [1988] 1 W.L.R. 692. *Herring v Boyle* (1834) 1 Cr. M. & R. 377; 149 E.R. 1126 must be regarded as wrongly decided.

[96]   Perhaps this is intended as a reference to the possibility of punitive damages where there is arbitrary, oppressive or unconstitutional action: see para.23-014.

is in a coma after an accident is not "detained" by the hospital. A more difficult case is *R. v Bournewood Community and Mental Health NHS Trust Ex p L*,[97] where a man who suffered from severe mental disabilities and who became agitated was admitted to the defendant hospital as a "voluntary" patient. The court held that the hospital's actions were justified at common law by necessity. The majority were of the view that the claimant was not "detained" by his being kept in an unlocked ward, even though he was sedated and closely supervised and despite the fact that had he attempted to leave the hospital would have considered detaining him compulsorily under the relevant legislation.[98]

Imprisonment "The essence of imprisonment is being made to stay in a particular place by another person".[99] However, the tort of false imprisonment is not committed unless motion be restrained in every direction. In *Bird v Jones*[100] the defendants wrongfully enclosed part of the public footway on Hammersmith Bridge, put seats in the enclosure for the use of spectators of a regatta on the river, and charged for admission to the enclosure. The claimant insisted on passing along this part of the footpath, and climbed over the fence of the enclosure without paying the charge. The defendants refused to let him go forward, but he was told that he might go back into the carriageway and cross to the other side of the bridge if he wished. He declined to do so and remained in the enclosure for half an hour. The defendants were held not to have committed false imprisonment.[101] Whether or not restraint is complete is a question of degree. A person would plainly be imprisoned if locked inside a large building,[102] even though he had full freedom to roam around inside it. Similarly, it would be false imprisonment to drive a person into the middle of a desert and leave him stranded there.[103] It has been suggested that unlawful conscription is theoretically capable of being false imprisonment[104] but it seems unlikely that an action for false imprisonment would lie if, for example, the claimant was wrongfully prevented from leaving this country.[105] It is entirely possible to restrain a

4-026

---

[97] *R. v Bournewood Community and Mental Health NHS Trust Ex p L* [1999] 1 A.C. 458.
[98] cf. Lord Steyn, dissenting on this issue: "The suggestion that L was free to go is a fairy tale" ([1999] 1 A.C. 458 at 495). Even the majority, however, were of the view that he was detained while being taken to the hospital by ambulance. The European Court of Human Rights held that he had been deprived of his liberty for the purposes of art.5 of the Convention: *HL v United Kingdom* (2004) 40 E.H.R.R. 761, which is (at least) strongly suggestive of there having been an imprisonment: see *R. (on the application of Jalloh) v Secretary of State for the Home Department* [2020] UKSC 4; [2020] 2 W.L.R. 418.
[99] *R. (on the application of Jalloh) v Secretary of State for the Home Department* [2020] UKSC 4; [2020] 2 W.L.R. 418 at [24] per Lady Hale.
[100] (1845) 7 Q.B. 742.
[101] Obstruction of the highway may be a public nuisance even though the claimant is not totally detained.
[102] By these standards, detaining people in Oxford Circus plainly constitutes imprisonment: *Austin v MPC* [2007] EWCA Civ 989; [2008] Q.B. 660 (on appeal on other issues [2009] UKHL 5; [2009] 1 A.C. 564).
[103] Or marooned on an island: Napoleon was certainly imprisoned on St Helena. cf. *Guzzardi v Italy* (1981) 3 E.H.R.R. 333.
[104] *Pritchard v MoD* [1995] C.L.Y. 4726.
[105] See *Louis v Commonwealth* (1986) 87 F.L.R. 277. Protocol 4, art.2 of the European Convention on Human Rights guarantees the rights to liberty of movement and to leave a country. However, these rights are not covered by the Human Rights Act 1998. There is no common law tort of imposing exile upon a person, even though it is forbidden by Magna Carta. It is necessary to show trespass to the person or some other tort: *Chagos Islanders v Attorney General* [2004] EWCA Civ 997.

person merely by threats or words, which is sometimes referred to as "constructive" imprisonment.[106]

4-027 **The duration of the imprisonment is irrelevant** Consistently with the fact that the tort of false imprisonment is actionable per se, if there is a total restraint upon the claimant's liberty, that is false imprisonment even though it lasts for only a brief period of time[107] and regardless of whether the restraint is intermittent, as when the claimant is subject to a daily curfew between certain hours.[108] This means that many acts which are "primarily" battery may also involve false imprisonment, as where C is raped by D. Of course, the duration of the detention, and whether it is periodic, will be highly relevant in connection with the assessment of damages.[109]

4-028 **Means of escape** If a person has reasonable[110] means of escape, but does not know it, it is submitted that his detention is nevertheless false imprisonment unless any reasonable person would have realised that he had an available outlet. Thus, if D pretends to turn the key of the door of a room in which you are situated and takes away the key, it would seem unreasonable if you made no attempt to see whether the door was in fact locked. A more difficult case is that in which you have a duplicate key in your pocket but have forgotten its existence. A reasonable person may suffer from a lapse of memory. A means of escape will not be regarded as one that should have been taken if C, had he availed himself of it, would have run the risk of incurring a criminal law sanction.[111]

4-029 **Reasonable condition** It is not false imprisonment to prevent a person from leaving your premises because he will not fulfil a reasonable condition subject to which he entered them. In *Robinson v Balmain Ferry Co Ltd*[112] the claimant paid a penny for entry to the defendants' wharf from which he proposed to cross the river by one of the defendants' ferry boats. A boat had just gone and, as there was not another one for 20 minutes, the claimant wished to leave the wharf and was directed to the turnstile which was its exit. There he refused to pay another penny which was chargeable for exit, as was stated on a noticeboard, and the defendant declined to let him leave the wharf unless he paid. The Privy Council held that this was not false imprisonment[113]:

---

[106] "Lord Coke, in his Second Institute (2 Inst 589), speaks of 'a prison in law' and 'a prison in deed': so that there may be a constructive, as well as an actual, imprisonment: and, therefore, it may be admitted that personal violence need not be used in order to amount to it": *Bird v Jones* (1845) 7 Q.B. 742 at 747–748.

[107] See, e.g., *Walker v Commissioner of Police of the Metropolis* [2014] EWCA Civ 897; [2015] 1 W.L.R. 312 (claimant detained for a matter of seconds by a police officer).

[108] *R. (on the application of Jalloh) v Secretary of State for the Home Department* [2020] UKSC 4; [2020] 2 W.L.R. 418.

[109] *R. (on the application of Jalloh) v Secretary of State for the Home Department* [2018] EWCA Civ 1260; [2019] 1 W.L.R. 394 at [92].

[110] See *McFadzean v Construction Forestry Mining and Energy Union* [2007] VSCA 289 for extensive discussion.

[111] *R. (on the application of Jalloh) v Secretary of State for the Home Department* [2018] EWCA Civ 1260; [2019] 1 W.L.R. 394 at [82] (affirmed [2020] UKSC 4; [2020] 2 W.L.R. 418).

[112] [1910] A.C. 295.

[113] [1910] A.C. 295 at 299. cf. Viscount Haldane LC in *Herd v Weardale Steel Co Ltd* [1915] A.C. 67 at 72.

"There is no law requiring the defendants to make the exit from their premises gratuitous to people who come there upon a definite contract which involves their leaving the wharf by another way ... The question whether the notice which was affixed to these premises was brought home to the knowledge of the plaintiff is immaterial, because the notice itself is immaterial."

The charge of a penny for exit was regarded as reasonable. It must be stressed that it was crucial to the decision in this case that the claimant had contracted to leave the wharf by a different route. Nonetheless, the decision is a striking one because it amounts, in effect, to recognising extra-judicial imprisonment as a method of enforcing contractual rights.[114]

Liability in false imprisonment distinguished from abuse of legal procedure   A defendant may be liable for false imprisonment even though he did not personally detain the claimant provided that he acted through an intermediary who exercised no independent discretion of his own. In *Austin v Dowling*[115] a police inspector refused to take the responsibility of arresting B on a charge made by A, but finally arrested B when A signed the charge sheet. It was held that A could be liable for false imprisonment. There can, however, be no false imprisonment if a discretion is interposed between the defendant's act and the claimant's detention. If, for example, A makes a charge against B before a magistrate and the magistrate then decides to order the arrest of B, A has set in motion not a ministerial but a judicial officer exercising a discretion of his own and A cannot be liable for false imprisonment.[116] In modern conditions it is very likely that where the police make an arrest on the basis of information or a complaint they will be held to be exercising an independent discretion[117] but that is not inevitably so, as, for example, where there is a request or encouragement to arrest on information provided solely by the defendant.[118] The liability of an informant for abuse of legal procedure[119] is an entirely different matter which is considered in detail below.[120]   **4-030**

6.   ACTS INTENDED TO CAUSE PHYSICAL HARM OTHER THAN TRESPASS TO THE PERSON

The action in Wilkinson v Downton   The action in trespass is confined to the intentional and direct infliction of harm. So what is the position in the situation where the harm is intentionally but indirectly inflicted? The central authority in this regard is *Wilkinson v Downton*.[121] In that case D, by way of a practical joke, falsely   **4-031**

---

[114] A right denied in *Bahner v Marwest Hotel* (1970) 12 D.L.R. (3d) 646. The claimant in *Robinson*'s case was, after a short time, allowed to leave by squeezing past the turnstile. Could the defendants have kept him there indefinitely?

[115] (1870) L.R. 5 C.P. 534.

[116] (1870) L.R. 5 C.P. 534 at 540 per Willes J; *Sewell v National Telephone Co Ltd* [1907] 1 K.B. 557.

[117] See, e.g., *Davidson v Chief Constable of North Wales* [1994] 2 All E.R. 597 (so held even though the informant was a store detective).

[118] *Ahmed v Shafique* [2009] EWHC 618 (QB); *Barkhuysen v Hamilton* [2016] EWHC 2858 (QB); [2018] Q.B. 1015 at [141]. cf. *Coles Myer Ltd v Webster* [2009] NSWCA 299; [2009] Aust. Torts Reports 82-033 (invention of allegation led to liability).

[119] A claim for defamation will fail because it is now held that even a malicious informant is protected by absolute privilege: see para.13-054.

[120] See Ch.20.

[121] *Wilkinson v Downton* [1897] 2 Q.B. 57.

told C that her husband had met with an accident in which both his legs had been broken. This caused C, who was found to be a person of normal fortitude, to suffer a violent shock "producing vomiting and other more serious and permanent physical consequences at one time threatening her reason, and entailing weeks of suffering and incapacity." In holding D liable to C, Wright J said that[122]:

> "[T]he defendant has ... wilfully done an act calculated to cause physical harm to the plaintiff – that is to say, to infringe her legal right to safety, and has in fact thereby caused physical harm to her. That proposition without more appears to me to state a good cause of action, there being no justification alleged for the act."

The principle was approved and applied by the Court of Appeal in *Janvier v Sweeney*[123] where a private detective, in order to get papers from the claimant, falsely represented that he was a police officer and that she was in danger of arrest for association with a German spy, thereby causing her psychiatric trauma.

Subsequently, however, the tort appears rarely to have been invoked,[124] and it came close to being formally eliminated in *Wainwright v Home Office*, where it was suggested that in modern conditions such cases could instead be dealt with in negligence.[125] This course was not pursued by the Supreme Court in *O v Rhodes*[126] although it nevertheless adopted a restrictive approach to the tort. In that case, a mother wished to prevent her former husband, a famous concert pianist, from publishing an autobiography that described sexual abuse that he had suffered as a school boy because she was concerned about the psychological impact that the book could have on their young son. The Supreme Court observed that, although the book had been dedicated to the son, it was not addressed to him but to the world at large, and determined that publishing the book was justified because of the father's legitimate interest in recounting his story and the public's corresponding interest in hearing it. Consequently, the Supreme Court held that there was no arguable case that publication would involve the commission of the tort in *Wilkinson v Downton* and discharged an interim injunction that had been granted by the Court of Appeal.

4-032   **The elements of the tort**   In *O*, the Supreme Court clarified that the tort has three elements: (1) "words or conduct directed towards the claimant for which there is no justification or reasonable excuse";[127] (2) the defendant by his conduct must intend to cause physical harm or "severe mental or emotional distress";[128] and (3) the claimant must as a result of the conduct concerned suffer physical harm or a recognised psychiatric illness. There is no need for the conduct concerned to be of general public interest in order for it to be justified.[129] In relation to the mental element, the Supreme Court made it clear that nothing short of an intention to cause harm would suffice, and that recklessness with respect to the risk of harm was not

---

122 [1897] 2 Q.B. 57 at 58–59. Described by Stuart-Smith LJ in *W v Essex CC* [1999] Fam. 90 at 114 as a "peculiar tort".
123 [1919] 2 K.B. 316.
124 "This is a case which has been far more often discussed than applied": *Wainwright v Home Office* [2003] UKHL 53; [2004] 2 A.C. 406 at [36] per Lord Hoffmann.
125 [2003] UKHL 53; [2004] 2 A.C. 406 at [36]–[47].
126 [2015] UKSC 32; [2016] A.C. 219.
127 [2015] UKSC 32; [2016] A.C. 219 at [74] per Lady Hale and Lord Toulson.
128 [2015] UKSC 32; [2016] A.C. 219 at [87] per Lady Hale and Lord Toulson.
129 [2015] UKSC 32; [2016] A.C. 219 at [76].

sufficient.[130] However, where the claimant has suffered a psychiatric illness, it is sufficient that the defendant intended to cause the severe distress that resulted in the illness as opposed to the illness itself.[131] Finally, and although it did not need to decide the point, the Supreme Court was inclined to the view that it was unnecessary for the claimant to prove that the defendant's conduct was "extreme, flagrant or outrageous".[132]

Unanswered questions *O* leaves several significant questions unanswered. One **4-033** is whether a claimant who suffers mental harm that falls short of a recognised psychiatric illness can sue in the tort.[133] Another is whether the tort adds anything as a practical matter to the tort of negligence. The Supreme Court clearly wished to reject any suggestion that the tort in *Wilkinson v Downton* had been absorbed by the cause of action in negligence. However, it seems that the circumstances in which it will be committed other than in tandem with the tort of negligence will be rare. In particular, the requirement that the words or conduct in issue be unjustified means that it will be unusual for the claimant to have a claim in the tort in *Wilkinson v Downton* if he does not also have a cause of action in negligence.[134] However, the possibility that a claim based on *Wilkinson v Downton* may be available for mental distress falling short of a recognised psychiatric illness means that such a claim may potentially be available where a claim would not lie in negligence (mere mental distress is not actionable in negligence).[135]

7. PROTECTION FROM HARASSMENT ACT 1997

Provision for a civil action Section 1 of the Protection from Harassment Act **4-034** 1997 makes it an offence to pursue a course of conduct[136] that the defendant knows or ought to know[137] amounts to harassment of another.[138] By s.3 this is civilly actionable, leading to "damages ... for (among other things) any anxiety caused by the harassment and any financial loss resulting from the harassment".[139] Damages may,

---

[130] [2015] UKSC 32; [2016] A.C. 219 at [87].

[131] [2015] UKSC 32; [2016] A.C. 219 at [87].

[132] [2015] UKSC 32; [2016] A.C. 219 at [88] per Lady Hale and Lord Toulson. cf. at [110] per Lord Neuberger; *Restatement (Third) of Torts: Liability for Physical and Emotional Harm*, §46.

[133] Lord Neuberger suggested that such a claimant should be able to sue: [2015] UKSC 32; [2016] A.C. 219 at [116].

[134] But see *C v WH* [2015] EWHC 2687 (QB); [2016] PIQR Q2 in which a teacher was held liable in battery and the tort in *Wilkinson v Downton* for abusing a pupil without a concurrent claim in negligence having been brought.

[135] See para.5-070.

[136] Conduct includes speech: s.7(3).

[137] But this is to be decided without reference to any mental illness or characteristic of the accused: *R. v C* [2001] EWCA Crim 1251; *Banks v Ablex Ltd* [2005] EWCA Civ 173; [2005] I.C.R. 819.

[138] A corporate body is incapable of being harassed within the meaning of the 1997 Act because it is not a "person" within the scope of that word in s.7(2): *Daiichi UK Ltd v Stop Huntingdon Animal Cruelty* [2003] EWHC 2337 (QB); [2004] 1 W.L.R. 1503 (but see *Smithkline Beecham Plc v Avery* [2009] EWHC 1488 (QB); [2011] Bus. L.R. D40).

[139] In accordance with general principle an employer is vicariously liable for conduct by an employee which contravenes the Act: *Majrowski v Guy's and St Thomas's NHS Trusts* [2006] UKHL 34; [2007] 1 A.C. 224. The standard of proof in civil cases of harassment is the ordinary civil one of the balance of probabilities: *Jones v Hipgrave* [2004] EWHC 2901 (QB). The "only real difference between the crime of s.2 and the tort of s.3 is standard of proof": *Ferguson v British Gas Trading Ltd* [2009] EWCA Civ 46; [2010] 1 W.L.R. 785 at [17] per Jacob LJ.

therefore, be awarded for the sort of psychiatric damage that was suffered by the victim in *R. v Ireland*,[140] but also for lesser degrees of psychic disturbance.[141] An injunction may also be granted to restrain the repetition of the conduct in issue in the future.[142]

4-035   **The meaning of "course of conduct"**   A "course of conduct" must involve conduct on at least two occasions.[143] This is a threshold requirement of actionability, and it does not follow that a claim will lie simply because conduct was engaged in on two occasions.[144] Whether or not a series of acts will comprise a "course of conduct" is a matter of fact and degree, and the more similar and temporally proximate the acts are to each other the more likely it is that they will amount to a "course of conduct".[145] Putting a person in fear of violence on at least two occasions by a course of conduct is a more serious offence under the 1997 Act but is not made civilly actionable as such. Plainly, however, the greater includes the lesser and such conduct will fall under the general crime of harassment and will therefore be civilly actionable by that route.

4-036   **The meaning of "harassment"**   The 1997 Act does not contain a detailed definition of harassment. It has been said that one has to draw a distinction between conduct which is "unattractive, even unreasonable, and conduct which is oppressive and unacceptable".[146] In doing this one must take account of the context in which the conduct takes place. As Gage LJ said in *Conn v Sunderland City Council* that: "What might not be harassment on the factory floor or in the barrack room might well be harassment in the hospital ward and vice versa."[147] For a course of conduct to constitute harassment it must "go beyond annoyances or irritations, and beyond the ordinary banter and badinage of life".[148] According to Lord Sumption in *Hayes v Willoughby*[149]:

> "Harassment is a persistent and deliberate course of unreasonable and oppressive conduct, targeted at another person, which is calculated to and does cause that person alarm, fear or distress."

It has been held that chanting intended to disrupt a graduation ceremony was not harassment because there was insufficient evidence that anyone was "alarmed, distressed, threatened or frightened" even though they were annoyed, though the

---

140   See para.4-019.
141   *S & D Property Investments Ltd v Nisbet* [2009] EWHC 1726 (Ch). However, such damages are likely to be modest: at [76].
142   The exercise of this power in a proper case does not infringe art.10 of the European Convention on Human Rights: *Howlett v Holding* [2006] EWHC 41 (QB).
143   By s.1(1A), where the harassment is of two or more persons there need only be conduct on one occasion in relation to each person, but s.1(1A) does not give rise to a civil claim for damages.
144   *Hourani v Thomson* [2017] EWHC 432 (QB) at [132].
145   "Whether two or more instances can be classified as a 'course of action' will depend on such factors as how similar they are in character, the extent to which they are linked, how closely in time they may have occurred, and so on": *Merelie v Newcastle PTC* [2004] EWHC 2554 (QB) at [22] per Eady J.
146   *Majrowski v Guy's and St Thomas's NHS Trusts* [2006] UKHL 34; [2007] 1 A.C. 224 at [30] per Lord Nicholls.
147   [2007] EWCA Civ 1492; [2008] I.R.L.R. 324 at [12].
148   *Iqbal v Dean Manson Solicitors* [2011] EWCA Civ 123 at [42] per Rix LJ.
149   [2013] UKSC 17; [2013] 1 W.L.R. 935 at [1].

line between distress and annoyance may be hard to draw.[150] At any rate, harassment goes well beyond causing fear of violence. It is capable of embracing, for example, persistent following, questioning or "doorstepping" by journalists; methods of debt collection which are humiliating, threatening or distressing[151] or persistent unjustified demands for payment;[152] newspaper articles,[153] abusive letters[154] or other publications;[155] uploading to the internet explicit photographs of the claimant;[156] bullying in the workplace;[157] bombarding the claimant with text messages or emails;[158] and conduct in the course of a neighbour dispute which is designed to distress,[159] for example, playing loud music or banging on walls. In determining whether a "course of conduct" constitutes harassment it is necessary to look at the course of conduct as a whole.[160] The mere fact that the conduct concerned is polite in tone and manner, while clearly a relevant consideration, does not prevent it from constituting harassment.[161] A request by the claimant that the defendant desist from continuing in the behaviour concerned is likely to be material[162] as will be the frequency with which the conduct occurred.

The defendant's state of mind   The defendant is liable only if he knew or should   **4-037**
have known that the course of conduct constituted harassment. The claimant's characteristics are relevant in this connection.[163] Harassment in its ordinary sense seems to imply something sustained and intended to distress. So if D quarrels with C in 2010 and makes an abusive telephone call to him on that occasion and this is repeated in 2011, but as a result of a wholly independent quarrel, that would not, it is submitted, fall within the 1997 Act.[164] Nor would one describe the constant playing of loud music, caused not by spite but by selfish indifference to neighbours, as harassment,[165] though it may amount to a private nuisance and an offence under other legislation governing noise. Although, for the reasons that have been given,

---

150 *University of Oxford v Broughton* [2008] EWHC 75 (QB) (an application for an interim injunction); but an injunction had earlier been granted against disruption of examinations: at [25].
151 *S & D Property Investments* [2009] EWHC 1726 (Ch). This may enable the claimant to set off the damages against the debt sought to be enforced.
152 *Allen v Southwark LBC* [2008] EWCA Civ 1478; *Ferguson v British Gas Trading Ltd* [2009] EWCA Civ 46; [2010] 1 W.L.R. 785.
153 *Thomas v News Group Newspapers Ltd* [2001] EWCA Civ 1233; [2002] E.M.L.R. 4. But press criticism which is robust and likely to cause distress is not harassment unless it is an abuse of press freedom.
154 *Iqbal v Dean Manson Solicitors* [2011] EWCA Civ 123; [2011] I.R.L.R. 428 at [31].
155 *Howlett v Holding* [2006] EWHC 41 (QB).
156 *AMP v Persons Unknown* [2011] EWHC 3454 (TCC).
157 *Majrowski v Guy's and St Thomas's NHS Trust* [2006] UKHL 34; [2007] 1 A.C. 224.
158 *APW v WPA* [2012] EWHC 3151 (QB).
159 *Jones v Ruth* [2011] EWCA Civ 804; [2012] 1 W.L.R. 1495.
160 *Iqbal v Dean Manson Solicitors* [2011] EWCA Civ 123 at [31].
161 *Roberts v Bank of Scotland Plc* [2013] EWCA Civ 882 at [48].
162 *Roberts v Bank of Scotland Plc* [2013] EWCA Civ 882 at [37].
163 *Banks v Ablex Ltd* [2005] EWCA Civ 173; [2005] I.C.R. 819 at [26].
164 Even where the incidents arise out of the same matter, it has been said that the fewer the incidents and the wider apart they are, the less likely they are to constitute harassment: *Lau v DPP*, *The Times*, 29 March 2000.
165 Section 1(2) of the 1997 Act provides that: "[T]he person whose course of conduct is in question ought to know that it amounts to harassment of another if a reasonable person in possession of the same information would think the course of conduct amounted to harassment of the other." This would cover, e.g., conduct directed at the victim which the defendant regards as a joke but which a reasonable person would regard as going beyond that.

it appears that the very concept of harassment means that the defendant must act with a certain intention,[166] it is unnecessary for the defendant to foresee that his conduct will cause the claimant to suffer damage.[167] However, while it is possible for the claimant to sue in respect of harassing conduct aimed at a third party, in such a case he will need to prove that he was "foreseeably, and directly" harmed by that conduct such that he could properly be described as a victim of it.[168]

4-038 **Defence of preventing or detecting a crime** Section 1(3)(a) of the 1997 Act provides for a defence to liability where the defendant was acting "for the purpose of preventing or detecting crime." The main aim of this provision is to shield statutory authorities from liability as a result of acts taken in connection with law enforcement, but it applies equally to private citizens.[169] In order for this defence to apply, it is unnecessary that the defendant establish that his conduct was objectively justified, although it has been suggested that, in view of the Human Rights Act 1998, s.1(3) of the 1997 Act would be interpreted as containing a requirement of necessity or proportionality.[170] The word "purpose" in s.1(3)(a) refers to a subjective state of mind.[171] Nevertheless, the defence is not solely contingent upon the defendant's thought processes. It is subject to a test of "rationality". In *Hayes v Willoughby* Lord Sumption explained that this test[172]:

> "imports a requirement of good faith, a requirement that there should be some logical connection between the evidence and the ostensible reasons for the decision, and (which will usually amount to the same thing) an absence of arbitrariness, of capriciousness or of reasoning so outrageous in its defiance of logic as to be perverse".

This means that the defendant[173]:

> ">must have thought rationally about the material suggesting the possibility of criminality and formed the view that the conduct said to constitute harassment was appropriate for the purpose of preventing or detecting it".

n irrational, obsessive vendetta will not satisfy these requirements,[174] and the defence does not give carte blanche to any citizen to set up as a vigilante.[175] The "purpose" that matters in relation to the defence is the defendant's dominant purpose.[176] Accordingly, the defence will not be excluded merely because the defendant had aims other than that of preventing or detecting crime.

4-039 **Criminal proceedings** If there are criminal proceedings for harassment, the court dealing with the offender may make a restraining order prohibiting the defendant

---

166 cf. *Trimingham v Associated Newspapers* [2012] EWHC 1296 (QB); [2012] 4 All E.R. 717 at [67] per Tugendhat J: "The 1997 Act does not require intent."
167 *Jones v Ruth* [2011] EWCA Civ 804; [2012] 1 W.L.R. 1495.
168 *Levi v Bates* [2015] EWCA Civ 206; [2016] Q.B. 91 at [34] per Briggs LJ.
169 *Hayes v Willoughby* [2013] UKSC 17; [2013] 1 W.L.R. 935 at [13].
170 *KD v CC Hampshire* [2005] EWHC 2550 (QB) at [144].
171 *Hayes v Willoughby* [2013] UKSC 17; [2013] 1 W.L.R. 935 at [14].
172 [2013] UKSC 17; [2013] 1 W.L.R. 935 at [14].
173 [2013] UKSC 17; [2013] 1 W.L.R. 935 at [15].
174 As in *Chief Constable of Surrey v Godfrey* [2017] EWHC 2014 (QB) (stalking police officers in the hope or expectation that some wrongdoing may be witnessed).
175 *Howlett v Holding* [2006] EWHC 41 (QB).
176 [2013] UKSC 17; [2013] 1 W.L.R. 935 at [17], [21].

from doing anything described in the order[177] and in practice this seems likely to be more important than civil claims under the 1997 Act for an injunction.

---

[177] See s.5.

CHAPTER 5

NEGLIGENCE: DUTY OF CARE

1. THE TORT OF NEGLIGENCE

5-001   **The tort of negligence**   This chapter is the first of several that analyse the tort of negligence. Its focus is on the duty of care concept. However, it is convenient to first make some general observations about the tort and the elements that constitute it.

5-002   **The elements of the tort**   The tort of negligence is by a very substantial margin the most important tort in terms of the volume of cases before the courts. It is a matter of some regret, therefore, that there is some doubt as to its elements. Judges and commentators describe its ingredients in a surprising diversity of ways.[1] For current purposes, however, we will proceed on the basis that the tort is constituted by: (1) a duty of care owed by the defendant to the claimant; (2) a breach of that duty; (3) damage suffered by the claimant; (4) which is caused by, and is a non-remote consequence of, the breach.

5-003   **The elements overlap with each other**   An important point to note at the outset is that the elements of the tort of negligence overlap extensively with each other in the sense that a given fact ual pattern can put several elements in issue simultaneously. This possibility exists partly because, as will be explained, the concept of foreseeability plays a role in relation to the questions of duty, breach and whether the claimant's damage is too remote to be compensable.[2] Suppose, for example, that D jostles X, causing X to drop something and this sets off a very unexpected train of events which causes injury to C, standing many feet away.[3] If one wished to hold that D was not liable to C, one might say that D owed him no duty of care because he could not foresee injury to him; or that he owed him a duty of care but had not breached it because he could not foresee that his conduct would cause C harm; or that he owed him a duty of care and had breached it but the damage was not legally attributable to him because no one could have foreseen it. All three ways of analysing the case are plausible.

5-004   **Criticism of the overlap**   The overlap between the elements of the tort of negligence raises the issue of redundancy. What is the point of having requirements that cover substantially the same territory as each other? The duplication has led many writers to attack some of the tort's elements as superfluous, especially the duty requirement. Buckland famously described the duty element as an "unnecessary fifth wheel on the coach, incapable of sound analysis and possibly productive of injustice".[4] Other scholars have been no less critical.[5] There is no doubt that many of the issues with which the duty requirement deals could be considered when other elements of the action in negligence are addressed.[6] For example, the rule that the police do not owe a duty of care to victims of crime in investigating criminal behaviour[7] could be reallocated to the causation element, which would see the act

---

1   See Owen (2007) 35 Hofstra L. Rev. 1671.
2   See paras 5-027, 6-020.
3   See *Palsgraf v Long Island RR* 162 N.E. 99 (N.Y. 1928), discussed at para.5-009.
4   Buckland (1935) 51 L.Q.R. 637.
5   See, e.g., Winfield (1934) 34 Col. L. Rev. 41; Howarth [1991] C.L.J 67; Nolan (2013) 129 L.Q.R. 559.
6   See Nolan (2013) 129 L.Q.R. 559.
7   The rule is exemplified by *Hill v Chief Constable of West Yorkshire Police* [1989] A.C. 53 although

of the criminal that injures the victim as an intervening cause. Because most issues that are presently dealt with at the duty stage could be accommodated by other elements of the tort of negligence, the duty element is arguably unnecessary. And even if it is thought that the duty element should be retained, it may well be that the issues that are currently dealt with by it could be better handled elsewhere.

The elements are interwoven In addition to the fact that the elements of the tort   5-005
of negligence overlap in the sense that a given fact pattern ual can raise issues under more than one element, the elements are fundamentally interlinked with each other. There is, for example, a significant connection between the duty of care and damage ingredients. It has been said to be meaningless to ask whether a defendant owes the claimant a duty of care without also considering the type of damage in question.[8] This is because a defendant may be under a duty to safeguard the claimant against one type of damage (for example, physical damage to his property) but not another type of damage (for example, pure economic loss). The duty and breach elements are similarly interwoven. A defendant may be required to take reasonable care to protect the claimant from certain risks of injury but not others depending on the nature of the duty owed. For example, ordinarily, a person who owes a duty of care can discharge it without taking any steps to safeguard the claimant from risks posed by third parties or from self-harm. However, the position may be different where, for example, the duty of care arises on account of the defendant taking the claimant into his custody.

Confusion between the elements Sometimes a given set of facts will engage   5-006
certain elements of the tort of negligence but not others. Suppose, for example, that it is alleged that a road accident occurred because the defendant, a user of a motor vehicle, failed to check with sufficient regularity that his vehicle's tyres were in a roadworthy condition A court, if it wished to reject the claim, could say that the defendant "owed no duty to check the tyres before each trip". However, the issue is clearly one of breach not of duty of care, it being clear that road users owe duties of care inter se.[9] Let us consider another example.[10] Imagine that C presents himself at a hospital that is run by D seeking treatment but leaves after he is wrongly told by the hospital's receptionist that he would need to wait for a lengthy period of time before being seen by a doctor. Suppose also that C's condition, which called for urgent medical treatment, then deteriorated but that by the time that C returned to the hospital and was treated he had suffered permanent injury. Were a court inclined to find in D's favour, it could say that D did not owe a duty of care to ensure that persons who present themselves for treatment are seen promptly. This choice of language characterises the facts as pertaining to the duty of care element. But this is quite wrong since it is well established that hospitals owe a duty of care to a

---

the reasoning in that case has been overtaken by subsequent developments. See further para.5-060.

[8]   "It is never sufficient to ask simply whether A owes B a duty of care. It is always necessary to determine the scope of the duty by reference to the kind of damage from which A must take care to save B harmless": *Caparo Industries Plc v Dickman* [1990] 2 A.C. 605 at 627 per Lord Bridge. See also *S v Gloucestershire CC* [2001] 2 W.L.R. 909 at 932.

[9]   Instances where the court wrongly treated a breach case as a duty case include *Orange v Chief Constable of West Yorkshire Police* [2001] EWCA Civ 611; [2002] Q.B. 347; *Fernquest v City & County of Swansea* [2011] EWCA Civ 1712.

[10]   This scenario is based on *Darnley v Croydon Health Services NHS Trust* [2018] UKSC 50; [2019] A.C. 831.

person accepted as a patient. Properly understood, the facts raise issues as to whether D's staff breached the duty that D undoubtedly owed.

5-007   **Sequence in which the elements are considered**   It is conventional for the courts to address the elements of the tort of negligence in sequence, beginning with duty of care,[11] then moving on to breach and finally considering the issues of damage, causation and remoteness. Taking the elements of the tort in this order can help judges to structure their decisions and to ensure that elements are not overlooked. Furthermore, the order in which the elements of the tort are considered is important because they form an integrated whole, in which one element can be defined and analysed only in terms of the other elements. For example, as questions of causation and remoteness concern the link between the breach of duty and the damage, it is important to look at fault and damage before looking at causation.

2.   DUTY OF CARE: GENERAL PRINCIPLES

A.   Introduction

5-008   **A duty of care is a central element of the tort of negligence**[12]   A person is not liable in the tort of negligence for every careless act that he commits. Indeed, a person is not liable even for every careless act that causes damage. Rather, a person is liable for negligence that causes damage only if he is under a legal duty to take care. This point was famously encapsulated by Lord Esher MR when he said: "A man is entitled to be as negligent as he pleases to the whole world if he owes no duty to them."[13]

5-009   **The duty of care must be owed to the claimant**   The duty of care must be owed specifically to the claimant. Negligence "in the air" is not enough: the claimant cannot build on a duty of care owed, or a wrong committed, to someone else.[14] The point is graphically illustrated by the famous United States case of *Palsgraf v Long Island Railroad*.[15] The facts as presented to the New York Court of Appeals were that D's employees negligently pushed X, who was attempting to board a moving train, and caused him to drop a package containing "fireworks". The resulting explosion knocked over a set of scales, many feet away, which struck C, injuring her. A majority of the court found for D. It might well have been the case that D's employees were negligent with regard to X, at least as far as his property was concerned. But there was nothing in the appearance of the package to suggest even to the most cautious mind that it would cause a violent explosion and hence injury to C. In the words of Cardozo CJ[16]:

---

[11]   "[D]uty is the threshold question": Robertson (2012) 33 O.J.L.S. 1 at 2.

[12]   Regarding the duty of care element, see generally Plunkett, *The Duty of Care in Negligence* (2018).

[13]   *Le Lievre v Gould* [1893] 1 Q.B. 491 at 497. In *Grant v Australian Knitting Mills Ltd* [1936] A.C. 85 at 103 Lord Wright said that "[i]t is essential in English law that the duty should be established. ... [I]f the act [of the defendant in respect of which the claimant complains] involves a lack of due care, ... no case of actionable negligence will arise unless the duty to be careful exists."

[14]   *Bourhill v Young* [1983] A.C. 92 at 108 per Lord Wright.

[15]   162 N.E. 99 (N.Y. 1928).

[16]   162 N.E. 99 at 99 (N.Y. 1928).

"If no hazard was apparent to the eye of ordinary vigilance, an act innocent and harmless, at least to outward seeming, with reference to [C], did not take to itself the quality of a tort because it happened to be a wrong, though apparently not one involving the risk of bodily insecurity, with reference to [someone] else."

Terminology   According to a famous analysis by Hohfeld, the idea of a duty correlates with that of a right.[17] However, it is doubtful whether the mere fact that C is owed a duty of care by D means that C has a right that is exigible against D. Strictly speaking, C has no right good against D unless and until D acts unreasonably with respect to C's interests and that unreasonable conduct causes C damage. It has, therefore, been argued that a duty of care is not really a duty at all and, hence, that it is misleading and confusing to use the language of duty in this context.[18]   **5-010**

Duty of care as a control device   A general liability for negligently causing harm to others would, at least as things are perceived by the courts, be far too onerous for a practical system of law and we shall see that there are areas of activity and types of loss where the law of negligence does not intervene or intervenes only in a limited way. Thus there is, for instance, no general liability for failing to assist or protect others.[19] Nor in general is there liability in respect of negligently inflicted pure economic loss.[20] The following remark by du Parcq LJ in 1946 is as true now as it was then (even though the range of recognised duties has increased substantially in the intervening years)[21]:   **5-011**

> "[I]t is not true to say that whenever a man finds himself in such a position that unless he does a certain act another person may suffer, or that if he does something another person will suffer, then it is his duty in the one case to be careful to do the act and in the other case to be careful not to do the act."

Duty is the primary "control device"[22] which allows the courts to keep liability for negligence within what they regard as acceptable limits and the controversies which have centred on the criteria for the existence of a duty reflect differences of opinion as to the proper ambit of such liability.

The two functions performed by the duty of care concept   The concept of the duty of care is arguably something of an arcane mystery. An Australian judge in 1998, having referred to the foundational speech of Lord Atkin in *Donoghue v Stevenson*,[23] remarked that, "the modern abundance of authority [on the duty of care] … would not make Lord Atkin much wiser".[24] Academic writers have been searing of their criticism of the quality of judicial reasoning in this area.[25] Nevertheless, much difficulty will be avoided if it is grasped that the duty of care element is fulfilling two functions. Because the courts do not decide academic issues but   **5-012**

---

17   Hohfeld (1913) 23 Yale L.J. 16 at 32.
18   Nolan (2013) 129 L.Q.R. 559 at 561–563.
19   See para.5-060.
20   See para.5-049.
21   *Deyong v Shenburn* [1946] K.B. 227 at 233.
22   This famous phrase was coined by Fleming: see Fleming (1953) 31 Can. Bar Rev. 471.
23   See para.5-017.
24   Priestley JA in *Avenhouse v Hornsby SC* (1998) 44 N.S.W.L.R. 1.
25   See, e.g., Stapleton in Cane and Stapleton (eds), *The Law of Obligations* (1998); Nolan (2013) 129 L.Q.R. 559.

disputes between parties, it is true that the question in every case in which the existence of a duty of care is contested is "did *this* defendant owe a duty of care to *this* claimant?" (the first function). Nevertheless, in most of the cases regarding the duty concept the courts have been concerned with broader questions that transcend the particular dispute and that are essentially directed at whether, and if so how far, the law of negligence should operate in a particular situation (the second function). Discussion is therefore couched in terms of general categories such as "Is there a duty of care not to cause pure economic loss by statements?" or "Is there a duty to prevent a third party from inflicting harm on another?". The court is ultimately concerned with mapping the limits of the law of negligence and identifying those areas in which there are factors that suggest that the law should not give a remedy for negligent conduct or at least should do so only to a limited extent. It was, therefore, perfectly possible for the House of Lords in *Hedley Byrne & Co Ltd v Heller & Partners Ltd*[26] to decide that: (1) the law recognised that a duty of care could arise in respect of statements; but (2) no duty was owed on the facts by the defendant to the claimant.[27] The twin functions served by the duty of care concept mean that the court is not concerned only with doing justice as between the parties to a particular case but in all cases of that type. As Lord Browne-Wilkinson explained in *Barrett v Enfield LBC*[28]:

"Once the decision is taken that, say, company auditors though liable to shareholders for negligent auditing are not liable to those proposing to invest in the company ... that decision will apply to all future cases of the same kind."

5-013 **Early disposal of claims** The issue of whether the defendant owed the claimant a duty of care is one of law. As such, the duty of care is often used by the courts as a mechanism for disposing of claims without a full trial. This is done via the power of the court to strike out[29] or order summary judgment[30] of claims that are bound to fail. The court can also order that the issue of whether a duty of care was owed be tried as a preliminary issue.[31] Where the matter can be dealt with at a preliminary stage as an issue of law the court should not hesitate to do so.[32] However, the question of whether a duty was owed may not lend itself to "bright line" rules established without close examination of the facts[33] and this is particularly so[34]:

"[I]n an area of the law which [is] uncertain and developing ... [where] it is not normally appropriate to strike out ... [I]t is of great importance that such development should be on the basis of actual facts found at trial not on hypothetical facts assumed (possibly wrongly) to be true for the purpose of the strike out."

---

[26] *Hedley Byrne & Co Ltd v Heller & Partners Ltd* [1964] A.C. 465, see para.12-027.
[27] On the facts this was because of a disclaimer and disclaimers are no longer automatically effective (see para.12-045).
[28] *Barrett v Enfield LBC* [2001] 2 A.C. 550 at 560. See also *Cooper v Hobart* [2001] SCC 79; [2001] 3 S.C.R. 537 at [37].
[29] CPR Pt.3.4(2).
[30] CPR Pt.24.2.
[31] CPR Pt.3.1(2)(l).
[32] *Kent v Griffiths* [2001] Q.B. 36 at 51.
[33] Even "quite feeble" particulars of negligence may prevent a striking out: *Strickland v Hertfordshire CC* [2003] EWHC 287 (QB).
[34] *Barrett v Enfield LBC* [2001] 2 A.C. 550 at 557 per Lord Browne-Wilkinson.

**A duty of care generally arises in cases of physical damage directly caused by 5-014
a positive act** The issue of duty features comparatively rarely in the day-to-day
business of the courts. That is because most cases of negligence result from acts
directly causing physical damage to persons or property and duty issues arise only
very occasionally in such claims.[35] In *Caparo Industries Plc v Dickman*[36] Lord
Oliver said that in the case of physical damage directly caused by the defendant,
"the existence of the nexus [of duty] between the careless defendant and the injured
plaintiff can rarely give rise to any difficulty".[37] It would, therefore, be wrong to
envisage negligence as a sea of non-liability surrounding islands of liability. If
anything, the true picture is the reverse, for as Lord Goff said[38]:

> "the broad general principle of liability for foreseeable damage is so widely applicable
> that the function of the duty of care is not so much to identify cases where liability is
> imposed as to identify those where it is not."

The need to demonstrate that a duty of care arises on the facts If a duty ex- 5-015
ists in the general sense there may sometimes be an issue as to whether it is applicable to the particular facts before the court or, in other words, whether it was
owed to the particular claimant. For example, the House of Lords in *Donoghue v
Stevenson*[39] was concerned with the general question whether a manufacturer owed
a duty of care to the ultimate user of his products and the conclusion was that he
did. If, however, the product had been stolen from his factory and taken to Australia
where, many years later, it caused injury to C, then it might be a difficult question
to determine whether a duty was owed to C, that is to say, whether C was a foreseeable victim of the initial negligence in manufacture.

Established duty categories and novel duties Many duties of care are long 5-016
established (for example, the duties owed by drivers to other road users and the duties that employers owe to their employees). Others are of more recent vintage but
nonetheless firmly fixed in the law, though they may still be in the course of
development (for example, the duty of a person who has "assumed responsibility"
for a task[40]). In a novel case, the court must make a decision as to whether a new
duty should be recognised. Is there any principle to guide it in this task? Four
periods in the history of the law must be distinguished.

B. The First Period: The Law Prior to Anns v Merton

Donoghue v Stevenson The first attempt to formulate a general principle was 5-017
made by Brett MR in *Heaven v Pender*[41] but by far the most important generalisation is that of Lord Atkin in *Donoghue v Stevenson*.[42] In the latter case, a

---

[35] But see *Langley v Dray* [1998] P.I.Q.R. P314, which involved an unsuccessful attempt to complicate
   a simple road traffic case with a duty issue.
[36] [1990] 2 A.C. 605 at 633.
[37] See also *Mobil Oil Hong Kong Ltd v Hong Kong United Dockyards Ltd* [1991] 2 Lloyd's Rep. 309
   at 328; *Sandhar v Dept of Transport* [2004] EWCA Civ 1440; [2005] P.I.Q.R. P13 at [38]; *Poole
   BC v GN* [2019] UKSC 25; [2019] 2 W.L.R. 1478 at [63].
[38] *Smith v Littlewoods Organisation Ltd* [1987] A.C. 241 at 280.
[39] *Donoghue v Stevenson* [1932] A.C. 562, see para.5-017.
[40] See para.5-040.
[41] (1883) 11 Q.B.D. 503 at 509.
[42] [1932] A.C. 562. For the history of the litigation and of Mrs Donoghue, see Rodger (1988) 41 C.L.P.

manufacturer sold ginger beer in an opaque bottle to a retailer. The retailer resold it to A, who treated a young woman of her acquaintance with its contents. It was alleged that these included the decomposed remains of a snail which had found its way into the bottle at the factory. The young woman alleged that she became seriously ill as a result and sued the manufacturer for negligence. The doctrine of privity of contract prevented her bringing a claim founded upon breach of the contract of sale, but a majority of the House of Lords held that the manufacturer owed her a duty to take care that the bottle did not contain noxious matter and that he would be liable in tort if that duty was breached. Lord Atkin said[43]:

> "In English law there must be, and is, some general conception of relations giving rise to a duty of care, of which the particular cases found in the books are instances. The liability for negligence, whether you style it such or treat it as in other systems as a species of 'culpa,' is no doubt based upon a general public sentiment of moral wrongdoing for which the offender must pay. But acts or omissions which any moral code would censure cannot, in a practical world, be treated so as to give a right to every person injured by them to demand relief. In this way rules of law arise which limit the range of complainants and the extent of their remedy. The rule that you are to love your neighbour becomes in law, you must not injure your neighbour; and the lawyer's question, Who is my neighbour? receives a restricted reply. You must take reasonable care to avoid acts or omissions which you can reasonably foresee would be likely to injure your neighbour. Who, then, in law is my neighbour? The answer seems to be—persons who are so closely and directly affected by my act that I ought reasonably to have them in contemplation as being so affected when I am directing my mind to the acts or omissions which are called in question."

5-018   **Limited initial significance of the neighbour principle**   There could be no denying that *Donoghue v Stevenson* established that manufacturers owe a duty not to cause physical damage to the ultimate consumers of their products but it seems plain from the structure of Lord Atkin's speech that what we may call the "neighbour principle" was a vital step on the road to this general conclusion of law.[44] Nevertheless, for a long time there was a marked judicial reluctance to accept that the "neighbour principle" had much relevance to determining whether a duty of care might exist in other areas of activity. There continued to be no duty of care in respect of making statements or in disposing of tumbledown houses—words were not like deeds and a dwelling was inherently different from a ginger beer bottle. Certainly, new "duty situations" continued to be recognised for, as Lord Macmillan had said in *Donoghue v Stevenson*, "the categories of negligence are never closed"[45] but little reliance was initially placed upon this generalised concept.

C.   The Second Period: The Law as Stated in Anns v Merton

5-019   **The Anns test**   In *Home Office v Dorset Yacht Co Ltd*[46] Lord Reid suggested that the time had come to regard the "neighbour principle" that had been developed in

---

1; and Chapman, *The Snail and the Ginger Beer* (2010).
[43]   [1932] A.C. 562 at 580.
[44]   The case came before the House of Lords from Scotland as what in modern English procedural terms would be called a preliminary issue and no trial of the truth of the averments seems to have taken place: see Rodger (1988) 41 C.L.P. 1 and Heuston (1957) 20 M.L.R. 2.
[45]   [1932] A.C. 562 at 619.
[46]   [1970] A.C. 1004 at 1027.

Donoghue v Stevenson as applicable in all cases where there was no justification or valid explanation for its exclusion. The suggestion was taken up by the House of Lords in *Anns v Merton LBC*,[47] where Lord Wilberforce famously said[48] that the matter should be approached in two stages.[49] First, one must ask whether there was a sufficient relationship of "proximity or neighbourhood" between claimant and defendant such that, in the defendant's reasonable contemplation, carelessness on his part might cause damage to the claimant. If so, a prima facie duty of care arose. Then, at the second stage, it was necessary to consider whether there were any considerations that ought to "negative, or to reduce or limit" that duty. This rationalisation of the law was eagerly used in several cases to attack previously well-entrenched principles of non-liability. One of the most radical manifestations of this expansive reliance on *Anns* was *Junior Books Ltd v Veitchi Co Ltd*,[50] where a majority of the House of Lords in dealing with a loss which was purely economic in nature, imposed a liability which appeared to conflict with hitherto well-established principles.[51]

D. The Third Period: The Caparo Test

The demise of the Anns test   In the 1980s, significant doubt was cast in several   **5-020**
cases on the *Anns* test. An important step in the "counter-revolution" was the decision of the Privy Council in *Yuen Kun Yeu v Attorney General of Hong Kong*,[52] in which *Anns* was reinterpreted.[53] A statutory officer, the Commissioner of Deposit-taking Companies, registered as a deposit-taker a company that subsequently went into liquidation with the result being that the claimants lost money that they had deposited with it. The claimants alleged that the Commissioner knew or ought to have known that the affairs of the company were being conducted fraudulently and speculatively, that he failed to exercise his statutory powers of supervision so as to ensure that the company complied with its obligations and that he should either never have registered the company or have revoked its registration. On a preliminary issue of law and assuming these allegations to be well founded, the Privy Council upheld the judgment of the Hong Kong Court of Appeal in favour of the Commissioner. It is hard to take exception to the decision itself, even though the Commissioner's function was of course the protection of depositors, for the facts were replete with characteristics which have been relied upon in many other cases as justifying the denial of a duty. The loss was purely economic in nature; the claimants were unascertained members of a huge class of persons depositing money with Hong Kong financial institutions and had no "special relationship" with the Com-

---

47   [1978] A.C. 728.
48   [1978] A.C. 728 at 751–752.
49   This test has been severely criticised. Stevens described it as "the greatest 20th century judicial disaster in the law of torts": Stevens in Degeling, Edelman and Goudkamp (eds), *Torts in Commercial Law* (2011), p.53.
50   [1983] 1 A.C. 520.
51   The case is dealt with more fully at para.5-056.
52   [1988] A.C. 175. See also *Governors of the Peabody Donation Fund v Sir Lindsay Parkinson Ltd* [1985] A.C. 210; *Candlewood Navigation Corp v Mitsui OSK Lines* [1986] A.C. 1; *Leigh and Sillavan Ltd v Aliakmon Shipping Co Ltd* [1986] A.C. 785.
53   The *Anns* test still has its defenders. A modified version of it is usually used in Canada: *Fullowka v Pinkerton's of Canada Ltd* [2010] SCC 5; [2010] 1 S.C.R. 132 at [18]. For an attempt to rehabilitate the *Anns* test, see Robertson (2011) 127 L.Q.R. 370.

missioner; the loss had been directly inflicted by the wrongful act of a third party and there is no general duty to confer protection against such loss; the Commissioner had neither the legal power nor the resources to control the day-to-day running of the many companies subject to this jurisdiction so that no duty which could fairly and practicably be imposed on him would be likely to forestall fraud by those determined to practise it; and the failure of Parliament to impose a civil sanction in the legislation was at least a pointer towards rejecting a common law duty of care. No doubt a court faithfully applying *Anns* might have rejected a duty at the second stage on any or all of these grounds[54] but the Privy Council held that it was not necessary to pass beyond the first stage because these were matters that on a proper view of the law were part of the notion of "proximity". There were, said the Privy Council, two possible interpretations of the first stage of the *Anns* formula: the first was that proximity meant merely reasonable foreseeability of injury, all matters of "policy" then being relegated to the second stage; the other, which was favoured by the Privy Council, was that proximity included other factors which should enter into the decision whether a duty of care should be imposed.

The House of Lords then dealt the *Anns* test a fatal blow in *Murphy v Brentwood DC*.[55] In this case, the defendant council had negligently signed off on flawed plans for the construction of a house. The claimant, who had purchased the defective house from its builders, sued the council claiming damages in respect of a diminution of the house's value once the defects came to light. In the course of holding that no duty of care was owed in respect of such pure economic loss, the House expressly overruled *Anns* and all other authorities in which *Anns* had been followed. It did so in large part on the basis that the *Anns* test was incompatible with the principles that had been established in *Donoghue v Stevenson*. However, the House was also influenced by several other factors including criticism of *Anns* by the High Court of Australia,[56] legislative developments regarding the liability of builders that provided for liability that was significantly more restrictive than that which the *Anns* test would countenance,[57] and concerns about the *Anns* test's potential to expose public authorities to "a large new area of responsibility ... in respect of defective buildings".[58]

5-021   **The Caparo test**   The rejection of the *Anns* test made room for the rise of the *Caparo* test. In *Caparo Industries Plc v Dickman*[59] the issue was whether a company auditor owed a duty of care to investors who suffered losses as a result of investing in the company. The House of Lords held that no duty of care was owed and the decision was subsequently regarded as having given rise to a tripartite test for the existence of a duty of care in a novel case. According to that test, it is necessary to ask whether: (1) the claimant was a type of person who may foreseeably be injured by negligence on the part of the defendant; (2) there was sufficient proximity between the parties; and (3) the imposition of a duty of care would be "fair, just and reasonable". Over time, this approach to the duty of care question became influential, particularly at first instance and in the Court of Appeal. Judges remarked

---

54   As, indeed, the Hong Kong Court of Appeal did: [1986] L.R.C. (Comm.) 300.
55   [1991] 1 A.C. 398.
56   *Sutherland Shire Council v Heyman* (1985) 157 C.L.R. 424.
57   Defective Premises Act 1972 (discussed at para.10-054ff).
58   [1991] 1 A.C. 398 at 457 per Lord Mackay LC.
59   [1990] 2 A.C. 605.

that it applied "to all claims in the modern law of negligence",[60] that it was "the most favoured test"[61] and that it "represents the modern backdrop against which to judge any putative negligence claim".[62] Although, as we will see below, the *Caparo* test has itself been consigned to the history books, it is necessary to address it briefly given that parts of it continue to play an important role in the tort of negligence.

The foreseeability stage The foreseeability stage of the *Caparo* test required it   **5-022** to have been reasonably foreseeable that someone such as the claimant might be injured if the defendant failed to exercise reasonable care. As Lord Russell of Kil-lowen put it, a duty of care would only arise "towards those individuals of whom it may reasonably be anticipated that they will be affected by the act which constitutes the alleged breach".[63] This stage of the *Caparo* test was rarely in issue on account of its having been exceptionally easy to satisfy. It was unnecessary that harm to the claimant specifically have been reasonably foreseeable. Rather, it was sufficient that the claimant was a member of a class that could foreseeably be injured as a result of negligence on the part of the defendant.[64] Further, the issue of foreseeability was tested objectively with the result that it was not a satisfactory answer for the defendant to say that he did not foresee that the claimant might be injured if the reasonable person would have appreciated that risk.

The proximity stage The proximity stage of the *Caparo* test was concerned with   **5-023** "nearness". Spatial propinquity between the parties was sometimes treated as important, but the concept of "nearness" was not, as Lord Atkin observed in *Donoghue v Stevenson*, "confined to mere physical proximity".[65] A closer nexus was required in some types of cases than in others. Where the defendant directly caused physical harm to the claimant or his property by an act, a duty was readily established by showing foreseeability and nothing else.[66] Where, however, there was a failure to act or the loss was purely economic or mental trauma or for some other reason the recognition of a duty based upon only foreseeability was perceived to be problematic, the law would, if it did not deny liability completely, insist on a substantially closer relationship between the parties.

The fair, just and reasonable stage Even if the first and second stage of the   **5-024** *Caparo* test were satisfied, a duty of care could still be denied if, in the court's view, it was not fair, just and reasonable to recognise a duty. A good illustration of a case in which this happened, and which demonstrates the types of factors that courts took into account in this regard, is *Marc Rich & Co AG v Bishop Rock Marine Co Ltd*.[67] The vessel *The Nicholas H* developed a crack while en route from South America

---

[60] *Robinson v Chief Constable of West Yorkshire Police* [2014] EWCA Civ 15; [2014] P.I.Q.R. P14 at [40] per Hallett LJ.
[61] *Van Colle v Chief Constable of the Hertfordshire Police* [2008] UKHL 50; [2009] 1 A.C. 225 at [42] per Lord Bingham.
[62] *Connor v Surrey CC* [2010] EWCA Civ 286; [2011] Q.B. 429 at [102] per Laws LJ.
[63] *Bourhill v Young* [1943] A.C. 92 at 102.
[64] He may join the class after the negligent act but before the damage is suffered: *Aiken v Stewart Wrightson Members Agency Ltd* [1995] 1 W.L.R. 1281.
[65] [1932] A.C. 562 at 581.
[66] *Mobil Oil Hong Kong Ltd v Hong Kong United Dockyards Ltd* [1991] 1 Lloyd's Rep. 309 at 368; *Caparo Industries Plc v Dickman* [1990] 2 A.C. 605 at 632; *Customs and Excise Commissioners v Barclays Bank Plc* [2006] UKHL 28; [2007] 1 A.C. 181 at [31].
[67] [1996] A.C. 211.

to Italy. A surveyor employed by a marine classification society[68] was called in by the master. The surveyor eventually pronounced that the vessel was fit to complete the voyage with temporary welding work. A few days later she sank together with her cargo. The claimants, who were owners of the cargo that was being shipped on board *The Nicholas H*, obtained US$500,000 pursuant to a settlement with the shipowners (this being the limit of the owners' liability under the conventions governing the carriage of goods by sea) and claimed the balance of US$5.7 million from the society. On a preliminary issue of law, for the purposes of which it was assumed that the surveyor was negligent and that the loss of the cargo was a foreseeable consequence of that negligence, a majority of the House of Lords held that the society did not owe a duty of care to the cargo owners. The majority proceeded upon the assumption that the requirement of proximity was satisfied, but concluded that the cumulative effect of several policy factors pointed against a decision in favour of the owners. The most important of these factors related to the structure of the network of transactions involved in carriage by sea. The liability of the shipowner was limited by statute to a specified sum per ton of the ship's tonnage and if the cargo owner were allowed to bypass this by the device of a claim against the classification society (which is beyond the protection of the tonnage limitation) such bodies would be likely to seek to pass on the cost of their liability insurance to shipowners or to seek indemnities against them, thereby disturbing the balance between cargo owners and carriers set by international convention. Even if this did not happen, another layer of insurance cover (namely, the liability cover of the classification society) would be wastefully introduced into the structure. Furthermore, there was a risk that classification societies would decline to survey high risk vessels, thereby causing damaging their function of acting for the public welfare in respect of safety at sea.

The fair, just and reasonable stage of the *Caparo* test encouraged litigants and judges to reach for more or less any policy argument available that weighed in favour of or against the existence or denial of a duty of care. Regard was, for example, had to the effect of recognising a duty on the way in which public money would be spent. In *Robinson v Chief Constable of West Yorkshire Police* the Court of Appeal held that[69]:

> "claims against the police in negligence for their acts or omissions in the course of investigating and suppressing crime and apprehending offenders will fail the third stage of the Caparo test".

In doing so the Court said that if police were placed under a duty of care in this regard their work would be undermined because police resources would in that event be spent not on policing but on paying compensation claims, meeting litigation costs and implementing measures that were aimed at avoiding liability.

In *Smith v Ministry of Defence*,[70] the concern was that recognising a duty of care would render the armed forces less effective in combat. The claimants in this case were servicemen who had been injured in the course of military operations in Iraq or dependants of such servicemen. It was alleged that the Ministry of Defence had

---

[68] These bodies inspect ships and give them certificates of seaworthiness for insurance purposes.
[69] [2014] EWCA Civ 15; [2014] P.I.Q.R. P14 at [46] per Hallett LJ. An appeal to the Supreme Court was allowed: [2018] UKSC 4; [2018] A.C. 736. The Supreme Court's decision, in which the *Caparo* test was decisively rejected, is discussed below: see para.5-027.
[70] [2013] UKSC 41; [2014] A.C. 52.

negligently failed to provide suitable equipment and training. The Ministry applied for the proceedings to be struck out for, relevantly, want of a duty of care. The Supreme Court held that the claims should not be struck out as the duty question could only be resolved once the evidence had been heard. However, it was acknowledged that it would be important to consider, in deciding whether a duty of care was owed, the public interest in the armed services being able to engage in operations without being distracted by the law of torts. As Lord Hope explained[71]:

> "[I]t is of paramount importance that the work that the armed services do in the national interest should not be impeded by having to prepare for or conduct active operations against the enemy under the threat of litigation if things should go wrong. The court [that will hear the claimants' proceedings] must be especially careful … to have regard to the public interest, to the unpredictable nature of armed conflict and to the inevitable risks that it gives rise to when it is striking the balance as to what is fair, just and reasonable."

Another factor to which reference was routinely made was the effect of imposing a duty of care on the law or the legal system more generally. Thus, where there was a statutory regime it was said that a[72]:

> "common law duty must not be inconsistent with the performance … of … statutory duties and powers in the manner intended by Parliament, or contrary in any other way to the presumed legislative intention".

In *CBS Songs Ltd v Amstrad Consumer Electrics Plc*[73] the defendants manufactured tape-to-tape domestic audio systems that facilitated the illegal copying of copyright material. In rejecting any duty of care by the manufacturers to the owners of the copyright, the House of Lords pointed out that in the copyright legislation Parliament had produced what could reasonably be regarded as a code governing the rights of copyright owners and that imposed liability only where copying had been authorised, a requirement plainly not satisfied on the facts since purchasers of the systems were warned against illegal copying by notices on the equipment. To impose liability for negligence would subvert the statutory regime.[74] Conversely, in other situations, the courts were prepared to provide a remedy in the tort of negligence even though doing so would cut across rules in another part of the law. Thus, in *Spring v Guardian Assurance Plc*[75] the House of Lords held that the writer of a reference might owe a duty of care to the subject of the reference notwithstanding that until then it had been assumed that the only liability arose in the torts of libel and malicious falsehood, both of which afford the writer a defence absent proof that the reference was written maliciously.

---

[71]   [2013] UKSC 41; [2014] A.C. 52 at [100].
[72]   *Stovin v Wise* [1996] A.C. 923 at 935 per Lord Nicholls.
[73]   [1988] A.C. 1013.
[74]   See further *Murdoch v Department for Work and Pensions* [2010] EWHC 1988 (QB); *Home Office v Mohammed* [2011] EWCA Civ 351; [2011] 1 W.L.R. 2862; *Desmond v Chief Constable of Nottinghamshire Police* [2011] EWCA Civ 3; *B v Home Office* [2012] EWHC 226 (QB); [2012] 4 All E.R. 276 at [128].
[75]   [1995] 2 A.C. 296, see para.12-050.

E.   The Fourth Period: The Current Law

5-025   **Objections to the Caparo test**   The *Caparo* test suffered from overwhelming objections. The concept of proximity was, essentially, empty and, hence, meaningless. According to the Privy Council in *Yuen Kun Yeu*, proximity meant "the whole concept of necessary [i.e., necessary to produce a duty of care] relationship between the plaintiff and defendant". However, this formulation gave no indication as to when the parties would be considered to be in a proximate relationship. In other words, the concept of proximity referred to that which was necessary in order to generate a duty of care but provided no way of ascertaining whether the requisite closeness existed. The "fair, just and reasonable" stage was to some extent redundant since it cannot ever have been "fair, just and reasonable" to have imposed a duty on a defendant with respect to a given claimant if the other stages of the *Caparo* test were unsatisfied. More fundamentally, the "fair, just and reasonable" formula has been criticised on the basis that it required judges to evaluate considerations of public policy in circumstances where, as Lord Reed recently put it, they "were not well equipped [to do so] in a convincing fashion".[76] To this it may be added that the "fair, just and reasonable" stage gave judges an essentially untrammelled discretion which was often exercised to deny a duty of care on spurious policy grounds including where doing so was contrary to authority that established that the parties' relationship attracted a duty. This injected an unacceptable amount of uncertainty into the duty analysis and derogated from the principle of *stare decisis*.

5-026   **The retreat from the Caparo test**   The Supreme Court's decision in *Michael v Chief Constable of South Wales*[77] was a milestone in the demise of the *Caparo* test.[78] In *Michael*, a woman, fearing that her former partner would attack her, telephoned the police seeking assistance before her partner arrived at her house. The call was wrongly classified by the call handler as not requiring an immediate response with the result that by the time the police reached the woman's house she had been murdered by her former partner. A majority of the Supreme Court held that the police did not owe the woman a duty of care. Two points of particular importance emerge from the decision for present purposes. The first was that Lord Toulson, delivering the majority reasons, criticised the understanding that the *Caparo* case had laid down a general test for the existence of a duty of care. He said[79]:

> "In *Caparo Industries Plc v Dickman* [1990] 2 AC 605 Lord Bridge (with whom Lords Roskill, Ackner and Oliver of Aylmerton agreed) emphasised the inability of any single general principle to provide a practical test which could be applied to every situation to determine whether a duty of care is owed and, if so, what is its scope. He said, at pp 617–618, that there must be not only foreseeability of damage, but there must also exist between the party owing the duty and the party to whom it is owed a relationship characterised by the law as one of 'proximity' or 'neighbourhood', and the situation should be one in which the court considers it fair, just and reasonable that the court should impose a duty of a given scope on one party for the benefit of the other. He added that the concepts

---

[76]   *Poole BC v GN* [2019] UKSC 25; [2019] 2 W.L.R. 1478 at [30].
[77]   [2015] UKSC 2; [2015] A.C. 1732. cf. *Kent v Griffiths* [2001] Q.B. 36 (ambulance service held to owe a duty of care upon ambulance being summoned).
[78]   See Goudkamp (2015) 131 L.Q.R. 519.
[79]   [2015] UKSC 2; [2015] A.C. 1732 at [106].

both of 'proximity' and 'fairness' were not susceptible of any definition which would make them useful as practical tests, but were little more than labels to attach to features of situations which the law recognised as giving rise to a duty of care. Paradoxically, this passage in Lord Bridge's speech has sometimes come to be treated as a blueprint for deciding cases, despite the pains which the author took to make clear that it was not intended to be any such thing."

Lord Toulson then proceeded, in stark contrast with the requirements of the supposed *Caparo* "test", to decide the appeal mainly on the basis of the general principle[80] that liability does not arise for failing to confer benefits on another person absent some exceptional circumstance, such as special control exercised by the defendant over a third party who caused the harm, or a relevant assumption of responsibility by the defendant towards the claimant.

The second point of significance is that Lord Toulson emphasised the importance of adhering closely to precedent and developing the law incrementally, which are matters that the *Caparo* formula sidelines. He said[81]:

"It is true that the categories of negligence are never closed ... , and it would be open to the court to create a new exception to the general rule about omissions. The development of the law of negligence has been by an incremental process rather than giant steps. The established method of the court involves examining the decided cases to see how far the law has gone and where it has refrained from going. From that analysis it looks to see whether there is an argument by analogy for extending liability to a new situation, or whether an earlier limitation is no longer logically or socially justifiable. In doing so it pays regard to the need for overall coherence. Often there will be a mixture of policy considerations to take into account."

Although the final sentence in this passage suggests a continuing role for consideration of policy, overall this incremental approach is a far cry from the analysis required by the *Caparo* test. That is because it does not track the familiar three-stage analysis, because it emphasises respect for precedent whereas existing authorities have no particular importance under the *Caparo* formula, and because it contemplates a conservative approach in deciding whether to extend the circumstances in which a duty of care exists which conservativism is absent on the *Caparo* analysis.

Rejection of the Caparo test   *Michael* was followed by the Supreme Court's   **5-027** decision in *Robinson v Chief Constable of West Yorkshire Police*,[82] in which the *Caparo* test was categorically rejected as an approach to the determination of the duty of care issue.[83] In this case, an elderly pedestrian was knocked over and injured by police officers as they attempted to arrest a suspected criminal. Since injury to the claimant was plainly a foreseeable consequence of negligence on the part of the officers and, in view of the fact that the conduct of the officers was in the nature of an act rather than an omission, it followed straightforwardly, the Supreme Court held, that the officers owed a duty of care to the pedestrian. In the course of reach-

---

80   See para.5-030.
81   [2015] UKSC 2; [2015] A.C. 1732 at [102].
82   [2018] UKSC 4; [2018] A.C. 736. For discussion, see Nolan in Clarry (ed), *The UK Supreme Court Yearbook*, Vol. 9 (2019).
83   Despite the rejection, courts occasionally still apply the *Caparo* test: e.g., *Kalma v African Minerals Ltd* [2020] EWCA Civ 144 at [138].

ing that conclusion, the Court clarified several important matters. The first was that the *Caparo* decision did not establish a universal test for the existence of a duty of care in novel situations. Lord Reed, delivering the principal reasons, emphasised that the understanding that *Caparo* had laid down a tripartite test (or, indeed, that the judges in *Caparo* had even attempted to establish a general duty test at all) was mistaken.[84] The second was that where a case falls within a category in which precedent establishes that a duty is owed (or is not owed), it is impermissible, subject to rules regarding the circumstances in which authority can be overruled, to ask *de novo* by reference to policy considerations whether a duty of care should be denied (or recognised).[85] The third was that in novel cases, the proper approach to deciding whether a duty of care was owed is to reason "incrementally and by analogy with established authority".[86] Finally, Lord Reed emphasised that discussions of policy considerations are "not a routine aspect of deciding cases in the law of negligence, and are unnecessary when existing principles provide a clear basis for the decision, as in the present appeal".[87] While policy considerations were thus relegated to a position of reduced importance, Lord Reed accepted that "the exercise of judgement about the potential consequences of a decision" had a part to play when a court was asked to decide whether a novel duty of care existed,[88] at least where "established principles" did not provide a clear answer to the duty question.[89] It will be apparent from the foregoing that, to some extent, *Robinson* simply applies the analysis endorsed in *Michael*. At the same time, however, the relevant principles in *Robinson* are articulated much more emphatically than in *Michael*, especially in terms of rejecting the *Caparo* test.

5-028   **Incrementalism**   Numerous points of importance arise in relation to the incremental approach to determining whether a duty of care should be recognised in a novel case.[90] First, it should be observed that *Michael* and *Robinson*, in endorsing the incremental approach, did not usher in a wholly new analysis. Indeed, in some ways, the decisions represent a return to a more traditional approach in circumstances where the courts have long stressed in negligence cases the importance of proceeding by analogy to existing authority and of refraining from making giant extensions to the circumstances in which a duty of care is owed. Second, the incremental approach is not (unlike the *Anns* and *Caparo* tests) a general test for the existence of a duty of care. Rather, it entails the application of the ordinary method of judicial reasoning that is adopted, both inside and outside of tort law, whenever the courts are confronted by a novel case. It is a general principle of the common law that judges should develop the law only by effecting modest accretions to it. The making of dramatic modifications to existing rules is the province not of the judiciary but the legislature. Third, the incremental approach does not mean that the circumstances in which a duty of care will arise will

---

84   In these circumstances, it is surprising that some courts continue to apply the *Caparo* test: see, e.g., *Seddon v Driver and Vehicle Licensing Agency* [2019] EWCA Civ 14; [2019] 1 W.L.R. 4593.
85   This principle was applied in in *Darnley v Croydon Health Services NHS Trust* [2018] UKSC 50; [2019] A.C. 831.
86   [2018] UKSC 4; [2018] A.C. 736 at [27].
87   [2018] UKSC 4; [2018] A.C. 736 at [69].
88   [2018] UKSC 4; [2018] A.C. 736 at [69].
89   [2018] UKSC 4; [2018] A.C. 736 at [42].
90   For an illustration of a case in which the incremental approach was applied, see *Sumner v Colborne* [2018] EWCA Civ 1006; [2019] Q.B. 430.

be inexorably enlarged. Incrementalism can apply "the other way round" so that it will be "particularly difficult to establish a duty of care in a situation closely analogous to one where the law has already denied the existence of such a duty".[91] Fourth, the incremental approach appears to leave some room for remnants of the *Caparo* test. For example, it clearly remains the law that a duty of care will arise only if the claimant belongs to a class of person who could foreseeably be injured by the defendant in the event that the defendant fails to exercise reasonable care. And it is also plain that policy factors will continue to have some resonance, as both Lord Toulson in *Michael* and Lord Reed in *Robinson* made explicit. The idea appears to be that such factors will colour the determination of whether it is just to extend (or refuse to extend) the circumstances in which a duty of care is owed (or denied) by analogy with existing authority. Fifth, the incremental approach places a premium on identifying prior decisions that have parallels with the case at hand. The incremental approach in principle brings enhanced certainty to this area of the law on account of its anchoring the duty enquiry firmly in existing authority. However, part of the price paid for that enhanced certainty is the encouragement that it gives to litigants to embark on extensive trawls of the case law. This incentive has the potential to drive up the cost of determining whether a duty of care exists in a novel case.

3. DUTY OF CARE: SPECIFIC PROBLEMS

Standard categories of case in which the duty of care arises as an issue The   **5-029** focus so far has been upon the general approach to determining whether a duty of care exists. Although the range of situations in which the "duty issue" may arise is almost infinite, there are several standard situations in which it has regularly fallen for consideration and it is necessary to say more about these since they are, to varying degrees, controlled by additional principles. Unfortunately, these standard situations are not watertight and there is a good deal of overlap between them.

A. Omissions

The omissions doctrine It is a general principle of tort law that there is no general   **5-030** duty to act for the benefit of others. The rule is that the defendant must not harm his neighbour (misfeasance) not that the defendant is required to save him from some peril (nonfeasance). The rule was stated starkly by Schiemann LJ in *Vellino v Chief Constable of Greater Manchester* when his Lordship said that "under our law two persons can stand aside and watch a third jump to his death: there is no legal duty to rescue".[92] It has also been suggested that the omissions doctrine prevents liability from arising where the defendant was only "negligibly" involved in what happened.[93] Dissatisfaction with the omissions rule has been ventilated periodically in some quarters[94] and in 1987 one member of the House of Lords, while accepting the existence of the rule, said that it might one day have to be

---

91   *M v MPC* [2007] EWCA Civ 1361 at [41] per Jacob LJ. Consider also *Home Office v Mohammed* [2011] EWCA Civ 351; [2011] 1 W.L.R. 2862 at [27].

92   [2001] EWCA Civ 1249; [2002] 1 W.L.R. 218 at [13].

93   *Kalma v African Minerals Ltd* [2020] EWCA Civ 144 at [128].

94   See, e.g., Linden (1971) 34 M.L.R. 241; Weinrib (1981) 90 Yale L.J. 247; Markesinis (1989) 105 L.Q.R. 104. cf. Honoré in Cane and Stapleton (eds), *Essays for Patrick Atiyah* (1991).

reconsidered.[95] More recently, however, the importance of the rule has been repeatedly and emphatically emphasised at the highest level,[96] and it has also been stressed that it applies to public bodies and to holders of public office as well as to private persons alike.[97] For example, in *Glaister v Appleby-in-Westmorland Town Council* a horse fair had been held in a small town for hundreds of years, and it was held that a local authority was under no obligation to take steps to ensure adequate arrangements for the control of horses or that horse traders had liability insurance against the risk of visitors to the fair being injured by horses. Toulson LJ said[98]:

"[T]he general policy of the law does not extend to holding D legally to blame for injury to C caused by the negligence of T on the ground that D could have prevented it ... As a matter of generality, to hold a person liable to a victim for injury for which the defendant was not directly to blame, but which was caused by the negligence of a third person which the defendant could have foreseen and prevented, would shift the basis of tort liability towards a system for the transfer of losses resulting from injuries not merely caused by the default of the defendant but which a defendant might have been able to prevent."

5-031   **Rationales**   In *Stovin v Wise* Lord Hoffmann said[99]:

"There are sound reasons why omissions require different treatment from positive conduct. It is one thing for the law to say that a person who undertakes some activity shall take reasonable care not to cause damage to others. It is another thing for the law to require that a person who is doing nothing in particular shall take steps to prevent another from suffering harm from the acts of third parties... or natural causes. One can put the matter in political, moral or economic terms. In political terms it is less of an invasion of freedom for the law to require him to consider the safety of others in his actions than to impose upon him a duty to rescue or protect. A moral version of this point may be called the 'Why pick on me?' argument. A duty to prevent harm to others or to render assistance to a person in danger or distress may apply to a large and indeterminate class of people who happen to be able to do something. Why should one be held liable rather than another? In economic terms, the efficient allocation of resources usually requires an activity should bear its own costs. If it benefits from being able to impose some of its costs on other people (what economists call 'externalities') the market is distorted because the activity appears cheaper than it really is. So liability to pay compensation for loss caused by negligent conduct acts as a deterrent against increasing the cost of the activity to the community and reduces externalities. But there is no similar justification for requiring a person who is not doing anything to spend money on behalf of someone else. Except in special cases (such as marine salvage) English law does not reward someone who voluntarily confers a benefit on another. So there must be some special reason why he should have to put his hand in his pocket."

These arguments obviously apply more forcefully in relation to some types of defendant than others. For example, it is difficult to see how they could apply to a public service the function of which is to guard the public against danger, which

---

[95]   Lord Goff in *Smith v Littlewoods Organisation Ltd* [1987] A.C. 241 at 271.

[96]   See, e.g., *Poole BC v GN* [2019] UKSC 25; [2019] 2 W.L.R. 1478 at [64].

[97]   See, e.g., *Poole BC v GN* [2019] UKSC 25; [2019] 2 W.L.R. 1478 at [64]–[65]. See, further, Nolan (2011) 127 L.Q.R. 260.

[98]   *Glaister v Appleby-in-Westmorland Town Council* [2009] EWCA Civ 1325; [2010] P.I.Q.R. P6 at [46]. *Furnell v Flaherty* [2013] EWHC 377 (QB) is another good illustration of the severe difficulties that claimants will often encounter in a claim against a public service for failing to confer benefits. For discussion of this case, see Nolan (2014) 130 L.Q.R. 21.

[99]   [1996] A.C. 923 at 943.

service will also be under some form of pre-existing public law duty (albeit not enforceable by a private law claim for damages) in respect of the performance of its functions.

The limited significance of the omissions doctrine The omissions doctrine is probably less significant in practice than might be thought to be the case for two main reasons. The first is that conduct which may from one point of view seem to be nonfeasance may be treated in law as misfeasance. The second is that the doctrine is subject to several exceptions.[100]   **5-032**

i. Cases Where There is Not a True Omission

An omission in the course of a wider activity may be regarded as an act An apparent omission may be treated as an item in a chain of active conduct. A driver must take positive steps to meet emergencies that arise and no one would seriously contend that his failure to brake at a junction was an omission in the sense here discussed.[101] However, starting something does not of itself impose a legal duty to finish it.[102] Thus, in *Stovin v Wise*[103] the defendant road authority had resolved to improve a junction and then let the matter go to sleep. Had the work been done, the claimant would probably not have been involved in the accident which occurred but, even if that were so, the accident was nevertheless caused by what the authority failed to do as opposed to by anything it did.   **5-033**

ii. Relationships

Introduction Even where there is a "true" omission the law may impose a duty to act. The discussion in this section canvasses a selection of situations where this occurs. Instances where the defendant comes under a duty of care because he has assumed responsibility for the claimant are considered separately later.[104]   **5-034**

Relationships of dependence A duty to act may be imposed where the claimant is under the care or control of the defendant and is incapable of protecting himself. Thus, claims have succeeded against schools for failing to safeguard pupils from injury[105] and against the police[106] and hospitals[107] for failing to protect mentally   **5-035**

---

[100] Regarding the exceptions, see Steel (2019) 135 L.Q.R. 484.

[101] Rigby LJ in *Kelly v Metropolitan Ry Co* [1895] 1 Q.B. 944 at 947 said of a train driver's failure to shut off steam so that his train ran into the dead end, "the proper description of what was done was that it was a negligent act in so managing the train as to allow it to come into contact with the dead-end".

[102] In *Capital & Counties Plc v Hampshire CC* [1997] Q.B. 1004 at 1035 Stuart-Smith LJ considered that if a doctor volunteers his assistance his only duty is not to make the patient worse, but presumably that may include making him worse by dissuading others from seeking to provide assistance. However, a hospital that admits a patient must treat him, not ignore him: *R. (on the application of Burke) v GMC* [2005] EWCA Civ 1003; [2006] Q.B. 273 at [32].

[103] [1996] A.C. 923.

[104] See paras 5-040—5-047.

[105] On the extent to which a school may have a duty to take action to prevent bullying out of school, see *Bradford-Smart v West Sussex CC* [2002] EWCA Civ 7; [2002] E.L.R. 139. Schools are not obliged to take out accident insurance for the child, or to advise the parents to do so: *Van Oppen v Bedford School* [1990] 1 W.L.R. 235.

[106] *Kirkham v Chief Constable of Greater Manchester* [1990] 2 Q.B. 283 (as to suicide by sane persons

disturbed persons in their custody from self-inflicted harm. In *Reeves v Metropolitan Police Commissioner*[108] the police were held liable for negligently failing to prevent the suicide of a sane person in custody in their cells. In fact, the existence of a duty of care was never challenged and the matter was fought in the House of Lords on the issue of whether the deliberate act of the deceased broke the chain of causation[109] but the clear implication is that the defendants' concession on the issue of duty was rightly made. However, a duty to prevent others of full age and capacity from harming themselves will be rare, for "on the whole people are entitled to act as they please, even if this will inevitably lead to their own death or injury".[110] So the existence of the duty turned on the fact that the deceased was in the police cells and the police had reason to know that he was a suicide risk.[111] It might seem obvious that a parent owes a duty to his child and this seems to be the law[112] although there is, perhaps due to the likely absence of liability insurance in this setting, a dearth of authority on the point.[113] However, it should be noted that the imposition of a duty would allow an insured defendant to seek contribution from an uninsured parent (e.g., in a case arising out of a road accident where the parent had failed to supervise the child).[114]

5-036 **Other relationships with the victim** A duty to act may be imposed on the defendant if he benefits or stands to benefit from his relationship with the claimant. Thus, an employer must not only take proper steps to secure safety in the workplace[115] but must look after a worker who is injured or falls ill at work even if the employer is not responsible for the emergency.[116] The same rule applies in relation to carriers with regard to their passengers.[117] Indeed, the Supreme Court of Canada has extended this so as to hold that a private boat owner was obliged to take steps to rescue a guest who fell overboard.[118] An occupier is required to take reason-

---

in custody, see para.5-035).

[107] *Savage v S Essex Partnership NHS Foundation Trust* [2008] UKHL 74; [2009] 1 A.C. 681 at [47].

[108] [2000] 1 A.C. 360.

[109] See para.7-058.

[110] *Reeves v Metropolitan Police Commissioner* [2000] 1 A.C. 360 at 379 per Lord Hope. "Under the domestic law of the United Kingdom there is no general legal duty on the state to prevent everyone within its jurisdiction from committing suicide": *Savage v S Essex Partnership NHS Foundation Trust* [2008] UKHL 74; [2009] 1 A.C. 681 at [25] per Lord Scott. See also para.10-021.

[111] By contrast, the police do not owe a duty of care to prevent a person who has just been arrested escaping and injuring himself in the process: *Vellino v Chief Constable of Greater Manchester* [2001] EWCA Civ 1249; [2002] 1 W.L.R. 218.

[112] *Surtees v Kingston on Thames BC* [1992] P.I.Q.R. P101 (foster parent). See also Saville LJ in *Marc Rich & Co AG v Bishop Rock Marine* [1994] 1 W.L.R. 1071 at 1077 (no duty on stranger to save blind man from road accident, but duty on parent to prevent child running into the road).

[113] Although see *XA v YA* [2010] EWHC 1983 (QB).

[114] Hence the caution of the High Court of Australia about imposing liability in *Hahn v Conley* (1971) 126 C.L.R. 378 unless the parent has embarked on some activity.

[115] See Ch.9. This duty does not however require employers to arrange accident insurance for workers abroad in a country with no developed system of motor insurance: *Reid v Rush and Tompkins Group Plc* [1990] 1 W.L.R. 212. cf. *Van Oppen v Clerk to the Bedford Charity Trustees* [1990] 1 W.L.R. 235.

[116] *Kasapis v Laimos* [1959] 2 Lloyd's Rep. 378. He is under no duty to safeguard the employee's property against theft: *Deyong v Shenburn* [1946] 1 K.B. 236.

[117] A duty to try to rescue a man overboard was conceded in *Davis v Stena Line Ltd* [2005] EWHC 420 (QB); [2005] 2 Lloyd's Rep. 13.

[118] *Horsley v Maclaren, The Ogopogo* [1971] 2 Lloyd's Rep. 410. But a taxi driver is not under a duty to assess the sobriety of his passenger and to set him down only where a drunken person would be

able care to ensure that his premises are reasonably safe for the purposes for which his visitor enters[119] and may also owe a duty to trespassers. Both of these duties may clearly require positive steps to be taken, such as the carrying out of repairs or putting up of warnings.[120] And the mere existence of a relationship between the parties does not mean that there is a protective duty: a social landlord who took action against an abusive tenant was not liable when the tenant responded by killing the person who had initiated the complaint.[121]

How far is a defendant providing an ordinary service, such as the sale of alcohol, under a duty to protect a claimant of full age and understanding against his own weakness? In *Barrett v Ministry of Defence*[122] the defendants operated a military base at an isolated site in northern Norway at which alcohol was available cheaply and drinking was a principal recreation. The claimant's husband died after consuming a large quantity of alcohol. The Court of Appeal rejected the contention that the defendants were under a duty to monitor and control the consumption of alcohol at the base, despite the fact that the disciplinary code contained provisions designed to curb excessive consumption. Beldam LJ, delivering the judgment of the Court of Appeal, pointed out that the level of consumption which might put a person in danger varied considerably from person to person and that it was[123]:

"[F]air, just and reasonable for the law to leave a responsible adult to assume responsibility for his own actions in consuming alcoholic drink. No one is better placed to judge the amount that he can safely consume or to exercise control in his own interest as well as in the interest of others. To dilute self-responsibility and to blame one adult for another's lack of self-control is neither just nor reasonable and in the development of the law of negligence is an increment too far."

The defendants were, however, liable for the death, subject to a two-thirds reduction in damages on account of contributory negligence, because of the way in which they had dealt with the deceased after he was found in a collapsed state.[124] Conversely, in *Jebson v Ministry of Defence*,[125] the defendants were held liable for an injury caused by their failure to supervise the claimant soldier during his return journey from an evening's drinking organised by the company commander. Perhaps that case is to be explained by the context that the soldiers were under military discipline.

The High Court of Australia has firmly rejected the view that a commercial seller of alcohol owes a duty of care to monitor the consumption of his customers or restrain them from leaving if he considers, for example, that they are unfit to drive. Such a duty would require surveillance and inquiries which would be seriously

---

safe: *Griffiths v Brown, The Times,* 23 October 1998.
[119] See, e.g., *Everett v Comojo Ltd* [2011] EWCA Civ 13; [2012] 1 W.L.R. 150 (nightclub).
[120] See generally Ch.10.
[121] *Mitchell v Glasgow CC* [2009] UKHL 11; [2009] 1 A.C. 874. See also *X v Hounslow LBC* [2009] EWCA Civ 286; [2009] P.T.S.R 1158.
[122] [1995] 1 W.L.R. 1217.
[123] [1995] 1 W.L.R. 1217 at 1224. Nor is a bookmaker under any general duty to safeguard punters against the risks of gambling: *Calvert v William Hill Credit Ltd* [2008] EWCA Civ 1427; [2009] Ch. 330.
[124] *Crocker v Sundance Northwest Resorts* [1988] 1 S.C.R. 1186 and *Jordan House v Menow* [1974] S.C.R. 239 were distinguished. In *Crocker*, the defendant had permitted the claimant to take part in a ski race as well as supplying drink. In *Jordan House*, the defendant had put the obviously intoxicated claimant out of the bar on a highway.
[125] [2000] 1 W.L.R. 2055.

invasive of customers' autonomy and potentially destructive to peaceful social relations. Gummow, Heydon and Crennan JJ wrote[126]:

> "To encourage interference by publicans, nervous about liability, with the individual freedom of drinkers to choose how much to drink and at what pace is to take a very large step. It is a step for legislatures, not courts, and it is a step which legislatures have taken only after mature consideration. It would be paradoxical if members of the public who may deliberately wish to become intoxicated and to lose the inhibitions and self-awareness of sobriety, and for that reason are attracted to attend hotels and restaurants, were to have that desire thwarted because the tort of negligence encouraged an interfering paternalism on the part of those who run the hotels and restaurants."

There may be exceptional cases where the drinker is beyond any rational action or mentally ill but the case was not made exceptional because the drinker had asked the bar owner to store his motorcycle and then demanded that it be returned to him.

5-037 **Relationship with the immediate wrongdoer** A relationship between the defendant and the person who harmed the claimant may lead to liability.[127] Accordingly, a school authority was liable for letting a small child out of school in circumstances where it was foreseeable that he would cause an accident in which a driver was killed trying to avoid him.[128] A parent company may also come under a duty of care to take reasonable steps to prevent one of its subsidiaries from causing damage.[129] The critical issue here will generally be the extent to which the parent company intervened in the management of the subsidiary company.[130] It is important to appreciate that where the parent company comes under a duty of care the courts are not, as has sometimes been suggested, disregarding the fact that the companies are separate legal persons. This principle of independent legal personality is not infringed because in the type of case under consideration the issue is not whether the parent company should be held liable for a breach of any duty of care owed by the subsidiary but whether the parent company is liable to the claimant for its own wrongdoing.[131] A relationship between the defendant and the person who harmed the claimant may result in a duty being imposed on the defendant to take reasonable care to prevent even wilful wrongdoing. Thus, in *Home Office v Dorset Yacht Co Ltd* authorities that failed in their duty of supervision of borstal inmates were responsible for damage done by the inmates to property in the immediate vicinity in the course of an escape.[132] Where the defendant has control over both the claimant and the immediate wrongdoer (for example, in a case where there is an assault on a prisoner by fellow inmates[133]) the case for the imposition of a positive duty of care is particularly strong. We have seen that the police incur no li-

---

[126] *CAL No 14 Pty Ltd v Scott* [2009] HCA 47; (2009) 239 C.L.R. 390 at [54]. See also *Cole v South Tweed Heads Rugby League Football Club Ltd* [2004] HCA 29; (2004) 217 C.L.R. 469.

[127] In some cases the relationship between the defendant and the immediate wrongdoer may make the defendant vicariously liable for the immediate wrongdoer's act: see Ch.21, below.

[128] *Carmarthenshire CC v Lewis* [1955] A.C. 549.

[129] *Chandler v Cape Plc* [2012] EWCA Civ 525; [2012] 1 W.L.R. 3111; *Okpabi v Royal Dutch Shell Plc* [2018] EWCA Civ 191; [2018] Bus. L.R. 1022; *AAA v Unilever Plc* [2018] EWCA Civ 1532; [2018] B.C.C. 959; *Vedanta Resources Plc v Lungowe* [2019] UKSC 20; [2019] 2 W.L.R. 1051.

[130] *Vedanta Resources Plc v Lungowe* [2019] UKSC 20; [2019] 2 W.L.R. 1051 at [44].

[131] For discussion, see Goudkamp (2017) 133 L.Q.R. 560.

[132] [1970] A.C. 1004.

[133] *Ellis v Home Office* [1953] 2 Q.B. 135.

ability for failing to apprehend criminals,[134] but there may be intermediate cases where there is a duty of supervision. In *Couch v Attorney General*[135] the Attorney General was sued as representing the New Zealand probation service on the basis that the service had allowed an offender, during his parole from a sentence for aggravated robbery, to take up employment at premises where there were large quantities of alcohol and cash and at which he had injured the claimant and murdered three other people during the course of theft. The Supreme Court of New Zealand held that these facts disclosed an arguable claim of negligence, although three members of the court considered that the claimant would have to establish that she was a member of a class especially vulnerable in view of the offender's record and her position as a fellow employee.

Occupiers and property owners   An occupier is not only under a duty to his visi-   **5-038**
tors but may also be obliged to take steps to remove a hazard on his land that threatens neighbouring property even though it has arisen from the act of nature or of a third party. In principle this can extend to taking steps to prevent a third party gaining access to the property and using it to inflict damage on the claimant, but such an obligation is in practice rare. Thus, in *Smith v Littlewoods Organisation Ltd*[136] the defendants were not liable when vandals entered an empty cinema scheduled for redevelopment and caused a fire which spread to adjacent properties.[137] Lord Griffiths said[138]:

"So far as Littlewoods knew, there was nothing significantly different about these empty premises from tens of thousands of others up and down the country. People do not mount 24-hour guards on empty properties and the law would impose an intolerable burden if it required them to do so save in the most exceptional circumstances."

iii.   Dangerous Situation Created by Defendant

A defendant who, with or without wrongdoing, creates a source of danger[139]   **5-039**
comes under a duty of care to take reasonable steps to safeguard others against it. For example, if the defendant's car breaks down on the highway the defendant must take steps to prevent it from endangering traffic.[140] Similarly, it has been held that

---

[134] See para.5-004. See further para.5-060.
[135] [2008] NZSC 45; [2008] 3 N.Z.L.R. 725.
[136] [1987] A.C. 241.
[137] What if the claim arises from criminal injury inflicted on the premises by some third party? It would be going too far to say that an occupier can never be under a duty to protect visitors against attack: see, e.g., *Everett v Comojo Ltd* [2011] EWCA Civ 13; [2012] 1 W.L.R. 150 (nightclub); *Al-Najar v The Cumberland Hotel (London) Ltd* [2019] EWHC 1593 (QB) (hotel). But it is unrealistic to expect the occupier to do much to prevent an assault in, say, its car park: *Modbury Triangle Shopping Centre v Anzil* [2000] HCA 61; (2000) 205 C.L.R. 254.
[138] [1987] A.C. 241 at 251. "Unless the needle that measures the probability of a particular result flowing from the conduct of a human agent is near the top of the scale it may be hard to conclude that it has risen sufficiently from the bottom to create the duty reasonably to foresee it": [1987] A.C. 241 at 261 per Lord Mackay.
[139] Steps taken to reduce a source of danger have been held not to qualify: *Kalma v African Minerals Ltd* [2020] EWCA Civ 144 at [133].
[140] *Wright v Lodge* [1993] 4 All E.R. 299. Consider also *Haynes v Harwood* [1934] 1 K.B. 146; *Ancell v McDermott* [1993] 4 All E.R. 355; *Topp v London Country Bus (South West) Ltd* [1993] 1 W.L.R. 976. For further discussion, see Rabin (1999) 49 DePaul L. Rev. 435; Goldberg and Zipursky (2009) 44 Wake Forest L. Rev. 1211.

where a police force allows an unstable and volatile police officer access to a loaded gun, a duty will arise to prevent the officer from using the weapon to injure others.[141] As Lord Scott explained[142]:

> "Sometimes the additional feature [necessary to found a duty of positive action] may be found in the manner in which the victim came to be at risk of harm or injury. If a defendant has played some causative part in the train of events that have led to the risk of injury, a duty to take reasonable steps to avert or lessen the risk may arise."

However, it is important that sensible limits be placed on this creation of danger principle, which has traditionally been strictly confined, especially in cases in which the immediate cause of the harm to the claimant was a third party. There is a clear risk that unless it is appropriately restricted, the creation of danger principle will erode to an unacceptable extent the fundamental rule that there is no liability for failure to control third parties, and result in a duty of care being placed on defendants who were involved in only a purely peripheral or historical way in the chain of events that led to the injury to the claimant. If tort law is to continue to be understood as a system of personal responsibility, liability should save in exceptional circumstances be placed on and only on immediate wrongdoers as opposed to on defendants whose actions merely enable or facilitate wrongdoing by others.

B. Assumption of Responsibility

5-040   **Hedley Byrne & Co Ltd v Heller & Partners Ltd**   In *Hedley Byrne & Co Ltd v Heller & Partners Ltd*[143] the House of Lords held that a duty of care could arise where the defendant had assumed responsibility for the claimant's interests. Although the "assumption of responsibility" notion[144] was not thereby elevated into a general test for the existence of a duty of care, the decision was nevertheless for various reasons a momentous one for tort law and, indeed, for private law more generally.[145] In the first place, *Hedley Byrne* established that the assumption of responsibility concept could be used to overcome the principle, discussed below,[146] that the tort of negligence does not impose liability for pure economic loss. Second, it quickly became plain that if a defendant assumed responsibility for the claimant's interests the defendant could thereby come under a duty to take positive action to safeguard those interests, so that the assumption of responsibility principle constituted a significant exception to omissions doctrine (indeed, to a considerable extent, the various exceptions to the omissions doctrine that have been discussed above today arguably fall to be understood, arguably as manifestations of the assumption of responsibility principle). Third, and relatedly, *Hedley Byrne* enabled a claimant to say that the defendant should have taken steps to benefit him even though, because of the absence of consideration, the parties did not stand in a contractual relationship. The principle in *Hedley Byrne*, when applicable, in a sense gave the claimant for free rights exigible against the defendant that the claim-

---

[141] *Attorney General of the British Virgin Islands v Hartwell* [2004] UKPC 12; [2004] 1 W.L.R. 1273.
[142] *Mitchell v Glasgow CC* [2009] UKHL 11; [2009] 1 A.C. 874 at [40].
[143] [1964] A.C. 465.
[144] See generally Nolan (2019) 72 C.L.P. 123.
[145] See Barker, Grantham and Swain (eds), *The Law of Misstatements* (2015).
[146] See para.5-049.

ant would normally need to buy. *Hedley Byrne* thus threatened to erode three fundamental principles of private law: the rule that liability does not ordinarily arise for negligently inflicted pure economic loss, the principle that there is no tort liability for omissions, and the (contractual) doctrine of consideration.

The significance of the principle in *Hedley Byrne* was increased in the years that followed on account of its scope being extended. On the facts, the House of Lords in *Hedley Byrne* was concerned with a negligent misstatement causing pure economic loss.[147] However, it quickly became clear that the principle that the House established is limited neither to misstatement cases (it is also capable of applying to cases in which the defendant is providing a service or performing a task[148]) nor to situations in which the claimant has suffered pure economic loss (it can also found a duty in physical damage cases[149]). The demise of the *Caparo* test for the existence of a duty of care has further enhanced the importance of the assumption of responsibility concept by depriving the courts of an alternative approach to the duty of care issue.

Illustrations   The principle in *Hedley Byrne* has been used to justify the imposition of a duty of care on an educational psychologist called in by a local authority to advise on a child,[150] on the British Boxing Board of Control in respect of the adequacy of medical arrangements at fights taking place under its aegis,[151] on a referee of an amateur rugby match with regard to the safety of a player,[152] on a solicitor acting for a borrower in connection with the adequacy of the security provided to an unrepresented lender[153] and on the provider of metal warehousing services in respect of the genuineness of receipts.[154] Conversely, an insurer that paid benefits under a health insurance scheme arranged with an employer did not assume responsibility to a worker in respect of the assessment of his condition—the worker's entitlement under the scheme was determined by the contract with his employer and if he contended that the payments had been wrongfully withheld, the proper course was an action against the employer.[155] Nor do fire fighters assume responsibility to the owners of property when they arrive at the scene of a fire.[156]

5-041

The voluntariness requirement   In order for a duty of care to arise on the basis of an assumed responsibility, the assumption of responsibility must have been voluntary. This requires that the defendant's decision to assume the responsibility be "'conscious', 'considered' or 'deliberate'".[157] However, it is unnecessary in order for a defendant to assume responsibility that he subjectively agree to incur the obligation to look out for the claimant's interests: "the touchstone of liability is not

5-042

---

[147] Liability for statements is treated in Ch.12.
[148] *Henderson v Merrett Syndicates Ltd* [1995] 2 A.C. 145.
[149] See, e.g., *W v Essex County Council* [2001] 2 A.C. 550, *Kent v Griffiths* [2001] Q.B. 36.
[150] *Phelps v Hillingdon LBC* [2001] 2 A.C. 619.
[151] *Watson v British Boxing Board of Control Ltd* [2001] Q.B. 1134. See also *Wattleworth v Goodwood Racing Co Ltd* [2004] EWHC 140 (motor sport association advising on safety at tracks).
[152] *Vowles v Evans* [2003] EWCA Civ 318; [2003] 1 W.L.R. 1607.
[153] *Dean v Allin & Watts* [2001] EWCA Civ 758; [2001] 2 Lloyd's Rep. 249. See also *Killick v Pricewaterhouse Coopers* [2001] Lloyd's Rep. P.N. 17 (valuation of shares).
[154] *Natixis SA v Marex Financial* [2019] EWHC 2549 (Comm); [2019] 2 Lloyd's Rep. 431.
[155] *Briscoe v Lubrizol* [2000] I.C.R. 694.
[156] *Capital & Counties Plc v Hampshire CC* [1997] Q.B. 1004 at 1036.
[157] *Customs and Excise Commissioners v Barclays Bank Plc* [2006] UKHL 28; [2007] 1 A.C. 181 at [73] per Lord Walker.

the state of mind of the defendant".[158] Rather, a defendant will be taken to have assumed responsibility if the reasonable person would understand that the defendant
had accepted responsibility for the claimant.[159]

5-043 **The significance of pre-existing obligations** It is a corollary of the fact that a
duty of care will arise on the basis of an assumption of responsibility only if
responsibility was voluntarily assumed that a duty will not be owed if the defendant was acting under compulsion sufficient to negate the existence of the requisite
voluntariness. For example, if the defendant is subjected to duress, responsibility
will not be assumed. However, it is important to appreciate that the mere fact that
the defendant is required by pre-existing obligations to act in a particular way will
not prevent the defendant from assuming responsibility. For example, in *Poole BC
v GN*, Lord Reed said that it is not the case that "an assumption of responsibility
can never arise out of the performance of statutory functions".[160] It is true that there
are several cases that may appear to suggest that pre-existing obligations point
against the defendant having assumed responsibility. In *Customs and Excise Commissioners v Barclays Bank Plc*[161] it was held that a bank did not assume
responsibility to a litigant who had obtained an injunction freezing a customer's account by writing to acknowledge that it had received notice of the injunction. The
House of Lords emphasised in this regard the fact that the bank owed obligations,
breach of which were punishable in committal proceedings, under the injunction.
For example, Lord Walker said, "[i]n this case the appellant bank has not, in any
meaningful sense, made a voluntary assumption of responsibility. It has by the
freezing order had responsibility thrust upon it."[162] However, it is a mistake to read
such cases as establishing that there will be no assumption of responsibility where
the defendant had "no choice" but to act in a particular way on account of other
obligations. Rather, no duty of care arose in cases like *Barclays Bank* because no
responsibility for the claimant's interests was assumed independently of the fact that
pre-existing obligations were owed. Thus, the bank in *Barclays Bank* simply did
nothing to suggest that it had voluntarily taken it upon itself to safeguard the
claimant's interests.

5-044 **The defendant must assume responsibility for the claimant as opposed to a
third party or the world at large** In order for a duty of care to arise based on
an assumption of responsibility, the defendant must have assumed responsibility for
the claimant or a group of persons of which the claimant is a member, as opposed
to some third party, or to the world at large. In *Playboy Club London Ltd v Banca
Nazionale del Lavoro SpA*[163] a casino wished to obtain a credit reference from the
bank of one of its customers. However, it did not make the request of the bank

---

158 *Williams v Natural Life Health Foods Ltd* [1998] 1 W.L.R. 830 at 835 per Lord Steyn.
159 *Smith v Eric S. Bush* [1990] 1 A.C. 831 at 862; *Henderson v Merrett Syndicates Ltd* [1995] 2 A.C.
    145 at 181; *Phelps v Hillingdon LBC* [2001] 2 A.C. 619 at 654.
160 [2019] UKSC 25; [2019] 2 W.L.R. 1478 at [72].
161 [2006] UKHL 28; [2007] 1 A.C. 181.
162 [2006] UKHL 28; [2007] 1 A.C. 181 at [74]. In the same case, Lord Bingham said: "I do not think
    that the notion of assumption of responsibility, even on an objective approach, can aptly be applied
    to the situation which arose between the commissioners and the bank on notification to it of the
    orders. Of course it was bound by law to comply. But it had no choice. It did not assume any
    responsibility towards the commissioners" (at [14]).
163 [2018] UKSC 43; [2018] 1 W.L.R. 4041.

directly but through an agent. The bank, which negligently stated that the customer was creditworthy despite its having had no relevant dealings with him, did not know that the request for a reference was ultimately emanating from the casino. The casino ended up being saddled with large losses when the customer disappeared after writing bad cheques in return for gambling chips. The casino sued the bank on the basis that the former had assumed responsibility for it by writing the credit reference. Lord Sumption said that[164]:

> "[i]t is fundamental to this way of analysing the duty that the defendant is assuming a responsibility to an identifiable (although not necessarily identified) person or group of persons, and not to the world at large or to a wholly indeterminate group."

In a statement case, Lord Sumption added that it must[165]:

> "be part of the statement's known purpose that it should be communicated and relied upon by [the claimant], if the representor is to be taken to assume responsibility to [the claimant]."

Because the casino was unable to establish that the bank had assumed responsibility to it specifically its claim against the bank failed.

Context Whether or not the defendant has assumed responsibility for the claimant's interests depends on the full circumstances of the case.[166] Highly relevant considerations in this regard will generally include the following. First, it may be important whether the defendant had or professed to have special skills.[167] This factor is relevant because possession of particular expertise makes it more likely than would otherwise be the case that the defendant would take it upon himself to look out for the claimant's concerns. Second, the nature of the occasion on which the parties dealt with each other will generally be significant. If the parties were interacting on a social occasion that will tend to point against responsibility having been assumed while the converse will be the case if the setting was a professional or commercial one.[168] Third, the existence of any representations made by the defendant to the claimant that are to the effect that the claimant can entrust the matter to the defendant may be of decisive importance. Fourth, and conversely, statements disclaiming responsibility or purporting to exclude liability will almost always establish that responsibility was not assumed[169] and it was because of such a disclaimer that the claim in *Hedley Byrne* itself failed.[170] Fifth, existing arrangements between the parties may militate against responsibility being assumed. For example, responsibility is unlikely to be assumed if it would be inconsistent with

5-045

---

164 [2018] UKSC 43; [2018] 1 W.L.R. 4041 at [7].
165 [2018] UKSC 43; [2018] 1 W.L.R. 4041 at [11].
166 Much depends on "the detailed circumstances of the particular case and the particular relationship between the parties in the context of their legal and factual situation as a whole": *Customs and Excise Commissioners v Barclays Bank Plc* [2006] UKHL 28; [2007] 1 A.C. 181 at [8] per Lord Bingham.
167 *Hedley Byrne & Co Ltd v Heller & Partners Ltd* [1964] A.C. 465 at 502–503.
168 *Lejonvarn v Burgess* [2017] EWCA Civ 254; [2017] B.L.R. 277 at [76].
169 Although a disclaimer should not be construed as though it were a contractual exclusion clause and is, instead, just one of several contextual matters to take into account: *McCullagh v Lane Fox & Partners Ltd* [1996] P.N.L.R. 205 at 237.
170 For another illustration of a case in which a disclaimer operated to prevent responsibility from being assumed in respect of certain matters, see *Natixis SA v Marex Financial* [2019] EWHC 2549 (Comm); [2019] 2 Lloyd's Rep. 431 at [359].

the terms of a contract between the parties,[171] or if the parties had taken other steps to structure their relationship so as to avoid their incurring liability directly to each other.[172] Sixth, a court is unlikely to recognise a duty of care on the basis of an assumed responsibility if doing so would be contrary to public policy.[173]

5-046   **Reliance**   In *Customs and Excise Commissioners v Barclays Bank Plc* Lord Bingham said that "reliance in the law is usually taken to mean that if A had not relied on B he would have acted differently".[174] Reliance by the claimant on an assumption of responsibility has sometimes been treated as a prerequisite to a duty of care arising. However, on other occasions, the courts have found a duty of care based on an assumed responsibility notwithstanding the absence of any reliance. A good illustration is *Barrett v Ministry of Defence*,[175] which is discussed above,[176] in which it was found that the defendant had assumed responsibility for a naval airman by taking him into its care. That finding was made even though the airman was incapable of relying on the defendant on account of his heavily intoxicated state.[177]

5-047   **Deemed assumption of responsibility**   The courts have sometimes found an assumption of responsibility even though it is quite clear that responsibility was not assumed.[178] The cases concerned are best categorised as instances of "deemed assumed responsibility". The leading illustration is *White v Jones*.[179] A testator, having made a will disinheriting his daughters after a family quarrel, reconciled with them and instructed his solicitor to prepare a new will restoring the daughters as beneficiaries. However, the solicitor negligently delayed in implementing that instruction and the testator died before the new will could be executed. Consequently, the "old" will governed the devolution of the testator's estate. The delay was a breach of the contract between the solicitor and the testator but, since the testator's estate was in no way diminished in size by the solicitor's failure promptly to implement the testator's instructions, the estate could have sued the solicitor only for nominal damages. And the daughters could not, of course, sue on the contract, as they were not parties to it. However, a majority of the House of Lords held that the solicitor owed the daughters a duty of care in the tort of negligence[180] on the basis of the assumption of responsibility concept. It is plain, however, that responsibility was not in fact assumed. The solicitor could hardly have assumed

---

[171] *Henderson v Merrett Syndicates Ltd* [1995] 2 A.C. 145 at 194–195; *Robinson v PE Jones (Contractors) Ltd* [2011] EWCA Civ 9; [2012] Q.B. 44 at [84].

[172] *Henderson v Merrett Syndicates Ltd* [1995] 2 A.C. 145 at 195; *Muirhead v Industrial Tank Specialities Ltd* [1986] Q.B. 507; *Simaan General Contracting Co v Pilkington Glass Ltd (No.2)* [1988] Q.B. 758 at 781, 785; *RM Turton & Co Ltd (in liq) v Kerslake and Partners* [2000] 3 N.Z.L.R. 406.

[173] For discussion, see Barker, "Economic Loss and the Duty of Care: A Study in the Exercise of Legal Justification" in Rickett (ed), *Justifying Private Law Remedies* (2008), p.195.

[174] [2006] UKHL 28; [2007] 1 A.C. 181 at [14].

[175] [1995] 1 W.L.R. 1217.

[176] See para.5-036.

[177] Consider, also, *Barrett v Enfield LBC* [2001] 2 A.C. 550, *Hedley Byrne & Co Ltd v Heller & Partners Ltd* [1964] A.C. 465 at 495.

[178] "There has sometimes been a tendency for courts to use the expression 'assumption of responsibility' when in truth the responsibility has been imposed by the court rather than assumed by D": *Michael v Chief Constable of South Wales* [2015] UKSC 2; [2015] A.C. 1732 at [100] per Lord Toulson.

[179] [1995] 2 A.C. 207.

[180] In *Hill v Van Erp* (1997) 188 C.L.R. 159 the majority of the High Court of Australia also concluded that a solicitor owed a duty to a disappointed beneficiary.

responsibility for the daughters since their interests could well have diverged from those of his client, the testator, to whom he had assumed responsibility. In these circumstances, the decision should be regarded as involving a deemed rather than actual assumption of responsibility. As Lord Goff said[181]:

> "In my opinion, therefore, your Lordships' House should in cases such as these extend to the intended beneficiary a remedy under the *Hedley Byrne* principle by holding that the assumption of responsibility by the solicitor towards his client *should be held in law* to extend to the intended beneficiary who (as the solicitor can reasonably foresee) may, as a result of the solicitor's negligence, be deprived of his intended legacy in circumstances in which neither the testator nor his estate will have a remedy against the solicitor."

As a side comment, it is worth noting that the House decided in *White* that a duty was owed to the daughters even though they had not been deprived of anything that they possessed or to which they had any right, since the testator could have cut them out of his will again for any or no reason at all and that the practical result was to increase the size of the testator's bounty at the expense of the solicitor, since the legatee under the unrevoked will could plainly keep what the testator did not intend to give him.[182] It is rather hard to explain why persons who foreseeably rely on an auditor's report cannot sue,[183] whereas those who find that they were the object of the intended bounty of a long-lost relative can. For Lord Goff, in the majority, the dominant factor seems to have been a strong "impulse for practical justice"[184] bolstered by a need for the law to recognise the role of solicitors in relation to testators and legatees and the fact that the courts in other major common law jurisdictions seemed all to have come down in favour of liability. It should also be noted that such a situation does not normally involve any possibility of wide-ranging or indeterminate liability. In such a case the defendant's contemplation of the claimant is: "actual, nominate and direct. It is contemplation by contract, though of course the contract is with the testator."[185]

C. Pure Economic Loss

The concept of "pure economic loss"　Much of the controversy about the role 　**5-048**
of the duty of care element of the tort of negligence has arisen in cases that have involved "pure economic loss". The expression "pure economic loss" is liable to mislead: if a car is negligently destroyed, that is "economic" in the sense that the owner's assets are thereby diminished, but in legal terms it is classified as damage to property and the owner is entitled to its value as damages. Further, even if a loss is unquestionably only financial in nature, no difficulty is felt about allowing its

---

181 [1995] 2 A.C. 207 at 268 (emphasis added).
182 "What is plain is that the family as a whole are better off because of the [solicitor's] negligence": [1995] 2 A.C. 207 at 293 per Lord Nolan. Hence the view of some that the answer lies in a modification of the law of succession: see Weir (1995) 111 L.Q.R. 357. cf. Cretney (1996) 112 L.Q.R. 54.
183 See para.5-021.
184 [1995] 2 A.C. 207 at 259.
185 *Ross v Caunters* [1980] Ch. 297 at 308 per Sir Robert Megarry VC. However, it is not wholly true to say that the quantum of the liability is certain. Suppose A intends to make a will leaving all his estate to B and A wins the National Lottery or discovers a Rembrandt in the attic. It is also possible in theory that there could be claims by persons who were unidentifiable at the time of the transaction (e.g., unborn members of a class). Lord Goff in *White v Jones* was content to leave such cases to be decided when they arose: [1995] 2 A.C. 207 at 269.

recovery if it is a *consequence* of physical injury to the claimant or damage to his property. For example, if the claimant suffers physical injuries due to the defendant's negligence and incurs medical expenses as a result, the claimant will be able to recover damages in respect of those expenses. In this part of this chapter, we are concerned with cases in which the economic loss is not consequential upon physical injuries or property damage inflicted on the claimant by the defendant.

5-049   **Situations in which pure economic loss is recoverable in tort are narrowly confined**   The circumstances in which the law of torts permits damages to be recovered for pure economic loss are narrowly confined. This is for various reasons. In the first place, it is possible to detect in the cases a perception among judges that pure economic loss is less serious, all other things being equal, than physical damage. Furthermore, there is a concern that if defendants are held responsible too readily for pure economic loss, the liability imposed will be disproportionate to the gravity of their wrongdoing. It is certainly the case that a single act of negligence can easily cause pure economic loss of great magnitude to many people, whereas negligent conduct that causes physical damage does not generally have the same potential. For example, if D interrupts the electricity supply to a whole neighbourhood a very substantial number of businesses may suffer significant financial losses. And if D causes pure economic loss to C, people from whom C bought goods might find that C buys fewer goods from them because less money is available to him, and those people might in turn have less money available to them and so on.

The restrictive approach to the recovery of damages for pure economic loss is most marked in the law of negligence, where the general rule is that one cannot recover damages for pure economic loss unless the defendant has assumed responsibility to safeguard the claimant from suffering such loss. There is significantly less difficulty about allowing the claimant to recover compensation for pure economic loss in the case of intentional torts such as deceit or intentionally inducing a breach of contract, since the requirement of intention sets the bar of culpability much higher, and because the defendant's liability for such torts will be limited to the persons whom he intended to harm. Another point to note is that tort law's restrictive attitude regarding the recovery of damages for pure economic loss is not mirrored in the law of contract. Thus, a claimant who can sue in contract will not face any special difficulty on account of the loss about which he complains being purely economic. Most claims for breach of contract involve only pure economic loss. Undoubtedly, a large part of the reason why the law of contract has no reservations about compensating pure economic loss is that, exceptions aside, the class of persons who can claim is limited by the doctrine of privity to contracting parties.

5-050   **Other considerations militating against the existence of a duty of care**   There are considerable difficulties in expounding the law in this area because cases involving pure economic loss often involve other factors that inhibit the imposition of a duty of care. For example, if a public authority fails to carry out an adequate inspection of a house in the course of its construction and is subsequently sued by the owner in respect of defects that later come to light at least three potential "problems" arise for the owner in relation to the duty of care issue. The first is that the loss suffered by the owner is purely economic. Although the loss manifests itself in physical defects in the building, the loss does not amount to property damage because nothing belonging to the owner has been made physically worse than it was previously. The second is that the authority's conduct concerned comprises a mere omission—failure to prevent the builder erecting a shoddy structure. And the third is that since the authority cannot devote infinite resources to such matters, the question arises of how far the courts will interfere with the authority's decision on allocation (although it may be said that this is more relevant to the breach element of the tort of negligence than the duty element). Some degree of overlap is therefore inevitable in any exposition of the law. In this section, we consider two situations: (1) where damage to the person or property of a third person causes pure economic loss to the claimant; and (2) where the claimant suffers pure economic loss because of defects in the quality of goods or property supplied to him.[186] The situation where pure economic loss is caused by the defendant's failure to fulfil an undertaking to perform a service has already been considered[187] and the liability for pure economic loss arising from statements is dealt with in Ch.12.

i. Pure Economic Loss Resulting from Injury to a Third Party

The general rule   Pure economic loss suffered because of damage to a third   **5-051**
party's person or property is generally irrecoverable for want of a duty of care. If D negligently damages X's property, X can sue D in negligence for that damage and foreseeable consequential economic loss resulting from it (for example, an unavoidable loss of revenue while the property is being repaired) but if C suffers loss because he is prevented from using that property as a result of the damage, C generally cannot sue D. Similarly, if D negligently kills X, who employs C, and C thereby loses his job C cannot recover damages from D,[188] though in the related context of loss of support from a deceased family member there is an important statutory modification of this.[189] In the words of Lord Oliver[190]:

> "[I]n an uninterrupted line of cases since 1875, it has consistently been held that a third party cannot successfully sue in tort for the interference with his economic expectations or advantage resulting from injury to the person or property of another person."

Spartan Steel & Alloys Ltd v Martin & Co (Contractors) Ltd   The general rule   **5-052**
is neatly illustrated by *Spartan Steel & Alloys Ltd v Martin & Co (Contractors) Ltd*.[191] The defendants negligently damaged a power cable owed by an electricity business resulting in a loss of power to the claimants' factory. This caused material to solidify in the claimants' furnace. The claimants recovered the reduction in value of the solidified "melt" (which had undergone a chemical change from partial processing (i.e., property damage)) and the profit they would have made from its sale as an ingot but for the negligence (i.e., consequential economic loss). However, but they recovered nothing for the loss of profit on four further melts which would normally have been processed during the period of time for which the power supply had been interrupted (i.e., pure economic loss), for this was not a consequence of any damage to their property but simply of the interruption of the electricity supply. In duty language, the defendants owed the claimants a duty in respect of

---

186 This is taken up in more detail in Chs 10–11.
187 See para.5-040.
188 *Islington LBC v University College London Hospital NHS Trust* [2005] EWCA Civ 596.
189 See Ch.24.
190 *Murphy v Brentwood DC* [1991] A.C. 398 at 485.
191 [1973] 2 Q.B. 27.

damage to their property[192] but did not owe them any duty with respect to mere loss of profits unconnected therewith. Of course, property damage was the source of the whole of the claimants' loss but with regard to the lost profits on the four melts it was a consequence of damage to the property of the electricity business, which had suffered no loss other than the cost of repairing the damaged cable and, perhaps, loss of revenue while the supply was interrupted. In other words, the claimant may only sue for damage to property and economic loss consequent on that if it is his property that is damaged[193] —though ownership is not necessary, possession (or even an immediate right to possession[194]) will suffice.[195] For this purpose an equitable owner of the property may recover, certainly if the legal owner is joined in the action and perhaps even without that formality.[196] It is not, however, enough that the claimant has merely contractual rights with respect to the property that are rendered less valuable as a result of the damage or that he has contractual obligations in respect of it which become more onerous.[197] If, therefore, the electricity supply in *Spartan Steel* had been speedily restored but the cooling had damaged the furnace, loss of production during the time taken to effect repairs to it would, it seems, have been recoverable. Equally the claimants would have succeeded if title to the electricity cable, at the point at which it was severed, had been vested in them.

5-053 **Candlewood Navigation Corp Ltd v Mitsui OSK Lines Ltd** This approach was affirmed by the Privy Council in *Candlewood Navigation Corp Ltd v Mitsui OSK Lines Ltd*[198] where time charterers of a damaged vessel (who did not have possession of it) failed to recover the hire which they had to pay even when the vessel was out of action and the revenue that they lost through being unable to make use of the vessel. It will be observed that there was nothing unforeseeable about the loss to the charterers (such loss being a highly likely consequence of damage to a cargo ship) and that the defendant escaped part of the liability that it would otherwise have incurred had the charterer been in possession of the vessel, for then the lost revenue would have been a consequence of damage to "their" property. The person from whom the charterer had hired the use of the vessel could not sue for this loss since he had not suffered it, nor did he suffer loss of hire, since the charterer had to go on paying it. Of course if the charterer had been relieved under the charter of their obligation to pay hire while the vessel was laid up, the shortfall would have been recoverable by the person from whom it had been hired. The extent of the

---

[192] Consider *Network Rail Infrastructure Ltd v Conarken Group* [2011] EWCA Civ 644; [2012] 1 All E.R. (Comm.) 692.

[193] This is the reason why if an insurer insures A's property and B negligently destroys it the insurer cannot sue the wrongdoer in its own name, though it may be subrogated to A's rights.

[194] *Colour Quest Ltd v Total Downstream UK Plc* [2009] EWHC 540 (Comm); [2009] 2 Lloyd's Rep. 1 and cases cited therein (upheld on this point in *Shell UK Ltd v Total UK Ltd* [2010] EWCA Civ 180; [2011] Q.B. 86).

[195] The common law equates possession and ownership for this purpose. Hence, at common law a bailee can sue for the full value of the goods bailed to him (even though his interest is limited) whether or not he is responsible to the owner for the loss. The amount that a bailee can recover may however now be restricted by statute: see para.18-034.

[196] *Shell UK Ltd v Total UK Ltd* [2010] EWCA Civ 180; [2011] Q.B. 86.

[197] *Cattle v Stockton Waterworks* (1875) L.R. 10 Q.B. 453. Thus, it would seem that fishermen who lost their livelihood as a result of oil pollution could not sue at common law: *Landcatch Ltd v International Oil Pollution Compensation Fund* [1999] 2 Lloyd's Rep. 316; *RJ Tilbury & Sons (Devon) Ltd v Alegrete Shipping Co Inc* [2003] EWCA Civ 65; [2003] 1 Lloyd's Rep. 327.

[198] [1986] A.C. 1.

tortfeasor's liability in such a case therefore turns on the contractual arrangements between the owner[199] of the damaged property and the person making use of it.

An exception to the general principle A principle of law of uncertain ambit   5-054
qualifies the general rule that has just been described. If the defendant negligently damages X's vessel, the owners of cargo in the vessel have to contribute rateably to expenditure necessary to meet the emergency (a "general average contribution") and a cargo owner may sue the defendant for this even though there is no physical damage to his portion of the cargo. In the leading case Lord Roche said[200]:

> "[I]f two lorries A and B are meeting one another on the road, I cannot bring myself to doubt that the driver of lorry A owes a duty to both the owner of lorry B and to the owner of goods then carried on lorry B. Those owners are engaged in a common adventure with or by means of lorry B and if lorry A is negligently driven and damages lorry B so severely, while no damage is done to the goods in it, the goods have to be unloaded for the repair of the lorry and then reloaded or carried forward in some other way and the consequent expense is (by reason of his contract or otherwise) the expense of the owner of the goods, then, in my judgment, the owner of the goods has a direct cause of action to recover such expense. No authority to the contrary was cited, and I know of none relating to land transport."

It seems that Lord Roche's "common adventure" principle is confined to the maritime context or at least to analogous situations involving carriage by land and it was therefore held inapplicable to the relationship between a power generator and an electricity supplier.[201] The question of whether another exception to the general principle arises in instances where expenditure is reasonably incurred by the claimant to prevent him from suffering physical damage as a result of the defendant's negligence has yet to receive a definitive answer, though the arguments in favour of recovery of such "preventive damages" seem strong.[202]

Merits and demerits of the current law The distinction that the law draws   5-055
between pure economic loss and physical damage is controversial and it has been rejected in other common law jurisdictions. The rule certainly rests in part upon the spectre of a liability, in Cardozo J's famous words, "in an indeterminate amount for an indeterminate time to an indeterminate class".[203] This risk is present in the case of interruption of public utility supplies, though it has been contended that it is exaggerated because individual losses may be small and unlikely to lead to much litigation.[204] However, the physical consequences of an accident may be very wide

---

[199] Confusingly, the claimant in Candlewood was the owner of the vessel. It had chartered it by demise to X (which gives possession to X) and then time chartered it back again. The claimant's losses were not suffered in its capacity as owner. In non-marine terms, a charter by demise is like hiring a self-drive van; a time (or voyage) charter is like engaging a removal firm.

[200] *Morrison SS Co Ltd v Greystoke Castle* [1947] A.C. 265 at 280.

[201] *Londonwaste Ltd v Amec Civil Engineering Ltd* (1997) 53 Con.L.R. 66.

[202] Nolan (2016) 132 L.Q.R. 68. See, e.g., *New Zealand Forest Products v Attorney General* [1986] 1 N.Z.L.R. 14.

[203] *Ultramares Corp v Touche* 174 N.E. 441 at 444 (1931).

[204] *New Zealand Forest Products v Attorney General* [1986] 1 N.Z.L.R. 14. In *Spartan Steel* itself it seems that there was no widespread interruption of supplies. However, for a case where more than a million households and businesses were affected (and where the pure economic loss claims failed) see *Johnson Tiles Pty Ltd v Esso Australia Pty Ltd* [2003] VSC 27; [2003] Aust. Torts Reports 81-692.

ranging[205] and in that context the courts do not (at least overtly) deny a remedy because it will be available to many and may bankrupt defendants. Furthermore, the rule applies even where there is no real risk of wide-ranging liability.[206] Conversely, one virtue of the present rule is that it provides a mechanical and fairly easily applied test for the resolution of disputes (and hence for the avoidance of prolonged litigation[207]) and in many cases where it would produce an unjust result it may be open to a potential claimant, if he chooses to do so, to restructure his arrangements to avoid its impact.

ii. Defects of Quality in Goods or Property Supplied

5-056   In *Muirhead v Industrial Tank Specialities Ltd*,[208] the claimant, an enterprising fishmonger, conceived a scheme to supply the market in lobsters at times of high demand by keeping them in tanks. He purchased the tanks from ITS but the pumps in the tanks failed to function properly. The result was that a large number of lobsters died and the claimant suffered loss in being unable to proceed with his project. There was a good claim for breach of contract against ITS but they were insolvent. Accordingly, the claimant sued the French manufacturers of the pumps (with whom he had no contract) alleging that they were negligent in supplying equipment which was not properly adapted for use under English voltages. Damages were recovered for the dead lobsters and for certain consequential losses but the claimant failed in his claim for the cost of the pumps and the profits that would have been made in the business had the pumps functioned properly because such losses were purely economic. It is certainly the law that the manufacturer of goods owes a duty of care to ultimate consumers who are not in a contractual relationship with him[209] but this duty is not to cause damage to persons or to property and the major part of the claimant's claim in this case was that he had suffered a loss of business because the pumps were unsuitable for their purpose, a claim which lay in contract against ITS but not in tort against the manufacturers.

Similarly in *Murphy v Brentwood DC*[210] the House of Lords ended a long period of controversy by reaffirming that defects in a building that cause it to be less valuable or even potentially dangerous constitute pure economic loss and do not at common law[211] give rise to any claim except via a contract with the defendant.[212] An important point to note here is that while a purchaser of a defective chattel will usually have a contract remedy against the seller[213] the purchaser of defective real

---

[205] See, e.g., *The Grandcamp* [1961] 1 Lloyd's Rep. 504, where an explosion caused 500 deaths and 3,000 personal injuries. The damages were US$70 million, though on appeal it was held that the explosion was not foreseeable to the defendants.

[206] See, e.g., *Leigh and Sillavan Ltd v Aliakmon Shipping Co Ltd* [1986] A.C. 786.

[207] "Bright line rules may be less than perfect because they are under-inclusive, but my impression is that most people who have been or are engaged in day-to-day practice of the law at the trial or advising stage prefer rules to indeterminate standards": *Perre v Apand Pty Ltd* [1999] HCA 36; (1999) 198 C.L.R. 180 at [81] per McHugh J.

[208] [1986] Q.B. 507.

[209] *Donoghue v Stevenson* [1932] A.C. 562, see para.11-002.

[210] [1991] 1 A.C. 398, see para.10-047.

[211] See the Defective Premises Act 1972 (discussed at para.10-054).

[212] The Contracts (Rights of Third Parties) Act 1999 will not generally affect either of these situations because: the contract (1) will not generally purport to confer a benefit on the third-party claimant; and (2) will not identify him.

[213] See the Sale of Goods Act 1979, ss.12–15 (and equivalent provisions of the Consumer Rights Act

property is unlikely to have a contractual remedy because sales of land are governed by the caveat emptor principle, which generally limits contractual liability to instances of misrepresentation. This means that there is more pressure for a tort remedy in cases of acquisition of defective premises and, as a result of this, in Australia, Canada and New Zealand the courts have not followed *Murphy* and have allowed some claims for pure economic loss in this type of case.[214]

D. Negligence and Public Authorities

i. Introduction

Three fundamental principles[215]   This section is concerned with the liability of   **5-057** public authorities in the tort of negligence and, more specifically, with the circumstances in which public authorities will owe a duty of care. There are three fundamental principles in this area that need to be borne in mind throughout the discussion. The first is that a public authority may incur liability in tort in the same way as a private individual. As Lord Reed observed in *Poole BC v GN*, it has been "traditionally understood" that public authorities are "subject to the same general principles of the law of tort, at common law, as private individuals and bodies".[216] The second principle is that the rule that tort law does not in general impose duties to confer gratuitous benefits on others[217] applies with its full rigour to claims against public authorities. That rule is not displaced merely because a public authority had a statutory power or duty to confer the benefit in issue. The third principle is that an act or decision that is invalid in public law terms does not for that reason become actionable in the tort of negligence. A public law wrong is not necessarily actionable in a private law claim since there is a clear distinction between a public law obligation and a private law obligation and, unless one is owed the latter, no claim will lie in tort.[218] Combined, these three fundamental principles dictate that no special rules govern the duty analysis in the context of negligence claims against public authorities. Such claims are subject to the ordinary rules that apply generally.

The multiplicity of actions that can arise in the context of public authori-   **5-058** **ties**   Proceedings against public authorities often involve a multiplicity of claims. In the first place, the claimant may sue the public authority for breach of a duty of care owed to him by the public authority. Second, the claimant may bring a claim for breach of statutory duty. The third possibility is that an agent of the public

---

2015 in a consumer sale).

[214] See *Winnipeg Condominium No 36 v Bird Construction* [1995] 1 S.C.R. 85; *Bryan v Maloney* (1995) 182 C.L.R. 609; *Body Corporate No 207624 v North Shore City Council* [2012] NZSC 83; [2013] 2 N.Z.L.R. 297.

[215] Fairgrieve and Squires, *The Negligence Liability of Public Authorities*, 2nd edn (2019); Fairgrieve, *State Liability in Tort* (2003); Harlow, *State Liability* (2004). The area of law was recently reviewed by the Law Commission, but in the end its proposals for reform were abandoned: see *Administrative Redress*, Law Com. No.332 (2010).

[216] [2019] UKSC 25; [2019] 2 W.L.R. 1478 at [26].

[217] See para.5-030.

[218] A duty of care in the tort of negligence cannot "grow parasitically out of a statutory duty not intended to be owed to individuals": *Gorringe v Calderdale MBC* [2004] UKHL 15; [2004] 1 W.L.R. 1057 at [71] per Lord Scott. See also *X v Bedfordshire CC* [1995] 2 A.C. 633; *Sandhar v Dept of Transport* [2005] EWCA Civ 1440; [2006] 1 W.L.R. 461 at [37]; *Neil Martin Ltd v Revenue and Customs Comrs* [2007] EWCA Civ 1041; [2007] S.T.C. 1802.

authority may owe a duty of care to the claimant, and the authority may be vicariously liable for a breach of that duty. Fourth, both the public authority and its employees may be liable for the tort of misfeasance in a public office. All four of these claims can in principle be brought concurrently with each other. The focus here is on the first type of claim. The others are dealt with in separate chapters.[219]

ii. Justiciability

5-059   Some decisions are non-justiciable in a private law action. These may be high political decisions ("shall we go to war?") but they may also extend to decisions on the allocation of resources or the infliction of risks. To take an example based loosely on *Home Office v Dorset Yacht Co*,[220] suppose that the Home Office institutes a policy of open, non-secure young offender institutions with a view to promoting the rehabilitation of young offenders. Claims in tort by neighbours of the institution whose homes are burgled by absconding offenders will plainly fail even if there is a sharp increase in burglaries in the area. This is because "the court cannot adjudicate on such policy".[221]

iii. Duty of Care

5-060   **The omissions doctrine**   If the hurdle of justiciability can be overcome, the next issue to address is whether a duty of care exists. Because the generally applicable rules regarding the duty of care element of the tort of negligence apply where the defendant is a public authority, it follows that if a public authority commits some positive act that results in the claimant suffering physical damage there will usually be little or no difficulty in finding that a duty of care was owed.[222] For example, if a public authority builds a dangerous intersection that leads to the claimant motorist suffering injury in a car accident it will normally be straightforward for the claimant to show that the authority owed him a duty of care. Similarly, if, by contrast, the public authority omits to take positive action to safeguard the claimant from damage, the omissions doctrine will apply with the result that no duty of care will have been owed, unless one of the exceptions to that doctrine is triggered.[223] As the Supreme Court confirmed in *Michael v Chief Constable of South Wales*, the general principle that there is no obligation to confer benefits on others is "equally applicable where D is a public body".[224] As discussed above,[225] that principle was applied in *Michael* to yield the conclusion that no duty of care was owed by the defendant chief constable to a woman who was murdered by her former partner. No duty existed because the police had simply failed to safeguard the woman from a third party, and because none of the exceptions to the omissions doctrine was applicable.

---

[219] See Chs 8 and 21.
[220] [1970] A.C. 1004.
[221] *X v Bedfordshire CC* [1995] 2 A.C. 633 at 738 per Lord Browne-Wilkinson.
[222] See para.5-014.
[223] See para.5-034.
[224] [2015] UKSC 2; [2015] A.C. 1732 at [101] per Lord Toulson.
[225] See para.5-060.

The omissions doctrine will not be displaced simply because the public author- 5-061
ity had a statutory duty or power to confer the relevant benefit In *Stovin v*
Wise[226] Mr Stovin was injured in an accident at a dangerous junction due to the
negligent driving of Mrs Wise. The junction was dangerous because visibility was
reduced by a bank of earth on the land of a third party. Mr Stovin recovered damages from Mrs Wise. Mrs Wise then sought contribution[227] from the highway
authority responsible for the junction, and a precondition of this was that the authority, if sued by Mr Stovin, would have been liable to him. There is a civilly actionable statutory duty to maintain the highway[228] but this was inapplicable because it
concerns the state of repair of the roadway and the danger at the junction arose from
poor visibility. There was a statutory power[229] to require the removal of an obstruction but after negotiations with the third party the council decided to remove the
bank of earth itself. However, the matter then "went to sleep" for nearly a year
before the accident. The majority of the House of Lords declined to find that the
authority owed a duty of care. There was no way, as Lord Hoffmann put it, in which
the statutory "may" could be turned into a common law "ought".[230] Although the
authority could have been compelled via public law remedies to consider whether
it should exercise the power, the duty did not give rise to a duty of care. *Stovin v*
Wise was followed by the House of Lords in *Gorringe v Calderdale MBC*.[231] This
case was based on a failure of the defendant highway authority to erect a sign warning the claimant driver of the need to reduce her speed. The claimant asserted that
the public law duty that the authority owed under s.39 of the Road Traffic Act 1988
to prepare and carry out a programme of measures designed to promote road safety
gave rise to a duty to act sounding in tort. However, this contention was rejected.
Lord Hoffmann remarked[232]:

> "I find it difficult to imagine a case in which a common law duty can be founded simply
> upon the failure (however irrational) to provide some benefit which a public authority has
> power (or a public law duty) to provide."

Of course, if the highway authority had installed misleading road markings or signs
there would be no difficulty about finding it liable because it would then have created a source of danger.

Incrementalism We described above[233] how the Supreme Court's decision in 5-062
Robinson had re-orientated the duty of care jurisprudence. In *Poole BC v GN*,[234] the
Supreme Court addressed how the principles that it had expounded in *Robinson* ap-
ply in the context of claims against public authorities. The defendant council in
Poole housed the claimants, two vulnerable children, and their mother adjacent to
another family that the council knew had persistently engaged in anti-social

---

226 [1996] A.C. 923. See also para.5-030.
227 Civil Liability (Contribution) Act 1978. See Ch.22.
228 Highways Act 1980. See para.15-085.
229 Highways Act 1980 s.79. The distinction between a power and a duty may not always be clear and
    in any event a duty may contain wide elements of discretion: *R. v Chief Constable of Sussex Ex p.*
    International Trader's Ferry Ltd [1999] 2 A.C. 418; *Larner v Solihull MBC* [2001] P.I.Q.R. P17.
230 [1996] A.C. 923 at 948.
231 [2004] UKHL 15; [2004] 1 W.L.R. 1057.
232 [2004] UKHL 15; [2004] 1 W.L.R. 1057 at [32].
233 See para.5-027.
234 [2019] UKSC 25; [2019] 2 W.L.R. 1478.

behaviour. The claimants were thereafter subjected to harassment and abuse for several years and they ultimately sued the council in negligence for physical and psychiatric harm suffered due to that behaviour. The negligence alleged, relevantly, was failing to protect them from harm by allowing them to continue to live in the house. The central issue in the proceedings was whether the council owed the claimants a relevant duty of care. Lord Reed, delivering reasons with which the other members of the Supreme Court agreed, emphasised that the case was one in which it was alleged that the defendant should have taken positive action to benefit the claimants and that *Robinson* required the claimants to establish that the case was analogous to one in which such a duty had been imposed. Lord Reed then focused on whether the authorities regarding assumed responsibilities supplied the required analogy but ultimately held that they did not. He said that[235]:

> "[i]n the present case, the council's investigating and monitoring the claimants' position did not involve the provision of a service to them on which they or their mother could be expected to rely".

The result was that the proceedings were struck out on the basis that they failed to disclose any recognisable basis for a cause of action. *Poole* confirms that the approach to the duty of care element that the Supreme Court had charted in *Robinson* is fully applicable to claims in negligence against public authorities, and also makes plain the heightened importance of the assumption of responsibility concept in the current era.

E. Lawyers and Negligence

5-063   **Introduction**   Solicitors will generally have a contract with their clients that will require them to exercise proper professional care and skill within the scope of the retainer.[236] There may be no contract where the client is legally aided and generally there is no contract between a barrister and a lay client[237] save, as is now permissible, where the barrister is acting without a solicitor. However, a tortious duty, identical in practical effect to a contractual duty, will arise by virtue of an assumption of responsibility.[238] Two matters have, however, proved controversial: the duty of the lawyer to third parties and the duty, even to his client, in the context of litigation.

i. Third Parties

5-064   **The principles established in White v Jones**   The paradigm case where a lawyer will owe a duty of care to a third party is where the lawyer is instructed to draft a will for X that will benefit C and the lawyer fails to carry out that task properly.[239]

---

[235] [2019] UKSC 25; [2019] 2 W.L.R. 1478 at [81].

[236] Lawyers are also required to warn their clients about risks and matters that are incidental to the tasks that they have been charged to perform. The duty to warn in this regard forms part of the retainer: *Lyons v Fox Williams LLP* [2018] EWCA Civ 2347; [2019] P.N.L.R. 9 at [41]–[42].

[237] Any rule of law (as opposed to professional conduct) forbidding a barrister entering into a contract was abolished by the Courts and Legal Services Act 1990 s.61.

[238] However, even where there is a contract there may be a parallel duty in tort: *Midland Bank Trust Co Ltd v Hett, Stubbs & Kemp* [1979] Ch. 384, approved in *Henderson v Merrett Syndicates Ltd* [1995] 2 A.C. 145.

[239] Where the will is in order and the deceased appoints A as his executor, leaving property to C, and

We have seen how in *White v Jones*[240] liability was imposed in such a case, but something more needs to be said by way of explanation of the scope of this duty.[241] Although the duty sounds in tort the underlying basis of it is the acceptance of the client's instructions and the scope of those instructions is obviously determinative of the duty to the beneficiary. While as a matter of principle there should be a duty in respect of gifts inter vivos, there is no liability if the donor is able to rectify the error made[242]: if he chooses not to do so, the effective cause of the failure of the transaction is not the negligence of the lawyer but the decision of his client.[243] The duty extends to the drafting of the instrument[244] and its execution[245] as well as a simple failure to implement the instructions.[246] There will generally be no liability to the estate because it will have suffered no loss by the bequest going to the wrong person, but the duty to the beneficiary is an independent one so that, while there must be no double liability,[247] there may be liability to the beneficiary and liability to the estate in respect of any further loss which it suffers.[248] However, the lawyer in such a situation is not the guardian of the interests of the object of the client's bounty[249] except to the limited extent of carrying out the client's instructions. For example, he does not owe a duty to the beneficiary to advise the testator on arranging his affairs so as to minimise the tax impact of the transaction on the beneficiary.[250] In *Clarke v Bruce Lance & Co*[251] the defendants in 1973 had drafted a will for the testator that left a petrol station to the claimant and some five years later they acted for the testator again in granting an option (at a fixed price) over the station to a tenant who was virtually certain to exercise it. The claimant's claim for negligence was struck out: if the defendants had owed him any duty of care they

---

the defendants culpably fail to carry out A's instructions to administer the estate promptly C may suffer loss because the property is not transferred to him expeditiously. However, in such a case A can sue for that loss (holding the damages in trust for C) since until the estate is administered the property is vested in A: *Chappell v Somers & Blake* [2003] EWHC 1644; [2004] Ch. 19.

[240] [1995] 2 A.C. 207, see para.5-047.

[241] The duty of care that was recognised in *White v Jones* is also owed by financial institutions that offer will-making services: *Esterhuizen v Allied Dunbar Assurance Plc* [1998] 2 F.L.R. 668.

[242] *Hemmens v Wilson Browne* [1995] Ch. 223. cf. *Hughes v Richards* [2004] EWCA Civ 266; [2004] P.N.L.R. 35.

[243] As to the effect of pre-death change of mind by the testator in the case of an ineffective will see *Humbleston v Martin Tolhurst Partnership* [2004] EWHC 151 (Ch); [2004] P.N.L.R. 26.

[244] *Horsefall v Haywards* [1999] Lloyd's Rep. P.N. 332; *Martin v Triggs Turner Bartons* [2009] EWHC 1920 (Ch); [2010] P.N.L.R. 3; cf. *Fraser v McArthur Stewart* [2008] CSOH 159; 2009 S.L.T. 31. Note that under s.20 of the Administration of Justice Act 1982 the court has jurisdiction, on application within six months of representation being taken out, to rectify a will so as to carry out the intentions of the testator, if it is satisfied that the will is so expressed that it fails to carry out the testator's intentions in consequence of a clerical error or of a failure to understand his instructions. Failure to take this course may amount to failure to mitigate loss and provide a defence to the claim against the solicitor: *Walker v Geo H Medlicott & Son* [1999] 1 W.L.R. 727.

[245] *Ross v Caunters* [1980] 1 Ch. 297; *Esterhuizen v Allied Dunbar Assurance Plc* [1998] 2 F.L.R. 668 (normally insufficient to leave accurate written instructions on attestation, but cf. *Gray v Richards Butler* [2000] W.T.L.R. 143).

[246] *White v Jones* [1995] 2 A.C. 207

[247] *Corbett v Bond Pearce* [2001] EWCA Civ 531; [2001] 3 All E.R. 769.

[248] *Carr-Glyn v Frearsons* [1999] Ch. 326.

[249] It is assumed that there is no direct assumption of responsibility to the third party, e.g., by answering questions from him.

[250] *Cancer Research Campaign v Ernest Brown* [1998] P.N.L.R. 592; *Woodward v Wolferstans, The Times,* 8 April 1997.

[251] *Clarke v Bruce Lance & Co* [1988] 1 W.L.R. 881.

could find themselves in the intolerable position of having to seek to dissuade their client (the testator) from carrying through a transaction upon which he had decided. The duty to third parties is not confined to carrying out instructions in relation to wills. For example, it has been held that a solicitor acting for a borrower may be under a duty to take care to ensure, for the benefit of an unrepresented lender, that the security given is effective.[252] However, in conducting litigation or negotiating in an adversarial situation neither client nor lawyer owes a duty of care to their opponent.[253]

ii. Litigation

5-065   **The lawyers' immunity for "in court" work and its abolition**   For many years the law took the view that a lawyer conducting litigation did not owe a duty of care even to his own client in the conduct of the case in court and matters closely connected therewith.[254] Various reasons were put forward for this immunity including: (1) the fact that lawyers have an overriding duty to the court and, in order to ensure that the lawyer did not neglect that duty, he had to be relieved of even the possibility that actions for negligence would be brought against him by a disgruntled client; (2) the difficulty or undesirability of retrying, in the action against the lawyer, the issue which arose in the original litigation; (3) the lawyers' immunity was analogous to the immunity granted to certain other participants involved in court proceedings (such as judges and jurors); (4) the "cab-rank" rule pursuant to which counsel must take any case within his field of competence; and (5) the existence of professional disciplinary procedures.[255] However, the immunity was jettisoned in civil proceedings by the House of Lords in *Arthur JS Hall & Co v Simons*.[256] None of the appeals in *Hall* involved criminal proceedings but four members of the House considered that lawyers should not be immune to liability in negligence in that context.

It is unsurprising that the House of Lords in *Hall* reached the conclusion that it did. The first of the abovementioned reasons for the immunity made no sense since a lawyer would never be found to be negligent in discharging his paramount duty to the court. The second reason was an appeal to the importance of litigation being final, but the House of Lords in *Hall* held that this interest could be adequately protected by the court's jurisdiction to strike out as an abuse of process actions that seek to re-litigate matters that have already been decided. The third reason is an incorrect analogy since the lawyer is the only person in the court who can fairly be said to have assumed responsibility to his client. The fourth reason did not explain why solicitors (who are not required to comply with the cab-rank rule) benefited from the immunity, and the fifth reason was unable to explain why lawyers should be treated differently from other professionals. An important factor that underpinned the decision to abolish the immunity, aside from the weakness of the arguments in

---

[252] *Dean v Allin & Watts* [2001] EWCA Civ 758; [2001] 2 Lloyd's Rep. 249; *Al Kandari v JR Brown & Co* [1988] Q.B. 665.

[253] *Business Computers International v Registrar of Companies* [1988] Ch. 229; *Connolly-Martin v D* [1999] Lloyd's Rep. P.N. 790.

[254] The leading decisions of the House of Lords were *Rondel v Worsley* [1969] 1 A.C. 191 and *Saif Ali v Sydney Mitchell & Co* [1980] A.C. 198.

[255] For discussion, see Goudkamp (2002) 10 Tort L. Rev. 188.

[256] [2002] 1 A.C. 615.

favour of it, was that it was a rule that must inevitably have been seen as lawyers giving special treatment to their own kind. There were also concerns that the immunity would have been vulnerable to attack under the European Convention on Human Rights. Finally, other jurisdictions with very similar legal systems had rejected the rule without undue effects.[257]

Solicitors who rely on barristers Where the claimant has been represented by solicitor and counsel and he sues the former the relationship between the two lawyers must be considered. A solicitor who has consulted counsel will prima facie be entitled to rely on his advice[258] (hence, it will be difficult to establish a breach of duty) but he cannot "rely blindly and with no mind of his own on counsel's view".[259]

5-066

Other participants in the judicial process Expert witnesses were once immune to liability in negligence but this immunity has also recently been removed.[260] Judges of superior courts cannot as a general rule be sued for negligence[261] although the precise scope of the immunity is uncertain.[262] Lay witnesses are immune, and this is an area where it is believed that immunity is necessary lest the witness be deterred from discharging his duty to the court. The prosecutor in a criminal case is simultaneously client, lawyer and also a minister of justice but the accused as a general rule has no cause of action for negligence[263] against those engaged in prosecuting him on behalf of the community.[264] This rests on general grounds of public policy and not on the former lawyer's immunity. However, in *Welsh v Chief Constable of Merseyside*[265] a claim that the Crown Prosecution Service had failed to inform the court that certain offences had been taken into consideration in other proceedings was held to disclose a cause of action based upon an assumption of responsibility via an undertaking given to the claimant.

5-067

F. Psychiatric Injury

Terminology and scope For many years it has been customary to refer to this form of damage as "nervous shock".[266] That terminology has the advantage of serv-

5-068

---

257 Most notably Canada (*Demarco v Ungaro* (1979) 95 D.L.R. (3d) 385) and New Zealand (*Chamberlains v Lai* [2006] NZSC 70; [2007] 2 N.Z.L.R. 1). However, the High Court of Australia has affirmed the immunity: *D'Orta Ekenaike v Victoria Legal Aid* [2005] HCA 12; (2005) 223 C.L.R. 1. See also *Attwells v Jackson Lalic Lawyers Pty Ltd* [2016] HCA 16; (2016) 259 C.L.R. 1.
258 *Matrix Securities Ltd v Theodore Goddard* (1997) 147 N.L.J. 1847; *McFaddens v Platford* [2009] EWHC 126 (TCC); [2009] P.N.L.R. 26 at [56].
259 *Davy-Chieseman v Davy-Chieseman* [1984] Fam. 48 at 64 per May LJ. See also *Locke v Camberwell HA* [1991] 2 Med. L.R. 249; *Bond v Royal Sun Alliance* [2001] P.N.L.R. 30. Where the solicitor is liable it is likely that counsel will bear the greater share of the damages for the purposes of contribution: *Pritchard Joyce & Hinds v Batcup* [2008] EWHC 20 (QB); [2008] P.N.L.R. 18.
260 *Jones v Kaney* [2011] UKSC 13; [2011] 2 A.C. 398.
261 "[T]he judges in the King's superior courts are not liable to answer personally for their errors in judgment ... [for] the protection in regard to the superior courts is absolute and universal": *Miller v Seare* (1777) 2 Wm. Bl. 1141 at 1145; 96 E.R. 673 at 674–675 per De Gray CJ.
262 For discussion, see Murphy (2013) 33 L.S. 455.
263 There may be liability for malicious prosecution or misfeasance in a public office (see Ch.20, and para.8-024 respectively) but these require "malice".
264 *Elguzouli-Daf v MPC* [1995] Q.B. 335.
265 [1993] 1 All E.R. 692.
266 Regarding liability for psychiatric injury, see further *Liability for Psychiatric Illness*, Law Com.

ing as a reminder that this head of liability has in most cases required something in the nature of a traumatic response to an *event*.[267] For example, it is still the law that the spouse of an accident victim who foreseeably succumbs to psychiatric illness from the strain of caring for the victim has no cause of action against the tortfeasor.[268] However, the expression seems to be falling into disuse[269] and the terms "psychiatric injury" or "mental injury"[270] are becoming more commonplace. Nevertheless, the new language is potentially misleading, since what marks out this category of case for special consideration at the duty stage is not the nature of the injury but the manner of its occurrence. For the common characteristic of the cases under discussion in this section is that they concern actions for *damage caused by psychiatric means*. Hence, if—as in the early cases[271]—the claimant has suffered a miscarriage, or a heart attack, as a result of seeing something traumatic, then, although the damage is physical, it is a "psychiatric injury" case because the damage is brought about through the medium of the mind, and so any claim for damages is subject to the restrictions to be described.

5-069 **Reasons why psychiatric injury is treated differently from other types of personal injury**   Although psychiatric injury is a form of personal injury special restrictions apply to the recovery of damages for psychiatric injury that do not extend to other types of personal injury. One reason why psychiatric injury is treated significantly less generously is that, despite advances in scientific knowledge regarding the working of the mind, there is still a belief, rightly or wrongly held, that it presents a greater risk of inaccurate diagnosis[272] and the incidence or the basis or even the very existence of some conditions is controversial. Another reason is that whereas the physical effects of an accident are limited by the laws of inertia, physical injury to one person, or even the threat of it, may produce mental trauma in many others—witnesses, relatives, friends and so on. The concern here is that if the circumstances in which liability for psychiatric injury are not narrowly confined, a single act of negligence may expose a defendant to liability that is unpredictable in its extent and potentially disproportionate relative to the seriousness of the defendant's wrongdoing.

i. A Recognised Psychiatric Illness

5-070 **It is necessary for the claimant to suffer a recognised psychiatric illness**   The early view was that mental injury unaccompanied by physical injury was not compensable at all[273] but that position was abandoned around the end of the 19th

---

No.249 (1998); Handford, *Tort Liability for Mental Harm*, 3rd edn (2017).

[267] This is not necessarily so where the claimant suffers a mental injury due to the direct act of the defendant: see para.5-083.

[268] *Alcock v Chief Constable South Yorkshire* [1992] 1 A.C. 310 at 396, 401, 416; *Jaensch v Coffey* (1984) 155 C.L.R. 549.

[269] See the criticism by Bingham LJ in *Attia v British Gas Plc* [1988] Q.B. 304 at 317.

[270] Evans LJ's preference in *Vernon v Bosley (No.1)* [1997] 1 All E.R. 577 at 597.

[271] See, e.g., *Dulieu v White* [1901] 2 K.B. 669; *Hambrook v Stokes* [1925] 1 K.B. 141. For a more recent example of such a case, see *Donachie v Chief Constable of Greater Manchester* [2004] EWCA Civ 405 (stroke).

[272] However, in *Frost v Chief Constable of South Yorkshire* [1997] 3 W.L.R. 1194 at 1217, Henry LJ put the risk of fraudulent shock claims as no greater than in "cases involving back injuries where there is often a wide gap between observable symptoms and complaints".

[273] *Victorian Ry Commissioners v Coultas* (1888) 13 App. Cas. 222.

century both for intentional wrongdoing[274] and for negligence.[275] However, it remains the law that mere sensations of fear or mental distress or grief[276] caused by negligence are not actionable.[277] Mental harm, unless it is consequential upon a physical injury, is not compensable unless it amounts to a recognised psychiatric illness.[278] Thus, where a claimant alleged negligence in the conduct of a police disciplinary investigation the submission that actionable damage had occurred in the form of anxiety and vexation was described by the House of Lords as unsustainable.[279] Similarly, a claim brought by persons who suffered claustrophobia and fear on account of their having become trapped in a lift was rejected.[280]

ii. The Distinction Between Primary and Secondary Victims

Attempts to define the distinction If the claimant can establish that he has suf-   5-071
fered a recognised psychiatric injury, the next step is to ask whether the claimant is a primary or secondary victim since different rules apply to the two categories of case. Broadly speaking, cases involving primary victims are those "in which the injured plaintiff was involved, either mediately or immediately, as a participant" in what happened whereas secondary victims are claimants who are "no more than a passive and unwilling witness of injury caused to others" or its immediate aftermath.[281] Another common way of expressing the distinction is to say that primary victims are persons who are themselves in the foreseeable "zone of danger" while secondary victims are those who are not. Thus, a passenger in a motor vehicle that is involved in an accident who emerges physically unscathed but develops a recognised psychiatric illness is a primary victim whereas a bystander who suffers a mental injury on account of observing the collision is a secondary victim.

Difficulty applying the distinction The dichotomy between primary and second-   5-072
ary victims can usually be straightforwardly applied but this is not always the case. Uncertainty arises because the courts have left the concept of "zone of danger" largely undefined. If the defendant drives furiously down a crowded street large numbers of people may foreseeably be imperilled yet it is unclear whether they would all be treated as being in the zone of danger. A person can be in the "zone of danger" even if D did not mean to put him in the zone of danger: thus where the negligence of the police force in failing to provide a functioning surveillance device required an officer to make repeated surreptitious visits to a car belonging to gangsters in order to make it work, the defendants were held liable when the stress of this, combined with his existing hypertension (of which they were unaware),

---

274 *Wilkinson v Downton* [1897] 2 Q.B. 57.
275 *Dulieu v White* [1901] 2 K.B. 669.
276 There is a limited statutory right of action for bereavement: see para.24-014.
277 *Page v Smith* [1996] A.C. 155 at 167. A claimant who suffers a physical injury can recover damages for adverse mental changes even though those changes do not amount to a recognisable psychiatric illness: see para.23-073.
278 Among many statements of this requirement, see *Hinz v Berry* [1970] 2 Q.B. 40 at 42; *Alcock v Chief Constable of South Yorkshire* [1992] 1 A.C. 310 at 401, 416; *Jaensch v Coffey* (1984) 155 C.L.R. 549 at 559, 587.
279 *Calveley v Chief Constable of Merseyside* [1989] A.C. 1228.
280 *Reilly v Merseyside RHA* [1995] 6 Med. L.R. 246. See also *Hicks v Chief Constable of South Yorkshire* [1992] 2 All E.R. 65.
281 *Alcock v Chief Constable of South Yorkshire* [1992] 1 A.C. 310 at 407 per Lord Oliver.

precipitated a psychiatric condition and a stroke.[282] It appears that a claimant will be regarded as a primary victim if he is in the zone of danger even if the mental injury is triggered by seeing others suffer injury. In *Chadwick v British Transport Commission*[283] the claimant was a volunteer helper at the scene of a rail disaster and suffered mental trauma as a result. For many years this case was regarded as resting on the basis that a duty was owed to him as a rescuer. However, the existence of any separate category of rescuers for this purpose was rejected in *Frost v Chief Constable of South Yorkshire*[284] and *Chadwick* was considered as having been correctly decided on the basis that the claimant had been in physical danger from the collapse of the wreckage even though the judge found that it was the horrific nature of the experience rather than the claimant's fear for himself which had affected him. This approach may be supported on the ground that in some cases it may be extremely difficult to determine whether or how far the claimant suffered shock from fear for himself or from the sight of what happened to others, and there may be cases in which there is a damaging impact on his psyche without his consciously suffering anything that could be called fear. Nevertheless, it is a mechanical approach and one can conceive of cases where it might operate in the claimant's favour even though he was at the time entirely unaware of any danger to himself.

iii.   Primary Victims

5-073   **The rule in Page v Smith**   Primary victims are treated significantly more generously than secondary victims. The courts have taken this approach due to the fact that the number of potential primary victims of any given act of negligence is necessarily limited whereas the same negligent conduct can cause mental injury to any number of secondary victims. The rule that governs the recoverability of damages by primary victims was established by the House of Lords in *Page v Smith*.[285] The claimant was involved in a collision caused by the defendant's negligence which resulted in property damage but no physical injury. However, the experience led the claimant to suffer a recurrence of myalgic encephalomyelitis, or chronic fatigue syndrome, which had affected him periodically for 25 years but which now became permanent. The issue before the House was whether the claimant had to prove that it was reasonably foreseeable that he would suffer psychiatric injury specifically or whether it was enough to establish that it was reasonably foreseeable that a person of "normal fortitude" would suffer personal injury. The majority held that it was sufficient to prove the latter.[286] Lord Lloyd wrote that "[s]ince the defendant was admittedly under a duty of care not to cause the plaintiff foreseeable physical injury, it was unnecessary to ask whether he was under a separate duty of care not to cause foreseeable psychiatric injury".[287]

5-074   **Perception of danger as opposed to actual danger sufficient**   The simplest situation where a primary victim will be able to recover damages is where the claim-

---

[282] *Donachie v Chief Constable of Greater Manchester* [2004] EWCA Civ 405; *The Times,* 6 May 2004. See also *A v Essex CC* [2003] EWCA Civ 1848; [2004] 1 W.L.R. 1881.
[283] [1967] 1 W.L.R. 912. See also *Young v Charles Church (Southern) Ltd* (1997) 39 B.M.L.R. 146.
[284] [1999] 2 A.C. 455.
[285] [1996] A.C. 155. For criticism, see Bailey and Nolan (2010) 69 C.L.J. 495.
[286] *Page v Smith* [1996] A.C. 155.
[287] [1996] A.C. 155 at 187.

ant suffers shock due to a reasonable fear for his own safety caused by the defendant's negligence (the "near miss"). For example, in *Dulieu v White*[288] the claimant succeeded in a claim for shock, resulting in a miscarriage, when a horse-drawn van was negligently driven into the bar of the public house where she was working. It is not necessary that the claimant should actually be in danger provided that he reasonably believes he is.[289] However, if the fear is not reasonably entertained (for example, if the claimant is a hyper-sensitive person who suffers shock from the noise of a collision on the other side of the street) there is no action.[290]

Rothwell v Chemical & Insulating Co Ltd   Suppose that the defendant exposes   **5-075**
the claimant to some risk of harm (a pollutant or some harmful chemical, for example) which has not caused any direct harm but that the claimant's knowledge of his exposure causes a deterioration in his mental state. Although he might be said to be in the "zone of danger", *Page v Smith* does not stretch this far. In *Rothwell v Chemical & Insulating Co Ltd*[291] one of the appellants, G, had been exposed to asbestos and developed asymptomatic pleural plaques. These did not in any way interfere with his physical health and would not themselves lead to any illness. But they were a signal that asbestos had penetrated the body and that there was increased risk of developing an asbestos-related condition, something which G discovered when he was told about it by a doctor over 30 years after the exposure, though he had been concerned about the risk of developing an asbestos-related disease for years before that. That would not amount to damage which created a cause of action (suffering a risk of damage is not damage).[292] However, G worried so much about the risk that he developed a clinical depressive condition. While it is obvious that this knowledge would cause anxiety to anyone, the case was conducted on the basis that there was no evidence that a person of reasonable fortitude would react so strongly as to become mentally ill. On that basis the House of Lords held that *Page v Smith* could not be extended to such a situation. The case is obviously very far removed on its facts from *Page*, not least because of the very long gap between the "exposure to danger" and the mental consequences of it, though the reasons for distinguishing that decision are variously expressed. Unlike *Rothwell*, *Page* was a case of psychiatric injury "arising as an immediate consequence of an obvious accident"[293]; the chain of causation in *Rothwell* was "stretched far beyond that which was envisaged in *Page*"[294]; and"it would be an unwarranted extension of [*Page*] to apply it to psychiatric illness caused by ap-

---

[288] [1901] 2 K.B. 669.
[289] *McFarlane v EE Caledonia Ltd* [1994] 2 All E.R. 1 at 10.
[290] *McFarlane v EE Caledonia Ltd* [1994] 2 All E.R. 1 at 11, although on the facts the Court of Appeal took the view that C was not in fact in fear for his own safety at the time. See also *Hegarty v E.E. Caledonia Ltd* [1997] 2 Lloyd's Rep. 259; *Monk v P.C. Harrington Ltd* [2008] EWHC 1879 (QB); [2009] P.I.Q.R. P3.
[291] [2007] UKHL 39; [2008] A.C. 281. See also *The Creutzfeldt-Jakob Disease litigation; Group B Plaintiffs v Medical Research Council* [2000] Lloyd's Rep. Med. 161; *Fletcher v Commissioners of Public Works* [2003] 1 I.R. 465
[292] See para.7-011.
[293] [2007] UKHL 39; [2008] A.C. 281 at [104] per Lord Mance. At [95], Lord Rodger spoke of "an immediate response to a past event".
[294] [2007] UKHL 39; [2008] A.C. 281 at [55] per Lord Hope.

prehension of the possibility of an unfavourable event which had not actually happened".[295]

iv. Secondary Victims

5-076   **Requirements where claimant is a secondary victim**   The leading case regarding secondary victims is *Alcock v Chief Constable South Yorkshire*.[296] The 10 appellants had suffered psychiatric injury due to the disaster in 1989 at Hillsborough Stadium in Sheffield, in which, because of the admitted negligence of the defendants, some 95 people were crushed to death and over 400 physically injured. None of the appellants had suffered any physical injury, nor been in any danger, indeed most of them were not at the ground, though they saw part of the events on television. All of the appeals before the House of Lords failed. The decision clearly assumes that there is a real need for the law to place some limitation going beyond reasonable foreseeability and proof of causation on the range of admissible claims by secondary victims. This limitation is to be found by reference to three elements: (1) there must have been close ties of love and affection between the claimant and the person endangered; (2) the claimant must have been in proximity to the event; and (3) the claimant must have perceived the event or its immediate aftermath by his unaided senses. The second and third elements obviously overlap with each other. In addition, applying ordinary negligence principles a secondary victim can recover only if it was reasonably foreseeable that a person of ordinary fortitude in his position would suffer psychiatric injury as a result of the events in question.[297]

5-077   **Close ties of love and affection with the person endangered**   As to the first element, the House of Lords rejected any arbitrary qualifying test by reference to particular relationships such as husband and wife or parent and child for, as Lord Keith pointed out[298]:

> "[T]he kinds of relationship which may involve close ties of love and affection are numerous, and it is the existence of such ties which leads to mental disturbance when the loved one suffers a catastrophe. They may be present in family relationships or those of close friendship, and may be stronger in the case of engaged couples than in that of persons who have been married to each other for many years."

The question is therefore whether there is in fact a sufficiently close relationship of love and affection between the claimant and the person injured or threatened subject to the practical qualification that such a relationship will be presumed in the case of the relationship of parent and child or husband and wife and perhaps engaged couples. The effect is that those falling outside these narrow categories have to show a relationship which is more intense than that usually found, and akin to a spousal or parental one. In *Alcock* three judges left open the possibility that a mere bystander without a close tie might have a claim if the circumstances of the accident were unusually horrific, as where a petrol tanker collided with a school in

---

[295] [2007] UKHL 39; [2008] A.C. 281 at [33] per Lord Hoffmann.
[296] [1992] 1 A.C. 310. See Nolan in Mitchell and Mitchell (eds), *Landmark Cases in the Law of Tort* (2009).
[297] *Liverpool Women's Hospital NHS Foundation Trust v Ronayne* [2015] EWCA Civ 588; (2015) 145 B.M.L.R. 110 at [13].
[298] [1992] 1 A.C. 310 at 397.

session and exploded in flame.[299] However, the Court of Appeal in *McFarlane v EE Caledonia Ltd*,[300] a case arising out of the Piper Alpha oil rig disaster, rejected this extension, on the ground that it ran counter to the general thrust of *Alcock* and would present practical problems since reactions to horrific events are subjective and variable.

Proximity in time and space to the event   The second element requires that there be sufficient proximity of time and space in relation to the event leading to the mental injury. This requirement was fatal to the claim in *Taylor v A Novo (UK) Ltd*.[301] The claimant in this case watched her mother who had been negligently injured by the defendant unexpectedly collapse and die three weeks later. The Court of Appeal said that the relevant event was the accident rather than the death and that the necessary proximity with the accident was lacking. However, this requirement will be satisfied if the claimant can establish sufficient proximity to the "immediate aftermath" of the event. In *McLoughlin v O'Brian*[302] a road accident caused by the defendant's negligence killed the claimant's young daughter and caused injuries of varying severity to other of her children and to her husband. At the time the claimant was at home two miles away. An hour later the accident was reported to the claimant by a friend who drove the claimant to a hospital at which the claimant was told of the death and saw the injured members of her family in circumstances which, it was found, were "distressing in the extreme and were capable of producing an effect going well beyond that of grief and sorrow".[303] The House of Lords held that this qualified as the "immediate aftermath" of the accident and, consequently, the proximity requirement was satisfied and the claim was upheld. *McLoughlin* was considered in *Alcock*, where a number of the claimants had seen the bodies of their loved ones in a temporary morgue set up at the stadium in the aftermath of the disaster. However, *McLoughlin* was distinguished because in *Alcock* the interval between the accident and the sight of the bodies by the claimants in question was longer (nine hours)[304] and (at least according to Lord Jauncey) because the purpose was formal identification rather than aid and comfort.[305]

5-078

The psychiatric injury must have been caused by sight or hearing of the shocking event or its immediate aftermath   The third element requires that the illness must have been caused by the "sudden appreciation by sight or sound of a horrifying event which violently agitated the mind".[306] Notification by third parties (including newspaper or broadcast reports) will not suffice. In practical terms, a claimant who fails on the second element will not be able to satisfy this requirement either although it is possible that there could be a case in which the claimant was in the vicinity but failed to satisfy the third requirement. However, in *Alcock* the House of Lords did not altogether rule out the possibility of liability where the

5-079

---

[299] Lord Ackner's example at [1992] 1 A.C. 310 at 403. See also Lord Keith at 397 and Lord Oliver at 416.
[300] *McFarlane v EE Caledonia Ltd* [1994] 2 All E.R. 1.
[301] [2013] EWCA Civ 194; [2014] Q.B. 150. See Nolan (2014) 30 P.N. 175.
[302] [1983] 1 A.C. 410. See also *Kelly v Hennessy* [1996] 1 I.L.R.M. 321.
[303] [1983] 1 A.C. 410 at 417 per Lord Wilberforce.
[304] See also *Palmer v Tees HA* [2000] P.I.Q.R. P1; *Spence v Percy* [1992] 2 Qd. R. 299.
[305] cf. *Galli-Atkinson v Seghal* [2003] EWCA Civ 697; [2003] Lloyd's Rep. Med 285.
[306] *Alcock v Chief Constable of South Yorkshire* [1992] 1 A.C. 310 at 401 per Lord Ackner. cf. *Walters v North Glamorgan NHS Trust* [2002] EWCA Civ 1792; [2003] Lloyd's Rep. Med. 49.

mental injury was induced by contemporaneous television transmission of the incident. Two members of the House referred in this regard to the example given by Nolan LJ in the Court of Appeal of a live television broadcast of a ballooning event for children, watched by parents, in which the balloon bursts into flames. In *Alcock* itself the television transmission showed the developing chaos in the stadium and no doubt provided the framework in which the fear of the claimants for their loved ones developed but it did not show the suffering of identifiable individuals and therefore lacked the immediacy necessary to found a claim.[307]

v. Participants other than Mere Bystanders

5-080   **Rescuers**   *Frost v Chief Constable of South Yorkshire*,[308] a second case that arose from the Hillsborough disaster, provides guidance as to the position of rescuers who suffer mental injury in the course of rendering assistance. This time the claimants were police officers who were not in physical danger from the crush in the pens (if they had been they would have been primary victims) but who tended the victims of the tragedy in various ways and who claimed to have suffered psychiatric harm as a result. The House of Lords held that there was no special category of rescuers and that the police officers were subject to the controls that apply to secondary victims. While it is well established that rescuers may be owed a duty of care by the person responsible for the danger,[309] it does not follow that rescuers are to be equated with primary victims (though of course they may fall into that category[310]) or that the requirement that they should have a relationship of love and affection with those threatened should be dispensed with. The claims of the relatives in the same disaster had failed in *Alcock* and the House of Lords considered that people in general[311]:

> "would think it wrong that policemen, even as part of a general class of persons who rendered assistance, should have the right to compensation for psychiatric injury out of public funds while the bereaved relatives are sent away with nothing".

The claimants in *Frost* sued additionally on the basis that the police officers were owed a duty of care by their employer,[312] which was responsible for the disaster. However, the House of Lords also rejected the proposition that a duty of care arose on this basis. Although it is certainly the case that the employer's duty of care may

---

[307] "It would be inaccurate and hurtful to suggest that grief is made any the less real or deprivation more tolerable by a mere gradual realisation, but to extend liability to cover injury in such cases would be to extend the law in a direction for which there is no pressing policy and in which there is no logical stopping point": *Alcock v Chief Constable of South Yorkshire* [1992] 1 A.C. 310 at 416 per Lord Oliver.

[308] [1999] 2 A.C. 455.

[309] See para.5-039.

[310] As in the case of the claimant in *Chadwick v British Transport Commission* [1967] 1 W.L.R. 912; cf. *Gregg v Ashbrae Ltd* [2006] NICA 17; [2006] N.I. 300. Claims by officers in *Frost v Chief Constable of South Yorkshire* who worked within the pens seem to have been settled on the basis that they were at risk of physical injury: [1999] 2 A.C. 455 at 466.

[311] *Frost v Chief Constable of South Yorkshire* [1999] 2 A.C. 455 at 510 per Lord Hoffmann.

[312] Strictly speaking, the police are not employees, but they are owed the same duty as those who are. Consider *James-Bowen v Commissioner of Police of the Metropolis* [2018] UKSC 40; [2018] 1 W.L.R. 4021 at [15].

extend to cases of psychiatric injury to a worker,[313] that does not dispense with the *Alcock* "control devices" where the claim is based on the worker's reaction to witnessing the injury or endangerment of a third party on a particular occasion.[314] Had the employment basis of the claims in *Frost* been accepted, the result would have been that the claims of the police officers would have succeeded, whereas those of ambulance crew performing the same function would have failed because their employers were not responsible for the disaster. The House indicated that the outcome might be different where the employer had reason to believe that a particular worker in an emergency service was susceptible to trauma from witnessing danger to others and took no steps to reduce this risk. In such a situation, it was suggested that it would be irrelevant whether the employer was responsible for the disaster.[315]

Involuntary participants in the event   In *Hunter v British Coal Corp*[316] the   **5-081**
claimant had triggered a series of events that led to a hydrant in a mine exploding and killing a co-worker. The accident occurred due to the negligence of the defendants, who owned the mine and employed the claimant to work at it. The claimant, who had left the scene in search of equipment to deal with the problem with the hydrant prior to its exploding, heard but did not see the explosion and subsequently suffered depression due to "survivor's guilt". The Court of Appeal rejected the claim on the basis that the claimant was neither a primary victim (because he was not in the zone of danger when the accident occurred) nor a secondary victim (since he was not at the scene of the accident, did not return to the scene until after it had been cleared up, and never saw the deceased's body). However, there may be liability where the employer negligently causes the employee who is present at the scene of the accident to think that he was an instrument of death or injury. In *Dooley v Cammell Laird & Co Ltd*[317] the claimant, a crane operator, suffered shock when, due to the negligence of his employers, the rope snapped and the load fell into the hold where the operator's colleagues were working.[318] Lord Oliver in *Alcock* regarded this as a case where the negligent act of the defendant had put the claimant in the position of thinking that he had been the involuntary instrument of death or injury to another and for that reason felt that it might not be subject to the *Alcock* restrictions.[319] In *Frost*, Lord Hoffmann made similar comments.[320] But there will be no liability where the psychiatric injury cannot be linked to a belief by the claimant that he was an unwitting cause of the accident. In *Robertson v Forth Road Bridge Joint Board*[321] the pursuers suffered psychiatric injury when they saw a work colleague of theirs blown over the side of a bridge by a gust of wind and fall to his

---

313 See para.5-084.
314 Thus in *Keen v Tayside Contracts* [2003] Scot CS 55; 2003 S.L.T. 500 the claim failed where the pursuer, a road worker, was required to remain at the scene while four burned bodies were removed from the wreckage of a crash. cf. *Harrhy v Thames Trains Ltd* [2003] EWHC 2286 (QB).
315 That, however, is more likely if the exposure is frequent (*Hartman v South Essex Mental Health etc. NHS Trust* [2005] EWCA Civ 6; [2005] I.R.L.R. 293) or prolonged (cf. *Harrhy v Thames Trains Ltd* [2003] EWHC 2120 (QB)).
316 [1999] Q.B. 140.
317 [1951] 1 Lloyd's Rep. 271. See also *Wigg v British Railways Board, The Times,* 4 February 1986; *Dillon v British Railways Board, The Times,* 18 January 1995.
318 In fact, none of them was injured.
319 [1992] 1 A.C. 310 at 408. See also *W v Essex CC* [2000] 2 W.L.R. 601 at 607.
320 [1999] 2 A.C. 455 at 508.
321 1995 S.C. 364.

death. The pursuers were not primary victims as they were not themselves in any danger (they were travelling inside motor vehicles at the time), and they were unable to satisfy the *Alcock* requirements since they were not in a relationship of love and affection with the deceased. *Dooley* and other cases in the same line of authority were regarded as being of no assistance to the pursuers since there was not "any basis in the evidence for attributing their illnesses to a belief that they had been the unwitting cause of [their colleague's] death".[322] The outcome was that no remedy was available.

vi.   Claimant Shocked by Defendant's Endangering Himself

5-082   In *Greatorex v Greatorex*[323] the defendant was seriously injured in a road accident due to his own fault. The claimant, a fire officer and the defendant's father, attended at the scene and contended that he had suffered post-traumatic stress disorder from seeing the defendant's injuries. The claimant, given the rather extraordinary circumstances, fulfilled the *Alcock* requirements for a secondary victim, but Cazalet J dismissed the claim on the ground that the defendant did not owe a duty of care to others not to shock them by the self-infliction of his injuries. Given that the "relationship" requirement in *Alcock* would confine such claims to cases between close family members, to admit a duty of care would open up the possibility of undesirable litigation arising from domestic accidents or deliberate self-harm.[324] Furthermore, a duty to take care of oneself so as not to shock others would, it was said, impinge upon the defendant's right of self-determination.[325] The force of these arguments is doubtful (as to the first, such litigation is very unlikely in the absence of liability insurance), and the result in *Greatorex* may not be entirely just where another defendant is involved. If the injury to D1 is caused by the combined fault of D1 and D2, D1's own personal injury claim against D2 would be reduced for contributory negligence, whereas D2 would be liable in full in respect of C's psychiatric injury and, because D1 would not be liable to C, D2 would be unable to recover any contribution from him.

vii.   Other Situations

5-083   **The primary/secondary victim distinction is not exhaustive**   The view is sometimes taken that in all psychiatric trauma cases claimants must be placed in one or other of the primary/secondary victim categories, but the distinction was created around the case where there is sudden danger to the claimant or a third party and there are situations of liability (or possible liability) which bear no resemblance to that. These situations are considered here.

5-084   **Prolonged exposure to a stressful situation**   Most psychiatric injury cases arise from accidents caused by the defendant's negligence that threaten injury to the

---

[322] 1995 S.C. 364 at 373–374 per Lord Hope.
[323] [2000] 1 W.L.R. 1970.
[324] This does not explain why there is no bar on a claim where one family member physically injures another, nor where family member A endangers member B in the presence of member C.
[325] This reasoning cannot explain why, if D negligently gets himself into danger and C is physically injured trying to rescue him, D may be liable to C: *Harrison v British Railways Board* [1981] 3 All E.R. 679.

claimant or, more usually, which injure or threaten injury to a third party. However, claims in other situations are possible. Liability has, for example, been imposed for mental trauma caused by prolonged exposure to stress,[326] usually at work. In these cases, there is no requirement that the injury must be a response to a sudden event or any other special control mechanisms. Rather, the issue is simply whether the employer fulfilled the general duty of care (which is a matter of contract as well as tort) that he owes not to injure his workers.[327] The employer must take account of the workers' individual weaknesses where these are known or ought to be known to the employer.[328] But the duty is still one of reasonable care and an employer is usually entitled to assume that the employee can withstand the normal pressures of the job unless he knows of some particular problem or vulnerability.[329] It has also been said that the employer will not incur liability if, having done what is reasonable[330] to reduce the risk, he declines to dismiss an employee who is willing to continue.[331] However, there may no longer be any absolute rule to this effect.[332]

Prior relationship between the parties In *Leach v Chief Constable of Gloucestershire*[333] the claimant agreed to act as the "responsible adult" required under the Police and Criminal Evidence Act 1984 where the police interview a person who may be mentally disordered. The claimant alleged that she suffered psychiatric injury and a stroke due to her involvement and that the police ought to have been aware of her susceptibility in this regard. The majority of the Court of Appeal struck out the claim on the basis that if the police owed a duty to safeguard the claimant's mental well-being that might impede their investigation of the offence. However, that aspect of her claim which was based on the failure of the police to offer counselling was allowed to proceed because such counselling was offered to police officers in the case and would not have interfered with the investigative process.[334] Another case that does not fit easily into the categories of primary and second victims is *W v Essex CC*.[335] In this case the House of Lords refused to strike out a claim based on parents' reaction to the discovery that they had taken into their home a foster child who abused their biological children even though the parents were neither secondary victims (because they had not witnessed a sudden event threaten-

5-085

---

[326] *Hatton v Sutherland* [2002] EWCA Civ 76; [2002] I.C.R. 613; *Walker v Northumberland CC* [1995] I.C.R. 702; *Cross v Highlands and Islands Enterprise* [2001] I.R.L.R. 336.

[327] *Hatton v Sutherland* [2002] EWCA Civ 76; [2002] I.C.R. 613 at [22].

[328] See para.6-021.

[329] *Hatton v Sutherland* [2002] EWCA Civ 76; [2002] I.C.R. 613 at [29]. And what must be foreseeable is psychiatric injury, not just anger or resentment: *Fraser v State Hospitals Board for Scotland* 2001 S.L.T. 1051.

[330] In the light of the terms of the contract, which is an essential part of the picture, though the relationship of the contract and the tort duty has not been explored much in the cases: *Barber v Somerset CC* [2004] UKHL 13; [2004] 1 W.L.R. 1089 at [35] per Lord Rodger. But see *Koehler v Cerebos (Australia) Ltd* [2005] HCA 15; (2005) 222 C.L.R. 44.

[331] *Hatton v Sutherland* [2002] EWCA Civ 76; [2002] I.C.R. 613 at [43].

[332] See *Coxall v Goodyear Great Britain Ltd* [2002] EWCA Civ 1010; [2003] 1 W.L.R. 536 and para.9-024.

[333] [1999] 1 W.L.R. 1421.

[334] In *Swinney v Chief Constable of Northumbria* [1997] Q.B. 464 the claimants claimed that they were suffering from psychiatric illnesses because they had been threatened with violence and arson after some confidential information furnished by the first claimant to the police had been stolen from a police vehicle broken into by criminals. The claim was allowed to proceed. The court did not pay any particular attention to the fact that the claims were for damages for psychiatric illness.

[335] [2001] 2 A.C. 592.

ing their biological children) nor primary victims (because the parents themselves were never in any danger). Damages have been recovered for psychiatric illness where a spouse's children were kidnapped due to the negligence of a solicitor engaged in the matrimonial proceedings,[336] where organs were removed from deceased children without the parents' consent[337] and where the claimant was falsely informed of the death of her child soon after birth.[338]

5-086   **Psychiatric injury resulting from damage to property**   Claims may be brought where psychiatric trauma is caused by damage to the claimant's property. In *Attia v British Gas Plc*[339] the Court of Appeal declined to strike out a claim for psychiatric illness arising from the defendant's negligent destruction of the claimant's house by fire. In *Attia* the claimant witnessed the fire. What would have happened if she had been abroad and had been told of it on the telephone and suffered the same trauma? It would be strange if she could recover when a person who is told of the death of his child cannot recover under the *Alcock* principles. Yet a person may recover damages for mental distress falling well short of psychiatric illness in certain types of claim for breach of a contract, e.g., to provide a holiday[340] or damages for inconvenience consequent on a negligent survey,[341] where peace of mind is an important element in the obligation undertaken, so it would be hard to support a principle that led to the automatic rejection of a claim by a householder whose home and possessions were destroyed before his eyes.[342] The same could perhaps be said of one who suffered shock by hearing of the destruction of his home. In *Yearworth v North Bristol NHS Trust*[343] some of the claimants claimed to have suffered psychiatric trauma from hearing of the destruction of sperm samples that they had deposited for storage before treatment that affected their fertility. Others suffered a lesser degree of mental distress. The Court of Appeal found it unnecessary to decide the fate of their claims in tort because there was a bailment which, although non-contractual, involved a specific promise to the claimants and should therefore be treated as akin to a claim in contract for this purpose. Accordingly, all the claimants would be able to recover if they showed that their loss was foreseeable.

---

[336] *Al-Kandari v JR Brown & Co* [1988] Q.B. 665.

[337] *Organ Retention Group Litigation, Re*, [2004] EWHC 644 (QB); [2005] Q.B. 506.

[338] *Allin v City & Hackney HA* (1996) 7 Med. L.R. 91 (but the duty issue was conceded).

[339] [1988] Q.B. 304.

[340] *Jarvis v Swans Tours Ltd* [1973] 1 Q.B. 233.

[341] *Farley v Skinner* [2001] UKHL 49; [2002] 2 A.C. 732

[342] It is difficult to know how to classify the strange case of *Owens v Liverpool Corp* [1939] 1 K.B. 394, where mourners recovered damages when they witnessed a collision involving the hearse, the overturning of the coffin and the threat that the contents might fall out. It seems unrealistic to treat it as a case of a threat to property (there is no property in a corpse). It does not fall within *Alcock* since no "third person" was endangered, yet one can imagine that such an event would be traumatic for the widow.

[343] [2009] EWCA Civ 37; [2010] Q.B. 1.

CHAPTER 6

NEGLIGENCE: BREACH OF DUTY

1. INTRODUCTION

Introduction   In order to establish a claim in the tort of negligence, the claimant   **6-001**
must prove that the defendant breached his duty of care, that is to say, acted
negligently with respect to him. In *Blyth v Birmingham Waterworks Co* Alderson
B said[1]:

> "Negligence is the omission to do something which a reasonable man, guided upon those
> considerations which ordinarily regulate the conduct of human affairs, would do, or do-
> ing something which a prudent and reasonable man would not do."

Put differently, a defendant will breach his duty of care if he takes less care of the
claimant than the reasonable person would have taken. The concept of the reasonable person, which is one of the most important and ubiquitous constructs in the law
of torts, has already been mentioned briefly.[2] This chapter develops that account.
The focus is on the reasonable person in the context of the tort of negligence.
However, the discussion is to a large extent applicable to the many other contexts
within tort law in which the reasonable person features.

An objective enquiry   The invocation of the reasonable person involves an objec-   **6-002**
tive enquiry as to the adequacy of the defendant's conduct. Accordingly, and as is
explained in greater detail below, the issue is not whether the defendant took as
much care as could reasonably have been expected of him given his shortcomings
and idiosyncrasies[3] but whether the defendant behaved at least as well as the
hypothetical prudent person would have performed. The fact that the standard of
care is determined objectively means that defendants who are incapable of achieving the benchmark set by the reasonable person may be held liable in negligence.
Whether or not this situation is fair is one of the most disputed points in the whole

---

[1]   (1856) 11 Ex. 781 at 784; 156 E.R. 1047 at 1049.
[2]   See para.3-013.
[3]   See para.6-007.

of the law of torts.[4] On the one hand, it seems unjust to hold a defendant liable for failing to achieve a level of care that he was incapable of achieving (although this unfairness may be partially mitigated on account of the fact that most defendants are insured). On the other hand, it is usually a matter of luck from the perspective of the claimant whether he was injured by a negligent but capable defendant or by a negligent but incapable defendant, and is it fair to the claimant to deny compensation simply because he had the misfortune of being injured by an incapable defendant?

6-003 Especially capable defendants What is the position in relation to defendants who are exceptionally capable[5] and are able easily to exceed the standard of the reasonable person? Are they permitted to "live down" to that standard? Or are they held, for example, to the standard of care that could reasonably be expected of them given their ability?[6] The position is unclear, although traces of authority suggest that provided the standard of the reasonable person is met, it is irrelevant that the defendant was capable of exceeding that standard but failed to do so.[7] This solution has the significant advantage of simplicity. It means that a single standard applies irrespective of the defendant's abilities.

6-004 Two stages to the breach analysis The process of determining whether the defendant breached his duty of care involves two steps. These steps are often not neatly separated from each other, but it is important to distinguish between them if one is to understand properly this area of the law. First, it is necessary to ascertain the qualities of the reasonable person. This is a question of law. Secondly, it must be asked whether the defendant took less care than the reasonable person, given the qualities attributed to him, would have taken in the circumstances. The law prescribes that certain factors fall to be considered in this regard but the amount of care that the reasonable person would have exercised, and whether the defendant took less care, are questions of fact.[8] If the defendant took less care than the reasonable person would have taken the breach element of the tort of negligence will be satisfied (and it makes no difference in this regard whether the defendant fell just short or far below the reasonable person standard). This chapter addresses these two steps in turn. As a practical matter, in the vast majority of cases in which the breach element is in issue only the second step is in contention.

2. THE REASONABLE PERSON

6-005 General characteristics The reasonable person does not suffer from defects in his constitution, but neither is he an individual of exceptional ability or skill. Thus, the reasonable person does not have the courage of Achilles, the wisdom of Ulysses

---

4   For discussion, see Honoré (1988) 104 L.Q.R. 530; Weinrib, *The Idea of Private Law* (1995), Ch.6; Cane, *Responsibility in Law and Morality* (2002), Ch.3; Goudkamp (2004) 28 M.U.L.R. 343; Goldberg and Zipursky (2007) 92 Cornell L. Rev. 1123.

5   As was the case in *Heydon v NRMA Ltd* (2000) 51 N.S.W.L.R. 1; *R. v Banister* [2009] EWCA Crim 1571 (noted in Goudkamp [2010] C.L.J. 8).

6   See Goudkamp (2004) 12 Tort L. Rev. 111.

7   *Rust v Needham* (1974) 9 S.A.S.R. 510 at 523; *Heydon v NRMA Ltd* (2000) 51 N.S.W.L.R. 1 at 53, 117, 236.

8   "What is reasonable care in a particular circumstance is a jury question": *Wooldridge v Sumner* [1962] 2 All E.R. 978 at 988 per Diplock LJ.

or the strength of Hercules. Nor does he have "the prophetic vision of a clairvoyant".[9] Because the reasonable person is not a perfect citizen or a "paragon of circumspection"[10] he will not anticipate folly in all its forms. However, he never puts out of consideration the teachings of experience and so will guard against the negligence of others when experience shows such negligence to be common.[11] While the reasonable person is not all-seeing and all-knowing and can therefore make reasonable mistakes, he is not the average person. Thus, whereas even the most careful person will on occasion act sub-standardly, the reasonable person takes reasonable care day in, day out.

The reasonable person is placed in the defendant's position The reasonable **6-006** person is placed into the shoes of the defendant at the time of the alleged breach of duty. Thus, if the defendant is a motorist, it is asked whether the defendant's conduct fell below the standard of the reasonable motorist, and if the defendant is a golfer, the question becomes whether the defendant fell below the standard of the reasonable golfer. In *Al-Najar v The Cumberland Hotel (London) Ltd* hotel guests were viciously attacked by an intruder who had snuck into the hotel and entered their rooms with a view to stealing valuables. In asking whether the defendant hotel had taken reasonable care of the guests' safety, the adequacy of the defendant's conduct was measured against the standard of a "a reasonable 4 star London hotel".[12] This principle can have important consequences. It means, for example, that a footballer is not expected to take as much care for another player's safety as if he were going on a leisurely walk with the latter in the countryside.[13] Similarly, if the defendant is undertaking some activity in a domestic context he will not be held to the standards that would be expected in a business setting.[14] Thus, a householder who does some repair work in his house is not required to show the skill which might be expected of a professional carpenter—he need only do his work with the skill of a reasonably competent householder doing the work in question.[15] Similarly, a jeweller who pierces ears is held to the hygiene standards of the reasonable jeweller, rather than those of the reasonable surgeon,[16] and a receptionist in an accident and emergency department need not achieve the standard of the reasonable medically trained person but only that of the "averagely competent and well-informed person performing the function of a receptionist at a department providing emergency medical care".[17] Where a defendant represents, expressly or by implication, that he possesses particular skills, those skills are attributed to the reasonable person, regardless of whether the defendant actually has the skills concerned. Thus, where a brewing company owned a ship it was held that the board of directors of the company must exercise the same degree of care and skill in the

---

[9]   *Hawkins v Coulsdon & Purley UDC* [1954] 1 Q.B. 319 at 341 per Romer LJ.
[10] *AC Billings & Sons Ltd v Riden* [1958] A.C. 240 at 255 per Lord Reid. For a brilliant caricature of "this excellent but odious creature" see Herbert, *Uncommon Law* (1935), pp.1–5.
[11] *London Passenger Transport Board v Upson* [1949] A.C. 155 at 173, 176; *Lang v London Transport Executive* [1959] 1 W.L.R. 1168 at 1175.
[12] [2019] EWHC 1593 (QB) at [196] per Dingemans J.
[13] *Condon v Basi* [1985] 1 W.L.R. 866.
[14] *Surtees v Kingston on Thames BC* [1991] 2 F.L.R. 559.
[15] *Wells v Cooper* [1958] 2 Q.B. 265.
[16] *Phillips v William Whiteley Ltd* [1938] 1 All E.R. 566
[17] *Darnley v Croydon Health Services NHS Trust* [2018] UKSC 50; [2019] A.C. 831 at [25] per Lord Lloyd-Jones.

management of the ship as would any other ship owner. "The law must apply a standard which is not relaxed to cater for their factual ignorance of all activities outside brewing: having become owners of ships, they must behave as reasonable shipowners."[18]

6-007   **Shortcomers**   Ordinarily, the defendant's shortcomings are not attributed to the reasonable person.[19] "The general rule is that the courts disregard them."[20] Accordingly, no allowance is made in determining the qualities of the reasonable person for the fact that the defendant was, for example, blind, deaf, intoxicated, dim-witted[21] or even insane.[22] Nor is any account normally taken of the fact that the defendant is a beginner or inexperienced. The leading authority on this point is *Nettleship v Weston* in which the Court of Appeal held that the defendant learner driver should be judged by reference to the standard of the reasonable experienced driver,[23] even where the claimant was her instructor.[24] The court was heavily influenced by the presence of compulsory insurance, but the holding is consistent with the general rule that the standard of the reasonable person eliminates the personal attributes of the defendant from consideration.

6-008   **The professional post occupied by the defendant**   The objective standard appears to make no allowance for the fact that everyone must, to some extent, learn by practical experience on the job. Novices must achieve the same benchmark as everyone else.[25] The potential for unfairness that this rule is liable to produce was pressed upon the Court of Appeal in *Wilsher v Essex Area Health Authority*.[26] In this case, one of the defendants was a junior doctor of limited experience. It was put to the court that what should be expected of an individual doctor was what was reasonably required of a person of his qualifications and experience. The majority rejected this argument on the ground that it would entail that "the standard of care which the patient is entitled to demand [would] vary according to the chance of recruitment and rostering".[27] Rather, the standard, the court held, was to be set by reference to the post held by the defendant in the unit in which he operated.[28] A junior member of the team could not be expected to show the skill of a consultant but, subject to that, no allowance would be made for the inexperience of the individual any more than for his domestic circumstances or his financial worries, either of which might equally contribute to an error. This principle means that a "general

---

18   *The Lady Gwendolen* [1965] P. 294 at 350 per Winn LJ.
19   For discussion of this rule, and departures from it, see Seavey (1927) 41 Harv. L. Rev. 1.
20   *FB v Rana* [2017] EWCA Civ 334; [2017] P.I.Q.R. P17 at [54] per Jackson LJ.
21   *Vaughan v Menlove* (1837) 3 Bing N.C. 468; 132 E.R. 490.
22   *Dunnage v Randall* [2015] EWCA Civ 673; [2016] Q.B. 639; Goudkamp (2012) 31 O.J.L.S. 727; Goudkamp and Ihuoma (2016) 32 P.N. 137.
23   [1971] 2 Q.B. 691.
24   cf. *Vowles v Evans* [2003] EWCA Civ 318; [2003] 1 W.L.R. 1607 at [28].
25   See para.6-007.
26   [1987] Q.B. 730. The decision was reversed by the House of Lords but not on this point: [1988] A.C. 1074. More recently, see *FB v Rana* [2017] EWCA Civ 334; [2017] P.I.Q.R. P17.
27   [1987] Q.B. 730 at 750 per Mustill LJ.
28   It has been held that a barrister "must conduct himself in his professional work with the competence (care and skill) of a barrister of ordinary skill who is competent to handle that type of and weight of work and a breach of that duty occurs when the error is one which no reasonably competent member of the profession possessing those skills should have made": *McFaddens v Platford* [2009] EWHC 126 (TCC); [2009] P.N.L.R. 26 at [49] per HHJ Toulmin QC.

practitioner" (whether in medicine, law, the valuation of pictures or any other trade or profession) will not be held to the standard of a specialist, but he should possess a sense of when it is necessary to take specialist advice.[29] It also follows that a specialist will be held to the higher standard of those practising within that specialism. *Wilsher* can be interpreted as affirming both the rule that no account will be taken of the fact that the defendant is a beginner,[30] and the principle that the reasonable person is placed in the position of the defendant.[31]

Childhood   If the defendant is a child, the adequacy of his conduct will be judged   **6-009**
against the standard of the reasonable child of the same age. In *Mullin v Richards* two 15-year-old schoolgirls engaged in a mock sword fight using plastic rulers. One of the rulers broke and the claimant suffered serious injury to one of her eyes when a fragment of plastic struck it. The claimant sued (relevantly) her classmate in negligence. Hutchinson LJ said[32]:

> "[t]he question for the judge is not whether the actions of the defendant were such as an ordinarily prudent and reasonable adult in the defendant's situation would have realised gave rise to a risk of injury, it is whether an ordinarily prudent and reasonable 15-year-old schoolgirl in the defendant's situation would have realised as much."

The reason for this rule has never been made sufficiently clear. Why should the fact that the defendant is a child be taken into account but not the defendant's other qualities? One possible answer to this question is that age is not truly idiosyncratic because everyone begins their life as a child. This answer, if accepted, suggests that an allowance should also be made for the elderly, although there is no suggestion in the case law that this is done. A possible exception to the rule that the conduct of child defendants is to be assessed by reference to the standard of the reasonable child of the same age concerns child defendants who were engaged in a dangerous adult activity at the time of the alleged wrongdoing. In this situation, it is arguable that the defendant's age should be ignored.[33] On this view, if, for example, a 10-year-old defendant takes his parents' car he will be held to the standard of the reasonable adult motorist.[34]

Taking childhood into account in defining the reasonable person can have important implications since the reasonable child may take less care than the reasonable adult. Consequently, the fact that the defendant is a child can operate to the defendant's advantage. This is particularly so where the defendant is, say, 10 years old or younger. Cases in which defendants of such tender years have been held liable are rare. Conversely, the standard of care will hardly be reduced at all where the defendant is just shy of the age of majority. Although infancy is not a defence to liability in tort,[35] if the defendant is so young that he is incapable of exercising

---

29   *Luxmore-May v Messenger May Baverstock* [1990] 1 W.L.R. 1009.
30   See para.6-007.
31   See para.6-006.
32   [1998] 1 W.L.R. 1304 at 1308. See also *Blake v Galloway* [2004] EWCA Civ 814; [2004] 1 W.L.R. 284; *Orchard v Lee* [2009] EWCA Civ 295; [2009] P.I.Q.R. P16.
33   An infant defendant is required to meet the standard set by the reasonable adult where he is engaged in a "dangerous activity that is characteristically undertaken by adults": *Restatement (Third) of Torts: Liability for Physical and Emotional Harm*, §10(c).
34   *Tucker v Tucker* [1956] S.A.S.R. 297.
35   See para.25-023.

any care, liability cannot arise. This is because it is impossible for a defendant to sink below such a standard.[36]

6-010   Other exceptions   In addition to childhood, the courts occasionally take account of other of the defendant's subjective qualities. A prominent example is *Goldman v Hargrave*.[37] In dealing with the liability of the defendant for failing to extinguish a fire started on his land by natural causes, the Privy Council said that "[l]ess must be expected of the infirm than of the able-bodied ... [and the defendant] should not be liable unless it is clearly proved that he could, and reasonably in his individual circumstances should, have done more."[38] *Goldman*, however, was a case in which the defendant was making no unusual use of his land and had a risk thrust upon him by no fault of his own. It seems, therefore, that this approach would not be employed where the danger arose from the defendant's activity.

6-011   Sudden incapacitation   If the defendant is suddenly incapacitated through no fault of his own (suppose that he suffers from a spontaneous blackout[39]) the defendant will not be liable in negligence for any damage that he inflicts. There are several ways of explaining this result. One way in which it can be accounted for is on the ground that the defendant did as well in the circumstances as the reasonable person who suffered from the same condition would have done.[40] This analysis attributes the defendant's condition to the reasonable person. Accordingly, it sits uncomfortably with the principle that the reasonable person eliminates from consideration the subjective qualities of the defendant. Furthermore, the notion of the reasonable incapacitated person is arguably contradictory. Another way of rationalising this outcome is to say that a defendant who is suddenly incapacitated is not acting at all, and that, in the absence of an act (or a failure to act where there is a duty to act), no one can incur liability in tort.[41] This line of reasoning is consistent with the fact that a breach of duty in negligence consists of *conduct* that falls below the standard of the reasonable person.

6-012   The doctrine of prior fault   The question of whether to attribute to the reasonable person conditions that suddenly incapacitate the defendant rarely arises in practice. This is probably at least partly because the issue can usually be sidestepped by invoking the doctrine of prior fault. This doctrine, when it applies, fixes liability on the defendant not in respect of what happened at the time of the injury but at some earlier point. Suppose that D carelessly fails to take his heart medication and, while driving, suffers from a heart attack that the medication would probably have prevented. In driving without having taken his medication, D breached his duty of care.[42] Liability can be straightforwardly pinned on him for any damage resulting from this carelessness and the issue of whether to attribute D's heart

---

[36]   For further discussion see Goudkamp, *Tort Law Defences* (2013), pp.50–51.
[37]   [1967] 1 A.C. 645.
[38]   [1967] 1 A.C. 645 at 663. See, further, para.15-045.
[39]   See, e.g., *Robinson v Glover* [1952] N.Z.L.R. 669; *Dessaint v Carriere* [1958] O.W.N. 481; [1958] 17 D.L.R. (2d) 222; *Jones v Dennison* [1971] R.T.R. 174. See also *Waugh v James K Allan Ltd* [1964] 2 Lloyd's Rep. 1 (lorry driver suffering fatal coronary thrombosis at the wheel of his lorry).
[40]   This analysis was adopted in *Mansfield v Weetabix Ltd* [1998] 1 W.L.R. 1263. See also *Dunnage v Randall* [2015] EWCA Civ 673; [2016] Q.B. 639 at [131].
[41]   See Goudkamp, *Tort Law Defences* (2013), pp.48–49.
[42]   *C (A child) v Burcombe* [2003] C.L.Y. 3030. See also *Kay v Butterworth* (1945) 110 J.P. 75.

condition to the reasonable person can be bypassed. The doctrine of prior fault also supplies a partial answer to the complaint that the objective standard of care can result in injustice to defendants. Shortcomers who cannot achieve the standard of the reasonable person cannot properly be blamed for failing to perform as well as the reasonable person, but it may be that they should have realised that they were inept, in which case they can fairly be criticised for having engaged in an activity that was beyond their ability.

Special knowledge possessed by the defendant   Usually, the reasonable person   6-013
will only possess such knowledge of the world as ordinary, competent people would possess. However, if the defendant enjoys relevant knowledge that is above and beyond that which most similarly situated people would possess such knowledge will be attributed to the reasonable person.[43] This rule is, essentially, an exception to the principle that it is permissible for defendants who are able to take an exceptional level of care to live down to the standard of the reasonable person.[44]

The rule in Roe v Minister of Health   The reasonable person is attributed with   6-014
such knowledge of the world as would have been reasonable to have at the time of the alleged breach of duty. Thus, if an accident occurred five years before the trial, the reasonable person would have had reasonable knowledge about the world according to the standards that prevailed at the time of the accident rather than according to the standards that existed at the time of the trial. In *Roe v Minister of Health*[45] the claimant had been admitted to hospital in 1947. An anaesthetist administered a spinal anaesthetic to the claimant in preparation for a minor operation. The anaesthetic was contained in a glass ampoule which had been kept in a solution of phenol. Unfortunately, some of the phenol had made its way into the ampoule through an "invisible crack". The phenol thus contaminated the anaesthetic, with the result that the claimant became permanently paralysed from the waist down. The anaesthetist was aware of the consequences of injecting phenol, and he therefore subjected the ampoule to a visual examination before administering the anaesthetic, but he was not aware of the possibility of invisible cracks. Had he been aware of this risk, the danger to the claimant could have been eliminated by adding a colouring agent to the phenol so that contamination of the anaesthetic could have been observed. However, it was held, at first instance and on an appeal that was heard in 1954, that the anaesthetist was not negligent in failing to take this step because the risk of invisible cracks had not been drawn to the attention of the profession until 1951. As Denning LJ said, "[w]e must not look at the 1947 accident with 1954 spectacles".[46]

General practice and new developments   The reasonable person takes account   6-015
of the general practice in the particular field in question. He also keeps his knowledge up to date.[47] However, the reasonable person is not necessarily an avid reader of scientific and technical periodicals,[48] and he may not learn of new

---

43   *Baker v Quantum Clothing Group Ltd* [2011] UKSC 17; [2011] I.C.R. 523 at [104].
44   This principle is discussed at para.6-003.
45   [1954] 2 Q.B. 66.
46   [1954] 2 Q.B. 66 at 84. See also at 92.
47   *Stokes v GKN (Bolts and Nuts) Ltd* [1968] 1 W.L.R. 1776 at 1783.
48   *Thompson v Smiths Shiprepairers (North Shields) Ltd* [1984] Q.B. 405.

knowledge until it becomes fairly widespread.[49] Even once the reasonable person acquires new knowledge, he may not put it into effect immediately. The fact that the defendant failed to comply or has complied with a general practice may be evidence for or against a finding of negligence. The use that can be made of such evidence is addressed below.[50]

3. APPLICATION OF THE STANDARD OF CARE

6-016   **A single standard of care**   According to conventional wisdom, there is only a single standard of care in the law of torts, namely, that of the reasonable person. Of course, the steps that constitute reasonable care will vary with the facts of each dispute. But the test is usually thought to be the same in all cases. Thus, whereas it would be possible for tort law to require gross negligence to be established on the part of a defendant in order to make out a breach of a duty of care in selected situations, that is not what tort law does. In other words, there are no degrees of negligence.[51] It has been questioned whether this traditional view is entirely accurate and whether the standard of care should not be varied in certain circumstances.[52] While there may be advantages in varying the standard of care on occasion, the current, single-standard approach does at least have the merit of simplicity.

6-017   **Foreseeability of risk as a threshold issue?**   Opinion is divided as to whether, before enquiring as to how much care the reasonable person in the defendant's position would have taken, it is necessary for the claimant to prove that the risk that materialised was one to which a reasonable person would have adverted. According to one line of cases, there is such a foreseeability filter, with the result that unless the claimant can establish that the reasonable person would have appreciated the risk that eventuated, the court will not proceed to enquire as to how much care the reasonable person would have exercised and the claim will fail. For example, in *Bussey v 00654701 Ltd* Underhill LJ said that "it is important to split out the question of the foreseeability of the risk from the question of what precautions it was reasonable to take against it",[53] and in *Jones v Whippey* Aikens LJ remarked that[54]:

> "Before holding that a person's standard of care has fallen below the objective standard expected and so finding that he acted negligently, the court must be satisfied that a reasonable person in the position of the Defendant (ie the person who caused the incident) would contemplate that injury is likely to follow from his acts or omissions".

These and other authorities to the same effect[55] are underpinned by the idea that the

---

[49]   *N v UK Medical Research Council* [1996] 7 Med. L.R. 309 (failure to undertake thorough reappraisal of human growth hormone programme after the discovery of Creutzfeldt-Jakob disease risk); *Bowman v Harland & Wolff Plc* [1992] I.R.L.R. 349 (vibration white finger).
[50]   See para.6-026.
[51]   See para.3-014.
[52]   Nolan (2013) 72 C.L.J. 651.
[53]   [2018] EWCA Civ 243; [2018] 3 All E.R. 354 at [63].
[54]   [2009] EWCA Civ 452 at [16]. See also Cane, *The Anatomy of Tort Law* (1997), pp.38–39.
[55]   Consider *Al-Najar v The Cumberland Hotel (London) Ltd* [2019] EWHC 1593 (QB) where the judge (at [191]–[195]) analyses the foreseeability of the risk of injury as an issue anterior to all of the other considerations relevant to the breach enquiry.

reasonable person cannot be expected to guard against unforeseeable risks. On this understanding it is nonsensical to enquire as to the precautions that the reasonable person would have taken in relation to risks that he could not foresee because the answer to that enquiry will always be "he would not have taken any precautions at all". By applying the forseeability filter, it is thought that the breach enquiry can in some cases be simplified and expedited.

According to the rival view, the law of negligence, properly understood, does not recognise a reasonable foreseeability filter and, instead, the foreseeability of the risk is simply a factor to be considered alongside all of the other relevant considerations that need to be addressed in asking how much care the reasonable person would have taken. In support of this second view, it may be said that it makes no sense to isolate just one of several factors that are relevant to the breach analysis and to take it as an initial matter. A preliminary filter is, on this view, at best superfluous and at worst supplies an illegitimate basis for rejecting claims.

The difference between these two views, although of some theoretical interest because it relates to a basic issue as regards the structure of the breach stage of the tort of negligence, is likely to be of minimal practical significance. This is partly because, if the breach element is subject to a foreseeability filter, the filter likely prevents only a modest number of claims from proceeding, it being rare for a court to conclude that a risk is not foreseeable to the reasonable person.[56] Only risks that are truly "fanciful"[57] are regarded as unforeseeable.

What does reasonable care require?   Several preliminary matters should be   **6-018** observed in relation to the concept of reasonable care. First, reasonable care can involve doing nothing in respect of a particular risk. The reasonable person will advert to risks that are reasonably foreseeable but, very often, he will take no steps to ameliorate the danger that they present, because that is what acting reasonably with respect to those risks entails. For instance, it is reasonably foreseeable that a person who enters an office may stumble and hit his head on the desk, but that does not mean that taking reasonable care involves (for example) eliminating desks from all offices or encasing them in bubble wrap. The reasonable thing to do in respect of this particular risk is nothing at all. As Gleeson CJ put it in the Australian case of *New South Wales v Fahy*: "There have been occasions when judges appear to have forgotten that the response of prudent and reasonable people to many of life's hazards is to do nothing."[58] A second point that is also sometimes overlooked is that taking reasonable care may involve discontinuing the activity in question, rather than merely taking additional precautions in the course of the activity concerned.[59] Thirdly, taking reasonable care with respect to a given risk will often involve doing nothing more than warning of its existence. Put differently, alerting persons to the existence of a risk may be sufficient in certain circumstances to meet the benchmark of the reasonable person.[60] Fourthly, the standard of the reasonable person, when it calls for precautions to be taken, does not necessarily require that

---

[56] For illustrations, see *Tacagni v Penwith DC* [2013] EWCA Civ 702; *Scott v Gavigan* [2016] EWCA Civ 544.
[57] *Rochester Cathedral v Debell* [2016] EWCA Civ 1094 at [12].
[58] [2007] HCA 20; (2007) 232 C.L.R. 486 at [6]. "[A]n ordinarily careful man does not take precautions against every foreseeable risk": *Bolton v Stone* [1951] A.C. 850 at 863 per Lord Oaksey.
[59] *Bolton v Stone* [1951] A.C. 850 at 867.
[60] Although the reasonable person may not warn of risks that are inherent and obvious in an activity on which the claimant is embarked: *Maylin v Dacorum Sports Trust* [2017] EWHC 378 (QB) at [29].

all of the risks in issue be eliminated. For example, the requirement to take reasonable care in respect of a footpath may require only that significant irregularities in its surface be addressed with it being permissible to ignore minor variations.[61]

6-019 **The negligence calculus** The enquiry as to how much care the reasonable person would have exercised is sometimes referred to as the "negligence calculus". It classically involves considering four factors: (1) the size of the risk; (2) the gravity of the risk (i.e., how serious would the likely harm be if the risk materialised); (3) the utility of the defendant's conduct; and (4) the cost of taking precautions. Describing this exercise as a calculus can be criticised on the ground that it suggests that it involves a mechanical or scientific process.[62] It is certainly true that the analysis involves the application of common sense and that there is no formula that can be applied to determine automatically the outcome in particular cases.

6-020 **The size of the risk** This factor refers to the probability of the risk of injury occurring. The lower the chance that the risk would materialise, the more likely it is that the reasonable person would ignore it (or not take increased precautions to guard against it) and vice versa. "The law in all cases exacts a degree of care commensurate with the risk."[63] In *Bolton v Stone*[64] the claimant was standing on the highway in a road adjoining a cricket ground when she was struck by a ball which a batsman had hit out of the ground. Such an event was reasonably foreseeable and, indeed, balls had to the defendant's knowledge occasionally been hit out of the ground before. Nevertheless, the House of Lords considered that the likelihood of injury to a person in the claimant's position was so slight that the cricket club was not negligent in allowing cricket to be played without having taken additional precautions. The House considered several factors including the distance from the pitch to the edge of the ground, the presence of a fence that was seven feet high and the upward slope of the ground in the direction in which the ball was struck.[65] In *Hilder v Associated Portland Cement Manufacturers Ltd*[66] the deceased was riding his motorcycle along a road outside a piece of open land occupied by the defendants where children were permitted to play football. A ball was kicked into the road which caused the deceased to crash. The conditions were such that the likelihood of injury to passers-by was much greater than in *Bolton v Stone* and, accordingly, the defendants were held liable for having permitted football to be played on their land without having taken any additional precautions.

---

[61] See *Rochester Cathedral v Debell* [2016] EWCA Civ 1094 at [9]–[12].
[62] "Reference to 'calculus', 'a certain way of performing mathematical investigations and resolutions', may wrongly be understood as requiring no more than a comparison between what it would have cost to avoid the particular injury that happened and the consequences of that injury": *New South Wales v Fahy* [2007] HCA 20; (2007) 232 C.L.R. 486 at [57] (footnote omitted); "What is involved ... is not a calculation; it is a judgment": *Mulligan v Coffs Harbour City Council* [2005] HCA 63; (2005) 223 C.L.R. 486 at [2] per Gleeson CJ.
[63] *Read v J. Lyons & Co Ltd* [1974] A.C. 156 at 173 per Lord Macmillan. "As the danger increases, so must the precautions increase": *Lloyds Bank Ltd v Ry Executive* [1952] 1 All E.R. 1248 at 1253 per Denning LJ.
[64] [1951] A.C. 850.
[65] Another case in which significant weight was placed on the fact that the size of the risk of injury was very low is *Al-Najar v The Cumberland Hotel (London) Ltd* [2019] EWHC 1593 (QB). See at [195].
[66] [1961] 1 W.L.R. 1434.

The gravity of the risk   The relevance of the seriousness of the risk is il-   **6-021**
lustrated by *Paris v Stepney BC*.[67] The claimant, a one-eyed man, was employed
by the defendants. The conditions in which he worked involved some risk of eye
injury. The likelihood of injury was regarded as insufficient to require the defendants to provide goggles to a two-eyed workman. However, the House of Lords held
that in the case of the claimant goggles should have been provided. This was
because the risk to which he was exposed was total blindness, whereas the risk to
a two-eyed man was a lesser one, namely, the loss of sight in one eye. In assessing
the gravity of the risk it is important to notice that the duty of care is owed to the
claimant himself and therefore if he suffers from some disability that increases the
gravity of the risk to him that disability must be taken into account so long as it is,
or should be, known to the defendant.[68]

The utility of the defendant's conduct   Account must be taken of the benefits of   **6-022**
the defendant's conduct that gave rise to the risk of injury that materialised.[69] As
Asquith LJ said[70]:

> "[I]f all the trains in this country were restricted to a speed of 5 miles an hour, there would
> be fewer accidents, but our national life would be intolerably slowed down. The purpose
> to be served, if sufficiently important, justifies the assumption of abnormal risk."

In *Watt v Hertfordshire CC*[71] the claimant, a fireman, was injured by the movement of a heavy jack when travelling with it in a lorry that was not specially
equipped to carry it. A woman had been trapped under a vehicle and the jack was
urgently required to save her. It was held that the fire authorities had not been
negligent in transporting the jack in the manner in which they did, bearing in mind
the reason why they proceeded in this way.[72] However, while rescuers are treated
sympathetically because of the value of their conduct,[73] the mere fact that a defend-

---

[67] [1951] A.C. 367. Consider, also, *Attorney General of the British Virgin Islands v Hartwell* [2004]
UKPC 12; [2004] 1 W.L.R. 1273 (loaded gun).

[68] *Haley v London Electricity Board* [1965] A.C. 778; *Baxter v Woolcombers* (1963) 107 S.J. 553
(claimant's low intelligence relevant to standard of care due to him); *Morrell v Owen, Times,* 14
December 1993 (coach of disabled athletes); *Walker v Northumberland CC* [1995] I.C.R. 702; *Hatton v Sutherland* [2002] EWCA Civ 76; [2002] I.C.R. 613 (susceptibility to stress).

[69] See s.2 of the Social Action, Responsibility and Heroism Act 2015 which provides: "The court must
have regard to whether the alleged negligence or breach of statutory duty occurred when the person
was acting for the benefit of society or any of its members." Regarding this statute, see Goudkamp
(2017) 37 L.S. 577; Mulheron (2017) 80 M.L.R. 88.

[70] *Daborn Bath Tramways* [1946] 2 All E.R. 333 at 336 (use of left-hand drive ambulance owing to
vehicle shortage in wartime not negligent). See also *Brisco v Secretary of State for Scotland* 1997
S.C. 14 (small risk of injury justified in training of prison officers); *Humphrey v Aegis Defence
Services Ltd* [2016] EWCA Civ 11; [2017] 1 W.L.R. 2937 (contractor acted reasonably in requiring Iraqi interpreters to participate in training exercise despite knowing that they were less fit than
the other participants given the importance of their role in rebuilding Iraq). cf. *Quinn v Scott* [1965]
1 W.L.R. 1004 (National Trust negligent in not felling dangerous tree near highway as safety of
public must take precedence over preservation of the amenities).

[71] [1954] 1 W.L.R. 835.

[72] The outcome would have been different if the jack had been carried in the course of a commercial
enterprise. "The commercial end to make profit is very different from the human end to save life or
limb": [1954] 1 W.L.R. 835 at 838 per Denning LJ.

[73] *Marshall v Osmond* [1983] Q.B. 1034 (police not liable for injury caused to suspect); *Scutts v MPC*
[2001] EWCA Civ 715; [2001] Po. L.R. 169 (police responding to emergency); *Craggy v CC
Cleveland* [2009] EWCA Civ 1128; [2009] Po. L.R. 349 (collision between emergency vehicles).

ant is a rescuer or otherwise proceeding altruistically does not mean that he cannot fall short of reasonable care.[74] Emergency services have no special exemption from liability in the tort of negligence.[75]

6-023   **The cost of taking precautions**   In determining how the reasonable person would have acted, it is necessary to take account of how practicable it would have been to eliminate or reduce the risk. As Lord Reid explained in *Morris v West Hartlepool Steam Navigation Co*, "the difficulty and expense and any other disadvantage of taking the precaution" must be factored into the standard of care.[76] In *Latimer v AEC*[77] a factory floor became slippery after a flood. The occupiers of the factory went to considerable lengths to ameliorate the effects of the flood, but the claimant was nevertheless injured and contended that the occupiers should have closed the factory. The House of Lords held that the reasonable person would not have taken this precaution.[78] However, the greater the risk, the less receptive a court is likely to be to a defence based simply upon the cost, in terms of money, of the required precautions[79] and some activities are so dangerous that they must be abandoned altogether.

Costs other than financial costs must be considered. This includes the inconvenience that the precautions may cause[80] and the possibility that taking precautions may create new risks.[81] Also relevant is the extent to which taking precautions would interfere with autonomy.[82] Because tea and coffee are palatable only when they are made with hot water, people generally want them to be served hot and a person who caters for that is not negligent merely because there is a risk of scalding.[83] If the law sets the standard of care too high the legitimate activities of people in general will be curtailed. This point was made with considerable force by the House of Lords in *Tomlinson v Congleton BC*.[84] The claimant had been catastrophically injured when he dived into an artificial lake on land occupied by the defendant. The House rejected the argument that the defendant should have

---

See also s.4 of the Social Action, Responsibility and Heroism Act 2015, which provides: "The court must have regard to whether the alleged negligence or breach of statutory duty occurred when the person was acting heroically by intervening in an emergency to assist an individual in danger."

[74]   See, e.g., *Ward v LCC* [1938] 2 All E.R. 341; *Wardell-Yerburgh v Surrey CC* [1973] R.T.R. 462; *Rigby v CC Northamptonshire* [1985] 1 W.L.R. 1242; *Purdue v Devon Fire and Rescue Service* [2002] EWCA Civ 1538.

[75]   Even though they may be exempt from criminal liability for, e.g., exceeding the speed limit. See *Gaynor v Allen* [1959] 2 Q.B. 403; *Griffin v Mersey Regional Ambulance* [1998] P.I.Q.R. P34.

[76]   [1956] A.C. 552 at 574.

[77]   [1953] A.C. 643. cf. *Bolton v Stone* [1951] A.C. 850 at 867 per Lord Reid: "I think that it would be right to take into account not only how remote is the chance that a person might be struck but also how serious the consequences are likely to be if a person is struck; but I do not think that it would be right to take into account the difficulty of remedial measures."

[78]   In *Gough v Upshire Primary School* [2002] E.L.R. 169 the fact that a child might slide down a banister was perfectly foreseeable, but that did not require alteration of the staircase.

[79]   See, e.g., *Morris v Luton Corp* [1946] 1 All E.R. 1 at 4 per Lord Greene MR (the report of this case at [1946] K.B. 116 is incomplete); *Christmas v General Cleaning Contractors* [1952] 1 K.B. 141 at 149 per Denning LJ (affirmed [1953] A.C. 180).

[80]   *Yorkshire Traction Co Ltd v Searby* [2003] EWCA Civ 1856.

[81]   *Morris v West Hartlepool Steam Navigation Co Ltd* [1956] A.C. 552

[82]   This is a relevant consideration pursuant to s.1 of the Compensation Act 2006. See, further, para.1-053.

[83]   *Bogle v McDonald's Restaurants Ltd* [2002] EWHC 490 (QB).

[84]   [2003] UKHL 47; [2004] 1 A.C. 46.

taken additional steps to keep people away from the water. Lord Hoffmann said[85]:

"I think that there is an important question of freedom at stake. It is unjust that the harmless recreation of responsible parents and children with buckets and spades on the beaches should be prohibited in order to comply with what is thought to be a legal duty to safeguard irresponsible visitors against dangers which are perfectly obvious. The fact that such people take no notice of warnings cannot create a duty to take other steps to protect them ... A duty to protect against obvious risks or self-inflicted harm exists only in cases in which there is no genuine and informed choice, as in the case of employees whose work requires them to take the risk, or some lack of capacity, such as the inability of children to recognise danger ... or the despair of prisoners which may lead them to inflict injury on themselves ...

It is of course understandable that organisations like the Royal Society for the Prevention of Accidents should favour policies which require people to be prevented from taking risks. Their function is to prevent accidents and that is one way of doing so. But they do not have to consider the cost, not only in money but also in deprivation of liberty, which such restrictions entail. The courts will naturally respect the technical expertise of such organisations in drawing attention to what can be done to prevent accidents. But the balance between risk on the one hand and individual autonomy on the other is not a matter of expert opinion. It is a judgment which the courts must make and which in England reflects the individualist values of the common law."

A cost/benefit analysis? The foregoing factors have sometimes been thought to create, or to call for, a cost/benefit analysis of the defendant's conduct. Especially in the United States, it has been argued that the breach element can be explained entirely in economic terms.[86] The idea, which is often referred to as the "Hand formula",[87] is that the negligence calculus can be interpreted as imposing liability where the burden of taking precautions is less than the likely cost of not doing so (assessed in the light of the probability of the risk materialising if the precautions are not taken and the likely gravity of the damage that will occur if it does). It is clear, however, that English courts and, indeed, Commonwealth courts generally, have not reduced the breach of duty element to an economic question. McHugh JA elegantly summarised the position in Commonwealth jurisdictions as follows: "Negligence is not an economic cost/benefit equation. Immeasurable 'soft' values such as community concepts of justice, health, life and freedom of conduct have to be taken into account."[88] One such additional factor is perhaps that which the courts must consider pursuant to s.3 of the Social Action, Responsibility and Heroism Act 2015, which requires the court to take account of whether the defendant at the time of the alleged breach "demonstrated a predominantly responsible approach towards protecting the safety or other interests of others". This provision seems to be aimed at providing some leniency for isolated errors. More generally, it can be said that the issue at this stage of the breach analysis is simply what reasonable care required, and that enquiry cannot be reduced to an equation. Whereas the

6-024

---

[85] [2003] UKHL 47; [2004] 1 A.C. 46 at [46]. See also *Keown v Coventry Healthcare NHS Trust* [2006] EWCA Civ 39; [2006] 1 W.L.R. 953 at [17].

[86] See, e.g., Posner, *Economic Analysis of Law*, 9th edn (2019), Ch.6. cf. Wright (2003) 4 Theoretical Inq. L. 1; Zipursky (2007) 48 Wm. & Mary L Rev. 1999; Stevens, *Torts and Rights* (2007), pp.92–97.

[87] See *US v Carroll Towing* 159 F.2d 169 (2d. Cir. 1947).

[88] *Western Suburbs Hospital v Currie* (1987) 9 N.S.W.L.R. 511 at 523.

probability of the harm occurring, its likely magnitude and the cost of avoiding it are all relevant considerations, they do not tell the whole story.

6-025 **Hindsight bias** Before leaving the issue of the standard of care that the reasonable person would have achieved it is worth emphasising that it is easy to be wise after the event. This must be kept in mind when asking what the reasonable person in the defendant's position would have done. The defendant should not be judged with the benefit of hindsight.[89] It is important to remember that the risk that materialised is just one of many that might have occurred and which consequently may have made calls on the reasonable person's attention. Accordingly, the court must resist the temptation to fixate on the risk that eventuated. The reasonable person acts reasonably and that involves turning one's mind to the full range of reasonably foreseeable risks. It might be reasonable to take no or minimal precautions in relation to the risk that resulted in injury to the claimant in order to address more pressing risks.

6-026 **General practice** The mere fact that the defendant complied with the general practice in a given activity does not necessarily mean that he took reasonable care. "Neglect of duty does not cease by repetition to be neglect of duty"[90] and it is for the courts, not a particular industry, to determine whether conduct complies with the standard of the reasonable person. As Lord Mance explained in *Baker v Quantum Clothing Group Ltd*[91]:

> "Respectable general practice is no more than a factor, having more or less weight according to the circumstances, which may ... guide the court [when determining whether the defendant complied with the standard of the reasonable person]."

Thus, the courts have sometimes held that following a general practice amounts to negligence.[92] That said, if it is shown that the defendant complied with widely accepted industry or professional standards the court is likely to find in his favour.[93] "When the court finds a clearly established practice ... the practice weighs heavily in the scale on the side of the defendant and the burden of establishing negligence, which the plaintiff has to discharge, is a heavy one."[94] Where the defendant has not complied with the general practice that is not of itself negligence for "otherwise all inducement to progress ... would then be destroyed".[95] But non-

---

[89]   *Marks and Spencer Plc v Palmer* [2001] EWCA Civ 1528 at [27].
[90]   *Bank of Montreal v Dominion Guarantee and Casualty Co Ltd* [1930] A.C. 659 at 666 per Lord Tomlin.
[91]   [2011] UKSC 17; [2011] 1 W.L.R. 1003 at [82].
[92]   See, e.g., *Lloyd's Bank Ltd v Savory* [1933] A.C. 201; *Markland v Manchester Corp* [1934] 1 K.B. 566; *Barkway v South Wales Transport Co Ltd* [1950] A.C. 185; *Paris v Stepney BC* [1951] A.C. 367; *General Cleaning Contractors v Christmas* [1953] A.C. 180; *Morris v West Hartlepool Steam Navigation Co Ltd* [1956] A.C. 552; *Cavanagh v Ulster Weaving Co Ltd* [1960] A.C. 145; *MacDonald v Scottish Stamping & Engineering Co* 1972 S.L.T. (Notes) 73; *Edward Wong Finance Co Ltd v Johnson Stokes & Master* [1984] A.C. 296; *Re Organ Retention Group Litigation* [2004] EWHC 644; [2005] Q.B. 506.
[93]   *Wright v Cheshire CC* [1952] 2 All E.R. 789; *Rich v LCC* [1953] 1 W.L.R. 895; *Simmons v Pennington & Sons* [1955] 1 W.L.R. 183; *Brown v Rolls-Royce Ltd* [1960] 1 W.L.R. 210; *Gray v Stead* [1999] 2 Lloyd's Rep. 559; *Baker v Quantum Clothing Group Ltd* [2011] UKSC 17; [2011] 1 W.L.R. 1003.
[94]   *Morris v West Hartlepool Steam Navigation Co Ltd* [1956] A.C. 552 at 579 per Lord Cohen.
[95]   *Hunter v Hanley* 1955 S.C. 200 at 206 per Lord Clyde.

compliance with a general practice may raise an inference of negligence.[96]

The Bolam principle   It has just been observed that the mere fact that the defend-   **6-027**
ant complied with the general practice in a particular industry will not establish that
the defendant met the standard of the reasonable person.[97] There is an important
exception to this rule, which is known as the *Bolam* principle.[98] The rule applies
where the defendant is a professional (although the courts have given little guidance as to what counts as a profession for this purpose) and it is alleged that the
damage was caused by his failure properly to discharge his professional obligations.
Paradigmatically, it is relevant in the context of medical professionals, but it is not
confined to that setting.[99] When the principle is applicable, the defendant will have
discharged his duty of care provided that what he did was supported by a
responsible body of opinion within his profession[100] and regardless of whether the
defendant achieved the standard of the reasonable person in his position. This means
that if there are, for instance, two views in a profession as to what should be done
in a given situation, and both views are endorsed by a responsible body of opinion,
no breach of duty will have been committed if the defendant's conduct was in accordance with one of the two views. The rationale for the *Bolam* principle is that it
avoids the need for courts to choose between competing professional opinions, as
expressed by expert witnesses, in circumstances in which judges may lack the
institutional competence to make such a choice. One response to this argument is
that judges are regularly required to choose between the views of experts in other
contexts, for example, when foreign law applies to a claim and the parties' expert
witnesses disagree about the content of the law in issue. More fundamentally, it can
be said that the *Bolam* principle is objectionable because it involves an abdication
by the courts of their responsibility to determine the amount of care that the law
requires people to exercise.[101]

Exceptions to the Bolam principle   There are two exceptions to the *Bolam*   **6-028**
principle. The first is that the principle does not apply where the body of opinion
with which the defendant complied is illogical.[102] This qualification to the *Bolam*
principle allows the courts to override professional views where they diverge too
far from the reasonable person standard. The other exception, which is significantly
more important, concerns cases of medical negligence in which the allegation
against the doctor is that he failed to warn the claimant about a risk of injury attendant upon a proposed medical procedure (as opposed to failing to take reason-

---

[96] *Lloyd Cheyham & Co Ltd v Littlejohn & Co* [1987] B.C.L.C. 303.
[97] *Natixis SA v Marex Financial* [2019] EWHC 2549 (Comm).
[98] *Bolam v Friern Hospital Management Committee* [1957] 1 W.L.R. 582.
[99] See, e.g., *Natixis SA v Marex Financial* [2019] EWHC 2549 (Comm); [2019] 2 Lloyd's Rep. 431
    (document authentication).
[100] It is not necessary that the defendant made a conscious choice between the two schools: *Adams v
    Rhymney Valley DC* [2000] Lloyd's Rep. P.N. 777.
[101] The *Bolam* test was rejected at common law in Australia by *Rogers v Whittaker* (1992) 175 C.L.R.
    479. The effect of that decision has, however, been disturbed by statute in some states: see, e.g., Civil
    Liability Act 2002 (NSW), s.5O.
[102] *Bolitho v City and Hackney HA* [1998] A.C. 232 at 243 ("incapable of withstanding logical
    analysis"). Regarding this exception, see Mulheron (2010) 69 C.L.J. 609. For a rare example of a
    case that fell within the exception, see *McGuinn v Lewisham and Greenwich NHS Trust* [2017]
    EWHC 88 (QB). The judge emphasised at [75] that a claimant who seeks to establish that the excep-
    tion applies has to surmount a "high hurdle".

able care in investigating and treating the claimant's ailments). In *Montgomery v Lanarkshire Health Board*[103] the Supreme Court held that the *Bolam* principle did not apply in that context and that instead medical professionals must "take reasonable care to ensure that a patient is aware of material risks of injury that are inherent in treatment".[104] A risk is material if "a reasonable person in the patient's position would be likely to attach significance to the risk, or the doctor is or should reasonably be aware that the particular patient would be likely to attach significance to it".[105] *Montgomery* reflects a move away from a paternalistic conception of the doctor/patient relationship and towards one that emphasises patient autonomy and the acceptance of responsibility by patients for the consequences of their choices. The reason for the different approach to failure to warn cases as opposed to matters involving negligent treatment is that the former category of case does not depend purely on medical considerations. There is a[106]:

"fundamental distinction between, on the one hand, the doctor's role when considering possible investigatory or treatment options and, on the other, her role in discussing with the patient any recommended treatment and possible alternatives, and the risks of injury which may be involved".

4. PROOF OF NEGLIGENCE

6-029 **Past decisions**   The question of whether the defendant fell short of the reasonable person standard is a question of fact. Each case must be decided according to its own individual circumstances, and the facts in two cases will never be identical.[107] Thus, strictly speaking, decisions regarding whether the defendant fell short of the objective standard of care have no precedential value.[108] So a decision in one case that, for example, the reasonable occupier would have installed a sign to warn of the risk presented by submerged rocks does not mean that all occupiers must install such signs where the danger posed by such rocks exists. Different judges confronted with similar conduct are at liberty to reach different conclusions as to whether the conduct concerned is reasonable. Nevertheless, situations tend to repeat themselves and, as a matter of practice, it is common to look to other decisions for guidance for the purposes of establishing that a given defendant took, or failed to take, reasonable care.

6-030 **Statutory standards**   Modern life is controlled by an endless array of regulatory provisions. These provisions touch on virtually every conceivable subject, including road transport, construction and industrial activities. It is relatively unusual for such rules to specify the consequences of a breach thereof for the purposes of the

---

[103] [2015] UKSC 11; [2015] A.C. 1430.

[104] [2015] UKSC 11; [2015] A.C. 1430 at [82] per Lord Kerr and Lord Reed.

[105] [2015] UKSC 11; [2015] A.C. 1430 at [87] per Lord Kerr and Lord Reed. Regarding the test of "materiality", see *A v East Kent Hospital University NHS Foundation Trust* [2015] EWHC 1038 (QB); [2015] Med. L.R. 262; *Tasmin v Barts Health NHS Trust* [2015] EWHC 3135 (QB); *Thefaut v Johnston* [2017] EWHC 497 (QB).

[106] *Montgomery v Lanarkshire Health Board* [2015] UKSC 11; [2015] A.C. 1430 at [82] per Lord Kerr and Lord Reed.

[107] "[N]o one case is exactly like another": *Baker v E Longurst & Sons Ltd* [1933] 2 K.B. 461 at 468 per Lord Wright.

[108] *Qualcast (Wolverhampton) Ltd v Haynes* [1959] A.C. 743; *Foskett v Mistry* [1984] R.T.R. 1.

law of torts.[109] However, breach of such rules (perhaps especially if they attract criminal liability) may be evidence of negligence on the part of the defendant. This is said expressly in, for example, the case of the Highway Code. Legislation provides that a failure to observe the Code may be relied upon to establish (or to negate) any tortious liability.[110] Equally, it is not difficult to imagine a case in which statutory requirements are met but the court finds negligence. With regard to the latter type of case, however, a distinction must be drawn between activities like driving, where there must be room for varying standards to meet varying circumstances, and matters such as the legally permissible level of toxic materials in products. For example, if statutory regulations lay down the amount of an ingredient which may be incorporated in petrol, it may be difficult to establish that it is negligent to incorporate this amount even in the face of evidence that it is potentially harmful to do so.[111]

Criminal convictions   In many cases (especially road accident cases) there may   **6-031** have been criminal proceedings that resulted in the conviction of the defendant. Section 11 of the Civil Evidence Act 1968 provides that a conviction can be used as evidence in civil proceedings, and that if a person has been convicted of an offence, then he shall be taken to have committed that offence unless he proves to the contrary. Accordingly, a conviction for dangerous driving in respect of the incident in which the claimant was injured is likely to be compelling evidence that the defendant fell short of the standard of the reasonable person.[112] However, the defendant may, if he can, show that he did not in fact commit the offence[113] or that for some reason his conduct did not amount to civil negligence.

Res ipsa loquitur   It is open to the court to infer negligence from the circum-   **6-032** stances in which the accident occurred, particularly if the defendant was in control of the situation that led to the damage, the damage is unlikely to have occurred in the ordinary course of things absent negligence, and the cause of the damage is not known.[114] Although this does not involve a reversal of the burden of proof,[115] if an inference of negligence is drawn the claimant will win unless the defendant offers an explanation consistent with due care.[116] This has traditionally been described by the phrase res ipsa loquitur—the thing speaks for itself. Morris LJ commented upon this phrase as follows[117]:

---

[109]   See Ch.8.
[110]   Road Traffic Act 1988 s.38(7). See further Ch.8.
[111]   See *Albery and Budden v BP Oil* [1980] J.P.L. 586.
[112]   An acquittal is of no evidential relevance to civil liability since the criminal standard of proof is higher.
[113]   This does not infringe the rule against collateral attacks on issues decided in criminal proceedings: *McCauley v Hope* [1999] P.I.Q.R. P185; *J v Oyston, The Times,* 11 December 1998. Care must be taken to distinguish s.11 from s.13, which makes proof of a conviction conclusive evidence of guilt for the purposes of defamation: see para.13-049.
[114]   Consider *Grace Electrical Engineering Pte Ltd v Te Deum Engineering Pte Ltd* [2017] SGCA 65 at [39].
[115]   *Ng v Lee* [1988] R.T.R. 296.
[116]   "The issue will be decided in the claimant's favour unless the defendants by their evidence provide some answer which is adequate to displace the prima facie inference": *Henderson v Henry E Jenkins & Sons* [1970] A.C. 282 at 310 per Lord Pearson.
[117]   *Roe v Minister of Health* [1954] 2 Q.B. 66 at 87.

"[T]his convenient and succinct formula possesses no magic qualities: nor has it any added virtue, other than that of brevity, merely because it is expressed in Latin. When used on behalf of a plaintiff it is generally a short way of saying: 'I submit that the facts and circumstances which I have proved establish a prima facie case of negligence against the defendant' ... There are certain happenings that do not normally occur in the absence of negligence, and upon proof of these a court will probably hold that there is a case to answer."

In the past, there was a tendency to elevate the phrase res ipsa loquitur to the status of a special rule of the law of negligence. The older cases should therefore be read cautiously and are of limited value. One had disputes as to whether res ipsa loquitur "could" apply to complex matters like surgery or the operation of an aircraft,[118] but to modern eyes these controversies are misplaced, because the question of drawing inferences from particular facts cannot be subject to rules of law and it is not possible to identify in advance the situations to which res ipsa loquitur will apply. It would be impossible to argue convincingly that if a patient dies during surgery or a child is born with brain damage that necessarily establishes a prima facie case of negligence against the doctors or the theatre staff. Conversely, if the procedure is simple and regarded as unattended by serious risk, an adverse outcome may well justify an inference of negligence. Even in such a case, however, the claimant will probably[119] need to lay a foundation with expert evidence about the procedure, whereas a court is not likely to require expert evidence before it concludes that a car veering across the carriageway suggests negligence on the part of the driver.[120] It has been said that in medical negligence cases the essential function of res ipsa loquitur is not so much to prove the claimant's case as to enable him, when he is not in possession of all the material facts "to be able to plead an allegation of negligence in an acceptable form and to force the defendant to respond to it at the peril of having a finding of negligence made against the defendant if the defendant does not make an adequate response".[121]

---

[118] It was held that in suitable circumstances res ipsa loquitur could be applied to air crashes in *George v Eagle Air Services* [2009] UKPC 21; [2009] 1 W.L.R. 2133.

[119] cf. *Ludlow v Swindon Health Authority* [1989] 1 Med. L.R. 104.

[120] In the case of a head-on collision in the middle of the road there may be no pointer one way or the other as to which driver was at fault and the correct inference will often be that both drivers were to blame: *Bray v Palmer* [1961] 1 W.L.R. 1455; *Baker v Market Harborough Co-operative Society* [1953] 1 W.L.R. 1472.

[121] *Ratcliffe v Plymouth and Torbay HA* [1998] P.I.Q.R. P170 at 189 per Hobhouse LJ.

CHAPTER 7

NEGLIGENCE: DAMAGE, CAUSATION AND REMOTENESS

1. INTRODUCTION

Four distinct concepts Once the claimant has established that the defendant **7-001** breached a duty of care owed to him, he must go on to show that that breach of duty caused him damage, and that the damage was not too "remote". Four distinct concepts are relevant in this regard: damage; causation in fact; causation in law; and remoteness. The *damage* issue is whether the claimant has suffered a form of harm which is actionable in negligence. The *factual causation* issue is whether there was a historical connection between the defendant's breach of duty and the claimant's damage, a question which is generally resolved by asking whether, if the defendant had not been negligent, the claimant would still have suffered the damage (the "but for" test). The *legal causation* issue is whether there was an intervening act

[147]

or omission of the claimant or a third party which "broke the chain of causation" between the defendant's negligent conduct and the claimant's damage (a "novus actus interveniens"). And the *remoteness of damage* issue is usually determined by asking whether the type of damage suffered by the claimant was a reasonably foreseeable consequence of the defendant's negligent conduct, although this principle is also supplemented by others.

These four concepts are not always properly separated out in judicial and academic analysis. Hence damage is frequently rolled up with factual causation, it is sometimes argued by judges that the separation between factual causation and legal causation is unnecessary, and many commentators conflate the questions of legal causation and remoteness, often under the catch-all heading of "scope of liability". However, it is clear from the case law that for the most part the courts do recognise that there are four different questions that may need to be answered, and that different concepts are used to answer them.[1] It should also be noted that some of these questions (or variations on them) can arise in connection with other torts, but most of the case law involves claims for negligence, so they are dealt with here, albeit that it may be necessary to consider them again at various later points.

7-002 **Liability and measure of damages** The issues dealt with in this chapter are in theory distinct from and anterior to the question of measure of damages, which will be dealt with at a later stage.[2] Thus, in one of the leading cases on remoteness, the issue was whether the defendants were liable for fire damage to a wharf which arose from a rather unusual chain of events after the defendants spilled oil into a harbour.[3] If they had been liable (in fact they were not) the prima facie measure of damages would have been the cost of repairing the wharf plus consequential losses like loss of business. However, in this case the remoteness question went to whether there was any liability *at all*, and so the separation between remoteness and measure of damages was clear. Frequently, however, questions of causation and remoteness arise even though it is not disputed that there is liability and, in these cases, the distinction between "causation/remoteness" and "measure" is not so easy to draw.[4] Consider, for example, *Baker v Willoughby*,[5] where the claimant suffered an injury to his left leg as a result of the defendant's negligence. Before the trial, the claimant was the victim of an armed robbery during which he suffered gunshot wounds to the same leg, as a result of which the leg had to be amputated. The defendant argued that his liability was limited to the loss suffered before the robbery, on the ground that all loss suffered thereafter was said to have merged in and flowed from the robbery. The case is usually dealt with as a case on factual causation (and will be so dealt with here[6]) but note that it was not disputed that the defendant was liable to the claimant: the argument between the parties was as to the extent of that liability. And similarly, in many of the leading cases on legal causation and remote-

---

[1] For an example of a clear line being drawn between legal causation and remoteness, see the speech of Lord Bingham in *Corr v IBC Vehicles Ltd* [2008] UKHL 13; [2008] A.C. 884. See also *Maitland Hudson v Solicitors Regulation Authority* [2017] EWHC 1249 (Ch) at [51].

[2] See *The Argentino* (1881) 13 P.D. 101 at 196.

[3] *The Wagon Mound* [1961] A.C. 388, para.7-062.

[4] Furthermore, "measure of damages" is sometimes used by judges when causation/remoteness is meant. See, e.g., *The Wagon Mound (No.2)* [1967] 1 A.C. 617 at 638.

[5] [1970] A.C. 467.

[6] See para.7-031.

ness, the defendant was undoubtedly liable in negligence to the claimant,[7] and the question was again the extent of that liability, in other words the quantum of the award to be made in respect of it. In such cases, it is doubtful whether a clear line can be drawn between causation/remoteness and assessment of damages, although the basic idea of that distinction is perhaps best understood as being the difference between the question of what the defendant is liable *for* and the question of how to quantify that liability.

2. DAMAGE

A. Damage in General

A neglected concept[8]   Despite being described as the "gist" of negligence,[9] the damage element of negligence has generally been under-emphasised by common lawyers. Issues concerning damage are frequently repackaged as questions of duty or causation,[10] important extensions of the categories of damage take place with little or no analysis or even acknowledgement of the fact, and the treatment given to the issue in the textbooks has hitherto generally been cursory or non-existent. One reason for the general neglect of the concept is that the question of what counts as damage has tended to arise only indirectly in negligence cases, rather than as an issue in its own right.[11] So, for example, because the requirement of damage completes the cause of action in negligence, with the result that the limitation period starts to run only when damage has been sustained, many of the older cases on damage are actually limitation cases,[12] where it was not in doubt that the claimant had suffered damage, but the outcome of the limitation issue depended on precisely when the damage was deemed to have occurred.[13]

7-003

Damage, damages and duty   It is important to distinguish between the forms of harm that are sufficient to establish a cause of action in negligence and the harms for which recovery is permitted once the cause of action has been established. For

7-004

---

7   See, e.g., *McKew v Holland & Hannen & Cubitts (Scotland) Ltd* [1969] 3 All E.R. 1621 (legal causation); *Spencer v Wincanton Holdings Ltd* [2009] EWCA Civ 1404; [2010] P.I.Q.R. P8 (legal causation); *Conarken Group Ltd v Network Rail Infrastructure Ltd* [2011] EWCA Civ 644; 136 Con L.R. 1 (remoteness).

8   Witting (2002) 61 C.L.J. 189; Nolan (2007) 70 M.L.R. 59; Nolan (2013) 4 J.E.T.L. 259; Fordham (2015) 27 S.Ac.L.J. 643; Cooper (2019) 25 Torts L.J. 128.

9   Stapleton (1988) 104 L.Q.R. 213, 389.

10   See, e.g., *ACB v Thomson Medical Pte Ltd* [2017] SGCA 20; [2017] 1 S.L.R. 918, where the Singapore Court of Appeal explicitly chose to categorise the issue of damage as a duty question. cf. *Harriton v Stephens* [2006] HCA 15; (2006) 226 C.L.R. 52 at [161] per Hayne J: "In this case a central, and the determinative, question is what does the law recognise as 'damage'? That question is separate and distinct from questions of duty or causation."

11   Although this has started to change: for important recent decisions addressing the question in its own right, see, e.g., *Rothwell v Chemical and Insulating Co Ltd* [2007] UKHL 39; [2008] A.C. 281 and *Dryden v Johnson Matthey Plc* [2018] UKSC 18; [2019] A.C. 403.

12   See, e.g., *Cartledge v E Jopling & Sons Ltd* [1963] A.C. 758.

13   The time at which the plaintiffs first sustained damage was also critical in *Alcan Gove Pty Ltd v Zabic* [2015] HCA 33; (2015) 257 C.L.R. 1, since it determined whether their claims in respect of disease caused by occupational asbestos exposure fell to be resolved under the common law or under a statutory workers' compensation scheme. The right to sue for property damage in negligence often also depends on when the damage occurred: see, e.g., *The Starsin* [2003] UKHL 12; [2004] 1 A.C. 715.

example, distress or upset do not themselves ground a negligence claim,[14] but if they are consequential on a harm that does—such as a broken leg—then compensation will generally be payable in respect of them. And it is also important to distinguish between forms of harm which are never actionable in negligence, and which therefore do not amount to "damage", and forms of harm which are actionable only in certain limited circumstances, where the harm does count as damage, but recovery for that harm is permitted only if there is a relevant duty of care. For example, mental harm falling short of a recognised psychiatric illness is in the former category, and so not damage, whereas recognised psychiatric illnesses themselves are in the latter category, so they do count as damage, although recovery for the negligent infliction of such an illness is severely constrained at the duty of care stage of the negligence enquiry. Unfortunately, however, there is a tendency to subsume the damage question into the duty of care question,[15] as in the psychiatric injury context, where the requirement of a "recognised psychiatric illness" is often treated as a duty issue.[16]

7-005 **Cases where damage was missing** The requirement of damage is best illustrated by cases where a negligence claim failed because the claimant was held not to have suffered any. One such decision is *Reilly v Merseyside Area Health Authority*,[17] where the claimants were an elderly couple who sued a health authority for the mental distress they experienced when they were trapped in an overcrowded hospital lift. Although the defendant was negligent in failing to install a device to prevent the lift from moving when overloaded, in the absence of a recognisable psychiatric illness it was held that the claimants had suffered no damage. Another illustrative case is *Calveley v Chief Constable of the Merseyside Police*[18] in which a police officer alleged that disciplinary proceedings brought against him had not been conducted properly. The claim was dismissed because the police officer's suspension from duty while the investigation was carried out was not in itself, and did not involve, injury of a kind capable of sustaining an action in negligence. And finally, in *A v A Health and Social Services Trust*[19] the white mother of the claimant infants had been inseminated with sperm from a donor of a Cape Coloured background in the course of in-vitro fertilisation treatment, with the result that the children were darker in complexion than their parents. Dismissing the children's claims in negligence against the provider of the treatment, the judge held that in a modern civilised society the colour of a person's skin could not amount to "damage" for legal purposes.[20]

7-006 **A legal construct** As an element of the cause of action for negligence, damage is a legal construct, rather than a purely factual phenomenon.[21] Suppose, for example, that D drives into C's parked car and writes it off. In ordinary parlance,

---

14   See para.5-070.
15   See Dias [1955] C.L.J. 198, 202.
16   See para.5-070.
17   (1995) 6 Med. L.R. 246.
18   [1989] 1 All E.R. 1025.
19   [2010] NIQB 108; [2012] N.I. 77.
20   cf. *ACB v Thomson Medical Pte Ltd* [2017] SGCA 20; [2017] 1 S.L.R. 918 (damages award for "loss of genetic affinity" when IVF treatment provider mistakenly fertilised the plaintiff's ovum with the sperm of a stranger instead of her husband).
21   *ACB v Thomson Medical Pte Ltd* [2017] SGCA 20; [2017] 1 S.L.R. 918 at [45].

we would say that it is the car itself that is damaged, but that is not to use the term in its legal sense. Rather, the legal concept of damage refers to the more intangible notion of an interference with a person's protected interests: it is *damage to the claimant* which grounds a negligence claim. Hence in the example, if C wishes to bring a negligence claim against D, it will not be enough for C simply to point to the written-off vehicle and say "that car is damaged": C will also have to establish that he had either legal ownership of or a possessory title to the car at the time D smashed into it.[22] The distinction between damage as a factual concept (the smashed car) and damage as a legal construct (the interference with a legally protected interest) is often lost sight of, because most negligence claims are for personal injury, and in such cases the distinction usually does not matter, since by injuring C's leg you by definition interfere with C's legally protected interest in bodily integrity. However, even in personal injury cases this distinction can become important, as is shown by the fact that an unwanted pregnancy is capable of amounting to a "personal injury" for the purposes of a negligence action,[23] whereas a desired pregnancy is not.[24] Hence despite the fact that the physical reality of the pregnancy is exactly the same in both cases, the claimant's feelings about it can turn something which would not otherwise be damage into something that is. It follows that to talk of "actionable damage" is a tautology. If a form of interference with the claimant's interests is actionable in negligence, then it is damage for negligence purposes, and if it is not actionable then it is not. In this context, in other words, "damage" is a technical legal term which itself connotes actionability.

Defining damage It is impossible to devise a general definition of damage that   **7-007**
avoids circularity.[25] The best we can do is to say that damage means a certain kind of interference with a person's protected interests, classically either bodily or mental injury, or property damage, such as will ground a claim in negligence. Although more elegant formulae have been suggested by judges, these give rise to difficulties. Take for example Lord Hoffmann's definition of damage in *Rothwell v Chemical and Insulating Co Ltd* as "an abstract concept of being worse off, physically or economically".[26] By limiting damage to physical and economic harms, this formula excludes psychiatric injury, which (if of sufficient severity) is undoubtedly capable of grounding a negligence claim,[27] and it also seems to preclude the possibility that, for example, a negligence action could lie in respect of loss of freedom of movement.[28] But even if we remove those limiting words, so that damage is simply defined as "an abstract concept of being worse off",[29] problems remain.[30] One is that

---

[22] See para.5-052.
[23] See para.7-013.
[24] See *R. v Croydon Health Authority* (1997) 40 B.M.L.R. 40; *Walkin v South Manchester HA* [1995] 1 W.L.R. 1543 at 1553.
[25] See *ACB v Thomson Medical Pte Ltd* [2017] SGCA 20; [2017] 1 S.L.R. 918 at [45] per Andrew Phang Boon Leong JA (damage "defies easy definition").
[26] [2007] UKHL 39; [2008] 1 A.C. 281 at [7].
[27] See Ch.5.
[28] See para.7-008.
[29] See the definition of damage as a "detrimental difference" to the claimant by Hayne and Bell JJ in *Tabet v Gett* [2010] HCA 12; (2010) 240 C.L.R. 537 at [66].
[30] In truth, formulae that refer to the claimant being "worse off", or "detrimentally affected" by the defendant's negligence work better as definitions of loss rather than damage, those two concepts being distinct for these purposes: see Nolan (2017) 37 O.J.L.S. 255. The distinction between damage and loss does, however, collapse in pure economic loss cases: see *DW Moore & Co Ltd v Ferrier*

not all forms of being worse off count as damage, as is shown by the fact that a claimant who has lost a loved one as a result of the defendant's negligence (and so is obviously "worse off") is not deemed to have suffered damage for these purposes. And another problem is that in some cases the claimant may be better off, not worse off, as a result of the defendant's negligence, but will none the less be considered to have suffered damage. Suppose, for example, that C is run over and injured by D while on his way to the airport, and that as a result C misses his plane, which then crashes on take-off, killing all those on board.[31] In this case, C is obviously better off as a result of D's negligence, and yet the physical injury C suffers still amounts to "damage" for the purposes of a negligence claim.[32]

7-008   **Categories of damage**   A more productive course of action than seeking to devise a general definition of damage is to consider the various kinds of harm which are and are not actionable in negligence. The paradigm cases are of course personal injury and property damage, and they will be addressed in the sections that follow, before we conclude by asking whether it is or should be possible to base a negligence action on the loss of a chance of avoiding injury. Before we turn to consider those categories, however, it should be noted that they do not exhaust the content of the concept of damage. In particular, while a wrongful invasion of personal autonomy is neither a free-standing cause of action nor a base on which a negligence action can be grounded,[33] more specific categories of autonomy loss can it seems constitute damage. A negligence action can be brought in respect of an extended period of imprisonment,[34] for example, and the conventional sum awarded to the parents in wrongful conception cases[35] is best understood as compensation for a loss of reproductive autonomy itself capable of forming the gist of a negligence claim.[36] Finally, it is important to remember that at the heart of the so-called "wrongful life" cases is the question of whether in cases of particularly severe disability life itself can amount to damage for the purposes of a negligence action,

---

[1988] 1 W.L.R. 267 at 280; and *Nykredit Mortgage Bank Plc v Edward Erdman Group Ltd (No.2)* [1997] 1 W.L.R. 1627 at 1638–1639.

[31]   See Weinrib (1989) 10 Cardozo L. Rev. 1283, 1283–1284.

[32]   Lest this example be thought far-fetched, a more routine one can be given. Suppose that C's house is damaged by vibrations attributable to D's negligence, but that the damage only becomes apparent after C has sold the house to X. In this case, because the damage was sustained, and so the cause of action arose, when C had the property in the house, C has a claim against D and X does not, even though it is X and not C who is left worse off. See *Leigh & Sillivan v Aliakmon Shipping Co Ltd (The Aliakmon)* [1986] A.C. 785.

[33]   *Shaw v Kovac* [2017] EWCA Civ 1028; [2017] 1 W.L.R. 4773; *ACB v Thomson Medical Pte Ltd* [2017] SGCA 20; [2017] 1 S.L.R. 918 (where there is extensive discussion of why this is so). See further Purshouse (2015) 22 Torts L.J. 226.

[34]   *De Freville v Dill* (1927) 96 L.J.K.B. 1056; *W v Home Office* [1997] Imm.A.R. 302; also implied in *McLoughlin v Jones* [2001] EWCA Civ 1743; [2002] Q.B. 1312 at [57]. See further, Heffey (1983) 14 Melb. U.L. Rev. 53; Nolan (2007) 70 M.L.R. 59, 62-70. Although the tort of false imprisonment is a possible source of redress in such a case, a negligence action may be required where the imprisonment is accidental, or, more importantly, where a deliberate imprisonment is the result of a mistake, but the jailer himself is not responsible for the mistake and has a defence of lawful authority against a false imprisonment claim.

[35]   *Rees v Darlington Memorial Hospital NHS Trust* [2003] UKHL 52; [2004] 1 A.C. 309, para.25-021.

[36]   See Nolan (2007) 70 M.L.R. 59, 77-80.

a question which the courts in most jurisdictions have answered in the negative, on the ground that there is no way of comparing existence and non-existence.[37]

B. Personal Injury

Impairment Although there is no judicial definition of personal injury, according to s.38(1) of the Limitation Act 1980, it "includes any disease and any impairment of a person's physical or mental condition".[38] This non-exhaustive definition suggests that the concept of "impairment" is central to the determination of whether or not someone has suffered personal injury. An impairment implies a characteristic of a thing that makes it a less good thing than it should be. So, for example, a broken leg is impaired because it is a less good leg than an undamaged leg: more difficult to stand on, walk on, perhaps painful and so forth. The law takes a broad approach to what constitutes an impairment. Hence, for instance, a condition such as back pain that causes the sufferer to feel discomfort amounts to a personal injury, as does a disfigurement, even if neither of them in any way affect the mechanical functioning of the body.

7-009

Disease The inclusion of "disease" as a separate element within the statutory definition of personal injury suggests that a disease may be a personal injury even if it does not (or does not yet) amount to an impairment. The claimants in *Cartledge v E Jopling & Sons Ltd*[39] were steel dressers who had contracted pneumoconiosis as a result of exposure to silica dust while working for the defendant. The nature of pneumoconiosis was such that serious damage could be caused to the victim's lungs before any symptoms became apparent. Whether the defendant had a limitation defence depended on when the claimants had first suffered actionable injury, and the claimants' argument that the damage necessary to bring a claim arose only when they became aware of the disease was rejected by the House of Lords. In the opinion of Lord Pearce, it was "impossible to hold that a man who has no knowledge of the secret onset of pneumoconiosis and suffers no present inconvenience from it cannot have suffered any actionable harm".[40] Similarly, it has been argued that a claimant who can prove by imaging evidence that he has contracted a cancer such as mesothelioma has suffered personal injury even if it has not yet resulted in overt disabling symptoms.[41]

7-010

Rothwell v Chemical and Insulating Co At the same time, *Rothwell v Chemical & Insulating Co Ltd*[42] shows that the courts have been careful to place limits on the concept of personal injury. As a result of having been negligently exposed

7-011

---

[37] See, e.g., *McKay v Essex AHA* [1982] Q.B. 1166, para.25-020.
[38] The same formula is used in other legislation: see, e.g., Consumer Rights Act 2015 s.65(3).
[39] [1963] A.C. 758.
[40] [1963] A.C. 758 at 778.
[41] Stapleton (1988) 104 L.Q.R. 213, 214. In *Alcan Gove Pty Ltd v Zabic* [2015] HCA 33; (2015) 257 C.L.R. 1, the High Court of Australia went further, and held that mesothelial cell changes that occurred shortly after the inhalation of asbestos fibres amounted to personal injury even though the plaintiffs had not developed malignant mesothelioma until many years later. However, with respect this decision rested on the drawing of questionable inferences from the scientific evidence, and arguably extended the concept of personal injury too far, since (unlike in the case of symptomless, but treatable, cancer) unobservable molecular changes are not in themselves a disease, and nor are they in any meaningful sense an impairment.
[42] [2007] UKHL 39; [2008] 1 A.C. 281.

to asbestos dust by an employer, the claimants in *Rothwell* had developed pleural plaques, a thickening of the lung lining indicative of asbestos exposure which may later manifest itself in asbestos-related injury. The House of Lords held that since pleural plaques were usually symptomless, had no effect on bodily function or appearance, and did not increase the claimant's susceptibility to disease or shorten the claimant's life expectancy, they would not in themselves generally amount to personal injury. According to Lord Hoffmann, symptomless bodily changes with no foreseeable consequences could not amount to damage for the purposes of a negligence claim. If we ask what the difference is in this respect between the pleural plaques in *Rothwell* and, say, a symptomless cancer, the answer is the likelihood that the cancer will develop into a disabling or potentially fatal condition, which among other things may mean that immediate and invasive treatment is required. By contrast, pleural plaques are not the early stages of an asbestos-related disease, but merely an indicator that the claimant may develop such a disease in the future. Being neither an impairment nor a disease, they do not amount to a personal injury.[43]

7-012 **Dryden v Johnson Matthey** While *Rothwell* was a relatively straightforward case, the facts of *Dryden v Johnson Matthey Plc*[44] show how difficult it can be to identify the limits of the personal injury concept. The defendant's factories were not properly cleaned and, as a result, the claimant employees were exposed to platinum salts to a greater extent than they should have been, which amounted to a breach of certain statutory obligations of the defendant. As a result of this the claimants developed platinum sensitisation. Although this is an asymptomatic condition which does not cause any health problems, it meant that further exposure of the claimants to platinum salts might trigger a platinum allergy, which it was accepted would constitute a personal injury. Once the claimants' sensitisation had been detected, therefore, the defendant either redeployed them to less well-paid jobs where they would not be exposed to platinum salts, or (if this was not possible) dismissed them and provided a payment under the terms of collective agreements with their trade union. The issue in the case was whether the development of platinum sensitisation was a personal injury. Jay J[45] and the Court of Appeal held that it was not. According to Sales LJ, who gave the sole substantive judgment in the Court of Appeal[46]:

> "[P]latinum sensitisation ... is a physiological change analogous to the development of pleural plaques in the lungs in the *Rothwell* case, and hence does not constitute actionable damage or injury. Unlike the lung scarring from pneumoconiosis in *Cartledge*, platinum sensitisation is not a 'hidden impairment' which has the potential by itself to give rise to detrimental physical effects in the course of ordinary life."

However, on appeal the Supreme Court held that the claimants had suffered a personal injury actionable in negligence. Lady Black rejected Sales LJ's proposi-

---

[43] Except in Northern Ireland and Scotland, by legislative decree: Damages (Asbestos-related Conditions) (Northern Ireland) Act 2011; Damages (Asbestos-related Conditions) (Scotland) Act 2009 (asp 4). Pleural plaques should be distinguished from pleural thickening, for which a claim may be made: *Sir Robert Lloyd & Co Ltd v Hoey* [2011] EWCA Civ 1060.

[44] [2018] UKSC 18; [2019] A.C. 403. Huang (2019) 82 M.L.R. 737.

[45] *Greenway v Johnson Matthey Plc* [2014] EWHC 3957 (QB).

[46] *Greenway v Johnson Matthey Plc* [2016] EWCA Civ 408; [2016] 1 W.L.R. 4487 at [30]–[31].

tion that the claimants had not suffered personal injury because they had not become sensitised to something in everyday life, like a person who developed a photosensitivity which prevented them going out in the sun[47]:

> "Ordinary everyday life is infinitely variable. For these claimants, their ordinary everyday life involved doing jobs of a type which, by virtue of their sensitisation, they can no longer do ... The physiological changes to the claimants' bodies may not be as obviously harmful as, say, the loss of a limb, or asthma or dermatitis, but harmful they undoubtedly are ... What has happened to the claimants is that their bodily capacity for work has been impaired and they are therefore significantly worse off."

Dryden is clearly a borderline case. A powerful argument in favour of the Court of Appeal's decision is that it is difficult to see how the claimants could have been awarded any general damages (as opposed to special damages for their economic loss), so that for example in the case of a retired employee who had become sensitised but who never suffered and would never suffer any loss of earnings, no damages at all would be recoverable, a surely impossible conclusion in a negligence case. Conversely, there is obvious force in Lady Black's observation that everyday life is infinitely variable. For example, does the logic of the Court of Appeal's position entail that a mountaineer suffers no personal injury if the defendant's negligence diminishes his lung capacity in a way that would not affect ordinary, everyday activities but does prevent him from undertaking the high altitude climbs on which his livelihood and general wellbeing depends? One point that does, however, seem clear is that whether a claimant has suffered personal injury cannot depend on whether the condition in question has made him worse off financially, for that would be to confuse the questions of damage and loss, or of injury and its consequences. Rather, the claimant must be "worse off" in a more abstract, physical sense,[18] because subject to an impairment or suffering from a disease.

Other issues The definition of personal injury in the Limitation Act 1980 refers to the impairment of a person's mental condition, and we have already seen that psychiatric harm can ground an action in negligence.[49] However, this is so only if the harm rises to the seriousness of a recognised psychiatric illness, such as clinical depression or post-traumatic stress disorder.[50] Normal human emotions, such as grief, sorrow, fear and anxiety, do not in themselves give rise to redress.[51] It has also been held that an untreated learning disorder such as dyslexia is a form of personal injury,[52] and the same is true of an unwanted pregnancy.[53] Conversely, damage to

7-013

---

[47] *Dryden v Johnson Matthey Plc* [2018] UKSC 18; [2019] A.C. 403 at [39]–[40].

[48] See *Dryden* [2018] UKSC 18; [2019] A.C. 403 at [26]–[27].

[49] See Ch.5.

[50] See para.5-070. In Canada, this restriction has been replaced with a lower threshold, viz. that the mental injury must be serious and prolonged and rise above the ordinary annoyances, anxieties and fears that come with living in civil society: *Saadati v Moorhead* 2017 SCC 28; [2017] 1 S.C.R. 543.

[51] In *Rothwell v Chemical & Insulating Co Ltd* [2007] UKHL 39; [2008] 1 A.C. 281, for example, the House of Lords held that no action lay for anxiety brought on by the knowledge that the claimants had been negligently exposed to asbestos, with the result that they were at heightened risk of contracting an asbestos-related disease. See also *Kimathi v The Foreign and Commonwealth Office* [2018] EWHC 1305 (QB) (fear without more not a personal injury).

[52] *Adams v Bracknell Forest BC* [2004] UKHL; [2005] 1 A.C. 76. But in the absence of a learning disorder, educational under-development is not damage: see Nolan (2007) 70 M.L.R. 59, 84–86.

[53] *Walkin v South Manchester HA* [1995] 1 W.L.R. 1543. See further, Nolan (2007) 70 M.L.R. 59, 71-77.

a part of the claimant's body, or to a bodily substance such as blood or semen, which has become physically separated from the rest of his body does not constitute personal injury.[54]

7-014 **De minimis** The concept of personal injury is subject to a de minimis requirement, so that "there is no cause of action if the damage suffered was negligible".[55] It follows that a negligence claim cannot be founded on a minor scratch without any untoward consequences;[56] or a "trifling, self-limiting, reversible reaction" to an irritant;[57] and that, although carelessly to subject another person to pain over a significant period of time is actionable in negligence, short-term pain and suffering is not, even when it presages death.[58] It may be difficult to say precisely when an injury becomes material for these purposes, as is shown by a body of recent county court case law on hearing loss caused by occupational noise exposure.[59] The courts have taken a pragmatic approach to the question of whether hearing loss is de minimis, holding that to recover damages a claimant must establish that it has affected him in concrete ways, so that, for example, he now finds it clearly more difficult to discern the spoken words of others in noisy environments, or that he has been required to make use of a hearing aid earlier than would otherwise have been necessary. Finally, it should be noted that where the defendant is sued for making a material contribution to a divisible injury,[60] the de minimis principle is applied to the injury, not the contribution.[61]

C. Property Damage

7-015 **Definition** Property damage is a physical change that impairs the value or utility of the property.[62] There are therefore two elements to the concept: a physical change, and what we can again refer to as an "impairment" of the value or utility of the article in question. Straightforward examples include the smashing of a valuable vase, the watering down of the wine in a barrel[63] and the impregnation of a cargo of basalt aggregate with sugar residue, with the result that it could not be used

---

[54] See *Yearworth v North Bristol NHS Trust* [2009] EWCA Civ 37; [2010] Q.B. 1 (loss of sperm caused by poor storage of semen samples).

[55] *Rothwell v Chemical & Insulating Co Ltd* [2007] UKHL 39; [2008] 1 A.C. 281 at [47] per Lord Hope. See also at [8].

[56] *Durham v BAI (Run Off) Ltd* [2010] EWCA Civ 1096; [2011] 1 All E.R. 605 at [92].

[57] *Saunderson v Sonae Industria (UK) Ltd* [2015] EWHC 2264 (QB) at [179] per Jay J.

[58] *Hicks v Chief Constable of the South Yorkshire Police* [1992] 2 All E.R. 65 (personal injury claims by estates of two girls who died of traumatic asphyxia at the Hillsborough football stadium disaster).

[59] See, e.g., *Holloway v Tyne Thames Technology Ltd* (Newcastle CC, 7 May 2015); *Hinchliffe v Six Continents Ltd* (Leeds CC, 12 May 2015); *Briggs v RHM Frozen Food Ltd* (Sheffield CC, 30 July 2015); *Childs v Brass & Alloy Pressings (Deritend) Ltd* (Birmingham CC, 21 December 2015).

[60] See para.7-027.

[61] *Mayne v Atlas Stone Co Ltd* [2016] EWHC 1030 (QB); [2016] I.C.R. 957 (diffuse pleural thickening).

[62] For judicial definitions along these lines, see *Ranicar v Frigmobile Pty Ltd* [1983] Tas. R. 113 at 116 per Green CJ ("a physical alteration or change ... which impairs the value or usefulness of the thing"); *Hunter v Canary Wharf Ltd* [1996] 2 W.L.R. 348 at 366 per Pill LJ ("a physical change which renders the article less useful or less valuable"). Such a definition is also used in criminal law: *R. v Whiteley* (1991) 93 Cr.App.R. 25 at 28–29 (relied on in the tort context in *The Orjula* [1995] 2 Lloyd's Rep. 395).

[63] As in the conversion case of *Richardson v Atkinson* (1723) 1 Stra. 576; 93 E.R. 710.

to manufacture concrete.[64] As with personal injury, property damage can occur without it being known about or even reasonably discoverable.[65]

Physical change   An impairment of the value or utility of property which is not   **7-016** accompanied by an alteration of its physical characteristics does not amount to damage. In *Perre v Apand Pty Ltd*,[66] the proximity of the plaintiffs' farms to land infected with bacterial wilt meant that it was impossible, due to export restrictions, for them to sell their potatoes on the Western Australian market, diminishing the value of their crops. The High Court of Australia held that this was pure economic loss, rather than physical damage to property, since the plaintiffs' potatoes were physically unchanged. Similarly, it is not enough for D simply to incapacitate C's property, as where D attaches a clamp to the wheel of C's car to prevent it from being moved, since the wheel in the clamp is in exactly the same physical condition.[67] The situation changes, of course, if the incapacitation of the property results in a physical deterioration.[68] In *D Pride & Partners v Institute for Animal Health*,[69] a number of claims were brought against the defendants for causing an outbreak of foot-and-mouth disease. One group of claimants complained that the outbreak had led to the introduction of restrictions on the movement of livestock which meant that by the time they were able to send their pigs to the abattoir the animals were in an "oversized" condition. Tugendhat J held that there was a real prospect of the claimants succeeding in their argument that this deleterious change in the physiology of the pigs amounted to damage for the purposes of a negligence claim.

Reversibility not a bar if damage material   Where there is a physical change to   **7-017** the claimant's property, its reversibility does not preclude a finding of damage; indeed, it would seem that the requirement of a physical change can be satisfied where a layer of foreign matter simply comes to rest on the property. In *Hunter v Canary Wharf Ltd*,[70] for example, the Court of Appeal accepted that the deposit of dust was capable of amounting to damage, if for example excessive dust deposits were in ordinary use trodden into the fabric of a carpet in such a way as to require it to be professionally cleaned. Similarly, where dredging caused the deposit of a layer of silt on mudflats which formed part of a nature reserve, this was held to be capable of amounting to damage to the land.[71] A de minimis principle applies in property damage cases, however, so that trivial or transient physical change will not count as damage for these purposes. The deposit of a thin layer of dust on the

---

64   *South Coast Basalt Pty Ltd v Miller & Co Pty Ltd* [1981] 1 N.S.W.L.R. 356 (obiter).
65   *Pirelli General Cable Works Ltd v Oscar Faber & Partners* [1983] 2 A.C. 1 (though this would now be analysed as a pure economic loss case: para.5-048ff).
66   [1999] HCA 36; (1999) 198 C.L.R. 180.
67   Though wheel-clamping may be a trespass to goods: *Vine v Waltham Forest London Borough Council* [2000] 1 W.L.R. 2383. See Ch.18.
68   See, e.g., the public nuisance case of *Maynell v Saltmarsh* (1664) 1 Keb. 847; 83 E.R. 1278 (D's obstruction of the highway prevented C from moving his corn, which was then spoilt by the rain).
69   [2009] EWHC 685 (QB); [2009] N.P.C. 56.
70   [1996] 2 W.L.R. 348 (not in issue on appeal: [1997] A.C. 655).
71   *Jan de Nul (UK) Ltd v Axa Royale Belge SA* [2002] EWCA Civ 209; [2002] 1 Lloyd's Rep. 583. See also *The Orjula* [1995] 2 Lloyd's Rep. 395 (ship physically damaged when deck doused in hydrochloric acid, which had to be neutralised and washed off by specialist contractors).

claimant's car would, for example, almost certainly not amount to damage.[72] Quite where the line is to be drawn in such cases is open to question.[73]

7-018   **Impairment**   There is no property damage unless the physical change is of a kind that tends to have a negative impact on the value or utility of items of property like the property in question. In general, of course, such a change will in fact render the particular item of property less valuable or less useful, but it need not do so, as long as that is the tendency of such a change[74]:

> "If a skilful painter overpaints X's daubs unasked, he inflicts property damage ... even if the world will pay more for the canvas now than it would have done before he came on the scene. If a lump of concrete is dropped on X's car, property damage has been inflicted even if someone can persuade an avant garde gallery owner curator that the resultant object is a work of art worth more than X paid for the car".

As with personal injury, "impairment" has a broad meaning in this context. Contamination of marshland by radioactive material requiring the removal of the topsoil has, for example, been held to be property damage.[75] And in *Ranicar v Frigmobile Pty Ltd*,[76] the Supreme Court of Tasmania held that an increase in the temperature of a consignment of scallops amounted to "damage" for insurance purposes because it meant that they no longer complied with export regulations and so had to be disposed of on the domestic market at a reduced price. Another instructive insurance case is *Quorum A/S v Schramm*,[77] where sub-molecular change to the chemical make-up of an artwork caused by exposure to heat from a warehouse fire was held to amount to physical damage because it shortened the life of the work and increased the risk of deterioration. Conversely, in the private nuisance case of *Smith v Inco Ltd*,[78] the Ontario Court of Appeal held that nickel particles deposited in the soil of a property did not constitute physical damage because even though public concern about the potential health consequences of the deposits had reduced the property's market value, the concern was baseless, and so objectively the deposits had had no detrimental effect on the land.

D.   Loss of a Chance

7-019   **The nature of the issue**[79]   A particularly controversial question pertaining to the damage requirement is whether the risk of harm, or the lost chance of avoiding it,

---

72   See *Hunter v Canary Wharf Ltd* [1996] 2 W.L.R. 348 at 366.

73   For a decision that arguably extends the concept of property damage too far, see *Attorney-General for Ontario v Fatehi* [1984] 2 S.C.R. 536 (scattering of vehicles, glass, oil and other debris over carriageway following a road accident actionable in negligence).

74   *Jan de Nul (UK) Ltd v Axa Royale Belge SA* [2002] EWCA Civ 209; [2002] 1 Lloyd's Rep. 583 at [92] per Schiemann LJ.

75   *Blue Circle Industries Plc v Ministry of Defence* [1999] Ch. 289 (liability under Nuclear Installations Act 1965). See also *Magnohard Ltd v United Kingdom Atomic Energy Authority* 2004 S.C. 247. cf. *Merlin v British Nuclear Fuels Plc* [1990] 2 Q.B. 557 (no property damage as radioactive material had not altered the physical characteristics of claimant's house).

76   [1983] Tas. R. 113.

77   [2002] 1 Lloyd's Rep. 249.

78   [2011] ONCA 628; 107 O.R. (3d) 321.

79   Lunney (1995) 15 L.S. 1; Reece (1996) 59 M.L.R. 188; Nolan in Robertson and Tang (eds), *The Goals of Private Law* (2009), pp.179-187; Turton, *Evidential Uncertainty in Causation in Negligence* (2016), pp.123-146.

can ground a negligence claim. Should, for example, a doctor be liable in damages to a cancer patient whose chances of recovery are reduced or eliminated as a result of the doctor's negligent failure to diagnose the cancer at an earlier stage, even if the patient cannot show on the balance of probabilities that an earlier diagnosis would have made a difference to the eventual outcome? The significance of this question derives from the problem of causal uncertainty—were the claimant able to demonstrate on the civil standard of proof the existence of a causal link between breach and physical injury, there would be no need to argue that the loss of a chance is itself damage, because the patient could then recover in full for the injury itself. The question, then, is whether the claimant who cannot establish causation of the injury can at least recover some lesser compensation by re-characterising the damage as the lost chance of avoiding the injury, rather than the injury itself. And note that the problem is one of *damage* not *damages*: where liability is not in question and the court is merely quantifying the claimant's losses, it is well established that unless a past fact is in issue (as opposed to a past or future hypothetical), the balance of probabilities test is abandoned, and proportionate recovery permitted.[80]

Hotson v East Berkshire Health Authority　The loss of a chance issue first came **7-020** before the House of Lords in *Hotson v East Berkshire Health Authority*.[81] The defendants negligently failed to diagnose the claimant's condition when he presented at their hospital after a fall, and there developed an avascular necrosis, a serious disability of the hip joint. On the facts there was, statistically, a 75 per cent probability that this disability would have developed even if the claimant had been treated properly, but the trial judge held that he was entitled to damages representing 25 per cent of his full loss and the Court of Appeal agreed. This was reversed by the House of Lords. In their Lordships' view it was wrong to say that the breach of duty had deprived the claimant of a one-in-four chance of recovery. The evidence was that the state of the claimant's leg at the time of his arrival at the defendants' hospital determined one way or the other whether prompt treatment would have prevented the disability (although there was no way of knowing in what state the leg had been, so while the metaphorical coin had been tossed and had landed, whether the result was heads or tails was unknown). As this was therefore a matter of past fact, it was to be resolved on the balance of probabilities in the usual way. In the words of Lord Mackay[82]:

"In the circumstances of this case the probable effect of delay in treatment was determined by the state of the facts existing when the plaintiff was first presented to the hospital. It is not, in my opinion, correct to say that on arrival at the hospital he had a 25 per cent chance of recovery. If insufficient blood vessels were left intact by the fall he had no prospect of avoiding complete avascular necrosis whereas if sufficient blood vessels were left intact on the judge's findings no further damage to the blood supply would have resulted if he had been given immediate treatment, and he would not have suffered the avascular necrosis".

Gregg v Scott　The issue was revisited in *Gregg v Scott*.[83] There was a negligent **7-021** delay in the diagnosis of the claimant's cancer and when treatment began he had

---

80　See, e.g., *Davies v Taylor* [1974] A.C. 207, para.24-018.
81　[1987] A.C. 750.
82　[1987] A.C. 750 at 785. See also at 792.
83　[2005] UKHL 2; [2005] 2 A.C. 176.

in statistical terms only a 25 per cent chance of recovery, whereas if it had been diagnosed promptly his chance would have been 42 per cent. It was therefore probable that he would not have survived even with prompt treatment. The majority of the House of Lords rejected the claimant's claim for the 17 per cent reduction in his chance of recovery. The case was different from *Hotson* in at least two respects. First, while in *Hotson* the adverse outcome (the avascular necrosis) had already occurred, in *Gregg* that was not so: the claimant was still alive. And, second, in *Hotson* the adverse outcome had been predetermined by the (unknown) amount of blood vessel damage which had been caused by the fall, whereas in *Gregg* the developments which reduced the claimant's life expectancy were potentially subsequent to the negligence. Nevertheless, for Lord Hoffmann and Lady Hale the claim was an attempt to reformulate the basis of the law in terms of lost chances rather than causal outcomes and in their view that should not be permitted. Lord Phillips agreed that the claim should be rejected, emphasising the difficulty of deciding cases about individual claimants on the basis of statistical evidence based on groups.[84] He contemplated that the law might allow a "chance-based" claim where the adverse outcome which due care might have averted had actually occurred,[85] although subsequent case law suggests that there is little appetite for permitting loss of a chance claims in cases of clinical negligence, and that in effect *Gregg v Scott* has shut the door on such actions, at least for the time being.[86]

For the minority, Lord Nicholls would have allowed recovery based on loss of a chance in those cases of medical negligence relating to the treatment of an existing illness where there was significant uncertainty about the outcome at the time of the negligence.[87] Lord Hope agreed with Lord Nicholls, although ultimately his view seems to have been that this was really a case of a proved physical injury (the enlargement of the tumour) which simply had to be *quantified*.[88] Whether this shift of focus from damage to damages was really justified on the facts is, however, open to question. For while there was no doubt that the growth of the tumour was itself a personal injury, it was by no means clear that, on the balance of probabilities, it would not have happened anyway.

---

[84] See para.7-045. Although the case had been treated below in terms of loss of the chance of a "cure" the medical definition of this was survival for 10 years. The trial took place five years after the negligence and the claimant was still alive at the time of the appeal decision, a little over 10 years after the negligence.

[85] [2005] UKHL 2; [2005] 2 A.C. 176 at [188]. The fact that the claimant had not died did not feature prominently in the reasoning of the other judges in the majority (Lord Hoffmann and Lady Hale), but has been emphasised in later cases: see *Barker v Corus UK Ltd* [2006] UKHL 20; [2006] 2 A.C. 572 at [48].

[86] *Wright v Cambridge Medical Group* [2011] EWCA Civ 669; [2013] Q.B. 312 at [84], [96].

[87] He would, therefore, exclude the *Hotson* situation: at [38]. Lord Nicholls's focus on whether the later occurrence of the adverse outcome was predetermined at the time of the breach of duty is understandable from a theoretical standpoint, as it marks the distinction between a "personal" and a purely "statistical" chance (see Hill (1991) 54 M.L.R. 511). However, it gives rise to considerable practical difficulties, as it will not always be known whether or not this was the case. On the facts of *Gregg*, for example, was the claimant's fate sealed, one way or the other, when he first went to see his doctor, or could subsequent events have also played a part in the development of the cancer?

[88] *Gregg v Scott* [2005] UKHL 2; [2005] 2 A.C. 176 at [118]. Lord Nicholls thought this approach was only "superficially attractive": at [58].

Evaluation   The general question of loss of a chance has been widely debated in   **7-022**
other jurisdictions and systems.[89] One complication of allowing such claims is that
it would then be hard to maintain the position that a claimant who can show causation on the balance of probabilities recovers damages in full. Hence if the House
of Lords had taken the opposite line in *Gregg* many currently successful claimants
would presumably receive less.[90] If that is correct, then although loss of a chance
recovery would mean fewer cases failing altogether, it would not necessarily follow that the global liability bill would be any greater, for the cutting back of
recovery in the claims which now succeed in full might offset (or even exceed) the
amount payable to claimants in cases like *Hotson* and *Gregg*. Since under the
present law there is no reason for a judge to put any figure on the probability of
causation, but only to decide whether or not it passes the point of balance, there is
no way of accumulating the data from which we could know what the effect would
be. In any event, moving from the current all-or-nothing approach to one based on
probabilistic recovery would certainly make the negotiation and adjudication of
claims a great deal more complicated and would result in more *claims* if not any
increase in the global liability bill.[91] Another difficulty with accepting loss of a
chance as damage is that taken to its logical conclusion this would open the door
to claims where the threatened physical injury has not, and perhaps may never,
occur. Even proponents of loss of a chance recovery accept that it may not be desirable to award compensation in such cases,[92] and yet limiting loss of a chance
recovery to cases where physical injury has materialised—as Lord Phillips suggested might be appropriate in *Gregg*—surely amounts to a tacit admission that the
gist of the claim is really the injury rather than the lost chance of avoiding it.
Conversely, in *Gregg* Lord Nicholls argued forcefully in favour of loss of a chance
recovery that to make the success or failure of a case turn on whether a probability
is, say, 45 per cent or 55 per cent is "irrational and indefensible.[93] Furthermore, he
pointed out, allowing recovery for loss of a chance may have beneficial deterrent
effects, particularly in cases where the patient's chance of recovery is always going to be less than 50 per cent, and where it will therefore always be impossible for
the patient to show on the balance of probabilities that the doctor's negligence
caused the physical injury he was duty-bound to take reasonable steps to prevent.

Loss of a chance of financial gain   Where the claimant loses a chance of mak-   **7-023**
ing a purely financial gain, fewer problems arise, since a chance of economic gain

---

[89]   After making some progress in Australia claims for loss of a chance of avoiding an adverse medical outcome were blocked in *Tabet v Gett* [2010] HCA 12; (2010) 240 C.L.R. 537. While the
Supreme Court of Canada rejected loss of a chance in *Laferrière v Lawson* [1991] 1 S.C.R. 541, the
decision in *Resurfice Corp v Hanke* [2007] SCC 7; [2007] 1 S.C.R. 333 contains passages which
can be read as supporting liability in a limited class of cases based on increase in risk. However, this
does not seem to have made any difference in the typical "loss of a chance of a better medical
outcome" situation: *Bohun v Segal* [2007] BCCA 23; 289 D.L.R. (4th) 614.

[90]   The claimant in *Gregg v Scott* accepted that any change to a "chance-based" system would have to
"cut both ways": [2005] UKHL 2; [2005] 2 A.C. 176 at [225]. How exactly would this work, though?
What is to stop the claimant whom it suits to do so pleading the injury as damage, rather than the
loss of the chance of avoiding it?

[91]   The potential impact on the National Health Service is prominent in the reasoning of Lord Hoffmann:
Gregg v Scott [2005] UKHL 2; [2005] 2 A.C. 176 at [90].

[92]   See, e.g., Stapleton (1988) 104 L.Q.R. 389, 395 (accepting that it might be possible to restrict loss
of a chance recovery to cases where the adverse outcome has occurred or is certain to do so).

[93]   [2005] UKHL 2; [2005] 2 A.C. 176 at [3].

is itself something of economic value, and hence its loss is itself an economic loss.[94] Many such cases are of course litigated in contract, where the question goes only to quantification rather than liability, breach of contract being actionable per se.[95] It is however clear that claims for a lost financial chance are also possible in tort, although the courts have limited such recovery to cases where the claimant's loss depends on what action would have been taken others, as opposed to the claimant himself. Hence in a case involving negligent professional advice, for example[96]:

"To the extent (if at all) that the question whether the client would have been better off depends upon what the client would have done upon receipt of competent advice, this must be proved by the claimant upon the balance of probabilities. To the extent that the supposed beneficial outcome depends upon what others would have done, this depends upon a loss of chance evaluation."

In *Allied Maples Group Ltd v Simmons & Simmons*[97] the facts assumed for the purpose of a preliminary issue were that the defendants had been negligent in advising the claimants about potential liabilities resulting from a purchase. The Court of Appeal held that it was not necessary for the claimants to show that if they had been properly advised they would have succeeded in persuading the seller to grant them protection or indemnity against these liabilities. Rather, they need show only that there was a substantial, rather than merely speculative, chance of success, the damages then being assessed by reference to the lost chance. The same approach would have been taken even if it had been more likely than not that the protection would have been obtained,[98] until it became a "near certainty",[99] when the chance that it would not have been could be ignored. Examples of other situations where this approach has been adopted are failure by a solicitor to proceed with a claim within the limitation period[100] and an inaccurate reference which deprives the claimant of an opportunity of employment.[101] It is however important to note that the *Allied Maples* principle applies only to what *others* would have done had the breach of duty not occurred; where the question whether the claimant would have been better off depends on what he himself would have done, this he must prove on the balance of probabilities though, if he does so, it is then treated as a certainty.[102] Quite what the justification is for drawing this sharp distinction between the hypothetical conduct of the claimant and of someone else remains something of a mystery.[103]

---

[94] "Losing a chance of [a financial] gain is a loss like the loss of the gain itself, alike in quality, just less in quantity: losing a chance of not losing a leg is not at all the same kind of thing as losing the leg": Weir, *An Introduction to Tort Law*, 2nd edn (2006), p.80. See also *Sellars v Adelaide Petroleum NL* (1994) 179 C.L.R. 332 at 355.

[95] See, e.g., *Chaplin v Hicks* [1911] 2 K.B. 786 (recovery for lost chance of winning a beauty contest).

[96] *Perry v Raleys Solicitors* [2019] UKSC 5; [2020] A.C. 352 at [20] per Lord Briggs.

[97] [1995] 1 W.L.R. 1602.

[98] *Assetco Plc v Grant Thornton UK LLP* [2019] EWHC 150 (Comm); [2019] Bus. L.R. 2291 at [406]–[411] (proportionate recovery under *Allied Maples* mandatory not permissive).

[99] *Allied Maples Group Ltd v Simmons & Simmons* [1995] 1 W.L.R. at 1614; *Charles v Hugh James Jones & Jenkins* [2000] 1 W.L.R. 1278.

[100] *Kitchen v Royal Air Force Association* [1958] 1 W.L.R. 563; *Pearson v Sanders Witherspoon* [2000] Lloyd's Rep. 151.

[101] *Spring v Guardian Assurance Plc* [1995] 2 A.C. 296 at 327.

[102] *Perry v Raleys Solicitors* [2019] UKSC 5; [2020] A.C. 352 (holding also that a legal claim alleged to have been lost would have had to have been made honestly).

[103] In *Gregg v Scott* [2005] UKHL 2; [2005] 2 A.C. 176 at [83], Lord Hoffmann said that "[t]his apparently arbitrary distinction obviously rests on grounds of policy", although he did not say what the

3. FACTUAL CAUSATION

We now turn to causation, which in negligence means the link between the fault of the defendant and the claimant's damage.[104] Causation is fundamental to a system of liability based on individual responsibility, or, as it sometimes styled, "corrective justice". It is conceivable that in another society or another time or in a different context it might be regarded as a good reason for saying that D must pay for damage suffered by C, that D was rich and C was poor, or that D was head of C's clan; or we might, as to some extent we do, via social security, decide that society as a whole should pay for it. However, the existence of a sufficient connection between D's fault and C's damage is a bedrock of negligence liability,[105] whatever other legal sanctions (such as criminal law penalties and professional discipline) may be directed at D's *behaviour*. In negligence, the question of causation divides into two, factual causation and legal causation.[106] In this part of the chapter we look at the former, and in the next part of the chapter, we look at the latter.

A. The "But For" Test

The "but for" test   Factual causation concerns the connection between the fault of the defendant and the damage of the claimant as a matter of historical fact. Since our concern here is with the link between fault and damage, factual causation must be considered only once we have decided what precisely the breach of duty is and what relevant damage the claimant has suffered. As for the causation question itself, while the nature of causation has exercised philosophers and more than one approach is possible,[107] the law takes a pragmatic approach. For legal purposes, the question of causation in fact is generally resolved by use of the so-called "but for" test, or in Latin, *causa* (or *conditio*) *sine qua non*.[108] In negligence, this means asking whether, if the defendant's breach of duty had not occurred, the claimant would still have suffered the relevant damage. It does not follow from a negative answer

7-024

7-025

---

policy was. Perhaps he had in mind the risk of the claimant giving self-serving testimony as to how he would have acted, but, if so, how does the use of a balance of probabilities test help? In *Perry v Raleys Solicitors* [2019] UKSC 5; [2020] A.C. 352 at [21], Lord Briggs described the distinction as "sensible, fair and practicable" but again provided no rationale for it.

[104] Green, *Causation in Negligence* (2015); Steel, *Proof of Causation in Negligence* (2015); Turton, *Evidential Uncertainty in Causation in Negligence* (2016).

[105] cf. *Sindell v Abbott Laboratories* 607 P. 2d 924 (1980), where the Supreme Court of California imposed a "market share" liability on manufacturers of a generic drug when the individual plaintiffs could not show which manufacturer had produced the batch that caused their injuries. This radical decision may be regarded either as an extreme modification of private law principles to cope with damage done by a group of defendants, or as an ad hoc, judicially created and industry-based compensation system.

[106] "The common law of negligence requires determination of causation for the purpose of attributing legal responsibility. Such a determination inevitably involves two questions: a question of historical fact as to how particular harm occurred; and a normative question as to whether legal responsibility for that particular harm occurring in that way should be attributed to a particular person": *Wallace v Kam* [2013] HCA 19; (2013) 250 C.L.R. 375 at [11]. The distinction between factual and legal causation is occasionally criticised by judges (see, e.g., Hoffmann (2005) 121 L.Q.R. 592) but because the issues involved are quite distinct it is convenient to disaggregate the two questions and to deal with them separately.

[107] Hart and Honoré, *Causation in the Law*, 2nd edn (1985), Pt I; Honoré in Owen (ed), *Philosophical Foundations of Tort Law* (1995).

[108] i.e., "a cause without which [the event would] not [have happened]".

[163]

to this question that responsibility for the damage should lie with the defendant, as we still have to consider legal causation and remoteness. But a positive answer—namely, that the damage would have happened anyway—is generally conclusive against liability. The test is therefore best understood as a preliminary filter to eliminate the irrelevant.

The application of the "but for" test is neatly illustrated by *Barnett v Chelsea and Kensington Hospital Management Committee*.[109] The claimant's husband, a night watchman, called early in the morning at the defendants' hospital and complained of vomiting after drinking tea. He was told to go home and consult his own doctor later, which amounted to a breach of the hospital's duty of care. Later that day he died of arsenical poisoning and the coroner's verdict was of murder by persons unknown. The hospital's breach of duty was held not to be a cause of the death because, even if the deceased had been examined and treated with proper care, the probability was that he would have died anyway. The claimant's action for damages therefore failed.

7-026 **Balance of probabilities** Part and parcel of the but for test is the fact that the question of historical connection is determined on the balance of probabilities, with the burden of proof lying on the claimant, so that in general the claimant must prove that it is more likely than not that the damage would not have occurred had it not been for the defendant's negligence. If he succeeds in showing this then the hypothetical non-occurrence of the damage is treated as being conclusively established, even though there may be a substantial chance that it would have happened just the same (and vice versa). In practice, the main difficulties in this area concern questions of proof (the problem of "causal uncertainty") but, before we turn to look at those difficulties, we must first consider some other matters relating to the operation of the but for test.

7-027 **Material contribution to the injury**[110] The but for test operates in a distinctive way in cases of "divisible" injury where it is possible to attribute different parts of the injury to different causes, for example because its severity varies according to the extent of the claimant's exposure to a toxic agent. In such a case, factual causation will be established if the defendant's negligent conduct made a "material contribution" to the injury.[111] Thus, in *Bonnington Castings Ltd v Wardlaw*[112] the defendant was held liable in a case where the claimant contracted the lung condition pneumoconiosis from the combination of dust which the defendants had created in breach of safety regulations and other dust which was an inevitable accompaniment of the claimant's work. Although in *Bonnington Castings* the claimant recovered in full,[113] it was subsequently held that in such a case the defendant is liable only for that part of the harm that he has been proved to have caused.[114] A

---

109 [1969] 1 Q.B. 428. See also *McWilliams v Sir William Arrol & Co Ltd* [1962] 1 W.L.R. 295 (death by falling; breach of employer's duty to provide safety harness; evidence showed that deceased would not have used it); *Deloitte Haskins & Sells v National Mutual Life Nominees Ltd* [1993] A.C. 774; *Chittock v Woodbridge School* [2002] EWCA Civ 915; [2003] P.I.Q.R. P6.
110 Bailey (2010) 30 L.S. 167.
111 Not material contribution to *the risk*. cf. the test used in *Fairchild v Glenhaven Funeral Services Ltd* [2002] UKHL 22; [2003] 1 A.C. 32, para.7-034.
112 [1956] A.C. 613.
113 No submission for an apportionment of liability was put to the court.
114 *Holtby v Brigham & Cowan (Hull) Ltd* [2000] 3 All E.R. 421; *Allen v British Rail Engineering Ltd*

contribution need not be substantial to count as "material" for these purposes; the requirement excludes only a de minimis contribution.[115]

Material contribution in indivisible injury cases?[116] It must be emphasised that **7-028** the material contribution test developed in the context of divisible injury, where different parts of the injury can be attributed to different causes. The concept is ill-suited to cases where the harm is indivisible, in the sense that there is no rational basis for an objective apportionment of causal responsibility for it (as, for example, with cancer and death).[117] In cases of this kind, by definition either the defendant's breach of duty was a cause of the entirety of the injury, applying the but for test, or it was not causative of the injury at all. There is no middle way. In this context, therefore, the language of "material contribution" adds nothing to the basic operation of the but for test and is liable to cause confusion.[118] Nevertheless, there are now two significant cases in which the test of material contribution has apparently been applied to an indivisible injury, and where this has resulted in recovery in full. The first is *Bailey v Ministry of Defence*,[119] where the claimant had suffered brain damage, an indivisible injury, as a result of a cardiac arrest triggered by her choking on her own vomit. The choking was the result of weakness which was caused by a combination of a naturally occurring disease and the defendant's negligent post-operative care. Although it was not clear whether or not the chain of events would still have occurred even without the defendant's negligence, the Court of Appeal held that the contribution of the negligence to the claimant's weakened condition was sufficient to establish causation of the brain damage. The second case of this kind is *Williams v Bermuda Hospitals Board*.[120] When the plaintiff had presented at the emergency department of the defendant's hospital with acute appendicitis, there was a negligent delay in carrying out an operation to remove his appendix. During the surgery, it became apparent that the appendix had ruptured and that this had caused a sepsis to develop. The sepsis caused surgical complications, and these led to heart and lung damage.[121] Although the trial judge had

---

[2001] EWCA Civ 242; [2001] I.C.R. 942; *BAE Systems (Operations) Ltd v Konczak* [2017] EWCA Civ 1188; [2018] I.C.R. 1 at [92] per Irwin LJ (as a matter of principle, where an injury is divisible "recompense must be limited to the consequences of identified injury attributable to the tort in question"). See further, Ch.22. This approach can lead to very small awards where the defendant's breach has made only a minor contribution to the overall injury: see, e.g., *Carder v University of Exeter* [2016] EWCA Civ 790; [2017] I.C.R. 392 (2.3 per cent; £1,552.50); *Mayne v Atlas Stone Co Ltd* [2016] EWHC 1030 (QB); [2016] I.C.R. 957 (0.4 per cent; £1,028).

[115] See *Bonnington Castings Ltd v Wardlaw* [1956] A.C. 613 at 621. In *Carder v University of Exeter* [2016] EWCA Civ 790; [2017] I.C.R. 392, it was conceded that a contribution of 2.3 per cent of the asbestos exposure causative of asbestosis was material.

[116] Bailey (2018) 38 L.S. 411.

[117] For this definition of an indivisible injury, see *BAE Systems (Operations) Ltd v Konczak* [2017] EWCA Civ 1188; [2018] I.C.R. 1.

[118] In *Heneghan v Manchester Dry Docks Ltd* [2016] EWCA Civ 86; [2016] 1 W.L.R. 2036 at [23], Lord Dyson MR implied that the material contribution test is limited to divisible injury (referring to a disease "caused by the cumulative effect of an agency part of which is attributable to" the defendant's negligence, and emphasising that the pneumoconiosis in *Bonnington* was "a divisible disease"). See also at [46] (material contribution test appropriate in the case of "divisible injuries ... whose severity is proportionate to the amount of exposure to the causative agent").

[119] [2008] EWCA Civ 883; [2009] 1 W.L.R. 1052.

[120] [2016] UKPC 4; [2016] A.C. 888.

[121] It is not entirely clear whether this damage was indivisible, but the award of damages in respect of the entirety of the injury suggests that it was treated as such by the Privy Council.

dismissed the plaintiff's claim on the ground that he had failed to establish a causal link between the delay and the complications, the Privy Council held that on the facts as found by the judge it was right to infer, on the balance of probabilities, that the delay had materially contributed to the development of the sepsis, and therefore materially contributed to the organ damage.

The reasoning in *Bailey* and *Williams* is not always easy to follow, and perhaps the best that can be said about them as authorities is that they are open to interpretation. One such interpretation is that they are based on factual inferences of but for causation, and hence do not involve any departure from settled principle, nor any extension of the material contribution concept to cases of indivisible harm. This interpretation seems to be consistent with the reasoning of Lord Toulson in *Williams*,[122] but it must be conceded that on the facts as found in the two cases it is difficult to see how such inferences could legitimately be made. An alternative interpretation of the decisions, which provides a better explanation of the outcomes, is that they involve an extension of the material contribution principle to situations where the defendant's negligence has contributed to a condition or state of affairs—the weakness in *Bailey*, and the sepsis in *Williams*—that was a but for cause of the damage.[123] However, since on this interpretation the court is clearly not holding that the negligence was a but for cause of the damage (but only that it contributed to a condition or state of affairs that was) there is then no escaping the conclusion that in this context the material contribution test is not merely an adaptation of the but for test but a departure from it. What is in any case clear is that these decisions have given rise to significant confusion and threaten unnecessarily to complicate the law in this area.[124] It is to be hoped that before long the Supreme Court will be given the opportunity to conduct a full review of this question.[125]

B. Multiple Causation

7-029 **More than one sufficient cause** Although the but for test is a useful rule of thumb, it may lead to unacceptable results where there is more than one sufficient cause of C's damage, as where A and B at the same moment inflict fatal injuries upon C.[126] In such a case, there is no doubt that, however we justify it,[127] both A and B are liable in full for the damage,[128] subject to the right of contribution against

---

[122] See in particular Lord Toulson's discussion of *Bailey*, which he denied was a departure from the but for test: *Williams v Bermuda Hospitals Board* [2016] UKPC 4; [2016] A.C. 888 at [47].

[123] See Plunkett (2016) 32 P.N. 158. The analysis of Stapleton and Steel (2016) 132 L.Q.R. 363 is similar. See also *Chetwynd v Tunmore* [2016] EWHC 156 (QB); [2017] Q.B. 188 at [31].

[124] See, e.g., *John v Central Manchester and Manchester Children's University Hospitals NHS Foundation Trust* [2016] EWHC 407 (QB); [2016] 4 W.L.R. 54.

[125] See also Bailey (2018) 38 L.S. 411, 425.

[126] A defendant cannot escape liability by saying that his breach of duty A was not a cause of the claimant's injury because he would anyway have committed breach of duty B which would have had the same effect: *Bolitho v City and Hackney HA* [1997] A.C. 232 at 240; cf. *Wright v Cambridge Medical Group* [2011] EWCA Civ 669; [2013] Q.B. 312 at [56]–[58]; *Robbins v Bexley LBC* [2013] EWCA Civ 1233; [2014] B.L.R. 11.

[127] See Wright (1985) 73 Cal. L. Rev. 1735 and (2001) 53 Vanderbilt L. Rev. 1071; Honoré in Owen (ed) *Philosophical Foundations of Tort Law* (1995); Stapleton in Cane and Gardner (eds), *Relating to Responsibility* (2001).

[128] "Where two people, acting independently, shoot simultaneously and kill another, each is still liable for the whole": *Barker v Corus (UK) Ltd* [2006] UKHL 20; [2006] 2 A.C. 572 at [122] per Lady Hale. This is what has become known as a "two-hit hunter" case; cf. the "one-hit hunter" case

the other (a matter which does not concern C).[129] A distinction must however be drawn between cases of cumulative wrongdoing and those where a tort combines with some factor for which no one is to blame. Where A and B both fatally wound C, the law treats both as having caused C's death because otherwise it would reach the absurd result that neither did. By contrast, where A's conduct combines with a non-tortious event which would in itself have been sufficient to cause all the damage, A is not liable.[130]

Successive events   It may also be that the claimant is affected by two successive events or that the act of the defendant precludes the operation of another cause which would otherwise have taken effect. If D injures or kills C then it is of course obvious that C would have one day died anyway and the law therefore limits the damages recoverable by C or his dependants by reference to C's pre-accident life expectancy. Likewise, if D tortiously kills a person who is very old or who is suffering from a terminal disease he is undoubtedly liable for the death, but the damages will be much lower than they would be in the case of a young, healthy victim.[131] So also, if D injures C and, before C's action comes to a trial, C dies from some wholly unrelated cause, the damages payable by D will be limited to those representing the loss incurred before the death.[132] But in other cases it may not be so easy to determine whether the later event obliterates the causative effect of the defendant's act.

7-030

Baker v Willoughby   In *Baker v Willoughby*,[133] the claimant suffered an injury to his left leg as a result of the defendant's negligence. Before the trial, however, the claimant was the victim of an armed robbery during which he suffered gunshot wounds to his left leg of such severity that the leg had to be amputated. The defendant argued that his liability was limited to the loss suffered before the robbery; all loss suffered thereafter was said to have merged in and flowed from the robbery.[134] This argument was rejected by the House of Lords because it would have produced a manifest injustice. Even if the robbers had been identified (and worth suing),[135] they would have been liable to the claimant only for depriving him of an already damaged leg[136] and the claimant would therefore have been left uncompensated in

7-031

---

discussed in para.7-033.

[129]   See Ch.22.

[130]   "If the evidence demonstrates on a balance of probabilities that the injury would have occurred as a result of the non-tortious cause or causes in any event, the claimant will have failed to establish that the tortious cause contributed": *Bailey v Ministry of Defence* [2008] EWCA Civ 883; [2009] 1 W.L.R. 1052 at [46] per Waller LJ.

[131]   *Smith v Cawdle Fen Commissioners* [1938] 4 All E.R. 64 at 71.

[132]   A well-known conundrum is the following: D injures C in a road accident while C is on the way to the airport, crippling him for life. The plane on which C was booked crashes, killing all on board. In such a scenario, there is a reluctance to accept that D is not required to compensate C for losses after the notional death.

[133]   [1970] A.C. 467.

[134]   Note that in a purely factual sense the accident was a cause of the injury in the robbery since the claimant changed his job as a result of the accident, but it could not possibly be contended that the defendant was liable in law for the consequences of the shooting: *Carslogie SS Co Ltd v Royal Norwegian Government* [1952] A.C. 292, para.7-072.

[135]   The speeches do not disclose whether the claimant made any claim under the Criminal Injuries Compensation Scheme.

[136]   *Performance Cars Ltd v Abraham* [1962] 1 Q.B. 33; *Baker v Willoughby* [1970] A.C. 467 at 495. An argument that the robbers would in theory be liable for the whole of the claimant's loss because

the period after the robbery for the "difference" between a sound leg and a damaged one. But although the justice of the outcome seems clear, their Lordships struggled to justify it convincingly. It was said that the defendant's argument contained a fallacy in its assertion that the first injury to the leg was obliterated by the subsequent amputation because, as Lord Reid put it,[137] a person:

> "[I]s not compensated for the physical injury: he is compensated for the loss which he suffers as a result of the injury. His loss is not in having a stiff leg: it is his inability to lead a full life, his inability to enjoy those amenities which depend on freedom of movement and his inability to earn as much as he used to earn or could have earned if there had been no accident. In this case the second injury did not diminish any of these. So why should it be regarded as having obliterated or superseded them?"

In other words, the claimant's loss after the removal of the leg was regarded as having two concurrent causes. However, this conclusion seems to rest on little more than assertion, and it is clear that if the robbers had shot the claimant dead the defendant's liability would not have extended beyond that point.[138]

7-032 **Jobling v Associated Dairies Ltd** The decision in *Baker v Willoughby* received a hard knock in *Jobling v Associated Dairies Ltd*.[139] The claimant suffered a back injury due to the defendants' negligence. Three years later, and before trial, the claimant was diagnosed as suffering from a condition (myelopathy), unrelated to, and arising after, the accident,[140] which of itself rendered him totally unfit for work. The defendants naturally contended that the onset of the myelopathy terminated the period in respect of which they were liable for loss of earnings; in reply, the claimant argued that the case should be governed by *Baker v Willoughby*. The House of Lords unanimously found for the defendants. The myelopathy was one of the "vicissitudes of life" in respect of which the courts regularly made discounts in the assessment of damages for future loss of earnings[141] and it followed that it must be taken into account in full when it had actually occurred before the trial[142]:

> "When the supervening illness or injury which is the independent cause of the loss of earning capacity has manifested itself before trial, the event has demonstrated that, even if the

---

they had reduced the value of his right of action against the defendant was rejected. However, an award of this nature was made in the fatal accident case of *Singh v Aitken* [1998] P.I.Q.R. Q37, though *Baker v Willoughby* is not mentioned in the judgment; cf. *Fox v British Airways* [2013] EWCA Civ 972; [2013] I.C.R. 1257; *Haxton v Philips Electronics UK Ltd* [2014] EWCA Civ 4; [2014] P.I.Q.R. P11 (husband killed by mesothelioma allowing dependency claim in favour of wife, but wife then also killed by mesothelioma; held wife had a claim against her employer for the diminution of her dependency claim caused by her shortened life expectancy).

[137] *Baker v Willoughby* [1970] A.C. 467 at 492.

[138] The robbers would (in theory) have been liable to his dependants under the Fatal Accidents Act 1976, but the damages would take account of any reduction in earning capacity attributable to the accident (subject to the argument rehearsed in fn.136). If the claimant had died of natural causes before the trial the liability of neither the defendant nor the robbers would have extended beyond that point.

[139] [1982] A.C. 794.

[140] The claimant conceded that if the myelopathy had been existing but dormant at the time of the accident it would have to have been taken into account in assessing damages.

[141] See Ch.23. If the case had come on quickly or been settled without anyone knowing about the impending illness then recovery for the injury would of course have been much more substantial and the matter could not have been reopened. See also *Dudarec v Andrews* [2006] EWCA Civ 256; [2006] 1 W.L.R. 3002; *Whitehead v Searle* [2008] EWCA Civ 285; [2009] 1 W.L.R. 549.

[142] [1982] A.C. 794 at 820 per Lord Bridge.

plaintiff had never sustained the tortious injury, his earnings would now be reduced or extinguished. To hold the tortfeasor, in this situation, liable to pay damages for a notional continuing loss of earnings attributable to the tortious injury, is to put the plaintiff in a better position than he would be in if he had never suffered the tortious injury."

This approach is inconsistent with the theory of the concurrent effect of consecutive causes advanced in *Baker v Willoughby* and, consequently, that case can no longer be regarded as a general authority on causation.[143] How far it is an authority on successive *tortious* injuries is less clear. In *Jobling*, Lord Russell suggested that *Baker* might have been correctly decided on the basis that a subsequent tortious injury was not to be regarded as within the "vicissitudes" principle, and hence should not be regarded as removing the effects of the first injury,[144] and Lord Keith, though not for the same reasons, also drew a distinction between tortious and non-tortious injuries.[145] However, Lord Bridge, while recognising the force of the argument that the claimant should not be under-compensated by reason of the fact that he is the victim of two torts rather than one, pointed out that the distinction between tortious and non-tortious causes had been implicitly rejected in *Baker*.[146]

C.   Causal Uncertainty

In practice, the most difficult problem facing the courts when it comes to factual causation is posed by cases in which it simply is not possible to establish whether or not there was a causal link between the defendant's negligent conduct and an injury to the claimant that fell within the risks created by that conduct.[147] This is the problem of "causal uncertainty". The classic scenario is the case of the two hunters who simultaneously shoot in the claimant's direction. One bullet hits him and the other misses, but the claimant is unable to prove which hunter fired which bullet. According to orthodox causation principles, the claimant fails against both hunters, since he cannot prove on the balance of probabilities that either shot him. However, courts in many jurisdictions, faced with this type of case, have departed from legal orthodoxy in order to allow the claimant to recover. In *Cook v Lewis*,[148] for example, the Supreme Court of Canada held that in a case like this the burden lies on each of the two defendants to exculpate himself and that, if both fail to discharge this burden, then both are liable.

7-033

---

143 [1982] A.C. 794 at 802, 809, 815, 821.
144 [1982] A.C. 794 at 810. See also *Penner v Mitchell* [1978] 4 W.W.R. 328.
145 [1982] A.C. 794 at 815.
146 [1982] A.C. 794 at 819. Lord Edmund Davies seemed to agree with Lord Bridge, for he said that he could "formulate no convincing juristic or logical principles supportive of the decision" in *Baker*. Lord Wilberforce in *Jobling* paid a good deal of attention to the fact that compensation is not merely a matter of tort damages and that the claimant's position with regard to other sources of money may determine whether he is under- or over-compensated. However, this is the general problem of offsets and deductions of collateral benefits (see Ch.23) and raises no more issues in multiple causation cases than in those where the issue of causation is clear.
147 Causation in fact may, of course, be established as a matter of inference: *Levicom International Holdings BV v Linklaters* [2010] EWCA Civ 494; [2010] P.N.L.R. 29 (solicitors advised C that it had a strong case to litigate rather than settle and C litigated; normal inference was that the advice was causative). See also: *Drake v Harbour* [2008] EWCA Civ 25; 121 Con. L.R. 18; *Vaile v Havering LBC* [2011] EWCA Civ 246; [2011] E.L.R. 274; *Schembri v Marshall* [2020] EWCA Civ 358; cf. *Saunders v Chief Constable of Sussex* [2012] EWCA Civ 1197.
148 [1951] S.C.R. 830. See also *Summers v Tice* 119 P. 2d 1 (1948).

i. The Fairchild Exception

7-034   **The Fairchild case**   A variation on the two hunters scenario came before the House of Lords in *Fairchild v Glenhaven Funeral Services Ltd*.[149] The claimant worked for differing periods of time for several employers, each of whom negligently exposed him to asbestos dust. As a result of this exposure, he contracted a mesothelioma (a form of cancer associated with asbestos).[150] However, such was the state of scientific knowledge concerning the aetiology of mesothelioma that it was impossible for the claimant to prove, on the balance of probabilities, that the mesothelioma was the result of any particular period of employment, whether separately or in combination with the others.[151] Nevertheless, the House of Lords held that in these circumstances, each employer was liable if the claimant could prove only that he had materially[152] increased the risk that the claimant would contract the disease. According to Lord Nicholls, "[a]ny other outcome would be deeply offensive to instinctive notions of what justice requires and fairness demands".[153] The real difficulty, as he went on to acknowledge, was to determine the precise basis for this exceptional departure from the normal requirement of proof of causation on the balance of probabilities.

7-035   **The Fairchild exception applies to a combination of tortious and non-tortious causes**   The House of Lords could have limited the *Fairchild* exception to cases where (as in the two hunters scenario) all potential causes of the defendant's injury are tortious. This would have kept the scope of the exception clear, and limited the departure from causal orthodoxy to cases where the injustice of denying recovery for lack of proof of causation seems most egregious.[154] However, any prospect that

---

[149] [2002] UKHL 22; [2003] 1 A.C. 32.

[150] There was said to be no doubt that the mesothelioma was the result of the occupational exposure because the disease is very rare and those exposed to asbestos at work have a thousand times greater incidence than the general population. However, contraction of the disease as a result of background environmental exposure cannot be ruled out, as is evident from *Sienkiewicz v Greif (UK) Ltd* [2011] UKSC 10; [2011] 2 A.C. 229, para.7-038.

[151] Although it seems that the day when this might be possible is getting closer, if not already here: see para.7-044.

[152] "Material" here means "more than de minimis": *Sienkiewicz v Greif (UK) Ltd* [2011] UKSC 10; [2011] 2 A.C. 229 at [176] (in *Greif* the increase in risk attributable to the defendant's breach of duty was 18 per cent (from 24 cases per million, to 28.39 cases per million) which was regarded as sufficient by the Supreme Court); see also *Cox v Rolls Royce Industrial Power* [2007] EWCA Civ 1189 (sufficient that C had only been exposed to asbestos by D for one year out of 24). In *Bannister v Freemans Plc* [2020] EWHC 1256 (QB), a dose of asbestos was said to be de minimis for these purposes if a doctor aware of the medical risks would regard it as something that the average patient should not worry about. On the facts, an exposure some 32.5 times smaller than the dose in *Sienkiewicz* was considered to satisfy that test, with the result that it was held not to have materially increased the risk of mesothelioma.

[153] [2002] UKHL 22; [2003] 1 A.C. 32 at [36].

[154] In other cases, the injustice which prompted the decision in *Fairchild* to some extent "loses its edge": *Barker v Corus (UK) Ltd* [2006] UKHL 20; [2006] 2 A.C. 572 at [117] per Lord Walker. For a careful exploration of the possible reasons why, see Steel (2015) 78 M.L.R. 729. In *Clements v Clements* 2012 SCC 32; [2012] 2 S.C.R. 181 at [46], McLachlin CJ, perhaps mindful of the complications to which the broader *Fairchild* exception has given rise, expressly limited the scope of the Canadian equivalent to cases where "(a) the plaintiff has established that her loss would not have occurred 'but for' the negligence of two or more tortfeasors, each possibly in fact responsible for the loss; and (b) the plaintiff, through no fault of her own, is unable to show that any one of the possible tortfeasors in fact was the necessary or 'but for' cause of her injury, because each can point to

the exception was so confined was effectively eliminated by the inclusion within it of the earlier House of Lords' decision in *McGhee v National Coal Board*,[155] where the injury might not have been the result of anybody's wrongful conduct. The pursuer in *McGhee* had developed dermatitis from brick dust to which he was exposed at work, and alleged that he would not have done so had the defender provided showers at his workplace, so that he could wash off the dust before cycling home. The defender admitted negligence in failing to provide these facilities but medical knowledge about the causes of dermatitis was such that it was not possible to say that had washing facilities been provided the pursuer would have escaped the disease; nor was it a case of cumulative causes where the breach of duty had made a material contribution. All that could be said was that the defender's negligence had materially increased the risk of dermatitis. On these facts the House held that the pursuer was entitled to succeed, and that decision was approved in *Fairchild*.

Confirmation that the *Fairchild* exception was not confined to cases where the claimant was undoubtedly the victim of a tort (but unable to pinpoint the tortfeasor) came in *Barker v Corus (UK) Ltd*,[156] where *Fairchild* was applied in circumstances where the claimant had been exposed to asbestos dust as a result both of the negligence of his employer (and other employers) and of his own negligence during a period of self-employment. Lord Hoffmann said that for the purpose of applying the *Fairchild* exception[157]:

> "[I]t should be irrelevant whether the other exposure [i.e., the exposure for which the defendant was not responsible] was tortious or non-tortious, by natural causes or human agency or by the claimant himself. These distinctions may be relevant to whether and to whom responsibility can also be attributed, but from the point of view of satisfying the requirement of a sufficient causal link between the defendant's conduct and the claimant's injury, they should not matter."

ii. The Limits of Fairchild

The "single agent" requirement[158]   Once it was decided by the House of Lords   **7-036**
in *Fairchild* that the exception to the usual but for rule encompassed the facts of *McGhee* their Lordships faced the challenge of how to limit the exception so that it did not swallow up the rule. In particular, the House was anxious to distinguish another causal uncertainty case where recovery had been denied, *Wilsher v Essex Area Health Authority*.[159] The claimant in *Wilsher* was born prematurely and succumbed to retrolental fibroplasia (RLF), a retinal condition causing serious damage to his sight. One possible cause of this was an excess of oxygen caused by a mistaken placing of a catheter. However, the conflicting expert evidence at the trial identified a number of other possible causes which were not attributable to the fault of the defendant and the failure of the trial judge to decide whether the mistake was

---

one another as the possible 'but for' cause of the injury, defeating a finding of causation on a balance of probabilities against anyone."

[155] [1973] 1 W.L.R. 1.
[156] [2006] UKHL 20; [2006] 2 A.C. 572.
[157] *Barker v Corus (UK) Ltd* [2006] UKHL 20; [2006] 2 A.C. 572 at [17]. See also Lord Rodger (at [97]).
[158] Wellington (2013) 20 Torts L.J. 1.
[159] [1988] A.C. 1074.

more likely as a cause than these others meant that there had to be a retrial on the causation issue. The argument that the claimant could succeed on the basis of the increased risk of RLF due to the excess of oxygen was firmly rejected by the House of Lords and the requirement of proof of a but for link on the balance of probabilities asserted.[160] *Wilsher* was approved in *Fairchild*, and distinguished on the basis that the *Fairchild* exception was confined to cases where the possible causes of the claimant's injury were all the same agent.[161] This meant that the exception covered the facts of *McGhee*, where the causal agent was brick dust, and *Fairchild*, where the causal agent was asbestos, but that it did not cover *Wilsher*, where the excess oxygen for which the defendant was responsible was only one of a number of agents that could have caused the damage.

This restriction, which became known as the "single agent" requirement, was approved in *Barker v Corus (UK) Ltd*, where Lord Hoffmann glossed it somewhat by saying that recovery under the *Fairchild* exception was limited to cases where "the impossibility of proving that the defendant caused the damage arises out of the existence of another potential causative agent which operated in the same way" as the agent for which the defendant was responsible.[162] So it did not matter that there was more than one possible causal agent, as long as they differed from each other only in some causally irrelevant respect, and the mechanism by which they could have caused the damage was the same. Even with this gloss, however, the limitation is not obviously a principled one,[163] and it appears to have been adopted simply because it places *some* limit on the *Fairchild* exception.[164] It also creates uncertainty as to the scope of the exception, since there are bound to be doubts as to whether or not two different agents have operated "in the same way".[165]

7-037   **Scientific impossibility of proving causation**   Another prerequisite for the application of the *Fairchild* exception is the scientific impossibility of drawing any conclusions as to causation even on the balance of probabilities. In *Hull v Sanderson*,[166] the Court of Appeal found that this prerequisite had not been met and that the trial judge should not have fallen back on the *Fairchild* exception as a way of avoiding making the necessary findings of fact to reach a decision on causation. It was clear that the claimant in the case had contracted campylobacter enteritis from the turkeys she plucked while working for the defendant, but whether the defendant's breach of duty in failing to advise her to take precautions against the risk of infection had been causative depended on how bacteria in the turkeys had been transferred to her mouth. It was up to the judge to make a finding on that on the balance of probabilities. By the same token, the *Fairchild* exception cannot be

---

[160]   The decision in *McGhee* was distinguished on the unsatisfactory basis, rejected in *Fairchild*, that it was no more than a "robust and pragmatic" application of the balance of probability test: [1988] A.C. 1074 at 1090 per Lord Bridge.

[161]   *Fairchild v Glenhaven Funeral Services Ltd* [2002] UKHL 22; [2003] 1 A.C. 32 at [22], [71].

[162]   [2006] UKHL 20; [2006] 2 A.C. 572 at [24] per Lord Hoffmann. See also at [64], [114].

[163]   As Lord Hoffmann pointed out in *Fairchild* (at [72]). It is true that in *Barker* (at [23]) he recanted, but in a subsequent book chapter on *Fairchild* he described the limitation as "absurd": Hoffmann in Burrows, Johnson and Zimmermann (eds), *Judge and Jurist: Essays in Memory of Lord Rodger of Earlsferry* (2013), p.66.

[164]   See Peel [2006] L.M.C.L.Q. 289.

[165]   Indeed in *Sienkiewicz v Greif (UK) Ltd* [2011] UKSC 10; [2011] 2 A.C. 229 at [187] Lord Brown said that he had "difficulty even in recognising the distinction" between "single agent" cases and "multiple agent" cases.

[166]   [2008] EWCA Civ 1211; [2009] P.I.Q.R. P7.

invoked in a routine accident case where the claimant simply has difficulty discharging the burden of proof.[167]

Fairchild exception not confined to mesothelioma cases In critical remarks   **7-038**
concerning the *Fairchild* exception in *Sienkiewicz v Greif*, Lord Brown referred to mesothelioma claims as "in a category all their own",[168] and said that that "save only for mesothelioma cases, claimants should henceforth expect little flexibility from the courts in their approach to causation".[169] These comments led to the observation that there was no "appetite in the appellate courts for extending the *Fairchild* exception to cases involving diseases other than mesothelioma",[170] and raised the possibility of the exception being confined to mesothelioma cases, notwithstanding the fact that it was said in *Fairchild* to encompass the facts of *McGhee*, which was not such a case. Subsequently, however, Lord Sumption said in *International Energy Group Ltd v Zurich Insurance Plc UK* that the House in *Fairchild* had recognised that the legal issue raised by the case "was not necessarily peculiar to mesothelioma",[171] and in *Heneghan v Manchester Dry Docks Ltd*,[172] the Court of Appeal applied the exception in a case involving lung cancer, thereby confirming its application beyond the mesothelioma context.

iii. Proportionate Liability?

The normal rule: joint and several liability The *Fairchild* appeals were   **7-039**
conducted on the basis that if the defendants before the court were liable at all, each was liable for all the damage suffered by the claimant in accordance with the normal rule applicable to contributing causes of indivisible injuries (joint and several liability).[173] Each defendant is, of course, entitled to seek contribution from any other persons liable for the same damage,[174] but under the normal rule the claimant is entitled to enforce the whole judgment against any one of them. This rule is particularly significant in the mesothelioma context as the asbestos exposure which attracts liability typically occurred decades ago, and many of the companies responsible for it have since become insolvent or ceased to exist. The result of this is that the combination of the *Fairchild* exception and the principle of joint and several liability may well lead to the burdening of a single solvent defendant with a very considerable liability, despite its being responsible for only a small proportion of the claimant's overall exposure to asbestos.

Barker v Corus (UK) Ltd In *Barker v Corus (UK) Ltd*[175] the House of Lords was   **7-040**
invited to depart from the normal rule and impose "proportionate" liability, that is to say liability quantified by reference to the amount of exposure for which the defendant was responsible. This invitation was accepted by the majority, es-

---

[167] See *Clough v First Choice Holidays and Flights Ltd* [2006] EWCA Civ 15; [2006] P.I.Q.R. P22 (slip-and-fall case).
[168] [2011] UKSC 10; [2011] 2 A.C. 229 at [186].
[169] [2011] UKSC 10; [2011] 2 A.C. 229 at [187].
[170] *Jones v Secretary of State for Energy and Climate Change* [2012] EWHC 2936 (QB) at [6.18].
[171] [2015] UKSC 33; [2016] A.C. 509 at [127].
[172] [2016] EWCA Civ 86; [2016] 1 W.L.R. 2036.
[173] See para.22-001.
[174] See para.22-005.
[175] [2006] UKHL 20; [2006] 2 A.C. 572.

sentially because this would "smooth the roughness of the justice" for defendants of a rule of joint and several liability in cases falling within the *Fairchild* exception.[176] Lord Hoffmann arrived at this outcome in an unexpected way, by holding that in such cases, the damage which the defendant should be regarded as having caused was not the disease itself, but the creation of a risk or chance of the disease coming about. Since chances are of course infinitely divisible, this meant that each defendant was liable only for the share of the claimant's exposure attributable to his negligence. By contrast, Lady Hale took a more conservative approach, making clear that in her view the damage was the disease and not the risk of it occurring, but reaching the same result as Lord Hoffmann by carving out an exception in cases within the *Fairchild* exception to the principle of joint and several liability. Lord Rodger dissented and said that the approach of the majority amounted to a rewriting of *Fairchild* (and *McGhee*). In his view *Fairchild* decided that, by showing that the defendant had materially increased the risk of the disease, the claimant had done enough for the court to deem that causation of the disease had been proved or, at least, that the defendant's breach of duty had made a material contribution, and the normal rule of joint and several liability should apply.

7-041   Compensation Act 2006, s.3   The decision in *Barker* proved politically unacceptable, and it was reversed by s.3 of the Compensation Act 2006, which reinstates joint and several liability in cases of mesothelioma induced by asbestos exposure where the defendant is found liable on the basis of the *Fairchild* exception.[177] However, *Barker* remains binding at common law, and so applies in cases which fall within the *Fairchild* exception but are not caught by s.3, as confirmed in *International Energy Group Ltd v Zurich Insurance Plc UK*,[178] a mesothelioma appeal from Guernsey, where no provision equivalent to s.3 is in force. In the UK itself, this means that proportionate recovery is still the rule in non-mesothelioma cases, which we have seen can still fall within the *Fairchild* exception.[179] Where the proportionate liability approach is applied, liability is calculated "according to each defendant's relative degree of contribution to the risk, usually measured by the duration and intensity of the exposure involved".[180]

7-042   Liability for risk exposure itself?   In *BAI (Run Off) Ltd v Durham (Employers' Liability Insurance "Trigger" Litigation)*,[181] the Supreme Court poured cold water on the idea that it followed from the reasoning of Lord Hoffmann in *Barker* that the damage for which the claimant recovers in cases within the *Fairchild* exception is the increased risk of disease rather than the disease itself. The issue in the *"Trigger" Litigation* case was the enforceability of employers' liability insurance

---

[176] [2006] UKHL 20; [2006] 2 A.C. 572 at [43] per Lord Hoffmann. See also at [109] per Lord Walker. In later extra-curial writing, Lord Hoffmann confirmed that the majority judgment in *Barker* was intended "to take some of the sting for defendants out of the *Fairchild* exception": Burrows, Johnson and Zimmermann (eds), *Judge and Jurist: Essays in Memory of Lord Rodger of Earlsferry* (2013), p.68.

[177] This provision was given retrospective effect, so as to apply to cases which had not come to judgment or been settled. On facts like *Barker*, where there was self-exposure, a reduction may still be made for contributory negligence.

[178] [2015] UKSC 33; [2016] A.C. 509.

[179] See para.7-038.

[180] *Equitas Insurance Ltd v Municipal Mutual Insurance Ltd* [2019] EWCA Civ 718; [2020] Q.B. 418 at [26] per Males LJ.

[181] [2012] UKSC 14; [2012] 1 W.L.R. 867.

policies in circumstances where cover was provided at the time of exposure but not at the time of onset of mesothelioma. The Court of Appeal had held that for policies where the insured risk was disease or injury "contracted" it was enough that the policy was in force at the time of exposure, but that for policies where the insured risk was disease or injury "sustained",[182] the policy must have been in force at the time the tumour developed.[183] In the Supreme Court a majority held that a claim could be made in both instances if the policy was in force at the time of the exposure for which the employer was held liable in accordance with the *Fairchild* exception. Lord Phillips dissented on the basis that, under the *Fairchild* exception, the employer is made liable for the increased risk of mesothelioma and that this form of liability could not satisfy either the concept of injury or of causation for the purposes of the insurance policies under consideration (whether defined in terms of injury sustained, or injury contracted). The majority disagreed, pointing out that, even after *Barker*, the employer is liable only if mesothelioma develops and holding that the liability of the employer is for *the mesothelioma*, not the increased risk of it eventuating.[184] This is a welcome clarification, as the alternative view threatened to drive a coach and horses through established principles governing the damage element of the negligence enquiry.[185]

iv. *Future Perspectives*

Fairchild in hindsight   As is suggested by the discussion of the *"Trigger" Litiga-*   **7-043**
tion case, one of the legacies of the *Fairchild* decision has been a myriad of very difficult questions in the law of liability insurance and reinsurance,[186] and indeed most of the recent cases touching on the exception have been concerned with such issues.[187] As Males LJ commented in one of those cases[188]:

"There is no doubt that the *Fairchild* decision together with the Compensation Act 2006 and the cases which have applied these principles have created significant anomalies in the law. That jurisprudence ... has extended into liability insurance and (now) reinsurance in ways which seem unlikely to have been intended or predicted."

Along with other considerations, these complications have caused judges in subsequent cases to question the wisdom of the House of Lords' decision to depart from orthodox principles governing proof of causation in *Fairchild*. In *Sienkiewicz v Greif*, for example, Lord Brown lamented the state of the law, describing the posi-

---

[182] cf. "occurring": *Bolton MBC v MMI Ltd* [2006] EWCA Civ 50; [2006] 1 W.L.R. 1492, where public liability insurance was in issue.

[183] *Durham v BAI (Run Off) Ltd* [2010] EWCA Civ 1096; [2011] 1 All E.R. 605.

[184] See also *International Energy Group Ltd v Zurich Insurance Plc UK* [2015] UKSC 33; [2016] A.C. 509 at [135] per Lord Sumption (in cases within the *Fairchild* exception, the defendant is liable "for the disease itself").

[185] See paras 7-019ff concerning denial of claims for "loss of a chance", a mirror image of "increased risk". For a critique of the idea of risk as damage, see Turton (2015) 35 L.S. 75.

[186] A "sort of juridical version of chaos theory": *International Energy Group Ltd v Zurich Insurance Plc UK* [2015] UKSC 33; [2016] A.C. 509 at [191] per Lord Neuberger and Lord Reed.

[187] See, e.g., *International Energy Group Ltd v Zurich Insurance Plc UK* [2015] UKSC 33; [2016] A.C. 509; *Equitas Insurance Ltd v Municipal Mutual Insurance Ltd* [2019] EWCA Civ 718; [2020] Q.B. 418. On the insurance implications of *Fairchild*, see Goudkamp [2015] L.M.C.L.Q. 443; Merkin (2016) 36 L.S. 302.

[188] *Equitas Insurance Ltd v Municipal Mutual Insurance Ltd* [2019] EWCA Civ 718; [2020] Q.B. 418 at [90].

tion after that case as "unsatisfactory" and the path by which it was reached as "quixotic".[189] The lesson of the *Fairchild* saga, he said, was that "the law tampers with the 'but for' test of causation at its peril".[190] And in the most recent Supreme Court decision in this area, *International Energy Group Ltd v Zurich Insurance Plc UK*, Lord Sumption referred to the problems associated with the adoption of special rules within what he called "the *Fairchild* enclave",[191] and Lord Neuberger and Lord Reed wondered whether, "with the wisdom of hindsight", it would not have been better if the House of Lords had decided *Fairchild* in favour of the defendants and left Parliament to sort out the problem through legislation creating a mesothelioma exception to the common law but for rule.[192] In any case the references to a "*Fairchild* enclave" in recent decisions[193] suggest that the current attitude of the courts is that this line of authority is very much an exception to the normal rule, that expansion of its scope is not to be countenanced,[194] and that further judicial experimentation in this area is not to be encouraged.

7-044   **Advances in medical science**   The *Fairchild* exception was introduced to deal with the evidential difficulty faced by claimants in the proof of causation. Such difficulty was due to the state of scientific knowledge at the time, but the science has moved on. The "single fibre" theory which featured prominently in *Fairchild* (i.e., the theory that mesothelioma could be caused by a single asbestos fibre) has been discredited[195] and it also seems that one can rule out inhalation of asbestos occurring in the period immediately prior to diagnosability.[196] More recently, it has been suggested that the understanding of the carcinogenesis of mesothelioma has reached a point where it is possible to conclude that the claimant's exposures to asbestos have a cumulative effect,[197] in which case he might be able to establish proof of causation against more than one defendant on the balance of probabilities. If this is the position which has been reached, or indeed if this is the position which is one day reached,[198] then given the uncertainty surrounding the *Fairchild* exception and

---

[189] [2011] UKSC 10; [2011] 2 A.C. 229 at [174].

[190] [2011] UKSC 10; [2011] 2 A.C. 229 at [186].

[191] [2015] UKSC 33; [2016] A.C. 509 at [187].

[192] [2015] UKSC 33; [2016] A.C. 509 at [209]–[211] (although they also pointed out (at [191]) that deciding against the claimants in *Fairchild* "would have required an exceptionally hard-headed (and, many people would say, hard-hearted) approach"). The suggestion that perhaps it would have been better to have left the issue to Parliament had previously been made extra-curially by Lord Hoffmann, who had himself sat in *Fairchild*: see Hoffmann in Burrows, Johnson and Zimmermann (eds), *Judge and Jurist: Essays in Memory of Lord Rodger of Earlsferry* (2013).

[193] See also *Equitas Insurance Ltd v Municipal Mutual Insurance Ltd* [2019] EWCA Civ 718; [2020] Q.B. 418 at [1] per Males LJ, describing it as "an area of law within which conventional principles have had to be adjusted to take account of the implications of [the *Fairchild*] decision".

[194] See *AB v Ministry of Defence* [2012] UKSC 9; [2013] 1 A.C. 78 at [157].

[195] *Sienkiewicz v Greif (UK) Ltd* [2011] UKSC 10; [2011] 2 A.C. 229 at [102].

[196] *BAI (Run Off) Ltd v Durham* [2012] UKSC 14; [2012] 1 W.L.R. 867 at [5] (roughly ten years prior); *Sienkiewicz* [2011] UKSC 10; [2011] 2 A.C. 229 at [19] (at least five years).

[197] This appears to have been the view expressed by one of the experts who appeared in *Fairchild* in the later case of *Jones v Secretary of State for Energy and Climate Change* [2012] EWHC 2936 (QB) at [8.21]: "Dr Rudd said that, if he were asked the same questions now as he had been asked in *Fairchild*, he would say that it was probable that the asbestos fibres from each source had contributed to the carcinogenic process".

[198] *Sienkiewicz v Greif (UK) Ltd* [2011] UKSC 10; [2011] 2 A.C. 229 at [142] per Lord Rodger: "If the day ever dawns when medical science can identify which fibre or fibres led to the malignant mutation and the source from which that fibre or fibres came, then the problem which gave rise to the exception will have ceased to exist".

the "quixotic process" it unleashed, it may be that the time has (or will have) come to abandon the exception and revert to causal orthodoxy.

Epidemiological evidence: "doubling of the risk" Just as the need for special **7-045**
rules on proof of causation may be reduced by advances in scientific understanding of the aetiology of certain conditions, it may also be that the courts can avoid the need for such rules by placing greater weight on epidemiological evidence in causal uncertainty cases. Epidemiology is the study of how disease is distributed in populations and the factors that influence or determine this distribution, and an important question for the courts going forward is the extent to which they can rely on evidence derived from work of this kind. Take the example used by Lord Mackay in *Hotson v East Berkshire Health Authority*[199]: if epidemiological evidence showed that of 100 men working in the same conditions as the claimant 30 would develop dermatitis even though they had showered after their shift, but the evidence also indicated that, if the men did not shower, 70 would develop dermatitis, the introduction of the defendant's breach of duty in failing to provide showers would have more than doubled the risk. Should this doubling of the risk suffice to prove that, on the balance of probability, the defendant's breach caused the dermatitis?

In *Sienkiewicz v Greif (UK) Ltd*,[200] the Supreme Court held that a "doubling of the risk" test should not be used in mesothelioma claims because the data then available on the incidence of the risk of mesothelioma from exposure to asbestos was either inadequate or unreliable.[201] But what if the data had been comprehensive and sound? Lord Rodger expressed scepticism on the basis that the only "fact" proved in Lord Mackay's example is that *in most cases* the dermatitis will be related to the lack of showers,[202] and that the test lacks the personal element which would allow the court to determine whether the claimant was one of the 30 who would have contracted dermatitis in any event, or one of the additional 40.[203] But, with respect, it is not clear why such significance is being attached to the "personal element" unless this is cautioning us to make sure that the epidemiological evidence on which reliance is placed is both relevant and reliable.[204] After all "the law of causation does not deal in certainties; it deals in probabilities"[205] and, as Lord Rodger himself acknowledged, unless there is evidence in Lord Mackay's example that the claimant is atypical "it is more probable than not that his dermatitis was caused by lack

---

[199] [1987] A.C. 750 at 786.
[200] [2011] UKSC 10; [2011] 2 A.C. 229. See Stapleton (2012) 128 L.Q.R. 221.
[201] But such unreliable data still have to be employed faute de mieux to deal with claims of contribution between joint tortfeasors: [2011] UKSC 10; [2011] 2 A.C. 229 at [106].
[202] *Sienkiewicz v Greif (UK) Ltd* [2011] UKSC 10; [2011] 2 A.C. 229 at [156]; cf. Lord Kerr (at [204]); Gold (1986) 96 Yale L.J. 376 at 382–384; *Merrell Dow Pharmaceuticals Inc v Havner* 953 S.W. 2d 706 (1997).
[203] In *Herskovits v Group Health Cooperative of Pugent Sound* 664 P. 2d 474 (1983) Brachtenbach J regarded it as an essential and minimal requirement that there be evidence connecting the relevant statistical information to the facts of the case; cf. *Amaca Pty Ltd v Ellis* [2010] HCA 5; (2010) 240 C.L.R. 111 at [70].
[204] See Stapleton (2012) 128 L.Q.R. 221; and *Amaca Pty Ltd v Ellis* [2010] HCA 5; (2010) 240 C.L.R. 111, where it was said that, when asked to draw a causal inference from epidemiological data, a court must: (1) relate the results of studies of populations to the case in hand; and (2) decide whether the case in hand should be treated as conforming to the pattern described by the studies (albeit that, unless there was evidence that the claimant's situation was atypical, such conformity might readily be assumed).
[205] [2011] UKSC 10; [2011] 2 A.C. 229 at [54] per Lord Phillips.

of showers".[206] There is therefore much to be said for Lord Dyson's view that "sufficiently compelling" epidemiological data should suffice to establish causation in an appropriate case,[207] and indeed the doubling of the risk test has been applied to resolve claims for lung cancer, bladder cancer and skin cancer caused by other types of carcinogen.[208] Furthermore, it has been suggested that in a multiple defendant case such as *Fairchild* the "doubling of the risk" test could potentially be used to establish but for causation as against a particular defendant responsible for the bulk of the relevant exposure.[209]

4. LEGAL CAUSATION

A. Introduction

7-046 **"Causation in law"** If we conclude that D's breach of duty was *a* cause of C's damage, we move on to consider whether it was a sufficiently significant cause to justify imposing liability on D. Suppose D leaves a loaded shotgun in an unlocked cupboard, X steals it and uses it to murder C (D knowing nothing of X's murderous intentions). D's breach of duty in failing to lock up the gun was a "factual cause" of C's death because, had the gun not been available, X would not have used it to kill C (though he might of course have done so at another time with another weapon). However, an English court is quite likely to say that if X is an adult of sound mind, then X, not D, is responsible for C's death and it may do so by speaking in terms of X's act being "the cause" or having "broken the chain of causation" between D's negligence and C's death.[210] On the other hand, if a young child

---

[206] *Sienkiewicz v Greif (UK) Ltd* [2011] UKSC 10; [2011] 2 A.C. 229 at [156]. Scepticism was also expressed about the "doubling of the risk" test in *Williams v Bermuda Hospitals Board* [2016] UKPC 4; [2016] A.C. 888 at [48], where Lord Toulson cautioned against a mechanistic approach to inferring causation from proof of a heightened risk, observing that "[a] doubled tiny risk will still be very small". However, the *overall* size of the risk is irrelevant to the inference of causation in a case where ex hypothesi that risk has materialised. If we were to change the figures in Lord Mackay's example so that the total population of men was 10,000 instead of 100, then on the same figures of 30 and 70 for contraction of dermatitis it would still be valid to infer causation on the balance of probabilities, even though the overall risk of contracting the disease has diminished from 30 per cent (with showers) and 70 per cent (without showers) to 0.3 per cent and 0.7 per cent respectively.

[207] [2011] UKSC 10; [2011] 2 A.C. 229 at [222]. The High Court of Australia had no qualms about relying on sound epidemiological evidence in *Amaca Pty Ltd v Ellis* [2010] HCA 5; (2010) 240 C.L.R. 111, where the issue was whether the deceased's lung cancer had been caused by smoking or by asbestos exposure for which the defendant was responsible. The trial of the case had centred on the implications of epidemiological studies of lung cancer, and the "relative risks" of lung cancer associated with smoking, asbestos exposure and a combination of the two. However, even on the most generous view of that evidence, the likelihood that the asbestos exposure had been causative of the cancer (whether acting alone or in combination with the smoking) was only 23 per cent, and so applying the balance of probabilities test the High Court dismissed the claim.

[208] *Novartis Grimsby Ltd v Cookson* [2007] EWCA Civ 1261; *Shortell v BICAL Construction Ltd* (QBD, 16 May 2008); *Jones v Secretary of State for Energy and Climate Change* [2012] EWHC 2936 (QB). Note also the reliance placed on statistical evidence in *Schembri v Marshall* [2020] EWCA Civ 358; and *Bannister v Freemans Plc* [2020] EWHC 1256 (QB).

[209] *Heneghan v Manchester Dry Docks Ltd* [2016] EWCA Civ 86; [2016] 1 W.L.R. 2036 at [55].

[210] See also Lord Hoffmann's illustration of the theft of a car radio in *Environment Agency v Empress Car Co (Abertillery) Ltd* [1999] 2 A.C. 22 at 29, where he points out that the meaning of "cause", like that of most words, depends on the context in which it is used. While at the trial of the thief we would unhesitatingly say that his act caused the loss of the radio, the owner's spouse might also properly say, by way of complaint, that the owner's negligence in leaving it in the car had caused

had taken the gun in our example and shot C while playing with it, we would probably readily agree that D ought to be responsible, even though what D did was just
as much an "historical" cause in one case as in the other. So if we are going to
distinguish between the two cases and still speak in the language of causation we
are now using a different concept and, despite a tendency even at this stage to use
mechanical metaphors about chains and links, the issue is much more obviously one
of ascription of responsibility as between D and X.[211] For while our notions of
individual responsibility would lead us to say in the first case that X bears sole
responsibility for C's death, in the second case the fact that X is not relevantly
responsible for his actions compels a different conclusion.[212]

Novus actus interveniens   The phrase "novus actus interveniens" signifies the   **7-047**
conclusion that although the defendant's breach of duty is a cause of the claimant's
damage in the sense that it satisfies the "but for" test of causation in fact, nevertheless in the eyes of the law some intervening conduct is regarded as the sole effective cause of that damage. Two classes of case fall to be considered, namely: (1)
where the intervening conduct was that of a third party; and (2) where the intervening conduct was that of the claimant himself. It should not be thought, however, that
in either of these cases the law will be particularly astute to attribute to the
claimant's damage a single legal cause. There is no objection to a finding that the
separate torts of two independent actors were both causes of the damage, and where
this is so the claimant may recover in full from either of them.[213] Nor is there any
objection to a finding that the defendant's breach of duty and the claimant's own
fault were both causes of the claimant's damage. On the contrary, such a finding is
a condition precedent to the operation of the law of contributory negligence.[214]

Relevant considerations   In *Clay v TUI UK Ltd*, Hamblen LJ said that in   **7-048**
determining whether intervening conduct broke the chain of causation, relevant
considerations include[215]:

"(1)   The extent to which the conduct was reasonably foreseeable—in general, the more
        foreseeable it is, the less likely it is to be a novus actus interveniens.

(2)   The degree of unreasonableness of the conduct—in general, the more unreason-
        able the conduct, the more likely it is to be a novus actus interveniens and a
        number of cases have stressed the need for a high degree of unreasonableness.

(3)   The extent to which it was voluntary and independent conduct—in general, the
        more deliberate the act, the more informed it is and the greater the free choice
        involved, the more likely it is to be a novus actus interveniens".

---

its loss. This is not to say, of course, that a negligent defendant can never be liable in tort for wilful
harm inflicted by another: paras 7-056ff.

[211] See, e.g., *Yorkshire Dale SS Co Ltd v Minister of War Transport* [1942] A.C. 691 at 706 per Lord
Wright (referring to "ordinary moral notions of when someone should be regarded as responsible
for something which has happened"); *Hughes-Holland v BPE Solicitors* [2017] UKSC 21; [2018]
A.C. 599 at [20] per Lord Sumption (referring to the concepts of legal causation and remoteness as
"concerned with assigning responsibility for the breach [of duty]").

[212] Hence the actions of young children and those not of sound mind are incapable of amounting to a
novus actus interveniens: see *Carmarthenshire CC v Lewis* [1955] A.C. 549 (four-year-old boy);
Kirkham v Chief Constable of Greater Manchester [1990] 2 Q.B. 283 (suicide of mentally ill
prisoner).

[213] See para.7-029. For contribution between tortfeasors, see, Ch.22.

[214] See para.23-040.

[215] [2018] EWCA Civ 1177; [2018] 4 All E.R. 672 at [28].

As that summary makes clear, while the degree to which the intervention was foreseeable is a relevant consideration, unlike in many remoteness scenarios foreseeability is not the sole determinant of legal causation[216] but only one factor among others. This point was made forcefully by Lord Reid in *McKew v Holland & Hannen & Cubitts (Scotland) Ltd*[217]:

> "I do not think that foreseeability comes into this. A defender is not liable for a consequence of a kind which is not foreseeable. But it does not follow that he is liable for every consequence which a reasonable man could foresee ... it is often easy to foresee unreasonable conduct or some other novus actus interveniens as being quite likely. But that does not mean that the defender must pay for damage caused by the novus actus."

B.   Intervening Act of a Third Party

7-049   **Introduction**   If the defendant's breach of duty has done no more than provide the occasion for an entirely independent act by a third party and that act is the immediate cause of the claimant's damage, then it will amount to a novus actus and the defendant will not be liable.[218] This, however, may not be the case if the act of the third party was not truly independent.[219] In *The Oropesa*[220] a collision occurred between the ship of that name and another ship, the *Manchester Regiment*, for which both ships were to blame. The *Manchester Regiment* was severely damaged and her master decided to cross to the *Oropesa* in one of the ship's boats to discuss salvage arrangements with the master of the *Oropesa*. The boat overturned in heavy seas before reaching the *Oropesa* and nine of the men on board, one of whom was the claimant's son, were drowned. The question was whether his death was caused by the negligence of those in control of the *Oropesa*,[221] or whether the action of the master of the *Manchester Regiment* in taking to the boat constituted a novus actus interveniens. It was held that that action could not be severed from the circumstances affecting the two ships, that the "hand of the casualty lay heavily" upon the *Manchester Regiment*, and so that the death was caused by and flowed from the collision.[222] According to Lord Wright[223]:

> "To break the chain of causation it must be shown that there is something which I will call ultroneous,[224] something unwarrantable, a new cause which disturbs the sequence of

---

[216]   *Maitland Hudson v Solicitors Regulation Authority* [2017] EWHC 1249 (Ch) at [69].

[217]   [1969] 3 All E.R. 1621 at 1623.

[218]   *Weld-Blundell v Stephens* [1920] A.C. 956; *Harnett v Bond* [1925] A.C. 669; *SS Singleton Abbey v SS Paludina* [1927] A.C. 16.

[219]   This appears to be the best explanation of the difficult case of *Wright v Cambridge Medical Group* [2011] EWCA Civ 669; [2013] Q.B. 312, in which the defendant medical practice negligently delayed C's referral to hospital, but the hospital then treated C negligently. The resolution of the claim was not assisted by the fact that no claim had been brought against the hospital, either by C or by the medical practice (by way of contribution) so that key issues had to be resolved on the basis of hypothesis rather than any finding of fact.

[220]   [1943] P. 32.

[221]   It is irrelevant to this question that the negligence of the *Manchester Regiment* leading to the collision may also have been a cause of the death.

[222]   *The Oropesa* [1943] P. 32 at 37 per Lord Wright.

[223]   *The Oropesa* [1943] P. 32 at 39.

[224]   "So Lord Wright found it necessary to go outside the dictionary, or at least to explore its furthest corners, in order to identify the kind of circumstances in which the defendant might cease to be liable for what could otherwise be regarded as the consequences of his act": *The Sivand* [1998] 2 Lloyd's Rep. 97 at 102 per Evans LJ.

events, something which can be described as either unreasonable or extraneous or extrinsic."

The intervening act of a third party need not be tortious   In *The Oropesa*, the   **7-050**
action of the master of the *Manchester Regiment* was not itself tortious: he was not
guilty of a breach of duty to the deceased in ordering him into the boat, but that fact
is not itself decisive one way or another. A non-tortious intervention may break the
chain of causation in one case while in another even deliberate tortious conduct may
not do so, though the further along the scale from innocent mistake to wilful
wrongdoing the third party's conduct moves the more likely it is to terminate the
defendant's liability.[225] In particular, there is a presumption that wilful wrongdoing will have this effect,[226] while in other cases reckless or grossly negligent
interventions are more likely to constitute a novus actus than instances of ordinary
negligence, where the more appropriate solution is likely to be to impose joint and
several liability on the defendant and the intervener, followed by apportionment of
responsibility between the two pursuant to contribution proceedings. Ultimately,
however, the matter is what in former times would have been regarded as a jury
question.[227] It calls for "common sense rather than logic"[228] and a "robust and
sensible approach".[229]

Illustrations   Decisions on legal causation are highly fact sensitive[230] as is shown   **7-051**
by some multiple collision cases. In *Rouse v Squires*[231] D1, driving negligently, jack-
knifed his lorry across a motorway; a following car collided with the lorry, and some
minutes later D2's lorry, also being driven negligently, collided with the other
vehicles, killing C, who was assisting at the scene. The Court of Appeal, reversing
the trial judge, held that D1's negligence was an operative cause of C's death,[232] for
if[233]:

> "[A] driver so negligently manages his vehicle as to cause it to obstruct the highway and
> constitute a danger to other road users, including those who are driving too fast or not
> keeping a proper lookout, but not those who deliberately or recklessly drive into the
> obstruction, then the first driver's negligence may be held to have contributed to the causa-
> tion of an accident of which the immediate cause was the negligent driving of the vehicle
> which because of the presence of the obstruction collides with it."

In contrast, in *Wright v Lodge*[234] D1's vehicle broke down and she negligently failed
to take steps to remove it from the highway. D2's lorry struck the car, injuring D1's
passenger C1, and then crossed into the opposite carriageway, where it collided with
cars being driven by C2 and C3, also injuring them. D1 was liable to C1, but not

---

[225] *Knightley v Johns* [1982] 1 W.L.R. 349 at 365.
[226] See para.7-056.
[227] *Wright v Lodge* [1993] 4 All E.R. 299 at 307.
[228] *Knightley v Johns* [1982] 1 W.L.R. 349 at 367 per Stephenson LJ.
[229] *Lamb v Camden LBC* [1981] Q.B. 625 at 647 per Watkins LJ.
[230] "[W]here there are successive tortfeasors, the contention that the causative potency of the negligence of the first is destroyed by the subsequent negligence of the second depends very much on the facts of the particular case": *Wright v Cambridge Medical Group* [2011] EWCA Civ 669; [2013] Q.B. 312 at [32] per Lord Neuberger MR.
[231] [1973] Q.B. 889; *Lloyds Bank Ltd v Budd* [1982] R.T.R. 80.
[232] For which D1 was held 25 per cent to blame under the Law Reform (Married Women and Tortfea-sors) Act 1935.
[233] *Rouse v Squires* [1973] Q.B. 889 at 898 per Cairns LJ.
[234] [1993] 4 All E.R. 299.

to C2 and C3, because the effective cause of the lorry being in the other car-riageway was the reckless manner in which D2 had been driving when he collided with D1's vehicle.[235] The chain of causation was also broken by intervening events in *Knightley v Johns*.[236] D1's negligent driving caused the blocking of a busy road tunnel. After a good deal of confusion as to the location of the accident, D2, a police inspector, took charge but did not immediately close the tunnel as he should have done. He then ordered C, a police constable, to drive back against the traffic for that purpose. While doing so C was struck and injured by D3, who was driving too fast into the tunnel. The Court of Appeal set aside a judgment for C against D1.[237] While it might be natural, probable and foreseeable that the police would come to deal with the accident in the tunnel and that there might be risk-taking[238] and even mistakes on their part, there had in fact been so many errors before C was ordered to ride back down the tunnel[239] that the subsequent collision with D3 was too remote a consequence of D1's original negligence.

7-052 **Negligent medical treatment** If C is knocked down and injured by D1 and a few moments later is struck and further injured by D2, also driving negligently, it is not difficult to conclude that D1 may bear some responsibility for the further injury. It is perhaps less intuitive to conclude that D1 is liable for the consequences of negligent medical treatment of the injury directly inflicted by him, but he usually will be unless the treatment is completely inappropriate.[240] Generally, of course, the matter will be one of contribution between the two defendants in respect of the second injury, and indeed, provided all defendants are claim-worthy, issues concern-ing the intervening acts of third parties will often be limited to contribution among defendants and of no direct concern to the claimant.[241]

C.   Intervening Act of the Claimant

7-053 **Introduction** Where, in combination with the defendant's breach of duty, the claimant's own act or omission has brought about his damage, then the problem is generally seen as one of contributory negligence.[242] Before there can be any ques-tion of contributory negligence, however, it is necessary that both the claimant's

---

[235] D2 was of course liable to C2 and C3 (and, along with D1, to C1). The issue was whether D2 could claim contribution from D1. D1's share in the liability to C1 was only 10 per cent. Note that these cases could equally well be analysed in terms of duty of care to the particular claimant—indeed *Wright v Lodge* has some affinities with *Palsgraf v Long Island Railroad* (para.5-009).

[236] [1982] 1 W.L.R. 349.

[237] However, D2 and D3 were liable to C.

[238] Taking risks to save others from danger does not normally break the chain of causation: see para.26-025.

[239] See in particular [1982] 1 W.L.R. 349 at 365–366.

[240] *Webb v Barclays Bank Plc* [2001] EWCA Civ 1141; [2002] P.I.Q.R. P8, following *Mahony v J Kruschich (Demolitions) Pty Ltd* (1985) 156 C.L.R. 522. In *Prendergast v Sam & Dee Ltd* [1989] 1 Med. L.R. 36, D1, a doctor, wrote an unclear prescription; D2, a pharmacist misread it, though he should have been put on inquiry. D2's negligence did not break the chain of causation but his rela-tive responsibility was assessed as 75 per cent. cf. *Horton v Evans* [2006] EWHC 2808 (QB); [2007] P.N.L.R. 17 (pharmacist liable for failing to question prescription, doctor prescribing repeat prescrip-tion not at fault).

[241] cf. the difficult case of *Rahman v Arearose Ltd* [2001] Q.B. 351, where it was conceded that the medical treatment was the sole cause of the loss of the eye; and see the divisions in the Court of Ap-peal in the equally difficult case of *Wright v Cambridge Medical Group* [2011] EWCA Civ 669; [2013] Q.B. 312.

[242] See Ch.23.

lack of care and the defendant's breach of duty be found to have been causes of the claimant's damage and in some cases, the defendant has been exonerated on the ground that the claimant's conduct amounted to a novus actus interveniens.[243]

Illustrations   No liability arises at all where conduct of the claimant occurring   **7-054** before any damage is done is held to amount to a novus actus interveniens. In *Clay v TUI UK Ltd*,[244] the claimant and members of his family had become trapped on the balcony of a hotel room in Tenerife when the door leading to the balcony inadvertently locked after being closed from the outside. After about 30 minutes the claimant tried to cross to an adjacent balcony, but a ledge on which he stood collapsed, and he fell some 20 feet to the ground, fracturing his skull. A majority of the Court of Appeal upheld the finding of the trial judge that a defect in the lock of the door was not a legal cause of the claimant's injuries because, by attempting a highly dangerous manoeuvre to escape a predicament that was no more than an inconvenience, he had broken the chain of causation.[245] In a second type of case, it is not disputed that the defendant is liable for the claimant's initial injury, but an intervening act of the claimant is held to be the sole legal cause of a subsequent injury, even though it would not have happened but for the first.[246] The pursuer in *McKew v Holland & Hannen & Cubitts (Scotland) Ltd*[247] suffered an injury in an accident for which the defenders were responsible, as a result of which his left leg occasionally gave way under him. Some days after this accident the pursuer went to inspect a flat which was approached by steep stairs between two walls and without a handrail. On leaving the flat he started to descend the stairs holding his young daughter by the hand and going ahead of his wife and brother-in-law. Suddenly he lost control of his left leg, threw his daughter back to protect her, and tried to jump so as to land in an upright position instead of falling down the stairs. As a result he sustained a severe fracture of his ankle. The House of Lords held that while the pursuer's act of jumping in the emergency in which he found himself did not break the chain of causation, it had been broken by his conduct in placing himself unnecessarily in a position where he might be confronted by just such an emergency, when he could have descended the stairs slowly and carefully by himself or sought the assistance of those accompanying him.

Unreasonable conduct necessary but not sufficient   In *McKew* it was critical to   **7-055** the conclusion that the pursuer's conduct broke the chain of causation that it was unreasonable. If he had had no real alternative but to act as he did then it would not have had that effect. Similarly, if it had been reasonable of the claimant in *Clay v TUI UK Ltd* to attempt to escape onto the adjacent balcony (because, for example, there was a fire in his room), then the defendant would almost certainly have been

---

[243] For discussion of this issue in the product liability context, see para.11-006.

[244] [2018] EWCA Civ 1177; [2018] 4 All E.R. 672.

[245] cf. *Sayers v Harlow Urban DC* [1958] 1 W.L.R. 623 (no break in chain of causation where claimant trapped in toilet cubicle tried to escape by climbing out, although damages reduced by 25 per cent for contributory negligence).

[246] Although it has been suggested that, as far as intervening conduct of the claimant is concerned, novus actus interveniens is limited to such cases (*Hicks v Young* [2015] EWHC 1144 (QB) at [23]–[24]), that is clearly incorrect, as is shown by decisions such as *Clay v TUI UK Ltd* [2018] EWCA Civ 1177; [2018] 4 All E.R. 672.

[247] [1969] 3 All E.R. 1621. See also *The San Onofre* [1922] P. 243; cf. *Wieland v Cyril Lord Carpets Ltd* [1969] 3 All E.R. 1006; *Dalling v RJ Heale & Co Ltd* [2011] EWCA Civ 365.

held liable for his injuries.[248] The principle that reasonable conduct is most unlikely to break the chain of causation is illustrated by *Emeh v Kensington and Chelsea and Westminster Health Authority*,[249] where the defendants negligently performed a sterilisation operation on the claimant and she became pregnant again, although she did not discover this until 20 weeks into the pregnancy. The Court of Appeal rejected the argument that her refusal to have an abortion broke the chain of causation between the negligence and the child's birth. It could not be right, Slade LJ said, for a court to declare it unreasonable for a woman to decline to have an abortion, "save in the most exceptional circumstances".[250] However, it does not follow that all unreasonable conduct will break the causal chain, for that would leave no possibility of an apportionment of responsibility between the parties pursuant to the doctrine of contributory negligence.[251] On the contrary, the conclusion that the claimant's conduct had this effect is likely only where it was *highly* unreasonable or he acted with reckless disregard for his own safety.

D. Intervening Wilful Conduct

7-056 **Wilful intervening conduct in general** Special considerations apply in cases where the intervening conduct of a third party is deliberately aimed at causing the damage in question. Since the doctrine of legal causation is centrally concerned with the ascription of responsibility for the damage as between the defendant and the intervening party, it is not surprising that[252]:

> "In general ... even though A is in fault, he is not responsible for injury to C which B, a stranger to him, deliberately chooses to do. Though A may have given the occasion for B's mischievous activity, B then becomes a new and independent cause."

Much of the case law in this area analyses the problem in terms of the existence of a duty of care to prevent wilful injury and the problem has already been considered in that context.[253] However, where the defendant has caused some initial injury to the claimant before the intervention of the third party the cases have continued to look at the question as one of legal causation. Whichever label is used to frame the analysis, the same reluctance to find the defendant liable for the wilful wrongdoing of others is observable. It has been said that the conduct of the third party must

---

[248] See [2018] EWCA Civ 1177; [2018] 4 All E.R. 672 at [33].

[249] [1985] Q.B. 1012.

[250] [1985] Q.B. 1012 at 1024. See also *The Calliope* [1970] P. 172 (maritime collision caused by negligence of claimant and defendant; claimant vessel sustaining further damage in turning because of Chief Officer's negligence; manoeuvre difficult but not unreasonable and did not break chain of causation; defendant liable for further damage, subject to further apportionment for contributory negligence: see para.23-040).

[251] See, e.g., *Spencer v Wincanton Holdings Ltd* [2009] EWCA Civ 1404; [2010] P.I.Q.R. P8, a case with facts not dissimilar to those of *McGhee*, where D was held liable for a second accident caused by a combination of an injury D had negligently inflicted on C and C's negligence. According to Aikens LJ at [45], the "line between a set of facts which results in a finding of contributory negligence and a set of facts which results in a finding that the 'unreasonable conduct' of the claimant constitutes a novus actus interveniens is not, in my view, capable of precise definition".

[252] *Weld-Blundell v Stephens* [1920] A.C. 956 at 986 per Lord Sumner. See also *Mitchell v Glasgow CC* [2009] UKHL 11; [2009] 1 A.C. 874 at [81].

[253] See para.5-037. According to Lord Goff in *Smith v Littlewoods Organisation* [1987] A.C. 241 at 280, "problems such as these are solved in Scotland, as in England, by means of the mechanism of the duty of care".

be something very likely to happen if it is not to break the chain of causation[254] but if anything, this formulation probably understates the burden on the claimant and "there may be circumstances in which the court would require a degree of likelihood amounting almost to inevitability before it fixes the defendant with responsibility for the act of a third party over whom he had and can have no control".[255] In *Lamb v Camden LBC*[256] the defendants' negligence caused the claimant's house to be damaged and become unoccupied but they were not liable for the further damage done by the depredations of squatters, notwithstanding a finding by the Official Referee that squatting was "foreseeable". On the other hand, in *Ward v Cannock Chase DC* on similar facts, but where the defendants had been guilty of wilful delay in effecting repairs and where the risk of damage by vandals was rather higher, they were found liable for the further loss.[257] A possible consequence of all of this is, of course, that precisely the same physical act may or may not break the chain of causation depending on the mental state of the actor.[258]

Where defendant is under a duty to guard against intervener's wrongdoing   7-057
The above principles apply where there are no special circumstances imposing on the defendant a duty to take care to guard against the wrongdoing of the third party. If such a duty exists, it would of course be nonsensical to bar recovery on the ground that the damage was wilfully inflicted.[259] A driver who knocks down a pedestrian would not be liable for theft of the pedestrian's wallet while he was lying injured, but a bailee, who is under an assumed obligation (normally, but not necessarily, arising from a contract) to safeguard his bailor's goods, is just as much liable where, by his default, they are stolen by a burglar as he is where they are destroyed in a flood. In *Stansbie v Troman*[260] a decorator was at work in a house and left it for two hours to get wallpaper. He was alone and had been told by the householder to close the front door whenever he left the house. Instead of doing so he left the door unlocked and during his absence a thief entered the house and stole a diamond bracelet and some clothes. The Court of Appeal held that the decorator was liable for the loss. The case has subsequently been explained as resting on the fact that the decorator had implicitly assumed a duty of reasonable care to safeguard the property against such dangers.[261]

Intervening wilful conduct of the claimant   We have seen that the wilful conduct   7-058
of a third party is more likely to break the chain of causation than negligence on his part but that the defendant may be liable in respect of wilful acts the guarding against which is the very foundation of his duty. The position is the same in the case

---

[254] *Home Office v Dorset Yacht Co Ltd* [1970] A.C. 1004 at 1030 per Lord Reid. Note, however, that the majority of the House of Lords regarded this case as about duty, not causation.
[255] *Lamb v Camden LBC* [1981] Q.B. 625 at 647 per Oliver LJ. cf. *Alexis v Newham LBC* [2009] EWHC 1323 (QB); [2009] I.C.R. 1517 (prank by school child; but no breach).
[256] [1981] Q.B. 625.
[257] *Ward v Cannock Chase DC* [1986] Ch. 546. But the defendants were not liable for theft of the claimant's goods, perhaps because he could himself have taken steps to secure those.
[258] *Environment Agency v Empress Car Co Ltd* [1999] 2 A.C. 22 at 30. See also *Philco Radio and Television Corp of Great Britain v J Spurling Ltd* [1949] 2 All E.R. 882.
[259] This principle is not limited to wilful interventions: see, e.g., *Scott v Gavigan* [2016] EWCA Civ 544 at [34]–[35] (pedestrian running into road in front of car unlikely to break the chain of causation as driver's duty of care encompasses an obligation to guard against such behaviour).
[260] [1948] 2 K.B. 48. The defendant was not a bailee.
[261] *Smith v Littlewoods Organisation Ltd* [1987] A.C. 241 at 272; *Mitchell v Glasgow CC* [2009] UKHL 11; [2009] 1 A.C. 874.

of wilful conduct by the claimant. In *Reeves v Metropolitan Police Commissioner*[262] the claimant committed suicide while in police custody. The case was fought on the basis that he was sane at the time. A majority of the House of Lords held that, since the defendants had conceded that they owed the claimant a duty of care to prevent him inflicting harm on himself,[263] it would make no sense at the next step to go on to hold that his suicide broke the chain of causation.[264] There was, however, a reduction of damages for contributory negligence.[265] Another possibility is that the defendant injures the claimant and the latter, because of depression brought about by the accident, commits suicide. Can the defendant be liable for his death? An affirmative answer was given by the House of Lords in *Corr v IBC Vehicles Ltd*,[266] even though the deceased was not insane in the legal sense. Lord Bingham accepted that a voluntary, informed decision taken by the claimant as an adult of sound mind was likely to be characterised as an independent, supervening cause. But on the facts, the suicide of the deceased was not a decision of that kind; rather, it was the response of a man suffering from a severe mental illness which impaired his capacity to make reasoned and informed decisions about his future, such illness being a consequence of the defendant's tort.

5. REMOTENESS OF DAMAGE

7-059 **Introduction** It is important to note that the phrase "remoteness of damage" will sometimes be used in such a way as to encompass both legal causation and (what we are calling) remoteness. Furthermore, our American counterparts would traditionally have used the language of "proximate cause" to encompass both concepts. In the *Third Restatement of Torts*, the language of "proximate cause" was abandoned in favour of "scope of liability",[267] although the fact that old habits die hard compelled the use of "proximate cause" in parentheses after the new expression. Like proximate cause, the language of "scope of liability", which is now also the preferred terminology in Australia,[268] tends to be used to encapsulate both legal causation and remoteness.

The question of remoteness in the narrower sense usually revolves around whether the damage suffered by the claimant was a reasonably foreseeable consequence of the defendant's negligent conduct, though even in cases where this is true recovery may yet be denied on the ground that the damage fell outside the "scope of the risk" that conduct created, and the enquiry may also be influenced by policy considerations. The discussion that follows is largely limited to negligence: where the remoteness rules applicable in other torts are different from those herein described they are discussed in the chapters on those torts.

A. The Reasonable Foreseeability Test

7-060 **Two competing views** In the 100 years or so until the middle of the 20th century two competing views of the test for remoteness were current in the law. According

---

[262] [2000] 1 A.C. 360.
[263] See para.5-035.
[264] Nor was volenti applicable (para.26-018) or the claim contrary to public policy (para.26-064).
[265] See para.23-040.
[266] [2008] UKHL 13; [2008] A.C. 884. A similar answer had been given in *Pigney v Pointer's Transport Services* [1957] 1 W.L.R. 1121.
[267] *Restatement of Torts 3d: Liability for Physical and Emotional Harm* (2011), Ch.6.
[268] This is particularly apparent in the civil liability legislation: see, e.g., Civil Liability Act 2002 (NSW) s.5D.

to the first, consequences were too remote if a reasonable man would not have foreseen them;[269] according to the second, if a reasonable man would have foreseen any damage to the claimant as likely to result from his act, then he was liable for the direct consequences of it suffered by the claimant, whether foreseeable or not.

Re Polemis   In 1921, the Court of Appeal apparently settled English law in favour   **7-061**
of the second rule in *Re Polemis*.[270] A chartered vessel was unloading in Casablanca when stevedores, who were employees of the charterers, negligently let a plank drop into the hold. Part of the cargo was a quantity of benzine in tins, which had leaked, and a rush of flames at once followed, destroying the ship. The Court of Appeal held that the charterers were responsible for all the direct consequences of the stevedores' negligence, even though they could not reasonably have been anticipated. Scrutton LJ said that damage was indirect if it was "due to the operation of independent causes having no connection with the negligent act, except that they could not avoid its results".[271]

The Wagon Mound   In *The Wagon Mound*[272] the Privy Council expressed its   **7-062**
disapproval of *Re Polemis*. The defendants were demise charterers[273] of *The Wagon Mound*, an oil-burning vessel which was moored in Sydney Harbour for the purpose of taking on fuel oil. Owing to the carelessness of the defendants' employees a large quantity of fuel oil was spilt on to the water, and after a few hours this had spread to the claimants' wharf about 600 feet away where welding operations were being carried out on another ship, the *Corrimal*. Two days later the oil caught fire and extensive damage was done to the claimants' wharf. Findings of fact were made to the effect that it was unforeseeable that fuel oil spread on water would ignite,[274] so that the fire damage to the wharf had not been foreseeable, although some foreseeable damage had been done to the wharf as the oil had fouled the slipways. The Privy Council held that *Re Polemis* was no longer good law and that the defendants were not liable for the fire damage. According to Viscount Simonds[275]:

"It is the foresight of the reasonable man which alone can determine responsibility. The *Polemis* rule by substituting 'direct' for 'reasonably foreseeable' consequence leads to a conclusion equally illogical and unjust."

Scope and significance of the Wagon Mound test   Although *The Wagon Mound*   **7-063**
was a decision of the Privy Council, it was immediately accepted as stating the law in England. The essence of the decision was that in proceedings in negligence foreseeability was relevant not only for the purpose of asking whether a duty of care

---

[269] First propounded by Pollock CB in *Rigby v Hewitt* (1859) 5 Ex. 240 at 243; 155 E.R.103 at 104; *Greenland v Chaplin* (1850) 5 Ex. 243 at 248; 155 E.R. 104 at 106.

[270] [1921] 3 K.B. 560.

[271] *Re Polemis* [1921] 3 K.B. 560 at 577.

[272] [1961] A.C. 388.

[273] That is, they were in full possession of it with their own crew.

[274] In *Overseas Tankship (UK) Ltd v Miller Steamship Co Pty Ltd (The Wagon Mound) (No.2)* [1967] A.C 617, an action by the owners of the *Corrimal* for damage caused to their ship by the same fire, the Privy Council, on somewhat different evidence, held that the fire damage was foreseeable: see para.7-062.

[275] *The Wagon Mound* [1961] A.C. 388 at 424. See also at 422: "It does not seem consonant with current ideas of justice or morality that for an act of negligence, however slight or venial, which results in some trivial foreseeable damage the actor should be liable for all consequences however unforeseeable and however grave, so long as they can be said to be 'direct'."

was owed and whether the defendant breached that duty but also in relation to remoteness of damage. It might have been thought from this that the effect of *The Wagon Mound* was restricted to actions for negligence but in *The Wagon Mound (No.2)*[276] the Privy Council held that foreseeability was also the test for remoteness of damage in cases of nuisance.[277] As for the significance of the decision to replace the test of directness with one of foreseeability, it will be seen below that frequently this has made little difference to the law in terms of practical result and, indeed, Viscount Simonds indicated that this would probably have been so in the case itself.[278] However, *The Wagon Mound* undoubtedly produced a change of principle and its merits as compared with those of *Re Polemis* have been much debated.

7-064   **Neither the extent of the damage nor the precise manner of its infliction need be reasonably foreseeable**   The test of foreseeability was from the beginning heavily qualified by the fact that neither the extent of the damage nor the precise manner of its infliction need be foreseeable. As Lord Denning MR put it[279]:

> "It is not necessary that the precise concatenation of circumstances should be envisaged. If the consequence was one which was within the general range which any reasonable person might foresee (and was not of an entirely different kind which no one would anticipate) then it is within the rule that a person who has been guilty of negligence is liable for the consequences."

In *Hughes v Lord Advocate*[280] employees of the Post Office opened a manhole in the street and in the evening negligently left the open manhole covered by a canvas shelter, unattended and surrounded by warning paraffin lamps. The claimant, a boy aged eight, took one of the lamps into the shelter and was playing with it there when he stumbled over and it fell into the manhole. A violent explosion followed and the claimant himself fell into the hole, sustaining terrible injuries from the burns. It was quite unpredictable that a lamp might explode, but the employees should have appreciated that children might take a lamp into the shelter and that, if the lamp fell and broke, they might suffer serious injury from burning. So although the lamp caused injury through a particular sequence of events which may not have been envisaged, the defendants were nevertheless held liable. A similar case is *Jolley v Sutton LBC*,[281] where the defendants had failed to take steps to remove an old, abandoned boat from land of theirs to which the public had easy access. The obvious risk (indeed the defendants conceded the point) was that a child might suffer injury from climbing on the boat and falling through the rotten planking; in fact the claimant and a friend embarked on a futile project to restore the boat and, while the claimant was working underneath it, it fell on him, breaking his back. The House of Lords restored the decision for the claimant by the trial judge, who it held had been entitled to conclude that the accident which occurred was within the range of

---

[276] [1967] 1 A.C. 617.

[277] See para.15-037. It has since been held that the test of liability under the rule in *Rylands v Fletcher* is also whether the type of damage done was a reasonably foreseeable consequence of the escape of the thing: see para.16-025.

[278] *The Wagon Mound* [1961] A.C. 388 at 422.

[279] *Stewart v West African Terminals Ltd* [1964] 2 Lloyd's Rep. 371 at 375. See also *Bradford v Robinson Rentals Ltd* [1967] 1 W.L.R. 337 at 344–345.

[280] [1963] A.C. 837. cf. *Doughty v Turner Manufacturing Co Ltd* [1964] 1 Q.B. 518; *Hadlow v Peterborough City Council* [2011] EWCA Civ 1329.

[281] [2000] 1 W.L.R. 1082. Nolan (2001) 9 Tort L. Rev. 101.

what was foreseeable, given the ingenuity of children, "in finding unexpected ways of doing mischief to themselves and others".[282] It is also clear from the decisions in *Hughes* and *Jolley* that if the accident occurs in a foreseeable way, as broadly defined, the defendant will be liable even though the damage is much greater in extent than might have been anticipated.[283]

The same "kind" of damage   *The Wagon Mound* requires that the foreseeable   **7-065**
damage must be of the same "kind" as the damage which actually occurred. In point of fact even under *Re Polemis* it was probably necessary to distinguish between three very broad "kinds" of damage, namely injury to the person, damage to property and pure financial loss, but *The Wagon Mound* demands a more elaborate classification of "kinds" of damage than that, at least in so far as property damage is concerned: in the case itself a distinction was drawn between fouling damage (which was foreseeable) and fire damage (which was not). The difficulty is to know how narrowly the kind of damage in question in any given case must be defined and, unfortunately, only minimal guidance can be gleaned from the case law on this point. In *Tremain v Pike*[284] the rat population on the defendant's farm was allowed to become unduly large and, as a result, the claimant, a herdsman on the farm, contracted Weil's disease. Even on the assumption that the defendants had been negligent in failing to control the rat population,[285] Payne J held that the claimant could not succeed. Weil's disease is extremely rare and is caused by contact with rat urine, and in Payne J's opinion it was therefore both unforeseeable and "entirely different in kind" from such foreseeable consequences of the alleged negligence as a rat bite or food poisoning from contaminated food. The claimant could not simply say that rat-induced disease was foreseeable and rat-induced disease occurred. However, while *Tremain v Pike* seems to require a rather high degree of precision in classifying kinds of damage, there are not many personal injury cases since *The Wagon Mound* where the claim has failed on the basis of remoteness, and in practice a more broad-brush approach has tended to be taken in later decisions,[286] so much so that in *Page v Smith*[287] the House of Lords rather surprisingly held that physical injury and psychiatric illness were not different "kinds" of damage for remoteness

---

[282] *Jolley v Sutton LBC* [2000] 1 W.L.R. 1082 at 1093 per Lord Hoffmann. See similarly, *Lear v Hickstead Ltd* [2016] EWHC 528 (QB); [2016] 4 W.L.R. 73 at [56] per Picken J: "[W]hat matters is not exactly how an injury might be sustained, nor the extent of the injury which is sustained, but the fact that it would have been reasonably foreseeable that some injury would, or might, be suffered in the event that a horse box ramp had to be lifted or lowered."

[283] One of the few clear examples of this is *Vacwell Engineering v BDH Chemicals* [1971] 1 Q.B. 88 (minor explosion foreseeable; huge explosion took place because claimants put a number of ampoules in the same sink). See also *Bradford v Robinson Rentals Ltd* [1967] 1 W.L.R. 337 (exposure causing frostbite). Where the loss is economic, this is in practical terms indistinguishable from the principle discussed in para.7-067.

[284] [1969] 1 W.L.R. 1556; cf. *Malcolm v Broadhurst* [1970] 3 All E.R. 508.

[285] The defendant's negligence in this respect was not actually made out.

[286] See, e.g., *Royal Opera House Covent Garden Foundation v Goldscheider* [2019] EWCA Civ 711; [2019] P.I.Q.R. P15 at [46] (long-term and sudden hearing loss not different "kinds" of damage). Such an approach is also discernible with regard to property damage: see *The Carnival* [1994] 2 Lloyd's Rep. 14.

[287] [1996] A.C. 155.

of damage purposes,[288] thereby apparently emasculating the foreseeability requirement in the personal injury context.[289]

7-066   **The egg-shell skull principle**   The practical significance of *The Wagon Mound* in personal injury cases is also limited by the continued application of what is known as the "egg-shell skull rule".[290] The gist of this (much misunderstood) principle is that the requirement of reasonable foreseeability applies only to the claimant's initial injury, so that provided the initial injury was of a kind that was foreseeable, it is irrelevant that the consequences of that injury were of a different, unforeseeable, kind.[291] The operation of the rule is illustrated by *Smith v Leech Brain & Co Ltd*,[292] where the claimant suffered a burn on his lip as a result of the negligence of the defendant, and which, because of a pre-malignant condition, triggered a cancer that ended up causing the claimant's death. Since the initial burn had been a reasonably foreseeable consequence of the defendant's negligence, the defendant was liable for all the damage that flowed from it, even though the cancer had not itself been reasonably foreseeable.[293] The same (or a similar) principle operates when the claimant's injury is exacerbated by a combination of his abnormality and some external force which foreseeably and naturally intervenes after the accident, for example medical treatment to which he is allergic.[294]

Misconceptions bedevil discussion of the egg-shell skull rule, largely because it is frequently expressed by saying that the defendant must "take the claimant as he finds him", a catchy phrase which unfortunately is far from accurate. The most important mistake made about the rule is its extension to the claimant's initial injury, with the reasoning being that where the initial injury only occurred because of an unforeseeable pre-existing susceptibility of the claimant, it is not considered to be too remote.[295] This extension of the rule is no part of English law: where no damage at all could have been foreseen to a person of normal sensitivity and the C's abnormal sensitivity was unknown to D, then D is not liable. Indeed, taking too literally the mantra that the defendant must "take the claimant as he finds him"

---

[288] For criticism of this aspect of the decision, see Bailey and Nolan (2010) 69 C.L.J. 495, 519-526.

[289] Though in practice full effect has not been given to the ramifications of *Page v Smith*: see, e.g., *Pratley v Surrey CC* [2003] EWCA Civ 1067; [2004] I.C.R. 159 (employer aware of risk of injury to health from over-work but not of the sudden collapse which occurred as a result of disappointment at non-implementation of palliative measures; not enough to categorise the risk as "risk of psychiatric illness").

[290] If a person is "negligently run over or otherwise negligently injured in his body, it is no answer to the sufferer's claim for damages that he would have suffered less injury ... if he had not had an unusually thin skull or an unusually weak heart": *Dulieu v White* [1901] 2 K.B. 669 at 679 per Kennedy J.

[291] The egg-shell skull rule is not needed in cases where it is only the *extent* of those consequences which is unforeseeable, as the extent of the injury need not be foreseeable applying a recognised gloss on the *Wagon Mound* rule: see para.7-064.

[292] [1962] 2 Q.B. 405. See also *Warren v Scruttons* [1962] 1 Lloyd's Rep. 497; *Lines v Harland and Wolff* [1966] 1 Lloyd's Rep. 400; *Boon v Thomas Hubback* [1967] 1 Lloyd's Rep. 281; *Wieland v Cyril Lord Carpets Ltd* [1969] 3 All E.R. 100.

[293] The claimant's weakness cuts both ways, however: his damages are likely to be less than those of a "normal" person suffering the same overall injury in order to reflect the greater risk to which he was exposed by the normal vicissitudes of life. In Canada, this is apparently known as the "crumbling skull" doctrine: *Athey v Leonati* (1996) 140 D.L.R. (4th) 235. The damages in *Page v Smith* [1996] A.C. 155 were reduced by some 40 per cent on account of this consideration.

[294] *Robinson v Post Office* [1974] 1 W.L.R. 1176. As to whether negligent treatment amounts to a novus actus interveniens, see para.7-052.

[295] See, e.g., *Page v Smith* [1996] A.C. 155 at 189; cf. *White v Chief Constable of the South Yorkshire Police* [1999] 2 A.C. 455 at 476.

would undermine not only the *Wagon Mound* remoteness principle but also the principles governing the "duty to the claimant" question and the question of fault—for if D cannot reasonably foresee any injury to C from D's actions, how can D either owe C a duty of care or be in breach of it?

Whether the egg-shell skull rule continues to have any practical effect depends on whether the courts take seriously the holding in *Page v Smith*[296] that personal injury is now an indivisible concept as far as the *Wagon Mound* foreseeability requirement is concerned, for if that is so then there is no longer any scope for the application of the rule, which rests on the assumption that for these purposes there are different "kinds" of personal injury.

Pecuniary amount of the damage Because the requirement of foreseeability is limited to the kind of damage, rather than its extent, if the defendant injures a high income earner or a piece of property with a high intrinsic value (such as an antique vase) he cannot argue that he had no reason to expect the amount of the loss to be so great.[297] The law is not, however, so clearly committed to this stand where the loss claimed is not "intrinsic" but arises from the fact that the damage to the claimant's goods renders him unable to earn profits with them.[298] Support can be found in the cases for the view that foreseeability is irrelevant,[299] but the better view is that where the loss is not "intrinsic" the defendant's liability is limited to "ordinary" or "foreseeable" losses.[300] The recoverability of such loss cannot be pre-determined by prior contractual arrangements made between the claimant and third parties who are affected by the damage done to the claimant's property.[301]

7-067

B. Impecuniosity of the Claimant

The Liesbosch decision: no liability for loss due to claimant's lack of means In *Liesbosch Dredger v Edison SS*[302] the claimant's dredger had been sunk as a result of the defendant's negligence. Because the claimant could not afford to purchase a substitute, he incurred extra expense in hiring one in order to complete his contracts. The House of Lords held that he could not recover that extra expense, which was

7-068

---

[296] [1996] A.C. 155. See also *Margereson v JW Roberts Ltd* [1996] P.I.Q.R. P154 (on appeal [1996] P.I.Q.R. P358).

[297] The point is perhaps so obvious that the only express authority for it appears to be a dictum of Scrutton LJ in *The Arpad* [1934] P. 189 at 202, although that case had nothing to do with negligence and the judgment was a dissenting one.

[298] The case of a claimant who is disabled from performing particular contracts (e.g., a musician) is perhaps analogous: see *The Arpad* [1934] P. 189 at 221.

[299] *The Star of India* (1876) 1 P.D. 466; *Liesbosch Dredger v SS Edison* [1933] A.C. 449 at 463–464 ("The measure of damages is the value of the ship to her owner as a going concern at the time and place of the loss. In assessing that value regard must naturally be had to her pending engagements, either profitable or the reverse"). This case is, of course, best known on the different point relating to the claimant's impecuniosity, para.7-068.

[300] *The Argentino* (1899) 14 App. Cas. 519 at 523; *The Arpad* [1934] P. 189; *The Daressa* [1971] 1 Lloyd's Rep. 60.

[301] *Conarken Group Ltd v Network Rail Infrastructure Ltd* [2011] EWCA Civ 644; 136 Con L.R. 1 (where the negligence of D caused damage to the rail network operated by C, C's losses included the sums it was contractually required to pay to train operating companies (T). Whether C was entitled to recover those sums from D was to be determined by ordinary principles of remoteness and mitigation, i.e. it did not follow automatically from C's obligation under contract to pay T. However, the losses in question were reasonably foreseeable and the sums payable under the C-T contracts were reasonable. They were therefore recoverable).

[302] [1933] A.C. 448.

an extraneous matter and too remote. The then leading case of *Re Polemis* was distinguished on the ground that it was concerned with the "immediate physical consequences of the negligent act".[303] It was never very clear why a distinction was drawn between the claimant's physical weakness, in which context the defendant took his victim as he found him, and his financial weakness.[304] Indeed, from a different point of view the defendant *did* take the claimant's financial position as he found it, for the claimant was always entitled to base his claim for lost earnings upon his pre-accident income, not some sort of national average.

7-069   **Lagden v O'Connor: no bar to recovery of loss due to claimant's lack of means**   The decision in the *Liesbosch* case was heavily criticised and frequently distinguished, and the House of Lords finally departed from it in *Lagden v O'Connor*.[305] The claimant's car was damaged by the defendant's negligence. On normal principles the claimant was entitled to the costs of repairs and the hire of a substitute vehicle while those were done.[306] However, being unable to afford the outlay on the hire of a car in the ordinary way, the claimant had contracted with a credit hire company, on terms that the company would take over the prosecution of his claim, he would receive a hire car on credit while his was repaired and the charges would be paid out of the damages recovered from the defendant. Due to the cost of handling the claim and the element of risk the charge for hire was about 30 per cent more than the standard "spot rate" for car hire in that area. The House of Lords unanimously held that there should no longer be any hard and fast rule that additional losses attributable to the claimant's impecuniosity were irrecoverable. However, the House was divided on whether the particular claim should succeed. For the majority this was a case where the defendant had failed to show that the claimant had behaved unreasonably in using the credit hire company. His financial position was such that he had no choice but to do so if he wished to obtain a car. That would not necessarily be so in other cases where the claimant had greater resources. The effect therefore is that a rule which was mechanical and "efficient" in terms of the disposition of claims is replaced with a test that is somewhat open-ended and therefore more likely to be productive of dispute. While the majority recognised this risk, they thought it exaggerated because it would be in the interests of motor insurers to keep down the costs of small claims.

7-070   **A question of remoteness, or of mitigation?**   In *Lagden v O'Connor* the majority of opinions were couched, as was *The Liesbosch*, mainly in terms of remoteness, but the placing of the burden on the defendant to show that the claimant had a realistic choice between taking an ordinary hire car and using credit hire matches the approach to mitigation,[307] and subsequent decisions have regarded it as a question of mitigation.[308]

---

[303]   [1933] A.C. 448 at 461.

[304]   The rule may have had some connection with the former rule that damages were not recoverable for non-payment of money, but this is no longer the law: *Sempra Metals Ltd v Commissioners of Inland Revenue* [2007] UKHL 34; [2008] 1 A.C. 561.

[305]   *Lagden v O'Connor* [2003] UKHL 64; [2004] 1 A.C. 1067.

[306]   *Bee v Jenson* [2007] EWCA Civ 923; [2007] 4 All E.R. 791.

[307]   The claimant must show that the damage is not too remote; the defendant must show that the claimant failed to take reasonable steps in mitigation: *Geest Plc v Lansiquot* [2002] UKPC 48; [2002] 1 W.L.R. 3111.

[308]   For Lord Walker in *Lagden* (at [101]) it was not a question of mitigation at all in that the hire was

C. Scope of the Risk

The risk principle[309] Although the starting point when considering remoteness   **7-071**
in negligence is that a defendant is not liable for a consequence of a kind which is
not reasonably foreseeable, "it does not follow that he is liable for all damage" that
was.[310] In particular, even a foreseeable consequence may be too remote if it is not
within the scope of the risk created by the defendant's negligence[311]:

> "[T]he scope of liability in negligence normally does not extend beyond liability for the
> occurrence of such harm the risk of which it was the duty of the negligent party to exercise
> reasonable care and skill to avoid."

The broader principle in play here is that liability in tort is generally limited to those
consequences, factually caused by the defendant and not otherwise too remote,
which are attributable to that which made the conduct complained of wrongful.[312]
This principle is most obvious in the tort of breach of statutory duty, so that, for
example, where a shipowner was under a statutory duty to provide pens for
livestock on his ship, he was not liable when the claimant's sheep were swept
overboard for lack of such pens, because the statutory purpose was prevention of
the spread of disease, not protection against perils of the sea.[313] However, the same
principle is applicable in common law negligence as well. Take Lord Hoffmann's
example[314] of a doctor negligently advising a mountaineer as to the fitness of his
knee. If the mountaineer were to be injured on an expedition because his knee gave
way, the doctor might be liable; but if the mountaineer were injured by a risk of
mountaineering unconnected with his knee (for example, being hit by a rock fall)
the doctor would not be liable for that since, although foreseeable, it is not within
the risk created by the doctor's negligence.[315]

Intervening natural events As the mountaineer example demonstrates, the   **7-072**
operation of the "scope of the risk" idea can best be illustrated by cases where the
claimant suffers damage as the immediate result of a natural event which occurs
independently of the defendant's breach of duty but which would have caused the
claimant no damage if the breach of duty had not occurred. In such a case, if the

---

not incurred in mitigating some greater loss. See also Lord Hobhouse in *Dimond v Lovell* [2002] 1
A.C. 384 at 406. On mitigation of damage, see Ch.23.
[309] Williams (1961) 77 L.Q.R. 179; Stauch (2001) 64 M.L.R. 191.
[310] *British Steel Plc v Simmons* [2004] UKHL 20; [2004] I.C.R. 585 at [67] per Lord Rodger.
[311] *Wallace v Kam* [2013] HCA 19; (2013) 250 C.L.R. 375 at [24].
[312] See *Hughes-Holland v BPE Solicitors* [2017] UKSC 21; [2018] A.C. 599 at [38]. See also *Restatement of Torts 3d: Liability for Physical and Emotional Harm* (2011) §29.
[313] *Gorris v Scott* (1874) L.R. 9 Exch. 125, para.8-017. This has obvious affinities with the notion of
the "protective purpose of the norm" which is found in Austrian and German law. See van Gerven,
Lever and Larouche, *Tort Law and Scope of Protection: Cases, Materials and Text (Casebooks for
the Common Law of Europe)* (1998), Ch.4.1.1.
[314] *Banque Bruxelles Lambert SA v Eagle Star Insurance Co Ltd* [1997] A.C. 191 at 213. "[O]ne of the
most celebrated legal parables of modern times": *Hughes-Holland v BPE Solicitors* [2017] UKSC
21; [2018] A.C. 599 at [1] per Lord Sumption.
[315] For an actual (as opposed to fictional) application of the principle in the medical negligence context,
see *Meadows v Khan* [2019] EWCA Civ 152; [2019] 4 W.L.R. 26 (doctor negligently failed to refer
patient for test to establish whether she was carrying the haemophilia gene; had he done so she would
have realised she was carrying the gene, and not had a child; when she subsequently had a child who
was diagnosed with both haemophilia and autism—the two conditions being unrelated—the doctor
was liable only for the loss associated with the haemophilia, and not for the loss associated with the
autism).

breach of duty has neither increased the likelihood that the claimant will suffer damage nor rendered him more susceptible to damage, the defendant will not be liable.[316] In *Carslogie Steamship Co Ltd v Royal Norwegian Government*[317] the claimant's ship was damaged in a collision for which the defendant was to blame. After temporary repairs which restored the ship to a seaworthy condition she set out on a voyage to the United States, a voyage which she would not have made had the collision not occurred. During her crossing of the Atlantic she suffered extensive damage due to heavy weather. The House of Lords held that the defendant was not liable for the heavy weather damage. It was true that if the collision had not taken place the storm damage also would not have occurred, but such damage was merely coincidental, as not within the risks created by the defendant's negligence.[318]

7-073   **SAAMCO**   The example of the mountaineer's knee was given in *Banque Bruxelles Lambert SA v Eagle Star Insurance Co Ltd* (or *SAAMCO*),[319] where the issue was whether a valuer who had negligently overvalued a property on which a lender advanced mortgage monies was liable for all of the losses suffered by the lender under the loan, including those caused by a precipitous fall in the property market. The lender would not have entered into the transaction if the valuation had been undertaken with reasonable care, and it could hardly be denied that falls in markets are foreseeable as a general rule.[320] However, the House of Lords held that where information had been provided to enable the claimant to decide on a course of action, the extent of negligence liability[321] was not to be determined by asking what position the claimant would have been in if the correct information had been given (the claimant would not have entered into the transaction). Rather, the extent of negligence liability was to be ascertained by reference to the consequence of the information being inaccurate (the claimant entered into the transaction with less security than he had been looking for). It was the risk of the claimant lending the money without adequate security that made the valuation negligent, not the risks associated with entering the transaction as a whole.[322]

The result of the *SAAMCO* decision is that the lender is prima facie entitled to

---

[316] "In law as in everyday life A's wrongful act is not normally regarded as having caused B's injury if the act made no difference to the probability of the injury occurring. In such a case the fact that injury would not have occurred but for the wrongful act is merely a coincidence": *Duce v Worcestershire Acute Hospitals NHS Trust* [2018] EWCA Civ 1307; [2018] P.I.Q.R. P18 at [84] per Leggatt LJ.

[317] [1952] A.C. 292.

[318] Distinguish the situation where the vessel is rendered less able to ride out the storm because of the damage inflicted on it by the defendant.

[319] *Banque Bruxelles Lambert SA v Eagle Star Insurance Co Ltd* [1997] A.C. 191. See also *Nykredit Mortgage Bank Plc v Edward Erdman Group Ltd (No.2)* [1997] 1 W.L.R. 1627; cf. *Kenny & Good Pty Ltd v MGICA (1992) Ltd* (1999) 199 C.L.R 413; Peel in Burrows and Peel (eds), *Commercial Remedies: Current Issues and Problems* (2003).

[320] In *John Grimes Partnership Ltd v Gubbins* [2013] EWCA Civ 37; 146 Con L.R. 26 an engineer (D) failed, in breach of contract, to do the work required of him by the agreed date with the result that a development was delayed during which time it declined in market value. Such loss was easily foreseen at the time of the contract and there was nothing to suggest that this was not a type of loss for which D assumed responsibility; he was therefore held liable.

[321] The position is different if the defendant is guilty of fraud, where he is liable for all losses flowing from the fraudulently induced transaction: *Smith New Court Securities Ltd v Scrimgeour Vickers (Asset Management) Ltd* [1997] A.C. 254 at 283. Indeed, in deceit the defendant is liable even for unforeseeable consequences.

[322] cf. *Haugesund Kommune v Depfa ACS Bank* [2011] EWCA Civ 33; [2011] 3 All E.R. 655 (D advised C that Norwegian municipalities had capacity to enter into swaps with C, but also advised that any claim against the municipalities could not be enforced. D's advice about capacity was negligent and

the whole of the loss flowing from his entry into the loan transaction, except for loss he would still have suffered had the valuation been accurate.[323] Suppose, for example, that property is valued at £500,000 when a true valuation would have been £400,000. When, on default, the property is sold, it realises only £200,000 because of a general fall in the market. The lender's loss is £300,000 but the valuer's liability is only £100,000 because the balance of £200,000 is the loss which the claimant would have suffered even if the valuation had been conducted with reasonable care.[324] Although what has come to be known as the "*SAAMCO* cap" has not proven universally popular,[325] it is in conformity with the "scope of the risk" principle and was recently reaffirmed in robust terms by the Supreme Court in *Hughes-Holland v BPE Solicitors*.[326]

"Information", or "advice"? *SAAMCO* was concerned with an obligation to provide information on the basis of which the claimant could take a decision. The position is different where the defendant undertakes to give general advice on the wisdom of entering into a transaction, for he will then be liable for all the foreseeable consequences of it.[327] In *Aneco Reinsurance Underwriting Ltd v Johnson & Higgins Ltd*[328] the defendant brokers, acting on behalf of the claimant reinsurers, negligently failed to disclose certain facts on a proposal for further reinsurance (or retrocession) of a US$10 million portion of a risk to be carried by the claimants. This meant that the retrocessionaires, who would have refused cover had they known the full facts, lawfully repudiated the claim. The claimants lost US$35 million on the risk as a whole. The majority of the House of Lords held that the brokers were liable for the full amount. Had the brokers carried out their duty properly they would have become aware that cover was not obtainable in the market on commercially sensible terms and the claimants would therefore have declined the main risk and suffered no loss at all. In the view of the majority the duty of the brokers was not merely to seek to obtain valid cover of US$10 million and report on having done so, but to advise on the market's estimation of the risk. For Lord Millett, dissenting, it was not enough that the brokers might have volunteered their estimation of the state of the market; the relevant question was whether such an estimation was within the scope of the duty they had undertaken and he thought that it was not.

The courts have not found it easy to draw the distinction between "information" and "advice",[329] and in *Hughes-Holland v BPE Solicitors*, Lord Sumption acknowledged the "descriptive inadequacy" of these labels, neither of which, he

7-074

---

wrong. C had a claim in restitution against the municipalities which was only part satisfied. C could not recover the balance from D. C's loss flowed either from the impecuniosity of the municipalities or the inability to pursue a claim: the credit risk was for C and did not fall within the scope of D's duty; and the enforcement risk fell within the scope of a duty which had not been breached, since D had advised correctly about the enforcement risk). See also *Capita Alternative Fund Services Ltd v Drivers Jonas* [2011] EWHC 2336 (Comm); 139 Con. L.R. 125; *Torre Asset Funding Ltd v Royal Bank of Scotland Plc* [2013] EWHC 2670 (Ch).

[323] *Hughes-Holland v BPE Solicitors* [2017] UKSC 21; [2018] A.C. 599 at [31].
[324] *Nykredit Mortgage Bank Plc v Edward Erdman Group Ltd (No.2)* [1997] 1 W.L.R. 1627 at 1631 per Lord Nicholls.
[325] See, e.g., the criticisms levelled at it by Stapleton (1997) 113 L.Q.R. 1.
[326] [2017] UKSC 21; [2018] A.C. 599.
[327] *Banque Bruxelles Lambert SA v Eagle Star Insurance Co Ltd* [1997] A.C. 191 at 214.
[328] [2001] UKHL 51; [2002] 1 Lloyd's Rep. 157.
[329] The cases are numerous, but in addition to those already cited in this part, see, e.g., *Harrison v Bloom Camillin* [2000] 1 Lloyd's Rep. P.N. 89 (Ch); *Intervention Board for Agricultural Produce v Leidig*

said, really corresponded "to the contents of the bottle".[330] The true nature of the distinction was said to be as follows[331]:

> "In ['advice' cases], it is left to the adviser to consider what matters should be taken into account in deciding whether to enter into the transaction. His duty is to consider all relevant matters and not only specific factors in the decision … By comparison, in ['information' cases] a professional adviser contributes a limited part of the material on which his client will rely in deciding whether to enter into a prospective transaction, but the process of identifying the other relevant considerations and the overall assessment of the commercial merits of the transaction are exclusively matters for the client (or possibly his other advisers)."

Furthermore, "the fact that the material contributed by the defendant is known to be critical to the claimant's decision" whether to enter into the transaction does not itself make it an "advice" case.[332] Finally, while Lord Sumption said that in all but the most clear-cut instances the appropriate characterisation of the case was "likely to depend on the range of matters for which the defendant assumed responsibility",[333] the Court of Appeal has since held that a judge should frame the enquiry in terms of whether the case is one of advice or information, rather than asking an open-ended question as to the extent of the responsibility assumed.[334]

D.   Special Rules

7-075   **Intended consequences**   Intended consequences are never too remote: "The intention to injure the plaintiff … disposes of any question of remoteness of damage."[335] However, the liability of an intentional wrongdoer is not limited to the intended consequences and will extend at least to such results as are foreseeable. *Scott v Shepherd*[336] is a well-known example. D threw a squib into a crowd. A, in alarm, threw it away and B did likewise. The squib ended its journey by falling upon C, exploding and putting out his eye. D certainly intended to scare somebody or other. With equal certainty he did not, in common parlance, "intend" to hurt C, much less to destroy his eye, but he was nevertheless held liable to C. The law insists that fools and mischievous persons must answer for consequences which common sense would unhesitatingly attribute to their wrongdoing.[337] Indeed, the intentional wrongdoer's liability may extend beyond the foreseeable because intentional torts have not necessarily been affected by *The Wagon Mound*. A fraudster is liable for unforeseeable consequences[338] and an intentional departure from the terms of a bailment may make the bailee subject to the liability of an insurer.

[2000] Lloyd's Rep. P.N. 144; *Lloyds Bank Plc v Crosse & Crosse* [2001] EWCA Civ 366; [2001] P.N.L.R. 830; *Petersen v Rivlin* [2002] EWCA Civ 194; [2002] Lloyd's Rep. P.N. 386.

[330] [2017] UKSC 21; [2018] A.C. 599 at [39].

[331] [2017] UKSC 21; [2018] A.C. 599 at [40]–[41].

[332] [2017] UKSC 21; [2018] A.C. 599 at [42]. See also *Haugesund Kommune v Depfa ACS Bank* [2011] EWCA Civ 33; [2011] 3 All E.R. 655 at [75].

[333] [2017] UKSC 21; [2018] A.C. 599 at [44].

[334] *Manchester Building Society v Grant Thornton UK LLP* [2019] EWCA Civ 40; [2019] 1 W.L.R. 4610. On the facts, it was held that the case was not one of "advice" because the defendant had not been responsible for guiding the whole decision-making process.

[335] *Quinn v Leatham* [1901] A.C. 495 at 537 per Lord Lindley.

[336] (1773) 2 Wm. Bl. 892; 96 E.R. 525.

[337] See para.3-004.

[338] See para.12-021.

Concurrent liability in contract for economic loss[339]   In the professional   **7-076**
negligence context contract and tort are essentially interchangeable. But while a
claimant may be able to gain certain advantages by framing his action in tort (such
as the benefit of a different limitation period[340]), in a case of concurrent liability he
will not thereby be able to avoid the stricter remoteness rules governing claims for
breach of contract. Earlier authorities to this effect[341] were confirmed in *Wellesley
Partners LLP v Withers LLP*.[342] According to Floyd LJ, where there are parallel
contractual and tortious duties of care, the test for recoverability of economic loss
is the same, and should be the contractual one. The basis for the formulation of the
contractual remoteness test (based on the "reasonable contemplation" of the parties when they entered into the contract) was "that the parties have the opportunity
to draw special circumstances to each other's attention" at the time of contract
formation, and that they are assumed to be contracting on the basis that "liability
will be confined to damage of the kind which is in their reasonable
contemplation".[343] It would make no sense for the existence of the concurrent tortious duty to upset that consensus, particularly given that it arose out of the same
assumption of responsibility as existed under the contract. Roth J agreed, and
inclined to the view that the contract remoteness rules should also apply in cases
where liability for negligent advice or professional services arose only in tort, there
being no parallel contractual obligation. There is certainly much to be said for that
view. After all, if the rationale for the narrower contract rule is the possibility of the
parties communicating special circumstances to each other at the time of contract
formation, then that rationale would seem to extend to a standalone tortious duty
of care arising out of a prior relationship between the parties, at least where the same
opportunity to communicate special circumstances existed at the time of the
defendant's assumption of responsibility towards the claimant.

Chester v Afshar[344]   Particularly difficult remoteness issues may arise in cases of   **7-077**
medical non-disclosure. A doctor owes a patient a duty to inform him of certain
risks attached to treatment[345] and if he breaches this duty and the patient can
establish that he would not have consented to the treatment but for this breach then
the doctor is liable for adverse consequences of the treatment, even though it was
carried out with reasonable care.[346] In *Chester v Afshar*[347] the defendant negligently
failed to warn the claimant of a 1–2 per cent unavoidable risk of paralysis in surgery
on her spinal column and this eventuated. Had the claimant been properly warned
the operation would not have taken place when it did since the claimant would have
sought another medical opinion, although she could not establish on the balance of
probabilities that she would not have submitted to the surgery at a later date. The
fact that the surgery would have been delayed if the risk had been disclosed meant
that the "but for" test of factual causation was satisfied (since the risk of paralysis

---

339 Burrows in Burrows and Peel (eds), *Commercial Remedies* (2003).
340 See, e.g., *Henderson v Merrett Syndicates Ltd* [1995] 2 A.C. 145, para.12-032.
341 See, e.g., *Rubenstein v HSBC Bank Plc* [2012] EWCA Civ 1184; [2013] P.N.L.R. 9.
342 [2015] EWCA Civ 1146; [2016] Ch. 529.
343 [2015] EWCA Civ 1146; [2016] Ch. 529 at [80]. See also at [68], [151], [157], [186]–[187].
344 Clark and Nolan (2014) 34 O.J.L.S. 659.
345 See para.26-011.
346 *Chatterton v Gerson* [1981] Q.B. 432.
347 [2004] UKHL 41; [2005] 1 A.C. 345. See also *Chappel v Hart* (1998) 195 C.L.R. 232.

in the later operation would still have been only 1–2 per cent).[348] However, applying orthodox remoteness principles,[349] since the policy underlying the duty to warn is "to protect the patient from the occurrence of physical injury the risk of which is unacceptable to the patient",[350] it seemed to follow that liability should be limited to injury of that kind.[351] Nevertheless, the majority of the House of Lords found in the claimant's favour, holding that it was necessary to modify the standard principles, albeit in a "narrow and modest"[352] way, in order to vindicate the claimant's autonomy interest and to recognise her freedom to make an informed choice over the treatment she was to receive. But if the infringement of the claimant's autonomy was the gist of the wrong, then there is much force in the suggestion of Lord Hoffmann, in the minority, that the appropriate award was a solatium to reflect the loss of autonomy, not damages for the paralysis.[353] The decision in *Chester* is unquestionably controversial, and it has been said that the matters with which it deals "may be thought ripe for further consideration by the Supreme Court when the opportunity arises".[354]

7-078 **Policy considerations** Sometimes policy comes to the surface and a loss is dismissed as too remote simply because the court does not think it reasonable or desirable to impose it on the defendant. Thus in *Pritchard v JH Cobden Ltd*,[355] it was held that where the claimant's marriage broke up as a result of wrongfully inflicted injuries, orders for financial provision made against him by the divorce court could not be the subject of a claim against the tortfeasor: quite apart from the point that redistribution of assets on divorce could not be regarded as a "loss", acceptance of such claims would risk confusion in the judicial process and be open to abuse.

---

[348] See *Wallace v Kam* [2013] HCA 19; (2013) 250 C.L.R. 375 at [20]. It follows that, "if a claimant is to rely on the exceptional principle of causation established by *Chester v Afshar*" it is necessary to plead that, if warned, the patient would have deferred the operation, and to support this by evidence: *Correia v University Hospital of North Staffordshire NHS Trust* [2017] EWCA Civ 356; [2017] E.C.C. 37 at [28] per Simon LJ. If this cannot be shown, the claim fails, as in *Duce v Worcestershire Acute Hospitals NHS Trust* [2018] EWCA Civ 1307; [2018] P.I.Q.R. P18.

[349] See para.7-059.

[350] *Wallace v Kam* [2013] HCA 19; (2013) 250 C.L.R. 375 at [36].

[351] See also *Duce v Worcestershire Acute Hospitals NHS Trust* [2018] EWCA Civ 1307; [2018] P.I.Q.R. P18 at [84] per Leggatt LJ: "The decision in *Chester* is ... problematic because on the facts ... the surgeon's failure to warn did not expose the claimant to a risk which she would not willingly have accepted."

[352] *Chester v Afshar* [2004] UKHL 41; [2005] 1 A.C. 345 at [24] per Lord Steyn.

[353] See also Leggatt LJ's criticism of this justification in *Duce v Worcestershire Acute Hospitals NHS Trust* [2018] EWCA Civ 1307; [2018] P.I.Q.R. P18 at [88].

[354] *Duce v Worcestershire Acute Hospitals NHS Trust* [2018] EWCA Civ 1307; [2018] P.I.Q.R. P18 at [92] per Leggatt LJ.

[355] [1988] Fam. 22.

CHAPTER 8

BREACH OF STATUTORY DUTY AND MISFEASANCE IN A PUBLIC OFFICE

TABLE OF CONTENTS

1.   BREACH OF STATUTORY DUTY

A.   Nature of the Action

The first part of this chapter is not concerned with statutes which have as their   **8-001**
principal objective the imposition of tort liability,[1] nor with the circumstances in
which the courts may regard to a statutory requirement or standard in deciding whether the defendant's conduct amounts to negligence.[2] It is instead concerned
with the circumstances in which a court will conclude that a statute which is primarily regulatory or criminal in its purpose should be treated as giving rise to a civil
action for damages at the suit of a person who is injured as a result of non-
compliance with it.[3] Although in such cases, the cause of action is founded on the
statute in question, it is nevertheless a common law claim, created by the courts.[4]
The question of whether the courts will recognise such a claim is conventionally
understood to be one of interpretation of the particular statute, though some scepticism has been expressed about this understanding, on the ground that it understates
the role of the courts in cases where the legislation is silent on the issue.[5]

Liability for breach of EU law   Earlier editions of this work included in this   **8-002**
chapter an overview of the principle of member state liability for breach of EU law,[6]
a liability treated by the English courts as in the nature of—or at least closely

---

[1]   For example, the Occupiers' Liability Act 1957 (Ch.10) and the Consumer Protection Act 1987 Pt.
      I (Ch.11).
[2]   See para.6-030.
[3]   Stanton et al, *Statutory Torts* (2003); Williams (1960) 23 M.L.R. 233; Buckley (1984) 100 L.Q.R.
      204; Stanton (2004) 120 L.Q.R. 324; Foster (2011) 33 Syd. L.R. 67.
[4]   *Campbell v Peter Gordon Joiners Ltd* [2016] UKSC 38; [2016] A.C. 1513 at [35].
[5]   *Campbell v Peter Gordon Joiners Ltd* [2016] UKSC 38; [2016] A.C. 1513 at [35].
[6]   The seminal ECJ authority is *Francovich v Italy* (C-6/90) [1995] I.C.R. 722.

analogous to—a breach of statutory duty.[7] However in the light of the UK's exit from the European Union on 31 January 2020, the relevant text has been removed from this edition, and reference should instead be made to comprehensive discussions elsewhere.[8]

8-003   **A tort independent of negligence**   Before examining the approach of the courts to the question of interpretation at the heart of the tort of breach of statutory duty, something should be said about the nature of the action itself. In terms of numbers of claims, the most important area of operation of the tort has been that concerned with work injuries[9] and there is, of course, no doubt that an employer owes his employee a duty of care for the purposes of the tort of negligence.[10] The English view is that liability for breach of statutory duty is a wholly separate tort superimposed on this, but this is not the approach of all common law countries. In the majority of jurisdictions in the United States, breach of a statute is "negligence per se" and this is tantamount to saying that the statute "concretises" the common law duty by putting beyond controversy the question whether in the circumstances reasonable care required that a particular precaution be taken. Other American states adopt the view that the statutory standard is compelling evidence of what reasonable care demands but in the last resort does not bind the court, a view also taken in Canada.[11] There are attractions in these views where a common law duty already exists, for they relieve the court of the task of searching for a legislative intention on civil liability. But where there is no common law duty it would amount to rejecting statutes as a source of civil liability, a view which is inconsistent with English law as it stands. In any event, even where there is a common law duty, the overwhelming weight of authority is to the effect that the action for breach of statutory duty is a separate tort. As Lord Wright put it in *London Passenger Transport Board v Upson*[12]:

> "A claim for damages for breach of a statutory duty intended to protect a person in the position of the particular plaintiff is a specific common law right which is not to be confused in essence with a claim for negligence ... I have desired before I deal specifically with the regulations to make it clear how in my judgment they should be approached, and also to make it clear that a claim for their breach may stand or fall independently of negligence. There is always a danger if the claim is not sufficiently specific that the due consideration of the claim for breach of statutory duty may be prejudiced if it is confused with the claim in negligence."

Thus, where the statute imposes strict liability it is possible for the defendant to be acquitted of negligence but still held liable for breach of the statute. Conversely, the defendant may have fulfilled his statutory duty but nevertheless be liable for negligence because the statute is not inconsistent with a common law duty broader in extent.

---

[7]   *R. v Secretary of State Ex p. Factortame Ltd (No.7)* [2001] 1 W.L.R. 942.

[8]   See Stanton et al, *Statutory Torts* (2003) Ch.6; Giliker, *The Europeanisation of English Tort Law* (2014) Ch.4.

[9]   Much of the statute law in this area has undergone radical amendment (para.9-007) but the proposition in the text remains true. Quaere the effect hereafter of the change made to the Health and Safety at Work etc. Act 1974 s.47(2): see para.8-006.

[10]   See Ch.9.

[11]   *R. v Saskatchewan Wheat Pool* (1983) 1 S.C.R. 205.

[12]   [1949] A.C. 155 at 168–169.

Relationship with negligence   In the modern law many claims for breach of statu-   **8-004**
tory duty have been advanced on the basis of legislation concerned with child
protection, education and other matters of social welfare. These actions have generally failed on the ground that the nature of the legislation did not support the inference of a Parliamentary intention to confer a civil right of action.[13] It may also be
the case that the circumstances are such that no common law duty of care will arise
either, in which case there is no liability at all.[14] However, it is wrong to assume that
because a statute in the area in question does not give rise to civil liability it
therefore also excludes a common law duty: the two questions are entirely
separate.[15] Any common law duty must be sought in the general principles of the
law of negligence, not in the non-actionable statute.[16] Equally, it does not follow
from the fact that a breach of a statute is actionable that it gives rise to a coexistent common law duty of care.[17]

B.   Existence of Liability

Establishing the intention of Parliament   Whether a private right of action in tort   **8-005**
is available to someone who is injured by the breach of a statutory duty depends
upon the intention of Parliament in imposing the duty in question. When Parliament has clearly stated its intention one way or the other no difficulty arises,[18] but
this is rarely the case. Until the 19th century the view seems to have been taken that
whenever a statutory duty is created, any person who can show that he has sustained
harm from its non-performance can bring an action against the person on whom the
duty is imposed.[19] During the first half of that century, however, a different view
began to be taken, and in *Atkinson v Newcastle Waterworks Co*[20] the Court of Appeal's doubts about the old rule were so strong as to amount to disapproval of it.
With the vast increase in legislative activity, the old rule was perceived to carry the
risk of liability wider than the legislature could have contemplated, particularly in
relation to public authorities. Since that time, therefore, the claimant has generally
been required to point to some indication in the statute that it was intended to give
rise to a civil action. If there is no such indication, the claimant is thrown back on
such other common law right of action as he may have.

   Although, as we have seen, a common law duty of care may co-exist with a statutory duty (whether or not the latter gives rise to a civil action) there is no common
law tort of "careless performance of a statutory duty". Either there is a duty of care
under the common law which has been breached, or breach of the statute gives rise

---

13   See para.8-008.
14   *X (Minors) v Bedfordshire CC* [1995] 2 A.C. 633 at 765; *Barrett v Enfield LBC* [2001] 2 A.C. 550;
      Phelps v Hillingdon LBC [2001] 2 A.C. 619.
15   *Gorringe v Calderdale MBC* [2004] UKHL 15; [2004] 1 W.L.R. 1057 at [3]. An obvious example
      is road accidents: road traffic legislation hardly ever gives rise to an action for breach of statutory
      duty but road accidents are a major source of negligence cases.
16   *Gorringe v Calderdale MBC* [2004] UKHL 15; [2004] 1 W.L.R. 1057 at [32]; *Neil Martin Ltd v
      Revenue and Customs Comrs* [2007] EWCA Civ 1041; [2007] S.T.C. 1802.
17   *Green v Royal Bank of Scotland Plc* [2013] EWCA Civ 1197; [2014] P.N.L.R. 6.
18   See, e.g. Health and Safety at Work etc Act 1974 s.47 (recently reformed: see para.8-006); Build-
      ing Act 1984 s.38 (actionable); Copyright, Designs and Patents Act 1988 s.103 (actionable);
      Financial Services and Markets Act 2000 s.71 (actionable); Railways Act 2005 s.44 (not actionable).
19   *Anon* (1703) 6 Mod. 26; 87 E.R. 791; *Ashby v White* (1703) 2 Ld. Raym. 938; 92 E.R. 710; *Couch
      v Steel* (1854) 3 El. & Bl. 402; 118 E.R. 1193.
20   (1877) 2 Ex. D. 441.

to liability in its own right, or both; but if there is no common law duty and the statute only operates in the public law sphere then the fact that the duty under the statute is carried out carelessly does not avail the claimant seeking damages.[21]

On the question whether the statute gives rise to a civil right of action, it has been said that "the only rule which in all circumstances is valid is that the answer must depend on a consideration of the whole Act and the circumstances, including the pre-existing law, in which it was enacted",[22] but also that "[t]his requires the court to pay due respect to the language and structure used by Parliament, rather than to preconceptions of what its objectives could or should have been".[23] Where the civil right of action is alleged to arise from subordinate legislation an intention to confer such a right (or at least authority to confer it) must be found in the enabling legislation.[24] Unfortunately, statutes all too rarely contain very much in the way of a clear indication of legislative intent and various presumptions have been developed by the courts.[25]

8-006   **Health and safety at work: a change of intention**   Before such presumptions are considered, a recent change in Parliament's express intention should be acknowledged. It has already been noted that, purely in terms of number of claims, the most important area of operation of the breach of statutory duty tort is that concerned with work injuries. In this area, there was previously an express indication of civil liability in s.47(2) of the Health and Safety at Work etc. Act 1974, which stated that breach of a duty imposed by health and safety regulations shall, so far as it causes damage, "be actionable except in so far as the regulations provide[26] otherwise".[27] However, this has been reversed for any breach of such regulations committed after 1 October 2013 which henceforward is regarded as "not actionable" unless otherwise provided.[28] The statement in the explanatory notes to the reforming legislation that "it will only be possible to claim for compensation in relation to breaches of affected health and safety legislation where it can be proved that the duty holder ... has been negligent" presumes that no amendments will be made to the regulations in question so that they might expressly provide for civil liability.[29] It follows that, even in cases where the statutory duty is an absolute one,[30] there will no longer be a claim without proof of fault by the duty holder.

---

[21]   *X (Minors) v Bedfordshire CC* [1995] 2 A.C. 633.

[22]   *Cutler v Wandsworth Stadium Ltd* [1949] A.C. 398 at 407 per Lord Simonds. See also at 412 and *Ministry of Housing and Local Government v Sharp* [1970] 2 Q.B. 223 at 272.

[23]   *Campbell v Peter Gordon Joiners Ltd* [2016] UKSC 38; [2016] A.C. 1513 at [18] per Lord Carnwath.

[24]   *R. v Deputy Governor of Parkhurst Prison Ex p. Hague* [1992] 1 A.C. 58. See also *Olotu v Home Office* [1997] 1 W.L.R. 328 at 339; *The Maraghetha Maria* [2002] EWCA Civ 509; [2002] 2 Lloyd's Rep. 293.

[25]   See paras 8-007—8-014.

[26]   Meaning "expressly provide": *Wembridge Claimants v Winter* [2013] EWHC 2331 (QB) at [188].

[27]   Under s.47(1) breach of the duties set out in ss.2–8 of the 1974 Act itself are not actionable and this is not affected by the 2013 reform.

[28]   Enterprise & Regulatory Reform Act 2013 s.69(3), (10); SI 2013/2227 art.2(f). The reform followed two reports on health and safety legislation (by Lord Young of Graffham, in 2010, and by Professor Löfstedt, in 2011). The author of the second report felt it necessary to state publicly that the approach taken in s.47(2) is "more far-reaching" than anticipated in his recommendations (*Progress Report*, January 2013, para.30); his principal recommendation was to remove any element of strict liability.

[29]   The principal regulations affected are: Personal Protective Equipment at Work Regulations 1992 (SI 1992/2996); Manual Handling Operations Regulations 1992 (SI 1992/2793); Workplace (Health, Safety and Welfare) Regulations 1992 (SI 1992/3004); Provision and Use of Work Equipment

The protection of a class   It has been said that an indication that the intention of   **8-007**
Parliament was to provide a civil action is that the statute was passed for the protection of a limited class of the public, rather than for the benefit of the public as a
whole. This was criticised many years ago by Atkin LJ on the ground that "it would
be strange if a less important duty, which is owed to a section of the public, may
be enforced by action, while a more important duty owed to the public at large
cannot".[31] Furthermore, the concept of a "class of persons" lacks clear definition[32]:
road users are not treated as a class of persons for this purpose since traffic legislation has generally not been interpreted as giving rise to a civil action, but workers
have been, the opposite conclusion having been consistently reached under
industrial safety legislation.[33] Nevertheless, the relevance of this consideration has
been reiterated in more modern statements of the law.[34] Perhaps it is more helpful
to put the matter negatively: it is not so much that the identifiability of a protected
class is a particularly powerful pointer towards liability, as that, where there is no
such class, it is inherently unlikely that Parliament would have intended that a
"general regulatory scheme intended for the benefit of the whole population"[35]
should sound in damages, in the absence of plain words.[36] This has some affinity
with the "special damage" requirement in public nuisance.[37]

In *Atkinson v Newcastle Waterworks Co*[38] a statute requiring a water company
to keep pipes, to which fire plugs were fixed, charged with a certain pressure of
water, was construed as in the nature of a bargain between the company and Parliament for the supply of water to the city in question rather than as creating a duty
actionable by householders. A modern example is the refusal by the Court of Appeal to find that the statutory duty owed by a fire authority to take reasonable
measures to ensure an adequate supply of water for fire-fighting gave rise to civil
liability.[39] In any event, the mere fact that the statute intends to confer some benefit
upon an identified group of persons is not conclusive. In one case it was contended

---

Regulations 1998 (SI 1998/2306); Lifting Operations and Lifting Equipment Regulations 1998 (SI
1998/2307); Management of Health and Safety at Work Regulations 1999 (SI 1999/3242); Control
of Substances Hazardous to Health Regulations 2002 (SI 2002/2677); Work at Height Regulations
2005 (SI 2005/735). For limited exceptions to the principle of non-actionability which have been
introduced, see: Health and Safety at Work etc. Act 1974 (Civil Liability) (Exceptions) Regulations 2013 (SI 2013/1667).

30   See para.8-019.

31   *Phillips v Britannia Hygienic Laundry Co Ltd* [1923] 2 K.B. 832 at 841. The oddness of this reasoning is illustrated by *Cullen v Chief Constable of the Royal Ulster Constabulary* [2003] UKHL 39;
[2003] 1 W.L.R. 1763, where the majority held that there was no action for breach of a duty which
went to, "a quasi-constitutional right of fundamental importance in a free society": at [67]. But quaere
the effect of the decision in *Cadder v HM Advocate* [2010] UKSC 43; [2010] 1 W.L.R. 2601.

32   It seems the class must be definable by reference to the type or status of its members, or in some
analogous way. "Victims of this offence" is not enough: *Issa v Hackney LBC* [1997] 1 W.L.R. 956.

33   But see now para.8-006.

34   *X (Minors) v Bedfordshire CC* [1995] 2 A.C. 633 at 731; *O'Rourke v Camden LBC* [1998] A.C. 188
at 194; *Ali v Bradford City MDC* [2010] EWCA Civ 1282; [2012] 1 W.L.R. 161 at [33]; *McDonald
v National Grid Electricity Transmission Plc* [2014] UKSC 53; [2015] A.C. 1128 at [101] (with the
caveat that while the class may be very wide, "there must be some limit").

35   *Campbell v Peter Gordon Joiners Ltd* [2016] UKSC 38; [2016] A.C. 1513 at [47] per Lady Hale.

36   Thus in *Mid Kent Holdings Plc v General Utilities Plc* [1997] 1 W.L.R. 14, a literal interpretation
of the Fair Trading Act 1973 s.93A, would have led to the extraordinary result of allowing any of
the whole population to bring proceedings to enforce an undertaking to the Minister.

37   See para.15-007.

38   (1877) 2 Ex. D. 441.

39   *Capital & Counties Plc v Hampshire CC* [1997] Q.B. 1004. See also para.5-041.

that bookmakers were a class of persons intended to be benefited by a provision in the Betting and Lotteries Act 1934 requiring the owner of a dog track to provide space for them. The action failed, for the purpose of the statute was not the conferring of private rights but the regulation of dog racing.[40] Ultimately, the question of the existence or nonexistence of an identifiable class does not provide an easy substitute for the fundamental question of what purpose the legislature intended to achieve by the particular legislation, taken as a whole.[41]

8-008   **Nature of the legislation**   Closely related to the "class" issue is the nature of the legislation. While a private law duty may more readily be inferred from legislation prescribing safety standards,[42] it is unlikely to be found in legislation on "social welfare", especially when that confers a wide discretion upon the body responsible for administering it. The proper remedy for maladministration is judicial review, not an action for damages. Thus, the House of Lords has rejected claims based upon child protection legislation,[43] the duty to provide sufficient and appropriate education under the Education Acts[44] and the duty to house homeless persons under the housing legislation.[45] As Lord Hoffmann put it in relation to the last issue[46]:

> "[T]he Act is a scheme of social welfare, intended to confer benefits at the public expense on grounds of public policy. Public money is spent on housing the homeless not merely for the benefit of people who find themselves homeless but on grounds of general public interest: because, for example, proper housing means that people will be less likely to suffer illness, turn to crime or require the attention of other social services. The expenditure interacts with expenditure on other public services such as education, the National Health Service and even the police. It is not simply a private matter between the claimant and the housing authority."

In the child protection context the House of Lords had rejected a common law duty of care because of the delicate nature of the local authority's function in investigating allegations of child abuse[47] and it was not, therefore, surprising that a private law action under the statute (which would not necessarily even have required proof of negligence) was also rejected. However, the European Court of Human Rights subsequently held[48] that the failure to intervene constituted a breach of art.3 of the Convention (torture or inhuman or degrading treatment) and that the failure of domestic law to afford a remedy for this was a violation of art.13. Although it is now clear that in such a case there is no common law duty of care,[49] damages may

---

[40]   *Cutler v Wandsworth Stadium Ltd* [1949] A.C. 398.
[41]   *R. v Deputy Governor of Brixton Prison Ex p. Hague* [1992] 1 A.C. 58 at 171; *Morrison Sports Ltd v Scottish Power* [2010] UKSC 37; [2010] 1 W.L.R. 1934.
[42]   *Roe v Sheffield CC* [2003] EWCA Civ 1; [2004] Q.B. 653. cf. *The Maraghetha Maria* [2002] EWCA Civ 509; [2002] 2 Lloyd's Rep. 293 (safety of trawlers legislation; designed to protect crew but indications that this was to be enforced by administrative means); similarly *Morrison Sports Ltd v Scottish Power* [2010] UKSC 37; [2010] 1 W.L.R. 1934 (safety of electricity supply).
[43]   *X (Minors) v Bedfordshire CC* [1995] 2 A.C. 633.
[44]   *Phelps v Hillingdon LBC* [2001] 2 A.C. 619.
[45]   *O'Rourke v Camden LBC* [1998] A.C. 188. See now the Housing Act 1996. Such duties may not involve individual civil rights so as to attract art.6(1) of the European Convention on Human Rights: *Ali v Birmingham CC* [2010] UKSC 8; [2010] 2 A.C. 39.
[46]   *O'Rourke v Camden LBC* [1998] A.C. 188 at 193.
[47]   *X (Minors) v Bedfordshire CC* [1995] 2 A.C. 633.
[48]   *Z v UK* (2001) 34 E.H.R.R. 3.
[49]   See *Poole BC v GN* [2019] UKSC 25; [2019] 2 W.L.R. 1478. See para.5-062.

be awarded by an English court (under the Human Rights Act 1998) for breach of the Convention, but there seems to be no direct impact on the actionability of the breach of statutory duty.

Remedy provided by the statute   A potential factor in deciding whether there is   **8-009**
a civil action is the nature of the remedy, if any, provided by the statute for its breach.[50] If the statute provides no such remedy and there is an intention to protect a limited class,[51] that may be an indication that Parliament intended a civil action, "since otherwise there is no method of securing the protection the statute was intended to confer".[52] In the great majority of cases, however, some machinery or sanction, whether administrative or criminal, will be contained in the statute and it has been said that "where an Act creates an obligation, and enforces the performance in a specified manner, we take it to be a general rule that performance cannot be enforced in any other manner".[53] Where the statute provides its own administrative machinery for redress (for example, by appeal to the minister) the court is likely to adopt this approach.[54] It now seems that on the parallel issue of whether there is a common law duty of care attaching to the performance of a statutory function, the court must take into account how far, if at all, the availability of an alternative remedy enables the claimant to gain financial redress,[55] but there is no indication that the principles applicable to breach of statutory duty are affected. The existence of the general remedy of judicial review may be an indication that no private law action for damages is available, though it is not conclusive.[56]

Criminal penalties   Statutes which are silent on civil liability frequently impose   **8-010**
criminal penalties. In principle the starting point is said to be the same as in the case of administrative remedies, that is to say that the criminal penalty is presumed to be the sole means of enforcement. However, it has to be pointed out that in the area where breach of statutory duty has historically been of most importance (safety at work) the express provisions of the legislation in question were, for over a century and almost without exception, based solely on criminal penalties.[57]

---

50   *Hall v Cable and Wireless Plc* [2009] EWHC 1793 (Comm); [2010] 1 B.C.L.C. 95 (no action for breach of the listing rules under s.74 of the Financial Services and Markets Act 2000 given the scheme of remedies provided by the statute).

51   This caveat is important: in practice the most likely case in which a statute will not provide a sanction is where it imposes a general duty owed to the public.

52   *X (Minors) v Bedfordshire CC* [1995] 2 A.C. 633 at 731. See also *Doe d Murray v Bridges* (1831) 1 B. & Ad. 847 at 859; 109 E.R. 1001 at 1005–1006; cf. *Poulton's Trustee v Ministry of Justice* [2010] EWCA Civ 392; [2011] Ch. 1.

53   *Doe d Murray v Bridges* (1831) 1 B. & Ad. 847 at 859; 109 E.R. 1001 at 1006.

54   *Wyatt v Hillingdon LBC* (1978) 76 L.G.R. 727; *Scally v Southern Health and Social Services Board* [1992] 1 A.C. 294; *X (Minors) v Bedfordshire CC* [1995] 2 A.C. 633.

55   *Phelps v Hillingdon LBC* [2001] 2 A.C. 619 at 672. See also the discussion of the relevance of alternative remedies to the negligence analysis in *Rowley v Secretary of State for Work and Pensions* [2007] EWCA Civ 598; [2007] 1 W.L.R. 2861.

56   *Calveley v Chief Constable of Merseyside Police* [1989] A.C. 1228. The possibility of judicial review of a complaints procedure was regarded as pointing away from a civil action because it reduced the possibility of damage being suffered by the person being investigated. So also in *Cullen v Chief Constable of the Royal Ulster Constabulary* [2003] UKHL 39; [2003] 1 W.L.R. 1763 the majority relied on the availability of judicial review to deny a claim for damages for being refused access to a lawyer; the minority adverted to the "formidable practical problems" in applying for judicial review when access to a lawyer is refused.

57   Thus the Factories Act 1961 and its predecessors contained no mention of civil liability. See now

8-011   **Wording or structure of the statute**   Sometimes an indication of an intention with regard to civil liability may be observable in the wording or structure of the statute. In *Keating v Elvan Reinforced Concrete Ltd*,[58] for example, the fact that the Public Utilities Street Works Act 1950 contained provisions creating civil liabilities in favour of public authorities was regarded as a reason for holding that it gave no right of action to individuals. On this basis the decision in *Groves v Wimborne*[59] is rather surprising. The statute made the occupier of a factory who did not properly fence dangerous machinery liable to a fine of £100 and provided that the whole or any part of the fine might be applied, if the Secretary of State should so determine, for the benefit of the person injured by the occupier's neglect. A boy employed in the defendant's factory was caught by an unfenced cog wheel and his arm had to be amputated. The Court of Appeal held that he was entitled to recover damages for breach of the statute in a civil action. The court reasoned that there was no certainty that any part of the fine would be awarded to the victim[60] and, even if it were awarded, its upper limit of £100, it was said, made it incredible that Parliament would have regarded that as a sufficient and exclusive compensation for mutilation or death.[61] Nevertheless, since Parliament had expressly adverted to the matter of compensation and the law of negligence applied as between employer and employee,[62] there was some force in the argument that no civil claim was intended. Nevertheless, *Groves v Wimborne* was the progenitor of hundreds of reported cases giving a civil remedy for breach of industrial safety legislation.

A common form of words in statutes creating offences is that "nothing in this Act shall be taken to prejudice any liability or remedy to which a person guilty of an offence thereunder may be subject in civil proceedings",[63] but such words do not create civil liability, they merely preserve whatever liability (for example, for negligence or trespass) may exist apart from the statute.[64] It has also been said, though the point is far from decisive, that it is easier to spell out a civil right of action if Parliament has expressly stated that something is unlawful and then provided a penalty, rather than merely saying, "it is an offence to do such-and-such",[65] but this seems a tenuous basis upon which to decide this issue.[66] Then again, civil liability will, it seems, be imposed only on those made directly responsible for compliance with a primary obligation, and not on those deemed criminally liable for consenting to or conniving at its breach.[67]

---

the position under the Health and Safety at Work etc. Act 1974: paras 8-006 and 9-007.

[58] *Keating v Elvan Reinforced Concrete Ltd* [1968] 1 W.L.R. 722.

[59] *Groves v Wimborne* [1898] 2 Q.B. 402.

[60] cf. *Richardson v Pitt-Stanley* [1995] Q.B. 123, where there was no such power to divert the penalty and where its potential quantum militated against a Parliamentary intention that breach of the statute give rise to a private cause of action.

[61] But the remedy provided by the statute need not be "complete" in order to infer the intention that no action is available: *Francis v Southwark LBC* [2011] EWCA Civ 1418; [2012] H.L.R. 16.

[62] Though then restricted by the doctrine of "common employment": para.9-003.

[63] See e.g. Protection from Eviction Act 1977 s.1(5).

[64] *McCall v Abelesz* [1976] Q.B. 585.

[65] *Rickless v United Artists Corp* [1988] Q.B. 40 at 51 (civil action found nonetheless); *Richardson v Pitt-Stanley* [1995] Q.B. 123 (action rejected).

[66] See the dissenting judgment of Sir John Megaw in *Richardson v Pitt-Stanley* [1995] Q.B. 123.

[67] *Campbell v Peter Gordon Joiners Ltd* [2016] UKSC 38; [2016] A.C. 1513 at [15]. For the context, see para.8-012, below.

Type of injury   The fact that the loss likely to be suffered as a result of the breach   **8-012**
of statutory duty is of a type not recoverable (or recoverable only on a restricted
basis) under the general law of tort is, it seems, a factor pointing away from the
implication of a civil right of action. In *Pickering v Liverpool Daily Post and Echo
Newspapers Plc*[68] the statutory provision related to the publication of information
about an application to a Mental Health Review Tribunal. The breach of this provision gave rise to no civil right of action because, although the publication might be
said to be against the applicant's interest in the sense that it involved the disclosure
of information he would prefer not to have ventilated in public, that was not then[69]
a form of harm actionable in the civil law. Similarly, the court will more readily
imply a civil action where the damage inflicted by the breach is physical harm,
rather than economic loss, reflecting the common law's more restrictive approach
to the latter.[70] However, this is not a universal rule,[71] for in *Monk v Warbey*[72] the
court imposed civil liability upon the owner of a vehicle who allowed an uninsured
driver to use it, and thereby committed an offence under s.35 of the Road Traffic
Act 1930.[73] The owner, who had no reason to doubt the driver's competence, had
not in any legally relevant sense caused the claimant to be injured,[74] but he had
caused the claimant to be in a position whereby his claim against the driver was
worthless.[75]

Other "adequate" remedies in law   The fact that the common law and other   **8-013**
statute law already contain adequate remedies to enforce private rights in the area
in question is an indication that a civil action does not arise from the statute. Thus

---

[68]   [1991] 2 A.C. 370; and see *Cullen v Chief Constable of the Royal Ulster Constabulary* [2003] UKHL
        39; [2003] 1 W.L.R. 1763 (no damage at all, not even substantial distress; it is not clear what the
        position would have been if there had been damage of a type generally recognised by the common
        law).
[69]   Nowadays there might of course be claims under the law of misuse of private information or under
        the data protection legislation: see Ch.13.
[70]   *Richardson v Pitt-Stanley* [1995] Q.B. 123.
[71]   That there may be liability for breach of statutory duty causing economic loss is expressly ac-
        cepted by Lord Bridge in *Pickering v Liverpool Daily Post and Echo Newspapers Plc* [1991] 2 A.C.
        370 at 420.
[72]   [1935] 1 K.B. 75. *Campbell v Peter Gordon Joiners Ltd* [2016] UKSC 38; [2016] A.C. 1513
        involved a rather similar situation, namely failure to comply with the Employers' Liability
        (Compulsory Insurance) Act 1969. However, the majority of the Supreme Court rejected a civil claim
        against the director of the employer for breach of statutory duty (the company itself having gone into
        insolvent liquidation). This was on the ground that the statutory duty is imposed only on the
        company, with the directors merely "deemed" to be criminally liable if they consent to or connive
        at the company's committing the offence. The minority regarded this approach as overly formalistic,
        with Lord Toulson arguing (at [27]) that the court should consider the "function, substance and ef-
        fect of the provision in real terms".
[73]   See now the Road Traffic Act 1988 s.143(1)(b).
[74]   But for limitation purposes, the claim is still one for damages for personal injuries: *Norman v Ali*
        [2000] R.T.R. 107. A permits B to drive A's car while uninsured. There is an accident caused by the
        combined fault of B, and C driving another vehicle (the proportions of fault being 25 per cent and
        75 per cent) in which A is injured. A sues C and recovers in full. C's counterclaim against A under
        Monk v Warbey will fail because the Act requires insurance only against personal injury and property
        damage and C's counterclaim is economic loss: *Bretton v Hancock* [2005] EWCA Civ 404; [2005]
        R.T.R. 22 (s.143(1)(a) rather than (b) was in issue but the point is the same).
[75]   It has been held that the court must look at the realities of the matter, and it is not necessary to show
        that the driver can never pay: *Martin v Dean* [1971] 2 Q.B. 208. However, in *Norman v Ali* [2000]
        R.T.R. 107 the court left open how far it was necessary to establish impecuniosity.

in *McCall v Abelesz*[76] the Court of Appeal, in denying that the crime of harassment of tenants in s.30 of the Rent Act 1965,[77] gave rise to civil liability, emphasised the fact that many acts of harassment by a landlord must inevitably involve trespass or breach of contract. Similarly, in rejecting the contention that regulations governing the construction and use of motor vehicles gave rise to civil liability Atkin LJ in *Phillips v Britannia Hygienic Laundry Co*,[78] spoke of highway accidents being "already well provided for" by the common law. Conversely, the fact that the general law of tort and the law of contract are applicable to the relationship between employer and employee has not prevented the courts from holding that an action lies for breach of industrial safety legislation. Perhaps more convincing, therefore (though once again industrial accident cases may have to be treated as an exception), is the view that the courts, in the absence of clear words, will tend to lean against a civilly actionable statutory duty which would contradict the general pattern of liability in a particular area of activity, but will tend to find one which will support or supplement it. This would explain why the courts have consistently[79] rejected road traffic legislation as a direct source of civil liability, for the effect would have been to introduce isolated pockets of strict liability into an area generally governed by negligence. At the same time, however, it would support the decision in *Monk v Warbey* because that case made it more likely that a victim of actionable negligence would recover.[80]

Again, in *Issa v Hackney LBC*[81] an attempt to bring a civil action on the basis of the "statutory nuisance" provisions of the Public Health Act 1936[82] was rejected. In the normal case of activities on land A causing disturbance to the occupiers of land B, the common law of nuisance would give an adequate remedy for harm suffered if that was still necessary after the operation of the statutory enforcement procedures and the exercise of the court's power to make a compensation order; but on the facts, the statute was being used in an attempt to outflank established principles governing the responsibility of a landlord for the upkeep of premises. Those principles were seriously deficient because of legislative inaction,[83] but the solution was to be sought in direct legislative amendment, not by the side-wind of straining the law of breach of statutory duty.

---

[76] [1976] Q.B. 585.

[77] Replaced by the Housing Act 1988 Pt I Ch.IV, which does give rise to civil liability. See also the more general statutory crime and tort of harassment under the Protection from Harassment Act 1997, para.4-034.

[78] [1923] 2 K.B. 832.

[79] *Phillips v Britannia Hygienic Laundry Co* [1923] 2 K.B. 832; *Clark v Brims* [1947] K.B. 497; *Coote v Stone* [1971] 1 W.L.R. 279; *Exel Logistics Ltd v Curran* [2004] EWCA Civ 1249. A rare exception is *London Passenger Transport Board v Upson* [1949] A.C. 155 (breach of the Pedestrian Crossing Places (Traffic) Regulations 1941 (St. R. & O. 1941, No. 397)). See also *Roe v Sheffield CC* [2003] EWCA Civ 1; [2004] Q.B. 653, though that related to the condition of the highway rather than the manner of using it.

[80] *Campbell v Peter Gordon Joiners Ltd* [2016] UKSC 38; [2016] A.C. 1613 certainly does not support the policy of *Monk v Warbey*, but the decision was based more on the wording of the statute than on policy.

[81] [1997] 1 W.L.R. 956.

[82] See now Pt III of the Environmental Protection Act 1990, para.15-002.

[83] As was devastatingly demonstrated in the judgment of Brooke LJ.

Public rights and special damage   In *Lonrho Ltd v Shell Petroleum Co Ltd*   **8-014**
(No.2)[84] Lord Diplock, having referred to the cases on statutes for the protection of
particular classes of persons, such as those dealing with industrial safety, said that
there was a further exception to the general rule that a statute was to be enforced
only by the means prescribed in it, namely[85]:

> "[W]here the statute creates a public right (i.e. a right to be enjoyed by all those of Her
> Majesty's subjects who wish to avail themselves of it) and a particular member of the
> public suffers what Brett J in *Benjamin v Storr*[86] described as 'particular, direct and
> substantial' damage 'other and different from that which was common to all the rest of
> the public'."

Benjamin v Storr was in fact a case on whether an individual can bring an action
for damages in respect of a public nuisance.[87] The principal authority relied on by
Lord Diplock in the context of statutory duty was not an action for damages but
concerned the question whether a member of the public could, without the assistance of the Attorney General, seek an injunction to restrain an interference with
public rights.[88] However, it was said in *Lonrho* that a "mere prohibition on members
of the public generally from doing what it would otherwise be lawful for them to
do is not enough" to create a public right for this purpose. It will not therefore be
enough for the claimant to point to the commission of a crime and say that he has
been damaged by it and he cannot escape by this route from the fundamental question of whether the statute is intended to give rise to a civil action.[89]

Assessment   The law on inferring civil actions from statutory duties is not very   **8-015**
satisfactory. The drastic reduction in the availability of a civil action in the one area
where it has hitherto consistently been available, i.e. industrial safety,[90] may revive
the suggestion that this form of liability should be abolished altogether.[91] As it is,
Lord Denning MR commented with perhaps a little pardonable exaggeration that
the legislature "has left the courts with a guess-work puzzle. The dividing line
between the pro-cases and the contra-cases is so blurred and so ill-defined that you
might as well toss a coin to decide it".[92] As Lord du Parcq pointed out[93] the drafts-
men of Acts of Parliament are aware of the principles—and lack of principles—

---

[84]   [1982] A.C. 173.
[85]   [1982] A.C. 173 at 185.
[86]   (1874) L.R. 9 C.P. 400 at 407.
[87]   See para.15-007. However, the connection is obvious. Public nuisance, like breach of statutory duty,
       is an example of civil liability arising out of what is primarily a crime, though in this case a com-
       mon law crime.
[88]   *Boyce v Paddington BC* [1903] 1 Ch. 109.
[89]   *Mid Kent Holdings Plc v General Utilities Plc* [1997] 1 W.L.R. 14 (whether the claim is for dam-
       ages, an injunction or a declaration).
[90]   See para.8-006.
[91]   The suggestion by the Law Commission that the action for breach of statutory duty should be
       abolished "in most contexts" (*Administrative Redress*, Law Com. CP No.187 (2008), para.4-105)
       was abandoned, along with the recommendation of an entirely new remedy, in its later report (Law
       Com No. 332 (2010)). But if Parliament does expressly indicate that an action for damages may be
       brought, what can the courts do other than to give effect to it?
[92]   *Ex p. Islands Records* [1978] Ch. 122 at 134–135. See also Schiemann J in *R. v Knowsley MBC Ex
       p. Maguire* (1992) 90 L.G.R. 653.
[93]   *Cutler v Wandsworth Stadium Ltd* [1949] A.C. 398 at 411; *Solomons v R Gertzenstein Ltd* [1954] 2
       Q.B. 243 at 267.

applied by the courts to fill the gaps left in legislation, and it can be argued, therefore, that the silence of a statute on the question of civil remedies for its breach is a deliberate invitation to the courts to decide the question for themselves. Certainly it should not be assumed that where the statute is silent this is because its promoters have not adverted to the point—much more likely that it would be politically inconvenient to attempt to answer the question one way or the other. If this is so, then the pretence of searching for the non-existent intention of Parliament should be abandoned.[94] Not only does it involve an unnecessary fiction, but it may lead to decisions being made on the basis of insignificant details of phraseology instead of matters of substance. If the question whether a person injured by breach of statutory duty is to have a right of action for damages is in truth one to be decided by the courts, then it should be acknowledged as such and some useful principles of law developed, if that is possible.[95] It is, however, debatable whether a clear overall presumption would help.[96] At least it can be said that there are numerous decisions on particular statutes so that in many cases it is already settled that a right of action does or does not exist.[97] Even where a right of action has been held to exist, however, it is not enough for the claimant simply to prove breach of the statute. There are other elements in the tort which we must now consider. It should, however, be noted that where the statute creates a criminal offence the victim may choose to seek a compensation order from the criminal court, a procedure which is not dependent upon the establishing of a civil right of action. Though applicable to all criminal offences outside the road traffic field, this mechanism has so far been of limited importance in the type of case considered in this chapter but its role in compensating losses may increase.[98]

C.   Elements of the Tort

8-016   **Duty must be owed to the claimant**   Some statutory duties are so expressed as to limit the classes of person for whose benefit they exist, and in such cases whether the claimant is a member of the protected class is a question of the construction of the relevant provision. If he is not, then his action for breach of statutory duty cannot succeed. In *Hartley v Mayoh & Co*,[99] for example, a firefighter was electrocuted while tackling a fire at the defendants' factory. His widow relied, inter alia, on a breach by the defendants of their obligations under certain statutory regulations but, since these existed only for the protection of "persons employed", the claim for breach of statutory duty failed.[100] And in *West Wiltshire DC v Garland*[101] it was held

---

94   Williams (1960) 23 M.L.R. 233.
95   For a case decided by reference to principle and policy rather than the supposed intention of Parliament, see *Hargreaves v Bretherton* [1959] 1 Q.B. 45 (no action in tort for perjury).
96   The Law Commission suggested a general presumption in favour of actionability: *The Interpretation of Statutes*, Law Com. No.21 (1969). But recent moves have been in the opposite direction: see para.8-006.
97   Williams (1960) 23 M.L.R. 233 argued that, as a very broad and oversimplified conclusion, legislation concerning industrial safety gave rise to civil liability while other legislation did not, but even in this area there is now a presumption of non-actionability: see para.8-006.
98   For the powers of the criminal court, see para.4-005.
99   [1954] 1 Q.B. 383.
100 cf. *McDonald v National Grid Electricity Transmission Plc* [2014] UKSC 53; [2015] A.C. 1128 (driver exposed to asbestos dust when visiting power station to collect fuel ash "person employed" there even if not servant of occupier).
101 [1995] Ch. 297.

that the statutory duty of a district auditor gave rise to a civil cause of action in the local authority whose accounts he audited, but not in an individual officer of the authority.

Injury must be of a kind which the statute was intended to prevent If the   **8-017** object of the statute was to prevent mischief of a particular kind, one who suffers from its non-observance loss of a different kind cannot twist its remedy into an action for his own recoupment. In *Gorris v Scott*[102] the defendant, a shipowner, was under a statutory duty to provide pens for cattle on his ship in order to lessen the risk of murrain (fever) among them. The claimant's sheep were swept overboard in consequence of lack of such pens. The defendant was held not liable, because it was no part of the purpose of the statute to protect cattle against the perils of the sea.[103] The modern tendency is, however, not to apply this decision too strictly, and it has been said that provided the claimant's damage is of a kind that the statute was designed to prevent, it is irrelevant that it occurred in a way that the statute did not contemplate.[104] Conversely, the House of Lords held that a worker who was injured by a dangerous part which flew out of a machine could not base a claim on the statutory obligation that dangerous parts of machinery "shall be securely fenced".[105] The object of this provision, it was said, was, "to keep the worker out, not to keep the machine or its product in".[106] It was only if he came into contact with the dangerous part of the machine, therefore, that the worker could rely upon breach of the obligation to fence, and an injury caused in a different way was not actionable.[107]

Scope of the statutory duty Many statutes and statutory regulations have strictly   **8-018** defined spheres of application and, outside such sphere, they are irrelevant.[108] For example, many actions for injury caused by conduct which would have amounted to a breach of the Factories Act had it taken place in a factory have failed on the ground that the place where the conduct in fact occurred was not a factory as defined.[109] The modification of much safety legislation so that it applies to workplaces in general reduces the likelihood of such cases[110] but the general point remains valid.[111] In *Chipchase v British Titan Products Co*,[112] a workman was

---

[102] (1874) L.R. 9 Exch. 125; *Larrimore v American National Insurance Co* 89 P.2d 340 (1939).

[103] The claimants relied on the statutory obligation and on nothing else, e.g. a claim in negligence. Yet even in a case of negligence, the defendant's liability may be limited by an approach similar to that in *Gorris v Scott*: see *Banque Bruxelles Lambert SA v Eagle Star Insurance Co Ltd* [1997] A.C. 191 in which Lord Hoffmann draws an analogy with *Gorris v Scott*, para.7-073.

[104] *Donaghey v Boulton & Paul Ltd* [1968] A.C. 1 at 26.

[105] Factories Act 1961 s.14; *Close v Steel Co of Wales Ltd* [1962] A.C. 367; *Sparrow v Fairey Aviation Co Ltd* [1964] A.C. 1019.

[106] *Nicholls v F Austin (Leyton) Ltd* [1946] A.C. 493 at 505 per Lord Simonds. See also *Fytche v Wincanton Logistics Plc* [2004] UKHL 31; [2004] I.C.R. 975 (steel toe-capped boot; purpose of regulations to protect from impact injury, not wet and cold).

[107] cf. *Young v Charles Church (Southern) Ltd* (1997) 39 B.M.L.R. 146 (regulation designed to prevent electrocution covered nervous shock at seeing workmate electrocuted).

[108] In addition to the cases discussed herein, see para.9-013.

[109] An example is *Longhurst v Guildford, etc. Water Board* [1963] A.C. 265.

[110] See para.9-013.

[111] See, e.g. *Kmiecic v Isaacs* [2011] EWCA Civ 451; [2011] I.C.R. 1269 where the occupier of premises was not liable for the injury suffered by a building contractor's employee because, under the relevant regulations, she did not control the way the construction work was carried out (the building contractor was potentially liable, but he was uninsured); contrast *Tafa v Matsim Properties Ltd* [2011] EWHC 1302 (QB) and *Ceva Logistics Ltd v Lynch* [2011] EWCA Civ 188; [2011] I.C.R. 746 (under

injured when he fell from a platform nine inches wide and six feet above the ground. Statutory regulations then required that "every working platform from which a person is liable to fall more than six feet and six inches shall be ... at least 34 inches wide" and it was argued that the case was so nearly within the ambit of the regulations that the court ought to take them into account. The argument was rejected and the defendants were held not liable either for breach of statutory duty or for negligence at common law.

8-019 **Content of the obligation**   The content of the defendant's obligation in every case must be found in the statute itself and generalisation is not possible.[113] In some cases the statute imposes an unqualified obligation, i.e. an absolute duty that a certain state of affairs shall exist and, in such cases, the nonexistence of that state of affairs constitutes the breach.[114] Historically, the best-known example was the provision of s.14 of the Factories Act 1961 requiring that "every dangerous part of any machinery ... shall be securely fenced".[115] This has been replaced by more complex regulations which create a less than absolute obligation, but there continue to be examples in industrial safety legislation of duties to secure a result, not merely to take care to do so. In such cases, the "result" which must be achieved will itself be open to interpretation, e.g. whether personal protective equipment is "suitable",[116] or whether a workplace is "safe".[117] Sometimes a duty is imposed "so far as is reasonably practicable", which has some similarity to the standard of common law negligence, though it is by no means identical and the burden is on the defendant to show that the requirement in question was not reasonably practicable.[118] Duties to secure something "so far as practicable" or to "take such steps as may be necessary" are more onerous but still not absolute.[119] There is no substitute for an analysis of the particular provision in its context.[120]

8-020 **Causation: conduct of the claimant**   In an action for breach of statutory duty, as in an action for common law negligence, the claimant bears the burden of proving the causal connection between the breach of duty and the damage.[121] There is,

---

different regulations, statutory duty owed to contractor's employee by owner and operator of a warehouse).

[112] [1956] 1 Q.B. 545.

[113] See further, para.9-010.

[114] *Galashiels Gas Co v Millar* [1949] A.C. 275.

[115] See, e.g. *John Summers & Sons Ltd v Frost* [1955] A.C. 740.

[116] See *Threlfall v Hull City Council* [2010] EWCA Civ 1147; [2011] I.C.R. 209; *Chief Constable of Hampshire v Taylor* [2013] EWCA Civ 496; [2013] I.C.R. 1150 ("suitability" of gloves under the Personal Protective Equipment at Work Regulations 1992 (SI 1992/2966)). See also *Hide v Steeplechase Co (Cheltenham) Ltd* [2013] EWCA Civ 545; [2014] 1 All E.R. 405, discussed in para.9-011.

[117] See *Baker v Quantum Clothing Group Ltd* [2011] UKSC 17; [2011] 1 W.L.R. 1003 (safety in the noise context held to be a "relative" concept to be judged by reference to the knowledge and standards of the time): see para.9-011.

[118] See para.9-012.

[119] See para.9-012.

[120] In the case of the industrial safety legislation which has provided the examples referred to in this paragraph, it should be noted that there may no longer be a civil action for breach of the relevant duty: see para.8-006.

[121] *Bonnington Castings Ltd v Wardlaw* [1956] A.C. 613; *McWilliams v Sir William Arrol & Co Ltd* [1962] 1 W.L.R. 295. These cases concern "factual causation"; factors which go to "legal causation" such as acts of a third party, may be relevant (*Horton v Taplin Contracts Ltd* [2002] EWCA

however, one rather special kind of case, peculiar to actions for breach of statutory duty, namely that in which the act or omission of the claimant himself has the legal result that both claimant and defendant are in breach of the same duty.

In *Ginty v Belmont Building Supplies Ltd*[122] the claimant was an experienced employee of the defendant roofing contractors. Statutory regulations binding on both parties required that crawling boards be used for work done on fragile roofs and, although boards had been provided by the defendants, the claimant neglected to use them and fell through a roof in consequence. In law both parties were in breach of their statutory duties, but Pearson J held that the claimant's action failed because the defendants' breach consisted of and was coextensive with his own wrongful act.[123] In other words, there was no wrongful act but the claimant's own, and[124]:

> "[I]t would be absurd if, notwithstanding the employer having done all he could reasonably be expected to do to ensure compliance, a workman, who deliberately disobeyed his employer's orders and thereby put the employer in breach of a regulation, could claim damages for injury caused to him solely by his own wrongdoing."

Although the result reached in *Ginty* has been judicially described as "obvious",[125] the scope of the decision is restricted. If the claimant shows a breach of the defendant's duty and that he suffered injury as a result, he establishes a prima facie case. The defendant will escape liability only if he can rebut that prima facie case by proof that the only act or default of anyone which caused the breach was that of the claimant himself.[126] It follows that where some fault is to be attributed to the defendant, as where an employer calls upon a worker to do a job beyond his proper competence,[127] fails to provide adequate instructions or supervision,[128] is responsible for some independent fault,[129] or encourages the worker in his own breach of statutory duty,[130] then the claimant is entitled to recover some damages, though they may be substantially reduced on account of his contributory negligence.

Volenti non fit injuria[131] It was long thought that the defence of volenti non fit injuria was not available in actions for breach of statutory duty and perhaps this is still generally so, though the law needs to be clarified. It is obviously open to Parlia-   **8-021**

Civ 1604; [2003] I.C.R. 179) but everything finally depends on the words of the statute.

[122] [1959] 1 All E.R. 414.
[123] [1959] 1 All E.R. 414 at 424.
[124] *Boyle v Kodak Ltd* [1969] 1 W.L.R. 661 at 665–666 per Lord Reid. "To say 'You are liable to me for my own wrongdoing' is neither good morals nor good law": at 673 per Lord Diplock.
[125] *Donaghey v Boulton & Paul Ltd* [1968] A.C. 1 at 24 per Lord Reid. See also *Brumder v Motornet Service and Repairs Ltd* [2013] EWCA Civ 195; [2013] 1 W.L.R. 2783 where the claimant was director and sole shareholder of the employer company.
[126] *Boyle v Kodak Ltd* [1969] 1 W.L.R. 661 at 672–673.
[127] *Byers v Head Wrightson & Co Ltd* [1961] 1 W.L.R. 961; *Ross v Associated Portland Cement Manufacturers Ltd* [1964] 1 W.L.R. 768; *Bhatt v Fontain Motors Ltd* [2010] EWCA Civ 863; [2010] P.I.Q.R. P17.
[128] *Jenner v Allen West & Co Ltd* [1959] 1 W.L.R. 554; *Ross v Associated Portland Cement Manufacturers Ltd* [1964] 1 W.L.R. 768; *Boyle v Kodak Ltd* [1969] 1 W.L.R. 661.
[129] *McMath v Rimmer Bros (Liverpool) Ltd* [1962] 1 W.L.R. 1; *Leach v Standard Telephones & Cables Ltd* [1966] 1 W.L.R. 1392; *Donaghey v Boulton & Paul Ltd* [1968] A.C. 1; *Keaney v British Railways Board* [1968] 1 W.L.R. 879. It appears that the fault for which the employer is responsible need not be such as to suffice as an independent ground of action.
[130] *Barcock v Brighton Corp* [1949] 1 K.B. 339; *Laszczyk v National Coal Board* [1954] 1 W.L.R. 1426.
[131] See para.26-018.

ment to create a statutory duty and to provide that the defence does not apply; but where, as is often the case, the actionable duty is conjured up by a process of construction somewhat akin to divination it is not easy to see why there should be any hard-and-fast rule. In 1964 the House of Lords held that the defence was available where a worker engaged with a colleague in flagrant breach of safety rules and sued the employer on the basis that there was a breach of statutory duty only via vicarious liability for the other worker's acts.[132] That was not a case where the employer was in breach of a duty directly imposed on *him*, and the case is consistent with the proposition that in that event the defence is still inapplicable.[133] It is certainly true that the courts are much less willing, even at common law, than they once were to apply the defence in the employment context and that there are often other routes (for example causation) to denying liability.[134] However, a blanket rule of exclusion of the defence based on the public policy of recognising the will of Parliament would be in the nature of a fiction.

8-022   **Contributory negligence**   Before the Law Reform (Contributory Negligence) Act 1945 the contributory negligence of the claimant was a complete defence to an action for breach of statutory duty[135] and it is therefore now a reason for reducing the damages he may recover. This matter is considered below.[136]

8-023   **Delegation of the duty to the claimant**   It is clear that in the ordinary way it is no defence for a person subjected to a statutory duty to claim that he has delegated the duty or its performance to another person.[137] In some cases, however, it seems to have been thought that delegation may be a defence where performance of the tasks necessary to secure compliance with the statutory obligation has been delegated to the claimant himself.[138] Nevertheless, although some specific requirements for the defence of delegation were laid down,[139] in no case did the claimant clearly fail in his action on the express ground that the defendant's statutory duty had been delegated to him[140] and the doctrine has now fallen into disrepute. In *Ginty*

---

132   *Imperial Chemical Industries Ltd v Shatwell* [1965] A.C. 656.
133   However, the dicta on the point are not perhaps entirely consistent: compare Lord Reid at 674 referring to, "an employer who is himself at fault in persistently refusing to comply with a statutory rule"; Lord Pearce at 687, seeming to accept a general rule of non-applicability of the defence and Lord Donovan at 693, referring to unequal bargaining strength.
134   There is no defence of "fireground immunity" in relation to fire officers and police officers injured at the scene of a fire: *Wembridge Claimants v Winter* [2013] EWHC 2331 (QB) (claims for breach of statutory duty and in negligence), but some regulations simply may not apply: e.g., the obligation on employers to ensure that work at height is carried out only when the weather conditions do not jeopardise health or safety (Work at Height Regulations 2005 (SI 2005/735)) is expressly disapplied "where members of the police, fire, ambulance or other emergency service are acting in an emergency" (reg.4(4)).
135   *Caswell v Powell Duffryn Associated Collieries* [1940] A.C. 152.
136   See para.26-039.
137   *Gray v Pullen* (1864) 5 B. & S. 970; 121 E.R. 1091; *Whitby v Burt, Boulton & Hayward Ltd* [1947] K.B. 918. See para.21-050.
138   See, e.g. *Vincent v Southern Railway Co* [1927] A.C. 430; *Smith v Baveystock & Co* [1945] 1 All E.R. 531.
139   See, e.g. *Beale v E Gomme Ltd* (1949) 65 T.L.R. 543; *Manwaring v Billington* [1952] 2 All E.R. 747.
140   However, the judgments of Lord Goddard in *Smith v Baveystock & Co* [1945] 1 All E.R. 531 at 533–534 and Hilbery J in *Barcock v Brighton Corp* [1949] 1 K.B. 339, could be taken as supporting this view.

v Belmont Building Supplies Ltd,[141] in a passage subsequently approved by the Court of Appeal,[142] Pearson J doubted its soundness[143]:

"There has been a number of cases ... in which it has been considered whether or not the employer delegated to the employee the performance of the statutory duty. In my view, the law which is applicable here is clear and comprehensible if one does not confuse it by seeking to investigate this very difficult and complicated question whether or not there was a delegation. In my view, the important and fundamental question in a case like this is not whether there was a delegation, but simply the usual question: Whose fault was it? ... If the answer to that question is that in substance and reality the accident was solely due to the fault of the plaintiff, so that he was the sole author of his own wrong, he is disentitled to recover."

It is submitted, therefore, that there is no special defence of delegation of a statutory duty and, indeed, that any other view would conflict with the general principle that no duty can be delegated.[144]

2. MISFEASANCE IN A PUBLIC OFFICE

Introduction[145]   This is a convenient point at which to outline the tort of misfeasance in a public office.[146] The only tort that can be committed by a public officer alone, misfeasance is frequently described as the "public law tort".[147] Although its roots are traceable back to the 17th century,[148] the misfeasance tort itself is relatively youthful—a child of two Commonwealth decisions in 1959.[149] And a definitive statement of the law in this jurisdiction was not forthcoming until the turn of the present century, when the House of Lords decided *Three Rivers DC v Bank of England (No.3)*,[150] a case arising out of allegations that the Bank of

8-024

---

[141] [1959] 1 All E.R. 414 at 423–424.

[142] *McMath v Rimmer Bros (Liverpool) Ltd* [1962] 1 W.L.R. 1 at 6. See also *Jenner v Allen West & Co Ltd* [1959] 1 W.L.R. 554.

[143] *Ginty v Belmont Building Supplies Ltd* [1959] 1 All E.R. 414 at 423–424 per Pearson LJ. See also *Ross v Associated Portland Cement Manufacturers Ltd* [1964] 1 W.L.R. 768 at 777 per Lord Reid ("Fault is not necessarily equivalent in this context to blameworthiness. The question really is whose conduct caused the accident").

[144] *Ross v Associated Portland Cement Manufacturers Ltd* [1964] 1 W.L.R. 768 at 776.

[145] Chamberlain, *Misfeasance in a Public Office* (2016); Aronson (2016) 132 L.Q.R. 427; Nolan in Barker et al (eds), *Private Law and Power* (2017); Fairgrieve and Squires, *The Negligence Liability of Public Authorities*, 2nd edn (2019), paras 6-02—6-38. The Law Commission provisionally proposed that the tort of misfeasance in a public office be abolished as part of a wider revamp of the law on damages claims against public bodies, but its proposals met with significant opposition and were subsequently abandoned: *Administrative Redress* Law Com. No.232 (2010).

[146] There is a comparable common law crime of misconduct in a public office: *R. v Bowden* [1996] 1 W.L.R. 98.

[147] For analysis of the tort in public law terms, see Nolan in Barker et al (eds), *Private Law and Power* (2017). Can a state entity itself bring a misfeasance claim? There is no English authority on this question, but for a thorough and helpful discussion see *Marin v Attorney-General* [2011] CCJ 9 (AJ); [2011] 5 L.R.C. 209, where a majority of the Caribbean Court of Appeal held that the Attorney General of Belize did have the right to sue for misfeasance former government ministers accused of selling state property at an undervalue.

[148] *Turner v Sterling* (1671) 2 Vent. 25; 86 E.R. 139. See also *Ashby v White* (1703) 2 Ld. Raym. 938; 92 E.R. 126.

[149] *Roncarelli v Duplessis* (1959) 16 D.L.R. (2d) 689; *Farrington v Thomson* [1959] V.R. 286.

[150] [2001] UKHL 16; [2003] 2 A.C. 1. This is an amalgam of two hearings, the first ([2003] 2 A.C. at 187) examining the law and the second applying it to the application to amend the particulars of

England had acted wrongfully in granting a banking licence to the Bank of Credit and Commerce International (or failing to revoke the existing licence), thereby causing loss to over 6,000 depositors. The purpose of the tort is to give compensation to those who have suffered loss as a result of improper abuse of public power,[151] it being based on the principle that such power may be exercised only for the public good and not for ulterior and improper purposes.[152] Restrictions on negligence claims against public authorities are such that the misfeasance tort is frequently pleaded,[153] but the hurdles a claimant must overcome are high, and successful claims are few and far between.

8-025   **Nature of the action**   Misfeasance in a public office consists of a purported exercise of some power or authority by a public officer otherwise than in an honest attempt to perform the functions of his office, whereby loss is caused to a claimant.[154] The essence of the cause of action is therefore a deliberate and dishonest wrongful abuse of the powers given to a public officer.[155] Lesser instances of maladministration, such as mere delay, the making of good faith mistakes, or the taking of good faith decisions on an erroneous or incomplete factual basis, do not constitute misfeasance.[156] An omission can amount to misfeasance in circumstances where there is a legal duty to act,[157] though it follows from the character of the tort that the failure to act must be the product of a deliberate decision, as opposed to mere inadvertence or oversight. Hence a police officer could be liable for misfeasance if he chose not to put a stop to an assault because he had a grudge against the victim, but not if he simply failed to notice it.

8-026   **Defendant must be a public officer**   The defendant in a misfeasance action must be the holder of a public office, a broad concept encompassing any person who, or body which, exercises governmental power.[158] It seems that neither susceptibility

---

claim ([2003] 2 A.C. at 237). Significant earlier cases were *Dunlop v Woollahra Municipal Council* [1982] A.C. 158 and *Bourgoin SA v Ministry of Agriculture, Fisheries and Food* [1986] Q.B. 716.

[151] Since *Kuddus v Chief Constable of Leicestershire Constabulary* [2001] UKHL 29; [2002] 2 A.C. 222, punitive damages may be available for this tort: para.23-018. The close correlation between the first of the categories of case identified in *Rookes v Barnard* [1964] A.C. 1129 where such damages may be awarded and the gist of the misfeasance action means that there will be considerable scope for such awards in this context.

[152] *Three Rivers DC v Bank of England (No.3)* at [2003] 2 A.C. 190 citing *Jones v Swansea CC* [1990] 1 W.L.R. 54 at 85. See the analogy with the tort of malicious prosecution drawn by Lord Sumption in *Crawford Adjusters v Sagicor General Insurance Ltd* [2013] UKPC 17; [2014] A.C. 366: para.20-024.

[153] For example, in the two most important misfeasance cases, *Bourgoin SA v Ministry of Agriculture, Fisheries and Food* [1986] Q.B. 716 and *Three Rivers DC v Bank of England (No.3)* [2001] UKHL 16; [2003] 2 A.C. 1, negligence actions would have failed because the claimants' losses were purely economic.

[154] *Northern Territory of Australia v Mengel* (1995) 185 C.L.R. 307 at 357. The requirement of causation means that if, for example, a cinema owner alleges (as in *David v Abdul Cader* [1963] 1 W.L.R. 834) that he was maliciously refused a licence to show films, his lost profits are recoverable only if he proves on the balance of probabilities that a licence would have been awarded had the malice not been present.

[155] *Three Rivers DC v Bank of England (No.3)* [1996] 3 All E.R. 558 at 582.

[156] *B v Home Office* [2012] EWHC 226 (QB); [2012] 4 All E.R. 276 at [130].

[157] *Three Rivers DC v Bank of England (No.3)* [2003] 2 A.C. 190 at 228, 230.

[158] Which is to say "the power to interfere with the way in which other citizens wish to conduct their affairs": *Society of Lloyd's v Henderson* [2007] EWCA Civ 930; [2008] 1 W.L.R. 2255 at [25]. Is the concept too broad as so defined? And is there a risk that the tort's application to unpaid council-

to judicial review nor classification as a "public authority" for the purposes of s.6 of the Human Rights Act 1998 is decisive in this context.[159] Misfeasance actions have been brought against police officers,[160] prison officers,[161] the Bank of England,[162] governors of a state school,[163] government departments[164] and local authorities.[165] By contrast, the Society of Lloyds was held not to be "public officer" for these purposes, since it was concerned with the internal commercial interests of its members, and the fact that it regulated their activities did not mean that it was exercising public functions.[166] The general principles of vicarious liability apply.[167]

An exercise of power by a public officer   For a misfeasance action to lie, the loss to the claimant must have been caused by the exercise of power by the defendant as a public officer. Again, the courts have adopted a broad approach to this issue, and it has been said that any act or omission by a public official in purported performance of the functions of his office can found an action for misfeasance.[168] While a malicious act of a public officer solely in his capacity as a private individual would fall outside the ambit of the tort, it seems that even the abuse of a private power by a public body may attract liability. In *Jones v Swansea City Council*,[169] it was alleged that the defendant council's refusal to allow one of its tenants to change the use of rented commercial property had been motivated by malice. Although the council's decision was not susceptible to judicial review, because the power to refuse permission derived not from statute but from the terms of the lease, the Court of Appeal held that it could nonetheless be the subject of an action in misfeasance. According to Slade LJ, in this context "it is not the juridical nature of the relevant power but the nature of the council's office which is the important consideration".[170] Conversely, it has been argued that, if the essence of the tort is an abuse of public power, then liability ought to be limited to cases where the defendant was engaged in the act of "governing" or "public regulation" when the misconduct occurred.[171]

8-027

---

lors and the like will discourage individuals from standing for office? (see Chamberlain, *Misfeasance in a Public Office* (2016), pp.86, 91).

[159] *Society of Lloyd's v Henderson* [2007] EWCA Civ 930; [2008] 1 W.L.R. 2255 at [37]–[41].

[160] *Darker v Chief Constable of the West Midlands Police* [2001] 1 A.C. 435; *Kuddus v Chief Constable of Leicestershire* [2001] UKHL 29; [2002] 2 A.C. 122.

[161] *Racz v Home Office* [1994] 2 A.C. 45.

[162] *Three Rivers DC v Bank of England (No.3)* [2003] 2 A.C. 190.

[163] *Brent LBC v Davies* [2018] EWHC 2214 (Ch).

[164] *Bourgoin SA v Ministry of Agriculture, Fisheries and Food* [1986] Q.B. 716. Though it has since been said that primary liability for misfeasance cannot attach to the state itself, and that in *Bourgoin* the department was vicariously liable for the misfeasance of a minister: *Chagos Islanders v Attorney General* [2004] EWCA Civ 997 at [26]–[27].

[165] *Jones v Swansea CC* [1990] 1 W.L.R. 1453.

[166] *Society of Lloyd's v Henderson* [2007] EWCA Civ 930; [2008] 1 W.L.R. 2255.

[167] See, e.g. *Racz v Home Office* [1994] 2 A.C. 45. Though the point is not uncontroversial: compare *Northern Territory of Australia v Mengel* (1995) 185 C.L.R. 307 at 357.

[168] *Northern Territory of Australia v Mengel* (1995) 185 CLR 307 at 355.

[169] [1990] 1 W.L.R. 54.

[170] [1990] 1 W.L.R. 54 at 71. The decision was reversed on the facts by the House of Lords ([1990] 1 W.L.R. 1453), but Lord Lowry (at 1458), with whom the other members of the House concurred, said that he was "inclined to agree" with the trial judge and the Court of Appeal on the question of the nature of the power exercised. See also Lord Steyn in *Three Rivers* [2003] 2 A.C. 1 at 191.

[171] Nolan (2019) 135 L.Q.R. 272 at 291.

8-028 **The two limbs of the tort** The House of Lords confirmed in *Three Rivers*[172] that the tort of misfeasance in a public office has two separate limbs, a targeted malice limb, where intent to injure is central, and an illegality limb, where the defendant's knowledge that his conduct is unlawful is central. It should however be noted that there is a substantial overlap between the two limbs. In particular, since it is unlawful for a public officer to use his powers to inflict injury, and since he will generally be aware of this, most cases of targeted malice will also be actionable under the illegality limb.

8-029 **The targeted malice limb** The targeted malice limb of the tort covers the case where the public officer acts with intent to harm the claimant or a class of which the claimant is a member. In actions under this limb, proof of recklessness is not enough. An example of such a case is *Roncarelli v Duplessis*[173] (decided under the civil law of Quebec) where the defendant, the Prime Minister and Attorney General of Quebec, deprived the claimant of his restaurant licence as an act of revenge for standing bail for members of the Jehovah's Witnesses, against whose activities there had been a Provincial government campaign. If in a case of this kind the decision under attack was made collectively, it is sufficient for the claimant to establish that a majority of those involved in the decision-making process were activated by malice. In the *Jones* case,[173] the ruling Labour group on the council had voted en bloc for the resolution rescinding the local authority's consent for the change in the use of the premises, and it was alleged that the leader of the group and its members had been motivated by hostility towards the claimant and her husband, a leading member of a rival party. The Court of Appeal held that to make out her claim of misfeasance, the claimant would have to establish that a majority of the councillors who voted on the resolution were infected by malice.[174]

8-030 **The illegality limb** The illegality limb of the tort covers the case where the public officer knows that, or is consciously indifferent to the fact that, his act or omission is unlawful, and will probably injure the claimant. In the seminal Australian case of *Farrington v Thomson*,[175] for example, the defendant police officers were liable for ordering the plaintiff to shut his hotel after his conviction for a licensing offence, since they knew that they had no right to do this under the relevant legislation. Misfeasance in public office is not, however, constituted solely by an act of a public officer which he knows is unlawful and which results in loss. It must also be shown that the public officer knew that his unlawful conduct would probably[176] cause damage of the type in fact suffered by the claimant. Reckless indif-

---

[172] [2003] 2 A.C. 190.

[173] [1990] 1 W.L.R. 54.

[174] The decision was reversed on the facts by the House of Lords ([1990] 1 W.L.R. 145), but while the House insisted on proof that all the Labour councillors had been infected by their leader's malice, this stricter approach was based solely on the way in which the claimant's case had been pleaded. For the suggestion that in such cases liability should be imposed if those whose votes were sufficient to turn the decision were affected by malice, see Arrowsmith, *Civil Liability and Public Authorities* (1992), p.234.

[175] [1959] V.R. 286.

[176] *Three Rivers DC v Bank of England (No.3)* [2003] 2 A.C. 1 at 191, 298. See also the second *Three Rivers* decision, where Lord Hope refers to awareness of "a serious risk of loss" (at 247). A more stringent approach was adopted by Lord Hobhouse, who spoke (at 230) of an "awareness that a certain consequence will follow as a result of the act unless something out of the ordinary intervenes", and by Lord Millett, who disapproved the test propounded by Lords Steyn and Hut-

ference as to the illegality and its probable consequences is sufficient to ground the tort in its second form.[177] This recklessness must, however, be subjective. It follows that the officer must be shown not to have had an honest belief that he was acting lawfully, meaning that he either knew his act was unlawful or wilfully disregarded the risk that it was.[178] Similarly, he will be liable only if he knew that his conduct would probably cause the claimant loss or wilfully disregarded the risk that it would.[179] The courts' insistence on subjective recklessness is consistent with the fact that the essence of the tort is bad faith or dishonest abuse of a public power, and is grounded in a perception that liability for inadvertent unlawfulness is best left to the law of negligence, with its attendant restrictions on recovery of economic loss and the like. Adoption of an objective standard would, it is feared, enable claimants to circumvent those restrictions, and might discourage officials from robust enforcement of rules and regulations.[180]

The requirement of damage[181]   In *Watkins v Home Office*,[182] the House of Lords   **8-031**
held that misfeasance in a public office is not actionable without proof of material damage. The claimant was a convicted prisoner who brought a misfeasance action against the Secretary of State and a number of prison officers for repeated interference with his legal correspondence in violation of the Prison Rules. It was found that three of the officers had breached the rules in bad faith, but the claim failed because no loss to the claimant had resulted.[183] While the Court of Appeal had taken the view that damage need not be proven because there had been a violation of one of the claimant's constitutional rights (the right of access to the courts and legal advice), according to the House material damage had always either been expressly recognised as an essential ingredient of the cause of action, or assumed to be one. As for what counts as "material damage" in this context, it is clear from *Watkins* that the concept includes physical damage,[184] mental injury amounting to a psychiatric illness, and financial loss, and in *Karagozlu v Metropolitan Police Commissioner*[185] it was held also to encompass loss of liberty.

No further restrictions on standing   Provided the claimant establishes that he has   **8-032**
suffered material damage as a result of the defendant's misfeasance, there are no further restrictions on standing. In particular, there is no requirement that the

---

ton, and said (at 236) that "the principle in play is that a man is presumed to intend the natural and probable consequences of his actions" (it should be noted in this connection that Lord Hope expressed his full agreement with Lords Steyn and Hutton on the misfeasance issues). Lord Hobhouse and Lord Millett were clearly influenced by the Commonwealth case law, where an analogy has been drawn with intentional interference with the person, and a relatively strict approach therefore adopted: see *Northern Territory of Australia v Mengel* (1995) 185 C.L.R. 307; and *Garrett v A-G* [1997] 2 N.Z.L.R. 332 at 349–350.

[177] *Three Rivers DC v Bank of England (No.3)* [2003] 2 A.C. 1 at 191.
[178] *Three Rivers DC v Bank of England (No.3)* [2003] 2 A.C. 1 at 230.
[179] *Three Rivers DC v Bank of England (No.3)* [2003] 2 A.C. 1 at 231.
[180] See *Northern Territory of Australia v Mengel* (1995) 185 C.L.R. 307 at 358; *Garrett v A-G* [1997] 2 N.Z.L.R. 332 at 350.
[181] See further, Chamberlain, *Misfeasance in a Public Office* (2016), pp.144–153.
[182] [2006] UKHL 17; [2006] 2 A.C. 395.
[183] The claimant would, however, probably have been entitled to redress under the Human Rights Act 1998 had the events in question taken place after it came into force.
[184] See, e.g. *Akenzua v Secretary of State for the Home Dept* [2002] EWCA Civ 1470; [2003] 1 W.L.R. 741.
[185] [2006] EWCA Civ 1691; [2007] 1 W.L.R. 1881.

defendant's conduct infringe an independent legal right vested in the claimant, nor that the defendant owed the claimant any particular duty over and above the duty not to cause loss through the deliberate abuse of a public power.[186] The majority of the Court of Appeal in *Three Rivers* held that the concept of proximity had a part to play in misfeasance, as it has sometimes been held to have in negligence, but the House of Lords disagreed. The requirement that the defendant must have acted in bad faith, and in the knowledge that his conduct would probably cause harm, was enough to keep the tort within reasonable bounds.[187]

---

[186] *Three Rivers DC v Bank of England (No.3)* [1996] 3 All E.R. 558 at 584 per Clarke J (approved by Lord Steyn on appeal to the House of Lords: [2001] UKHL 16; [2003] 2 A.C. 1 at 193).

[187] See [2003] 2 A.C. 1 at 193, 228. What was described as an attempt to introduce a proximity requirement by the back door failed in *Akenzua v Secretary of State for the Home Dept* [2002] EWCA Civ 1470; [2003] 1 W.L.R. 741, where it was held that in cases falling within the illegality limb, the claimant need not establish the probability of harm to him or a class of which he was a member. In cases falling within the targeted malice limb, there is of course a de facto "proximity" requirement, since liability rests on the very fact that the misconduct was directed at the claimant.

CHAPTER 9

EMPLOYERS' LIABILITY

1. INTRODUCTION

Statutory compensation for injury at work Since 1948,[1] a system of national **9-001** insurance has been in operation under which benefits are payable to the victims of industrial accidents and to sufferers from certain prescribed industrial diseases. Both employer and worker make national insurance contributions and, generally speaking, any person employed under a contract of service or apprenticeship is entitled to the benefits provided by the system. The scheme of benefits provided for industrial injuries is largely assimilated with the general social security system, but disablement benefit remains special to this area. This is paid when, as a result of an accident, the claimant suffers disablement amounting to at least a 14 per cent loss of physical or mental faculty.[2] Benefit is payable in respect of personal injury by accident, "arising out of and in the course of insurable employment". An accident arising in the course of the employment is deemed, in the absence of evidence to the contrary, to have arisen out of that employment.[3] If the employee was, at the time of the accident, disobeying any statutory or other regulations applicable to his employment, or disobeying his employer's order, the accident is nevertheless deemed to have arisen out of and in the course of the employment, provided: (1) the accident would be deemed so to have arisen if there had been no disobedience; and (2) the act was done for the purpose of, and in connection with, the employer's trade or business.[4] The employee is insured against injuries sustained while travelling to and from work in transport provided by his employer[5] or while acting in an

---

[1] National Insurance (Industrial Injuries) Act 1946. The principal Act is now the Social Security (Contributions and Benefits) Act 1992. On employers' liability generally, see Bennett (ed), *Munkman on Employer's Liability*, 17th edn (2019).
[2] Social Security (Contributions and Benefits) Act 1992 s.103(1).
[3] Social Security (Contributions and Benefits) Act 1992 s.94(3).
[4] Social Security (Contributions and Benefits) Act 1992 s.98.
[5] Social Security (Contributions and Benefits) Act 1992 s.99.

emergency (actual or supposed) on his employer's premises, for instance, averting damage by fire. The legislation in question is administered on behalf of the government and not by the ordinary courts. Claims under it are not a matter for the employer, but are made against the State, and their validity in no way depends upon proof of the fault or breach of duty of the employer.

9-002 **Relationship with other claims against employers** The legislation that came into force in 1948 replaced the Workmen's Compensation Acts, the first of which was enacted in 1897, and these Acts also provided compensation to an injured worker without requiring him to prove fault or any breach of duty by his employer. It has thus been possible since the end of the 19th century for an injured worker to receive some compensation independently of the ordinary law governing the civil liability of his employer. Under the law now in force the worker is entitled to retain his benefits under the scheme and also to bring an action for damages against his employer.[6] Actions by workers against their employers are, in fact, amongst the most numerous to be dealt with by the courts. In earlier times cases nearly always concerned physical injury by accident; nowadays a much greater proportion of claims against employers arise from illness and disease. Many cases now concern mental illness caused by stress[7] and these present formidable problems of risk assessment for employers and of adjudication for the courts.

9-003 **Liability of the employer in negligence: the doctrine of common employment** The recorded history of employers' liability does not start until 1837, and then it began by denying the worker a remedy. *Priestley v Fowler*,[8] decided in that year, is generally regarded as the *fons et origo* of the doctrine of common employment, which held that the employer was not liable to his employee for injury caused by the negligence of another employee, but the case really went further than that. It came close to denying that an employer could be liable to his workers on any grounds,[9] and there can be no doubt that the judges of the first half of the 19th century viewed with alarm the possibility of widespread liability for industrial accidents.[10] Nevertheless, by 1858, if not earlier, common employment was recognised to be an exception to the ordinary principle that an employer is liable for torts committed by his servants in the course of their employment.[11] The doctrine was said to rest upon the theory that the contract of service contained an implied term to the effect that the servant agreed to run the risks naturally incident to the employment, including the risk of negligence on the part of his fellow employees, but it did not follow that he agreed to take the risk of negligence on the part of the

---

6 However, since 1990 there has existed a "clawback" system whereby certain benefits payable in the first five years are deductible from damages with a concomitant obligation on the defendant to reimburse the Secretary of State: para.23-097. There is no such deduction in fatal accident cases in respect of benefits payable on death.

7 See para.5-083.

8 (1837) 3 M. & W. 1; 150 E.R. 1030; *Farwell v Boston and Worcester Railroad Corp* 4 Met. 49 (1842).

9 "The mere relation of the master and the servant can never imply an obligation on the part of the master to take more care of the servant than he may reasonably be expected to do of himself": *Priestley v Fowler* (1837) 3 M. & W. 1 at 6; 150 E.R. 1030 at 1032 per Lord Abinger CB.

10 Striking instances are the judgments of Pollock CB in *Vose v Lancashire and Yorkshire Railway Co* (1858) 2 H. & N. 728; 157 E.R. 300 and of Bramwell B in *Dynen v Leach* (1857) 26 L.J.(N.S.) Ex. 221.

11 See Ch.21.

employer himself. If the employer had been negligent the worker's claim was still defeated if he had been guilty of contributory negligence, or even if he merely knew of the danger,[12] but something of a general principle had emerged. If the worker was injured by the employer's own negligence he could recover, but if he was injured by the negligence of a fellow employee he could not.[13]

The advent of the employer's non-delegable duty of care　During the second half of the 19th century judicial opinion veered in favour of the worker, and efforts began to be made to limit the scope of common employment. The doctrine was not finally abolished, however, until 1948[14] and, though much restricted in scope before that date,[15] the harshness of the law was chiefly modified by the evasion of common employment through the development of the rule that an employer was liable for an injury to his worker caused by his own negligence or breach of statutory duty.[16] So far as the latter was concerned, no particular difficulty existed: if a duty was placed directly upon the employer by statute, then he did not discharge that duty by entrusting its performance to another.[17] Nonetheless, how could an employer be personally negligent unless he actually took a hand in the work himself, a physical impossibility where the employer was not a human individual but, as was increasingly the case during the 19th century and is now the general rule, a company with independent legal personality? Such an employer could only act through its servants and, if they were negligent, the doctrine of common employment applied and relieved the employer of liability.

9-004

The answer to this difficulty was found in the concept of duties personal to the employer, for the careful performance of which the employer remained responsible even though the tasks necessary to discharge the duties were entrusted to a servant.[18] "It is quite clear", said Lord Herschell[19]:

> "[T]hat the contract between employer and employed involves on the part of the former the duty of taking reasonable care to provide proper appliances, and to maintain them in a proper condition, and so to carry on his operations as not to subject those employed by him to unnecessary risk. Whatever the dangers of the employment which the employed undertakes, amongst them is certainly not to be numbered the risk of the employer's negligence and the creation or enhancement of danger thereby engendered."

The employer's threefold duty of care　In the famous case of *Wilsons and Clyde Coal Co Ltd v English*,[20] Lord Wright redefined the employer's duty as threefold, "the provision of a competent staff of men, adequate material, and a proper system and effective supervision". The duty is a non-delegable duty of care, so that the employer must not only take reasonable care and skill himself, but must also ensure

9-005

---

[12]　In *Smith v Baker & Sons* [1891] A.C. 325 the House of Lords finally held that mere knowledge did not defeat the workman's claim: para.26-022.

[13]　The negligent employee was, of course, liable, but he was seldom worth suing.

[14]　Law Reform (Personal Injuries) Act 1948 s.1(1). It is not possible to contract out of the Act: s.1(3).

[15]　See, e.g., *Radcliffe v Ribble Motor Services* [1939] A.C. 215; *Graham v Glasgow Corp* [1947] A.C. 368; *Lancaster v London Passenger Transport Board* [1948] 2 All E.R. 796.

[16]　It was settled in *Groves v Wimborne* [1898] 2 Q.B. 402 that common employment afforded no defence in an action brought against the employer for breach of his statutory duty.

[17]　See para.8-023.

[18]　On the scope of non-delegable duties generally, see Ch.21.

[19]　*Smith v Baker* [1891] A.C. 325 at 362.

[20]　[1938] A.C. 57.

that such care and skill is taken by those to whom he entrusts the fulfilment of the duty.[21]

9-006   **The present position**   With the abolition of the doctrine of common employment in 1948,[22] the employer became vicariously liable for the negligence of a fellow servant of the claimant acting in the course of his employment as well as for breach of his personal duty, and it thus became unnecessary always to distinguish between the two kinds of case. Nevertheless the concept of the employer's personal non-delegable duty was survived.[23] There are also numerous and detailed statutory duties which are imposed directly upon employers and these have, at least previously,[24] had the effect of increasing his overall liability for injury suffered by his workers. Vicarious liability is the subject of a separate chapter and here we shall consider the employer's personal duty to his employees, but in view of the mass of statutory duties in existence, to consider the common law alone would give a false picture of the present law of employer's liability. We shall also, therefore, consider first some of the more significant of these duties and their effect upon employers' liability as a whole.

2.   STATUTE LAW

9-007   The Health and Safety at Work, etc. Act 1974 was passed as a result of the report of a Royal Commission which recommended a thorough review of the then existing patchwork of industrial safety legislation.[25] The Act contains a generalised duty upon employers to ensure, so far as is reasonably practicable, the health, safety and welfare at work of all employees. This duty is in some respects reminiscent of the employer's common law duty of care towards his workers, but the duty is supported only by penal sanctions and does not give rise to any civil liability.[26] However, the Act also gave power to repeal existing statutes governing safety and replace them with regulations which would continue to give rise to civil liability unless they provided otherwise.[27] This process made comparatively slow progress until the arrival on the scene of European Community legislation. As a result of a series of EC Directives, implemented by a number of important Regulations, there was a radical reform of the statutory law in this area. It would be entirely out of place in a book of this kind to attempt to consider these provisions in detail but they are (or have been)[28] an important source of civil liability and without some sketch it is not possible to see the general common law in its wider context.

9-008   **Reform: no civil liability for breach of the regulations**   While it is still relevant to sketch out the operation of the regulations which govern the workplace, it must be stressed at the outset that they will, or may, no longer lead to the civil liability of the employer based on breach of the regulations alone. This is the result of an

---

[21]   The duty "is not fulfilled by entrusting its fulfilment to employees, even though selected with due care and skill": [1938] A.C. 57 at 78 per Lord Wright.

[22]   Law Reform (Personal Injuries) Act 1948 s.1(1).

[23]   See *Staveley Iron & Chemical Co v Jones* [1956] A.C. 627.

[24]   See the significant reform referred to in para.9-008.

[25]   Cmnd.5034.

[26]   1974 Act s.47(1).

[27]   1974 Act s.47(2), but see now para.9-008.

[28]   See para.9-008.

amendment to the operative provision of the 1974 Act, which came into force on 1 October 2013, the effect of which is that the breach of any provision after that date shall not be actionable unless the regulations themselves so provide.[29] One consequence of this reversal in the presumption of actionability is that the question of the precise relationship between breach of the regulations and any liability of the employer in negligence will become more significant.[30]

The Regulations   The Management of Health and Safety at Work Regulations 1999[31] are, from an administrative point of view, the central element in the scheme and implement the so-called "framework" EC Directive[32] in so far as the general provisions of the Health and Safety at Work, etc. Act 1974 do not already incorporate the principles of the Directive into English law. Perhaps the most significant feature of the 1999 Regulations is the duty of every employer to make a "suitable and sufficient assessment" of the risks to the health and safety of workers and of other persons likely to be affected. The 1999 Regulations, unlike the others, did not at first generally give rise to civil liability and a later provision for liability[33] has now been reversed,[34] as a result of the reform referred to above.[35] Broadly speaking, the scheme was to replace the old system of legislating separately for each type of trade by a unified set of regulations governing particular aspects of employment, so that, for example, the Workplace (Health, Safety and Welfare) Regulations 1992[36] deal with ventilation, cleanliness and working facilities in offices and shops as well as in factories.[37]

9-009

The nature of the obligations imposed   As was previously the case, the regulations impose a mixture of unqualified, or absolute, obligations and obligations which are qualified in some way. Broadly speaking, such obligations may be divided as follows: (1) to ensure a result; (2) to do what is practicable to ensure a result; and (3) to do what is reasonably practicable to ensure a result. A further distinction to be borne in mind is that while the burden is on the employee to prove that the employer has not ensured a particular result, the burden of proving that this was not practicable, or reasonably practicable, rests on the employer.[38] The decisions of the courts on the interpretation of the obligations imposed by the regulations and the earlier provisions regulating health and safety at work are not easy to

9-010

---

[29]   See s.47(2) as amended by Enterprise and Regulatory Reform Act 2013 s.69(3), (10).
[30]   See para.9-015.
[31]   SI 1999/3242 (replacing SI 1992/2051).
[32]   Directive 89/391.
[33]   SI 2003/2457.
[34]   SI 2013/1667 reg.3.
[35]   See para.9-008.
[36]   SI 1992/3004. Other regulations include: Personal Protective Equipment at Work Regulations 1992 (SI 1992/2966); Manual Handling Operations Regulations 1992 (SI 1992/2793); Workplace (Health, Safety and Welfare) Regulations 1992 (SI 1992/3004); Provision and Use of Work Equipment Regulations 1998 (SI 1998/2306); Lifting Operations and Lifting Equipment Regulations 1998 (SI 1998/2307); Control of Substances Hazardous to Health Regulations 2002 (SI 2002/2677); Work at Height Regulations 2005 (SI 2005/735).
[37]   However, the coverage is not universal: e.g., SI 1992/3004 does not apply to ships, building sites or mines and quarries.
[38]   *Nimmo v Alexander Cowan & Sons Ltd* [1968] A.C. 107; *Egan v Central Manchester etc. NHS Trust* [2008] EWCA Civ 1424; [2009] I.C.R. 585. After all the evidence has been produced the initial burden of proof is rarely of importance: *Dorman Long (Steel) Ltd v Bell* [1964] 1 W.L.R. 333 at 335; *Jenkins v Allied Ironfounders Ltd* [1970] 1 W.L.R. 304 at 312.

reconcile. The only general proposition that can be stated with any confidence is that it is a question of the proper construction of the regulation in each case.

9-011   **The obligation to ensure a result**   Where the obligation is an unqualified one to ensure a result, it may be regarded as absolute. One of the best known provisions of the old law was s.14 of the Factories Act 1961, which required that every dangerous part of machinery should be securely fenced and which was construed as imposing an absolute duty in the sense that difficulty or even impossibility of complying and at the same time leaving the machine in a usable condition afforded no defence.[39] But in relation to other results, the concept of reasonable foreseeability which is relevant to a claim in negligence may be imported, even without the qualification of practicality or reasonable practicality. This is one of the issues on which it is not easy to reconcile the decisions of the courts. For example, in *Hide v Steeplechase Co (Cheltenham) Ltd*[40] the relevant obligation under the Provision and Use of Work Equipment Regulations 1998[41] was to ensure that work equipment was "suitable".[42] This was defined in the Regulations to mean "suitable in any respect which it is reasonably foreseeable will affect the health or safety of any person".[43] The Court of Appeal overturned the finding of the judge that this imported the common law test of "reasonably foreseeable" in negligence. It referred only to the limited defences available under the Directives which are implemented by the Regulations, under which the burden is on the defendant to prove either: (1) occurrences due to unforeseeable circumstances beyond his control; or (2) occurrences due to exceptional events, the consequences of which were unavoidable despite the exercise of all due care.[44] By contrast, in *Baker v Quantum Clothing Group Ltd*,[45] where claims for hearing loss were made by those who had worked in the knitting industry, the issue was whether the workplace was "safe" within the meaning of s.29 of the Factories Act 1961.[46] A majority of the Supreme Court held that, while safety must be determined objectively, it is a relative and not an absolute concept; foreseeability of the risk of hearing loss was therefore relevant and it had to be judged by the level of knowledge and standards prevailing at the time.[47] Similarly, it has been

---

[39]   *John Summers & Sons Ltd v Frost* [1955] A.C. 740.

[40]   [2013] EWCA Civ 545; [2014] 1 All E.R. 405 (not strictly a case of employer liability; the claim was brought by a jockey injured by colliding with a railing post against the owners and operators of the racecourse on the basis of their "control" of the work equipment, i.e., the rail); cf. *Willock v Corus UK Ltd* [2013] EWCA Civ 519; [2013] P.I.Q.R. P21.

[41]   SI 1998/2306.

[42]   See also *Robb v Salamis (M & I) Ltd* [2006] UKHL 56; [2007] I.C.R. 175 (in determining suitability the employer has to bear in mind that workers may be inattentive).

[43]   Regulation 4(4)(a).

[44]   Directive 89/391 art.5(4).

[45]   [2011] UKSC 17; [2011] 1 W.L.R. 1003.

[46]   It was the provisions of the 1961 Act which were in force at the time of the relevant exposure to noise.

[47]   Overruling *Larner v British Steel Plc* [1993] I.C.R. 551. Lord Kerr and Lord Clarke dissented, but agreed with the majority that the test of safety is not confined to some structural or permanent feature of the workplace: it can extend to operations constantly and regularly carried on in it. According to Lord Clarke, s.29 of the 1961 Act is "a results provision" (at [204]). It does not create an absolute liability because of the defence that the employer took all reasonably practical steps (see para.9-012), but it is only that defence which involves consideration of what risks are reasonably foreseeable (at [213]). See also the differing views expressed by Lord Brodie and Lord Drummond Young on the relevance of foreseeability at this stage of the enquiry in *Dow v Amec Group Plc* [2017] CSIH 75; 2018 S.C. 247.

held that for there to be a breach of the strict obligation imposed by the Workplace (Health, Safety and Welfare) Regulations 1992[48] to maintain the workplace in "an efficient state", the condition complained of must have posed a real or material risk of injury to those working there.[49]

The obligation to do what is "practicable" or "reasonably practicable" It seems likely that an obligation to do what is "practicable" to ensure a result is intended to be more onerous than an obligation to do what is "reasonably practicable" to ensure a result.[50] Beyond that, the case law on the meaning of these formulations is, again, not easy to reconcile.[51] In *Baker v Quantum Clothing Group Ltd*, the obligation to make the workplace "safe" was in fact one to do so "so far as is reasonably practicable" and Lord Mance expressed the view that "the criteria relevant to reasonable practicability must on any view very largely reflect the criteria relevant to satisfaction of the common law duty to take care".[52] This was, however, said in circumstances where the correctness of the approach taken by the Court of Appeal did not arise for consideration given the finding that the workplace had not been found to be unsafe in any event.[53] The Court of Appeal had followed an earlier decision in which it was suggested that the test of whether steps were not reasonably practicable required there to be "gross disproportion" between the risk of injury[54] and the steps necessary to avoid it, or for the risk to be "insignificant" in relation to the cost.[55] Whatever the meaning given to reasonably practicable, one difference between the statutory requirement and common law negligence is that, as noted above, it is for the employer to prove that he has done what was reasonably practicable. Once the employee has proved that a result has not been achieved, he is not required to aver what measures the defendant should have taken to comply with the regulation.

9-012

Scope of the obligations imposed In some cases any civil liability of the employer has turned not on the nature and meaning of the obligation imposed, but on whether the relevant obligation is owed at all. For example, under the Provision and Use of Work Equipment Regulations 1998[56] "work equipment" means, "any machinery, appliance, apparatus, tool or installation for use at work (whether exclusively or not)" and the requirements of the Regulations apply to "such equipment provided for use or used by an employee at his work". The Regulations

9-013

---

48 SI 1992/3004.
49 *Cruz v Chief Constable of Lancashire Police* [2016] EWCA Civ 402.
50 "Likelihood or foresight of injury does not come into the matter. Nor is it of any relevance to consider whether [the measures to be taken] would be sensible (as opposed to impractical) ... This is a sea-change from the old concepts of common law negligence": *Blair v Chief Constable of Sussex Police* [2012] EWCA Civ 633; [2012] I.C.R. D33 at [14] per Longmore LJ.
51 See, e.g., *Sanderson v National Coal Board* [1961] 2 Q.B. 244; *Brown v National Coal Board* [1962] A.C. 574; *Jayne v National Coal Board* [1963] 2 All E.R. 220.
52 *Baker v Quantum Clothing Group Ltd* [2011] UKSC 17; [2011] 1 W.L.R. 1003.
53 On the basis of the test referred to in para.9-011.
54 i.e., both "the gravity of the harm which might occur as well as the likelihood of its occurrence": *Mann v Northern Electric Distribution Ltd* [2010] EWCA Civ 141 at [12] (risk of steps taken to enter sub-station not foreseeable).
55 [2009] EWCA Civ 499 at [82]–[87] citing *Edwards v National Coal Board* [1949] 1 All E.R. 743 at 747. See also *Austin Rover Group Ltd v HM's Inspector of Factories* [1990] 1 A.C. 619 at 626—627.
56 SI 1998/2306.

present formidable problems in determining how far they extend beyond the "direct sphere of [the employer's] undertaking or control"[57] since they plainly do not require that the equipment should have been provided by the employer or even specifically approved by him.[58] In *Smith v Northamptonshire CC*[59] the claimant was injured when a ramp at the house from which she was collecting a person confined to a wheelchair collapsed. Her employers knew of the ramp, indeed they had inspected it properly and that had revealed no defect. A majority of the House of Lords held that there had been no breach of the Regulations. There had to be "some specific nexus (beyond the mere fact of use) ... between the equipment and the employer's undertaking",[60] such that the equipment had been[61]:

> "[I]ncorporated into and adopted as part of the employer's business or other undertaking, whether as a result of being provided by the employer for use in it or as a result of being provided by anyone else and being used by the employee in it with the employer's consent and endorsement."

As for the requirement that the equipment be for use "at work", in *Kennedy v Cordia (Services) LLP*,[62] the Supreme Court held that this condition was met whenever the employee was acting in the course of his employment, and that it was not necessary that the risks ameliorated by the equipment be associated with the job the claimant was employed to do. It followed that the employer of a home carer who injured her wrist after slipping on an icy path leading to a client's house could be liable under the Regulations for not supplying her with anti-slip attachments for her footwear. The position where the employer's business is to deal with equipment submitted for repair by third parties is unclear.[63] In *Wembridge Claimants v Winter*[64] the court also felt some difficulty in applying the concept of control of the "workplace" in the context of the scene of a fire.

9-014 **The compensatory role of the Regulations** The old legislation was primarily regulatory in its nature, that is to say it provided an administrative mechanism, backed by the enforcement powers of bodies like the Factory Inspectorate and the Health and Safety Executive, and, if necessary, by criminal prosecution,[65] to promote safety by preventing accidents and disease. That remains true under the

---

57   *Smith v Northamptonshire CC* [2009] UKHL 27; [2009] I.C.R. 734 at [64].
58   cf. the wording of para.3(1) of the underlying Directive.
59   [2009] UKHL 27; [2009] I.C.R. 734.
60   [2009] UKHL 27; [2009] I.C.R. 734 at [63] per Lord Mance.
61   [2009] UKHL 27; [2009] I.C.R. 734 at [65] per Lord Mance. See also *Spencer-Franks v Kellogg Brown and Root Ltd* [2008] UKHL 46; [2008] I.C.R. 863; *PRP Architects v Reid* [2006] EWCA Civ 1119; [2007] I.C.R. 78; *Couzens v T McGee & Co Ltd* [2009] EWCA Civ 95; *Mason v Satelcom* [2008] EWCA Civ 494; [2008] I.C.R. 971.
62   [2016] UKSC 6; [2016] 1 W.L.R. 597.
63   In *Spencer-Franks v Kellogg Brown and Root Ltd* [2008] UKHL 46; [2008] I.C.R. 863, Lord Hoffmann at [26] doubted whether the Regulations would make an employer liable for defects in equipment submitted by a third party for repair but thought that, since the Regulations extended the scope of the liability to persons having "control" of the equipment, the third party might be liable. It seems extraordinary that a person taking his car to a garage for repair could incur liability without fault for a vehicle about which he has no expertise to a mechanic with whom he has no relationship whatever.
64   [2013] EWHC 2331 (QB).
65   The regulations themselves say nothing about criminal penalties; those are to be found in the 1974 Act s.33. See the remarks of Ormrod LJ in *Mirza v Ford Motor Co Ltd* [1981] I.C.R. 757 at 761, on the tension between the penal purposes and the compensatory effect of the Factories Act 1961.

present regime.[66] There has always therefore been a tension between the regulatory and compensatory roles. The Regulations were never designed as a code of compensation in private law; that was merely their incidental effect as a result of the long tradition of treating industrial safety legislation as giving rise to a civil cause of action. The result has been that, rather than a coherent system of employer's civil liability, English law has consisted of a patchwork of statutory duties overlaying general common law liability for negligence. There do seem to have been differences of approach to the balance of these elements of liability, one seeking to reconcile them with the common law approach, the other emphasising compensation.

In *Fytche v Wincanton Logistics Plc*[67] the claimant was a tanker driver who had been issued with steel-capped boots by his employers because there was a risk of heavy objects falling on his feet. During freezing weather in which the claimant had had to dig to extricate his tanker, some water got into one of the boots through a tiny hole and he suffered mild frostbite to a toe. The employers were not negligent in failing to provide weatherproof boots because as a rule he would not be exposed to freezing conditions. However, because the boots had been provided as a precaution against the risk of falling objects they were safety equipment under the Personal Protective Equipment at Work Regulations 1992[68] and had to be, "maintained … in an efficient state, in efficient working order and in good repair". So, it was argued, the tiny hole meant that they were not in this state and this had caused his injury, leading to liability. The majority of the House of Lords regarded such a result as "very strange and arbitrary"[69] and they rejected the argument: the equipment only had to be efficient and in good repair in respect of the risk against which it was provided. For the minority, however, this involved reading a restriction into the legislation which was not there.[70]

The new liability regime Questions about how expansively the Regulations should be interpreted will continue to be just as relevant so far as any penal sanctions are concerned, but in terms of civil liability they have become less significant in light of the change from a presumption of actionability to a presumption of non-actionability.[71] What significance, if any, remains will depend on their relevance to the claims in negligence to which employees will henceforward be confined.[72] It has always been possible to rely on statutory infringements as evidence of common law negligence,[73] but where all that has been established is infringement of an absolute obligation that, in and of itself, will not suffice for a successful claim in negligence.

9-015

---

[66] The various regulations, "are there primarily to promote a culture of good practice with a view to preventing injury": *Smith v Northamptonshire CC* [2009] UKHL 27; [2009] I.C.R. 734 at [4] per Lord Hope.

[67] [2004] UKHL 31; [2004] I.C.R. 975.

[68] SI 1992/2966.

[69] [2004] UKHL 31; [2004] I.C.R. 975 at [7] per Lord Hoffmann.

[70] See to similar effect the division of opinion in the Supreme Court in *Baker v Quantum Clothing Group Ltd* [2011] UKSC 17; [2011] 1 W.L.R. 1003, para.9-011.

[71] See para.9-008.

[72] See, e.g., *Cockerill v CXK Ltd* [2018] EWHC 1155 (QB) at [17]: "in considering the nature of the modern common law employers' duty it is still permissible to have regard to the statutory duties, to understand in more detail what steps reasonable and conscientious employers can be expected to take".

[73] See *Lochgelly Iron and Coal Co Ltd v M'Mullan* [1934] A.C. 1; *Franklin v Gramophone Co Ltd* [1948] 1 K.B. 542; *National Coal Board v England* [1954] A.C. 403.

It is in relation to such cases of strict liability that the change in the law will be felt most keenly.[74] In some cases, however, the regulations (and their associated codes of practice)[75] may come very close in practice to being treated as the standard measure of what is required under the common law,[76] albeit the burden of proof will remain on the employee throughout.[77] In cases other than those involving breach of an absolute obligation, this shift in the burden of proof may prove to be the most significant effect of the change in the law.[78]

3. COMMON LAW

9-016   **The utility of the employer's personal duty**   Although, as we have seen,[79] the employer is now liable to his employee for an injury caused by a fellow employee in the course of his employment, the concept of the personal duty continues to serve a useful purpose. In many cases it is obviously much more convenient to say that a given state of affairs or a given event proves a breach by the employer of his personal duty than to say that some employee must somehow have been negligent for that state of affairs to exist or for that event to have come about. If a worker is injured because no one has taken the trouble to provide him with an obviously necessary safety device, it is sufficient and in general satisfactory to say that the employer has not fulfilled his duty, even if the employer is a company. It is unnecessarily complicated to say that someone whose duty it was to provide the device in question, or someone whose duty it was to see that there was someone else to

---

[74] For example, see *Stark v Post Office* [2000] I.C.R. 1013 where a postman was injured because the brakes on his bicycle failed. The fault could not reasonably have been detected, but the employer was liable under the applicable regulations (Provision and Use of Work Equipment Regulations 1992 (SI 1992/2932)) on the basis of the failure to ensure the bicycle was in "good condition" and "properly maintained"; cf. *Ball v Street* [2005] EWCA Civ 76. The shift away from strict liability may be welcomed by some: "the relative inflexibility of the regulations seem to me to be less apt to do justice than the suppleness of the common law": *Wembridge Claimants v Winter* [2013] EWHC 2331 (QB) at [197] per Irwin J.

[75] Though not a code of practice, the statutory duty to conduct a risk assessment may begin to play an even bigger role in negligence claims. In *Threefall v Hull City Council* [2010] EWCA Civ 1147; [2011] I.C.R. 209 Smith LJ (at [35]) observed that: "Such a requirement (whether statutory or not) has to a large extent taken the place of the old common law requirement that an employer had to consider (and take action against) those risks which could reasonably be foreseen. The modern requirement is that he should take positive thought for the risks arising from his operations"; and see *Uren v Corporate Leisure (UK) Ltd* [2011] EWCA Civ 66; [2013] EWHC 353 (QB); *Kennedy v Cordia (Services) LLP* [2016] UKSC 6; [2016] 1 W.L.R. 597 at [89], [110]; cf. *Blair-Ford v CRS Adventures Ltd* [2012] EWHC 2360 (QB) at [46].

[76] The Manual Handling Operations Regulations 1992 (SI 1992/2793) may provide an example because the Regulations themselves are (necessarily, given their subject-matter) rather less precise than the others. On the application of these Regulations see *O'Neill v DSG Retail Ltd* [2002] EWCA Civ 1139; [2003] I.C.R. 222. See also the extent to which the negligence concept of reasonably foreseeable may be imported into the result which must be ensured (para.9-011) and the meaning given to "reasonably practicable" (para.9-012).

[77] cf. the position under the regulations themselves where the burden is on the employer to show that it was not "reasonably practicable" to ensure a particular result: para.9-012.

[78] *Galashiels Gas Co v Millar* [1949] A.C. 275 at 282 per Lord Morton: "[The] sub-section must have been so worded in order to relieve the injured workman from the burden of proving that there was some particular step which the employers could have taken and did not take. This would often be a difficult matter, more especially if the cause of the failure of the mechanism to operate could not be ascertained. The statute renders the task of the injured workman easier by saying 'You need only prove that the mechanism failed work efficiently and that this failure caused the accident'."

[79] See para.9-006.

consider what safety devices were required and to provide them, must have been negligent and therefore that the employer is vicariously liable. Again, in many cases the only person involved in the sequence of events leading up to the accident is the claimant himself and yet his employer is liable, for example because the claimant should not have been left alone to do the job. In terms of vicarious liability this would have to be explained by saying that some other employee had somehow failed in his duty of organising the work. It is simpler, and no less accurate, to say that the employer himself was in breach of his duty.[80]

It is not only for its convenience, however, that the continued use of the employer's personal duty is justified. True vicarious liability exists only where an employee has committed a tort in the course of his employment,[81] but the employer's liability is not so restricted, so that there are cases in which the worker's injury is attributable to the negligence of an independent contractor and yet the employer is liable for breach of his personal duty to the worker.[82] Moreover, though employers' liability is most commonly dealt with as a matter of tort, it is also a matter of contract,[83] and the worker's contract of service is made with his employer, not with his fellow employees. Duties which exist by virtue of express or implied terms in the contract of employment must, therefore, be duties owed by the employer himself.

A. The Employer's Duty

One general duty We have already noted Lord Wright's threefold division of the employer's duty—"the provision of a competent staff of men, adequate material and a proper system and effective supervision"[84] —and, making due allowance for its being expressed in terms contemplating industrial work, it is convenient to adhere approximately to this in the exposition which follows. In truth, however, there is but one duty, a duty to take reasonable care so to carry on operations as not to subject employees to unnecessary risk.[85]

9-017

The majority of the reported cases concern accidents, but that is only because in earlier times there was less awareness of the risks to health (as opposed to safety) presented by employment. The development of knowledge about matters like the

---

[80] *McCafferty v Metropolitan Police Receiver* [1977] 1 W.L.R. 1073 is a good example of this approach.

[81] See Ch.21.

[82] See para.9-029.

[83] *Matthews v Kuwait Bechtel Corp* [1959] 2 Q.B. 57; *Reid v Rush & Tompkins* [1990] 1 W.L.R. 212; *Johnstone v Bloomsbury HA* [1992] Q.B. 333; *Scally v Southern Health & Social Services Board* [1992] 1 A.C. 294; and see para.1-004.

[84] *Wilsons and Clyde Coal Co v English* [1938] A.C. 57 at 78; see para.9-005.

[85] i.e., risk of injury: it is not the employer's duty to insure his employee nor to advise him to insure himself (*Reid v Rush & Tompkins* [1990] 1 W.L.R. 212); nor, in the absence of some specific assumption of responsibility, to take steps to safeguard the employee's economic well-being: *Crossley v Faithful & Gould Holdings Ltd* [2004] EWCA Civ 293; [2004] I.C.R. 1615; *Greenway v Johnson Matthey Plc* [2016] EWCA Civ 408; [2016] 1 W.L.R. 4487 (not in issue on appeal: [2018] UKSC 18; [2019] A.C. 403). In *Greenway*, Sales LJ said (at [37]) that: "The classic formulation of the duty owed by an employer to an employee is focused on protection of the employee from physical injury, not protection from economic harm." cf. *Rihan v Ernst & Young Global Ltd* [2020] EWHC 901 (QB): no duty to safeguard partner in accountancy firm against pure economic loss caused by his having to cease working to protect his physical safety; but on facts a narrower duty of care was recognised in respect of loss of earnings caused by the defendants' failure to perform an audit in an ethical and professional manner.

effects of asbestos,[86] noise,[87] vibration[88] and the effects of repetitive manual movements,[89] coupled with a relaxation of the former strict provisions on limitation of actions,[90] has produced much litigation in recent decades, sometimes on a very large scale indeed. Furthermore, it is now recognised that the employer's duty extends to the effect of working conditions on the mental health of his employees.[91]

In many respects, therefore, the duty is similar to the duty of care in the tort of negligence generally, but expressed in terms appropriate to the relationship of employer and employee.[92] As we shall see, the duty of the employer cannot, as can an ordinary duty of care, always be discharged by the employment of an independent contractor,[93] but it is nevertheless a duty of care, not an absolute duty,[94] and it is for the claimant to prove its breach.[95]

9-018   **Scope of the employer's duty of care**   The employer's duty of care concerns not only the actual work of his employees, but also all such acts as are normally and reasonably incidental to a day's work,[96] and the mere fact that an employee disobeys an order does not necessarily deprive him of the protection of his employer's duty, though he may, of course, be guilty of contributory negligence.[97] The special duty we are now considering arises only when the relationship of employer and employee exists[98] and so an independent contractor employed to do work in a factory, or a visitor, cannot rely upon it. Such a person will, however, generally be owed a duty of care on some other basis.[99]

9-019   **Emergency services and armed forces**   The same general duty will be owed in relationships which are not, strictly speaking, governed by a contract of employment but which are closely analogous to those that are, such as that between a police

---

[86] See, e.g., *Jameson v Central Electricity Generating Board* [2000] 1 A.C. 455.
[87] See, e.g., *Thompson v Smith's Shiprepairers (North Shields) Ltd* [1984] Q.B. 405; *Baker v Quantum Clothing Group Ltd* [2011] UKSC 17; [2011] 1 W.L.R. 1003.
[88] See, e.g., *Bowman v Harland & Wolff* [1992] I.R.L.R. 349.
[89] See, e.g., *Pickford v ICI Plc* [1998] 1 W.L.R. 1189.
[90] See Ch.26.
[91] *Hatton v Sutherland* [2002] EWCA Civ 76; [2002] I.C.R. 613; *Yapp v Foreign and Commonwealth Office* [2014] EWCA Civ 1512; [2015] I.C.R. D13. See para.5-084.
[92] The special relationship of employer and employee may impose positive duties of assistance or protection: thus an employer may be obliged to provide medical assistance in cases of illness or injury in no way attributable to him (*Kasapis v Laimos* [1959] 2 Lloyd's Rep. 378) or to warn his workers to be medically examined if he learns that past working conditions, which were then regarded as proper, have caused a danger of disease (*Wright v Dunlop Rubber Co* (1971) 11 K.I.R. 311).
[93] See para.9-028.
[94] *Winter v Cardiff RDC* [1950] 1 All E.R. 819 at 823; *Davie v New Merton Board Mills* [1959] A.C. 604.
[95] Where difficulty of proof is the result of the defendant's breach, the claimant's evidence will be judged benevolently: *Keefe v Isle of Man Steam Packet Co Ltd* [2010] EWCA Civ 683 (employer failed to take noise measurements in the workplace).
[96] *Davidson v Handley Page Ltd* [1945] 1 All E.R. 235. cf. *Vaughan v Ministry of Defence* [2015] EWHC 1404 (QB) (no breach of defendant's duty of care qua employer to a marine injured in a swimming accident while off duty on a training week).
[97] *Rands v McNeil* [1955] 1 Q.B. 253 (but no breach of duty on the facts).
[98] The importance of safety may lead the court to emphasise the substance rather than the form of the relationship: *Lane v Shire Roofing (Oxford) Ltd* [1995] I.R.L.R. 493; see *Mullaney v Chief Constable of the West Midlands* [2001] EWCA Civ 700 (police—"quasi-employment"); and see para.9-019.
[99] For example, under the Occupiers' Liability Act 1957.

officer and a chief constable.[100] In the case of the emergency services generally, whether the relationship is strictly one of employment or analogous thereto, the operational requirements of the job may mean that the employee accepts the risks which are inherent in the nature of the work, but the duty owed by the employer remains the same[101]:

> "The starting point is that an Ambulance Service owes the same duty of care towards its employees as does any other employer. There is no special rule in English law qualifying the obligations of others towards firefighters, or presumably police officers, ambulance technicians and others whose occupations in the public service are inherently dangerous ... Such public servants accept the risks which are inherent in their work, but not the risks which the exercise of reasonable care on the part of those who owe them a duty of care could avoid."

While, therefore, "there is no established 'battle immunity' in relation to decisions taken in the heat of the moment by those in charge in the emergency services",[102] those circumstances will be relevant in determining whether there was any breach of duty, so that, for example, "it is incumbent on the Courts ... to make every allowance for the difficulty of exercising command and making swift decisions on a fireground"[103] In relation to the armed forces, however, a "combat immunity" is recognised to exclude the existence of a duty of care in "the conduct of an active military operation or act of war", albeit that this policy-based exception to the normal common law liability regime is narrowly construed.[104]

Competent staff   The duty to take reasonable care to provide a competent staff is less significant in the modern law than it was in the days of the common employment doctrine, but it may still play a role. If, for example, an employer engages a person with insufficient experience or training for a particular job and as a result another worker is injured, it may well be that there is a breach of this branch of the employer's duty.[105] Furthermore, if one employee is injured by the violent horseplay of another, or is actually assaulted by him, the employer may escape vicarious liability on the basis that the conduct in question was not in the course of the wrongdoer's employment.[106] It may be, however, that the employer should have known of the wrongdoer's playful or vicious propensities and taken steps to prevent

9-020

[100] *Mullaney v Chief Constable of the West Midlands* [2001] EWCA Civ 700; *Waters v MPC* [2000] 1 W.L.R. 1607.
[101] *Sussex Ambulance NHS Trust v King* [2002] EWCA Civ 953 per Hale LJ, cited as "an authoritative exposition of the relevant principles" concerning the duties owed by employers to their staff in the context of the delivery of emergency services: *Smith v Ministry of Defence* [2013] UKSC 41; [2014] A.C. 52 at [171] per Lord Carnwath. cf. *Burn v Ministry of Justice* [2012] EWHC 876 (QB).
[102] *Wembridge Claimants v Winter* [2013] EWHC 2331 (QB) at [225].
[103] *Wembridge Claimants v Winter* [2013] EWHC 2331 (QB) at [225].
[104] *Smith v Ministry of Defence* [2013] UKSC 41; [2014] A.C. 52, see para.5-024.
[105] See *Butler v Fife Coal Co* [1912] A.C. 149.
[106] *O'Reilly v National Rail and Tramway Appliances Ltd* [1966] 1 All E.R. 499. This might be thought to be less likely applying the modern "close connection" test to the "course of employment" question, but in fact even when this test has been applied intentional assaults by co-workers have not generally attracted vicarious liability: see, e.g., *Wilson v Exel UK Ltd* 2010 S.L.T. 671; *Vaickuviene v J Sainsbury Plc* 2014 S.C. 147; *Graham v Commercial Bodyworks Ltd* [2015] I.C.R. 665. cf. *Weddall v Barchester Healthcare Ltd* [2012] EWCA Civ 25; [2012] I.R.L.R. 307 (employer vicariously liable for assault by junior employee on senior employee when reacting to instructions); *Bellman v Northampton Recruitment Ltd* [2018] EWCA Civ 2214; [2019] 1 All E.R. 113.

them from resulting in injury to another, in which case he may be liable for breach of his personal duty.[107]

9-021 **Adequate plant and equipment** The employer must take reasonable care to provide his workers with the necessary plant and equipment,[108] and is therefore liable if an accident is caused through the absence of some such item which a reasonable employer would have recognised was needed.[109] He must also take reasonable care to maintain the plant and equipment in proper condition, and the more complex and dangerous it is the more frequent must be the inspection.[110] What is required in each case, however, is reasonable care according to the circumstances, and in some cases it may be legitimate to rely upon the worker himself to rectify simple defects in the plant he is using.[111] The duty extends to the installation of necessary safety devices on dangerous machinery[112] and the provision of protective equipment when required,[113] but the employer does not warrant the safety of plant and equipment. At common law, therefore, he is not liable if an accident is caused by some latent defect in equipment which could not have been discovered by the exercise of reasonable care on the part of the persons for whose negligence he is answerable.[114] By the Employer's Liability (Defective Equipment) Act 1969,[115] however, if an employee is injured in the course of his employment as a result of a defect in equipment provided by his employer and the defect is due to the fault of a third party, whether identified or not, then the injury is deemed to be also attributable to the negligence of the employer. If a worker can show, for example, that a tool he was using was defective in such a way that there must, on the balance of probabilities, have been negligence or other fault in its manufacture, and that his injury was caused by that defect, then the employer as well as the manufacturer will be liable to him, whether or not the employer was in any way to blame.[116] The

---

[107] *Hudson v Ridge Manufacturing Co* [1957] 2 Q.B. 348. cf. *Smith v Crossley Bros* (1951) 95 S.J. 655; *Coddington v International Harvester Co of Great Britain Ltd* (1969) 6 K.I.R. 146. The principle may extend to victimisation or bullying where there is sufficient injury: *Waters v MPC* [2000] 1 W.L.R. 1607.

[108] While a defendant who engages a contractor is generally entitled to look to the contractor to safeguard the latter's employees, he may owe the employees a duty if he assumes some responsibility, for example by providing unsuitable equipment: *McGarvey v Eve NCI Ltd* [2002] EWCA Civ 374.

[109] *Williams v Birmingham Battery and Metal Co* [1892] 2 Q.B. 338; *Lovell v Blundells & Crompton & Co* [1944] 1 K.B. 502; *Ross v Associated Portland Cement Manufacturers Ltd* [1964] 1 W.L.R. 768. It is not always necessary, however, for the employer to adopt the latest improvements: *Toronto Power Co v Paskwan* [1915] A.C. 734 per Sir Arthur Channell. See also *O'Connor v BTC* [1958] 1 W.L.R. 346.

[110] For example, *Murphy v Phillips* (1876) 35 L.T. 477; *Baxter v St Helena Hospital Management Committee, The Times,* 14 February 1972. Even inspection may not always be sufficient: *Barkway v S Wales Transport Co* [1950] A.C. 185; *Pearce v Round Oak Steel Works Ltd* [1969] 1 W.L.R. 595.

[111] *Bristol Aeroplane Co v Franklin* [1948] W.N. 341; *Richardson v Stephenson Clarke Ltd* [1969] 1 W.L.R. 1695.

[112] *Jones v Richards* [1955] 1 W.L.R. 444; *Lovelidge v Anselm Odling & Sons Ltd* [1967] 2 Q.B. 351.

[113] *Qualcast Ltd v Haynes* [1959] A.C. 743 per Lord Denning but cf. *Brown v Rolls-Royce* [1960] 1 W.L.R. 210. See also *McGhee v NCB* [1973] 1 W.L.R. 1 (washing facilities).

[114] *Davie v New Merton Board Mills* [1959] A.C. 604. Contrast the position under statute in *Stark v Post Office* [2000] I.C.R. 1013.

[115] "Equipment" has been held to include a 90,000-tonne ship: *Coltman v Bibby Tankers Ltd* [1988] A.C. 276. The word extends to material which is used in the employment and is not confined to tools with which that material is processed: *Knowles v Liverpool CC* [1993] 1 W.L.R. 1428.

[116] *Clarkson v Jackson, The Times,* 21 November 1984. The employer is entitled to raise the defence

principal advantage of this from the worker's point of view is that he is relieved of any need to identify and sue the manufacturer of defective equipment provided by his employer. Under the Consumer Protection Act 1987,[117] the manufacturer is subject to a stricter liability not dependent on proof of negligence. Since "fault" is defined in the 1969 Act as, "negligence, breach of statutory duty or other act or omission which gives rise to liability in tort"[118] it seems that in such a case the employer may also be liable even if there is no fault on anyone's part. Since there is no longer any civil liability for breach of the statutory regulations which regulate work equipment,[119] the prospect of such "no fault" claims under the 1969 Act may have renewed significance.

Safe place of work   Though not expressly mentioned by Lord Wright in *Wilsons and Clyde Coal Co v English*,[120] it is clear that the employer's duty of care extends to the place of work[121] and in some cases may even apply to the means of access to that place.[122] No particular difficulty exists where the place of work is in the occupation or control of the employer, but it must be recalled that the duty is one of reasonable care only and thus the employer is not obliged to take unreasonable precautions even against foreseeable risks.[123] It used to be thought that because an employer had no control over premises in the occupation of a third party he could owe no duty in respect of those premises, but it is now clear that this is wrong.[124] The duty of care remains, but what is required for its performance may well be different where the place of work is not under the employer's control.[125] Even if the employer is not responsible for defects in someone else's premises under this heading, he may be under a duty to give advice, instructions or orders about commonly encountered hazards (a matter which would fall under the next heading). Thus it has been held that in modern conditions[126] the employer of a window cleaner should

9-022

---

of contributory negligence against the worker and may seek to recover indemnity or contribution from the person to whose fault the defect is attributable. He cannot, however, contract out of the liability imposed by the Act.

[117] See para.11-016 (strict liability of manufacturer).

[118] 1969 Act s.1(3).

[119] The Provision and Use of Work Equipment Regulations 1998 (SI 1998/2306): see para.9-008. The Regulations would not cover the case where the complaint is that there has been a failure to provide necessary equipment.

[120] [1938] A.C. 57.

[121] For example, *Cole v De Trafford (No.2)* [1918] 2 K.B. 535 per Scrutton LJ; *Davidson v Handley Page* [1945] 1 All E.R. 235 at 236. At the lowest, the employer's duty to his employee in respect of premises occupied by the employer must be the common duty of care under the Occupiers' Liability Act 1957. Most workplaces are now likely to be covered by the Workplace (Health, Safety and Welfare) Regulations 1992 (SI 1992/3004), but there is no longer any civil liability for breach of the regulations alone: see para.9-008.

[122] *Ashdown v Samuel Williams & Sons* [1957] 1 Q.B. 409 at 430–432; *Smith v National Coal Board* [1967] 1 W.L.R. 871. The employer cannot be subject to a duty of maintenance in so far as the means of access consists of a public highway, but if the employee has to cross private property, whether the employer's own or that of a third party, the duty should exist.

[123] *Latimer v AEC Ltd* [1953] A.C. 643; *Thomas v Bristol Aeroplane Co* [1954] 1 W.L.R. 694.

[124] *Wilson v Tyneside Window Cleaning Co* [1958] 2 Q.B. 110; *Smith v Austin Lifts* [1959] 1 W.L.R. 100; *Clay v AJ Crump & Sons Ltd* [1964] 1 Q.B. 533.

[125] *Wilson v Tyneside Window Cleaning Co* [1958] 2 Q.B. 110 at 121–122; *Kilbride v Scottish & Newcastle Breweries* 1986 S.L.T. 642.

[126] cf. *General Cleaning Contractors Ltd v Christmas* [1953] A.C. 180, where the House of Lords was not prepared to go so far.

place an embargo on cleaning upper floor windows by standing on the sill unless there are anchorage points for a safety harness.[127]

9-023   **Safe system of working**   This, the most frequently invoked branch of the employer's duty, is also the most difficult to define, but it includes[128]:

> "[T]he physical lay-out of the job—the setting of the stage, so to speak—the sequence in which the work is to be carried out, the provision in proper cases of warnings and notices and the issue of special instructions. A system may be adequate for the whole course of the job or it may have to be modified or improved to meet the circumstances which arise; such modifications or improvements ... equally fall under the head of system."

The employer's duty in respect of the system of working is most evident where the work is of a regular or routine nature, but its application is not limited to such cases. The concept is a flexible one, which can be applied as much to a police operation as to work in a factory.[129] Even where a single act of a particular kind is to be performed, the employer may have an obligation to organise the work, for example if it is of a complicated or unusual kind or if a large number of people are involved.[130] In each case it is a question of fact whether a reasonable employer would have left it to his workers to decide for themselves how the job should be done.[131]

In devising a system of working the employer must take into account the fact that workers are often heedless of their own safety,[132] and this has two implications. First, the system should so far as is reasonably possible minimise the danger of a worker's own foreseeable carelessness. Secondly, the employer must also exercise reasonable care to see that his system of working is complied with by those for whose safety it is instituted and that the necessary safety precautions are observed.[133] Lord Denning said in one case,[134] however, (and others have agreed[135]) that this is a proposition not of law but of good sense, so that proof that a worker was never actually instructed to wear necessary protective clothing is not of itself proof of negligence. The employer's personal duty is not confined to devising a safe system, but also extends to its implementation, so that the employer is liable even if the system itself is safe but A fails to follow it and causes injury to B.[136] It is clear that

---

[127] *King v Smith* [1995] I.C.R. 339.

[128] *Speed v Thomas Swift & Co* [1943] K.B. 557 at 563–564.

[129] *Mullaney v Chief Constable of the West Midlands* [2001] EWCA Civ 700; *French v Sussex CC* [2006] EWCA Civ 312 (claim failed on other grounds).

[130] *Winter v Cardiff RDC* [1950] W.N. 193 at 200; *Boyle v Kodak Ltd* [1969] 1 W.L.R. 661.

[131] Since the abolition of common employment the employer is liable vicariously for the negligence of the person in charge of the operation, but this cannot assist the claimant if he was himself in charge or if no worker was guilty of negligence.

[132] *General Cleaning Contractors v Christmas* [1953] A.C. 180 at 189–190; *Smith v National Coal Board* [1967] 1 W.L.R. 871 at 873; *Kerry v Carter* [1969] 1 W.L.R. 1372.

[133] *General Cleaning Contractors v Christmas* [1953] A.C. 180. cf. *Woods v Durable Suites* [1953] 1 W.L.R. 857; *Bux v Slough Metals Ltd* [1973] 1 W.L.R. 1358; *Birch v Ministry of Defence* [2013] EWCA Civ 676 (Ministry of Defence liable for allowing soldier to drive when unqualified to so).

[134] *Qualcast (Wolverhampton) Ltd v Haynes* [1959] A.C. 743 at 760.

[135] *Smith v Austin Lifts* [1959] 1 W.L.R. 100 at 105. In *Smith v Scot Bowyers* [1986] I.R.L.R. 315 it was held to be enough to inform workers about the availability of replacement boots; it was not necessary to inspect boots in use from time to time.

[136] *McDermid v Nash Dredging and Reclamation Co Ltd* [1987] A.C. 906; *Chandler v Cape Plc* [2012] EWCA Civ 525; [2012] 1 W.L.R. 3111.

the duty to provide a safe system of work includes the duty to conduct an appropriate risk assessment.[137]

B. Standard of Care

Common practice[138]   As has been emphasised in the foregoing paragraphs and constantly reiterated by the courts, the employer's duty is a duty of care only and there are limits to the protection which the employer must provide, even against foreseeable risk to his employee[139]:

> "He must weigh up the risk in terms of the likelihood of injury occurring and the potential consequences if it does; and he must balance against this the probable effectiveness of the precautions that can be taken to meet it and the expense and inconvenience they involve. If he is found to have fallen below the standard to be properly expected of a reasonable and prudent employer in these respects, he is negligent."

9-024

The common practice of other employers is relevant in determining whether the defendant employer has fallen below the standard of care, but is not necessarily determinative.[140] For example, it is not sufficient to follow common practice if "in the light of common sense or newer knowledge it is clearly bad",[141] or if a risk which was previously "acceptable" is, at the time of injury, no longer so.[142] When considering the relevance of common practice a distinction may be drawn between the "average employer" and larger employers with additional resources who perhaps should have altered their practice at an earlier stage.[143] The same is true of any code of practice[144]:

> "[T]o follow a relevant code of practice or regulatory instrument will often afford a defence to a claim in negligence. But there are circumstances where it does not do so. For example, it may be shown that the code of practice or regulatory instrument is compromised because the standards that it requires have been lowered as a result of heavy lobbying by interested parties; or because it covers a field in which apathy and fatalism has prevailed amongst workers, trade unions, employers and legislators ... or because the instrument has failed to keep abreast of the latest technology and scientific understanding."

---

[137] See, e.g., *Vaile v Havering LBC* [2011] EWCA Civ 246; [2011] E.L.R. 274. The source of the duty to conduct the assessment may be statutory.

[138] See, generally, para.6-026.

[139] *Stokes v Guest, Keene and Nettlefold (Bolts and Nuts) Ltd* [1968] 1 W.L.R. 1776 at 1783 per Swanwick J. See, e.g., *Latimer v AEC Ltd* [1953] A.C. 643; *Coates v Jaguar Cars Ltd* [2004] EWCA Civ 337; and *Mitchell v United Co-operatives Ltd* [2012] EWCA Civ 348 (not negligent not to have fitted security screens or installed a security guard in a shop to deter robbery)

[140] *Morris v West Hartlepool Steam Navigation Co Ltd* [1956] A.C. 552.

[141] *Stokes v Guest, Keene and Nettlefold (Bolts and Nuts) Ltd* [1968] 1 W.L.R. 1776 at 1783 per Swanwick J.

[142] *Thompson v Smiths Shiprepairers (North Shields) Ltd* [1984] Q.B. 405 at 415–416 per Mustill J; *Williams v University of Birmingham* [2011] EWCA Civ 1242; [2012] E.L.R. 47.

[143] *Baker v Quantum Clothing Group Ltd* [2011] UKSC 17; [2011] 1 W.L.R. 1003 (the "larger employers" should have departed from the applicable code of practice on noise levels five years earlier than the "average employers". Lord Mance dissented on this issue, on the ground that it made employers liable not "for not ploughing a lone furrow" (see *Thompson v Smiths Shiprepairers (North Shields) Ltd* [1984] Q.B. 405 at 415–416 per Mustill J), but "for ploughing a lone furrow but not doing so deeply enough" (at [25])).

[144] *Baker v Quantum Clothing Group Ltd* [2011] UKSC 17; [2011] 1 W.L.R. 1003 at [101] per Lord Dyson.

9-025 **The employee's individual circumstances** It is important to notice that although the employer's duty springs from the relationship of employment, the duty is owed individually to each worker, so that circumstances concerning the particular worker which are known or which ought to be known to the employer may determine the precautions the employer must take to fulfil his duty. Thus in *Paris v Stepney BC*[145] the claimant had only one eye and it was therefore held that he should have been provided with goggles even though the risk involved in his work was not so great as to require the provision of goggles to a two-eyed man doing a similar job. In the same way, "an experienced man dealing with a familiar and obvious risk may not reasonably need the same attention or the same precaution as an inexperienced man who is likely to be more receptive of advice or admonition".[146] The need for the employer to take into account the individual circumstances of the employee is particularly important in the context of mental harm caused by stress.[147]

9-026 **Protecting the employee from himself**[148] In *Withers v Perry Chain Co*[149] the claimant had previously contracted dermatitis from contact with grease in the course of her work and was therefore given the driest work her employers had available. This work she accepted without protest but nevertheless she again contracted dermatitis and sued her employers on the ground that, knowing that she was susceptible to dermatitis, they should not have permitted her to do work carrying a risk of causing that disease. Her action was dismissed by the Court of Appeal because the employers had done everything they reasonably could have done to protect the claimant short of refusing to employ her at all[150]:

> "In my opinion there is no legal duty on an employer to prevent an adult employee from doing work which he or she is willing to do. If there is a slight risk ... it is for the employee to weigh it against the desirability, or perhaps the necessity, of employment. The relationship of master and servant is not that of a schoolmaster and pupil[151] ... It cannot be said that an employer is bound to dismiss an employee rather than allow her to run a small risk."

There is a tension here between the stance of the common law in giving primacy to the worker's personal autonomy and the expanding responsibility of employers. While what is said in *Withers* is probably still the starting point, there is no absolute rule that an employer may expose a willing worker to *any* risk by continuing to employ him: it has been said that to employ someone known to suffer from vertigo as a "spiderman" would be a plain breach of the employer's duty.[152] That is not necessarily good news from the worker's point of view, for it follows that dismissal

---

[145] [1951] A.C. 367. cf. *Hatton v Sutherland* [2002] EWCA Civ 76; [2002] I.C.R. 613 (stress; employer's legitimate expectations about capacity), para.5-084.

[146] *Qualcast (Wolverhampton) Ltd v Haynes* [1959] A.C. 743 at 754 per Lord Radcliffe. But the employer cannot necessarily accept at face value the worker's assertion of previous experience: *Tasci v Pekalp of London Ltd* [2000] I.C.R. 633.

[147] *Hatton v Sutherland* [2002] EWCA Civ 76; [2002] I.C.R. 613. See para.5-084.

[148] The issue here is whether the employer fulfils the standard of care by leaving the decision whether to run the risk of injury to the employee. Whether the employer's breach was the cause of the injury when it is based on the conduct of the claimant (see, e.g., *Ginty v Belmont Building Supplies Ltd* [1959] 1 All E.R. 414) is dealt with in para.8-020.

[149] [1961] 1 W.L.R. 1314.

[150] [1961] 1 W.L.R. 1314 at 1320 per Devlin LJ.

[151] See, e.g., *Rozario v Post Office* [1997] P.I.Q.R. P15 (simple lifting task).

[152] *Coxall v Goodyear Great Britain Ltd* [2002] EWCA Civ 1010; [2003] 1 W.L.R. 536 at [26].

may be fair for the purposes of employment protection legislation.[153] In the case of stress, even where the risk to health is substantial, it has been said that it is for the employee to decide whether or not to carry on: it should not be for the law to say that the employer must sack a worker to protect his mental health.[154]

Volenti non fit injuria   The defence of volenti is rarely available in employers'   **9-027**
liability cases because the courts are unwilling to infer an agreement by the worker to run the risk of his employer's negligence merely because he remains in unsafe employment.[155] However, in *Johnstone v Bloomsbury Health Authority*,[156] where the claimant was contractually committed to work up to an average of 88 hours a week if the employer so required, it was contended that the express term of the contract limited or overrode the employer's duty of care not to injure his health. On a strike-out application, this was accepted in principle by Browne-Wilkinson VC and Leggatt LJ[157] but the majority of the court (Stuart-Smith LJ and Browne-Wilkinson VC) held that the contractual right to call for long hours was, on the proper construction of the contract of employment, limited to calling for work that was compatible with the employer's duty of care.

C.   Nature of the Duty

A non-delegable duty of care   It might be supposed that an employer who   **9-028**
entrusts some task to a third party (not an employee), whose competence he has taken reasonable care to ascertain, has thereby discharged his own duty of reasonable care. To state the law in this way, however, would be to deny the ruling in *Wilsons and Clyde Coal Co v English*[158] that the employer's duty is personal and is not discharged simply by the appointment of a competent person to carry out the necessary tasks.[159] In that case the defendant employers were held liable in respect of an injury sustained by a miner because the system of working was not reasonably safe. The system had been devised by the manager of the mine, a fellow servant of the claimant, to whom the employers were obliged by statute to leave the matter, but yet, despite the existence of common employment and despite the fact that the employers personally had done everything they possibly could, they were held to be in breach of their duty to the claimant. Their duty was[160]:

---

153 *Lane Group Plc v Farmiloe* [2004] P.I.Q.R. 22. cf. *Canterbury CC v Howletts* [1997] I.C.R. 925 (duty under the Health and Safety at Work etc. Act 1974 s.2, to ensure safety to employees was duty to do what could be done in the context of the job and did not prohibit work—entering a tiger's cage—which could not be done without danger; but on the civil liability in such a situation, see the Animals Act 1971 s.6(5), para.17-008).
154 *Hatton v Sutherland* [2002] EWCA Civ 76; [2002] I.C.R. 613 at [43](12); but see *Barber v Somerset CC* [2004] UKHL 13; [2004] 1 W.L.R 1089 at [30].
155 See para.26-022.
156 [1992] Q.B. 333.
157 In fact, Stuart-Smith LJ also accepted that what he called an "express term of volenti non fit injuria" would exclude the employer's duty.
158 [1938] A.C. 57, para.9-005.
159 In *Uren v Corporate Leisure UK Ltd* [2011] EWCA Civ 66; [2011] I.C.R. D11, the Court of Appeal inclined to the view that the duty to conduct a risk assessment under reg.3(1) of the Management of Health and Safety at Work Regulations 1999 (which may be relevant to a claim in negligence: see para.9-023) was itself non-delegable.
160 *Wilsons and Clyde Coal v English* [1938] A.C. 57 at 83–84 per Lord Wright. See also at 64–65, 75 and 87–88.

"[T]he employer's personal duty, whether he performs or can perform it himself, or whether he does not perform it or cannot perform it save by servants or agents. A failure to perform such a duty is the employer's personal negligence."

The employer's liability, therefore, not being a vicarious liability, was not defeated by the doctrine of common employment.

9-029 Liability for independent contractors Although the non-delegable nature of the employer's personal duty was developed to avoid the now defunct doctrine of common employment, its practical effect goes beyond cases formerly covered by that doctrine because it involves the proposition that the employer's duty is not so much a duty to take care as a duty to ensure that care is taken and therefore the employer may be liable for damage caused by independent contractors. A person can only be vicariously liable for the torts of his employees committed in the course of employment, but a duty that care will be taken is not fulfilled if there is fault on the part of anyone to whom the employer entrusts its performance.[161] This view of the law was confirmed by *McDermid v Nash Dredging and Reclamation Co Ltd*.[162] The defendants were a wholly owned subsidiary of S, a Dutch company, and their function was to employ British staff engaged in S's dredging work in Sweden. While the claimant, an employee of the defendants, was aboard a tug owned by S he was seriously injured as a result of the negligence of the skipper (an employee of S) in putting the engines astern without warning to the claimant. The defendants were liable because they had delegated the performance of their duty to take care for the claimant's safety to S and its employees on the tug and could not escape liability when that duty was not fulfilled.[163] Given the close connection between the defendants and S the decision was not surprising, for if the law were otherwise the claimant's rights would be at risk from the chances of corporate organisation.[164]

In deciding not to impose liability upon an employer for injury suffered by an employee working in Saudi Arabia the Court of Appeal distinguished *Nash* on the basis that it was confined to cases where there was some sort of "joint venture"[165] but this seems an unsatisfactory distinction and the principle of *Nash* has been applied at first instance[166] and by the Court of Appeal[167] to cases where the employer was a "labour only" contractor and in one of which[168] the injury took place abroad.[169] However, it has been said that the "suggestion that the homebased

---

[161] Non-delegable duties are not confined to defendants who stand in the position of employer of the claimant. Employment has been explained as but one application of a wider test based on an antecedent relationship, in particular one where the defendant assumes responsibility for those who are in a "vulnerable position": *Woodland v Swimming Teachers Association* [2013] UKSC 66; [2014] A.C. 537, para.21-047.

[162] *McDermid v Nash Dredging and Reclamation Co Ltd* [1987] A.C. 906; cf. *Hopps v Mott Macdonald Ltd* [2009] EWHC 1881 (QB).

[163] It was not regarded as important whether the case was one of failing to devise a safe system of work or failing to operate a safe system.

[164] Where the claimant has a contract with one member of a corporate group it may be that on the facts other members of the group have assumed responsibility for his safety: *Newton-Sealey v Armor Group Services Ltd* [2008] EWHC 233 (QB); *Chandler v Cape Plc* [2012] EWCA Civ 525; [2012] 1 W.L.R. 3111; cf. *Thompson v Renwick Group Plc* [2014] EWCA Civ 635; [2014] P.I.Q.R. P18.

[165] *Cook v Square D Ltd* [1992] I.C.R. 262.

[166] *Johnson v Coventry Churchill International Ltd* [1992] 3 All E.R. 15.

[167] *Morris v Breaveglen Ltd* [1993] I.R.L.R. 350.

[168] *Johnson v Coventry Churchill International Ltd* [1992] 3 All E.R. 15.

[169] cf. *A v MoD* [2004] EWCA Civ 641; [2005] Q.B. 183, para.21-047.

employers have any responsibility for the daily events of a site in [another country] has an air of unreality"[170] and it may be that the question of how far the employer has control of the distant site is a critical factor in such cases.[171] Where no actual fault is attributable to the employer, that may justify awarding him a complete indemnity in contribution proceedings against the person at fault.[172]

The need for delegation   The employer's non-delegable duty of care does not mean that he is liable whenever his employee is injured at work as a result of the negligence of a third party: the employer is only responsible if it can be fairly said that he has delegated the performance of his duty of care to the third party. Thus, if a lorry driver delivering goods to a factory were negligently to run over a factory worker, the worker's employer would not be liable—the negligence of the lorry driver (and the vicarious responsibility of his employer) does not negative the exercise of care in the employer's personal duty for it is unrelated to any aspect of that duty, and the employer has delegated nothing to him.[173] Similarly, although the effect of the case has been reversed by the Employer's Liability (Defective Equipment) Act 1969,[174] the underlying ratio of *Davie v New Merton Board Mills*,[175] denying the liability of the employer for a latent defect in a tool, was that the employer had discharged rather than delegated his duty by buying from a reputable supplier. If, conversely, a gas fitter negligently installs a gas appliance at the employer's premises with the result that a worker is injured by an explosion, the better view is that the employer's personal duty with regard to the safety of the place of work has not been fulfilled and he is liable, whether or not the worker is entitled to rely on the 1969 Act.[176]

9-030

---

[170] *Cook v Square D Ltd* [1992] I.C.R. 262 at 271. However, it was accepted that in some cases it might be incumbent on the employer of someone working abroad to inspect the site and satisfy himself that the occupiers were conscious of safety obligations.

[171] See *DIB Group Pty Ltd v Cole* [2009] NSWCA 210, in which the use of the concept of non-delegable duty is criticised.

[172] *Nelhams v Sandells Maintenance Ltd, The Times,* 15 June 1995.

[173] This is an example of the "collateral negligence" of the independent contractor which is discussed generally at para.21-051.

[174] See para.9-021.

[175] *Davie v New Merton Board Mills* [1959] A.C. 604.

[176] In *Knowles v Liverpool CC* [1993] 1 W.L.R. 1428 *Davie* is given a broad interpretation so as to include material with which the employee is working. However, this is done for the purpose of justifying an equally wide meaning of "equipment" in the 1969 Act. It is accepted in *Coltman v Bibby Tankers Ltd* [1988] A.C. 276 that the Act does not extend to the factory premises themselves.

CHAPTER 10

LIABILITY FOR LAND AND STRUCTURES

1. INTRODUCTION

The greater part of this chapter concerns the liability of an occupier of premises **10-001**
for injury suffered by visitors on the premises[1] and the main source of the law is
the Occupiers' Liability Act 1957. However, consideration is also given to the liability of occupiers to non-visitors (usually trespassers), as regulated by the Occupiers' Liability Act 1984, and to the liability of non-occupiers (vendors and lessors) for damage caused by defects in premises.[2] Where things done on premises
affect other premises, that is the province of the law of nuisance, which is dealt with
in Ch.15. To speak of "liability for premises" in this context is potentially misleading, for the rules now to be discussed are not limited to immovable property like
open land, houses, railway stations and bridges, but have been extended to mov-

---

[1] i.e., persons who have entered the premises. It is conceivable that an occupier may "assume
     responsibility" at common law in respect of the safety of the approach to the premises, which may
     be the explanation of *Dodkins v West Ham Utd* [2000] C.L.Y. 4226 (season ticket holder fell on
     broken manhole cover outside gate to ground).
[2] North, *Occupiers' Liability*, 2nd edn (2014).

able structures like ships, gangways and scaffolding.[3] However, henceforth we shall use the expression "premises" because it covers the vast majority of cases.

2. LIABILITY OF OCCUPIERS TO VISITORS

10-002 **Common Law before the Occupiers' Liability Act 1957** At common law the duties of an occupier were cast in a descending scale to four different kinds of person and a brief account is necessary to gain a full understanding of the 1957 Act. The highest degree of care was owed by the occupier to one who entered in pursuance of a contract with him (for example, a guest in a hotel): in that case there was an implied warranty that the premises were as safe as reasonable care and skill could make them. A lower duty was owed to the "invitee", that is to say, a person who (without any contract) entered on business of interest both to himself and the occupier (for example, a customer coming into a shop to view the wares): he was entitled to expect that the occupier should prevent damage from unusual danger, of which he knew or ought to have known.[4] Lower still was the duty to the "licensee", a person who entered with the occupier's express or implied permission but without any community of interest with the occupier: the occupier's duty towards him was to warn him of any concealed danger or trap of which he actually knew. Finally, there was the trespasser, to whom under the original common law there was owed only a duty to abstain from deliberate or reckless injury.[5] With regard to lawful visitors the tripartite classification into contractual entrants, invitees and licensees did not provide a complete picture of the law for the courts sometimes showed themselves willing to confine these categories to cases arising from the static condition of the premises, and to treat accidents arising from an activity on the premises as governed by the general law of negligence. As Denning LJ graphically put it[6]:

> "If a landowner is driving his car down his private drive and meets someone lawfully walking upon it, then he is under a duty to take reasonable care so as not to injure the walker and his duty is the same, no matter whether it is his gardener coming up with his plants, a tradesman delivering his goods, a friend coming to tea, or a flag seller seeking a charitable gift."

The law was widely thought to be unsatisfactory and to have ossified in the form in which it was stated in *Indermaur v Dames*[7] at a time when the general law of negligence was undeveloped. It was, therefore, referred to the Law Reform Committee in 1952 and, as a result of the Committee's Report,[8] the Occupiers' Liability Act 1957 was passed.[9]

---

3   The relevant legislation encompasses not only land and buildings but any "fixed and movable structure": Occupiers' Liability Act 1957 s.1(3)(a); Occupiers' Liability Act 1984 s.1(2). See, e.g., *Bunker v Charles Brand & Son Ltd* [1969] 2 Q.B. 480 (tunnelling machine); *Furmedge v Chester-le-Street DC* [2011] EWHC 1226 (QB) (inflatable art installation). See also *Wheeler v Copas* [1981] 3 All E.R. 405 at 408 (ladder).
4   *Indermaur v Dames* (1866) L.R. 1 C.P. 274; affirmed (1867) L.R. 2 C.P. 311.
5   *Robert Addie & Sons (Collieries) Ltd v Dumbreck* [1929] A.C. 358.
6   *Slater v Clay Cross Co Ltd* [1956] 2 Q.B. 264 at 269.
7   (1866) L.R. 1 C.P. 274; affirmed (1867) L.R. 2 C.P. 311.
8   (1954) Cmnd. 9305.
9   On the history of the legislation, see Bailey in Arvind and Steele (eds), *Tort Law and the Legislature* (2013).

A. Scope of the Occupiers' Liability Act 1957

A single duty of care The 1957 Act abolished the common law distinction **10-003**
between invitees and licensees and substituted for it a single common duty of care
owed by the occupier to his "visitors". The definition of "occupier" remains the
same as at common law, and "visitors" are those persons who would at common
law have been treated as either invitees or licensees.[10] The law therefore continues
to treat contractual entrants as a separate category, but this is now of less
significance than formerly: if there is an express provision in the contract warrant-
ing the safety of the premises, that will govern the case,[11] but if, as is usual, the
contract is silent on the matter, the Act provides that there shall be implied into the
contract a term that the occupier owes the entrant the common duty of care.[12] There
may, of course, be obligations under a contract which are wholly outside the scope
of the law of occupiers' liability: if, for example, a lease requires the landlord to
maintain a lift, failure to do so, so that it becomes inoperative, would be a breach
of contract but it would not be a breach of the common duty of care,[13] except in the
unlikely event that there was no other reasonably safe access to accommodation in
the building.

"Occupancy" and "activity" duties[14] We saw above how the courts utilised the **10-004**
concept of the "activity duty" to blur the distinction between invitees and licensees
at common law and it may be asked whether this concept remains relevant. On the
one hand, it is enacted that the rules provided by the Act "shall have effect, in place
of the rules of the common law, to regulate the duty which an occupier of premises
owes to visitors in respect of dangers due to the state of the premises or to things
done or omitted to be done on them."[15] But on the other hand, it is said that those
rules "shall regulate the nature of the duty imposed by law in consequence of a
person's occupation or control of premises",[16] and the "activity duty" does not seem
to be aptly described in this way. It rather arises by the application of the ordinary
principles of negligence and applies equally to occupiers and non-occupiers.[17]

Where there is a defect in the premises which was not created by the occupier
but which he has failed to remedy, the case must fall within the scope of the Act
and the Act alone if there is no other relationship between him and the claimant,
for it is then only his role as occupier that puts the defendant under any positive duty
with regard to the safety of the premises. However, in other cases, the position is
less clear. In *Fairchild v Glenhaven Funeral Services*,[18] it was held that the Act did

---

[10] 1957 Act s.1(2).
[11] In the majority of personal injury cases an express provision can now only be effective if it favours
the entrant, as a term reducing the occupier's duty below the common duty of care will be unenforceable under the Unfair Contract Terms Act 1977 or Consumer Rights Act 2015: para.10-023.
[12] 1957 Act s.5(1). *Maguire v Sefton MBC* [2006] EWCA Civ 316; [2006] 1 W.L.R. 2550. A contractual
entrant may frame his claim in the alternative as a non-contractual visitor: *Sole v WJ Hallt* [1973]
Q.B. 574.
[13] *Berryman v Hounslow LBC, The Times,* 18 December 1996.
[14] North, *Occupiers' Liability*, 2nd edn (2014) Ch.6.
[15] 1957 Act s.1(1).
[16] 1957 Act s.1(2).
[17] *Riden v Billings & Sons* [1957] 1 Q.B. 46 at 56, affirmed [1958] A.C. 240; *Ogwo v Taylor* [1988]
A.C. 431 at 434, affirmed at 441.
[18] [2001] EWCA Civ 1881; [2002] 1 W.L.R. 1052 (approving the speech of Lord Goff in *Ferguson v
Welsh* [1987] 1 W.L.R. 1553).

not apply to an activity carried out on the premises by a third party who was there with the occupier's consent.[19] Brooke LJ distinguished between "the static condition of the premises" (governed by the 1957 Act) and "what was going on in those premises" (governed by the common law).[20] And common law negligence, rather than the 1957 Act, was also considered applicable when the defendant failed to warn his children against playing with lighted candles,[21] and in a claim arising out of the defendant's carelessness in setting fire to his house.[22] However, in *Tomlinson v Congleton BC*,[23] it was suggested obiter that liability under the 1957 Act could extend to activities conducted by the occupier, or by others with his consent, that create a risk to persons on the premises (e.g., shooting), and there are other cases in which the distinction between occupancy and activity duties has not been drawn.[24] Overall, the better view is that the distinction has survived, though it may not always be easy to make.

10-005 **Merits and significance of the distinction** When assessing the merits of the distinction between occupancy and activity duties, it must be recalled that one reason for separating out occupiers' liability cases from the ordinary law of negligence is that they tend to involve duties of positive conduct, so that this an area where omissions liability—otherwise unusual in the law of tort[25]—is commonplace. Drawing on this observation, it has been argued[26] that "it is the nature of the occupier's responsibility" that should determine the applicability of the 1957 Act, which should be limited to cases where: (1) the risk arises from a natural deterioration in the state of the premises; (2) the risk arises from conduct of the occupier that was not careless when carried out; or (3) the negligent act of a third party (not being the occupier's employee) creates a risk on the premises, whether by changing the physical state of the premises or otherwise, such as by careless driving. These are situations where, it is argued, the gist of the complaint against the occupier is a failure to act to protect the safety of the visitor, the core concern of occupiers' liability.

The issue is anyway unlikely to be of much practical significance in most cases, for there will typically be little if any difference between the duty of care in negligence and the common duty of care as applied to current activities. From a pleading point of view the answer would seem to be to plead the Act and negligence

---

[19] cf. *Cunningham v Reading Football Club Ltd* [1992] P.I.Q.R. P141, where a duty under both the Act and the common law was held to extend to taking care to ensure that the state of a football stadium was not such as to enable hooligans to cause harm to other visitors by ripping up lumps of concrete from the terraces for use as projectiles. Although this was imposing liability for an activity of a third party, the circumstances are distinguishable from *Fairchild* because the third parties were taking advantage of a feature of the premises (loose concrete) to inflict injury.

[20] [2001] EWCA Civ 1881; [2002] 1 W.L.R. 1052 at [149]. See also *Macarthy v Marks & Spencer Plc* [2014] EWHC 3183 (QB) at [81]. Note that the "static condition" test does not connote any degree of permanence. A patch of ice or some spilled liquid would count as such. There are many such examples in the case law on the 1957 Act.

[21] *Jauffar v Akhbar, The Times,* 10 February 1984.

[22] *Ogwo v Taylor* [1988] A.C. 431. The case was pleaded in the alternative under both heads. See also *Revill v Newbery* [1996] Q.B. 567 (Occupiers' Liability Act 1984 does not govern the liability of the occupier for his activities on the land).

[23] [2003] UKHL 47; [2004] 1 A.C. 46.

[24] See, e.g., *Maguire v Sefton MBC* [2006] EWCA Civ 316; [2006] 1 W.L.R. 2550.

[25] See paras 5-030ff.

[26] Bailey in Arvind and Steele (eds), *Tort Law and the Legislature* (2013), pp.207–208.

as alternatives[27] wherever there is any doubt. The Act may also overlap with other statutory liabilities: for example, it is quite possible to hold that the occupier/ employer is not negligent in a claim by a worker for an injury caused by the state of the premises but that he is liable on the basis of some stricter liability in employment safety regulations.[27]

"Dangers due to the state of the premises" Whatever the precise relationship **10-006** between the Act and general negligence law with regard to activities on the premises, the heart of the 1957 Act is liability for "dangers due to the state of the premises".[28] In *Tomlinson v Congleton BC*[29] the claimant was injured when he dived from a standing position into the shallow water of a lake occupied by the defendants in a country park. Because swimming was forbidden by notices it was held by the majority of the House of Lords that he was a trespasser,[30] but the same words appear in the Occupiers' Liability Act 1984 dealing with trespassers. It is clear therefore that the same decision in favour of the defendants would have been reached even if the claimant had been a lawful visitor[31] and the case is as relevant to the 1957 Act as it is to the later Act. The risk, such as it was, was obvious to any sensible person. There was no concealed hazard or trap and the lake presented no dangers other than those inherent in any substantial body of water. In the view of the majority of the House of Lords the injury could not fairly be said to have been caused by a danger due to the state of the premises.[32] Similarly, it has been held that there is no liability in respect of some artificial thing like a building which is in good repair if the claimant chooses to use it in order to carry out some hazardous activity.[33] It has been said that it follows from these authorities that "it is necessary to identify what danger(s) there is/are before one can see to what (if anything) the occupier's duty in each case attaches"[34] This does not of course mean that the occupier cannot be liable in respect of a natural feature: one could not rent out a hotel room with a balcony overlooking a cliff without incorporating an adequate guard rail. The underlying idea seems to be: was there something wrong with the premises, given the purposes for which visitors were invited?[35] But there is a risk of straying into the territory of breach of duty here, and many of the claims which have been rejected on the ground that there was no "danger due to the state of the premises" might more straightforwardly have been dealt with by saying that it was not reasonable to require the occupier to take protective steps.[36] Saying that the Act

---

27 See, e.g., *Irvine v MPC* [2004] EWHC 1536 (QB); [2005] P.I.Q.R. P11. But civil liability for breach of such regulations is now severely curtailed: see para.8-006.
28 1957 Act s.1(1).
29 [2003] UKHL 47; [2004] 1 A.C. 46.
30 See para.10-040.
31 See at [1] (Lord Nicholls agreeing with Lord Hoffmann), [50], [67], [92] (Lord Scott, who thought that the claimant was not a trespasser).
32 At [1], [28] and [69]. Lord Scott does not address the state of the premises issue directly but he agreed with Lord Hoffmann, save as to whether the claimant was a trespasser. Contra, Lord Hutton at [53].
33 *Keown v Coventry Healthcare NHS Trust* [2006] EWCA Civ 39; [2006] 1 W.L.R. 953 (another trespasser case; climbing up underside of fire escape).
34 *Edwards v Sutton LBC* [2016] EWCA Civ 1005; [2017] P.I.Q.R. P2 at [38].
35 The last phrase is important. The murky condition of natural waters presents an obvious hazard. A municipal swimming pool with water so murky one could not see the bottom might be a different matter.
36 *Grimes v Hawkins* [2011] EWHC 2004 (QB).

is not engaged at all has the obvious advantage of enabling the claim to be dismissed without close consideration of the circumstances, but that comes at a price: not only a somewhat strained reading of the legislation, but also the difficulty of drawing the line in such a way as to exclude hopeless claims while not foreclosing the outcome where closer scrutiny of the facts is actually appropriate.

B. Occupier

10-007 **A test of "control"** The duty under the 1957 Act is imposed upon the "occupier," but that is a word which may vary considerably in its meaning according to the context in which it is used. Its meaning in the context of landlord and tenant legislation, for example, is not necessarily the same as in the context of the 1957 Act.[37] Here the word "occupier" is simply a convenient one to denote a person who "has a sufficient degree of control over premises that he ought to realise that any failure on his part to use care may result in injury to a person coming lawfully there."[38] An owner in possession is, no doubt, an "occupier";[39] an owner who has let the premises to another and parted with possession is not;[40] but an absentee owner may "occupy" through his employee and remain subject to the duty[41] and he may also be subject to it though he has contracted to allow a third party to have the use of the premises.[42] On the other hand, it is not necessary that an "occupier" should have any estate in land[43] or even exclusive occupation.[44] The foundation of occupiers' liability is occupational control, i.e., control associated with and arising from presence in and use of or activity in the premises.[45] Whether this exists is a question of degree: a builder undertaking a large development would be an occupier of the site, but a decorator painting a house would not.[46] Such occupational control may perfectly well be shared between two or more people but, where this is so, though each is under the same common duty of care, it does not follow that what that duty requires of each of them is necessarily itself the same.[47]

---

[37] *Graysim Holdings Ltd v P&O Property Holdings Ltd* [1996] A.C. 329.

[38] *Wheat v Lacon & Co Ltd* [1966] A.C. 552 at 577 per Lord Denning.

[39] In *Harvey v Plymouth CC* (13 November 2009, QBD) the defendants admitted that they were occupiers even though they were not conscious they owned the land (appeal allowed ([2010] EWCA Civ 860; [2010] P.I.Q.R. P18) on the basis that the claimant was not a visitor).

[40] A landlord may, nevertheless, be liable if the conditions of the Defective Premises Act 1972 s.4, are fulfilled. See para.10-058.

[41] *Wheat v Lacon & Co Ltd* [1966] A.C. 552; *Stone v Taffe* [1974] 1 W.L.R. 1575.

[42] *Wheat v Lacon & Co Ltd* [1966] A.C. 552; *Fisher v CHT Ltd (No.2)* [1966] 2 Q.B. 475. See also *Greene v Chelsea BC* [1954] 2 Q.B. 127, where requisitioning authorities were held to occupy requisitioned houses which were being lived in by persons they had placed in them; cf. *Kearney v Eric Waller Ltd* [1967] 1 Q.B. 29.

[43] *Humphreys v Dreamland (Margate) Ltd* (1930) 144 L.T. 529.

[44] *Hartwell v Grayson Rollo and Clover Docks Ltd* [1947] K.B. 901; *Donovan v Cammell Laird & Co* [1949] 2 All E.R. 82. A local authority which has made a compulsory purchase order and served a notice of entry becomes an occupier when the former owner vacates the premises, and it is unnecessary that there should be any actual or symbolic taking of possession: *Harris v Birkenhead Corp* [1976] 1 W.L.R. 279.

[45] *Wheat v Lacon & Co Ltd* [1966] A.C. 552 at 589.

[46] *Page v Read* (1984) N.L.J. 723.

[47] *Wheat v Lacon & Co Ltd* [1966] A.C. 552 at 581, 585–587. Hence, ownership of the land on which a hotel is situated might entail some responsibility for the building's structural condition, but not for the hotel's operations: *Shtern v Cummings* [2014] UKPC 18.

C. Visitors

A single category   The common duty of care is owed by the occupier to his "visi-   **10-008**
tors" and they are those persons who would at common law have been treated as
invitees or licensees.[48] The distinction between invitees and licensees has therefore
been abolished.[49] A visitor is usually a person to whom the occupier has given
express or implied permission to enter and the principal category opposed to visitor is that of trespasser, whose rights are governed not by the 1957 Act but by the
Occupiers' Liability Act 1984.[50]

Implied permission   Where there is no express permission, it is a question of fact   **10-009**
in each case whether the occupier has impliedly permitted a person to enter upon
his premises, and the onus of proving an implied permission rests upon the person
who claims that it existed.[51] The simplest example of implied permission is also the
commonest in practice. Any person who enters the occupier's premises for the
purpose of communicating with him[52] will be treated as having the occupier's tacit
permission unless he knows or ought to know that he has been forbidden to enter,[53]
for example by a notice.[54] The occupier may, of course, withdraw this licence by
refusing to speak or deal with the entrant, but if he does so the entrant has a reasonable time in which to leave the premises before he becomes a trespasser.[55]

Other cases depend very much on their particular facts and it is difficult to state
any general rule. It is, however, clear that the facts must support the implication
from the occupier's conduct that he has permitted entry,[56] not merely tolerated it,
for knowledge is not tantamount to consent and failure to turn one's premises into
a fortress does not confer a licence on anyone who may seek to take advantage of
one's inaction.[57] That said, the courts have sometimes gone to surprising lengths in
implying licences in the teeth of the facts.[58] In many cases the court has been astute
to find an implied licence because of the severity of the law relating to liability to

---

48   1957 Act s.1(2).
49   Lord Browne-Wilkinson in *McGeown v Northern Ireland Housing Executive* [1995] 1 A.C. 233 at-
      tempted to revive the distinction in relation to public rights of way, but see *Campbell v Northern
      Ireland Housing Executive* [1996] 1 B.N.I.L. 99.
50   See para.10-034.
51   *Edwards v Railway Executive* [1952] A.C. 737.
52   Not necessarily in connection with business of the occupier: *Brunner v Williams* [1975] Crim. L.R.
      250.
53   *Robson v Hallett* [1967] 2 Q.B. 393. cf. *Dunster v Abbott* [1954] 1 W.L.R. 58 at 59–60; *Great Central
      Railway Co v Bates* [1921] 3 K.B. 578.
54   For example, "no canvassers, hawkers or circulars". Less clear is the effect of "Private" or "Keep
      Out" in such cases: cf. *Christian v Johanesson* [1956] N.Z.L.R. 664 at 666.
55   *Robson v Hallett* [1967] 2 Q.B. 393; *Kay v Hibbert* [1977] Crim. L.R. 226. Dismissive words may
      sometimes be abuse rather than revocation of the licence: *Snook v Mannion* [1982] Crim. L.R. 601.
56   *Edwards v Railway Executive* [1952] A.C. 737; *Phipps v Rochester Corp* [1955] 1 Q.B. 450 at 455;
      Faulkner v Willetts [1982] R.T.R. 159. It is what may properly be inferred that counts, not the oc-
      cupier's actual intention. Where O licenses A to enter his land to do work, A may have ostensible
      authority to invite B to enter as a sub-contractor even though the contract between O and A forbids
      this: *Ferguson v Welsh* [1987] 1 W.L.R. 1553.
57   *Edwards v Railway Executive* [1952] A.C. 737 at 746 per Lord Goddard CJ ("Repeated trespass itself
      confers no licence").
58   See, e.g., *Lowery v Walker* [1911] A.C. 10 and *Cooke v Midland Great Western Railway of Ireland*
      [1909] A.C. 229. More supportable are the decisions in *Oldham v Sheffield Corp* (1927) 136 L.T.
      681; *Coleshill v Manchester Corp* [1928] 1 K.B. 776; *Purkis v Walthamstow BC* (1934) 151 L.T.
      30; *Phipps v Rochester Corp* [1955] 1 Q.B. 450.

trespassers.[59] The trespasser's position is now much improved,[60] and it is likely that implied permission will be rather less readily found, but the courts will still have to grapple with the problem of the implied licence, for the position of a trespasser is by no means identical to that of a visitor under the 1957 Act.

10-010 **Exceeding permission** The duty owed to a visitor does not extend to anyone who is injured as a result of going where he is expressly or impliedly warned by the occupier not to go, as where a person falls over a cliff by getting on the wrong side of railings erected by the proprietor who has also put up a notice of the danger of going near the cliff[61] or where a tradesman's boy deliberately chooses to go into a pitch dark part of the premises not included in the invitation and falls downstairs there.[62] Further, the duty does not protect a visitor who goes to a part of the premises where no one would reasonably expect him to go.[63]

Again the claimant cannot succeed if, although rightly on the structure, he makes a use of it alien to the invitation.[64] So, where a stevedore in loading a ship was injured by making use of the hatch covers for loading, although he knew that a statutory regulation forbade this practice in his own interests, it was held that he had no remedy.[65] In fact, in all these cases the claimant ceases to be a visitor and becomes a trespasser.[66] Where, however, the negligence of the occupier causes the visitor to take an involuntary step outside the area in which he is permitted to be, he does not thereby cease to be a visitor to whom a duty of care is owed,[67] and the position is probably the same even if the involuntary step is not caused by the occupier's negligence.[68] A person may equally exceed his licence by staying on premises after the occupier's permission has expired but the limitation of time must be clearly brought home to him. Thus, a person on licensed premises who remained there when drinks were being consumed long after closing time was held to continue to be a visitor in the absence of evidence that he knew of instructions from the brewers to their manager forbidding this practice.[69]

---

[59] *British Railways Board v Herrington* [1972] A.C. 877 at 933.
[60] See para.10-034.
[61] *Anderson v Coutts* (1894) 58 J.P. 369.
[62] *Lewis v Ronald* (1909) 101 L.T. 534, distinguished in *Prole v Allen* [1950] 1 All E.R. 476.
[63] *Mersey Docks and Harbour Board v Procter* [1923] A.C. 253, where there was a great difference of opinion as to the application of this principle to the facts; *Lee v Luper* [1936] 3 All E.R. 817; *Gould v McAuliffe* [1941] 2 All E.R. 527. By contrast, the suggestion that an entrant's "state of mind and intention is an important additional factor" (*Spearman v Royal United Bath Hospitals NHS Foundation Trust* [2017] EWHC 3027 (QB) at [56]) seems, with respect, to be questionable. The unintentional trespasser is after all a commonplace legal phenomenon: para.14-001.
[64] "When you invite a person into your house to use the staircase you do not invite him to slide down the bannisters": Scrutton LJ in *The Calgarth* [1927] P. 93 at 110 (a hypothetical example now made real: *Geary v JD Wetherspoon Plc* [2011] EWHC 1506 (QB); [2011] N.P.C. 60). But, e.g., a hotel guest does not become a trespasser merely because he smokes in a non-smoking room: *James v White Lion Hotel* (9 January 2020, QBD) at [107]–[110]. In any case, the content of the common duty of care is determined by reference to the purposes for which the visitor is invited or permitted to be on the premises: s.2(2), below and *Harvey v Plymouth CC* [2010] EWCA Civ 860; [2010] P.I.Q.R. P18 at [22].
[65] *Hillen v ICI (Alkali) Ltd* [1936] A.C. 65.
[66] *Hillen v ICI (Alkali) Ltd* [1936] A.C. 65 at 69–70.
[67] *Braithwaite v S Durham Steel Co* [1958] 1 W.L.R. 986.
[68] See the difference of opinion in the High Court of Australia in *Public Transport Commission (NSW) v Perry* (1977) 137 C.L.R. 107. Quaere as to the claimant whose initial entry is involuntary. He cannot be sued for trespass, but that does not necessarily make him a visitor.
[69] *Stone v Taffe* [1974] 1 W.L.R. 1575. The manager, as agent of the brewers, had authority to invite

An extended category The 1957 Act extends the concept of visitor to include   **10-011**
persons who enter the premises for any purpose in the exercise of a right conferred
by law, for they are to be treated as permitted by the occupier to be there for that
purpose, whether they in fact have his permission or not.[70] The occupier therefore
owes the common duty of care to firefighters attending a fire, to police officers
executing a search warrant and to members of the public entering recreation
grounds under rights guaranteed by law.

Rights of way Despite the wide wording of the Act, a person using a public[71] or   **10-012**
private[72] right of way is not a visitor for the purposes of the Act. The user of a
private right of way may be owed a duty under the Occupiers' Liability Act 1984,[73]
but at common law the owner of the highway[74] or servient tenement has no obligation to the user to maintain its safety, as opposed to not creating dangers on it. While
it is true that public rights of way pass over so many different types of property and
in such varying circumstances that any blanket duty of care would be impracticable[75] the present state of the law may lead to results which might be considered
arbitrary. For example, the owners of shopping malls commonly take steps to ensure
that the public do not acquire rights of way through them, but if such a right is
acquired by user,[76] or by express dedication, entrants to the property, who may know
nothing of this, will lose the protection of the Occupiers' Liability Act 1957,
whereas if they were outside on the pavement they would be likely to have the
protection of the highway authority's duty to maintain under the Highways Act
1980.[77] Persons exercising access rights under the National Parks and Access to the
Countryside Act 1949 or the Countryside and Rights of Way Act 2000 are not visitors[78] but a duty is potentially owed to them under the 1984 Act.[79]

D. Common Duty of Care

The common duty of care, owed to all visitors and also where the duty of the oc-   **10-013**
cupier depends upon a term to be implied in a contract, is defined as[80]:

> "[A] duty to take such care as in all the circumstances of the case is reasonable to see that
> the visitor will be reasonably safe in using the premises for the purposes for which he is
> invited or permitted to be there."

---

the claimant on to the premises in the first place.
[70] 1957 Act s.2(6).
[71] *Greenhalgh v British Railways Board* [1969] 2 Q.B. 286.
[72] *Holden v White* [1982] 2 Q.B. 679.
[73] See para.10-043.
[74] *McGeown v Northern Ireland Housing Executive* [1995] 1 A.C. 233. A highway authority may
however be liable for breach of its duty to maintain a highway under the Highways Act 1980:
para.15-085.
[75] Lord Keith in *McGeown*'s case at [1995] 1 A.C. 243.
[76] As in *Cumbernauld and Kilsyth DC v Dollar Land (Cumbernauld) Ltd* 1993 S.L.T. 1318.
[77] See Lord Browne-Wilkinson in *McGeown v Northern Ireland Housing Executive* [1995] 1 A.C. 233.
See generally Barker and Parry (1995) 15 L.S. 335.
[78] 1957 Act s.1(4), as substituted by s.13 of the Countryside and Rights of Way Act 2000.
[79] See para.10-043.
[80] 1957 Act s.2(2).

The question whether the occupier has fulfilled his duty to the visitor is thus dependent upon the facts of the case,[81] and, though the purpose of the visit may be a relevant circumstance, it can no longer be conclusive as it so often was when it governed the status of the entrant.[82] All the circumstances must be taken into account.[83] If, for example, the owner of an inn permits the resident manager to accept paying guests, both are "occupiers" in relation to such guests but, while the owner may be liable for injury caused to them by a structural defect such as the collapse of a staircase, the manager alone would be liable for injury caused by a defect in his own furnishings, such as a dangerous hole in the carpet of the living room.[84] Where professional expertise is involved, the standard of care to be observed is subject to the *Bolam* test,[85] i.e., it is sufficient if the occupier has acted in accordance with a practice accepted as proper by a responsible body of opinion in the particular field.[86]

10-014 **The particular visitor** Section 2(3) of the 1957 Act provides that the relevant circumstances in applying the common duty of care include the degree of care and of want of care that may be looked for in the particular visitor:

> "[S]o that (for example)[87] in proper cases:
> (a) an occupier must be prepared for children to be less careful than adults and
> (b) an occupier may expect that a person, in the exercise of his calling, will appreciate and guard against any special risks ordinarily incident to it, so far as the occupier leaves him free to do so."

10-015 **Children** We have seen above that one cannot say there is a danger due to the state of the premises simply because a visitor may choose to take obviously hazardous risks, but children may lack the awareness of danger which can be expected of an adult: an ordinary, well-maintained staircase may present a significant hazard to a toddler. It is not right to disregard someone's choice to ignore a danger simply

---

81 The similarity of the duty to the common law duty of care is demonstrated in *Simms v Leigh Rugby Football Club Ltd* [1969] 2 All E.R. 923. In the era of the "risk assessment", the carrying out of such an assessment, or the failure to conduct one, appears to be of increasing importance, itself creating a risk that the duty of care will be transformed into a box-ticking exercise: *Bowen v National Trust* [2011] EWHC 1992 (QB); *Hufton v Somerset CC* [2011] EWCA Civ 789; [2011] E.L.R. 482; *Furmedge v Chester-le-Street DC* [2011] EWHC 1226 (QB). cf. *West Sussex CC v Pierce* [2013] EWCA Civ 1230; [2014] P.I.Q.R. P5 at [12].

82 Where premises are hired for a purpose about which the hirer knows more than the occupier, the latter may be entitled to leave it to the hirer's judgment whether the premises are suitable: *Wheeler v St Mary's Hall, The Times,* 10 October 1989.

83 Including the period when the building was constructed: *Hogg v Historic Buildings and Monuments Commission* [1988] 3 C.L. 285.

84 *Wheat v Lacon & Co Ltd* [1966] A.C. 552 at 585–587.

85 See para.6-027.

86 *Bowen v National Trust* [2011] EWHC 1992 (QB) (tree inspectors).

87 The two categories which follow are therefore not exhaustive. It has been suggested, for example, that an occupier of licensed premises should take account of the fact that its patrons may be under the influence of alcohol (*AB v Pro-Nation Ltd* [2016] EWHC 1022 (QB)), while decisions that have turned on the heightened foreseeability of injury to a particular visitor include *Pollock v Cahill* [2015] EWHC 2260 (QB) (blind house guest falling from open window) and *G4S Care and Justice Services (UK) v Manley* [2016] EWHC 2355 (QB) (prisoner with mobility problems falling in cell during power cut). Strictly speaking, these latter two cases did not fall within s.2(3) because they were concerned not with the degree of care to be expected of the visitor, but rather his greater vulnerability. However, nothing turns on the point since the subsection merely emphasises what is in any case breach of duty orthodoxy: see para.6-021.

because he is a child,[88] but even where there is no capacity for discernment at all it would be unrealistic to expect that all land must be made safe enough for unaccompanied toddlers. A person who owns a mountain in the vicinity of a town is not obliged to fence it off in case small children come there.[89] What Lord M'Laren said more than a hundred years ago about the Scots common law remains true under the Occupiers' Liability Act 1957[90]:

"In a town, as well as in the country, there are physical features which may be productive of injury to careless persons or to young children against which it is impossible to guard by protective measures. The situation of a town on the banks of a river is a familiar feature; and whether the stream be sluggish like the Clyde at Glasgow, or swift and variable like the Ness at Inverness, or the Tay at Perth, there is always danger to the individual who may be so unfortunate as to fall into the stream. But in none of these places has it been found necessary to fence the river to prevent children or careless persons from falling into the water. Now, as the common law is just the formal statement of the results and conclusions of the common sense of mankind, I come without difficulty to the conclusion that precautions which have been rejected by common sense as unnecessary and inconvenient are not required by the law."

This simply reflects the fact that the law of occupiers' liability is not an insurance scheme to compensate people for any misfortune which may occur on another's land.

Parental responsibility The reason for saying that there is no relevant danger due   **10-016** to the state of the premises in such cases involving children no doubt reflects the fact that society expects parents to take care of their children. That is the basis of the decision in *Phipps v Rochester Corp*.[91] The claimant, a boy aged five, was collecting blackberries with his sister, aged seven, and they walked across a large open space which formed part of a housing estate being developed by the defendants. The defendants had dug a long deep trench in the middle of the open space, a danger obvious to an adult. The claimant fell into it and broke his leg. On the facts it was held that a prudent parent would not have allowed two small children to go alone on the open space in question or would at least have first satisfied himself that the place held no dangers for them. The defendants were entitled to assume that parents would behave in this way and therefore the defendants were not in breach of their duty to the claimant. Devlin J's judgment squarely placed the primary responsibility for the safety of small children on their parents. The occupier will have discharged his duty towards a child if the place is reasonably safe for a child accompanied by the sort of guardian the occupier is entitled to expect the child to be accompanied by. In an appropriate case, the child's injury may be attributed either to both the occupier's breach of his common duty of care and the negligence of the guardian (rendering them both liable) or to neither.[92]

---

88 *Keown v Coventry Healthcare NHS Trust* [2006] EWCA Civ 39; [2006] 1 W.L.R. 953 (a trespasser case, but the same must apply to visitors).
89 *Simkiss v Rhondda BC* (1983) 81 L.G.R. 460.
90 *Stevenson v Glasgow Corp* 1908 SC 1034 at 1039.
91 [1955] 1 Q.B. 450.
92 Neither: *Marsden v Bourne Leisure Ltd* [2009] EWCA Civ 671 (two-year-old drowned in holiday park pond).

10-017 **Injury to contractors** Paragraph (b) of s.2(3) of the 1957 Act clearly preserves such decisions as *Bates v Parker*,[93] to the general effect that[94]:

> "[W]here a householder employs an independent contractor to do work, be it of cleaning or repairing, on his premises, the contractor must satisfy himself as to the safety or condition of that part of the premises on which he is to work."

In *Roles v Nathan*[95] two chimney sweeps were killed by carbon monoxide gas while attempting to seal up a "sweep hole" in the chimney of a coke-fired boiler, the boiler being alight at the time, but the occupier was held not liable for their deaths, partly at least on the ground that s.2(3)(b) applied.[96] As Lord Denning MR said[97]:

> "When a householder calls in a specialist to deal with a defective installation on his premises, he can reasonably expect the specialist to appreciate and guard against the dangers arising from the defect."

The result might no doubt have been different if, for example, the stairs leading to the cellar where the boiler was situated had given way,[98] for that would not have been a special risk ordinarily incidental to the calling of a sweep. In any case, it is important to note that the fact that the claimant is an expert is only a factor to be considered when determining whether there has been a breach of duty: his calling is not in itself a defence. Thus an occupier who negligently starts a fire may be liable to a firefighter injured by even an ordinary risk of fighting it if that risk is one which remains even when all proper skill is used.[99] Furthermore, the fact that there is someone else whose duty it is to safeguard the visitor, for example his employer, does not of itself insulate the occupier from liability, though the occupier may be able to seek contribution from the other if he is also at fault.[100]

10-018 **Warnings** Section 2(4)(a) of the 1957 Act provides that[101]:

> "Where damage is caused to a visitor by a danger of which he had been warned by the occupier, the warning is not to be treated without more as absolving the occupier from liability, unless in all the circumstances it was enough to enable the visitor to be reasonably safe."

Although a warning of the danger may enable the visitor to be reasonably safe, thereby discharging the duty of care, if it is not then the occupier may be liable. This

---

[93] [1953] 2 Q.B. 231; *Christmas v General Cleaning Contractors* [1952] 1 K.B. 141 (affirmed [1953] A.C. 180); *Roles v Nathan* [1963] 1 W.L.R. 1117 at 1123.

[94] *Bates v Parker* [1953] 2 Q.B. 231 at 235.

[95] [1963] 1 W.L.R. 1117.

[96] [1963] 1 W.L.R. 1117 at 1123–1125.

[97] [1963] 1 W.L.R. 1117 at 1123; *Clare v Whittaker & Son (London) Ltd* [1976] I.C.R. 1; *Kealey v Heard* [1983] 1 W.L.R. 573.

[98] *Roles v Nathan* [1963] 1 W.L.R. 1117; *Bird v King Line* [1970] 2 Lloyd's Rep. 349; *Eden v West & Co* [2002] EWCA Civ 991; [2003] P.I.Q.R. Q2.

[99] *Ogwo v Taylor* [1988] A.C. 431; *Salmon v Seafarers Restaurant Ltd* [1983] 1 W.L.R. 1264. As to the position of "rescuers" generally, see para.26-025. Where there is no negligence by the defendant in starting the fire, he may still be liable for not warning of unusual risks in the premises: *Bermingham v Sher Bros* (1980) 124 S.J. 117. Strictly, perhaps, only the second type of case falls within the Act, the other involving the common law: see para.10-004.

[100] *Intruder Detection etc Ltd v Fulton* [2008] EWCA Civ 1009.

[101] The warning may be given by the occupier's agent: *Roles v Nathan* [1963] 1 W.L.R. 1117.

can be contrasted with the position before the 1957 Act, whereby an invitee could not succeed if he had full knowledge of the nature and extent of the danger.[102] Whether a warning is sufficient will depend on all the circumstances, including the purposes for which the visitor was permitted onto the premises, the nature of the danger, and the feasibility of mitigating or eliminating it. In *Roles v Nathan*, Lord Denning MR gave the following instructive example[103]:

> "Suppose, for instance, that there was only one way of getting into and out of premises, and it was by a footbridge over a stream which was rotten and dangerous. According to [the law before the 1957 Act] the occupier could escape all liability to any visitor by putting up a notice: 'This bridge is dangerous', even though there was no other way by which the visitor could get in or out, and he had no option but to go over the bridge. In such a case, s.2(4)(a) makes it clear that the occupier would nowadays be liable. But if there were two footbridges, one of which was rotten, and the other safe a hundred yards away, the occupier could still escape liability, even today, by putting up a notice: 'Do not use this footbridge. It is dangerous. There is a safe one further upstream'. Such a warning is sufficient because it does enable the visitor to be reasonably safe."

It is of course also possible that the absence of a warning will itself constitute a breach of the common duty of care,[104] though this will generally not be the case if the risk is obvious. In *Darby v National Trust*,[105] the husband of the claimant had drowned while swimming in a pond on the defendant's property. It was held that the failure to put up signs warning against the danger of swimming was not negligent since the risks of doing so were obvious and such signs would not have told people anything that they did not already know.[106]

Dangers due to the fault of independent contractors[107]   Section 2(4)(b) of the **10-019** 1957 Act states that:

> "where damage is caused to a visitor by a danger due to the faulty execution of any work of construction, maintenance or repair by an independent contractor[108] employed by the occupier, the occupier is not to be treated without more as answerable for the danger if in all the circumstances he had acted reasonably in entrusting the work to an independent contractor and had taken such steps (if any) as he reasonably ought in order to satisfy himself that the contractor was competent[109] and that the work had been properly done."

This provision is designed to afford some protection for the occupier who engages

---

102 *London Graving Dock Co v Horton* [1951] A.C. 737.
103 [1963] 1 W.L.R. 1117 at 1124.
104 Conversely, could a badly positioned warning amount to such a breach? See *Beaton v Ocean Terminal Ltd* [2018] CSOH 74 (pursuer alleged to have slipped on a "wet floor" sign).
105 [2001] EWCA Civ 189; [2001] P.I.Q.R. P27.
106 Similarly a commercial operator of a climbing wall is not obliged to point out to users that matting does not provide complete security in the event of a fall: *Poppleton v Portsmouth Youth Activities Committee* [2008] EWCA Civ 646; [2009] P.I.Q.R. P1. cf. *English Heritage v Taylor* [2016] EWCA Civ 448; [2016] P.I.Q.R. P14 (liability for not warning of sheer drop at castle; but "not to be interpreted as requiring … unsightly warning signs in prominent positions all over sensitive historic sites" (at 30])).
107 North, *Occupiers' Liability*, 2nd edn (2014), Ch.9.
108 The burden of proving that the danger was due to the fault of an independent contractor rests with the occupier: *Christmas v Blue Star Line* [1961] 1 Lloyd's Rep. 94; *AMF International Ltd v Magnet Bowling Ltd* [1968] 1 W.L.R. 1028 at 1042–1043.
109 On the content of this duty see para.10-020.

an independent contractor who does the work in a faulty manner and was intended to reverse the decision of the House of Lords in *Thompson v Cremin*[110] in so far as that laid down that an invitor was responsible for his contractor's shortcomings. The paragraph therefore makes the law relating to occupiers accord with the general law, under which there is generally no liability for the default of independent contractors.[111] Although limited to works of "construction, maintenance and repair", those words have been given a broad, purposive, interpretation,[112] and the courts have relied on s.2(4)(a) by analogy in cases that do not fall within its terms,[113] which seems appropriate since the logic of the provision appears to extend to all cases where an independent contractor has been employed.

The operation of the paragraph is illustrated by two cases from the period before the 1957 Act. In *Haseldine v Daw*[114] H was going to visit a tenant in a block of flats belonging to D and was injured when the lift fell to the bottom of its shaft as a result of the negligence of a firm of engineers employed by D to repair the lift. It was held that D, having employed a competent firm of engineers to make periodical inspections of the lift, to adjust it and report on it, had discharged the duty owed to H, whether H was an invitee or licensee.[115] In *Woodward v Mayor of Hastings*,[116] on the other hand, a pupil at a school for which the defendants were responsible fell and was injured on an icy step which had been negligently left in a dangerous condition by a cleaner. Even assuming that the cleaner was an independent contractor, it was held that the defendants were liable and *Haseldine v Daw* was distinguished. Technical knowledge was required in the maintenance and repair of a lift, but such considerations were not relevant in *Woodward's* case: "The craft of the charwoman may have its mysteries, but there is no esoteric quality in the nature of the work which the cleaning of a snow-covered step demands."[117]

10-020   **Obligations of the occupier in respect of the contractor and his work**   Where an independent contractor has been employed, therefore, the question today is whether the occupier himself has done all that reasonable care requires of him. He must take reasonable steps to satisfy himself that the contractor he employs is competent, and, if the character of the work permits, he must take similar steps to see that the work has been properly done. In fact, where the work is especially complex, as with the construction of a large building or a ship, he may even have to cause the independent contractor's work to be supervised by a properly instructed architect or other professional person.[118] There are many cases in which the technical nature of the work to be done will require the occupier to employ an independent contractor and he will be negligent if he attempts to do it himself. This does not

---

[110] [1953] 2 All E.R. 1181.

[111] *AMF International Ltd v Magnet Bowling Ltd* [1968] 1 W.L.R. 1028. See para.21-041.

[112] *Ferguson v Welsh* [1987] 1 W.L.R. 1553 at 1560 ("construction" includes demolition).

[113] See, e.g., *Gwilliam v West Hertfordshire NHS Trust* [2002] EWCA Civ 1041; [2002] Q.B. 443 (provider of "splat-wall").

[114] [1941] 2 K.B. 343.

[115] *Haseldine v Daw* [1941] 2 K.B. 343 at 356, 374.

[116] [1954] K.B. 174.

[117] *Woodward v Mayor of Hastings* [1954] K.B. 174 at 813 per du Parcq LJ. See also *Alexander v Freshwater Properties Ltd* [2012] EWCA Civ 1048 (landlord liable for failing to ensure repair to front door had been done properly).

[118] *AMF International Ltd v Magnet Bowling Ltd* [1968] 1 W.L.R. 1028 at 1044–1047; *Kealey v Heard* [1983] 1 All E.R. 973.

mean, however, that a householder must not himself undertake some ordinary domestic repair such as the fixing of a new door handle. Provided that he does the work with the care and skill of a reasonably competent carpenter he has fulfilled his duty.[119]

One justification for a general rule of non-liability for independent contractors is that the contractor (who is of course personally liable) is more likely to be claim-worthy than an individual employee of the occupier. That prompts the question, "Is the occupier therefore obliged to investigate the liability insurance position of the contractor?" In *Gwilliam v West Hertfordshire NHS Trust*,[120] the claimant was injured due to the negligence of an independent contractor while attending a charity fair organised by the defendant occupier. The liability insurance of the independent contractor having expired, the claimant sued the occupier for carelessly failing to ensure that the contractor had adequate insurance cover. Lord Woolf CJ and Waller LJ held that the defendant had been obliged to inquire into the contractor's insurance position, but that on the facts it had taken all reasonable steps in that regard. However, Sedley LJ considered that the scope of the occupier's duty of care did not extend so far, since any default of the occupier in this regard would cause a visitor only a pure economic loss, and such losses were not recoverable under the Act. Sedley LJ's reasoning on this issue has since been preferred,[121] and it has been held that there is no general requirement that an occupier check on the insurance position of an independent contractor.[122] With respect, that seems right. Not only would an obligation to investigate the contractor's insurance position be difficult to reconcile with the wording of the statute—which refers only to the "competence" of the contractor, and imposes a duty only in respect of the "safety" of the visitor, a concept that does not obviously extend to his economic interests—it would also be impracticable: consider, for example, the position of the householder who engages a tradesman to do a small job around the house or garden.

Where an occupier engages a contractor to do work on his premises and the claimant suffers injury not from the condition in which the contractor leaves the premises but from the manner in which the operation is carried out,[123] any liability arises under the general law and not under the 1957 Act.[124] However, there may be circumstances where the occupier is required to intervene because he has failed to take care in selecting a competent contractor[125] or because it is obvious that the contractor is using an unsafe system of work.

Personal responsibility: Tomlinson's case   It must be emphasised that the provisions dealt with in the preceding paragraphs are no more than explanations or il-   **10-021**

---

[119] *Wells v Cooper* [1958] 2 Q.B. 265.
[120] [2002] EWCA Civ 1041; [2002] Q.B. 443.
[121] *Glaister v Appleby in Westmorland Town Council* [2009] EWCA Civ 1325; [2010] P.I.Q.R. P6 at [63].
[122] *Payling v T Naylor (Trading as Mainstreet)* [2004] EWCA Civ 560; [2004] P.I.Q.R. P36. See also *Mackin v SV Drumgarth Parish and RCB* [2008] NIQB 118.
[123] For example, removing asbestos lagging without taking the recognised precautions.
[124] "It would not ordinarily be reasonable to expect an occupier of premises having engaged a contractor whom he has reasonable grounds for regarding as competent, to supervise the contractor's activities in order to ensure that he was discharging his duty to his employees to observe a safe system of work": *Ferguson v Welsh* [1987] 1 W.L.R. 1553 at 1560. See also *Fairchild v Glenhaven Funeral Services Ltd* [2001] EWCA Civ 1881; [2002] 1 W.L.R. 1052.
[125] *Bottomley v Todmorden Cricket Club* [2003] EWCA Civ 1575; [2004] P.I.Q.R. P18.

lustrations of the fundamental rule, which is that the occupier must do what is reasonable in the circumstances of the case and that standard, as in any other case of negligence, will be arrived at by the court's weighing the relative risks and burdens.[126] The burdens are not only those that would be directly imposed on the particular occupier if he were required to take the action contended for by the claimant, but include the restrictions on the freedom of the majority of people which will be imposed if what is required of the occupier is set at a level which will prevent the foolhardy encountering obvious risks.[127] This is the basis of *Tomlinson v Congleton BC*,[128] where Lord Hobhouse said[129]:

> "It is not, and should never be, the policy of the law to require the protection of the foolhardy or reckless few to deprive, or interfere with, the enjoyment by the remainder of society of the liberties and amenities to which they are rightly entitled. Does the law require that all trees be cut down because some youths may climb them and fall? Does the law require the coastline and other beauty spots to be lined with warning notices? Does the law require that attractive waterside picnic spots be destroyed because of a few foolhardy individuals who choose to ignore warning notices and indulge in activities dangerous only to themselves? The answer to all these questions is, of course, no. But this is the road down which your Lordships, like other courts before, have been invited to travel and which the councils in the present case found so inviting. In truth, the arguments for the claimant have involved an attack upon the liberties of the citizen which should not be countenanced. They attack the liberty of the individual to engage in dangerous, but otherwise harmless, pastimes at his own risk and the liberty of citizens as a whole fully to enjoy the variety and quality of the landscape of this country. The pursuit of an unrestrained culture of blame and compensation has many evil consequences and one is certainly the interference with the liberty of the citizen."

E.   Damage to Property

10-022   Section 1(3)(b) of the 1957 Act provides that the rules which it enacts shall apply:

> "[I]n like manner and to the like extent as the principles applicable at common law to an occupier of premises and his invitees or licensees would apply, to regulate … the obligations of a person occupying or having control over any premises or structure in respect of damage to property, including the property of persons who are not themselves his visitors."

Clearly, therefore, where property lawfully on the premises is damaged by a structural defect of the premises,[130] whether it actually belongs to a visitor or not,

---

[126]   See, e.g., *Lewis v Six Continents Plc* [2005] EWCA Civ 1805 (no need to make upper storey hotel window unopenable). See also *Neindorf v Junkovic* [2005] HCA 75; (2005) 222 A.L.R. 631 at [8].

[127]   Indeed, even where the risk is not obvious and the claimant not foolhardy there is a danger of inhibiting ordinary activities if the standard of care is set too high: *Cole v Davis-Gilbert* [2007] EWCA Civ 396.

[128]   [2003] UKHL 47; [2004] 1 A.C. 46, para.10-006. See also *Darby v National Trust* [2001] EWCA Civ 189; [2001] P.I.Q.R. P27.

[129]   [2003] UKHL 47; [2004] 1 A.C. 46 at [81]. See also Lord Hoffmann at [46]. The sentiment expressed by Lord Hobhouse and Lord Hoffmann is now enshrined in the Compensation Act 2006 s.1, but it does "not add anything to the common law position": *Uren v Corporate Leisure UK Ltd* [2011] EWCA Civ 66; [2011] I.C.R. D11 at [13] (though the case was remitted where Foskett J ([2013] EWHC 353 (QB)) drew as much, if not more so, on the speeches in *Tomlinson* than on s.1 of the 2006 Act).

[130]   For example, if, with your permission, I leave my car in the drive outside your house and a tile falls

the question in each case is whether the occupier has discharged the common duty of care. Where there has been a bailment, however, as where goods are deposited in a warehouse, the liability of the warehouse-keeper will not depend upon the common duty of care but upon his duty under the bailment or special contract. The rules contained in the 1957 Act replace only the principles of the common law formerly applicable between the occupier and his invitee or licensee. They do not affect the relationship of bailor and bailee.[131] Where there is no bailment, the common law rule was that there was no duty on the occupier to protect the goods of his visitors from theft by a third party[132] and the Act did not change this. A mere licence to put goods on land (as in the case of most car parks) does not make the occupier a bailee.[133]

F. Exclusion of Liability

Exclusion of liability by contract or notice   Under s.2(1) of the 1957 Act the **10-023** common duty of care is owed by the occupier "except in so far as he is free to and does extend, restrict, modify or exclude his duty ... by agreement or otherwise".[134] No contract is necessary for this purpose, for s.2(1) gives statutory force to the decision of the Court of Appeal, shortly before the Act, in *Ashdown v Samuel Williams & Sons*.[135] The claimant was a licensee on land belonging to the defendants when she was knocked down and injured by railway trucks which were being negligently shunted along a railway line on the land. Various notices had been posted by the defendants to the effect that every person on the land was there at his own risk and should have no claim against the defendants for any injury whatsoever, and it was found as a fact that they had taken reasonable steps to bring the conditions contained in the notices to the claimant's attention. It was held, therefore, that the claimant could not recover.[136] Despite criticism to the effect that the absence of a contract should have been fatal to the defence,[137] the decision seems to accord with general principle. If I can exclude you from my property altogether, why can I not permit you to enter upon any terms that I wish to make? The result might, indeed, be construed as a contract whereby you give up what would otherwise be your legal rights in return for my allowing you to enter, but this construction is not essential to the validity of the conditions.[138]

As with any purported exclusion of liability any term to this effect must have been validly incorporated in the contract and in the case of a non-contractual notice

---

off the roof and damages it: see *AMF International Ltd v Magnet Bowling Ltd* [1968] 1 W.L.R. 1028.

[131] cf. *Fairline Shipping Corp v Adamson* [1975] Q.B. 180.

[132] *Tinsley v Dudley* [1951] 2 K.B. 18. See also *Ashby v Tolhurst* [1937] 2 K.B. 242; *Deyong v Shenburn* [1946] K.B. 227; *Edwards v West Herts Group Hospital Management Committee* [1957] 1 W.L.R. 418.

[133] *Tinsley v Dudley* [1951] 2 K.B. 18; *John C. Dogherty v Drogheda Harbour Commissioners* [1993] 1 I.R. 315.

[134] We are not concerned here with the question of whether the occupier has *discharged* his duty, e.g., by the use of an appropriate warning: see para.10-018.

[135] [1957] 1 Q.B. 409; see also *White v Blackmore* [1972] 2 Q.B. 651.

[136] Since the case was concerned with the activities of the occupier, the power to exclude liability is clearly not limited to the static condition of the premises, even if it is less easy to justify the existence of that power with regard to current activities: Odgers [1957] C.L.J. 39 at 54.

[137] See Gower (1956) 19 M.L.R. 536.

[138] It was rejected by Lord Greene MR in *Wilkie v LPTB* [1947] 1 All E.R. 258 at 260. cf. *Gore v Van Der Lann* [1967] 2 Q.B. 31; Odgers (1970) 86 L.Q.R. 69.

reasonable steps must have been taken to bring it to the attention of the visitor, though he need not actually be aware of it.[139] In both cases the wording will be construed *contra proferentem*, i.e., in favour of the visitor in the event of any ambiguity.[140]

10-024 **Common law limits on the power to exclude liability** The occupier may only exclude the common duty of care "in so far as he is free to" do so. The principal restrictions are now provided by statute,[141] but clearly the 1957 Act does not enlarge the power to exclude which existed at common law. It is submitted, for example, that there could be no exclusion of liability to a person entering in exercise of a right conferred by law and the same may be true of those who do not enter as of right, but have no "free choice" in the matter.[142]

10-025 **Statutory controls on the power to exclude liability** The power of the occupier to exclude or restrict his liability to a visitor may be subject to the controls set out in the Unfair Contract Terms Act 1977 (UCTA 1977), or, in the case of a consumer relationship, by the Consumer Rights Act 2015 (CRA 2015). It will be convenient to consider UCTA 1977 first.

10-026 **Unfair Contract Terms Act 1977** Section 2 of UCTA 1977 provides[143]:

> "(1) A person cannot by reference to any contract term or to a notice[144] ... exclude or restrict his liability for death or personal injury resulting from negligence.
> (2) In the case of other loss or damage, a person cannot so exclude or restrict his liability for negligence except in so far as the term or notice satisfies the requirement of reasonableness."

The definition of "negligence" under the 1977 Act expressly includes the breach of the common duty of care imposed by the Occupiers' Liability Act 1957,[145] but the limitations on exclusion of liability apply only to breach of obligations or duties arising from things done in the course of a business or from the occupation of premises used for the business purposes of the occupier.[146] A business probably requires at least some degree of regularity, so that an isolated transaction whereby access to land was granted for payment would probably not fall within the scope of s.2, but UCTA 1977 contains a broad definition which extends the concept to activities which would not ordinarily be thought of in those terms.[147] Since the operator of a farm or commercial forest is occupying land for business purposes, the Act as originally formulated caused restrictions to be placed on public access to such locations, and to avoid this it was amended by s.2 of the Occupiers' Li-

---

[139] *Ashdown v Samuel Williams & Sons* [1957] 1 Q.B. 409 at 425.
[140] *Ashdown v Samuel Williams & Sons* [1957] 1 Q.B. 409 at 429—430.
[141] See para.10-026.
[142] See *Burnett v British Waterways Board* [1973] 1 W.L.R. 700 (lighterman required to bring employer's barge into dock).
[143] See s.11 of UCTA 1977.
[144] Defined in s.14 of UCTA 1977, e.g., a sign at the entry to the premises.
[145] Section 1(1)(c) of the 1957 Act. By virtue of s.1(4) it is immaterial whether liability "arises directly or vicariously".
[146] Section 1(3) of the 1957 Act.
[147] By s.14 of UCTA 1977 "'business' includes a profession and the activities of any government department or local or public authority".

ability Act 1984, as a result of which s.1(3)(b) of UCTA 1977 now provides that:

> "[L]iability of an occupier of premises for breach of an obligation or duty towards a person obtaining access to the premises for recreational or educational purposes, being liability for loss or damage suffered by reason of the dangerous state of the premises, is not a business liability of the occupier unless granting that person such access for the purposes concerned falls within the business purposes of the occupier."

Hence, if a farmer has on his property a ruinous castle he may allow access on condition that he is not liable for death or personal injury caused by the state of the premises,[148] but were the ancient monuments body English Heritage to impose such a condition it would be ineffective because admission of the public for recreation or education falls within its business purposes within the meaning of the Act. The liberty to exclude liability is, however, confined to damage suffered by reason of the dangerous state of the premises, so that if the visitor is run over by the farmer's tractor, s.2(1) applies and so any exclusion, no matter how widely drawn, is ineffective.

Consumer Rights Act 2015   Where the occupier seeks to exclude liability towards a visitor by a term in a "consumer contract" or by a "consumer notice", s.2 of UCTA 1977 is inapplicable,[149] and the position is instead governed by the Consumer Rights Act 2015. A consumer contract is defined[150] as a contract between a "trader"[151] and a "consumer",[152] and there is an equivalent definition of a consumer notice.[153] The relevant provisions roughly mirror of those of UCTA 1977, so that the occupier cannot exclude his liability for death or personal injury resulting from negligence,[154] while attempts to limit liability for other types of damage are not binding on the visitor if "unfair".[155] There is a parallel provision to s.1(3)(b) of UCTA 1977, though this is limited to access for "recreational purposes".[156]   **10-027**

G.   Other Defences

Contributory negligence   Although the Occupiers' Liability Act 1957 does not expressly incorporate the Law Reform (Contributory Negligence) Act 1945, there is no doubt that the 1945 Act applies when claims are brought under the former and judges have in numerous cases discounted the damages awarded to visitors against occupiers for contributory negligence.[157] Where the claimant's fault is extreme it may, of course, amount to the sole legal cause of his loss.[158]   **10-028**

---

[148] If the farmer charges the public even a small sum for admission there is likely to be a business occupation.

[149] UCTA 1977 s.2(4).

[150] CRA 2015 s.61.

[151] A "person acting for purposes relating to that person's trade, business, craft or profession": CRA 2015 s.2(2). The definition of "business" mirrors that in UCTA 1977: CRA 2015 s.2(7).

[152] An "individual acting for purposes that are wholly or mainly outside that individual's trade, business, craft or profession": CRA 2015 s.2(3).

[153] CRA 2015 s.61.

[154] CRA 2015 s.65(1). "Negligence" again expressly includes breach of the common duty of care in the Occupiers' Liability Act 1957: CRA 2015 s.65(4)(c).

[155] CRA 2015 s.62.

[156] CRA 2015 s.66(4).

[157] See Goudkamp and Nolan, *Contributory Negligence in the Twenty-First Century* (2019), paras 4.43–4.45. Sometimes the discount is very high: see, e.g., *Poppleton v Portsmouth Youth Activities Com-*

10-029   **Volenti non fit injuria**   Section 2(5) of the 1957 Act provides that:

> "The common duty of care does not impose on an occupier any obligation to a visitor in respect of risks willingly accepted as his by the visitor (the question whether a risk was so accepted to be decided on the same principles as in other cases in which one person owes a duty of care to another)."

This provision has generally been understood as making available the defence of volenti non fit injuria in claims under the 1957 Act,[159] and has been described as "indistinguishable from the common law defence".[160] It is true that strictly speaking the wording of s.2(5) goes to the conceptually distinct issue of breach of duty,[161] but the words in parentheses support the conventional view of the effect of the subsection. The legislation regulating the power of the occupier to exclude or restrict his liability[162] provides that a person is not to be taken to have voluntarily accepted any risk merely by virtue of his agreement to or awareness of an exempting condition or notice.[163]

H.   Effect of Contract on Occupier's Liability to Third Parties

10-030   **Occupiers' Liability Act 1957 s.3**   It was the opinion of the Law Reform Committee[164] that where a person contracts with the occupier for the use of premises on the footing that he is to be entitled to permit third parties to use them, the duty owed by the occupier to those third parties was the same as that owed to the other party to the contract. This could lead to a person being deprived of his rights by a contract to which he was not a party and the content of which he was unaware. It was therefore provided by s.3(1) of the 1957 Act that:

> "[W]here an occupier of premises is bound by contract to permit persons who are strangers to the contract[165] to enter or use the premises, the duty of care which he owes to them as his visitors cannot be restricted or excluded by that contract, but (subject to any provision of the contract to the contrary) shall include the duty to perform his obligations under the contract, whether undertaken for their protection or not, in so far as those obligations go beyond the obligations otherwise involved in that duty."

Furthermore, where a tenancy, including a statutory tenancy which does not in law amount to a tenancy, requires either the landlord or the tenant to permit persons to enter premises of which he is the occupier, the section applies as if the tenancy were a contract between the landlord and the tenant.[166]

10-031   **Effect of the section**   Section 3 of the 1957 Act has a twofold effect. First, the occupier cannot by contract reduce his obligations to visitors who are strangers to the

---

mittee [2008] EWCA Civ 646; [2009] P.I.Q.R. P1 (75 per cent).

[158]   See, e.g., *Brayshaw v Leeds CC* [1984] 2 C.L. 234.

[159]   Section 2(5) of the 1957 Act.

[160]   *Geary v JD Wetherspoon Plc* [2011] EWHC 1506 (QB); [2011] N.P.C. 60 at [36].

[161]   See *James v White Lion Hotel* (9 January 2020, QBD) at [78].

[162]   See para.10-026.

[163]   UCTA1977 s.2(3); CRA 2015 s.65(2).

[164]   (1954) Cmd. 9305, paras 55, 79. Reliance was placed on the authority of *Fosbroke-Hobbes v Airwork Ltd* [1937] 1 All E.R. 108.

[165]   "Stranger to the contract" is defined in s.3(3) of the 1957 Act.

[166]   Section 3(4) of the 1957 Act.

contract to a level below that imposed by the common duty of care.[167] Second, where the contract requires the occupier to take some precaution not required in the circumstances by that duty, the visitor shall have the benefit of that precaution. If, for example, A contracts with B to allow B and C to use his premises and the contract provides that the premises shall be lit during the hours of darkness, C has a right of action against A for injury due to A's failure to light the premises, whether or not such a failure would amount to a breach of the common duty of care. It is provided, however, that the section shall not have the effect, unless the contract so provides, of making an occupier who has taken all reasonable care liable for dangers due to the faulty execution of any work of construction, maintenance or repair or other like operation by persons other than himself, his servants or persons acting under his direction and control.[168]

Contracts (Rights of Third Parties) Act 1999   There may now be cases where **10-032** a visitor can rely on the provisions of the Contracts (Rights of Third Parties) Act 1999 in order to enforce a term in the contract between the occupier and another under which the visitor is allowed entry, and which imposes a higher duty than the common duty of care. However, in practice s.3 of the 1957 Act may continue to be relied on, not least because it will not then be necessary to satisfy the conditions laid down in the 1999 Act that the visitor be expressly identified in the contract[169] and that the relevant term purports to confer a benefit on him.[170]

Effect of a non-contractual notice   Can an occupier, though unable to restrict his **10-033** duty to third parties by a provision in the contract itself, do so by publishing a notice? Such a notice will of course be subject to the usual restrictions on the purported exclusion or limitation of the occupier's liability,[171] but it is also arguable that the occupier is in any case not "free to" restrict or exclude his duty of care under s.2(1) of the 1957 Act, on the grounds that the alternative view would tend to defeat the object of s.3. However, the effect of this interpretation would be to put a visitor entering pursuant to a contractual right covered by s.3 in a better position than other visitors, and it has been questioned whether this is justifiable.[172]

---

[167] As far as personal injuries are concerned much the same effect may be achieved by the Unfair Contract Terms Act 1977 s.2(1) and Consumer Rights Act 2015 s.65, but s.3 of the 1957 Act is more favourable to the claimant since: (1) it is not confined to business occupation; and (2) the limits imposed by UCTA 1977 and the CRA 2015 on the exclusion or limitation of liability for property damage are qualified, not absolute.

[168] 1957 Act s.3(2). The wording of this subsection differs from that of s.2(4)(b) (see para.10-019), but the effect of the two subsections is probably the same and if s.2(4)(b) includes demolition (*Ferguson v Welsh* [1987] 1 W.L.R. 1153) so should s.3(2).

[169] 1999 Act s.1(3). This requirement would not be met if, for example, the obligation to admit the third party was implied.

[170] 1999 Act s.1(1)(b). For other possible complications, see North, *Occupiers' Liability*, 2nd edn (2014), paras 10.38-10.41, who concludes that "it seems very unlikely" that a visitor will be aided by recourse to the 1999 Act.

[171] See paras 10-025ff.

[172] North, *Occupiers' Liability*, 2nd edn (2014), para.10-36. An argument in favour of this view is that while such a visitor will or should be aware of the notice, being a "stranger to the contract" pursuant to which he enters, he may not know of its contents: Payne (1958) 21 M.L.R. 359, 369–370.

3. LIABILITY TO TRESPASSERS AND OTHER NON-VISITORS

10-034 The common law The duty of an occupier to a trespasser was unaffected by the Occupiers' Liability Act 1957. The original common law rule was that the occupier was only liable to a trespasser in respect of some wilful act, "done with deliberate intention of doing harm ... or at least some act done with reckless disregard of the presence of the trespasser",[173] but the law underwent substantial alteration and development by the House of Lords in 1972 in *British Railways Board v Herrington.*[174] As a result of that case the occupier owed to the trespasser a "duty of common humanity" which, generally speaking, was lower than the common duty of care but substantially higher than the original duty. *Herrington*'s case was applied by the Court of Appeal on a number of occasions without undue difficulty[175] but the Law Commission considered that no sufficiently clear principle emerged from the case and recommended legislative action. After a long delay, this was done by the passing of theOccupiers' Liability Act 1984.[176]

10-035 Scope of the 1984 Act Though in this section we shall continue to speak of trespassers, for that is the commonest case, the Act in fact covers liability to all persons who are not the occupier's visitors. It applies, for example, to persons exercising private rights of way,[177] and persons exercising access rights under National Parks legislation[178] but not to persons using a public right of way,[179] whose rights, if any, must be sought in the highways legislation.[180]

10-036 "Activity duties" Although the 1984 Act is in terms as ambiguous as the 1957 Act on the relationship between the "occupancy" and "activity" duties, it has been said that it is confined to the liability of "an occupier as occupier".[181] On this basis it does not therefore apply to a case where the occupier negligently[182] shoots a trespasser.[183] However, both the wording of the statute and history show that it must apply to some activities carried out on the land—some of the leading cases on the common law involved activities, such as operating winding gear[184] or running trains.[185] These cases are perhaps distinguishable from that of the shooting since the pursuit of the activity was the very reason for the occupation of the land.[186] Where

---

173 *Robert Addie & Sons (Collieries) Ltd v Dumbreck* [1929] A.C. 358 at 365.

174 [1972] A.C. 877.

175 See, e.g., *Pannett v P McGuinness & Co Ltd* [1972] 2 Q.B. 599; *Harris v Birkenhead Corp* [1976] 1 W.L.R. 279.

176 Law Com. No.75.

177 *Vodden v Gayton* [2001] P.I.Q.R. P4 (owners of servient tenement across which fenced track ran occupiers of the track; no breach of duty on facts).

178 See para.10-012. As to persons exercising rights under the Countryside and Rights of Way Act 2000, see para.10-043.

179 Section 1(7).

180 See para.15-084.

181 *Revill v Newbery* [1996] Q.B. 567 at 576 per Neill LJ.

182 If the injury is inflicted deliberately the question will not be one of occupiers' liability but of whether a defence applies to a claim in respect of an intentional tort such as battery: see Ch.26.

183 *Revill v Newbery* [1996] Q.B. 567.

184 *Robert Addie and Sons (Collieries) Ltd v Dumbreck* [1929] A.C. 358.

185 *Videan v British Transport Commission* [1963] 2 Q.B. 650; *Herrington* [1972] A.C. 877.

186 Consider the case of the trespasser shot on a grouse moor. In *Revill* [1966] Q.B. 567 Neill LJ admitted that if the claim were framed as the negligent organisation of a shooting party by the owner of the estate, it would plainly fall within the 1984 Act.

the common law is applicable it should, as a matter of precedent, be that stated by the House of Lords in *Herrington*'s case[187]—in summary, the occupier was not obliged to institute checks for the presence of trespassers or dangers but a duty arose if on the facts of which he knew there was a likelihood of serious harm to the trespasser sufficient to make it inhumane to fail to take steps against it. Putting aside the point that *Herrington*'s case made some allowance for the ability and resources of the individual occupier and that the 1984 Act may not do that,[188] this is very similar to the approach of the Act and in *Revill v Newbery*[189] Neill LJ suggested that the Act might provide useful guidance on the nature of the duty owed at common law. If this is so, then where the precautions required do not involve significant effort or expenditure there will be little, if any, practical difference between the two sources of liability.[190]

When duty is owed   Section 1(3) of the 1984 Act provides that a duty is owed **10-037** by an occupier to a trespasser in relation to a risk of their suffering injury by reason of any danger due to the state of the premises[191] or things done or omitted to be done thereon[192] if:

"(a)   [The occupier] is aware of the danger or has reasonable grounds to believe that it exists;

(b)   he knows or has reasonable grounds to believe that the other is in the vicinity of the danger concerned or that he may come into the vicinity of the danger …; and

(c)   the risk is one against which, in all the circumstances of the case, he may reasonably be expected to offer the other some protection."

The expression "has reasonable grounds to believe" in paras (a) and (b) requires actual knowledge of facts which would lead a reasonable person to be aware of the danger or the presence of the trespasser[193] and simple ignorance, though blameworthy, is not enough, though it would be under the 1957 Act.[194] As for para.(c), it was held in *Tomlinson v Congleton BC*[195] that it was not reasonable for a teenager who defied a prohibition on swimming in a lake in a country park to expect protection against the obvious risks involved in that activity, while it has been queried whether it was reasonable of a child trespasser to expect protection against the risk of falling off an unfenced and unguarded hospital fire escape.[196] There is a danger when considering s.1(3)(c) of straying into the question of fault

---

[187] [1972] A.C. 877.
[188] See para.10-036.
[189] [1996] Q.B. 567.
[190] So it seems that the common law is to be looked at to interpret the Act (*Ratcliffe v McConnell* [1999] 1 W.L.R. 670, para.10-036) and that the Act is to be looked at to determine the common law.
[191] As we saw above (para.10-006), courts have relied on this phrase to exclude claims on the basis that there was nothing wrong with the premises in question, quite apart from any question of fault on the occupier's part. Some of the cases there cited concerned trespassers; see also *Burke v Southern Education & Library Board* [2004] NIQB 13 and *Phillips (A Child) v South Eastern Education and Library Board* [2015] NIQB 91 (children climbing fences); *Buckett v Staffordshire CC* (13 April 2015, QBD) (trespasser falling through skylight on school roof).
[192] See s.1(1)(a) of the 1984 Act.
[193] *Swain v Puri* [1996] P.I.Q.R. P442. See also *Rhind v Astbury Water Park Ltd* [2004] EWCA Civ 756; [2004] N.P.C. 95. The question is whether the occupier has reason to expect the trespasser at that time: *Donoghue v Folkestone Properties Ltd* [2003] EWCA Civ 231; [2003] Q.B. 1008.
[194] Consciously closing one's eyes to an obvious risk should however suffice.
[195] [2003] UKHL 47; [2004] 1 A.C. 46. See para.10-006.
[196] *Keown v Coventry Healthcare NHS Trust* [2006] EWCA Civ 39; [2006] 1 W.L.R. 953 at [17].

which ought rightfully to be dealt with under s.1(4), but one advantage of the wording of the former is that it enables a court to distinguish between different classes of non-visitor. Hence while a user of a private right of way, or an innocent trespasser (particularly a child), might reasonably expect some protection against a given risk, the same might not be true of a burglar or trespasser intent on criminal damage.[197]

10-038 **The duty of care** Where all three conditions in s.1(3) of the 1984 Act are satisfied, the duty that arises is to take such care as is reasonable in all the circumstances to see that the trespasser does not suffer injury[198] on the premises by reason of the danger concerned[199] and it may, in appropriate circumstances, be discharged by taking such steps as are reasonable to give warning of the danger concerned or to discourage persons from incurring the risk.[200] The standard is objective and so not conditioned by the occupier's own resources, unlike the common law duty of common humanity.[201]

10-039 **Warnings** While the giving of a warning will not necessarily discharge the occupier's duty under s.1(4) of the 1984 Act,[202] it is more likely to do so than in the case of a visitor. The latter may have no choice but to encounter the danger and the warning must therefore make him reasonably safe in using the premises for the purposes for which he was permitted to enter; a trespasser who continues to intrude after passing a prominent warning notice may be thought to have only himself to blame for any injury he then suffers.

10-040 **Obvious risks** Even where no effective warning is given, an adult trespasser (or even a child with sufficient understanding[203]) who took a risk which should have been obvious to him cannot complain that the occupier did not take more rigorous steps to discourage his folly.[204] The leading case of *Tomlinson v Congleton BC*[205] has been considered above in the context of the 1957 Act. In fact the majority of the House of Lords considered that the claimant was a trespasser in the lake and if the occupier was not liable under the 1957 Act then a fortiori this was true under the 1984 Act. In such a case it is unnecessary to rely on volenti non fit injuria as an answer to the claim, though the defence is expressly preserved.[206]

10-041 **Property damage** The 1984 Act is plainly inapplicable to damage to the property of the trespasser. If therefore, C trespasses on D's property and he is hurt when his car falls into a concealed crater, he may be able to recover damages for his personal injuries but not for the damage to his vehicle. However, the Act seems to leave the

---

[197] See further *Donoghue v Folkestone Properties Ltd* [2003] EWCA Civ 231; [2003] Q.B. 1008.
[198] For the definition of injury, see s.1(9) of the 1984 Act.
[199] 1984 Act s.1(4).
[200] 1984 Act s.1(5).
[201] *Herrington* [1972] A.C. 877 at 899, 920–921, 942. It might be argued that the occupier's resources are to be taken into account as part of "all the circumstances of the case", but the same words appear in s.2(2) of the 1957 Act and it has not been suggested that the occupier's "personal equation" forms part of the standard of care owed to visitors.
[202] For example, where the likely trespassers are young children; but the principle that the occupier must be entitled to look to parents to take principal responsibility for the safety of their children must apply here, too: para.10-016.
[203] *Keown v Coventry Healthcare NHS Trust* [2006] EWCA Civ 39; [2006] 1 W.L.R. 953.
[204] *Ratcliffe v McConnell* [1999] 1 W.L.R. 670.
[205] [2003] UKHL 47; [2004] 1 A.C. 46, para.10-006.
[206] 1984 Act s.1(6).

common law untouched on this point.[207] There can be little doubt that where an occupier is in breach of his common law duty of common humanity his liability would extend beyond the personal injuries suffered by the trespasser to, say, the destruction of his clothing. It is not, however, easy to apply the concept of "common humanity" to a situation where there is not at least a threat of personal injury.

Claims against non-occupiers One more situation appears to be governed by the **10-042** common law. Suppose the defendant is not the occupier but the occupier's contractor or guest, a situation to which the 1984 Act is plainly inapplicable. There was authority that, as between the trespasser and the non-occupier, trespassory status as such[208] was irrelevant,[209] but the balance of the dicta in *Herrington*'s case pointed towards the removal of any sharp distinction between occupiers and others in this respect,[210] and in *Revill v Newbery*[211] it was assumed that a non-occupier would be in the same position as the occupier.

Other non-visitors Those who enter premises in the exercise of private rights of **10-043** way are not visitors, but are owed the more limited duty of care under the 1984 Act.[212] As for public rights of way, the Countryside and Rights of Way Act 2000 introduced a general right of public access to open land for recreational purposes. Persons exercising this right, like those taking advantage of the access agreements under the more limited National Parks and Access to the Countryside Act 1949, are not visitors of the occupier[213] but they are potentially owed a duty under the 1984 Act. However, any such duty is specifically excluded in respect of[214]:

"(a)   [A] risk resulting from the existence of any natural feature of the landscape, or any river, stream, ditch or pond whether or not a natural feature, or

(b)   a risk of [the entrant] suffering injury when passing over, under or through any wall, fence or gate, except by proper use of the gate or of a stile."

This restriction seems to have been designed to head off any argument that, the duty under the 1984 Act being a flexible one, it should embrace such hazards in relation to the lawful entrant exercising his statutory "right to roam". However, in the light of *Tomlinson*'s case[215] it is not very likely that these matters would attract liability in any case. It is also provided that in determining whether any, and if so what, duty is owed to an entrant under the 2000 Act regard is to be had to the fact that the existence of the right to roam ought not to place an undue burden (whether financial or otherwise) on the occupier, and to the importance of maintaining the

---

[207] Section 1(1) of the 1984 Act provides that the Act is to replace the rules of the common law in respect of personal injury. Section 1(8), preventing recovery in respect of "loss of or damage to property", applies only to breaches of duty under s.1.

[208] On the facts, a trespasser might of course be unforeseeable when a lawful visitor would not.

[209] *Buckland v Guildford Gas Light and Coke Co* [1949] 1 K.B. 410; *Davis v St Mary's Demolition and Excavation Co Ltd* [1954] 1 W.L.R. 592; *Creed v McGeogh & Sons Ltd* [1955] 1 W.L.R. 1005.

[210] *Herrington* [1972] A.C. 877 at 914, 929. cf. at 943.

[211] [1996] Q.B. 567.

[212] *Vodden v Gayton* [2001] P.I.Q.R. P4.

[213] Occupiers' Liability Act 1984 s.1(4)(a) (as substituted by s.13(1) of the Countryside and Rights of Way Act 2000).

[214] Occupiers' Liability Act 1984 s.1(6A) (as inserted by s.13(2) of the Countryside and Rights of Way Act 2000). See also s.306 of the Marine and Coastal Access Act 2009. The restriction does not apply to dangers arising from anything done by the occupier with the intention of creating the risk, or reckless as to whether the risk is created: s.1(6C).

[215] See para.10-006.

character of the countryside.[216]

10-044 **Exclusion of liability** The 1984 Act is silent when it comes to the power of the occupier to exclude his liability to a trespasser.[217] As a consequence, the law in this respect cannot be stated with any certainty. The omission from the 1984 Act of any express reference to a power to exclude liability appears to have been deliberate,[218] and this may have been attributable to the conceptual problem of how a non-contractual exclusion notice[219] can bind a trespasser in the first place (the "condition of permitting entry" analysis used in the case of a visitor[220] being obviously inapplicable where no permission is given at all). It is also the case that the law's original level of duty to trespassers—not to injure them deliberately or recklessly—represented a minimum standard of conduct which could not be excluded. However, the protection now afforded to trespassers is much greater and, if it is non-excludable, then a trespasser could potentially be in a more favourable position than a visitor where any exclusion is not caught by the Unfair Contract Terms Act 1977 or the Consumer Rights Act 2015.[221] What does at least seem clear is that any power to exclude liability under the 1984 Act would not itself be caught by those enactments, since the definition of "negligence" in both references only common law negligence and the 1957 Act.[222] This may be a further argument in favour of the occupier having no power to exclude liability in the first place.

4. LIABILITY OF NON-OCCUPIERS

10-045 We are concerned here with the situation where a person who is not an occupier of premises is sued in respect of damage or loss caused by a danger or defect in the premises. Possible defendants under this heading include builders, vendors and owners out of occupation. The common law was at first solicitous to such persons but then swung sharply against them in the 1970s, albeit at the price of getting into a quite extraordinary state of complexity and uncertainty. A complicating strand in the story was the imposition of liability on local authorities for negligent exercise of their statutory functions of approval and inspection; indeed, since the builder had often gone into liquidation by the time the problem became apparent, local authorities frequently ended up with the bill. One of the principal features of the case law in this period was a tendency to blur the distinction between contract and tort. From 1988 there was a sharp reaction, culminating in the decision in *Murphy v Brentwood DC*[223] and scores of cases in the middle period must now be regarded as wrongly decided.

---

[216] Occupiers' Liability Act 1984 s.1A (as inserted by s.13(3) of the Countryside and Rights of Way Act 2000). Regard is also to be had to any guidance issued under the 2000 Act.

[217] The same is true of the Consumer Rights Act 2015.

[218] It had been allowed for in the draft bill put forward by the Law Commission (Law Com No.75), but was dropped in Parliament.

[219] A contractual exclusion is of course unlikely in the case of a trespasser, though a contract allowing access to only part of the premises might seek to exclude liability where the limits laid down are exceeded.

[220] See para.10-003.

[221] See para.10-023.

[222] See para.10-026.

[223] [1991] 1 A.C. 398.

A. Builder or Vendor

i. Claims in Contract

There is, of course, a contract between vendor and purchaser of land but the **10-046** implied contractual obligations as to quality are very much less extensive than they are in contracts for the sale of goods even if the vendor is a builder or developer, and hence "in the business" of selling houses. The basic rule is caveat emptor though this may be displaced by express terms in the contract or misrepresentations. In one situation, however, there is a limited implied obligation, namely, when there is a contract for the sale of a house to be built or completed by the vendor.[224] There is then a threefold implied warranty: that the builder will do his work in a good and workmanlike manner,[225] that he will supply good and proper materials and that it will be reasonably fit for human habitation.[226] This warranty avails only the first purchaser from the builder and the limitation period (six years) will start to run when the defective work is done, not when it comes to the purchaser's notice. The latter rule is, however, somewhat mitigated by the fact that if the builder knowingly covers up defective work this will constitute concealment of the cause of action so that time will not run until the purchaser discovers, or could with reasonable diligence have discovered, the defect.[227] In practical terms, the National House Building Council (NHBC) insurance scheme, which is considered below, is a good deal more important than the implied contractual warranties. While the law of contract may be of limited importance in the context of dwellings it may have a larger role to play in respect of defects in commercial buildings and in such cases recovery by, or for the benefit of, a subsequent transferee may be possible, either by the transferee if the original contracting party's claim is assigned to him[228] or by the contracting party for the benefit of the transferee.[229]

ii. Liability in Tort

No liability for mere defect in quality   The question which has given rise to difficulty in tort is for what type of loss is the builder liable? Personal injuries caused **10-047** by structural defects in premises, though not unknown,[230] are rare in comparison with complaints that the premises are inadequately built and are deteriorating, perhaps with a long-term threat of collapse. It was to just such cases that the courts in cases like *Anns v Merton LBC*[231] extended the liability of the builder.[232] This was despite the fact that a building which threatens to collapse (or even one which does

---

[224] Thus there is no implied warranty if the house is already completed before sale.
[225] The Supply of Goods and Services Act 1982 s.13, seems to apply but not to add anything of substance.
[226] *Hancock v BW Brazier (Anerley) Ltd* [1966] 1 W.L.R. 1317.
[227] Limitation Act 1980 s.32(1)(b); *King v Victor Parsons & Co* [1973] 1 W.L.R. 29.
[228] *Darlington BC v Wiltshier Northern* [1995] 1 W.L.R. 68.
[229] See *Linden Gardens Trust Ltd v Lenesta Sludge Disposal* [1994] 1 A.C. 85 and *Alfred McAlpine Construction Ltd v Panatown Ltd* [2001] 1 A.C. 518. As the latter case shows, the builder may give some direct undertaking to the third party. In some cases, the Contracts (Rights of Third Parties) Act 1999 may also be applicable.
[230] See, e.g., *Otto v Bolton* [1936] 2 K.B. 46; *Sharpe v ET Sweeting & Son Ltd* [1963] 1 W.L.R. 665.
[231] [1978] A.C. 728.
[232] Though in many of these cases, including *Anns*, the actual defendant was a local authority accused of negligent inspection of a building under construction.

collapse, causing no injury to person or other property) is legally speaking analogous to a manufactured article which is fragile and inferior in quality, in that the loss is properly characterised as purely economic, despite the manifestation of the defect in physical symptoms such as cracks in the walls. Cases of this kind have traditionally been looked on as the province of contract rather than tort, and orthodoxy was restored by the House of Lords in *Murphy v Brentwood DC*.[233] The defendant in the case was a local authority accused of negligently approving a flawed design for the foundations of a house but the reasoning extended to the builder of defective premises—indeed much of the discussion is couched directly in terms of the builder's liability.[234] It is now clear that in the absence of a special relationship of proximity such as existed in *Junior Books v Veitchi*[235] (and which, it appears, does not normally exist between the builder and even the first purchaser of a standard house)[236] there is no liability in tort for quality defects in the building. In fact, even the previous case law had not gone so far as to impose such liability in all cases[237] but had done so only where the defect presented an imminent danger to the health or safety of those occupying it.[238]

A key argument for recovery in respect of dangerous defects had been that, if the defect had not been discovered and someone had been injured, the defendant would have been liable for that injury on the principle of *Donoghue v Stevenson*, and so it would be absurd to deny liability for the cost of preventing that injury from arising in the first place.[239] However, that reasoning was rejected in *Murphy*, on the ground that once the defect becomes apparent (which is, ex hypothesi, the first point at which any claim can be made) it no longer presents a danger[240]:

> "The injury will not now ever occur unless the claimant causes it to do so by courting a danger of which he is aware and his expenditure [in removing the danger] is incurred not in preventing an otherwise inevitable injury but in order to enable him to continue to use the property."

---

[233] [1991] 1 A.C. 398. Cooke (1991) 107 L.Q.R. 46; Howarth (1991) 50 C.L.J. 58; Markesinis and Deakin (1992) 55 M.L.R. 619; Wallace (1991) 107 L.Q.R. 228.

[234] *DoE v Thomas Bates & Son Ltd* [1991] A.C. 499, decided on the same day, is a direct authority applying *Murphy* to a builder.

[235] [1983] 1 A.C. 520. See para.5-057.

[236] It is not entirely clear why this should be so with regard to the first purchaser. If even in the absence of a contract there may be a special relationship of proximity sufficiently akin to contract to attract liability for economic loss (*Junior Books*), should there not be such liability where there is a contract? Nevertheless, in *Lancashire and Cheshire Association of Baptist Churches Inc v Howard & Seddon Partnership* [1993] 3 All E.R. 467, liability in tort was denied even though there would seem to have been a clear contractual duty (the right of action for which was assumed to be statute-barred for the purpose of the proceedings). The decision in *Robinson v PE Jones* [2011] EWCA Civ 9; [2012] Q.B. 44 can be explained on the basis that the terms of the contract negated the assumption of responsibility. But the CA went further to deny that the contract could be the source of any such assumption in cases "beyond the realm of professional retainers" (at [76] per Jackson LJ).

[237] At least after *Anns v Merton LBC* [1978] A.C. 728.

[238] *Anns v Merton LBC* [1978] A.C. 728 at 760. This requirement was tied to the fact that the local authority's duty of care (with which the relevant cases were primarily concerned) originated in its functions under the public health legislation. Though the measure of damages is not much discussed in the case law, it seems that liability would only have been in such an amount as was necessary to avert the danger.

[239] See *Murphy v Brentwood DC* [1991] 1 A.C. 398 at 488. In *Dutton v Bognor Regis UDC* [1972] 1 Q.B. 373 at 396 (overruled in *Murphy*) Lord Denning MR described any attempted distinction between the two scenarios as "impossible".

[240] *Murphy v Brentwood DC* [1991] 1 A.C. 398 at 488 per Lord Oliver. See also *DoE v Thomas Bates & Son Ltd* [1991] 1 A.C. 499 (building safe if used below design loading).

The argument that the loss is in truth economic and that the "averting of danger" does not change its nature is logically compelling, though it raises severe difficulties for an owner who simply cannot afford to abandon his house. The justification that if the claimant does not abandon the property and suffers injury he is the author of his own loss may, however, mislead if it is divorced from the underlying nature of his complaint. Suppose, for example, that the claimant owns property which is initially sound and the defendant by negligence causes it damage which renders it dangerous. It may well be that if the claimant chooses to remain in the property (unrepaired because he cannot immediately afford to repair it) rather than move into temporary accommodation, he is the author of his own loss if the property collapses on him,[241] but no one would suggest that he was therefore precluded from recovering the cost of repairs from the defendant. In such a case he had something which was perfect and which was rendered imperfect by what the defendant did. In *Murphy* the essence of the complaint was that the property was imperfect from the beginning. It was not "damaged"; it was simply worth less than was paid for it.

Personal injury caused by a known defect   The argument that if the occupier **10-048** remained and suffered injury he would be the author of his own loss was advanced in a slightly different context in *Targett v Torfaen BC*[242] where the claimant was a weekly tenant of a council house and was aware of the defect and the danger it presented, but had failed to persuade the council to repair it before it caused him injury. In finding for the claimant, the Court of Appeal distinguished *Murphy* on the ground that the House of Lords was there concerned with the nature of the loss and could not be taken to have intended to lay down any absolute rule to the effect that a claim by someone suffering personal injury from a defective building was automatically barred by his prior knowledge of the defect.[243] So to hold would be absurdly unrealistic[244] for many householders and the question should rather be determined by asking whether in all the circumstances it was reasonable, in the light of the danger, to remain in the house.[245]

Damage to "other property"   *Murphy v Brentwood* in no way casts doubt upon **10-049** the proposition that if a negligently constructed building causes damage to other property, whether of the claimant or a third party, the defendant is liable for that.[246] So if the claimant's house collapses he can, at least on the assumption that he was unaware of imminent danger, recover damages for loss of the contents. However, difficulties may arise in determining what counts as "other property" in this context.

---

[241] The case is more obvious with continued use of a chattel, e.g., an unroadworthy car.

[242] [1992] 3 All E.R. 27.

[243] The Court of Appeal pointed out that its own decision in *Rimmer v Liverpool CC* [1985] Q.B. 1, which was inconsistent with this view, had not been referred to in *Murphy*.

[244] *Targett v Torfaen BC* [1992] 3 All E.R. 27 at 37.

[245] Both *Targett* and *Rimmer* concerned lettings but no distinction can be drawn between tenants and purchasers. If anything, the former are likely to be in a better position to find alternative accommodation than the latter.

[246] Illustrated by *Bellefield Computer Services v E Turner & Sons* [2000] B.L.R. 97 and [2002] EWCA Civ 1823; [2003] Lloyd's Rep. P.N. 53.

In *D&F Estates Ltd v Church Commissioners*[247] (which had anticipated many of the issues in *Murphy*) Lord Bridge had, to use his words in *Murphy*[248]:

> "[M]ooted the possibility that in complex structures or complex chattels one part of a structure or chattel might, when it caused damage to another part of the same structure or chattel, be regarded in the law of tort as having caused damage to 'other property' for the purpose of the application of *Donoghue v Stevenson* principles."

This theory of the complex structure was not embraced with any enthusiasm in the *D&F Estates* case, but rather offered as a possible explanation of the line of decisions centring on *Anns v Merton*, which the House of Lords was at that stage unwilling to overrule without further argument. It is clear as a result of *Murphy* that those decisions cannot be supported in this way. When a single builder builds a house from the foundations upwards he is creating a single, integrated unit and it is completely unrealistic to argue that the foundations (the usual source of problems) are an item of property distinct from the rest of the house, so that, when they fail, they cause damage to "other" property—the walls, floors, etc.[249] However, the "complex structure theory" does point to the fact that in some cases the distinction between property damage and pure economic loss may be difficult to draw.[250] Where the thing which causes the damage has been incorporated into an existing building owned by the claimant, a property damage analysis is straightforward,[251] but otherwise matters may be less clear. If, for example, a central heating boiler, which is in a sense ancillary to the building, malfunctions and sets the building on fire, then the negligent manufacturer of the boiler (or the negligent installer) would potentially be liable for the damage to the building.[252] Conversely, where part of a building burnt down due to deficiencies in a firewall, there was held to be no damage to "other property", but only pure economic loss,[253] and the same conclusion was reached when chilled water pipework corroded because its insulation was defective.[254]

10-050 **Exceptional recovery of "pre-emptive repairs" to the defective property?** Even where no physical damage has been done it was suggested by Lord Bridge in *Murphy* that the cost of "pre-emptive repairs" might be recoverable in one situation[255]:

> "[I]f a building stands so close to the boundary of the building owner's land that after discovery of the dangerous defect it remains a potential source of injury to persons or property on neighbouring land or on the highway, the building owner ought, in principle, to be entitled to recover in tort from the negligent builder the cost of obviating the danger."

---

[247] [1989] A.C. 177.

[248] [1991] 1 A.C. 398 at 476.

[249] *Broster v Galliard Docklands Ltd* [2011] EWHC 1722 (TCC); [2011] B.L.R. 569 (no distinction between roof and rest of the building).

[250] Hence the suggestions in *The Orjula* [1995] 2 Lloyd's Rep. 395 and *Payne v John Setchell Ltd* [2002] P.N.L.R. 146 that *Murphy* "disapproves" the complex structure theory is, with respect, something of an over-simplification.

[251] See, e.g., *Jacobs v Morton & Partners* (1996) 72 B.L.R. 92, where the defendants inserted underpinning (itself defective) to cure an existing defect.

[252] *Murphy v Brentwood DC* [1991] 1 A.C. 398 at 497.

[253] *Bellefield Computer Services Ltd v E Turner & Sons* [2000] B.L.R. 97.

[254] *Linklaters Business Services v Sir Robert McAlpine Ltd (No.2)* [2010] EWHC 2931 (TCC); 133 Con. L.R. 211.

[255] [1991] A.C. 398 at 475.

His Lordship did not set out the reasoning behind this possible exception, but it could perhaps be justified on the basis that the building would constitute a nuisance in respect of which the adjoining landowner[256] would be able to obtain an injunction requiring repair or demolition.[257] Alternatively, it may represent a rather broader principle whereby the claimant is entitled to recover the cost of removing a danger which threatens others[258] (for example, members of his family, visitors and even trespassers) and for which the defendant is responsible.[259] If this were confined to the cost of demolition where that is less than the cost of repairs it would not represent too serious a derogation from the reasoning upon which *Murphy* was based. Nevertheless, the proposed exception has met with a lukewarm reception in the lower courts,[260] and in *Thomas v Taylor Wimpey Developments Ltd*[261] it was held not to represent the law.

The position in other jurisdictions   While *Murphy v Brentwood* certainly clari-   **10-051**
fied the law, it has been the subject of widespread criticism and three major Commonwealth courts have declined to accept it. In *Winnipeg Condominium Corp v Bird Construction Co*[262] the Supreme Court of Canada held that a remote purchaser might recover in negligence against a builder the cost of remedying dangerous defects in a building. In *Bryan v Maloney*[263] the majority of the High Court of Australia held that such a purchaser might recover in respect of defects in quality which rendered a house less valuable even though they presented no danger, though later decisions have refused to extend the duty of care to purchasers of commercial or investment property.[264] In the New Zealand case of *Invercargill CC v Hamlin*,[265] as in *Murphy* itself, the liability of the builder was not directly in issue because he had gone out of business, but the Court of Appeal rejected the whole line of English development leading up to *Murphy* by imposing liability upon the local authority for negligence in inspection during construction.[266] The decision was upheld by the Privy Council[267] on the bases that: (1) New Zealand courts were entitled to develop their version of the common law in accordance with local policy

---

[256] Or the local authority under the "statutory nuisance" procedure: para.15-007.

[257] Though the builder may be said to have created the nuisance, no injunction could be obtained against him because he is not in occupation. Though the building owner's loss is still "economic", it seems just that the builder should have to pay the cost, imposed on the house owner by law, of averting the threatened collapse.

[258] See *The Orjula* [1995] 2 Lloyd's Rep. 395, where Mance J held it arguable that it could apply to the cost of decontamination work on a cargo ordered by harbour authorities.

[259] On the issues raised by such claims for "preventive damages" where the danger is to the claimant or his property, rather than a third party, see Nolan (2016) 132 L.Q.R. 68.

[260] In *Morse v Barratt (Leeds) Ltd* (1992) 9 Constr. L.J. 158, a claim for pre-emptive repairs was allowed, but cf. *George Fischer Holding Ltd v Multi Design Consultants Ltd* (1998) 61 Con. L.R. 85 at 110–111.

[261] [2019] EWHC 1134 (TCC); [2019] P.N.L.R. 26. HHJ Keyser QC considered the proposed exception to be inconsistent with the decision in *Robinson v PE Jones* [2011] EWCA Civ 9; [2012] Q.B. 44. Sed quaere.

[262] (1995) 1 S.C.R. 85 (thereby reviving the reasoning in the dissent in *Rivtow Marine Ltd v Washington Iron Works* [1974] S.C.R. 1189).

[263] (1995) 182 C.L.R. 609. Brennan J, dissenting, would have imposed liability, in line with the *Winnipeg* case, if the expenditure had been to remove a danger.

[264] *Woolcock St Investments Pty Ltd v CDG Pty Ltd* [2004] HCA 16; (2004) 216 C.L.R. 515; *Brookfield Multiplex Ltd v Owners Corp Strata Plan No 61288* [2014] HCA 36; (2014) 254 C.L.R. 185.

[265] [1994] 3 N.Z.L.R. 513.

[266] In New Zealand, unlike in Australia, the duty is not limited to residential purchasers: *Body Corporate No 207624 v North Shore CC* [2012] NZSC 83.

[267] *Invercargill City Council v Hamlin* [1996] A.C. 624.

considerations and community expectations, of which they were the best judge; and (2) there were differences in the statutory backgrounds, in particular the existence in England of the Defective Premises Act 1972, which had been an important factor in the *Murphy* decision.

10-052 Claims against local authorities As we have seen, *Murphy v Brentwood*, like most of the earlier building cases, was a claim against the local authority. The House of Lords in *Murphy* agreed with the reasoning in *Anns v Merton* in so far as it had held that any liability of the local authority could not be more extensive than that of the builder, but was prepared to assume that where the builder would still be liable (i.e., in the comparatively rare case where there was personal injury or damage to other property), the local authority might also be so if it had negligently approved defective plans or inspected the building work and failed to discover the defect.[268] However, it has since been made clear that a public body cannot be held liable in negligence for the failure to exercise a statutory power or duty except in accordance with general private law principles.[269] The result is that recovery from a local authority in a case of this kind is only possible if its involvement made matters worse than they otherwise would have been (for example, because the defect is attributable to compliance with a recommendation made by its inspector), or in the unlikely event that it had assumed a relevant responsibility towards those who suffered injury or damage.

10-053 Claims against the house owner for defective work Finally, what of the house owner himself? If he does work on his house in a negligent manner and this results in injury to a subsequent owner then there would be liability.[270] If, however, he has not created the danger by his own action but knew or ought to have known about it at the time of sale it is unlikely that any liability would attach to him. It is true that such a liability has been imposed upon a trader disposing of goods[271] but such a significant departure from the principle of caveat emptor would, in the case of realty, be open only to the ultimate appellate court[272] or the legislature.[273]

iii. Statute

10-054 Defective Premises Act 1972 s.1 A recurrent theme of the speeches in *Murphy v Brentwood* is the need for the courts not to trespass upon ground already covered by parliamentary action. Some years before the decision of the Court of Appeal in *Dutton v Bognor Regis UDC*[274] started the short-lived revolution in the common law, the issue of liability for defective premises was referred to the Law Commission and the result was the Defective Premises Act 1972, which was passed more

---

[268] [1991] 1 A.C. 398 at 479 per Lord Bridge (though "by no means satisfied" that the assumption was correct).
[269] See para.5-059.
[270] *Hone v Benson* (1978) 248 E.G. 1013; Defective Premises Act 1972 s.3. For mere defects of quality there is of course no liability because of *Murphy v Brentwood*.
[271] *Andrews v Hopkinson* [1957] 1 Q.B. 229 (dealer selling goods to a finance company to be let by it to the claimant on hire-purchase terms).
[272] See *Rimmer v Liverpool CC* [1985] Q.B. 1 (a landlord-tenant case).
[273] It may be significant that cl.3 of the Defective Premises Bill would have made the "mere" vendor liable in respect of defects of which he knew, but this was rejected by Parliament.
[274] [1972] 1 Q.B. 373.

or less contemporaneously with *Dutton*'s case.[275] The common law developments had the effect of making the Act something of a dead letter[276] but *Murphy v Brentwood* has now restored it to primacy. The provisions of the Act cannot be excluded or restricted by any agreement.[277]

The duty owed   Section 1 of the 1972 Act imposes upon persons who undertake   **10-055**
work[278] for, or in connection with, the provision[279] of a dwelling[280] a statutory duty to see that the work taken on is done[281] in a workmanlike or professional manner, with proper materials and so that as regards that work the dwelling will be fit for habitation[282] when completed. This is a single composite duty,[283] owed to any person to the order of whom the dwelling is provided or who acquires an interest in the dwelling. It is in some ways stricter than a duty of care. It corresponds closely with the implied warranty at common law in a contract for the construction of a house[284] and in that context it has been held that the warranty in relation to materials is strict.[285] Breach of an applicable building regulation will amount to breach of the duty, compliance with which must be judged by reference to the prevailing standards at the time the work is done.[286]

   The range of persons on whom the duty is imposed goes beyond the builder

---

[275]   See Law Com. No.40 (1970).

[276]   It is also worth noting that in its early years the operation of the Act was substantially restricted because it has no application to houses protected by an "approved scheme" (s.2), and the scheme operated by the NHBC, which covers the great majority of newly-constructed dwellings, was such a scheme. The NHBC scheme (now known as "Buildmark"), though by no means unlimited, generally provides superior cover than the Act because claims for major structural defects may be made for up to 10 years. However, the NHBC scheme is no longer an approved scheme, and so the Act now has a much wider field of operation.

[277]   Section 6(3).

[278]   Or arrange the work in question "in the course of a business" (s.1(4)(a)): see *Zennstrom v Fagot* [2013] EWHC 288 (TCC); 147 Con. L.R. 162.

[279]   This does not include work of rectification (*Jacobs v Morton & Partners* (1996) 72 B.L.R. 92) or improvement (*Jenson v Faux* [2011] EWCA Civ 423; [2011] 1 W.L.R. 3038) to an existing building.

[280]   Hence industrial and commercial premises are excluded from the protection afforded by s.4. "Exclusive possession of a particular space for the purpose of living" was said in *Rendlesham Estates Plc v Barr Ltd* [2014] EWHC 3968 (TCC); [2015] 1 W.L.R. 3663 at [42] to be indicative of what constitutes a dwelling, so that it is the apartments in a block of flats which are the dwellings, and not the block itself. However, while it follows that the common parts of such a block do not themselves form part of a dwelling, on the facts the construction of the common parts and basement car park nevertheless constituted "work carried out for or in connection with the provision of a dwelling" (viz. each individual flat).

[281]   The 1972 Act applies as much to failing to do necessary work as to doing work badly: *Andrews v Schooling* [1991] 1 W.L.R. 783.

[282]   On the meaning of "fit for habitation", see *Rendlesham Estates Plc v Barr Ltd* [2014] EWHC 3968 (TCC); [2015] 1 W.L.R. 3663 at [60]–[81]. It is made clear there that, among other things: (1) the dwelling must be fit for habitation by all the classes of people who might reasonably be expected to occupy it; (2) where there is more than one defect, the question of whether the dwelling is fit for habitation should be addressed holistically (rather than with reference to each individual defect); and (3) the question of fitness for habitation must be judged at the time the dwelling is built.

[283]   *Alexander v Mercouris* [1979] 1 W.L.R. 1270; *Harrison v Shepherd Homes Ltd* [2011] EWHC 1811 (TCC); 27 Con. L.J. 709; *Bole v Huntsbuild Ltd* [2009] EWCA Civ 1146; 127 Con. L.R. 154.

[284]   See para.10-046.

[285]   *Hancock v BW Brazier (Anerley) Ltd* [1966] 1 W.L.R. 1317; see also Supply of Goods and Services Act 1982 s.4.

[286]   *Rendlesham Estates Plc v Barr Ltd* [2014] EWHC 3968 (TCC); [2015] 1 W.L.R. 3663 at [55]–[57].

himself and includes the architect[287] and surveyor and any sub-contractors involved,[288] though the manufacturer of standard components is not covered.[289] The duty is owed not only to the persons ordering the work but also to every person who then or later acquires an interest (whether legal or equitable) in the dwelling. The duty is therefore a statutory hybrid, having characteristics of both contract and tort: on the one hand, it covers mere defects of quality (provided they make the house unfit for human habitation) without any necessity for imminent danger of personal injury; on the other hand it may pass along a chain of purchasers notwithstanding the lack of privity between them and the builder. A claimant is entitled to recover only for foreseeable loss and damage attributable to the fact that the dwelling is unfit for habitation.[290]

10-056 **Limitation of actions** Despite the strictness of the duty under the 1972 Act the protection it affords to purchasers is still less extensive than the common law liability struck down by *Murphy v Brentwood* because the six-year limitation period begins to run when the dwelling is completed,[291] whereas at common law time might start to run at a later date, when some physical symptoms appeared (though they might not then necessarily be observable by the owner). Indeed, by the Latent Damage Act 1986 Parliament sought to improve the claimant's common law position still further by providing, in actions for negligence, an alternative limitation period of three years running from the time when the claimant could reasonably have known about the damage (subject to a "long-stop" of 15 years from the last act of negligence) and specifically providing for the case where the property was acquired by a subsequent purchaser.[292] The 1986 Act is not confined to building cases but they were undoubtedly the primary motivation for its enactment and *Murphy v Brentwood* greatly reduced its significance by deciding that in those cases there is simply no cause of action in the first place.[293]

B. Landlord

10-057 **Common law** A lease is a contract as well as an estate in land, but at common law the range of implied terms relating to the fitness of the premises is very limited. There is an implied warranty in the letting of furnished premises that they are fit

---

[287] *Payne v John Setchell Ltd* [2002] P.N.L.R. 146 (structural engineer).

[288] See also s.2(4) (developers), but note the important provisions of s.1(2), (3), which will generally relieve a person of liability if he does the work properly in accordance with instructions given by another. This would appear to cover not only the builder on whom the client imposes detailed specifications, but also the sub-contractor who receives instructions from the builder. However, "a person shall not be treated ... as having given instructions for the doing of work merely because he has agreed to the work being done in a specified manner".

[289] He may, however, be liable under the Consumer Protection Act 1987 Pt.1 (para.11-020) and if he were negligent he might be in breach of a common law duty. Furthermore, a builder held liable under s.1 might seek a contractual indemnity from him. The emphasis is "on those who do work which positively contributes to the creation of the dwelling", and so no duty is owed by approved inspectors exercising their (essentially negative) statutory function of ensuring compliance with building regulations: *Lessees and Management Co of Herons Court v Heronslea Ltd* [2019] EWCA Civ 1423; [2019] 1 W.L.R. 5849.

[290] *Rendlesham Estates Plc v Barr Ltd* [2014] EWHC 3968 (TCC); [2015] 1 W.L.R. 3663 at [78].

[291] Section 1(5).

[292] See para.26-098.

[293] Where there is personal injury or damage to other property time will run under the general law of limitation from the date when that injury or damage occurs.

for occupation at the commencement of the tenancy[294] and the House of Lords has held that in the case of a "high rise" block, obligations may be implied with regard to the maintenance of such necessary things as stairs and lifts.[295] These obligations sound in contract and hence avail only the tenant, unless the Contracts (Rights of Third Parties) Act 1999 applies. As for tort, the lessor's position was equated with that of the vendor and he was immune from liability for negligence in respect of defects created by him before the demise.[296] This immunity has now died along with that of the vendor,[297] subject to the point that the range of damage recoverable is restricted by *Murphy v Brentwood*. However, where the landlord did not create the defect, the position remains that there is no liability at common law,[298] and this is so even if he undertakes to maintain and repair the demised premises.[299]

Defective Premises Act 1972 s.4 According to s.4 of the Defective Premises Act 1972, where premises arc let under a tenancy which puts on the landlord an obligation to maintain or repair the premises,[300] the landlord owes to all persons who might reasonably be expected to be affected by defects in the state of the premises a duty to take such care as is reasonable in all the circumstances to see that they are reasonably safe from personal injury or damage to their property caused by a defect within the maintenance or repairing obligation.[301] **10-058**

The duty of care is not limited by requirements of notice which might be relevant to the contractual obligation.[302] Most significant of all, a landlord who has a power, express or implied, to enter and repair is to be treated for the purposes of the section (but no other[303]) as if he were under an obligation to repair.[304] The obvious beneficiaries of s.4 are the tenant's family and visitors, but other persons who might reasonably be expected to be affected include trespassers,[305] neighbours and passers-by and even the tenant himself, notwithstanding the existence of a

---

[294] *Collins v Hopkins* [1923] 2 K.B. 617.

[295] *Liverpool CC v Irwin* [1977] A.C. 239. As to licences for occupation of business premises, see *Wettern Electric Ltd v Welsh Development Agency* [1983] Q.B. 796.

[296] *Robbins v Jones* (1863) 15 C.B.(N.S.) 221 at 240; 143 E.R. 768 at 776 per Erle CJ ("Fraud apart, there is no law against letting a tumbledown house"). See also *Cavalier v Pope* [1906] A.C. 428.

[297] This was implicit in *Anns v Merton LBC* [1978] A.C. 728, and made explicit in *Rimmer v Liverpool CC* [1985] Q.B. It seems to have survived the overruling of *Anns* in *Murphy*.

[298] *Boldack v East Lindsey DC* (1999) 31 H.L.R. 41.

[299] *Essex CC v Davies* [2019] EWHC 3443 (QB). Though this is the case where a duty of care is likely to arise under the Defective Premises Act 1972 s.4.

[300] "A first step, therefore, is to ascertain the landlord's duties under the tenancy agreement or by imposition of law": *Rogerson v Bolsover DC* [2019] EWCA Civ 226; [2019] Ch. 450 at [35].

[301] The duty to repair arises only where the premises are in a state of disrepair. It is not a more general duty to make the premises safe where, for example, there is a steep staircase without a handrail or bannister (*Sternbaum v Dhesi* [2016] EWCA Civ 155; [2016] H.L.R. 16; *Dodd v Raeburn Estates Ltd* [2017] EWCA Civ 439; [2017] 2 P.&C.R. 14) or a front door without safety glass (*Alker v Collingwood Housing Association* [2007] EWCA Civ 343; [2007] 1 W.L.R. 2230).

[302] *Sykes v Harry* [2001] EWCA Civ 167; [2001] Q.B. 1014. At the same, it does not necessarily require a landlord to carry out regular inspections: *Rogerson v Bolsover DC* [2019] EWCA Civ 226; [2019] Ch. 450.

[303] Thus the tenant could not compel such a landlord to repair under the Landlord and Tenant Act 1985 s.17.

[304] Section 4(4). See *Smith v Bradford Metropolitan Council* (1982) 44 P.&C.R. 171; *Barrett v Lounova Ltd* [1989] 1 All E.R. 351. Such a power is said to exist in the case of small houses let on periodic tenancies (*Mint v Good* [1951] 1 K.B. 517). The effect of this subsection is that the duty of reasonable care in s.4(1) applies; it does not impose a stricter duty: *Lafferty v Newark & Sherwood DC* [2016] EWHC 320 (QB); [2016] H.L.R. 243.

[305] cf. the position of the tenant-occupier himself: para.10-034.

contractual obligation to him.[306] The tenant, however, is not owed any duty in respect of a defect arising from, or continuing because of, a failure to carry out an obligation expressly imposed on the tenant by the tenancy.[307]

---

[306] *Sykes v Harry* [2001] EWCA Civ 167; [2001] Q.B. 1014.
[307] Section 4(4).

CHAPTER 11

LIABILITY FOR DEFECTIVE PRODUCTS

Introduction[1]   This chapter is concerned with 'product liability', by which is   **11-001**
meant liability imposed on the producer or other supplier of a product in respect of
any personal injury or property damage attributable to a defect in the product.[2] Such

---

[1] Stapleton, *Product Liability* (1994); Whittaker, *Liability for Products* (2005); Howells (ed), *The Law of Product Liability*, 2nd edn (2007); Fairgrieve and Goldberg, *Product Liability*, 3rd edn (2020). On liability for harm caused by medical and pharmaceutical products, see Goldberg, *Medicinal Product Liability and Regulation* (2013).

[2] In addition to providing civil remedies for harm caused by defective products, the law also seeks to enhance consumer protection by regulatory measures backed up by criminal penalties for non-compliance. An example is provided by the General Product Safety Regulations 2005 (SI 2005/1803), which make it an offence for a producer to place a product on the market that is not safe. In general, a person who suffers loss as a result of the commission of an offence of this type is not entitled to bring a civil claim for breach of statutory duty (see *Square v Model Farm Dairies Ltd* [1939] 1 All E.R. 259), but occasionally the statute in question expressly confers a right of action: see, e.g., Consumer Protection Act 1987 s.41(1). However, it has now been held that s.41(1) cannot be relied upon if and to the extent that the breach of duty in question is covered by the strict li-

liability is capable of arising in contract, common law negligence, and under the Consumer Protection Act 1987, and on a given set of facts it may be that one, two, or even all three of these distinct causes of action will be available. The scope of product liability is limited to injury or loss caused by movables—where the harm results from defective premises a separate body of law applies.[3]

A realistic picture of the incidence of product liability can only be obtained if the relevant contractual principles are borne in mind. Where a claimant is injured by a product transferred to him under a contract of sale he may rely upon the seller's implied undertakings as to compliance with description, satisfactory quality and fitness for purpose under the Sale of Goods Act 1979 and the Consumer Rights Act 2015. These undertakings give rise to absolute obligations, i.e., the seller is liable if the goods do not come up to the standard required by the legislation even though he has taken all possible care that they should do so and is in no way to blame for the defect.[4] Though the purpose of these undertakings when they were being developed at common law was probably to allow the buyer a remedy for the financial loss he suffered in acquiring goods of inferior quality, it has been accepted for many years that they also allow recovery for personal injury and for damage to property other than the defective product itself.[5]

The existence of this strict liability in the seller (often, in modern conditions, a much larger organisation than the manufacturer) means that as far as the purchaser is concerned his right of action in tort is often of academic interest and may only be utilised where the seller is insolvent or cannot, for some other reason, be successfully sued.[6] Where a contractual action is successfully pursued then, in theory, the implied terms in the chain of contracts between manufacturer and retailer will lead to the manufacturer bearing the ultimate responsibility, though it should be noted that this chain may be broken in practice by the insolvency of a "middleman" or by some valid exemption clause. However, the contractual liability of the seller is of no assistance to persons injured by the product who were not parties to the sale contract—members of the purchaser's family,[7] passers-by[8] or donees from the buyer[9]—and nor will such persons generally be assisted by the Contracts (Rights of Third Parties) Act 1999.[10] It is this class of "ultimate consumers" who are most likely to seek to rely on a tort claim, typically against the producer.

---

ability regime set out in Pt.I of the 1987 Act, since this would deprive defendants of the defences etc. recognised in that regime: *Wilson v Beko Plc* [2019] EWHC 3362 (QB). This seems essentially to kill off the possibility of reliance on breach of statutory duty in this context.

3   See Ch.10.
4   He may, of course, have an indemnity under the contract of sale between him and his supplier, and so on up the chain to the manufacturer.
5   *Godley v Perry* [1960] 1 W.L.R. 9; *Grant v Australian Knitting Mills Ltd* [1936] A.C. 85.
6   There is nothing to prevent the claimant suing both seller (in contract) and manufacturer (in tort): *Grant v Australian Knitting Mills Ltd* [1936] A.C. 85.
7   *Evans v Triplex Safety Glass Co* [1936] 1 All E.R. 283.
8   *Stennett v Hancock* [1939] 2 All E.R. 578.
9   *Donoghue v Stevenson* [1932] A.C. 562; *Fisher v Harrods* [1966] 1 Lloyd's Rep. 500.
10 The 1999 Act allows a third party expressly identified in a contract to sue on the contract if it expressly provides that he may do so, or if it purports to confer a benefit on him and the parties intended it to be enforceable by him. But the Law Commission's view was that these requirements would not generally be met in the case of a purchaser seeking redress from a manufacturer (*Privity of Contract: Contracts for the Benefit of Third Parties* Law Com. No.242 (1996), para.7.18), while bystanders and donees are unlikely to meet the requirement that the third party be expressly identified in the relevant contract. A purchaser may be able to sue on a manufacturer's guarantee (a form of collateral contract), though such guarantees do not necessarily extend to compensation for personal

1. LIABILITY AT COMMON LAW

The origin of the ordinary claim in negligence Before *Donoghue v Stevenson*[11]   **11-002**
was decided in 1932, it was doubtful whether the manufacturer of a product owed
any duty of care in negligence to the ultimate consumer unless the product belonged
to the class of "dangerous chattels"[12] or was actually known by the manufacturer
to be dangerous. However, the classification of products into those which were
dangerous and those which were not was an unsatisfactory one and in *Donoghue v
Stevenson* the House of Lords held, by a majority of three to two, that, quite apart
from contract and without reference to any special rule about dangerous chattels,
a manufacturer could owe a duty of care to those injured by a defect in one of his
products. Lord Atkin laid down the following principle[13]:

> "A manufacturer of products, which he sells in such a form as to show that he intends them
> to reach the ultimate consumer in the form in which they left him with no reasonable pos-
> sibility of intermediate examination and with the knowledge that the absence of reason-
> able care in the preparation or putting up of the products will result in an injury to the
> consumer's life or property, owes a duty to the consumer to take that reasonable care."

Scope of the Donoghue v Stevenson rule In effect the majority in *Donoghue v*   **11-003**
Stevenson held that the producer of any article was under a duty to all those who
might foreseeably be injured by a defect in it to exercise due care in its design,
manufacture and marketing. Since the rule laid down in that case is merely a
specific manifestation of the general principles of negligence, it is not limited to any
particular subject-matter. Liability under the rule has been extended from articles
of food and drink and has been applied to, inter alia, kiosks,[14] tombstones,[15] hair
dye,[16] industrial chemicals,[17] lifts,[18] cars[19] and even poisonous pants.[20] Likewise the
liability is not limited to the ultimate user of the article, but includes anyone in
physical proximity to it.[21] Furthermore, it is clear that the duty of care extends
beyond the product itself to encompass any container,[22] package or pipe[23] in which
it is distributed, its labelling,[24] and the warnings and instructions for use that accompany it.[25]

---

injury and property damage.
[11]   [1932] A.C. 562.
[12]   The "privity of contract fallacy" held that because the manufacturer (A) had a contract with the
        retailer (B) he could not owe a tort duty to the consumer (C).
[13]   [1932] A.C. 562 at 599.
[14]   *Paine v Colne Valley Electricity Supply Co* [1938] 4 All E.R. 803.
[15]   *Brown v Cotterill* (1934) 51 T.L.R. 21.
[16]   *Watson v Buckley* [1940] 1 All E.R. 174.
[17]   *Vacwell Engineering Co Ltd v BDH Chemicals Ltd* [1971] 1 Q.B. 88.
[18]   *Haseldine v Daw* [1941] 2 K.B. 343.
[19]   *Herschtal v Stewart & Ardern* [1940] 1 K.B. 155; *Andrews v Hopkinson* [1957] 1 Q.B. 229.
[20]   *Grant v Australian Knitting Mills* [1936] A.C. 85.
[21]   *Brown v Cotterill* (1934) 51 T.L.R. 21 (child injured by falling tombstone); *Stennett v Hancock*
        [1939] 2 All E.R. 578 (pedestrian hit by flange of lorry wheel).
[22]   *Donoghue v Stevenson* [1932] A.C. 562 at 585.
[23]   *Barnes v Irwell Valley Water Board* [1938] 2 All E.R. 650.
[24]   *Kubach v Hollands* [1937] 3 All E.R. 907 (no liability on facts).
[25]   *Vacwell Engineering Co Ltd v BDH Chemicals Ltd* [1971] 1 Q.B. 88 (warning).

11-004   Effect of the Consumer Protection Act 1987   Liability under *Donoghue v Stevenson* stands completely untouched by the enactment of the principle of strict liability in the Consumer Protection Act 1987[26] but in most cases claimants will prefer the statutory route to redress, since fault need not be proven. However, there are a number of circumstances in which resort to the common law will still be necessary. Damage to property not intended for private use lies outside the scope of the legislation, as do claims for property damage of less than £275.[27] If the product was never put into circulation,[28] or if the production or supply of the product was non-commercial,[29] then there is a defence under the Act, and so any claim would have to be in negligence. Those who repair, certify or inspect products cannot be sued under the Act, but may be liable at common law. Furthermore, the limitation rules are more favourable in negligence.[30]

A.   Intermediate Examination

11-005   Intermediate examination no longer a restriction in itself   As originally formulated by Lord Atkin the principle in *Donoghue v Stevenson* applied where there was "no reasonable possibility of intermediate examination".[31] However, this requirement was not rigidly adhered to by the courts, and it soon became clear that even a probability of an intermediate examination would not exonerate the defendant unless it gave him reason to expect that it would reveal the defect and that this would result in the elimination of the defect or at least the claimant's being warned of it in such a way as to make him safe.[32] Hence in *Griffiths v Arch Engineering Co Ltd*,[33] where a worker was injured by a defective grinding tool he borrowed from sub-contractors, the plant hire firm that had supplied the tool was held liable because, although the sub-contractors had had an opportunity to examine the machine when it was handed over to them, the hirers could not reasonably have anticipated that they would do so.

11-006   Relevance of intermediate examination to breach and legal causation   Although Lord Atkin clearly conceived the intermediate examination requirement as a stand-alone restriction, going to duty, the modern view is that the significance of the probability (or indeed the occurrence) of such an examination lies in the impact it may have on the inquiries into breach and legal causation.[34] As

---

26   See para.11-016.
27   See para.11-021.
28   See para.11-045.
29   See para.11-046.
30   No claim can be brought under the 1987 Act more than ten years after the supply of the product (Limitation Act 1980 s.11A(3)), but in personal injury cases there is no such restriction at common law, while in property damage cases the cut-off point is a more generous 15 years, this time from the date of breach (Limitation Act 1980 s.14B). And while the basic limitation period applicable to property damage claims is six years in negligence (Limitation Act 1980 s.2), under the Act it is only three (Limitation Act 1980 s.11A(4)).
31   See also [1932] A.C. 585 at 622.
32   *McIlveen v Charlesworth Developments* [1982] N.I. 216 at 221; *Pearson Education Ltd v Charter Partnership Ltd* [2007] EWCA Civ 130; [2007] B.L.R 324. It may not be so much a matter of intermediate examination as of intermediate treatment.
33   [1968] 3 All E.R. 217; *Lambert v Lewis* [1978] 1 Lloyd's Rep. 610 (point not in issue on appeal [1982] A.C. 225). cf. *Taylor v Rover Co Ltd* [1966] 1 W.L.R. 1491.
34   *M/S Aswan Engineering Establishment Co v Lupdine Ltd* [1987] 1 W.L.R. 1 at 23.

regards breach, the manufacturer may be able to shelter behind the probability of intermediate inspection if his expectation of such an inspection justified his regarding it as an adequate safeguard to persons who might otherwise suffer harm. In *Kubach v Hollands*,[35] for example, a manufacturer sold a chemical to an intermediary with an express warning that it had to be tested before use. When no such test was conducted and injury to a user resulted, the intermediary was liable but the manufacturer was not.[36] Similarly, the manufacturer of a prescription drug generally fulfils his duty under *Donoghue v Stevenson* by giving adequate warning to the prescribing physician (who is far more likely than is the patient to be able to understand the warning)[37]: if the physician fails to heed the warning his default may properly be regarded as the sole cause of injury to the patient.[38] As regards legal causation, a third party's negligent failure to inspect a product—or negligent failure to discover a defect on inspection—may constitute a novus actus interveniens.[39] However, the conduct of the intermediary will generally have to amount to gross negligence if it is to be regarded as the sole legal cause of the damage—a merely careless failure to inspect will usually entitle the manufacturer only to contribution from the third party as a joint tortfeasor.[40]

B. Persons Liable

Manufacturers, repairers, assemblers, inspectors etc. Where a defective **11-007** product gives rise to a common law negligence action, the defendant is usually the manufacturer or producer of the product in question, but the principle laid down in *Donoghue v Stevenson* has also been extended to include repairers,[41] fitters, erectors,[42] assemblers,[43] and inspectors.[44] A manufacturer whose product is incorporated into a larger product may be liable if his component is defective, but the manufacturer of a composite product (such as a car) must also take reasonable care to ensure the suitability of components supplied by others and cannot simply rely on them to produce a good design.[45]

---

35 [1937] 3 All E.R. 907.
36 See also *Holmes v Ashford* [1950] 2 All E.R. 76 (hairdresser failed to heed instruction to test hair dye before application).
37 *Hollis v Dow Corning* (1996) 129 D.L.R. (4th) 609 (breast implants).
38 But what if there is no warning? In *Hollis v Dow Corning* (1996) 129 D.L.R. (4th) 609 the Supreme Court of Canada held that in such a case the manufacturer cannot escape liability by giving evidence tending to show that the doctor would not have passed the information on. That would leave the claimant in the position of failing against the doctor (who is not negligent because he received no warning) and against the manufacturer. cf. *Walker Estate v York Finch General Hospital* [2001] SCC 23; [2001] 1 S.C.R. 647.
39 *Clay v AJ Crump & Sons Ltd* [1964] 1 Q.B. 533 at 558.
40 *Clay v AJ Crump & Sons Ltd* [1964] 1 Q.B. 533; *Lambert v Lewis* [1978] 1 Lloyd's Rep. 610 (point not in issue on appeal [1982] A.C. 225). If the claimant himself neglects an opportunity of examination, his damages may be reduced for contributory negligence, though again the possibility exists that his omission may be so extreme as to break the chain of causation: *Nitrigin Eireann Teoranta v Inco Alloys Ltd* [1992] 1 All E.R. 854 at 862.
41 *Stennett v Hancock* [1939] 2 All E.R. 578; *Haseldine v Daw* [1941] 2 K.B. 343.
42 *Brown v Cotterill* (1934) 51 T.L.R. 21.
43 *Howard v Furness-Houlder Argentine Lines Ltd* [1936] 2 All E.R. 296.
44 *Driver v William Willett (Contractors) Ltd* [1969] 1 All E.R. 665.
45 *Winward v TVR Engineering* [1986] B.T.L.C. 366.

11-008   **Suppliers**   Where a distributor or supplier has actively created or accentuated the danger a product poses by, for example, selling a dangerous item to a child,[46] or misreading a prescription and so dispensing the wrong drug,[47] then his position is similar to that of a manufacturer, and negligence liability may readily follow. But even where this is not the case, a distributor or supplier may be under a duty to make inquiries or carry out an inspection of the product and, if it is dangerous for some reason of which he should have known, his failure to warn of it may amount to negligence.[48] In *Andrews v Hopkinson*,[49] by arrangement with the claimant the defendant car dealer sold a second-hand car to a finance company, which the company hired to the claimant under a hire-purchase agreement. The car was some 18 years old and the defendant had taken no steps to see that it was in a roadworthy condition. In fact the car had a defective steering mechanism which caused the claimant to have an accident a week after he took delivery. McNair J held that the defendant was liable and said[50]:

> "Having regard to the extreme peril involved in allowing an old car with a defective steering mechanism to be used on the road, I have no hesitation in holding that the defendant was guilty of negligence in failing to make the necessary examination, or at least in failing to warn the plaintiff that no such examination had been carried out."[51]

Similarly, suppliers may be liable if they carelessly represent the goods to be harmless without having made any adequate tests,[52] but it should not be thought that these cases impose a general duty on suppliers to subject all their goods to an exhaustive examination. The duty to examine will only arise if in all the circumstances they could reasonably be expected to carry out an examination. A second-hand car dealer may be expected to discover a patent defect in the steering mechanism of one of his cars, and a manufacturer and supplier of chemicals must take reasonable care to discover and give warning of industrial hazards arising out of the chemicals he supplies.[53] But a retail grocer, for example, cannot be expected to institute inspections to discover whether his tinned food is contaminated. He may be obliged to satisfy himself as to the reputation of his supplier[54] and he must certainly follow

---

46   *Burfitt v A & E Kille* [1939] 2 All E.R. 372; *Yachuk v Oliver Blais Co Ltd* [1949] 2 All E.R. 150. See also *Faisal v Younis (t/a Safa Superstore)* [2018] EWHC 1111 (QB) (shopkeeper liable for displaying dangerous product within reach of child). cf. *Ricketts v Erith Borough Council* [1943] 2 All E.R. 629.

47   *Prendergast v Sam and Dee Ltd* [1989] 1 Med. L.R. 36.

48   In the case of a gratuitous transfer, it is true that older authorities held that, unless the product was in the class of dangerous things, the transferor was liable only for wilful or reckless conduct, i.e., when he actually knew of the danger: *Gautret v Egerton* (1867) L.R. 2 C.P. 371 at 375; *Coughlin v Gillison* [1899] 1 Q.B. 145. The validity of these cases is now very doubtful (see *Griffiths v Arch Engineering Co Ltd* [1968] 3 All E.R. 217 at 220; *Marsh* (1950) 66 L.Q.R. 39) and the better view is that in the modern law the gratuitous nature of the transfer is simply a factor to be taken into account in assessing what is reasonable care by the transferor.

49   [1957] 1 Q.B. 229. See also *White v John Warwick & Co* [1953] 1 W.L.R. 1285; *Griffiths v Arch Engineering Co Ltd* [1968] 3 All E.R. 217.

50   [1957] 1 Q.B. 229 at 237. cf. *Rees v Saville* [1983] R.T.R. 332 (duty of private purchaser; MOT certificate).

51   He was also prepared to hold the dealer liable on a collateral contract with the claimant.

52   *Watson v Buckley, Osborne, Garrett & Co* [1940] 1 All E.R. 174 (distributors of a dangerous hair dye held liable because they advertised it as positively harmless and requiring no tests); *Devilez v Boots Pure Drug Co* [1962] C.L.Y. 2015; *Goodchild v Vaclight* [1965] C.L.Y. 2669.

53   *Vacwell Engineering Co Ltd v B.D.H. Chemicals Ltd* [1971] 1 Q.B. 88.

54   *Fisher v Harrods* [1966] C.L.Y. 8148.

proper practices in keeping his wares but otherwise, unless the contamination was caused by his negligence or he actually knew of it, his only liability is to the actual purchaser under the contract of sale. If a third party becomes ill on eating the contaminated food, his remedy, if any, is against the manufacturer.

C. Proof of Negligence

Burden of proof   The duty owed is that of reasonable care and the burden of proving negligence is on the claimant. Although in *Donoghue v Stevenson*[55] itself Lord Macmillan said that in a case such as that[56] there was no justification for applying res ipsa loquitur,[57] the practice of the courts is to draw inferences of negligence in suitable product liability cases as much as in any other.[58] The question in each case is whether the claimant has provided sufficient evidence to justify the inference of negligence against the defendant and he is not necessarily required to specify what the defendant did wrong.[59] Indeed, any other rule would stultify the principle of *Donoghue v Stevenson*, for it will often be impossible for a claimant to bring evidence of particular negligent acts or omissions occurring in the defendant's manufacturing processes. However, since it has been held that the claimant need not pinpoint precisely how the defect arose,[60] in practice it is usually sufficient for him to establish that the product was defective when it left the defendant's hands.[61] This should present few difficulties where interference with the product en route to the consumer is unlikely, because, for example, it is stored in a sealed container.[62] On the other hand, where the product is vulnerable to tampering, the court may hold that the manufacturer is absolved.

11-009

In *Mason v Williams & Williams Ltd*[63] the claimant was injured while using a cold chisel manufactured by the defendants and which was too hard for its purpose. Finnemore J held that since the claimant had established that nothing had happened to the chisel after it left the defendants' factory which could have caused the excessive hardness, the defendants' negligence was established. It is suggested that the claimant will generally discharge his burden of proof by showing that the article was defective and that, on a balance of probabilities, the defect arose in the course of manufacture by the defendant. In many cases in practice this comes very close to the imposition of a strict liability, for even if the defendant gives evidence that the quality control system in his factory complies with approved practice, there is still the possibility—indeed it perhaps becomes stronger by this very evidence— that one of his employees was careless and prevented that system operating cor-

---

[55]   *Donoghue v Stevenson* [1932] A.C. 585 at 622.
[56]   Decomposed snail allegedly found in a bottle of ginger beer.
[57]   See para.6-032.
[58]   *Carroll v Fearon* [1998] P.I.Q.R. P416; *Divya v Toyo Tire & Rubber Co Ltd* [2011] EWHC 1993 (QB).
[59]   *Grant v Australian Knitting Mills* [1936] A.C. 85 at 101 per Lord Wright: "The appellant is not required to lay his finger on the exact person in all the chain who was responsible, or to specify what he did wrong. Negligence is found as a matter of inference from the existence of the defects taken in conjunction with all the known circumstances."
[60]   *Grant v Australian Knitting Mills* [1936] A.C. 85 at 101; *Lockhart v Barr* 1943 S.C. 1 at 2.
[61]   *Mason v Williams and Williams Ltd* [1955] 1 All E.R. 808 at 810.
[62]   As in *Donoghue v Stevenson* [1932] A.C. 562. See also *Grant v Australian Knitting Mills* [1936] A.C. 85 at 105.
[63]   [1955] 1 W.L.R. 549.

rectly, in which case he remains liable, though vicariously rather than for breach of his personal duty.[64]

11-010 **Possibility of alternative cause** In *Grant v Australian Knitting Mills Ltd*,[65] the Privy Council held that the defendants were liable to the ultimate purchaser of some pants which they had manufactured and which contained a chemical that gave the claimant a skin disease when he wore them. It was argued for the defendants that as they dispatched the pants in paper packets of six sets there was a greater likelihood of intermediate tampering with the goods before they reached the user than there was with the sealed bottle in *Donoghue*'s case, but the court held that[66]:

> "[T]he decision in that case did not depend on the bottle being stoppered and sealed; the essential point in this regard was that the article should reach the consumer or user subject to the same defect as it had when it left the manufacturer."

While the mere possibility of interference will not necessarily shield a manufacturer from liability, there must be sufficient evidence that the defect existed when the article left his hands and that it was not introduced later on. In *Evans v Triplex Safety Glass Co Ltd*,[67] the claimant bought a car fitted with a "Triplex Toughened Safety Glass" windscreen of the defendants' manufacture. A year later, when the car was being used, the windscreen suddenly and for no apparent reason broke into many fragments and injured the occupants of the car. The defendants were held not liable in negligence for the following reasons: (1) the lapse of time between the purchase and the accident; (2) the possibility that the glass may have been strained when screwed into its frame; (3) the opportunity of intermediate examination by the intermediate seller; and (4) the fact that the breaking of the glass might have been caused by something other than a defect in manufacture. By contrast, in *Carroll v Fearon*,[68] although the tyre, the bursting of which caused the accident, was seven years old and three-quarters worn, there was evidence of a manufacturing defect and the action against the manufacturer succeeded.

D. Nature of the Damage

11-011 **Pure economic loss generally not recoverable** Liability under *Donoghue v Stevenson* clearly covers personal injury and damage to other property: if, for example, a defectively wired heater causes a fire which burns down the consumer's house he could sue for the value of the house. It does not, however, normally cover purely financial loss caused by the failure of a product to fulfil the function for which it was acquired.[69] Such loss is properly claimable only in an action by the

---

[64] See *Grant v Australian Knitting Mills* [1936] A.C. 85 at 101. The inference of negligence in these circumstances is difficult to resist, and in reality, the manufacturer can probably escape liability only by establishing that the defect was in a component supplied by another, or was caused by a third party to whom an aspect of the manufacture was contracted out.

[65] [1936] A.C. 85.

[66] [1936] A.C. 85 at 106–107.

[67] [1936] 1 All E.R. 283. cf. *Mason v Williams & Williams Ltd* [1955] 1 W.L.R. 549.

[68] *Carroll v Fearon* [1998] P.I.Q.R. P416.

[69] *Finesse Group Ltd v Bryson Products* [2013] EWHC 3273 (TCC); [2013] 6 Costs L.R. 991 at [24]–[29]. cf. the case where the product's failure to perform a preventive function leads to personal injury or property damage, as in *Howmet Ltd v Economy Devices Ltd* [2016] EWCA Civ 847; 168 Con. L.R. 27 (where a relevant duty of care was owed, but the claim failed on causation grounds).

buyer against the seller in contract. In other words, *Donoghue v Stevenson* is about dangerous products, not merely defective ones and a modern Mrs Donoghue could not sue Stevenson if her bottle of "ginger beer" contained only water. And even where the defect is a dangerous one, recovery is denied if the danger comes to light before harm is done, so that the loss is limited to the cost of replacement or repair,[70] or if the damage it causes is restricted to the defective product itself.[71] Having said all that, it is of course possible for a duty of care to arise by means of an assumption of responsibility in respect of pure economic loss caused by the acquisition of a defective chattel,[72] albeit that such an analysis is unlikely as between manufacturer and ultimate consumer, even if the manufacturer is aware of the destination of his product.[73]

The rule precluding recovery of pure economic loss in the defective chattels context must be evaluated in the light of the earlier discussions of the general no-recovery rule in respect of such loss[74] and the operation of that rule in the related area of defective premises.[75] However, it is worth noting that the rule causes fewer problems here than in other types of case, since where the claimant is a purchaser of the article and the usual chain of contractual indemnities functions fully it is the manufacturer, as the originator of the defect, who ultimately carries responsibility, even if he is not negligent. Furthermore, the creation of a direct tortious liability from manufacturer to consumer in respect of "safe but shoddy" products might itself raise formidable difficulties. For example, how would a standard of "defectiveness of quality" be set, since that is something which must be related to the terms of the contract (in particular, the price) between the manufacturer and the intermediary (the seller or some more remote person in the distribution chain)? And what would be the effect of exclusions or limitations of liability in the contract between the manufacturer and that intermediary?[76]

Damage to other property: "complex products" The undoubted proposition **11-012** that *Donoghue v Stevenson* applies where the product causes damage to other property of the claimant causes some difficulty where failure of a component in a complex product causes damage to the rest of the product in which it is incorporated.[77] Suppose for example that you buy a car and that one of the tyres on the car bursts and causes a crash that damages the rest of the car: is this a case where "the car" has simply damaged itself (a form of pure economic loss, and so unlikely to be actionable), or is it a case where one item of property (the tyre) has damaged

---

[70] See further Nolan (2016) 132 L.Q.R. 68 at 76–78. But where the claimant must incur expenditure safely to dispose of a dangerous chattel, it has been suggested that recovery may be possible: *The Orjula* [1995] 2 Lloyd's Rep. 395 at 403.

[71] *D&F Estates Ltd v Church Commissioners for England* [1989] A.C. 117; *Murphy v Brentwood DC* [1991] 1 A.C. 398.

[72] See, e.g., *Chaudhry v Prabhakar* [1989] 1 W.L.R. 29 (gratuitous agent inspecting car liable to purchaser for defects, though the existence of a duty of care was conceded). On assumption of responsibility as a basis for duties of care, see para.5-040ff.

[73] In *Hamble Fisheries Ltd v Gardner* [1999] 2 Lloyd's Rep. 1, for example, it was held that on the facts the defendant manufacturers had not assumed a responsibility to warn users of a known defect in their product.

[74] See para.5-056.

[75] See para.10-047.

[76] For example, in *Junior Books v Veitchi Co Ltd* Lord Fraser thought that the claimant in tort could be in no better position than the purchaser from the manufacturer: [1983] 1 A.C. 520 at 534.

[77] See Tettenborn [2000] L.M.C.L.Q. 333.

another (the rest of the car) so that it gives rise to a straightforward claim for property damage? This is essentially the same issue as that of the "complex structure" problem which was discussed earlier in connection with *Murphy v Brentwood DC*,[78] and it is suggested that in the case of a "complex product" similar principles apply.

The easy case here is where the negligently manufactured component is a replacement or added part which is acquired separately and attached to a product that already belongs to the claimant (as where a new tyre is fitted to the claimant's car), since any damage it causes to the remainder of the product is clearly damage to "other property".[79] More difficult is the case where the claimant acquires the product with the defective component already attached. In this scenario, it is submitted that the characterisation of the damage should be governed by the extent to which the component is physically integrated into the larger item: the greater the degree of integration, the less appropriate it is to characterise the damage as damage to other property.[80] And finally, a helpful test of physical integration is whether the component can be removed without damaging the parts of the product that remain.[81] If this test is used, then, for example, a tyre fitted to a car would be "other property", but a replacement panel welded to a car would not. This analysis is consistent with *M/S Aswan Engineering Establishment Co v Lupdine Ltd*,[82] where the claimants lost a quantity of waterproofing compound when the pails in which it was contained collapsed because of the high temperatures to which they were exposed on a dockside in Kuwait. Although an action against the manufacturer of the pails failed on the ground that the damage had not been reasonably foreseeable, Lloyd LJ expressed the provisional view that had that not been the case the loss of the compound caused by the collapse of the pails would have been damage to the property of the claimants for which the manufacturer would have been liable.

E. Other Issues

11-013 **Post-sale duties** A manufacturer's duty of care extends to dangers discovered only after the product has gone into circulation. Hence if he becomes aware of a risk posed by goods already on the market, he must take reasonable steps to alert past customers, however lacking in negligence he may have been at the time the product in question was supplied. In *E Hobbs v Baxenden Chemical Co*,[83] for example, a manufacturer failed to alert its customers after it became clear that

---

[78] See para.10-049.

[79] See, e.g., *Nitrigin Eireann Teoranta v Inco Alloys Ltd* [1992] 1 All E.R. 854, where defective tubing installed in a chemical production plant ruptured, leading to an explosion that damaged the plant. But where the claimant mixed together a number of ingredients to create a new product, and a defect in one of the ingredients rendered the product defective, this was characterised as pure economic loss: *Bacardi-Martini Beverages Ltd v Thomas Hardy Packaging Ltd* [2002] EWCA Civ 549; [2002] 2 Lloyd's Rep. 379 (contaminated carbon dioxide rendered fizzy drinks unsaleable).

[80] See *Murphy v Brentwood DC* [1991] 1 A.C. 398 at 478; *Restatement (Third) of the Law of Torts: Products Liability* (1998), §21, comment e.

[81] cf. Tettenborn [2000] L.M.C.L.Q. 333 at 342–345. Although Tettenborn agrees with the physical integration test, he considers it satisfied whenever the component is attached to the complex chattel with some degree of permanence, as with a roof-rack fixed to a car. In addition he argues that even if this test is not satisfied, there is no damage to other property where the component and the complex chattel may not ordinarily be used independently of each other.

[82] [1987] 1 W.L.R. 1.

[83] [1992] 1 Lloyd's Rep. 54.

insulation foam described as "self-extinguishing" was nothing of the sort. The claimant recovered damages when the foam he had fitted in his warehouse caught fire, leading to extensive damage. In exceptional cases, a manufacturer may even be required to recall a defective product for replacement or repair.[84] Nor are post-sale duties of this kind limited to manufacturers. Retailers may also be subject to them,[85] and in *Hamble Fisheries Ltd v Gardner*,[86] Nourse LJ said that a firm which took over an engine manufacturer had a duty to inform users of reports of faulty pistons on engines produced before the business changed hands.[87]

Misuse of the product A product perfectly suitable for its intended purpose may **11-014** become dangerous if used in other ways, and tales of misuse—like the cat dried in the microwave—abound in product liability folklore. Where misuse is foreseeable, a product may be defective unless appropriate precautions are taken, such as fitting a bottle of dishwasher powder with a child-proof cap,[88] or issuing a suitable warning. However, manufacturers are not always responsible for the consequences of misuse. The conduct of the consumer may be so unpredictable or so costly to forestall that failing to design or warn against it is not negligent. If, for example, a sound tyre clearly intended for use on a car is fitted not to a car but to a bus, the producer is unlikely to be held liable if an accident ensues.[89] Nor is the significance of misuse limited to the issue of breach of duty: even where the danger of misuse was so obvious that the failure to pre-empt it was culpable the misuse itself may nevertheless constitute contributory negligence.[90]

Causation The general principles of factual and legal causation discussed earlier[91] **11-015** of course apply to product liability as elsewhere in negligence. In certain types of product liability case, the requirement of factual causation may present the claimant with significant evidential difficulties. For example, a claimant who alleges that his injury resulted from use of a defective drug may be unable to establish that other possible causes were not in fact responsible.[92] And where an action is brought for failure to warn of a risk associated with a product's use, the claimant must establish that if an adequate warning had been provided his injury would not have occurred—in other words, that the warning would have been followed. This may be difficult to do.[93]

Even where a causal connection between the defective product and the claimant's injury has been established, liability may be denied on legal causation grounds. If, for example, the claimant uses a product in the knowledge that it is defective this

---

84 *Walton v British Leyland UK Ltd, The Times,* 13 July 1978. For the (more developed) US position on product recalls, see *Restatement (Third) of the Law of Torts: Products Liability* (1998), §11.

85 *Rivtow Marine Ltd v Washington Ironworks* (1973) 40 D.L.R. (3d) 530.

86 [1999] 2 Lloyd's Rep. 1.

87 [1999] 2 Lloyd's Rep. 1 at 10. The claim failed because the claimant's losses were purely economic.

88 See *Pollard v Tesco Stores Ltd* [2006] EWCA Civ 393.

89 *M/S Aswan Engineering Establishment Co v Lupdine Ltd* [1987] 1 W.L.R. 1 at 23.

90 Hence if a manufacturer fails to install an automatic shut-off switch on an iron, and the claimant is burnt after forgetting to turn the iron off, the claimant's carelessness would not necessarily absolve the manufacturer of liability but would likely amount to contributory fault: *Resurfice Corp v Hanke* 2007 SCC 7; [2007] 1 S.C.R. 333 at [17]. cf. *Barry v Black-Cawson International Ltd* (1996) 2 K.I.R. 237 (not negligent of factory workers to use handrail as hoist).

91 See Ch.7.

92 See, e.g., *Loveday v Renton* (1990) 1 Med. L.R. 117.

93 See, e.g., *Coal Pension Properties Ltd v Nu-Way Ltd* [2009] EWHC 824 (TCC).

will break the chain of causation,[94] unless it was reasonable for the claimant to run the risk, either because he was unaware of the full extent of the danger or because in the circumstances he was unable to avoid it.[95] As Jackson LJ said in *Howmet Ltd v Economy Devices Ltd*[96]:

"Once the end user is alerted to the dangerous condition of a chattel, if he voluntarily continues to use it thereby causing personal injury or property damage, he normally does so entirely at his own risk. I say 'normally' rather than 'always', because ... there are some situations in which the claimant may have no choice but to continue using the chattel as before."

Furthermore, we have seen that, in extreme cases, the failure of the claimant or a third party to carry out a proper examination of the product, or the misuse of a product, may also amount to a novus actus interveniens.[97]

2. LIABILITY UNDER THE CONSUMER PROTECTION ACT 1987

11-016 **The trend towards strict liability** Looked at against the background of the general law of tort the level of protection given to victims of dangerous products by *Donoghue v Stevenson* may appear reasonable, though it may be thought hard to justify the differential treatment of a purchaser who benefits from strict liability in respect of death or personal injury[98] by virtue of his contract of sale, and a donee or bystander who must prove negligence. Concerns over that disparity were central to the move towards strict liability for defective products in the United States that took place in the middle of the 20th century, a move best conceived as an attempt to extend contract-type protections to third parties previously hamstrung by the doctrine of privity.[99] The first step was liability for express warranty, shorn of the privity restriction and based on advertising claims,[100] but this was soon overtaken by the idea of the implied warranty of safety.[101] The culmination was *Greenman v Yuba Power Products Inc*[102] in which the Supreme Court of California abandoned the idea of warranty and imposed a straightforward strict liability in tort. Most other American jurisdictions followed California's lead, and the move to strict liability was confirmed in § 402A of the *Restatement (Second) of the Law of Torts*, which stated that the seller of a product "in a defective condition unreasonably dangerous" was strictly liable for harm thereby caused to the consumer or his property.[103]

Various arguments have been advanced in favour of these developments[104] but

---

[94] *Farr v Butters Bros & Co* [1932] 2 K.B. 606; *Gledhill v Liverpool Abattoir Ltd* [1957] 3 All E.R. 117; *Howmet Ltd v Economy Devices Ltd* [2016] EWCA Civ 847; 168 Con. L.R. 27.

[95] By analogy with the defective premises cases of *Rimmer v Liverpool CC* [1985] Q.B. 1 and *Targett v Torfaen BC* [1992] 3 All E.R. 27, discussed above, para.10-048.

[96] [2016] EWCA Civ 847; 168 Con. L.R. 27 at [92].

[97] See paras 11-006 and 11-014 respectively.

[98] As opposed to the liability for financial loss caused by the failure of the goods to function.

[99] See, e.g., Prosser (1960) 69 Yale L.J. 1099 (the title of the article is "The Assault Upon the Citadel", the citadel being privity).

[100] *Baxter v Ford Motor Co* 12 P. 2d. 409 (1932). This has obvious affinities with the collateral contract.

[101] *Henningsen v Bloomfield Motors* 161 A. 2d. 69 (1960).

[102] *Greenman v Yuba Power Products Inc* (1963) 27 Cal. Rptr. 697.

[103] *Restatement (Second) of the Law of Torts* (1977), §402A(1). It is noteworthy that the *Restatement (Third) of the Law of Torts: Products Liability* (1998), reverts to a negligence standard in design and marketing defect cases, retaining strict liability only for manufacturing defects.

[104] See, e.g., *Liability for Defective Products* Law Com. No.82 (1977), para.38.

the most commonly occurring ones are that the manufacturer, as creator of the risk, should bear its consequences; that he is in the best position to insure that risk and to cover the cost of that insurance in his price;[105] that strict liability is even more of an incentive than fault to the taking of adequate precautions;[106] and that strict tort liability only achieves in one action what the law of contract achieves in many cases by the chain of indemnities stretching back from the consumer-purchaser to the manufacturer.

Developments in the EU In numerical terms the problem of injuries caused by   **11-017**
product defects is small when compared with those attributable to other risks[107] and the difficulty of establishing a case under the law of negligence can be exaggerated,[108] but by the 1970s there was in the United Kingdom a powerful tide in favour of change, prompted not only by developments in the United States, but also by the Thalidomide tragedy and pressure for harmonisation of laws within Europe. The adoption by the Council of the EEC of a Directive on liability for defective products[109] meant that the UK was required, by virtue of its treaty obligations, to legislate to implement the Directive and this was done by Pt.I of the Consumer Protection Act 1987.[110] The liability imposed by the Act is additional to liability that might arise at common law.[111]

General effect of the Act The general effect of the 1987 Act is to establish a   **11-018**
system of strict liability for damage caused by defective products. The focus is on the product's safety, as opposed to its quality (the issue in a contract action) or the producer's conduct (the issue in a negligence action).[112] The central provisions are in s.2, and these impose liability on the producer, apparent producer or importer for damage caused wholly or partly by a defect in a product. The onus is on the claimant to establish the damage, the defect, and the causal link between the two. He must also establish that the defendant is a person liable for the damage under the terms of the Act. The burden of proof then shifts to the defendant, for whom several defences are available.

The overall impact of the legislation should not be exaggerated.[113] Where the flaw in the product is attributable to a problem in the manufacturing process, the common law approximates to strict liability in any case, and in so-called "design" and

---

[105] A sufficiently bad claims record should raise his premium costs to such a level that he is driven off the market.

[106] Though this argument seems to rest on some questionable assumptions, since the negligence standard already requires producers to take reasonable precautions. Should they be incentivised to take unreasonable ones?

[107] On the basis of its personal injury survey the Pearson Commission in 1978 estimated that between 30,000 and 40,000 injuries per year (about 1 per cent of all injuries) might be attributable to defective products other than drugs and that the risk of death was lower than for other categories of risk: *Civil Liability And Compensation For Personal Injury*, Cmnd.7054 (1978), Vol.1, para.1201. The 1987 Act hardly figured in case law for 12 years but there have been some important decisions since 2000.

[108] See para.11-009.

[109] See *Whittaker* (1985) 5 Y.E.L. 233; Whittaker, *Liability for Products* (2005).

[110] For a highly critical account of the changes produced by the Directive, see Stapleton, *Product Liability* (1994).

[111] Consumer Protection Act 1987 s.2(6).

[112] See *Wilkes v DePuy International Ltd* [2016] EWHC 3096 (QB); [2018] Q.B. 627 at [63]–[64].

[113] See Stapleton (1986) 6 O.J.L.S. 392.

"marketing" defect cases, liability under the Act will often in practice require evidence of fault. Nevertheless, it is possible to identify categories of case where the strict liability created by the Act offers consumers genuine advantages over a negligence regime,[114] and the legislation also strengthens the hand of claimants by giving them a wide range of possible defendants to target, including apparent producers, importers, and (in some circumstances) suppliers of the product.

11-019 **Relationship of Act and Directive**[115]   Section 1(1) of the 1987 Act states that Pt.I was enacted in order to implement the 1985 Directive, and that it should be construed accordingly. It follows that any ambiguities in the legislation should be resolved in a manner consistent with the provisions of the Directive, and in interpreting the Directive for this purpose account should be taken of its recitals and of decisions in other jurisdictions interpreting its provisions. The duty to interpret the 1987 Act in a "purposive" way is, not, however, absolute, and if it is not possible to construe the domestic legislation in such a way as to accord with the Directive, then the wording of the former must be followed.[116]

A.   Products

11-020   A product is any goods or electricity[117] and "goods" is further defined as including, "substances,[118] growing crops[119] and things comprised in land by virtue of being attached to it and any ship, aircraft or vehicle".[120] Components of a building are, therefore, covered, so that a manufacturer of defective steel joists would be liable for injury caused by the collapse of a block of flats. Conversely, the building as a whole is not "goods",[121] although where damage is caused by a defective building, an action may of course lie in negligence or under the Defective Premises Act 1972.[122] Since the Act applies to products, but not to services, defective software would not in itself attract strict liability, but if a flaw in the software contained in a physical device (such as a mobile phone or laptop) made the device unsafe, then a claim under the Act would be possible.[123] Similarly, the better view is that where

---

[114] See para.11-034 with respect to design defects.

[115] Following the United Kingdom's withdrawal from the European Union, the 1987 Act continues to have effect, despite its derivation from an EU Directive: European Union (Withdrawal) Act 2018 s.1B.

[116] cf. *A v National Blood Authority* [2001] 3 All E.R. 289, where Burton J bypassed the 1987 Act altogether, and applied the Directive instead. This highly unorthodox approach, which renders the wording of the Act entirely otiose, was not followed in *Wilkes v DePuy International Ltd* [2016] EWHC 3096 (QB); [2018] Q.B. 627, where it was said that the focus should "be on the Act, not the Directive" (at [53]).

[117] Section 1(2). That sub-section also makes clear that the definition of a product includes a product comprised in another product as, for example, a component part or a raw material.

[118] It was conceded in *A v National Blood Authority* [2001] 3 All E.R. 289 that blood and blood products for transfusion were within the Act.

[119] Until 2000 the producer of primary agricultural produce and game was exempt from liability under the 1985 Directive if he supplied them before they had undergone an industrial process. This exemption was removed by the Consumer Protection Act 1987 (Product Liability) (Modification) Order 2000 (SI 2000/2771), implementing Directive 1999/34.

[120] Section 45(1).

[121] See the Directive, art.2, which defines "product" as "all movables".

[122] See Ch.10.

[123] For endorsement of this distinction between the software itself and the device that carries it, see *St Albans DC v ICL* [1996] 4 All E.R. 481 at 493.

damage is caused by reliance on false information conveyed by a physical product—such as inaccurate instructions in a chemistry textbook or a misleading aviation chart—a claim lies under the 1987 Act,[124] but that if such information is conveyed in other ways (on a web page, for example) any claim would have to lie in negligence. This may not seem logical or indeed defensible, but since there is no clear basis in the legislation for limiting the "safety" of a product to its physical characteristics,[125] the conclusion appears to follow inevitably from the line drawn by the legislation between products and services. Furthermore, were so-called "information products" to be excluded from the ambit of the Act, this would itself give rise to problems when it came to traffic lights, smoke alarms and the like, where the product's safety is inextricably bound up with the information it does or does not convey, and where the case for strict liability seems stronger than in the case of a book or a map.[126]

B. Damage

Damage is defined in the 1987 Act as "death or personal injury or any loss of or **11-021** damage to any property (including land)".[127] Pure economic loss is therefore excluded, as is ordinarily the case in negligence.[128] Claims for loss of or damage to property are subject to three restrictions. First, no liability for property damage arises unless the amount of the award would be at least £275.[129] Secondly, there is no liability in respect of loss of or damage to the defective product itself or the whole or any part of any product which has been supplied with the defective product comprised in it.[130] If, therefore, my defective car radio catches fire and burns out the car, no liability arises under the Act,[131] unless it was installed after I bought the car, in which case the car would not have been "supplied" with the radio comprised in it.[132] Thirdly, the Act is inapplicable unless the property damaged or lost is of a description ordinarily intended for private use and is mainly so intended by the claimant.[133] The qualification "mainly" means that damage to a private car used for the odd business trip is recoverable, but damage to a company car can never be

---

[124] Presumably against the book's printer (its "producer"), as opposed to the author or publisher, even though the printer is hardly responsible for the content of the work.

[125] It had been the Government's intention to exclude information products from the Act, but two sub-clauses in the Bill which were designed to achieve this were dropped because of drafting difficulties: see Whittaker (1989) 105 L.Q.R. 125 at 128.

[126] For helpful discussion of the problems posed by "information products", see Whittaker (1989) 105 L.Q.R. 125 and Stapleton (1989) 9 Tel Aviv Univ. Stud. in Law 147. This type of case should not be confused with a marketing defect case, where the information accompanying a product (or the lack of it) renders the product itself physically unsafe. Marketing defects are undoubtedly covered by the Act: see para.11-038.

[127] Section 5(1). The concept of personal injury under the Directive was given a broad interpretation in *Boston Scientific Medizintechnik GmbH v AOK Sachsen-Anhalt-Die Gesundheitskasse* [2016] 3 C.M.L.R. 6, where it was held to encompass surgical interventions to replace faulty pacemakers.

[128] See para.11-011.

[129] Section 5(4).

[130] Section 5(2).

[131] Compare the rather uncertain position at common law: para.11-012.

[132] What if a defective cork ruins a bottle of wine? The cork is not comprised in the wine itself, of course, but could not the damage be said to be to "the bottle of wine", in which it is comprised?

[133] Section 5(3). A golf clubhouse is not of a description ordinarily intended for private use, as it is used by a large number of people who have usually paid to do so: *Renfrew Golf Club v Motocaddy Ltd* [2016] CSIH 57; 2016 S.C. 860.

actionable, since the company that owns it does not intend the car for *its* private use at all.

C. Who is Liable?

11-022   Producers   The three principal categories of persons liable under the 1987 Act are listed in s.2(2) and the first is the producer of the product,[134] who is further defined in s.1(2) as:

> "(a)   the person who manufactured it;
> (b)   in the case of a substance which has not been manufactured but has been won or abstracted, the person who won or abstracted it;
> (c)   in the case of a product which has not been manufactured, won or abstracted but essential characteristics of which are attributable to an industrial or other process having been carried out (for example, in relation to agricultural produce), the person who carried out that process."

The first class within s.1(2) is largely self-explanatory,[135] but it is important to note that if a product causes damage as a result of failure of a component part then both the manufacturer of the component and the final manufacturer/assembler are treated as producers.[136] Paragraph (b) covers, for example, those who mine coal, drill for oil, or bottle mineral water. Paragraph (c), which covers things not falling within either of the two previous categories,[137] raises some awkward questions of degree as to what is an "essential characteristic": presumably, the packing of vegetable crops does not bring this paragraph into play but their canning does, as would, for example, the processing and freezing of poultry.

11-023   Apparent producers   The second category identified in s.2(2)(b) of the 1987 Act is the "own brander" or, as the Act puts it "any person who by putting his name on the product or using a trade mark or other distinguishing mark in relation to the product, has held himself out to be the producer of the product". This provision may be of narrower effect than it has often been assumed to be, for it is not enough to put your name on the goods; you must do so in such a way as to hold yourself out as the producer. Does anyone really believe that, for example, Tesco actually makes the products marketed under its own label? The matter is, of course, fundamentally a question of fact, but labelling which clearly states that the product is made for and not by the store might be thought to have the effect of circumventing s.2(2). Then again, there is a powerful case for adopting a broad approach based on consumer expectations, so that where consumers may have relied on a reasonable belief that

---

[134]   Section 2(2)(a).

[135]   One would not expect a mere entity in the chain of distribution to be regarded as a manufacturer, even if closely connected to the producer, but according to the ECJ, such an analysis would be plausible if said entity carried out "different production activities": *O'Byrne v Sanofi Pasteur MSD Ltd* [2006] 1 W.L.R. 1606, paras 29–30. cf. *Aventis Pasteur SA v OB* [2010] All E.R. (EC) 522, Opinion of AG Trstenjak, paras 39ff, which however surely extends the notion of a manufacturer too far. See further, *O'Byrne v Aventis Pasteur MSD Ltd* [2010] UKSC 23; [2010] 1 W.L.R 1412.

[136]   This is because both the component and the composite product are defective products that have caused the damage, applying the definition of "product" in s.1(2).

[137]   If X extracts oil and Y refines it into petroleum, X falls within para.(b). Does Y fall within para.(a) or para.(c)? If (c), it is presumably irrelevant that the product has been abstracted in another form.

the own brander influenced and controlled the production process, liability should follow.[138]

Importers At the time of writing, the third category set out in s.2(2)(c) **11-024** encompasses any person who imports the product into a member state of the European Economic Area[139] from a place outside the EEA in order to supply it to another in the course of his business. Hence, if A, a Belgian company, imports goods into Belgium from China and then sells them to B, who imports them into the United Kingdom, where they are sold to C, A (but not B) is liable under this head. However, from the end of the Brexit transition period[140] s.2(2)(c) will apply instead to importers into the UK,[141] so that in the example, it will then be B (and not A) who will be liable under this head.

Suppliers The supply of goods does not attract primary liability under the 1987 **11-025** Act, but under s.2(3) a supplier[142] who is asked by an injured person to identify one or more of the persons who are primarily liable (i.e., the producer, the apparent producer and the importer) is himself liable if he does not within a reasonable time either comply with the request or identify the person who supplied the product to him. The idea of this secondary liability is to enable the claimant to trace "anonymous" goods back along the chain of distribution to a producer or importer who carries primary liability under the Act, and to incentivise suppliers to facilitate this by keeping adequate records.[143]

Multiple defendants It will be apparent from the above that under the 1987 Act **11-026** a number of different persons may be liable for the same damage. Where this is so, the defendants are jointly and severally liable,[144] but existing rights of contribution and indemnity are preserved.[145]

D. Defect

The test of defectiveness[146] The core of the strict liability regime established by **11-027** the 1987 Act is to be found in the proposition that the damage must be caused, not

---

138 Simoes [2013] J.R. 469, 476.
139 The EU plus Liechtenstein, Norway and Iceland.
140 At the time of writing, 31 December 2020.
141 Product Safety and Metrology etc. (Amendment etc.) (EU Exit) Regulations 2019 (SI 2019/696), Sch.3, para.3.
142 "Supply" is defined in s.46(1) and is a broad concept that includes not only selling the product, but also bartering it, hiring it, lending it, letting it on hire-purchase, and even making a gift of it. But a finance company is not a supplier for the purposes of this Act; the "effective supplier" (e.g., the garage in a car hire-purchase transaction) is: s.46(2). Note also that the supplier of a product is not treated by virtue of that supply as having supplied any of the product's components: s.1(3). It follows that a car dealer can be asked to identify the manufacturer of a vehicle he sold, but not the manufacturer of its defective brake pads.
143 Hence the supplier's potential liability seems to be premised on the assumption that the supply of the defective product by the supplier was subsequent to an earlier supply of the product to the supplier by a producer or intermediate supplier, so that for example a blood donor would not be a supplier of the blood under the legislation (see in particular the wording of s.2(3)(c)).
144 Section 2(5).
145 Section 2(6). On possible complications in the contribution position, see Stapleton, *Products Liability* (1994), pp.299–302.
146 Griffiths [1987] J.B.L. 222; Stoppa (1992) 12 L.S. 210.

(as in negligence) by the fault of the defendant, but by a defect in the product.[147] According to s.3(1):

> "[T]here is a defect in a product ... if the safety of the product is not such as persons generally are entitled to expect; and ... safety, in relation to a product, shall include safety with respect to products comprised in that product and safety in the context of risks of damage to property, as well as in the context of risks of death or personal injury."

Section 3 goes on to provide that all the circumstances are to be taken into account in determining whether the product is as safe as persons generally are entitled to expect, specifically drawing attention to the following:

"(a) [T]he manner in which, and the purposes for which, the product has been marketed, its get-up, the use of any mark in relation to the product and any instructions for, or warnings with respect to, doing or refraining from doing anything in relation to the product;

(b) what might reasonably be expected to be done with or in relation to the product;[148] and

(c) the time when the product was supplied by its producer to another; and nothing ... shall require a defect to be inferred from the fact alone that the safety of a product which is supplied after that time is greater than the safety of the product in question."

It has been said that whether a product has a defect is determined by reference to the condition of the product itself (viz., its failure to meet the required level of safety), so that the court's focus "should be on whether the product is safe ... rather than on whether there is a specific fault in it".[149]

11-028 **An empty vessel** The basic test of defectiveness laid down in the Act—whether the safety of the product is not such as persons generally are entitled to expect—is wholly objective. In *Wilkes v DePuy International Ltd*, a case involving a medical device, Hickinbottom J said that[150]:

> "[T]he relevant level of safety is not that which a particular patient considers the product should provide; nor even the level of safety which members of the public generally may consider it ought to provide. The level of safety is not assessed by reference to actual expectations of an actual or even a notional individual or group of individuals. [The test of defectiveness] can only be a reference to an entitlement as a matter of law, not actual individual or even general expectation ...."

The question then is what persons generally are *entitled* to expect, not what they actually do expect.[151] In the case of complex and technological products, for example, ordinary people may not know what to expect, but the courts, aided by

---

[147] Although the burden of proof is on the claimant, it is possible that the existence of the defect and its causal relationship with the damage may be established by inference: *Ide v ATB Sales Ltd* [2008] EWCA Civ 424; [2008] P.I.Q.R. P13. See also *Gee v DePuy International Ltd* [2018] EWHC 1208 (QB); [2018] Med. L.R. 347 at [99]–[100]. On the American "malfunction doctrine", which operates to similar effect, see *Restatement (Third) of the Law of Torts: Products Liability* (1998), §3.

[148] "Whilst [s.3] is not intended to produce an entitlement to protection for each and every possible use, regard must be had to likely use, and indeed reasonably foreseeable misuse, by a representative cross-section of the target population, which may include some consumers at heightened risk": *Busby v Berkshire Bed Co Ltd* [2018] EWHC 2976 (QB) at [139] per HHJ Cotter QC.

[149] *Gee v DePuy International Ltd* [2018] EWHC 1208 (QB); [2018] Med. L.R. 347 at [86]–[87].

[150] *Wilkes v DePuy International Ltd* [2016] EWHC 3096 (QB); [2018] Q.B. 627 at [69].

[151] See also *A v National Blood Authority* [2001] 3 All E.R. 289 at [31]. Unfortunately, the courts

expert evidence, are in a position to decide what they are entitled to expect. Most importantly, once it is appreciated that the test of defectiveness is not a subjective "consumer expectation" test, it becomes apparent that in substantive terms it is an "empty"[152] vessel, the eventual content of which will derive from the decisions made in cases brought under the 1987 Act.

Threefold classification   American product liability law draws a distinction **11-029** between the "production or manufacturing defect" (a dangerous departure from the product's intended design), the "design defect" (the case where the product is unreasonably dangerous when manufactured as intended) and the "marketing defect" (the case where the product is not accompanied by adequate warnings or instructions).[153] While completely routine in other jurisdictions, there has been some resistance to the use of this classification in the United Kingdom, based on the fact that neither the 1987 Act nor the Directive refers to it. Nevertheless, in *A v National Blood Authority*[154] Burton J drew a distinction between "standard" and "non-standard" products that roughly tracked the design/manufacturing defect distinction, and even though the importance of this distinction was subsequently downplayed in *Wilkes v DePuy International Ltd*,[155] Hickinbottom J accepted that it was a relevant consideration when addressing the defectiveness issue and in fact employed it when applying the defectiveness test on the facts.[156] In any case, there are important differences between the two situations of the product which is dangerous only because it is non-standard and the product every example of which carries a risk,[157] and experience elsewhere indicates that the use of a classification along these lines is essential if a regime of strict product liability is to function effectively.

i.   Non-standard Products

In the case of the non-standard product (that is to say, one which is not in the **11-030** condition in which the manufacturer intended it to be distributed to the public[158]) the claimant will generally succeed by showing the non-standard nature of the article and that that made it dangerous and caused his damage. Although in many cases the mere existence of the defect would provide powerful indirect evidence of

---

sometimes lose sight of this: see, e.g., *Pollard v Tesco Stores Ltd* [2006] EWCA Civ 393 at [16]–[17].

152 [2016] EWHC 3096 (QB); [2018] Q.B. 627 at [68].

153 A classification maintained by *Restatement (Third) of the Law of Torts: Products Liability* (1998), §2.

154 [2001] 3 All E.R. 289.

155 [2016] EWHC 3096 (QB); [2018] Q.B. 627.

156 See also *Gee v DePuy International Ltd* [2018] EWHC 1208 (QB); [2018] Med. L.R. 347 at [158] (no reason the distinction "should not be adopted as a useful starting point in the analysis"); *Hastings v Finsbury Orthopaedics Ltd* [2019] CSOH 96; 2019 S.L.T. 1411 at [105] ("almost inevitable" that in applying the defectiveness test "there will be some focus" on the distinction).

157 Though there are also some cases which resist categorisation in this way, such as *Boston Scientific Medizintechnik GmbH v AOK Sachsen-Anhalt-Die Gesundheitskasse* [2015] 3 C.M.L.R. 6, concerning a brand of pacemaker particularly susceptible to failure, where it was held that the existence of a potential defect in some products in a particular product line could amount to a defect in all products in that line.

158 Difficulties arise in the case of food products, since these often lack a specific design against which individual product units can be assessed. See *Restatement (Third) of the Law of Torts: Products Liability* (1998), §7.

negligence[159] the claimant is no longer required to rely on this and will succeed even if there is no fault. In the *A v National Blood Authority* case the claims arose from Hepatitis C infections from blood products at a time when no reasonable and effective methods of screening for the virus were available—indeed, in the case of the earlier claims the products had been administered before the virus had even been identified. In concluding that the products were defective within the meaning of the Act, Burton J held that the focus was upon the individual item which caused the damage and that the cost and practicability of eliminating the "rogue product" were not elements in the "circumstances of the case" in determining what the user was entitled to expect in the way of safety. Even if (which was not the case) the public had been generally aware of the risk of untraced infected samples of blood, the individual user was entitled to expect that his bag of blood was infection-free and was not to be taken to be participating in a form of Russian roulette.[160]

National Blood Authority therefore stands for the proposition that a product which fails to offer the level of safety intended because it deviates from its design specification will generally be defective for that reason.[161] However, it is important to note that Burton J refused to accept that non-standard products were automatically defective. In particular, he posited that a given non-standard product might be held not to be defective on the basis that the public at large accepted that a proportion of products of the same type would be flawed. With respect, however, this possible exception is problematic, since it seems to look to what the public *actually* expect, rather than what they are *entitled to* expect,[162] and it would therefore be preferable if the courts were to adopt a simpler approach, under which a manufacturing defect would *always* render a product defective for the purposes of the 1987 Act.

ii. Standard Products

11-031 **Defectiveness turns on a risk-benefit analysis**   When it comes to standard products, the defectiveness issue presents greater difficulties. Unlike in non-standard product cases, there is no objective standard against which the product can be assessed: its features are the result of conscious choices by the producer, which the court is being asked to second-guess. An additional problem is that safety is "inherently and necessarily a relative concept".[163] No product is perfectly safe, because safety must be traded off against cost and convenience. If all cars were required to be four-wheel drive, for example, there would be no cheap cars available. It follows that in standard product cases, "whether a product has an acceptable level of safety... necessarily involves some balancing of risks and potential benefits",[164] with the court ultimately having to determine whether the risks associ-

---

[159] See, e.g., *Mason v Williams & Williams Ltd* [1955] 1 W.L.R. 549, para.11-009.

[160] *A v National Blood Authority* [2001] 3 All E.R. 289 at [65]. cf. *Richardson v LRC Products* [2000] Lloyd's Rep. 280.

[161] In Burton J's words, in such a case a finding of defectiveness is "likely to be straightforward": [2001] 3 All E.R. 289 at [66].

[162] Burton J's reasoning seems to have been based on a concept of "social acceptability" of the risk put forward by certain commentators, but they appear to have had in mind the rather different problem (discussed in para.11-035) of inherently dangerous products, such as kitchen knives.

[163] *Wilkes v DePuy International Ltd* [2016] EWHC 3096 (QB); [2018] Q.B. 627 at [65].

[164] [2016] EWHC 3096 (QB); [2018] Q.B. 627 at [13].

ated with the product in its present form are outweighed by the benefits it brings.[165] And while scientific evidence is no doubt relevant and often helpful there is no escaping the fact that in the last resort the judgment is a "value" one.[166]

Relevant considerations   A useful way of testing the risk–benefit balance in a   **11-032**
design defect case may be to ask whether the risks of harm posed by the product could have been avoided or materially reduced by the adoption of a feasible alternative design.[167] It follows that, unlike in non-standard product cases, "the ease and extent to which a risk can be eliminated or mitigated" may be relevant in a standard product case.[168] With some kinds of product, most obviously prescription drugs, it may also be necessary to apply a more general test of whether the danger the product poses outweighs its utility.[169] In applying the feasible alternative design test, the court should take into account the cost and general feasibility of the alternative design, the degree to which it would have obviated the risk, and any impact it would have had on the effectiveness of the product.[170] Comparisons can usefully be made with similar products on the market, though it does not follow from the fact that a particular product is "worst in class" that it is defective.[171] Other, more general, indications of defective product design include post-accident changes in design; post-sale warnings or recall notices; and failure to comply with general industry practice. Liability will usually be imposed if applicable mandatory standards or regulatory requirements have been violated;[172] conversely, it may be difficult to establish that a product which complies with such standards or requirements is defective.[173]

---

[165] In *Wilkes v DePuy International Ltd* [2016] EWHC 3096 (QB); [2018] Q.B. 627 at [66], Hickinbottom J said that what had to be balanced "are, or at least include, the potential benefits of the medicinal product for the specific patient against the risks for that patient, at the time the product is used". Sed quaere. In a standard product case, the question is whether the entire product range is defective, a determination that can be made only by assessing the risk–benefit issue in the round (i.e., with respect to *all* patients).

[166] The question "must be one of fact and degree": *Gee v DePuy International Ltd* [2018] EWHC 1208 (QB); [2018] Med. L.R. 347 at [465].

[167] *Restatement (Third) of the Law of Torts: Products Liability* (1998), §2(b). See, e.g., *Abouzaid v Mothercare (UK) Ltd* (21 December 2001, CA), where it was held that a pushchair accessory was defective since the risk of eye injury from a hook on an elastic strap could have been avoided by using a non-elasticated method of attachment. On the requirement that the risk would have been *materially* reduced by the adoption of the alternative design, see *Gee v DePuy International Ltd* [2018] EWHC 1208 (QB); [2018] Med. L.R. 347 at [463]–[465].

[168] *Wilkes v DePuy International Ltd* [2016] EWHC 3096 (QB); [2018] Q.B. 627 at [89]; see also *Gee v DePuy International Ltd* [2018] EWHC 1208 (QB); [2018] Med. L.R. 347 at [146], [165]–[166].

[169] See *Restatement (Third) of the Law of Torts: Products Liability* (1998), §6(c). Suppose a drug causes brain damage as a side-effect. The drug is likely to be defective even if there is no feasible alternative design available, though the position ultimately depends on the frequency of the side-effect and the benefits offered by the drug: see *Gee v DePuy International Ltd* [2018] EWHC 1208 (QB); [2018] Med. L.R. 347 at [161]ff.

[170] In *Bogle v McDonald's Restaurants Ltd* [2002] EWHC 490 (QB), for example, very hot drinks were held not to be defective because avoiding the risk of serious burns would have meant serving the drinks at temperatures unacceptable to customers.

[171] *Gee v DePuy International Ltd* [2018] EWHC 1208 (QB); [2018] Med. L.R. 347 at [463].

[172] The same is not true of voluntary standards: in *Pollard v Tesco Stores Ltd* [2006] EWCA Civ 393, it was held that a child-resistant cap on a bottle of dishwasher powder was not defective even though it did not comply with the British Standard torque measure.

[173] See *Wilkes v DePuy International Ltd* [2016] EWHC 3096 (QB); [2018] Q.B. 627 at [98] (in an appropriate case, compliance with mandatory standards "will have considerable weight"); see similarly at [99]–[101] regarding regulatory compliance. See also *Gee v DePuy International Ltd* [2018]

11-033 **Wilkes v DePuy International Ltd**   A good illustration of the application of the defectiveness test to a standard product is provided by the leading case on the subject, *Wilkes v DePuy International Ltd*.[174] The claimant had hip-replacement surgery, which involved insertion of an artificial hip joint comprised of metal components manufactured by the defendant. One of these was a steel femoral shaft (a "C-Stem"), the neck of which featured a fine groove at the point where it was connected to the metal femoral head. Three years later, the C-Stem fractured in the grooved area, and the claimant brought a claim under the 1987 Act. Hickinbottom J rejected the claimant's argument that there was a defect in the C-Stem because the groove created an excessive concentration of stress at its neck which gave rise to a risk of early fracture. In so deciding, the judge was influenced by a number of considerations, including: (1) that the alternative design proposed by the claimant might have proved more expensive, and made the prosthesis less comfortable; (2) that other producers had made the same design choice; (3) that the product had received the necessary regulatory approvals; (4) that adequate warning was given of the fracture risk, and factors that increased it; (5) that the risk was small, and there was no evidence that the product carried a higher such risk than equivalent products; and (6) that the consequences of a fracture were relatively limited. A similar weighing of risk and benefit was also undertaken in the subsequent case of *Gee v DePuy International Ltd*,[175] where Andrews J concluded that the inherent propensity of metal-on-metal artificial hips to shed metal debris through normal use, thereby potentially triggering an immunological reaction in some patients, was not a "defect" under the Act.

11-034 **Comparison with negligence**   The risk–benefit approach employed in standard product cases is reminiscent of the breach of duty inquiry in negligence, but a defectiveness test is distinct from fault liability in this context, because knowledge acquired since the time the product was marketed is imputed to the manufacturer.[176] Admittedly, the significance of this distinction is reduced by the presence of the development risks defence[177] but the Act still offers claimants in defective design cases some advantages when compared with a negligence regime. After all, the defendant bears the burden of establishing that a product risk was not discoverable at the relevant time for the purposes of the development risk defence, while the test of discoverability under that defence—whether the knowledge in question was "accessible"—can apparently be satisfied even though a reasonable producer would not have discovered the risk.[178] Furthermore, it may be that a reasonable producer would not have identified the risk, not because it was undiscoverable in the light of the state of scientific and technical knowledge, but simply because it would not have crossed his mind. In such a scenario, there would be no liability in

---

EWHC 1208 (QB); [2018] Med. L.R. 347 at [170]–[178]. In the unlikely event that the defect is *attributable to* compliance with a legislative requirement, s.4(1)(a) of the 1987 Act provides a defence: see para.11-044.

[174] [2016] EWHC 3096 (QB); [2018] Q.B. 627. Nolan (2018) 134 L.Q.R. 176.

[175] [2018] EWHC 1208 (QB); [2018] Med. L.R. 347.

[176] In determining whether the product met the standard of safety set out in s.3, "the Court is entitled to have regard to everything now known about it that is relevant to that enquiry, irrespective of whether that information was available at the time it was put on the market or has come to light subsequently": *Gee v DePuy International Ltd* [2018] EWHC 1208 (QB); [2018] Med. L.R. 347 at [84] per Andrews J.

[177] See para.11-039.

[178] See para.11-042.

negligence, but where the risk, if identified, could readily have been eliminated, then there would be liability under the 1987 Act, since the product would be defective and the development risk defence would not be available.[179] And finally, where the defective characteristic of the product was the result of the work of a component manufacturer or an out-of-house designer, the producer can still be liable under the Act, but will not be so liable in negligence unless he was at fault in either selecting or supervising that person.

Inherently dangerous products   Some products are dangerous without being   **11-035** defective. The risks they create are part and parcel of the benefits they offer. Examples include kitchen knives, fireworks and cigarettes. Since the characteristic that poses the danger—the sharpness, the explosiveness, the nicotine—is essential to the proper functioning of the item in question, the most that can be expected of manufacturers of such products is that they provide adequate warnings and reduce the inherent risks where possible. Theoretically, the courts could go beyond this, and rule that the overall social harm caused by, say, alcohol, outweighs the enjoyment it gives to those who partake of it, but it is important that we respect people's right to self-determination. Hence a Scottish court refused to make this call in the case of cigarettes, on the grounds that the judiciary are ill-equipped to make such a judgement, and that such a serious inroad into consumer autonomy is best left to the legislature.[180]

Allergic reactions and side-effects   A product which carries an unavoidable risk   **11-036** of an allergic reaction in susceptible persons is not defective if its overall benefits outweigh that risk,[181] and it carries a suitable warning. In *Buckley v Henkel Ltd*,[182] for example, a hair dye which triggered a severe allergic reaction was held not to be defective under the 1987 Act, account being taken of the presence of adequate warnings and the instruction to users to carry out a "patch" test to see if an allergic reaction was likely.[183] A similar approach will be taken in the case of pharmaceutical products with unavoidable side-effects.

Time element   The proposition in s.3(2) of the 1987 Act that the safety of a   **11-037** product is to be judged by reference to standards prevailing when it was put into circulation[184] (so that a 2015 car is not defective merely because subsequent models are produced with more advanced safety features) seems to be an inevitable concomitant of the concept of "defect" and if the rule were otherwise there might be a positive disincentive to an industry to introduce safety improvements. The "product" in question for this purpose is, of course, the individual item which causes

---

179   See, e.g., *Abouzaid v Mothercare (UK) Ltd* (21 December 2001, CA), where the producer of a pushchair accessory was held liable under the 1987 Act after a hook on its elastic strap caused an eye injury, even though the risk of this happening would not have been identified by a reasonable manufacturer before the accident occurred.

180   *McTear v Imperial Tobacco Ltd* [2005] CSOH 69; 2005 2 S.C. 1. See also *Pou v British American Tobacco (New Zealand) Ltd* (3 May 2006, NZHC). Both cases were litigated in negligence.

181   This will depend, inter alia, on whether a safer alternative product is available, and on whether those with the allergy are likely to be aware of it, and hence able to mitigate the risk.

182   25 November 2013, Liverpool CC.

183   See also *Gee v DePuy International Ltd* [2018] EWHC 1208 (QB); [2018] Med. L.R. 347 at [110].

184   i.e., the time of supply by the manufacturer, not the time of manufacture or of supply to the end user.

the damage,[185] not the product "line" or design—one cannot go on forever producing cars to 2015 standards when everyone else's safety standards have improved—but except in cases where legislative requirements are imposed (for example, as to the fitting of safety belts) it may be very difficult for the court to decide at what point a development becomes necessary to satisfy the requirement of safety, as opposed to being merely desirable. However, neither industry practice at the time nor the fact that it was possible to incorporate the safety feature in question is necessarily decisive. The question is always whether persons generally were entitled to expect incorporation of the feature in the light of the state of scientific knowledge, the feasibility of incorporation, and prevailing attitudes towards the relevant risk.

iii.   Warnings and Instructions

11-038   A standard product may be perfectly safe if used properly but unsafe if used in an improper way or for an improper purpose. To take from the demonology of American product liability law the (apocryphal) case of the claimant who attempted to dry her cat in a microwave oven, the oven would not for that reason be defective. However, where a risk is not obvious to the user, the product may be defective because it is not accompanied by adequate warnings or instructions, as is made clear by s.3(2)(a).[186] The standard here would seem to be indistinguishable from negligence, since persons are presumably entitled to expect only that producers will exercise reasonable care in bringing product hazards to the attention of consumers.[187] There can therefore be no liability unless it is shown that the producer knew or ought to have known of the risk of which he failed to warn, and that the damage would have been avoided if steps which ought reasonably to have been taken to alert users had in fact been taken.[188]

E.   The Development Risks Defence

11-039   **The defence**[189]   By s.4(1)(e) of the 1987 Act it is a defence for the defendant to prove that:

> "the state of scientific and technical knowledge at the relevant time[190] was not such that a producer of products of the same description as the product in question might be expected to have discovered the defect if it had existed in his products while they were under his control."

This defence is distinguishable from "state of the art" arguments that go to defectiveness when marketed: here, it is accepted that the product was defective, but it is argued that the risk that made it so was not discoverable at the relevant time.

---

[185]   *Hastings v Finsbury Orthopaedics Ltd* [2019] CSOH 96; 2019 S.L.T. 1411 at [91].

[186]   Schlechtriem (1989) 9 Tel Aviv Univ. Stud. in Law 33.

[187]   In *Worsley v Tambrands Ltd* [2000] P.I.Q.R. P95, where a warning was held to be adequate for the purposes of the 1987 Act, the analysis was essentially negligence-based.

[188]   There is no blanket rule that the manufacturer may safely ignore a danger which is "obvious", for the product may foreseeably get into the hands of children or other incompetents and if a simple design change will reduce the danger to them, the law may require it. But warnings of obvious dangers may detract from safety by diminishing the significance of warnings about non-obvious risks.

[189]   Newdick [1988] C.L.J. 455 and (1992) 20 Anglo-American L.R. 309; Mildred in Fairgrieve (ed), *Product Liability in Comparative Perspective* (2005).

[190]   The time of the supply by the producer: s.4(2).

This defence was optional under the Directive and the decision to include it controversial. The policy among Member States has not been uniform: Germany, for example, allows such a defence generally, but not for pharmaceuticals.

The terms of s.4(1)(e) do not accord completely with the equivalent provision of the Directive, art.7(e), which requires that "the state of scientific and technical knowledge at the time when [the producer] put the product into circulation was not such as to enable the existence of the defect to be discovered ...." While the Directive seems to speak in terms of scientific possibility, the references in s.4(1)(e) to comparable producers and what might have been expected come closer to a traditional negligence formula. A challenge to the wording of s.4(1)(e) by the European Commission was however rejected by the European Court of Justice[191] on the grounds that the provision did not plainly and irremediably fail to comply with art.7(e) and that the United Kingdom courts would have to interpret it in the light of the Directive.

Non-standard products Section 4(1)(e) asks whether the defect might be **11-040** expected to have been discovered if "it had existed in [the producer's] *products* while they were under his control", and the use of the plural here seems to rule out the possibility of the defence operating where there is no way of discovering a defect in an individual non-standard product.[192] This interpretation was confirmed in *A v National Blood Authority*,[193] where blood products had been infected with the Hepatitis C virus. Burton J held that the development risks defence was not available on these facts since, although the risk of infection had been unavoidable, the defendants had been aware of the danger.[194] The result is that the defence applies only in non-standard product cases where is no knowledge of the existence of the risk in a generic sense.[195] Once this knowledge exists, the manufacturer loses the protection of the defence, even if it is impossible to identify the individual, non-standard products in which the risk has manifested itself.

The "state of scientific and technical knowledge"[196] In *EC Commission v United* **11-041** *Kingdom*, the ECJ made it clear that the development risks defence is concerned not with the state of scientific and technical knowledge in the industrial sector in which the producer is operating, but with the state of such knowledge more generally. Furthermore, AG Tesauro made it clear that the state of scientific and technical knowledge should be identified with the "most advanced level of research" at the relevant time.[197] Hence a discovery which came to be accepted as orthodoxy counted as such knowledge even if at the relevant time it was merely an "isolated opinion".[198] It has been said that a database of previous accidents would not count as "scientific and technical knowledge" for these purposes, since that phrase "contemplates scientific and technical advances" of some kind.[199]

---

[191] *EC Commission v United Kingdom* [1997] All E.R. (EC) 481.
[192] Contrast in this respect the wording of art.7(e) of the Directive, which refers to the singular "product".
[193] [2001] 3 All E.R. 289.
[194] See also *Richardson v LRC Products* [2000] Lloyd's Rep. 280 at 285.
[195] [2001] 3 All E.R. 289 at [77].
[196] Pugh and Pilgerstorfer [2004] J.P.I.L. 258.
[197] *EC Commission v United Kingdom* [1997] All E.R. (EC) 481, Opinion of AG Tesauro at [21].
[198] Opinion of AG Tesauro at [22].
[199] *Abouzaid v Mothercare (UK) Ltd* (21 December 2001, CA) at [29].

11-042 **Accessibility of the knowledge** The wording of s.4(1)(e) of the 1987 Act has been described as laying down a discoverability test "close to negligence principles",[200] but in *EC Commission v United Kingdom* the ECJ held that the art.7(e) defence laid down a stricter standard of "accessibility". It follows that the defence is not available where the relevant scientific and technical knowledge was accessible to the producer at the relevant time, even if a reasonable producer would not have been aware of it. The requirement that the knowledge be accessible is unlikely to be satisfied in the case of unpublished research,[201] and even published work might not qualify if, for example, the publication was in a foreign-language scientific journal with which a producer would not be expected to be familiar.[202]

11-043 **Assessment** The principal justification for the defence is that development risks are difficult to insure against, and the absence of adequate insurance protection could stifle beneficial product innovation by the makers of high-risk products, like pharmaceuticals. A subsidiary point is that any deterrence argument for strict liability loses its force where the defect is not discoverable. On the other hand, opponents of the defence argue that it is incompatible with the loss-spreading rationale of strict liability, and it has been suggested that another thalidomide-type tragedy might slip through the liability net under the 1987 Act, for which reason both the Law Commission[203] and the Pearson Commission[204] rejected any exemption for development risks.

F. Other Defences

11-044 **Compliance with a legislative requirement** It is a defence to an action under the 1987 Act that the defect "is attributable to compliance with any requirement imposed by or under any enactment or with any EU obligation".[205] For example, suppose that legislation required all wine to contain sulphur dioxide. Suppose also that this was later found to be harmful. The producer would have a defence without reference to the "development risks" defence of s.4(1)(e). It should be emphasised that it is not enough that the product *complies with* such an enactment or obligation.[206] Rather, the defendant must establish that the defect was the *inevitable result* of that compliance—in other words, that it was not possible to comply with the provision without rendering the productive defective.

11-045 **No supply** It is a defence to show that the defendant "did not at any time supply the product to another".[207] The meaning of supply is broad, and encompasses the hiring out, lending, and gift of the product.[208] It follows that this defence is not available to, for example, a shampoo manufacturer who distributes free samples. The defence is, however, applicable to goods stolen from the factory, waste products,

---

[200] Griffiths, De Val and Dormer (1988) 62 Tulane L.R. 354, 390.
[201] *A v National Blood Authority* [2001] 3 All E.R. 289 at [49].
[202] *EC Commission v United Kingdom* [1997] All E.R. (EC) 481, Opinion of AG Tesauro at [23]–[24].
[203] See Law Com. No.82, para.105.
[204] Cmnd. 7054, Vol.1, para.1259.
[205] Section 4(1)(a). "Enactment" here means any primary or secondary domestic legislation. After the Brexit transition period ends, "EU obligation" changes to "retained EU obligation": Product Safety and Metrology etc. (Amendment etc.) (EU Exit) Regulations 2019 (SI 2019/696), Sch.3, para.4.
[206] Though this may be relevant to the defectiveness issue: see para.11-032.
[207] Section 4(1)(b).
[208] Section 46.

prototypes and medicinal products used in clinical trials. The defence is also available if a product causes injury to an employee in the course of production.[209]

"Non-commercial" production or supply   Section 4(1)(c) excludes non-commercial production or supply from the ambit of the 1987 Act, an exclusion that can be justified on the ground that the policy reasons for strict product liability, in particular the loss-spreading rationale, are weaker where the defendant is not engaged in a business activity.[210] If the supplier of the product is sued, it is a defence for him to prove that the supply by him was not in the course of his business, as where a private individual sells a used car. By contrast, a producer[211] must establish both that the supply by him was not in the course of his business and that he made the product other than with a view to profit.[212] This would exempt, for example, the home baker who donates a cake to a village fête, but not the home brewer who sells damson wine to his neighbours.   **11-046**

Subsequent defect   It is a defence to show that the defect did not exist in the product at the "relevant time".[213] If the defendant is a producer, apparent producer or importer, the "relevant time" is the time he supplied the product to another; if the defendant is a supplier, it is the time the product was last supplied by a producer, apparent producer or importer. This protects the producer from liability for defects which have arisen as a result of criminal tampering,[214] a botched repair, fair wear and tear etc.[215] The defence is configured so as to protect a supplier who is himself responsible for the introduction of the defect, as where a grocer fails to refrigerate a meat pie. However, in these circumstances, the injured party may well be entitled to damages from the supplier outside the 1987 Act, either in contract or in negligence.   **11-047**

Component manufacturers   When a component is incorporated into a composite product, the component itself remains a "product" under the 1987 Act and the component's manufacturer is therefore liable, along with the manufacturer of the composite product, for any damage caused by a defect in the component. By virtue of s.4(1)(f), however, the component manufacturer has a defence if the defect in the component was wholly attributable to the design of the composite product or to compliance by the defendant with instructions given by the producer of the composite product. Where the plea is that the defect was due to compliance with the other manufacturer's instructions, the component's producer will have to show that it was impossible to comply with those instructions without introducing the   **11-048**

---

[209] cf. *Veedfald v Arhus Amtskommune* [2001] E.C.R. I-3569, an ECJ decision on the equivalent defence in art.7(a) of the Directive (that the defendant "did not put the product into circulation"), which would appear to exclude from the ambit of the defence any case where the defendant himself has used the product after the completion of the manufacturing process. However, this is hard to square with the defence as worded in the 1987 Act, since in such a scenario the defendant would not have supplied the product to another: see Whittaker, *Liability for Products* (2005), pp.517–519.

[210] "Business" is a broad concept, not limited to profit-making activity: see s.46. See also *Veedfald v Arhus Amtskommune* [2001] E.C.R. I-3569 (art.7(a) defence did not extend to a medical product manufactured and used by a public health provider).

[211] Or (as the case may be) apparent producer or importer.

[212] This is the joint effect of s.4(1)(c) and s.2(2) (to which the former provision refers).

[213] Section 4(1)(d).

[214] Unless, of course, the alleged defect was that the product's packaging was not tamper-proof.

[215] For a successful invocation of the defence, see *Piper v JRI (Manufacturing) Ltd* [2006] EWCA Civ 1344; 92 B.M.L.R. 141 (flaw in prosthesis probably not present when it left the factory).

defect. As for the alternative scenario, it frankly makes no sense. If the "defect" in the component is wholly attributable to the design of the composite product, how can it constitute a defect *in the component* in the first place?

G. Contributory Negligence

11-049   Where damage is caused partly by a defect in a product and partly by the fault of the claimant, the defence of contributory negligence applies and the damages payable are reduced accordingly.[216]

H. Causation and Remoteness

11-050 **Causation**   Whether the defect caused the claimant's damage for the purposes of a claim under the 1987 Act is determined by general causation principles.[217] So, for example, applying the "but for" test of factual causation, where the defect is the absence of a warning, it must be shown that a warning would have been heeded. Furthermore, the defect must have been the cause in law of the damage, and deliberate, reckless or grossly negligent conduct by the claimant[218] may amount to a novus actus interveniens. Arguments of this latter kind could be met with the objection that liability is said to arise under the Act where damage "is caused wholly *or partly* by a defect in a product",[219] but the answer to this is that where the intervening conduct constitutes a novus actus it is in law the *sole* cause of the damage.

11-051 **Remoteness of damage**   It is unclear whether the remoteness rules applicable in negligence cases govern liability under the 1987 Act, so that recovery is restricted to damage of a kind that was a reasonably foreseeable consequence of the defect in question.[220] How, for example, would the courts respond to the claim that a defective washing machine had shaken so violently that the claimant had developed a traumatic neurosis?[221] Perhaps the better view is that a foreseeability test should indeed be applied, since the tendency has been to extend the negligence remoteness rules to other unintentional torts, including those where liability is strict.[222]

I. Exclusion of Liability

11-052   Section 7 of the 1987 Act enacts a simple rule invalidating any limitation or exclusion of liability "by any contract term, by any notice or by any other provision", no matter what the nature of the damage.[223] Of course, care must be taken to distinguish substance from form: "manufacturers will not be responsible unless this product is earthed" is not an exclusion of liability but a warning which goes to the safety of the product under s.3.

---

[216] Section 6(4).
[217] See Ch.7.
[218] But probably not third-party conduct, a defendant's reliance on which is expressly excluded by art.8(1) of the Directive.
[219] Section 2(1) (emphasis added).
[220] See Newdick (1987) 103 L.Q.R. 288, 297–300.
[221] *Barnette v Dickens* 135 S.E. 2d. 109 (Va. 1964).
[222] See, e.g., *Cambridge Water Co v Eastern Counties Leather Plc* [1994] 2 A.C. 264 (liability under the rule in *Rylands v Fletcher*).
[223] Contrast s.2 of the Unfair Contract Terms Act 1977 (para.26-017), which makes exclusion of liability for property damage caused by negligence subject to a reasonableness test.

J.   Limitation

This is dealt with in Ch.26. At this stage, however, it is worth noting the "cut-   **11-053**
off" provision whereby any liability is extinguished 10 years after the product has
been put into circulation, thus smothering to some extent the risk of mass disaster
litigation arising from defects which come to light only after many years.[224] This
does not, however, affect the common law of negligence.

---

[224] For example, asbestosis. On when a product is put into circulation, see *O'Byrne v Sanofi Pasteur
MSD Ltd* [2006] 1 W.L.R. 1606 (ECJ) and *O'Byrne v Aventis MSD Ltd* [2010] UKSC 23; [2010] 1
W.L.R. 1412.

CHAPTER 12

LIABILITY FOR STATEMENTS

1. INTRODUCTION

The title of this chapter raises the difficulty of arranging a general account of tort **12-001** law, for a good deal of the law about liability for damage done by statements will be found elsewhere in this book. Statements may cause harm even if true, as where they involve invasions of a person's privacy or breach of his confidences. Liability for untrue statements has a wider canvas. First, a statement may injure a person's reputation, if defamatory and published to a third party; secondly, it may cause direct injury by shock to the person to whom it is addressed; third, it may cause him to act to his detriment; or, fourth, it may cause him loss because it is addressed to other persons whom it causes to act (perhaps perfectly lawfully) to his detriment. The first is covered by the tort of defamation, the subject of a separate chapter, which also looks at privacy and confidence.[1] The second is the liability under *Wilkinson v Downton*, which has been considered in connection with intentional wrongs to the person.[2] This chapter is concerned with the third category and part of the fourth; only part of the fourth, because that category includes malicious falsehood, which is considered with defamation because it often overlaps with it.

Even on this basis the arrangement is still to a certain extent arbitrary. Deceit typically involves deliberate interference with economic interests in a business or contractual context and could be placed in the chapter on the economic torts.[3] "Negligent misstatement" is certainly not a tort in its own right (though deceit is) and liability is often (though not wholly)[4] based upon a broader concept of assumption of responsibility, which we have examined in the context of the duty of care in negligence[5]: if a professional person undertakes a task in respect of which he owes a duty to the claimant he is liable whether he performs that task incompetently or negligently advises the claimant on the action he should take. Nevertheless, "statement" cases throw up enough commonly recurring features (such as legitimacy of reliance and the range of persons to whom a duty is owed) to justify some further, separate treatment.

2. DECEIT

12-002   **Nature of the tort**[6]   Since the decision in *Pasley v Freeman*[7] in 1789, it has been the law that A is liable in tort to B if he knowingly or recklessly (i.e., not caring whether it is true or false) makes a false statement to B with the intention that it shall be acted upon by B, who does act upon it and thereby suffers loss. In other words, liability in deceit requires proof that the defendant acted dishonestly.[8]

12-003   **The effect of the introduction of liability for negligent misrepresentation**   It was long thought that there could be no liability in tort for a false statement honestly made, however negligent its maker may have been and however disastrous its consequences were. Eventually, however, the House of Lords held that there may in certain circumstances be a duty of care upon the maker of a statement in respect of a purely economic loss,[9] and thus that a person may be liable for a false statement honestly but negligently made. Such claims cannot of course be brought in the tort of deceit—they are for negligence and not for fraud—but the existence of negligence liability has a profound bearing on liability for statements as a whole. The possibility of a claim in negligence has to some extent reduced the significance of deceit, but the latter cause of action is still of great importance.[10] There are many

---

1   Ch.13.
2   *Wilkinson v Downton* [1897] 2 Q.B. 57, para.4-031.
3   Ch.19.
4   *Caparo Industries Plc v Dickman* [1990] 2 A.C. 605, para.5-021.
5   See para.5-030.
6   MacDonald Eggers, *Deceit: The Lie of the Law* (2009); Murphy (2016) 75 C.L.J. 301.
7   (1789) 3 Term Rep. 51; 100 E.R. 450.
8   *Derry v Peek* (1889) 14 App. Cas. 337.
9   *Hedley Byrne & Co Ltd v Heller & Partners Ltd* [1964] A.C. 465. See also Misrepresentation Act 1967 s.2.
10   It is, for example, frequently employed by insurers against those who have made fraudulent personal injury claims: see, e.g., *UK Insurance Ltd v Gentry* [2018] EWHC 37 (QB); *Axa Insurance UK Plc*

reasons why a claimant may still seek to establish a case of deceit: there is, for example, no need to establish a duty of care;[11] it may enable him to avoid a disclaimer which would otherwise be valid;[12] his claim cannot be met by an allegation of contributory negligence;[13] and the test for remoteness is more favourable to him.[14] However, a case based on deceit should not be advanced without clear instructions and credible material to support it;[15] it must be unequivocally pleaded[16] and put to the defendant;[17] and it must be distinctly proved,[18] for fraud is inherently less likely than negligence.[19] Summary judgment is now in principle available in a case of deceit[20] but is rather unlikely in practice.

Liability within intimate relationships   Statements made within intimate or family settings are not exempt from liability for deceit. The issue has arisen several times in connection with allegations of paternity fraud made by men against their former partners. It was first held that such a claim could lie as between cohabitees.[21] Subsequently, in *FRB v DCA*,[22] a husband embroiled in divorce proceedings brought a deceit action against his wife, having discovered that he was not the biological father of the child of the marriage. Cohen J rejected the wife's argument that the tort of deceit could not be relied upon as between husband and wife in relation to intimate matters, while striking out the claim as an abuse of process on the ground that where the parties to a marriage were engaged in financial remedy proceedings under the Matrimonial Causes Act 1973, allocation of their resources and bad behaviour by either party was to be dealt under the terms of that legislation and not by way of common law remedies. Courts in other jurisdictions have however been less receptive to the use of deceit in relation to intimate matters.[23]

12-004

Summary requirements   The requirements for the action of deceit may be summarised as follows[24]: (1) there must be a representation of fact made by words or

12-005

---

v Financial Claims Solutions Ltd [2018] EWCA Civ 1330; [2019] R.T.R. 1.

11   *Noel v Poland* [2001] B.C.L.C 645 at [48].
12   See para.12-024.
13   See para.23-060.
14   See para.12-021.
15   Though not necessarily admissible evidence at the pleading stage: *Medcalf v Weatherill* [2002] UKHL 27; [2003] 1 A.C. 120.
16   *Armitage v Nurse* [1998] Ch. 241 at 257.
17   *Haringey LBC v Hines* [2010] EWCA Civ 1111; [2011] H.L.R. 6 at [39].
18   *Hornal v Neuberger Products Ltd* [1957] 1 Q.B. 247.
19   *H (Minors), Re* [1996] A.C. 563 at 586, but on principle it would not seem necessary for the claimant to establish loss to the same elevated standard: *GE Commercial Finance Ltd v Gee* [2005] EWHC 2056 (QB); [2006] 1 Lloyd's Rep. 367 at [122].
20   CPR r.24.3; *Cheshire Building Society v Dunlop Haywards (DHL) Ltd* [2008] EWHC 51 (Comm); [2008] P.N.L.R. 19.
21   *P v B (Paternity: Damages for Deceit)* [2001] 1 F.L.R. 1041; *A v B (Damages: Paternity)* [2007] EWHC 1246 (QB); [2007] 2 F.L.R. 1051.
22   [2019] EWHC 2816 (Fam); [2020] Fam. 211.
23   See *Magill v Magill* [2006] HCA 51; (2006) 226 C.L.R. 551 ("private matters" not amenable to analysis by reference to the elements of deceit). See also *PP v DD* 2017 ONCA 180, though there the concern centred on the damages issues arising in the context of an "involuntary parenthood" claim against a woman alleged to have lied to her ex-boyfriend about using contraception.
24   A principal may recover damages for "fraud" in respect of a transaction into which his agent is bribed (*Mahesan v Malaysia Government Officers' Co-operative Housing Society* [1979] A.C. 374) although there will not usually be any representation to the principal. This has been described as, "not ... deceit, but a special form of fraud": *Petrotrade Inc v Smith* [2001] 1 Lloyd's Rep. 486 at 490.

conduct;[25] (2) the representation must be made with knowledge that it is or may be false, or at least made in the absence of any genuine belief that it is true;[26] (3) the representation must be made with the intention that it should be acted upon by the claimant, or by a class of persons which includes the claimant, in the manner which resulted in loss to him;[27] (4) the claimant must have acted upon the false statement;[28] and (5) the claimant must have suffered loss by so doing.[29]

A. A False Representation of Fact

12-006 **An objective test** For liability in deceit to arise, there must be a representation of fact, or possibly of law.[30] It need not be the representation of the defendant himself, as for example where he knowingly participates in a scheme to defraud and the representations in question are made by another party to the scheme.[31] The representation may be made by words, or by conduct[32] and it follows from the latter that it may be implied as well as express. In determining whether and what representation has been made, the courts adopt an objective test[33]:

> "In determining whether there has been an express representation, and to what effect, the court has to consider what a reasonable person would have understood from the words used in the context in which they were used. In determining what, if any, implied representation has been made, the court has to perform a similar task, except that it has to consider what a reasonable person would have inferred was being implicitly represented by the representor's words and conduct in their context."

12-007 **Promises and other representations of intention** It is commonly said that mere promises are not representations of fact, but this is misleading, for every promise involves a representation of present intention as to future conduct: "There must be a misstatement of an existing fact: but the state of a man's mind is as much a fact as the state of his digestion."[34] If, then, I make a promise believing that I shall keep it, the reason that I am not liable for deceit if I do not keep it is that the representation of fact implied by the promise was true. By contrast, if at the time I made it I had no intention of keeping my promise, I may be liable for deceit. So in *Edgington v Fitzmaurice*[35] directors of a company were held liable for deceit in procuring the public to subscribe for debentures by falsely stating in a prospectus that the loan secured by the debentures was for the purpose of completing buildings of the

---

[25] See para.12-011.
[26] See para.12-014.
[27] See para.12-015.
[28] See para.12-016. The most likely act of the claimant in reliance on a fraudulent misrepresentation is to enter into a contract with the misrepresentor. For detailed consideration of fraud, and misrepresentation in general, in this context, see *Treitel: The Law of Contract*, 15th edn (2020), Ch.9.
[29] See para.12-020.
[30] See para.12-009.
[31] *Dadourian Group International Inc v Simms* [2009] EWCA Civ 169; [2009] 1 Lloyd's Rep. 601 at [72]-[94].
[32] i.e., "active" conduct. There is no representation from mere silence unless there is a prior duty to speak: see para.12-012.
[33] *IFE Fund SA v Goldman Sachs International* [2006] EWHC 2887 (QB); [2007] 1 Lloyd's Rep. 264 at [50] per Toulson J.
[34] *Edgington v Fitzmaurice* (1885) 29 Ch. D. 459 at 483 per Bowen LJ. See also *Clydesdale Bank Ltd v Paton* [1896] A.C. 381 at 394; cf. at 397.
[35] (1885) 29 Ch. D. 459; cf. *East v Maurer* [1991] 1 W.L.R. 461.

company, purchasing horses and vans and developing the trade of the company; in fact the directors intended to use it to pay off pressing liabilities.

Statements of opinion   In the same way, a statement of opinion carries within **12-008** itself a representation of fact, namely that it is in fact the opinion of the person making it. Hence a person who says "I believe X to be honest" is making a representation of fact as to his state of mind and, if it is untrue, there is no reason why, if the other requirements of the tort are met, he should not be held liable for deceit. An expression of opinion also often carries the implication that the person making it has reasonable grounds for it, and where this is not the case he may be guilty of a misrepresentation of fact.[36] On the other hand, there must be some latitude for "sales talk" and a seller's imprecise commendations of his wares do not give rise to liability merely because even the seller might, on careful reflection, think them exaggerated.

Representations of law   As a matter of general principle a misstatement of law **12-009** ought to be a sufficient misstatement of fact for the purposes of deceit.[37] A great many statements which we should not hesitate to describe as statements of fact involve inferences from legal rules and the distinction between law and fact is by no means as precise as might at first appear. So, in *West London Commercial Bank Ltd v Kitson*,[38] where directors of a company, knowing that the private Act of Parliament which incorporated the company gave them no legal power to accept bills of exchange, nevertheless represented to the claimant that they had such authority, there was held to have been deceit. Bowen LJ put the point as follows[39]:

> "Suppose I were to say I have a private Act of Parliament which gives me power to do so and so. Is not that an assertion that I have such an Act of Parliament? It appears to me to be as much a representation of a matter of fact as if I had said I have a particular bound copy of 'Johnson's Dictionary'."

Even if the representation is of a pure proposition of law and not a deduction from a rule of law it is not easy to see what argument can be produced the other way. To urge that everyone is presumed to know the law is to carry into the law of deceit a distinction between law and fact which, artificial enough in any event, was never intended to shield swindlers.[40]

Half-truths   While the general rule is that there must be a statement or representa- **12-010** tion by words or conduct, this does not mean that there must be a direct lie; it is sufficient that there is "such a partial and fragmentary statement of fact, as that the withholding of that which is not stated makes that which is stated absolutely false".[41] For example, where a husband whose income is £80,000 a year is under

---

[36] *Brown v Raphael* [1958] Ch. 636, a case of innocent misrepresentation in contract: see further *Treitel: The Law of Contract*, 15th edn (2020), para.9-015.

[37] A deliberate false statement of law is sufficient for the crime of fraud under s.2(3) of the Fraud Act 2006.

[38] (1884) 13 Q.B.D. 360.

[39] (1884) 13 Q.B.D. 360 at 363.

[40] Furthermore, money may now be recovered for mistake of law as well as fact (*Kleinwort Benson v Lincoln CC* [1999] 2 A.C. 349) and it has been held that a statement of law can fall within the Misrepresentation Act 1967 (*Pankhania v Hackney LBC* [2002] EWHC 2441 (Ch)).

[41] *Peek v Gurney* (1873) L.R. 6 H.L. 377 at 392 per Lord Chelmsford ("Half the truth will sometimes

agreement to pay half to his wife and writes to her saying, "I send £30,000, half my income"—that would be a lie. It makes no difference if he sends her £30,000 and says nothing, for it would be an implied representation that it is half his income and he is guilty of deceit.[42]

12-011 Conduct A representation may be implied from conduct, e.g., a customer's conduct in sitting down in a restaurant amounts to a representation that he is able to pay for his meal.[43] If the defendant deliberately acts in a manner calculated to deceive the claimant and the other elements of the tort are present, the defendant is as much liable for deceit as if he had expressly made a false statement of fact.[44] Deliberate concealment, too, amounts to deceit,[45] but subject to what is said below[46] mere silence, however morally wrong, will not support an action for deceit.[47]

12-012 Mere silence Silence will not normally support an action for deceit in the absence of any conduct which carries with it an implied representation. Sometimes, however, a person is under a legal duty to disclose facts[48] and Lord Blackburn said that in such a case if he deliberately held his tongue with the intention of inducing the other party to act on the belief that he did not speak because he had nothing to say, that would be fraud.[49]

12-013 Continuing representations Related to the above is the situation where D makes a true statement to C and then discovers, before C acts upon it, that it has become false.[50] Does the law permit D to remain silent or does it compel him to correct C's false impression under pain of an action of deceit? It is submitted that the latter answer is in general correct. The tort of deceit is not complete when the representation is made. It only becomes complete when the misrepresentation—not having been corrected in the meantime[51]—is acted upon by the representee.[52] The proper

---

amount to a real falsehood"), at 403; *Smith New Court Securities Ltd v Scrimgeour Vickers (Asset Management) Ltd* [1997] A.C. 254 at 274 per Lord Steyn ("A cocktail of truth, falsity and evasion is a more powerful instrument of deception than undiluted falsehood"). See also *Briess v Woolley* [1955] A.C. 333.

[42] *Legh v Legh* (1930) 143 L.T. 151 at 152.

[43] See *DPP v Ray* [1974] A.C. 370 at 379 (cited by Longmore LJ when refusing to strike out claims based on the implied representations alleged to have been made by banks simply by proposing transactions on the basis of the manipulated LIBOR rate of interest: *Graiseley Properties Ltd v Barclays Bank Plc* [2013] EWCA Civ 1372).

[44] *Ward v Hobbs* (1878) 4 App. Cas. 13 at 16; *Bradford Building Society v Borders* [1942] 1 All E.R. 205 at 211; *Advanced Industrial Technology Corp Ltd v Bond Street Jewellers Ltd* [2006] EWCA Civ 923.

[45] *Gordon v Selico* (1984) 275 E.G. 899.

[46] See paras 12-012—12-013.

[47] *Bradford Building Society v Borders* [1942] 1 All E.R. 205 at 211.

[48] For established categories where there is a duty of disclosure, see *Treitel: The Law of Contract*, 15th edn (2020), paras 9-157—9-182. Beyond them, the precise scope of any "duty to speak" is far from certain: see *Graiseley Properties Ltd v Barclays Bank Plc* [2013] EWCA Civ 1372 at [26].

[49] *Brownlie v Campbell* (1880) 5 App. Cas. 925 at 950; *Conlon v Simms* [2006] EWCA Civ 1749; [2008] 1 W.L.R. 484 at [130].

[50] In *Cramaso LLP v Ogilvie Grant* [2014] UKSC 9; [2014] A.C. 1093 (a case of negligent misrepresentation) the representation was initially made by D to C1, but continued until it was later relied upon by C2, a limited liability partnership incorporated by C1 for the purpose of entering into the contract.

[51] See, e.g., *Mortgage Express v Countrywide Surveyors Ltd* [2016] EWHC 224 (Ch) (no deceit action in relation to mortgage transactions completed after correspondence served to correct earlier

question in any case, therefore, is whether the statement was false when it was acted upon, not when it was made, and so a person whose true statement becomes false to his knowledge before it is acted upon should be liable in deceit if he does not correct it.[53]

Closely akin to this is another problem. Suppose that D's statement was false from the very beginning, but that, when he made it, he honestly believed it to be true and then discovers later and before C has acted upon it that it is false. Must he acquaint C with this? Here equity has a decided answer, whereas the common law is short of any direct decision. In *Reynell v Sprye*[54] a deed was cancelled by the Court of Chancery because D had not communicated the falsity of his belief. As to the wider liability to an action of deceit, it might be inferred from a dictum of Lord Blackburn that it exists,[55] and this was the view taken in a recent Australian decision where auctioneers discovered after selling a painting that their claims prior to its sale as to its authenticity had been inaccurate.[56]

However we treat the question, there is no substantial difference between the two problems just put,[57] so that D is guilty of deceit in both of them if he withholds from C the further information. This certainly ought to be the law where there is plenty of time to retract the statement and where the result of not doing so is certain to be widespread loss or damage (as in the case of a company prospectus) or physical danger or serious business loss to even one person; but it must not be taken too far. As we have seen, a false statement of present intention is a sufficient misrepresentation of fact to support an action of deceit, and the difference between a false statement of intention and a breach of a promise is that in the latter case the promisor believes what he says about his intention. The subsequent breach of promise shows, however, that at some time his intention must have changed, but it does not follow that his failure to inform the promisee of his change of intention is fraudulent. Suppose that C has booked (but not paid for) a seat on D's coach at 9.00, and that D tells him correctly that he intends to start the journey at 11.00. Suppose that D, finding it more convenient to start at 10.30, starts then without informing C of his change of plans, because it would take nearly half an hour to find C. Here, D has certainly committed a breach of contract, but it is wrong to style his silence as to the changed circumstances deceit, even though it is admittedly intentional. It is re-

---

fraudulent valuations). Where it is claimed that a correction was operative, the burden of establishing that a correction was made rests on the defendant and the correction must be sufficiently clear (at [194]).

[52] *Briess v Woolley* [1954] A.C. 333 at 353, 349; *Diamond v Bank of London & Montreal* [1979] Q.B. 333 (service out of jurisdiction); *Lindsay v O'Loughnane* [2010] EWHC 529 (QB); [2012] B.C.C. 153.

[53] See *Incledon v Watson* (1862) 2 F. & F. 841; 175 E.R. 1312; *With v O'Flanagan* [1936] Ch. 575 at 584; *Bradford Building Society v Borders* [1941] 2 All E.R. 205 at 220; cf. *Arkwright v Newbold* (1881) 17 Ch.D. 301 at 325, 329.

[54] (1852) 1 De G.M. & G. 660 at 708–709; 42 E.R. 710 at 728–729.

[55] *Brownlie v Campbell* (1880) 5 App. Cas. 925 at 950. It was not necessary to decide the point in *Henry Ansbacher & Co Ltd v Binks Stern* [1998] P.N.L.R. 221.

[56] *McBride v Christie's Australia Pty Ltd* [2014] NSWC 1729. But was there a misrepresentation of fact in this case at all? Claims as to the authenticity of works of art are generally considered mere statements of opinion, and if the opinion is honestly held when given then there is no implied misrepresentation of fact: see para.12-008.

[57] Except that in the latter case the statement was false from the moment it was made, while in the former it was not. Since it is impossible for a person to make a false statement of his intention while believing it to be true, it would appear that the qualification stated below has no application to the solution of the second problem put.

ally no more than a churlish indifference to a breach of contract. On the other hand, where D induced C to embark on the development of a shopping centre by representing that it proposed to restrict the "tenant mix" at a nearby development by X and then made a secret agreement with X to relax that, D was liable in deceit for loss suffered by C when, a few months later, C irrevocably committed itself to the work. In fact, there were further, positive misrepresentations of D's intention after the secret agreement, but it seems that the result would have been the same if D had kept silent. Certainly it seems realistic in this situation to treat D as making a continuing representation up to the time when C is induced to act on it.[58]

One more possible case of silence raises no difficulty. If D knowingly makes a false statement to C, but before C acts upon it subsequent events have turned the statement into a true one, this is not deceit. Thus, in *Ship v Crosskill*,[59] a false claim in a prospectus, that applications for more than half the capital of the company had been subscribed, had become true before the claimant made his application for shares, and it was held that there was no misrepresentation for which relief could be given to him. "If false when made but true when acted upon there is no misrepresentation."[60]

B.   The Fraudulent State of Mind

12-014   **Derry v Peek**   The representation must be made with knowledge that it is or may be false, or at least in the absence of any genuine belief that it is true. This rule is the result of the decision in *Derry v Peek*,[61] where the House of Lords made it clear that a blundering but honest belief in the truth of a representation cannot be deceit. In Lord Herschell's classic formulation[62]:

> "[F]raud is proved when it is shewn that a false representation has been made (1) knowingly,[63] or (2) without belief in its truth, or (3) recklessly,[64] careless whether it be true or false. Although I have treated the second and third as distinct cases, I think the third is but an instance of the second, for one who makes a statement under such circumstances can have no real belief in the truth of what he states. To prevent a false statement being fraudulent, there must, I think, always be an honest belief in its truth."

The facts of *Derry v Peek* were that the directors of a tramway company issued a prospectus in which they stated that they had parliamentary powers to use steam in propelling their trams. In fact, the grant of such powers was subject to the consent of the Board of Trade. The directors honestly but mistakenly believed the giving of this consent to be a merely formal matter; it was, however, refused. The company was wound up in consequence and the claimant, who had bought shares in it on the

---

58   *Slough Estates Plc v Welwyn Hatfield DC* [1996] 2 P.L.R. 50.
59   (1870) L.R. 10 Eq. 73.
60   *Briess v Woolley* [1954] A.C. 333 at 353 per Lord Tucker.
61   (1889) 14 App. Cas. 337.
62   (1889) 14 App. Cas. 337 at 374.
63   *Armstrong v Strain* [1951] 1 T.L.R. 856 at 871 per Devlin J: "A man may be said to know a fact when once he has been told it and pigeonholed it somewhere in his brain where it is more or less accessible in case of need. In another sense of the word a man knows a fact only when he is fully conscious of it. For an action of deceit there must be knowledge in the narrower sense and conscious knowledge of falsity must always amount to wickedness and dishonesty".
64   For recklessness, see *Angus v Clifford* [1891] 2 Ch. 449 at 471; *Derry v Peek* (1889) 14 App. Cas. 337 at 371.

faith of the prospectus, instituted an action for deceit against the directors. The House of Lords, reversing the decision of the Court of Appeal, gave judgment for the defendants, holding that a false statement made carelessly and without reasonable ground for believing it to be true could not be fraud, though it might furnish evidence of it. However, the defendant is not excused by a belief that such a misrepresentation is common practice or will facilitate the transaction.[65] It must be noted that Lord Herschell's formulation of the law as requiring an honest belief in the truth of the statement was made in the context of a statement by promoters, who had a completely free choice as to what they said. It has been suggested that it does not necessarily follow that an employee is personally guilty of deceit where he makes a statement on the instruction of a senior officer and has some uncertainty as to its accuracy.[66]

C. The Protected Claimant

The representation must be made with the intention that it should be acted upon **12-015** by the claimant, or by a class of persons which includes the claimant, in the manner which resulted in loss to him. So long as that is the case, it need not be made to him either literally,[67] or in particular. In *Langridge v Levy*,[68] the seller of a defective gun, which he had falsely and knowingly warranted to be sound, was held liable to the claimant who was injured by its bursting, although it was the claimant's father to whom the gun had been sold, he having acquainted the seller with the fact that he intended his sons to use it. The claimant need not be individually identifiable,[69] but if the statement is intended for a limited class of persons, only members of that class can sue upon it. Thus, because at common law a company prospectus was ordinarily confined in its scope to the original shareholders, they could sue for false statements in it, but purchasers of the shares from them could not.[70] Intention is not to be confused in this context with motive: it is immaterial whether or not the defendant wished the claimant to rely on the representation as long as he realised that he would almost inevitably do so.[71] There need be no intent to cause loss to the claimant: it is enough that the claimant was intended to act on the misrepresentation and did so act in the manner contemplated.[72]

---

[65]   *Standard Chartered Bank v Pakistan National Shipping Corp* [2000] 1 Lloyd's Rep. 218 (appealed on other grounds [2002] UKHL 43, [2003] 1 A.C. 959); *Brown Jenkinson & Co Ltd v Percy Dalton (London) Ltd* [1957] 2 Q.B. 621.

[66]   *GE Commercial Finance Ltd v Gee* [2005] EWHC 2056 (QB); [2006] 1 Lloyd's Rep. 337. However, if there is the requisite state of mind the fact that a person purports to speak on behalf of a company does not insulate him from personal liability: para.25-034.

[67]   It may, for example, be made to a machine, such as a computer, under his control: *Renault UK v Fleetpro Technical Services Ltd* [2007] EWHC 2541 (QB); [2008] Bus L.R. D17.

[68]   (1837) 2 M. & W. 519; 150 E.R. 863; 4 M. & W. 337; 150 E.R. 1458.

[69]   *Abu Dhabi Investment Co v H Clarkson & Co* [2008] EWCA Civ 699.

[70]   *Peek v Gurney* (1873) L.R. 6 H.L. 377. But the statutory remedy under the Financial Services and Markets Act 2000 s.90, is not so limited. As to the position in common law negligence, see para.12-039.

[71]   *Shinhan Bank Ltd v Sea Containers Ltd* [2000] 2 Lloyd's Rep. 406.

[72]   *Polhill v Walter* (1832) 3 B. & Ad. 114; 110 E.R. 43; *Edgington v Fitzmaurice* (1885) 29 Ch. D. 459 at 482; *Brown Jenkinson & Co Ltd v Percy Dalton (London) Ltd* [1957] 2 Q.B. 621.

D. Inducement

12-016   The claimant[73] must prove that he was induced by the defendant's false representation to act[74] as he did, which usually is to have entered into a transaction.[75] In such cases, the issue of inducement is assessed at the time when the claimant irrevocably committed himself to the transaction that later caused him to suffer loss.[76] Whether he was so induced is a question of fact. It is rare for a person to enter into a transaction solely on the basis of one factor and it is no bar to a deceit claim that the claimant was influenced by other things beside the defendant's misrepresentation.[77] Nor need the misrepresentation be even the decisive factor, so long as it influenced his decision.[78] The materiality of the representation—i.e., the likelihood that it would induce a reasonable person to enter into the transaction—is evidence of inducement,[79] but the presumption that the claimant was induced by a material representation is one of fact which can be rebutted, even if (as has been said) it will be "very difficult" to do so.[80] It is not necessary to prove that the claimant would have acted differently had he known the truth,[81] but only that he was induced by the lie.[82]

12-017   **Lack of belief in the truth irrelevant**   Although the claimant must have been induced to act as he did by the defendant's statement, he need not have believed it to be true. In *Hayward v Zurich Insurance Co Plc*[83] the claimant insurer had settled a personal injury action brought by the defendant against his employer despite nursing suspicions that he was exaggerating the extent of his injuries. When those suspicions were later proven to have been justified, the insurer was held to be entitled to rescind the settlement agreement for the defendant's fraudulent misrepresentation and to recover the sums paid under it.[84] According to the Supreme Court, the claimant's belief in the truth of the statement was not a standalone requirement of liability in deceit, and nor was it a necessary condition of establishing inducement. Generally speaking, it would of course be difficult to prove inducement without such a belief, but even that was not true in this case, because what had driven the insurer's decision-making was not their own belief in the defendant's

---

[73]   Or, where appropriate, a machine under his control: *Renault UK v Fleetpro Technical Services Ltd* [2007] EWHC 2541 (QB); [2008] Bus. L.R. D17.

[74]   Or fail to act, since an omission can amount to reliance for these purposes: see, e.g., *McBride v Christie's Australia Pty Ltd* [2014] NSWC 1729.

[75]   *Downs v Chappell* [1997] 1 W.L.R. 426.

[76]   See, e.g., *Mortgage Express v Countrywide Surveyors Ltd* [2016] EWHC 224 (Ch) at [186] (reliance on fraudulent valuations had to be shown when claimant completed mortgage loans rather than when revocable mortgage offers made).

[77]   *Edgington v Fitzmaurice* (1885) 29 Ch. D. 459.

[78]   *Hayward v Zurich Insurance Co Plc* [2016] UKSC 48; [2017] A.C. 142.

[79]   "[W]hat is material tends to induce": *Hayward v Zurich Insurance Co Plc* [2016] UKSC 48; [2017] A.C. 142 at [29] per Lord Clarke.

[80]   *Zurich Insurance Co Plc v Hayward* [2016] UKSC 48; [2017] A.C. 142 at [37] per Lord Clarke.

[81]   Though this may be relied on by the claimant as evidence of inducement: *Parabola Investments Ltd v Browallia Cal Ltd* [2009] EWHC 901 (Comm); [2009] 2 All E.R. (Comm) 589 at [105] (affirmed [2010] EWCA Civ 486; [2011] Q.B. 477).

[82]   *Downs v Chappell* [1997] 1 W.L.R. 426; *Smith v Kay* (1859) 7 H.L. Cas. 750 at 759.

[83]   [2016] UKSC 48; [2017] A.C. 142.

[84]   Although the claim was not a deceit action but a contractual rescission action, it was assumed that the same principles applied. For criticism of that assumption, see Davies and Day [2019] L.M.C.L.Q. 390.

veracity, but its assessment of the probability that a judge would believe him if the action went to trial. Logically, it follows that a claim can lie in deceit even if the claimant not only lacked a belief in the statement's truth but positively knew it be false, though the court chose to leave that point open.[85]

Ambiguous statements   In the case of an ambiguous statement the claimant must prove: (1) the sense in which he understood the statement; (2) that in that sense it was false; and (3) that the defendant intended him to understand it in that sense or deliberately made use of the ambiguity with the express purpose of deceiving him.[86] It does not follow from the fact that the defendant uses ambiguous language that he is conscious of the way in which the claimant will understand it. Unless the defendant "is conscious that it will be understood in a different manner from that in which he is honestly though blunderingly using it, he is not fraudulent".[87] In *Smith v Chadwick*[88] the prospectus of a company alleged that "the present value of the turnover or output of the entire works is over £1,000,000 sterling per annum". Did this mean that the works had turned out in one year produce worth more than that amount? If so, it was untrue. Or did it mean only that the works could turn out that amount of produce? If so, it was true. The claimant failed to prove that he had interpreted the words in the sense in which they were false, so he lost his action.

12-018

Opportunity to discover the truth   If the claimant is induced to act by the defendant's statement it is irrelevant that he acted incautiously and failed to take those steps to verify its truth which a prudent person would have taken.[89] In *Central Ry of Venezuela v Kisch*[90] directors of a company made deceitful statements in a prospectus and were held liable to a shareholder defrauded thereby, although the prospectus stated that certain documents could be inspected at the company's office and, if the shareholder had taken the trouble to do so, he would have discovered the fraud.[91] This rule is consistent with the fact that contributory negligence is not a defence to deceit.[92]

12-019

---

[85]   Though Lord Clarke inclined to the view that knowledge of falsity would not necessarily be a bar to recovery: [2016] UKSC 48; [2017] A.C. 142 at [44]–[45]. See further Lee [2017] L.M.C.L.Q. 150, 157-158.

[86]   *Smith v Chadwick* (1884) 9 App. Cas. 187 at 201; *Arkwright v Newbold* (1881) 17 Ch. D. 301 at 324; *AIC Ltd v ITS Testing Services (UK) Ltd* [2006] EWCA Civ 1601; [2007] 1 Lloyd's Rep. 555 at [253]. The meaning placed by the defendant on the representation may however be so far removed from the sense in which it would be understood by any reasonable person as to make it clear that the defendant cannot honestly have understood it to bear that meaning: *Henry Ansbacher & Co Ltd v Binks Stern* [1998] P.N.L.R. 221.

[87]   *Angus v Clifford* [1891] 2 Ch. 449 at 472 per Bowen LJ. See also *Smith v Chadwick* (1892) 20 Ch. D. 27 at 79; *Gross v Lewis Hillman Ltd* [1970] Ch. 445.

[88]   (1884) 9 App. Cas. 187.

[89]   "[T]he representee has no duty to be careful, suspicious or diligent in research": *Hayward v Zurich Insurance Co Plc* [2016] UKSC 48; [2017] A.C. 142 at [39] per Lord Clarke.

[90]   (1867) L.R. 2 H.L. 99.

[91]   So too, *Dobell v Stevens* (1825) 3 B. & C. 623; 107 E.R. 864; *Mellor v Partridge* [2013] EWCA Civ 477 at [20].

[92]   *Standard Chartered Bank v Pakistan National Shipping Corp (Nos 2 and 4)* [2002] UKHL 43; [2003] 1 A.C. 959. See para.23-060.

E. Loss

12-020   **Requirement of loss**   Loss is the gist of the action for deceit. In the words of Lord Toulson[93]:

> "It is essential to show that the defendant's false representation caused the claimant to act to [his] detriment. It stands to reason that this should be so. The vice of the defendant's conduct consists in dishonestly making a false representation with the intention of influencing the representee to act on it to [his] detriment. If it does not cause the representee to do so, the mischief against which the tort provides protection will not have occurred. A misrepresentation which has no impact on the mind of the representee is no more harmful than an arrow which misses the target."

The loss which must be induced by the representation will usually be financial but it may consist of personal injury[94] or mental distress[95] or damage to property; and it has also been held that the inconvenience occasioned by loss of possession of a regulated tenancy, even without actual financial loss, will suffice.[96]

12-021   **Recoverable loss**   The measure of damages in deceit is the loss directly flowing from the action of the claimant induced by the defendant's fraudulent misrepresentation.[97] Although the misrepresentation will commonly have induced the claimant to enter a contract, the damages recoverable in deceit differ from the damages recoverable for breach of contract in that the claimant can recover only the money he has lost by entering into the transaction, and not the gains he would have made from it had it worked out. However, he may be able to recover for the loss of the opportunity to lay out his money in other, more profitable, ways, including other contracts,[98] and even a better deal with the defendant himself.[99]

12-022   **Time of assessment**   Where the claimant has been induced to buy property by a fraudulent representation the normal measure of damages is the difference between the price he paid and the market value of the property at the time of acquisition absent the deceit.[100] This general rule is not displaced by evidence that the buyer's

---

[93]   *Hayward v Zurich Insurance Co Plc* [2016] UKSC 48; [2017] A.C. 142 at [62].

[94]   *Langridge v Levy* (1837) 2 M. & W. 519; 150 E.R. 863; (1838) 4 M. & W. 337; 150 E.R. 1458; *Burrows v Rhodes* [1899] 1 Q.B. 816. See also *Allan v Ellis & Co* [1990] 11 E.G. 78 (misdescription in survey causative of claimant's subsequent fall); *Banks v Cox* [2002] EWHC 2166 (Ch) (depression).

[95]   *Shelley v Paddock* [1979] Q.B. 120 (affirmed [1980] Q.B. 348); *Saunders v Edwards* [1987] 1 W.L.R. 1116; *A v B* [2007] EWHC 1246 (QB); [2007] 2 F.L.R. 1051. In *F v Wirral MBC* [1991] Fam. 69 it is suggested that deceit leading to loss of parental "rights" could be actionable.

[96]   *Mafo v Adams* [1979] 1 Q.B. 548.

[97]   Hence where the representation is a continuing one, the loss is to be assessed at the time that it was acted upon: *Inter Export LlC v Townley* [2018] EWCA Civ 2068.

[98]   *East v Maurer* [1991] 1 W.L.R. 461; *4 Eng Ltd v Harper* [2008] EWHC 915; [2009] Ch. 91. The claimant does not need to identify a specific alternative transaction: *Parabola Investments Ltd v Browallia Cal Ltd* [2009] EWHC 901 (Comm); [2009] 2 All E.R. (Comm) 589 (affirmed [2010] EWCA Civ 486; [2011] Q.B. 477). It would seem to follow that damages should be reduced if the defendant can prove that the claimant would have invested in another *loss-making transaction*, but this point is not free from doubt: see *Yam Seng Pte Ltd v International Trade Corp Ltd* [2013] EWHC 111 (QB); [2013] 1 Lloyd's Rep. 526, where the contrary position is described as "impossible to defend" (at [217]).

[99]   *Clef Aquitaine SARL v Laporte Materials (Barrow) Ltd* [2001] Q.B. 488.

[100]   *Smith New Court Securities Ltd v Scrimgeour Vickers (Asset Management) Ltd* [1997] A.C. 254 at 267, as explained in *OMV Petrom SA v Glencore International AG* [2016] EWCA Civ 778; [2017]

"true" loss was less than that sum, for example because the property was used by him for its intended purpose without any ill consequences.[101] He paid more than he should have done because of the deceit, and that is the measure of his loss.[102] However, the rule can be departed from if its application would lead to the claimant being under-compensated.[103] Thus, if a fraud does not come to light for some time the claimant is not necessarily barred from recovering his full loss because the property might have been disposed of at its "false" value immediately after the sale.[104]

In *Smith New Court Securities Ltd v Scrimgeour Vickers (Asset Management) Ltd*[105] C was induced to bid 82p a share for a parcel of 28 million or so Ferranti shares by a fraudulent misrepresentation that there were other buyers in the market. At that time the shares had a market value of 78p. Unknown to D, Ferranti had itself been defrauded on a massive scale by one G, and when this came out the shares fell in value to 44p. The House of Lords restored the trial judge's decision that C was entitled to damages based on the difference between 82p and 44p and did not have to give credit for the "value" of the shares at the time of purchase.[106] The shares in *Smith New Court* were "fatally flawed" or "pregnant with loss"[107] at the time of acquisition. If D induced C to buy a racehorse by representing that it had a good record as a winner and then it died as a result of some latent disease it already had, C would be able to recover all he had paid for it.[108] The case would have been different if the slump in value had been caused by a subsequent fraud, for then the fraud practised by D would have been a cause of C's loss only in the sine qua non sense, not an effective cause: it would have been like a case where a person buys a horse for 200 per cent of its true value as the result of a fraudulent misrepresentation about its record and then it *later* catches a disease (wholly unrelated to the fraud) from which it dies.[109] It may be, however, that the fraudster bears the risk of subsequent general falls in the market.[110]

---

3 All E.R. 157 at [84].

[101] See, e.g., *OMV Petrom SA v Glencore International AG* [2016] EWCA Civ 778; [2017] 3 All E.R. 157 (inferior blended oil passed off by seller as superior branded oil).

[102] *OMV Petrom SA v Glencore International AG* [2016] EWCA Civ 778; [2017] 3 All E.R. 157 at [40].

[103] But not, it seems, because it would lead to him being over-compensated: *OMV Petrom SA v Glencore International AG* [2016] EWCA Civ 778; [2017] 3 All E.R. 157 at [39].

[104] *Peek v Derry* (1887) 37 Ch. D. 541 at 591 (reversed on other grounds: (1889) 14 App. Cas. 337).

[105] [1997] A.C. 254.

[106] Note that if C had been able to rescind the contract, he would have recovered the price in exchange for the shares and the quantum of loss would have been irrelevant. A claim to rescind seems to have been abandoned because the shares had been sold, but Lord Browne-Wilkinson was of the tentative opinion that C might have rescinded by tendering an equivalent quantity of other Ferranti shares.

[107] *Smith New Court Securities Ltd v Scrimgeour Vickers (Asset Management) Ltd* [1997] A.C. 254 at 267 per Lord Browne-Wilkinson.

[108] Cockburn CJ's example in *Twycross v Grant* (1877) 2 C.P.D. 469 at 544–545. See also *MAN Nutzfahrzeuge AG v Freightliner Ltd* [2005] EWHC 2347 (Comm) at [242].

[109] The other example in *Twycross v Grant*, approved by Lord Steyn in *Smith New Court*. Both he and Cockburn CJ plainly thought that D would be liable for the difference between the price paid and the "true" value, but should D be liable at all in such a case? Has the supervening event prevented his fraud having damaging effect? The view that D is liable for the difference between the price paid and the true value can of course be defended by reference to a mechanical rule based on assessment of damages at the time of the sale but such a rule is rejected in *Smith New Court*.

[110] See *Slough Estates Plc v Welwyn Hatfield DC* [1996] 2 P.L.R. 50. It was held in *Banque Bruxelles Lambert SA v Eagle Star Insurance Co Ltd* [1997] A.C. 191 that a negligent valuer did not bear this risk because his liability was confined to the consequences of the information which he gave being wrong (see para.7-073), but different considerations apply where deceit is proven. In *Downs v Chap-*

12-023 Mitigation and remoteness   The claimant must, of course, give credit for any benefit he may have received from the transaction into which he entered as a result of the deceit, provided it may fairly be said to be causally related to the transaction.[111] He is also required to take all reasonable steps to mitigate his loss once he is aware of the fraud.[112] Subject to this the claimant may also[113] recover consequential loss which is directly caused by the fraud, for example liabilities reasonably incurred in seeking to run a business[114] or damage to other property caused by a fraudulently concealed danger.[115] As an intentional wrongdoer the fraudster is not entitled to the benefit of the reasonable foreseeability test of remoteness applicable in negligence,[116] but has to pay for all actual loss directly flowing from the transaction his misrepresentation induced.[117]

F.   Excluding Liability

12-024   A person cannot exclude liability for his own deceit,[118] though it may be that it is possible to exclude liability for the fraud of an agent.[119] The bar on exclusion of liability for personal deceit extends to non-reliance clauses.[120]

G.   Lord Tenterden's Act

12-025   By the Statute of Frauds 1677 promises that are guarantees to answer for another's debts are actionable only if in writing and signed by the party to be charged or his agent. To prevent the statute being evaded by means of the comparatively new action of deceit, s.6 of the Statute of Frauds Amendment Act 1828 (commonly called Lord Tenterden's Act) was passed, providing, in effect, that

---

pell [1997] 1 W.L.R. 426, Hobhouse LJ applied what seemed to be the negligence principle in a fraud case, but in *Smith New Court* Lord Steyn (and perhaps Lord Browne-Wilkinson) said that this was wrong.

[111] cf. *Hussey v Eels* [1990] 2 Q.B. 227 (not a case of fraud).

[112] *Smith New Court Securities Ltd v Scrimgeour Vickers (Asset Management) Ltd* [1997] A.C. 254 at 267.

[113] As to punitive damages, see para.23-012.

[114] *Doyle v Olby (Ironmongers) Ltd* [1969] 2 Q.B. 158; *Downs v Chappell* [1997] 1 W.L.R. 426. In *Hornal v Neuberger Products Ltd* [1957] 1 Q.B. 247, the claimant was induced to buy a lathe by a fraudulent representation that it was fit for immediate use. Although it was worth what he paid for it, he was put to seven weeks delay in preparing it for use and recovered damages for this delay.

[115] See, e.g., *Mullett v Mason* (1866) L.R. 1 C.P. 559; *Nicholls v Taylor* [1939] V.L.R. 119.

[116] See para.7-064.

[117] *Doyle v Olby (Ironmongers) Ltd* [1969] 2 Q.B. 158; *Smith New Court Securities Ltd v Scrimgeour Vickers (Asset Management) Ltd* [1997] A.C. 254.

[118] *HIH Casualty and General Insurance Ltd v Chase Manhattan Bank* [2003] UKHL 6; [2003] 2 Lloyd's Rep. 61. The Statute of Frauds Amendment Act 1828, which may provide a defence to a claim in deceit, is considered below in terms of its application to both deceit and negligence: see para.12-025.

[119] This was the view of the Court of Appeal in *HIH Casualty and General Insurance Ltd v Chase Manhattan Bank* [2001] EWCA Civ 1250; [2001] 2 Lloyd's Rep. 483. However, the House of Lords did not have to decide the point since the clause did not cover such a situation. It is "extraordinarily unlikely" that parties to a contract will agree such a term "with sufficient clarity to raise squarely the question of whether it should be lawful to do so": [2003] UKHL 6; [2003] 2 Lloyd's Rep. 61 at [81] per Lord Hoffmann. cf. *Frans Maas (UK) Ltd v Samsung Electronics (UK) Ltd* [2004] EWHC 1502 (Comm); [2004] 2 Lloyd's Rep. 251 (wilful wrongdoing of servants in performance of contract).

[120] *FoodCo UK LLP v Henry Boot Developments Ltd* [2010] EWHC 358 at [166].

a false representation as to credit cannot be sued upon unless it is made in writing and signed by the party to be charged.[121] The section clearly covers fraudulent representations as to a person's credit[122] but it does not apply to an action between contracting parties in respect of advice negligently given,[123] nor a claim in tortious negligence.[124]

3. LIABILITY FOR NEGLIGENT MISSTATEMENT

The introduction of liability in negligence *Derry v Peek* settled that liability for deceit is liability for fraudulent and not for careless statements, but for many years the case was treated as authority for more than that, for the House of Lords was taken to have held that there could be no tortious liability for a misstatement unless it was fraudulent.[125] In 1914 the House itself, in *Nocton v Lord Ashburton*,[126] pointed out that *Derry v Peek* had not ruled out every form of liability (independent of statute) but that for fraud. Not only would there be liability in contract but it could exist in equity as well, where there was a fiduciary relationship, for advice which was not "dishonest" in the common law sense. Fifty years later, in *Hedley Byrne & Co Ltd v Heller & Partners Ltd*,[127] the House was able to rely on *Nocton v Lord Ashburton* as showing that *Derry v Peek* governed only liability for deceit so that they were not precluded from holding that when making a statement a tortious duty of care might exist. In the period between these cases it was also recognised that there could be liability for physical damage caused by a misleading statement.[128] Many cases which are primarily thought of in terms of acts also contain elements of misstatement: no harm would have come to the pursuer in *Donoghue v Stevenson*, for example, if there had been no implied representation that the ginger beer was fit for human consumption. Indeed, in some cases the distinction between word and deed is for all practical purposes non-existent. Quite apart from contract, a doctor is as much liable for negligently advising his patient to take a certain drug as he is for negligently injecting the drug himself. However, in *Hedley Byrne* the loss was solely pecuniary.

12-026

Hedley Byrne v Heller The facts of *Hedley Byrne* were that the claimants, who were advertising agents, were anxious to know whether they could safely give credit to a company, Easipower, on whose behalf they had entered into various advertising contracts, and they therefore sought bankers' references about Easipower. For

12-027

---

[121] See *Contex Drouzhba Ltd v Wiseman* [2006] EWCA Civ 1201; [2008] 1 B.C.L.C. 631; *Lindsay v O'Loughnane* [2010] EWHC 529 (QB); [2012] B.C.C. 153.
[122] Given a narrow construction: *Lindsay v O'Loughnane* [2010] EWHC 529 (QB); [2012] B.C.C. 153; *Roder UK Ltd v West* [2011] EWCA Civ 1126; [2012] Q.B. 752.
[123] *Banbury v Bank of Montreal* [1918] A.C. 626.
[124] *WB Anderson & Sons Ltd v Rhodes (Liverpool) Ltd* [1967] 2 All E.R. 850. It does however apply to the Misrepresentation Act 1967 s.2(1), because of the form of that provision: *UBAF Ltd v European Banking Corp* [1984] Q.B. 713.
[125] However, the year after *Derry v Peek*, Parliament imposed liability for false statements in prospectuses by the Directors' Liability Act 1890. See now Financial Services and Markets Act 2000 s.90.
[126] [1914] A.C. 932.
[127] [1964] A.C. 465.
[128] See, e.g., *Watson v Buckley, Osborne, Garrett & Co Ltd* [1940] 1 All E.R. 174. See also *Clayton v Woodman & Son (Builders) Ltd* [1962] 2 Q.B. 533 (reversed on the facts: [1962] 1 W.L.R. 585) and *The Apollo* [1891] A.C. 499.

this purpose, the claimants' bankers approached the defendants, who were Easipower's bankers, and on two occasions the defendants gave favourable references. These were passed on to the claimants by their bankers and, although the defendants did not know who the claimants were and had in fact marked their communications to the claimants' bankers "Confidential. For your private use …", they did know the inquiry was made in connection with an advertising contract. They must also have known that the references were to be passed on to a customer.[129] In reliance on these references the claimants incurred expenditure on Easipower's behalf and, when Easipower went into liquidation, they suffered substantial loss. This loss they sought to recover from the defendants in an action based upon the defendants' alleged negligence in giving favourable references concerning Easipower.

At first instance McNair J held that the defendants owed no duty to the claimants, and this decision was affirmed in the Court of Appeal[130] both on the ground that the case was covered by authority and also on the ground that it would not be reasonable to impose upon a banker an obligation to exercise care when informing a third party of the creditworthiness of his client. In the House of Lords the decision in favour of the defendants was affirmed, but none of their Lordships based his decision on a general rule of non-liability for negligent misstatement. On the contrary, Lords Reid, Devlin and Pearce held that, assuming the defendants to have been negligent, the only reason for exonerating them was that the references had been given "without responsibility".[131] Lord Hodson and, perhaps, Lord Morris considered that even without this denial of responsibility there was no duty of care on the facts, but nevertheless agreed that a duty of care in making statements was a possibility.

A. A Special Relationship

12-028   We have seen that *Hedley Byrne* has been regarded as the progenitor of the principle of "assumption of responsibility", which has now been extended beyond liability for statements.[132] In that broader context the decision has really become part of the background to the House of Lords cases in the 1990s concerning services to be performed for the claimant or a third party.[133] However, we are now concerned with *Hedley Byrne* in the particular context of statements and advice and it should not be assumed that all cases based upon assumption of responsibility have common characteristics: for example, in the situations dealt with in this section it is always necessary that the claimant should have relied on the statement, whereas reliance is not always necessary in other types of case.[134]

It is clear from *Hedley Byrne* that for a duty of care to arise in respect of speech or writing, something more is required than in the straightforward case of physical damage caused by an act where, generally speaking, foreseeability of harm will be sufficient.[135] This is very largely because a statement is likely to cause economic

---

129   [1964] A.C. 465 at 482, 503.
130   *Hedley Byrne & Co Ltd v Heller & Partners Ltd* [1962] 1 Q.B. 396.
131   See para.12-045.
132   See para.5-040.
133   See para.5-041.
134   See para.5-046.
135   See para.5-014.

loss rather than physical harm and the risk of crushing liability is exacerbated by the fact that information is likely to be disseminated among a large number of persons even if it was originally addressed only to a small group. In some activities, for example auditing or financial advice, the potential liability is so great that it is beyond the capacity of the insurance market.[136] Their Lordships in *Hedley Byrne* were in general agreement that *Donoghue v Stevenson* had little, if any, direct bearing on the problem of negligent misstatement and that a duty of care would exist in relation to statements only if there was a "special relationship" between the parties. Indeed, Lord Devlin spoke in terms of a relationship "equivalent to contract"[137] and in a later case where liability was imposed on a valuer engaged by a mortgagee for loss incurred by the mortgagor as a result of a negligent report, the relationship between the valuer and mortgagor was described as "akin to contract".[138] While expressly disclaiming any intention to lay down conditions which were either conclusive or exclusive, Lord Oliver in *Caparo Industries Plc v Dickman*[139] described the necessary relationship as typically having four characteristics:

"(1) the advice is required for a purpose, whether particularly specified or generally described, which is made known, either actually or inferentially, to the adviser at the time when the advice is given; (2) the adviser knows, either actually or inferentially, that his advice will be communicated to the advisee, either specifically or as a member of an ascertained class, in order that it should be used by the advisee for that purpose; (3) it is known, either actually or inferentially, that the advice so communicated is likely to be acted upon by the advisee for that purpose without independent inquiry[140]; and (4) it is so acted upon by the advisee to his detriment."

B. Professional Advisers

There is a view that liability under *Hedley Byrne* is further restricted to professional advisers or those claiming equivalent skills. This is based on the majority opinion in the Privy Council in *Mutual Life and Citizens' Assurance Co Ltd v Evatt*.[141] The claimant, a policyholder in the defendant company, sought advice from it as to the financial soundness of another company, "Palmer", with which it was closely associated. The information he was given was incorrect and he lost his money. It was held by the majority that the omission from the claimant's declaration of any allegation that the defendant was in the business of supplying information or advice or had claimed to possess the necessary skill to do so was fatal. However, the minority took a broader approach[142]:

"[O]ne must assume a reasonable man who has that degree of knowledge and skill which facts known to the inquirer (including statements made by the adviser) entitled him to

12-029

---

[136] See para.5-024.
[137] *Hedley Byrne & Co Ltd v Heller & Partners Ltd* [1964] A.C. 465 at 530.
[138] *Smith v Eric S Bush* [1990] 1 A.C. 831 at 846 per Lord Templeman.
[139] [1990] 2 A.C. 605 at 638.
[140] See *Patchett v Swimming Pool and Allied Trades Association Ltd* [2009] EWCA Civ 717; [2010] 2 All E.R. (Comm) 138 (trade association website; advice to seek further information). cf. *HSBC Bank Plc v So* [2009] EWCA Civ 296; [2009] 1 C.L.C. 503 (no reason to investigate where other party had made unqualified statement about matter within its own knowledge).
[141] [1971] A.C. 793.
[142] [1971] A.C. 793 at 812 per Lord Reid and Lord Morris.

expect of the adviser, and then inquire whether a reasonable man could have given the advice which was in fact given if he had exercised reasonable care."

This approach has recommended itself to judges at first instance[143] and in the Court of Appeal,[144] though strictly perhaps it has not been necessary for them to choose between the majority and minority views in *Evatt*'s case.[145] The issue was also really irrelevant when the House of Lords considered *Hedley Byrne* in *Smith v Eric S Bush*[146] and in *Caparo Industries Plc v Dickman*.[147] In fact, the extent of the practical difference between the two camps very much depends upon the way in which the court interprets the majority test in *Evatt* and its qualifications.[148] Thus, it seems clear that the expression "business or profession" is not meant to confine liability to those engaged in private enterprise or the pursuit of profit, but may extend to a public authority supplying information and in *Spring v Guardian Assurance Plc*,[149] where the claim arose from an incorrect reference, Lord Goff, having referred to the criticisms of *Evatt*, said that in any event it did not stand in the way of a decision in favour of the claimant, for the skill of preparing a reference in respect of an employee falls as much within the expertise of an employer as the skill of preparing a bank reference fell within the expertise of the bank.

C. Voluntariness

12-030   There is a clear thread running through *Hedley Byrne* that the duty arises from an "undertaking", express or implied, to use due care, a voluntary assumption of responsibility, but it is plain that these expressions should not be understood as requiring any actual or subjective acceptance of legal liability by the defendant. In *Smith v Eric S Bush*, Lord Griffiths said that[150]:

"[T]he phrase 'assumption of responsibility' can only have any real meaning if it is understood as referring to the circumstances in which the law will deem the maker of the statement to have assumed responsibility to the person who acts upon the advice."

Indeed, where a surveyor carried out a valuation of an ordinary dwelling house on the instructions of a building society he thereby "assumed responsibility" to the intending purchaser who, as he knew, would rely upon his skill, even though in fact he attempted (unsuccessfully) to exclude his liability.[151] The test is an objective one

---

[143] *Argy Trading Development Co Ltd v Lapid Developments Ltd* [1977] 1 W.L.R. 444.

[144] *Esso Petroleum Co Ltd v Mardon* [1976] Q.B. 801 at 827; *Howard Marine and Dredging Co Ltd v A Ogden (Excavations) Ltd* [1978] Q.B. 574.

[145] See the differing views expressed in *Shaddock v Parramatta CC* (1981) 151 C.L.R. 590 about the extent to which the facts could be covered by the *Evatt* formula.

[146] [1990] 1 A.C. 831.

[147] [1990] 2 A.C. 605.

[148] Namely, that a duty may arise if the defendant holds himself out as possessing a skill equivalent to that of a "professional" or if he has a financial interest in the transaction. The former case in particular seems capable of almost infinite expansion.

[149] [1995] 2 A.C. 296. Note that this case does not represent a straightforward *Hedley Byrne* situation since the statement was made by D to X about C: see para.12-049. See also *Lennon v MPC* [2004] EWCA Civ 130; [2004] 1 W.L.R. 2594.

[150] *Smith v Eric S Bush* [1990] 1 A.C. 831 at 862.

[151] *Smith v Eric S Bush* [1990] 1 A.C. 831. Note that the building society does not assume responsibility for the accuracy of the report of an independent valuer: its duty is to take care in selecting the valuer. cf. *Harris v Wyre Forest DC* [1990] 1 A.C. 831 (appeal heard with *Smith v Bush*) where the

applied to the context and what passes between the claimant and the defendant.[152] The assumption of responsibility is certainly voluntary in the sense that at common law the defendant can normally displace the duty by disclaimer, although this possibility is often barred by the Unfair Contract Terms Act 1977 or the Consumer Rights Act 2015.[153]

D. Public Officers and Bodies

We have already seen that a certification or inspection authority may incur liability for personal injury to a member of the public even without any direct communication or reliance.[154] Even where there is a direct statement, however, matters are not so simple with regard to economic loss. If, for example, an inspection authority has told the claimant to spend more than was necessary on safety precautions, he may have difficulty in establishing a duty of care because there would appear to be no relevant assumption of responsibility towards him.[155] And while persons undertaking development of land may make inquiries of the planning authorities before embarking on the project, it has been held that "the ordinary process of giving routine advice to an applicant for planning permission and answering such questions as he or she may raise, especially when the applicant is one known to have her own professional advisers" does not give rise to any duty of care.[156] Nevertheless, it was accepted that a local authority could owe a duty of care when answering search enquiries,[157] and a local land registry was held liable when its inaccurate answer to an inquiry caused an incumbrancer to lose his rights.[158] More recently, in *Sebry v Companies House* the Registrar of Companies was held to owe a duty of care when entering a winding-up order on the company register to take reasonable care to ensure that the order was not registered against the wrong company.[159] Edis J rightly rejected the idea that a public authority which has made a representation pursuant to a statutory duty cannot be said to have *voluntarily* assumed a responsibility when, as a matter of public law, it had no choice but to do so.[160]

12-031

---

valuer was an employee of the lender and the lender was vicariously liable for his negligence.

[152] *Williams v Natural Life Health Foods Ltd* [1998] 1 W.L.R. 830 at 835; *Electra Private Equity Partners v KPMG Peat Marwick* [2001] B.C.L.C. 589.

[153] See para.12-046.

[154] See para.5-024.

[155] See *Harris v Evans* [1998] 1 W.L.R. 1285. In fact the case involved not advice but the making of a prohibition notice, which brought into play the statutory appeal process. In *Welton v North Cornwall DC* [1997] 1 W.L.R. 570, where the defendants' environmental health officer imposed wholly excessive hygiene requirements on the claimants' guest house, the claim was described as "well within" Hedley Byrne and "incontrovertible". The court in *Harris* was able to distinguish *Welton* because in the latter case the "advice" was directly given to the claimant, whereas in *Harris* the officer caused the local authority to impose the prohibition notice, but it clearly had doubts about *Welton*.

[156] *Haddow v Secretary of State for the Environment* [2000] Env. L.R. 212; *Tidman v Reading BC* [1994] E.G.C.S. 180; *Fashion Brokers Ltd v Clarke Hayes* [2000] Lloyd's Rep. P.N. 398.

[157] *Gooden v Northamptonshire CC* [2001] EWCA Civ 1744; [2002] P.N.L.R. 18.

[158] *Ministry of Housing and Local Government v Sharp* [1970] 2 Q.B. 223.

[159] [2015] EWHC 115 (QB); [2016] 1 W.L.R. 2499.

[160] [2015] EWHC 115 (QB); [2016] 1 W.L.R. 2499 at [108]–[109].

E.   Hedley Byrne and Contract Relations

12-032   Concurrent liability   Negligent misstatement very often takes place in the context of a contract. It was established in *Henderson v Merrett Syndicates Ltd*[161] that a duty of care in tort could co-exist with a contractual obligation where there had been an assumption of responsibility in relation to the provision of services and the same is true in relation to a statement.[162] Where there is a contract between the parties there is no reason in principle why there should not be a tort duty of care, during the currency of the contract, which involves a matter outside the scope of the contract,[163] but the fact that the proposed duty is inconsistent with the terms of the contact is, of course, reason for rejecting it.[164]

12-033   Section 2(1) of the Misrepresentation Act 1967   In relation to the negotiations leading to a contract the importance of *Hedley Byrne* was very much diminished by s.2(1) of the Misrepresentation Act 1967. This provides that where a person has entered into a contract after a misrepresentation has been made to him by another party to the contract then, if the representor would have been liable in damages if the representation had been made fraudulently, he shall be so liable unless he proves that he had reasonable grounds to believe that the statement was true.[165] This is more favourable to the claimant than *Hedley Byrne* because there can be no argument about duty and the defendant bears the burden of proving that he had reasonable grounds to believe in the truth of his statement. However, there may still be pre-contractual negotiation cases where the claimant will seek to rely on *Hedley Byrne*, for example because no contract was in the end concluded (but the claimant still suffered loss), because he seeks to impose liability on an agent,[166] or because the representation was made by someone who is not a party to the contract and is therefore not caught by s.2(1).[167]

12-034   Duty owed to non-contracting parties   The fact that D, in relation to the statement which causes damage to C, is performing a task under contract for X does not mean that D may not owe a duty of care to C—this is, after all, the "statement" equivalent of *Donoghue v Stevenson*. Hence a valuer engaged to value an ordinary dwelling on behalf of the mortgagee may owe a duty of care to the mortgagor (purchaser) to whom he knows the report will be shown,[168] and where accountants or financial advisers provide information to persons contemplating a transaction

---

[161] [1995] 2 A.C. 145.

[162] *Esso Petroleum Co Ltd v Mardon* [1976] Q.B. 801; *Howard Marine and Dredging Co Ltd v A Ogden & Son (Excavations) Ltd* [1978] Q.B. 574; *Hagen v ICI* [2002] I.R.L.R. 31.

[163] *Holt v Payne Skillington* (1995) 49 Con. L.R. 99 (where, however, there was no sufficient pleaded case).

[164] *J Nunes Diamonds Ltd v Dominion Electric Co* (1972) 26 D.L.R. (3d) 699. Though not a *Hedley Byrne* case, *Tai Hing Cotton Mill Ltd v Liu Chong Hing Bank Ltd* [1986] A.C. 80 is another example of the principle.

[165] Since the liability created by s.2(1) is tortious, the measure of damages is the tort measure, not the contractual one: *Royscott Trust v Rogerson* [1991] 2 Q.B. 297. The application in that case of the deceit rule of remoteness—based on a doubtful interpretation of the wording of s.2(1)—is regrettable.

[166] See para.12-035.

[167] See *Taberna Europe CDO II Plc v Selskabet at 1 September 2008 A/S (formerly Roskilde Bank A/S)* [2016] EWCA Civ 1262; [2017] Q.B. 633 at [33]–[47].

[168] *Smith v Eric S Bush* [1990] A.C. 831.

with their client they may owe a duty to those persons.[169] However, the nature of the contractual arrangements between the various parties[170] or the nature of the transaction may lead to the conclusion that no duty of care arises. Thus, the valuer for the mortgagee may not owe a duty to the purchaser where the sale involves a commercial[171] or industrial property and the same will be true where for other reasons it is legitimate to expect that the claimant will undertake his own inquiries.[172]

F. Agents

Personal liability of the agent   The statement may be made by the agent of one **12-035** party to a transaction, in the sense of representing that party in the matter. The principal will incur liability for what the agent says if it is within the scope of his authority and, depending on the terms of any contract between them, the principal may in turn have recourse against the agent. The agent may also incur personal liability in tort to the recipient of the statement[173] and this will be relevant, for example, if the principal is insolvent. However, this will happen only if the agent assumed a personal responsibility to the recipient of the statement. In *Williams v Natural Life Health Foods Ltd*[174] the House of Lords held that a director of a company did not owe a duty of care to its franchisees merely because he worked on the fulfilment of the contract which they made with the company—it was the company that had assumed a responsibility towards them and not the director personally.[175] Nor will a solicitor acting for one party to an arm's length transaction generally owe a duty of care to the other party.[176] Hence a vendor's solicitor owed no duty of care to the buyer when answering inquiries before contract;[177] a solicitor acting for a borrower, who had mistakenly drawn up documents under which the lender discharged its security on all the properties on which the loan was

---

[169] See the dissenting judgment of Denning LJ (which was approved in *Hedley Byrne*) in *Candler v Crane, Christmas & Co* [1951] 2 K.B. 164; *Morgan Crucible v Hill Samuel Bank Ltd* [1991] Ch. 295; *Electra Private Equity Partners v KPMG Peat Marwick* [2001] B.C.L.C. 589.

[170] As in *Pacific Associates Inc v Baxter* [1990] 1 Q.B. 993 and *Galliford Try Infrastructure Ltd v Mott MacDonald Ltd* [2008] EWHC 1570 (TCC); 120 Con. L.R. 1. But there is certainly no rule that the fact that the parties have arranged their relationships so that there is no direct contractual link precludes a duty of care: *Henderson v Merrett Syndicates Ltd* [1995] 2 A.C. 181; *Riyad Bank v Ahli United Bank (UK)* [2006] EWCA Civ 780; [2006] 2 Lloyd's Rep. 292.

[171] No duty was found to be owed where the mortgagor was purchasing a residential house as part of a buy-to-let scheme: *Scullion v Bank of Scotland Plc* [2011] EWCA Civ 693; [2011] 1 W.L.R. 3212.

[172] *James McNaughton Paper Group Ltd v Hicks Anderson & Co* [1991] 2 Q.B. 295 (draft accounts requested as quickly as possible for use in negotiation; buyers aware of poor state of client's affairs).

[173] The agent will generally not be party to any contract with the recipient. Nor will the agent incur a personal liability under the Misrepresentation Act 1967 s.2(1): *Resolute Maritime v Nippon Karji Kyokai* [1983] 1 W.L.R. 857.

[174] [1998] 1 W.L.R. 830. See para.25-034.

[175] See further the discussion in *Trevor Ivory Ltd v Anderson* [1992] 2 N.Z.L.R. 517. The reasoning in *Williams* is difficult to reconcile with *Merrett v Babb* [2001] EWCA Civ 214; [2001] Q.B. 1174, where a surveyor whose employer was insolvent and uninsured was held to be personally liable to an intended purchaser of a house, even though the house buyer had never had any communication with him. May LJ at [45] regarded *Williams* as turning on the fact that it involved a director, but with respect that is doubtful.

[176] *Steel v NRAM Ltd* [2018] UKSC 13; [2018] 1 W.L.R. 1190 at [25]. A fortiori in the case of adversarial matters, where there is no doubt that one should deny a duty of care in the agent to the third party: see, e.g., the position of lawyers in connection with litigation, para.5-065.

[177] *Gran Gelato Ltd v Richcliff (Group) Ltd* [1992] Ch. 560.

secured instead of just one, owed no duty of care to the lender;[178] and the solicitors acting for a fraudster purporting to sell property belonging to another assumed no responsibility to the defrauded buyer in respect of the checks they made as to the identity of their client.[179] This rule is however open to exceptions. In *Dean v Allin & Watts*,[180] for example, a solicitor acting for a borrower on a loan transaction was held to have owed a duty of care to the lender to create the effective security which was fundamental to the transaction and which the borrower was willing to grant to the lender. This decision has been justified on the ground that the instructions the solicitor had received were intended to benefit both their own client and the claimant third party.[181]

G. Failure to Speak

12-036   Failure to speak raises the same issues as omissions generally in the law of negligence.[182] There is therefore no general duty to volunteer information for the protection of others, even as between contracting parties.[183] However, everything turns on the responsibility which the defendant has assumed towards the claimant. If, as is clear, D may be liable for an omission if he has undertaken the management of C's affairs,[184] there is no reason why he should not be equally liable if he fails to perform an undertaking to warn C of hazards or problems.[185] If a statement is made in circumstances where there is a duty of care which at the time is fulfilled (because the statement is true or the maker has reasonable cause to believe it to be true) then, by analogy with the law on rescission for misrepresentation and deceit there should be a duty to take steps to bring a change of circumstances to the notice of the recipient where this occurs before he acts upon it.[186] The defendant may, however, make it clear that he is not undertaking to inform of any future developments.[187]

---

[178] *Steel v NRAM Ltd* [2018] UKSC 13; [2018] 1 W.L.R. 1190. Central to the reasoning in this case was the fact that it had not been reasonable of the lender to rely on the representation by the borrower's solicitor, but with respect it is difficult to see how the question of whether a duty of care is owed when a statement is made can depend on whether it was reasonable of the representee thereafter to rely on it. The result is nonetheless perfectly defensible since there was nothing to suggest on the facts that the solicitor was assuming any direct responsibility towards the lender.

[179] *P & P Property Ltd v Owen White & Catlin LLP* [2018] EWCA Civ 1082; [2019] Ch. 273.

[180] [2001] EWCA Civ 758; [2001] 2 Lloyd's Rep. 249.

[181] *P & P Property Ltd v Owen White & Catlin LLP* [2018] EWCA Civ 1082; [2019] Ch. 273 at [79].

[182] See para.5-030.

[183] The relationship between banker and customer is not fiduciary and in the absence of some positive assumption of responsibility the bank does not owe a duty to advise the customer on the wisdom of a transaction in respect of which he seeks a loan: *Williams & Glyns Bank Ltd v Barnes* [1981] Com. L.R. 205; *Murphy v HSBC Plc* [2004] EWHC 467 (Ch). In other contexts, the existence and scope of any "duty to speak" is uncertain: *ING Bank NV v Ros Roca SA* [2011] EWCA Civ 353; [2012] 1 W.L.R. 472 at [90]-[96]; cf. *Graiseley Properties Ltd v Barclays Bank Plc* [2013] EWCA Civ 1372 at [26].

[184] *Henderson v Merrett Syndicates* [1995] 2 A.C. 145 at 181.

[185] *Holt v Payne Skillington* (1995) 49 Con. L.R. 99 (no duty on facts). cf. *Van Oppen v Bedford School* [1989] 1 All E.R. 273 and *Reid v Rush & Tompkins Group Plc* [1990] 1 W.L.R. 212 where, despite an existing relationship, there was no implied undertaking to advise about insurance and *Tai Hing Cotton Mill Ltd v Liu Chong Hing Bank Ltd* [1986] A.C. 80 (no duty to check bank statements for evidence of fraud). In *Hamble Fisheries Ltd v L Gardiner & Sons Ltd* [1999] 2 Lloyd's Rep. 1 there was no relationship at all, simply the fact that C owned an engine made by D's predecessor.

[186] cf. *McCullagh v Lane Fox & Partners Ltd* [1996] 1 E.G.L.R. 35.

[187] *IFE Fund SA v Goldman Sachs International* [2007] EWCA Civ 811; [2007] 2 Lloyd's Rep. 449.

H.   Advice Informally Given

No duty on "social occasions"   It is unlikely that a duty of care will arise in   **12-037**
respect of advice requested and given on a purely social occasion, since in such a
scenario there will rarely be a relevant assumption of responsibility. The boundaries
of this type of case, where the informality of the transaction leads to a denial of duty,
cannot be drawn with precision. In *Chaudhry v Prabhakar*[188] liability was imposed
on a friend who had assessed a used car for the claimant. The friend had some
expertise in relation to cars and the task undertaken was related to a specific
purchase, but the existence of a duty was conceded and one judge doubted the correctness of that concession. And in *Burgess v Lejonvarn*,[189] it was held that an
architect who had agreed to assist friends with the design and project management
of a domestic landscaping project had owed them a duty of care. Although her
services were provided gratuitously, the context was not informal or social but
professional, and there was an expectation that she would be paid for subsequent,
related, work. Finally, in *Howard Marine and Dredging Co Ltd v A Ogden (Excavations) Ltd*[190] the defendant answered an inquiry as to the carrying capacity of barges
on the basis of his (accurate) recollection of the Lloyd's Register figure, which was
incorrect, and without checking the barge's papers. The actual decision went on
s.2(1) of the Misrepresentation Act 1967 but, as far as the common law was
concerned, two members of the court were of the view that, given the impromptu,
"off the cuff" circumstances of the response, the defendant's only duty was to give
an honest answer.[191]

Standard of care   The fear of imposing an unreasonably onerous duty in respect   **12-038**
of responses to comparatively informal inquiries may, in the alternative, be met by
manipulation of the standard of care required. If it is unreasonable to expect a
banker answering a query about a customer to spend time and trouble in searching
records and so on, then a duty to take such care as is reasonable in all the
circumstances of the case does not require him to do so. The duty of care is not a
duty to take all possible care, still less is it a duty to be right. Similarly, a surveyor
conducting a valuation for mortgage purposes is not expected to go to the lengths
required in an expensive structural survey; but if his inspection reveals grounds for
suspicion he must take reasonable steps to follow the trail, even though he is working to a standard fee—he must "take the rough with the smooth" or decline to
proceed.[192]

I.   The Protected Claimant

A test of purpose   It is not necessary that the defendant know the identity of the   **12-039**
claimant for a duty of care to be owed, for in *Hedley Byrne* itself the inquiry was

---

[188] [1989] 1 W.L.R. 29.
[189] [2017] EWCA Civ 254; [2017] B.L.R. 277. The claim was however dismissed.
[190] [1978] Q.B. 574.
[191] See also *Titan Steel Wheels Ltd v Royal Bank of Scotland Plc* [2010] EWHC 211 (Comm); [2010]
      2 Lloyd's Rep. 92 (mere sales conversation). There was a difference of opinion in *Hedley Byrne* as
      to whether on the facts a duty of care would have been owed in the absence of the disclaimer.
[192] *Roberts v J Hampson & Co* [1990] 1 W.L.R. 94; *Smith v Eric S Bush* [1990] 2 A.C. 831. cf. *Cross v
      Davis Martin & Mortimer* [1989] 10 E.G. 110.

made and the response received via an intermediary bank.[193] However, in a case like this it must at least be known (as it was there) that the inquiry is being made on behalf of a third party. In *Playboy Club London Ltd v Banca Nazionale del Lavoro SpA*,[194] a bank provided a credit reference to a company called Burlington Street Services, not knowing that the company was acting on behalf of the Playboy Club, a casino frequented by the subject of the reference. It was held that the bank did not owe a duty of care to the club in respect of the contents of the reference because it had assumed no responsibility towards it. Furthermore, Lord Sumption made it clear that in such a case it is not enough for the defendant to know that the statement is likely to be communicated to and relied on by the third party: that must be part of the statement's known purpose.[195]

What is the position where information is foreseeably relied on by a larger group of persons? It has been said that the defendant must have assumed a responsibility "to an identifiable (although not necessarily identified) person or group of persons, and not to the world at large or to a wholly indeterminate group".[196] Most of the relevant cases have concerned accountants and auditors and the key decision is *Caparo Industries Plc v Dickman*,[197] which concerned the statutory audit of the accounts of a public company, which, it was alleged, was performed negligently and gave a misleading impression of the company's financial position and upon which the claimants relied to make a successful bid to acquire the company's shareholding. The House of Lords held that the claim failed. While it was perfectly foreseeable that the accounts of a public company (which are public documents) might be relied upon by a vast range of persons in an almost infinite variety of dealings with the company, the liability of the auditors had to be considered against the background of the statutory purpose of the audit and this was to enable shareholders to exercise their rights in the management of the company; it was not to provide information to investors, least of all predators. Accordingly, a duty of care was owed neither to persons investing in the company for the first time in reliance on the accounts, nor to existing shareholders who acquired further shares.[198] The auditors are, of course, liable to the company with which they have contracted for losses caused by a negligent audit (for example failure to expose an employee who has been defrauding the company).

To be contrasted with *Caparo* is the "auditing" situation in *Law Society v KPMG Peat Marwick*.[199] The defendants supplied to a firm of solicitors, DF, a report required by the Solicitors Act 1974 to the effect that the firm had complied with the

---

[193] Lord Reid (at 482) and Lord Morris (at 493) regarded it as sufficient that it was obvious that the inquiry was being made by someone thinking of doing business with Easipower, but the later cases suggest that some more specific knowledge of the nature of the transaction is necessary.

[194] [2018] UKSC 43; [2018] 1 W.L.R. 4041.

[195] [2018] UKSC 43; [2018] 1 W.L.R. 4041 at [11]. The claimant's invocation by analogy of contractual principles concerning undisclosed principals was rejected. For critical analysis of that aspect of the reasoning, see Grower and Sherman (2019) 135 L.Q.R. 177.

[196] *Playboy Club London Ltd v Banca Nazionale del Lavoro SpA* [2018] UKSC 43; [2018] 1 W.L.R. 4041 at [7] per Lord Sumption.

[197] [1990] 2 A.C. 605. See also the decisions of the High Court of Australia in *Esanda Finance Corp Ltd v Peat Marwick Hungerfords* (1997) 188 C.L.R. 241 and the Supreme Court of Canada in *Hercules Management Ltd v Ernst & Young* (1997) 146 D.L.R. (4th) 577.

[198] The HL did not decide whether shareholders who, in reliance on an under-valuation, sold existing holdings could sue, but since the basis of the decision is that any duty is owed to the shareholders as a whole it is thought the answer should be "No".

[199] [2000] 1 W.L.R. 1921.

professional accounting rules and, as the defendants knew, this report was to be sent to the Law Society. It was subsequently discovered that two partners in DF had taken large amounts of clients' money and this led to payments of £8.5 million out of the compensation fund administered by the Law Society. On a preliminary issue based on an allegation that the report was insufficiently qualified, the Court of Appeal held that the defendants owed a duty of care to the Society: although the report was obtained and paid for by DF, the whole purpose of the reporting system was to allow the Law Society to intervene in the running of a firm in order to protect the compensation fund.[200]

Identifying the purpose of a statement It is clear from the cases already **12-040** considered that the purpose of a statement is not to be equated with the reliance which may foreseeably be placed on it. Thus, a marine surveyor or certifier does not owe a duty to a potential purchaser of the vessel surveyed,[201] even if he is aware that it may be sold,[202] since the purpose of the survey is to promote safety at sea. Similarly, one of the reasons why the Driver and Vehicle Licensing Agency was held not to owe a duty of care to a purchaser of a car with respect to the information contained in the vehicle's registration document was that the purpose of providing such documents was to collect tax and ensure the registration of vehicles operating on the roads, and not to inform "the commercial decisions of those who may choose to purchase registered vehicles".[203]

However, the purpose test is not always easy to apply, for it may often be arguable that there is an additional purpose beyond the primary purpose for which the information is given and *Caparo*, it will be recalled, turned on the court's interpretation of the statutory scheme underlying the audit. A clear example of a secondary purpose giving rise to a duty of care is *Smith v Eric S Bush*,[204] where the immediate purpose of the valuation was to enable the mortgagees to decide whether the property valued provided adequate security for the loan. The knowledge that the report would probably be passed on to the prospective purchaser, who would use it to confirm his decision to buy the house, was sufficient to impose on the valuer a duty of care to him. The pointers towards a finding in favour of the claimant were, however, very strong in this case: the sum at stake was modest because the house was at the lower end of the market and liability in such cases would not place an unmanageable burden on valuers; it was virtually certain that the purchaser would have no form of independent advice;[205] and the purchaser was in effect paying the valuer's fee because he was reimbursing the mortgagees in respect of it.[206] Even

---

[200] cf. *Royal Bank of Scotland v Bannerman Johnstone Maclay* [2005] CSIH 39; [2005] P.N.L.R. 43.
[201] *Reeman v DoT* [1997] 2 Lloyd's Rep. 648.
[202] *Mariola Marine Corp v Lloyd's Register of Shipping* [1990] 1 Lloyd's Rep. 547.
[203] *Seddon v Driver and Vehicle Licensing Agency* [2019] EWCA Civ 14; [2019] 1 W.L.R. 4593 at [66] per Hamblen LJ.
[204] [1990] 1 A.C. 831, para.12-034.
[205] No duty was found to be owed where the claimant was purchasing a residential house as part of a buy-to-let scheme, in part because it was reasonable for the valuer to expect that the purchaser would commission his own report because of the need to verify other matters such as rental prospects: *Scullion v Bank of Scotland Plc* [2011] EWCA Civ 693; [2011] 1 W.L.R. 3212. See also *Seddon v Driver and Vehicle Licensing Agency* [2019] EWCA Civ 14; [2019] 1 W.L.R. 4593 (buyer of classic car not owed duty of care by the DVLA because, inter alia, in the light of the high purchase price he could have been expected to protect himself by stipulating for contractual protection or arranging an expert inspection).
[206] Compare the audit situation, where the claimant is relying on something paid for by someone else.

here, however, a line is drawn at the purchaser in pursuance of whose application the report is prepared—the duty does not extend to subsequent buyers.[207]

12-041 **Purpose distinguished from knowledge of reliance** If the reliance by the claimant takes place outside the relevant purpose, the defendant's knowledge of the reliance is irrelevant: it would have made no difference in *Caparo* if at the time of the audit a partner in the defendant firm had been aware, as a result of a conversation in the pub, that his next-door neighbour was interested in acquiring Fidelity shares. At the opposite extreme, a bidder for a company may extract from the auditors a warranty that the accounts are an accurate view of the company's financial health, in which case there can be no possible defence to a claim if they are not. However, something less may do, as where the defendant is aware of the claimant's interest in the transaction and supplies information relating to it directly to the claimant[208] or expressly or impliedly confirms information he has supplied before for another purpose. In principle a duty may arise even where an auditor simply repeats what he has said in his audit report, provided it can be said that in the circumstances the defendant assumed responsibility to an identified person, which may be possible where he is aware that that person contemplates a transaction with the client and makes no qualification or disclaimer.[209]

12-042 **Ultimately a fact-specific enquiry** While concepts such as purpose may be employed to determine the outcome, detailed examination of the facts will usually be required to see if the provider of the information can fairly be said to have behaved in such a way as to indicate that he was assuming responsibility to the particular person relying on it.[210] In *Precis (521) Plc v William M Mercer Ltd*[211] the defendant actuaries prepared a valuation report on the pension fund of the SG company and this turned out to have seriously underestimated the fund's deficit. Later the claimants made a successful offer for SG and sued the defendants when they discovered the scale of the deficit. The defendants were held not liable. They had prepared the valuation for the information of SG (it expressly declared that its purpose was to enable SG to review its contribution rate) and even though they had provided a copy of the valuation for SG to pass to the claimants that could just as well have been done by SG, in which case there would have been no shadow of a

---

In *Preston v Torfaen BC* (1993) Con. L.R. 48 a surveyor engaged to do a site survey for a housing development was held not to owe a duty to the purchasers of houses.

[207] *Smith v Eric S Bush* [1990] 1 A.C. 831 at 865. For other examples of decisions that turned on the purpose of the representation, see *Al Nakib Investments (Jersey) Ltd v Longcroft* [1990] 1 W.L.R. 1390 (purpose of prospectus inviting shareholders to subscribe for shares was to invite participation in a rights issue, not guide later market dealings); *Possfund Custodian Trustee Ltd v Diamond* [1996] 1 W.L.R. 1351 (arguable that prospectus in the unlisted securities market was intended to influence after-market purchases as well as applications for allotment of shares; see now Financial Services and Markets Act 2000 s.90A); and *Morgan Crucible Co Plc v Hill Samuel Bank Ltd* [1991] Ch. 295 (arguable that profit forecasts in circulars to shareholders advising them to reject a takeover bid were also intended to persuade the bidders to increase the amount of their bid).

[208] See the dissenting judgment of Denning LJ in *Candler v Crane, Christmas & Co* [1951] 2 K.B. 164.

[209] *Andrew v Kounis Freeman* [1999] 2 B.C.L.C. 641; cf. *Peach Publishing Ltd v Slater & Co* [1998] P.N.L.R. 364. See also *Galoo Ltd v Bright Grahame Murray* [1994] 1 W.L.R. 1360.

[210] See, e.g., *Schubert Murphy v Law Society* [2017] EWCA Civ 1295; [2017] 4 W.L.R. 200 (whether the Law Society owed a duty of care to users of its "Find a Solicitor" service was a fact-sensitive question which required a trial of the action).

[211] [2005] EWCA Civ 114; [2005] P.N.L.R. 28.

claim. There was no direct contact between the claimants and the defendants and the knowledge that there was some sort of "corporate transaction" on foot between SG and the claimants was not enough to justify treating them as having assumed any responsibility to the claimants.[212]

Reliance on statement for a transaction different in nature from that contem- **12-043** **plated** Even if the adviser has a particular person in mind as likely to rely on his statement he will not be liable if the reliance takes place in the context of a transaction different from that which the adviser contemplated. However, it is possible that the provider of, say, a credit reference takes a relaxed approach and has no specific purpose in mind.[213] Nor should too literal a congruence between the transaction contemplated and that which in fact takes place be required, so long as this does not increase the liability to which the adviser would be exposed. Where, for example, a valuer provides a report knowing that it will be shown to a particular intending purchaser of a property it ought not to matter that, say, the recipient eventually takes a long lease rather than buying the freehold.[214] Conversely, even if the transaction is exactly what was contemplated, the defendant only owes a duty of care in respect of a type of loss arising from it which he ought to have in contemplation. For example, if a local authority receives from a potential purchaser an inquiry about the maintenance obligations governing a way fronting a property, the fact that its answer is incorrect does not make it responsible for losses which are attributable to the impact on the development value of the site.[215]

J.   Immunities

As with any other head of negligence, there may be reasons of public policy **12-044** which prevent a duty of care arising. *Hedley Byrne* has not affected the immunity from suit of a judge[216] but there is no reason for extending that immunity to a person appointed as a valuer[217] or to an architect granting certificates of completion of work under a building contract[218] and the immunity which expert witnesses had previously enjoyed in relation to their participation in legal proceedings has been

---

[212] Furthermore, SG had supplied the valuation report on the basis that neither SG nor its advisers had any responsibility for its accuracy and the defendants had "accepted" the benefit of this for the purposes of the Contracts (Rights of Third Parties) Act 1999. See also *MAN Nutzfahrzeuge AG v Freightliner Ltd* [2007] EWCA Civ 910; [2008] P.N.L.R. 6, where it was held that while auditors might have been under a duty to the purchaser of a company in respect of losses arising from statements in the accounts used in the share-purchase agreement, no responsibility would have arisen in respect of fraudulent statements about the accounts made during the negotiations by the parent company's financial controller, even if these had been foreseeable.

[213] See *Playboy Club London Ltd v Banca Nazionale del Lavoro SpA* [2018] UKSC 43; [2018] 1 W.L.R. 4041 at [22].

[214] In *JEB Fasteners Ltd v Marks, Bloom & Co* [1981] 3 All E.R. 289 it was held that a duty was owed by accountants to a person whom they believed might be approached by the company for financial support even though in fact he effected a takeover rather than making a loan. The claim failed for lack of causative reliance (affirmed on appeal: [1983] 1 All E.R. 583). It was said in *Caparo* that the case might have been correctly reasoned on its facts and it seems that the accountants had in fact been aware of developments right up to the acquisition.

[215] *Gooden v Northamptonshire CC* [2001] EWCA Civ 1744; [2002] P.N.L.R. 18 (where there was a difference of opinion on what the authority ought to have foreseen).

[216] See para.25-009.

[217] *Arenson v Casson Beckman Rutley & Co* [1977] A.C. 405.

[218] *Sutcliffe v Thackrah* [1974] A.C. 727.

removed.[219] Although there was some doubt about the position of an arbitrator at common law, s.29 of the Arbitration Act 1996 provides that an arbitrator "is not liable for anything done or omitted to be done in the discharge or purported discharge of his functions as arbitrator unless the act or omission is shown to have been in bad faith".

K.   Excluding Liability

12-045   It must not be overlooked that, in the result, judgment in *Hedley Byrne* went to the defendants and that this was because they had supplied the information "without responsibility". There is therefore the possibility in this context of the defendant using a suitable disclaimer to protect himself from liability, or, for example, to limit the persons to whom a duty of care is owed.[220] In such cases, the correct analysis is that the disclaimer prevents a duty from arising (or limits its scope), rather than excluding or limiting a duty that exists.[221] Nevertheless, the freedom of a defendant to avoid liability in this manner is now severely curtailed by the Unfair Contract Terms Act 1977 and Consumer Rights Act 2015.

12-046   **Statutory controls on disclaimers**   By s.2(2) of the Unfair Contract Terms Act 1977, a person cannot by means of any contract term or notice restrict his liability for loss or damage other than personal injury[222] caused by negligence in the course of a business[223] unless he shows that the term or notice is reasonable. Section1(1)(b) defines "negligence" as including the breach of any common law duty to take reasonable care or exercise reasonable skill. It may be objected that this is not apt to catch a statement given "without responsibility"[224] since the defendant is then making it clear that he does not undertake a duty in the first place but this objection is met by the provision in s.13 that s.2 also prevents, "excluding or restricting liability by reference to terms and notices which exclude or restrict the relevant obligation or duty".[225] However, there is a distinction between such a case and one where there cannot fairly be said to be any assumption of responsibility at all and this is said to be a matter of substance rather than form.[226] Where the disclaimer is

---

[219] *Jones v Kaney* [2011] UKSC 13; [2011] 2 A.C. 398.

[220] See, e.g., *Barclays Bank Plc v Grant Thornton UK LLP* [2015] EWHC 320 (Comm); [2015] 1 C.L.C. 180 (no duty owed by auditors to third parties).

[221] See, e.g., *McCullagh v Lane Fox & Partners Ltd* [1996] P.N.L.R. 205 at 223; *Barclays Bank Plc v Grant Thornton UK LLP* [2015] EWHC 320 (Comm); [2015] 1 C.L.C. 180 at [41]. Hence, as was made clear in *Hedley Byrne*, such a disclaimer is not necessarily subject to the same restrictions as operate where a defendant seeks to exclude or limit an existing duty, such as interpretation *contra proferentem*.

[222] Such loss or damage is typical of claims for negligent statements. Liability for death and personal injury cannot be excluded: s.2(1).

[223] Section 1(3).

[224] Or as now seems more common, statements made against the background of an acknowledgement by the recipient that "no representations" are being made, or that the recipient "has not relied" on any representations made.

[225] See *Smith v Eric S Bush* [1990] 1 A.C. 831; but cf. Nourse LJ in *First National Commercial Bank v Loxleys* [1997] P.N.L.R. 211.

[226] *IFE Fund SA v Goldman Sachs International* [2007] EWCA Civ 811; [2007] 2 Lloyd's Rep. 449. See also the approach of Christopher Clarke J in *Raiffeisen Zentralbank Osterreich AG v Royal Bank of Scotland Plc* [2010] EWHC 1392 (Comm); [2011] 1 Lloyd's Rep. 123 of asking whether the clause attempts to "re-write history", i.e., where representations clearly have been made and have been relied upon (dealing mainly with the application of s.3 of the Misrepresentation Act 1967, which

in a consumer contract or consumer notice, s.2 of the 1977 Act is inapplicable,[227] and the position is instead governed by the Consumer Rights Act 2015. Under s.62 of that Act, a disclaimer in a consumer contract or consumer notice is not binding on the consumer if it is "unfair".

L. Reliance and Contributory Negligence

Reliance by the claimant must be a cause of the loss Although reliance by the claimant is not necessary in all cases based upon assumption of responsibility,[228] it is plainly required where the damage arises from a statement by the defendant to the claimant and this reliance must be a cause of the loss. Although here, as in the case of deceit, the law allows for mixed motives, if the claimant, though aware of the defendant's statement, did not believe it[229] or was uninfluenced by it, there is no liability.

12-047

Contributory negligence As to contributory negligence, the case law shows that there are situations in which the claimant's careless failure to look after his own interests justifies a reduction in the damages awarded for negligent misrepresentation.[230] At the same time, many negligent misrepresentation cases involve professional defendants, and empirical evidence suggests that it may be particularly difficult for such a defendant to establish contributory negligence on the part of a client.[231] If the fault alleged against the claimant was subsequent to the point at which he had irrevocably committed himself to a transaction in reliance on the defendant's advice,[232] that might be a case of failure to mitigate rather than contributory negligence properly so called.[233]

12-048

M. Injury to Persons Not Relying on the Statement

The nature of the claim A statement made by D to X may cause X to act in a manner that is detrimental to C, but in respect of which C has no redress against X. The question then arises whether D is liable to C. Putting aside the case where the statement is defamatory of C there is no doubt that D incurs liability where the statement was made with "malice" and causes loss to C, as where D knowingly published a false story that C had ceased to trade.[234] This is the tort of malicious

12-049

---

applies the same test of reasonableness to pre-contractual misrepresentations that induce the representee to contract with the representor); cf. *Springwell Navigation Corporation v JP Morgan Chase Bank* [2010] EWCA Civ 1221; [2010] 2 C.L.C. 705.

[227] Section 2(4).

[228] See para.5-047.

[229] *Rushmer v Smith* [2009] EWHC 94 (QB).

[230] There are, for example, several cases involving reliance on negligent valuations where the claimant's conduct fell below the standard of a reasonable commercial lender: see, e.g., *Paratus AMC Ltd v Countrywide Surveyors Ltd* [2011] EWHC 3307 (Ch); [2012] P.N.L.R. 12; *Webb Resolutions Ltd v E.Surv Ltd* [2012] EWHC 3653 (TCC); [2013] P.N.L.R. 15; *Barclays Bank Plc v Christie Owens & Davies Ltd* [2011] EWHC 3307 (Ch); [2017] P.N.L.R. 8.

[231] Goudkamp and Nolan, *Contributory Negligence in the Twenty-First Century* (2019), Ch.8.

[232] For example, C buys a house in reliance on D's negligently conducted survey but C then negligently fails to notice warning signs so that the loss is greater than it would otherwise have been.

[233] *Webb Resolutions Ltd v E.Surv Ltd* [2012] EWHC 3653 (TCC); [2013] P.N.L.R. 15 at [144]-[146].

[234] *Ratcliffe v Evans* [1892] 2 Q.B. 525.

falsehood, which is discussed later.[235] It is also possible that D may incur liability to C for loss caused by lies told to X under the head of unlawful interference with trade;[236] but neither of these wrongs is committed by mere negligence. That there may, however, be liability for negligence in some such situations is established by the decision of the House of Lords in *Spring v Guardian Assurance Plc*.[237]

12-050   **Spring v Guardian Assurance Plc**   The claimant had been employed by A and had been a "company representative" of G, selling G's policies. He was dismissed by G when G took over A. The claimant then went into business and sought to gain authority to sell SA's policies. In accordance with the rules of the regulatory body under the Financial Services Act 1986, SA sought a reference on the claimant and this was very uncomplimentary, asserting inter alia that the claimant was "of little or no integrity and could not be regarded as honest".[238] SA thereupon declined to authorise the claimant to sell its policies. The trial judge held that while the claimant had certainly been guilty of incompetence he had not been dishonest and that the sources in G who had supplied information to the compiler of the reference had failed to exercise reasonable care, although they were not malicious.[239]

The words were plainly defamatory but the provision of a reference at the request of a prospective employer is the classic occasion of qualified privilege[240] and the finding of lack of malice was therefore fatal to the claimant's libel claim, as it was to the alternative claim for malicious falsehood. However, a majority of the House of Lords held that if causation of loss could be established[241] the claimant had a cause of action in negligence. The argument (which had convinced the Court of Appeal) that the imposition of liability for negligence would subvert the protection which the law of defamation had deliberately cast around referees was rejected by the House of Lords because there were significant differences between the two heads of liability: on the one hand, negligence required proof of fault and damage; on the other, an inaccurate statement might be damaging without being defamatory, in that it reflected on a person's suitability for employment without being defamatory of him. Furthermore, it was argued in favour of a duty of care being recognised that in the light of the requirement of malice the law of defamation provided a "wholly inadequate" remedy in such cases, and that the threat of negligence liability "would encourage the adoption of appropriate standards when preparing references".[242]

It has subsequently been held that a referee can be liable for making misleading (as opposed to simply untrue) statements,[243] but that the duty of care does not extend

---

[235] See para.13-124.

[236] See para.19-020.

[237] [1995] 2 A.C. 296.

[238] [1995] 2 A.C. 296 at 306.

[239] The above is a somewhat simplified account, since the reference was in fact compiled by an employee of GRE, the parent company of G, on the basis of information supplied by other employees of GRE and an employee of A (which was itself two associated companies) but this was treated as the responsibility of G. Lord Goff did not think GRE were under any duty of care to the claimant but the other members of the majority treated all four companies as one unit.

[240] See para.13-057.

[241] For which purpose the case had to be remitted to the Court of Appeal.

[242] *Spring v Guardian Assurance Plc* [1995] 2 A.C. 296 at 346 per Lord Woolf. Similar reasoning applies to malicious falsehood, which is wider than defamation in that the statement need not be defamatory, but which still requires malice.

[243] *Bartholomew v Hackney LBC* [1999] I.R.L.R. 246.

to an obligation to write a "full" reference.[244] The majority of the judges in *Spring* considered that there would be a parallel liability based on the (terminated) contract between the former employer and the claimant.[245]

Other relationships It is clear from *Spring* that because a former employer is li- **12-051** able to the subject of a reference it by no means follows that the same applies to a reference written by a social acquaintance.[246] The speeches focus very much on the particular "reference situation" and emphasise the close degree of proximity between the parties. It therefore seems most unlikely that the law will be developed so as to create liability for damaging but non-malicious and non-defamatory statements which are published generally (for example that a company has ceased to trade or that its sales are lower than in fact they are),[247] albeit that a different result has been arrived at where the entity that makes such a statement does so pursuant to a statutory duty and the claimant has no way of protecting himself against the inaccurate information which operates to his prejudice.[248] However, there are other relationships which are arguably as "proximate" as those of referee and subject. Consider, for example, the case of a doctor who is commissioned by an insurer to report on the health of a proposer or by an employer on the health of a prospective employee. Both cases seem similar to the case of a reference, save that they are carried out under contract with a person other than the claimant.[249] Nevertheless, it has been held that a doctor employed by a company owed no duty of care to a prospective employee when reporting on his health.[250]

---

[244] *Kidd v Axa Equity and Law* [2000] I.R.L.R. 301.
[245] There is some discussion in the case of whether there could be a duty on the employer to provide a reference (as opposed to taking care when he does provide one).
[246] *Spring v Guardian Assurance Plc* [1995] 2 A.C. 296 at 319, 336, 345.
[247] *Smeaton v Equifax Plc* [2013] EWCA Civ 108; [2013] 2 All E.R. 959 (no duty of care owed by credit reference agency for misleading credit report which prevented C from raising a business loan).
[248] See *Ministry of Housing and Local Government v Sharp* [1970] 2 Q.B. 223 (inaccurate certificate issued by land registry); *Sebry v Companies House* [2015] EWHC 115 (QB); [2016] 1 W.L.R. 2499 (winding-up order registered against wrong company). See para.12-031.
[249] Even this is not necessarily true: a family doctor may receive an inquiry from an insurer which is to be answered briefly on the basis of the patient's records.
[250] *Kapfunde v Abbey National* [1999] I.C.R. 1. Of course even if one took the alternative view the purpose of the examination has to be borne in mind. It is one thing to say that the doctor should be liable for causing the claimant to lose his job; it is another to say that he should be liable for failing to warn of abnormalities, at least so long as they are not life-threatening. See *R. v Croydon HA* (1997) 40 B.M.L.R. 40.

CHAPTER 13

DEFAMATION, PRIVACY AND RELATED MATTERS

1.   DEFAMATION

A.   Elements of the Cause of Action

13-001   The elements of the cause of action in defamation are: (1) a defamatory statement; (2) that refers to the claimant; (3) that is published (i.e., communicated to at least one person other than the claimant); and (4) that causes damage to the claimant. The claimant must also be a type of person who can bring proceedings in defamation. It should be noted at the outset that a distinction is drawn between two forms of defamation: libel and slander. The distinction will be explored in detail later, but for the moment it suffices to say that libel is defamation in permanent form whereas slander is defamation in non-permanent form. Damage is presumed in the case of libel and in certain types of slander.

i.   A Defamatory Statement

13-002   **General tests**   A comprehensive definition of a defamatory statement has eluded courts and commentators.[1] According to Parke B in *Parmiter v Coupland* a statement is defamatory if it tends to bring a person into "hatred, contempt or ridicule".[2] Although this famous definition has stood the test of time, it has been said that a statement is defamatory not only "if it brings the plaintiff into hatred, ridicule, or contempt by reason of some moral discredit on her part, but also if it tends to make the plaintiff be shunned and avoided and that without any moral discredit on her part".[3] Another frequently quoted test is that the words must tend to lower the claimant in the estimation of right-thinking members of society generally.[4] Regardless of the test used, it is clear that a statement, in order to be defamatory, must tend to give rise to the feelings mentioned above, even if it does not actually do so. For example, if D defames C to C's best friend who does not believe a word of it C has still been defamed.[5]

13-003   **Whether a statement is defamatory is determined objectively**   The question is whether the statement induces the relevant feelings in the mind of the reasonable person, here transformed into the reasonable reader or viewer or listener. This rules out on the one hand those persons who are so cynical that they would think none the worse of a person whatever was imputed to him, and on the other hand those who are so censorious as to regard even trivial accusations as lowering a person's

---

[1]   Eight definitions are collected in *Berkoff v Burchill* [1996] 4 All E.R. 1008 at 1011–1013.
[2]   (1840) 6 M. & W. 105 at 108; 151 E.R. 340 at 342.
[3]   *Youssoupoff v Metro-Goldwyn-Mayer Pictures Ltd* (1934) 50 T.L.R. 581 at 587 per Slesser LJ.
[4]   *Sim v Stretch* [1936] 2 All E.R. 1237 at 1240 per Lord Atkin.
[5]   *Hough v London Express Newspaper* [1940] 2 K.B. 507 at 515. In *Morgan v Odhams Press Ltd* [1971] 1 W.L.R. 1239 at 1246 Lord Reid referred to this as a proposition so obvious that no one had had the hardihood to dispute it. However, in modern practice such a claim is unlikely to satisfy the "serious harm" requirement: see para.13-011.

reputation. The way in which the claimant or defendant would regard the statement is also irrelevant for the purposes of determining whether it is defamatory. The reasonable person is the "right-thinking member of society generally"[6] and, in reality, he is of course the personification of the judge's view of the state of public feelings and opinion. The reasonable person is a layman not a lawyer and the judge must therefore try to put himself in the position of someone who may be guilty of a certain amount[7] of loose thinking and who may not reflect fully and carefully upon a newspaper story or a television programme.

Changing public views   Plainly, public views change over time. In the reign of   **13-004**
Charles II it was defamatory to accuse someone of being a Roman Catholic or a witch but neither would be defamatory now. Seventy years ago to say that a man was a homosexual would have been regarded as a very serious defamation whereas it is highly unlikely that such an allegation would be regarded as defamatory today.[8]

The issue of truth is irrelevant for the purposes of determining whether a state-   **13-005**
ment is defamatory   Truth is normally a complete defence to an action for defamation.[9] But the issue of whether a statement is true is separate from the question of whether it is defamatory, which looks solely to the effect of the statement on the claimant's reputation.[10] Thus, the statement "C is a thief" is defamatory of C even if D can show that C is a thief.

Statements that disparage a person professionally   A statement that dispar-   **13-006**
ages a person in his reputation in relation to his office, profession, calling, trade or business may be defamatory. This will be the case, for example, with statements that impute breaches of widely recognised canons of business ethics[11] and fraudulent or dishonest conduct.[12] However, an imputation made in a business or employment setting will not be defamatory unless it reflects on the claimant's reputation at least in a broad sense. Thus, it is not defamatory to say that a trader has ceased to trade.[13]

The statement must be defamatory in the eyes of persons generally   A state-   **13-007**
ment will not be defamatory merely because it tends to disparage the claimant in the eyes of a particular class or group of persons. Rather, to be actionable, the statement in question must have had that effect in the eyes of persons "generally". In

---

6   *Sim v Stretch* [1936] 2 All E.R. 1237 at 1240 per Lord Atkin.
7   Lord Devlin's view in *Lewis v Daily Telegraph* [1964] A.C. 234 at 277 was that the "layman reads in an implication much more freely; and unfortunately, as the law of defamation has to take into account, is especially prone to do so when it is derogatory". This view has been described as perhaps rather patronising to the modern way of thinking: *Armstrong v Times Newspapers* [2005] EWHC 2816 (QB) at [31].
8   In *Brown v Bower* [2017] EWHC 2637 (QB); [2017] 4 W.L.R. 197 at [50] the parties agreed that the allegation that the claimant was homosexual was not defamatory.
9   See para.13-041.
10   "The fact that words are false … is not germane to the question whether they are defamatory": *Daniels v British Broadcasting Corporation* [2010] EWHC 3057 (QB) at [46] per Sharp J. See further Descheemaeker (2011) 31 L.S. 1.
11   See, e.g., *Clark v Express Newspapers* [2004] EWHC 481 (QB) (politician "ratted" on manifesto promise).
12   See, e.g., *Turner v MGM Pictures Ltd* [1950] 2 All E.R. 449; *Angell v HH Bushell & Co Ltd* [1968] 1 Q.B. 813; *Drummond-Jackson v British Medical Association* [1970] 1 W.L.R. 688.
13   *Ratcliffe v Evans* [1892] 2 Q.B. 524.

practice this requirement is not quite as restrictive as it may seem because in many cases where a claimant is charged with offending against the tenets of a group to which he belongs there may be an implication of disloyalty or hypocrisy, which is actionable in its own right, even though ordinary people are indifferent to the direct charge against him.[14] Thus, to say of a person that he drinks alcohol in moderation is not defamatory, but to say it of a temperance crusader may very well be.[15] However, to say of someone that he has reported a crime to the police is not defamatory, since the law cannot admit that a reasonable person would think less of the claimant for doing so (even though real people might well do so where the crime was a minor one).[16]

13-008 **Statements that are defamatory by implication** A statement may be defamatory by implication: just as it is defamatory of C to say that he murdered X, it is defamatory of C to say that justice miscarried when C was acquitted of murdering X.[17] As Lord Morris put it in *Jones v Skelton*, "[t]he ordinary and natural meaning [of words] may ... include any implication or inference which a reasonable reader guided not by any special but only by general knowledge, and not fettered by any strict legal rules of construction would draw from the words".[18] Juxtaposition of material about the claimant with other material may make an otherwise innocent statement defamatory. A famous instance is *Monson v Tussauds Ltd*.[19] The defendants, who kept a waxwork exhibition, placed an effigy of the claimant, with a gun, in a room adjoining the "Chamber of Horrors". The claimant had been tried for murder in Scotland and released on a verdict of "Not Proven" and a representation of the scene of the alleged murder was displayed in the Chamber of Horrors. The Court of Appeal considered that the exhibition was capable of being found by a jury to be defamatory. On the other hand, the mere fact that an article about the claimant appeared in a newspaper where numerous articles attacking dishonest businessmen had appeared on other occasions was held incapable of carrying a defamatory imputation.[20] If reliance is placed upon juxtaposition it must be shown that a reasonable person, seeing the two objects together, would draw from their relative positions an inference defamatory of the claimant.

13-009 **Innuendo** In ordinary English any implied or allusive meanings are called "innuendoes" but the technical legal meaning is narrower.[21] An innuendo in the legal sense arises only when the defamatory nature of the statement depends upon facts or circumstances which are not part of general knowledge but which are known to the persons to whom the statement is published. So to state that the claimant is "no Mother Theresa" might imply to the ordinary reader that she was wanting in kindness or charity because people generally know about Mother Theresa; but to say of a surgeon that he had carried out 10 private operations last week would convey

---

14   *Leetham v Rank* (1912) 57 Sol. Jo. 111; *Myroft v Sleight* (1921) 90 L.J.K.B. 883.
15   Compare *Peck v Tribune Co* 214 U.S. 185 (1909).
16   *Byrne v Deane* [1937] 1 K.B. 818.
17   See, e.g., Lord Reid and Lord Devlin in *Lewis v Daily Telegraph* [1964] A.C. 234 at 258 and 280 respectively.
18   [1963] 1 W.L.R. 1362 at 1370–1371.
19   [1894] 1 Q.B. 671.
20   *Wheeler v Somerfield* [1966] 2 Q.B. 94.
21   Lord Devlin in *Lewis v Daily Telegraph* [1964] A.C. 234 at 279 doubted the value of the technical distinction.

nothing defamatory at all except to people who know that he is contracted full time to the National Health Service, in which case it might carry the implication that he was "moonlighting". Each innuendo is a separate cause of action[22] and the claimant must identify the persons with knowledge of the special facts to whom he alleges the words were published and prove their knowledge[23] and publication to them. So if it is stated that the claimant was seen entering a particular house that is a brothel, but the nature of the house is not specified, the words are defamatory only in so far as it is proved that they were published to persons who knew the character of the house.[24] If, however, the claimant fails to establish the supporting facts for the innuendo he may, of course, still fall back on the ordinary meaning of the words if those are defamatory. The line between what is and is not innuendo may be very difficult to draw because it turns on the general knowledge possessed by ordinary people and this changes from time to time.[25] Nowadays most people know what the Mafia is and so words alleging that a company is controlled by the Mafia are defamatory in their ordinary meaning,[26] but, "cony-catcher" is unlikely to convey much to people today, though it was once a common word for a swindler; and a knowledge of biblical allusions and characters is probably far less common now than would have been assumed by Victorian judges.

Mere vulgar abuse   It is commonly said that mere vulgar spoken abuse is not   **13-010**
defamation[27] but this needs some explanation. Spoken words that are prima facie defamatory are not actionable if it is clear that they were uttered merely as general vituperation *and* were so understood by those who heard them,[28] and the same applies to words spoken in jest.[29] The burden is on the defendant to show that his listeners understood the words in a non-defamatory sense.[30] This makes the manner and context in which the words were spoken very important—for example, whether they are used deliberately in cold blood or bawled out at the height of a violent quarrel. It is generally said that written words cannot be protected as abuse because the defendant had time for reflection before he wrote and his readers may know nothing of any dispute or other circumstances which caused him to write as

---

22   *Grubb v Bristol United Press Ltd* [1963] 1 Q.B. 309 at 327.
23   At the time of the publication: *Grappelli v Derek Block (Holdings) Ltd* [1981] 1 W.L.R. 822.
24   Lord Devlin's example in *Lewis v Daily Telegraph* [1964] A.C. 234 at 278. It seems that in principle a defendant may contend that words which are defamatory in their ordinary sense are not so because of special knowledge possessed by the persons to whom they were published, but he will have to show that all the persons to whom the words were published knew those facts, which might be very difficult, and indeed impossible in the case of a generally circulated libel: *Hankinson v Bilby* (1847) 16 M. & W. 422; 153 E.R. 1262.
25   In *Lennon v Scottish Daily Record and Sunday Mail Ltd* [2004] EWHC 359 (QB); [2004] E.M.L.R. 18 it was suggested that the ordinary reader must now be credited with having achieved a level of education which was not widely accessible to earlier generations.
26   Even "Mafia" may be used in a non-defamatory, metaphorical sense meaning a close-knit group: *Brooks v Lind, The Times,* 26 March 1997.
27   "For mere general abuse spoken no action lies": *Thorley v Kerry* (1812) 4 Taunt. 355 at 365; 128 E.R. 367 at 371 per Mansfield CJ. See also *Parkins v Scott* (1862) 1 H. & C. 153 at 158–159; 158 E.R. 839 at 841–842; *Trimingham v Associated Newspapers* [2012] EWHC 1296 (QB); [2012] 4 All E.R. 717 at [69]. Abuse may of course be a crime. It might also give rise to an action for harassment: see paras 4-034ff.
28   For entertaining cases on abuse see *Rambo v Cohen* 587 N.E. 2d 147 (Ind. 1992) and *Ralston v Fomich* [1994] 2 W.W.R. 284.
29   *Donoghue v Hayes* (1831) Hayes (Ir. Ex.) R. 265.
30   *Penfold v Westcote* (1806) 2 B. & P.N.R. 335; 127 E.R. 656.

he did. However, it is hard to see why there should be any absolute rule and it is submitted that the same should be true where a jest is expressed in writing or in a cartoon.

13-011 **Serious harm requirement** By virtue of s.1(1) of the Defamation Act 2013, a "statement is not defamatory unless its publication has caused or is likely to cause serious harm to the reputation of the claimant".[31] Section 1(2) provides that in the case of a body that trades for profit, the serious harm requirement will not be satisfied unless the statement "has caused or is likely to cause the body serious financial loss".[32] The existence of such harm, or the likelihood thereof, must be proven as a matter of fact,[33] and this is an additional requirement to the need to establish that the statement complained of has the tendency to lower the claimant in the estimation of others.[34] Put differently, the existence of serious harm must be ascertained by reference to its impact and not solely in view of the meaning of the words.

"Serious harm" is greater harm than, for example, "substantial harm".[35] In determining whether serious harm has been caused, the relevant time for the enquiry is the date on which the claim was issued.[36] The mere fact that a statement has been published to just a few people will not mean that the serious harm requirement is unsatisfied.[37] But where a seriously defamatory statement has been republished by the mass media the requirement is very likely to be met,[38] although difficult questions of causation may well arise where a publication contains several defamatory statements only some of which are the subject of litigation (because of, for example, limitation bars).[39] In such circumstances, it is likely to be challenging to ascertain whether the harm complained of is traceable to the defamatory statement or statements in respect of which proceedings have been brought. In deciding the question of serious harm, weight will ordinarily be placed on any apology that the defendant has made.[40] A claimant cannot satisfy the serious harm requirement by referring to two or more defamatory imputations neither of which independently satisfy the requirement.[41]

---

[31] Claims in which the claimant had suffered only trivial harm can be struck out as an abuse of process: *Jameel v Dow Jones & Co Inc* [2005] EWCA Civ 75; [2005] Q.B. 946; *Khader v Aziz* [2010] EWCA Civ 716; [2010] 1 W.L.R. 2673. However, it is expected that this jurisdiction will be of reduced significance in view of the serious harm requirement, and it has been said that the court should start by considering the latter: *Ames v Spamhaus Project Ltd* [2015] EWHC 127 (QB); [2015] 1 W.L.R. 3409 at [50]–[51].

[32] As to s.1(2), see *Brett Wilson LLP v Persons Unknown* [2015] EWHC 2628 (QB); [2016] 4 W.L.R. 69; *Undre v London Borough of Harrow* [2016] EWHC 931 (QB); [2017] E.M.L.R. 3

[33] However, a case on serious harm can be established on the basis of inference, especially where the imputation is serious and its publication widespread: *Hourani v Thomson* [2017] EWHC 432 (QB) at [125].

[34] *Lachaux v Independent Print Ltd* [2019] UKSC 27; [2020] A.C. 612.

[35] *Cooke v MGN Ltd* [2014] EWHC 2831 (QB); [2015] 1 W.L.R. 895 at [37].

[36] *Cooke v MGN Ltd* [2014] EWHC 2831 (QB); [2015] 1 W.L.R. 895 at [32].

[37] "Very serious harm to reputation can be caused by publication to a relatively small number of publishees": *Turley v Unite the Union* [2019] EWHC 3547 (QB) at [109] per Nicklin J.

[38] *Sobrinho v Impress Publishing SA* [2016] EWHC 66; [2016] E.M.L.R. 12 at [47].

[39] *Sobrinho v Impress Publishing SA* [2016] EWHC 66; [2016] E.M.L.R. 12 at [49].

[40] *Cooke v MGN Ltd* [2014] EWHC 2831 (QB); [2015] 1 W.L.R. 895 at [44].

[41] *Sube v News Group Newspapers Ltd* [2018] EWHC 1961 (QB); [2018] 1 W.L.R. 5767 at [22].

ii. Reference to the Claimant

The claimant need not be named The tort of defamation is not committed un- **13-012**
less the defamatory statement refers to the claimant. If the claimant is mentioned
by name there is usually no difficulty in establishing this requirement, but the claimant need not be named, for the issue is whether the statement may be understood
by reasonable people as referring to the claimant. For example, the claimant might
be referred to by a nickname or by initials[42] or by his job or by reference to some
allegorical or historical character. In *J'Anson v Stuart*[43] a newspaper paragraph
stated: "This diabolical character, like Polyphemus the man-eater, has but one eye,
and is well-known to all persons acquainted with the name of a certain noble
circumnavigator." It was clear that the claimant was the person referred to on his
giving proof that he had only one eye and bore a name similar to that of a famous
admiral named Anson.

A statement may refer to more than one person A reference to A may by **13-013**
implication also refer to B, so that, for example, a derogatory statement about the
conduct of a company may impute wrongdoing or incompetence to its directors or
officers.[44]

The claimant may rely on innuendo to satisfy the reference requirement In **13-014**
many cases there is at least some "peg" in the article that points to the claimant but
this is not necessary. In *Morgan v Odhams Press Ltd*[45] a newspaper article alleged
that a young woman had been kidnapped by a dog-doping gang. At the relevant time
the woman had been staying at the claimant's flat and the claimant produced six witnesses who swore that they understood from the article that he was connected with
the gang. A majority of the House of Lords held that these facts constituted sufficient material to leave to the jury. The test of whether the words "refer to the
claimant" in this situation is whether a hypothetical, sensible reader, having
knowledge of the special circumstances, would believe that the defendant was referring to the claimant. In such a case it is, of course, essential that the claimant shows
that the material was published to persons who knew the special facts. Where, on
the other hand, the article identifies the claimant on its face, so that no true innuendo is necessary, it seems that the claimant does not need to show that anyone
who read it knew him and therefore was actually put in mind of him. Provided there
is evidence that the words were published to others, the question is whether
ordinary, sensible readers, knowing of the claimant, would consider that the words
referred to him (although evidence that people actually did so may of course inflate
the damages). Thus, in *Shevill v Presse Alliance SA*[46] the court refused to strike out
a claim by a claimant in Yorkshire in respect of an issue of *France Soir*, of which
perhaps 10 copies had been sold in Yorkshire and 230 in England and Wales.

---

[42] See *Heller v Bianco* 244 P. (2d) 757 (Cal. 1952) (Christian name and telephone number on toilet
wall).
[43] (1787) 1 Term Rep. 748; 99 E.R. 1357.
[44] *Aspro Travel Ltd v Owners Abroad Group* [1996] 1 W.L.R. 132. For the reverse case of imputations about officers reflecting on the company, see *Jameel v Times Newspapers Ltd* [2004] EWCA
Civ 983; [2004] E.M.L.R. 31.
[45] [1971] 1 W.L.R. 1239.
[46] [1992] 1 W.L.R. 1. A minimal publication may mean that the serious harm requirement is unsatisfied:
see para.13-011.

13-015 Circumstances in which recourse may be made to subsequent publications Where a defamatory publication does not sufficiently identify the claimant, he may rely for identification purposes on a subsequent publication by the same defendant,[47] or on a forthcoming publication by another to which the defendant draws attention.[48] It has been said that were the law otherwise, it would be open to a newspaper to publish a virulent libel without identifying the person defamed but adding a statement that the victim would be identified in a week's time.[49]

13-016 The defendant's intention is irrelevant As is the case in relation to the requirement that the statement be defamatory,[50] the ultimate question with respect to the requirement of reference to the claimant is not what the defendant intended but what the words can reasonably be understood as conveying. Therefore, the reference requirement may be satisfied even if the defendant intended to write about a fictitious character. In *Hulton & Co v Jones*[51] H were newspaper proprietors who published a humorous account of a motor festival at Dieppe in which imputations were cast on the morals of one Artemus Jones, a churchwarden at Peckham. The writer of the article and the editor of the paper maintained that this individual was intended to be purely fictitious.[52] In fact there was a barrister named Artemus Jones, who was not a churchwarden, did not live in Peckham and had taken no part in the Dieppe motor festival. He sued H for libel and friends of his swore that they believed the article referred to him. In affirming a verdict for the claimant the House of Lords held that there was evidence upon which the jury could have come to the conclusion that reasonable people would believe the claimant was referred to and that it was immaterial that the defendants did not intend to defame him. It logically follows from *Hulton* that if D intends to defame X, about whom the statement is true, and reasonable people might take it as referring to C, then D has defamed C. This was accepted by the Court of Appeal in *Newstead v London Express*,[53] where a report of the conviction of "Harold Newstead, thirty year old Camberwell man" for bigamy was held to be actionable by another Harold Newstead in Camberwell of about the same age.

A minor qualification to the foregoing concerns so-called "look-alike cases". In *O'Shea v MGN Ltd*[54] the defendants published an advertisement for pornographic internet services that contained a photograph of a woman who was alleged to be the "spit and image" of the claimant. Morland J held that the reference requirement was satisfied according to the law as articulated by *Hulton* and *Newstead*. However, he concluded that such a result would be incompatible with art.10 of the European Convention on Human Rights and, consequently, the claim was dismissed as having no reasonable prospect of success. Morland J said[55]:

> "It would impose an impossible burden on a publisher if he were required to check if the true picture of someone resembled someone else who because of the context of the picture

---

[47] *Hayward v Thompson* [1982] Q.B. 47.
[48] *Baltinos v Foreign Language Publications Ltd* (1986) 6 N.S.W.L.R. 85.
[49] *Hayward v Thompson* [1982] Q.B. 47 at 72.
[50] See para.13-002.
[51] [1910] A.C. 20.
[52] Though whether that was true is open to question: see Mitchell (1999) 20 J.L.H. 64.
[53] [1940] 1 K.B. 377.
[54] [2001] E.M.L.R. 40.
[55] [2001] E.M.L.R. 40 at [43].

was defamed. Examples are legion—unlawful violence in street protest demonstrations, looting, hooliganism at football matches, people apparently leaving or entering Court with criminal defendants and investigative journalism into drug dealing, corruption, child abuse and prostitution."

References to a group of persons   Whether an individual can sue in respect of **13-017** words directed against a group, or body, or class of persons generally was considered by the House of Lords in *Knuppfer v London Express Newspaper Ltd*,[56] and the law may be summarised as follows: (1) the crucial question is whether the words were published "of the claimant" in the sense that he can be said to be personally pointed at; (2) normally, where the defamatory statement is directed at a class of persons, no individual belonging to the class is entitled to say that the words were published of him;[57] (3) words that appear to apply to a class may be actionable if there is something in them, or in the circumstances in which they were published, that indicates a particular claimant or claimants;[58] (4) in practice the smaller the group upon which the attack is directed the more likely it is that the claimant will be able to make out a case; and (5) where the charge is very specific and levelled against an entire group it is possible that the reference requirement would be satisfied in relation to each member of the group, irrespective of the group's size.[59] A conundrum arises where a charge is made in terms like "one of these people stole my watch". It might be argued that the statement does not impute the wrongdoing to any individual, but it is not clear that this is the law[60] and the statement would seem to impute suspicion, which is itself defamatory, though to a lesser degree.[61]

iii.   Publication

Generally   The tort of defamation is not committed unless the statement **13-018** concerned is communicated to at least one person other than the claimant. Thus, simply making a statement to the claimant alone is not actionable. This is because the tort of defamation is concerned with protecting reputation rather than one's opinion of oneself.

Any statement is capable of being a publication   Publication in the com- **13-019** mercial sense, as in a book or newspaper or broadcast, is not necessary, although these are of course likely to attract larger damages. A statement made by any means whatsoever is in principle capable of satisfying the publication requirement.

The statement need not be published to more than a single person   Publica- **13-020** tion to one person will suffice to give rise to liability. However, the fact that a statement has been published to only one person may mean that the court would strike

---

[56]   [1944] A.C. 116.
[57]   "[I]f a man wrote that all lawyers were thieves, no particular lawyer could sue him unless there was something to point to the particular individual": *Eastwood v Holmes* (1858) 1 F. & F. 347 at 349; 175 E.R. 758 at 759 per Willes J.
[58]   *Le Fanu v Malcolmson* (1848) 11 H.L.C. 637.
[59]   *Knuppfer v London Express Newspaper Ltd* [1944] A.C. 116 at 124.
[60]   *Farrington v Leigh, The Times,* 10 December 1987.
[61]   *Lewis v Daily Telegraph* [1964] A.C. 234.

any claim brought out as an abuse of process.[62] Further, the claimant may have difficulty satisfying the "serious harm" requirement.[63]

13-021 **Each publication gives rise to a separate cause of action subject to statutory exceptions** At common law, each time a defamatory statement is published a separate cause of action arises.[64] This rule is highly significant since it means that every time a statement is republished a new limitation period commences. Section 8 of the Defamation Act 2013 creates an exception to this rule. Section 8 applies when D publishes a statement "to the public" and subsequently republishes the statement or a statement that is substantially the same, whether or not to the public. When s.8 is enlivened, new limitation periods will not be triggered by the republication. Section 8 was enacted principally to deal with the perceived problem of online archives. At common law, each time a website is accessed and material downloaded, the material in question is treated as republished and the republication triggers a fresh limitation period. The concern was therefore that website operators would purge archived material or not establish archives in the first place due to a fear of incurring liability in defamation indefinitely. It is important to note that s.8(6)(a) provides that s.8 does not affect the court's discretion to extend the limitation period under s.32A of the Limitation Act 1980.[65] This discretion may significantly reduce the importance of s.8.

13-022 **Statements made to and by one's assistant** When a printer or typist hands back to the author a defamatory document processed by the former on the latter's instructions, that is not a publication by the printer or typist,[66] but there is, of course, publication to them when the author sends the document to them in the first place. Unless a defence applies, it follows that if a manager of a company in the course of his duties dictates to a secretary a memorandum defamatory of a fellow employee, not only has the manager committed libel but the company is also vicariously liable.[67]

13-023 **Communications between spouses** Communication of defamatory matter by a husband to his wife or vice versa is not a publication: that which passes between them is protected on the ground that any other rule "might lead to disastrous results to social life".[68] This rule probably emerged as a result of the doctrine of unity (which is now largely a relic of a bygone age)—namely, the idea that husband and wife are one person in the eyes of the law. This supported the rule that communications between spouses could not satisfy the publication requirement on the logic that a person could not publish a statement to himself. In modern conditions a broader rule based on "domestic relations", however hard to define, might be more apt. Communication by a third party to one spouse of matter defamatory of the other is a publication.

---

[62] See para.26-082.
[63] See para.13-011.
[64] *Duke of Brunswick v Harmer* (1849) 14 Q.B. 185.
[65] See para.26-111.
[66] *Eglantine Inn Ltd v Smith* [1948] N.I. 29.
[67] *Riddick v Thames Board Mills Ltd* [1977] Q.B. 881.
[68] *Wennhak v Morgan* (1888) 20 Q.B.D. 635 at 639 per Manisty J.

The statement must be one that can be understood by the recipient The state- **13-024** ment must be intelligible to the recipient of it.[69] There is no publication if it is in a foreign language the recipient does not understand or if he is too deaf to hear it or too blind to read it, although in the case of books, newspapers or broadcasts it will of course be inferred that it was intelligible to the majority of recipients.

Passive role in facilitating the transmission of information Persons who play **13-025** a merely passive role in transferring information do not publish the statements transmitted. Thus, a telephone company or internet service provider does not publish information that they transmit.[70]

Responsibility for publication by a third party If X publishes a statement in **13-026** premises controlled by D and D fails to remove it (where it is not merely transi-tory material), D (as well as, of course, X) may be taken to have published the state-ment from the point in time at which D acquired knowledge of it. This principle, which is a striking exception to the doctrine that liability in tort does not arise in respect of omissions, is nicely illustrated by *Byrne v Deane*.[71] In this case T published a statement regarding C on a notice board at D's golf club where it remained for several days. D had control of the notice board and it was held that D published it because it failed to remove it. In *Tamiz v Google Inc*[72] an issue arose as to how this principle may operate in relation to a blog. It was held that once the host of the blog, Google, became aware that a blog created by a third party on that service was defamatory it was arguable that it became a publisher of the material concerned.

The statement must be published intentionally or negligently Unless the state- **13-027** ment is communicated intentionally or negligently, the publication requirement will not be satisfied. A defendant will publish a statement negligently if he should have foreseen that it would be read by someone. For example, the publication require-ment will not be established if D locked in a safe a defamatory note which was then read by a burglar who broke into it. However, the position is likely to be otherwise if D sends a letter to C containing defamatory imputations about C (which would not be actionable if read by C alone) and it is opened in the ordinary course of busi-ness by C's employee.[73] If the defendant leaves his correspondence about for people to read, or if he inadvertently puts a letter in the wrong envelope or if he speaks too loudly so that he is overheard he will have published the material.[74]

Secondary publishers The common law spreads the net of liability very wide. **13-028** In the case of an article in a newspaper, for example, not only is the author treated as a publisher, but so is the editor, the printer, the proprietor and, indeed, anyone who participated in the publication. However, those who are concerned with the

---

[69] *Daniels v British Broadcasting Corporation* [2010] EWHC 3057 (QB) at [46].

[70] *Bunt v Tilley* [2006] EWHC 407; [2007] 1 W.L.R. 124; *Metropolitan International Schools Ltd v DesignTechnica Corp* [2009] EWHC 1765 (QB); [2009] E.M.L.R. 27.

[71] [1937] 1 K.B. 818.

[72] [2013] EWCA Civ 68; [2013] 1 W.L.R. 2151.

[73] *Pullman v Hill* [1891] 1 Q.B. 524. Consider also *Theaker v Richardson* [1962] 1 W.L.R. 151. Where it is no part of the employee's duties to read the letter liability will not arise: *Huth v Huth* [1915] 3 K.B. 32 (inquisitive butler).

[74] *Pullman v Hill* [1891] 1 Q.B. 524 at 527.

mere mechanical distribution of material, such as newsagents, libraries and booksellers, may be entitled to the defence of innocent dissemination.[75] There is a further defence that is available to secondary publishers where it is not reasonably practical to sue the primary publisher.[76]

iv. Damage

13-029 **Introduction** The tort of defamation requires proof that the statement caused the claimant to suffer damage. However, damage is presumed in the case of libel and in certain types of slander. When the presumption of damage applies it is irrebuttable.[77] The significance of the distinction between libel and slander is less important today than it was in the past.[78] Among other reasons, this is because, since the Defamation Act 2013 was enacted, a claimant must prove that the statement has caused or is likely to cause him to suffer serious harm.[79] Where serious harm can be shown, damage will usually exist. However, this will not always be the case since the serious harm requirement can be established upon proof that it is "likely" that the claimant will suffer serious harm. It follows that there may be cases in which the claimant can satisfy the serious harm test but cannot prove damage. This means that the serious harm requirement has not rendered the distinction between libel and slander entirely otiose.

13-030 **The distinction between libel and slander** It used to be thought that the distinction between libel and slander was that between written words (which were libel) and spoken words (which were slander). Today, however, the general view is that libellous statements are statements in permanent form whereas slanderous statements are statements in non-permanent form. Examples of libel are a piece of writing, printed material, or other mark or sign exposed to view, or a picture, waxwork, statue or effigy. On the other hand, defamation in sign language, and mimicry and gesticulation generally (e.g., holding up an empty purse to indicate that the claimant has been robbed by the defendant[80]) would be slander, because the movements are transient. However, some arbitrary lines have to be drawn: it is thought that chalk marks on a wall would be libel even though they may be quickly washed away by the rain. Far more important in practice are the statutory provisions that state that broadcasting, both radio and television,[81] and theatrical performances,[82] are libel. The Court of Appeal in *Youssoupoff v Metro-Goldwyn-Mayer Pictures Ltd*[83] held that the showing of defamatory matter embodied in a film with a soundtrack was libel. Obviously, if a defamatory oral utterance is communicated to a person it is slander and if a written statement is shown it is libel, but an oral statement by A may be written down by D and shown by D to B. In that case D publishes a libel. No doubt A's original uttering of the words to D was slander, but

---

[75] See para.13-080.
[76] See para.13-086.
[77] *Jameel (Yousef) v Dow Jones & Co Inc* [2005] EWCA Civ 75; [2005] Q.B. 946.
[78] Libel but not slander used to be a common law offence. However, the offence was abolished by s.73(b) of the Coroners and Justice Act 2009.
[79] See para.13-011.
[80] *Cook v Cox* (1814) 3 M. & S. 110 at 114; 105 E.R. 552 at 553–554.
[81] Broadcasting Act 1990 s.166.
[82] Theatres Act 1968 s.4.
[83] (1934) 50 T.L.R. 581.

the communication to B is not by word of mouth. Conversely, if A writes to D something defamatory of C and D reads it aloud to B, that ought logically to be slander, but the balance of authority is the other way.[84] If D dictates a defamatory letter to a secretary D publishes a slander in doing so, but when the secretary reads or hands it back to D it seems that there is no publication at all by him.[85]

Consequences of the distinction The significance of the distinction between libel **13-031**
and slander is that libel is always actionable per se (damage is presumed), whereas in most cases of slander "special damage" must be shown. "Special damage" is a phrase that has been rightly criticised as either meaningless or misleading and "actual" damage has been suggested as a more accurate expression.[86] It involves loss of money or of some temporal or material advantage estimable in money. The mere loss of society of one's friends, even ostracism, is insufficient. Hence, while the loss of your friend's hospitality is special damage, exclusion from the religious congregation to which you belong is not, for a dinner has a temporal and material value, while spiritual communion has none in this connection.[87]

The special damage must not be too remote a consequence of the slander. It was once held that if D slandered C so that C was wrongfully dismissed from X's employment, D was not liable because the damage was not the "legal and natural consequence" of the words spoken: X's wrongful act was regarded as breaking the chain of causation.[88] However, this is no longer necessarily so. In *Lynch v Knight* Lord Wensleydale said[89]:

> "To make the words actionable by reason of special damage, the consequence must be such as, taking human nature as it is, with its infirmities and having regard to the relationship of the parties concerned, might fairly and reasonably have been anticipated and feared would follow from the speaking of the words."

In other words, if D slanders C, the chain of causation may possibly be broken by the unlawful act of X, but it does not follow that it must necessarily be severed thereby.[90] Illness arising from worry induced by the slander is too remote.[91]

Situations where slander is actionable per se There are two types of case where **13-032**
slander is actionable without proof of special damage.[92] These may have originated in the idea that the nature of the allegation made damage so likely that it should be presumed. The first situation is where the statement is to the effect that the claimant is guilty of a criminal offence punishable with imprisonment.[93] There must be

---

[84] *Forrester v Tyrrell* (1893) 9 T.L.R. 257; *Robinson v Chambers* [1946] N.I. 148; cf. *Osborne v Boulter* [1930] 2 K.B. 226.

[85] See para.13-022.

[86] Bowen LJ in *Ratcliffe v Evans* [1892] 2 Q.B. 524. For other meanings of the phrase, see Jolowicz [1960] C.L.J. 214.

[87] *Roberts v Roberts* (1864) 5 B. & S. 384; 122 E.R. 874; *Davies v Solomon* (1871) L.R. 7 Q.B. 112.

[88] *Vicars v Wilcocks* (1806) 8 East 1; 103 E.R. 244.

[89] (1861) 9 H.L.C. 597 at 600.

[90] See also *Bowen v Hall* (1881) 6 Q.B.D. 333.

[91] *Allsop v Allsop* (1865) 5 Hurl. & N. 534; 157 E.R. 1292.

[92] There were previously four but two were abolished by the Defamation Act 2013 s.14.

[93] A company cannot be imprisoned but in *D&L Caterers v D'Ajou* [1945] K.B. 210 Stable J thought that an imputation of a crime to a company which would be punishable by imprisonment in the case of a natural person was actionable per se. The Court of Appeal left the point open.

a direct imputation of the commission of the offence, not merely of suspicion of it,[94] and the offence must be punishable by imprisonment in the first instance[95] and not merely because, for example, a fine imposed on conviction has not been paid.[96] The statement does not need to identify the offence in question,[97] and technical language need not be used,[98] but if the words as a whole in their context do not impute a crime punishable by imprisonment they do not fall within the rule.[99] It seems that the basis of this exception is the probability of social ostracism of the claimant and not his jeopardy of imprisonment.[100]

The second exception to the rule that slander requires proof of damage is much more important in practical terms. It is actionable per se to impute to any person unfitness, dishonesty or incompetence in any office,[101] profession,[102] calling, trade or business[103] carried on by him at the time when the slander was published. At common law the exception's scope was severely restricted by the rule that the slander must be spoken of the claimant in the way of his office so that it was not, for example, slander actionable per se to say of a schoolteacher that he had committed adultery with one of the school's cleaners.[104] This requirement, however, has been jettisoned by statute.[105] Although there is no decisive authority, "calculated to" probably means "likely to". That which will fall within the exception is, of course, going to turn on the nature of the office and the nature of the charge: a charge of uncharitable behaviour against a member of the clergy may be more likely to be damaging than the same charge against another person, and to say of a judge that he could not stay awake on the bench would be actionable per se, although to say that he had an extramarital affair would not be.

13-033 **The distinction between libel and slander is anachronistic** The distinction between libel and slander has few friends and it has been abolished in several jurisdictions.[106] The distinction appears to have arisen for historical reasons which are to some extent obscure, although it was firmly set in the law by the end of the 18th century.[107] Even then it was subject to criticism and its abolition was advocated by a Select Committee of the House of Lords in 1843. Rationalisations such as that libel has a greater potential for harm or is more likely to be premeditated do not alter the fact that, as Sir James Mansfield CJ said long ago, "an assertion made in a public

---

94   *Simmons v Mitchell* (1880) 6 App. Cas. 156.
95   *Hellwig v Mitchell* [1910] 1 K.B. 609.
96   *Ormiston v Great Western Railway Co* [1917] 1 K.B. 598.
97   *In Curtis v Curtis* (1834) 10 Bing. 477; 131 E.R. 980, the statement that "You have committed an act for which I can transport you" was held to suffice.
98   *Webb v Beavan* (1883) 11 Q.B.D. 609.
99   *Jackson v Adams* (1835) 2 Bing. N.C. 402; 132 E.R. 158.
100 *Gray v Jones* (1939) 160 L.T. 361.
101 A distinction used to be drawn between offices of profit and offices of honour, but this is no longer the case: *Maccaba v Liechtenstein* [2004] EWHC 1580 (QB).
102 All professions count: *Terry v Hooper* (1663) 1 Lev. 115 at 115; 83 E.R. 325 at 325 (lime burner).
103 The exception was held not to apply to performance of a duty imposed on citizens in war time: *Cleghorn v Sadler* [1945] K.B. 325 (fire watching).
104 *Jones v Jones* [1916] 2 A.C. 481; *Hopwood v Muirson* [1945] K.B. 313 ("the slander was upon the solicitor as a man; not upon the man as a solicitor").
105 Defamation Act 1952 s.2.
106 The distinction has been removed in Australia and New Zealand. It does not exist in Scots law, although the expressions "libel" and "slander" are in common use in Scotland.
107 *Thorley v Kerry* (1812) 4 Taunt. 355; 128 E.R. 367. For detail, see Holdsworth (1924) 40 L.Q.R. 302; Holdsworth (1925) 41 L.Q.R. 13; Kaye (1975) 91 L.Q.R. 524.

place, as upon the Royal Exchange, concerning a merchant in London, may be much more extensively diffused than a few printed papers dispersed or a private letter".[108] Had it not been for the intervention of the legislature in the case of broadcasting the distinction would probably have come under greater pressure. The Faulks Committee recommended in 1975[109] that it be abolished and fears that this might lead to a flood of petty actions for spoken words appear not to be borne out by the experience in other parts of the world.

Republication　If D slanders C and the case is not within one of the categories of slander that are actionable per se C will have no action against D unless he can establish that he suffered special damage. However, if C is unable to show that D's slander resulted in special damage, C will nevertheless be able to sue D if D's statement was foreseeably republished by X and X's republication caused special damage (C will, of course, also be able to sue X).[110] Republication will usually be foreseeable where, for example, D speaks at a press conference.[111] The starting position, however, is that D is not liable for the republication by another person by virtue of the general principle that the voluntary act of another will break the chain of causation.[112] **13-034**

v.　Standing to Sue

Any living human being can sue for defamation.[113] There is no doubt that a trading corporation may bring an action in respect of words affecting its trading reputation or property[114] and the same is probably true of non-trading corporations in so far as they raise funds and own property. However, a governmental body (whether a local authority or an organ of central government) cannot sue even if the statement in no way concerns its "governing" reputation.[115] The reason for this rule, which probably applies regardless of whether or not the governmental body is popularly elected, is that in a democratic society it is important that people be free to criticise the government. A political party also lacks standing to sue.[116] It remains to be seen whether public utility suppliers, which in legal form are now generally ordinary trading companies, although regulated in their activities, can sue. Of course, an attack on a governmental body may be defamatory of individual members or officers and there is no restriction on an individual who manages a governmental body suing in respect of a statement that is defamatory of him in relation to his work for it.[117] **13-035**

---

[108]　*Thorley v Kerry* (1812) 4 Taunt. 355 at 365; 128 E.R. 367 at 371.

[109]　*Report on the Committee of Defamation* (Cmnd. 5909, 1975), Ch.2.

[110]　*McManus v Beckham* [2002] EWCA Civ 939; [2002] 1 W.L.R. 2982 at [44]; *Slipper v BBC* [1991] 2 Q.B. 283 at 301.

[111]　*Sims v Wran* [1984] 1 N.S.W.L.R. 317; cf. *Barron v Vines* [2015] EWHC 1161 at [11] (press interview).

[112]　*Ward v Weeks* (1830) 7 Bing. 211; 131 E.R. 81; *Weld-Blundell v Stephens* [1920] A.C. 956.

[113]　One cannot be liable for defaming the dead: see para.24-004.

[114]　*Metropolitan Saloon Omnibus Co (Ltd) v Hawkins* (1859) 4 Hurl. & N. 87; 157 E.R. 769; *South Hetton Coal Co v North Eastern News Association Ltd* [1894] 1 Q.B. 133.

[115]　*Derbyshire CC v Times Newspapers Ltd* [1993] A.C. 534 (management of local authority pension fund).

[116]　*Goldsmith v Boyruhl* [1998] Q.B. 459.

[117]　*McLaughlin v London Borough of Lambeth* [2010] EWHC 2726 (QB) at [46].

vi. Meaning

13-036 **Generally** It is common for disputes to arise about the meaning of the words in relation to which the claimant complains. This is especially so where the defendant raises the defence of truth since, as we will see below,[118] the defendant will enjoy that defence only if he can establish that the meaning of the statement for which he contends was substantially true. However, because the meaning of the statement can be relevant to the elements of the cause of action in defamation (including, for example, in connection with whether the statement in issue is defamatory), it is convenient to address the rules on meaning before turning to defences.

13-037 **The single meaning rule** The judge must arrive at a single meaning of the words in issue.[119] If one of the potential meanings that the words can bear is not defamatory, "the court is not impelled to select that meaning".[120] Nor is the judge confined to the meanings for which the parties contend, although he will not usually select a different one.[121] Rather, "[t]he touchstone remains what would the ordinary reasonable reader consider the words to mean".[122] None of this is to say, of course, that, for example, a newspaper article cannot convey more than one defamatory allegation. The effect of the single meaning rule is simply that the same "words cannot be treated as conveying two or more charges which are different from and inconsistent with each other".[123]

13-038 **The meaning of the statement is determined objectively** That which the defendant intended the words to mean is irrelevant.[124] Here, again, the test is the meaning that would be conveyed to the reasonable person.[125] The reasonable person is neither unusually suspicious[126] nor unusually naive and he does not always interpret the meaning of words as would a lawyer. He "is not inhibited by knowledge of the rules of construction".[127] However, the reasonable person is fair-minded and will be taken, at least in the case of an article in a popular newspaper, to have read the piece as a whole. The allegedly defamatory statement will, in other words, be read in context. Thus, where pictures in an article might have given the impression that the claimants had participated in the making of a pornographic video game, it was held that the defendants were not liable because the article made it plain that they had not and it was irrelevant that many readers of the newspaper might just have seen the "bane" in the photographs and not the "antidote" in the text.[128] In *Stocker v Stocker* the issue was the meaning of the words written in a

---

[118] See para.13-042.
[119] *Stocker v Stocker* [2019] UKSC 17; [2020] A.C. 593 at [32]–[34].
[120] *Stocker v Stocker* [2019] UKSC 17; [2020] A.C. 593 at [37] per Lord Kerr.
[121] *Yeo v Times Newspapers* [2014] EWHC 2853 (QB); [2015] 1 W.L.R. 971 at [82].
[122] *Stocker v Stocker* [2019] UKSC 17; [2020] A.C. 593 at [37] per Lord Kerr.
[123] *Yeo v Times Newspapers* [2014] EWHC 2853 (QB); [2015] 1 W.L.R. 971 at [85] per Warby J.
[124] "Trite law": *Berkoff v Burchill* [1996] 4 All E.R. 1008 at 1018 per Neill LJ.
[125] "The governing principle is reasonableness": *Jeynes v News Magazines Ltd* [2008] EWCA Civ 130 at [14] per Sir Anthony Clarke MR.
[126] In *Bennison v Hulton, The Times,* 13 April 1926 Scrutton LJ said that "suspicious people might get a defamatory meaning out of 'chop and tomato sauce'".
[127] *Lewis v Daily Telegraph Ltd* [1964] A.C. 234 at 258 per Lord Reid.
[128] *Charleston v News Group Newspapers Ltd* [1995] 2 A.C. 65. *Charleston* was strongly criticised by Kirby J in *Chakravarti v Advertiser Newspaper* [1998] HCA 37; (1998) 193 C.L.R. 519 at [134]. He said that "it ignores the realities of the way in which ordinary people receive, and are intended

social media post: "He tried to strangle me". The Supreme Court held that the reasonable social media user reading the post "would unquestionably have interpreted the post as meaning that [the defendant] had grasped [the claimant] by her throat and applied force to her neck rather than that he had tried deliberately to kill her".[129]

vii. Non-elements

It is important to reflect upon matters that are not elements of the action in defamation. Falsity is not an element,[130] although truth is a defence.[131] Malice is not an element either. It is perfectly possible to succeed in an action in defamation without showing that the defendant was acting out of spite, for example. However, malice is relevant to certain defences, and the claimant will often endeavour to prove that the defendant published the statement concerned maliciously in the hope that doing so will increase his recovery,[132] by, for example, opening the door to an award of aggravated damages. **13-039**

B. Defences

It is very easy for the elements of the tort of defamation to be satisfied. The fact that the elements of the cause of action are so readily established means that defences to liability in defamation are particularly important. They play a much more significant role in delimiting liability than is the case with most other torts. **13-040**

i. Truth

Generally Although falsity of the statement in question is not an element of the action in defamation, truth is a defence. This defence used to be known by the label "justification". However, that term has been banished and the defence put on a statutory footing by s.2 of the Defamation Act 2013. **13-041**

The statement must be substantially true The defendant does not need to show that the statement is precisely true in every aspect: what matters is whether it is substantially true[133] and it has been said that journalists "need to be permitted a degree of exaggeration even in the context of factual assertions".[134] Subject to that, it is a general principle that the defence must be as broad as the charge, and must cover the precise charge. **13-042**

The defendant's belief and motive are irrelevant This defence is concerned simply with whether the statement was substantially true. Thus, there is no requirement that D knew that the statement was true or reasonably believed that the statement was true. Indeed, the defence may be available even if D thought that the state- **13-043**

---

to receive, communications of this kind. It ignores changes in media technology and presentation".
[129] [2019] UKSC 17; [2020] A.C. 593 at [49] per Lord Kerr.
[130] "A claimant does not have to prove that the words complained of were untrue": *Barron v Vines* [2015] EWHC 1161 at [15] per Warby J.
[131] See para.13-041.
[132] For discussion, see *Adelson v Anderson* [2011] EWHC 2497 (QB) at [81].
[133] Defamation Act 2013 s.2(1).
[134] *Turcu v News Group Newspapers Ltd* [2005] EWHC 799 (QB) at [108] per Eady J.

ment was false. Similarly, D's motive is also irrelevant. It is immaterial that the defendant published the statement out of ill-will or spite, provided that the statement is true. It is not that the law has any special relish for the indiscriminate infliction of truth on other people, but defamation is an injury to a person's reputation, and if people think the worse of C when they hear the truth about him that merely shows that C's reputation has been reduced to its proper level.

13-044 **Unknown facts and facts that post-date the publication** Because the sole focus of the defence of truth is whether the statement is substantially true, the defendant can rely on any facts to prove the truth of that which was said. Thus, the facts relied on need not be referred to in the statement.[135] The defendant is entitled to rely on facts unknown to him at the time of publication and even facts occurring after the publication.[136]

13-045 **Repetition rule** Suppose that X publishes the defamatory statement "C is a thief" and that D says "X said that C is a thief". D cannot avoid liability by showing that it is true that X published the defamatory statement as he will be treated as having made "a direct statement to the same effect".[137] D must, therefore, show that the facts asserted in the statement are themselves true in order to obtain the defence of truth, i.e., that C is a thief. In other words, D must prove that the content of the statement was true, not merely that it was made.[138] This principle is commonly known as the "repetition rule".

13-046 **Distinct charges** If the defamatory statement contains distinct charges and D can only show that one or some of them are substantially true, the defence of truth will not fail provided that the imputations that are not proved to be substantially true do not seriously harm the claimant's reputation in the light of those that are.[139] To give a simple example: if D were to allege of C (1) that he had participated in genocide during a war, and (2) while so serving had made certain dishonest expenses claims, proving that (1) is true would entitle the court to deliver a verdict for D on the whole article even if there was no evidence at all that (2) is true. However, this rule only applies where the claimant sues in respect of two or more distinct charges. If the claimant chooses to sue only in respect of one charge (and the initiative is his) the defendant cannot adduce evidence of truth relating to the other charge or charges.[140] "It is no defence to a charge that 'You called me A' to say 'Yes, but I also called you B on the same occasion and that was true'".[141]

13-047 **Common sting** As has just been indicated, it is for the claimant to decide in respect of which statements he will bring proceedings, and the defendant cannot plead that a different statement that he made was true. However, despite this general rule, where several defamatory allegations have a common sting the defendant is entitled to show that the sting is true even though it amounts to a charge of more

---

[135] *Doyle v Smith* [2018] EWHC 2935 (QB) at [75].
[136] *Doyle v Smith* [2018] EWHC 2935 (QB) at [75].
[137] *Lachaux v Independent Print Ltd* [2019] UKSC 27; [2020] A.C. 612 at [23] per Lord Sumption.
[138] *Shah v Standard Chartered Bank* [1999] Q.B. 240.
[139] Defamation Act 2013 s.2(3).
[140] *Polly Peck (Holdings) Plc v Trelford* [1986] Q.B. 1000; *Bookbinder v Tebbit* [1989] 1 W.L.R. 640; *McKeith v News Group Newspapers Ltd* [2005] EWHC 1162 (QB).
[141] *Cruise v Express Newspapers Plc* [1999] Q.B. 931 at 954 per Brooke LJ.

general wrongdoing in respect of which the claimant has not sued.[142] In *Williams v Reason*[143] the allegation was that the claimant had written a book for money and had thereby compromised his amateur status as a Rugby Union player. The defendants obtained leave to allege that the claimant had taken money for wearing the boots of a named manufacturer, for the sting of the libel was "shamateurism", not merely the writing of the book. However, in *Bookbinder v Tebbit*,[144] where a local politician was accused of squandering public money by overprinting stationery in support of "nuclear free zones", the defendant was not allowed to introduce several other alleged instances of irresponsibility with public money. Had the charge been made in the context of a broader political attack on maladministration the position might have been different but on the facts to accept the defendant's contention would be tantamount to saying that a particular charge of wrongdoing necessarily included a general charge of that sort of wrongdoing, thereby considerably widening the field in the defendant's favour.

The defendant's pleadings The defendant must make clear the defamatory meaning that he says is true.[145] This is not quite the same thing as requiring him to specify what the words mean: he may give notice in his defence of his preparedness to prove the truth of two or three different meanings and he is not obliged to pick out one of those as his exclusive defence. **13-048**

Burden and standard of proof The defendant carries the burden of proving that the statement in question is true. Nevertheless, claimants routinely seek to establish that the statement about which they complain is false since unless it is shown that the statement is untrue they are unlikely to be awarded a remedy, and especially not substantial damages.[146] The standard of proof is the balance of probabilities although the more serious the defendant's allegation the greater the proof that is needed to show that it is true to the civil standard.[147] Where the defamatory allegation was that the claimant had committed a criminal offence, the common law rule was that his criminal conviction was not even prima facie evidence of guilt for the purpose of the defamation proceedings, and this meant that the defendant had to prove the guilt of the claimant all over again if the defence of truth was to succeed.[148] However, it is provided by s.13 of the Civil Evidence Act 1968 that in an action for libel or slander in which the question whether the claimant committed a criminal offence is relevant, proof that he stands convicted of the offence is conclusive evidence that he committed it.[149] **13-049**

Criminal convictions The only qualification to the proposition that truth is a complete defence is to be found in the Rehabilitation of Offenders Act 1974. The Act seeks to rehabilitate convicted offenders by restricting or forbidding the **13-050**

---

[142] *Khashoggi v IPC Magazines Ltd* [1986] 1 W.L.R. 1412.
[143] [1988] 1 W.L.R. 96.
[144] [1989] 1 W.L.R. 640.
[145] *Lucas-Box v News Group Newspapers Ltd* [1986] 1 W.L.R. 147.
[146] For discussion, see *Adelson v Anderson* [2011] EWHC 2497 (QB) at [76]–[78].
[147] *Laurence v Chester Chronicle, The Times,* 8 February 1986.
[148] This he did not always succeed in doing: *Hinds v Sparks* [1964] Crim. L.R. 717; *Goody v Odhams Press Ltd* [1967] 1 Q.B. 333.
[149] It appears that s.13 applies only to domestic convictions and that foreign convictions are not admissible as evidence of guilt: *Harrath v Stand for Peace Ltd* [2016] EWHC 665 (QB) at [23].

disclosure of "spent convictions". The Act provides that D cannot adduce evidence of C's conviction in support of a plea of truth if the conviction is spent and D published the statement maliciously.[150] Malice here means that the publication is made with some spiteful, irrelevant or improper motive.[151]

ii. Absolute Privilege

13-051 Generally In certain situations, it is thought to be so important that people can speak freely that the law confers complete protection from liability in defamation, including in respect of false statements maliciously made. The logic is that unless total protection is given, people might be fearful of speaking in case what they say turns out to be untrue and they are consequently unable to avoid liability on the basis of the defence of truth. When the law of defamation confers such protection it gives what is known as "absolute privilege". The term privilege is apt to be misleading because of the diversity of ways in which it is used in the law of torts. For the moment it prevails, but in the future it might be replaced by "immunity". As we will see below, the law of defamation also recognises a defence of qualified privilege. Unlike absolute privilege, qualified privilege is lost if the defendant published the statement concerned maliciously.

13-052 Statements made in Parliament The Bill of Rights 1688 provides: "the freedom of speech and debates or proceedings in Parliament ought not to be impeached or questioned in any court or place out of Parliament".[152] This provision confers absolute privilege on statements made in the chamber of either House of Parliament.[153] The purpose of this head of privilege is to ensure that Parliament is not restricted in its functions by the law of defamation.[154] If a member of either House repeats outside the House what he said inside it, the second statement is not protected,[155] although this rule is subject to an exception where the following three conditions are met[156]: (1) it is in the public interest that the member repeat or refer to his earlier utterance in Parliament; (2) there is such a close connection between the Parliamentary and extra-Parliamentary utterances that it was reasonably foreseeable that there might be an obligation, expectation or promise to speak outside of Parliament; and (3) the purpose of speaking on both occasions is the same or very

---

[150] Section 8(5).

[151] *Herbage v Pressdram Ltd* [1984] 1 W.L.R. 1160.

[152] The Bill of Rights was declared law by 2 W. & M., c.1 (1689). For an unsuccessful challenge under the European Convention on Human Rights, see *A v UK* (2003) E.H.R.R. 51.

[153] The meaning of "proceeding in Parliament" is not free from doubt. See, for example, *Re Parliamentary Privilege Act 1770* [1958] A.C. 331, on a letter written by an MP to a Minister. Section 13(5) of the Defamation Act 1996 makes it clear that the privilege extends to, among other things, giving evidence before either House or a committee and the presentation or submission of a document to either House or a committee. See also *Hamilton v Al Fayed* [2001] A.C. 395 (proceedings before the Parliamentary Commissioner for Standards).

[154] Consequently, it may also have the effect of blocking a libel action *by* a member of either House of Parliament if a significant element of the defendant's case turns on what happened in Parliament: see *Prebble v Television New Zealand* [1995] 1 A.C. 321.

[155] Even if he repeats it by reference rather than *in extenso*: *Buchanan v Jennings* [2004] UKPC 36; [2005] 1 A.C. 115.

[156] *Church of Scientology v Johnson-Smith* [1972] 1 Q.B. 522.

closely related.[157] The claimant may not use statements in Parliament as evidence of malice in respect of statements made outside it.[158]

Reports, papers, votes and proceedings ordered to be published by either House of Parliament   These are the subject of absolute privilege under s.1 of the Parliamentary Papers Act 1840.[159] Extracts from or abstracts of Parliamentary papers and reports of Parliamentary proceedings (e.g., in the press) enjoy qualified privilege.[160]   **13-053**

Judicial proceedings   Anything said, whether orally or in documentary form, in judicial proceedings[161] is absolutely privileged. It does not matter how false or malicious the statement may be. Nor does it matter who makes it—the judge,[162] the jury, the parties, the advocates,[163] or the witnesses.[164] The function of this head of privilege is to ensure that the administration of justice is not frustrated. Justice could not be done if, for example, judges could not write freely in their opinions, and if witnesses could not give evidence unconstrained by the threat that, if they defame someone, they might be sued.   **13-054**

The absolute privilege applies not only to proceedings before an ordinary court of law but also whenever there is an authorised inquiry which, although not before a court of justice, is before a tribunal that has similar attributes[165]—for example, an employment tribunal,[166] a military court of inquiry[167] or the Disciplinary Committee of the Law Society.[168] However, an industrial conciliation procedure,[169] a social security adjudication,[170] and an investigation by the Commission of the European Union into breaches of the competition provisions of the Treaty[171] have been held not to possess these attributes. In any case, it is essential that the tribunal be one "recognised by law".[172]

---

[157] *Makudi v Baron Triesman of Tottenham* [2014] EWCA Civ 179; [2014] Q.B. 839 at [21]–[28].

[158] *Church of Scientology v Johnson-Smith* [1972] 1 Q.B. 522.

[159] Passed as a result of *Stockdale v Hansard* (1839) 9 Ad. & El. 1; 112 E.R. 1112.

[160] See para.13-068.

[161] The judgment and the reasons for it are part of the proceedings, so neither the judge nor court officials who disseminate the judgment need rely on the reporting privilege (as to the reporting privilege, see para.13-068).

[162] *Glick v Hinchcliffe* (1967) 111 S.J. 927 is a modern example. The privilege appears to be broader than the general immunity of judges for acts done in the execution of their office (see para.25-009) in that no distinction is drawn between the various steps in the judicial hierarchy.

[163] *Munster v Lamb* (1883) 11 Q.B.D. 588 at 603–604. This is unaffected by the removal of the immunity from suit for negligence enjoyed by advocates in relation to the conduct of a case in court: see para.5-065.

[164] *Seaman v Netherclift* (1876) 2 C.P.D. 53.

[165] *Royal Aquarium Society Ltd v Parkinson* [1892] 1 Q.B. 431 at 442. See also *Trapp v Mackie* [1979] 1 W.L.R. 377.

[166] *Wilson v Westney* [2001] EWCA Civ 839.

[167] *Dawkins v Lord Rokeby* (1873) L.R. 8 Q.B. 255, affirmed (1875) L.R. 7 H.L. 744. *Heath v MPC* [2004] EWCA Civ 943; [2005] I.C.R. 329 (police disciplinary tribunal).

[168] *Addis v Crocker* [1961] 1 Q.B. 11. That the Committee sits in private makes no difference provided that its functions are similar to those of a court of justice: *Marrinan v Vibart* [1963] 1 Q.B. 234, affirmed [1963] 1 Q.B. 528 (barrister). Compare an organisation or company's internal disciplinary committee: *Gregory v Portsmouth CC* [2000] 1 A.C. 419.

[169] *Tadd v Eastwood* [1985] I.C.R. 132.

[170] *Purdew v Serres-Smith, The Times*, 9 September 1992.

[171] *Hasselblad (GB) Ltd v Orbinson (No.2)* [1985] Q.B. 475.

[172] *Trapp v Mackie* [1979] 1 W.L.R. 377 at 379. See also *Gregory v Portsmouth CC* [2000] 1 A.C. 419.

The absolute privilege is not confined to what is said in the presence of the court or tribunal but extends to statements made in preparation for judicial proceedings. In *Watson v McEwan*, where privilege was held to apply to what was said by a witness to a solicitor taking a proof of his evidence, Lord Halsbury said that[173]:

"[I]f the law were otherwise ... the object for which the privilege exists is gone, because then no witness could be called; no one would know whether what he was going to say was relevant to the question in debate between the parties. A witness would only have to say: 'I shall not tell you anything; I may have an action brought against me tomorrow if I do; therefore I shall not give you any information at all'."

In *Evans v London Hospital Medical College* Drake J said that absolute privilege covered any "statement or conduct ... that can fairly be said to be part of the process of investigating a crime or a possible crime with a view to a prosecution or a possible prosecution in respect of the matter being investigated".[174] Where people answer police questions it may be unclear whether they will be called to give evidence or whether any crime has been committed at all, but it is necessary, in order to ensure that they speak freely, that they should know where they stand when they answer. Similarly, it is necessary for the investigating officers to share information among themselves. This immunity from suit is not confined to defamation—it extends, for example, to malicious falsehood—but it does not extend to malicious prosecution,[175] nor does it apply to a claim (e.g., for conspiracy to injure or misfeasance in a public office) involving the fabrication of a case or the "planting" of evidence[176] and it is unlikely that a case will be struck out where such allegations are made.[177]

Traditionally, a mere complaint[178] or the voluntary giving of information[179] attracted only qualified privilege for they were not regarded as a "step in judicial or quasi-judicial proceedings". Now, however, this head of absolute privilege has been extended to those who make a complaint to the police in respect of a crime said to have been committed against them.[180] It is debatable whether this is a desirable development. Of course, the previous law may have deterred the making of some honest complaints, but the burden of proving malice to defeat qualified privilege is a heavy one. A person's life may be ruined by a false accusation of crime but now any claim against the complainant will be automatically struck out. Perhaps not all whose good name has been maliciously traduced would agree that they should be satisfied with the fact that the Crown Prosecution Service has decided not to prosecute them. If a prosecution takes place and there is an acquittal it is possible in theory to sue the complainant for malicious prosecution but there may be great difficulty in showing that he is a "prosecutor" for this purpose.[181]

It is important to distinguish privilege for the purposes of the law of defamation from legal professional privilege. Legal professional privilege is a right to refuse

---

[173] [1905] A.C. 480 at 487; *Beresford v White* (1914) 30 T.L.R. 591.
[174] [1981] 1 W.L.R. 184 at 192. Approved in *Taylor v Director of the Serious Fraud Office* [1999] 2 A.C. 177.
[175] *Darker v Chief Constable of the West Midlands* [2001] 1 A.C. 435.
[176] *Darker v Chief Constable of the West Midlands* [2001] 1 A.C. 435.
[177] *L v Reading BC* [2001] 1 W.L.R. 1575.
[178] See *Lincoln v Daniels* [1962] 1 Q.B. 237, especially the judgment of Devlin LJ.
[179] *Hasselblad (GB) Ltd v Orbinson (No.2)* [1985] Q.B. 475.
[180] *Westcott v Westcott* [2008] EWCA Civ 818; [2009] Q.B. 407.
[181] See para.20-007.

to disclose information. There are two quite separate varieties of legal professional privilege. First, there is what is known as litigation privilege. Litigation privilege applies to communications between solicitors, their clients and third parties (such as experts) made for the dominant purpose of pending or contemplated litigation. Secondly, there is legal advice privilege. Legal advice privilege confers a right to keep private communications between lawyers and their clients made for the dominant purpose of obtaining advice in relation to one's legal rights and obligations. Legal professional privilege is quite separate in origin from privilege in the law of defamation. However, both types of privilege can apply to the same communication. Thus, the Court of Appeal in *More v Weaver*[182] considered that any professional communication between solicitor and client was protected by absolute privilege in the defamation sense. The House of Lords in *Minter v Priest*[183] found it unnecessary to decide whether any such privilege should be absolute or qualified and left the matter open. In *Waple v Surrey CC*[184] the Court of Appeal said that, at least in non-contentious matters, communications between a solicitor and his client would be adequately protected from liability in defamation by qualified privilege.

Communications between certain officers of state   In *Chatterton v Secretary of*   **13-055** *State for India*[185] the Court of Appeal held that an action for libel based on a letter from the defendant Secretary of State to the Under-Secretary of State concerning the claimant's removal to the list of half-pay officers (i.e., officers in retirement or not in active service) was rightly dismissed, on the ground that to allow any judicial inquiry into such matters would tend to deprive officers of State of their freedom of action "in matters concerning the public weal". The decision in *Isaacs & Sons Ltd v Cook*[186] shows that the fact that a report relates to commercial matters does not preclude it from falling within this principle. The extent of this head of absolute privilege is, however, somewhat uncertain, although there is certainly no blanket immunity for communications between civil servants. It has been suggested that it does not extend to officers of state below ministerial level,[187] and in *Merricks v Nott-Bower*[188] the Court of Appeal refused to strike out a claim for libel based on a report regarding two police officers written by a Deputy Commissioner of the Metropolitan Police to the Commissioner. The position is equally uncertain in relation to military affairs. In *Dawkins v Lord Paulet*[189] it was held that a report concerning a lieutenant-colonel made by a major-general to the adjutant-general of the Army was covered by absolute privilege, but in *Dawkins v Lord Rokeby*[190] the Exchequer Chamber regarded the matter as open for consideration by the House of Lords.

The argument generally advanced for absolute rather than qualified privilege is that a person will perform his duties better if he is released from the fear of being

---

[182] [1928] 2 K.B. 520.
[183] [1930] A.C. 558.
[184] [1998] 1 W.L.R. 860.
[185] [1895] 2 Q.B. 189.
[186] [1925] 2 K.B. 391.
[187] Henn-Collins J in *Szalatnay-Stacho v Fink* [1946] 1 All E.R. 303. The Court of Appeal made no reference to this point: [1947] K.B. 1.
[188] [1965] 1 Q.B. 57; *Richards v Naum* [1967] 1 Q.B. 620.
[189] (1869) L.R. 5 Q.B. 94.
[190] (1873) L.R. 8 Q.B. 255. On appeal the decision was on the basis of witness immunity: (1875) L.R. 7 H.L. 744.

sued altogether than given an easily substantiated defence if he is sued. On this view, absolute privilege should be reserved for those cases in which complete freedom of communication is so important that it is right to deprive the citizen of his remedy for all defamatory statements made about him including even those made maliciously. However, no one could claim that this is true of all communications between all servants of the Crown. The caution of the Court of Appeal in *Merricks v Nott-Bower* was therefore fully justified and care should be taken not to extend absolute privilege further than is unambiguously necessary.

13-056   **Reports of court proceedings**   By s.14 of the Defamation Act 1996 absolute privilege is accorded to fair and accurate contemporaneous reports of court[191] proceedings in public in the United Kingdom and of certain supranational tribunals.[192] In practice the requirement of contemporaneity probably restricts this privilege to reports in the news media. "Contemporaneous" likely means at the first reasonable opportunity after the event (which will vary with the frequency of the journal or broadcast involved) but if publication is restricted by law[193] time will not begin to run until that restriction is removed. It is not necessary that the report be verbatim,[194] nor that it await the outcome of a trial lasting several days,[195] and a report in the press cannot be judged by the standards of a law report.[196] Nonetheless, it should be impartial and should not give the evidence for one side and suppress that of the other.[197] The basis of the privilege is that the reporter is merely the eyes and ears of the public, who have the right to attend and therefore it is said that it is confined to what passes in open court,[198] and does not extend to the publication of the contents of documents such as pleadings and affidavits, which are not brought up in court.[199] However, this may need reconsideration in view of changes in the way litigation is conducted and the provision in rules of court for public access to documents.

iii.   Qualified Privilege at Common Law

13-057   **Generally**   Like absolute privilege, qualified privilege protects the maker of an untrue defamatory statement from liability. However, unlike absolute privilege, qualified privilege is lost if the maker of the statement acted maliciously. If, therefore, the claimant can establish malice, the defence will not apply and (assuming that no other defence is available) the claimant will be able to recover damages. It falls to the claimant to prove malice.[200] Heads of qualified privilege are provided for both by the common law and by statute. This section deals with qualified privilege at common law.

---

[191]   This "includes any tribunal or body exercising the judicial power of the State": s.14(3).

[192]   The Court of Justice of the European Union or any court attached to it, the European Court of Human Rights and certain international criminal tribunals: s.14(3)

[193]   See, e.g., Contempt of Court Act 1981 s.4.

[194]   *McDougall v Knight* (1886) 17 Q.B.D. 636 at 642.

[195]   *Kimber v Press Association Ltd* [1893] 1 Q.B. 65 at 71.

[196]   *Hope v Leng Ltd* (1907) 23 T.L.R. 243.

[197]   *Wright v Outram* (1890) 17 R. 596.

[198]   On irrelevant matters such as interruptions, see *Hope v Leng Ltd* (1907) 23 T.L.R. 243 and *Farmer v Hyde* [1937] 1 K.B. 728.

[199]   This was common ground in *Stern v Piper* [1997] Q.B. 123.

[200]   *Adam v Ward* [1917] A.C. 309.

Two principal tests The common law confers qualified privilege on statements **13-058** made by D to X about C where: (1) the statement is one which D is under a legal, moral or social duty to communicate to X and which X has a corresponding interest in receiving (the "duty/interest test"); and (2) X has an interest to be protected and D has a corresponding interest or has a duty to protect the interest of X (the "common interest test"). The position was stated as follows by Parke B in *Toogood v Spyring*[201]:

> "In general, an action lies for the ... publication of statements which are false in fact, and injurious to the character of another ... unless it is fairly made by a person in the discharge of some public or private duty whether legal or moral, or in the conduct of his own affairs, in matters where his interest is concerned. In such cases the occasion ... affords a qualified defence depending on the absence of actual malice."

It is impossible to classify the cases precisely according to the two tests and there is a good deal of overlap between them, so that where the Bar Council issued a circular on the propriety of accepting instructions from the claimants it was said that it mattered "not at all whether the ... Bar Council are properly to be regarded as owing a duty to the Bar to rule on questions of professional conduct such as arose here, or as sharing with the Bar a common interest in maintaining professional standards".[202]

Both tests involve reciprocity and, normally, some relationship between the **13-059** **defendant and the recipient of the statement** Regardless of which test is in play, there must be "reciprocity" and, generally, a prior relationship between the defendant and the recipient. "Reciprocity" means that, in the case of the duty/interest test, the duty corresponds to the interest and, in the case of the common interest test, the interests of both parties are aligned with each other. As Lord Atkinson put it in *Adam v Ward*[203]:

> "A privileged occasion is ... an occasion where the person who makes a communication has an interest, or a duty, legal, social or moral, to make it to the person to whom it is made, and the person to whom it is so made has a corresponding interest or duty to receive it. This reciprocity is essential."

Watt v Longsdon[204] illustrates these principles. B was a manager of a company. He wrote a letter to D, a director of the company, alleging gross charges of immorality, drunkenness and dishonesty on the part of C, who ran the company abroad. D wrote a reply to B in which he stated his own suspicions of C's immorality and asked B to get confirmation of B's allegations in order that D might communicate them to C's wife whom D stated to be an old friend of his. Then, without waiting for any corroboration of B's statement, D showed B's letter to S, the chairman of the board of directors and largest shareholder in the company and also to C's wife. All of the allegations against C were false. C sued D for libel in respect of: (1) his reply to B; (2) his communication of B's letter to S; and (3) his communication of B's letter to C's wife. D pleaded qualified privilege. The Court of Appeal held that:

---

[201] (1834) 1 Cr. M. & R. 181 at 193; 149 E.R. 1044 at 1049–1050.
[202] *Kearns v General Council of the Bar* [2003] EWCA Civ 331; [2003] 1 W.L.R. 1357 at [39] per Simon Brown LJ.
[203] [1917] A.C. 309 at 334.
[204] [1930] 1 K.B. 130.

(1) D's letter to B was privileged, because both B and D had a common interest in the affairs of the company, and that entitled them to discuss the behaviour of C as another employee of the company and to collect further information for the chairman of the company; and (2) D's communication of B's letter to S was privileged, because a duty to make it arose both from the fact of employment in the same company and from the possibility that S might be asked by C for an employment reference. But the court held that (3) the communication of the letter to C's wife was not privileged. Although she had the strongest possible interest in hearing a statement about C's moral conduct, and although there may be occasions on which a friend of a wife is under a duty, or has a corresponding interest, in informing her of statements about her husband,[205] here D had no sufficient interest or duty to pass the letter to C's wife.

13-060 **What is a duty?** The question of whether there is a duty to communicate the facts concerned is one of law. It is easy enough to answer where there is a legal duty but, in this context, "duty" embraces "moral" or "social" duties that could not be enforced by legal means. Lindley LJ said in *Stuart v Bell* that[206]:

> "each judge must decide [the question of moral or social duty] as best he can for himself. I take moral or social duty to mean a duty recognised by English people of ordinary intelligence and moral principle, but at the same time not a duty enforceable by legal proceedings, whether civil or criminal".

Scrutton LJ in *Watt v Longsdon*[207] referred to the difficulties in this area when he asked:

> "Is the judge merely to give his own view of moral and social duty, although he thinks that a considerable portion of the community hold a different opinion? Or is he to endeavour to ascertain what view the great mass of right-minded men would take?"

The classic example of a moral or social duty is that which former employers are under to give a reference in respect of a former employee. A distinction has been drawn between a statement made in response to an enquiry and one that is merely volunteered. Where there has been a request for information that may show that a duty exists. One is a poor citizen if one stays silent when one sees the safety or property of another person imperilled and it has therefore been held that "when a person has reason to believe that a crime has been committed it is his duty and his right to inform the police".[208]

13-061 **What is an interest?** In most of the reported cases the interest is a business or financial one, such as where a complaint is made about the quality of work done,[209] where an employer informs employees about the reason for the dismissal of a colleague,[210] where an insurance company writes to policyholders about an agent,[211]

---

205 [1930] 1 K.B. 130 at 149 per Scrutton LJ.
206 [1891] 2 Q.B. 341 at 350.
207 [1930] 1 K.B. 130 at 144.
208 *Croucher v Inglis* (1889) 16 R. 774 at 778. If a person reports a crime against himself he may be regarded as acting in protection of an interest, although nowadays this situation attracts absolute privilege: see para.13-054.
209 *Toogood v Spyring* (1834) 1 Cr. M. & R. 181; 149 E.R. 1044.
210 *Hunt v Great Northern Railway Co* [1891] 2 Q.B. 189.

where a creditor informs an auctioneer holding funds from a sale of a suspected act of bankruptcy by the seller,[212] and where information is given to hoteliers about the imminent collapse of a travel firm so as to minimise claims on a travel insurance fund.[213] But any legitimate interest worthy of protection by the law will suffice. "So long as the interest is of so tangible a nature that for the common convenience and welfare of society it is expedient to protect it, it will come within the rule."[214] So it was held that a complaint to the Home Secretary that a magistrate had incited breaches of the peace,[215] to a bishop that a clergyman had got into a fight with a schoolteacher[216] and a statement by an invigilator to examinees that one of their number had cheated[217] were privileged.

Reality of duty or interest   The question is whether the law recognises a duty or **13-062** interest, not whether the defendant believes there is one. For example, if a defendant submits a complaint to a body that he mistakenly believes has jurisdiction to receive it the complaint will not be privileged.[218] However, it might be enough to attract the protection of qualified privilege that the reasonable person would believe that there is a duty or interest. If a person receives a request for a reference from someone who represents that he is a prospective employer but in fact is a busybody, it would be odd if the giver of the reference would lose the protection of qualified privilege because the recipient has no legitimate interest. However, the defendant can only rely on matters which were known to him at the time when he published the statement for the purposes of establishing a duty.[219]

In deciding whether there is a sufficient common interest in respect of a communication it may be important to consider the stage which has been reached in the matter upon which the statement is made. In *De Buse v McCarthy*[220] a committee of the council had been charged to inquire into the loss of petrol from depots and the report of the committee was placed in public libraries in the borough as part of the agenda papers for the meeting of the council at which it was to be considered. The Court of Appeal held that, at that stage, the report being still a matter of internal administration upon which no decision or resolution had been made, the council had neither a duty nor an interest in making the contents known to the body of ratepayers. Although it was not necessary to decide the matter, the court accepted that the position might have been different once the council had come to a decision on the matter.

Relevance   A statement made on a privileged occasion may contain material **13-063** which is unrelated to the purpose for which the law grants the privilege. One view

---

211   *Nevill v Fine Art and General Insurance Co* [1897] A.C. 68.
212   *Baker v Carrick* [1894] 1 Q.B. 838; *Boston v WS Bagshaw & Sons* [1966] 1 W.L.R. 1126.
213   *Aspro Travel v Owners Abroad Group* [1996] 1 W.L.R. 132 (interest arguable).
214   *Howe v Lees* (1910) 11 C.L.R. 361 at 377 per O'Connor J. Not a "matter of gossip or curiosity": at 398 per Higgins J.
215   *Harrison v Bush* (1855) El. & Bl. 355; 119 E.R. 509.
216   *James v Boston* (1846) 2 Car. & K. 4; 175 E.R. 2.
217   *Bridgman v Stockdale* [1953] 1 W.L.R. 704.
218   *Blagg v Stuart* (1846) 10 Q.B. 899; *Hebditch v MacIlwaine* [1894] 2 Q.B. 54; cf. *Beach v Freeson* [1972] 1 Q.B. 14 (Lord Chancellor having no formal disciplinary powers over solicitors but having an interest in receiving complaints in view of his position in the legal system).
219   *GKR Karate (UK) Ltd v Yorkshire Post Newspapers Ltd* [2000] 1 W.L.R. 2571; *Loutchansky v Times Newspapers Ltd* [2001] EWCA Civ 536; [2002] Q.B. 321.
220   [1942] 1 K.B. 156.

is that this goes only to malice[221] but the judgments in *Adam v Ward*[222] are to the effect that the inclusion of irrelevant material may take the case outside the protection of privilege altogether. Either way, a statement that contains material that is not logically connected to the privileged occasion will not be protected by privilege. For example, if A were to make an enquiry of D about C's creditworthiness and D were to give a reply on this subject and to add the imputation that C was a sex offender the latter imputation would not be privileged. In *Warren v Warren*[223] D wrote a letter to the manager of property in which D and C were jointly interested that was principally about C's conduct in relation to the property but which also contained charges against C in relation to his conduct towards his family. It was held that the latter were not privileged.

It seems that the test of relevance is applied leniently. In *Watts v Times Newspapers*[224] the defendant solicitors negotiated, on behalf of their client, an apology to be published in a newspaper for a libel that had arisen from a confusion of identity between their client and C.[225] The apology contained a defamatory reference to C, upon which the defendant solicitors insisted. This reference went beyond that which was objectively necessary as an apology to the client but was still protected by privilege, for the content of the apology was not "unconnected with the theme" and did not include "entirely irrelevant and extraneous material".[226]

13-064 **Range of publication** The requirement of reciprocity[227] means that a publication which reaches uninterested persons and is therefore wider than is reasonably necessary to serve the interest underlying the protection may take the case outside the protection of privilege.[228] A simple example is *Williamson v Freer*[229] where a communication which would have been privileged if sent by sealed letter was not so protected when sent by telegram. Another illustration is *Clift v Slough Borough Council*.[230] In this case a council placed the claimant on a register of violent persons and published that register to 66 council employees and also to "partner organisations" that provided services on behalf of the council, such as environmental management services. It was held that such publication was wider than necessary. While the council was under a duty to protect its employees, not all of its employees had contact with members of the public in their work, and publishing the register in the indiscriminate way that it did deprived the council of its claim to qualified privilege. "[I]f a business communication is privileged ... the privilege covers all the incidents of the transmission and treatment of that communication which are in accordance with the reasonable and usual course of business."[231] Suppose, for example, that D decides to write a letter to X which is defamatory of C and that

---

[221] *Horrocks v Lowe* [1975] A.C. 135 at 151.

[222] [1917] A.C. 309 at 318, 339–340, 348.

[223] (1834) 1 Cr.M. & R. 250; 149 E.R. 1073.

[224] [1997] Q.B. 650.

[225] On the position of a solicitor speaking in defence of his client's interests, see also *Regan v Taylor* [2000] E.M.L.R. 549.

[226] The newspaper failed on the issue of privilege for its position had to be judged independently of that of the solicitors' client.

[227] See para.13-059.

[228] See e.g., *Brady v Norman* [2008] EWHC 2481 (QB) (union journal with circulation of 18,000; about 130 subscribers not connected with union).

[229] (1884) L.R. 9 C.P. 393. See also *De Buse v McCarthy* [1942] 1 K.B. 156.

[230] [2010] EWCA Civ 1484; [2011] 1 W.L.R. 1774.

[231] *Edmondson v Birch & Co Ltd* [1907] 1 K.B. 371 at 382 per Cozens-Hardy LJ.

publishing the letter to X would be privileged. If D dictates the letter to his secretary the publication to the secretary is likely to be privileged too.[232] Such a privilege may be regarded as ancillary to that which protects the communication to X.[233] In some cases, of course, there may be an independent, "original" privilege between the sender of the letter and the secretary based on a common interest. In *Bryanston Finance Ltd v de Vries* it was said that "[t]he businessman has an interest in dictating the letter to [the secretary] – so as to get it written – and [the secretary] has an interest or duty to take it down – so as to type it out for him to sign".[234] A further possibility is that D sends a letter to C that is defamatory of C himself[235] and in the usual course of business first dictates the letter to a typist. The "ancillary privilege" explanation will hardly serve here for the only publication apart from that to the typist is to C and that needs no privilege for it is not tortious.[236] Nonetheless, the Court of Appeal in *Osborne v Thomas Boulter & Sons*[237] assumed that there was some sort of privilege in such a situation.

The foregoing issues have been important because the classical qualified privilege at common law has, by virtue of the requirement of reciprocity, tended to be confined to communications of a private nature and not those directed at the public. However, there are sometimes situations where a much wider range of communication is necessary and justifiable: the issue of a circular to all members of the Bar was held to be a privileged occasion[238] and it was held arguable that the same was true of the publication of material on a website directed at the Jewish community in Britain and warning them about terrorism: "[it] could hardly be suggested that the Board [of Deputies] should address their information by individual letters to each and every Jew in the country".[239] In such cases the fact that the communication is likely to come to the attention of "uninterested" persons is irrelevant.

Miscellaneous heads of qualified privilege   It has been seen that at common law   **13-065**
qualified privilege principally arose (or was denied) pursuant to the duty/interest test or the common interest test. However, there are several miscellaneous heads of qualified privilege recognised by the common law. Most of these have been rendered redundant by statutory heads of qualified privilege and will not be discussed. However, one common law head that has not been superseded by statute concerns statements made in "self-defence" or "defence of others". Such statements are privileged. For example, it was held that a statement by a bishop justifying conduct of his that had been attacked in public was privileged,[240] and the same was true of a reply by a daughter to a statement in the press about her father.[241] The basic rule here is that the defendant "is entitled to protect his reputation by a

---

232   *Boxsius v Goblet Frères* [1894] 1 Q.B. 842; *Lawless v Anglo-Egyptian Co* (1869) L.R. 4 Q.B. 262 (delivery of company circular to printer).
233   *Bryanston Finance Ltd v de Vries* [1975] Q.B. 703 at 727, 736.
234   [1975] Q.B. 703 at 719–720 per Lord Denning MR.
235   If the intended publication is to a third party but this never in fact takes place (e.g., because it is restrained by injunction) it is "the use which the author ... intends to make of it ... that attracts whatever ancillary privilege there may be": *Bryanston Finance Ltd v de Vries* [1975] Q.B. 703 at 729 per Diplock LJ.
236   See para.13-018.
237   [1930] 2 K.B. 226.
238   *Kearns v General Council of the Bar* [2003] EWCA Civ 331; [2003] 1 W.L.R. 1357.
239   *Hewitt v Grunwald* [2004] EWHC 2959 (QB) at [74] per Eady J.
240   *Laughton v Bishop of Sodor and Man* (1872) L.R. 4 P.C. 495.
241   *Bowen-Rowlands v Argus Press, The Times,* 26 March 1926.

proportionate response".[242] It seems that this head of qualified privilege is governed by similar principles to those that apply to the defence of self-defence in cases of trespass to the person.

13-066 **Malice** Malice defeats qualified privilege both at common law and under statute. In this context, malice means use of the privileged occasion for some improper purpose. It was described as follows by Brett LJ in *Clarke v Molyneux*[243]:

> "If the occasion is privileged it is so for some reason, and the defendant is only entitled to the protection of the privilege if he uses the occasion for this reason. He is not entitled to the protection if he uses the occasion not for the reason which makes the occasion privileged but for an indirect or wrong motive."

Of course people often act with mixed motives and to constitute malice in law the improper purpose must be the dominant one: D does not lose the protection of qualified privilege if D receives information that a person D dislikes has committed a crime and D takes pleasure in reporting it to the police. "It is only where [D's] desire to comply with the relevant duty or to protect the relevant interest plays no significant part in his motives for publishing what he believes to be true that ... malice can properly be found."[244] Although a desire to injure the claimant constitutes malice, it is not a prerequisite of it. Thus, malice will be present where the defendant's motive is to advance his own interests or to injure some third person. The central issue is whether the defendant used the privileged occasion for an improper purpose. Lack of belief in the truth of what is said is generally conclusive evidence of malice, except where the defendant is obliged to pass on defamatory statements made by another, such as where he receives a complaint or is under a duty to protect the interests of a third party.[245] Mere carelessness in arriving at a belief, or even belief produced by unreasoning prejudice, is not malice: "despite the imperfection of the mental process by which the belief is arrived at it may still be 'honest'. The law demands no more."[246] Even an honest belief will not, however, protect the defendant if he uses the occasion for some purpose other than that for which the privilege is accorded by law.

Evidence of malice may be found in the publication itself. The use of gratuitous language may lead to an inference of malice,[247] but the law does not weigh words with a jeweller's scales and it does not follow that merely because the words are excessive there is therefore malice.[248] "Malice is not established by forensic imagination, however, eloquently and subtly expressed."[249] Malice may also be inferred from the relations between the parties before or after publication or from the conduct of the defendant in the course of the proceedings themselves, as, for example, where the defendant persisted in a plea of truth while nevertheless making no attempt to prove it.[250] However, the mere pleading of truth is not of itself evidence of malice even though the plea ultimately fails: on the contrary, it may

---

[242] *Hamilton v Clifford* [2004] EWHC 1542 at [65] per Eady J.
[243] (1877) 3 Q.B.D. 237 at 246.
[244] *Horrocks v Lowe* [1975] A.C. 135 at 151 per Lord Diplock.
[245] See, e.g., *Stuart v Bell* [1891] 2 Q.B. 341.
[246] *Horrocks v Lowe* [1975] A.C. 135 at 150 per Lord Diplock.
[247] *Adam v Ward* [1917] A.C. 309 at 327, 330, 335.
[248] *Nevill v Fine Arts and General Insurance Co* [1895] 2 Q.B. 156 at 170.
[249] *Broadway Approvals Ltd v Odhams Press Ltd (No.2)* [1965] 1 W.L.R. 805 at 815 per Sellers LJ.
[250] *Simpson v Robinson* (1848) 12 Q.B. 511.

point more to honesty than to malice.[251] There may also be evidence of malice in the mode of publication.

Malice is "individual". Thus, when a defamatory communication is made by several persons (e.g., partners or a committee) on an occasion of qualified privilege, only those against whom malice is proved are liable.[252] It was for a long time thought that where a defamatory communication was published by an agent (e.g., a clerk or a printer), the agent was liable if the principal was actuated by malice, for the agent's privilege was "ancillary" to or "derivative" from that of the principal and the malice of the principal therefore destroyed the protection of the agent.[253] However, in *Egger v Viscount Chelmsford*[254] the Court of Appeal declared this to be wrong. The malice of an agent may make the innocent principal liable in some cases on the ordinary principles of vicarious liability, but the malice of the principal cannot do the same for the innocent agent: it is *respondeat superior*, not *respondeat inferior*. It may be argued that there are difficulties in a derivative privilege standing alone in this way and that the Court of Appeal in effect created a new head of privilege—namely, publication by an agent in circumstances in which the principal has a prima facie privilege to make the defamatory communication, but the decision accords well with common sense (it would be absurd to hold a secretary liable because the employer was malicious).[255]

iv. Qualified Privilege under Statute

Generally   Various heads of qualified privilege are created by statute. The most **13-067** important provisions are in Sch.1 of the Defamation Act 1996. This Act confers a qualified privilege on "fair and accurate reports" of a wide range of proceedings. The privilege is not limited to publications in the news media although it is confined to reports of what others have said on public occasions or in statements of an "official" or "quasi-official" nature. Thus, it does not cover the newspaper's own conclusions from its inquiries or "reports" that are heavily editorialised with comment.[256] The reports and other statements of proceedings that are privileged are divided into two categories: the first (Pt.I) comprises those which are privileged "without explanation or contradiction"; and the second (Pt.II) those which are privileged "subject to explanation or contradiction". As regards matters in the second category, the defence of qualified privilege is lost if[257] the defendant has been asked by the claimant to publish in a suitable manner a reasonable letter or statement by way of explanation or contradiction, and has refused or neglected to do so. In other words, in some cases, the defendant must accord the claimant a "right of reply" if he wishes to rely on the defence. The idea behind this two-category system is that it is more important that reports of matters in the first category be published, all other things being equal, than matters in the second category. Fairness and ac-

---

[251] *Broadway Approvals Ltd v Odhams Press Ltd (No.2)* [1965] 1 W.L.R. 805 at 825.

[252] *Longdon-Griffiths v Smith* [1951] 1 K.B. 295; *Meekings v Henson* [1964] 1 Q.B. 472.

[253] *Smith v Streatfield* [1913] 3 K.B. 764.

[254] [1965] 1 Q.B. 248. See also *Richardson v Schwarzenegger* [2004] EWHC 2422 (QB).

[255] Even though the secretary could recover a full indemnity under the Civil Liability (Contribution) Act 1978: see Ch.22. In some of these cases the agent might have an alternative defence under s.1 of the Defamation Act 1996 (see para.13-080) but that is narrower than privilege since negligence is in issue.

[256] *Henry v BBC* [2005] EWHC 2787 (QB).

[257] See Defamation Act 1996 s.15(2).

curacy are approached in a manner similar to that under the absolute privilege that attaches to reports of judicial proceedings[258]—that is to say, the report need not be verbatim (indeed it may be a very brief summary[259]) and need only be substantially accurate. The law should take care not to impose too high a duty on the press and thereby to transform "investigative journalism from a virtue to a necessity".[260] Protection is not given to the publication of any matter which is not of "public interest" and the publication of which is not for the "public benefit",[261] nor to the publication of matter which is prohibited by law.[262]

13-068 **Statements privileged without explanation or contradiction** Part I of Sch.1 provides that a fair and accurate report of the following matters benefits from qualified privilege "without explanation or contradiction": (1) proceedings in public of a legislature anywhere in the world; (2) proceedings in public before a court anywhere in the world; (3) proceedings in public of a person appointed to hold a public inquiry by a government or legislature anywhere in the world;[263] (4) proceedings in public anywhere in the world of an international organisation or an international conference; (5) a copy or an extract from any register or other document required by law to be open to public inspection; (6) a notice or advertisement published by or on the authority of a court, or of a judge or officer of a court, anywhere in the world; (7) a copy of or extract from matter published by or on the authority of a government or legislature anywhere in the world; and (8) a copy of or extract from matter published anywhere in the world by an international organisation or an international conference.

13-069 **Statements privileged subject to explanation or contradiction** Part II of Sch.1 is lengthy and unnecessarily convoluted. It will be described leaving out most of the detail. It refers to fair and accurate reports of the following matters:

(1) a notice or other matter issued[264] for the information of the public by or on behalf of:
    (a) a legislature anywhere in the world;
    (b) an authority anywhere in the world performing governmental functions; or
    (c) an international organisation or international conference;
(2) a copy of or extract from a document made available by a court anywhere in the world for the discussion of a matter of public interest;
(3) proceedings at any public meeting or sitting in the United Kingdom of a local authority, before a justice of the peace acting otherwise than as a court, a commission, tribunal, committee or person appointed for the purposes of any inquiry, and before any tribunal, board, committee or body constituted by or under any statutory provision;

---

[258] See para.13-054.
[259] *Tsikata v Newspaper Publishing Plc* [1997] 1 All E.R. 655 (decided under previous legislation).
[260] *Tsikata v Newspaper Publishing Plc* [1997] 1 All E.R. 655 at 671 per Ward LJ.
[261] Defamation Act 1996 s.15(3). These are, at least in theory, distinct requirements: *Kelly v O'Malley* (1889) 6 T.L.R. 62; *Crossley v Newsquest (Midlands South) Ltd* [2008] EWHC 3054 (QB).
[262] Section 15(4).
[263] The fact that there are doubts about the correctness of the conclusions does not remove the privilege: *Tsikata v Newspaper Publishing* [1997] 1 All E.R. 655.
[264] That is, volunteered rather than extracted by questioning: *Blackshaw v Lord* [1984] Q.B. 1.

(4) proceedings at a press conference held anywhere in the world for the discussion of a matter of public interest;
(5) proceedings at any "public meeting"[265] held anywhere in the world;[266]
(6) proceedings at a general meeting of a listed company and copies and extracts from any document circulated to members of a public company in the United Kingdom;
(7) any finding or decision of certain associations; and
(8) proceedings of a scientific conference held anywhere in the world.

Section 6 of the Defamation Act 2013   Section 6 of the Defamation Act 2013   **13-070** provides that statements in scientific or academic journals enjoy qualified privilege. This privilege obtains only if the journal concerned is peer-reviewed. Section 6 does not protect academic speech generally. It would not, for example, apply when an academic writes an opinion piece in a newspaper or in a book, even if the book is peer-reviewed.[267]

Malice   As with common law qualified privilege, malice will defeat statutory   **13-071** qualified privilege. Malice has been discussed above.[268]

v.   Publication on a Matter of Public Interest

Generally   Section 4 of the Defamation Act 2013 provides for a defence of   **13-072** publication on a matter of public interest.[269] The defence has three elements: (1) the statement must have been on a matter of public interest; (2) the defendant must have believed that publication of the statement was in the public interest; and (3) the defendant's belief must have been reasonable.[270] The defendant carries the onus of proof in relation to these matters.[271] Section 4(2) instructs the court to consider all of the circumstances of the case in determining whether the defence is applicable. Pursuant to s.4(4), the court must, in deciding whether the defendant reasonably believed that publishing the statement was in the public interest, make such allowance for editorial judgement as it considers appropriate. Two points are noteworthy in this regard. First, this provision suggests that the courts should apply the test of reasonableness fairly leniently. Secondly, although s.4(4) implies that the focus of the defence is on media defendants, it is clear that it is not confined to such defendants, or to particular types of publications or publications in particular formats.[272]

Purpose   The purpose of this defence is to ensure that people are not unduly fear-   **13-073** ful of publishing statements on matters of public interest which they think are in the public interest simply because the statement might turn out to be false. Provided

---

[265] A "public meeting" means "a meeting bona fide and lawfully held for a lawful purpose and in the furtherance or discussion of a matter of public interest, whether admission to the meeting is general or restricted": para.12(2).
[266] A public meeting does not require any participation or opportunity for participation by those attending it: *McCartan Turkington Breen v Times Newspapers Ltd* [2001] 2 A.C. 227.
[267] Numerous ambiguities in s.6 are explored in Mullis and Scott (2014) 77 M.L.R. 87 at 98–99.
[268] See para.13-066.
[269] The genesis of s.4 is discussed in *Serafin v Malkiewicz* [2020] UKSC 23; [2020] 1 W.L.R. 2455 at [52]–[66].
[270] *Serafin v Malkiewicz* [2020] UKSC 23; [2020] 1 W.L.R. 2455 at [74].
[271] *Hourani v Thomson* [2017] EWHC 432 (QB) at [167].
[272] "The defence is available to anyone who publishes material of public interest in any medium": *Turley v Unite the Union* [2019] EWHC 3547 (QB) at [138] per Nicklin J.

that publishers act sufficiently carefully in publishing a defamatory statement on a matter of public interest they will be protected from liability in defamation even if it transpires that the statement was false. The defence expresses a preference for an increased number of statements on matters of public interest that appear likely to be true at the time of publication being made at the expense of leaving more people who have untrue defamatory things said about them without redress.

13-074 **The creation and abolition of the Reynolds defence** The defence in s.4 replaces[273] what was known as the *Reynolds* defence. However, because the s.4 defence substantially restates[274] and shares the same objectives[275] as the *Reynolds* defence, it is necessary to consider the latter defence in some detail. Indeed, the Supreme Court has confirmed that the principles "that underpinned the *Reynolds* defence are … relevant to the interpretation of the statutory defence".[276] In *Reynolds v Times Newspapers Ltd*[277] the House of Lords created a new defence—a new form of qualified privilege[278]—for the general communication of matters of public concern.[279] It was not confined to publications by the news media but they were almost always the persons relying on it. The defence had two elements: (1) the defendant must have acted responsibly in publishing the statement; and (2) the statement must have been on a matter of public interest. The issue of whether the defendant acted maliciously was incorporated within the first element, on the logic that a defendant who acts maliciously does not act responsibly.[280] The House of Lords created the *Reynolds* defence primarily because of concerns about the compatibility of the pre-existing law of defamation with art.10 of the European Convention on Human Rights. The concerns had arisen mainly because traditional qualified privilege did not apply to publications to the world generally because of the requirement of reciprocity,[281] which meant that, except in unusual situations, the media could not take advantage of that defence.

Lord Nicholls delivered the leading speech in *Reynolds*. He set out the following non-exhaustive list of circumstances which would be relevant to the question of whether the defendant acted responsibly[282]:

"1.   The seriousness of the allegation. The more serious the charge, the more the public is misinformed and the individual harmed, if the allegation is not true.

2.   The nature of the information, and the extent to which the subject-matter is a matter of public concern.

---

273 Section 4(6).
274 *Economou v de Freitas* [2018] EWCA Civ 2591 at [76], [86]. However, according to Lord Wilson in *Serafin v Malkiewicz* [2020] UKSC 23; [2020] 1 W.L.R. 2455 at [66] it would be going too far to say that s.4 codifies the *Reynolds* defence. Lord Wilson added at [72] that "[i]t is wrong to consider that the elements of the statutory defence can be equiparated with those of the *Reynolds* defence."
275 *Economou v de Freitas* [2018] EWCA Civ 2591 at [86].
276 *Serafin v Malkiewicz* [2020] UKSC 23; [2020] 1 W.L.R. 2455 at [68] per Lord Wilson.
277 [2001] 2 A.C. 127.
278 Although described in *Reynolds* as a type of qualified privilege, it is doubtful whether the new defence was truly a form of qualified privilege. The latest word on this debate is that, properly understood, the defence is not an offshoot of qualified privilege: *Serafin v Malkiewicz* [2020] UKSC 23; [2020] 1 W.L.R. 2455 at [73].
279 The House of Lords and the Supreme Court elaborated on the application of the *Reynolds* defence in *Jameel (Mohamed) v Wall Street Journal Europe Sprl* [2006] UKHL 44; [2007] 1 A.C. 359 and *Flood v Times Newspapers Ltd* [2012] UKSC 11; [2012] 2 A.C. 273 respectively.
280 *Jameel (Mohamed) v Wall Street Journal Europe Sprl [2006] UKHL* [2007] 1 A.C. 359 at [46].
281 See para.13-059.
282 [2001] 2 A.C. 127 at 205.

3. The source of the information. Some informants have no direct knowledge of the events. Some have their own axes to grind, or are being paid for their stories.
4. The steps taken to verify the information.
5. The status of the information. The allegation may have already been the subject of an investigation which commands respect.
6. The urgency of the matter. News is often a perishable commodity.
7. Whether comment was sought from the claimant. He may have information others do not possess or have not disclosed. An approach to the claimant will not always be necessary.
8. Whether the article contained the gist of the claimant's side of the story.
9. The tone of the article. A newspaper can raise queries or call for an investigation. It need not adopt allegations as statements of fact.
10. The circumstances of the publication, including the timing.

The list is not exhaustive. The weight to be given to these and any other relevant factors will vary from case to case. Any disputes of primary facts will be a matter for the jury, if there is one. The decision on whether, having regard to the admitted or proved facts, the publication was subject to qualified privilege is a matter for the judge. This is the established practice and seems sound. A balancing operation is better carried out by a judge in a reasoned judgment than by a jury. Over time, a valuable corpus of case law will be built up."

Public interest In order for the defence in s.4 to apply, the statement in question **13-075** must be a statement on a matter of public interest.[283] This hurdle, which involves an objective enquiry,[284] is relatively low.[285] Lord Nicholls in *Reynolds* said that the "court should be slow to conclude that a publication was not in the public interest and, therefore, the public had no right to know, especially when the information is in the field of political discussion".[286] There is no reason to think that the matter is any different under s.4. In *Doyle v Smith* Warby J opined that "[t]he governance of public bodies is invariably a matter of public concern, but the governance of private clubs not so".[287]

The continuing relevance of the Reynolds factors Depending on the individual **13-076** circumstances of each case, some or all of the *Reynolds* factors that Lord Nicholls identified will be relevant to whether the requirement of reasonable belief in s.4 is satisfied.[288] For example, in *Doyle v Smith* Warby J said that[289]:

"Several points from the *Reynolds* checklist of considerations relevant to the availability of the common law privilege are pertinent here: the Court will consider (among other things) (a) the reliability or credibility of the defendant's source(s); (b) what steps were taken by the defendant to verify the truth of the allegations before he made them; (c) whether the defendant sought any comment from the claimant; (d) whether the defendant included the claimant's side of the story. Where the target of a publication has given an explanation, but the publisher fails to report it, it will be difficult if not impossible to claim the protection of the privilege."

---

[283] The test is whether the statement was on a matter of public interest not whether the statement was in the public interest: *Serafin v Malkiewicz* [2020] UKSC 23; [2020] 1 W.L.R. 2455 at [75].
[284] *Doyle v Smith* [2018] EWHC 2935 (QB) at [64].
[285] Events occurring overseas may be a matter of public interest: *Hourani v Thomson* [2017] EWHC 432 (QB) at [166].
[286] [2001] 2 A.C. 127 at 205.
[287] [2018] EWHC 2935 (QB) at [70].
[288] *Serafin v Malkiewicz* [2020] UKSC 23; [2020] 1 W.L.R. 2455 at [76].
[289] [2018] EWHC 2935 (QB) at [82].

Needless to say, the appropriate weight to place on a given factor will vary from case to case. The factors should not be approached as though they are a checklist despite their sometimes being referred to as such.[290]

13-077 **The reasonable belief requirement** The reasonable belief requirement has two parts. First, the defendant must actually believe that the statement is on a matter of public interest. This involves a subjective enquiry.[291] Second, the belief that the statement is on a matter of public interest must be reasonably held. According to Warby J in *Hourani v Thomson*[292]:

> "A belief will be reasonable for this purpose only if it is one arrived at after conducting such enquiries and checks as it is reasonable to expect of the particular defendant in all the circumstances of the case. Among the circumstances relevant to the question of what enquiries and checks are needed, the subject-matter needs consideration, as do the particular words used, the range of meanings the defendant ought reasonably to have considered they might convey, and the particular role of the defendant in question."

The reasonable belief requirement is tested at the time at which the statement was published.[293] A s.4 defence will not necessarily fail simply because the publication contained some minor misstatements that the defendant did not believe.[294]

13-078 **Fact and comment** One change in the law effected by s.4 is that the s.4 defence is capable of applying both to statements of fact and to comments.[295] By contrast, the *Reynolds* defence applied only to statements of fact.[296] It has been held that the s.4 defence can apply to defamatory comments to which the defence of honest comment[297] does not.[298]

13-079 **Reportage** As we have seen, the "repetition rule"[299] says that if D repeats a statement made by X then D is treated as publishing the imputations in it even if D makes it clear that he is only repeating what X said. Since *Reynolds* was decided, however, there has been some modification of this. In *Al-Fagih v HH Saudi Research & Marketing (UK) Ltd*[300] the *Reynolds* defence was held to apply to the publication in a newspaper circulating among Saudis living in England of developments in a feud in a group seeking political change in Saudi Arabia. This was so even though it was obvious that an informant had an axe to grind and no steps were taken to verify the story. The court held that the defendants had in no way adopted or endorsed the allegation: this was a report of a stage in an ongoing political dispute of legitimate interest to the readership and the failure of the defendants to

---

290 *Serafin v Malkiewicz* [2020] UKSC 23; [2020] 1 W.L.R. 2455 at [68].
291 *Hourani v Thomson* [2017] EWHC 432 (QB) at [169].
292 [2017] EWHC 432 (QB) at [173].
293 *Economou v de Freitas* [2016] EWHC 1853 (QB) at [139].
294 *Doyle v Smith* [2018] EWHC 2935 (QB) at [85].
295 Section 4(5).
296 *Reynolds v Times Newspapers Ltd* [2001] 2 A.C. 127 at 201, 237–238.
297 See para.13-089.
298 *Barron v Vines* [2015] EWHC 1161 at [59].
299 See para.13-045.
300 [2001] EWCA Civ 1634; [2002] E.M.L.R. 13.

take steps to verify the allegation did not in such a case prevent the report from being protected by the *Reynolds* defence. Simon Brown LJ said that there[301]:

"will be circumstances where, as here ... both sides to a political dispute are being fully, fairly and disinterestedly reported in their respective allegations and responses. In this situation ... the public is entitled to be informed of such a dispute without having to wait for the publisher, following an attempt at verification, to commit himself to one side or the other".

This rule is known as the doctrine of reportage. In *Roberts v Gable* Ward LJ offered the following guidance as to when it will apply[302]:

"To qualify as reportage the report, judging the thrust of it as a whole, must have the effect of reporting, not the truth of the statements, but the fact that they were made ... If upon a proper construction of the thrust of the article the defamatory material is attributed to another and is not being put forward as true, then a responsible journalist would not need to take steps to verify its accuracy. He is absolved from that responsibility because he is simply reporting in a neutral fashion the fact that it has been said without adopting the truth."

What remains unclear is how far this is confined to the reporting of a dispute. It has been said that "the reportage doctrine ... cannot logically be confined to the reporting of reciprocal allegations. A unilateral libel, reported disinterestedly, will be equally protected".[303] But if we travel far down this road it will change the balance between claimants and the media quite dramatically. It has subsequently been said that the doctrine has no application to ordinary investigative journalism.[304]

Just as the reportage doctrine (rightly or wrongly) was seen as part of the *Reynolds* defence,[305] the Defamation Act 2013 has absorbed it within the s.4 defence. Section 4(3) provides that if the statement in question "was, or formed part of, an accurate and impartial account of a dispute to which the claimant was a party", the court must in determining whether the reasonable belief requirement is satisfied "disregard any omission of the defendant to take steps to verify the truth of the imputation conveyed by it". The case law that preceded the enactment of the Defamation Act 2013 suggests that the reportage doctrine will apply relatively rarely.[306]

---

301 [2001] EWCA Civ 1634; [2002] E.M.L.R. 13 at [52].
302 [2007] EWCA Civ 721; [2008] Q.B. 502 at [61].
303 *Charman v Orion Publishing Ltd* [2007] EWCA Civ 972; [2008] 1 All E.R. 750 [2007] EWCA Civ 721; [2008] Q.B. 502 at [91] per Ward LJ.
304 *Charman v Orion Publishing Ltd* [2007] EWCA Civ 972; [2008] 1 All E.R. 750 at [49].
305 In *Flood v Times Newspapers Ltd* [2012] UKSC 11; [2012] 2 A.C. 273 at [35] Lord Phillips said that reportage is "a special example of *Reynolds* privilege" and warned against "putting reportage in a special box of its own". However, it is doubtful whether reportage is a sub-species of the *Reynolds* privilege. The test that governs the reportage doctrine is quite different from that which controlled the *Reynolds* defence.
306 See the comments of Lord Phillips in *Flood v Times Newspapers Ltd* [2012] UKSC 11; [2012] 2 A.C. 273 at [77].

vi. Innocent Dissemination

13-080 **Generally**   Under s.1 of the Defamation Act 1996, it is a defence for the defendant to show that: (1) he was not the author,[307] editor or publisher of the statement; (2) he took reasonable care in relation to the publication; and (3) he did not know, and had no reason to believe, that what he did caused or contributed to the publication of a defamatory statement.

13-081 **Meaning of "publisher"**   For the purposes of s.1 of the Defamation Act 1996, a "publisher" is defined as a "commercial publisher",[308] which is in turn defined as "a person whose business is issuing material to the public". It was held in *Tamiz v Google Inc*[309] that Google was not a "publisher" of material on a blogging service that it hosted since it did not "issue" information on the service to the public.

13-082 **Determining whether a person took reasonable care or had reason to believe that he was contributing to the publication**   In determining whether a person took reasonable care or had reason to believe that he was contributing to the publication of a defamatory statement, the court will consider the extent of his responsibility for the content of the statement and the decision to publish it, the nature and circumstances of the publication and the previous conduct or character of the author, editor or publisher.[310] Obvious examples of questions which may arise in litigation are: at what point does a publication acquire a "reputation for libel" and what steps does a distributor have to take to check new issues? What steps should a radio company running a live phone-in programme take to "vet" potential contributions? And should the broadcaster in such a case utilise a delay mechanism on transmission? In the case of material which is not of a transitory nature the distributor who receives notice of its defamatory nature will of course be liable for further publications if he then fails to withdraw it.[311]

13-083 **The Electronic Commerce (EC Directive) Regulations**   Internet service providers have further protection under the Electronic Commerce (EC Directive) Regulations 2002.[312] One acting as a mere conduit (e.g., for the transmission of email or access to the site where the information sought is stored) is simply not liable in damages at all. One who hosts information (e.g., stores on its servers web pages produced by others) is not liable in damages if he is not aware of facts from which it is apparent to him that the information is "unlawful" and acts expeditiously to remove it when he acquires such knowledge. Although not identical to the 1996 Act, this is at least similar to it.

13-084 **Internet search engines**   This complex web of domestic and European legislation has not proved easy to apply to internet publications. Take, for example, a

---

[307] "Author" is defined as the originator of the statement: s.1(2).

[308] That is, whose business is issuing material to the public or a section of the public: s.1(2)

[309] [2013] EWCA Civ 68; [2013] 1 W.L.R. 2151 at [40].

[310] See s.1(5). For consideration, see *Tamiz v Google Inc* [2013] EWCA Civ 68; [2013] 1 W.L.R. 2151 at [41]–[43].

[311] *Godfrey v Demon Internet Ltd* [2001] Q.B. 201. Although he must have a reasonable opportunity to make inquiry into the complaint.

[312] SI 2002/2013. Strangely described in the Directive and Regulations as "information society service providers". See *Bunt v Tilley* [2006] EWHC 407; [2007] 1 W.L.R. 1243; *Davison v Habeeb* [2011] EWHC 3031 (QB).

search engine that leads the user to a defamatory publication originally published by another. Does the search engine operator publish the communication to which it leads? Does it make any difference if the "snippet" that the operator shows contains defamatory words? Does the operator provide its service "for remuneration" (a requirement of the Regulations) when it obtains its funds from advertising rather than direct charges to users? How is the concept of reasonable care to be applied when the information collected by the search engine is obtained by web-crawling "robots" that simply look for particular words? English courts have so far shown an inclination instead to deal with these problems via the common law concept of publication.[313] In *Bunt v Tilley*[314] Eady J held that any service provider playing only a passive role in facilitating internet transactions was not a "publisher" at common law and in *Metropolitan International Schools Ltd v DesignTechnica Corp*[315] the same approach was applied to a search engine.

Does s.1 of the Defamation Act 1996 go far enough?   While the defence in s.1 **13-085** of the Defamation Act 1996 gives a distributor a degree of protection, the fact that he is presumptively liable may lead him to refuse to distribute given material. In *Goldsmith v Pressdram*[316] the claimant, who considered that he had been defamed by *Private Eye*, brought a criminal prosecution (as was then possible) against the magazine in respect of one article and a civil action in respect of two others but he also sued 37 distributors of the magazine. Many settled by an undertaking not to distribute *Private Eye* again, but some sought an order that the actions against them be stayed as an abuse of the process. The Court of Appeal dismissed this application because, whilst it was undoubtedly an abuse of process to pursue by legal action a collateral advantage which the law would not allow, the claimant believed that the magazine was carrying on a defamatory campaign against him and the terms of the settlements were thus directly related to the grievances which had caused him to sue. His purpose was not to shut down *Private Eye* (although the proceedings might, conceivably, have had that effect) but to protect his reputation.

vii. Secondary Publishers

It was noted above that, essentially, everyone who is involved in the distribu- **13-086** tion of a defamatory statement is regarded as a publisher and therefore potentially liable in defamation.[317] However, secondary publishers may be entitled to rely on the defence created by s.10 of the Defamation Act 2013, which provides that the court does not have jurisdiction to hear an action for defamation brought against a person who is not the "author, editor or publisher" of the statement unless it is not reasonably practicable for the "author, editor or publisher" to be sued.

viii. Website Operators

Generally   One of the main reasons for the enactment of the Defamation Act 2013 **13-087** was to bolster the protection afforded to website operators. There was a concern that

---

[313] See para.13-018.
[314] [2006] EWHC 407 (QB); [2007] 1 W.L.R. 1243.
[315] [2009] EWHC 1765 (QB); [2009] E.M.L.R. 27. Email carriers must fall within the "passive role" concept.
[316] [1977] Q.B. 83.
[317] See para.13-021.

website operators were removing information posted by other persons out of a concern that, if they failed to do so, they might be liable in defamation as secondary publishers of the information. This worry is addressed in s.5 of the Act, which provides "the operator of a website" (a term that is not defined[318]) with a defence in respect of statements posted on its website in the following circumstances. First, the operator must not have been the person who posted the statement on the website. Secondly, the defence will be excluded if the claimant proves that: the person who posted the statement cannot be identified; the claimant gave the operator notice of the statement; and the operator failed to respond to the notice in accordance with any regulations. Thirdly, the defence will be lost if the operator acted maliciously, but the mere fact that the operator moderates statements posted on its website does not strip the operator of the defence. Where the defence in s.5 applies, a website operator may leave the defamatory statement on its website unless the court orders its removal.[319]

13-088 **The regulations** The only regulations that have been made to date under s.5 of the Defamation Act 2013 are the Defamation (Operator of Websites) Regulations 2013.[320] These Regulations are verbose and complex. Describing them at the highest level of generality, they provide as follows. First, the claimant must in his notice describe the meaning that he attributes to the statement about which he complains and identify the aspects of it that are factually inaccurate or are opinions not supported by fact. Secondly, where the operator can contact the poster, the operator must notify him within 48 hours of the fact that a complaint has been made and the poster must, if he does not consent to the statement being removed, provide the operator with his full correspondence details. Thirdly, if the operator cannot contact the poster, the operator must remove the statement within 48 hours. Fourthly, if the poster fails to respond within five days, the operator must remove the statement within 48 hours. Fifthly, if the poster responds but does not consent to the removal of the statement and to his contact details being passed to the claimant the operator must remove the statement within 48 hours. Because of the highly cumbersome nature of the regulations, it is suspected that few website operators will make use of the defence in s.5. Other defences that might be particularly useful to website operators include the defence of innocent dissemination[321] and the defence granted to secondary publishers.[322]

ix.   Honest Opinion

13-089 **Generally** The common law provided for a defence which was originally known as fair comment. It was rebranded in *Joseph v Spiller* as "honest comment"[323] and then replaced with the defence of "honest opinion" by s.3 of the Defamation Act 2013. The defence in s.3 is similar in many ways to the common law defence that it superseded, and some of the common law principles inform the operation of s.3. The basic function of the defence is to ensure that people are free to express their

---

[318] Difficulties caused by the failure to define this term are discussed in Mullis and Scott (2014) 77 M.L.R. 87 at 100–101.
[319] See para.13-121.
[320] SI 2013/3028.
[321] See para.13-080.
[322] See para.13-086.
[323] [2010] UKSC 53; [2011] 1 A.C. 852 at [117].

opinions, which is an important aspect of a democratic society. As Diplock J put it in *Silkin v Beaverbrook Newspapers Ltd*, "[t]he basis of our public life is that the crank, the enthusiast, may say what he honestly thinks".[324]

Elements of the defence　The defence has three elements. First, the statement in 　**13-090** question must be a statement of opinion (as opposed to a statement of fact). Secondly, the statement must indicate, in general or specific terms, the basis of the opinion. Thirdly, it must be shown that an honest person could have held the opinion based on any fact that existed at the time that the statement was published or anything asserted to be a fact in a privileged statement. The defence will be lost if the claimant proves that the defendant did not hold the opinion.[325] In a case where the statement was republished by someone other than the author, the defence will be unavailable if the person who republished it knew or ought to have known that the author did not hold the opinion. In contrast with the position at common law, it is not necessary for the defence of honest opinion to apply that the statement be on a matter of public interest.

The statement must be one of opinion　The honest opinion defence applies only 　**13-091** to statements of opinion. Unfortunately, the borderline between fact and opinion is difficult to draw, which is why a critic should take pains to keep his facts and his opinions on them separate from each other, for if it is not reasonably clear that the matter purports to be an opinion, he cannot succeed on the honest opinion defence,[326] and will need to rely on another defence, such as truth or privilege. Every statement must be taken on its merits and the very same words may be fact or opinion according to the context.

A hallmark of an opinion is that it is an evaluative statement which is not readily susceptible to being shown to be true or false. Thus, to describe the line "A Mr. Wilkinson, a clergyman",[327] as the worst in English poetry is obviously an opinion, for verification of it as exact is impossible. Reviews of films and theatrical performances are paradigmatic illustrations of statements of opinion. Similarly, comments upon a person's competence are treated as opinion. In *Dakhyl v Labouchere*[328] the claimant identified himself as "a specialist for the treatment of deafness, ear, nose, and throat diseases". By contrast, the defendant described him as a "quack of the rankest species". The House of Lords held that the common law predecessor to the defence in s.3 (i.e., the defence of fair comment) should be left to the jury.

In *British Chiropractic Association v Singh*[329] the defendant, a science writer, wrote an article in *The Guardian* about chiropractors. He said that the British Chiropractic Association claimed that their members could treat various conditions "even though there is not a jot of evidence" that their treatments are effective. The Court of Appeal concluded that this was an opinion on the ground that it

---

[324] [1958] 1 W.L.R. 743 at 747.
[325] Section 3(5).
[326] *Hunt v Star Newspaper Co Ltd* [1908] 2 K.B. 309 at 320; *London Artists Ltd v Littler* [1969] 2 Q.B. 375 at 395.
[327] A parody of Wordsworth in Benson's *Life of Fitzgerald*.
[328] [1908] 2 K.B. 325n.
[329] [2010] EWCA Civ 350; [2011] 1 W.L.R. 133.

constituted a "value judgment".[330] It is doubtful whether this was correct. It is argu-able that the court reached this conclusion partly because if it had held that the state-ment was one of fact, courts may, in cases such as this, be required to decide whether the statement was true, which would see them resolving scientific disputes.

Although it is classically concerned with "evaluation", the defence of honest opinion may also embrace certain inferences drawn from other facts stated or to which reference is made. Thus, in *Branson v Bower*[331] a statement that the claimant's motive for his actions was revenge fell within the scope of the defence. However, the defence will not apply to statements of fact which are verifiable in the ordinary way, such as the statement that there are reasonable grounds to suspect that the claimant is guilty of an offence.[332]

In *Telnikoff v Matusevitch*[333] it was held that where a defendant writes a letter to a newspaper refuting an article published in it, then, in deciding whether state-ments in the letter were opinion, the court is confined to the letter itself because the readers of the letter may include a substantial number of people who have not read the article. The court denied that this meant that the whole of the material about which an opinion is expressed would have to be repeated in the letter containing the opinion (a situation obviously unacceptable to any newspaper editor) as long as some form of words was used that made it plain that the letter was an opinion and nothing else.

13-092 **The statement must indicate, in general or specific terms, the basis of the opinion** This element of the defence of honest opinion in s.3 tracks the decision of the Supreme Court in *Joseph v Spiller*.[334] In that case, the court indicated that the common law ancestor to s.3 required the defendant to identify in his statement "at least the general nature of the facts that have led him to make the criticism".[335] Lord Phillips supplied the following example[336]:

> "[i]f [the defendant] states that a barrister is 'a disgrace to his profession' he should make it clear whether this is because he does not deal honestly with the court, or does not read his papers thoroughly, or refuses to accept legally aided work, or is constantly late for court, or wears dirty collars and bands".

That which qualifies as a sufficient reference to the facts upon which the opinion purports to be made is something on which no hard and fast rule can be laid down. Certainly, it is unnecessary that the defendant should set out verbatim in his state-ment all of the facts upon which he expresses his opinion. The question is whether there is a sufficient substratum of facts indicated in the words that are the subject matter of the action to show that an opinion is being expressed. The substratum of facts may be indicated impliedly. In *Kemsley v Foot*[337] the claimant newspaper owner sued the defendant, which had published a newspaper article under the head-ing "Lower than Kemsley". The article was violently critical of the conduct of a newspaper owned by a third party and contained no reference to the claimant other

---

330 [2010] EWCA Civ 350; [2011] 1 W.L.R. 133 at [26].
331 [2001] EWCA Civ 791.
332 *Hamilton v Clifford* [2004] EWCA Civ 1407.
333 [1992] 2 A.C. 343.
334 [2010] UKSC 53; [2011] 1 A.C. 852.
335 [2010] UKSC 53; [2011] 1 A.C. 852 at [103].
336 [2010] UKSC 53; [2011] 1 A.C. 852 at [103].
337 [1952] A.C. 345.

than in the heading. The House of Lords found for the defendant because, in the circumstances, the conduct of the Kemsley press in its publications was sufficiently indicated as the fact on which the opinion was expressed. However, in determining whether a statement is opinion the court must not voyage beyond what is said expressly or by implication in the defendant's words.

The factual basis of the opinion must be true or privileged   For an opinion to **13-093** be protected by the defence of honest opinion, it must be such that an honest person could have held it on the basis of any true or privileged fact that existed at the time that the statement was published. Thus, opinions that are based on facts which are neither true nor privileged are not protected, and facts which emerge after the statement was published cannot be taken into consideration when asking whether this requirement is satisfied.[338] Section 3(7) states (in outline) that for the purposes of the defence "privileged statements" are: (1) statements protected under the public interest defence in s.4; (2) statements covered by the qualified privilege enjoyed by academic publications; (3) the absolute privilege that covers reports of court proceedings; and (4) the heads of qualified privilege provided for by the Defamation Act 1996. The foregoing rules do not apply where the defendant bases his opinion on a statement of another person. Where this is the case, pursuant to s.3(6), the defence will be lost only if the claimant shows that the defendant knew or ought to have known that the original author did not hold the opinion.

Malice irrelevant   It is immaterial that the defendant held the opinion maliciously. **13-094** The sole question here is whether the defendant believed the opinion that he expressed.[339] The unreasonableness of the defendant's opinion would seem to be irrelevant save in so far as the more unreasonable it is the more likely it may be that the defendant did not hold it.

x. Apology and Payment into Court

Under s.2 of the Libel Act 1843, a newspaper that publishes a libel without **13-095** malice and without gross negligence may plead in its defence the publication of a full apology and payment of money into court. This provision has fallen into complete disuse because it is more advantageous for the defendant to make a "Part 36 offer" under the general provisions applicable to all actions for damages.[340]

xi. Offer of Amends

Generally   Sections 2–4 of the Defamation Act 1996 provide for a defence of of- **13-096** fer of amends. This defence requires the defendant to make a suitable correction and a sufficient apology, to publish those in a manner that is reasonable and practicable in the circumstances and to pay to the claimant such compensation (if any), and such costs, as may be agreed or determined to be payable.[341] An offer may only be made before service of a defence,[342] although once a defence has been served the defendant may still of course offer to settle the dispute under the general law.

---

338 *Cohen v Daily Telegraph Ltd* [1968] 1 W.L.R. 916.
339 Section 3(5).
340 See para.1-041.
341 Section 2(4).
342 Section 2(5).

13-097 **Situation where the offer is accepted** If the offer is accepted the claimant may not bring an action for defamation or continue one that he has commenced. This is so even if the parties have not agreed the details of what should be done under the offer. Where that is the case, there is no question of the court being able to compel the defendant to do anything in particular by way of correction, apology or publication—in the absence of agreement that is a matter for the defendant to decide. If, however, the parties have also failed to agree on the amount of the compensation to be paid, that is something which will be settled by the court "on the same principles as damages in defamation proceedings"[343] and account may be taken in setting the figure of the suitability and sufficiency of what the defendant has done by way of correction and apology.[344] An early and unqualified offer of amends followed by an agreed apology will attract a "discount" on the damages. The discount has been said to be approximately 50 per cent,[345] although this might be regarded as the top of the scale.[346]

13-098 **Situation where the offer is not accepted** If the offer is not accepted the action will proceed but the defendant may use the making of the offer as a defence unless the claimant is able to show[347] that the defendant knew at the time of publication or had reason to believe that the statement referred to the claimant (or was likely to be understood as referring to him) and was both false and defamatory of him.[348] "Had reason to believe" is not to be equated with "failed to take reasonable care"—it is equivalent to the recklessness or conscious indifference as to truth which constitutes malice for the purpose of qualified privilege.[349]

13-099 **Qualified offer of amends** Since defamatory words are often capable of more than one interpretation, it is open to the defendant to make a qualified offer in relation to a specific defamatory meaning which he accepts the words bear. If, for example, the allegation against a company director is that his conduct has caused the company to get into difficulties the defendant might concede that this imputed incompetence and make an offer in respect of that meaning. The claimant, however, might contend that the words in their context carried the implication that he had been dishonest. If the offer of amends in respect of the lesser meaning is not accepted then it will be for the court at the trial to determine what the words mean. If, though untrue, they bear only the lesser meaning and the claimant is unable to show that the defendant had reason to believe them to be untrue the defence based on the offer of amends will succeed. Conversely, if the court considers that the words were to be understood in the more serious sense, the claimant will win.

---

[343] Section 3(6).
[344] *Nail v News Group Newspapers Ltd* [2004] EWCA Civ 1708; [2005] 1 All E.R. 1040 at [19].
[345] *Nail v News Group Newspapers Ltd* [2004] EWCA Civ 1708; [2005] E.M.L.R. 12.
[346] *Cairns v Modi* [2012] EWCA Civ 1382; [2013] 1 W.L.R. 1015 at [50].
[347] The burden is on the claimant: s.4(3).
[348] Section 4(3).
[349] *Milne v Express Newspapers* [2004] EWCA Civ 664; [2004] E.M.L.R. 24.

Defence is mutually exclusive of other defences The defendant cannot rely on **13-100** an offer by way of defence in combination with any other defence,[350] although this is subject to an exception where the defendant makes a qualified offer of amends.[351]

Offer of amends cannot be accepted after a reasonable time The provisions **13-101** of the Defamation Act 1996 merely speak of the consequences of the offer being accepted or not accepted, but the claimant cannot simply sit on the offer and pursue his case with a view to accepting it at the last moment if things go badly. Thus, a claimant cannot accept an offer after a reasonable period of time has elapsed.[352]

Rationale The purpose of the offer of amends procedure is to encourage **13-102** settlement. A claimant accepting an offer has his reputation vindicated and obtains compensation without the worry and expense of trial, while a defendant who makes an offer gets to put the claimant to the difficult burden of proof of malice if it is not accepted. Further, and as noted above, the fact that an offer of amends has been made will have a significant deflationary effect on the amount of compensation that is payable if proceedings are needed to determine that issue.

xii. Consent

Consent is a defence to liability in defamation, but it is very rarely engaged. In **13-103** *Chapman v Lord Ellesmere*[353] the claimant, a horse trainer, complained about a report regarding doping allegations that had been published by the stewards of a horse racing club of which he was a member. It was held that the claimant had consented to the publication of this report as he had agreed to be governed by the club's rules (which permitted the stewards to publish the report in question) when he joined the club.

xiii. Apology is Not a Defence

It is open to the defendant to a claim for defamation, as in the case of any other **13-104** tort, to settle out of court. This may involve an apology, which may be incorporated in a statement in open court (approved by the judge).[354] However, generally speaking, an apology is not, as such, a defence, although it may go to reduce the damages if the claimant wins.[355] An apology need not be an abject one, but it should at least withdraw completely the imputation and express regret for having made it. To say that someone has manners not fit for a pig and then to retract that by saying that his manners are fit for a pig would merely aggravate the damages.

C. Procedure

The demise of the jury The law of defamation has for much of its history been **13-105** subjected to severe criticism. Few commentators have had kind words to say about

---

[350] Section 4(4). But even if not relied on by way of defence the offer may be relied on in mitigation of damages: s.4(5).
[351] The defendant may rely on any other defence in respect of a meaning to which a qualified offer does not relate: s.4(4).
[352] *Tesco Stores Ltd v Guardian News & Media Ltd* [2009] E.M.L.R. 5.
[353] [1932] 2 K.B. 431.
[354] CPR PD 53, para.6.1.
[355] See para.13-114.

it. Many of the attacks on the tort have been made in the public arena, and successive governments have changed the law with a view to making it more difficult to sue for defamation. An important change effected by the Defamation Act 2013 is effectively to eliminate juries in defamation cases. Section 11(1) of the Act provides that defamation cases will be tried without a jury unless the court orders otherwise.[356] In practice, this means that juries are no longer used in this setting,[357] thereby removing what was one of the last refuges of the jury in tort law. This shift in the law was prompted primarily by a belief that the use of juries lay behind many of the problems from which the law of defamation was perceived to suffer. Juries had in several cases made very large awards even though no measurable financial loss was suffered. This created the impression that the law of defamation was a bonanza for claimants. The Court of Appeal had sought to combat this concern[358] but evidently its efforts were thought to be insufficient by Parliament. There was also a perception that juries drove up the cost of defamation actions on the assumption that it was slower to try a case before a jury than before a judge sitting alone.

13-106   **Summary judgment**   Pursuant to s.8 of the Defamation Act 1996, the court may enter summary judgment for the claimant and grant him summary relief if it appears that there is no defence that has a realistic prospect of success and there is no other reason why the claim should be tried. Similarly, summary judgment can be entered for the defendant if the claim appears to lack realistic prospects of success and there is no other reason why it should be tried. The granting of summary judgment to the claimant involves a declaration that the statement was false and defamatory, an order that the defendant publish a suitable correction and apology, and an order that the defendant pay damages not exceeding £10,000.[359] This provision may mislead on a superficial reading of it for the court cannot in fact dictate the terms of any correction and apology: if the defendant is intransigent the court can only compel him to publish a summary of the court's judgment.[360] For the claimant who desires a cheaper and speedier vindication of his reputation than is offered by a full trial this provides a "fast track" route,[361] but it should not be looked on solely in this light for the court may force this solution on the claimant and deny him a trial only if it is satisfied that the summary relief "will adequately compensate him for the wrong he has suffered".[362] It is therefore clearly contemplated that there is a distinction between "minor" and "serious" libels, with the former considered suitable for summary disposition even if the claimant wishes to go to trial. The judicial declaration of falsity under the summary procedure goes some way to meeting that element of libel damages which is concerned with vindicating the claimant's reputa-

---

[356] As to the discretion to order a jury trial, see *Yeo v Times Newspapers Ltd* [2014] EWHC 2853 (QB); [2015] 1 W.L.R. 971.

[357] In *Stocker v Stocker* [2019] UKSC 17; [2020] A.C. 593 at [32] Lord Kerr referred to the "almost complete abolition" of trial by jury in defamation proceedings.

[358] See, e.g., *John v Mirror Group Newspapers Ltd* [1997] Q.B. 586.

[359] Defamation Act 1996 s.9(1).

[360] Defamation Act 1996 s.9(2), which contemplates that the content and venue will normally be agreed by the parties.

[361] A defendant wishing to take advantage of the summary procedure may legitimately waive a triable defence: *Milne v Telegraph Group Ltd* [2001] E.M.L.R. 30. The origin of the summary procedure is a Bill drafted by Lord Hoffmann in 1989.

[362] Defamation Act 1996 s.8(3)

tion[363] so that the procedure may extend further up the scale than libels which are "worth" £10,000 in damages terms.[364]

Costs From the point of view of claimants, the bonanza image was never the **13-107** whole story, and if the law of defamation has presented a harsh face to media defendants it can present an even harsher one to claimants, as costs in defamation cases can be very high[365] and legal aid has never been available in this setting.[366] Most defamation defendants are media corporations and most claimants are individuals and under the traditional system of funding litigation whereby clients paid their lawyers by the hour the cards were necessarily stacked in favour of the former. The picture changed to some extent under the system of conditional fees.[367] Provided that the claimant can find lawyers who are willing to conduct his claim on a no-win/no-fee basis he avoids the risk of having to pay his own legal costs if he loses although he will still be exposed to the risk that he will be ordered to bear the defendant's costs.

From the perspective of defendants, the high costs in defamation cases can have a "chilling effect" on free speech.[368] One major concern here is that defendants will refrain from publishing statements because of the fear that they might lose a libel case and be faced with very significant costs. The present system also has the potential to "chill" speech because even victorious defendants may be unable to recover their costs where the claimant is impecunious and decides not to secure after-the-event insurance. The irrecoverable costs of defending the action may be so significant that it is not worth publishing a given statement even if doing so is unlikely to attract liability.

Actions involving persons not domiciled in the United Kingdom or a Member **13-108** **State** There is a concern that English defamation law, because it has traditionally provided the right to reputation with robust protection, has resulted in proceedings being commenced in the United Kingdom rather than elsewhere in circumstances where the case has little connection with the United Kingdom. This concern has been heightened by publications on the internet. Internet publications accessed within the United Kingdom are treated as published here. This means that if D, who is domiciled in another jurisdiction, writes something defamatory about C, who is also resident in that jurisdiction, but the statement is accessed by X in the United Kingdom, D will in principle be liable for defamation in the United Kingdom. Although the abuse of process doctrine enables the courts to stay proceedings brought by claimants based overseas where there is minimal publication within the United Kingdom,[369] and although the courts have the power to stay proceedings on the basis of *forum non conveniens* where the United Kingdom is not

---

[363] See para.13-109.

[364] *Mawdsley v Guardian Newspapers Ltd* [2002] EWHC 1780 (QB).

[365] It has been suggested that even an award of £30,000 damages against a solvent defendant might leave a claimant out of pocket on irrecoverable costs: *Clarke v Bain* [2008] EWHC 2636 (QB) at [54].

[366] In *Steel v UK* (2005) 41 E.H.R.R. 22 the European Court of Human Rights held that the absence of legal aid violated the rights of the applicant libel defendants under arts 6 and 10 of the European Convention on Human Rights. The applicants, who were unwaged, had been sued by the fast-food chain McDonald's in litigation that became known as the "McLibel" case, and which was said to be the longest-running libel case in English legal history.

[367] See para.1-029.

[368] For discussion, see *Times Newspapers Ltd v Flood* [2017] UKSC 33; [2017] 1 W.L.R. 1415 at [68].

[369] See fn.31.

an appropriate jurisdiction in which to hear the case, the legislature did not think that these mechanisms were sufficient to deal with "libel tourism". Consequently, s.9 of the Defamation Act 2013 was enacted. In outline, s.9 denies jurisdiction to the courts of England and Wales where the defendant is based outside the United Kingdom and the European Union unless the court considers that England and Wales "is clearly the most appropriate place in which to bring an action in respect of the statement".[370] The burden is on the claimant to show that the test in s.9 is satisfied.[371] To discharge this onus, the claimant "has to show that the scales come decisively down in his/her favour".[372]

D. Remedies

i. Damages

13-109 **Generally** A claimant who establishes liability in defamation is entitled to compensatory damages in respect of the harm caused by the publication. The leading case in this regard is *John v MGN Ltd*.[373] Sir Thomas Bingham MR, giving the judgment of the Court of Appeal, said[374]:

> "The successful plaintiff in a defamation action is entitled to recover, as general compensatory damages, such sum as will compensate him for the wrong he has suffered. That sum must compensate him for the damage to his reputation; vindicate his good name; and take account of the distress, hurt and humiliation which the defamatory publication has caused."

In *Cairns v Modi* the Court of Appeal said that these three purposes of awarding compensatory damages—repairing damage to the claimant reputation, vindicating his name, and compensating him for the distress caused—are always relevant, "but the emphasis to be placed on each will vary from case to case".[375]

The fact that a judge has delivered a reasoned judgment in which he explains why he has found in favour of the claimant may be (but will not necessarily be) its own vindication of his name, such as to render it unnecessary to award damages to achieve this purpose.[376] The issue of whether or not a judgment provides sufficient vindication without more is one of fact.[377] A judgment alone is unlikely to serve as sufficient vindication where the defamatory statement was disseminated widely and a substantial award is necessary to convince interested bystanders of the claimant's good name. The trial judge has significant leeway in terms of deciding the sum to be awarded, although he should not award more than is necessary to compensate the claimant for the injury done to him, and so the damages should be proportionate to the harm.[378]

13-110 **Gravity of the libel** A central consideration when calculating damages is the gravity of the defamatory statement. This refers to how closely "it touches the

---

[370] Section 9(2).
[371] *Wright v Ver* [2019] EWHC 2094 (QB) at [22].
[372] *Wright v Ver* [2019] EWHC 2094 (QB) at [36] per Nicklin J.
[373] [1997] Q.B. 586.
[374] [1997] Q.B. 586 at 607.
[375] [2012] EWCA Civ 1382; [2013] 1 W.L.R. 1015 at [22].
[376] *Cairns v Modi* [2012] EWCA Civ 1382; [2013] 1 W.L.R. 1015 at [30]–[31].
[377] *Cairns v Modi* [2012] EWCA Civ 1382; [2013] 1 W.L.R. 1015 at [32].
[378] *Cairns v Modi* [2012] EWCA Civ 1382; [2013] 1 W.L.R. 1015 at [34]–[35].

plaintiff's personal integrity, professional reputation, honour, courage, loyalty and the core attributes of his personality".[379] The closer the connection between the defamatory statement and the claimant's "core attributes" the greater the damages will be, all other things being equal. An example of a statement that will strike at the core of the claimant's character is where the claimant is a professional cricketer and the statement alleges that he is guilty of match-fixing.[380]

Extent of the publication   Another significant factor to consider when assessing damages is the extent of the publication. The more widely the statement is published the greater the award that will be merited.[381] As the Court of Appeal explained in *Cairns v Modi*[382]:   **13-111**

> "[I]t is virtually self-evident that in most cases publication of a defamatory statement to one person will cause infinitely less damage than publication to the world at large, and that publication on a single occasion is likely to cause less damage than repeated publication and consequent publicity on social media."

It is important to bear in mind in this connection that publication of a defamatory statement will rarely end with the person to whom it is originally published.[383] This "percolation phenomenon" is likely to be particularly significant in the modern world where communications systems enable stories to be spread widely virtually instantaneously.[384] Thus, damages may be sought not only for the original publication but also in respect of loss that flows from that publication, provided it is reasonably foreseeable.[385]

It may be important to consider not only the extent of the publication but also the number of people who realised that the publication referred to the claimant. In one of the appeals in *Cairns v Modi*[386] the claimant, whom the defendant newspaper had mistakenly alleged to be a paedophile, remained anonymous throughout the proceedings, and only a handful of people, such as the claimant's relatives, understood that the article was referring to him. Taking this factor into account, the Court of Appeal considered that damages should be reduced by a third (from £150,000 to £100,000).[387]

Relationship of the claimant to the publishees   It is relevant to consider the nature of the relationship between the claimant and the persons to whom the defamatory statement was published. For example, publication to persons with whom the claimant is in a business relationship might call for a greater award of damages than publication to persons with whom the claimant is unlikely to enter into such a relationship.[388]   **13-112**

---

[379] *John v MGN Ltd* [1997] Q.B. 586 at 607 per Sir Thomas Bingham MR.
[380] *Cairns v Modi* [2012] EWHC 756 (QB) at [121] (not doubted on appeal [2012] EWCA Civ 1382; [2013] 1 W.L.R. 1015).
[381] *John v MGN Ltd* [1997] Q.B. 586 at 607.
[382] [2012] EWCA Civ 1382; [2013] 1 W.L.R. 1015 at [24].
[383] *Slipper v British Broadcasting Corpn* [1991] 1 Q.B. 283 at 300.
[384] *Cairns v Modi* [2012] EWCA Civ 1382; [2013] 1 W.L.R. 1015 at [26]–[27].
[385] *McManus v Beckham* [2002] EWCA Civ 939; [2002] 1 W.L.R. 2982.
[386] [2012] EWCA Civ 1382; [2013] 1 W.L.R. 1015 at [46]–[49].
[387] Damages were further reduced to £50,000 because the defendant had promptly made an offer of amends.
[388] *Cooper v Turrell* [2011] EWHC 3269 (QB) at [96]–[97].

13-113 **Unsuccessful reliance on plea of truth** A defendant who unsuccessfully invokes the defence of truth is likely to be met with a heavier award of damages than would have been the case had he accepted that the statement was false.[389]

13-114 **Retraction and apology** A defendant who withdraws a defamatory statement and apologises, especially if he does so promptly, will reduce the damage caused to the claimant and will consequently be liable for a smaller sum.[390] The more effective the apology, the greater the reduction.

13-115 **Evidence of general bad reputation** The defendant may adduce evidence of general bad reputation on the issue of damages. The idea here is that the law should prevent the recovery of substantial damages by a person whose reputation is unworthy of protection. However, the defendant is not permitted to adduce evidence of specific acts of misconduct[391] for it would be oppressive to allow the defendant (perhaps a newspaper with large financial resources) to lengthen a trial with detailed evidence of the claimant's past conduct. Despite this restriction, the defendant is entitled to rely in mitigation of damages on any evidence that has properly been put before the court and this may include evidence of specific acts of misconduct advanced under an unsuccessful plea of truth.[392] However, the court will not countenance the pleading of such specific acts under the guise of a plea of truth with the sole purpose of mitigating damages.[393]

The rule that evidence of specific misconduct is generally inadmissible in mitigation of damages does not prevent the admission into evidence of matters concerning the background context which is directly relevant to the publication. In *Burstein v Times Newspapers Ltd*,[394] for example, while the defendant could not prove that the claimant had organised bands of hecklers to wreck musical performances, it did provide evidence of an incident in which the claimant had booed after one performance. This principle applies equally to the situation where the claimant has accepted the defendant's offer of amends under the Defamation Act 1996[395] and the court has to assess compensation because the amount thereof has not been agreed[396]—indeed, it is particularly important that it should apply in such a case because the defendant will have had no opportunity to raise the claimant's conduct under a plea of truth or honest opinion. There will inevitably be cases where it is difficult to decide whether the evidence relates to the "directly relevant background context" and hence the principle should be applied with some caution.

13-116 **Maximum allowable compensatory damages** In an effort to bring greater consistency to damages awards, the courts have placed a "ceiling" on allowable damages, leaving aside punitive damages and damages for financial loss. The ceiling is the prevailing maximum level of damages for pain and suffering and loss of amenity in personal injury cases. It has been said that the relevant sum would be

---

[389] *John v MGN Ltd* [1997] Q.B. 586 at 607–608.

[390] Libel Act 1843 s.1; *John v MGN Ltd* [1997] Q.B. 586 at 607–608.

[391] *Plato Films v Speidel* [1961] A.C. 1090. The restriction on such evidence is commonly known as the rule in *Scott v Sampson* (1882) 8 Q.B.D. 491.

[392] *Pamplin v Express Newspapers Ltd (Note)* [1988] 1 W.L.R. 116.

[393] *Atkinson v Fitzwalter* [1987] 1 W.L.R. 201; *Prager v Times Newspapers Ltd* [1988] 1 W.L.R. 77.

[394] [2001] 1 W.L.R. 579.

[395] See para.13-096.

[396] *Turner v News Group Newspapers Ltd* [2006] EWCA Civ 540; [2006] 1 W.L.R. 3469.

in the region of £300,000,[397] and that awards "[a]t that level are reserved for the gravest of allegations, such as imputations of terrorism or murder. One must seek to place an individual case in its proper position on the scale that leads up to this maximum".[398]

Corporations   Corporations which establish that they have been defamed are entitled to substantial damages.[399] Generally speaking, the principles that determine the award of damages to a corporation are the same as those governing awards to natural persons. However, corporations, since they have no feelings, are not entitled to damages for distress, hurt and humiliation.[400]   **13-117**

Aggravated and punitive damages   An award of damages for defamation may include aggravated or punitive damages. These are considered elsewhere.[401]   **13-118**

ii.   Injunctive Relief

The availability of injunctive relief is discussed elsewhere in this book.[402]   **13-119**

iii.   Publication of Summary of the Court's Judgment

Under s.12 of the Defamation Act 2013, the court has the power to order the defendant to publish a summary of its judgment. If the parties cannot agree on the time, manner, form and place of the summary's publication, the court is to settle those matters. The court cannot exercise this power when it disposes summarily of a claim.[403]   **13-120**

iv.   Removal of Statements

Section 13 of the Defamation Act 2013 empowers the court to order the operator of a website on which a defamatory statement is posted to remove the statement. The court can also order any person who is not the "author, editor or publisher" of the defamatory statement to stop "distributing, selling or exhibiting material contained in the statement".   **13-121**

v.   Remedies that are Not Available

The court has no power to order the defendant to publish a correction or to issue a retraction or to give the claimant a right of reply. Nor can it compel the defendant to apologise.   **13-122**

vi.   Is the Focus on Damages Satisfactory?

It is arguable that the heavy emphasis on damages as a remedy militates against what a claimant will (or should, according to some conventional wisdom) regard   **13-123**

---

[397] *Raj v Bholowasia* [2015] EWHC 382 (QB) at [179].
[398] *Barron v Vines* [2016] EWHC 1226 (QB) at [79] per Warby J.
[399] *Cooper v Turrell* [2011] EWHC 3269 (QB) at [95].
[400] *Cooper v Turrell* [2011] EWHC 3269 (QB) at [99].
[401] See paras 23-012, 23-025.
[402] See para.23-124.
[403] See para.13-106.

as the major purpose of his claim—that is, the vindication of his good name. The recovery of damages, whether by judgment or settlement, will not necessarily achieve this end unless the fact of recovery is widely publicised. Furthermore, the defences available in a defamation action, while undoubtedly necessary to protect freedom of speech, may have the effect that the issue of the truth of the allegations is wholly or partly suppressed and an entirely unfounded and very damaging accusation may still lead to a verdict for the defendant. Even where the claimant's reputation is vindicated it will only be after protracted litigation, the expense of which is at least in part produced by the necessity to hold the balance between the protection of reputation and free speech. On the face of it, therefore, there is much attraction in a system for media defamation whereby there would be a speedy procedure for requiring a correction of a defamatory statement or the publication of a counter-statement by the complainant.

It must also be borne in mind that a person aggrieved by inaccurate statements may complain to the Independent Press Standards Organisation (a self-regulatory body for the press) or Ofcom (a statutory body) which do not award compensation but which may require the offending newspaper or broadcaster to publish a summary of any adjudication. However, there are some difficulties with such remedies if they are made the exclusive or even the primary form of redress. From the claimant's point of view "mud sticks" and the possibility of being required to publish an apology and correction would not be a very powerful deterrent against the dissemination of the careless or even reckless falsehoods which are undoubtedly from time-to-time published by the media.[404] From the defendant's perspective, it would be a new and perhaps dangerous step to impose upon a newspaper a legal requirement (which presumably would have to be backed by criminal sanctions) to publish a statement "extolling the complainant's non-existent virtue".[405] In any event, forced publication might not convince the reader that the smoke really had no underlying fire.

2. MALICIOUS FALSEHOOD

13-124 **Introduction**[406]   A false statement may be damaging even though it is not defamatory. It may be relied on by others to their detriment, in which case it may be actionable as deceit if made knowingly or recklessly[407] or, if there is a "special relationship", as negligence.[408] But a false, non-defamatory statement may also cause damage by influencing the way in which other persons behave towards the claimant. For example, a newspaper may state incorrectly that a trader has closed his business, with the result that potential customers do not approach him; or a manufacturer may circulate false information that because of technological development his product is now twice as effective as the claimant's and thereby take business away from him; alternatively, the manufacturer may represent that his goods are in fact the goods of the claimant, which enjoy a good reputation. None of these representations is, on the face of it, defamatory, for they do not impute anything derogatory, indeed in the final case the position is quite the reverse. The final case

---

[404] See, e.g., *John v Mirror Group Newspapers* [1997] Q.B. 586.
[405] The phrase is the Faulks Committee's: *Report on the Committee of Defamation* (Cmnd. 5909, 1975).
[406] Injurious falsehood is an alternative name.
[407] See para.12-002.
[408] See para.12-026.

is covered by the tort of passing off, which is dealt with elsewhere in this book,[409] but the other two may constitute malicious falsehood, which overlaps considerably with defamation.

Elements of the action   The tort of malicious falsehood has the following **13-125** elements: (1) the making of a false statement; (2) maliciously; (3) to some person other than the claimant; and (4) damage is suffered by the claimant as a result of the making of the statement. It is for the claimant to prove that the statement is false. There is no presumption in his favour.[410] If the statement is true, no liability can arise. It is not, therefore, malicious falsehood for a businessperson to utter true but damaging remarks about a competitor. The serious harm requirement applicable in claims for defamation by virtue of s.1 of the Defamation Act 2013 does not extend to the tort of malicious falsehood.

A.   The Making of a False Statement

Statements   For the purposes of malicious falsehood, the statement may be oral **13-126** or written, and even conduct conveying a false impression will be sufficient.[411]

Actionable statements often affect the claimant's trade or business but this is **13-127** **not required**   Actionable statements usually affect the claimant's trade or business. For example, in the leading case of *Ratcliffe v Evans*[412] an action succeeded in respect of a statement by a newspaper that the claimant had ceased to trade. However, it does not matter that it affects the claimant in other ways. In one of the earliest malicious falsehood cases the false statement was that the claimant was already married, whereby she lost a proposed marriage.[413] In an American case the defendant gave false information that the claimant was not a citizen which resulted in his being subjected to deportation proceedings.[414] In *Kaye v Robertson*[415] the tort was established where a newspaper published what was falsely claimed to be an interview to which a television personality had consented, thereby depriving him of the chance to sell his story as an "exclusive".

The statement must relate to the claimant or his property   The tort does not **13-128** extend to statements that have no connection with the claimant or his property: it is not malicious falsehood (although it may be another tort) if, for example, A tells B lies in order to obtain B's property and thereby deprives C of the opportunity to bid for it.[416]

Statement by D about the purported superiority of his goods to C's   A state- **13-129** ment by a trader that his goods are superior to those of a rival (mere "puffing") is

---

[409] See para.19-051.
[410] cf. the position in defamation, where the defendant carries the burden of establishing truth: see para.13-049.
[411] *Wilts United Dairies v Robinson & Sons* [1958] R.P.C. 94.
[412] [1892] 2 Q.B. 524.
[413] *Sheperd v Wakeman* (1662) 1 Sid. 79; 82 E.R. 982.
[414] *Al Raschid v News Syndicate Co* 191 N.E. 713 (N.Y. 1934). The deportation proceedings were not "judicial proceedings" for the purposes of the tort of malicious prosecution.
[415] [1991] F.S.R. 52.
[416] *Lonrho Plc v Fayed* [1988] 3 All E.R. 464 (though no claim for malicious falsehood appears to have been made). On appeal on another point [1992] 1 A.C. 448.

not actionable, even if it is known to be false and causes damage, since courts of law cannot be converted into agencies for trying the relative merits of rival products.[417] However, this is only the case with respect to those imprecise commendations that are a common part of advertising and to which a reasonable person does not attach much importance. Accordingly, if a defendant chooses to frame his comparison in the form of scientific tests or other statements of ascertainable fact, he will be liable if they are proved untrue and the other elements of the tort are present.[418]

13-130 The single meaning rule in defamation does not apply in malicious falsehood In defamation, the words about which the claimant complains must be given a single meaning.[419] This rule does not apply in malicious falsehood.[420] Thus, it does not matter for the purposes of malicious falsehood if the false meaning of the words relied upon by the claimant is not the only meaning that they might be capable of bearing.

13-131 Each publication gives rise to a separate cause of action Each publication of the statement complained of generates a fresh cause of action and, consequently, a fresh limitation period. The changes to the law in this connection in relation to defamation[421] do not apply to malicious falsehood.

B. Malice

13-132 Malice exists if the defendant knows that the statement is false or if he makes the statement not caring whether it is true or false, but mere negligence is not enough.[422] Scrutton LJ said[423]:

> "Honest belief in an unfounded claim is not malice, but the nature of the unfounded claim may be evidence that there is not an honest belief in it. It may be so unfounded that the particular fact that it is put forward may be evidence that it is not honestly believed."

However, even if the defendant believes the untrue statement there will still be malice if he is actuated by some indirect, dishonest or improper motive, which seems here to mean the purpose of injuring the claimant rather than defending his own interests or pushing his own business.[424] Where the statement in question has more than one meaning, the existence of malice must be ascertained by reference to the meaning that the defendant intended to convey.[425]

---

[417] *White v Mellin* [1895] A.C. 154 at 164; *Hubbuck & Sons Ltd Wilkinson* [1899] 1 Q.B. 86.
[418] *De Beers Products Ltd v International General Electric Co of New York* [1975] 1 W.L.R. 972. Even imprecise assertions of superiority may be actionable if they denigrate the claimant's wares in a manner that a reasonable person would take seriously: *White v Mellin* [1895] A.C. 154 at 171; *Alcott v Miller's Karri etc. Ltd* (1904) 91 L.T. 722.
[419] See para.13-037.
[420] *Ajinomoto Sweeteners Europe SAS v Asda Stores Ltd* [2010] EWCA 609; [2011] Q.B. 497.
[421] See para.13-021.
[422] *Shapiro v La Morta* (1923) 40 T.L.R. 39 (Div Ct); (1923) 40 T.L.R. 201 (CA).
[423] *Greers Ltd v Pearman & Corder Ltd* (1922) 39 R.P.C. 406 at 417.
[424] *Dunlop v Maison Talbot* (1904) 20 T.L.R. 579.
[425] *Cruddas v Calvert* [2015] EWCA Civ 171; [2015] E.M.L.R. 16 at [111]–[112].

C. Damage

The default position is that proof of special (that is, actual, pecuniary) damage **13-133** is required,[426] though this is satisfied by proof of a general loss of business where the falsehood is in its very nature intended, or is reasonably likely, to produce such loss and actually does so in the ordinary course of things.[427] By s.3(1) of the Defamation Act 1952 it is no longer necessary to allege or prove special damage if: (1) the words complained of are published in writing or other permanent form; or (2) the words are calculated to cause pecuniary damage to the claimant in respect of any office, profession, calling, trade or business carried on by him at the time of the publication. The words "calculated to cause pecuniary damages" mean "more likely than not to cause pecuniary damage".[428] Distress and injury to feelings do not amount to special damage for the purpose of malicious falsehood. However, where special damage is established (or where s.3 of the Defamation Act 1952 applies) the claimant can recover aggravated damages for injury to feelings as in an action for defamation. The award may take account of the conduct of the defendant during the litigation, for example, in trying to blacken the claimant's name.[429]

D. Varieties of the Tort

Two particular varieties of malicious falsehood have acquired names of their **13-134** own: slander of goods (where the defendant disparages the claimant's goods); and slander of title (where he questions the claimant's ownership of property). These are not separate torts and have nothing to do with "slander" in the defamation sense. It would be better if the expressions were dropped.

E. Defences

Generally speaking, the rules concerning absolute privilege in the law of defama- **13-135** tion apply also to malicious falsehood. Thus, if a judge disparages C's business in the course of court proceedings C will not be able to recover damages from the judge. Qualified privilege is not a defence to malicious falsehood. Because malice is one of the elements of the action in malicious falsehood, where the action is constituted, the defence will necessarily be excluded since it is forfeited if the defendant acted maliciously. The defence of abuse of process is available, and might be triggered where, for example, the claim is for trivial loss.[430]

3. PRIVACY

Introduction[431] English law does not recognise any direct action for the inva- **13-136** sion of privacy.[432] However, the technically correct proposition that there is no tort of invasion of privacy would be seriously misleading if it were not substantially

---

[426] *White v Mellin* [1895] A.C. 154; *Royal Baking Powder Co v Wright & Co* (1900) 18 R.P.C. 95 at 99.

[427] *Ratcliffe v Evans* [1892] 2 Q.B. 524 at 533; cf. *Joyce v Sengupta* [1993] 1 W.L.R. 337 at 347.

[428] *Tesla Motors Ltd v British Broadcasting Corporation* [2011] EWHC 2760 (QB) at [7].

[429] *Khodaparast v Shad* [2000] 1 W.L.R. 618.

[430] Consider the remarks in *Tesla Motors Ltd v British Broadcasting Corporation* [2013] EWCA Civ 152 at [47]–[49].

[431] See generally Tugendhat and Christie, *The Law of Privacy and the Media*, 3rd edn (2016).

[432] *Wainwright v Home Office* [2003] UKHL 53; [2004] 2 A.C. 406. The law in the United States took

qualified. Privacy is a value recognised by the law and protected in several ways. First, there is indirect protection afforded by torts such as trespass and nuisance. Secondly, protection is provided by various statutory provisions, most particularly those relating to data protection and the behaviour of public authorities under the Human Rights Act 1998. Thirdly, recent years have seen the substantial development of the old law of breach of confidence, resulting in an offshoot that is sometimes called the tort of misuse of private information.

A.   The Indirect Impact of Other Torts

13-137   **Trespass to land and nuisance**   Where there is a trespass to land it is quite likely that one of the claimant's grievances will be the invasion of his privacy and in a suitable case there is no reason why damages for trespass should not reflect that.[433] It is also possible to imagine circumstances in which the fact that the defendant is clearly observing persons on private land would constitute a nuisance.[434] However, the torts of trespass and private nuisance operate only in favour of persons with a proprietary interest in the premises entered or affected.[435] Further, neither tort is apt to deal with modern means of electronic and optical surveillance, which may be carried on from a great distance. There is no trespass in watching or listening from outside and it is difficult to see how the law of nuisance could be stretched to cover an "interference" of which the occupier was wholly unaware at the time.

13-138   **Defamation**   It is perhaps an oversimplification to say that the law of defamation is not concerned with the invasion of privacy: the distress which is felt by the victim of a libel may be as much due to the torrent of intrusive publicity that descends upon him as to the affront he feels at having untrue things said about him. However, the protection given to privacy by the law of defamation is limited. This is partly because truth is a complete defence to liability in defamation. If, therefore, a defendant publishes private information he will not incur liability in defamation provided that it is true. And even where the statement is untrue there is no liability in defamation unless the statement in question can properly be said to reflect on the reputation of the person about whom it is made. Thus, it is not difficult to conceive of statements about, say, a person's health which would be distressing but not defamatory.

13-139   **Copyright**   Another actionable form of interference with proprietary rights that may indirectly involve a court in protecting privacy is breach of copyright. In *Williams v Settle*[436] the claimant's father-in-law had been murdered in circumstances that attracted publicity. The defendant, who had taken the photographs at the claimant's wedding two years previously, sold one that showed the claimant's father-in-law for publication in the national press. The copyright in the photographs was the claimant's and therefore the court was able to award him heavy damages

---

a different course at the end of the 19th century, largely as a result of a famous article: Warren and Brandeis (1890) 4 Harv. L.R. 193. But, like the law of defamation there, the protection of privacy has been significantly curtailed by the constitutional protection afforded to freedom of speech by the First Amendment.

[433]   *Morris v Beardmore* [1981] A.C. 446 at 464.
[434]   Though this will not necessarily be the case, as famously illustrated by *Victoria Park Racing & Recreation Grounds Co Ltd* (1937) 58 C.L.R. 479.
[435]   *Hunter v Canary Wharf* [1997] A.C. 655.
[436]   [1960] 1 W.L.R. 1072.

for the defendant's "scandalous conduct", which was "in total disregard not only of the legal rights of the claimant regarding copyright but of his feelings and his sense of family dignity and pride".[437] Under current copyright law the rights in such a photograph would probably be in the photographer but, ironically, this is one instance in which the law addresses the issue of privacy head on, since under s.85 of the Copyright, Designs and Patents Act 1988, breach of which is actionable as a breach of statutory duty, a person who for private and domestic purposes commissions the making of a photograph or film has the right to prevent the issue of copies to the public.

B. The Human Rights Act 1998 and the Data Protection Act 2018

The right to private and family life in art.8 and its protection generally One **13-140** of the effects of the Human Rights Act 1998 has been to some extent to create a free-standing right of privacy in English law. Article 8 of the Convention provides:

> "1. Everyone has the right to respect for his private and family life, his home and his correspondence.
> 2. There shall be no interference by a public authority with the exercise of this right except such as is in accordance with the law and is necessary in a democratic society in the interests of national security, public safety or the economic well-being of the country, for the prevention of disorder or crime, for the protection of health or morals, or for the protection of the rights and freedoms of others."

Section 6 of the Human Rights Act 1998 makes it unlawful for a public authority to act in a way which is incompatible with a Convention right and a breach of s.6 gives rise to such remedy as the court considers just and appropriate, including damages if the court considers them necessary to afford just satisfaction.[438] Accordingly, bodies like the police, central and local government departments and statutory regulatory bodies that contravene art.8 in their dealings with a citizen are exposed to a claim for damages in the English courts, whether or not there is a parallel common law liability based on misuse of private information. It follows that as far as public authority defendants are concerned, there may fairly be said to be a wrong of "invasion of privacy", although a warning has been sounded against the assumption that this would extend to cases where an intrusion which the victim in fact found offensive was the result of sloppiness rather than malice. It is one thing to wander carelessly into the wrong hotel bedroom and another to hide in the wardrobe to take photographs.[439]

Data Protection Act 2018 It is not possible to give any extended account here **13-141** of the complex data protection regime established by the Data Protection Act 2018, most of which is of a regulatory nature albeit with significant civil liability consequences. Though by no means confined to privacy, the protection of that interest is the primary purpose of the Act. Sections 168 and 169 provide for compensation for damage (pecuniary and non-pecuniary) suffered as a result of contravention of the General Data Protection Regulation or "by reason of a contravention of a requirement of the data protection legislation". The "data protection principles"

---

[437] [1960] 1 W.L.R. 1072 at 1082 per Sellers LJ. Compare *Bradley v Wingnut Films* [1994] E.M.L.R. 195 (use of C's family gravestone in "comedy horror" film disclosed no cause of action).
[438] Section 8.
[439] *Wainwright v Home Office* [2003] UKHL 53; [2004] 2 A.C. 406 at [51].

which must be complied with by the data controller include that data be processed fairly and lawfully, that they be obtained only for the means which the data controller specified, that they be not excessive or retained for longer than is necessary and that they be accurate. There is a wide-ranging exemption from many requirements of the Act for the processing of journalistic material for publication where the data controller reasonably believes that publication would be in the public interest.[440]

C.   Misuse of Private Information

13-142   Evolution of the action   The action for misuse of private information derives from the equitable action for breach of confidence. Although the foundational case regarding breach of confidence[441] may fairly be said to have been, in modern terms, one concerned with "privacy", the primary focus of the law of confidence was for many years on commercial (and then governmental) secrets. Even where it was applied to personal information[442] it was typically conceived of in terms of information having been imparted in a relationship that expressly or impliedly created an obligation of confidence. However, it became accepted that an obligation of confidence might arise from wrongful taking of confidential material or from accidentally coming across an obviously confidential document.[443] Under the influence of the Human Rights Act 1998 and European Convention on Human Rights a cause of action that has now come to be described as "misuse of private information" was thus born. As Lord Nicholls put it in the landmark decision in *Campbell v MGN Ltd*[444]:

> "This cause of action has now firmly shaken off the limiting constraint of the need for an initial confidential relationship. In doing so it has changed its nature ... Now the law imposes a 'duty of confidence' whenever a person receives information he knows or ought to know is fairly and reasonably to be regarded as confidential. Even this formulation is awkward. The continuing use of the phrase 'duty of confidence' and the description of the information as 'confidential' is not altogether comfortable. Information about an individual's private life would not, in ordinary usage, be called 'confidential'. The more natural description today is that such information is private. The essence of the tort is better encapsulated now as misuse of private information."

In a later case Lord Nicholls said that we now have "two distinct causes of action, protecting two different interests: privacy and secret ('confidential') information".[445]

13-143   The decision in Campbell v MGN Ltd   *Campbell* is the leading case in relation to the action for misuse of private information. The claimant, a famous model, publicly denied having a drug addiction. She was later photographed leaving a Narcotics Anonymous meeting. The defendant printed these photographs in its

---

[440] See Sch.2 Pt.5.

[441] *Prince Albert v Strange* (1849) 2 De G. & Sm. 652; 64 E.R. 293 (catalogue of etchings by Queen Victoria and Prince Albert).

[442] As in *Argyll v Argyll* [1967] Ch. 302 and *Stephens v Avery* [1988] Ch. 449 (sexual behaviour).

[443] *Attorney General v Guardian Newspapers Ltd (No.2)* [1990] A.C. 109 at 281.

[444] [2004] UKHL 22; [2004] 2 A.C. 457 at [14]. It has been held that the cause of action for misuse of private information is a "tort" for the purposes of the tort gateway in CPR PD 6B: *Vidal-Hall v Google Inc* [2015] EWCA Civ 311; [2016] Q.B. 1003.

[445] *Douglas v Hello! Ltd (No.3)* [2007] UKHL 21; [2008] 1 A.C. 1 at [255]. See also *Vidal-Hall v Google Inc* [2015] EWCA Civ 311; [2016] Q.B. 1003 (confirming that the cause of action for misuse of private action is separate from that for breach of confidence).

newspaper and details of the meetings that she attended. The claimant accepted that the defendant was entitled to report the bare fact that she suffered from an addiction to drugs and was receiving treatment, but contended that the publication of the photographs and details of the meetings was actionable. A majority of the House of Lords found for the claimant. The majority held that the photographs and details of the meetings were private information and that the defendant, in publishing them, did more than was necessary to lend credibility to its story that the claimant had misled the public.

Elements of the action   The action for misuse of private information consists of **13-144** the following elements[446]: (1) the defendant must have disclosed private information; and (2) the defendant's interest in publishing the information must be less important than the claimant's interest in the information remaining private. Dishonesty is not an element of the action and the defendant's state of mind more generally is not relevant either.[447] Similarly, if the twin elements of the tort are present, it will not assist the defendant to show that he acted in good faith.[448]

Private information   It is difficult to define private information without a degree **13-145** of circularity: it is information that the "holder" does not intend to be imparted to the public[449] and in respect of which he has a reasonable expectation of privacy. The determination of whether information is private information involves an objective enquiry[450] that needs to be made based on all the circumstances of the case, including[451]:

"the attributes of the claimant, the nature of the activity in which the claimant was engaged, the place at which it was happening, the nature and purpose of the intrusion, the absence of consent and whether it was known or could be inferred, the effect on the claimant and the circumstances in which and the purposes for which the information came into the hands of the publisher".

Information about a person's sexual life[452] or health[453] or financial affairs or (at least where disclosure might expose him to some danger) his address or whereabouts[454] qualifies. It has been said that information stored on a person's mobile telephone will generally be regarded as private information.[455] It should not be assumed that the information must relate to something discreditable or embarrassing to the claimant: for example, it has been suggested that a donor to charity might restrain the disclosure of his gifts.[456]

Information that is already in the public domain is not private information but this should not be taken too literally—something may still be private even though

---

[446] *McKennitt v Ash* [2006] EWCA Civ 1714; [2008] Q.B. 73 at [11].
[447] *HRH The Duchess of Sussex v Associated Newspapers Ltd* [2020] EWHC 1058 (Ch) at [36], [40].
[448] *HRH The Duchess of Sussex v Associated Newspapers Ltd* [2020] EWHC 1058 (Ch) at [37].
[449] *Douglas v Hello! Ltd (No.3)* [2005] EWCA Civ 595; [2006] Q.B. 125 at [83].
[450] *HRH The Duchess of Sussex v Associated Newspapers Ltd* [2020] EWHC 1058 (Ch) at [37]–[38].
[451] *Murray v Express Newspapers Plc* [2008] EWCA Civ 446; [2009] Ch. 481 at [36].
[452] *Stephens v Avery* [1988] Ch. 449; *Mosley v News Group Newspapers Ltd* [2008] EWHC 1777 (QB); [2008] E.M.L.R. 2; *AMP v Persons Unknown* [2011] EWHC 3454 (TCC); *Ferdinand v MGN Ltd* [2011] EWHC 2454 (QB).
[453] *W v Egdell* [1990] Ch. 359; *Campbell v MGN Ltd* [2004] UKHL 22; [2004] 2 A.C. 457.
[454] *Venables v News Group Newspapers Ltd* [2001] Fam. 430; *Mills v News Group Newspapers Ltd* [2001] E.M.L.R. 41.
[455] *AMP v Persons Unknown* [2011] EWHC 3454 (TCC).
[456] *Attorney General v Guardian Newspapers Ltd (No.2)* [1990] 1 A.C. 109 at 256.

it could be traced by extensive and determined research and it has been suggested that publication of improperly obtained photographs could be restrained even though they had been widely circulated.[457] Nor does the fact that certain aspects of the information are public knowledge prevent other aspects of it being private and secret. So, in *Douglas v Hello! Ltd (No.3)*,[458] the upcoming glamorous wedding of the claimants had received widespread coverage in the tabloid press but that did not mean that they were not entitled to control the taking and use of photographs at the event. The fact that a person is a public figure who speaks out on controversial matters does not deprive him of his right to confidentiality over his thoughts on those matters committed to a private journal, even if that has been circulated among associates,[459] still less to his right of privacy in matters unrelated to his public activities.[460] In contrast, a person who ran a blog containing criticisms, made from an insider's point of view, of the management of police services and a journalist who wrote under a pseudonym had no reasonable expectation that their identities might not be revealed when discovered by investigation.[461]

13-146 Justified disclosure Disclosure will be justified when the defendant's interest in publishing the information outweighs the claimant's interest in the information remaining private. Essentially, this issue involves balancing the claimant's art.8 Convention right to privacy with the defendant's art.10 right to freedom of expression. In *Re S (a Child)* Lord Steyn offered the following guidance as to how this balancing exercise should proceed. He isolated four propositions[462]:

> "First, neither article has *as such* precedence over the other. Secondly, where the values under the two articles are in conflict, an intense focus on the comparative importance of the specific rights being claimed in the individual case is necessary. Thirdly, the justifications for interfering with or restricting each right must be taken into account. Finally, the proportionality test must be applied to each. For convenience I will call this the ultimate balancing test."

Mosley v News Group Newspapers Ltd[463] illustrates the operation of the balancing test. In this case the defendant newspaper published photographs of the claimant, who played a leading role in the organisation of motor racing, engaging in sadomasochistic activities. The photographs had been clandestinely taken by one of the women who had been involved in the activities, using a camera supplied by the newspaper. The newspaper contended that the activities had a "Nazi" or "death camp" theme to them. Had this been true, the defendant might have been justified in disclosing those activities because that would have cast doubt on the suitability of the claimant for the organisational role that he was discharging. However, since this theme was not established the disclosure was not justified. It was insufficient

---

[457] *Douglas v Hello! Ltd (No.3)* [2005] EWCA Civ 595; [2006] Q.B. 125 at [105].

[458] [2007] UKHL 21; [2008] A.C. 1.

[459] *Prince of Wales v Associated Newspapers Ltd* [2006] EWCA Civ 1776; [2008] Ch. 57.

[460] Even well-known people are entitled to some private life: *X v Persons Unknown* [2006] EWHC 2783 (QB); [2007] E.M.L.R. 10.

[461] *Author of a Blog v Times Newspapers Ltd* [2009] EWHC 1359 (QB); *Mahmood v Galloway* [2006] EWHC 1286; [2006] E.M.L.R. 26.

[462] *In re S (A Child) (Identification: Restrictions on Publication)* [2004] UKHL 47; [2005] 1 A.C. 593 at [17] (emphasis in original). See also *PJS v News Group Newspapers Ltd* [2016] UKSC 26; [2016] A.C. 1081 at [20].

[463] [2008] EWHC 1777 (QB); [2008] E.M.L.R. 2.

that many people might regard the defendant's behaviour as immoral. It is[464]:

> "not for the state or for the media to expose sexual conduct which does not involve any significant breach of the criminal law. That is so whether the motive for such intrusion is merely prurience or a moral crusade. It is not for journalists to undermine human rights, or for judges to refuse to enforce them, merely on grounds of taste or moral disapproval".

Disclosure may be justified where it is necessary to correct a false image that the claimant has projected to the public.[465] The claimant in *Campbell v MGN Ltd* accepted that the defendant newspaper was entitled to publish information that corrected the false image that she had cultivated. Her action succeeded only because the newspaper had gone too far in publishing a photograph and details of her attendance at the drug counselling meetings. Conversely, in *PJS v News Group Newspapers Ltd*[466] it was said that the starting point is that disclosure of "purely private sexual encounters, even though they involve adultery or more than one person at the same time"[467] will be unjustified and hence amount to the tort of misuse of private information. Lord Mance regarded the disclosure of such information as tortious even if it was made to someone to whom the information had already been imparted especially if the disclosure occurred in a different medium.[468]

Photographs taken in public places   *Campbell v MGN Ltd* raises a more general   **13-147**
issue about photographs taken in public places. Some legal systems give a person, as part of the general "right of personality", the right to control the use of their "image". Hence, while a person might not object to the publication of a photograph in which he is merely an incidental "face in a crowd" he might object if he is the subject of the photograph, even if it is innocuous and entirely non-derogatory.[469] The general thrust of the decision in *Campbell* is against any such right in English law. However, in *Weller v Associated Newspapers Ltd*[470] the Court of Appeal held that three child claimants who were photographed in California while in public with their father, a famous musician, had a reasonable expectation of privacy and that the balance of interests came down in favour of the claimants' right to privacy. In deciding that there was a reasonable expectation of privacy, the court considered it critical that the claimants were children and that they were identified by surname in the article which the photographs accompanied. In relation to the balancing stage of the enquiry, weight was placed on various considerations including the fact that: (1) the children had no public profile in their own right; (2) their father had not consented to the photographs being taken (much less published, and had been told, incorrectly as it turned out, that the children's faces would be pixelated in the event that the photographs were published); and (3) the trial judge had found that one of the children was genuinely embarrassed by the photographs.

Damages   Compensatory damages for misuse of private information are as-   **13-148**
sessed according to general principles. The purpose of awarding such damages is

---

[464] [2008] EWHC 1777 (QB); [2008] E.M.L.R. 2 at [127] per Eady J.
[465] *Campbell v MGN Ltd* [2004] UKHL 22; [2004] 2 A.C. 457; *Ferdinand v MGN Ltd* [2011] EWHC 2454 (QB) at [65].
[466] [2016] UKSC 26; [2016] A.C. 1081.
[467] [2016] UKSC 26; [2016] A.C. 1081 at [32].
[468] [2016] UKSC 26; [2016] A.C. 1081 at [32].
[469] See, e.g., *Aubry v Editions Vice-Versa Inc* [1998] 1 S.C.R. 591, under the Civil Code of Québec.
[470] [2015] EWCA Civ 1176; [2016] 1 W.L.R. 1541.

to acknowledge the wrong committed by the defendant and to compensate for the loss of control of information as well as the injury to feelings, embarrassment and distress caused.[471] In assessing damages, judges should consider the levels of awards made in personal injury cases.[472] The award in *Mosley v News Group Newspapers Ltd*[473] was £60,000. For a time, because it was difficult to think of more damaging revelations than had occurred in that case disclosure of which would not be justified in the public interest, it was thought that this sum must be near the maximum. However, in *Gulati v MGN Ltd*[474] awards ranging between £72,500 and £260,250 were made for misuse of private information derived from extensive and serious phone hacking by journalists. Aggravated damages are available[475] whereas punitive damages are not.[476]

13-149 Injunctive relief A court may grant an injunction to restrain the wrongful disclosure of personal information, understandably so, since once it is out in the open the harm is done and the award of damages may be a poor consolation prize.[477] Here the law on misuse of private information differs radically from that applicable in defamation cases. It is practically impossible to obtain an interim injunction against defamation if the defendant asserts that he will raise one of the standard defences like truth or privilege,[478] but such injunctions are regularly granted in cases of alleged misuse of private information. The fact that it is easier to obtain an interim injunction against misuse of private information than against defamation raises an interesting point. Private information may be defamatory. If faced with threatened disclosure, can a claimant say "I deny that what you are about to say is true but whether it is true or not makes no difference because publication would invade my privacy" and seek an injunction against misuse of private information? Indeed, can he go further and, even when the information has been disclosed, sue for damages for misuse of private information rather than defamation and deprive the defendant of the opportunity to prove that what he said was true? Of course it might require a certain hardihood to do that because many people would no doubt conclude that the unwillingness of the claimant to sue for defamation showed that it *was* true. Furthermore, a court assessing damages for misuse of private information would surely have to proceed on the basis that the allegation was true and award lower damages. The point is unresolved but the Court of Appeal said in *McKennett v Ash* that the "question in a case of misuse of private information is whether the information is private not whether it is true or false. The truth or falsity

---

[471] *Gulati v MGN Ltd* [2015] EWCA Civ 1291; [2017] Q.B. 149 at [45], [48].
[472] *Gulati v MGN Ltd* [2015] EWCA Civ 1291; [2017] Q.B. 149 at [61].
[473] [2008] EWHC 1777 (QB); [2008] E.M.L.R. 20.
[474] [2015] EWCA Civ 1291; [2017] Q.B. 149.
[475] *HRH The Duchess of Sussex v Associated Newspapers Ltd* [2020] EWHC 1058 (Ch) at [54].
[476] *Mosley v News Group Newspapers Ltd* [2008] EWHC 1777 (QB); [2008] E.M.L.R. 20.
[477] However, in *PJS v News Group Newspapers Ltd* [2016] UKSC 26; [2016] A.C. 1081 the Supreme Court continued an interim injunction to restrain disclosure of alleged extra-marital sexual activity by a celebrity even though details of the allegations had already been published in several countries (including Scotland) and on the internet. Lord Mance remarked (at [1]) that the defendant's purpose in seeking to have the injunction lifted was to "add extensively and in a qualitatively different medium to such invasions".
[478] *Bonnard v Perryman* [1891] 2 Ch. 269; *Khuja v Times Newspapers Ltd* [2017] UKSC 49; [2019] A.C. 161 at [19]. See, further, para.23-128.

of the information is an irrelevant inquiry in deciding whether the information is entitled to be protected".[479] However, in the same case the court added that[480]:

"[I]f it could be shown that a claim in [misuse of private information] was brought where the nub of the case was a complaint of the falsity of the allegations, and that that was done in order to avoid the rules of the tort of defamation, then objections could be raised in terms of abuse of process. That might be so at the interlocutory stage in an attempt to avoid the rule [about interim injunctions in defamation cases]".

Despite the foregoing it is doubtful whether the defence of abuse of process should be available here. No reasons were given by the court as to why the claimant should not be able to exercise his right to choose which action to bring. It is a familiar feature of the common law that a single act will generate liability in one action but not in another. This is ordinarily thought to be entirely unproblematic.[481] The difficulty with the court's suggestion regarding abuse of process is that it intimates that where it would be defamatory to publish the private information the case should be seen as a defamation case and subject to the restrictions on liability recognised by the law of defamation. However, more is needed than a mere assertion that the case should be analysed only as one in defamation.

---

[479] [2006] EWCA Civ 1714; [2008] Q.B. 73 at [86]. See also at [80].
[480] [2006] EWCA Civ 1714; [2008] Q.B. 73 at [79].
[481] See para.1-009.

CHAPTER 14

TRESPASS TO LAND

1. TRESPASS DEFINED

Trespass to land is the name given to that form of trespass which is constituted **14-001** by unjustifiable interference with the possession of land. Contrary to popular belief trespass is not criminal in the absence of some special statute which makes it so.[1] Since the decision in *Fowler v Lanning*,[2] it may be asked whether tortious liability for trespass to land, like that for trespass to the person, requires proof of intention or at least negligence on the part of the defendant. We must, however, be careful to define what that intention or negligence goes to, for it is clear law that an entry upon another's land is tortious whether or not the entrant knows that he is trespassing.[3] Thus it is no defence that the only reason for his entry was that he had lost his way or even that he genuinely but erroneously believed that the land was his. It follows that the great majority of trespasses to land are, for legal purposes, self-evidently intentional—I intend to enter upon your land if I consciously place

---

[1]   There are a number of exceptions to the basic rule: see, e.g., Criminal Law Act 1977 ss.6–9; Criminal Justice and Public Order Act 1994 ss.61, 68; Serious Organised Crime and Police Act 2005 s.128; Legal Aid, Sentencing and Punishment of Offenders Act 2012 s.144.

[2]   [1959] 1 Q.B. 426. See para.4-003.

[3]   *Conway v George Wimpey & Co Ltd* [1951] 2 K.B. 266 at 273–274; *Jolliffe v Willmett & Co* [1971] 1 All E.R. 478.

myself upon what proves to be your land, even though I neither knew nor could reasonably have known that it was not mine.

14-002 Liability for involuntary entry We are left with those cases where the defendant's entry was involuntary, whether caused by his fault or not. Where he is thrown or pushed on to the land he is not liable for trespass simply because there is no act on his part.[4] As for other situations it is clear that where land adjoining the highway is unintentionally entered, as a result, for example, of a road accident, the claimant must prove negligence, a proposition established long before *Fowler v Lanning*.[5] In *League Against Cruel Sports v Scott*,[6] Park J had to deal with trespass by hounds in pursuit of a stag and he concluded that the law was that the master of the pack was liable if he intended the hounds to enter the claimant's land or if, knowing that there was a real risk that they would enter, their entry was caused by his failure to exercise proper control of them.[7] The burden of proof as to either condition is upon the claimant.[8]

14-003 Actionable per se Trespass is actionable per se, i.e., whether or not the claimant has suffered any damage. This rule may seem harsh but in earlier times trespass was so likely to lead to a breach of the peace that even trivial deviations on to another person's land were reckoned unlawful. The theoretical severity of the rules as to land trespass is in any case rarely exploited in practice. An action will not normally be brought for trespass without damage unless the claimant wishes to deter persistent trespassing or there are disputes over boundaries or rights of way.[9]

2. POSSESSION

14-004 A contextual meaning Trespass to land, like the tort of trespass to goods, which is considered in a later chapter, consists of interference with possession, and it is necessary to say something here of this concept.[10] Our law has, however, not worked out a consistent theory of possession, and its meaning turns upon the context in which it is used.[11]

14-005 Physical presence or de facto control Mere physical presence on the land or the use[12] or de facto control of it does not necessarily amount to possession sufficient to bring an action of trespass. It is, for example, generally said that a lodger in another's house does not have possession,[13] nor does an employee occupying a

---

4 *Smith v Stone* (1647) Style 65; 82 E.R. 533.
5 See, e.g., *River Wear Commissioners v Adason* (1877) 2 App. Cas. 743.
6 [1986] Q.B. 240.
7 Despite the reference to "knowing", this is a negligence standard, though it is not the tort of negligence since no damage is required.
8 cf. *Fowler v Lanning* [1959] 1 Q.B. 426, para.4-003.
9 In the modern law an action for a declaration might be used to settle disputed rights.
10 See further Pollock and Wright, *An Essay on Possession in the Common Law* (1888); Wonnacott, *Possession of Land* (2006).
11 *Towers & Co Ltd v Gray* [1961] 2 Q.B. 351 at 361; *Greenmanor Ltd v Pilford* [2012] EWCA Civ 756 at [27].
12 A person who has been granted a right to grow crops on another's land has sufficient possession to sue for trespass to land in respect of damage to them: *Monsanto Plc v Tilly* [2000] Env. L.R. 313.
13 *Allan v Liverpool Overseers* (1874) L.R. 9 Q.B. 180 at 191–192, adopted in *Appah v Parncliffe Investments Ltd* [1964] 1 W.L.R. 1064 at 1069–1970.

room in his employer's house,[14] since possession lies in another, i.e., the owner of the house, or the employer.

Possession under a lease On the other hand, a lessor of land gives up posses- **14-006** sion to his tenant so that a tenant can bring trespass during the currency of the lease—even against the lessor unless, of course, the lessor's entry was effected in accordance with the provisions of the lease.[15] Most of the cases on the distinction between a tenant and a licensee (who does not have possession) have arisen in the context of security of tenure under the Rent Acts, but it is clear that the matter is to be determined by the substance of the agreement between the parties rather than by the label which they have chosen to attach to their relationship[16] and the hallmark of a tenancy is the right in the tenant to "exclusive possession".[17] It is, however, possible that in modern conditions there may be rare cases in which a person has sufficient possession to bring trespass against a third party even though he is not a tenant.[18] As for the lessor, he cannot bring proceedings for a wrongful entry during the currency of the lease except in so far as it has caused permanent damage to the land, leading to a reduction in the value of his reversion, such as would result from the cutting of trees or the pulling down of buildings.[19]

Relevance of a legal interest in the land It is not necessary that the claimant **14-007** should have some lawful estate or interest in the land so that there is no doubt, for example, that a squatter occupying the land without any claim of right may have sufficient possession to bring a claim for trespass and, generally speaking, a stranger who enters the land without the squatter's consent cannot rely in his defence upon another person's superior right (the jus tertii) unless he can prove that he acted with that person's authority.[20] This is not to say that legal title is irrelevant, for where the facts leave it uncertain which of several competing claimants has possession it is in him who can prove title, i.e., the right to possess.[21] More generally, "in the absence of evidence to the contrary, the owner of land with the paper title is deemed to be in possession of the land".[22] That which will amount to possession varies according to the nature of the property, so that possession of a flat with a front door which can be locked is obviously different from possession of part of an unfenced moor or hillside.[23] Possession once acquired is not, however, ended by sending the

---

14 *White v Bayley* (1861) 10 C.B. (N.S.) 227; 142 E.R. 438.
15 *Lane v Dixon* (1847) 3 C.B. 776; 136 E.R. 311.
16 *Street v Mountford* [1985] A.C. 809; *Antoniades v Villers* [1990] A.C. 417; *Aslan v Murphy* [1990] 1 W.L.R. 766.
17 That is to say, the right to exclude the landlord during the currency of the term except in so far as a right of entry is reserved for a limited purpose, e.g., to repair. See *Radaich v Smith* (1959) 101 C.L.R. 209 at 222, adopted in *Street v Mountford* [1985] A.C. 809.
18 *Mehta v Royal Bank of Scotland* [1999] 3 E.G.L.R. 153 seems to be an example (very long-term occupancy of hotel room).
19 *Ward v Macauley* (1791) 4 Term. Rep. 489; 100 E.R. 1135; *Mayfair Property Co v Johnson* [1894] 1 Ch. 508; *Jones v Llanrwst UDC* [1911] 1 Ch. 393.
20 *Chambers v Donaldson* (1809) 11 East. 65; 103 E.R. 929; *Nicholls v Ely Beet Sugar Factory* [1931] 2 Ch. 84. As to the jus tertii in relation to trespass to goods, see para.18-032.
21 *Jones v Chapman* (1849) 2 Ex. 803 at 821; 153 E.R. 717 at 724.
22 *Powell v McFarlane* (1977) 38 P. & C.R. 452 at 470 per Slade J; *Star Energy Weald Basin Ltd v Bocardo SA* [2010] UKSC 35; [2011] 1 A.C. 380 at [30] (where the claimant, as owner of the surface, had done nothing to reduce the subsoil to its actual possession).
23 *Simpson v Fergus* (1999) 79 P. & C.R. 398; *Ocean Estates Ltd v Pinder* [1969] 2 A.C. 19.

defendant a letter demanding delivery-up of the land.[24] Some estate or interest in the land may also lead the court to find possession in the claimant in other circumstances. For example, it is probably still the law that a spouse who is merely occupying a matrimonial home along with the other spouse does not have possession so as to maintain trespass,[25] but a spouse who has a share in the ownership (as would normally be the case today) would certainly have it.

14-008 Continuous physical control not necessary Possession may obviously extend to things which are beyond a person's immediate physical control. I do not lose possession of my house and its contents when I leave them to go to the office or even to go away on holiday.

14-009 Immediate right to possess: trespass by relation The immediate right to possess, sometimes also known as constructive possession,[26] signifies the lawful right to retain possession when one has it or to acquire it when one has not. Without possession it is not sufficient to support an action of trespass[27] but, owing to the willingness of the courts to extend the superior protection afforded by the older law to possession as distinct from ownership, it has for long been the law that once a person entitled to immediate possession actually enters upon the land and so acquires possession, he is deemed to have been in possession from the moment that his right to it accrued.[28] This fiction, known as trespass by relation, has the result that he can sue for acts of trespass committed while he was actually out of possession and it also provides the foundation for the claim in respect of "mesne profits", that is, the claim for the damage suffered by a person as a result of having been kept out of the possession of his land.[29]

3. INTERFERENCE

14-010 Must be direct and immediate Interference with the possession of land sufficient to amount to trespass may occur in many ways. The most obvious example is unauthorised walking upon it or going into the buildings upon it, but it is equally trespass if I throw things on to your land,[30] deliberately discharge water[31] or allow my cattle to stray on to it, and even if I do no more than place my ladder against your wall.[32] If you have given me permission to enter your land and I act in excess of the permission or remain on your land after it has expired, then, again, I am a trespasser.[33] The one restriction is that for trespass the interference must be direct

---

[24] *Mount Carmel Investments Ltd v Peter Thurlow Ltd* [1988] 1 W.L.R. 1078.

[25] *Hunter v Canary Wharf Ltd* [1997] A.C. 655 (a case of nuisance but, it is thought, still in point).

[26] For an explanation of this term, see *Alicia Hosiery Ltd v Brown Shipley & Co Ltd* [1970] 1 Q.B. 195 at 207.

[27] It is, however, sufficient for an action of conversion and is explained more fully in connection with that tort, para.18-026.

[28] See *Dunlop v Macedo* (1891) 8 T.L.R. 43.

[29] The action for mesne profits is explained in para.14-033.

[30] For a modern, power-assisted example, see *Rigby v CC Northamptonshire* [1985] 1 W.L.R. 1242.

[31] *Manchester Ship Canal Co Ltd v United Utilities Water Plc* [2014] UKSC 40; [2014] 1 W.L.R. 2576 at [2]. This would include discharging water into another's flowing watercourse.

[32] *Westripp v Baldock* [1938] 2 All E.R. 779, affirmed [1939] 1 All E.R. 279; *Home Brewery Co Ltd v William Davis & Co (Leicester) Ltd* [1987] Q.B. 339.

[33] *Hillen v ICI (Alkali) Ltd* [1936] A.C. 65; *Canadian Pacific Ry v Gaud* [1949] 2 K.B. 239 at 249, 254–255; but a lessee holding over after the termination of his lease is no trespasser, for trespass can only

and immediate. If it is indirect or consequential, it may be a nuisance, but will not be a trespass. So if I plant a tree on your land, that is trespass; but if the roots or branches of a tree on my land project into or over your land, that is a nuisance.[34]

A. Trespass on Highway

It is obvious that a person who uses a highway for the purpose of travelling from one place to another commits no trespass against anyone, but at one time it was held that the right of user of the highway was confined to use for passage and matters incidental thereto, like resting, and that otherwise there was a trespass against the owner of the subsoil.[35] However, in *Director of Public Prosecutions v Jones*[36] (where the civil law issue arose in the context of a charge of taking part in a trespassory assembly under the Public Order Act 1986) the majority of the House of Lords held that it was not a trespass to participate in a peaceful assembly on the highway so long as it was reasonable and caused no obstruction. Lord Irvine LC went so far as to say that any reasonable use of the highway, not involving nuisance or obstruction, was lawful. However, he did not seem to regard as wrongly decided earlier cases in which it had been held to be trespass to use the highway to disrupt shooting[37] or to gain information about racehorse trials[38] on land crossed by the highway. It has since been held that to conduct commercial operations on the highway without the consent of the landowner is in and of itself unreasonable.[39]

14-011

B. Trespass to Subsoil

Any intrusion upon the subsoil is just as much a trespass as entry upon the surface, and subsoil and surface may be possessed by different persons.[40] If A is in possession of the surface and B of the subsoil, and I walk upon the land, that is a trespass against A, but not against B. If I dig holes vertically in the land, that is a trespass against both A and B. If I bore a tunnel from my land into B's subsoil, that is a trespass against B only.[41] Even if the landowner has been deprived of ownership of minerals by statute, intrusions beneath the surface to obtain them, such as

14-012

---

be committed against the person in present possession of the land: *Hey v Moorhouse* (1839) 6 Bing. N.C. 52; 133 E.R. 20. cf. *Minister of Health v Bellotti* [1944] K.B. 298 (licensee holding over after termination of licence and after lapse of reasonable time becomes a trespasser).

34 *Smith v Giddy* [1904] 2 K.B. 448 at 451; *Davey v Harrow Corp* [1958] 1 Q.B. 60.

35 At common law this is the person whose land abuts on the highway. cf. *Tithe Redemption Commission v Runcorn UDC* [1954] Ch. 383, and Highways Act 1980 ss.263–265. Where the top surface is vested in a highway authority, there would seem no reason why that authority could not bring proceedings for trespass: see the comment of Collins LJ in *DPP v Jones* [1998] Q.B. 563 on the view of Lord Denning MR in *Hubbard v Pitt* [1976] Q.B. 142.

36 [1999] A.C. 240.

37 *Harrison v Duke of Rutland* [1893] 1 Q.B. 142.

38 *Hickman v Maisey* [1900] 1 Q.B. 752.

39 *Cambridge City Council v Traditional Cambridge Tours Ltd* [2018] EWHC 1304 (QB) (punting trips on River Cam using slipway owned by local authority without permission).

40 Although, according to Lord Hope in *Star Energy Weald Basin Ltd v Bocardo SA* [2010] UKSC 35; [2011] 1 A.C. 380 at [27], "There must obviously be some stopping point, as one reaches the point at which physical features such as pressure and temperature render the concept of the strata belonging to anybody so absurd as to be not worth arguing about." On the facts, however, that "stopping point" was not reached at a depth of 2,900 feet.

41 *Cox v Glue* (1848) 5 C.B. 533; 136 E.R. 987.

pipelines, still amount to trespass, though in such a case the quantum of damages may be limited.

C. Interference with Airspace

14-013   Invasion of the air space above a person's land can amount to trespass. In *Kelsen v Imperial Tobacco Co*[42] McNair J held that an advertising sign erected by the defendants on their own property, which projected into the airspace above the claimant's shop, was a trespass.[43] The issue arises not infrequently as a result of the operation of tower cranes on building sites, which swing over adjoining land. There is no doubt that this amounts to trespass[44] and the claimant will normally be entitled to an injunction[45] even though this state of the law allows him to take a "dog in the manger" attitude[46] and force the defendant to pay him a sum in excess of any damage he has suffered.

14-014   **Extent of the landowner's rights**   Although an intrusion into air space at a relatively low height constitutes trespass,[47] the landowner's rights in airspace extend only to such height as is necessary for the ordinary use and enjoyment of the land and structures on it,[48] so that the flight of an aircraft "several hundred feet" above a house is not wrongful at common law.[49] Quite apart from the common law position, it is provided by statute that to fly a civil aircraft at a reasonable height (having regard to wind, weather and all the circumstances of the case) it is not a trespass.[50] A landowner is not, however, without protection from persistent aerial surveillance from a height outside his zone of user, for such conduct may constitute a nuisance.[51]

D. Continuing Trespass

14-015   Trespass, whether by way of personal entry or by placing things on the claimant's land, may be "continuing" and give rise to actions from day-to-day so long as it lasts. In *Holmes v Wilson*,[52] highway authorities supported a road by wrongfully building buttresses on the claimant's land, and they paid full compensation in an action for trespass. They were nevertheless held liable in a further action for trespass, because they had not removed the buttresses. Nor does a transfer of the

---

[42] [1957] 2 Q.B. 334.

[43] See also *Stadium Capital Holdings v St Marylebone Properties Company Plc* [2010] EWCA Civ 952.

[44] *Woollerton & Wilson Ltd v Richard Costain Ltd* [1970] 1 W.L.R. 411; *Anchor Brewhouse Developments Ltd v Berkley House (Docklands Developments) Ltd* (1987) 284 E.G. 625.

[45] In the *Woollerton & Wilson* case the injunction was suspended for long enough to allow the defendant to complete the works but this cannot be supported: *Jaggard v Sawyer* [1995] 1 W.L.R. 269.

[46] *Anchor Brewhouse Developments Ltd v Berkley House (Docklands Developments) Ltd* (1987) 284 E.G. 625 at 633.

[47] *Liaquat v Majid* [2005] EWHC 1305 (QB); 26 E.G. 130 (C.S.) (75cm projection 4.5m above ground).

[48] *Didow v Alberta Power* [1988] 5 W.W.R. 606 (power lines 50 feet up within zone of user).

[49] *Bernstein v Skyviews & General Ltd* [1978] Q.B. 479.

[50] Civil Aviation Act 1982 s.76(1). It is conceivable that s.76 confers a wider exemption than the common law and might, in certain circumstances, justify an entry even into the zone of normal user.

[51] Or harassment under the Protection from Harassment Act 1997.

[52] (1839) 10 A. & E. 50; 113 E.R. 190.

land by the injured party prevent the transferee from suing the defendant for continuing trespass.[53]

Trespass by omission   At one time it may have been the law that trespass did not **14-016** lie for omission to remove something from the land which was lawfully there to begin with,[54] although if the thing did damage to the land after it ought to have been removed an action on the case would lie. However, more modern authority imposes liability for trespass[55] and there is a close analogy with the situation where a visitor's stay exceeds the duration of his licence. But there is no trespass if the defendant merely fails to restore land to the condition in which he found it. So while to dig a pit on another's land is, of course, a trespass, a subsequent failure to fill it in is not.[56]

4.   DEFENCES

A.   Licence

Pollock defined a licence as "that consent which, without passing any interest in **14-017** the property to which it relates, merely prevents the acts for which consent is given from being wrongful".[57] A person is not a trespasser if he is on land with the permission, express or implied,[58] of the possessor. Whether that permission is given is a matter for the possessor, even if the public generally have free access to the property (such as a shopping mall) and regardless of whether he has a good reason for exclusion.

Revocable licences   A bare licence, i.e., one granted otherwise than for valuable **14-018** consideration, may be revoked at any time,[59] and so may many contractual licences, even though revocation may render the licensor liable for breach of contract.[60] After revocation the licensee becomes a trespasser, but he must be allowed a reasonable time in which to leave and to remove his possessions.[61]

---

[53]   *Hudson v Nicholson* (1839) 5 M. & W. 437; 151 E.R. 185, followed in *Konskier v Goodman Ltd* [1928] 1 K.B. 421.

[54]   *Shapcott v Mugford* (1696) 1 Ld. Raym. 187 at 188; 91 E.R. 1021 at 1022: trespass vi et armis does not apply to nonfeasance.

[55]   *Konskier v Goodman Ltd* [1928] 1 K.B. 421. cf. *Penarth Dock Co v Pounds* [1963] 1 Lloyd's Rep. 359 (breach of contract).

[56]   *Clegg v Dearden* (1848) 12 Q.B. 576 at 601; but a tenant who removes fixtures and does not make good may be liable for waste. This is a tort, but not one of much importance, since the landlord will normally rely on covenants in the lease: *Mancetter Developments Ltd v Garmanson Ltd* [1986] Q.B. 1212.

[57]   *Pollock's Law of Torts*, 15th edn (1951), p.284. It necessarily follows that the acts of the licensee must not exceed the terms of the licence: *Seeff v Ho* [2011] EWCA Civ 186.

[58]   See *Robson v Hallett* [1967] 2 Q.B. 939 at 950–951, 953–954.

[59]   On a licence granted by one co-occupier and revoked by another, see *Robson-Paul v Farrugia* (1969) 20 C.C.R. 820.

[60]   *Thompson v Park* [1944] K.B. 408. cf. *Kerrison v Smith* [1897] 2 Q.B. 445; *King v David Allen & Sons Ltd* [1916] 2 A.C. 54. In *Stokes v Brent LBC* [2009] EWHC 1426 (QB) C was unable to challenge the revocation of the licence granted to her by the defendant council on the basis of a violation of art.8 of the ECHR.

[61]   *Cornish v Stubbs* (1870) L.R. 5 C.P. 334; *Canadian Pacific Ry v The King* [1931] A.C. 414; *Minister of Health v Bellotti* [1944] K.B. 289; *Robson v Hallett* [1967] 2 Q.B. 939.

14-019 Irrevocable licences Some contractual licences are, however, irrevocable because revocation in breach of contract would be prevented by the grant of an equitable remedy to the licensee. A licence coupled with an interest is irrevocable because, although the licence itself—the bare permission to enter—is only a right in personam, it confers a right in rem to something when you have entered[62]:

> "[A] licence to hunt in a man's park, and carry away the deer killed to his own use; to cut down a tree in a man's ground, and to carry it away the next day after to his own use, are licences as to the acts of hunting and cutting down the tree; but as to the carrying away of the deer killed, and tree cut down, they are grants."

Until the tree or deer is carried away the licence is irrevocable.[63]

14-020 Uncertain cases A contractual licence may also be irrevocable even if it is not coupled with an interest, but the circumstances in which this will be so are unclear. It seems, however, that the following propositions are warranted by the cases.[64] Whether a contractual licence is revocable is a question of construction of the contract.[65] It will be irrevocable if such is the intention of the parties, and it may be inferred from the terms of the contract, the character of the transaction, and the attendant circumstances that the licence is intended to endure for a definite or ascertainable period. Where a licence is granted for a limited period and for a definite purpose, it will be irrevocable until the accomplishment of the purpose.[66] If the licensee is prepared to observe the terms of the contract the licensor may be restrained by injunction from revoking the licence[67] and even where there is no opportunity to seek such a remedy (for example, where the claimant is ejected from a cinema) the equitable right which the licensee has destroys the defence of "trespasser" which the licensor might otherwise plead to an action for assault.[68]

14-021 Executed licence If a licence has been executed, it cannot be revoked in the sense that the licensee can be compelled to undo that which he has lawfully done. If I allow you to post bills on my hoarding, I can cancel my permission, but I cannot force you to remove bills that you have already stuck there. So in *Liggins v Inge*[69] where

---

[62] *Thomas v Sorrell* (1672) Vaughan 330 at 351; 124 E.R. 1098 at 1109 per Vaughan CJ.

[63] *Wood v Leadbitter* (1845) 13 M. & W. 838 at 844–845; 153 E.R. 351 at 354–355; *Jones & Sons Ltd v Tankerville* [1909] 2 Ch. 440 at 442. cf. *Frank Warr & Co Ltd v LCC* [1904] 1 K.B. 713; *Clore v Theatrical Properties Ltd* [1936] 3 All E.R. 483.

[64] See especially *Hurst v Picture Theatres Ltd* [1915] 1 K.B. 1; *Winter Garden Theatre (London) Ltd v Millennium Productions Ltd* [1948] A.C. 173; *Bendall v McWhirter* [1952] 2 Q.B. 466; *Hounslow LBC v Twickenham Garden Developments Ltd* [1971] Ch. 233. cf. *Wood v Leadbitter* (1845) 13 M. & W. 838; 153 E.R. 351.

[65] *Winter Garden Theatre (London) Ltd v Millennium Productions Ltd* [1946] 1 All E.R. 678 at 680; *Re Spenborough UDC's Agreement* [1968] Ch. 139. cf. *Winter Garden* case [1948] A.C. 173 at 193; Wade (1948) 64 L.Q.R. 57 at 69.

[66] *Winter Garden Theatre (London) Ltd v Millennium Productions Ltd* [1948] A.C. 173 at 186, 189.

[67] *Winter Garden Theatre (London) Ltd v Millennium Productions Ltd* [1946] 1 All E.R. 678 at 685; *Bendall v McWhirter* [1952] 2 Q.B. 466 at 478–483. In a proper case, revocation of the licence may be restrained even though performance has not yet commenced: *Verrall v Great Yarmouth BC* [1981] Q.B. 202.

[68] Wade (1948) 64 L.Q.R. 57 at 76; *Errington v Errington* [1952] 1 K.B. 290 at 297–299; *Bendall v McWhirter* [1952] 2 Q.B. 466 at 479–483. *Bendall v McWhirter* was overruled in *National Provincial Bank Ltd v Ainsworth* [1965] A.C. 1175 but, it is submitted, without affecting the propositions in the text.

[69] (1831) 3 Bing. 683; 131 E.R. 263; *Davies v Marshall* (1861) 10 C.B.(N.S.) 697; 142 E.R. 627. See

an oral licence had been given to lower a riverbank and make a weir above the licensor's mill, it was held that the licensor could not sue the licensee for continuing the weir which the latter had erected; but the rule that an executed licence is irrevocable applies only where the licence can be construed as authorising the doing of exactly what has been done. It does not apply where there has been mere acquiescence in something which was never authorised before it was done.[70] Nor does it apply if its application would amount to the creation of an easement in favour of the licensee. An easement cannot be granted by parol and therefore, after the licence has been revoked, the claimant is prima facie entitled to an injunction restraining the continuation of the trespass.[71]

Public law restrictions The power of a public body to revoke a licence to enter **14-022** its premises may be restricted by the requirements of public law, for example by requiring it to hear the licensee first,[72] but there is no basis for restricting the power of revocation of occupiers of shopping malls, public utility showrooms or the like on the ground that they are "quasi-public" places.[73]

B. Legal Authority

Acts which would otherwise be trespasses are frequently prevented from being **14-023** so by the existence of some justification provided by the law. The majority of such justifications are provided by statute.

Entry by law officers Most important are the innumerable instances in which of- **14-024** ficers of the law are authorised to enter land, but these belong more to public than to private law and, accordingly, only one or two illustrations can be given here. The police have no general common law power to enter private premises without consent or warrant but their most important statutory powers are those conferred by the Police and Criminal Evidence Act 1984. Under s.17[74] a constable may enter[75] and search premises (if need be, by force) for the purpose of arresting a person for an indictable offence and for various other purposes (including to save life or limb or prevent serious damage to the property)[76] and under s.18 there is power to enter premises after an arrest for an indictable offence and search for evidence of the commission of that offence or connected or similar offences.[77] A police officer also has a power of entry to premises to prevent a breach of the peace.[78]

Wade (1948) 64 L.Q.R. 57 at 68–69.

[70] *Canadian Pacific Ry v The King* [1931] A.C. 414 at 428–429.

[71] *Armstrong v Sheppard & Short Ltd* [1959] 2 Q.B. 384. The right to an injunction is not unqualified and an injunction may be refused on the ground that the injury is trivial.

[72] *Wandsworth LBC v A* [2000] 1 W.L.R. 1246 (parent's licence to enter child's school).

[73] *CIN Properties Ltd v Rawlins* [1995] E.G.L.R. 30; *Porter v MPC* unreported 20 October 1999, CA.

[74] For search warrants, see ss.8–16.

[75] The officer must, unless the circumstances make it impracticable or undesirable, give the occupier the reason for exercising the power of entry: *O'Loughlin v CC Essex* [1998] 1 W.L.R. 364. For emergency powers of entry of firefighters see the Fire and Rescue Services Act 2004 s.44.

[76] For the power to enter in pursuit of persons "unlawfully at large", see the Prisoners (Return to Custody) Act 1995.

[77] Only premises occupied by the arrested person: *Khan v MPC* [2008] EWCA Civ 723; [2008] Po L.R. 112 (arrestee giving false address). See also s.32, as amended.

[78] *Thomas v Sawkins* [1935] 2 K.B. 249.

14-025   **Entry by private persons in furtherance of the law**   Nor is it only officers of the law who may be thus empowered. A private person may in certain circumstances arrest a criminal, and it is no trespass if he breaks into the house of another person in order to prevent him from murdering his wife,[79] or (probably) from committing other serious offences.[80]

14-026   **Entry under statute: other examples**   In addition to the powers granted to law officers, other forms of entry may be authorised by statute and so not amount to trespass. For example, a person entering land in pursuance of arrangements made for the public to have access to open country is not a trespasser so long as he does no damage and complies with the specified restrictions.[81] Under the Access to Neighbouring Land Act 1992 the court may make an order allowing access to land for the purpose of carrying out works which are reasonably necessary for the preservation of adjoining land and which cannot be carried out, or would be substantially more difficult to carry out, without entry upon the land. No such order is to be made, however, if it would cause unreasonable interference with the enjoyment of the land sought to be entered or unreasonable hardship. The 1992 Act does not permit entry for development or improvement as such but does permit entry for the purpose of work of "alteration, adjustment or improvement [or] demolition if merely incidental to the work necessary for preservation".[82] More generally, the scope of the entry authorised by the statute concerned is a question of its proper construction.[83]

14-027   **Abuse of authority: trespass ab initio**   Where an entry upon land or other prima facie trespass is justified by legal authority, then, according to an ancient doctrine of the common law, if the actor abuses that authority he becomes a trespasser ab initio and his act is treated as unlawful from the very beginning, however innocent his conduct may have been up to the moment of the abuse.[84] The doctrine applies only if the authority is that of the law,[85] not that of the other party concerned,[86] and the abuse must be by a positive act, not a mere omission.[87] The explanations of these restrictions on the doctrine are historical,[88] but they show that its purpose, derived from its origin in the law of distress, was to provide protection against abuses of authority. Seen in this light it would seem to be unduly optimistic to suppose that

---

[79]   *Handcock v Baker* (1800) 2 Bos. & P. 260; 126 E.R. 1270.

[80]   *Handcock v Baker* (1800) 2 Bos. & P. 260 at 265; 126 E.R. 1270 at 1273. Such cases would now fall under the Criminal Law Act 1967 s.3.

[81]   Countryside and Rights of Way Act 2000 s.2.

[82]   See s.1(5). See also the Party Wall, etc., Act 1996.

[83]   *Manchester Ship Canal Co Ltd v United Utilities Water Plc* [2014] UKSC 40; [2014] 1 W.L.R. 2576 (general right to discharge into private watercourses could not be implied into the Water Industry Act 1991, although rights of discharge which had accrued in relation to existing outfalls under previous statutory regimes survived). See also *Star Energy Weald Basin Ltd v Bocardo SA* [2010] UKSC 35; [2011] 1 A.C. 380 on the construction of s.9(2) of the Petroleum Act 1998. cf. the defence of statutory authority in nuisance: para.15-056.

[84]   *Six Carpenters Case* (1610) 8 Co. Rep. 146a; 77 E.R. 695.

[85]   Where entry takes place by virtue of an access order under the Access to Neighbouring Land Act 1992 the doctrine is excluded by s.3(6) of the Act.

[86]   *Delta Holdings Ltd v Magrum* (1975) 59 D.L.R. (3d) 126.

[87]   *Delta Holdings Ltd v Magrum* (1975) 59 D.L.R. (3d) 126.

[88]   Holdsworth, *A History of English Law*, vol. vii, pp.499–501.

the doctrine has outlived its usefulness,[89] even given the modern limitation that partial abuse of an authority does not render everything done under it unlawful. For example, in *Elias v Pasmore*[90] police had lawfully entered the claimant's premises in order to arrest a man and, while there, they seized a number of documents, some of them unlawfully. It was held that this did not render their original entry a trespass. However, in *Chic Fashions (West Wales) Ltd v Jones*,[91] though no point involving trespass ab initio was in fact in issue, the Court of Appeal criticised the doctrine as offending against the principle that subsequent events cannot render unlawful an act which was lawful when it was done. This principle is, in general, a sound one, but it should not be over-stressed. Not only may subsequent events illuminate the intent with which an act was originally done and thus assist in determining its lawfulness or unlawfulness,[92] but there are, and should continue to be, cases in which, in effect, the law withholds judgment on the lawfulness of an act for a time and allows it to depend upon subsequent events.[93] The doctrine of trespass ab initio enables this to be done in the important area of the protection of one's person, goods and land against abuse of official power.[94]

5. REMEDIES

The action for trespass, besides being used to remedy trespass as a pure tort, has **14-028** also some varieties which are employed for the recovery of land and the profits thereof.

A. Re-entry

The remedies for trespass as a pure tort[95] need no special mention except the right **14-029** of re-entry. The person entitled to possession can enter or re-enter the premises, but the Criminal Law Act 1977 makes it an imprisonable offence for anyone (other than a displaced residential occupier) to use or threaten violence for the purposes of securing entry to any premises occupied by another.[96] This replaces earlier criminal legislation in a series of Forcible Entry Acts, beginning in 1381. However, in *Hemmings v Stoke Poges Golf Club*[97] the Court of Appeal held that whatever might be his criminal liability under such statutes, a landowner was not civilly liable if he used no more force than was necessary to remove the other party and his property.

---

89   cf. *Chic Fashions (West Wales) Ltd v Jones* [1968] 2 Q.B. 299.
90   [1934] 2 K.B. 164; *Harvey v Pocock* (1843) 11 M. & W. 740; 152 E.R. 1003; *Canadian Pacific Wine Co Ltd v Tuley* [1921] 2 A.C. 417.
91   [1968] 2 Q.B. 299.
92   This was one of the explanations of the doctrine of trespass ab initio itself given by Coke: 8 Co. Rep. 146b. Winfield ridiculed it (see the eighth edition of this book, p.346) but even though it contains an element of fiction, it perhaps has some merit.
93   *Southam v Smout* [1964] 1 Q.B. 308 provides one example, and there are others too. The power of a private person to arrest on reasonable suspicion of an offence exists only if the offence suspected has actually been committed (Police and Criminal Evidence Act 1984 s.24A), and this cannot be known until further investigations have been carried out.
94   Lord Denning MR, a member of the court in *Chic Fashions*, subsequently referred to the doctrine with approval in *Cinnamond v British Airports Authority* [1980] 1 W.L.R. 582.
95   As to damages in respect of land, see para.23-119.
96   Note that the proposition in the text is a summary of a complex provision.
97   [1920] 1 K.B. 720, where the earlier authorities are considered.

It is contended that the law remains the same under the Criminal Law Act 1977[98] and it has been said in the Supreme Court that "self-help is a remedy still available, in principle, to a landowner against trespassers (other than former residential tenants)",[99] even if the risk of criminal liability has curtailed its utility.[100]

B.   Action for the Recovery of Land

14-030   **Introduction**   By the action of ejectment, or, as it is now known, the action for the recovery of land, a person dispossessed of land can recover it specifically. Although the history is complex,[101] an action for the recovery of land differs in no formal respect from any other action. A special summary procedure has, however, been devised to enable a claimant to obtain an order for possession against persons in occupation of his land if they entered or remained there without his licence or consent, whether or not he is able to identify all, or even any, of those persons.[102]

14-031   **Requirements to be met**   A person seeking to recover land under the modern procedure must show that he has a "better title" than the defendant, as where he is a purchaser from an owner who has been excluded by the defendant. However, nothing approaching a paper title is necessary. Although it was said that for ejectment it was insufficient to set up the mere de facto possession which, as we have seen, will usually enable the claimant to sue for trespass as a tort,[103] this distinction is now very tenuous in view of *Asher v Whitlock*,[104] where it was held that if A takes possession of wasteland without any other title than such seizure, he could get possession against B who subsequently enters on the land.[105] When, therefore, it is said that A's former possession raises only a presumption of title it must be admitted that this presumption is not easily rebutted.[106] Indeed, it may now be that the law goes further and allows the claimant to succeed in a claim for possession where he would fail in an action of pure trespass. In *Manchester Airport Plc v Dutton*[107] the operators of an airport needed to lop and fell trees in a nearby wood in order to build a new runway. With a view to preventing the construction, the wood was occupied by protestors and the owner then granted the airport a licence to "enter

---

[98]   This was the view of Clarke LJ in *Ropaigealach v Barclays Bank Plc* [2000] Q.B. 263.

[99]   *Secretary of State for Environment, Food and Rural Affairs v Meier* [2009] UKSC 11; [2009] 1 W.L.R. 2780 at [66] per Lord Neuberger.

[100]   *Malik v Fassenfelt* [2013] EWCA Civ 798; [2013] 28 E.G. 84 (C.S.) at [25].

[101]   See Holdsworth, *A History of English Law*, vol. iii, pp.213–217, vol. vii, pp.4–23. The best account is in Maitland, *Equity: A Course of Lectures* (1909), pp.352–355.

[102]   CPR Pt 55. The court's jurisdiction extends to making an order for possession of the whole premises, not just that part presently under adverse occupation, provided an intention to decamp can be inferred: *University of Essex v Djemal* [1980] 1 W.L.R. 1301. Where the defendants are in occupation of land A it is possible to grant an injunction restraining them from going on to other, separate land B to which the claimant fears they may decamp, but the special procedure for possession is not available in such a case. This is because a possession order would require the defendants to do what they cannot then do, surrender possession of land B: *Secretary of State for Environment, Food and Rural Affairs v Meier* [2009] UKSC 11; [2009] 1 W.L.R. 2780. On the potential application of the Human Rights Act 1998 in such a case, see *Malik v Fassenfelt* [2013] EWCA Civ 798; [2013] 28 E.G. 84 (C.S.).

[103]   *Harper v Charlesworth* (1825) 4 B. & C. 574 at 589, 592–594; 107 E.R. 1174 at 1179–1181.

[104]   (1865) L.R. 1 Q.B. 1. See, too, *Doe d. Hughes v Dyeball* (1829) 3 Car. & P. 610; 172 E.R. 567.

[105]   Approved in *Perry v Clissold* [1907] A.C. 73 at 79.

[106]   *Whale v Hitchcock* (1876) 34 L.T. 136.

[107]   [2000] Q.B. 133.

and occupy" the site. An order for possession against the protestors was upheld by the majority of the Court of Appeal. For Laws LJ, modern proceedings for the recovery of land were no longer subject to the requirements of ejectment so the fact that that remedy had not concerned itself with the position of the licensee out of occupation was not decisive[108]:

> "[A] licensee not in occupation may claim possession against a trespasser if that is a necessary remedy to vindicate and give effect to such rights of occupation as by contract with his licensor he enjoys."

Although the airport would not have been able to sue for damages for trespass, nevertheless, for the purpose of gaining possession it had a "superior right" to that of the defendants. However, the same court has subsequently declined to extend this decision to a situation where the licence was to enter and carry out work on the land but not to occupy it.[109]

The defence of jus tertii   The modern cases on recovery of land have not ad-   **14-032**
dressed another question, which has been controversial: if the claimant relies on his title to the land, how far may the defendant defeat his claim by showing a superior right in a third party? In an ordinary action of trespass the defendant cannot as a general rule set up the defence of jus tertii,[110] but is this rule applicable to the defendant to an action for the recovery of land? If the claimant must prove his title,[111] it would seem to be a corollary that if the evidence shows that some third person is entitled to the land, the claimant ought not to succeed: in other words, the defendant ought to be allowed to plead jus tertii. The position is, however, not necessarily the same where the claimant relies on prior possession of the land. Although the title of the third party (the lord of the manor) was not directly in issue in *Asher v Whitlock*[112] the reasoning seems inconsistent with the view that the defendant could have raised that title and in *Perry v Clissold*[113] Lord Macnaghten thought that the earlier case of *Doe d. Carter v Barnard*[114] could not stand with *Asher v Whitlock*. Although the matter has been greatly debated[115] and is perhaps not finally settled, the better view seems to be that the jus tertii cannot be raised in this case.[116] Whether or not jus tertii is in general a defence in such cases, it cannot be relied upon where the defendant has acquired possession from the claimant himself or from one through whom the claimant claims. The rule that a tenant is estopped from denying his landlord's title is well known, but a licensee is similarly estopped from denying the title of his licensor,[117] and indeed this rule of estoppel

---

108   [2000] Q.B. 133 at 150.
109   *Countryside Residential (North Thames) Ltd v Tugwell* [2000] 34 E.G. 87.
110   See para.14-007.
111   For example, where he is someone who has purchased or inherited the property.
112   (1865) L.R. 1 Q.B. 1.
113   [1907] A.C. 73 at 79.
114   (1849) 13 Q.B. 945.
115   For full discussion of the question, see Wiren (1925) 41 L.Q.R. 139; Hargreaves (1940) 56 L.Q.R. 376; Holdsworth (1940) 56 L.Q.R. 479.
116   See *Mayor of London v Hall* [2010] EWCA Civ 817; [2011] 1 W.L.R. 504, where, however, there was an implied statutory right to obtain possession. Winfield was firmly of the contrary view: see early editions of this book.
117   *Doe d. Johnson v Baytup* (1835) 3 Ad. & El. 188; 111 E.R. 384. A general denial in a pleading by a tenant does not amount to a sufficient denial of the landlord's title to cause a forfeiture of the lease:

extends to anyone who is sued in ejectment by one from whom he derived his interest.[118]

C. Damages

14-033 **Mesne profits** The action for mesne profits is another species of the action for trespass and lies for the damage which the claimant has suffered through having been out of possession of his land. By Blackstone's time, nothing but a shilling or some trivial sum was usually recoverable in the action of ejectment because it had been "licked into the form of a real action"[119] and its chief purpose had become the trial of the title to land.[120] If the claimant was successful, he got possession of the land but no compensation for having been kept out of it. The action for mesne profits enables the claimant to claim a reasonable rent for the possession of the property by the defendant[121] up to the time when possession is surrendered[122] and damages for any deterioration, as well as the reasonable costs of getting possession.[123] It remains a matter of debate whether the sum payable by way of a reasonable rent is based on the claimant's loss or the defendant's gain,[124] but the method adopted is to calculate the sum which the parties would have agreed by way of a rent or a licence fee on a hypothetical basis as a willing seller and buyer at the time of the trespass.[125] Such a hypothetical calculation must take account of the context, so that where the defendant trespassed on the substrata below the claimant's land in drilling for oil, damages were assessed by reference to the principles governing compulsory purchase in recognition of the defendant's statutory entitlement[126] to enforce the right to drill.[127] The claimant in an action for the recovery of land may join with it a claim for mesne profits, and if he does so it is unnecessary for him to

---

Warner v Sampson [1959] 1 Q.B. 297.
[118] *Dalton v Fitzgerald* [1897] 2 Ch. 86 at 93.
[119] *Goodtitle v Tombs* (1770) 3 Wils. K.B. 118 at 120; 95 E.R. 965 at 967 per Wilmot CJ.
[120] Blackstone, Commentaries, vol.ii, p.205.
[121] It does not matter that the claimant cannot show that he could have let the property while he was out of possession, nor that the defendant has not profited from the property: *Inverugie Investments Ltd v Hackett* [1995] 1 W.L.R. 713.
[122] *Jones v Merton LBC* [2008] EWCA Civ 660; [2009] 1 W.L.R. 1269 (tenant found to have surrendered possession before landlord became aware of surrender).
[123] In *Ramzan v Brookwide Ltd* [2011] EWCA Civ 985; [2012] 1 All E.R. 903, where the trespass took the form of the appropriation of a store room which had also provided access to a fire escape, the claimant was required to elect between alternative heads of loss: the loss of profits from his inability any longer to use an adjoining room as a restaurant or mesne profits, since he could not both use the room himself and let it out.
[124] Or whether this even matters: see *Inverugie Investments Ltd v Hackett* [1995] 1 W.L.R. 713 at 718. See also *MoD v Ashman* (1993) 66 P. & C.R. 195 at 201 where Hoffmann LJ would leave it to the election of the claimant; cf. *Penarth Dock Engineering Co Ltd v Pounds* [1963] 1 Lloyd's Rep. 359. In *Stadium Capital Holdings v St Marylebone Properties Company Plc* [2010] EWCA Civ 952 the trial judge was held to have erred in awarding damages equivalent to the total revenue generated by the defendant in the employment of advertising hoardings which trespassed on the airspace above the claimant's land, but the Court of Appeal remitted the question of damages without indicating which of the possible bases for assessment should have been adopted.
[125] *Eaton Mansions (Westminster) Ltd v Stinger Compania De Inversion SA* [2013] EWCA Civ 1308; [2014] 1 P. & C.R. 5, in which the Court of Appeal held that the parties were only to be taken to be negotiating for a licence period equivalent to the actual duration of the trespass which had occurred.
[126] Under the Mines (Working Facilities and Support) Act 1966.
[127] *Star Energy Weald Basin Ltd v Bocardo SA* [2010] UKSC 35; [2011] 1 A.C. 380.

have entered the land before he sues.[128] If he prefers he can still bring the action for mesne profits separately[129] but in that event he must first enter the land. That is because that action is one of trespass, trespass is a wrong to possession, and until he enters the claimant does not have possession. Once he has entered, however, then by the fiction of trespass by relation[130] the claimant is deemed to have been in possession during the whole period for which he claims the mesne profits.

Aggravated and punitive damages   Aggravated damages may be awarded in **14-034** cases of trespass where the defendant's conduct has been high-handed, insulting or oppressive.[131] Similarly, where the requisite conditions are met,[132] the court may award punitive damages.[133]

---

[128] If the claimant's title to the land has been extinguished by adverse possession, so is his claim for mesne profits: *Mount Carmel Investment Ltd v Peter Thurlow Ltd* [1988] 1 W.L.R. 1078.

[129] A later claim for mesne profits is not defeasible by the doctrine of res judicata, since the two claims rest on distinct causes of action: *Farrar v Leongreen Ltd* [2017] EWCA Civ 2211; [2018] 1 P. & C.R. 17.

[130] See para.14-009.

[131] *Horsford v Bird* [2006] UKPC 3; [2006] 1 E.G.L.R. 175; *Eaton Mansions (Westminster) Ltd v Stinger Compania De Inversion SA* [2013] EWCA Civ 1308; [2014] 1 P. & C.R. 5 at [26] (not awarded in the case of a company). For aggravated damages generally, see paras 23-025—23-032.

[132] See paras 23-012—23-024.

[133] *Eaton Mansions (Westminster) Ltd v Stinger Compania De Inversion SA* [2012] EWHC 3354 (Ch); [2012] 49 E.G. 66 (C.S.) at [75]–[77] (appeal dismissed but without any appeal against the judge's decision not to award punitive damages: [2013] EWCA Civ 1308; [2014] 1 P. & C.R. 5).

CHAPTER 15

NUISANCE

1. INTRODUCTION

The law of nuisance consists of the tort of private nuisance and public nuisance, **15-001**
a crime which in some circumstances gives rise to tort liability.[1] In modern parlance,

---

[1] Murphy, *The Law of Nuisance* (2010).

nuisance is that branch of the law of tort most closely concerned with "protection of the environment".[2] Thus nuisance actions have concerned pollution by oil[3] or noxious fumes,[4] interference with leisure activities,[5] offensive smells from premises used for keeping animals[6] and noise from industrial installations.[7] Three important qualifications must be made, however, to this broad generalisation. First, there are areas of nuisance, such as obstruction of the highway or of access thereto,[8] which have no "environmental" flavour. Secondly, the prevailing stance of nuisance liability is that of protection of private rights in the enjoyment of land,[9] so that control of injurious activity for the benefit of the whole community is incidental. Thirdly, the common law of nuisance has been supplemented and to a large extent replaced by an array of statutory powers designed to control environmental damage.

15-002 **Statutory protection of the environment** A full account of the statutory powers in question would be beyond the scope of a book on tort[10] but a brief sketch of the principal provisions may help the reader to put the common law in context. The main statute is the Environmental Protection Act 1990, which consolidated and restated much previous law as well as introducing a new administrative system for pollution control. Under Pt III of this Act[11] various matters[12] are "statutory nuisances". A local authority which is satisfied that such a nuisance exists is under a duty to serve an abatement notice requiring the nuisance to be terminated and failure, without reasonable excuse, to comply with the notice is a criminal offence.[13] Part II of the Act contains wide-ranging powers to control the deposit of waste and contravention of these provisions causing damage may give rise to civil liability.[14] The statutory nuisance provisions do not, as such, give rise to civil liability,[15] though conviction of the criminal offence would entitle the criminal court in a straightforward case to make a compensation order under the Powers of Criminal Courts

---

[2] On nuisance and the environment, see McLaren (1972) 10 Osgoode Hall L.J. 505; Steele (1995) 15 L.S. 236.

[3] *Esso Petroleum Co Ltd v Southport Corp* [1956] A.C. 218.

[4] *St Helen's Smelting Co v Tipping* (1865) 11 H.L.C. 642.

[5] *Bridlington Relay v Yorkshire Electricity Board* [1965] Ch. 436.

[6] *Rapier v London Tramways Co* [1893] 2 Ch. 588.

[7] *Halsey v Esso Petroleum Co Ltd* [1961] 1 W.L.R. 683.

[8] See para.15-079.

[9] *Hunter v Canary Wharf Ltd* [1997] A.C. 655, para.15-039. There is, however, a strong public law element in the shape of the power of public authorities to bring proceedings for an injunction to restrain a public nuisance: see para.15-007.

[10] See Malcolm and Pointing, *Statutory Nuisance: Law and Practice*, 2nd edn (2011); McCracken et al, *Statutory Nuisance*, 3rd edn (2012).

[11] As amended, particularly by the Noise and Statutory Nuisance Act 1993 and the Environment Act 1995. For earlier provisions see the Public Health Act 1936 Pt II. Much of the case law on that Act remains relevant.

[12] Section 79. Examples are premises in a state prejudicial to health or constituting a nuisance, and similar states of affairs in relation to smoke, fumes, dust, noise or accumulations or deposits. If the complaint is that the premises constitute a nuisance there must be a nuisance in the common law sense, i.e., the matter has to affect neighbouring land: *National Coal Board v Neath BC* [1976] 2 All E.R. 478; but this is not necessary if, e.g., the premises are in a state prejudicial to health, though even then the statute is concerned with the condition of the premises, not the layout or facilities: *Birmingham CC v Oakley* [2001] 1 All E.R. 385.

[13] If the local authority considers that summary proceedings would afford an inadequate remedy it may proceed in the High Court: s.81(5).

[14] See para.16-006.

[15] *Issa v Hackney LBC* [1997] 1 W.L.R. 956.

(Sentencing) Act 2000. However, the principal remedy sought by most victims of nuisance is an order to prevent its continuance and a complaint to the local authority under the 1990 Act will often be a considerably cheaper and more expeditious way of getting redress than a common law action for an injunction. Indeed, even if the local authority declines to take proceedings in the matter it is possible under s.82 for summary proceedings to be brought by a "person aggrieved".

The residuary role of the common law   Complaint to the local authorities which **15-003** enforce this legislation will generally be a cheaper and quicker route to redress for the victim of a nuisance than action at common law. The common law remedies do, however, play an important residuary role: they remain useful in situations where the interference in question is not covered by a statutory provision, where the local authority refuses to act, and where civil action will be more advantageous for the victim than the statutory procedure.[16] Civil actions for nuisance certainly continue to be brought[17] and it would be wrong to think that the role of the common law is insignificant but the reader should be aware that some of the older cases in this chapter might now be dealt with by other means.

Human rights[18]   Article 8 of the European Convention on Human Rights requires **15-004** respect for private and family life and the home and breach of that requirement by a public authority is actionable in damages under the Human Rights Act 1998. Since the Strasbourg case law makes it clear that severe environmental pollution, noise etc. may amount to a violation of art.8,[19] it follows that a public authority which causes a very serious nuisance may be liable to those affected under the 1998 Act.[20] In such a scenario, the 1998 Act may be more advantageous than a common law claim. In particular, standing under art.8 is not limited (as in nuisance) to those with a proprietary right in the land affected by the interference but extends to all those who count it as their home,[21] and the defendant public authority will not be able to invoke a defence of statutory authority.[22] Where the same set of facts gives rise to liability to the same claimant at common law and under the 1998 Act, it has been said to be "most improbable, if not inconceivable" that nuisance damages would be exceeded by damages for a violation of art.8, so that the former would normally

---

[16] Possible reasons for this include: (1) an injunction may be more effective than a criminal fine (even though there are "topping-up" provisions where the nuisance continues), see, e.g., *City of London Corp v Bovis Construction Ltd* [1992] 3 All E.R. 697; (2) where damage has been suffered the case may be too complex for a compensation order; (3) under s.80(7) it is in some cases a defence to a prosecution that the "best practicable means" have been used to prevent it. This may be more favourable to the defendant in some cases than the common law (but see *Wivenhoe Port v Colchester BC* [1985] J.P.L. 175).

[17] Sometimes on a large scale. In *Hunter v Canary Wharf Ltd* [1997] A.C. 655 there were 690 claimants.

[18] Nolan in Hoffman (ed), *The Impact of the UK Human Rights Act on Private Law* (2011).

[19] See, e.g., *Lopez Ostra v Spain* (1994) 20 E.H.R.R. 277 (fumes and smells from waste treatment plant); *Guerra v Italy* (1998) 26 E.H.R.R. 357 (toxic emissions from chemical factory); *Moreno Gómez v Spain* (2005) 41 E.H.R.R. 40 (noise from bars and clubs).

[20] *Dennis v Ministry of Defence* [2003] EWHC 793 (QB); [2003] Env. L.R. 34 (noise from military jets flying over stately home); *Andrews v Reading BC* [2005] EWHC 256 (QB) (traffic noise caused by closure of alternative route); *Dobson v Thames Water Utilities Ltd* [2011] EWHC 3523 (TCC); 140 Con. L.R. 135 (foul odour from sewage treatment works). cf. *Marcic v Thames Water Utilities Ltd* [2004] UKHL 66; [2004] 2 A.C. 42.

[21] *Khatun v UK* (1998) 26 E.H.R.R. CD212.

[22] On the defence, see paras 15-056ff.

constitute "just satisfaction" for the purposes of s.8(3) of the 1998 Act, and no additional award would be necessary.[23] Furthermore, the recovery of common law damages by the owner or occupier has also been said to be relevant to whether damages are necessary to provide just satisfaction under the 1998 Act to a person living in the same property who has no standing in nuisance, and to the quantum of any such award made.[24] However, in such a case the extent to which the 1998 Act claim is affected by the common law damages award will depend on the circumstances, and in particular the degree of community of interest between the owner/occupier and the claimant.[25] In addition to providing an alternative cause of action to nuisance where the interference is caused by a public authority, the 1998 Act may also affect the law of nuisance itself, by virtue of its "horizontal effect" on disputes between private parties. This possibility is however best considered when we come to look at the rules of nuisance law in question.

15-005 **Public and private nuisance**   Nuisances are divided into public and private, but beyond the fact that both may arise from the same state of affairs,[26] the two forms of nuisance have little in common. The terminological resemblance has nevertheless resulted in a failure adequately to differentiate between them, which in turn has caused much confusion. To avoid this, the following judicial admonition should always be borne in mind[27]:

> "It is … important to recall that the crime of common or public nuisance and the tort of [private] nuisance were and are distinct. There can be no automatic transposition of the learning in one area to the other."

The differences between the two forms of nuisance are too numerous to list them all here, but four can be highlighted. First, public nuisance is a crime which may give rise to tort liability, while private nuisance is only a tort. Second, to be actionable in public nuisance the defendant's conduct must affect the public generally, whereas a claim may lie in private nuisance even if only a single individual is affected. Third, private nuisance is firmly rooted in the protection of real property rights, whereas public nuisance represents a rather unsuccessful attempt to link the criminal law with compensation for damage.[28] And finally, although it has long been the case that damages for personal injury may be recovered in public nuisance,[29] this is not the case in the private variety.[30] Notwithstanding these and other differences between the two forms of liability, however, some cases of public nuisance are really just aggregated private nuisances, as where fumes from a factory have a

---

[23]   *Dobson v Thames Water Utilities Ltd* [2009] EWCA Civ 28; [2009] 3 All E.R. 319 at [52]. But for some complexities, see Bagshaw (2004) 120 L.Q.R. 37, 41.

[24]   [2009] EWCA Civ 28; [2009] 3 All E.R. 319 at [45]–[46].

[25]   At the trial of the *Dobson* action, for example, Ramsey J held that for household members who lacked standing in nuisance it was not necessary to award damages under the 1998 Act: *Dobson v Thames Water Utilities Ltd* [2011] EWHC 3523 (TCC); 140 Con. L.R. 135.

[26]   *Colour Quest Ltd v Total Downstream UK Plc* [2009] EWHC 540 (Comm); [2009] 2 Lloyd's Rep. 1.

[27]   *Brodie v Singleton Shire Council* [2001] HCA 29; (2001) 206 C.L.R. 512 at [257]. See also *Claimants in Corby Group Litigation v Corby BC* [2008] EWCA Civ 463; [2009] Q.B. 335 at [30].

[28]   Hence in public nuisance there is no equivalent of the private nuisance standing requirement of an interest in affected land.

[29]   *Claimants in Corby Group Litigation v Corby BC* [2008] EWCA Civ 463; [2009] Q.B. 335.

[30]   See para.15-078.

detrimental effect on a whole neighbourhood, and in these instances individual householders may be able to sue on both bases. In addition, whether private or public, a nuisance is typically an ongoing situation, so the injunction remedy is significant throughout the law of nuisance, while the defences available to actions in private and public nuisance are not dissimilar.

2. PUBLIC NUISANCE

Introduction[31]   According to Lord Bingham in *R. v Rimmington*, a public nuisance   **15-006**
is[32]:

> "[An act or omission which] endanger[s] the life, health, property ... or comfort of the public, or ... obstruct[s] the public in the exercise or enjoyment of rights common to all Her Majesty's subjects."

A public or common nuisance is one which materially affects the reasonable comfort and convenience of life of a class of the public who come within the sphere or neighbourhood of its operation.[33] The question whether the number of persons affected is sufficient to constitute a class is one of fact in every case, and it is sufficient to show that a representative cross-section of that class has been.[34] Furthermore, interference with a right enjoyed by the public generally is a public nuisance no matter how many people are actually affected,[35] so that, for example, obstruction of a highway is a public nuisance even if the highway is a footpath used by only one or two people.

Public nuisance is a vague concept which it has rightly been said "covers a multitude of sins, great and small".[36] Public nuisances at common law include such diverse activities as carrying on an offensive trade, keeping a disorderly house, selling food unfit for human consumption, obstructing public highways, and throwing fireworks about in the street. In many cases such conduct will now be covered by a specific statutory offence and where this is so a criminal prosecution should normally be brought for that rather than at common law.[37] Subject to this, however, the common law of public nuisance meets the requirement of certainty prescribed by the European Convention on Human Rights.[38]

---

[31]   Spencer [1989] C.L.J. 55; Neyers [2017] C.L.J. 87.
[32]   [2005] UKHL 63; [2006] 1 A.C. 549 at [36].
[33]   Since a public nuisance must affect members of the public *as a whole*, rather than merely a number of different individuals, sending offensive mail to many people does not qualify: *R. v Rimmington* [2005] UKHL 63; [2006] 1 A.C. 459.
[34]   *Attorney General v PYA Quarries Ltd* [1957] 2 Q.B. 169 at 184 (blasting, stones and splinters projected from quarry, dust, noise and vibration). Provided it affects the public it does not matter that only a small number of people in fact use the facility: *Jan de Nul (UK) Ltd v Axa Royal Belge* [2000] 2 Lloyd's Rep. 700 (on appeal, [2002] EWCA Civ 209; [2002] 1 Lloyd's Rep. 583).
[35]   *News Group Newspapers Ltd v SOGAT '82 (No.2)* [1987] I.C.R. 181 at 202.
[36]   *Southport Corp v Esso Petroleum Co Ltd* [1954] 2 Q.B. 182 at 196 per Denning LJ. The Law Commission has recommended wholesale reform of the crime of public nuisance and its codification in statute: Law Commission, *Simplification of Criminal Law: Public Nuisance and Outraging Public Decency*, Law Com. No.358 (2015).
[37]   *R. v Rimmington* [2005] UKHL 63; [2006] 1 A.C. 459.
[38]   *R. v Rimmington* [2005] UKHL 63; [2006] 1 A.C. 459.

15-007   Civil liability for particular damage[39]   So long as the public only or some section of it is injured no civil action can be brought by a private individual for public
nuisance. Where a public highway is obstructed, I cannot sue the person responsible
merely because my passage is delayed or I am obliged either to pursue my journey
by a devious route or to remove the obstruction, for these are inconveniences common to everyone else.[40] The reason normally given for the rule is that it prevents
multiplicity of actions, for if one were allowed to sue a thousand might do so and
this would lead to harsh results. If, for instance, a public body obstructed a highway
temporarily for the purpose of draining, paving or lighting it and it was then
discovered that owing to some technical error they had no authority to do so, they
would be sufficiently punished by a criminal prosecution.[41] If, for some reason, a
criminal prosecution is an inadequate sanction, the Attorney General may, on the
information of a member of the public, bring a civil action for an injunction (known
as a "relator" action), but if he refuses to do so the courts are not at liberty to inquire
into the propriety of his actions or to grant declarations at the suit of the individual
instead of injunctions.[42] By statute, a local authority may however bring proceedings for an injunction where they "consider it expedient for the promotion or protection of the interests of the inhabitants of their area".[43]

But where any private person is injured in some way peculiar to himself, that is,
if he can show that he has suffered some particular or special loss over and above
the ordinary inconvenience suffered by the public at large, then he can sue in tort,
for example if he falls into a trench unlawfully opened in a street and breaks his leg.
Particular damage is not limited to special damage in the sense of pecuniary loss
actually incurred. It may consist of proved general damage, such as inconvenience
and delay, provided it is substantial and appreciably different in nature or extent
from that suffered by the general public, although in another sense it is "general"
and not "special" to him.[44] Personal injury[45] and property damage[46] will also always
suffice. The distinction between public and private nuisance and the meaning of
particular damage are illustrated by *Tate & Lyle Industries Ltd v GLC*.[47] Ferry
terminals constructed by the defendants in the Thames caused silting which
obstructed the access of large vessels to the claimants' jetty and the claimants had
to spend large sums in dredging operations. Their claim in private nuisance was
dismissed because the jetty itself was unaffected and they had no private rights of
property in the river bed, but the silting had caused interference with the public right

---

[39]   Prosser [1966] Va. L. Rev. 997; Kodilinye (1986) 6 L.S. 182.
[40]   *Winterbottom v Lord Derby* (1867) L.R. 2 Ex. 316 at 321–322.
[41]   *Winterbottom v Lord Derby* (1867) L.R. 2 Ex. 316.
[42]   *Gouriet v Union of Post Office Workers* [1978] A.C. 435 (not a case of public nuisance).
[43]   Local Government Act 1972 s.222. And if a public nuisance affects the public right to use a highway,
the highway authority can bring proceedings: Highways Act 1980 s.130.
[44]   *Walsh v Ervin* [1952] V.L.R. 361 at 368–369 per Sholl J reviewing the English authorities; *Jan de
Nul (UK) Ltd v Axa Royal Belge* [2000] 2 Lloyd's Rep. 700. Particular damage includes injury to
the claimant's person, loss of custom, depreciation in the actual value of the property by reducing
or cutting off the approach to it: *Boyd v GN Ry* (1895) 2 I.R. 555 (doctor held up at level crossing
for 20 minutes, recovered).
[45]   *Fowler v Sanders* (1617) Cro. Jac. 446; 79 E.R. 382; *Harrold v Watney* [1898] 2 Q.B. 320.
[46]   *Southport Corp v Esso Petroleum Co Ltd* [1954] 2 Q.B. 182; *Halsey v Esso Petroleum Co Ltd* [1961]
1 W.L.R. 683.
[47]   [1983] 2 A.C. 509.

of navigation and the expenditure the claimants incurred was particular damage sufficient to entitle them to bring an action for public nuisance.[48]

Who can be liable The rules governing who can be liable for public nuisance **15-008**
mirror those governing the same issue in private nuisance.[49] In particular, an occupier is liable for continuing or adopting a public nuisance that emanates from his property, whether its origins lie in the forces of nature,[50] the actions of a previous occupier,[51] or the unauthorised act of a third party.[52]

Public nuisance and negligence Public nuisance and negligence may overlap in **15-009**
cases of damage to person or property caused by a danger on or near the highway. For example, persons injured after running into stationary vehicles obstructing the highway have occasionally sued in public nuisance in the belief that this might be more advantageous than a negligence claim.[53] This duplication of actions arose through an unfortunate series of historical accidents, and serves only to sow confusion.[54] It is in any case doubtful whether such imaginative pleading will make any difference. A defendant is after all responsible only for a public nuisance which he knew, or ought to have known, would be the consequence of his act or omission.[55] And since there is no reason why a plea of public nuisance should confer an advantage on the claimant, in this type of case the better view is that the claimant ought to be required to establish fault, no matter what the cause of action.[56]

3.   Private Nuisance

A.   Introduction

Nature of private nuisance[57] A private nuisance is an unlawful interference with **15-010**
a person's use or enjoyment of land, or some right over, or in connection with it.[58]

---

48   See also *Jan de Nul (UK) Ltd v Axa Royal Belge* [2002] EWCA Civ 209; [2002] 1 Lloyd's Rep. 583; *Rose v Miles* (1815) 4 M. & S. 101; 105 E.R. 773; *News Group Newspapers Ltd v SOGAT'82* [1986] I.R.L.R. 337 (cost of "bussing-in" employees because of picketing). Note that in these cases the loss was "economic" but though that may be a bar to a claim for negligence it is not to one for public nuisance. cf. the position where the claim relates to failure to repair the highway: para.15-084.

49   See paras 15-042ff.

50   *Wandsworth LBC v Railtrack Plc* [2001] Env. L.R. 441 (pigeons roosting under bridge over highway).

51   *Coupland v Hardingham* (1813) 3 Camp. 398; 170 E.R. 1424; *British Road Services v Slater* [1964] 1 W.L.R. 498.

52   *Barker v Herbert* [1911] 2 K.B. 633 (trespassers); *R. v Shorrock* [1994] Q.B. 279 (licensees).

53   See, e.g., *Ware v Garston Haulage Co Ltd* [1943] 2 All E.R. 558; *Dymond v Pearce* [1972] 1 Q.B. 496.

54   See Newark (1949) 65 L.Q.R. 480.

55   This being the mens rea of the crime: *R. v Rimmington* [2005] UKHL 63; [2006] 1 A.C. 459 at [39], [56].

56   The High Court of Australia has held that, in its application to highway cases, public nuisance is to be treated as absorbed by the principles of ordinary negligence: *Brodie v Singleton Shire Council* [2001] HCA 29; (2001) 206 C.L.R. 512 at [129].

57   Nolan in Agnew and McFarlane (eds), *Modern Studies in Property Law vol.10* (2019).

58   Adopted by Scott LJ in *Read v Lyons & Co Ltd* [1945] K.B. 216 at 236; by Lord Goddard CJ in *Howard v Walker* [1947] 2 All E.R. 197 at 199; by Evershed J in *Newcastle-under-Lyme Corp v Wolstanton Ltd* [1947] Ch. 92 at 107; and by Windeyer J in *Hargrave v Goldman* (1963) 110 C.L.R. 40 at 59 (affirmed [1967] 1 A.C. 645).

To be unlawful, the interference must be unreasonable.[59] If the interference consists of a direct incursion onto the claimant's land, then trespass to land, rather than private nuisance, is the appropriate cause of action.[60] Interference with the use and enjoyment of land is a broad concept, though it has limits: conduct that merely diminishes the market value of property,[61] or the profitability of a business conducted on it,[62] but without affecting the utility of the land itself, is not a nuisance.[63] It has been said[64] that the tort takes three forms: encroachment on a neighbour's land;[65] direct physical injury to the land; or interference with the enjoyment of the land. However, these are merely examples of the kinds of violations of real property rights that can ground an action in nuisance, and any "rigid categorisation" along these lines should be avoided.[66] Not every slight annoyance is actionable. Whether an interference with amenity caused by noise, odours, smoke, the escape of effluent and a multitude of other things constitutes an actionable nuisance will depend on a variety of considerations, including the nature and extent of the interference, the locality and the character of the defendant's conduct.

15-011 **A tort against land**[67] Private nuisance always protects the same interest, namely the interest of an owner or occupier in the use and enjoyment of real property. It is, therefore, a "tort against land".[68] As Lord Hoffmann pointed out in *Hunter v Canary Wharf Ltd*,[69] while this is obvious in cases of physical damage to the claimant's property, it is less so when the interference is with its amenity. But here too the injury is to the property, not the person, for the gist of the action is not the discomfort of those affected, but the diminished utility of the land on which they live.[70] The practical implications of this analysis are threefold. First, since the tort is to the land, the right to sue is limited to those with an interest in the affected property.[71] Second, in amenity nuisance cases, because the focus is the impact on the utility of the land itself, as opposed to the particular occupiers, an objective approach is taken when assessing both the gravity of the interference and the dam-

---

59 See paras 15-016ff.
60 Keeton (1959) 59 Col. L. Rev. 457 at 464–70.
61 *Network Rail Infrastructure Ltd v Williams* [2018] EWCA Civ 1514; [2019] Q.B. 601 at [46]–[51]. See also *Smith v Inco Ltd* [2011] ONCA 628; 107 O.R. (3d) 321.
62 The classic example is *Victoria Park Racing and Recreation Grounds Ltd v Taylor* (1937) 58 C.L.R. 479, where the High Court of Australia dismissed a nuisance claim brought by a racecourse owner when attendances dropped after the defendants began broadcasting live commentaries on the races, which they observed from neighbouring land. See Lunney, *A History of Australian Tort Law 1901–1945* (2018), pp.266–276.
63 In *Anglian Water Services Ltd v Crawshaw Robbins Ltd* [2001] B.L.R. 173 it was held that interrupting the supply of gas to a property is not actionable in nuisance. One of the reasons given for this conclusion was that the interference could be regarded as being with the use of gas appliances on the claimant's land, rather than with the use and enjoyment of the land itself. Sed quaere.
64 *Hunter v Canary Wharf Ltd* [1997] A.C. 655 at 695.
65 e.g., by spreading roots or overhanging branches.
66 *Network Rail Infrastructure Ltd v Williams* [2018] EWCA Civ 1514; [2019] Q.B. 601 at [41].
67 Nolan in Nolan and Robertson (eds), *Rights and Private Law* (2012).
68 *Hunter v Canary Wharf Ltd* [1997] A.C. 655 at 702 per Lord Hoffmann. This characteristic of the tort is also emphasised in *Network Rail Infrastructure Ltd v Williams* [2018] EWCA Civ 1514; [2019] Q.B. 601 at [40].
69 [1997] A.C. 655.
70 "A sulphurous chimney in a residential area is not a nuisance because it makes householders cough and splutter but because it prevents them taking their ease in their gardens": Newark (1949) 65 L.Q.R. 480 at 489.
71 See para.15-039.

ages to be awarded.[72] And finally, claims for damage to chattels are limited to cases where the damage is consequential on damage to the land, while claims for personal injury are excluded altogether.[73]

Types of interference that are never actionable In most nuisance cases, the interference consists of a physical emanation, such as a noise or smell, but there is no requirement that the interference take this form.[74] For example, persistent phone calls have been held to be actionable in nuisance,[75] as has the picketing of the claimant's property,[76] the use of neighbouring premises as a brothel,[77] and a withdrawal of lateral support that causes the claimant's land to collapse.[78] Even the claim that only in exceptional cases will there be liability in nuisance in the absence of an invasion of a substance or form of energy onto the claimant's land[79] is doubtful, particularly if acquired rights to light and air are borne in mind. There are, however, three types of interference with the use and enjoyment of land which cannot amount to a nuisance, no matter how substantial or unreasonable the interference is. It follows that in cases of this kind even malicious interference is lawful.[80] The first such category is obstruction of a view. There is no natural right to the view from a property, and nor can such a right be acquired as an easement.[81] Second, the House of Lords held in *Hunter v Canary Wharf Ltd*[82] that the mere presence of a building in the line of sight between a television transmitter and other properties is not actionable in private nuisance. It does not, however, necessarily follow that the same is true of some activity (for example, the generation of electricity) on the defendant's land which interferes with television signals.[83] In *Hunter* an analogy was drawn with the rule denying liability for the ruination of a prospect, and that rule and the decision in *Hunter* can now be seen as applications of a broader principle of the common law that (in the absence of agreement to the contrary) a landowner may build what he likes on his own land.[84] And finally, an owner or occupier has an absolute right at common law to appropriate or divert water which

15-012

---

[72] See para.15-028.

[73] See para.15-078.

[74] *Barratt Homes Ltd v Welsh Water (No.2)* [2013] EWCA Civ 233; [2013] 1 W.L.R. 3486 at [60], [81].

[75] *Khorasandjian v Bush* [1993] Q.B. 727.

[76] *Hubbard v Pitt* [1976] Q.B. 142.

[77] *Thompson-Schwab v Costaki* [1956] 1 W.L.R. 335. See also *Laws v Florinplace Ltd* [1981] 1 All E.R. 659 (sex shop). These cases are however controversial, and their significance was downplayed in *Network Rail Infrastructure Ltd v Williams* [2018] EWCA Civ 1514; [2019] Q.B. 601 at [50]–[51].

[78] *Hunt v Peake* (1860) John 705; 70 E.R. 603; *Backhouse v Bonomi* (1861) 9 H.L. Cas. 503.

[79] *Anglian Water Services Ltd v Crawshaw Robbins Ltd* [2001] B.L.R. 173 at 197.

[80] *Bradford Corp v Pickles* [1895] A.C. 587 (malicious appropriation of percolating water).

[81] *Dalton v Angus* (1881) 6 App. Cas. 740 at 824; cf. Pontin (2018) 38 L.S. 627.

[82] [1997] A.C. 655.

[83] The point was left open in *Hunter*, though the level of enthusiasm for the possibility varied. In *Bridlington Relay Ltd v Yorkshire Electricity Board* [1965] Ch. 436, Buckley J doubted whether interference with such a purely recreational amenity was capable of being a nuisance, but the centrality of television in modern life means that his reasoning now looks dated: contrast *Nor-Video Services Ltd v Ontario Hydro* (1978) 84 D.L.R. (3d) 221. Then again, the rise of new television technologies (cable, satellite, broadband etc.) have served to reduce the significance of television signals, so the issue is perhaps now less likely to arise than in the past.

[84] This principle is subject to the qualification that by prescription one may acquire an easement of light or to the passage of air through a definite aperture or channel, but consistent with the rule that no nuisance action lies for blocking the free passage of air to neighbouring property: see *Webb v Bird* (1862) 13 C.B.N.S. 841; 143 E.R. 332 (no remedy when new school reduced flow of air to windmill).

percolates through undefined channels on or under his land, with the result that no nuisance action will lie for the abstraction of such water,[85] even if the effect is to dry up a well or spring on neighbouring land.[86]

15-013 **Interference with privacy** English law has traditionally not recognised a right not to be overlooked.[87] Hence it has been said that it is not a nuisance to open (i.e., create) a new window which commands a view of neighbouring property,[88] and, in his article on privacy, Winfield cited an unreported case in which a dentist in Balham was denied redress against neighbours who used an array of large mirrors to observe events in his surgery.[89] Despite the fact that other areas of the law of tort have come to accord greater significance to privacy as an interest worthy of protection,[90] the traditional approach of the law of nuisance in this regard was strongly reasserted in *Fearn v Tate Gallery Board of Trustees*.[91] The defendant art gallery had opened a new viewing platform from which members of the public could see directly into the living areas of the claimants' flats in a luxury residential development 35 metres away. The claimants sought an injunction requiring the defendants to close the part of the platform facing their apartments. At first instance,[92] Mann J held that the tort of nuisance was capable of operating so as to protect the privacy of a home, although he went on to decide for a variety of reasons—including the nature of the locality and the "particularly sensitive" nature of the flats, which had floor-to-ceiling windows—that the interference was not unreasonable on the facts. However, while affirming the result below, the Court of Appeal went further, holding that it had been a mistake to open the door to privacy claims at all. As a matter of authority and principle an invasion of privacy by overlooking was simply not capable of being actionable in private nuisance. The court acknowledged that in an extreme case of the kind described by Winfield, other causes of action might afford the claimant redress,[93] but considered that further extensions of the legal protection of privacy interests were a matter for Parliament.

15-014 **Nuisance to servitudes**[94] Private nuisance encompasses both unlawful interference with a man's use and enjoyment of his own land and unlawful interference with his rights over the land of others, that is to say with easements and profits à prendre. So the right to light, for example, is "no more than a right to be protected

---

85 It may however be tortious to pollute an underground stratum from which neighbours draw water: *Ballard v Tomlinson* (1885) 29 Ch. D. 115; *Cambridge Water Co Ltd v Eastern Counties Leather Plc* [1994] 2 A.C. 264.

86 *Acton v Blundell* (1842) 12 M. & W. 324; 152 E.R. 1223; *Chasemore v Richards* (1859) 7 H.L. Cas. 349; *Bradford Corp v Pickles* [1895] A.C. 587. Indeed, it has even been held that no action lies in either nuisance or negligence where the abstraction of such water causes physical damage to neighbouring land or buildings: *Langbrook Properties Ltd v Surrey CC* [1970] 1 W.L.R. 161; *Stephens v Anglian Water Authority* [1987] 1 W.L.R. 1381. The extension of this principle to negligence is however questionable: see Fleming (1988) 104 L.Q.R. 183.

87 See, e.g., *Dalton v Angus* (1881) 6 App. Cas. 740 at 764.

88 *Tapling v Jones* (1865) 11 H.L. Cas. 290 at 305.

89 (1931) 47 L.Q.R. 23, 27.

90 See Ch.13.

91 [2020] EWCA Civ 104; [2020] 2 W.L.R. 1081.

92 [2019] EWHC 246 (Ch); [2019] Ch. 369.

93 Most obviously the Protection from Harassment Act 1997: see para.4-034.

94 The discussion of servitudes in a text on tort law must necessarily be cursory. For fuller treatment, see *Gale on Easements*, 20th edn (2016); Sara, *Boundaries and Easements*, 7th edn (2019); and texts on the law of real property.

against a particular form of nuisance",[95] and in the same way it is to nuisance that one must turn for a remedy when faced with the obstruction of a private right of way.[96] The nuisance action for interference with servitudes is no different from other nuisance claims. In particular, the requirement that the interference be unreasonable (or substantial) applies in cases on rights of way and rights of light,[97] just as it does in cases on interference by noise or smell, and once substantial interference has been established the usual nuisance remedies are available.

Isolated events   The typical private nuisance is an ongoing interference with the claimant's use and enjoyment of his land. As Windeyer J said in *Hargrave v Goldman*, "[g]enerally speaking, the term 'nuisance' denotes a state of affairs that is either continuous or recurrent".[98] In amenity nuisance cases an element of continuance or recurrence is almost inevitable, as otherwise the requirement of unreasonable interference would not be satisfied. But when it comes to property damage, the possibility arises of a claimant framing a claim in respect of a one-off event in nuisance, perhaps with a view to circumventing the more onerous demands of a more obvious cause of action, such as negligence. This manoeuvre was successful in *Spicer v Smee*,[99] where a fire caused by defective wiring in the defendant's house spread to the claimant's bungalow and burned it to the ground. It was held that on these facts a nuisance action lay. However, more recent authority indicates that a claim in respect of an isolated occurrence is unlikely to succeed without either fault or a non-natural use bringing the case within the ambit of the rule in *Rylands v Fletcher*.[100] It follows that there is little to be gained by framing such a claim in nuisance, the cause of action for which is therefore effectively limited to scenarios where there is a degree of continuity in the interference.[101]

15-015

---

[95] *Colls v Home and Colonial Stores Ltd* [1904] A.C. 179 at 212 per Lord Lindley.

[96] This would, however, change if the Law Commission has its way. A key plank of the Commission's reform proposals in this area is replacement of the role of private nuisance in servitude cases with a new cause of action for "breach of a land obligation": *Making Land Work: Easements, Covenants and Profits à Prendre*, Law Com. No.327 (2011).

[97] This is made particularly clear in the law on light: see *Colls v Home and Colonial Stores Ltd* [1904] A.C. 179.

[98] (1963) 110 C.L.R. 40 at 59.

[99] [1946] 1 All E.R. 489. Two other cases are regularly cited for the proposition that nuisance can lie in respect of a one-off event, but neither is convincing. The facts of *Midwood & Co Ltd v Manchester Corp* [1905] 2 K.B. 597 surely came within the rule in *Rylands v Fletcher*, as then understood, and in *British Celanese Ltd v AH Hunt (Capacitors) Ltd* [1969] 1 W.L.R. 959, recovery in negligence was straightforward, and it was unnecessary for Lawton J to hold that liability arose in nuisance as well.

[100] *Northumbrian Water Ltd v Sir Robert McAlpine Ltd* [2014] EWCA Civ 685; [2014] B.L.R. 605. See also *Crown River Cruises v Kimbolton Fireworks* [1996] 2 Lloyd's Rep. 533.This position has long been advocated by commentators: see Newark (1949) 65 L.Q.R. 480 at 489; Gearty [1989] C.L.J. 214 at 222.

[101] It remains to be seen whether this principle applies when an occupier is sued in respect of a nuisance he did not create (see paras 15-043ff). Some of the cases of this kind, e.g., *Sedleigh-Denfield v O'Callaghan* [1940] A.C. 880, concerned one-off events, but since an occupier is liable only if he "adopts" or "continues" the nuisance, the requirement of fault is likely to be satisfied. Indeed, in one of the leading authorities on this issue the Privy Council thought it unnecessary to decide whether the cause of action lay in nuisance or negligence: *Goldman v Hargrave* [1967] 1 A.C. 645.

B.   Unreasonable Interference

15-016   "Give and take, live and let live"   The rights and duties created by the tort of private nuisance are not framed in absolute terms, and so not every interference with another's use and enjoyment of his land is actionable. A rule that, for example, you may not make a noise which irritates your neighbour would be totally unworkable. Some intrusion by noise (or smells or dust, etc.) is the inevitable price of living in an organised society in proximity to others. In the words of the *Restatement (Second) of the Law of Torts*[102]:

"Practically all human activities unless carried on in a wilderness interfere to some extent with others or involve some risk of interference, and these interferences range from mere trifling annoyances to serious harms. It is an obvious truth that each individual in a community must put up with a certain amount of annoyance, inconvenience and interference and must take a certain amount of risk in order that all may get on together. The very existence of organized society depends upon the principle of "give and take, live and let live', and therefore the law of torts does not attempt to impose liability or shift the loss in every case where one person's conduct has some detrimental effect on another. Liability is imposed only in those cases where the harm or risk to one is greater than he ought to be required to bear under the circumstances, at least without compensation."

In the law of nuisance the principle of "give and take, of live and let live"[103] is encapsulated in the requirement that the interference with another's use and enjoyment must be unreasonable. An interference is unreasonable if in all the circumstances "an ordinary person could not reasonably be expected to put up with it".[104] As the use of the word "ordinary" signifies, when applying this test, the courts have regard to "the ordinary usages of mankind living in ... a particular society".[105] And so, in deciding whether there has been unreasonable interference, the court must consider whether the inconvenience ought[106]:

"[T]o be considered in fact as more than fanciful, more than one of mere delicacy or fastidiousness, as an inconvenience materially interfering with the ordinary comfort, physically, of human existence, not merely according to elegant or dainty modes and habits of living, but according to plain and sober and simple notions among the English people."

15-017   A claimant-sided test   The test of unreasonable interference is claimant-sided: the question being addressed is whether the threshold degree of interference necessary to maintain an action has been crossed. Although, in a general sense, the court must balance the competing interests of the two parties, it is not engaged in a cost–benefit analysis, in which the harm to the claimant is weighed against the utility of the defendant's conduct. On the contrary, the courts have consistently held that no matter how beneficial the defendant's activity is to society, if the effect on his neighbours is intolerable it is an actionable nuisance.[107] Nor is the question of actionability resolved by considering whether the defendant's use of his property

---

[102] *Restatement (Second) of the Law of Torts* (1977), §822, comment g.
[103] *Bamford v Turnley* (1862) 3 B. & S. 66 at 83; 122 E.R. 27 at 33 per Bramwell B.
[104] *Barr v Biffa Waste Services Ltd* [2012] EWCA Civ 312; [2013] Q.B. 455 at [74] per Carnwath LJ.
[105] *Sedleigh-Denfield v O'Callaghan* [1940] A.C. 880 at 903 per Lord Wright.
[106] *Walter v Selfe* (1851) 4 De G. & Sm. 315 at 322; 64 E.R. 849 at 852 per Knight Bruce V-C.
[107] See para.15-026.

is reasonable.[108] Although it is sometimes said that there must be "unreasonable user" of the defendant's land for a nuisance to be actionable, it is the interference with the claimant, rather than the conduct of the defendant, which must be unreasonable. "Unreasonableness" in nuisance therefore signifies what is legally right between the parties taking account of all the circumstances of the case; unlike in negligence, liability is not contingent on the *defendant's conduct* being unreasonable. This is far short of saying that lack of reasonable care is irrelevant to liability for nuisance, for the claimant cannot reasonably be expected to put up with interference which could be reduced by the adoption of reasonable ameliorative measures.[109] But if the court considers that the interference is excessive then the fact that the defendant has taken all reasonable care and reduced it to a minimum provides no defence.[110]

A question of fact There is no precise or universal formula by which it can be   **15-018**
determined whether a given interference is unreasonable. The question "so entirely depends on the surrounding circumstances ... as to make it impossible to lay down any rule of law of law applicable to every case".[111] Hence the question of actionability cannot generally be determined by the application of a rigid threshold, such as the test applied at first instance in an odour nuisance case that claimants must have made one complaint about the smell each week to recover damages.[112] Rather, it is a question of fact which can be determined only by reference to all the circumstances of the particular case. In determining the answer to that question[113]:

> "[R]egard is had to a variety of factors including: the nature and extent of the harm or interference; the social or public interest value in the defendant's activity; the hypersensitivity (if any) of the user or use of the claimant's land; the nature of established uses in the locality (eg residential, industrial, rural); whether all reasonable precautions were taken to minimise the interference; and the type of damage suffered."

Certain of these factors will now be discussed in greater detail.

i. The Type of Harm

The distinction between "material injury" and personal discomfort In the   **15-019**
leading case of *St Helen's Smelting Co v Tipping*,[114] where trees on the claimant's estate were injured by fumes from a copper smelter, the House of Lords drew a distinction between matters producing "sensible injury to the value of property" or "material injury"[115] on the one hand and those causing personal discomfort on the

---

108 *Bamford v Turnley* (1862) 3 B. & S. 66 at 77–78; 122 E.R. 27 at 31; *Broder v Saillard* (1876) 2 Ch. D. 692 at 701; *Reinhardt v Mentasti* (1889) 42 Ch. D. 685 at 690; *Barr v Biffa Waste Services Ltd* [2012] EWCA Civ 312; [2013] Q.B. 455 at [66]–[72]. See Cross (1995) 111 L.Q.R. 445, 447–458.
109 *Southwark LBC v Tanner* [2001] 1 A.C. 1 at 16.
110 *Rapier v London Tramways Co* [1893] 2 Ch. 588.
111 *Bamford v Turnley* (1862) 3 B. & S. 66 at 79; 122 E.R. 27 at 31 per Pollock CB.
112 See *Barr v Biffa Waste Services Ltd* [2011] EWHC 1003 (TCC), disapproved on appeal on the grounds that it deprived the claimants of their right to have their individual cases decided on their merits: [2012] EWCA Civ 312; [2013] Q.B. 455 at [46].
113 *Southern Properties (WA) Pty Ltd v Executive Director of the Dept of Conservation and Land Management* [2012] WASCA 79; 42 W.A.R. 287 at [118] per McLure P.
114 *St Helen's Smelting Co v Tipping* (1865) 11 H.L.C. 642.
115 *St Helen's Smelting Co v Tipping* (1865) 11 H.L.C. 642 at 651.

other. Only when assessing whether the latter constitute an actionable nuisance was it necessary to take into account the character of the locality, for example. The distinction is not free from difficulty and its consequences do not seem to have been fully investigated by the courts,[116] but it has been reiterated on several occasions.[117]

15-020 **Physical damage to the land or other property**   One way of interpreting *St Helen's Smelting Co v Tipping* is that it emphasises the ease of finding an interference to be unreasonable where it causes physical damage to the claimant's property. In many such cases it will be appropriate for the court to disregard, not only the locality,[118] but also the duration of the interference (so that an isolated event will potentially be actionable),[119] and the utility of the defendant's activity.[120] Indeed, it has even been suggested that once physical damage has been proven, liability is established, and there is no need to consider any of the surrounding circumstances.[121] However, although there are clear differences in the courts' treatment of physical damage and amenity cases, it is as well not to over-emphasise the distinction, which can be difficult to draw.[122]

ii.   The Nature and Extent of the Interference

15-021   Most amenity nuisance cases turn on the nature and extent of the interference. Where the interference is by smell or noise, there are at least three elements to be considered under this heading: the character of the smell or noise, the degree of interference (the intensity of the smell, or the volume of the noise), and the duration of the interference. In considering the character of the interference, the court will take account of the fact that some smells and noises are generally regarded as being more objectionable than others. But one man's music is another man's din, and the defendant cannot impose his own tastes, however refined, on the ears of his neighbours. In cases of discomfort or inconvenience—as opposed to physical damage[123]—some element of continuity is of course essential if the interference is to count as unreasonable, and its duration is an important factor in determining its actionability. But all the circumstances must be considered, and an interference that

---

[116] It seems clear from Lord Westbury's speech that he did have in mind physical damage (including visible deterioration). Noises or smells primarily cause only personal discomfort but they may seriously reduce the selling value of the property affected by them and injure a business (e.g., a hotel) carried on therein.

[117] See, e.g., *Halsey v Esso Petroleum Co* [1961] 1 W.L.R. 683; *Miller v Jackson* [1977] Q.B. 966 at 986.

[118] As in *Halsey v Esso Petroleum Co* [1961] 1 W.L.R. 683, where the nature of the locality was not taken into account when it came to the property damage aspect of the claim.

[119] *Colwell v St Pancras BC* [1904] 1 Ch. 707; *Crown River Cruises Ltd v Kimbolton Fireworks Ltd* [1996] 2 Lloyd's Rep. 533 at 545.

[120] *Schenck v Ontario* (1981) 131 D.L.R. (3d) 310 (liability where orchards partially destroyed by salt used to de-ice adjacent road).

[121] *Kent v Dominion Steel & Coal Corp Ltd* (1964) 49 D.L.R. (2d) 241 at 248; *Clearlite Holdings Ltd v Auckland City Corp* [1976] 2 N.Z.L.R. 729 at 740–741. cf. *Antrim Truck Centre Ltd v Ontario (Transportation)* 2013 SCC 13; [2013] 1 S.C.R. 594 at [46]–[51].

[122] Is the deposit of dust physical damage, for example? In theory, it seems that the answer is "it depends" (see *Hunter v Canary Wharf Ltd* [1996] A.C. 655 at 676) though in practice the courts in nuisance cases treat it as amenity damage: *Pwllbach Colliery Co Ltd v Woodman* [1915] A.C. 634; *Matania v National Provincial Bank Ltd* [1936] 2 All E.R. 633; *Andreae v Selfridge & Co* [1938] Ch. 1.

[123] See para.15-015.

is relatively short-lived may be unreasonable, particularly if the defendant could easily have prevented it from happening at all.[124] Two further points should be made. First, when assessing the gravity of the interference in noise cases, the timing of the disturbance is critical: for obvious reasons the courts come down particularly hard on nocturnal noise.[125] And second, the predictability of the interference may be a relevant consideration, since if it is possible to predict when one's property is going to be affected by, say, noise or odour, this is likely to prove less disruptive than interference that is unpredictable, and hence less easy to work around.[126]

iii. The Character of the Locality

The locality principle[127]   In the case of an amenity nuisance, the character of the   **15-022**
neighbourhood is a relevant consideration in determining the actionability of the defendant's activity: as was once said, "What would be a nuisance in Belgrave Square would not necessarily be so in Bermondsey."[128] After all, the reasonable expectations of the owner or occupier cannot be assessed in the abstract, but must reflect the nature of the area in which he chooses to buy or lease his property.[129] Sometimes, then, a nuisance is, in the words of an American judge, merely "a right thing in the wrong place—like a pig in the parlor instead of the barnyard".[130] Usually, the courts applying the locality principle are concerned with the dominant land use: is the area primarily residential, commercial, industrial or agricultural? However, the courts have also distinguished between different types of residential areas, according to the "quality" of the neighbourhood,[131] and it has been said that the "occupiers of low cost, high density housing must be expected to tolerate higher levels of noise from their neighbours than others in more substantial and spacious premises".[132] The locality is only one factor in the substantial interference inquiry, however, and a person who lives in an industrial area is entitled to complain if an interference is excessive even according to the minimal standard of comfort he can reasonably expect. The claimant in *Rushmer v Polsue & Alfieri Ltd*[133] lived in a locality devoted to printing and other noisy trades, but nevertheless obtained an injunction to stop the defendants operating printing machinery in the house next

---

[124] See, e.g., *Metropolitan Properties Ltd v Jones* [1939] 2 All E.R. 202, where damages were awarded for a three-week period during which the claimant was disturbed by the noise from a badly installed electric motor in a neighbouring flat.

[125] *De Keyser's Royal Hotel Ltd v Spicer Bros Ltd* (1914) 30 T.L.R. 257; *Halsey v Esso Petroleum Co Ltd* [1961] 1 W.L.R. 683. Noise is also more serious on a Sunday than on a weekday: *Dewar v City and Suburban Racecourse Co* [1899] 1 I.R. 345.

[126] See *Barr v Biffa Waste Services* [2012] EWCA Civ 312; [2013] Q.B. 455 at [115].

[127] Penner (1993) 5 J.E.L. 1; Steel [2017] C.L.J. 145.

[128] *Sturges v Bridgman* (1879) 11 Ch. D. 852 at 865 per Thesiger LJ.

[129] "[T]his is an industrial area. The local inhabitants are not entitled to expect to sit in a sweet-smelling orchard": *Shoreham-by-Sea UDC v Dolphin Canadian Proteins Ltd* (1972) 71 L.G.R. 261 at 266 per May J.

[130] *Village of Euclid v Amber Realty Co* 272 U.S. 365 (1926) at 388 per Sutherland J.

[131] See, e.g., *Adams v Ursell* [1913] 1 Ch. 269 (fried fish shop a nuisance in a "high-class" street). See also *Thompson-Schwab v Costaki* [1956] 1 W.L.R. 365; and *Laws v Florinplace Ltd* [1981] 1 All E.R. 659. These decisions are however surely out of step with current social attitudes.

[132] *Baxter v Camden LBC (No.2)* [2001] Q.B. 1 at 10 per Tuckey LJ (affirmed [2001] 1 A.C. 1). See also in respect of "an inner city urban environment", *Fearn v Tate Gallery Board of Trustees* [2019] EWHC 246 (Ch); [2019] Ch. 369 at [190] (affirmed on other grounds [2020] EWCA Civ 104; [2020] 2 W.L.R. 1081).

[133] [1906] 1 Ch. 234 (affirmed [1907] A.C. 121).

door, since this created a degree of "discomfort by night in excess of that which an ordinary person could reasonably be expected to put up with in a printing neighbourhood".[134]

15-022A **Relevance of defendant's own activity** In *Coventry v Lawrence*[135] the Supreme Court was required to consider whether a nuisance was committed as a result of the noise generated by the defendants' motoring events: speedway and stock car racing (held in a stadium) and moto-cross (held on a track at the rear of the stadium). One issue was the extent to which the defendants' own activities could be taken into account in determining the character of the locality. According to Lord Neuberger they were to be taken into account, but not to the extent that they constituted a nuisance to the claimant, i.e., the court could take into account that motoring events were held and that they generated noise, but not noise at the level which constituted a nuisance.[136] The circularity involved in this proposition was not lost on Lord Neuberger but he considered it preferable to either of the alternatives—namely, to ignore the defendants' activities altogether or to take them into account without modification (as the Court of Appeal had done)[137] which would mean that there could rarely be a successful claim for nuisance. As for the circularity involved, while this gave "cause for concern", the court would be required to go through an "iterative process" when assessing the character of the locality and what noise within it constituted a nuisance.[138] Lord Carnwath noted that in earlier cases involving noise[139] the courts did not find it necessary to undertake an "iterative process". Rather, they proceeded "on the basis that a change in the intensity or character of an existing activity may result in a nuisance, no less than the introduction of a new activity". Whether it did so was a matter for the judge to determine "as an issue of fact or degree".[140] Understandably, this aspect of the reasoning in *Coventry v Lawrence* has been criticised,[141] and it has been said that it is unlikely to be the final word on the subject.[142] In our respectful opinion, there is no escaping the fundamental contradiction inherent in Lord Neuberger's approach, and it would be better if the courts were simply to discount the defendant's activity when assessing the character of the neighbourhood for the purposes of the locality principle.

15-023 **Relevance of planning permission**[143] It may be that in the course of time Belgrave Square declines and Bermondsey goes up in the world. Nowadays, a major factor in such changes in the character of the locality will be the planning process, but in *Coventry v Lawrence* the Supreme Court criticised the Court of Appeal and a number of earlier cases for overstating the significance of the grant of

---

134 [1906] 1 Ch. 234 at 249 per Stirling LJ.
135 [2014] UKSC 13; [2014] A.C. 822.
136 [2014] UKSC 13; [2014] A.C. 822 at [65].
137 [2012] EWCA Civ 26; [2012] 1 W.L.R. 2127.
138 [2014] UKSC 13; [2014] A.C. 822 at [65].
139 *Kennaway v Thompson* [1981] Q.B. 88; *Watson v Croft Promo-Sport Ltd* [2009] EWCA Civ 15; [2009] 3 All E.R. 249.
140 *Coventry v Lawrence* [2014] UKSC 13; [2014] A.C. 822 at [190].
141 See, e.g., Lee [2014] J.P.L. 705.
142 Reid [2015] Edin. L.R. 383, 386.
143 Lee [2011] J.P.E.L. 986; Nolan in Dyson, Goudkamp and Wilmot-Smith (eds), *Defences in Tort* (2015).

permission for the defendant's activities.[144] According to Lord Neuberger, the granting of permission is "normally of no assistance to the defendant in a claim brought by a neighbour who contends that the activity causes a nuisance to her land in the form of noise or other loss of amenity".[145] He acknowledged that there will be "occasions" when the *terms* of a planning permission could be relevant,[146] but Lord Carnwath went a little further (and a little closer to the earlier authorities) when he accepted that, in "exceptional cases", planning permission cannot sensibly be ignored when assessing the character of the locality.[147] Such cases are those in which the project is exceptional in scale and where the permission is the "result of a considered policy decision by the competent authority leading to a fundamental change in the pattern of uses" in the locality,[148] as opposed to a single grant, such as permission to expand a pig farm.[149] It should be emphasised that, at this stage, we are concerned with the question of *liability* for nuisance. When it comes to the question of the appropriate *remedy* if a nuisance has been established, the justices in *Coventry v Lawrence* were agreed that the grant of planning permission is of potentially greater significance. This is dealt with below.[150]

iv. The Reasonableness of the Defendant's Conduct

The more unreasonable the defendant's behaviour is, the less the claimant can be expected to put up with the interference that results, so the reasonableness of the defendant's conduct is a factor in determining whether an interference is unreasonable. It follows that the motive of the defendant, the utility of the defendant's activity, and the failure of the defendant to take reasonable care to eliminate or minimise the interference can all be taken into account in the unreasonable interference inquiry. **15-024**

Motive of the defendant[151]   If A's legitimate use of his own property causes to B annoyance which does not amount to a nuisance, will the fact that A's acts are done solely for the purpose of annoying B turn them into a nuisance? In *Christie v Davey*,[152] the defendant, exasperated by a considerable number of music lessons given by the claimant, a teacher of music whose residence was separated from that **15-025**

---

[144] *Gillingham BC v Medway (Chatham) Dock Co Ltd* [1993] Q.B. 343; *Watson v Croft Promo-Sport Ltd* [2009] EWCA Civ 15; [2009] 3 All E.R. 249; *Hirose Electrical UK Ltd v Peak Ingredients Ltd* [2011] EWCA Civ 987; [2011] Env. L.R. 34. See also the earlier criticism of Peter Gibson LJ in *Wheeler v JJ Saunders* [1996] Ch. 19 and Pill LJ in *Hunter v Canary Wharf Ltd* [1997] A.C. 655.
[145] *Coventry v Lawrence* [2014] UKSC 13; [2014] A.C. 822 at [94].
[146] *Coventry v Lawrence* [2014] UKSC 13; [2014] A.C. 822 at [96].
[147] Lord Mance agreed with Lord Neuberger (at [165]–[166]); Lord Sumption said that the grant of permission would "at best" provide some evidence of the reasonableness of the particular use of the land in question (at [156]); Lord Clarke said that it is "capable of being relevant" but the facts of cases are so varied "that it is difficult to lay down hard and fast rules" (at [169]).
[148] Such as in the *Gillingham* case above; cf. the reference by Staughton LJ in *Wheeler v JJ Saunders Ltd* [1996] Ch. 19 at 30 to "a strategic planning decision affected by considerations of public interest"; and see the observations of Lord Cooke in *Hunter v Canary Wharf Ltd* [1997] A.C. 655 at 722.
[149] *Wheeler v JJ Saunders* [1996] Ch. 19; cf. *Watson v Croft Promosport Ltd* [2009] EWCA Civ 15; [2009] 3 All E.R. 249.
[150] See para.15-073.
[151] Fridman (1954) 40 Va. L. Rev. 583.
[152] [1893] 1 Ch. 316. See also *Ibbotson v Peat* (1865) 3 H. & C. 644 (exploding fireworks to drive game off neighbour's land). On the relationship between malice and abnormal sensitivity, see *Hollywood Silver Fox Farm Ltd v Emmett* [1936] 2 K.B. 468, discussed below, para.15-032.

of the defendant only by a party-wall, interrupted the claimant's lessons by knocking on the party-wall, beating on trays, whistling and shrieking. North J issued an injunction because the defendant had acted deliberately and maliciously for the purpose of annoying the claimant. The learned judge added[153]:

> "If what has taken place had occurred between two sets of persons both perfectly innocent, I should have taken an entirely different view of the case."

The courts, in judging what constitutes a nuisance, take into consideration the purpose of the defendant's activity,[154] and acts otherwise justified on the ground of reciprocity, if done wantonly and maliciously with the object of injuring a neighbour are devoid of any social utility and so the resultant interference cannot be regarded as "reasonable".

In *Christie v Davey* the defendant interfered with a legally protected interest of the claimant and the issue was whether the interference was unreasonable. If, however, the defendant's activity has not infringed any such right or interest, the claimant has no cause of action[155] and the defendant's motive is irrelevant. This was the position in *Bradford Corpn v Pickles*,[156] where the defendant deliberately drained his land so as to diminish the water supply reaching the land of the claimants. His purpose was to coerce the claimants into purchasing his land. It had previously been established that no interest in percolating waters exists until appropriation, and as no interest or right could therefore have been infringed, the motive of the defendant was immaterial.

15-026 **Utility of the defendant's activity** Since nuisance is the law of give and take the court is inevitably concerned to some extent with the utility or general benefit to the community of the defendant's activity. Thus if we live in a commercial area, we must put up with the noise of trucks making early morning deliveries, though probably not with the same amount of noise made by drunken neighbours.[157] This approach, however, will only justify an injurious activity up to a certain point, and that point is reached when serious damage is being done to the claimant's use and enjoyment of his property. In such a case the court will not accept the argument that the claimant should put up with the harm because it is beneficial to the community as a whole, for that would amount to requiring him to carry the burden alone of an activity from which many others benefit.[158] Even in such cases, however, the "public interest" in the continuation of the defendant's activity may be taken into account when it comes to determining the appropriate remedy.[159]

---

[153] *Christie v Davey* [1893] 1 Ch. 316 at 326–327.

[154] *Harrison v Southwark and Vauxhall Water Co* [1891] 2 Ch. 409 at 414; *Grant v Fynney* (1872) L.R. 8 Ch. App. 8 at 12.

[155] See para.15-012.

[156] [1895] A.C. 587. See Taggart, *Private Property and Abuse of Rights in Victorian England* (2002).

[157] This is demonstrated most clearly where the activity is actuated by malice, for malicious conduct can have no utility: see para.15-025.

[158] In *Miller v Jackson* [1977] Q.B. 966, where the interference took the form of balls escaping from a cricket ground, Lord Denning MR referred to the contribution the defendant cricket club made to the social cohesion of the village, and held that for this reason the playing of cricket was not a nuisance to adjacent householders; but the majority disagreed and their reasoning of the majority was followed in *Kennaway v Thompson* [1981] Q.B. 88, where it was held that the noise from motor boat races was actionable even though large numbers of people came to watch them.

[159] See para.15-073. On the public interest and nuisance, see Lee [2015] C.L.J. 329.

Failure to exercise reasonable care or to comply with relevant statutory   **15-027**
norms   Although the exercise of reasonable care is not generally a defence to an
action for private nuisance,[160] whether the defendant took reasonable precautions
to eliminate or minimise the interference his activity caused is a factor in the
unreasonable interference inquiry.[161] Failure by the defendant to take reasonable
care will usually lead to the conclusion that the interference is actionable, since there
is no reason why the claimant should have to put up with discomfort or inconvenience that the adoption of proper measures would eliminate. Similarly, although
compliance with relevant regulatory norms or planning controls is not a defence to
a nuisance action,[162] it may be relevant in determining whether an interference is
unreasonable.[163]

v. Gravity of the Interference Assessed Objectively

Whether a particular use of land unreasonably interferes with the use and enjoy-   **15-028**
ment of another's land is to be judged objectively.[164] This follows from the fact that
in private nuisance the injury is strictly speaking to the land, not the persons occupying it. In considering what is reasonable the law does not therefore take account of abnormal sensitivity in persons, uses or property. If the only reason why
a person complains of fumes is that he has an unusually sensitive nose or that he
grows particularly exotic flowers, he cannot expect any sympathy from the courts.

Sensitive persons   In *Heath v Mayor of Brighton*[165] the incumbent and trustees of   **15-029**
a Brighton church sought an injunction to restrain noise from the defendants' power
station. There was no proof of diminution of the congregation or of any personal
annoyance to anyone except the incumbent and he was not prevented from preach-
ing or conducting his services, nor was the noise such as to distract the attention
of ordinary healthy persons attending the church. An injunction was not granted.
It seems that no regard should be had to the special needs of invalids, or to special
occupational needs, for there is no redress for damage due solely to the exceptionally delicate nature of the operations carried on by an injured party.[166]

Sensitive uses   You cannot increase the liabilities of your neighbour by applying   **15-030**
your property to special uses, whether for business or pleasure.[167] In *Robinson v
Kilvert*[168] the defendant began to manufacture paper boxes in the cellar of a house
the upper part of which was in the occupation of the claimant. The defendant's business required hot and dry air and he heated the cellar accordingly. This raised the

---

[160] See para.15-017.
[161] See, e.g., *Moy v Stoop* (1909) 25 T.L.R. 262 (crying of children in nursery not actionable but might be if neglected by nurse).
[162] See para.15-067.
[163] *Hirose Electrical UK Ltd v Peak Ingredients Ltd* [2011] EWCA Civ 987; [2011] Env. L.R. 34 at [40].
[164] *Network Rail Infrastructure Ltd v Williams* [2018] EWCA Civ 1514; [2019] Q.B. 601 at [43]; *Fearn v Tate Gallery Board of Trustees* [2020] EWCA Civ 104; [2020] 2 W.L.R. 1081 at [46].
[165] (1908) 98 L.T. 718.
[166] *Bloodworth v Cormack* [1949] N.Z.L.R. 1058 at 1064; cf. *Stretch v Romford Football Club* (1971) 115 S.J. 741.
[167] *Eastern and SA Telegraph Co v Cape Town Tramways* [1902] A.C. 381 at 383.
[168] (1889) 41 Ch. D. 88. See also the famous American case of *Amphitheaters Inc v Portland Meadows* 198 P. 2d 847 (Or. 1948), where the court refused to issue an injunction to protect a drive-in cinema from the glare of floodlights on an adjacent racetrack.

temperature on the claimant's floor and dried (and thereby diminished the value of) brown paper which the claimant warehoused there, but it did not inconvenience the claimant's employees nor would it have harmed paper generally. It was held that the defendant was not liable for nuisance. A person who carries on an exceptionally delicate trade cannot complain because it is injured by his neighbour doing something on his property which would not injure anything but an exceptionally delicate trade.[169] But once the nuisance is established, the remedies by way of damages or an injunction will extend to sensitive operations such as the growing of orchids.[170]

15-031 Sensitive property   This objective principle also extends to the physical make-up of buildings and other fixtures on the claimant's land. In *Hirose Electrical UK Ltd v Peak Ingredients Ltd*,[171] for example, it was held that no claim lay where the manufacture of food additives on an industrial estate generated odours that seriously affected the adjoining unit because the party wall was porous, and the same should be true where vibrations from the defendant's factory cause the claimant's house to collapse only because it is particularly old and unstable.[172] The application of the hypersensitivity principle to the claimant's property also provides the best explanation for the decision in *Southwark LBC v Tanner*,[173] though the principle was not relied upon by the House of Lords in that case. The claimant rented a flat in a converted house owned by the defendant council. When the conversion work had been done, sound insulation had not been installed and, as a result, the noise generated by the residents of the flat above was excessive. It was held that no action lay in these circumstances, since the ordinary use of residential premises was not actionable in nuisance. However, with respect this reasoning is difficult to reconcile with other authorities,[174] and is at odds with the claimant-sided approach to the actionability of the interference usually adopted in nuisance cases. The decision could however have been justified on the grounds that the absence of adequate soundproofing made the flat abnormally sensitive to noise. This would explain why liability has been imposed in cases where the interference caused by ordinary use of residential premises is attributable to the physical make-up of the *defendant's* property.[175]

15-032 The limits of the objective approach   Quite how thoroughly the principle of objectivity is to be applied in nuisance cases remains unclear. Certainly, the objec-

---

[169] A uses his land to produce organic cereal crops. His neighbour B uses genetically modified canola seed which strays onto A's land and causes him to lose his organic certification. Since organic farming was not common in the locality, A's use was judged abnormally sensitive: *Marsh v Baxter* [2015] WASCA 169; (2015) 49 W.A.R. 1. See also the discussion of similar issues in *Hoffmann v Monsanto Canada Inc* [2005] SKQB 225.

[170] *McKinnon Industries Ltd v Walker* [1951] 3 D.L.R. 577.

[171] [2011] J.P.L. 429 (affirmed [2011] EWCA Civ 987; [2011] Env. L.R. 34).

[172] See *Cremidas v Fenton* 111 N.E. 855 (Mass. 1916); cf. *Anger v Northern Construction Co* [1938] 4 D.L.R. 70 (affirmed [1938] 4 D.L.R. 738). See also *Grosvenor Hotel Co v Hamilton* [1894] 2 Q.B. 836 (where however the point was left open); *Hoare & Co v McAlpine* [1923] 1 Ch. 167.

[173] [2001] 1 A.C. 1.

[174] *Sampson v Hodson-Pressinger* [1981] 3 All E.R. 710; *Toff v McDowell* (1993) 25 H.L.R. 650; *Stannard v Charles Pitcher Ltd* [2002] B.L.R. 441.

[175] *Sampson v Hodson-Pressinger* [1981] 3 All E.R. 710 (poorly constructed roof terrace); *Toff v McDowell* (1993) 25 H.L.R. 650; *Stannard v Charles Pitcher Ltd* [2002] B.L.R. 441 (changes to layout and floor coverings increased noise in flat below).

tive standard is jettisoned in cases where the defendant acts maliciously. In *Hollywood Silver Fox Farm Ltd v Emmett*,[176] the defendant deliberately caused guns to be fired near the boundary of the claimant's land in order to scare the claimant's silver foxes during breeding time. Even though—as counsel for the defendant pointed out—silver foxes are abnormally sensitive to noise at breeding time, Macnaghten J held that the fact that the shooting was intended to cause the claimants harm made it actionable. Nor is it apparent whether the objective standard would be employed by the courts in circumstances where the claimant is not more but *less* susceptible to the interference than the average person. Could, for example, a deaf person bring a nuisance action for noise? Since strictly speaking it is the damage to the land (not the damage to the occupier) that is the foundation of the claim, it is difficult to see on what basis such an action could be dismissed.[177] Indeed, logically, a claim for amenity nuisance could even be brought by the owner of a vacant property. Nor is it an easy answer to allow the claim and award nominal damages, since the assessment of damages in nuisance cases is also subject to the objectivity principle.[178]

An unnecessary principle?   It has been suggested that it is difficult to see any   **15-033**
further life in the principle about abnormal sensitivity.[179] With respect, that does not seem correct: the principle flows from the very nature of the cause of action for private nuisance as a property tort. Besides, why should the freedom of action of one's neighbours be restricted by the fact that you, or your use of your property, are especially sensitive?[180] Of course, that is not to say that the law's response to what were once regarded as abnormally sensitive activities may not change over time: for example, the use of sensitive electronic equipment is now part of everyday life and there are detailed regulatory controls designed to minimise interference.[181]

C.   Standard of Liability

The question of the extent to which fault (in the sense of negligence) is neces-   **15-034**
sary to establish liability in damages for nuisance has given rise to great difficulty.[182] There are many judicial statements of various vintages asserting that liability in

---

[176] [1936] 2 K.B. 468.
[177] In *Fearn v Tate Gallery Board of Trustees* [2020] EWCA Civ 104; [2020] 2 W.L.R. 1081 at [46], Sir Terence Etherton MR referred to "undue sensitivities or insensitivity on the part of the claimant" being disregarded. See also the *Restatement (Second) of the Law of Torts* (1977), §821F, comment d.
[178] See para.15-077.
[179] *Network Rail Infrastructure Ltd v Morris* [2004] EWCA Civ 172; [2004] Env. L.R. 41 at [35] per Buxton LJ. Buxton LJ's scepticism was rooted in an approach to nuisance centred on an openended test of reasonableness as between neighbours, but this approach has not taken hold in later decisions. See, e.g., *Fearn v Tate Gallery Board of Trustees* [2020] EWCA Civ 104; [2020] 2 W.L.R. 1081 at [38]: "Whether or not there has been a private nuisance does not turn on some overriding and free-ranging assessment by the court of the respective reasonableness of each party in the light of all the facts and circumstances."
[180] A point emphasised in *Fearn v Tate Gallery Board of Trustees* [2020] EWCA Civ 104; [2020] 2 W.L.R. 1081 and *Network Rail Infrastructure Ltd v Williams* [2018] EWCA Civ 1514; [2019] Q.B. 601, in both of which the abnormal sensitivity principle was reaffirmed. At first instance in *Fearn*, Mann J expressed his agreement with academic commentary critical of the questioning of the principle: [2018] EWHC 246 (Ch); [2019] Ch. 369 at [231].
[181] *Network Rail Infrastructure Ltd v Morris* [2004] EWCA Civ 172; [2004] Env. L.R. 41 at [18].
[182] Keeton (1959) 59 Col. L. Rev. 457; Cross (1995) 111 L.Q.R. 445.

nuisance is "strict" but there are very few cases in which the meaning of that expression has really been explored. It is impossible to reconcile everything that has ever been said on this subject, but it is submitted that the current law may be summarised as follows.

15-035 Remedy by way of an injunction Where the claimant seeks an injunction to restrain a nuisance the purpose of the remedy is to protect him from future damage. As the Law Commission has pointed out[183]:

> "[C]onsideration of the strictness of the duty is then out of place—all that the court is concerned with is the question, 'Should the defendant be told to stop this interference with the claimant's rights?' Whether or not the defendant knew of the noise or smell or the like when it first began to annoy the plaintiff does not matter; he becomes aware of it at the latest when the plaintiff brings his claim before the court."

In such a case, as we have seen in the previous section, the court is concerned with determining the permissible extent of an interference which, since the defendant ex hypothesi knows about it, is deliberate. If the stench of my pig farm fouls your air, I am liable because I have knowingly created an intolerable situation for you—and if it is intolerable for you by ordinary, sensible standards it is unnecessary to ask whether I was negligent in creating the smell. Accordingly, great care must be taken in transferring statements in injunction cases to the different context of claims for damages for past harm.[184]

15-036 Creation of a nuisance distinguished from continuing a nuisance When it comes to a claim for damages, we must draw a distinction between the creation or adoption of a nuisance by the defendant and the continuance of a nuisance[185] created by a third party or an act of nature. An occupier "continues" a nuisance, for the initial creation of which he is not responsible, if, once he knows or ought to know of its existence, he fails to take reasonable precautions to abate it and it is clear that he is not liable in damages if these conditions are not satisfied.[186] Here fault is therefore required and there is a "sort of condominium" with the law of negligence.[187]

15-037 Requirement of reasonable foreseeability Even where the defendant has created the situation which interferes with the claimant's land, there is no liability in damages where the possibility of interference of the type which occurs could not reasonably have been foreseen by a person in the defendant's position when he did the relevant acts. In *Cambridge Water Co v Eastern Counties Leather Plc*[188] the defendants had for some years used a chemical called PCE in their tanning factory.

---

[183] *Civil Liability for Dangerous Things and Activities*, Law Com. No.32 (1970), 25.
[184] *Cambridge Water Co v Eastern Counties Leather Plc* [1994] 2 A.C. 264 at 300.
[185] *Sedleigh-Denfield v O'Callaghan* [1940] A.C. 880 at 904–908, 913.
[186] This situation is discussed further in para.15-043. The burden of proof in this respect would appear to lie on the claimant (*Sedleigh-Denfield v O'Callaghan* [1940] A.C. 880 at 887, 899, 908; *Green v Lord Somerleyton* [2003] EWCA Civ 198; [2004] 1 P. & C.R. 520) and it is significant that in *Goldman v Hargrave* [1967] 1 A.C. 645 the Privy Council thought it unnecessary to decide whether the cause of action lay in nuisance or negligence. See also *Smith v Littlewoods Organisation Ltd* [1987] A.C. 241 at 274.
[187] *Transco Plc v Stockport MBC* [2003] UKHL 61; [2004] 2 A.C. 1 at [96] per Lord Walker.
[188] [1994] 2 A.C. 264.

Continual small spillages had gradually built up a pool of PCE under the land and contaminated the aquifer from which the claimants drew their supply of water, forcing them to find another source at a cost of nearly £1 million. When the contamination was taking place it was not foreseeable that quantities of the chemical would accumulate in the aquifer nor, even if this could have been foreseen, was it foreseeable that there would be any significant damage to the claimants' water. The House of Lords held that the defendants were not liable in damages under the rule in *Rylands v Fletcher* but speaking for the House Lord Goff made it clear that "foreseeability of harm is ... a prerequisite of the recovery of damages in private nuisance".[189] In *Cambridge Water* the issue of foreseeability arose because the interference was caused by an ongoing interference of which the defendant had been unaware, as was also true of a later case where the nuisance damages claim failed because it had not been foreseeable that electromagnetic interference caused by a signalling system would affect the sound made by electric guitars in a nearby recording studio.[190] The issue may also arise where the claimant seeks damages for a one-off interference, such as physical damage caused by flooding or fire. However, it now seems clear that in this type of case fault is required (unless the facts fall within the rule in *Rylands v Fletcher*),[191] and since fault requires foreseeability, foreseeability does not here operate as an additional condition of liability.

Reasonable foreseeability: further points   Three further points should be made   **15-038**
about the foreseeability requirement in nuisance. First, the requirement goes to both liability and damages. The defendant will not be liable at all unless some interference with the claimant's interests was reasonably foreseeable as a result of his activity. And where liability is established, the claimant will be compensated only for harm of a type which was reasonably foreseeable.[192] Suppose, for example, that it was foreseeable that factory emissions would interfere with the comfort of the occupiers of neighbouring properties, but not that they would lead to physical damage. In that case, damages might be recoverable for the amenity harm, but not for shrubs or flowers killed by chemicals in the smoke. Second, the foreseeability of the interference is assessed objectively. Where the use of fertiliser led to contamination of the claimant's water supply, for example, the question of foreseeability was determined according to the viewpoint of the "hypothetical good farmer" competent to run a farm such as the defendant's.[193] Finally, where interference with the claimant's land is not reasonably foreseeable when the defendant creates the state of affairs which leads to the nuisance, but subsequently becomes so, the defendant is not strictly liable, but merely comes under a duty to take reasonable steps to remove or reduce the danger.[194]

---

189 [1994] 2 A.C. 264 at 290. See also *Arscott v The Coal Authority* [2004] EWCA Civ 892; [2005] Env. L.R. 6, where an increased risk of flooding was not foreseeable when infilling works were done.
190 *Network Rail Infrastructure v Morris* [2004] EWCA Civ 172; [2004] Env. L.R. 41. See also *Ilford UDC v Beal* [1925] 1 K.B. 671; *Savage v Fairclough* [2000] Env. L.R. 183; *Northumbrian Water Ltd v Sir Robert McAlpine Ltd* [2014] EWCA Civ 685; [2014] B.L.R. 605.
191 See para.15-015.
192 Note, however, that where the defendant is an occupier accused of adopting or continuing the nuisance, both the type *and the extent* of the harm must have been foreseeable: *Holbeck Hall Hotel Ltd v Scarborough BC* [2000] Q.B. 836.
193 *Savage v Fairclough* [2000] Env. L.R. 183.
194 See *Cambridge Water Co v Eastern Counties Leather Plc* [1994] 2 A.C. 264 at 307. See, e.g., *Anthony v The Coal Authority* [2005] EWHC (QB) 1654; [2006] Env. L.R. 17.

D. Who can Sue?

15-039 **Interest in land**[195] "He alone has a lawful claim [for private nuisance] who has suffered an invasion of some proprietary or other interest in land."[196] After a period of doubt, this proposition was reaffirmed by the House of Lords in *Hunter v Canary Wharf Ltd*.[197] As far as encroachment on or damage to the land is concerned the proposition is self-evident, but it is equally applicable to nuisances like smells and noise which affect the enjoyment of the land, for what is being remedied by the law is not the personal discomfort of the persons on the land but the diminution in the utility of the land. It follows that even in such cases a claim may only be brought by a person with a sufficient interest in the land (whom for the moment we shall call the occupier) and not by members of the occupier's family, guests, lodgers or live-in employees. Where the object of the complaint is to obtain an injunction to put an end to the nuisance, this is unlikely to cause hardship and a contrary rule might be productive of practical difficulties. If the occupier sues, then the other persons using the premises will benefit from the grant of the injunction; if the others were allowed to sue it would complicate post-injunction negotiations and mean that a person on adjoining land who wished to come to an arrangement with the occupier whereby the latter would license some temporary nuisance (for example during repairs or improvements) could not safely rely on it.[198]

15-040 **Qualifying interests** To sue in private nuisance the claimant must have a right to the land, for example as owner[199] or reversioner, or be in exclusive occupation of it as a tenant[200] or under a licence to occupy.[201] No distinction is made in this respect between legal and equitable interests, so a spouse with a beneficial but not legal interest in the matrimonial home can sue in nuisance for damage to that interest.[202] But because the basic test is whether the claimant is in exclusive occupation, licensees—such as lodgers and domestic employees—will usually not be able

---

[195] Kodilinye (1989) 9 L.S. 284; Malcolm in Jackson and Wilde (eds), *Contemporary Property Law* (1999).

[196] *Read v J Lyons & Co Ltd* [1947] A.C. 156 at 183 per Lord Simonds.

[197] [1997] A.C. 655. The doubts were created by *Khorasandjian v Bush* [1993] Q.B. 727 (overruled in *Hunter*), which had departed from the previous orthodoxy as observable in *Malone v Laskey* [1907] 2 K.B. 141.

[198] See Pontin, *Nuisance Law and Environmental Protection* (2013), pp.168–170.

[199] In subsidence cases, only the owner of the property at the time it was damaged is entitled to bring a claim: *Jeffries v Williams* (1850) 5 Exch. 792. However, where there is a continuing nuisance (e.g., intrusion of tree roots) an owner can recover damages for remedial work even if the damage may have been done before he acquired the property: *Masters v Brent LBC* [1978] Q.B. 841; *Delaware Mansions Ltd v Westminster CC* [2001] UKHL 55; [2002] 1 A.C. 321.

[200] Though if an injunction is granted to a tenant, it may be limited to the duration of the tenancy: *Simper v Foley* (1862) 2 J. Cohn. & H. 555.

[201] *Foster v Warblington UDC* [1906] 1 K.B. 648; *Crown River Cruises Ltd v Kimbolton Fireworks Ltd* [1996] 2 Lloyd's Rep. 533 (licensee with exclusive use and occupation of river mooring); *Pemberton v Southwark LBC* [2000] 1 W.L.R. 1672 ("tolerated trespasser"); *Tinsel Time Ltd v Roberts* [2011] EWHC 1199 (TCC); [2011] B.L.R. 515; cf. *Jan de Nul (UK) Ltd v Axa Royale Belge* [2000] 2 Lloyd's Rep. 700 at 719 (contractual mooring rights insufficient).

[202] *Hunter v Canary Wharf Ltd* [1997] A.C. 655 at 708. Does the statutory right of occupation granted to a spouse by s.30 of the Family Law Act 1996 constitute an interest in land for these purposes? It has been argued that it may depend on which of the "home rights" recognised by the Act a spouse or civil partner enjoys: Murphy, *The Law of Nuisance* (2010), paras 4.20–4.24.

to bring claims in private nuisance,[203] and the same is true of children living in their parents' home. The owner of an incorporeal hereditament such as an easement or profit can sue for disturbance of his right.[204] A reversioner can bring an action in nuisance if he can show that there is a likelihood that permanent injury will be caused to the property and his right is then coexistent with that of the occupier.[205] A permanent injury is one which will continue indefinitely unless something is done to remove it,[206] for example a building which infringes the right to ancient lights,[207] vibrations causing structural damage,[208] or keeping locked a gate across a path over which the reversioner has a right of way;[209] but the emission of noise or fumes or other invasions of a temporary nature, even if they cause the tenants to leave, or reduce the letting value, has been said not to suffice.[210] However, more recently it was held to be arguable that where third party interference entitles a tenant to damages for breach of the landlord's covenant for quiet enjoyment, this might amount to an injury to the reversion that gives the landlord standing to sue the third party in nuisance.[211] It is certainly difficult to see why a landlord should be unable to bring an action in such a case, or where he suffers loss because a nuisance makes it difficult to re-let or sell the affected property.[212]

Article 8 ECHR   In the aftermath of *Hunter v Canary Wharf Ltd* it was suggested that the restriction on the right to sue in nuisance to those with an interest in the land affected could violate the rights of other household members under art.8 of the ECHR,[213] but in the light of the close connection between this restriction and the underlying nature of the cause of action such an argument is unlikely to succeed. More recently it has been said that "overlaying" private nuisance with art.8 "would significantly distort the tort in some important respects", with the question of who can sue being given as an example[214] (on the basis that extending the standing rules so as to encompass those lacking proprietary rights is difficult to reconcile with the essential nature of private nuisance as a property tort).   **15-041**

E.   Who can be Sued?

i.   Creator of the Nuisance

Creator of nuisance always liable[215]   The creator of the nuisance is always liable, even if he is neither the owner nor the occupier of the land from which the   **15-042**

---

203 See, e.g., *Malone v Laskey* [1907] 2 K.B. 141.
204 *Nicholls v Ely Beet Sugar Factory Ltd* [1936] 1 Ch. 343 (destruction of fish by pollution).
205 The damages will have to be divided according to the relative interests of reversioner and occupier: *Hunter v Canary Wharf Ltd* [1997] A.C. 655 at 707.
206 *Jones v Llanrwst UDC* [1911] 1 Ch. 393 at 404.
207 *Jesser v Gifford* (1767) 4 Burr. 2141.
208 *Colwell v St Pancras BC* [1904] Ch. 707.
209 *Kidgill v Moor* (1850) 9 C.B. 364; 137 E.R. 934.
210 *Simpson v Savage* (1856) 1 C.B.(N.S.) 347; 140 E.R. 143; *Cooper v Crabtree* (1882) 20 Ch. D. 589.
211 *John Smith & Co (Edinburgh) Ltd v Hill* [2010] EWHC 1016 (Ch); [2010] 2 B.C.L.C. 566. See also *Hampstead and Suburban Properties Ltd v Diomedous* [1968] 3 All E.R. 545 at 550 (where, however, the older authorities had not been cited).
212 See Kidner [1998] Conv. 267 at 273–275.
213 *McKenna v British Aluminium Ltd* [2002] Env. L.R. 30.
214 *Fearn v Tate Gallery Board of Trustees* [2020] EWCA Civ 104; [2020] 2 W.L.R. 1081 at [91].
215 On who can be sued in private nuisance, see generally Friedmann (1943) 59 L.Q.R. 63.

interference emanates.[216] In *Hussain v Lancaster CC*[217] certain persons engaged in a campaign of racial harassment against the claimant shopkeepers. Various acts of trespass and intimidation were committed which were no doubt torts in their own right. However, the Court of Appeal said that there was no nuisance because the acts did not involve the primary wrongdoers' use of their land, even though they affected the claimants' enjoyment of theirs.[218] With respect, this seems an unnecessary restriction: to say that nuisance is a tort to the claimant's land does not require the additional proposition that it must involve the defendant's use of his. Suppose, for example, that D, in pursuit of a vendetta against C, repeatedly disturbs C in his remote farmhouse by parking outside, shining his headlights on full beam through the windows and playing his car stereo at full volume. Is there any reason why that should not be a private nuisance? Furthermore, the issue in *Hussain* was not the liability in tort of the wrongdoers, but whether their landlord could be held responsible for their actions. A perfectly adequate basis for the negative answer would have been that the relationship of landlord and tenant between the defendant and the primary wrongdoers had no connection with what was going on at the claimants' shop.[219]

The approach in *Hussain* would also insulate from liability persons like independent contractors who may create a nuisance affecting the land of C while working on the land of B but who have no possession of the latter. In a later decision the Court of Appeal held that a local authority which had undertaken as the agent of the highway authority to maintain trees was liable for a "nuisance of omission" in allowing encroachment by roots, whether or not it was the occupier of the land on which the trees stood, and said that there was no authority "for the proposition that a person cannot be liable in nuisance unless he is in occupation of the land or has some legal interest in it".[220] In other cases it has simply been assumed that the creator of the nuisance is liable even though he has no interest in any relevant land.[221]

ii. Occupier

15-043 **Liability for "adopting" or "continuing" the nuisance** An occupier is not liable for a state of affairs created by a trespasser or resulting from an act of nature unless either he "adopts" the nuisance by using the state of affairs for his own purposes or he "continues" the nuisance. An occupier continues a nuisance if once he has actual or constructive knowledge of its existence he fails to take reasonably

---

[216] *Thompson v Gibson* (1841) 7 M. & W. 456; 151 E.R. 845. See also *The Church of Jesus Christ of Latter Day Saints v Price* [2004] EWHC 3245 (QB) at [154]; *Barratt Homes Ltd v Welsh Water (No. 2)* [2013] EWCA Civ 233; [2013] 1 W.L.R. 3486 at [57]. Indeed, a private nuisance may originate on public land: see, e.g., *Halsey v Esso Petroleum Co Ltd* [1961] 1 W.L.R. 683 (noise from lorries in highway); *Hubbard v Pitt* [1976] 2 Q.B. 142 (picketing); *LE Jones (Insurance Brokers) Ltd v Portsmouth CC* [2002] EWCA Civ 1723; [2003] 1 W.L.R. 427 (roots encroaching from the highway).

[217] [2000] Q.B. 1. Criticised by Bagshaw (2000) 8 Tort. L. Rev. 165; O'Sullivan [2000] C.L.J. 11.

[218] [2000] Q.B. 1 at 23.

[219] *Lippiatt v South Gloucestershire Council* [2000] Q.B. 51 at 61.

[220] *LE Jones (Insurance Brokers) Ltd v Portsmouth CC* [2002] EWCA Civ 1723; [2003] 1 W.L.R. 427.

[221] *Fennell v Robson Excavations Pty Ltd* [1977] 2 N.S.W.L.R. 486 is directly in point and reviews the authorities. See also *Southport Corp v Esso Petroleum Ltd* [1954] 2 Q.B. 182 at 204; [1956] A.C. 218 at 225.

prompt and efficient steps to abate it. He cannot of course be liable unless he is in a position to take effective steps to abate the nuisance.[222]

Trespassers   This principle was enunciated by the House of Lords in relation to **15-044**
a nuisance created by a trespasser in the leading case of *Sedleigh-Denfield v O'Callaghan*.[223] The defendant occupied land on which there was a ditch. A trespasser laid a pipe in the ditch with a grating designed to keep out leaves, but which was placed in such an ill-chosen position that it caused a blockage of the pipe when a heavy rainstorm occurred, as a result of which the claimant's adjacent land was flooded. The storm occurred nearly three years after the erection of the grating and the defendant was held liable both because during that period the employee responsible for clearing the ditch ought to have realised the risk of flooding presented by the obstruction, and because it had used the ditch to get rid of water from its property. Although there is much to be said for the view that the principle of *Sedleigh-Denfield* should be confined to cases where the trespasser interferes with the physical state of the land itself,[224] this is not currently the law. For example, a local authority was held liable for failing to take steps to remove from its land travellers whose objectionable behaviour damaged the claimants' business next door,[225] and an occupier has even been held liable where the wrongdoers used his land as a base from which they made damaging forays onto the claimant's land.[226]

Acts of nature   The old rule was that an occupier was never under a duty to abate **15-045**
a natural nuisance.[227] However, this rule was decisively rejected by the Privy Council in *Goldman v Hargrave*,[228] where the defendant was held liable for his failure to take adequate steps to extinguish a fire in a redgum tree on his land which had been struck by lightning, the fire having then spread to his neighbour's property. The principle of *Goldman v Hargrave* was formally accepted as part of English law by the Court of Appeal in *Leakey v National Trust*,[229] which involved damage done by movement of the land itself onto adjoining land below it. As regards such nuisances of omission, therefore, it is no longer relevant whether the state of affairs was originally created by a third party or by nature.[230] Once the occupier either becomes aware of the nuisance, or ought to become aware of it, he is liable for any damage it may cause if he fails to take reasonable ameliorative measures.[231]

---

[222] *Smeaton v Ilford Corp* [1954] Ch. 450 at 462; *Goldman v Hargrave* [1967] 1 A.C. 645.
[223] [1940] A.C. 880; *Leanse v Egerton* [1943] K.B. 323.
[224] As argued by Bright (2001) 21 O.J.L.S. 311.
[225] *Page Motors Ltd v Epsom and Ewell BC* (1982) 80 L.G.R. 337.
[226] *Lippiatt v South Gloucestershire Council* [2000] Q.B. 51.
[227] *Giles v Walker* (1890) 24 Q.B.D. 656; *Pontardawe UDC v Moore-Gwyn* [1929] 1 Ch. 656; *Neath R.D.C. v Williams* [1951] 1 K.B. 115. See Goodhart (1931) 4 C.L.J. 13.
[228] [1967] 1 A.C. 645.
[229] [1980] Q.B. 485.
[230] It is therefore no longer the law that a higher occupier owes no duty in any circumstances to prevent the natural, unconcentrated flow of water from his land to lower land: *Green v Lord Somerleyton* [2003] EWCA Civ 198; [2004] 1 P. & C.R. 520.
[231] As a result of this principle the rule that the owner of a servient tenement subject to an easement of support owes no duty to incur expenditure has been outflanked: *Holbeck Hall Hotel Ltd v Scarborough BC* [2000] Q.B. 836 at 856; *Rees v Skerrett* [2001] EWCA Civ 760; [2001] 1 W.L.R. 1541. Indeed, it has even been held that, applying this principle, the occupier of supporting land may have to contribute to the maintenance of that support where no easement exists in the first place: *Ward v Coope* [2015] EWCA Civ 30; [2015] 1 W.L.R. 4081.

15-046 **A subjective standard of care** In determining the standard of care required of an occupier sued for continuing a nuisance the fact that he was confronted with a nuisance not of his own creation cannot be disregarded, and because of this the court is entitled to consider the occupier's individual circumstances. As Lord Wilberforce said[232]:

> "The law must take account of the fact that the occupier on whom the duty is cast has, *ex hypothesi*, had this hazard thrust upon him through no seeking or fault of his own. His interest, and his resources, whether physical or material, may be of a very modest character either in relation to the magnitude of the hazard, or as compared with those of his threatened neighbour. A rule which required of him in such unsought circumstances in his neighbour's interest a physical effort of which he is not capable, or an excessive expenditure of money, would be unenforceable or unjust. One may say in general terms that the existence of a duty must be based upon knowledge of the hazard, ability to foresee the consequences of not checking or removing it, and the ability to abate it ... The standard ought to be to require of the occupier what is reasonable to expect of him in his individual circumstances."

This partly subjective test is an exception to the general rule in negligence[233] and is carefully limited by Lord Wilberforce to cases where the defendant was not himself responsible for the creation of the source of danger.[234] In these cases it is immaterial whether the cause of action is termed "nuisance" or "negligence": the duty of the defendant to his neighbours and the standard imposed on him is the same.[235]

15-047 **Scope of liability** The magnitude of the hazards which may be involved in cases of this type is illustrated by *Holbeck Hall Hotel Ltd v Scarborough BC*.[236] The lower part of the South Cliff at Scarborough was vested in the council and the cliff became unstable, leading to the collapse of the claimants' hotel at the top. The Court of Appeal held that *Leakey's* case was in principle applicable[237] but although the problem had been apparent in a general way for years and there had been progressive landslides, which might continue and foreseeably affect the grounds of the hotel, on the facts it was found that the council did not have reason to be aware of the likelihood of a comparatively sudden, catastrophic collapse such as took place and it was held not liable. Despite the general rule that when a defendant could foresee

---

[232] *Goldman v Hargrave* [1967] 1 A.C. 645 at 663.

[233] See para.6-002; but in applying this test, "I do not think that, except perhaps in a most unusual case, there would be any question of discovery as to [the] means of the plaintiff or the defendant, or evidence as to their respective resources. The question of reasonableness ... would fall to be decided on a broad basis, in which on some occasions, there might be included an element of obvious discrepancy of financial resources": *Leakey v National Trust* [1980] Q.B. 485 at 527 per Megaw LJ.

[234] Doubt was cast on the subjective standard of care in *Abbahall Ltd v Smee* [2002] EWCA Civ 1831; [2003] 1 W.L.R. 1472, where the Court of Appeal overturned a decision limiting the defendant's share of the cost of repairing a common roof to one quarter on the grounds of her poverty, holding instead that the expense should be divided equally between the two parties. However, Munby J expressly limited the scope of the decision to cases involving common roofs, and added (at [77]) that different considerations might apply if the properties were side by side, or if the cost of repair were of a "wholly different and very much greater order of magnitude" than the bill of around £20,000 in the case.

[235] See para.15-036.

[236] *Holbeck Hall Hotel Ltd v Scarborough BC* [2000] Q.B. 836.

[237] *Leakey* was a case of the collapse of the upper property on to the lower. *Holbeck* [2000] Q.B. 836 involved the collapse of the lower property damaging the upper.

some injury to the claimant he was liable for all damage of that type,[238] it was not appropriate to impose such an onerous requirement in respect of the "measured duty of care" which arose in these cases. Furthermore, in a case of this kind it was made clear that liability could be imposed only in respect of dangers that were patent, rather than latent, in other words only if the occupier either saw or should have seen the problem on his land, but not where the threat to neighbouring property was discoverable only by further investigation. But should such a duty be recognised at all in such a case? If the problem is not caused by an isolated event like a lightning strike, why should the defendant (whose own property may also be under threat) owe *any* duty to put his hand in his pocket to protect the claimant?[239] Although obiter, the Court of Appeal contemplated that it might not necessarily have been incumbent on someone in the council's position to carry out extensive and expensive remedial work and that the scope of the duty might have been limited to warning of the risk and sharing information.[240]

When assessing the content of the measured duty, the court must have regard not only to the physical and financial resources of the occupier, but to all the relevant circumstances, including the resources of the claimant. In *Lambert v Barratt Homes Ltd*,[241] the work of a developer on land sold by D, the local authority, led to water collecting on land which had been retained by D and which occasionally flooded C's neighbouring property. D's duty was limited to co-operating in a solution which involved the construction of suitable drainage and a catch pit on their retained land, for example, by allowing access and the necessary consents, but it was required to carry out and pay for the work itself. Considerations that were taken into account included the fact that most local authorities were under financial pressure; that the cost of remedial work might be met by the claimants' insurers; and that the claimants should be able to recover the cost of the work from the developer. By contrast, in *Vernon Knight Associates v Cornwall Council*[242] a highway authority was held liable for its failure to prevent damage to neighbouring property caused by flooding at a previously identified "hotspot" on one of the roads for which it was responsible. Whether it had been appropriate for the court in the *Lambert* case to attach significance to insurance considerations was doubted.[243] In any case, the occupier's duty to take ameliorative measures may be dependent on the claimant's contributing to the cost,[244] in which case the claimant's failure to pay his share will relieve the defendant of liability.[245]

---

[238] See para.7-065.

[239] Parts of the east coast of England are subject to rapid and continuous erosion. Suppose D has a field half a mile wide on the edge of the sea and that this is eaten away by the waves, which then begin to erode C's land. It seems bizarre to suggest that D can be under any liability to C.

[240] *Holbeck Hall Hotel Ltd v Scarborough BC* [2000] Q.B. 836 at 863. In *Willis v Derwentside DC* [2013] EWHC 738 (Ch); [2013] Env. L.R. 31, it was held that where the nuisance consisted of the escape of poisonous gas from disused mine workings, the occupier had been obliged (on request) to provide information about the escape and planned remedial works, and must reimburse the claimants for the costs they incurred in obtaining advice on these matters from a third party expert.

[241] [2010] EWCA Civ 681; [2010] B.L.R. 527.

[242] [2013] EWCA Civ 950; [2014] Env. L.R. 6 at [50], where the approach required of the court was referred to as a "multi-factorial assessment".

[243] [2013] EWCA Civ 950; [2014] Env. L.R. 6 at [47], [70].

[244] e.g, where work on a common roof will be to the benefit of both parties: *Abbahall Ltd v Smee* [2002] EWCA Civ 1831; [2003] 1 W.L.R. 1472. Generally equal division of the cost will be appropriate: [40]–[42].

[245] *Abbahall Ltd v Smee* [2002] EWCA Civ 1831; [2003] 1 W.L.R. 1472 at [44]–[45].

15-048 **Sewerage undertakers** The development of the law in this line of cases was thought to mean that a public authority engaged in drainage or sewerage could no longer necessarily rely on the principle that it escapes liability if its facilities were adequate when installed and have failed to keep pace with increased demand. However, such activities are carried out under statutory schemes and the position is not the same as it is between two adjoining landowners. In *Marcic v Thames Water Utilities Ltd*[246] the claimant's property was repeatedly flooded due to overloading of the sewerage system. The relevant statutory scheme entrusted the industry regulator with the decision as to the expenditure required to increase sewerage provision. The regulator set limits on what the sewerage undertakers could charge for their services and was better able than the courts to take account of the various competing interests.[247] Accordingly, the House of Lords declined to hold the defendant liable and in so doing placed weight on the fact that imposing liability for nuisance would cut across the statutory scheme.[248] It was open to persons aggrieved by flooding to complain to the regulator, who had the power to issue enforcement notices against the sewerage undertaker, and its decisions in that regard were subject to judicial review.

15-049 **Independent contractors** As a general rule, a principal is not liable for the acts or defaults of an independent contractor engaged by him, but there are certain exceptions to this rule. In some cases, for instance, the principal is said to be under a "non-delegable" duty to see that care is taken and if, in fact, damage is caused to a third party by the activity of the contractor, the principal will be liable, because he himself is thereby in breach of his duty of care.[249] There seem to be nuisance cases where the idea of the non-delegable duty has been applied. Thus, in *Bower v Peate*[250] the defendant was held liable when he engaged a contractor to do construction work on his land in the course of which the contractor undermined the support for the claimant's adjoining house. And in *Matania v National Provincial Bank*[251] the occupier of the first floor of a building was held liable to the occupier of the higher floors for a nuisance by dust and noise created by his independent contractor. In both cases the nature of the work was such that there was a special danger of a nuisance being caused by it. However, in so far as these cases are understood as manifestations of a wider principle imposing a non-delegable duty on those who engage others to carry out particularly hazardous tasks,[252] the recent curtailment of that wider principle may be expected to limit its future significance.[253]

---

[246] [2003] UKHL 66; [2004] 2 A.C. 42.
[247] The estimated cost of remedial work for the defendants' whole area, without taking account of new house building, was £1 billion: [2003] UKHL 66; [2004] 2 A.C. 42 at [23].
[248] In *Welsh Water v Barratt Homes Ltd* [2013] EWCA Civ 23; [2013] 1 W.L.R. 3486, it was held that no cause of action lay in nuisance for wrongfully refusing connection to the public sewers under s.106 of the Water Industry Act 1991 since the court found that Parliament had not intended to confer a right to compensation for the breach of that provision, and it followed that such a breach could not form the essential basis of a cause of action for nuisance.
[249] See para.21-049.
[250] (1876) 1 Q.B.D. 321; *Dalton v Angus* (1881) 6 App. Cas. 740.
[251] [1936] 2 All E.R. 633; *Duncan's Hotel (Glasgow) Ltd v J&A Ferguson Ltd* 1972 S.L.T. (Notes) 84.
[252] See Ch.21.
[253] *Biffa Waste Services Ltd v Maschinenfabrik Ernst Hese GmbH* [2008] EWCA Civ 1257; [2009] Q.B. 725. See para.21-044.

Licensees   Where the nuisance is created by a person who is licensed to be on the   **15-050**
premises for his own purposes rather than to do work for the occupier, the occupier is liable only if he had knowledge, or means of knowledge, of the nuisance
and failed to take steps to control the licensee.[254] However, if those conditions of
liability are satisfied, it is irrelevant that the occupier lives elsewhere: what matters is that the occupier (unlike a landlord) has control and possession of the
property. In *Cocking v Eacott*,[255] a mother allowed her daughter to live in a house
she owned rent free, while the mother resided elsewhere. Because the daughter was
a licensee rather than a tenant the mother was liable for a nuisance caused by the
daughter's dog, which the mother had known about but done nothing to abate.[256]

Nuisance created by predecessor in title   Where the nuisance existed before the   **15-051**
occupier acquired the property he will be liable if it can be proved that he knew, or
ought reasonably to have known, of its existence but not otherwise.[257] In *St Anne's
Well Brewery Co v Roberts*,[258] C owned an ancient inn, one side of which was
bounded by the old city wall of Exeter. D owned part of the wall. On either side of
C's kitchen fireplace, recesses had at some time been formed by excavations in the
wall. Part of the wall belonging to D collapsed and demolished the inn. D was held
not liable because he neither knew of the defect nor could have discovered it by
reasonable diligence. It is arguable that the special standard of care discussed in
Goldman v Hargrave should apply also to this situation.[259] If the predecessor in title
created the nuisance he may remain liable for injury done by it after he disposes
of the land.[260] If, however, he did not create it his liability ceases upon disposal. The
duty to remedy a nuisance created by another or by natural causes is part of the price
of the occupation of land but there is no reason why it should continue after that
occupation has ceased.[261]

iii.   Landlord

Nuisance authorised by landlord   A landlord out of occupation is liable if he has   **15-052**
expressly or impliedly authorised his tenant to create the nuisance. Where D let a
field to B for working it as a lime quarry and B's acts in blasting the limestone and
letting kiln smoke escape constituted a nuisance to C, D was held liable, for B's
method of working the quarry was the usual way of getting lime and D was taken

---

[254] *White v Jamieson* (1874) L.R. 18 Eq. 303. In *Lippiatt v South Gloucestershire Council* [2000] Q.B.
51 at 56 it was regarded as irrelevant whether the wrongdoers were licensees or trespassers but it
was made plain that there was no question of any liability for acts of which the defendant occupier
had no knowledge.

[255] [2016] EWCA Civ 140; [2016] Q.B. 1080.

[256] It was however possible that a purported licence might either be held to be a tenancy or so much
akin to one that the licensor could not properly be regarded as an occupier for these purposes: [2016]
EWCA Civ 140; [2016] Q.B. 1080 at [29].

[257] *Montana Hotels v Fasson Pty* (1986) 69 A.L.R. 258 (a Privy Council decision where the defendant
was lessee of a newly completed building with a latent defect).

[258] (1929) 140 L.T. 1. Followed in *Wilkins v Leighton* [1932] 2 Ch. 106. cf. *Hall v Duke of Norfolk*
[1900] 2 Ch. 493.

[259] See para.15-046.

[260] *Roswell v Prior* (1701) 12 Mod. 635; 88 E.R. 1570.

[261] This is the position of the vendor/lessor with regard to injuries occurring on the premises: *Rimmer
v Liverpool CC* [1985] Q.B. 1, para.10-053.

to have authorised it.[262] Similarly, a local authority was liable when it let land for go-karting and a nuisance was a natural and necessary consequence of that activity.[263] By contrast, where the creation of a nuisance is not an "inevitable, or nearly certain"[264] consequence of the lease of the land, but only a possible or probable one, the landlord is not liable. Hence a local authority which let a house to a "problem" family was not liable for a nuisance created by the family,[265] and when a stadium and track were leased for use as a motorsports facility, the owners were not liable for the resultant noise nuisance because the activities in question could have been conducted without causing a nuisance.[266] The concept of authorisation also encompasses a landlord's active involvement or participation in the activity that is causing the nuisance.[267] But mere inaction is not enough: a landlord is not liable for his tenant's nuisance because with knowledge of its existence he refrained from exercising his right to determine the tenancy, or took no active steps to prevent or discourage the continuation of the interference.[268] And nor is it enough to attract liability on this footing that the landlord took steps to mitigate the interference in question, countered allegations of nuisance directed at his tenant or sought to persuade a local authority not to take action in respect of such allegations.[269]

15-053 **Liability for nuisance caused by disrepair**[270]   The occupier of premises is always liable for nuisance caused by their disrepair. In the case of demised premises, the landlord is liable in addition to the tenant where the condition giving rise to the nuisance existed at the date of the letting, and the landlord either knew or should have known about it at that time.[271] If the condition that causes the nuisance arises after the lease is granted, then whether the landlord is liable depends on whether he has, as against the tenant, either a duty or power to repair. Thus, the owner can be sued if he has covenanted to repair,[272] or if he has expressly or impliedly reserved the right to enter for the purposes of repair.[273] If the landlord has undertaken to

---

262 *Harris v James* (1876) 45 L.J.Q.B. 545.
263 *Tetley v Chitty* [1986] 1 All E.R. 663. Note that: (1) it is irrelevant whether or not a covenant against nuisance is included in the lease; and (2) it need not be shown that the landlord knew or should have known that a nuisance was likely to result from the intended activity, as long as he was aware of the aspects of that activity from which a nuisance arose: *Coventry v Lawrence (No.2)* [2014] UKSC 46; [2015] A.C. 106 at [17] and [55] respectively.
264 *Coventry v Lawrence (No.2)* [2014] UKSC 46; [2015] A.C. 106 at [15].
265 *Smith v Scott* [1973] Ch. 314.
266 *Coventry v Lawrence (No.2)* [2014] UKSC 46; [2015] A.C. 106. See also *Rich v Basterfield* (1847) 4 C.B. 783; 136 E.R. 715.
267 [2014] UKSC 46; [2015] A.C. 106 at [59].
268 *Malzy v Eichholz* [1916] 2 K.B. 308; *Smith v Scott* [1973] Ch. 314; *Hussain v Lancaster CC* [2000] Q.B. 1. A challenge to this principle on human rights grounds failed in *Mowan v Wandsworth LBC* [2001] L.G.R. 228, where a social landlord was held not liable for a nuisance caused by a mentally ill tenant.
269 *Coventry v Lawrence (No.2)* [2014] UKSC 46; [2015] A.C. 106 at [24]–[26].
270 In addition to any liability that may arise at common law, a landlord who has a duty or power to repair demised premises owes to persons who might reasonably be expected to be affected by defects in the premises a statutory duty of reasonable care: Defective Premises Act 1972, s.4. See para.10-054.
271 *Todd v Flight* (1860) 9 C.B.N.S. 377; 142 E.R. 148. On the requirement of actual or constructive knowledge, see *St Anne's Well Brewery Co v Roberts* (1928) 140 L.T. 1. "Letting" includes re-letting to the same tenant: *Sandford v Clarke* (1888) 21 Q.B.D. 398; *Bowen v Anderson* [1894] 1 Q.B. 164.
272 *Payne v Rogers* (1794) 2 H. Bl. 350; 126 E.R. 590.
273 *Heap v Ind Coope & Allsopp Ltd* [1940] 2 K.B. 476 (express right); *Mint v Good* [1951] 1 K.B. 517

repair, or has the right to enter and repair, his liability does not affect that of the tenant, who is still liable as occupier,[274] though the latter will, of course, be able to obtain an indemnity if sued.

F. Damage

Since private nuisance is an action on the case it follows that the claimant must **15-054** have suffered damage in order to establish liability, but in practice this is not a significant limitation on liability as the "concept of damage in this context is a highly elastic one".[275] In cases founded upon physical damage to the claimant's land, the requirement of damage will not normally prove problematic, though the harm must be more than trivial.[276] In encroachment cases, physical damage is generally required for actionability,[277] though in a case involving Japanese knotweed roots it was held that this is not always required, and that diminution in amenity value may suffice.[278] When the claimant brings an action in respect of noise, smoke, smells and the like, the damage is the effect on the amenity value of the land[279]: he does not have to prove that the interference is injurious to his health,[280] or that it affects the market value of his property.[281] No nuisance action lies where the claimant alleges only that there is a risk of future damage,[282] though a quia timet injunction may be granted if there is a strong probability of actionable interference occurring, and the harm to the claimant would likely be irreparable.[283]

Nuisance to servitudes It has been suggested that where the interference is with **15-055** a servitude of the claimant, nuisance may be actionable without proof of damage. In *Nicholls v Ely Beet Sugar Factory Ltd*,[284] for example, where refuse and effluent were alleged to have been discharged from the defendants' beet sugar factory into the river in which the claimant owned two several and exclusive fisheries, Lord Wright MR stated that damage was not the gist of the action.[285] However, the bet-

---

(implied right). The Landlord and Tenant Act 1985 s.11 provides that in any lease of a dwelling house for a term of less than seven years or any lease which is terminable by the lessor in less than seven years, there is an implied covenant by the lessor to keep in repair the structure and exterior and certain installations.

274 *Wilchick v Marks* [1934] 2 K.B. 56. Conversely, the landlord can be liable even though the tenant has expressly covenanted to repair: *Brew Bros Ltd v Snax (Ross) Ltd* [1970] 1 Q.B. 612.

275 *Network Rail Infrastructure Ltd v Williams* [2018] EWCA Civ 1514; [2019] Q.B. 601 at [42].

276 *Salvin v North Brancepeth Coal Co* (1874) 9 Ch. App. 705 at 709. Though, e.g., contamination of a drinking water supply such that it no longer complies with complex regulatory standards is capable of grounding a nuisance action: *Savage v Fairclough* [2000] Env. L.R. 183 (where the claim failed on foreseeability grounds). See further on the concept of property damage, paras 7-015ff.

277 *Lemmon v Webb* [1894] 3 Ch. 1 at 11; *Smith v Giddy* [1904] 2 K.B. 448.

278 *Network Rail Infrastructure Ltd v Williams* [2018] EWCA Civ 1514; [2019] Q.B. 601.

279 *Network Rail Infrastructure Ltd v Williams* [2018] EWCA Civ 1514; [2019] Q.B. 601 at [43].

280 *Crump v Lambert* (1867) L.R. 3 Eq. 409.

281 *Bone v Seale* [1975] 1 W.L.R. 797.

282 *Midland Bank Plc v Bardgrove Property Services Ltd* (1992) 65 P. & C.R. 153; *Yorkshire Water Services Ltd v Sun Alliance & London Insurance Plc (No.2)* [1998] Env. LR 204 (not in issue on appeal: [1997] 1 Lloyd's Rep. 420). Naturally, the position is different where it is the threat of damage that itself constitutes the alleged interference: see, e.g., *Birmingham Development v Tyler* [2008] EWCA Civ 859; [2008] B.L.R. 445 (where, however, liability was denied since the claimant's concern that the defendant's wall would collapse onto its land was unfounded).

283 See para.23-129.

284 [1936] Ch. 343.

285 [1936] Ch. 343 at 349.

ter view is that even in these cases actionable damage, in the form of substantial interference with the servitude in question, must be established.[286] In *Nicholls* itself, Lord Wright accepted that there must be substantial interference with the claimant's rights,[287] while Romer LJ said only that the claimant need not have suffered financial loss.[288] An argument sometimes made against a requirement of damage in servitudes cases is that it may enable the defendant to continue the interference without interruption, and so to acquire by prescription a right in derogation of the claimant's right.[289] However, this seems to assume the very point in issue, for a prescriptive right will only arise if the interference is an actionable nuisance,[290] and hence if damage is required to make a nuisance actionable, the claimant's rights cannot be threatened until damage is sustained.

G. Defences

i. Statutory Authority

15-056   When a statute authorises the commission of what would otherwise be a tort, then the party injured has no remedy. Although this defence applies to any tort,[291] it is most often illustrated in the nuisance context.[292] Usually, the statute in question will make provision for compensation of those most seriously affected,[293] but while the absence of such provision is evidence that Parliament did not intend to exclude the right to sue at common law, it is not conclusive in this regard.[294] In the leading case of *Allen v Gulf Oil Refining Ltd*,[295] for example, the defence applied even though no provision for compensation had been made in the relevant legislation.[296] Since we are dealing with a defence, the burden of proof falls throughout on the defendant.[297]

---

[286] On the requirement of substantial interference in servitude cases, see Jackson, *The Law of Easements and Profits* (1978), p.207. See, e.g., *Colls v Home and Colonial Stores* [1904] A.C. 179; *Kine v Jolly* [1905] 1 Ch. 480 at 489 (right to light). In *Network Rail Infrastructure Ltd v Williams* [2018] EWCA Civ 1514; [2019] Q.B. 601 at [42] it was said that there is no need for "specific damage" in this context, but it is not clear what was meant by that phrase.

[287] [1936] Ch. 343 at 353.

[288] [1936] Ch. 343 at 356.

[289] *Harrop v Hirst* (1868) L.R. 4 Ex. 43 at 46.

[290] See para.15-060A.

[291] See para.26-063.

[292] Linden (1966) 4 Osgoode Hall L.J. 196; Kodilinye (1990) 19 Anglo-Am. L. Rev. 72. Some statutes go beyond merely authorising the activity that causes the interference, and specifically provide that the right to sue in nuisance is taken away: see, e.g., Civil Aviation Act 1982 s.76(1), which gives immunity from nuisance and trespass liability to civil aircraft flying at a reasonable height, and was held to apply to helicopters conducting training exercises at an aerodrome in *Peires v Bickerton's Aerodromes Ltd* [2017] EWCA Civ 273; [2017] 1 W.L.R. 2865.

[293] A major general compensation provision is that for "injurious affection" in s.10 of the Compulsory Purchase Act 1965, which is the successor of Victorian legislation dating back to the construction of railways. This provision is reviewed in *Wildtree Hotels Ltd v Harrow LBC* [2001] 2 A.C. 1. For other such general provisions, see Land Compensation Act 1973; Planning Act 2008 s.152(3).

[294] *Metropolitan Asylum District v Hill* (1881) 6 App. Cas. 193 at 203; *Edgington v Swindon BC* [1939] 1 K.B. 86 at 89–90. For the contrary view that the defence ought not to apply in the absence of compensation, see *Hammersmith and City Rly Co v Brand* (1869) L.R. 4 H.L. 171 at 191–192; *Allen v Gulf Oil Refining Ltd* [1980] Q.B. 156 at 168–169.

[295] [1981] A.C. 1001.

[296] Though this rule could now be challenged on human rights grounds: see para.15-059.

[297] *Metropolitan Asylum District v Hill* (1881) 6 App. Cas. 193 at 208 (requirement that activity be

Activity must be authorised   The defence of statutory authority applies only if,   **15-057**
on the proper construction of the statute in question, Parliament is deemed to have
authorised the activity that is causing the interference. Such authorisation may be
express or implied. A good example of express authorisation is provided by s.158
of the Planning Act 2008, which confers statutory authority on all "nationally
significant infrastructure projects" granted planning permission under the special
procedures laid down in that legislation. As for implied authorisation, the presumption that statute does not authorise interference with private rights[298] can be rebutted by sufficient evidence of a legislative intention to the contrary. In *Allen v Gulf
Oil Refining Ltd*,[299] a private Act of Parliament authorised the defendant oil
company to buy land near Milford Haven for the purpose of constructing an oil
refinery, but did not specifically authorise the operation of the refinery once built.
When a nuisance action was brought against the company for interference caused
by the refinery, the House of Lords held by a majority that the defence of statutory
authority applied, since it was not credible to suppose that Parliament intended to
authorise only the construction of the refinery, and not its operation as well.[300]

Activity must be intra vires the statute   Since we are dealing with statutory pow-   **15-058**
ers the primary question where what is complained of is damage arising from the
exercise of the powers must be whether that exercise is intra vires the statute.[301]
Work causing substantial interference with neighbouring property will not normally
be intra vires the statute unless that interference is the "inevitable" consequence of
the work, i.e., unless it must arise even though the work is carried on with reasonable care and with approved techniques. Where the statute contains a "nuisance
clause",[302] then if the authority is merely permissive there may be liability even for
the inevitable consequences of the works, but this is not so if the undertaker is under
a statutory duty to carry them out.[303] A more rational distinction is probably between
statutes which require works to be done in a particular place and those which give
the undertaker a wide discretion in this respect. In the former case, there is no liability provided that the work is undertaken with reasonable care;[304] in the latter,
the undertaker may be liable if he chooses to carry out the works in a place where

---

authorised); *Manchester Corp v Farnworth* [1930] A.C. 171 (requirement that interference be
inevitable).
[298] See *Manchester Ship Canal Co Ltd v United Utilities Water Plc* [2014] UKSC 40; [2014] 1 W.L.R.
2576 at [1].
[299] [1981] A.C. 1001. See Wilde in Bishop and Stallworthy (eds), *Environmental Law and Policy in
Wales* (2013).
[300] cf. *Jones v Festiniog Rly Co* (1868) L.R. 3 Q.B. 733 (statutory power to operate railway not authority for use of locomotive steam engines); *Pigot v Environment Agency* [2020] EWHC 930 (Ch)
(statute did not authorise keeping fish pass in river open at low water).
[301] See *Home Office v Dorset Yacht Co Ltd* [1970] A.C. 1004 at 1064–1071.
[302] e.g., "Nothing in this Act shall exonerate the undertakers from any indictment, action, or other
proceedings for nuisance in the event of any nuisance being caused by them."
[303] See the summary in *Dept of Transport v NW Water Authority* [1983] 3 W.L.R. 105 and in the HL
[1984] A.C. 336. It might be argued that even without a nuisance clause the granting of merely
permissive powers showed an intention not to take away any private rights, particularly since we
are here commonly dealing with private Acts, to which the *contra proferentem* approach may fairly
be applied, but this would be inconsistent with the authorities. Similarly, the absence of a provision
for compensation in the relevant legislation is no more than a weak indication of an intention to
preserve private rights: *Allen v Gulf Oil Refining Ltd* [1981] A.C. 1001 at 1016.
[304] *Manchester Corp v Farnworth* [1930] A.C. 171; *Allen v Gulf Oil Refining Ltd* [1981] A.C. 1001.

they cause a nuisance to neighbours when he could have carried them out elsewhere without such consequences.[305]

However, where the discretion conferred by the statute cannot reasonably be exercised without a nuisance resulting, the defence is still available. In *London, Brighton and South Coast Rly Co v Truman*,[306] cattle in the defendant railway company's station yard disturbed local residents. The company had legislative authority to accommodate cattle awaiting transportation in a station yard, and since the yard had realistically to be next to a station, and the stations were in built-up areas, it was bound to end up being a nuisance to someone. Similarly, where a statute confers on an undertaker a broad discretionary power to carry out works as it sees fit, and some resultant interference with private rights is inevitable, the undertaker cannot be challenged by those affected on the ground that the interference caused on any particular occasion was unnecessary.[307]

15-059 **Human rights** The defence of statutory authority must be applied in the light of the Human Rights Act 1998. Article 8 of the European Convention on Human Rights requires respect for private and family life and the home. Although at common law the courts have been mindful of the need to protect private rights when applying the defence of statutory authority, this value is subsidiary to the meaning of the statutory words. However, s.3 of the 1998 Act requires legislation to be read and given effect to in a way which is compatible with the Convention rights "so far as it is possible to do so", which goes beyond merely relying on those rights to resolve an ambiguity in the statute.[308] It is possible that the courts will invoke art.8 in circumstances where the defendant would previously have been able to call upon the statutory authority defence. In particular, it may be that in the absence of a provision in the relevant legislation providing for compensation of those most seriously affected, a court would either refuse to apply the defence on the grounds that the statute should be read down so as to protect the claimant's Convention rights, or apply the defence but issue a declaration of incompatibility under s.4 of the 1998 Act.[309]

ii. Acquired Right

15-060 **General** The right to commit what would otherwise amount to a private nuisance can be acquired as an easement, either by prescription or by reservation and grant. In cases involving express easements by way of reservation and grant, the precise scope of the acquired right is determined by construction of the language of the reservation or grant in conjunction with the circumstances surrounding its

---

[305] *Metropolitan Asylum District v Hill* (1881) 6 App. Cas. 193; but if Parliament had specified the site there would have been no liability: *Allen v Gulf Oil Refining Ltd* [1981] A.C. 1001 at 1014. See also *Pigot v Environment Agency* [2020] EWHC 930 (Ch) at [58] per Stephen Jourdan QC (defendant must prove "no practical way" of performing the authorised act without causing a nuisance).

[306] (1885) 11 App. Cas 45. See also *Hammersmith and City Rly Co v Brand* (1868) L.R. 4 H.L. 171.

[307] *Marriage v East Norfolk Rivers Catchment Board* [1950] 1 K.B. 284 at 308 (while making it clear that nuisance liability remains if: (1) the defendant's exercise of its discretion is capricious; or (2) an act of negligence in the course of carrying out the work produces some unintended consequence).

[308] *R. v A (No.2)* [2001] UKHL 25; [2002] 1 A.C. 45 at [44]. For a tort example, see *Cachia v Faluyi* [2001] EWCA Civ 998; [2002] 1 All E.R. 192.

[309] See Nolan in Hoffman (ed), *The Impact of the UK Human Rights Act on Private Law* (2011), pp.188–191.

creation.[310] An easement of drainage, for example, was held not to permit the discharge of sewage into a septic tank on neighbouring property when the sewage regularly overflowed, flooding the neighbour's garden.[311]

Prescription Acquisition of the right to commit what would otherwise be a **15-060A** nuisance by prescription is in practice rare, but in principle a landowner can, for example, acquire by long user a right to discharge rainwater from his eaves onto neighbouring land,[312] or to pollute[313] or divert[314] a stream. For a right to arise by prescription, there must be 20 years' uninterrupted user, and—since the scope of the right must be clear for it to be accepted as an easement—certainty and uniformity of use are necessary.[315] This requirement of certainty casts doubt on the possibility of acquiring by prescription a right to commit a nuisance by noise, smell etc., since the nature and extent of the interference is likely to vary over time,[316] but if there is sufficiently consistent interference of this kind, then in principle such a right can be acquired.[317] As the doctrine of prescription is based on acquiescence, time does not begin to run until the claimant has both knowledge of the interference and the power to put an end to it.[318] In *Sturges v Bridgman*[319] a confectioner had for more than 20 years used large pestles and mortars in the back of his premises which abutted on the garden of a physician, but these did not cause an actionable interference with the physician's enjoyment of his property during that period. Then, however, the physician built a consulting room in his garden and, for the first time, found that the noise and vibration materially interfered with the pursuit of his practice.[320] He was granted an injunction against the confectioner, whose claim to a prescriptive right failed because the interference had not been an actionable nuisance for the required period.[321]

iii. Other Defences

Consent Although it is no defence that the claimant came to the nuisance,[322] the **15-061** consent of the claimant or of someone whose consent binds the claimant can be a defence to a nuisance action. In most such cases, consent is based on the express or implied terms of a contract between the parties. In *Lyttelton Times Co Ltd v*

---

[310] *Gardner v Davis* [1999] E.H.L.R. 13 at 24.

[311] *Gardner v Davis* [1999] E.H.L.R. 13.

[312] *Thomas v Thomas* (1835) 2 Cr. M. & R. 34; 150 E.R. 15; *Harvey v Walters* (1873) L.R. 8 C.P. 162.

[313] *Baxendale v McMurray* (1867) 2 Ch. App. 790.

[314] *Cox v Matthews* (1673) 1 Vent. 239; 86 E.R. 160.

[315] Hence the courts will not recognise a right to pollute a stream if the intensity of the pollution has changed during the period of prescription: *Hulley v Silversprings Bleaching and Dyeing Co* [1922] 2 Ch. 268.

[316] See, e.g., *Dennis v Ministry of Defence* [2003] EWHC 793 (QB); [2003] Env. L.R. 34, where a prescription defence failed because the noise created by military jets had fluctuated over the years.

[317] See *Coventry v Lawrence* [2014] UKSC 13; [2014] A.C. 822 (noise).

[318] So the secret discharge of pollution cannot prejudice a claimant's rights: *Liverpool Corp v Coghill & Son Ltd* [1918] 1 Ch. 307.

[319] (1879) 11 Ch. D. 852.

[320] See *Bliss v Hall* (1838) 4 Bing. N.C. 183; 132 E.R. 758.

[321] See also *Coventry v Lawrence* [2014] UKSC 13; [2014] A.C. 822 (operators of motorsports facility did not show that the resultant noise amounted to a nuisance for 20 years).

[322] See para.15-065.

Warners Ltd,[323] the claimant agreed to rent the upper floors of a printing house from the defendant, who would use the ground floor to operate printing machinery. The claimant's action in respect of noise and vibration caused by the presses failed because he had agreed that the defendant could operate them, and there was no evidence that they were being used improperly.[324] Consent may also be inferred from, for example, the implied term in all landlord and tenant contracts that the tenant takes the property as he finds it;[325] or the principle that if A takes a grant over B's property and it is in the contemplation of both parties that B's property is going to be used for a particular purpose, A cannot complain of anything arising in the ordinary course of the contemplated user.[326] The defence of consent is however only available if it is established that the activity consented to cannot practically be conducted without causing the interference concerned.[327]

15-062   Contributory negligence[328]   In the typical private nuisance case involving ongoing interference intentionally caused, there is unlikely to be scope for a plea of contributory negligence. But where a nuisance results from negligent conduct on the defendant's part, as where he is an occupier who has continued a nuisance created by another, the defence can be invoked.[329]

15-063   Mitigation   A claimant in nuisance has the usual duty to mitigate his loss, and so cannot recover damages for harm suffered after the commission of the tort that he could have avoided by the exercise of reasonable care.[330] The claimant is not, however, required himself to remedy the defendant's wrong by forgoing the right to enjoy his property to the full. Hence, an occupier need not keep his windows shut to keep out noises or smells,[331] and nor need he hide behind shutters to avoid stray balls from the cricket ground next door,[332] though his ability to shut out the interference may be relevant to whether it is serious enough to be actionable in the first place.[333]

15-064   Common enemy and necessity   The "common enemy" rule entitles an occupier to take steps to protect his property against an external threat, even if the effect is to divert the threat onto the land of another. Most of the cases involve flood

---

323 [1907] A.C. 476. See also *Kiddle v City Business Properties Ltd* [1942] 1 K.B. 269 (right to have water pass from landlord's to tenant's premises).

324 Similarly, when a landowner gave his neighbour the right to mine under his property, he had no cause for complaint when, through no fault of the neighbour, the operations caused subsidence: *Rowbotham v Wilson* (1860) 8 H.L. Cas. 348.

325 *Cheater v Cater* [1918] 1 K.B. 247.

326 *Thomas v Lewis* [1937] 1 All E.R. 137.

327 *Pwllbach Colliery Co Ltd v Woodman* [1915] A.C. 634.

328 Seavey (1952) 65 Harv. L. Rev. 984.

329 *Trevett v Lee* [1955] 1 W.L.R. 113 at 122; *Gilson v Kerrier RDC* [1976] 1 W.L.R. 904.

330 See, e.g., *Taylor v Auto Trade Supply Ltd* [1972] 2 N.Z.L.R. 102.

331 *Webster v Lord Advocate* [1984] S.L.T. 13 at 15.

332 *Miller v Jackson* [1977] Q.B. 966.

333 *Bank of New Zealand v Greenwood* [1984] 1 N.Z.L.R. 525 at 532. In *Fearn v Tate Gallery Board of Trustees* [2019] EWHC 246 (Ch); [2019] Ch. 369, Mann J said that it was relevant to the actionability of an interference with privacy that the occupiers of the affected flats could install blinds, privacy film or net curtains. Although the Court of Appeal seemed to think this was contrary to principle ([2020] EWCA Civ 104; [2020] 2 W.L.R. 1081 at [99]), it is hard to see why such considerations should not be factored into the analysis if appropriate.

defences,[334] though in *Greyvensteyn v Hattingh*[335] the principle protected a farmer who had driven a swarm of locusts away from his land and towards a neighbour's. The possibility of a more general defence of necessity in nuisance was discussed in *Southport Corpn v Esso Petroleum Ltd*, where at first instance Devlin J expressed the view that such a defence would be available if the interference with the claimant's land arose out of conduct intended to protect life.[336] In the Court of Appeal, Singleton and Denning LJJ agreed,[337] with the caveat that the defence would be lost if the danger arose out of the defendant's fault, an analysis endorsed by Lord Radcliffe when the case reached the House of Lords.[338]

iv. Non-defences

Coming to the nuisance   It is usually said that it is no defence that the claimant   **15-065**
came to the nuisance or that the place is a convenient one for committing it. As Lord Halsbury put it in *Fleming v Hislop*[339]:

> "It is clear that whether the man went to the nuisance or the nuisance came to the man, the rights are the same."

What this means is that, if the annoyance is unreasonable in that particular district, then the claimant can recover even if it had been going on long before he came there. In *Bliss v Hall*,[340] the defendant had set up a tallow chandlery which emitted "divers noisome, noxious, and offensive vapours, fumes, smells and stenches" to the discomfort of the claimant, who had taken a house near it. It was held to be no defence that the business had been in existence for three years before the claimant's arrival, for he "came to the house ... with all the rights which the common law affords, and one of them is a right to wholesome air".[341] This rule is grounded in good sense since, if the law were otherwise, an easement to commit a nuisance would effectively arise as soon as the affected property changed hands, rather than by the 20 years' prescription currently required. However, where the claim does not relate to "material injury" to property, the rule is qualified by the locality principle.[342] If you choose to make your home in the heart of a manufacturing district, you can expect no more freedom from the discomfort usually associated with such a place than any other resident.[343]

The principle that coming to the nuisance is no defence also encompasses a

---

[334] See, e.g., *Maxey Drainage Board v Great Northern Rly Co* (1912) 106 L.T. 429 (defendants entitled to raise embankment around their land to protect against flooding even if floodwaters thereby diverted onto the claimant's land). On the limits of the principle in this context, see *Arscott v The Coal Authority* [2004] EWCA Civ 892; [2005] Env. L.R. 6.

[335] [1911] A.C. 355.

[336] [1953] 3 W.L.R. 773 at 779. However, Lord Devlin doubted that a threat to property interests would suffice.

[337] [1954] 2 Q.B. 182 at 194, 197–198.

[338] [1956] A.C. 218 at 242. On necessity more generally, see paras 26-045ff.

[339] (1886) 11 App. Cas. 686 at 697.

[340] (1838) 4 Bing. N.C. 183; 132 E.R. 758 (followed, with some reluctance, by the majority of the Court of Appeal in *Miller v Jackson* [1977] Q.B. 966).

[341] (1838) 4 Bing. N.C. 183 at 186; 132 E.R. 758 at 759 per Tindal CJ. See also *Elliotson v Feetham* (1835) 2 Bing. N.C. 134; 132 E.R. 53.

[342] See para.15-022.

[343] A tenant takes the building as it is in respect of defects present at the commencement of the lease: *Jackson v JH Watson Property Investment Ltd* [2008] EWHC 14 (Ch); [2008] Env. L.R. 30.

second rule, namely that a claimant can still maintain an action where the defendant's activity only becomes a nuisance because of a change in the use or configuration of the claimant's property, as in *Sturges v Bridgman*,[344] where we have seen that a physician built a consulting room in his garden, hard up against the noisy kitchen of a neighbouring confectioner. However, this second rule was not always good law,[345] and it was questioned by Lord Neuberger in *Coventry v Lawrence*,[346] at least in cases where the defendant's activity is carried on in a reasonable manner and affects only the senses of those on the claimant's land. If these (obiter) remarks herald a change in the law, then the result will be that those who arrive first in a place are to some extent able to dictate the uses to which later arrivals can put their properties.

15-066   **Utility of the defendant's activity**   The mere fact that a process or business is useful to persons generally, while not irrelevant in determining whether a nuisance has been committed,[347] is no defence once a nuisance has been proved. One who keeps a pigsty, a tannery, a limekiln or an iron foundry is pursuing a laudable occupation and possibly one of benefit to the public, yet that by itself will not excuse him. In *Adams v Ursell*[348] a fried-fish shop was held to be a nuisance in the residential part of a street where it was carried on. It was argued unsuccessfully that an injunction would cause great hardship to the defendant and his customers. Nor does the need to maintain an air force for national defence excuse serious and continual noise caused by training exercises, though that is a case where damages rather than an injunction is likely to be the proper remedy.[349]

15-067   **Planning permission and regulatory compliance**[350]   The defence of statutory authority is limited to direct expressions of legislative will, and does not extend to decisions of administrative authorities acting under statutory powers, such as regulatory agencies and planning authorities.[351] As regards planning permission, it is a well-established rule that the grant of planning permission for the defendant's activity is not equivalent to statutory authorisation and so confers no immunity.[352] The obtaining of planning permission simply makes lawful what would otherwise be a criminal offence, and there is "neither necessity nor justification for regarding such a licence as negativing established principles of civil liability".[353] As for regulatory compliance, the leading case is *Barr v Biffa Waste Services Ltd*,[354] where nuisance actions were brought by residents affected by the odours emanating from

---

[344] (1879) 11 Ch. D. 852, para.15-060.
[345] See to the contrary *Lawrence v Obee* (1814) 3 Camp. 514; 170 E.R. 1465 (claimant brought nuisance upon herself by opening a new window near her neighbour's privy); II Bl. Comm. 402–403.
[346] [2014] UKSC 13; [2014] A.C. 822 at [51]–[58].
[347] See para.15-026.
[348] [1913] 1 Ch. 269.
[349] *Dennis v Ministry of Defence* [2003] EWHC 793 (QB); [2003] Env. L.R. 34.
[350] Nolan in Dyson, Goudkamp and Wilmot-Smith (eds), *Defences in Tort* (2015).
[351] There might be thought to be a tension between this proposition and the decision in *Marcic v Thames Water Utilities Ltd* [2003] UKHL 66; [2004] 2 A.C. 42 (see para.15-048), but the general significance of that case is limited since it concerned an omission rather than positive conduct, and because the reasoning of the House of Lords was inextricably linked to the traditional immunity of sewerage authorities for nonfeasance.
[352] *Wheeler v JJ Saunders Ltd* [1996] Ch. 19.
[353] Tromans [1995] C.L.J. 494, 495.
[354] [2012] EWCA Civ 312; [2013] Q.B. 455.

the defendant's landfill site. The deposit of waste at the site was assumed to have been in compliance with the conditions attached to a waste management permit issued by the Environment Agency, and the defendant argued that it followed that the nuisance actions must fail. The Court of Appeal disagreed. According to Carnwath LJ, it would be quite wrong for the terms of a waste permit issued under regulatory legislation to be treated as "cutting down the common law rights of local residents",[355] when they had neither agreed to, nor even been consulted on, its terms. His overall conclusion was as follows[356]:

"An activity which is conducted in contravention of planning or environmental controls is unlikely to be reasonable. But the converse does not follow. Sticking to the rules is an aspect of good neighbourliness, but it is far from the whole story—in law as in life."

It should however be noted that whether the defendant has acted in compliance with a relevant regulatory regime or obtained planning permission may be a relevant consideration for the purposes of the unreasonable interference enquiry, and may also militate against the issuing of an injunction.

Nuisance due to many   It is no defence that the nuisance was created by independent acts of different persons, although the act of any one of them was not per se unlawful; for example where 100 people independently leave 100 wheelbarrows in a place and the obstruction consists in the accumulation and not in the presence of any one of them.[357] This rule has been applied in the context of streams polluted by a number of different sources,[358] and also in a case where a noise nuisance was caused by the combined effect of two organs used by rival caterers to drum up business.[359] It may appear paradoxical that a defendant is held liable although his act alone would not be a tort, but the explanation may be said to lie in the fact that the standard of what is reasonable is governed by the surrounding circumstances, including the conduct of the others.[360] In such a case each defendant is liable only to the extent of his contribution and, if there is no satisfactory basis on which to apportion responsibility, the liability is divided equally.[361] **15-068**

Jus tertii   If the claimant has exclusive possession of the land affected by the interference he can sue on the strength of his possession and need not prove his title. The defendant cannot therefore plead jus tertii (i.e., that some third party has a better claim to the property than the claimant).[362] In *Foster v Warblington UDC*,[363] the **15-069**

---

[355] [2012] EWCA Civ 312; [2013] Q.B. 455 at [102].
[356] [2012] EWCA Civ 312; [2013] Q.B. 455 at [76]. In *Coventry v Lawrence* [2014] UKSC 13; [2014] A.C. 822 at [198], Lord Carnwath said that his comments on the relationship between regulatory compliance and nuisance law in *Barr v Biffa* were open to the criticism that they were "unduly simplistic", but we would respectfully demur.
[357] *Thorpe v Brumfitt* (1873) L.R. 8 Ch. App. 650 at 656.
[358] *Crossley v Lightowler* (1867) 2 Ch. App. 478; *Pride of Derby & Derbyshire Angling Association Ltd v British Celanese Ltd* [1953] Ch. 149.
[359] *Lambton v Mellish* [1894] 3 Ch. 163.
[360] Might this mean that the liability of each contributor is dependent on his awareness of what the others are doing? See *Lambton v Mellish* [1894] 3 Ch. 163 at 166; *Restatement (Second) of Torts* (1977) §840E, comment b.
[361] *Bank View Mills Ltd v Nelson Corp* [1942] 2 All E.R. 477 at 483 (not considered on appeal: [1943] 1 All E.R. 299).
[362] *Hunter v Canary Wharf Ltd* [1997] A.C. 655 at 688, 703.
[363] [1906] 1 K.B. 648.

claimant had been storing oysters in oyster ponds on the foreshore for over 20 years. The defendants discharged sewage into the sea near the ponds, and thereby rendered the oysters unfit for consumption. It was held that, irrespective of who had title to the soil, the claimant was in exclusive occupation of the ponds and so could maintain a nuisance action. Since a profit à prendre confers a possessory right, the person in possession of a profit is similarly entitled to protection without proving his title.[364] However, in cases of interference with an easement, there is no possession of the servient tenement, so the claimant will have to establish his title if challenged.[365]

H. Remedy

15-070   Two remedies are available for private nuisance: damages at common law for past harm and equitable relief by way of an injunction or damages in lieu where the harm is ongoing.[366] The general principles governing damages and injunctions are dealt with elsewhere,[367] but some discussion of the operation of these remedies in the particular context of nuisance is required.

i.   Injunctions and Damages in Lieu

15-071   **Injunction or damages in lieu?**[368]   The normal remedy in respect of any further commission of the tort of nuisance is injunctive relief, but the circumstances in which the court should be willing to award damages in lieu of an injunction[369] in such cases were fundamentally re-assessed by the Supreme Court in *Coventry v Lawrence*.[370] The justices all considered that the courts should be more flexible than they had previously been,[371] but with varying degrees of emphasis as to how far that flexibility should be taken.[372]

15-072   **An "unfettered discretion"?**   According to Lord Neuberger, the court's power to award damages in lieu of an injunction should not, as a matter of principle, be fet-

---

[364]   *Nicholls v Ely Beet Sugar Factory* [1931] 2 Ch. 84 (pollution of a private fishery).

[365]   *Paine & Co Ltd v St Neots Gas & Coke Co* [1939] 3 All E.R. 812 at 823.

[366]   Abatement is often said to be a "self-help remedy" for nuisance, but it is dealt with in this book as a defence: see paras 26-040ff.

[367]   See Ch.23.

[368]   Pontin, *Nuisance Law and Environmental Protection* (2013); Nolan in Day and Worthington (eds), *Challenging Private Law* (2020).

[369]   Now under s.50 of the Senior Courts Act 1981.

[370]   [2014] UKSC 13; [2014] A.C. 822. The facts and circumstances of the case (nuisance by noise) are considered above: para.15-022A.

[371]   For observations to the effect that damages should only be awarded in an exceptional case, see, e.g., *Kennaway v Thompson* [1981] Q.B. 88; *Regan v Paul Properties Ltd* [2006] EWCA Civ 1391; [2007] Ch. 135; *Watson v Croft Promo-Sport Ltd* [2009] EWCA Civ 15; [2009] 3 All E.R. 249. For dicta adopting a more flexible approach, particularly in the right to light context, see *Colls v Home & Colonial Stores Ltd* [1904] A.C. 179; *Kine v Jolly* [1905] 1 Ch. 480; *Fishenden v Higgs & Hill Ltd* (1935) 153 L.T. 128.

[372]   Since this represented a departure from previous decisions, the defendants had not raised the point that the judge should have awarded damages at trial and they were criticised for not having at least reserved their position. They were refused permission to raise the issue in the Supreme Court, but it was held that they should be free to make the argument before the trial judge on the reinstatement of his order for an injunction under the provision therein giving the parties permission to apply: [2014] UKSC 13; [2014] A.C. 822 at [151].

tered but while firm guidance was "likely to do more harm than good" it was nonetheless necessary to provide as much guidance as possible as to the relevant factors in the interest of predictability.[373] The prima face position was said to be that an injunction should be granted, so that the legal burden is on the defendant to show why it should not be. While in each case the outcome should depend on all the evidence and arguments, Lord Neuberger suggested a continued role for the test which had been laid down by A.L. Smith LJ in *Shelfer v City of London Electric Lighting Co*, namely[374]:

"(1) If the injury to the plaintiff's legal rights is small, (2) And is one which is capable of being estimated in money, (3) And is one which can be adequately compensated by a small money payment, (4) And the case is one in which it would be oppressive to the defendant to grant an injunction—then damages in substitution for an injunction may be given."

Lord Neuberger emphasised that the application of this test only offered some guidance as to how the courts might exercise their discretion.[375] While it would normally be right to refuse an injunction if all four criteria were satisfied, in the absence of additional relevant circumstances pointing the other way, the fact that they were not did not necessarily mean that an injunction should be granted.[376]

Public interest and planning permission The most important development in **15-073** *Coventry v Lawrence* was the extent to which the Supreme Court was willing to take into account the public interest in the continuation of the defendant's activity when determining whether to grant an injunction. It was also in this connection that the Court regarded any grant of planning permission as having the greatest likely salience, having significantly restricted its relevance to the question of liability.[377] If there is any such public interest, it should be regarded as a relevant factor in all cases and not, as had previously been held, only where the damage done to the claimant was minimal. Lord Neuberger said[378]:

"[T]he court may well be impressed by a defendant's argument that an injunction would involve a loss to the public or a waste of resources on account of what may be a single claimant, or that the financial implications of an injunction for the defendant would be disproportionate to the damage done to the claimant if she was left to her claim in damages. In many such cases, particularly where an injunction would in practice stop the defendant from pursuing the activities, an injunction may well not be the appropriate remedy."

---

[373] [2014] UKSC 13; [2014] A.C. 822 at [120]–[121].

[374] [1895] 1 Ch. 287 at 322–323.

[375] It is debatable how much reliance is likely to be placed on the *Shelfer* criteria in the future. Lord Sumption (at [161]) described *Shelfer* as "out of date", and said that it was unfortunate that it had been followed "so recently and so slavishly". Lord Clarke (at [171]) concurred. However, reference continues to be made to the criteria in the lower courts, where it seems that the more conservative approach adopted by Lord Neuberger in *Coventry v Lawrence* has prevailed: *Beaumont Business Centres Ltd v Florala Properties Ltd* [2020] EWHC 550 (Ch) at [330].

[376] *Coventry v Lawrence* [2014] UKSC 13; [2014] A.C. 822 at [124].

[377] See para.15-023.

[378] [2014] UKSC 13; [2014] A.C. 822 at [126]. A decision which may be easier to explain in the light of this development is *Dennis v Ministry of Defence* [2003] EWHC 793 (QB); [2003] Env. L.R. 34, where Buckley J refused to grant a declaration against the flying of military jets in close proximity to the claimant's stately home because of the needs of national defence and the enormous inconvenience and cost of relocating the training in question.

This is a significant departure from an earlier view which emphasised that damages in lieu of an injunction amount in effect to a forced sale of the claimant's rights without the sanction of Parliament.[379] As for the grant of planning permission, Lord Neuberger regarded it as a factor which would have "real force in cases where it was clear that the planning authority had been reasonably and fairly influenced by the public benefit of the activity, and where the activity cannot be carried out without causing the nuisance complained of.[380] Lord Sumption suggested that, in future, it may be appropriate to go further: "it may well be that an injunction should as a matter of principle not be granted in a case where a use of land to which objection is taken requires and has received planning permission.[381]

15-074   **Assessment of damages in lieu**   A greater willingness of the courts to award damages in lieu of an injunction inevitably throws a sharper focus on the basis for assessing such damages. According to Lord Neuberger in *Coventry v Lawrence*[382]:

> "It seems to me at least arguable that, where a claimant has a prima facie right to an injunction to restrain a nuisance, and the court decides to award damages instead, those damages should not always be limited to the value of the consequent reduction in the value of the claimant's property. While double counting must be avoided, the damages might well, at least where it was appropriate, also include the loss of the claimant's ability to enforce her rights, which may often be assessed by reference to the benefit to the defendant of not suffering an injunction."

In assessing the "benefit to the defendant", Lord Neuberger suggested that the courts might begin to adopt a similar approach to that taken in trespass cases of determining the "licence fee" which a willing claimant might reasonably have demanded for the continuation of the nuisance.[383] Lord Carnwath was reluctant to open up this possibility without fuller argument. He noted that cases relating to a clearly defined interference with a specific property right could not readily be transferred to claims for nuisance relating to interference with the enjoyment of land. Such an approach would also be a "radical departure" from the normal basis for assessment regarded by Parliament as appropriate in relation to injury done by activities carried out under statutory authority.[384]

---

[379] *Shelfer v City of London Electric Co* [1895] 1 Ch. 287; *Watson v Croft Promo-Sport Ltd* [2009] EWCA Civ 15; [2009] 3 All E.R. 249. Indeed, in *Bellew v Cement Co* [1948] Ir. R. 61 the court enjoined a nuisance even though the order would have the effect of closing for three months the only cement factory in Ireland at a time when building was an urgent public necessity. In *Miller v Jackson* [1977] Q.B. 966, Lord Denning MR had held that the public interest must prevail over private property rights when it came to the remedy issue, this view was subsequently rejected in *Kennaway v Thompson* [1981] Q.B. 88. See Tromans [1982] C.L.J. 87.

[380] [2014] UKSC 13; [2014] A.C. 822 at [125].

[381] [2014] UKSC 13; [2014] A.C. 822 at [161]. Lord Mance (at [167]–[168]) thought this put the significance of planning permission and public benefit "too high" and agreed with Lord Carnwath (at [246]–[247]) that the grant of permission could not give rise to a presumption that there should be no injunction. Lord Clarke (at [169]) noted only that the grant of permission may be "particularly relevant" to the remedy to be granted.

[382] [2014] UKSC 13; [2014] A.C. 822 at [128].

[383] See para.14-033.

[384] [2014] UKSC 13; [2014] A.C. 822 at [248]. Lord Clarke preferred to leave this question open (at [172]) but also noted that there may be scope for the award of general damages, citing the contract case of *Farley v Skinner* [2002] 2 A.C. 732.

Injunctions: further points   Two further points should be made about injunc-   **15-075**
tive relief in this context. The first is that, if an injunction is awarded in a nuisance
case, the court should be careful to limit its terms to the interference that is
actionable. In *Kennaway v Thompson*,[385] for example, an injunction restraining a
nuisance caused by the noise of power-boat racing did not bar the activity
altogether, but merely restricted the frequency and duration of the races so that the
noise would diminish to a lawful level. And the second point is that a court which
decides to issue an injunction can soften the blow by suspending its operation.[386]
This course of action may be appropriate where there are strong public interest arguments against granting an injunction with immediate effect, or where the impact on
the defendant of such an injunction would be wholly disproportionate to the interference in question.

ii.   Damages for Past Harm

Measure of damages   When damages are awarded for past harm in a nuisance   **15-076**
case, the prima facie measure is the diminution in the value of the affected land attributable to the nuisance. In cases of encroachment or physical damage to the
property, the focus is on diminution in market value (which often equates to the cost
of reinstatement[387]), and in amenity nuisance cases on diminution in utility value.
In addition to the diminution in value measure, the claimant can recover the cost
of his own reasonable efforts to abate the nuisance or prevent future injury. So, for
example, where encroaching tree roots had caused structural cracking in a block of
flats, the owners were entitled to recover the cost of underpinning the building to
prevent further damage.[388] In such a case the defendant is however entitled to be
informed of the problem and given a reasonable opportunity to abate the nuisance
before remedial expenditure is incurred.[389]

Damages for amenity nuisance   In nuisance, loss of amenity damages are "dam-   **15-077**
ages for the diminution in the value of the right to occupy the affected property",
rather than the personal distress or inconvenience of the occupiers.[390] Since the injury is to the property, not the occupiers, the quantum of damages in an amenity nuisance case does not depend on the number of people enjoying the land in question[391]:

> "The damages for nuisance recoverable by the … occupier may be affected by the size,
> commodiousness and value of his property but cannot be increased merely because more
> people are in occupation and therefore suffer greater collective discomfort. If more than
> one person has an interest in the property, the damages will have to be divided among them
> … But the damages cannot be increased by the fact that the interests in the land are
> divided; still less according to the number of persons residing on the premises."

---

[385] [1981] Q.B. 88. See also *Watson v Croft Promosport Ltd* [2009] EWCA Civ 15; [2009] 3 All E.R.
249 (use of motor circuit for noisy activities limited to 40 days a year).

[386] See, e.g., *Pennington v Brinsop Hall Coal Co* (1877) 5 Ch. D. 769; *Pride of Derby & Derbyshire
Angling Association Ltd v British Celanese Ltd* [1953] Ch. 149.

[387] See, e.g., *Dodd Properties (Kent) Ltd v Canterbury CC* [1980] 1 W.L.R. 433. Cost of reinstatement
may even be awarded where it is greater than the value lost, if repair is nonetheless reasonable: *Ward
v Cannock Chase DC* [1986] Ch. 546.

[388] *Delaware Mansions Ltd v Westminster CC* [2001] UKHL 55; [2002] 1 A.C. 321.

[389] [2001] UKHL 55; [2002] 1 A.C. 321 at [34].

[390] *Raymond v Young* [2015] EWCA Civ 456; [2015] H.L.R. 456 at [27].

[391] *Hunter v Canary Wharf Ltd* [1997] A.C. 655 at 706 per Lord Hoffmann.

An impressionistic approach is necessarily required, and evidence of the actual impact on persons living in the premises is relevant.[392] In some cases, it may be appropriate to award as loss of amenity damages a reduction in the notional rental value of the property caused by the nuisance.[393] Finally, only losses attributable to wrongful interference are recoverable. In *Andreae v Selfridge & Co Ltd*,[394] the noise and dust generated by construction work was held to be excessive and therefore actionable. Some degree of interference would, however, have been caused even if the operations had been conducted in a lawful manner, and it was emphasised that when assessing damages the court must take that into account.

15-078   **Consequential loss**   In addition to an award for the diminution in the value of his property, the claimant is entitled to recover any foreseeable consequential loss attributable to the nuisance.[395] Hence, economic losses that result from the unlawful interference are recoverable in a nuisance action, such as rental income lost due to the flooding of tenants' houses[396] and a drop in hotel takings attributable to the noise and dust from building works next door.[397] Similarly, in *Hunter v Canary Wharf Ltd*, Lord Hoffmann indicated that damages would be recoverable for harm to chattels that is consequential on a nuisance, as where livestock are lost when pastures are flooded.[398] It is difficult to see why the same approach should not be taken in cases of personal injury consequential on a nuisance, but here it would appear that the bar on recovery is absolute.[399] Furthermore, no separate award of damages for distress or discomfort should be made, since this is covered by the basic award for loss of amenity.[400]

4. HIGHWAYS

15-079   In *Jacobs v LCC* Lord Simonds said that[401]:

"Nuisance may be defined, with reference to highways, as any wrongful act or omission upon or near a highway, whereby the public are prevented from freely, safely, and conveniently passing along the highway."

In considering the general law of public nuisance we have to some extent considered its application to highways. We must now discuss some of the ap-

---

[392] *Dobson v Thames Water Utilities Ltd* [2009] EWCA Civ 28; [2009] 3 All E.R. 319 at [33]. It is also said there that if the premises were empty the damages would be nominal. However, that observation is difficult to reconcile with the objective approach laid down in *Hunter*.

[393] See [2009] EWCA Civ 28; [2009] 3 All E.R. 319 at [32]–[33]; *Raymond v Young* [2015] EWCA Civ 456; [2015] H.L.R. 456 at [29]. A reduction in rental value is not however a prerequisite of recovery: *Barr v Biffa Waste Services Ltd* [2011] EWHC 1003 (TCC); [2011] 4 All E.R. 1065 at [545].

[394] [1938] Ch. 1.

[395] *Hunter v Canary Wharf Ltd* [1997] A.C. 655 at 706.

[396] *Rust v Victoria Graving Dock Co* (1887) 36 Ch. D. 113 (though on the facts the loss was too remote).

[397] *Andreae v Selfridge & Co Ltd* [1938] Ch. 1.

[398] [1997] A.C. 655 at 706. On this analysis, however, it seems that if, e.g., the paintwork of a car parked on the claimant's property is damaged by acid emitted by the defendant's factory, then any claim would have to be in negligence, since the damage to the car is not consequential on the damage to the land.

[399] [1997] A.C. 655 at 696, 706. See also *Transco Plc v Stockport MBC* [2004] 2 A.C. 1.

[400] *Raymond v Young* [2015] EWCA Civ 456; [2015] H.L.R. 456.

[401] [1950] A.C. 361 at 375.

plicable rules in greater detail and also certain other matters which have not yet been mentioned.[402]

A. Actionable Obstructions

Not every obstacle on the highway constitutes an actionable nuisance, for the **15-080** highway would be scarcely usable if it were. The law requires of users of the highway a certain amount of "give and take" and each person is deemed to assume the normal risks of passage along the highway by way of inconvenience and even danger.[403] It is only when the defendant does something which in the circumstances is unreasonable that it becomes actionable. For this reason, the repair of the water, gas and electric mains which run under the street, of the surface of the street itself, and the building and alteration of the houses bordering on it, all constitute lawful occasions, either under statutory powers or by the common law, for temporary interference with its free passage and its amenities; and if shops and houses are to get any supplies, vehicles and persons must pause on the highway to deliver them. A temporary obstruction, provided it is reasonable in amount and duration, is permissible.[404] Nor is every permanent obstruction a nuisance.[405]

Accidents Continuing obstructions are one thing, highway accidents are another. **15-081** In a number of cases the courts have been faced with accidents arising from the parking or stopping of vehicles on the highway. If the vehicle is left[406] in such a position that it is a foreseeable source of danger to other road users, then there may be liability in nuisance but the defendant's conduct would probably amount to negligence in any case. It has been said, however, that, quite apart from foreseeability of danger, the defendant will be liable in nuisance if he so leaves his vehicle as to constitute an obstruction of the highway even though it does not constitute a risk to other road users.[407] There are though several authorities that seem to require proof of fault,[408] and in Australia the High Court has said that public nuisance should be treated as having been absorbed into negligence in this type of case.[409] That seems the better view.

---

[402] *Encyclopedia of Highway Law and Practice*; Sauvain, *Highway Law*, 5th edn (2013). Navigable waters are analogous to highways on land. As to ferries see *Gravesham BC v British Railways Board* [1978] Ch. 379.

[403] *Fletcher v Rylands* (1866) L.R. 1 Ex. 265 at 286. See also *River Wear Commissioners v Adamson* (1877) 2 App. Cas. 743 at 767.

[404] *Harper v Haden & Sons Ltd* [1933] Ch. 298 at 304.

[405] *Attorney General v Wilcox* [1938] Ch. 934.

[406] It is important to distinguish between one who deliberately parks a vehicle and one who stops temporarily, e.g., to deal with an emergency: *Dymond v Pearce* [1972] 1 Q.B. 496 at 504. Thus, if the driver, on finding his lights are out, stops the vehicle, this is not of itself a nuisance, though it may be so if he leaves it on the highway for an unreasonable time or without giving warning of its presence there or if the vehicle became unlit because of some fault on his part: *Maitland v Raisbeck* [1944] K.B. 689, explaining and distinguishing *Ware v Garston Haulage Co Ltd* [1944] K.B. 30.

[407] *Dymond v Pearce* [1972] 1 Q.B. 496; but see the contrary view of Edmund Davies LJ at 503.

[408] *Crane v South Suburban Gas Co* [1916] 1 K.B. 33; *Dollman v Hillman* [1941] 1 All E.R. 355; *Maitland v Raisbeck* [1944] K.B. 689. Another view is that fault is necessary, but the burden of disproving it on the defendant: *Southport Corp v Esso Petroleum Co Ltd* [1954] 2 Q.B. 182 at 197.

[409] *Brodie v Singleton Shire Council* [2001] HCA 29; (2001) 206 C.L.R. 512.

B. Access To and From the Highway

15-082 **Impeding access to the highway**   It is clear that the right of passage along the highway is a public right[410] and that interference with it is remediable by an action for public, not private, nuisance. As we have seen,[411] this means that the claimant can only sue if he has suffered damage over and above that suffered by the rest of the public. However, the owner of property adjoining the highway has a common law right of access to the highway which is a private right remediable by an action of private nuisance, so that anything which prevents his access (as opposed to making it less convenient for his purposes)[412] enables the recovery of at least nominal damages.[413] Any tension between the private right of access and the public right of passage is resolved on the ordinary principle that a reasonable exercise of both must be allowed.

15-083 **Impeding access to business premises**   In some cases the gist of the claimant's complaint has been not so much that his access to and from the highway has been impeded but that the obstruction has prevented other people coming on to his premises and doing business with him. It seems that such a state of affairs is both a private and a public nuisance, though as far as the latter is concerned the loss of trade will amount to special damage.[414] Picketing in pursuance of a trade dispute is, in certain circumstances, made lawful by statute[415] but otherwise it is certainly capable of amounting to a nuisance if it involves violence or intimidation[416] and perhaps even if it is carried on so as to exert pressure to regulate and control access to and from the claimant's premises.[417] Such conduct may also now fall within the Protection from Harassment Act 1997.[418]

C. Condition of the Highway

15-084 **Development of the law**[419]   At common law a highway authority could not be liable for injury suffered by a user of the highway and resulting from the authority's failure to discharge its duty to keep the highway in repair.[420] The remedy for breach

---

[410]   *Boyce v Paddington BC* [1903] 1 Ch. 109 at 114.

[411]   See para.15-007.

[412]   See *Attorney General v Thames Conservators* (1862) 1 Hem. & M. 1; 71 E.R. 1; *Tate & Lyle Industries Ltd v GLC* [1983] A.C. 509 (siltation preventing large vessels approaching claimants' jetty; an interference with the public right of navigation rather than with a private right); *Deepcliffe Pty Ltd v Council of the City of Gold Coast* [2001] QCA 342; (2001) 118 L.G.E.R.A. 117 (parking restrictions near restaurant); *Shogunn Investments Pty Ltd v Public Transport Authority of Western Australia* [2016] WASC 42 (changes to road layout near entrance to commercial car park).

[413]   *Walsh v Ervin* [1952] V.L.R. 361.

[414]   *Wilkes v Hungerford Market Co* (1835) 2 Bing. N.C. 281; 132 E.R. 110; *Lyons, Sons & Co v Gulliver* [1914] 1 Ch. 631; *Blundy, Clark & Co v L & NE Ry* [1931] 2 K.B. 342 at 352, 362 (cf. at 372); *Harper v Haden & Sons Ltd* [1933] Ch. 298 at 306–307; *Colour Quest Ltd v Total Downstream UK Plc* [2009] EWHC 540 (Comm); [2009] 2 Lloyd's Rep. 1 at [459].

[415]   Trade Union and Labour Relations (Consolidation) Act 1992 s.220.

[416]   *Messenger Newspapers Group Ltd v N.G.A.* (1982) [1984] I.R.L.R. 397; *News Group Newspapers Ltd v SOGAT '82* [1987] I.R.L.R. 337.

[417]   *Mersey Docks & Harbour Co v Verrinder* [1982] I.R.L.R. 152; *Hubbard v Pitt* [1976] Q.B. 142.

[418]   See para.4-034.

[419]   On the law relating to the condition of the highway, see Fairgrieve and Squires, *The Negligence Liability of Public Authorities*, 2nd edn (2019), Ch.10.

[420]   *Russell v Men of Devon* (1788) 2 Term Rep. 667; 100 E.R. 359; *Cowley v Newmarket Local Board*

of the duty was proceedings on indictment. This civil law immunity did not extend to misfeasance on the highway nor to acts of repair improperly performed. The distinction between misfeasance and nonfeasance and the rule of immunity were criticised and eventually the latter was abrogated by statute.[421] The law is now to be found in the Highways Act 1980.

Highways Act 1980 A highway authority may now be liable for physical injury to person or property[422] arising out of breach of its statutory duty to maintain the highway as laid down in s.41 of the Highways Act 1980. The duty to maintain is a duty only to repair and keep in repair, so no liability arises under the Act in respect of, for example, an unsafe highway layout,[423] or material lying on the surface of the highway,[424] nor for failure to improve the highway, by for example painting or erecting traffic signs or removing obstructions in the line of sight.[425] To recover damages, the claimant must prove that the highway was dangerous, that this was due to the authority's failure to maintain it, and that this failure caused damage to the claimant's person or property. The onus then shifts on to the authority, which has a defence under s.58 if it can prove that it took such care as in all the circumstances was reasonably required to secure that the relevant part of the highway was not dangerous for traffic. In assessing whether reasonable care was taken in a particular case, the financial resources available to the authority are not taken into account.[426] The end result is broadly speaking a negligence regime with the burden of proof as to fault on the defendant, though the authority is liable for the default of its contractors,[427] and it has also been said that proof that the accident would have happened even if due care had been taken would not be a defence.[428]

15-085

[1892] A.C. 345.

[421] Highways (Miscellaneous Provisions) Act 1961 s.1.

[422] Hence the Act does not give an action to an adjoining owner whose business is ruined because the condition of the highway means that vehicles cannot get to his premises: *Wentworth v Wilts CC* [1993] Q.B. 654 (dairy farm made inaccessible to milk tankers).

[423] *Thompson v Hampshire CC* [2004] EWCA Civ 1016; [2005] L.G.R. 467.

[424] *Valentine v Transport for London* [2010] EWCA Civ 1358; [2011] B.L.R. 89.

[425] *Gorringe v Calderdale MBC* [2004] UKHL 15; [2004] 1 W.L.R. 1057; *Stovin v Wise* [1996] A.C. 923. For the equivalent common law rule, see para.5-061. Parliament has, however, added to the duty an obligation "to ensure, as far as reasonably practicable, that safe passage along a highway is not endangered by snow or ice": Highways Act 1980 s.41(1A), inserted by s.111 of the Railways and Transport Safety Act 2003. The relationship between this provision and the statutory defence under s.58 is unclear.

[426] *Wilkinson v City of York Council* [2011] EWCA Civ 207.

[427] Section 58(2).

[428] *Griffiths v Liverpool Corp* [1967] 1 Q.B. 374 at 391, 395. However, Diplock LJ said at 391 that it: "may be that if the highway authority could show that no amount of reasonable care on its part could have prevented the danger the common law defence of inevitable accident would be available to it".

CHAPTER 16

THE RULE IN RYLANDS V FLETCHER

1. THE RULE IN RYLANDS V FLETCHER

Although it is now judicial orthodoxy that the rule in *Rylands v Fletcher*[1] is a **16-001** "sub-species of nuisance",[2] for most of its existence it was treated as a distinct principle of liability, and the rule still calls for separate treatment, since it remains the case that "the criteria or ingredients of the two causes of action are in some important respects different".[3] Liability under the rule is strict in the sense that it relieves the claimant of the burden of showing fault; however, it is far from absolute since there are several important defences.

---

[1] (1865) 3 H. & C. 774; 159 E.R. 737 (Court of Exchequer); (1866) L.R. 1 Ex. 265 (Court of Exchequer Chamber); (1868) L.R. 3 H.L. 330 (House of Lords). See generally *Civil Liability for Dangerous Things and Activities*, Law Com. No.32 (1970); Murphy (2004) 24 O.J.L.S. 643; Nolan (2005) 121 L.Q.R. 421; Oliphant in Koziol and Steininger (eds), *European Tort Law 2004* (2005).

[2] *Transco Plc v Stockport MBC* [2003] UKHL 61; [2004] 2 A.C. 1 at [9] per Lord Bingham.

[3] *Colour Quest Ltd v Total Downstream UK Plc* [2009] EWHC 540 (Comm); [2009] 2 Lloyd's Rep. 1 at [411] per David Steel J.

A. Genesis and Nature of the Principle

16-002 **The case** The facts in *Rylands v Fletcther* were as follows. B, a mill owner, employed independent contractors, who were apparently competent, to construct a reservoir on his land to provide water for his mill. While excavating the bed of the reservoir the contractors discovered some old shafts, filled in with soil. Neither B nor the contractors knew that the shafts led to old workings under the reservoir site, which were in turn connected, by means of other underground workings, to the mines of A. Some days after the reservoir was filled with water, one of the shafts burst downwards and the water passed through the old workings and flooded A's mines. It was found as a fact that B had been free of fault, but that it had been negligent of the contractors not to block up the shafts. On these facts, the Court of Exchequer held, by a majority, that A could not recover his losses from B.[4] However, that decision was reversed by the Court of Exchequer Chamber, where Blackburn J laid down what came to be known as the "rule in *Rylands v Fletcher*"[5]:

> "We think that the true rule of law is, that the person who for his own purposes brings on his lands and collects and keeps there anything likely to do mischief if it escapes, must keep it in at his peril, and, if he does not do so, is prima facie answerable for all the damage which is the natural consequence of its escape. He can excuse himself by shewing that the escape was owing to the plaintiff's default; or perhaps that the escape was the consequence of vis major, or the act of God; but as nothing of this sort exists here, it is unnecessary to inquire what excuse would be sufficient."

Liability under this rule rested on causation rather than fault. The act of building the reservoir was lawful, but once the water escaped and did damage A was entitled to recover without establishing negligence. B's only hope would have been a causation argument: that the harm was caused not by B, but by an act of God, the claimant, or a stranger. However, since the contractors were not strangers, no such defence was available. According to Blackburn J, this rule of strict liability was just, because the person who suffers damage from such an escape is[6]:

> "damnified without any fault of his own; and it seems but reasonable and just that the neighbour, who has brought something on his land which was not naturally there, harmless to others so long as it is confined to his own property, but which he knows to be mischievous if it gets on his neighbour's, should be obliged to make good the damage which ensues if he does not succeed in confining it to his property"

On appeal to the House of Lords, the decision of the Exchequer Chamber was affirmed.[7] Lord Cairns LC and Lord Cranworth, who gave the only speeches, both approved Blackburn J's statement of the law. However, Lord Cairns chose to put his own gloss on the governing principle by saying that if the defendants had been using their land for a purpose for which it might in the ordinary course of the enjoyment of land be used (in other words, for a natural user of the land) no liability would have arisen. It was only because their use was "non-natural" that they were acting at their peril.[8] Whether Lord Cairns intended to qualify the rule as stated by

---

4   *Fletcher v Rylands* (1865) 3 H. & C. 774; 159 E.R. 737.
5   *Rylands v Fletcher* (1866) L.R. 1 Ex. 265 at 279–280.
6   (1866) L.R. 1 Ex. 265 at 280.
7   (1868) L.R. 3 H.L. 330.
8   (1868) L.R. 3 H.L. 330 at 338–339.

Blackburn J is not clear, but in later cases this idea of a non-natural use of land came to be treated as a significant limitation on the scope of liability under the rule, additional to the requirements laid down in the Exchequer Chamber.[9] It follows that the true "rule in *Rylands v Fletcher*" must be sought in the decisions of both the Exchequer Chamber and the House of Lords.

A new principle or an application of nuisance to isolated escapes? The earlier   **16-003** cases from which Blackburn J derived his statement of the law concerned cattle trespass, overflowing privies and noisome fumes from alkali works, and the last two are clear instances of nuisance. Nevertheless, it was Winfield's view that *Rylands v Fletcher* should not be regarded as merely an application of the law of nuisance but as laying down a new principle governing a rather ill-defined category of "exceptional" or "unusual" risks.[10] English courts displayed an ambivalent attitude towards the rule but in the United States it contributed (after an initially hostile reception) towards the creation of a category of liability for damage caused by ultra-hazardous or abnormally dangerous activities that present an unavoidable risk even when due care is taken.[11] This was justified on the basis that persons carrying on such activities should bear all the risks associated with them and not merely those arising from negligence. However, there was another view, advanced by Newark,[12] that all *Rylands v Fletcher* did was to apply a general rule of strict liability in nuisance to situations where there was an isolated escape rather than the more usual ongoing state of affairs. Nevertheless, the strictness of the liability was brought into sharper focus because in the normal situation of a trickle from a watercourse or pollution from a factory the interference will usually have been apparent for some time before a claim is brought, with the result that the defendant's conduct can be described as intentional.

The close relationship between the rule and nuisance was demonstrated by the decision of the House of Lords in *Read v J Lyons & Co*[13] to the effect that in order for liability in *Rylands v Fletcher* to arise there must be an "escape", that is to say that the rule was applicable only to damage occurring outside the place in which the dangerous thing was kept,[14] and by doubts expressed in the case as to the applicability of the rule to personal injuries. In *Cambridge Water Co v Eastern Counties Leather Plc*[15] the House of Lords firmly accepted Newark's view of the origin of the rule.[16] However, it also accepted that in several respects the law had moved on since 1868. Lord Goff's speech emphasises the close connection between the rule and the law of nuisance and at one point he says that: "[I]t would ... lead to a more coherent body of common law principles if the rule were to be regarded as essentially an extension of the law of nuisance to isolated escapes from land."[17]

---

9   See paras 16-012—16-020.
10   (1931) 4 C.L.J. 189.
11   See *Restatement (Third) of the Law of Torts: Liability for Physical and Emotional Harm* (2010), §20.
12   (1949) 65 L.Q.R. 480.
13   [1947] A.C. 156.
14   *Transco Plc v Stockport MBC* [2003] UKHL 61; [2004] 2 A.C. 1 at [9].
15   [1994] 2 A.C. 264.
16   cf. Murphy (2004) 24 O.J.L.S. 643 and Nolan (2005) 121 L.Q.R. 421, who both reject what Nolan calls the "nuisance offshoot theory" and maintain, as Winfield had done, that the rule is a separate basis of liability which overlaps with nuisance, but is not subsumed by it.
17   *Cambridge Water Co v Eastern Counties Leather Plc* [1994] 2 A.C. 264 at 306.

16-004 **Current relevance of the rule** The rule in *Rylands v Fletcher* has rarely been the basis of a successful claim in the English courts since 1900[18] and it has been said that "it is hard to escape the conclusion that the intellectual effort devoted to the rule by judges and writers over many years has brought forth a mouse".[19] This has been largely because of the defences of act of a third party and statutory authority and, above all, the very restrictive attitude taken by many 20th century cases to the concept of non-natural use. The tendency was to say that common large-scale activities, especially services such as the supply of gas or water, do not constitute a non-natural use of land even though their potential for causing damage is very great. Moreover, in determining whether there is a non-natural use, the courts had regard to the benefit accruing to the public from the activity and this was an important element in the rejection of the rule in some of the leading cases.[20]

The important decision of the House of Lords in *Transco Plc v Stockport MBC*[21] indicates that the future role of *Rylands v Fletcher* is likely to be a yet more limited one. Although it had been suggested in *Cambridge Water* that non-natural use should perhaps be given a rather broader meaning than had been the case hitherto, in *Transco* their Lordships adopted a narrow definition of the concept that seemed destined to condemn the rule to further atrophy.[22] Furthermore, while the rule is an example of strict liability for abnormal risk, it does not now amount to a general rule of strict liability for ultra-hazardous activities, and in *Cambridge Water* and *Transco* the House of Lords declined to turn it into one. It is rather a narrow rule that requires an escape from one property onto another, protects only real property interests, and is inapplicable to personal injuries. The last point looks odd to the modern way of thinking, which tends to place bodily integrity at the top of the tree of protected interests; but it makes sense on the assumption that the rule is an offshoot of the law of private nuisance, which was (and still is) concerned only with the protection of the use and enjoyment of land.[23]

16-005 **No general strict liability for exceptional risk** The English common law contains a good deal less in the way of strict liability for physical damage than most other European legal systems.[24] In *Cambridge Water* the House of Lords did not disagree with the proposition that strict liability might be justifiable but it inclined to the view that[25]:

---

[18] See *Civil Liability for Dangerous Things and Activities*, Law Com. No.32 (1970) p.7.

[19] *Transco Plc v Stockport MBC* [2003] UKHL 61; [2004] 2 A.C. 1 at [39] per Lord Hoffmann. However, the assertion that no claimant had successfully relied on *Rylands v Fletcher* since the Second World War was incorrect: see *LMS International Ltd v Styrene Packaging Ltd* [2005] EWHC 2065 (TCC); [2006] T.C.L.R. 6 at [26].

[20] *Read v J Lyons & Co Ltd* [1947] A.C. 156; *Dunne v NW Gas Board* [1964] 2 Q.B. 806.

[21] *Transco Plc v Stockport MBC* [2003] UKHL 61; [2004] 2 A.C. 1.

[22] See para.16-021.

[23] In *Burnie Port Authority v General Jones Pty Ltd* (1994) 179 C.L.R. 520, the majority of the High Court of Australia went even further than the House of Lords and cast *Rylands v Fletcher* out from the Australian common law on the ground that adequate protection was afforded by the "non-delegable duty" under developed negligence law: para.21-049.

[24] See Koziol and Koch (eds), *Unification of Tort Law: Strict Liability* (2002). See also Reid (1999) 48 I.C.L.Q. 731.

[25] [1994] 2 A.C. 264 at 305 per Lord Goff. See also *Transco Plc v Stockport MBC* [2003] UKHL 61; [2004] 2 A.C. 1 at [7].

"[A]s a general rule, it is more appropriate for strict liability in respect of operations of high risk to be imposed by Parliament than by the courts. If such liability is imposed by statute, the relevant activities can be identified, and those concerned can know where they stand. Furthermore, statute can where appropriate lay down precise criteria establishing the incidence and scope of such liability."

However, the prospects of legislative intervention to impose wide-ranging strict liability on high-risk activities look dim. In the 1970s, the Pearson Commission recommended that there should be a statutory scheme making the controller of any stipulated dangerous thing or activity strictly liable for personal injury or death the thing or activity occasioned.[26] At the time, this recommendation was not followed and there is no reason to suppose that Parliament will be any more receptive to such ideas in the foreseeable future.

Strict liability under modern legislation Although neither common law nor **16-006** statute currently recognise a general principle of strict liability for ultra-hazardous activity, Parliament has enacted several statutes imposing such liability in particular areas. These enactments go some way towards avoiding the likelihood of protracted litigation inherent in the ill-defined nature of the rules of strict liability at common law. Thus, statutory water undertakers are strictly liable for damage (including personal injury) caused by escapes of water from mains,[27] and strict liability also attaches to damage caused by the underground storage of gas,[28] to injury or damage caused by a nuclear incident,[29] to damage caused by waste deposited on land unless under and in accordance with a waste management licence,[30] and to pollution damage caused by the discharge or escape of oil from ships at sea.[31] Full accounts of the relevant statutory provisions must be sought elsewhere.[32]

The present law Given the various shifts in the fortunes of *Rylands v Fletcher* **16-007** over the years earlier cases must be approached with more than usual caution but, with this in mind, we may attempt to state the present law.

B. Summary Requirements

In *Transco*, Lord Bingham summed up the effect of the modern-day rule in **16-008** *Rylands v Fletcher* as follows[33]:

"An occupier of land who can show that another occupier of land has brought or kept on his land an exceptionally dangerous or mischievous thing in extraordinary or unusual circumstances is in my opinion entitled to recover compensation from that occupier for

---

26 Cmnd.7054 (1978), Vol.1, Ch.31.
27 Water Industry Act 1991 s.209.
28 Gas Act 1965 s.14.
29 Nuclear Installations Act 1965.
30 Environmental Protection Act 1990 s.73.
31 Merchant Shipping Act 1995 Pt VI, Ch.III. Note also s.76(2) of the Civil Aviation Act 1982, which provides that, if material loss or damage is caused to any person or property by, or by a person in, or an article or person falling from, an aircraft while in flight, taking off or landing, then damages are recoverable without proof of negligence or intention or other cause of action as if the loss or damage had been caused by the wilful act, neglect, or default of the owner of the aircraft.
32 Stanton et al, *Statutory Torts* (2003), Ch.16; Oliphant (ed), *The Law of Tort*, 3rd edn (2015), paras 23-50—23-57.
33 *Transco Plc v Stockport MBC* [2003] UKHL 61; [2004] 2 A.C. 1 at [11] per Lord Bingham.

any damage caused to his property interest by the escape of that thing, subject to defences of act of God or of a stranger, without the need to prove negligence."

The treatment of the rule in this chapter begins with an analysis of the sorts of "dangerous things" that have been held to come within the rule. Analysis of the core elements of escape, non-natural user and actionable damage follows, and consideration is then given to who can sue and who is liable, and remoteness of damage. The remainder of the chapter deals with defences to a claim under the rule and liability for fire.

C. Dangerous Things

16-009   *Rylands v Fletcher* has been applied (or said to apply, because the cases sometimes turned on other points) to a remarkable variety of things: fire;[34] gas;[35] blasting and munitions;[36] electricity;[37] oil and petrol;[38] noxious fumes;[39] colliery spoil;[40] rusty wire from a decayed fence;[41] vibrations;[42] poisonous vegetation;[43] a flag pole;[44] a "chair-o-plane" in a fairground;[45] and even (in a case of very questionable validity) noxious persons.[46] Conversely, in *Noble v Harrison*,[47] where a branch of a beech tree had fallen on the claimant's car, it was held that the tree was not a dangerous thing within the rule, and it should also be noted that, although in principle strict liability could be imposed for damage done by escaping animals under *Rylands v Fletcher*,[48] in practice the courts seem unlikely to go beyond the specific instances of strict liability imposed by the Animals Act 1971.[49]

16-010   **A requirement of dangerousness?**   In his formulation of the rule in *Rylands v Fletcher*, Blackburn J referred to the defendant bringing onto his land "something

---

[34]   See para.16-036.
[35]   *Batchellor v Tunbridge Wells Gas Co* (1901) 84 L.T. 765.
[36]   *Miles v Forest Rock Co* (1918) 34 T.L.R. 500; *Rainham Chemical Works Ltd v Belvedere Fish Guano Co Ltd* [1921] 2 A.C. 465.
[37]   *National Telephone Co v Baker* [1893] 2 Ch. 186; *Eastern SA Telegraph Co Ltd v Cape Town Tramways Cos Ltd* [1902] A.C. 381.
[38]   *Smith v GW Ry* (1926) 135 L.T. 112; *Colour Quest Ltd v Total Downstream UK Plc* [2009] EWHC 540 (Comm); [2009] 1 Lloyd's Rep. 1.
[39]   *West v Bristol Tramways Co* [1908] 2 K.B. 14.
[40]   *Attorney General v Cory Bros Ltd* [1921] 1 A.C. 521.
[41]   *Firth v Bowling Iron Co* (1878) 3 C.P.D. 254.
[42]   *Hoare & Co v McAlpine* [1923] 1 Ch. 167. It is however most unlikely that vibrations would attract strict liability nowadays, since they are not themselves brought on to the land, and yet, according to *Stannard v Gore* [2012] EWCA Civ 1248; [2014] Q.B. 1, it is the very thing that is brought on to the land that must escape: see *Lindsay v Berkeley Homes (Capital) Plc* [2018] EWHC 2042 (TCC) at [39].
[43]   *Crowhurst v Amersham Burial Board* (1878) 4 Ex. D. 5; *Ponting v Noakes* [1894] 2 Q.B. 281.
[44]   *Shiffman v Order of St John* [1936] 1 All E.R. 557 (though the case was decided on the ground of negligence).
[45]   *Hale v Jennings Bros* [1938] 1 All E.R. 579.
[46]   *Attorney General v Corke* [1933] Ch. 89; but cf. *Smith v Scott* [1973] Ch. 314, where it is suggested that this case could at least equally well have been decided on the basis that the landowner was in possession of the property and was himself liable for nuisances created by his licensees. Liability in nuisance was imposed in similar circumstances in *Lippiatt v South Gloucestershire Council* [2000] Q.B. 51, para.15-042.
[47]   *Noble v Harrison* [1926] 2 K.B. 332.
[48]   North, *Civil Liability for Animals* (2012), pp.164–165.
[49]   See Ch.17.

dangerous" that was "likely to do mischief" if it escaped.[50] However, "dangerousness" is an elastic concept and, in practice, this requirement has rarely been applied to exclude liability under the rule,[51] with the focus instead being on the requirement of non-natural user. Nevertheless, in his speech in *Transco v Stockport*, Lord Bingham expressed the view that this requirement remained applicable, and that the test of mischief or danger should not "be at all easily satisfied"; it must be shown that the defendant had done something which he recognised, or ought reasonably to have recognised, gave rise to "an exceptionally high risk of danger or mischief if there should be an escape".[52] But he also acknowledged that this issue could not be considered in complete isolation from the question of non-natural use, and the courts might in future be better off following the advice of Lord Walker in *Transco*, and considering the two issues together.[53] On this approach, it is the fact that the defendant's activity gives rise to an extraordinary risk which makes it a non-natural use.

D. Escape

The requirement of escape was firmly set in the law by the House of Lords' in **16-011** *Read v J Lyons & Co Ltd*.[54] The claimant was employed by the Ministry of Supply as an inspector of munitions in the defendants' munitions factory and, in the course of her employment, was injured by the explosion of a shell that was being manufactured. Though it was admitted that high explosive shells were dangerous, the defendants were held not liable. There was no allegation of negligence on their part and *Rylands v Fletcher* was inapplicable because there had been no "escape" of the thing that inflicted the injury. "Escape" was defined as, "escape from a place where the defendant has occupation or control over land to a place which is outside his occupation or control".[55] For the purposes of the escape requirement, the material that escapes and does the damage need not be the thing that the defendant actually accumulated. Hence, where the damage is caused by an explosion, it is not the explosive that escapes, but other matter, propelled from the defendant's land by the blast.[56] This principle used also to apply in fire cases, so that the thing brought onto the land did not itself have to escape: it was enough that it caught fire, and the *fire* escaped. However, that is no longer so, for the Court of Appeal has held that the fire that escapes must *itself* have been brought onto the land by the defendant.[57]

---

[50] *Rylands v Fletcher* (1866) L.R. 1 Ex. 265 at 279.

[51] "[I]t is difficult to identify anything which, accumulated either in sufficient quantity or under sufficient pressure, might not be a dangerous substance": *Burnie Port Authority v General Jones Pty Ltd* (1994) 179 C.L.R. 520 at 538 per Mason CJ, Deane, Dawson, Toohey and Gaudron JJ.

[52] *Transco Plc v Stockport MBC* [2003] UKHL 61; [2004] 2 A.C. 1 at [10]. See also at [67] per Lord Hobhouse.

[53] [2003] UKHL 61; [2004] 2 A.C. 1 at [103]. See also at [49], where Lord Hoffmann dealt with Lord Bingham's "criterion of exceptional risk" as going to the issue of non-natural use.

[54] [1947] A.C. 156; *Transco Plc v Stockport MBC* [2003] UKHL 61; [2004] 2 A.C. 1 at [9], [34], [77].

[55] [1947] A.C. 156 at 168 per Viscount Simon. See also at 177 per Lord Porter: "Escape from the place in which the dangerous object has been maintained by the defendant to some place not subject to his control." Note that since a defendant under the rule need not be the owner or occupier of the land to which he has brought the dangerous thing (see para.16-028), a more precise way of expressing the escape requirement may be to say that there must be an escape from land in which the claimant has no proprietary interest to land in which he does: see Bagshaw (2004) 120 L.Q.R. 388 at 391.

[56] See, e.g., *Miles v Forest Rock Granite Co* (1918) 34 T.L.R. 500.

[57] *Stannard v Gore* [2012] EWCA Civ 1248; [2014] Q.B. 1. See para.16-037.

Whether that change affects the general principle remains to be seen. In the case of a voluntary release or discharge of a dangerous thing, as opposed to an inadvertent "escape", trespass may lie, but if (because the thing is not aimed at the claimant or his property) it does not, there is no reason why an action under *Rylands v Fletcher* should not be available.[58] The escape requirement has in the past been criticised for creating arbitrary distinctions,[59] but can now be explained as following from the limitation of the rule in *Rylands v Fletcher* to the protection of the claimant's real property interests.[60]

E.   Non-natural Use

16-012   **Significance of the requirement**[61]   For an escape to be actionable under the rule in *Rylands v Fletcher* it must be the consequence of a non-natural use of land. This requirement of non-natural use is additional to the requirement that the agent of the harm must be a "dangerous thing" that comes within the rule. The non-natural use concept performs an important role in the modern law of *Rylands v Fletcher*, and the distinction between natural and non-natural use lends the rule a desirable degree of flexibility, by enabling the courts to infuse notions of social and economic needs prevailing at a given time and place.[62]

16-013   **History of the requirement**   We have already noted that Blackburn J in the Court of Exchequer Chamber made no mention of the requirement of non-natural use. He did, however, make it plain that the principle he stated applied only to things which the defendant collected for his own purposes. Hence, a defendant cannot be liable under the rule merely for permitting a spontaneous accumulation (for example, of water, vegetation or birds) on his land,[63] or even for inducing a spontaneous accumulation as an undesired by-product of the normal working of the land.[64] However, as a practical matter these principles have been much reduced in importance by the recognition that an occupier may owe a duty of care to abate a nuisance arising naturally on his land.[65]

It may well be that Lord Cairns in the House of Lords in *Rylands v Fletcher* did not intend to add anything to Blackburn J's requirement that the defendant should have accumulated the dangerous thing by positive action but the law developed so as to give the expression he used a meaning which excluded from the rule deliberate accumulations resulting from "ordinary" uses of the land. A key milestone was *Rickards v Lothian*,[66] where the Privy Council refused to apply *Rylands v Fletcher* to an overflowing toilet bowl. According to Lord Moulton[67]:

---

[58]   *Crown River Cruises Ltd v Kimbolton Fireworks Ltd* [1996] 2 Lloyd's Rep. 533 at 547; cf. *Rigby v CC Northamptonshire* [1985] 1 W.L.R. 1242 (CS gas canister fired into claimant's shop).

[59]   See, e.g., *Burnie Port Authority v General Jones Pty Ltd* (1994) 179 C.L.R. 520 at 548.

[60]   See *Transco Plc v Stockport MBC* [2003] UKHL 61; [2004] 2 A.C. 1 at [9].

[61]   Newark (1961) 24 M.L.R. 557; Williams [1973] C.L.J. 310.

[62]   *Fleming's The Law of Torts*, 10th edn (2011), p.389.

[63]   *Giles v Walker* (1890) 24 Q.B.D. 656 (thistledown); *Pontardawe RDC v Moore-Gwyn* [1929] 1 Ch. 656 (falls of rocks); *Seligman v Docker* [1949] Ch. 53.

[64]   *Wilson v Waddell* (1876) 2 App. Cas. 95; *Smith v Kenrick* (1849) 7 C.B. 515; 137 E.R. 205.

[65]   However, they remain relevant where there is a sudden disaster against which the occupier cannot take steps: *Ellison v MoD* (1997) 81 B.L.R. 101 (flood produced by works at airfield).

[66]   *Rickards v Lothian* [1913] A.C. 263.

[67]   *Rickards v Lothian* [1913] A.C. 263 at 279–280.

"It is not every use to which land is put that brings into play [the *Rylands v Fletcher*] principle. It must be some special use bringing with it increased danger to others, and must not merely be the ordinary use of the land or such a use as is proper for the general benefit of the community."

This statement rapidly came to be seen as authoritative, and the courts thereafter interpreted the words "non-natural use" to mean a use that was extraordinary, unusual, abnormal or exceptional.[68]

Rationale of the requirement The logic of the restriction of the strict liability **16-014** rule to the extraordinary or abnormal is that if the activity is one carried on by a large proportion of persons, then the incidence of harm and responsibility are so nearly co-extensive that nothing is gained by the imposition of strict liability. Unless there is a special danger created by a small minority at the expense of the general public, strict liability merely substitutes a risk of liability for a risk of loss. Besides, the very rationale of *Rylands v Fletcher* liability is that it is only fair that, if the defendant wants to engage in an activity that creates exceptional risks, he should at least pay his way.[69] Where the activity is ordinary and commonplace, so too are the risks it creates, and so (in the absence of negligence) "mutual sufferance" can reasonably be expected.[70]

Transco Plc v Stockport MBC The leading modern authority on the meaning **16-015** and application of the non-natural use requirement is the decision of the House of Lords in *Transco Plc v Stockport*.[71] The facts were that water had escaped from the service pipe to a block of flats owned by the defendant, causing a nearby embankment to collapse, with the result that the claimant's gas main was left exposed and unsupported. The claimant sought recovery of the expenditure it had incurred to avert the risk of damage to the main and, since the escape was found to have occurred without any negligence on the defendant's part, reliance was placed on the rule in *Rylands v Fletcher*. The House of Lords dismissed the claim on the ground that the supply of water to the tower block had been a natural use of land. According to Lord Bingham, "ordinary user" was a preferable test to natural user, since it made it clear that the strict liability rule was engaged only where the defendant's use was shown to be "extraordinary and unusual". The test of non-natural use was: "[W]hether the defendant has done something which he recognises, or ought to recognise, as being quite out of the ordinary in the place and at the time when he does it."[72] Lord Bingham had little difficulty in concluding that this test was not satisfied on the facts of the case. The piping of a water supply from the mains to the storage tanks in the tower block was "a routine function which would not have struck anyone as raising any special hazard".[73] Even though the pipe in question supplied 66 flats, and was much larger than an ordinary domestic pipe, the council's

---

68 See, e.g., *Rainham Chemicals Works Ltd v Belvedere Fish Guano Co Ltd* [1921] 2 A.C. 465 at 471.
69 *Transco Plc v Stockport MBC* [2004] UKHL 61; [2004] 2 A.C. 1 at [55].
70 Stallybrass (1929) 3 C.L.J. 376 at 396. See also *Restatement (Third) of the Law of Torts: Liability for Physical and Emotional Harm* (2010), § 20, comment j.
71 *Transco Plc v Stockport MBC* [2003] UKHL 61; [2004] 2 A.C. 1.
72 [2004] 2 A.C. 1 at [11].
73 [2004] 2 A.C. 1 at [13].

use of its land was in no way extraordinary or unusual, but "entirely normal and routine".[74]

16-016 Comparison with Cambridge Water The treatment of the non-natural use issue in *Transco Plc v Stockport MBC* can fruitfully be compared with the approach to the requirement taken in the earlier *Cambridge Water* case.[75] Lord Goff there expressed the opinion that, bearing in mind the other controls on *Rylands v Fletcher*, an overly restrictive approach to the concept of non-natural use ought not to be taken, and described the use in that case—storage of substantial quantities of chemicals on industrial premises—as "an almost classic case of non-natural use".[76] In *Transco*, by contrast, the House conceived of the non-natural use requirement in very narrow terms. According to Lord Hoffmann, for example, the "criterion of exceptional risk must be taken seriously and creates a high threshold for the claimant to surmount".[77] This more restrictive approach suggested that the future field of operation of the strict liability rule would be very limited, and indeed little has been heard of the rule in the courts since *Transco* was decided.[78]

16-017 Relevance of time and place Lord Porter said in *Read v J Lyons & Co Ltd* that in deciding the question of non-natural user: "[A]ll the circumstances of time and practice of mankind must be taken into consideration so that what may be regarded as dangerous or non-natural may vary according to the circumstances."[79] For this reason that which may seem extraordinary to one generation may seem ordinary to its successor. At the time of the First World War the Court of Appeal held that keeping a motor car in a garage with petrol in a tank was a non-natural use of land,[80] a decision which may well have been dubious even at that time but, it is submitted, would be inconceivable today notwithstanding the doctrine of precedent.[81] In the same way, a use that may be extraordinary and unusual in one place may not be in another.[82]

16-018 Common or domestic use It follows from the characterisation of non-natural use as connoting the extraordinary or unusual that common or domestic uses which have some potential for danger are excluded from the scope of the rule. So the following have been regarded as natural or ordinary uses of land: water installations in a house or office;[83] the main water supply to a block of flats;[84] a fire in a domestic

---

74   [2004] 2 A.C. 1 at [13]. See also at [48] per Lord Hoffmann ("a perfectly normal item of plumbing").
75   *Cambridge Water Co v Eastern Counties Leather Plc* [1994] 2 A.C. 264.
76   [1994] 2 A.C. 264 at 309.
77   *Transco Plc v Stockport MBC* [2003] UKHL 61; [2004] 2 A.C. 1 at [49].
78   For an example of a restrictive approach to the non-natural use concept in the aftermath of *Transco Plc v Stockport MBC*, see *Stannard v Gore* [2012] EWCA Civ 1248; [2014] Q.B. 1. In *Lindsay v Berkeley Homes (Capital) Plc* [2018] EWHC 2042 (TCC) at [38] Jefford J described the rule in *Rylands v Fletcher* as "a rule of limited utility".
79   [1947] A.C. 156 at 176.
80   *Musgrove v Pandelis* [1919] 2 K.B. 43.
81   See *Transco Plc v Stockport MBC* [2003] UKHL 61; [2004] 2 A.C. 1 at [107]. See also *Mackenzie v Sloss* [1959] N.Z.L.R. 533 (internal combustion engine a natural and ordinary use of property).
82   See *Hazelwood v Webber* (1934) 52 C.L.R. 268 (burning off stubble a non-natural use in Australia during the summer months); *Canadian Forest Products Ltd v Hudson Lumber Co Ltd* (1959) 20 D.L.R. (2d) 712 (logging a natural use of land in British Columbia).
83   *Rickards v Lothian* [1913] A.C. 263.
84   *Transco Plc v Stockport MBC* [2003] UKHL 61; [2004] 2 A.C. 1.

grate;[85] electric wiring;[86] gas pipes in a house or shop;[87] erecting or pulling down houses or walls;[88] burning stubble in the normal course of agriculture;[89] the ordinary working of mines or minerals;[90] the possession of trees whether planted or self-sown;[91] or generating steam on a ship.[92] The risks posed by these things are commonplace ones, with which people must put up unless there is fault. There has, however, been a greater willingness to apply the rule to the bulk storage or transmission of water[93] or gas or electricity,[94] or to the bulk storage of chemicals,[95] or combustible materials,[96] though in such cases the defence of statutory authority has often prevented a decision in the claimant's favour.

The relevance of public benefit Blackburn J's reference to the defendant col- **16-019**
lecting the dangerous thing "for his own purposes" does not mean that he must be seeking to profit from the activity; indeed, in one case the phrase was said not to be a sufficient reason to refuse to apply the rule to a local authority which was required by statute to receive sewage into its sewers.[97] However, there has sometimes been a tendency to say that a use is natural where it leads to a public benefit,[98] a course which requires the court either to make very difficult value judgments or to deprive the rule of all practical effect. In *Rainham Chemical Works Ltd v Belvedere Fish Guano Co Ltd*[99] it was assumed without argument that the manufacture of military explosives during the First World War was a non-natural use but, on similar facts occurring during the Second World War in *Read v J Lyons & Co Ltd* suggested that this might not be so because of the urgent public necessity for munitions in wartime.[100] In the years that followed, that suggestion proved influential and, on the rare occasions when *Rylands v Fletcher* was pleaded, the public benefit riposte was much in evidence.[101] Orthodoxy was however restored in *Cambridge Water*,[102] where Lord Goff said that if general benefit to the com-

---

85 *Sochacki v Sas* [1947] 1 All E.R. 344.
86 *Collingwood v Home and Colonial Stores Ltd* [1936] 3 All E.R. 200.
87 *Miller v Addie & Sons (Collieries) Ltd* 1934 S.C. 150.
88 *Thomas and Evans Ltd v Mid-Rhondda Co-operative Society* [1941] 1 K.B. 381.
89 *Perkins v Glyn* [1976] R.T.R. ix (note).
90 *Rouse v Gravelworks Ltd* [1940] 1 K.B. 489.
91 *Noble v Harrison* [1926] 2 K.B. 332. cf. *Crowhurst v Amersham Burial Board* (1878) 4 Ex. D. 5 (poisonous yew tree).
92 *Howard v Furness Ltd* [1936] 2 All E.R. 781; *Miller Steamship Co Pty Ltd v Overseas Tankship (UK) Ltd* [1963] 1 Lloyd's Rep. 402 at 426.
93 *Rylands v Fletcher* (1866) L.R. 1 Ex. 265 (affirmed (1868) L.R. 3 H.L. 330); cf. *Transco Plc v Stockport MBC* [2003] UKHL 61; [2004] 2 A.C. 1.
94 *Charing Cross Electricity Supply Co v Hydraulic Power Co* [1914] 3 K.B. 772; *Northwestern Utilities v London Guarantee and Accident Co* [1936] A.C. 108.
95 *Cambridge Water Co v Eastern Counties Leather Plc* [1994] 2 A.C. 264.
96 *Mason v Levy Auto Parts of England Ltd* [1967] 2 Q.B. 530; *Hobbs (Farms) Ltd v Baxenden Chemical Co Ltd* [1992] 1 Lloyd's Rep. 54; *LMS International Ltd v Styrene Packaging and Insulation Ltd* [2005] EWHC 2065 (TCC); *Colour Quest Ltd v Total Downstream UK Plc* [2009] EWHC 540 (Comm); [2009] 1 Lloyd's Rep. 1.
97 *Smeaton v Ilford Corp* [1954] 1 Ch. 459 at 469, 472.
98 For the first judicial intimation to this effect, see *Rickards v Lothian* [1913] A.C. 263 at 280.
99 [1921] 2 A.C. 465.
100 [1947] A.C. 156 at 169, 174.
101 See *Pride of Derby and Derby Angling Association Ltd v British Celanese Ltd* [1953] Ch. 149; *Dunne v NW Gas Board* [1964] 2 Q.B. 806; *British Celanese Ltd v AH Hunt Ltd* [1969] 1 W.L.R. 959 at 963–964.
102 *Cambridge Water Co v Eastern Counties Leather Plc* [1994] 2 A.C. 264.

munity were taken into account, it was difficult to see how the natural user exception could be kept within reasonable bounds, and, in particular, that the creation of employment was not of itself sufficient to establish a use as natural or ordinary. That is surely correct. Benefit to the community was not a consideration in the early case law on the rule, and such reasoning is incompatible with the rationale of strict liability, which is that—although the carrying on of the activity is reasonable and lawful—the defendant must pay his way by compensating those whom it harms.

16-020 **Insurance considerations** In *Transco Plc v Stockport MBC*, Lord Hoffmann said that a useful guide in deciding whether a particular risk was created by a non-natural use was to ask whether the resultant damage was something against which the occupier could reasonably be expected to have insured himself.[103] Property insurance was cheap and accessible, and people should be encouraged to insure their property rather than to seek to transfer the risk to others by expensive litigation. However, his reasoning was criticised by Lord Hobhouse, who pointed out that some risks might be insurable only at prohibitive rates, that the allocation of the risk determines who bears the economic burden of insuring against the risk, and that the same argument could be used to justify abolishing negligence actions in road traffic cases, since all drivers could take out comprehensive car insurance.[104] It is respectfully suggested that Lord Hobhouse's analysis is to be preferred. The courts are not necessarily in a position to know which risks are, and are not, routinely insured against and, besides, it would seem very strange that if an escape of water flooded both domestic premises (often not insured) and a council-owned adventure playground (often not insured), then there might be recovery in the latter case but not the former.[105] In *LMS International Ltd v Styrene Packaging and Insulation Ltd*, Lord Hobhouse's reasoning was preferred, and the insurance position of the claimant treated as irrelevant.[106]

F. Actionable Damage

16-021 Damage to real property is of course actionable under *Rylands v Fletcher*, and in several cases damages have been awarded under the rule for injury to chattels,[107] although following the assimilation of the rule into private nuisance, it is arguable that only damage to chattels consequential on damage to the land ought now to be recoverable, as in that tort.[108] Where the escape causes personal injury, the position used to be less clear, but the assimilation of the rule into private nuisance has clarified matters. In *Transco Plc v Stockport MBC*, Lord Hoffmann described the rule as "a remedy for damage to land or interests in land",[109] and it followed that recovery for personal injury was not possible.[110] Whether this is a satisfactory outcome is another matter. As one commentator has pointed out[111]:

---

[103] *Transco Plc v Stockport MBC* [2003] UKHL 61; [2004] 2 A.C. 1 at [46].
[104] [2004] 2 A.C. 1 at [60].
[105] Bagshaw (2004) 120 L.Q.R. 388, 390.
[106] [2005] EWHC 2065 (TCC); [2006] T.C.L.R. 6 at [228].
[107] See, e.g., *Jones v Festiniog Rly Co* (1868) LR 3 Q.B. 733 (haystacks); *Halsey v Esso Petroleum Co Ltd* [1961] 1 W.L.R. 683 (car and clothing).
[108] See para.15-078.
[109] *Transco Plc v Stockport MBC* [2003] UKHL 61; [2004] 2 A.C. 1 at [39].
[110] [2003] UKHL 61; [2004] 2 A.C. 1 at [35]. See also at [9], [52].
[111] Tylor (1947) 10 M.L.R. 396 at 400.

"The suggestion that I can recover for an explosion wrecking my conservatory or a horse trespassing on my rose bed, but not for an explosion blowing me out of my deck chair in my own garden, or a horse treading on my face as I sleep on my lawn, has little to commend it."

Pure economic loss Damages are not recoverable under *Rylands v Fletcher* for **16-022** economic loss caused by injury to the person or property of another. In *Weller & Co v Foot and Mouth Disease Research Institute*,[112] for example, a firm of auctioneers were denied damages for the losses they suffered when cattle markets were closed after the foot and mouth disease virus escaped from the defendant's research facility and infected local cattle. However, as in nuisance,[113] economic losses consequential on actionable damage to the claimant's land ought to be recoverable under the rule. Furthermore, damages are apparently recoverable for financial loss the claimant reasonably incurs in protecting his property from the escaping thing.[114] In *Transco Plc v Stockport MBC*, for example, it was assumed that if the elements of a *Rylands v Fletcher* claim had been made out then the claimant would have been entitled to recover the cost of measures taken to safeguard its gas main after the escaping water caused the embankment supporting the main to collapse.[115]

G.   Who Can Sue and Who is Liable

Who can sue Following the assimilation of the rule in *Rylands v Fletcher* into **16-023** private nuisance, it seems that, as in that tort,[116] the claimant in an action under the rule must have a proprietary interest in the land where the damage occurs.[117] As in nuisance, the requirement of an interest in land is satisfied where the interference is with an easement which the claimant has over another's land,[118] although no claim will lie against the servient owner himself in the absence of negligence or intentional conduct.[119]

Who is liable Primary liability under the rule attaches to the person who ac- **16-024** cumulates the thing that escapes, not the person who causes the escape to occur. Hence when bystanders were injured after a car taking part in a stock car race crashed through the fence surrounding the track, the organiser of the race was held liable under *Rylands v Fletcher*, but the driver's liability rested on negligence.[120] Conversely, where—as in *Rylands v Fletcher* itself—an occupier employs contractors to bring the thing onto his land, the occupier rather than the contractor is liable, since the accumulation is for his purposes, not theirs. There is no require-

---

[112] [1966] 1 Q.B. 569. See also *Cattle v Stockton Waterworks Co* (1875) L.R. 10 Q.B. 453 at 457; *D Pride and Partners v Institute for Animal Health* [2009] EWHC 685 (QB); [2009] N.P.C. 56.
[113] See para.15-078.
[114] *New Zealand Forest Products Ltd v O'Sullivan* [1974] 2 N.Z.L.R. 80.
[115] See *Transco Plc v Stockport MBC* [2003] UKHL 61; [2004] 2 A.C. 1 at [47]. On such "preventive damages" more generally, see Nolan (2016) 132 L.Q.R. 68.
[116] See para.15-039.
[117] *Transco Plc v Stockport MBC* [2003] UKHL 61; [2004] 2 A.C. 1 at [47]. This was not the case prior to the reformulation of the rule as a land tort: see Nolan (2005) 121 L.Q.R. 421, 432–434.
[118] [2004] 2 A.C. 1 at [47], [78].
[119] [2004] 2 A.C. 1 at [80]. See also at [68]. In such circumstances, the requirement of an "escape" would in any case not be met.
[120] *Aldridge v Van Patter* [1952] 4 D.L.R. 93.

ment that the defendant be the owner or occupier of the land to which he has brought the dangerous thing.[121] Here, the rule is the same in nuisance,[122] so convergence with that tort will not be a catalyst for change. An occupier is liable under the rule if the thing is brought onto his land by a third party for his purposes, or with his permission, but not otherwise.[123] And a landowner who is not in occupation of the land when the thing escapes is probably liable if (but only if) he has authorised the accumulation.[124]

H.   Remoteness of Damage

16-025   In Blackburn J's formulation of the rule in *Rylands v Fletcher* he said that the defendant "is prima facie answerable for all the damage which is the natural consequence" of the escape of the dangerous thing, but concrete guidance on remoteness of damage was not forthcoming until *Cambridge Water*.[125] The defendant in that case was a leather manufacturer which used a chemical solvent in its tanning process. Over the years, solvent that spilled onto the tannery floor seeped into the soil and contaminated the supply of underground water to a borehole used by the claimant water company. As a result, the claimant had to develop a new source of supply, and it sought recovery of the added expense from the defendant under *Rylands v Fletcher*. Lord Goff held that the first instance finding that the defendant could not reasonably have foreseen that the spilled solvent would sensibly affect the claimant's water supply was fatal to the action, since, as in negligence and nuisance, "foreseeability of damage of the relevant type should be regarded as a prerequisite of liability under the rule".[126]

The test which should be applied is whether it was reasonably foreseeable that, *in the event of an escape*, damage of the relevant type would occur. In other words, the escape itself need not be foreseeable, but only the harm that follows. Although Lord Goff's speech in *Cambridge Water* was somewhat opaque on this question, this interpretation is the one most consistent with the general tenor of his remarks, and was expressly adopted by Lord Hoffmann in *Transco Plc v Stockport MBC*.[127] Finally while it was previously unclear whether recovery was possible under the rule where damage occurred only because the property or activity affected by the escaping thing was abnormally sensitive,[128] the requirement of foreseeability can now be used to resolve this question. If the defendant could reasonably have

---

[121] Hence utilities that lay mains or cables under the highway are liable for escapes that cause damage: *Charing Cross Electricity Supply Co v Hydraulic Power Co* [1914] 3 K.B. 772; *Northwestern Utilities Ltd v London Guarantee and Accident Co Ltd* [1936] A.C. 108. And the rule has also been applied to escapes from the surface of the highway on to neighbouring land: *Powell v Fall* (1880) 5 Q.B.D. 597; *Mansell v Webb* (1918) 88 L.J.K.B. 323. See also *Crown River Cruises Ltd v Kimbolton Fireworks Ltd* [1996] 2 Lloyd's Rep. 533 at 547 (escape from vessel in a navigable river).

[122] See para.15-042.

[123] See *Rainham Chemical Works Ltd v Belvedere Fish Guano Co Ltd* [1921] 2 A.C. 465 at 480.

[124] *Rainham Chemical Works Ltd v Belvedere Fish Guano Co Ltd* [1921] 2 A.C. 465 at 476, 489. As to what constitutes authorisation in this context, see para.15-052.

[125] *Cambridge Water Co v Eastern Counties Leather Plc* [1994] 2 A.C. 264.

[126] [1994] 2 A.C. 264 at 302.

[127] *Transco Plc v Stockport MBC* [2003] UKHL 61; [2004] 2 A.C. 1 at [33]. See also *Stannard v Gore* [2012] EWCA Civ 1248; [2014] Q.B. 1 at [67]. As Lord Hoffmann implied, a requirement that the escape itself be foreseeable would not have been satisfied on the facts of *Rylands v Fletcher*.

[128] cf. *Eastern SA Telegraph Co Ltd v Cape Town Tramways Co Ltd* [1902] A.C. 381 at 393 and *National Telephone Co v Baker* [1893] 2 Ch. 186 at 202.

foreseen the harm then he will be liable, irrespective of any abnormal sensitivity, but of course the abnormal sensitivity may itself affect the foreseeability of the damage that occurs.[129]

I. Defences

Of the five established defences to an action under the rule in *Rylands v Fletcher*, **16-026** three—act of God, act of a stranger and default of the claimant—go to causation.[130] The event that gives rise to one of these defences is a novus actus interveniens and so, in law, the proximate cause of the claimant's injury. The recognition of these defences is in keeping with the philosophy underpinning the rule, which is that liability is based on causation rather than fault. In the words of Lord Hobhouse in *Transco Plc v Stockport MBC*[131]:

> "[The defences recognised in *Rylands v Fletcher* and in cases following it] were the same as those used elsewhere in the common law in relation to strict liabilities and related to the causal connection between the relevant damage and the conduct of the defendant."

The other established defences, consent and statutory authority, are defences of general application in the law of tort. In this context, they have the effect of removing the protection of the strict liability rule, and remitting the claimant to the general negligence standard. If *Rylands v Fletcher* applies to the deliberate release of a dangerous thing,[132] then a defence of necessity ought also to be available, as in trespass.[133]

i. Consent of the Claimant

Where the claimant expressly or impliedly consented to the presence of the **16-027** source of danger and there was no negligence on the defendant's part, the defendant is not liable.[134] Almost always, consent is implied,[135] most frequently from the fact that the accumulation is for the common benefit of the claimant and the defendant. In *Carstairs v Taylor*,[136] the claimants leased the ground floor of a warehouse from the defendant, who occupied the floor above. The water from the roof was collected by gutters into a wooden box, from which it was discharged by a pipe into the drains. A rat gnawed a hole in the box, and the water leaked into the claimants' premises and damaged their goods. Bramwell B distinguished *Rylands v Fletcher* on the ground that "the conducting of the water was no more for the benefit of the defendant than of the [claimants]", and that therefore the claimants

---

[129] See, e.g., *Hamilton v Pakapura DC* [2002] UKPC 9; [2002] 3 N.Z.L.R. 308 (not reasonably foreseeable that low levels of herbicide residue in water supply would prove toxic to hydroponically grown tomato plants).

[130] See *Benning v Wong* (1969) 122 C.L.R. 249 at 306.

[131] [2003] UKHL 61; [2004] 2 A.C. 1 at [59].

[132] See para.16-011.

[133] As suggested in *Rigby v CC Northamptonshire* [1985] 1 W.L.R. 1242.

[134] *Gill v Edouin* (1894) 71 L.T. 762 at 763; *Attorney General v Cory Bros Ltd* [1921] 1 A.C. 521 at 539.

[135] For a rare example of express consent, see *Pattison v Prince Edward Region Conservation Authority* (1984) 23 D.L.R. (4th) 201.

[136] (1871) L.R. 6 Ex. 217.

must be taken to have consented to it.[137] Where the element of common benefit is missing, the claimant may still be subject to the consent argument if he leased the premises from the defendant in full knowledge of the defendant's accumulation for, in these circumstances, the rule that a tenant must take the premises as he finds them applies.[138] Many of the actions which in the past were dismissed on consent grounds would now also fall foul of the requirement that there be a non-natural use of land, so the practical importance of the defence has diminished in modern times.

ii. Act of Stranger

16-028   It is a defence to an action under *Rylands v Fletcher* that the escape was due to an act of a stranger which the defendant could not reasonably have anticipated and guarded against. In *Box v Jubb*[139] the defendant's reservoir overflowed partly because of the acts of a neighbouring reservoir owner and for this reason the defendant escaped liability. The claimant also failed in his claim in *Rickards v Lothian*[140] where some third person deliberately blocked up the waste pipe of a toilet bowl in the defendant's premises, thereby flooding the claimant's premises. Unlike in negligence, where much rests on the nature of the third party's conduct, in *Rylands v Fletcher* it is irrelevant whether the stranger acted deliberately or only negligently.[141] This is because the basis of the defence is the absence of any control by the defendant over the acts of a stranger on his land.[142]

16-029   **Foreseeable act of a stranger**   To avail himself of this defence, the defendant must show that the escape was due to the unforeseeable act of a stranger without any negligence on his own part. This requirement was not satisfied in *Northwestern Utilities Ltd v London Guarantee and Accident Co Ltd*,[143] where gas that escaped from one of the defendants' mains ignited and destroyed a hotel. Although the immediate cause of the leak was the operations of the municipality in constructing a storm sewer, it was held that the defendants were nonetheless liable to the insurers of the building, since they ought to have foreseen the danger the city's operations represented and taken appropriate precautions. By contrast, in *Perry v Kendricks Transport Ltd*,[144] the owners of a disued coach were held not to be responsible for injuries the claimant suffered when a young boy threw a match into the petrol tank, since they could not reasonably have been expected to anticipate the boy's action.

16-030   **Meaning of "stranger"**   For the purposes of this defence a stranger is someone over whose activities the defendant had no control. The actions of trespassers clearly qualify,[145] as do actions off the defendant's land by persons beyond his control.[146]

---

[137] (1871) L.R. 6 Ex. 217 at 221–222. See also *Ross v Fedden* (1872) L.R. 7 Q.B. 661; *Blake v Woolf* [1898] 2 Q.B. 426; *Kiddle v City Business Properties Ltd* [1942] 1 K.B. 269.

[138] (1871) L.R. 6 Ex. 217 at 222.

[139] (1879) 4 Ex. D. 76

[140] [1913] A.C. 263.

[141] See, e.g., *Smith v Great Western Rly Co* (1926) 42 T.L.R. 391, where a third party's negligent act (failing to notice a defect in an oil tank) was held to be a good defence. cf. *Perry v Kendricks Transport Ltd* [1956] 1 W.L.R. 85 at 87.

[142] *Perry v Kendricks Transport Ltd* [1956] 1 W.L.R. 85 at 90.

[143] [1936] A.C. 108.

[144] [1956] 1 W.L.R. 85.

[145] *Mandraj v Texaco Trinidad Inc* (1969) 15 W.I.R. 251.

On the other hand those the defendant engages to do work on his behalf are not strangers, regardless of whether they be employees or independent contractors, as they are invited onto the defendant's premises, and he can order them to leave at any time.[147] In the closely related context of liability for fire it has been held that the occupier is liable for the fault of his licensees or guests unless the act is wholly alien to the licence or invitation[148] and this seems also to be the position more generally.

iii. Statutory Authority

A question of the proper construction of the statute The rule in *Rylands v Fletcher* may be excluded by statute. Whether it is so or not is a question of construction of the particular statute concerned. In *Green v Chelsea Waterworks Co*,[149] for instance, a main belonging to a waterworks company, which was authorised by Parliament to lay the main, burst without any negligence on the part of the company and the claimant's premises were flooded; the company was held not liable. Conversely, in *Charing Cross Electricity Co v Hydraulic Power Co*,[150] where the facts were similar, the defendants were held to have no exemption on the proper interpretation of the relevant statute. The distinction between the cases is that the Hydraulic Power Co were empowered by statute to supply water for industrial purposes, that is, they had permissive power but not a mandatory authority, and they were under no obligation to keep their mains charged with water at high pressure, or at all. By contrast, the Chelsea Waterworks Co were authorised by statute to lay mains and were under a statutory duty to maintain a continuous supply of water; it was an inevitable consequence that damage would be caused by occasional bursts and so by necessary implication the statute exempted them from liability where there was no "negligence".[151]

Where a statutory authority is under a mandatory obligation to supply a service, whether or not with a savings or nuisance clause (that nothing shall exonerate it from proceedings for nuisance), the authority is under no liability for anything expressly required by statute to be done, or reasonably incidental to that requirement, if it is done without negligence.[152] Where the statutory authority is merely permissive, with no clause imposing liability for nuisance, the authority is not liable for doing what the statute authorises, provided it is not negligent; but it is liable when there is a clause imposing liability for nuisance, even if it is not negligent.[153]

16-031

---

[146] See, e.g., *Box v Jubb* (1879) 4 Ex. D. 76.

[147] See *Balfour v Barty-King* [1957] 1 Q.B. 496 at 505–506 (contractors). See also *Hobbs (Farms) Ltd v Baxenden Chemical Co Ltd* [1992] 1 Lloyd's Rep. 54.

[148] See para.16-036.

[149] (1894) 70 L.T. 547.

[150] [1914] 3 K.B. 772.

[151] *Smeaton v Ilford Corp* [1954] Ch. 450 at 475–477. "Negligence" in this connection is not a very appropriate word for it means, "adopting a method which in fact results in damage to a third person, except in a case where there is no other way of performing the statutory duty": per Farwell J in *Provender Millers (Winchester) Ltd v Southampton CC* [1940] Ch. 131 at 140.

[152] *Department of Transport v NW Water Authority* [1984] A.C. 336.

[153] *Dunne v North Western Gas Board* [1964] 2 Q.B. 806 at 833–837.

16-032 **Burden of proof?**   One important question in this area awaits a final answer: if, on its proper construction, the statutory authority exempts the undertaker from *Rylands v Fletcher* liability and imposes only an obligation to use due care, upon whom does the burden of proof as to fault lie? Although a bare majority of the High Court of Australia held otherwise,[154] the better view is that it is up to the defendant to show that he took all reasonable care to prevent an escape. The statutory authority is dependent on the absence of negligence, and the burden of establishing the elements of a defence falls on the party prima facie liable.[155]

iv.   Act of God

16-033 **Extraordinary acts of nature**[156]   Where the escape is caused directly by natural causes without human intervention in "circumstances which no human foresight can provide against and of which human prudence is not bound to recognise the possibility",[157] the defence of act of God applies. This was recognised by Blackburn J in *Rylands v Fletcher*[158] itself and the defence was applied in *Nichols v Marsland*.[159] In this case the defendant for many years had been in possession of some artificial ornamental lakes formed by damming up a natural stream. An extraordinary rainfall, "greater and more violent than any within the memory of witnesses", broke down the artificial embankments and the rush of escaping water carried away four bridges in respect of which damage the claimant sued. Judgment was given for the defendant; the jury had found that she was not negligent and the court held that she ought not to be liable for an extraordinary act of nature which she could not reasonably anticipate and guard against.

16-034 **A restricted approach**   The ambit of the act of God defence is narrow, so much so that *Nichols v Marsland* appears to be the only domestic case in which it has operated to defeat an action under the rule.[160] In *Greenock Corp v Caledonian Railway Co*,[161] the House of Lords criticised its application in *Nichols v Marsland*, and cast doubt on the finding of facts by the jury in the earlier case.[162] The defendants in the *Greenock Corp* case constructed a concrete paddling pool for children in the bed of a stream and to do so they had to alter the course of the stream and obstruct the natural flow of the water. Owing to a rainfall of extraordinary violence, the stream overflowed at the pond, and a great volume of water, which would normally have been carried off by the stream, poured down a public street into the town and caused damage to the pursuers' property. The House of Lords held that the rainfall was not an act of God and that the defendants were liable. It was their duty "so to work as to make proprietors or occupiers on a lower level as secure

---

[154]   *Benning v Wong* (1969) 122 C.L.R. 249.
[155]   (1969) 122 C.L.R. 249 at 257–258.
[156]   Hall (1993) 13 O.J.L.S. 227.
[157]   *Tennent v Earl of Glasgow* (1864) 2 M. (HL) 22 at 26–27 per Lord Westbury, approved by the House of Lords in *Greenock Corp v Caledonian Railway Co* [1917] A.C. 556.
[158]   (1866) L.R. 1 Ex. 265 at 280.
[159]   (1876) 2 Ex. D. 1.
[160]   Though it was one of several grounds on which the claim in *Carstairs v Taylor* (1871) L.R. 6 Ex. 217 was dismissed. For a modern Irish decision applying the defence, see *Superquinn Ltd v Bray UDC* [1998] 3 I.R. 542.
[161]   [1917] A.C. 556.
[162]   [1917] A.C. 556 at 573–574, 575, 580–581.

against injury as they would have been had nature not been interfered with".[163] Similar considerations apply to an extraordinary high wind[164] and an extraordinary high tide.[165] Lightning, earthquakes, cloudbursts and tornadoes may be acts of God but there seems to be no English decision in which they have been involved. Finally, although the mere fact that it was physically possible to provide against the occurrence does not defeat a plea of act of God,[166] if reasonable precautions would have protected against the forces of providence the defence will not apply.[167]

v. Default of the Claimant

It is a defence to an action in *Rylands v Fletcher* that the claimant was wholly **16-035** to blame for the escape or the harm that resulted from it. If, for example, a person knows that there is a danger of his mine being flooded by his neighbour's operations on adjacent land, and courts the danger by doing some act which renders the flooding probable, he cannot complain.[168] So, too, in *Ponting v Noakes*,[169] the claimant's horse reached over the defendant's boundary, nibbled some poisonous tree there and died, and it was held that the claimant could recover nothing, for the damage was due to the horse's own intrusion. Where the claimant is merely contributorily negligent, the apportionment provisions of the Law Reform (Contributory Negligence) Act 1945 will apply.[170]

2. FIRE

A. Common Law

Winfield traced the history of the earlier forms of action available as remedies **16-036** for damage caused by the spread of fire.[171] The usual remedy was the special action of trespass on the case for negligently allowing one's fire to escape in contravention of the general custom of the realm which we first hear of in *Beaulieu v Finglam*.[172] The allegation in the action for fire that the defendant *tam negligenter ac improvide* "kept his fire that it escaped", referred to negligence in its older sense—one mode of committing a tort. Centuries later remedies became available under the rule in *Rylands v Fletcher*,[173] in nuisance,[174] and in negligence.[175]

---

163 [1917] A.C. 556 at 579 per Lord Shaw.
164 *Cushing v Walker & Sons* [1941] 2 All E.R. 693 at 695.
165 *Greenwood Tileries Ltd v Clapson* [1937] 1 All E.R. 765 at 772.
166 *Nichols v Marsland* (1875) L.R. 10 Ex. 255 at 258–259.
167 See *AMF International Ltd v Magnet Bowling Ltd* [1968] 1 W.L.R. 1028 at 1039.
168 *Lomax v Stott* (1870) 39 L.J. Ch. 834; *Dunn v Birmingham Canal Co* (1872) L.R. 7 Q.B. 244.
169 *Ponting v Noakes* [1894] 2 Q.B. 281; cf. *Cheater v Cater* [1918] 1 K.B. 247.
170 See Ch.23. For a contrary view, see *Burnie Port Authority v General Jones Pty Ltd* (1994) 179 C.L.R. 520 at 590.
171 Winfield (1931) 4 C.L.J. 203; Newark (1945) 6 N.I.L.Q. 134; Ogus [1969] C.L.J. 104.
172 (1401) Y.B. Pashc. 2 Hen. 4, f.18, pl.6, translated in Fifoot, *History and Sources of the Common Law: Tort and Contract* (1970), p.166.
173 *Jones v Festiniog Ry* (1866) L.R. 1 Ex. 265; *Powell v Fall* (1880) 5 Q.B.D. 597; *Musgrove v Pandelis* [1919] 2 K.B. 43; *Job Edwards Ltd v Birmingham Navigations* [1924] 1 K.B. 341 at 351–352; *Balfour v Barty-King* [1957] 1 Q.B. 496 at 505.
174 *Spicer v Smee* [1946] 1 All E.R. 489.
175 *Musgrove v Pandelis* [1919] 2 K.B. 43; *Job Edwards Ltd v Birmingham Navigations* [1924] 1 K.B. 341 at 361.

Exactly what "negligenter" meant can only be conjectured, for the old authorities are confused, but it certainly excluded liability where the fire spread or occurred (1) by the act of a stranger[176] over whom the defendant had no control, such as a trespasser,[177] and (2) by the act of nature. He is responsible for the default of his servant,[178] his guest[179] or one entering his house with his leave[180] and for his independent contractor,[181] unless the act done is wholly alien to the permission to enter. The second exception was established in *Tuberville v Stamp*,[182] where it was held that liability extended to a fire originating in a field as much as to one beginning in a house, but that if the defendant kindled it at a proper time and place and the violence of the wind carried it to his neighbour's land, that was fit to be given in evidence.

16-037 **Strict liability?** Although it is repeatedly said that at common law a person must keep his fire "at his peril", we cannot be sure that at any period in the history of the common law he was absolutely liable for the escape of his fire.[183] He is liable for damage done by his fire if it has been caused wilfully,[184] or by his negligence, or by the escape without negligence of a fire which has been brought into existence by some non-natural use of the land. In some cases, the latter type of liability could not strictly speaking be brought within the rule in *Rylands v Fletcher* in that the thing accumulated on the land did not itself escape. It was suggested that the rule had to be adapted so that the criterion of liability was: "Did the defendants ... bring to their land things likely to catch fire, and keep them there in such conditions that if they did ignite the fire would be likely to spread to the claimant's land?"[185] However, in *Stannard v Gore*[186] the Court of Appeal held that such an extension of the rule could no longer stand following the emphasis in *Transco Plc v Stockport MBC*[187] on, first, the need to re-state the principles of liability with certainty and, second, the requirement within those re-stated principles that it is the dangerous "thing" which has been brought on to the land which must have escaped. On this basis, the defendant can only be liable for a fire which he deliberately or negligently started on his land, or perhaps where fire is an "essential part" of the dangerous

---

[176] *Balfour v Barty-King* [1957] 1 Q.B. 496 at 504; *Tuberville v Stamp* (1697) 1 Ld. Raym. 264; 92 E.R. 671; *HN Emanuel Ltd v GLC* [1971] 2 All E.R. 835.

[177] Unless the occupier has knowledge of the fire and fails to take steps to extinguish it within a reasonable time.

[178] An employee acting outside the course of his employment is a stranger: *MacKenzie v McLeod* (1834) 10 Bing. 385; 131 E.R. 953.

[179] *Crogate v Morris* (1617) 1 Brownl. 197; *Iverson v Purser* (1990) 73 D.L.R. (4th) 33.

[180] *Ribee v Norrie* [2001] P.I.Q.R. P128.

[181] *Balfour v Barty-King* [1957] 1 Q.B. 496; *HN Emanuel Ltd v GLC* [1971] 2 All E.R. 835; *Johnson v BJW Property Developments Ltd* [2002] EWHC 1131 (TCC); [2002] 3 All E.R. 574; *Spicer v Smee* [1946] 1 All E.R. 489 (as explained in *Johnson*).

[182] (1697) 1 Ld. Raym. 264; 92 E.R. 671.

[183] Winfield (1926) 42 L.Q.R. 46.

[184] If the damage is intentional it is a trespass or assault, e.g., deliberately throwing a lighted match on a haystack or a lighted firework in a person's face.

[185] *Mason v Levy Auto Parts of England Ltd* [1967] 2 Q.B. 530 at 542 per MacKenna J. If the damage is to persons or goods on the property on which the fire starts the only liability is for negligence: *Johnson v BJW Property Developments Ltd* [2002] EWHC 1131 (TCC); [2002] 3 All E.R. 574 at [32].

[186] [2012] EWCA Civ 1248; [2014] Q.B. 1. See Steele and Merkin (2013) 25 J.E.L. 305.

[187] [2003] UKHL 61; [2004] 2 A.C. 1.

thing.[188] In *Stannard v Gore* itself the defendant ran a business fitting tyres and stored large quantities of them on his land. A fire which started in the electrical wiring of his workshop, without fault on the defendant's part, became hot enough to ignite the tyres and the more intense fire which resulted spread to and damaged the claimant's neighbouring property. The court that found that the defendant's use of his land was not non-natural and the quantity of tyres and the method of storing them did not amount to a dangerous thing in the sense that they were "likely to catch fire", but even if those requirements had been met, it was the fire which "escaped" and not the tyres. Ward LJ observed that only very rarely will damage caused by fire fall within the *Rylands v Fletcher* rule,[189] and the decision does indeed seem largely to emasculate the rule in this context, particularly when the now very restrictive approach to the non-natural use requirement is also weighed in the balance.

B. Statute

Fires beginning accidentally on the defendant's land The common law liability has been modified in respect of fires spreading from the defendant's land by s.86 of the Fires Prevention (Metropolis) Act 1774, which provides that no action shall be maintainable against anyone in whose building or on whose estate a fire shall accidentally begin. This section of the Act is of general application and is not limited to London.[190] In *Filliter v Phippard*[191] the word "accidentally" was interpreted restrictively so as to cover only "a fire produced by mere chance or incapable of being traced to any cause".[192] In other words, a fire caused by negligence[193] or due to a nuisance[194] will give rise to a cause of action. **16-038**

The immunity of a defendant under the statute is illustrated by *Collingwood v Home and Colonial Stores Ltd.*[195] A fire broke out on the defendants' premises and spread to those of the claimant. It originated in the defective condition of the electrical wiring on the defendants' premises but, as there was no negligence on their part, they were held not liable. Nor was the rule in *Rylands v Fletcher* applicable, for the installation of electric wiring, whether for domestic or trade purposes, was a reasonable and ordinary use of premises.[196] Where that rule is applicable, the Act of 1774 does not provide a defence and the defendant will be liable.[197]

---

[188] See e.g., Ward LJ's explanation in *Stannard v Gore* (at [36]) of *Jones v Festiniog Ry* (1866) L.R. 1 Ex. 265 as a readily understandable example of the rule in *Rylands v Fletcher*: "The dangerous thing which the defendant railway company brought onto their land was a steam engine which depended for its locomotion on the burning of coal, particles of which would be belched forth from its maw onto the haystack adjoining the railway line. Although the engine itself remained on the defendant's land the sparks, which were an essential part of the machine, escaped and the danger posed by such an escape was high and it was foreseeable" (emphasis added).

[189] [2012] EWCA Civ 1248; [2014] Q.B. 1 at [47].

[190] *Filliter v Phippard* (1847) 11 Q.B. 347 at 355.

[191] (1847) 11 Q.B. 347.

[192] (1847) 11 Q.B. 347 at 357 per Denman CJ.

[193] For example, *Mulholland and Tedd Ltd v Baker* [1939] 3 All E.R. 253 at 255 (liability in negligence and under the rule in *Rylands v Fletcher* when lit paper was inserted in a drainpipe to smoke out a rat, and the fire spread to a packing case and exploded a drum of paraffin).

[194] For example, *Spicer v Smee* [1946] 1 All E.R. 489 at 495 (owner liable in nuisance or negligence when defective electric wiring negligently installed by contractor caused fire; see the comments on this case in *Johnson v BJW Property Development Ltd* [2002] EWHC 1131 (TCC); [2002] 3 All E.R. 574 at [51]).

[195] (1936) 155 L.T. 550.

[196] cf. *Stannard v Gore* [2012] EWCA Civ 1248; [2014] Q.B. 1. Even if the fire is lit intentionally,

However, the statute does not confer protection on one who was not at fault so far as the origin of the fire is concerned but who was negligent in letting it spread. In *Musgrove v Pandelis*,[198] the claimant occupied rooms over a garage and let part of the garage to the defendant, who kept a car there. The defendant's employee, who had little skill as a chauffeur, started the engine of the car and without any fault on his part the petrol in the carburettor caught fire. If he had acted like any chauffeur of reasonable competence, he could have stopped the fire by turning off the tap connecting the petrol tank with the carburettor. He did not do so and the fire spread and damaged the claimant's property. The defendant was held liable, for the fire which did the damage was not that which broke out in the carburettor but that which spread to the car and this second or continuing fire did not "accidentally" begin.[199] The same principle applies where the origin of the fire lies in an act of nature so that in *Goldman v Hargrave*,[200] the statute provided no defence: the fire in the tree caused by the lightning strike was not the defendant's fault, but that which spread after his inadequate attempts to extinguish it was. The burden of proving such negligence is on the claimant: it is not for the defendant to prove that the fire was accidental.[201]

---

providing it is lit properly, there is no liability if it spreads without negligence and causes damage, for example a spark jumps out of an ordinary household fire and causes it to spread: *Sochacki v Sas* [1947] 1 All E.R. 344. It would be different, of course, if the fire were made too large for the grate.

[197] *Mason v Levy Auto Parts of England Ltd* [1967] 2 Q.B. 530 at 540–541. In *Stannard v Gore* [2012] EWCA Civ 1248; [2014] Q.B. 1, Lewison LJ concluded that s.86 defeated any claim in *Rylands v Fletcher* but this view was not shared by the other members of the court: cf. Etherton LJ at [71].

[198] [1919] 2 K.B. 43.

[199] See also *Sturge v Hackett* [1962] 1 W.L.R. 1257.

[200] [1967] 1 A.C. 645. See para.15-045.

[201] *Mason v Levy Auto Parts of England Ltd* [1967] 2 Q.B. 530 at 538.

CHAPTER 17

ANIMALS

Introduction[1] At common law a person might be liable for damage caused by an **17-001** animal on one or more of three distinct grounds, namely ordinary liability in tort, liability under the strict *scienter* rule[2] and liability for cattle trespass. The law was substantially modified with regard to the latter two forms of liability by the Animals Act 1971[3] but its structure is still in large measure the same and it is convenient to retain the common law headings for the purposes of exposition.[4]

1. ORDINARY LIABILITY IN TORT

There are many possible ways in which one may incur ordinary liability in tort **17-002** through the instrumentality of an animal under one's control, but the fact that the agent happens to be animate rather than inanimate is immaterial, for while the common law, like other legal systems, developed special or additional rules of liability for animals, it did not deny the applicability to them of general law.

Nuisance A good example of this is nuisance, for you can be liable for nuisance **17-003** through the agency of your animals, just as you can be for nuisance through the

---

[1] Williams, *Liability for Animals* (1939); North, *Civil Liability for Animals* (2012).
[2] This expression is properly confined to liability for animals which do not belong to a dangerous species, but is commonly used in the wider sense employed here.
[3] The 1971 Act was based on a Law Commission report: *Civil Liability for Animals*, Law Com. No.13 (1967). For an illuminating analysis of the Act, see Bagshaw in Arvind and Steele (eds), *Tort Law and the Legislature* (2012).
[4] For the previous law, see the eighth edition of this work, Ch.17, and Law Com. No.13 (1967).

agency of anything else you own. A person who keeps pigs too near his neighbour's house may commit a nuisance by smell, but that is not solely because they are pigs. He would commit a nuisance just as much if what he owned were a manure heap.[5] Indeed, nuisance may be the only appropriate remedy where there is no "escape" and where the animal is not dangerous, for example obstruction of the highway by large numbers of animals,[6] or stench from pigs[7] or the crowing of cockerels.[8] At one time there was no liability for the escape of noxious animals on the defendant's land in the ordinary course of nature, such as rabbits, rats or birds,[9] unless damage they caused to neighbouring owners was the result of "extra-ordinary, non-natural or unreasonable action".[10] However, it seems that the modern law follows the principle that a landowner may be required to take steps against a situation which is not attributable to his actions.[11]

17-004 **Other torts** Again, if a dog owner deliberately sets his dog on a peaceable citizen he is guilty of assault and battery in the ordinary way just as if he had flung a stone or hit him with a cudgel.[12] So, too, if a person teaches his parrot to slander anyone, that is neither more nor less the ordinary tort of defamation than if he prefers to say it with his own tongue rather than with the parrot's. Similarly, ordinary trespass can be committed by means of animals. Trespass by beasts so often takes the form of "cattle trespass" (with which we deal separately) that one does not meet with many ordinary actions for trespass in the reports. However an indirect example is *Paul v Summerhayes*[13] where fox hunters persisted in riding over the land of a farmer in spite of his protests and were held to have committed trespass.

17-005 **Negligence** Liability for animals may also be based on the ordinary rules of negligence.[14] The action for negligence for harm done through animals was quite distinct from both the cattle trespass rule and the *scienter* rule at common law[15] and now is distinct from the various forms of strict liability imposed by the Animals Act 1971.[16]

In one respect, however, the common law failed to extend the principles of negligence to cases involving animals. It was the rule for centuries that if animals

---

5   *Pitcher v Martin* [1937] 3 All E.R. 918 illustrates negligence and nuisance committed through the agency of a dog; *Farrer v Nelson* (1885) 15 Q.B.D. 258 nuisance through the agency of pheasants (distinguished in *Seligman v Docker* [1949] 1 Ch. 53).
6   *Cunningham v Whelan* (1917) 52 Ir. L.T. 67.
7   *Aldred's Case* (1610) 9 Co. 57b; 77 E.R. 816;; *Wheeler v JJ Saunders Ltd* [1996] Ch. 19.
8   *Leeman v Montagu* [1936] 2 All E.R. 1677.
9   *Brady v Warren* [1900] 2 I.R. 636 (rabbits); *Seligman v Docker* [1949] 1 Ch. 53 (wild pheasant increasing in numbers owing to favourable weather conditions).
10   *Farrer v Nelson* (1885) 15 Q.B.D. 258 at 260 (nuisance by unreasonable number of pheasants brought onto the land); *Peech v Best* [1931] 1 K.B. 1 at 14; *Seligman v Docker* [1949] 1 Ch. 53 at 61–63.
11   *Wandsworth LBC v Railtrack Plc* [2001] EWCA Civ 1236; [2002] Q.B. 756.
12   *Roberts v CC Kent* [2008] EWCA Civ 1588; [2009] Po L.R. 8 (where the action was justified under s.3 of the Criminal Law Act 1967).
13   (1878) 4 Q.B.D. 9. See also *League Against Cruel Sports v Scott* [1986] Q.B. 240.
14   *Fardon v Harcourt-Rivington* (1932) 146 L.T. 391 at 392; *Searle v Wallbank* [1947] A.C. 341 at 359–360.
15   See *Draper v Hodder* [1972] 2 Q.B. 556 (where a claim based upon *scienter* failed at the trial). Similarly, a claim might in some cases be founded upon the statutory variant of negligence created by the Occupiers' Liability Act 1957.
16   *Jones v Whippey* [2009] EWCA Civ 452; *Addis v Campbell* [2011] EWCA Civ 906.

(or at least, ordinary tame animals) strayed from adjacent land onto the highway neither the owner of the animals nor the occupier of the land was liable for any ensuing damage even though it could have been prevented by controlling the animal or by fencing.[17] This immunity was abolished by s.8 of the Animals Act 1971, so that where damage is caused by animals straying on the highway the question of liability is now to be decided in accordance with the ordinary principles of negligence. It is provided, however, that if a person has a right to place animals on unfenced land, he is not to be regarded as in breach of a duty of care by reason only of his placing them there, so long as the land is in an area where fencing is not customary or is common land or a town or village green.[18] It is important to note that the Act does not require all landowners to fence against the highway: in moorland areas this would be an intolerable burden and in such areas a motorist must be expected to be on the look-out for straying livestock. That is not to say that the burden imposed by s.8 is trivial: the Court of Appeal has held that the duty of care of the farmer extends to guarding against the carelessness of hikers lawfully on his land, and may require the provision of stiles, so enabling a stock gate to be secured.[19] Furthermore, there are situations in which the escape of animals attracts strict liability under s.2(2).[20]

2. LIABILITY FOR DANGEROUS ANIMALS

Animals Act 1971   At common law the keeper of an animal was strictly liable, **17-006** independently of negligence, for damage done by the animal if: (1) the animal was *ferae naturae* (i.e., belonged to a dangerous species); or (2) the animal was *mansuetae naturae* (i.e., did not belong to a dangerous species) but he knew of its vicious characteristics. These forms of strict liability have been retained by the Animals Act 1971 and, though they have been subjected to considerable modification, some of the old learning may continue to be relevant. It is, however, important to remember that the law is now to be found in the words of the Act and these must always prevail.[21]

No escape or attack necessary   For the purpose of imposing liability animals are **17-007** divided into two categories of dangerousness but, with regard to both, the 1971 Act, unlike the common law,[22] contains no requirement that the animal must escape from

---

[17]   *Searle v Wallbank* [1947] A.C. 341. The immunity had no application where the animal was brought onto the highway and then got out of control: *Gomberg v Smith* [1963] 1 Q.B. 25.

[18]   Section 8(2). Like many "by reason only" exceptions, this subsection is a fertile source of difficulties. Even without it, the owner would not be liable by reason only of placing his animals there, for there would have to be sufficient traffic to create a serious danger. The subsection was applied in *Davies v Davies* [1975] Q.B. 172 but the case turned largely on the right of a commoner to license others to graze animals.

[19]   *Wilson v Donaldson* [2004] EWCA Civ 972.

[20]   See para.17-010.

[21]   The Guard Dogs Act 1975 governs the keeping of guard dogs and the Dangerous Dogs Act 1991 controls the breeding and keeping of fighting dogs or other dogs appearing to the Secretary of State to have the same characteristics. The first does not impose civil liability (s.5(2)(a)). The second is silent on the point. No doubt certain contraventions of either Act would be almost conclusive evidence of negligence, e.g., the condition of muzzling in s.1(2)(d) of the 1991 Act.

[22]   *Behrens v Bertram Mills Circus Ltd* [1957] 2 Q.B. 1; *Fitzgerald v AD and EH Cooke Bourne Farms Ltd* [1964] 1 Q.B. 249 at 270; Williams, *Liability for Animals* (1939), p.341.

control, nor that there must be any sort of attack.[23] If, therefore, an elephant slips or stumbles or a cow known to be prone to escape stands stock still in the road and is struck by a car,[24] the strict liability imposed by the Act will apply.

A.   Animals Belonging to a Dangerous Species

17-008 **Dangerous species**   Under s.2(1) of the 1971 Act, where any damage is caused by an animal which belongs to a dangerous species, any person who is a keeper of the animal is liable for the damage.[25] A dangerous species is defined as[26]:

> "[A] species[27] (a) which is not commonly domesticated in the British Islands and (b) whose fully grown animals normally have such characteristics that they are likely, unless restrained, to cause severe damage or that any damage they may cause is likely to be severe."

A number of points arise on this definition. First, it seems that, as was the case at common law, in classifying animals as *ferae naturae*, the question of whether an animal belongs to a dangerous species is one of law. It is therefore to be expected that where an animal had been classified as *ferae naturae* at common law it will be regarded as belonging to a dangerous species under the Act (for example a lion,[28] an elephant[29] and at least certain types of monkeys).[30] In two respects, however, the definition is wider than at common law in that the Act: (1) renders a species dangerous if it poses a threat to property;[31] and (2) allows for a species to be considered dangerous if it is not commonly domesticated in Britain, even though it may be so domesticated overseas.[32]

Secondly it remains the case that once a species has been judicially classified as dangerous, then, subject to the doctrine of precedent, there is no room for distinctions based upon the fact that some variants or individual animals within the species may not in fact be at all dangerous. In other words, the law ignores "the world of difference between the wild elephant in the jungle and the trained elephant in the

---

[23] *Wallace v Newton* [1982] 1 W.L.R. 375. cf. *Smith v Ainger, The Times,* 5 June 1990 (no abnormal characteristic).

[24] *McKenny v Foster* [2008] EWCA Civ 173 (though the claim failed for want of knowledge of the relevant characteristic); *Williams v Hawkes* [2017] EWCA Civ 1846; [2018] R.T.R. 16 at [38]. There is an obvious tension with s.8 (para.17-005), which is based on negligence.

[25] Section 2(1). For the definition of "keeper", see para.17-009.

[26] Section 6(2).

[27] By s.11 "species" includes sub-species and variety: see further para.17-011.

[28] *Murphy v Zoological Society of London* [1962] C.L.Y. 68.

[29] *Behrens v Bertram Mills Circus Ltd* [1957] 2 Q.B. 1.

[30] Hale 1 P.C. 101. cf. *Brooke v Cooke* (1961) 105 S.J. 684. As to other animals, see Williams, *Liability for Animals* (1939), pp.292–294. The Dangerous Wild Animals Act 1976 provides for a system of licensing of keepers of dangerous wild animals. Such animals are those listed in the Schedule to the Act and it is thought that such listing would be almost conclusive on the issue of whether the animal belonged to a dangerous species under the 1971 Act (none of the listed animals appears to be commonly domesticated here). Omission from the list should not, however, be particularly persuasive that the animal is not dangerous under the 1971 Act; some species were omitted because it was not thought likely that any attempt would be made to keep them privately (HL Vol. 371 col.1180).

[31] The definition of "damage" in s.11 is not exhaustive, and clearly includes damage to property.

[32] Thus a camel is dangerous under the Act, though not *ferae naturae* at common law: *Tutin v Chipperfield Promotions Ltd* (1980) 130 N.L.J. 807, not following *McQuaker v Goddard* [1940] 1 K.B. 687 (which probably applied the wrong test at common law, anyway).

circus ... [which] is in fact no more dangerous than a cow".[33] Furthermore, the 1971 Act clearly adopts as the test of danger either "the greater risk of harm" or "the risk of greater harm": an elephant may not in fact be very likely to get out of control and do damage but, if it does so, its bulk gives it a great capacity for harm.

Keeper   For the purposes of this form of liability a person is a "keeper" of the   **17-009**
animal if[34]:

> "(a) [H]e owns the animal or has it in his possession or (b) he is the head of a household of which a member under the age of 16 owns the animal or has it in his possession and if at any time an animal ceases to be owned by or to be in the possession of a person, any person who immediately before that time was a keeper thereof ... continues to be a keeper of the animal until another person becomes a keeper thereof ..."

B.   Other Animals

Section 2(2) of the 1971 Act provides: **17-010**

> "Where damage is caused by an animal which does not belong to a dangerous species, a keeper[35] of the animal is liable for the damage if:
>
> (a)   the damage is of a kind which the animal, unless restrained, was likely to cause or which, if caused by the animal, was likely to be severe; and
>
> (b)   the likelihood of the damage or of its being severe was due to characteristics of the animal which are not normally found in animals of the same species or are not normally so found except at particular times or in particular circumstances; and
>
> (c)   those characteristics were known to that keeper or were at any time known to a person who at that time had charge of the animal as that keeper's servant or, where that keeper is the head of a household, were known to another keeper of the animal who is a member of that household and under the age of sixteen."

The purpose of this rather complex provision is to preserve a liability akin to the old rule of *scienter* liability for tame animals: while you are strictly liable in any case for damage done by your tiger you are only strictly liable for damage done by your dog or your horse if you have knowledge of some special dangerous characteristic.[36] This provision has come before the courts more frequently than other parts of the Act and has proved troublesome, as witnessed by the fact that it produces a regular stream of appellate decisions.[37]

---

[33]   *Behrens v Bertram Mills Circus Ltd* [1957] 2 Q.B. 1 at 14. However, it is not clear to what extent the common law was prepared to distinguish among sub-species and the same problem arises under the Act: see para.17-011.

[34]   1971 Act s.6(3). It is provided, however, by s.6(4) that where an animal is taken into and kept in possession for the purpose of preventing it from causing damage or of restoring it to its owner, a person is not a keeper of it by virtue only of that possession.

[35]   One keeper may be liable to another keeper: *Flack v Hudson* [2001] Q.B. 698 (owner liable to bailee/ rider of horse who did not know of its characteristics).

[36]   The old *scienter* rule might be regarded as a primitive form of negligence under which the defendant was, subject to certain defences, irrebuttably presumed to be negligent in keeping the animal after he discovered its character. There is now liability for negligence under the general law but there is no doubt that the defendant may be liable under s.2(2) even if he is not negligent (in the modern sense) on the occasion in question: *Curtis v Betts* [1990] 1 W.L.R. 459.

[37]   "Unfortunately the language of section 2(2) is... opaque ... Over the years section 2(2) has attracted much judicial obloquy": *Mirvahedy v Henley* [2003] UKHL 16; [2003] 2 A.C. 491 at [9] per

17-011 **Range of animals covered** The first problem is the range of animals to which s.2(2) of the 1971 Act applies. Common experience shows that, say, rottweilers are a good deal fiercer than spaniels, but it has been stated in the Court of Appeal (though the point was not argued) in a case concerning a bull mastiff that the category is "dogs",[38] the generality of which could not possibly be said to belong to a dangerous species under s.2(1). However, the Act defines "species" as including "sub-species and variety"[39] and it has been held in the rather different context of determining what are "abnormal characteristics" under s.2(2)(b) that the proper comparators are other dogs of that breed.[40] However, even in the case of dogs of a breed commonly perceived to be fierce the argument that they are covered by s.2(1) would nearly always be defeated by the condition in that subsection requiring that such animals are not commonly[41] domesticated here.[42] Once it has been determined whether s.2(2) applies at all, it is necessary to consider each of the requirements in turn.

17-012 **Damage: s.2(2)(a)** Paragraph (a) follows the pattern of s.2(1) of the 1971 Act in adopting the likelihood (which means the foreseeable likelihood)[43] of damage or likelihood that any damage that may be caused will be severe. The second limb of this is not to be read as imposing any requirement that the likelihood that the damage will be severe must be related to any abnormality in the animal. Alsatians are powerful dogs and, if a member of that breed does bite someone, it is likely that the injury will be severe[44]: it is unnecessary to show that the particular Alsatian is unusually large or has unusually big teeth.[45] Paragraph (a) has given rise to comparatively little difficulty.[46] It seems plain that something can be "likely" even though it does not reach the level of being "more likely than not" but it is not clear exactly how far down the scale of probability we can go: perhaps we can do no better than say that the damage (or, where relevant, its severity) is something which "might well happen"[47] or which is "reasonably to be expected".[48] One might break one's neck by falling downstairs after tripping over an escaped pet dormouse[49] but

---

Lord Nicholls; "The drafting ... is grotesque": *Turnbull v Warrener* [2012] EWCA Civ 412; [2012] P.I.Q.R. P16 at [4] per Maurice Kay LJ; "[T]he wording of the section is marked by both linguistic and conceptual obscurity": *Williams v Hawkes* [2017] EWCA Civ 1846; [2018] R.T.R. 16 at [4] per Davis LJ.

[38] *Curtis v Betts* [1990] 1 W.L.R. 459 at 462.

[39] Section 11.

[40] *Hunt v Wallis*, *The Times,* 10 May 1991. Indeed, this was in effect the approach to the same issue in *Curtis v Betts* [1990] 1 W.L.R. 459.

[41] Presumably, however, the test of whether a breed is commonly domesticated here would not be satisfied by showing that there were a tiny number here all kept as pets.

[42] If it be the case that there is a species (or sub-species or variety) which: (1) normally and in all circumstances has dangerous characteristics; and (2) is commonly domesticated here there would seem to be an illogical gap in the legislation since such animals fall under neither subsection.

[43] *Curtis v Betts* [1990] 1 W.L.R. 459 at 469.

[44] Note that the actual injury suffered does not have to be severe.

[45] *Curtis v Betts* [1990] 1 W.L.R. 459.

[46] But see the difference of opinion in the Court of Appeal in *Turnbull v Warrener* [2012] EWCA Civ 412; [2012] P.I.Q.R. P16.

[47] One of the interpretations offered by Neill LJ in *Smith v Ainger*, *The Times,* 5 June 1990.

[48] Lord Scott's preference in *Mirvahedy v Henley* [2003] UKHL 16; [2003] 2 A.C. 491 at [95]; but he thought this meant much the same as Neill LJ's suggestion. He did not accept Neill LJ's alternative of "such as might happen".

[49] Lord Scott's example in *Mirvahedy v Henley* [2003] UKHL 16; [2003] 2 A.C. 491 at [95].

no one would suggest that a dormouse was likely to cause death or injury. Conversely, the requirement was satisfied where a Charolais steer escaped on to a dual carriageway, because of the size and weight of the animal,[50] and the same was conceded where horses had entered the highway.[51]

Abnormal characteristics: s.2(2)(b) Paragraph (b) has been the source of the **17-013** problems under s.2(2) of the 1971 Act.[52] The first limb deals with the straightforward case where the animal has "permanent" characteristics which depart from the norm of the species, for example a dog which has a propensity to attack humans in all situations and without discrimination; the second limb is a further, alternative, basis for a claim and imposes liability for damage caused by characteristics which may be normal to the species but only manifest themselves at particular times or in particular circumstances, for example a bitch being aggressive when she has pups[53] or a breed of dog having a tendency aggressively to defend its "territory".[54] In other words, "in such a case the animal's normal behaviour in abnormal circumstances is equated with a more vicious [animal's] abnormal behaviour in normal circumstances".[55]

Mirvahedy v Henley In the leading case of *Mirvahedy v Henley*[56] horses owned **17-014** by the defendants were terrified at night by persons unknown, broke down the fence and galloped onto a dual carriageway where one of them collided with the claimant's car, causing him injury. Horses are not normally in a state of mindless panic but they will be when they are frightened and, for the majority of the House of Lords, their being frightened was "particular circumstances" for the purposes of the second limb of s.2(2)(b).[57] There is[58]:

"[A]n implicit assumption of fact in section 2(2) that domesticated animals are not normally dangerous. But the purpose of paragraph (b) is to make provision for those that are. It deals with two specific categories where that assumption of fact is falsified. The first is that of an animal which is possessed of a characteristic, not normally found in animals of the same species, which makes it dangerous. The second is an animal which, although belonging to a species which does not normally have dangerous characteristics, nevertheless has dangerous characteristics at particular times or in particular circumstances. The essence of these provisions is the falsification of the assumption, in

---

50 *Williams v Hawkes* [2017] EWCA Civ 1846; [2018] R.T.R. 16 at [35].
51 *Mirvahedy v Henley* [2003] UKHL 16; [2003] 2 A.C. 491 (though Lord Scott reserved his opinion on this issue).
52 It is not in the same form as the Law Commission's original draft: see *Mirvahedy v Henley* [2003] UKHL 16; [2003] 2 A.C. 491 at [37].
53 *Barnes v Lucille Ltd* (1907) 96 L.T. 680 (common law).
54 *Curtis v Betts* [1990] 1 W.L.R. 459. See also *Cummings v Grainger* [1977] Q.B. 397.
55 *Mirvahedy v Henley* [2003] UKHL 16; [2003] 2 A.C. 491 at [142] per Lord Walker.
56 [2003] UKHL 16; [2003] 2 A.C. 491.
57 Similarly, a horse which bucked when alarmed: *Goldsmith v Patchcott* [2012] EWCA Civ 183; [2012] P.I.Q.R. P11 (irrelevant that the bucking may have been more violent than anticipated); a horse which refused to respond to instructions given through a bitless bridle with which it was unfamiliar: *Turnbull v Warrener* [2012] EWCA Civ 412; [2012] P.I.Q.R. P16; and a steer which behaved erratically after being spooked by various adverse stimuli, including the lights and noise of cars on a road: *Williams v Hawkes* [2017] EWCA Civ 1846; [2018] R.T.R. 16. cf. *Freeman v Higher Park Farm* [2008] EWCA Civ 1185; [2009] P.I.Q.R. P6.
58 *Mirvahedy v Henley* [2003] UKHL 16; [2003] 2 A.C. 491 at [71] per Lord Hobhouse.

the first because of the departure of the individual from the norm for its species, in the second because of the introduction of special factors."

The rival, unsuccessful interpretation, that the "second limb" is not an alternative basis of liability but merely explains the basic requirement of abnormality by recognising that in some circumstances even placid animals will react dangerously, is less consistent with the statutory wording but may be thought to reflect better policy, bearing in mind that the law of negligence is available as a fallback. Suppose, for example, that a road accident is caused by a panic-stricken deer which has escaped from a deer park. Although there are deer parks, deer are presumably not commonly domesticated in this country, yet it would be impossible to say that deer in general satisfied the requirement of a dangerous species as defined in s.6(2)(b). Yet, on the basis that the owner of this particular deer can hardly deny that he knows that deer may panic on the highway at night, we have[59]:

"[T]he paradoxical situation in which on the one hand deer are removed by section 6(2)(b) from being categorised as a 'dangerous species' but on the other hand an individual deer may impose strict liability on its keeper under section 2(2)(b) for damage caused by behaviour entirely normal for the species."

17-015 **Assessment** As things stand, the owner of the animal is in danger of finding himself in a cleft stick: either the behaviour was abnormal by the general standards of the species or, even if it was normal in that sense, the behaviour was produced by the particular circumstances. Suppose, for example, that the claimant kicks a dog and the dog bites him. The owner can hardly be heard to deny that he knew that dogs are likely to bite when they are kicked, as a propensity to bite is a characteristic found in dogs in the particular circumstances of being kicked and therefore the requirements of para.(b) are fulfilled. Of course in such a case the owner would not be *liable*, for it is a defence to show that the damage was wholly due to the fault of the claimant[60] but it seems strange to treat the animal as "dangerous" in the first place.[61] It seems that once one attempts to bring in some cases where the ordinary or average animal of the species would behave in that way, s.2(2) becomes very difficult to operate, even more so when it is held that "normally" in s.2(2)(b) is to be read in the sense of "natural" or "conforming to type" even though on most occasions such animals would have reacted differently.[62] It would be better either to abandon it and to make liability for domesticated animals turn on negligence in the keeper or to have a simple, general rule of strict liability for damage done by animals.[63] The latter might be justified on the ground that, while no one would regard a horse or a dog as presenting the same risk as a tiger, yet they have "minds of their own" and are prone to behave unpredictably.[64]

---

59 *Mirvahedy v Henley* [2003] UKHL 16; [2003] 2 A.C. 491 at [117] per Lord Scott.
60 See para.17-017. See *Nelms v CC Avon & Somerset* unreported 9 February 1993 CA.
61 See Lord Scott's example at [115] in *Mirvahedy* of the police horse attacked by a demonstrator and the horse's defensive kick connecting with someone other than the attacker.
62 *Welsh v Stokes* [2007] EWCA Civ 796; [2008] 1 W.L.R. 1224; cf. *Freeman v Higher Park Farm* [2008] EWCA Civ 1185; [2009] P.I.Q.R. P6.
63 Such is French law: art.1243, Code Civil; but German law, while imposing strict liability for pets does not apply this to "working" animals.
64 A consultation process by the Department for Environment Food and Rural Affairs in 2009 did not lead to any concrete proposals for reform.

Knowledge of the keeper: s.2(2)(c)[65]   The strict liability under s.2(2) of the 1971   **17-016**
Act only arises if the characteristics of the animal were known to the keeper under
para.(c). The requirement of knowledge is clearly of "actual" rather than of
constructive knowledge,[66] though a person who ought to know of his animal's vicious characteristics may, of course, still be liable for negligence. Where the claim
is based on the second limb of s.2(2)(b), the situation where the characteristic is
common in the species in particular circumstances, it is sufficient that the keeper
knows that animals of that type may react in the way which led to the damage: he
does not need to have additional knowledge about the particular animal.[67] However,
where the individual animal displays a common characteristic which would not
normally be dangerous in such an exaggerated form as to make it so, the defendant will not be liable if he does not know of this particular propensity.[68] In some
cases the knowledge of an employee of the keeper, or of a person under the age of
16 in the keeper's household, will fulfil the requirement of knowledge under
para.(c). Furthermore, if, for example, the keeper's spouse knew of the animal's
propensities it may be proper for the court to infer that the keeper also knew of
them.[69]

C. Defences

Conduct of the claimant   Under s.5(1) of the 1971 Act it is a defence to an ac-   **17-017**
tion brought under s.2 that the damage was wholly due to the fault of the person
suffering it.[70] By definition, this defence is inapplicable where the fault of both the
claimant and the keeper is causative,[71] though in such a case the partial defence of
contributory negligence will apply.[72]

Under s.5(2) it is a defence that the person suffering damage voluntarily assumed the risk of it (though a person employed as an employee by a keeper of the
animal is not to be treated as accepting voluntarily risks incidental to his
employment).[73] Although s.5(2) no doubt reflects the common law defence of

---

65 The definition of "keeper" for this head of liability is the same as that for animals belonging to a
   dangerous species, i.e., the owner or the person in possession. See the appeal in *Hole v Ross-
   Skinner* [2003] EWCA Civ 774, which seems to have been pursued solely to absolve the possessor
   from negligence and allow him to seek contribution against the owner.
66 *Chauhan v Paul* [1998] C.L.Y. 3990. There is nothing in the Act to support the view that he must
   know, at the time of the incident, of the circumstances which bring the characteristic into play. The
   damage must be attributable to the characteristics referred to in para.(b): if the keeper knows that
   the animal becomes aggressive in certain conditions he is liable if a bite is inflicted in those conditions, but not for an unexpected attack in quite different conditions: *Curtis v Betts* [1990] 1 W.L.R.
   459; but if a dog is prone to attack other dogs but not humans there may still be a likelihood of injury
   to a human being, namely the owner of the other dog: *Smith v Ainger, The Times,* 5 June 1990.
67 *Welsh v Stokes* [2007] EWCA Civ 796; [2008] 1 W.L.R. 1224.
68 *McKenny v Foster* [2008] EWCA Civ 173 (cow so distressed at being separated from her weaned
   calf that she was able to leap a six-bar gate and a 12ft cattle grid).
69 As in *Gladman v Johnson* (1867) 36 L.J.C.P. 153.
70 *Nelms v CC Avon & Somerset* unreported 9 February 1993, CA, where the claimant kicked the dog.
   A person who ignores police warnings to come out and who is then bitten by a police dog brings
   his injury upon himself: *Dhesi v Chief Constable of the West Midlands, The Times,* 9 May 2000.
71 *Turnbull v Warrener* [2012] EWCA Civ 412; [2012] P.I.Q.R. P16. In some cases both defences may
   apply: *Smith v Harding,* unreported 26 November 2013, Manchester CC.
72 Section 10.
73 Section 6(5). So if the lion tamer is eaten by the lion, his dependants can sue. cf. *Canterbury CC v
   Howletts & Port Lympne Estates Ltd* [1997] I.C.R. 925.

volenti non fit injuria, it is to be interpreted according to the ordinary meaning of the words used.[74] The defence is engaged where the claimant has assumed the relevant *type* of risk. Thus, in *Goldsmith v Patchcott*[75] the claimant was aware of the risk that the horse she was riding would rear and buck if startled and s.5(2) applied even though the particularly violent bucking which occurred was not foreseen.

17-018   **Injury to trespassers**   There is special provision for injury to trespassers by dangerous animals. Section 5(3) of the 1971 Act provides that a person is not liable under s.2 for any damage by an animal kept on any premises or structure[76] to a person trespassing there, if it is proved either: (1) that the animal was not kept there for the protection[77] of persons or property; or (2) (if the animal was kept there for the protection of persons or property) that keeping it there for that purpose was not unreasonable. It would seem unreasonable to protect your premises with a lion or a cobra, but not, perhaps, with a fierce dog.[78] This subsection does not, of course, affect any liability for negligence which the defendant may incur qua occupier of the premises or keeper of the animal, but it is thought that the keeping of guard dogs is not per se inconsistent with the occupier's duty to trespassers,[79] provided at least some warning of their presence is given.

3.   LIABILITY FOR STRAYING LIVESTOCK

17-019   **Common law**   At common law the possessor of "cattle"[80] was strictly liable, independently of *scienter*, for damage done by them when they trespassed on the land of his neighbour. Whatever may have been the original rationale of this form of liability, it was certainly not the same as that of *scienter*, for agricultural animals present no peculiar risk. However, the Law Commission recommended the retention of strict liability for this type of harm on the ground that it provided a simple method of allocating liability for what were usually comparatively small damages.[81] The law was, however, in need of considerable modification and the modern form of "cattle trespass" is found in s.4 of the 1971 Act.

17-020   **Animals Act 1971 s.4**   Section 4 of the 1971 Act provides:

> "(1)   Where livestock[82] belonging[83] to any person strays[84] on to land in the ownership or occupation of another and—

---

74   *Freeman v Higher Park Farm* [2008] EWCA Civ 1185; [2009] P.I.Q.R. P6.

75   [2012] EWCA Civ 183; [2012] P.I.Q.R. P11.

76   Not necessarily animals owned by or kept by the occupier.

77   This probably does not have to be a dominant purpose. Thus the old lady who keeps a dog partly for companionship and partly for protection would fail on (1), though her conduct would certainly be reasonable under (2).

78   So held in *Cummings v Grainger* [1977] Q.B. 397: "True it was a fierce dog. But why not? A gentle dog would be no good. The thieves would soon make friends with him": at 405 per Lord Denning MR. Since 1975 it is an offence to have a guard dog roaming about the premises unless under the control of a handler: Guard Dogs Act 1975. It has been suggested that contravention might make the keeping unreasonable under the 1971 Act: *Cummings v Grainger* [1977] Q.B. 397 at 406.

79   See para.10-038.

80   "Cattle" or avers was a class virtually identical with livestock under the Act: see Williams, *Liability for Animals* (1939), pp.2–3.

81   Law Com. No.13 (1967), paras 62–63.

82   Defined in s.11 as, "cattle, horses, asses, mules, hinnies, sheep, pigs, goats and poultry [which is further defined as the domestic varieties of fowls, turkeys, geese, ducks, guinea-fowls, pigeons,

(a) damage is done by livestock to the land or to any property on it which is in the ownership or possession of the other person or

(b) any expenses[85] are reasonably incurred by that other person in keeping the livestock while it cannot be restored to the person to whom it belongs or while it is detained in pursuance of section 7 of [the] Act,[86] or in ascertaining to whom it belongs;

the person to whom the livestock belongs is liable for the damage or expenses, except as otherwise provided by [the] Act."

The reference in s.4(1)(a) to "damage ... to the land or to any property on it" makes it clear that damages are not recoverable for personal injuries under this section, as they had been under the common law rule.[87] However, with regard to property damage, the range of potential claimants and their claimable losses is rather wider than at common law.

A. Defences

Conduct of the claimant The 1971 Act provides that there is no liability under   **17-021**
this head for damage which is due wholly to the fault of the person suffering it[88] and that contributory negligence is a partial defence.[89] In this context default of the claimant is often closely bound up with fencing obligations and the Act therefore provides that damage shall not be treated as due to the fault of the claimant "by reason only that he could have prevented it by fencing", but also that the defendant is not liable "where it is proved that the straying of the livestock on to the land would not have occurred but for a breach by any other person, being a person having an interest in the land, of a duty to fence."[90]

Lawful use of the highway One other common law defence is preserved by the   **17-022**
1971 Act: the defendant is not liable under this form of liability if his livestock strayed on to the claimant's property from the highway and its presence there was a lawful use[91] of the highway.[92] *Tillet v Ward* illustrates the principle.[93] D owned an ox which, while his servants were driving it with due care through a town, entered the shop of C, an ironmonger, through an open door. It took three-quarters of an

---

83 By s.4(2) livestock belongs to the person in whose possession it is.
84 The marginal note to s.4 refers to "trespassing", but the enacting words do not. "Stray" is probably wide enough to cover the facts of *Ellis v Loftus Iron Co* [1874] L.R. 10 C.P. 10 and *Wiseman v Booker* (1878) 3 C.P.D. 184.
85 A local authority operating a pound for animals straying on its land may properly impose a standard charge: *Morris v Blaenau Gwent DC* (1982) 80 L.G.R. 793.
86 See para.17-024.
87 *Wormald v Cole* [1954] 1 Q.B. 614.
88 Section 5(1).
89 Section 10.
90 Section 5(6). The law relating to the obligation to fence is notoriously complex and the Law Commission thought it inappropriate to deal with it other than by providing a relatively simple rule: Law Com. No.13 (1967), fn.98. It should be noted that there is no requirement under s.5(6) that the duty in question be owed to the defendant.
91 Hence, the defence is inapplicable if the animals had been allowed to stray on to the highway: *Matthews v Wicks, The Times,* 25 May 1987.
92 Section 5(5). This does not, of course, remove any liability for negligence in such a case: *Gayler and Pope Ltd v Davies & Son Ltd* [1924] 2 K.B. 75.
93 (1882) 10 Q.B.D. 17.

The text at the top of the footnotes reads: peacocks and quails] and also deer not in the wild state".

hour to get it out and meanwhile it did some damage. D was held not liable to X, for this was one of the inevitable risks of driving cattle on the streets. It would have made no difference if the ironmonger's door had been shut instead of open, and the ox had pushed its way through, or had gone through a plate-glass window.[94]

B. Detention and Sale of Straying Livestock

17-023 **Common law** The common law provided a form of self-help remedy to a person harmed by straying livestock by way of distress damage feasant.[95] The Law Commission concluded that some remedy of this type should be retained but considered that the old remedy was so hedged about with limitations (in particular, it provided no power of sale) and obscurities that it should be replaced. Under s.7 of the 1971 Act the right of distress damage feasant is therefore abolished in relation to animals and is replaced by a new statutory right.[96]

17-024 **Statutory right of detention** The occupier of land may detain any livestock which has strayed on to his land and which is not then under the control of any person.[97] The right to detain the livestock ceases[98] at the end of a period of 48 hours (unless within that period the detainer gives notice of the detention to the police and, if he knows the person to whom the livestock belongs, to that person), or when the detainer is tendered sufficient money to satisfy any claim he may have for damage and expenses in respect of the straying livestock,[99] or if he has no such claim when the person to whom the livestock belongs claims it.[100] The detainer is liable for any damage caused to the livestock by failure to treat it with reasonable care and supply it with adequate food and water.[101]

17-025 **Statutory right of sale** Where the livestock has been rightfully detained for not less than 14 days, the person detaining it may sell it at a market or by public auction, unless proceedings are then pending for the return of the livestock or for any claim for damages done by it or expenses incurred in detaining it.[102] Where the net proceeds of sale exceed the amount of any claim the detainer may have for damages and expenses, the excess is recoverable from him by the person who would be entitled to the livestock but for the sale.[103]

---

[94] *Gayler and Pope Ltd v Davies & Son Ltd* [1924] 2 K.B. 75. The driver of beasts which stray without his fault into property adjoining the highway is entitled to enter the property in order to get them out, and for that purpose he must be allowed such time as is reasonable in the circumstances: *Goodwin v Cheveley* (1895) 28 L.J. Ex. 298.
[95] See Williams, *Liability for Animals* (1939), Pt I.
[96] Section 7(1). The right is abolished for all animals and the new remedy applies only in the case of livestock.
[97] Section 7(2). The latter requirement was also a condition of the exercise of the common law right and is designed to prevent breaches of the peace.
[98] In the absence of a request for the return of the livestock, however, the detainer will not necessarily be liable for conversion.
[99] i.e., under s.4.
[100] Section 7(3).
[101] Section 7(6).
[102] Section 7(4).
[103] Section 7(5).

4. REMOTENESS OF DAMAGE AND STRICT LIABILITY UNDER THE 1971 ACT

Common law At common law both forms of *scienter* liability and cattle trespass   **17-026**
had close affinities with *Rylands v Fletcher* and were probably governed by the
remoteness principle applicable to that rule—was the consequence a "natural" one,
a question of causation. There were, however, at least two exceptions to the generality of this principle. First, in the case of *scienter* liability for animals *mansuetae
naturae*, the keeper was only liable if the animal caused some harm of the kind to
be expected from its known vicious characteristics;[104] secondly, in the case of cattle trespass, there was a rule that the damage had to be in accordance with the
natural characteristics of the animals.[105]

Animals Act 1971 The 1971 Act contains no provisions relating to remoteness   **17-027**
of damage and the position thereunder is to some extent speculative. The rule in
Rylands v Fletcher was not considered in *The Wagon Mound (No.1)* though, as has
been stated elsewhere in this book, it is governed by the principles of foreseeability as developed since *The Wagon Mound*.[106] Those principles should also be applicable to the 1971 Act. However, the form of s.2(2) means that with regard to liability for animals not belonging to dangerous species the position will be
fundamentally the same as at common law, since the damage must be of a kind attributable to the characteristics known to the keeper.[107] As for animals belonging to
a dangerous species, even though a camel was held to be such because it may cause
severe injury by kicking and biting, strict liability was imposed for injuries suffered by falling off the camel because of its irregular gait.[108] Whether or not any
special rule survives for straying cattle is not likely to be of any importance now
that damages for personal injuries cannot be recovered under that head.[109]

5. PROTECTION OF LIVESTOCK AGAINST DOGS

Liability for attacks on livestock Section 3 of the 1971 Act re-enacted, with   **17-028**
some modification, the form of strict liability formerly found in the Dogs Acts 1906
to 1928 and provides that where a dog causes damage by killing or injuring
livestock,[110] any person who is a keeper[111] of the dog is liable for the damage.[112] The
1971 Act provides the following defences: that the damage was wholly due to the
fault of the person suffering it[113] and that the livestock was killed or injured on land
on which it had strayed and either the dog belonged to the occupier or its presence

---

[104] See Williams, *Liability for Animals* (1939), p.301. If, however, the animal committed a "direct"
       wrong of the type to be expected, the keeper was probably liable for other losses stemming from
       that injury, e.g., a disease caught from the bite of a vicious dog: Williams, p.320.
[105] *Wormald v Cole* [1954] 1 Q.B. 614.
[106] See para.16-025.
[107] See para.17-016.
[108] *Tutin v Chipperfield Promotions Ltd* (1980) 130 N.L.J. 807.
[109] See para.17-020.
[110] "Livestock" for this purpose is slightly wider than under s.4, including pheasants, partridges and
       grouse in captivity: s.11.
[111] "Keeper" has the same meaning as in s.2: see para.17-009.
[112] Section 3.
[113] Section 5(1).

on the land was authorised by the occupier.[114] Contributory negligence is a partial defence.[115]

17-029 **Killing or injuring dogs to protect livestock** It may, in certain circumstances, be lawful for a person to kill or injure an animal belonging to another if this is necessary for protection of his livestock or crops. The common law rule on this was laid down by the Court of Appeal in *Cresswell v Sirl*[116] but this rule has been modified, so far as the protection of livestock against dogs is concerned,[117] by s.9 of the Animals Act 1971. It is a defence[118] to an action for killing or injuring a dog to prove that the defendant acted for the protection of livestock and was a person entitled so to act and, within 48 hours thereafter, notice was given to the officer in charge of a police station.[119] A person is entitled to act for the protection of livestock if either the livestock or the land on which it is belongs[120] to him or to any person under whose express or implied authority he is acting[121] and he is deemed to be acting for their protection if and only if,[122] either the dog is worrying or is about to worry the livestock and there are no other reasonable means of ending or preventing the worrying or the dog has been worrying livestock, has not left the vicinity and is not under the control of any person and there are no practicable means of ascertaining to whom it belongs.[123]

---

[114] Section 5(4).

[115] Section 10.

[116] *Cresswell v Sirl* [1948] 1 K.B. 241.

[117] The rule in *Cresswell v Sirl* continues to govern in the case of animals other than dogs, e.g., pigeons damaging crops, as in *Hamps v Darby* [1948] 2 K.B. 311. See the eighth edition of this work, pp.761–762.

[118] Not the only defence. A defendant who fails to make out the statutory defence (e.g., because he has not informed the police) may presumably fall back on the common law.

[119] Section 9(1).

[120] For this purpose an animal belongs to a person if he owns it or has it in his possession and land belongs to the occupier thereof: s.9(5).

[121] Section 9(2)(a). If the livestock have strayed on to the land of another, there is no right under this section to shoot a dog which is lawfully on that land: s.9(2)(b).

[122] The two following conditions are satisfied by reasonable belief on the defendant's part: s.9(4).

[123] Section 9(3). This right to take punitive action in respect of an attack which is over is the major difference between s.9 and *Cresswell v Sirl* [1948] 1 K.B. 241.

CHAPTER 18

INTERFERENCE WITH GOODS

1. HISTORY

Introduction[1] The English law governing remedies for interference with goods **18-001** is exceedingly technical, partly because of the long survival and overlap of a number of different heads of liability and partly because the law, though tortious in form, is largely proprietary in function. The Torts (Interference with Goods) Act 1977 simplified matters somewhat by abolishing one head of liability but it was only a piecemeal attempt to deal with certain deficiencies in the common law and is in no way a code governing interference with goods.[2] Accordingly, the law must still

---

[1] Green and Randall, *The Tort of Conversion* (2009); Douglas, *Liability for Wrongful Interference with Chattels* (2011).

[2] The Act was based upon the *Report of the Law Reform Committee*, Cmnd.4774 (1971). See Bentley

be sought mainly in the decisions of the courts and it is impossible to give an intelligible account of the developed law without first providing a brief historical sketch.

18-002 **Trespass** The most obvious forms of interference, such as removing or damaging goods, were covered in early law by trespass *de bonis asportatis*, the forerunner of the modern "trespass to goods". Trespass was (and still is) essentially a wrong to possession and the defendant need not have asserted any right to deal with the goods or indulged in any "appropriation" of them.

18-003 **Detinue** Trespass was unsuitable to deal with the case where the owner had voluntarily put his goods into another's possession and the other refused to redeliver them, but this situation was covered by the remedy of detinue. In neither form of action could the claimant be sure of recovering his goods *in specie* since the judgment in trespass was for damages and in detinue gave the defendant the option of redelivery or paying damages. Indeed, the remedy of specific restitution of chattels has remained unusual right up to modern times.[3] However, detinue was open to the serious objection from the claimant's point of view that the defendant could insist on the method of trial known as wager of law, i.e., getting compurgators to swear that they believed him to be oath-worthy, although they knew nothing of the facts of the case. This was the principal reason why detinue was all but wiped out by the encroachment of trover.

18-004 **Trover** Trover began as an action of trespass on the case in which it was alleged that the defendant had converted the claimant's goods to his own use.[4] By the mid-16th century it had emerged as a distinct species of case involving four allegations[5]: (1) that the claimant was possessed of the goods; (2) that he accidentally lost them; (3) that the defendant found them; and (4) that the defendant converted them to his own use. The losing and finding were soon treated as pure fictions and the defendant was not allowed to deny them.[6] The new remedy rapidly encroached on the sphere of trespass, though the law never went quite so far as to say that touching or damaging or moving goods was conversion.

The difficulty in extending trover to cases covered by detinue was that conversion could only be committed by a positive act. Detinue lay where a person was in possession of another's goods and refused to give them up but could such a refusal be said to be a positive act? The line between misfeasance and nonfeasance is apt to be a fine one and the courts after some hesitation took advantage of this and held mere refusal to redeliver to be conversion.[7] Detinue, with its procedural disadvantages, wilted considerably under this treatment though it retained a place in the law because inability to redeliver as a result of loss or destruction of the goods was not regarded as conversion.[8]

(1972) 35 M.L.R. 171. The Report proposed rather more thoroughgoing reforms than the Act in fact produced.

3   See para.18-054.
4   See Douglas (2009) 68 C.L.J. 198.
5   Milsom [1954] C.L.J. 105, 114; Simpson (1959) 75 L.Q.R. 364.
6   *Gumbleton v Grafton* (1600) Cro. Eliz. 781; 78 E.R. 1011 (losing); *Isaack v Clark* (1614) 2 Bulst. 306; 80 E.R. 1143 (finding).
7   Holdsworth, *A History of English Law*, vol. vii, pp.405–415.
8   *Owen v Lewyn* (1673) 1 Vent. 223; 86 E.R. 150.

The modern action for conversion Nineteenth-century legislation swept away **18-005** the fictions on which trover was based and it became the modern action for conversion, though no change was made to the substance of the law. The abolition of wager of law in 1833 caused some revival in detinue but in view of the expansion of conversion, detinue only really remained necessary where the defendant was unable to redeliver the goods. The process of simplification was carried a stage further by s.2 of the Torts (Interference with Goods) Act 1977, which abolished detinue and provided that conversion also covered the only case that was formerly the exclusive province of detinue—i.e., inability to redeliver goods as a result of their loss or destruction.[9] However, one still needs to look back at the common law of detinue to determine what constitutes the new form of conversion, and the action for conversion still overlaps considerably with trespass to goods.[10]

Replevin and interim relief Replevin is an ancient cause of action which was **18-006** originally a tenant's remedy for wrongful distress by his lord. By the 15th century it had been extended to other forms of unlawful taking of goods[11] but in practice it tended to be used only for unlawful distress and the modern procedure in the action was regulated by statute.[12] As a form of interim relief, replevin was largely overtaken by s.4 of the Torts (Interference with Goods) Act 1977, which added a new and more important form of interim relief, available in the county courts and High Court, whereby goods the subject of present or future proceedings for wrongful interference may be ordered to be delivered up to the claimant, or a person appointed by the court, on such terms and conditions as may be specified. The procedure is particularly apt if there is a risk that the goods may be destroyed or disposed of before trial of the action but is not confined to such situations. An order was made under it in *Howard E Perry & Co Ltd v British Railways Board*[13] even though the goods were in no danger and the defendants recognised the claimants' title: the shortage of stock caused by industrial action was acute and damages would not adequately have compensated the claimants for the injury to their business. However, it has been said that the facts of that case were "very specific", and that the "usual position [is] that a risk of disposal, destruction or damage will be necessary before an order will be made".[14] The rules of replevin themselves have now been displaced by the Tribunals, Courts and Enforcement Act 2007 Pt 3.[15]

---

9 See para.18-024.
10 The Law Reform Committee recommended a new, all-embracing tort of "wrongful interference with chattels" (Cmnd.4774 (1971)). The Act uses this terminology (see s.1) but only as a convenient label for the various reforms made by it on ancillary matters. As such, it does not merge the three torts of conversion, trespass and replevin (now all but displaced: para.18-006). cf. the assertion in *HSBC Rail (UK) Ltd v Network Rail Infrastructure Ltd* [2005] EWCA Civ 1437; [2006] 1 W.L.R. 643 at [1] that there is a tort of wrongful interference with goods and that trespass and conversion are "now old-fashioned terms".
11 Thus it does not lie against a carrier who detains them, for he did not obtain possession by trespass, though he may be liable in conversion: *Galloway v Bird* (1827) 4 Bing. 299; 130 E.R. 782; *Mennie v Blake* (1856) 6 El. & Bl. 842; 119 E.R. 1078.
12 County Courts Act 1984 s.144 and Sch.1.
13 [1980] 1 W.L.R. 1375.
14 *Bear Necessities Daycare Ltd v Lancashire Fuels 4 U Ltd* [2015] EWHC 721 (QB) at [33] per Swift J.
15 Section 65(1).

2. TRESPASS TO GOODS

18-007 **Direct interference required but not damage** Trespass to goods is a wrongful physical interference with them. It may take innumerable forms, such as scratching the panel of a vehicle,[16] removing a tyre from it[17] or the vehicle itself from a garage,[18] the cutting of nets and fish cages,[19] or, in the case of animals, beating[20] or killing[21] them. Putting out poison for an animal to take[22] is probably not trespass since the interference is not direct, a requirement of all true forms of trespass; a defendant engaging in such conduct would, of course, be liable if injury to the animals ensued but his liability would be in negligence rather than trespass. Trespass is actionable per se, and so although there is some authority to the effect that trespass to goods requires proof of some damage or asportation[23] the better view is to the contrary[24] and otherwise the result would be that in the case of mere touching of objects like waxworks or paintings in a gallery or museum, their possessor would be without remedy.[25]

18-008 **Unintentional contacts** The considerations of policy which point to making intentional meddling actionable even without damage have no application to unintended contacts. And even assuming that some damage has been caused, in the case of unintentional contact negligence is also necessary for liability.[26] In *Fowler v Lanning*,[27] it was held that in an action for unintentional trespass to the person the claimant must prove negligence on the part of the defendant, and the same must now be true of trespass to goods. An alternative analysis, and one to be preferred, is that in the modern law trespass to goods is confined to intentional interference and that unintentional interference is remediable only by the tort of negligence.[28] Trespass, however, obviously remains appropriate where a person takes another's goods in the mistaken belief that he is entitled to do so, for the act is intentional towards the goods. In *Wilson v Lombank Ltd*[29] the claimant had "purchased" a car from a person who had no title to it and had sent it to a garage for repair. In the false

---

16   *Fouldes v Willoughby* (1841) 8 M. & W. 538 at 549; 151 E.R. 1153 at 1157.
17   *GWK Ltd v Dunlop Rubber Co Ltd* (1926) 42 T.L.R. 376 at 593.
18   *Wilson v Lombank Ltd* [1963] 1 W.L.R. 1294.
19   *Fish & Fish Ltd v Sea Shepherd UK* [2013] EWCA Civ 544; [2013] 1 W.L.R. 3700.
20   *Slater v Swann* (1730) 2 Str. 872; 93 E.R. 906.
21   *Sheldrick v Abery* (1793) 1 Esp. 55; 170 E.R. 278.
22   As opposed to forcing it down its throat.
23   *Slater v Swann* (1730) 2 Str. 872; *Everitt v Martin* [1953] N.Z.L.R. 298.
24   *Transco Plc v United Utilities Water Plc* [2005] EWHC 2784 (QB); *UK Oil and Gas Investments Plc v Persons Unknown* [2018] EWHC 2252 (Ch) (climbing on vehicles, or "lorry-surfing", a trespass to goods). See also *Leitch & Co Ltd v Leydon* [1931] A.C. 90 at 106.
25   Even an intentional touching is surely not actionable if it is the sort of trivial interference to which people do not object, like moving a coat on a stand to get at one's own: see *White v Withers LLP* [2009] EWCA Civ 1122; [2009] 3 F.C.R. 435; cf. *Collins v Wilcock* [1984] 1 W.L.R. 1172.
26   *National Coal Board v Evans* [1951] 2 K.B. 861.
27   [1959] 1 Q.B. 426, para.4-003.
28   See Douglas, *Liability for Wrongful Interference with Chattels* (2011), Ch.6. In *Letang v Cooper* [1965] 1 Q.B. 232 at 240 Lord Denning said that negligence is the only cause of action for unintended injury to the person and the logic of that view extends to unintended damage to goods. In truth, once it is conceded that the burden of proof of negligence lies on the claimant (a point on which the court in *Letang v Cooper* was unanimous) the traditional distinction between trespass and negligence loses much of its significance and Lord Denning's solution is the more satisfactory.
29   [1963] 1 W.L.R. 1294. See also *Colwill v Reeves* (1811) 2 Camp. 575; 170 E.R. 1257.

belief that it was his, the defendant had removed it from the garage. The defendant was liable in trespass.[30]

Possession essential Since trespass is an interference with possession, if the **18-009** claimant was not in possession at the date of the alleged meddling, he cannot sue for trespass. He may be able to sue for conversion, but that is a different matter: "The distinction between the actions of trespass and trover is well settled: the former is founded on possession the latter on property."[31]

Exceptions? It is said that there are exceptions to the rule that possession is es- **18-010** sential and that the following persons can sue for trespass despite not being in possession: (1) a trustee against any third person who commits a trespass to trust chattels in the hands of the beneficiary; (2) an executor or administrator for trespasses committed to goods of the deceased after his death but before probate is granted to the executor or before the administrator takes out letters of administration; and (3) the owner of a franchise (for example a right to take wreck or treasure trove) against anyone who seizes the goods before he himself can take them. However, it is questionable whether any of these exceptions is genuine. The language used in the authorities relating to the trustee is obscure, but it indicates that the trustee has possession of chattels in the hands of the beneficiary, and not merely the right to possess them.[32] It does not follow from this that the beneficiary himself cannot sue, for if he holds the chattels he seems to have joint possession with the trustee. Again, it has long been considered that the executor and administrator have the deceased's possession continued in them, and that when they assume office their title relates back to his death. In other words, they do not merely have the right to possess but are in possession.[33] Similarly, in the case of the franchise, possession is deemed to be with the owner of the franchise.[34] In a simple bailment determinable at will the bailor does not lose possession and may sue any wrongdoer

---

[30] See para.18-034 as to the possible effect of the Torts (Interference with Goods) Act 1977 on this case.

[31] *Ward v Macauley* (1791) 4 Term Rep. 489 at 490; 100 E.R. 1135 at 1135 per Lord Kenyon CJ. It does not follow that D is not liable for trespass to C where X wrongfully takes C's goods and then passes them to D: *White v Withers LLP* [2009] EWCA Civ 1122; [2009] 3 F.C.R. 435 at [48]. If the goods are damaged or destroyed the owner out of possession will have an action on the case for injury to his reversionary interest: *Mears v London & South Western Ry* (1862) 11 C.B.(N.S.) 850; 142 E.R. 1029; *East West Corp v DKBS 1912* [2003] EWCA Civ 83; [2003] Q.B. 1509; *HSBC Rail (UK) Ltd v Network Rail Infrastructure Ltd* [2005] EWCA Civ 1437; [2006] 1 W.L.R. 643 (where, however, the claim failed, the owner having been indemnified under contract by the bailee). See further Tettenborn [1994] C.L.J. 326.

[32] *White v Morris* (1852) 11 C.B. 1015; 138 E.R. 778; approved in *Barker v Furlong* [1891] 2 Ch. 172, a case of conversion.

[33] *Tharpe v Stallwood* (1843) 5 Man. & G. 760 at 770; 134 E.R. 766 at 771; Pollock & Wright, *Possession in the Common Law* (1888), pp.146–147.

[34] *The Bailiffs, Burgesses and Commonalty of the Borough of Dunwich v Sterry* (1831) 1 B. & Ad. 831; 109 E.R. 995 (franchise of wreck; cask taken before franchisee could get it).

other than his bailee[35] in trespass,[36] though the bailee may also have sufficient possession to bring trespass.[37]

3. CONVERSION

18-011   Conversion at common law can be committed in so many different ways that any comprehensive definition is probably impossible[38] but the wrong is committed by dealing with the goods of a person in such a way as to deprive him of the use or possession of them (though to "deprive" the owner does not necessarily require that the defendant should himself take the goods from him[39]). Thus it may be committed by wrongfully taking possession of goods, by wrongfully disposing of them, by wrongfully misusing them, by wrongfully destroying them or simply by wrongfully refusing to give them up when demanded. At common law there must be some deliberate act[40] depriving the claimant of his rights: if this element is lacking there is no conversion. Thus if a bailee negligently allows goods in his charge to be destroyed the claimant's loss is just the same as if the bailee had wrongfully sold them to a third party but there is no conversion. Such conduct is now conversion by statute but this is merely for the draftsman's terminological convenience and has no effect on the concept of conversion at common law: for this reason, it must be kept separate in our analysis.

A.   What Can be Converted?

18-012   Any corporeal, movable property can be converted.[41] This includes money in the form of coins or notes, though once the taker has paid them to another they become currency and the payee and subsequent recipients cannot be sued for conversion by the original owner. There can be no conversion of a chose in action, so when invalidly appointed receivers dealt with a company's contracts they did not commit this tort.[42] Although the true value of cheques and other negotiable instruments or share certificates lies in their character as evidence of non-corporeal rights,

---

[35]   If the act is licensed by the bailee it seems it is not trespass as against a bailor: Palmer, *Bailment*, 2nd edn (1991), p.206—the general chapter on the chattel torts is not included in the third edition.

[36]   *Lotan v Cross* (1810) 2 Camp. 464; 170 E.R. 1219; *Ancona v Rogers* (1876) L.R. 1 Ex. D. 285 at 292. The authorities are discussed in *Penfolds Wines Pty Ltd v Elliott* (1946) 74 C.L.R. 204 at 214–220, 226–236, 239–244; *USA v Dollfus Mieg et Cie* [1952] A.C. 582 at 605, 611–613; *Wilson v Lombank Ltd* [1963] 1 W.L.R. 1294.

[37]   *Nicolls v Bastard* (1835) 2 Cr. M. & R. 659 at 660; 150 E.R. 279 at 280.

[38]   See *Kuwait Airways Corp v Iraqi Airways Co (Nos 4 and 5)* [2002] UKHL 19; [2002] 2 A.C. 883 at [39]; *Howard Perry & Co Ltd v British Railways Board* [1980] 1 W.L.R. 1375 at 1380; *Hiort v London & North Western Ry Co* (1879) 4 Ex. D. 188 at 194.

[39]   *Kuwait Airways Corp v Iraqi Airways Co (Nos 4 and 5)* [2002] UKHL 19; [2002] 2 A.C. 883 at [40].

[40]   The defendant may still be liable even if he is motivated by some innocent mistake: para.18-039. However, innocently taking goods into one's custody (e.g., to transport them) is not conversion unless one is aware of the owner's rights: para.18-041.

[41]   Hence not wild animals which have not been reduced into possession (as they are not anyone's property) nor land. However, where material is wrongfully severed from land the owner may sue in conversion.

[42]   *OBG Ltd v Allan* [2007] UKHL 21; [2008] 1 A.C. 1 (though the House of Lords was divided on both the feasibility and desirability of change). See also, concerning electronic documents, *Thunder Air Ltd v Hilmarsson* [2008] EWHC 355 (Ch); *Environment Agency v Churngold Recycling Ltd* [2014] EWCA Civ 909; [2015] Env. L.R. 13.

the owner may sue in conversion for their face value,[43] though not where a cheque has been materially altered, for then it ceases to be valid and becomes a worthless piece of paper.[44] There have been a number of cases about rights of ownership in corpses and body parts,[45] though generally in contexts other than conversion. There is said to be no property in a corpse (as opposed to e.g., a preserved specimen[46] or skeleton prepared for anatomical purposes) but in some circumstances a person may have ownership of parts of or products obtained from his own body.[47] Hence a tort claim may lie in respect of the destruction of sperm stored for potential future use or of a body part severed in an accident which had been capable of being reattached.[48]

B. What Constitutes Conversion at Common Law

i. Taking Possession

A matter of degree Whether taking another's goods is conversion is a matter of   **18-013** degree. Generally it will constitute the tort but there will be no conversion where the interference is merely temporary and unaccompanied by any intention to assert rights over the goods. Thus in *Fouldes v Willoughby*[49] it was not conversion (though no doubt it was trespass) to remove the claimant's horses from a ferry boat to the shore. If I snatch your hat from your head with intent to steal it or destroy it that is conversion as well as trespass, but if I throw it at another person that is trespass only.[50] It is sometimes said that this is because I am not questioning your title to it but a better explanation seems to be that it is because the interference is temporary and trivial[51] for it is clearly not necessary in cases of conversion that the defendant should assert ownership over the goods: taking for the purpose of acquir-

---

43 *Morrison v London County and Westminster Bank* [1914] 3 K.B. 356; *Rugby Football Union v Viagogo Ltd* [2011] EWHC 764 (QB); [2011] N.P.C. 37 at [46] (rugby tickets).
44 *Smith v Lloyd's TSB Group Plc* [2001] Q.B. 541.
45 See, generally, Hardcastle, *Law and the Human Body: Property Rights, Ownership and Control* (2007).
46 See *R. v Kelly* [1999] Q.B. 621. In *Dobson v North Tyneside HA* [1997] 1 W.L.R. 596 it was held that conversion did not lie in respect of a brain which had been extracted and preserved for an inquest rather than research. The claim seems to have been linked to the claimants' action for medical negligence causing the death. The Court of Appeal in *Yearworth v North Bristol NHS Trust* [2009] EWCA Civ 37; [2010] Q.B. 1 regarded *Dobson* as depending on the fact that the pathologist had never undertaken to preserve the brain. Where a post-mortem is lawfully carried out the removal of organs is lawful and the person who does that may have the initial right to possession of them. However, failure to explain the possibility of removal and retention of organs may give rise to a claim for negligence or under art.8 of the European Convention on Human Rights: *Re Organ Retention Group Litigation* [2004] EWHC 644 (QB); [2005] Q.B. 506.
47 Wall (2011) 31 O.J.L.S. 783.
48 *Yearworth v North Bristol NHS Trust* [2009] EWCA Civ 37; [2010] Q.B. 1 (sperm; this was despite the fact that legislation deprived the "owners" of the prime sign of ownership, viz. the power to *direct* what should be done with the material. It would have been possible to decide the case on the basis that the skill used in preserving the sperm made it analogous to the cases on anatomical specimens but the court did not wish to proceed on such a narrow basis).
49 (1841) 8 M. & W. 540; 151 E.R. 1153.
50 *Price v Helyar* (1828) 4 Bing. 597; 130 E.R. 898.
51 cf. *The Playa Larga* [1983] 2 Lloyd's Rep. 171 (diversion of goods by seller at the behest of a third party was conversion). To be conversion the conduct must be "so extensive an encroachment on the rights of the owner as to exclude him from use and possession of the goods": *Kuwait Airways Corp v Iraqi Airways Co (Nos 4 and 5)* [2002] UKHL 19; [2002] 2 A.C. 883 at [39].

ing a lien,[52] or even for temporary use[53] have been held to be conversion. On the other hand, some of the cases talk in terms of "exercising dominion"[54] or of "denying the owner's right".[55] These expressions should not be taken too literally but if that is how the defendant's conduct would appear to an observer that is certainly a pointer towards its being conversion rather than trespass.[56]

18-014 **Trespass or conversion: significance**   The distinction between trespass to goods and conversion may be significant on the question of remedy. If there is a conversion the claimant's damages are prima facie measurable by the value of the goods; in other words the judgment is a sort of forced sale. This may be thought a draconian remedy for a temporary deprivation and points towards keeping conversion within narrower bounds than trespass.[57] Yet if goods are destroyed while in the possession of a wrongdoer it would surely be wrong to allow him to escape by showing that it was not his fault, for that would be to treat him like a bailee. However, these problems can be solved without taking an artificial approach to what amounts to conversion. Where there is a temporary deprivation and the goods are returned to the claimant there is no doubt that this goes in reduction of the damages. If the claimant should refuse to take the goods back then the court has power to stay the action before judgment if they are tendered undamaged.[58] As to the second situation, since the law imposes the liability of an insurer upon a person who came lawfully into the possession of another's goods but who deviates from the terms of his permission[59] it must inevitably do the same to a defendant who takes the goods wrongfully.

18-015 **Third-party recipients**   Where A, without lawful authority, transfers B's goods to C, the mere voluntary receipt of them by C is in general conversion, however innocent C may be. This is abundantly supported by decisions with respect to receipt of goods by a buyer[60] and receipt of a cheque by a banker.[61] Some qualifications of

---

52   *Tear v Freebody* (1858) C.B.(N.S.) 228; 140 E.R. 1071. Unlawful wheelclamping is plainly trespass (*Vine v Waltham Forest LBC* [2000] 1 W.L.R. 2383) but is it also conversion? In *Arthur v Anker* [1997] Q.B. 564 the cause of action was described as "tortious interference" with the car. See now Protection of Freedoms Act 2012 s.54 (criminal offence without lawful excuse to immobilise a vehicle on private land with a view to preventing its removal by the owner).

53   e.g., "joyriding": Rolle Abr. tit. *Action Sur Case*, p.5 (equine variety).

54   *Hollins v Fowler* (1875) L.R. 7 H.L. 757; *Oakley v Lister* [1931] 1 K.B. 148 at 156.

55   *Lancashire and Yorkshire Ry v MacNicholl* (1919) 88 L.J.K.B. 601 at 605; *Oakley v Lister* [1931] 1 K.B. 148 at 153.

56   In *White v Withers LLP* [2009] EWCA Civ 1122; [2009] 3 F.C.R. 435 at [53], it was suggested that copying a document could constitute conversion of it. But as the copies belong to the person who makes them, the owner of the originals naturally has no conversion claim in respect of *them*: *Environment Agency v Churngold Recycling Ltd* [2014] EWCA Civ 909; [2015] Env. L.R. 13.

57   Of course in another sense conversion is *wider* than trespass. D can convert goods without touching them or even seeing them, as where D sells them.

58   *Fisher v Prince* (1762) 3 Burr. 1363; 97 E.R. 876; *Kuwait Airways Corp v Iraqi Airways Co (Nos 4 and 5)* [2001] 3 W.L.R. 1117 at 1235; on appeal [2002] UKHL 19; [2002] 2 A.C. 883.

59   See, e.g., *Roberts v McDougall* (1887) 3 T.L.R. 666; *Mitchell v Ealing LBC* [1979] Q.B.1; *Toor v Bassi* [1999] E.G.C.S. 9.

60   *Wilkinson v King* (1809) 2 Camp. 335; 170 E.R. 1175; *Farrant v Thompson* (1822) 5 B. & Ald. 826; 106 E.R. 1392; *Dyer v Pearson* (1824) 3 B. & C. 38; 107 E.R. 648; *Hilbery v Hatton* (1864) 2 H. & C. 822; 159 E.R. 341.

61   *Fine Art Society v Union Bank of London* (1886) 17 Q.B.D. 705; *Orbit Mining & Trading Co Ltd v Westminster Bank Ltd* [1963] 1 Q.B. 794. Under the Cheques Act 1957 s.4, the banker has a defence if he has acted in good faith and without negligence.

this where the defendant acts bona fide are discussed below.[62] It was once held that receipt of goods by way of pledge did not amount to conversion even though the same receipt by way of purchase would have.[63] Whether or not this decision was ever good law it was reversed by the Torts (Interference with Goods) Act 1977.[64]

Involuntary receipt of goods Involuntary receipt of goods is not conversion.[65] **18-016** Such is the case where a thief, in order to escape detection, slips a purse he has stolen into the pocket of an innocent person. Even where the receiver knows that the thing belongs to someone else,[66] he incurs no liability by having it thrust upon him. The recipient cannot, without his consent, be made a bailee in the strict sense of that term and mere negligence on his part with respect to the safe custody of the thing will not make him liable. So, in *Howard v Harris*,[67] where a playwright sent the manuscript of a play to a theatrical producer who had never asked for it and who lost it, the producer was held not liable. Similarly, the involuntary bailee does no wrong if he acts reasonably in trying to return the goods. In *Elvin and Powell Ltd v Plummer Roddis Ltd*,[68] X, a swindler, directed the claimants to supply the defendants with coats worth £350. X then forged a telegram to the defendants: "Goods dispatched to your branch in error.—Sending van to collect. Elvin and Powell." Then a confederate of X called on the defendants, who delivered the coats to him under the impression that he was the claimants' agent. The confederate disappeared. Hawke J held that there was no conversion, for the defendants had acted reasonably.[69] Contrast with this case *Hiort v Bott*,[70] where A mistakenly sent an invoice for barley to B (who had ordered none), which stated that B had bought the barley of A through G as broker and A also sent B a delivery order which made the barley deliverable to the order of A or of B. G then told B there had been a mistake and got B to endorse the delivery order to G. G thereby got hold of the barley, disposed of it and absconded. Here B was held liable to A for conversion. Had he merely handed the delivery order to G for return to A, the decision might have been otherwise, but by endorsing it to G he had gone beyond what was necessary to secure its return to A.

Wilful damage or destruction by involuntary recipient The involuntary recipi- **18-017** ent must not wilfully damage or destroy the thing.[71] The law has not, however, been

---

62 See para.18-040.
63 *Spackman v Foster* (1883) 11 Q.B.D. 99.
64 Section 11(2).
65 See Burnett (1958) 76 L.Q.R. 364; Palmer, *Bailment*, 3rd edn (2009), Ch.13.
66 According to the Court of Appeal in *Marcq v Christie Manson & Woods Ltd* [2003] EWCA Civ 731; [2004] Q.B. 286 one cannot be a bailee without some knowledge of the existence of one's bailor but if one mistakenly destroys goods which are self-evidently someone else's one is negligent whether or not there is a bailment. Where one finds goods in property which one has acquired the nature of them will determine what inquiries one should make before concluding that they have been abandoned: *Robot Arenas Ltd v Waterfield* [2010] EWHC 115 (QB).
67 (1884) Cababe & Ellis 253; *Lethbridge v Phillips* (1819) 2 Stark. 544; 171 E.R. 731. cf. Palmer, *Bailment*, 3rd edn (2009), para.13-013.
68 (1933) 50 T.L.R. 158.
69 See also *Batistoni v Dance* (1908) 52 S.J. 202.
70 (1874) L.R. 9 Ex. 86. Note that the defendant was not, strictly, a bailee since he never had actual possession of the barley.
71 "I am not bound to warehouse it, nor am I entitled to turn it into the street": *Hiort v Bott* (1874) L.R. 9 Ex. 86 at 90 per Bramwell B.

fully explored here. It is simple enough with a small and imperishable article like a book or a fountain pen, but what of a parcel of fish or a piano which is delivered to D's house in D's absence? D may want to get rid of them and is certainly not bound to incur the expense of packing and returning them. If the sender is traceable, probably the most sensible thing for D to do is to notify him that the goods are at his risk and to request him to fetch them and if (as is likely with perishables) the goods become a problem, D would surely be justified in destroying them, even without notice to the sender, if the emergency were so pressing as to leave him no time to give it.[72]

18-018 **Detention of goods by involuntary recipient** A related question arises if the involuntary recipient wishes to detain the goods as security for the payment of his expenses or for the inconvenience caused to him, a situation exemplified by the modern practice of wheel clamping of vehicles. The ancient right of distress damage feasant applies only where the landowner has suffered actual damage, though this extends to inconvenience, as well as physical injury to the property.[73] The cost of clamping or of towing to another location is not "damage".[74] However, the display of a prominent notice warning of clamping may mean that the car owner consents to the risk.[75]

ii. Abusing Possession

18-019 **Numerous forms** Abuse of possession which the defendant already has may take many forms,[76] such as sale accompanied by delivery of the claimant's goods or their documents of title to another,[77] pawning them,[78] or otherwise disposing of them, even by innocently delivering them to a fraudster with forged delivery documents.[79] The use of a borrowed car to transport smuggled watches has been held a conversion of the car, for such conduct if discovered leads to the forfeiture of the car under the Customs and Excise legislation and its consequent loss to the owner.[80] In less extreme cases of unauthorised use by a bailee the question whether his act amounts to conversion probably depends upon the degree of departure from the terms of the bailment,[81] though it must be remembered that in any event the departure will

---

[72] The position is rather different when the goods came into the defendant's hands by reason of a genuine, voluntary bailment for then the bailee has a statutory power of sale of the goods if the bailor fails to collect them: see the Torts (Interference with Goods) Act 1977 ss.12, 13. The 1977 Act does not define "bailment" but it is thought that these provisions would not extend to an involuntary recipient: *Taylor v Diamond* [2012] EWHC 2900 (Ch) at [106].

[73] *Arthur v Anker* [1997] Q.B. 564.

[74] *Arthur v Anker* [1997] Q.B. 564. The landowner may remove the car, but that may cause him other problems: *Lloyd v DPP* [1992] 1 All E.R. 982.

[75] *Arthur v Anker* [1997] Q.B. 564; *Vine v Waltham Forest LBC* [2000] 1 W.L.R. 2383. It seems from the latter case that it is not necessarily enough that the notices are sufficiently prominent to bring the matter to the attention of a reasonably alert entrant.

[76] See, e.g., *Tower Hamlets LBC v Bromley LBC* [2015] EWHC 1954 (Ch); [2015] 2 P. & C.R. DG23 (council converted Henry Moore sculpture located on one of its housing estates by removing it from its site, loaning it to a museum, restoring it, etc.).

[77] *Hollins v Fowler* (1875) L.R. 7 H.L. 757.

[78] *Parker v Godin* (1728) 2 Str. 813; 93 E.R. 866.

[79] *Motis Exports Ltd v Dampskibsselskabet AF 1912 A/S* [2000] 1 Lloyd's Rep. 211.

[80] *Moorgate Mercantile Co Ltd v Finch* [1962] 1 Q.B. 701. cf. *BMW Financial Services (GB) Ltd v Bhagwanani* [2007] EWCA Civ 1230.

[81] Palmer, *Bailment*, 3rd edn (2009), para.21–07.

expose the bailee to strict liability for damage or loss. At common law an omission on the part of the defendant (for example, negligently allowing the goods to be stolen) would not make him liable for conversion[82] though if he were a bailee of the goods he might be liable in detinue in such circumstances.[83] Since this type of detinue has by statute been assimilated to conversion the bailee may now be liable in conversion.[84]

Disposition without transfer of possession   A mere sale or other attempted **18-020** disposition of goods is not a conversion without a transfer of possession, i.e., delivery: the act is void and does not change the property or the possession.[85] However, in those situations where a person in possession of goods to which he has no title can confer a good title on someone else by selling, pledging, or otherwise disposing of the goods,[86] then, since the true owner is thereby deprived of his title, such a disposition constitutes conversion whether or not the goods are actually delivered.[87]

Destruction or alteration   The destruction of goods amounts to conversion and **18-021** so does the alteration of their nature. If I make an omelette out of your eggs or a statue out of your block of marble, that is conversion.[88] The owner of the original material may wish to assert ownership in the product, but that is a different question. If the materials can still be identified in the new product, which is wholly or substantially composed of them[89] (leather turned into shoes,[90] skins turned into a fur coat[91]) the owner of the materials is owner of the product. Where the property of A is wrongfully mixed with that of B which is of substantially the same nature and quality and they cannot practicably be separated (grain in a bin, oil in a tank) the mixture is owned in common in proportion to the quantity contributed by each;[92] and it has been held that the same is true where the components are of different grades, so as to produce a commercially different mixture.[93]

---

82 *Ashby v Tolhurst* [1937] 2 K.B. 242; *Tinsley v Dudley* [1951] 2 K.B. 18. In both cases the claimant's vehicle had been stolen from the defendant's car park.

83 It is important to note that there is no bailment where a vehicle is placed in an ordinary car park: *Chappell v National Car Parks*, *The Times*, 22 May 1987. The cases do not seem to have been affected by the Occupiers' Liability Act 1957: para.10-022; but cf. *Fairline Shipping Corp v Adamson* [1975] Q.B. 180.

84 See para.18-024. Thus a carrier who negligently allows goods to be stolen may now be liable for conversion of the goods as well as negligent breach of bailment.

85 *Lancashire Waggon Co v Fitzhugh* (1861) 6 H. & N. 502; 158 E.R. 206.

86 i.e., the exceptions to the rule *nemo dat quod non habet*.

87 Though most of the exceptions require a delivery.

88 The bottling of wine entrusted to a person in cask may be evidence of conversion even if none of the wine is drunk, but much will depend on the circumstances of the bottling. If done to preserve the wine from deterioration it is not conversion: see *Philpott v Kelley* (1835) 3 Ad. & El. 106; 111 E.R. 353.

89 *Glencore International AG v Metro Trading International Inc* [2001] 1 Lloyd's Rep. 284 at 328.

90 *Case of Leather* Y.B. 5 Hen.VII fol.15.

91 *Jones v de Marchant* (1916) 28 D.L.R. 561, approved in *Foskett v McKeown* [2001] 1 A.C. 102 at 132.

92 *Indian Oil Corp Ltd v Greenstone Shipping SA* [1988] Q.B. 345.

93 *Glencore International AG v Metro Trading International Inc* [2001] 1 Lloyd's Rep. 284.

iii. Demand and Refusal

18-022   Merely keeping someone else's goods, while it may be a breach of contract,[94] is not a conversion of them for it does not necessarily show an intention to exclude the rights of the owner. However, in such a case proof of a demand by the claimant for the return of the goods met by a refusal of the defendant will usually establish conversion.[95] Yet it is not the only way of doing so. In *Kuwait Airways Corp v Iraqi Airways Co (Nos 4 and 5)*[96] aircraft were seized by Iraqi forces in the invasion of Kuwait and transferred to the defendants, who were held to have converted them by resolving to register them in their name, using them to the limited extent possible in the circumstances and generally treating them as their own.[97] Where there is a demand, there is no conversion if the refusal is conditional and the condition is reasonable. An example would be a refusal to give up a banknote you found in the street to the first stranger who alleges it to be his, on the ground that either he must authenticate his claim or you must make further inquiries.[98] Whether the duration, extent and form of such inquiries are reasonable may be nice questions.[99] Similarly, delivery in response to a demand need not be immediate if it is necessary first to separate the claimant's goods from others to which he is not entitled.[100] However, the defendant cannot justify a refusal on the ground that compliance with the demand may have unpleasant consequences for him. In *Howard E Perry & Co Ltd v British Railways Board*[101] it was held that D's refusal to allow C to enter D's premises to collect goods belonging to C could not be justified by D's fear of intensified industrial action in this eventuality.

iv. Residual Forms of Conversion

18-023   Though most cases of conversion at common law fall within the categories of taking or abusing possession, or refusing to return the goods, such acts on the part of the defendant are not a necessary element of liability provided he has dealt with the goods in a way inconsistent with the claimant's rights, such as by signing a delivery order for goods which are delivered under that order,[102] or by refusing access to his premises to a lessor of goods brought onto the premises by the lessee.[103]

---

[94]   A bailee is not, in the absence of special contract, obliged to return the chattel to his bailor; he must merely allow the bailor to collect it: *Capital Finance Co Ltd v Bray* [1964] 1 W.L.R. 323.

[95]   On the question of whether refusal may be inferred from mere inactivity in the face of a demand compare *R. (on the application of Atapattu) v Home Secretary* [2011] EWHC 1388 (Admin) with *Schwarzchild v Harrods Ltd* [2008] EWHC 521 (QB).

[96]   *Kuwait Airways Corp v Iraqi Airways Co (Nos 4 and 5)* [2002] UKHL 19; [2002] 2 A.C. 883.

[97]   The initial seizure by the state of Iraq was not actionable in tort because of sovereign immunity: para.25-008.

[98]   *Alexander v Southey* (1821) 5 B. & Ald. 247; 106 E.R. 1183; *Clayton v Le Roy* [1911] 2 K.B. 1031.

[99]   See, e.g., *Burroughes v Bayne* (1860) 5 H. & N. 296; 157 E.R. 1196, where the court was not unanimous; *Pillott v Wilkinson* (1864) 3 H. & C. 345; 159 E.R. 564; *Spencer v S Franses Ltd* [2011] EWHC 1269.

[100]   *Metall Market OOO v Vitorio Shipping Co Ltd* [2013] EWCA Civ 650; [2013] 1 C.L.C. 979.

[101]   [1980] 1 W.L.R. 1875.

[102]   *Hiort v Bott* (1874) L.R. 9 Ex. 86; *Van Oppen v Tredegars* (1921) 37 T.L.R. 504; *Douglas Valley Finance Co Ltd v S Hughes (Hirers) Ltd* [1969] 1 Q.B. 738; *Ernest Scragg & Sons Ltd v Perseverance Banking and Trust Co Ltd* [1973] 2 Lloyd's Rep. 101.

[103]   *London Trocadero Ltd v Family Leisure Holdings Ltd* [2012] EWCA Civ 1037 at [36]–[40] (the lessee was bankrupt).

It has even been held that refusing to hand over the registration book of the claimant's car amounts to conversion of the car since the absence of the book makes it difficult to deal with the car.[104] However, a mere denial of title without more is not conversion.[105]

Where the defendant is in possession of the claimant's goods there is no doubt that an unjustified refusal to return them generally constitutes conversion but it has been held that where the claimant has possession there is no conversion if the defendant simply refuses to allow the claimant to remove them. In *England v Cowley*[106] M owed money to both the claimant and the defendant, her landlord. The claimant held a bill of sale over M's furniture and put a man into M's house to take charge of it. When the claimant then attempted to remove the furniture the defendant forbade him to do so and stationed a policeman at the gate to make sure he did not. The defendant was held not liable for conversion. Bramwell B said[107]:

"In order to maintain trover, a plaintiff who is left in possession of the goods must prove that his dominion over his property has been interfered with, not in some particular way, but altogether that he has been entirely deprived of the use of it. It is not enough that a man should say that something shall not be done by the plaintiff he must say that nothing shall."

C. Conversion Under the Torts (Interference with Goods) Act 1977

Apart from one or two minor matters[108] the 1977 Act did not interfere with the concept of conversion at common law. However, the Act abolished detinue,[109] which was wrongful retention of a chattel. In most cases of detinue there would be a concurrent liability in conversion based upon a demand and refusal to return[110] but as we have seen conversion required a positive act and had never lain where the defendant once had the claimant's goods but was unable to return them because they had been lost or negligently destroyed.[111] Accordingly, to deal with this situation, the Act provides[112] that an[113]: **18-024**

"action lies in conversion for loss or destruction of goods which a bailee[114] has allowed to happen in breach of his duty to his bailor (that is to say it lies in a case which is not otherwise conversion, but would have been detinue before detinue was abolished)".

---

[104] *Bryanston Leasings Ltd v Principality Finance Ltd* [1977] R.T.R. 45. See also *Douglas Valley Finance Co Ltd v S Hughes (Hirers) Ltd* [1969] 1 Q.B. 738. In *Martin v Norbury*, 21 July 1999, CA, wrongfully registering a car with HPI, rendering it unsaleable, was held to be conversion.

[105] Torts (Interference with Goods) Act 1977 s.11(3).

[106] *England v Cowley* (1873) L.R. 8 Exch. 126; *Club Cruise, etc BV v Department of Transport* [2008] EWHC 2794 (Comm); [2009] 1 Lloyd's Rep. 201.

[107] *England v Cowley* (1873) L.R. 8 Exch. 126 at 128.

[108] Receipt by way of pledge (para.18-015); conversion by denial of title (para.18-023); co-ownership (para.18-025).

[109] Section 2(1).

[110] See para.18-004.

[111] See para.18-004. In cases where before the Act there was a concurrent liability in conversion and detinue the claimant might claim in detinue in the hope that this would enable him to get specific restitution. See, now, s.3 of the Act.

[112] Section 2(2).

[113] The claimant must, therefore, show a right to immediate possession since this was necessary for detinue at common law. As to the jus tertii, see para.18-032.

[114] Not, therefore, in a situation like that in *Ashby v Tolhurst* [1937] 2 K.B. 242, para.18-019.

D. Conversion and Co-owners

18-025   As between co-owners there is unity of possession, each is entitled to possession and use of the chattel, and mere enjoyment in one way or another by one co-owner cannot amount to conversion against the other. The assertion of exclusive rights will, however, be actionable in tort. By s.10 of the Torts (Interference with Goods) Act 1977 co-ownership is no defence to an action in conversion[115] where one co-owner, without the authority of the other[116]:

> "(a) destroys the goods,[117] or disposes of the goods in a way giving a good title to the entire property in the goods,[118] or otherwise does anything equivalent to the destruction of the other's interest in the goods,[119] or (b) purports to dispose of the goods in a way which would give a good title to the entire property in the goods if he was acting with the authority of all co-owners of the goods".

Paragraph (a) is by way of restatement of the common law;[120] para.(b) extends it so as to make the disposition conversion even if it does not confer a good title on the disponee.[121]

E. Title of Claimant

18-026 **Possession or an immediate right to possess**   What kind of right to the goods must the claimant have in order to sue in conversion? The answer is that he can maintain the action if at the time of the defendant's act he had: (1) ownership and possession of the goods; (2) possession of them; or (3) an immediate right to possess them, but without either ownership or actual possession.[122] Some of the older cases suggest that the claimant must have "a right of property in the thing and a right of possession" and that unless both these rights concur the action will not lie[123] but the Court of Appeal has stated that an immediate right of possession, even if based on contract, is sufficient.[124] The fact that ownership is not necessary is demonstrated

---

[115] The same rules apply to trespass.

[116] The position is different where co-ownership arises because the parties are buyers of portions of goods in bulk (e.g., oil in a tank) who have paid in full or in part. If there is delivery in full to one and then there is a shortfall as to the rest, the others are deemed to have authorised the first delivery, though they retain their contractual rights against the seller: Sale of Goods Act 1979 s.20B.

[117] This does not, presumably, cover acts of the normal user which change the form of the property as in *Fennings v Grenville* (1808) 1 Taunt. 241; 127 E.R. 825 (cutting up and boiling down a whale).

[118] e.g., not a valid pledge under the Factors Act 1889, s.2, since that does not transfer the "entire property".

[119] *Adventure Films Ltd v Tully, The Times,* 14 October 1982 (detention of television film).

[120] On which see *Baker v Barclays Bank Ltd* [1955] 1 W.L.R. 822.

[121] In *Nyberg v Handelaar* [1892] 2 Q.B. 202, A and B were co-owners of a gold enamel box under an agreement that A was to have possession until it was sold. A entrusted it to B for a limited purpose but B pledged it to C. In A's successful action against C, Lopes LJ gave his opinion that A could have maintained conversion against B because of the agreement, but B's pledge would not now purport to dispose of the entire property.

[122] *Rogers v Kennay* (1846) 9 Q.B. 594 at 596 per Patteson J: "Any person having a right to the possession of goods may bring trover in respect of the conversion of them, and allege them to be his property: and lien, as an immediate right of possession, was held to constitute such a property".

[123] *Gordon v Harper* (1796) 7 Term Rep. 9 at 12; 101 E.R. 828 at 829; *Bloxam v Sanders* (1825) 9 B. & C. 941 at 950; 107 E.R. 1309 at 1312; *Owen v Knight* (1837) 4 Bing. N.C. 54 at 57; 132 E.R. 709 at 710; *Bradley v Copley* (1845) 1 C.B. 685; 135 E.R. 711.

[124] *Iran v Barakat Galleries Ltd* [2007] EWCA Civ 1374; [2009] Q.B. 22, explaining *Jarvis v Wil-*

by the fact that it has never been doubted that a bailee (who has possession but not ownership) can sue.[125]

Examples of immediate right to possess The immediate right to possess must **18-027** be briefly examined. A reversionary owner out of possession certainly has not got it, for example in the case of a landlord of premises let together with furniture to a tenant whose term is still unexpired: hence if the furniture is wrongfully seized by the sheriff, it is the tenant and not the landlord who can sue for conversion.[126] Again, an employee with custody of his employer's goods does not have possession of them, for possession is constructively in the employer;[127] but if the employer has made him a bailee of them so as to vest him with exclusive possession, then, like any other bailee of this sort, he has it. Similarly, if goods are delivered to an employee to hand to his employer, the employee has possession of them until he has done some act which transfers it to his employer, for example a shop assistant has possession of money paid to him by a customer until he puts it in the till. Up to that moment the employer has only the right to possess.

These examples are tolerably clear, but it must depend to a large extent on the facts of each case whether the law will attribute to a person the immediate right to possess. A bailor had it against a mere bailee at pleasure[128] even if he never himself had actual possession of the goods and only acquired title by virtue of an illegal but completely executed contract of sale.[129] Similarly, where furniture dealers transferred furniture on hire-purchase to X with an express proviso that the hiring was to terminate without any notice if the goods were taken in execution for debt, they could sue the sheriff for conversion when he levied execution on them.[130] The wrongful sale of goods subject to a hire-purchase agreement will constitute a repudiation and hence vest a right to immediate possession in the finance company even though the agreement does not expressly provide for this.[131] However, in modern conditions legislation may restrict the enforcement of the creditor's rights under a hire-purchase agreement.[132]

---

liams [1955] 1 W.L.R. 71.
[125] *Burton v Hughes* (1842) 2 Bing. 173 at 175; 130 E.R. 272 at 273.
[126] *Gordon v Harper* (1796) 7 Term Rep. 9; 101 E.R. 828.
[127] See Holmes, *The Common Law* (1881), pp.227–228; Pollock and Wright, *Possession in the Common Law* (1888), pp.58–60.
[128] *Manders v Williams* (1849) 4 Ex. 339 (brewers could maintain trover against a sheriff in respect of empty barrels in charge of publican). cf. *Bradley v Copley* (1845) 1 C.B. 685; 135 E.R. 711, where, upon the construction of a bill of sale, a demand was held to be necessary to confer the immediate right to possess.
[129] *Belvoir Finance Co Ltd v Stapleton* [1971] 1 Q.B. 210 (claimant finance company buys car from dealer and lets it on hire-purchase to defendant's employer. Contracts of sale and hire-purchase both illegal. Defendant "sells" car on behalf of employer. Liable for conversion).
[130] *Jelks v Hayward* [1905] 2 K.B. 460, applied in *North General Wagon and Finance Co Ltd v Graham* [1950] 2 K.B. 7; *Alexander v Ry Executive* [1951] 2 K.B. 882; distinguished in *Reliance Car Facilities Ltd v Roding Motors* [1952] 2 Q.B. 844 (hiring terminable on notice, but no notice given).
[131] *Union Transport Finance Ltd v British Car Auctions Ltd* [1978] 2 All E.R. 385. It may be necessary to identify the point in time when the conversion takes place since the right to possession must exist then. In *Smith v Bridgend CBC* [2001] UKHL 58; [2002] 1 A.C. 336, D's power of sale of C's plant was void as an unregistered floating charge. D contracted to sell the plant to X at a time when D had a contractual right to retain it to complete the works. This did not prevent the delivery of the plant to X when the works had been completed being a conversion.
[132] See, e.g., *Barclays Mercantile Business Finance Ltd v Sibec Developments Ltd* [1993] 2 All E.R. 195, where the restriction was regarded as only procedural. For hire-purchase transactions by individu-

18-028 **Simple bailment** In a simple bailment, i.e., one which does not exclude the bailor from possession, an action for conversion against a third person is maintainable by either bailor or bailee[133]: by the bailee because he is in possession, by the bailor because it is said that his title to the goods draws with it the right to possession, that the bailee is something like his employee and that the possession of the one is equivalent to that of the other.[134]

18-029 **Sale of goods** A buyer of goods can sue the seller or a third party for conversion if he has ownership of the goods even though he has not yet got possession of them,[135] but he cannot sue the third party if the latter has a better title than the buyer by reason of exceptions to the rule *nemo dat quod non habet*, under ss.21–25 of the Sale of Goods Act 1979 or under the Factors Act 1889;[136] however, in this instance, the seller is liable for conversion to the buyer.

18-030 **Temporary possession** A person who is entitled to the temporary possession of a chattel and who delivers it back to the owner for a special purpose may, after that purpose is satisfied and during the existence of his temporary right, sue the owner for conversion of it;[137] a fortiori he can sue anyone else.

18-031 **Equitable interest** A person who has a merely equitable right in property and who lacks possession,[138] does not have an immediate right to possession for the purposes of conversion, even though the legal owner is a mere nominee who has to transfer the property to the beneficiary on demand.[139] Though there may in some cases be little practical difference between them, the legal distinction between bailor and bailee, on the one hand, and beneficiary and trustee, on the other hand, is fundamental.[140]

F. Jus Tertii

18-032 **Common law** Once a system of law accepts possession as a sufficient foundation for a claim for recovery of personal property it is faced with the question of how far the defendant should be allowed to raise the issue that a third party has a better right to the property than the claimant—the jus tertii. There are arguments either way. On the one hand, refusal to admit the jus tertii allows recovery by a claimant who may have himself wrongfully dispossessed the true owner and also exposes the wrongdoer to the risk of multiple liability. On the other hand, it may be argued that a person who has dispossessed another should have no right to raise

---

als see the Consumer Credit Act 1974.

[133] *Nicolls v Bastard* (1835) 2 Cr.M. & R. 659; 150 E.R. 279.

[134] *Manders v Williams* (1849) 4 Ex. 339 at 344. As to the avoidance of double liability in such cases, see para.18-034.

[135] See, e.g., *North West Securities Ltd v Alexander Breckon Ltd* [1981] R.T.R. 518. Note that if the goods remain in the seller's possession subject to his lien for their unpaid price, the buyer cannot sue a wrongdoer for conversion: *Lord v Price* (1874) L.R. 9 Ex. 54.

[136] See para.18-040.

[137] *Roberts v Wyatt* (1810) 2 Taunt. 268; 127 E.R. 1080.

[138] cf. *Healey v Healey* [1915] 1 K.B. 938, where the beneficiary had actual possession, which was disturbed by the trustee.

[139] *MCC Proceeds Ltd v Lehman Bros* [1998] 4 All E.R. 675, rejecting a contrary view in *International Factors v Rodriguez* [1979] 1 Q.B. 351.

[140] See further Tettenborn [1996] C.L.J. 36.

such issues concerning the relationship between the dispossessed and some other party having a claim over the goods, for there is a serious risk of abuse and of the interminable prolongation of actions. The common law compromised: if the claimant was in possession at the time of the conversion, the defendant could not set up the jus tertii,[141] unless he was acting under the authority of the true owner.[142] Where, however, the claimant was not in possession at the time of the conversion but relied on his right to possession, jus tertii could be pleaded by the defendant.[143] To this latter rule there was an exception where the defendant was the claimant's bailee, for the bailee was regarded as being estopped from denying the bailor's title[144] unless evicted by title paramount[145] or defending the action on behalf of the true owner.[146]

Fundamental change introduced by the 1977 Act   These rules were fundamentally changed by the Torts (Interference with Goods) Act 1977. According to s.8, in an action for "wrongful interference" with goods[147] the defendant is entitled to show, in accordance with the rules of court,[148] that a third party has a better right than the claimant as respects all or any part of the interest claimed by the claimant, or in right of which he sues.[149] The rules of court require the claimant to identify any other person whom he knows to have a claim on the goods. The defendant may apply for directions as to whether any third person with a competing claim should be joined and if that person fails to appear on such a successful application the court may deprive him of any right of action against the defendant.[150]   **18-033**

Avoiding double liability   The general purpose of these provisions is to allow the court so far as possible to settle competing claims in one set of proceedings. Where all the claimants are before the court, then the relief granted is to be "such as to avoid double liability of the wrongdoer",[151] which presumably means that the court is to apportion the damages representing the value of the chattel according to the   **18-034**

---

[141] Assumed rather than decided in the famous case of *Armory v Delamirie* (1721) 1 Str. 505; 93 E.R. 664 where a chimney-sweep's boy who had found a jewel recovered in conversion against a goldsmith who took it for valuation and refused to return it. The rule was the same for trespass to goods, where, of course, the claimant's possession was a pre-condition to his right to sue.

[142] However, the fact that he had returned the property to the owner was not of itself a defence: *Wilson v Lombank Ltd* [1963] 1 W.L.R. 1294.

[143] *Leake v Loveday* (1842) 4 Man. & G. 972; 134 E.R. 399. cf. Atiyah (1955) 18 M.L.R. 97 and the reply of Jolly (1955) 18 M.L.R. 371.

[144] *Henderson v Williams* [1895] 1 Q.B. 521.

[145] *Shelbury v Scotsford* (1602) Yelv. 23; 80 E.R. 17.

[146] *Rogers, Sons & Co v Lambert & Co* [1891] 1 Q.B. 318.

[147] Defined in s.1 as conversion, trespass, negligence so far as it results in damage to goods or to an interest in goods and "any other tort so far as it results in damage to goods or to an interest in goods". How far can the change in the law on jus tertii be evaded by framing the claim as breach of bailment or in contract? The courts may be able to block the former (cf. *American Express Co v British Airways Board* [1983] 1 W.L.R. 701) but the latter will be more difficult to deal with. See further Palmer (1978) 41 M.L.R. 629.

[148] See CPR r.19.5A.

[149] Section 8(1). This provision applies even though the third party has disposed of the alleged interest before proceedings are begun: *De Franco v MPC, The Times*, 8 May 1987.

[150] Section 8(2). See also s.9, which provides machinery to deal with concurrent claims in different courts.

[151] Section 7(2).

respective interests of the claimants.[152] The 1977 Act is perhaps not so clear where only the claimant with a possessory title is before the court, for example, because the true owner does not appear or cannot be found. A literal interpretation of s.8 might suggest that the ability to plead the jus tertii provides the defendant with a defence,[153] but it seems clear that in such a case the provisions of s.7 preserve the common law rule that a claimant relying on a possessory interest may recover the full value of the thing converted.[154] In such a situation the true owner may have been divested of his claim against the wrongdoer under s.8(2)(d) but, if not, he might still be entitled to sue by virtue of his title. Two provisions of the Act are aimed at this problem. By s.7(3)[155]:

> "on satisfaction, in whole or in part, of any claim for an amount exceeding that recoverable if subsection (2) applied [i.e., where both claimants are parties], the claimant is liable to account over to the other person having a right to claim to such extent as will avoid double liability".

And by s.7(4): "where, as a result of enforcement of a double liability, any claimant is unjustly enriched to any extent, he shall be liable to reimburse the wrongdoer to that extent." Thus, if A loses his goods, which are found by C and then converted by D, both C and A might bring successive claims against D. If C accounts to A under s.7(3), A must then reimburse D. If C does not so account, C is liable to reimburse D. A "double liability" would, however, still exist if both A and C were insolvent.[156]

18-035 **Double liability in cases of bailment** A central difficulty in construing the provisions of the 1977 Act on jus tertii is the position where there is a bailment, which is presumably far and away the commonest source of a "possessory title". As we have seen, at common law the bailee could recover the full value of the goods on the basis of his possession. If he did so, he had to account to the bailor for the amount by which the damages exceeded his (the bailee's) interest.[157] In such a case the wrongdoer, having paid full damages to the bailee, had a complete answer to

---

[152] As between finder and true owner, the interest of the finder would presumably be nil.

[153] Or at least reduce the claimant's damages to the value of his interest.

[154] *The Winkfield* [1902] P. 42 (a strong case since the bailee claimant would have been under no liability to the owners for loss of the goods); *Chabbra Corp Pte Ltd v Jag Shakti (owners)* [1986] A.C. 337. This was certainly the intention of the Law Reform Committee: Cmnd.4774 (1971), para.75 and was the view taken in *Costello v CC Derbyshire* [2001] EWCA Civ 381; [2001] 1 W.L.R. 1437 at [15]. Some cases, e.g., *The Winkfield*, are claims for negligence but the position is the same.

[155] As to the bailee, see para.18-035.

[156] What is the effect of the Act on the facts of *Wilson v Lombank Ltd* [1963] 1 W.L.R. 1294? C purchased a car from a person who had no title, the car in fact belonging to X. While the car was at a garage after undergoing repairs, D's agents passed by and, mistakenly thinking it belonged to D, took it away. D discovered the truth and returned the car to X. C sued D for trespass to goods and recovered the full value of the car (£470) because, in Hinchcliffe J's opinion, D could not set up the title of X against C's possessory title. Since it is inconceivable that, the car having been returned to X, X could have sued D for anything other than nominal damages, it seems somewhat strained to talk of a "double liability" under s.7. Could this be a case where s.8(1) is to be taken at its face value?

[157] Among the many statements to this effect see *The Winkfield* [1902] P. 42 at 55; *Eastern Construction Co Ltd v National Trust* [1914] A.C. 197 at 210; *Hepburn v A Tomlinson (Hauliers) Ltd* [1966] A.C. 451 at 467–468, 480.

any action by the bailor.[158] Conversely, if the bailor sued first and recovered full value,[159] the bailee was equally barred.[160]

These principles cast some doubt upon the reality of the risk of double liability which lies at the root of ss.7 and 8 of the 1977 Act but the Act may still provide a useful means of enabling the court to apportion the full range of loss which could arise from the conversion or destruction of goods and to avoid the risk that, say, the bailor might have difficulties in getting the bailee to account for part of the judgment sum.[161] Curiously, the common law principles have been applied in a modern case in which the Act is not even mentioned[162] and it is to be hoped that certain statements in the case will not present obstacles to the application of the Act's machinery.

Claim based on possession of stolen goods It has been seen above that where **18-036** the true owner of goods cannot be involved in the proceedings the common law rule that a mere possessory interest entitles the claimant to recover the full value of the goods against a wrongdoer still applies. Does this mean that if there is clear evidence that the goods were stolen by C from X (who has since disappeared) C may nevertheless recover from D, who converted them by taking them from C? In *Costello v Chief Constable of Derbyshire*[163] the police seized a car in C's possession and refused to return it when their investigations were complete. The trial judge found that the car was stolen (though not by C) and that C was aware of that, though the person from whom it had been stolen remained unidentified. The Court of Appeal held that the refusal to return the car to C was conversion of it: his prior possession gave him a better claim to it than the police[164] and he was not required to rely on any illegal transaction to establish that.[165] Where the owner could not be

---

[158] *Nicolls v Bastard* (1835) 2 Cr. M. & R. 659 at 660; 150 E.R. 279 at 280; *The Winkfield* [1902] P. 42 at 61.

[159] It was held in *Chabbra Corp Pte Ltd v Jag Shakti (Owners)* [1986] A.C. 337 that a person with a mere right to possession might recover full value but this is controversial: Palmer, *Bailment*, 3rd edn (2009), para.4-138.

[160] *Nicolls v Bastard* (1835) 2 Cr. M. & R. 659 at 660; 150 E.R. 279 at 280; *O'Sullivan v Williams* [1992] 3 All E.R. 385, where there was a non-contractual bailment at will and the bailee therefore had no right to look to the bailor. Complications which could arise from the fact that the bailee might sustain losses not covered by the bailor's claim do not seem to have been fully explored in the cases: Palmer, *Bailment*, 3rd edn (2009), para.4-099.

[161] See, e.g., Palmer, *Bailment*, 3rd edn (2009), para.4-138: "It is submitted that s.7(2) should be construed expansively to enable the court, in all cases where two or more claimants are parties, to divide the damages according to the value of their respective interests, whether this is strictly necessary to save the wrongdoer from a [double liability] or not."

[162] *O'Sullivan v Williams* [1992] 3 All E.R. 385. Perhaps this was because the claim arose from a (very unusual) vehicle collision and at the time these were not subject to the court rules then applicable.

[163] [2001] EWCA Civ 381; [2001] 1 W.L.R. 1437. See also *Webb v Chief Constable of Merseyside* [2000] Q.B. 427 (even if it could be established that money seized from the claimant was the product of drug trafficking, that provided no basis for refusing to return it); *Gough v Chief Constable of the West Midlands* [2004] EWCA Civ 206; and *Jaroo v Attorney General of Trinidad and Tobago* [2002] UKPC 5; [2002] 1 A.C. 871 (where the claim was brought under a constitutional guarantee of the right to enjoyment of property); *Ecclestone v Khyami* [2014] EWHC 29 (QB) at [125]–[129].

[164] There are powers under the Police and Criminal Evidence Act 1984 to retain property for the purposes of investigation or as evidence but the conditions for the exercise of these were not satisfied in this case. The Police Property Act 1897 gives magistrates power to make orders for the disposition of property in the hands of the police but that does not override civil rights under the general law.

[165] See *Tinsley v Milligan* [1994] 1 A.C. 340 and the general discussion of illegality at para.26-064.

identified, the only ground for refusing to treat the claimant as entitled to the goods would be that it was inherently unlawful to possess them, as in the case of controlled drugs.[166] However, in cases of this kind, consideration must now be given to the enormously extensive powers of confiscation and forfeiture under the Proceeds of Crime Act 2002,[167] s.329 of which makes it an offence for a person to be in possession of property which constitutes a benefit from his criminal conduct.

G. Finding

18-037   **The finder has a limited title**[168]   "Finders keepers" is a dangerous half-truth, which needs a good deal of expansion and qualification to make it square with the law. A finder of a chattel has a title which enables him to keep it against everyone,[169] with two exceptions. The first is that the finder acquires no title as against the rightful owner. Hence if the finder appropriates the chattel he not only commits the tort of conversion,[170] but is also guilty of the crime of theft unless he did so in the belief that the owner could not be discovered by taking reasonable steps.[171]

18-038   **The relative rights of finder and occupier of the land**   The second exception is that the occupier[172] of the land on which the chattel[173] was found may in some cases have a title superior to that of the finder. The Court of Appeal in *Parker v British Airways Board*[174] took the opportunity to restate the law in a comprehensive manner and bring order to an area in which there were numerous conflicting precedents. The cases in which the occupier of the land has the superior title[175] are: (1) where the finder is a trespasser on the land;[176] (2) where the property is embedded in or attached to the land, as in *Waverley BC v Fletcher*,[177] where a medieval gold brooch

---

[166]   In *Chief Constable of Merseyside v Owens* [2012] EWHC 1515 (Admin), it was held that there is no entitlement to retain property only because the defendant reasonably suspects that the claimant may commit a crime with it. But cf. *McCarthy v Chief Constable of the PSNI* [2016] NICA 36; [2018] N.I. 158 at [31] (public policy defence to claims for return of goods in certain circumstances).

[167]   Various public authorities (see the Serious Crime Act 2007) may take civil proceedings for the recovery of the proceeds of criminal activity (on a civil standard of proof and with assumptions against the defendant if he has a "criminal lifestyle"). See *Fletcher v Leicestershire Constabulary* [2013] EWHC 3357 (Admin); [2014] Lloyd's Rep. F.C. 60.

[168]   Palmer, *Bailment*, 3rd edn (2009), Ch.26; Hickey, *Property and the Law of Finders* (2010).

[169]   Like the person in possession of stolen goods, the finder's claim is based on his possession alone.

[170]   *Moffatt v Kazana* [1969] 2 Q.B. 152.

[171]   Theft Act 1968 ss.1, 2(1)(c).

[172]   Not an owner out of occupation: *Hannah v Peel* [1945] K.B. 509.

[173]   Different rules apply where the property is "treasure", as to which, see the Treasure Act 1996, replacing the common law of treasure trove. The Crown's rights in treasure override those of the finder and the occupier, with a discretion in the Secretary of State to compensate either or both of them up to the value of the goods found. The definition of treasure under the Act is a good deal wider than at common law.

[174]   [1982] Q.B. 1004.

[175]   It is assumed that the finder is not employed by the occupier, for an employee who finds in the course of his employment must account to his employer. The same may be true of an agent of the occupier acting within the scope of his authority.

[176]   Where the finder is not a trespasser but dishonestly intends to retain the property even against the true owner, he "probably has some title, albeit a frail one, because of the need to avoid a free-for-all": *Parker v British Airways Board* [1982] Q.B. 1004 at 1010.

[177]   [1996] Q.B. 334. See also *South Staffordshire Water Co v Sharman* [1896] 2 Q.B. 44, the result in which can however also be justified on the ground that the finders were employed by the claimants: *Parker v British Airways Board* [1982] Q.B. 1004 at 1013.

was found embedded nine inches deep in the soil of a park; and (3) where, before the finding, the occupier "has manifested an intention to exercise control over the [premises] and the things which may be upon it or in it".[178] The burden of proof of this rests upon the occupier, though in some cases the matter speaks for itself[179]:

> "If a bank manager saw fit to show me round a vault containing safe deposits and I found a gold bracelet on the floor, I should have no doubt that the bank had a better title than I, and the reason is the manifest intention to exercise a very high degree of control. At the other extreme is the park to which the public has unrestricted access during daylight hours. During those hours there is no manifest intention to exercise any such control. In between these extremes are the forecourts of petrol filling stations, unfenced front gardens of private houses, the public parts of shops and supermarkets as part of an almost infinite variety of land, premises and circumstances."

In *Parker*'s case itself the claimant found a gold bracelet on the floor of the executive lounge at Heathrow Airport and was held entitled to it as against the occupiers. That they restricted entry to the lounge to certain classes of passenger and gave their staff instructions as to what to do with lost property was insufficient to manifest an intention to exercise the requisite degree of control.[180] It is, of course, open to the occupier to regulate the right to possession of lost property by contract with the entrant; it remains to be seen whether merely putting up notices at the entrance declaring that lost property is to vest in the occupier will be an effective manifestation of the intent to control required by *Parker*'s case.

4. STRICT LIABILITY AND CONVERSION

Mistake no defence   Mistake does not usually provide a defence to a claim in conversion,[181] for liability is strict[182]:   **18-039**

> "At common law one's duty to ... the owner ... of any goods is to refrain from doing any voluntary act in relation to his goods which is a usurpation of his proprietary or possessory rights in them. Subject to some exceptions ... it matters not that the doer of the act of usurpation did not know, and could not by the exercise of any reasonable care have known of [the owner's] interest in the goods. This duty is absolute; he acts at his peril."

The classic illustration is the auctioneer, who is liable in conversion if he innocently effects the sale of another's goods[183] and of whom it has been said that conversion is one of "the risks of their profession".[184]

This rule was set solidly into law by the House of Lords in *Hollins v Fowler*.[185] B fraudulently obtained possession of cotton from Fowler. Hollins, a cotton broker who was ignorant of the fraud, bought it from B and resold it to another person,

---

[178] *Parker v British Airways Board* [1982] Q.B. 1004 at 1018 per Donaldson LJ.

[179] *Parker v British Airways Board* [1982] Q.B. 1004 at 1019 per Donaldson LJ.

[180] The much-criticised decision in *Bridges v Hawkesworth* (1851) 21 L.J.Q.B. 75, where an occupier failed against the finder of banknotes on the floor of a shop, was approved in *Parker*'s case.

[181] Licence and the exercise of a right of distress are defences to an action for conversion but these have already been touched on in relation to trespass to land.

[182] *Marfani & Co Ltd v Midland Bank Ltd* [1968] 1 W.L.R. 956 at 971 per Diplock LJ.

[183] *Consolidated Co v Curtis & Son* [1892] 1 Q.B. 495; *RH Willis & Sons v British Car Auctions Ltd* [1978] 1 W.L.R. 438, doubting *National Mercantile Bank Ltd v Rymill* (1881) 44 L.T. 767.

[184] *Sachs v Miklos* [1948] 2 K.B. 23 at 37 per Lord Goddard CJ.

[185] (1875) L.R. 7 H.L. 757.

receiving only broker's commission. Hollins was held liable to Fowler for the conversion of the cotton. The justification for such a rule is not obvious, particularly in a case where the claimant has handed his goods over to a rogue on some flimsy excuse while the defendant has acquired the goods not only in good faith but from some reputable dealer who has himself been deceived. One solution which has been suggested would be to apportion the loss between claimant and defendant in such a case[186] but this was rejected as impracticable by the Law Reform Committee.[187] An alternative approach would be to apply the "ready-made" system of apportionment in the Law Reform (Contributory Negligence) Act 1945 to liability in conversion.[188] There was previously some authority for this but the matter is now governed by s.11(1) of the Torts (Interference with Goods) Act 1977, which states that contributory negligence is no defence in proceedings founded on conversion, or on intentional trespass to goods.[189]

18-040 Exceptions   There are, however, exceptions to the rule that an innocent mistake is no defence to an action in conversion. The first group of these consists of the exceptions to the rule *nemo dat quod non habet*, whereby a bona fide purchaser of goods from A obtains a good title to them even though the goods really belonged to B. In these cases, no action lies against the bona fide purchaser in conversion and B's remedy is against A alone. The law here seeks to strike a compromise between the competing principles that ownership of property must be protected and that speedy commerce in goods should be facilitated. The details of the relevant law must be sought elsewhere[190] but the principal exceptions are as follows: (1) estoppel by representation or by negligence;[191] (2) sale under a voidable title;[192] (3) disposition in the ordinary course of business by a mercantile agent in possession of the goods or documents of title with the owner's consent;[193] (4) second sale by seller in possession;[194] (5) sale by buyer in possession;[195] and (6) private purchaser of vehicle subject to a hire-purchase agreement.[196]

18-041 No conversion in ministerial handling   We have seen above that a person commits conversion if he sells the goods to another, whether on his own behalf or as an agent (e.g., an auctioneer), but the position is different where the defendant innocently interferes with the claimant's goods by doing an act that amounts to no

---

186 *Ingram v Little* [1961] 1 Q.B. 31 at 73–74.
187 Twelfth Report, *Transfer of Title to Chattels*, Cmnd.2958 (1966).
188 This would not have gone so far as Devlin LJ's proposal since the claimant's damages could only have been reduced if he was at fault.
189 However, under s.47 of the Banking Act 1979 a "defence of contributory negligence" is available to a banker converting a cheque if the circumstances are such that he would be protected by s.4 of the Cheques Act 1957 if he were not negligent.
190 *Benjamin's Sale of Goods*, 10th edn (2017), Ch.7.
191 Such a plea is extremely difficult to establish, no doubt because it would soon eat up all the other exceptions. Carelessness in allowing goods to be stolen or putting the goods in the hands of a third party will not found the estoppel. See *Moorgate Mercantile Co Ltd v Twitchings* [1977] A.C. 890.
192 e.g., *Lewis v Avery* [1972] 1 Q.B. 198.
193 Factors Act 1889 s.2.
194 Sale of Goods Act 1979 s.24.
195 Sale of Goods Act 1979 s.25.
196 Hire Purchase Act 1964 Pt III. See also Twelfth Report of the *Law Reform Committee*, Cmnd.2958 (1966).

more than transportation, custody or redelivery of the goods.[197] So in *Marcq v Christie, Manson & Woods Ltd*[198] a painting was deposited by S with the defendant auctioneers for sale. Unknown to the auctioneers the painting had been stolen some years previously from M. It failed to sell at auction and was eventually returned by the defendants to S. A claim for conversion against the auctioneers in redelivering it failed and it was irrelevant that the terms of contract gave the auctioneers a lien for their charges against S.[199] Similarly there is no liability where a railway company, acting upon A's directions, carries B's goods, honestly believing that A has B's authority to give such directions,[200] nor where a finder removes them to a place of safety.[201]

This principle would protect all those persons in *Hollins v Fowler* who merely handled the cotton ministerially, such as a carrier who received and delivered the cotton in the ordinary way,[202] but it would not save the person who sold the cotton to another. Unfortunately, it is unclear how far the principle goes. Does it protect the defendant if A wrongfully gives him B's wheat to grind into flour and he innocently does so? In *Hollins v Fowler* Blackburn J thought not (and indeed a mere finder of lost wheat could not authorise the grinding of it), and yet he felt that it would be hard to hold the defendant liable. In any case, a finder of perishable commodities would no doubt be justified in taking any reasonable steps to preserve them pending the ascertainment of their owner—for example he would not commit conversion by making jam of strawberries if that were the only means of preserving them.

5. RETAKING OF GOODS

A species of self-help Retaking of goods is a form of self-help. It may now be an oversimplification to say that if A's goods are wrongfully in B's possession there is no need for A to go to the expense of litigation to recover them.[203] No doubt there are still cases where this is so, as where A catches B immediately after he has seized A's property and retakes it.[204] It would be a hard rule (and an unrealistic one) which said that a person who caught a bag snatcher had to sue to recover his bag and committed a battery if he laid hands on the thief. In such a case there may anyway be the further justification of preventing crime or effecting an arrest. Beyond that simple case it is not easy to state the law with certainty. Perhaps there is also a right to retake goods wherever the holder came into possession of them wrongfully (even by an innocent purchase from a thief conferring no title) but there is authority both

18-042

---

[197] *Hollins v Fowler* (1875) L.R. 7 H.L. 757 at 766–767.

[198] [2003] EWCA Civ 731; [2004] Q.B. 286.

[199] Of course, if M had demanded the painting from the auctioneers their refusal by assertion of the lien against him *would* have been conversion.

[200] See *Hollins v Fowler* (1875) L.R. 7 H.L. 757 at 767; cf. *The Pioneer Container* [1994] 2 A.C. 324 (bailee "assumes responsibility" only to person of whose interest he is aware).

[201] *Sorrell v Paget* [1950] 1 K.B. 252.

[202] In *Hollins v Fowler* (1875) L.R. 7 H.L. 757, Blackburn J speaks of the delivery as merely "changing the custody" but it is hard to see why, as he suggests, it would be "very difficult, if not impossible" to fix the carrier with knowledge that the goods had been sold to the consignee. Yet to impose liability on the carrier who had such knowledge would seem to be wholly unreasonable. See *Re Samuel (No.2)* [1945] Ch. 408.

[203] Delay may mean destruction or carrying away of the goods by B, who may be quite incapable of paying damages: III Bl. Comm. 4.

[204] See, e.g., *Whatford v Carty, The Times,* 29 October 1960.

ways on the situation where the taker initially consented to the possession of the holder but then withdrew it.[205] Criminal cases arising out of wheel clamping have shown a hostile attitude to self-help by the vehicle owner, though on the facts the vehicles were not lawfully on the property where the clamp was applied.[206] Even where the owner is justified in using force it must be no more than is reasonably necessary and that varies with the facts of each case and the view of the court after the event, so self-help is likely to be just as dangerous a course of action here as elsewhere in the law. Moreover, there are other qualifications of A's right to retake goods.[207]

18-043 **Retaking and trespass to land** Further difficulty arises over the circumstances in which a person can enter premises to retrieve his goods without committing a trespass. There is no doubt that the person entitled to goods may enter and take them from the land of the first taker if the taker himself wrongfully put them there;[208] but it is by no means certain what the law is when the goods are on the premises of one who was not responsible for bringing them there and who has committed no tort with respect to them. The only case of any real assistance is *Anthony v Haney*,[209] but the dicta are obiter and, although of considerable weight, do not probe the question of recaption very deeply. Tindal CJ in that case gave as examples of permissible retaking by A from the land of an innocent person, C: (1) where the goods have come there by accident; (2) where they have been feloniously taken by B and A follows them to C's land; and (3) where C refuses to deliver up the goods or to make any answer to A's demand for them.

18-044 **Retaking goods accidentally on another's land** In this first category, the examples given were A's fruit falling on C's land, or A's tree falling on it by decay or being blown upon it by the wind. By "accident" it seems clear that "inevitable accident" was meant, rather than, say, negligence. Where the entry of the goods was inevitable, not only is there no liability for trespass on the part of their owner, but the view that he can retake them seems to be right, even if there is no direct decision to that effect.

18-045 **Following goods taken criminally on to another's land** The distinction between felonies and misdemeanours no longer exists[210] but there seems no reason why the rule, if it is a rule at all, should not apply wherever B's taking is criminal.

18-046 **Retaking goods when occupier refuses to deliver up the goods or answer a demand** Tindal CJ thought that where C refused to deliver up the goods or to answer A's demand "a jury might be induced to presume a conversion from such silence, or at any rate the owner might in such case enter and take his property

---

[205] The matter is reviewed at length in *Toyota Finance Australia Ltd v Dennis* [2002] NSWCA 369; (2002) 58 N.S.W.L.R. 101.
[206] *Lloyd v DPP* [1992] 1 All E.R. 982 ("no reasonable alternative"); *R. v Mitchell* [2003] EWCA Crim 2188; [2004] R.T.R. 14. See also *Arthur v Anker* [1996] 1 W.L.R. 602.
[207] There are certain important statutory restrictions on the retaking of goods, the best known of which are in the Consumer Credit Act 1974.
[208] *Patrick v Colerick* (1838) 3 M. & W. 483; 150 E.R. 1235.
[209] (1832) 8 Bing. 186; 131 E.R. 372.
[210] Abolished by the Criminal Law Act 1967 s.1(1).

subject to the payment of any damage he might commit",[211] though there are cases suggesting that mere refusal to allow collection would not be conversion.[212] As a matter of policy it is arguable that where the owner of goods is under no tortious liability in respect of their appearance on the occupier's land, he ought to be able to retake them in any event, provided he does no injury to the premises or gives adequate security for making good any unavoidable injury. Conversely, it may be urged that self-help ought to be strictly limited even against one who is a wrongdoer and forbidden altogether against one who is not, except that retaking might be permitted in circumstances of inevitable accident or of necessity (for example, where the goods are perishable or are doing considerable damage to the land and it is impossible to communicate speedily enough with the occupier or his agent).

The need for an explanation from the retaker   The retaker, before he attempts   **18-047**
to retake, must, if required to do so, explain to the occupier of the land or the person in possession of the goods the facts upon which his proposed action is based. A mere allegation that the goods are his, without any attempt to show how they came on the premises, will not do, for "to allow such a statement to be a justification for entering the soil of another, would be opening too wide a door to parties to attempt righting themselves without resorting to law, and would necessarily tend to breach of the peace".[213]

<h3 style="text-align:center">6.   REMEDIES FOR INTERFERENCE WITH GOODS</h3>

<h2 style="text-align:center">A.   Damages</h2>

Damages the primary remedy   In practice damages are, as elsewhere in the law   **18-048**
of torts, the primary remedy for wrongful interference with goods. This is necessarily so where the defendant is no longer in possession because he has destroyed the goods or disposed of them or they have been returned, but even where the defendant is still in possession it is comparatively rare for him to be ordered specifically to return them, though he may be given the option of returning them or paying their value.

Assessment of damages   In most cases the judgment for damages will be for the   **18-049**
value[214] of the goods at the time of the conversion[215] together with any consequential

---

[211] *Anthony v Haney* (1832) 8 Bing. 186 at 192–193; 131 E.R. 372 at 374–375. The report in 1 L.J.C.P. 81 at 84 omits the passage about the right to enter, subject to payment of damages; the report in 1 Moo. & Sc. 300 at 308 omits any reference to the obligation to pay for the damage done. Since Tindal CJ had already dealt with accidental entry and wrongful appropriation it is not wholly clear what type of case he had in mind.

[212] *British Economical Lamp Co Ltd v Empire Mile End Ltd* (1913) 29 T.L.R. 386. Maule J in *Wilde v Waters* (1855) 24 L.J.C.P 193 at 195 thought that if a former tenant of a house left a picture on a wall and the new tenant refused to admit him and merely said "I don't want your chattel, but I shall not give myself any trouble about it", that would not be conversion. This seems to be a sort of permanent legal stand-off, though since the former tenant undoubtedly remains the owner of the picture he must surely be able to obtain an order allowing collection. See also *Moffatt v Kazana* [1969] 2 Q.B. 152 at 156–157 and Palmer (1980) 9 Anglo-Am. L.R. 279.

[213] *Anthony v Haney* (1832) 8 Bing. 186 at 191–192; 131 E.R. 372 at 374 per Tindal CJ.

[214] For the value of documents such as negotiable instruments, see para.18-012. Punitive damages may be awarded where the defendant calculates to make a profit exceeding compensatory damages: *Borders (UK) Ltd v MPC* [2005] EWCA Civ 197; [2005] Po. L.R. 1 and para.23-015.

loss which is not too remote, or which the claimant failed to mitigate.[216] The value of the goods is prima facie their market price, though where they cannot be obtained in the market the cost of replacement may be allowed where the claimant has replaced them or will do so.[217] If there is doubt as to the value of the chattel the claimant will get the benefit of it for *omnia praesumuntur contra spoliatorem*,[218] though pressing this too far would negate the principle that it is for the claimant to prove his loss.[219] Damages for conversion are however ultimately assessed on the basis of what is necessary to give the claimant just compensation for his loss[220] and the test of value will therefore have to give way to that where the claimant's loss is smaller. Thus a finance company letting goods on hire-purchase is limited to recovering the amount owing under the agreement;[221] and a person who uses raw materials for processing rather than trading in them and who does not replace them during the period they are wrongfully detained cannot recover damages by reference to the fall in the market price during that period.[222]

18-050 **Allowance for the value of returned goods**   Where the goods (or an exact equivalent) are returned, one plainly cannot ignore the value of what the claimant receives. In *BBMB Finance (Hong Kong) Ltd v Eda Holdings Ltd*[223] D converted C's share certificates by selling the shares for HK $5.75 each. D later replaced these with equivalent shares at HK $2.40 each. On the basis that both these figures represented the market value of the shares at the relevant time, the Privy Council held that C was entitled to the value of the shares sold at the time of conversion, less the value of the replacements.

18-051 **Consequential loss**   The recovery of consequential losses is illustrated in a very simple way by *Bodley v Reynolds*,[224] where a carpenter's tools were converted and he was thereby prevented from working: £10 above the value of the tools was awarded as special damage. Such loss may include personal inconvenience, such as loss of a hobby,[225] and the costs of seeking out the goods.[226] On a rather grander

---

[215] This is the general rule and reflects the claimant's duty to mitigate his loss, but the position would be different if the claimant were unaware of the conversion until later: *Sachs v Micklos* [1948] 2 K.B. 23; *BBMB Finance (Hong Kong) Ltd v Eda Holdings Ltd* [1990] 1 W.L.R. 409. cf. *Scheps v Fine Art Logistic Ltd* [2007] EWHC 541 (QB), which simply allows the claimant to add on any subsequent notional rise in value to judgment as consequential loss.

[216] *Uzinterimpex JSC v Standard Bank Plc* [2008] EWCA Civ 819; [2008] 2 Lloyd's Rep. 456.

[217] *Hall v Barclay* [1937] 3 All E.R. 620; *Wilson v Robertsons (London) Ltd* [2006] EWCA Civ 1088; and see para.23-115 (damage and destruction).

[218] Everything is presumed against a wrongful taker: *Armory v Delamirie* (1721) 1 Str. 505; 93 E.R. 664.

[219] *Zabihi v Janzemini* [2009] EWCA Civ 851; *Malhotra v Dhawan* [1997] Med. L.R. 319; *Colbeck v Diamanta (UK) Ltd* [2002] EWHC 616 (QB).

[220] *Kuwait Airways Corp v Iraqi Airways Co (Nos 4 and 5)* [2002] UKHL 19; [2002] 2 A.C. 883 at [67].

[221] *Wickham Holdings Ltd v Brooke House Motors Ltd* [1967] 1 W.L.R. 295. For the position of the claimant with a possessory interest, see para.18-034.

[222] *Brandeis Goldschmidt & Co Ltd v Western Transport Ltd* [1981] Q.B. 864. The same would likely be true where the goods are a family heirloom which the owner would never have sold: *Glenbrook Capital LP v Hamilton (t/a Hamiltons)* [2014] EWHC 2297 (Comm) at [55].

[223] [1990] 1 W.L.R. 409. See also *Solloway v McLaughlin* [1938] A.C. 247.

[224] (1846) 8 Q.B. 779. cf. *Chubb Cash Ltd v John Crilley & Son* [1983] 1 W.L.R. 599 (market value recoverable, not higher sum that claimant owed on the goods).

[225] *Graham v Voigt* (1989) 89 A.C.T.R. 11.

[226] *Aziz v Lim* [2012] EWHC 915 (QB) (converted diamonds tracked to Geneva).

scale, when a fleet of airliners was converted during the Gulf War damages for consequential losses such as repairs, chartering substitutes and lost operating profits ran into hundreds of millions of US dollars.[227] Generally, however, loss incurred as a result of the claimant's inability to deliver the goods under a lucrative contract of sale is too remote unless the defendant is aware of the contract.[228]

Damages not governed by the "but for" test   Damages for conversion are not   **18-052** governed by the application of the simple "but for" test of causation. Property may be successively converted by A and B and C and the claimant may sue all or any of them for the value of the goods. It has never been suggested that B or C might seek to reduce or extinguish the damages because A had already deprived the claimant of his goods or by showing that if A had not transferred them to B he would probably have transferred them to someone else[229]:

> "By definition, each person in a series of conversions wrongfully excludes the owner from possession of his goods. This is the basis on which each is liable to the owner. That is the nature of the tort of conversion. The wrongful acts of a previous possessor do not therefore diminish the plaintiff's claim in respect of the wrongful acts of a later possessor."

In *Kuwait Airways Corp v Iraqi Airways Co (Nos 4 and 5)*[230] the state of Iraq seized ten aircraft belonging to the claimants and the defendants subsequently converted them by incorporating them into their fleet pursuant to a decree which was not recognised by English law. Four were then destroyed on the ground by Allied bombing, something which would probably have happened even if the defendants had not taken them over. Six were spirited away to Iran and eventually recovered by the claimants. As the law then stood,[231] the matters were only actionable in England if they: (1) amounted to a tort in English law; and (2) were civilly actionable under the law of Iraq. The claim failed in regard to the first four aircraft because in a case of destruction Iraqi law applied a "but for" test, though the Court of Appeal (this matter was not considered in the House of Lords) thought there was liability in conversion in English law, unless perhaps it could be shown that the destruction was inevitable.[232] However, in the case of the other six aircraft the requirements of Iraqi law were no more stringent than those of the English law of conversion and accordingly it was no answer to the claim that if the defendants had not taken them the Iraqi Government would have retained them and probably flown them to Iran anyway.

---

[227] *Kuwait Airways Corp v Iraqi Airways Co (Nos 4 and 5)* [2002] UKHL 19; [2002] 2 A.C. 883. Detention of a stallion turned out to be expensive in *Cash v Chief Constable of Lancashire* [2008] EWHC 396 (Ch).

[228] *The Arpad* [1934] P. 189; *Saleslease Ltd v Davis* [1999] 1 W.L.R. 1664; *Checkprice (UK) Ltd (in administration) v Revenue & Customs Commissioners* [2010] EWHC 682 (Admin); [2010] S.T.C. 1153; cf. *France v Gaudet* (1871) L.R. 6 Q.B. 199, distinguished in *The Arpad*.

[229] *Kuwait Airways Corp v Iraqi Airways Co (Nos 4 and 5)* [2002] UKHL 19; [2002] 2 A.C. 883 at [82] per Lord Nicholls.

[230] [2002] UKHL 19; [2002] 2 A.C. 883.

[231] See para.18-022.

[232] See [2001] 3 W.L.R. 1251 at [606]. Suppose that a week after the conversion of an aircraft a design defect in the type was discovered and all such aircraft had to be scrapped. Is the defendant liable for their full market value at the date of the conversion?

18-053 **Remoteness** The question may also arise, in relation to consequential losses,[233] whether the damage suffered is too remote. In the *Kuwait Airways* case Lord Nicholls (with the explicit agreement of Lord Hoffmann and Lord Hope) expressed the view that where the defendant converts the goods knowingly the test in deceit applies—namely, that the loss must be the "direct and natural consequence" of the conversion.[234] Yet, where the conversion is innocent, although *liability* may be strict, the defendant is liable only for consequences which would be foreseeable on the basis of knowledge that the goods had been misappropriated.[235] On the facts, the cost of hiring substitute aircraft and loss of business were clearly to be expected; but when the claimants went into the market to buy replacement aircraft they not only sought equivalent substitutes, but also made significant changes in the structure of their fleet and while this was a commercially reasonable decision they were unable to recover the finance costs associated with it.[236]

B. Delivery Up

18-054 The only remedy for conversion at common law was the purely personal one of damages. However, when the defendant was in possession of the goods and refused to deliver them up on demand his act was not only conversion but also detinue and the form of judgment in detinue might include an order for the delivery up of the goods.[237] Detinue has now been abolished but the remedies for conversion where goods are detained by the defendant[238] are set out in s.3 of the Torts (Interference with Goods) Act 1977, which is modelled on the common law remedies available for detinue.[239]

18-055 **Relief available under s.3 of the Torts (Interference with Goods) Act 1977** The relief available under s.3 is as follows[240]: (1) an order for the delivery of the goods, and for payment of any consequential damages;[241] or (2) an order for delivery[242] of

---

[233] Recovery of loss relating to the proprietary or possessory interest itself (e.g., legal costs incurred in protecting that interest) is not subject to rules of remoteness or legal causation: *Maitland Hudson v Solicitors Regulation Authority* [2017] EWHC 1249 (Ch).

[234] See para.12-023.

[235] *Kuwait Airways Corp v Iraqi Airways Co (Nos 4 and 5)* [2002] UKHL 19; [2002] 2 A.C. 883 at [100]–[104].

[236] See also *Sandeman Coprimar SA v Transitos y Transportes Integrales SL* [2003] EWCA Civ 113; [2003] Q.B. 1270 (loss of cartons; carrier unaware of consequent liability of consignor for customs duty).

[237] See the full discussion in *General and Finance Facilities Ltd v Cook Cars (Romford) Ltd* [1963] 1 W.L.R. 644 at 650–651. There were in fact three forms: (1) for the value of the chattel and damages for detention; (2) for the return of the chattel or recovery of its value as assessed and damages for detention; and (3) for the return of the chattel and damages for detention.

[238] Except perhaps in the case of a "one-man company", a director is not "in possession or control" of goods in the possession or control of the company: *Thunder Air Ltd v Hilmarsson* [2008] EWHC 355 (Ch); *Joiner v George* [2002] EWHC 90 (Ch); cf. *Mainline Private Hire Ltd v Nolan* [2011] EWCA Civ 189; [2011] C.T.L.C. 145 (possession of the defendant by way of possession of his bailee).

[239] *IBL Ltd v Coussens* [1991] 2 All E.R. 133 at 141. The section applies if the defendant ceases to be in possession between issue of proceedings and judgment: *Hillesden Securities Ltd v Ryjack Ltd* [1983] 1 W.L.R. 959.

[240] Section 3(2).

[241] See *Brandeis Goldschmidt Ltd v Western Transport Ltd* [1981] Q.B. 864, a case of detinue before the Act.

[242] At common law the form of judgment for detinue was that the claimant "do have delivery up" of

the goods, but giving the defendant the alternative of paying damages by reference to the value of the goods, together in either alternative[243] with payment of any consequential damages; or (3) damages.[244] Relief under (1) is at the discretion of the court, but the claimant may choose between (2) and (3).[245] If the claimant chooses damages the defendant cannot satisfy the judgment by returning the goods.[246]

Though there is nothing in s.3 to compel this conclusion, it has traditionally been said that option (1), specific restitution, is apt only for rare articles or articles having a special value to the claimant and not for "ordinary articles of commerce".[247] Option (2) is said to be the commonest order in practice[248] but the value of the goods may have changed between wrong and judgment and the statute contains no guidance as to the time at which the goods should be valued for the purpose of quantifying the damages which the defendant may choose to pay.[249] It has been said that the "general prima facie rule" is assessment at the date of conversion,[250] but in *IBL Ltd v Coussens* (which concerned cars which appreciated in value up to the time of trial) it was held that there is no hard-and-fast rule, and that the value should be calculated by reference to such date as will fairly compensate the claimant for his loss if the defendant chooses to pay damages rather than return the goods.[251] There may be cases in which it will be found that the claimant could and should have replaced the converted goods at the time of the wrong or that he would have disposed of them at some later time, facts which would point towards taking the value at the time of the conversion or some intermediate time.[252] If, however, the claimant does not trade

---

the goods and while the defendant might have to facilitate their collection (*Metals & Ropes Co Ltd v Tattersall* [1966] 1 W.L.R. 1500) it was up to the claimant to go and get his goods. Query whether the rule is the same under the Act. Manchester (1977) 127 N.L.J. 1219 suggests that the court could order an actual redelivery by virtue of its power to impose conditions (s.3(6)) and it seems to be implied in *Howard E Perry & Co Ltd v British Railways Board* [1980] 1 W.L.R. 1375 that a delivery could be ordered. Nonetheless, the wording of s.3(6) seems more apt for the imposition of conditions on the claimant.

[243] In *Tanks and Vessels Industries Ltd v Devon Cider Co Ltd* [2009] EWHC 1360 (Ch), consequential loss of use damages were payable only if the defendant returned the goods; if he chose to pay their value, only interest was payable. On damages for loss of use, see also *Al-Khyami v El-Muderris* [2018] EWHC 24 (QB) at [76].

[244] i.e., assessed by reference to the value and the consequential loss. There is no reason to think that the Act has changed the common law on consequential loss: *Trafigura Beheer BV v Mediterranean Shipping Co SA* [2007] EWCA Civ 794; [2007] 2 Lloyd's Rep. 622 at [41].

[245] Section 3(3)(b).

[246] Section 3(5). But where there has been no fall in value it is thought that upon return of the goods the court would still stay the action before judgment: *Fisher v Prince* (1762) 3 Burr. 1363.

[247] See *Tanks and Vessels Industries Ltd v Devon Cider Co Ltd* [2009] EWHC 1360 (Ch); *Blue Sky One Ltd v Mahan Air* [2009] EWHC 3314 (Comm).

[248] If the defendant is in financial difficulties a judgment for damages alone is obviously unattractive to the claimant but this form of order if made for a specific date protects him: *Blue Sky One Ltd v Mahan Air* [2009] EWHC 3314 (Comm) at [323].

[249] At common law it was said that in conversion the value was taken at the time of the conversion, but in detinue at the time of the judgment.

[250] *Kuwait Airways Corp v Iraqi Airways Co (Nos 4 and 5)* [2002] UKHL 19; [2002] 2 A.C. 883 at [67]; *BBMB Finance (Hong Kong) v Eda Holdings* [1990] 1 W.L.R. 409.

[251] *IBL Ltd v Coussens* [1991] 2 All E.R. 133; *Trafigura Beheer BV v Mediterranean Shipping Co SA* [2007] EWHC 944 (Comm); [2007] 2 All E.R. (Com) 149 (affirmed on this point [2007] EWCA Civ 794; [2007] 2 Lloyd's Rep. 622).

[252] In *Irving v Keen* unreported 3 March 1995, CA, C was "incredibly lackadaisical" about getting his classic car back from D, a repairer, and settling the bill. D detained it for some years, during which it increased in value, but finally sold major parts of it and returned the remainder as scrap. Since there

in the goods in question and acts reasonably[253] in seeking their return[254] it may be proper to take the value at the time of the trial.

C. Improvement of Goods

18-056   The problem of a converter improving goods is illustrated by *Munro v Willmott*.[255] The claimant was given a temporary licence to leave her car in the defendant's yard. After the car had been there for some years the defendant wished to convert the yard into a garage but was unable to communicate with the claimant. Accordingly, he "did up" the car (then worth £20) at a cost of £85 and then sold it for £100. In proceedings for conversion Lynskey J felt obliged to assess the value of the car at the date of judgment (£120) but he gave credit for the sum expended by the defendant, leaving £35 as the damages recoverable by the claimant.[256]

18-057   **Torts (Interference with Goods) Act 1977 s.6**   Improvement of the goods is now governed by s.6 of the Torts (Interference with Goods) Act 1977, which provides that if the improver acted in the mistaken but honest belief that he had a good title, an allowance is to be made for the extent to which the value of the goods, at the time at which it falls to be assessed, is attributable to the improvement.[257] The requirement of good faith would seem to make the law somewhat narrower than it was previously.[258]

D. Effect of Judgment

18-058   Where damages for wrongful interference are assessed on the basis that the claimant is being compensated for the whole of his interest in the goods[259] (including a case where judgment is subject to a reduction for contributory negligence)[260]

---

was no conversion until the sale of the parts, that was the earliest point at which damages could be set; cf. *Sachs v Micklos* [1948] 2 K.B. 23.

[253] cf. *Radford v De Froberville* [1977] 1 W.L.R. 1262.

[254] If the claimant replaces the goods and goes for damages only, he obviously takes a risk in respect of the defendant's solvency when the matter comes to trial.

[255] *Munro v Willmott* [1949] 1 K.B. 295; *Reid v Fairbanks* (1853) 13 C.B. 692; 138 E.R. 1371.

[256] It is contended that the correct approach on the conversion count (there was an alternative count for detinue) would have been to assess the value at the date of conversion. On the basis of *Greenwood v Bennett* [1973] Q.B. 195 it seems that the defendant committed two acts of conversion (beginning work on the car and selling it) and that the claimant could rely on either. It has been held that where a series of acts of conversion constitute a continuous course of conduct the claimant can claim only the value at the beginning: *Highland Leasing v Paul Field* [1986] 2 C.L. 276. cf. *The Saetta* [1994] 1 All E.R. 851 at 859.

[257] Section 6(1).

[258] See, however, Palmer, *Bailment*, 3rd edn (2009), para.4-156, arguing that s.6 is in addition to, rather than in replacement of, the common law. It must also be pointed out that under s.12 of the 1977 Act the defendant in *Munro v Willmott* might now have a lawful power of sale though this does not help with the cost of improvement. The Act also provides for an allowance in favour of a defendant who is a bona fide purchaser of the car from the improver (who in this instance need not act bona fide), since though not an improver he will normally have paid a price reflecting the improved value (s.6(2)). See also s.6(3) (allowance in action for recovery of purchase price on total failure of consideration).

[259] e.g., where the defendant's trespass or negligence has destroyed them or where they have been wrongfully disposed of. A judgment in respect of mere damage has no effect upon title.

[260] As where the defendant has negligently destroyed the goods. Contributory negligence is no defence to conversion or intentional trespass: para.18-039.

payment of the damages or of any settlement[261] in full extinguishes the claimant's title to that interest in the goods.[262] Until payment of the damages, however, the claimant retains his property in the goods and may exercise all his rights as owner even after judgment has been given in his favour. In *Ellis v John Stenning & Son*[263] A sold land to B, reserving to himself the right to cut and sell the uncut timber on the land. He then sold the timber to E. B wrongfully removed some of the timber and E obtained judgment against him for conversion but took no steps to enforce his judgment, because B was insolvent. B sold the timber to S. E then sued S for conversion of the timber. It was held that S was liable because, the judgment against B not having been satisfied, title to the timber remained with E.

---

[261] See s.5(2). Where a claimant settles with one of two or more defendants the onus is upon him to establish that the settlement was not one which compensated him for the whole of his interest in the goods: *Macaulay v Screenkarn Ltd* [1987] F.S.R. 257.

[262] Section 5. This provision has no application, however, where the damages paid are limited to some lesser amount by virtue of any enactment or rule of law. The claimant's title is, therefore, presumably extinguished where there is a valid limitation of liability clause in a contract not governed by such statutory codes.

[263] [1932] 2 Ch. 81.

CHAPTER 19

INTENTIONAL INTERFERENCE WITH ECONOMIC INTERESTS

1.   INTRODUCTION

Scope of the chapter   This chapter is concerned with a group of torts the func-   **19-001**
tion of which is to protect some of a person's economic interests from unlawful

interference.[1] As we have observed, tort law is less ready to protect these interests from negligently inflicted harm than it is to secure interests in bodily security and tangible property.[2] However, the law is more willing to safeguard economic interests from harm where that harm is intentionally caused. It is not possible, however, to say simply that a person commits a tort whenever he intentionally harms another's economic interests since, as we have already seen, the mere fact that D's motive in performing an otherwise lawful act is to cause damage to another will not without more make D's act tortious.[3] There is more truth in the proposition that it is tortious intentionally to cause damage to a person's economic interests by an *unlawful* act although even that would go too far as an unqualified statement.

19-002 **The principal heads of liability** The law in this area has developed around five situations that must be distinguished from each other. First, it is a tort for D to induce the breach of A's contract with C. This, according to prevailing thinking, is a form of "accessory liability" for A's breach of contract and requires nothing independently unlawful on D's part. Second, D may be liable to C if, with the intention of injuring C, he uses unlawful means against A in order to affect A's ability to deal with C. We will refer to this form of liability as the "unlawful means tort". Third, D may be liable to C if, with the intention of injuring C, he uses unlawful means directly against C even if those unlawful means are not in themselves some other tort. According to one view, this third form of liability, which is sometimes called the tort of intimidation, is a sub-species of the second. Fourth, where D1 and D2 combine to injure C they may be liable for the tort of conspiracy. This tort comes in two forms: lawful means (or simple) conspiracy and unlawful means conspiracy. Where the conspiracy does not involve the use of unlawful means, liability will not arise unless D1 and D2 conspired with the predominant intention of injuring C. But where unlawful means are used, there is no need for C to prove the existence of such an intention. Fifth, it is a tort for D to exploit or endanger the goodwill in C's name or business: the tort of passing off.

19-003 **A disparate collection of torts?** Although the torts that are under consideration in this chapter are concerned with intentional interference with economic interests, they are not the only torts that are so concerned. For example, liability in the tort of deceit[4] may arise in respect of damage intentionally caused to economic interests although it is not exclusively so concerned as it extends to fraudulent representations that result in the claimant's suffering physical harm. Further, it is important to recognise that the torts addressed in this chapter are not solely concerned with economic interests, although that is their principal province. For example, if D1 and D2 conspire to inflict physical injury upon C and that agreement is carried out, both D1 and D2 will be liable to C for the tort of conspiracy. Likewise, if C uses unlawful means against A with the intention of injuring C, damage to any of C's interests, whether or not economic, is actionable.[5]

---

[1] See, further, Cane, *Tort Law and Economic Interests*, 2nd edn (1996); Weir, *The Economic Torts* (1997); Carty, *An Analysis of the Economic Torts*, 2nd edn (2010); Hoffmann in Degeling, Edelman and Goudkamp (eds), *Torts in Commercial Law* (2011).
[2] See para.5-049.
[3] See para.3-017.
[4] Ch.12.
[5] "The [unlawful means] tort protects all interests, not just economic ones": Davies and Sales (2018)

What, then, is the rationale for dealing collectively with the five torts on which this chapter is focused? In truth, they are treated together in part because it is traditional to do so rather than because there is any unity to the torts, although, as we will see, they are governed, to a limited extent, by common principles. Indeed, it has often been argued that there is no general idea that underpins the five torts addressed and that they lack their "Atkin".[6] Accordingly, the courts have regularly issued warnings about the dangers of endeavouring to determine the rules governing one of the torts in issue by reference to the principles that control another, and in seeking to formulate a "unified theory" to explain the various causes of action.[7]

Opposing interests at stake   Major issues arise as to the precise way in which the torts that are considered in this chapter are calibrated and there are powerful countervailing interests at stake in this regard. On the one hand, it is thought to be unacceptable for people deliberately to inflict economic injury on others in certain ways. On the other hand, the courts are anxious to avoid imposing tort liability for economic injury too readily since doing so risks stifling legitimate competition. Most if not all commercial activity is carried out with the knowledge that it will harm one's business rivals, and the courts are particularly chary of imposing tort liability if to do so would erode the clear public interest in competition. In *JSC BTA Bank v Ablyazov (No.14)*, Lord Sumption and Lord Lloyd-Jones summarised the position as follows[8]:   **19-004**

> "Along with tortious misrepresentation (fraudulent or negligent), passing off, slander of title and infringement of intellectual property rights, the economic torts are a major exception to the general rule that there is no duty in tort to avoid causing a purely economic loss unless it is parasitic upon some injury to person or property. The reason for the general rule is that, contract apart, common law duties to avoid causing pure economic loss tend to cut across the ordinary incidents of competitive business, one of which is that one man's gain may be another man's loss. The successful pursuit of commercial self-interest necessarily entails the risk of damaging the commercial interests of others. Identifying the point at which it transgresses legitimate bounds is therefore a task of exceptional delicacy. The elements of the four established economic torts[9] are carefully defined so as to avoid trespassing on legitimate business activities or imposing any wider liability than can be justified in principle."

The modern role of the economic torts   Many of the early cases on the economic torts were concerned with disputes involving trade unions and this context should be borne firmly in mind when reading historical decisions in this field. However, since the Trade Disputes Act 1906 was passed trade unions and their officials have enjoyed an immunity from liability in the economic torts where the acts were done in contemplation or furtherance of a trade dispute. The statutory framework, which is highly complex, has undergone many significant revisions over the years and the current scheme is that established by, principally, the Trade Union and Labour Rela-   **19-005**

---

6   134 L.Q.R. 69 at 83.
6   Wedderburn (1983) 46 M.L.R. 224 at 226.
7   *JSC BTA Bank v Ablyazov* [2018] UKSC 19; [2018] 2 W.L.R. 1125 at [6] per Lord Sumption.
8   [2018] UKSC 19; [2018] 2 W.L.R. 1125 at [6]. See also *Starbucks (HK) Ltd v British Sky Broadcasting Group Plc* [2015] UKSC 31; [2015] 1 W.L.R. 2628 at [61].
9   Although this chapter treats passing off, Lord Sumption and Lord Lloyd-Jones evidently do not regard passing off as one of the "established economic torts" although they do see it as allied to those torts in that it also derogates from the general rule to which they refer.

tions (Consolidation) Act 1992 (as amended). This chapter does not address the details of the law in this regard for two main reasons. First, because of the immunity, the economic torts are much less significant in industrial disputes than they were in the past. Indeed, in the 21st century the primary domain of the economic torts is not labour disputes but commercial litigation, often involving allegations of fraud. And second, labour law has long been a specialised area of study in its own right and the particular rules governing the operation of the economic torts in the context of industrial disputes can therefore be found in works in that field.

2. INDUCING A BREACH OF CONTRACT

19-006 Origins D is liable to C if, without lawful justification, he induces or procures A to break A's contract with C.[10] The origin of this form of liability lies in the mid-19th century decision in *Lumley v Gye*.[11] C alleged that he had contracted with Johanna Wagner,[12] a famous operatic singer, for her to perform exclusively in C's theatre for a certain time and that D, the owner of a rival theatre, wishing himself to obtain Miss Wagner's services, "knowing the premises and maliciously intending to injure the plaintiff ... enticed and persuaded [her] to refuse to perform". The claim succeeded on demurrer[13] on the basis, according to the majority of the court, that the (now long since extinct) action for enticement could be extended beyond the strict relation of master and servant to embrace other contracts for personal services, but support was also given in varying degrees to a broader view that a claimant might sue for the knowing violation of any contractual right.

19-007 A form of accessory liability? Liability arising under the principle in *Lumley v Gye* has sometimes been said to rest on a property analogy.[14] The idea here is that contractual relations are valuable rights that are entitled to at least some of the protection given by the law to property. However, the analogy can only be taken so far because the requirements of knowledge and intent, discussed below, make this form of liability considerably more restrictive than the actions for conversion or trespass. The current view of the courts is that the principle in *Lumley v Gye* imposes a form of "accessory" liability, that is to say, the person who induces the breach incurs an additional liability in tort for the consequences of the "primary" breach of contract.[15]

If the accessory theory is correct it means that the principle in *Lumley v Gye* is not an independent tort but a cause of action that is parasitic upon a breach of A's contract with C. However, the accessory theory is open to question. Were the accessory theory sound, one would, for example, expect the remedies awarded under

---

[10] However, A cannot sue D for D's having procured him to break his contract with C. "[A] has no right at law to restrain [D] from attempting to suborn him from his duty to C. He must resist A's efforts by strength of will": *Boulting v Association of Cinematograph, Television and Allied Technicians* [1963] 2 Q.B. 639 at 640 per Upjohn LJ.

[11] (1853) 2 El. & Bl. 216; 118 E.R. 749.

[12] Students of contract will be familiar with *Lumley v Wagner* (1852) 1 De G.M. & G. 604; 42 E.R. 687, in which the claimant obtained an injunction against Miss Wagner.

[13] C ultimately lost at trial with the jury finding that D believed that Ms Wagner's contract was not binding. See, further, Waddams (2001) 117 L.Q.R. 431.

[14] See Bagshaw (1998) O.J.L.S. 729 and the discussion in *Zhu v Treasurer of NSW* [2004] HCA 56; (2004) 218 C.L.R. 530 at [123]ff.

[15] *OBG Ltd v Allan* [2007] UKHL 21; [2008] 1 A.C. 1 at [3], [172], [320].

the principle in *Lumley v Gye* substantially to mirror those available to C in a contract claim against A, whereas there are important differences between the remedial regimes. Thus, the rules regarding remoteness differ, with the claim in contract but not the claim based on the principle in *Lumley v Gye* being subject to the test for remoteness that is applicable in the law of contract. Similarly, punitive damages are in principle available in a claim for inducing a breach of contract[16] but are unavailable in a claim for breach of contract itself.[17] Conversely, there are other aspects of the law that the accessory theory explains, most significantly the rule that liability will arise under the principle in *Lumley v Gye* only where A in fact breaches his contract with C: the mere fact that D sought to persuade A to do so will not suffice.

A. A Breach of Contract

D will be liable under the principle in *Lumley v Gye* only if A breaches his contract with C.[18] In *Allen v Flood*[19] D, an official of the boilermakers' trade union, told shipyard owners that his members would not work unless C, a non-member who had done ironwork, was discharged. C was dismissed but, since he was engaged by the day, the owners committed no breach of contract and so this tort was not committed by D.[20]   **19-008**

No liability for "interference" without any breach   At one time it was thought that there was a wider liability, even if no unlawful means were used, of "interference" with the performance of a contract short of procuring a breach[21] at least if the interference was "direct" (though it was never very clear what that meant). That view was exploded by *OBG Ltd v Allan*.[22] No one suggests that, without the use of unlawful means, it is a tort for D to persuade A not to contract with C, for that is what competitors in business do every day (and are encouraged to do). It cannot be different if there is an existing contract between A and C and without unlawful means D persuades A to terminate it by proper notice.   **19-009**

Void and voidable contracts   If the contract between A and C is void for contravention of the law C cannot sue D for inducing breach of it.[23] The same result obtains if the contract is voidable and D persuades A to exercise his right to avoid.[24]   **19-010**

---

16 In *East England Schools CIC v Palmer* [2013] EWHC 4138 (QB), which concerned a claim for inducing a breach of contract, the judge proceeded on the understanding that punitive damages were in principle available but concluded that they should not be awarded on the facts.

17 *Addis v Gramophone Ltd* [1909] A.C. 488.

18 *OBG Ltd v Allan* [2007] UKHL 21 [2008] 1 A.C. 1 at [44]. C may, of course, obtain a quia timet injunction to restrain a threatened inducement. It has been said that the tort is capable of extending to interference with a "secondary right to a remedy", but only where violation of the secondary right is itself an actionable wrong: *Law Debenture Trust Ltd v Ural Caspian Oil Corp Ltd* [1995] Ch. 152.

19 [1898] A.C. 1.

20 Nor was there any unlawful means (see the next section) by a threat of breach of contract by the boilermakers since they, too, were employed by the day.

21 See, e.g., *Torquay Hotel Co Ltd v Cousins* [1969] 2 Ch. 106 at 138.

22 [2007] UKHL 21; [2008] 1 A.C. 1 at [185].

23 *De Francesco v Barnum* (1890) 45 Ch. D. 430; *Joe Lee Ltd v Dalmeny* [1927] 1 Ch. 300; *Said v Butt* [1920] 3 K.B. 497; *Associated British Ports Ltd v Transport and General Workers Union* [1989] 3 All E.R. 796 at 816.

24 *Greig v Insole* [1978] 1 W.L.R. 302.

It has also been held that D is not liable where he induces A not to perform the voidable contract without any formal avoidance.[25] If, conversely, it is C who has the right to avoid the contract there seems to be no reason why D should be allowed to rely upon its voidability in a claim by C.

B. Knowledge and Intention of the Defendant

19-011 **Knowledge of the contract and of its breach** There is no liability under this tort for negligently interfering with a person's contractual rights (though the law of negligence may give limited protection in certain circumstances[26]). But while the tort presupposes knowledge of the contract, that does not mean knowledge of all its details. As Lord Denning MR said in *Emerald Construction Co Ltd v Lowthian*[27]:

> "Even if [the union officials] did not know the actual terms of the contract, but had the means of knowledge—which they deliberately disregarded—that would be enough. Like the man who turns a blind eye. So here, if the officers deliberately sought to get this contract terminated, heedless of its terms, regardless whether it was terminated by breach or not, they would do wrong. For it is unlawful for a third person to procure a breach of contract knowingly, or recklessly, indifferent whether it is a breach or not."

This state of mind of conscious indifference is not the same as negligence,[28] although the required state of mind may be inferred from circumstances which would have caused suspicion to a reasonable person. There is no general duty actively to inquire about contracts with others[29] and a supplier of services is not obliged to infer, from the fact that the services are obviously already being supplied by another, that there is a continuing contract, breach of which he must be careful not to induce.[30] In *Mainstream Properties Ltd v Young*, which was one of the three appeals reported as *OBG Ltd v Allan*,[31] D had provided finance for a development venture by A and B, employees of C, a development company. The risk that the venture conflicted with A and B's duties to C was obvious and D raised this issue with them but it was held that he was entitled to accept their assertion that the land concerned had been offered to C and that it had declined.[32] At one time the view was taken that there would be liability if D intended to bring about a situation where there would as a matter of law be a breach of contract even though he mistakenly believed there would not.[33] However, that view was rejected in *OBG Ltd v Allan* with Lord Hoffmann remarking that[34]:

---

[25] *Proform Sports Management Ltd v Proactive Sports Management Ltd* [2006] EWHC 22903 (Ch); [2007] 1 All E.R. 542.

[26] See para.5-048.

[27] [1966] 1 W.L.R. 691 at 700. See also *Greig v Insole* [1978] 1 W.L.R. 302.

[28] *OBG Ltd v Allan* [2007] UKHL 21; [2008] 1 A.C. 1 at [41]; *Kallang Shipping SA Panama v Axa Assurances Senegal* [2008] EWHC 2761 (Comm); [2009] 1 Lloyd's Rep. 124; *Wolff v Trinity Logistics USA Inc* [2018] EWCA Civ 2765; [2019] 1 W.L.R. 3997 at [51].

[29] *Leitch & Co v Leydon* [1931] A.C. 90.

[30] *Schindler Lifts Australia Pty Ltd v Debelak* (1989) 89 A.L.R. 275; *Unique Pub Properties Ltd v Beer Barrels and Minerals (Wales) Ltd* [2004] EWCA Civ 586; [2005] 1 All E.R. (Comm.) 181.

[31] [2007] UKHL 21; [2008] 1 A.C. 1.

[32] Perhaps to be seen as another case where, in accepting the defendant's evidence the court had "vindicated [his] honesty ... at the expense of his intelligence": *British Industrial Plastics Ltd v Ferguson* [1938] 4 All E.R. 504 at 513.

[33] See, e.g., *Solihull MBC v National Union of Teachers* [1985] I.R.L.R. 211.

[34] [2007] UKHL 21; [2008] 1 A.C. 1 at [39]. Lord Nicholls made similar remarks at [202]. See also

"[i]t is not enough that you know that you are procuring an act which, as a matter of law or construction of the contract, is a breach. You must actually realize that it will have this effect. Nor does it matter that you ought reasonably to have done so".

Intention   D must intend to bring about a breach of the contract but that is not   **19-012**
necessarily the same thing as intending to cause damage to C. Thus, in *South Wales Miners' Federation v Glamorgan Coal Co Ltd*[35] it did not help the union, when it induced breaches of employment contracts by calling a strike, to argue that its intention "was, OPEC-like, to restrict production of coal and thereby raise its price"[36] thus benefiting the coal owners as well as the workers. Further, it does not matter that D has no desire to injure C and was simply seeking to benefit himself: it is sufficient that D intended to bring about a breach as a means to an end, if not as an end in itself.[37]

C.   The Inducement

The need for persuasion   Simply doing something that causes A to commit a   **19-013**
breach of contract does not give rise to liability. Rather, liability will accrue only when D persuades A not to comply with his contractual obligations. A distinction can be drawn between persuasion and mere advice. Advice in the sense of "a mere statement of, or drawing of the attention of the party addressed, to the state of facts as they were"[38] is not actionable.[39] The position is otherwise if the advice is intended to have persuasive effect.[40] Further, "the fact that an inducement to break a contract is couched as an irresistible embargo rather than in terms of seduction does not make it any the less an inducement".[41] Ultimately, the issue is one of intention and causation.[42] If D's words were intended to cause and did in fact cause A to break his contract with C, then they are actionable by C whatever their precise form. If so, and bearing in mind that intention in this context is not the same as motive and that the tort may be committed without any ill will towards C, it will be rare for D to escape liability on the ground that his words were only "advice" if they caused A's breach. If D's inducement of A takes the form of wrongful threats against A there will be an overlap with the torts of intentionally causing damage by unlaw-

---

Meretz Investments NV v ACP Ltd [2007] EWCA Civ 1303; [2008] Ch. 244.

[35]   [1905] A.C. 239.

[36]   *OBG Ltd v Allan* [2007] UKHL 21; [2008] 1 A.C. 1 at [8] per Lord Hoffmann.

[37]   "Mr Gye would very likely have preferred to be able to obtain Miss Wagner's services without her having to break her contract. But that did not matter": *OBG Ltd v Allan* [2007] UKHL 21; [2008] 1 A.C. 1 at [42] per Lord Hoffmann.

[38]   *DC Thomson & Co Ltd v Deakin* [1952] Ch. 646 at 686.

[39]   A direction to do something which may be done lawfully or unlawfully cannot be said to induce wrongs committed by those who respond unlawfully and that is so even if the person giving the direction harbours a secret desire that the thing be done unlawfully: *Sanders v Snell* (1998) 196 C.L.R. 329; *CBS Songs Ltd v Amstrad Consumer Electronics Plc* [1988] A.C. 1013 (provision of machines capable of being used for breach of copyright).

[40]   *Camden Nominees Ltd v Forcey* [1940] Ch. 352 at 366; *DC Thomson & Co Ltd v Deakin* [1952] Ch. 646 at 686; cf. *Stocznia Gdanska SA v Latvian Shipping Co* [2002] EWCA Civ 889; [2002] 2 All E.R. (Comm) 768 at [107].

[41]   *JT Stratford & Co Ltd v Lindley* [1965] A.C. 269 at 333 per Lord Pearce. See also *Greig v Insole* [1978] 1 W.L.R. 302.

[42]   "[D]id the defendant's acts of encouragement, threat, persuasion and so forth have a sufficient causal connection with the breach by the contracting party to attract accessory liability?": *OBG Ltd v Allan* [2007] UKHL 21; [2008] 1 A.C. 1 at [36] per Lord Hoffmann.

ful means and unlawful means conspiracy,[43] which are considered later. It has been said that "even silence in certain circumstances can be persuasive in encouraging a breach of contract" and can be intended to do so.[44]

19-014 **Entering into inconsistent contracts** Liability may arise where D enters into a contract with A knowing that the contract is inconsistent with an existing contract between A and C. This occurred in *BMTA v Salvadori*[45] where D bought a car from A knowing that the sale constituted a breach by A of his contract with C that he would not sell the car within a year. However, while statements of principle are often couched in terms that merely knowingly entering into the transaction amounts to the tort,[46] it is not wholly clear that this is so where D simply accedes to an initiative of the contracting party.[47] Where the prior contract of A and C is specifically enforceable it would create an equitable interest in the subject matter in favour of C, which C could enforce against D even if D had only constructive notice of C's rights.[48] In many cases this would render consideration of D's tort liability in a case of actual knowledge otiose, but it seems possible to assert such a claim where there is some additional loss.[49]

19-015 **Inducement by an employee** If D's employee, acting bona fide within the scope of his authority, procures D to break a contract between D and C, C cannot sue the employee for interference with the contract.[50] This is because the employee is D's alter ego here, and D cannot be sued for inducing himself to break a contract. In *Said v Butt*[51] C wanted to obtain a ticket for A's theatre but knew that A would not sell him one because they had quarrelled. C therefore persuaded a friend to procure a ticket for him without disclosing C's identity. When C presented himself at the theatre, D, who was the manager of the theatre, detected C and refused to admit him. C sued D for procuring a breach of his contract with A. The action was dismissed because there was no contract, since the identity of C was, in the circumstances, material to the formation of the alleged contract. However, it was held, alternatively, that even if there had been a valid contract, the principle stated above would have prevented liability from arising.[52]

---

43 Since the breach induced can constitute unlawful means, D and A may also be guilty of conspiracy by unlawful means: *Aerostar Maintenance International Ltd v Wilson* [2010] EWHC 2032 (Ch) at [171]–[172].

44 *Lonmar Global Risks Ltd v West* [2010] EWHC 2878 (QB); [2011] I.R.L.R. 138 at [220] per Hickinbottom J; cf. *Premier Model Management Ltd v Bruce* [2012] EWHC 3509 (QB) at [57] (silent receipt of information by D sent by A in breach of his contract with C, but there were also findings that D was not guilty of mere silence).

45 [1949] Ch. 556.

46 *DC Thomson & Co Ltd v Deakin* [1952] Ch. 646 at 694; *Law Debenture Trust Ltd v Ural Caspian Oil Corp Ltd* [1993] 1 W.L.R. 138 at 151.

47 *Batts Combe Quarry Ltd v Ford* [1943] Ch. 51.

48 Unless D was a bona fide purchaser for value without notice.

49 See *Pritchard v Briggs* [1980] Ch. 338 (although on the facts the majority of the court rejected a claim for damages).

50 This passage was approved in *DC Thomson & Co Ltd v Deakin* [1952] Ch. 646 at 681.

51 [1920] 3 K.B. 497.

52 The rule in *Said v Butt* also protects company directors who vote to cause a breach of contract from liability for inducing breach of contract: *Crystalens Ltd v White* [2006] EWHC 3357 (Comm); *O'Brien v Dawson* (1942) 66 C.L.R. 18. However, it should be noted that the rule is not absolute. It does not apply where the director acts mala fide in relation to the company: *Antuzis v DJ Houghton Catching Services Ltd* [2019] EWHC 843 (QB); [2019] Bus. L.R. 1532. As regards receivers, see

D. Defence of Justification

An inexact definition Justification is a defence to this tort,[53] but what constitutes **19-016** justification is incapable of exact definition. Regard must be had to the nature of the contract broken, the position of the parties to the contract, the grounds for the breach, the means employed to procure it, the relation of the person procuring it to the person who breaks the contract and the object of the person procuring the breach.[54] The advancement of one's own interests will not suffice, nor will that of the interests of one's own group[55] and D cannot avoid liability by showing that his motives are impersonal, disinterested and altruistic.[56] However, in *Brimelow v Casson*,[57] persuasion of theatre proprietors by a theatrical performers' protection society to break their contracts with a theatrical manager was justified on the ground that the wage paid by the manager to chorus girls was so low that they were obliged to supplement it by resorting to prostitution.[58] It has been suggested that pressure of a moral[59] obligation as justification is the basis of *Brimelow v Casson*, though the case has been said to stand alone[60] and there are conflicting dicta on moral obligation.[61] Presumably there is justification when a doctor urges[62] his patient to give up fixed-term employment because it is a danger to his health, but what of the tutor who insists that his student give up a vacation job because it will interfere with his studies?

Inconsistent contracts The question of justification may also arise where D seeks **19-017** to assert rights under a contract with A which is inconsistent with another contract between A and C. The question here is whether D has a right equal or superior to that of C and, if he has, he is justified in persuading A to break his contract with C. So if A enters into a contract to sell property to D for £10,000 and then the next day enters into a contract to sell the same property to C for £15,000, by persuading A to perform the first contract D commits no wrong against C.[63] D will also be justified in reaching an accommodation with A rather than exercising his strict legal rights under the contract. In *Edwin Hill & Partners v First National Finance Corp*[64] a finance company which had a legal charge over A's property to secure a loan came

Welsh Development Agency v Export Finance Co Ltd [1992] B.C.C. 270.
53 *Palmer Birch (A Partnership) v Lloyd* [2018] EWHC 2316 (TCC); [2018] 4 W.L.R. 164 at [185].
54 *Glamorgan Coal Co Ltd v South Wales Miners' Federation* [1903] 2 K.B. 545 at 574–575.
55 *South Wales Miners' Federation v Glamorgan Coal Co Ltd* [1905] A.C. 239; *Camden Nominees Ltd v Forcey* [1940] Ch. 352; *Greig v Insole* [1978] 1 W.L.R. 302.
56 *Greig v Insole* [1978] 1 W.L.R. 302; *Posluns v Toronto Stock Exchange* (1964) 46 D.L.R. (2d) 210 at 270 (affirmed (1968) 67 D.L.R. (2d) 165); *Slade & Stewart Ltd v Haynes* (1969) 5 D.L.R. (3d) 736.
57 [1924] 1 Ch. 302.
58 cf. *Stott v Gamble* [1916] 2 K.B. 504 (banning of film under statutory powers).
59 *Pritchard v Briggs* [1980] Ch. 338 at 416.
60 *Camden Nominees Ltd v Forcey* [1940] Ch. 352 at 366; *Pritchard v Briggs* [1980] Ch. 338 at 416; *Timeplan Education Group Ltd v National Union of Teachers* [1997] I.R.L.R. 457 at 460.
61 See, e.g., *South Wales Miners' Federation v Glamorgan Coal Co Ltd* [1905] A.C. 239 at 245–246, 249, 255; *Crofter Hand-Woven Harris Tweed Co v Veitch* [1942] A.C. 435 at 443, where the example is given of a man inducing his daughter not to marry a "scoundrel" (but engagement is no longer a contract).
62 It is assumed that the advice is "persuasive" in the sense explained in para.19-013
63 *Smithies v National Association of Operative Plasterers* [1909] 1 K.B. 310 at 337.
64 [1989] 1 W.L.R. 225; cf. *Meretz Investments NV v ACP Ltd* [2007] EWCA Civ 1303; [2008] Ch. 244 at [142]; *Sar Petroleum Inc v Peace Hills Trust Co* [2010] NBCA 22; (2010) 318 D.L.R. (4th) 70.

to an arrangement with A whereby they would develop the property themselves rather than exercise their power of sale under the charge. A condition in this arrangement whereby C was to be replaced as architect for the scheme was not actionable in the *Lumley v Gye* tort.

E.   Inducing Breaches of Other Obligations

19-018   Although the principle of *Lumley v Gye* commonly appears under the heading of inducing breach of contract it has been regarded as a wider principle covering violation of other legal rights.[65] It has been said that there is no need to rely upon the tort where the wrong procured is itself a tort against C, for the procurer is then himself liable as a joint tortfeasor,[66] but the courts have recognised causes of action for inducing a breach of statutory duty where the statutory duty gives rise to a private right on behalf of C[67] actionable by him in the courts,[68] and for inducing a violation of rights in a judgment debt.[69] There is no tort of inducing breach of trust because a person who procures such an act becomes himself, by the doctrines of equity, liable as a trustee and it is said that that is sufficient to protect the beneficiary under the trust.[70] The tort liability probably extends to procuring breaches of equitable obligations such as that of confidence but the readiness of the courts to restrain the use of confidential information by the third party who acquires it makes the point of limited importance in most cases. However, these issues were not discussed in the leading decision in *OBG Ltd v Allan* and Lord Nicholls said in that case that he left "open the question of how far the *Lumley v Gye* principle applies equally to inducing a breach of other actionable obligations such as statutory duties or equitable or fiduciary obligations".[71]

F.   Remedies

19-019   Damages in this tort are said to be "at large".[72] This expression seems to mean that C's recovery is not confined to those losses that can be strictly proven. It has been held that "the conduct of the defendant and the nature of the wrongdoing is

---

[65]   "It is clear that the procurement of the violation of a right is a cause of action in all instances where the violation is an actionable wrong, as in violations of a right to property, whether real or personal, or to personal security ...": *Lumley v Gye* (1853) 2 El. & Bl. 216 at 232; 118 E.R. 749 at 755 per Erle J; cf. *Quinn v Leathem* [1901] A.C. 495 at 510; *F v Wirral Metropolitan Council* [1991] Fam. 69 at 107.

[66]   *CBS Songs Ltd v Amstrad Consumer Electronics Plc* [1988] A.C. 1013 at 1058; cf. *Belegging, etc. BV v Witten Industrial Diamonds Ltd* [1979] F.S.R. 59 at 66.

[67]   *Meade v Haringey LBC* [1979] 1 W.L.R. 637; *Associated British Ports v Transport and General Workers Union* [1989] 1 W.L.R. 939 (reversed on other grounds [1989] 1 W.L.R. 939). See Ch.8.

[68]   *Wilson v Housing Corp* [1998] I.C.R. 151 (no tort of inducing unfair dismissal).

[69]   In *Marex Financial Ltd v Sevilleja Garcia* [2017] EWHC 918 (Comm); [2017] 4 W.L.R. 105 (the case went on appeal to the Supreme Court on other issues: [2020] UKSC 31; [2020] 3 W.L.R. 255) it was held there was a good arguable case that the tort existed for the purposes of an application for permission to serve the claim form out of the jurisdiction.

[70]   *Metall und Rohstoff AG v Donaldson Lufkin & Jenrette Inc* [1990] 1 Q.B. 391. However, liability for "knowing assistance" in a breach of trust (as opposed to receipt of trust property) requires dishonesty: *Twinsectra Ltd v Yardley* [2002] UKHL 12; [2002] 2 A.C. 164; *Barlow Clowes International Ltd v Eurotrust International Ltd* [2005] UKPC 37; [2006] 1 W.L.R. 1476.

[71]   [2007] UKHL 21; [2008] 1 A.C. 1 at [189].

[72]   *Palmer Birch (A Partnership) v Lloyd* [2018] EWHC 2316 (TCC); [2018] 4 W.L.R. 164 at [242]–[244] per Judge Russen QC.

likely to form a significant part of [the] assessment" as to the heads of financial loss that the claimant has sustained.[73]

3. THE UNLAWFUL MEANS TORT

A. Introduction

A tort of "primary liability"   This tort was the source of much confusion in the 20th century but its nature and its relationship with inducing breach of contract were considerably clarified by *OBG Ltd v Allan*, at least in "three-party" situations. D commits this tort where, intending to cause loss to C, he uses unlawful means against A which affect A's liberty to deal with C. The cause of action is a good deal older than the tort of inducing breach of contract and an early example is to be found in *Tarleton v M'Gawley*.[74] D, the master of the *Othello*, was trading on the coast of West Africa and when A put off from the shore to trade with another vessel, the *Bannister*, belonging to C, D fired his guns at A, driving A away. C's action against D succeeded. The short judgment is largely concerned with refuting the argument that C's claim should fail because he had no licence from the local ruler but, looked at in the light of *OBG Ltd v Allan*, the wrongful act (assault or battery) committed against A made D's conduct tortious against C even though C had no subsisting contract with A. In any event even if there had been a contract between A and C, A's retreat under artillery fire could hardly have been a breach of that contract: it was rather as if Johanna Wagner had been kidnapped by Gye rather than enticed away. This is a tort based on the primary liability of D for his wrongdoing and is in no sense, unlike the *Lumley v Gye* principle, parasitic on a liability of A. Both torts, it is true, involve D striking at C through acts directed at A,[75] but that does not make them the same. Of course, a given act may trigger liability in both torts, such as where A breached a contract with C on account of threats that D had made against A.

19-020

B. Background

Earlier confusion   In earlier cases the relationship between the torts of inducing a breach of contract and unlawful means became very confused. In *GWK Ltd v Dunlop Rubber Co Ltd*[76] C made tyres and had a contract with A, motor manufacturers, that all new cars would be fitted with tyres of C's manufacture and displayed with them at shows. D, a rival tyre company, surreptitiously removed C's tyres from the cars displayed at the Glasgow motor show and substituted its own. D was held liable to C but on the basis that D had interfered without justification with the contractual relationship between A and C, thereby making it at least an offshoot, though not a direct application, of *Lumley v Gye*. In fact of course it was a simple case falling under the *Tarleton v M'Gawley* principle: D committed trespass to A's goods when it removed the tyres and used that as a means to inflict damage on C. Lord Hoffmann in *OBG Ltd v Allan* suggested that one reason for the confusion is

19-021

---

73   *Palmer Birch (A Partnership) v Lloyd* [2018] EWHC 2316 (TCC); [2018] 4 W.L.R. 164 at [246] per Judge Russen QC.
74   (1793) 1 Peake 270; 170 E.R. 153. See also *Garret v Taylor* (1620) Cro. Jac. 567; 79 E.R. 485.
75   *OBG Ltd v Allan* [2007] UKHL 21; [2008] 1 A.C. 1 at [306].
76   (1926) 42 T.L.R. 376.

that situations like *Tarleton* had been labelled "intimidation" because they commonly involved threats and this label did not easily fit the case where the unlawful means had taken another form.[77] If in *Tarleton* D had warned A that he would sink him if he approached C that would have been "intimidation"; if he had simply sunk A with his broadside before A could become aware of any threat it is inconceivable that the result of the case would have been different or even that it would have been a different tort against C. It is an irresistible inference from the existence of liability for intimidation that there is liability on the same basis where unlawful conduct of the kind that might have been threatened is simply carried out.[78]

In the latter part of the 20th century a process[79] occurred whereby the *Lumley v Gye* tort was regarded as extending beyond simple inducement to: (1) "prevention" (the *GWK* situation); (2) "indirect" procurement of a breach (as where D persuaded X to break his contract with A so that A could not perform his contract with C);[80] and even (3) interference falling short of breach, although all these situations were generally regarded as requiring some independently unlawful means. Now, it seems, after *OBG Ltd v Allan*, we can dispense with these complexities: the *Lumley v Gye* tort is confined to the simple situation where D persuades A to break his contract with C and all the others constitute the unlawful means tort. It is true that even before *OBG Ltd v Allan* it was recognised that some varieties of "interference with contract" where unlawful means were involved could be regarded as species of a wider "genus" tort of interference with business by unlawful means.[81] However, this recognition was befogged by the insistence on classifying the categories described above as offshoots of the principle in *Lumley v Gye*. The problem here is that it was impossible to bring that tort within the genus because liability arising pursuant to *Lumley v Gye* did not require proof that D had used independently unlawful means.

C.   Unlawful Means

19-022   **Unlawful means confined to civil wrongs**   According to one view, "unlawful means" embraces anything "a defendant is not permitted to do, whether by the civil law or the criminal law" and this is supported by Lord Nicholls in *OBG Ltd v Allan*[82] but the majority view is narrower: it covers only acts or threats of acts which are civilly wrongful against and actionable by A (or would be actionable by him if he suffered loss).[83] It does not therefore include criminal breaches of statutory duty which do not give rise to a civil action.[84] Nor does it cover common law crimes, though many of them will be torts in their own right and "unlawful" under that head. However, even those who would extend the concept beyond matters actionable in their own right would not go so far as to include all incidental infringements of the

---

77   [2007] UKHL 21; [2008] 1 A.C. 1 at [25].
78   *Rookes v Barnard* [1964] A.C. 1129 at 1168.
79   The leading authority was *DC Thomson & Co Ltd v Deakin* [1952] Ch. 646.
80   Exemplified by *JT Stratford & Son Ltd v Lindley* [1965] A.C. 269.
81   *Merkur Island Shipping Corp v Laughton* [1983] 2 A.C. 581 at 610; *JT Stratford & Son Ltd v Lindley* [1965] A.C. 269 at 324, 329.
82   [2007] UKHL 21; [2008] 1 A.C. 1 at [162].
83   *National Phonograph Co Ltd v Edison-Bell Consolidated Phonograph Co Ltd* [1908] 1 Ch. 335 and *Lonrho Plc v Fayed* [1992] 1 A.C. 448 seem to be examples of this situation (D fraudulently inducing A to act to C's detriment).
84   *OBG Ltd v Allan* [2007] UKHL 21; [2008] 1 A.C. 1 at [57].

criminal law. The example often given is of a pizza delivery business that manages to gain a larger share of the market by constantly infringing the traffic speed limits. For Lord Nicholls that would not amount to a tort actionable by its competitor because it would not be an "offence committed against the rival company in any meaningful sense of that expression".[85] Perhaps the most significant point in practice is that the concept of unlawful means includes breaches of contract and threats thereof,[86] that being the means of coercion most commonly used.[87]

The unlawful means must hinder the third party's ability to deal with the claimant The majority in *OBG Ltd v Allan* imposed a further requirement beyond the fact that there must be a wrong actionable or potentially actionable by A: the wrong (or the threat of it) must also hinder A's ability to deal with C. Thus, the mere fact that D's conduct is wrongful against A will not suffice if it does not affect A's freedom to deal with C and that is so even if D's actions affect A in a way in which C has an economic interest.[88] In an earlier case approved on this basis by the majority[89] C had an exclusive licence to exploit A's registered design and D sold articles alleged to infringe the design right. The relevant legislation gave A, but not C, the right to sue D and C's claim against D in the unlawful means tort was said to have been rightly struck out. Although C's sales may have been less than they would otherwise have been, the performance of the contractual relations between A and C were unaffected.[90]   19-023

The requirement of unlawful means excludes the defence of justification The need to establish unlawful means in order for liability to arise leaves no space for any defence of justification. Any considerations of justification are already "wrapped up in the element ... of unlawfulness".[91]   19-024

---

85 *OBG Ltd v Allan* [2007] UKHL 21; [2008] 1 A.C. 1 at [160].

86 *Rookes v Barnard* [1964] A.C. 1129.

87 Some doubt exists as to whether contempt of court comprises unlawful means: *Acrow (Automation) Ltd v Rex Chainbelt Inc* [1971] 1 W.L.R. 1676 at 1683; cf. *Chapman v Honig* [1963] 2 Q.B. 502. Contempt of court can, however, constitute unlawful means for the purposes of the tort of unlawful means conspiracy: see para.19-041.

88 For detailed discussion on this point, see *Secretary of State for Health v Servier Laboratories Ltd* [2019] EWCA Civ 1160; [2019] 3 W.L.R. 938.

89 *Oren v Red Box Toy Factory Ltd* [1999] F.S.R. 785. See also *RCA Corporation v Pollard* [1983] Ch. 135; *Secretary of State for Health v Servier Laboratories Ltd* [2019] EWCA Civ 1160; [2019] 3 W.L.R. 938.

90 According to Lord Hoffmann this requirement would have been determinative in one of the appeals heard in *OBG Ltd v Allan* [2007] UKHL 21; [2008] 1 A.C. 1 (i.e., *Douglas v Hello! Ltd*) had it been necessary to consider the claim for causing loss by unlawful means. D was a celebrity magazine which published photographs of A's wedding, where A had agreed to give C, another celebrity magazine, exclusive access. While D did cause loss to C (i.e., lower circulation) and intended it as a means to an end (i.e., D's own higher circulation) and did use unlawful means as against A (i.e., breach of confidence), those means did not interfere with A's freedom of action to deal with C. In the result, the claim in the unlawful means tort was unnecessary because C had its own claim against D for breach of confidence.

91 *Palmer Birch (A Partnership) v Lloyd* [2018] EWHC 2316 (TCC); [2018] 4 W.L.R. 164 at [186] per Judge Russen QC.

D. Intention

19-025 **An intention to injure the claimant** This tort requires that D strike intentionally at C through A. So if Gye had kidnapped Johanna Wagner in order to damage Lumley's theatre she would no doubt have had a defence to any action for breach of contract by Lumley but Gye would (according to current thinking) have been liable to Lumley for causing loss by unlawful means. Conversely, if Johanna Wagner had been a passenger in Gye's car, and Gye had carelessly injured her in a road accident so that she could not sing, he would not be liable to Lumley, even if he was aware of her contract with him, because he had no intention to injure him. Nor is it enough that D's wrong is intentional towards A, if there is not the necessary intention to injure C. In *Millar v Bassey*[92] it was alleged that D, a popular singer, entered into a contract with A, a recording company, to produce an album and that C contracted with A to perform various services in connection with the album. D, in breach of contract, failed to turn up for rehearsals and then withdrew from the project. Since her services were irreplaceable, this inevitably caused A to be in breach of its contract with C. The Court of Appeal refused to strike out C's claim against D. However, in *OBG Ltd v Allan* the House of Lords regarded that decision as wrong. Although it may have been obvious to D that her action would prevent the performance of the contract between A and C she did not intend to injure C. As Lord Nicholls put it[93]:

> "a defendant's foresight that his unlawful conduct may or will probably damage the claimant cannot be equated with intention for this purpose … Miss Bassey did not breach her recording contract with the intention of thereby injuring any of the plaintiffs".

19-026 **Intention to injure as an end, or as a means to an end** Although foresight of probable harm to C is not sufficient, it is not necessary that an intention to injure C should be D's sole purpose[94]:

> "[T]he master of the Othello in *Tarleton v M'Gawley* may have had nothing against the other trader. If he had gone off to make his fortune in other waters, he would have wished him well. He simply wanted a monopoly of the local trade for himself. But he nevertheless intended to cause him loss."

So disinterested malice towards C is not necessary: D's purpose may be to advance his own interests by diverting business from C to himself but in that case C's loss and D's gain are two sides of the same coin and in law he intends to injure C.[95] Conversely, D is not liable where he believes that he is entitled to act as he does in protection of his own interests.[96]

---

[92] [1994] E.M.L.R. 44.
[93] [2007] UKHL 21; [2008] 1 A.C. 1 at [166]. See also *Barretts & Baird (Wholesale) Ltd v Institution of Professional Civil Servants* [1987] I.R.L.R. 3.
[94] *OBG Ltd v Allan* [2007] UKHL 21; [2008] 1 A.C. 1 at [63] per Lord Hoffmann.
[95] *OBG Ltd v Allan* [2007] UKHL 21; [2008] 1 A.C. 1 at [167]; *Sorrell v Smith* [1900] A.C. 700 at 742.
[96] *Meretz Investments NV v ACP Ltd* [2007] EWCA Civ 1303; [2008] Ch. 244. The proposition is made in the context of a claim for unlawful means conspiracy, but it must equally apply to the unlawful means tort which may be committed by an individual. This is, in effect, the defence of justification articulated as part of the requirement of intention.

E. Trade or Business

The tort is not necessarily confined to trade or business It has long been **19-027** customary to call this tort the wrong of interference with business (or trade) by unlawful means and *OBG Ltd v Allan* is replete with references to that or similar formulae.[97] This may simply be because the overwhelming majority of cases are likely to arise in a business context, but it is doubtful that the tort is so confined.[98] If it is actionable to use unlawful means to drive away C's prospective customers[99] why should it not equally be actionable to use such means against a person who proposes to buy C's house but has not yet signed a contract to do so?[100]

F. Two-party Cases: Intimidation

Intimidation as a sub-species of the unlawful means tort? If there is no third **19-028** party and D uses unlawful means to inflict harm directly on C, then in very many cases D will have committed one of the specific intentional torts dealt with in this book such as deceit, conversion or assault. Nonetheless, there may be situations in which C succumbs to the *threat* of unlawful action in which none of the torts considered so far in this book will have been committed. Such cases have often been, and still are, discussed on the basis that "intimidation" amounts to a separate tort but Lord Hoffmann in *OBG Ltd v Allan*[101] seemed to consider intimidation to be a "two-party" variety (perhaps the most common variety) of the unlawful means tort. It is worth noting, however, that the House of Lords squarely recognised intimidation as an established tort in *Rookes v Barnard*.[102] Also militating against Lord Hoffmann's view is the fact that the courts continue to define the elements of intimidation in rather different terms than the ingredients of the unlawful means tort.

Elements In *Berezovsky v Abramovich* Longmore LJ, with whom the other two **19-029** members of the Court agreed, said that[103]:

> "the essential ingredients of the tort of intimidation are: (1) a threat by the defendant to do something unlawful or 'illegitimate'; (2) the threat must be intended to coerce the claimant to take or refrain from taking some course of action; (3) the threat must in fact coerce the claimant to take such action; (4) loss or damage must be incurred by the claimant as a result".

A threat can be express or implied, and this perhaps explains the decision that the tort was committed where a young girl was kept in coercive and exploitative conditions as a domestic servant, since there was an implicit threat of more abuse.[104] The

---

97 See, e.g., *OBG Ltd v Allan* [2007] UKHL 21; [2008] 1 A.C. 1 at [139], [141], [180], [247], [261].
98 cf. *Revenue and Customs Commissioners v Total Network SL* [2008] UKHL 19; [2008] 1 A.C. 1174 at [100].
99 *Tarleton v M'Gawley* (1793) Peake N.P. 270; 170 E.R. 153. See para.19-020.
100 cf. Deakin and Randall (2009) 72 M.L.R. 519. Most cases of inducing breach of contract will also occur in a business context, but it seems to be assumed that the tort could apply to a non-commercial property transaction (*Smith v Morrison* [1974] 1 W.L.R. 659) though the result may be affected by the statutory provisions on registration of land charges.
101 [2007] UKHL 21; [2008] 1 A.C. 1 at [47].
102 [1964] A.C. 1129.
103 [2011] EWCA Civ 153; [2011] 1 W.L.R. 2290 at [5].
104 *Godwin v Uzoigwe* [1993] Fam. Law 65. See also *News Group Newspapers Ltd v Society of Graphi-*

concept of unlawfulness arguably has the same meaning as in the unlawful means tort,[105] particularly if Lord Hoffmann's view that intimidation is a sub-species of that tort is accepted. In any event, it clearly includes breaches or threatened breaches of contract.[106] It has been held that the test of causation is the same as that which applies in the tort of deceit and the threshold is, consequently, "low" given the "policy of English law to impose more extensive liability on intentional wrongdoers than on careless or other less culpable defendants".[107]

19-030 **No tort claim where there has been an actual breach of contract** It has been suggested above[108] that in a three-party situation an actual breach of contract by D against A is as much unlawful means as a threatened breach in the context of D's liability in tort to C. Is it therefore the law that if D deliberately breaks his own contract with C he is liable in the tort of intimidation as well as in contract? It seems that it is not, at least where there was no threat that preceded the breach. The remedies provided to C by the law of contract are as effective, if not more so, than in the case where D threatens to break the contract; and there would be something very odd in turning every profit-motivated breach of contract into a tort.[109] English law is not unfriendly to concurrent liability[110] but this would be taking it a step too far.

19-031 **Should the claimant be confined to his contractual remedies?** Whereas in the three-party situation, if C cannot sue in tort, he cannot sue at all, because D's threat of breach is made to A,[111] in the two-party situation there is normally a contractual remedy available to C. Thus, if D threatens C with a breach of contract C may be able to treat the contract as repudiated and sue for damages or, of course, he may wait for the breach and then do so (C may sometimes also be able to obtain an injunction to restrain the breach). C will be adequately compensated by his remedy in damages for breach of contract as his loss can scarcely be other than financial. It is thus arguable that where D threatens C with a breach of his contract with C, C should be restricted to his contractual remedies. What is the position where D threatens C with the commission of a tort? Here C may, of course, bring an action for damages for the tort concerned if it is committed (or apply for an injunction to restrain its commission). However, it is perhaps less realistic to say that these legal remedies afford him adequate protection against the consequences of resisting in the face of the threat, especially where the threat is of violence.[112]

---

cal and Allied Trades '82 [1986] I.R.L.R. 337 at 347 with reference to the seventh claimant.
[105] See para.19-020. However, in *OBG Ltd v Allan* [2007] UKHL 21; [2008] 1 A.C. 1 at [61] Lord Hoffmann warned that he did "not intend to say anything about the question of whether a claimant who has been compelled by unlawful intimidation to act to his own detriment, can sue for his loss. Such a case of 'two-party intimidation' raises altogether different issues".
[106] *Rookes v Barnard* [1964] A.C. 1129.
[107] *Al Nehayan v Kent* [2018] EWHC 333 (Comm); [2018] 1 C.L.C. 216 at [233].
[108] See para.19-021.
[109] The remedy of requiring the defendant to account for his profits from the breach to the claimant is very restricted and this is no accident: *Attorney General v Blake* [2001] 1 A.C. 268. Punitive damages for profit-motivated torts go wider (para.23-015). The fact that it would suit the claimant to dress up his claim as tort rather than contract is not necessarily a reason for allowing him to do so.
[110] See para.1-009.
[111] Hoffmann (1965) 81 L.Q.R. 116 at 127–128.
[112] A point demonstrated clearly by *Godwin v Uzoigwe* [1993] Fam. Law 65.

Economic duress Pursuant to the doctrine of economic duress, C can avoid a **19-032** contract into which he entered as a result of pressure applied by D if that pressure was "illegitimate" and a significant cause of C entering into the contract.[113] Thus, not every threat to break a contract will amount to duress. Where such a threat does not amount to duress, it cannot be the case that C can avoid the binding nature of the contract by counter-claiming for damages for intimidation. Accordingly, it seems that for the purposes of a claim for intimidation C should be required to show unlawful coercion at least of such a degree as would enable him to avoid a contract.[114] Although the doctrine of duress is mainly concerned with threats of unlawful action, it is thought to be capable exceptionally of extending to unfair pressure that falls short of illegal conduct. In such cases, it seems that there is no possibility of concurrent liability in intimidation given that it is an ingredient of the tort that the threatened conduct be unlawful.[115]

Harassment and the tort in Wilkinson v Downton The Protection from Harass- **19-033** ment Act 1997 created a tort (and crime) of "harassment" by conduct (which includes speech) on at least two occasions which a reasonable person would think amounted to harassment.[116] While this is plainly wider than the tort of intimidation because, among other things, it is not confined to threats of wrongful acts, it overlaps with it to a considerable degree. The same is also true of the tort in *Wilkinson v Downton*.[117]

4. CONSPIRACY

A. History

Although our early law knew a writ of conspiracy, this was restricted to abuse **19-034** of legal procedure and the action on the case in the nature of conspiracy, which came into fashion in the reign of Elizabeth I, developed into the modern tort of malicious prosecution.[118] Conspiracy as a crime was developed by the Star Chamber during the 17th century and, when taken over by the common law courts, came to be regarded by them as not only a crime but also as capable of giving rise to civil liability provided that damage resulted to the claimant. As a tort, however, it was little developed until the second half of the 19th century[119] and the law remained obscure until the decision of the House of Lords in *Crofter Hand-Woven Harris Tweed Co Ltd v Veitch*.[120] Conspiracy remains a crime as well as a tort, but the scope of the crime has been curtailed by the Criminal Law Act 1977 so that, broadly speaking, the only conspiracies that are now indictable are those to commit a

---

[113] *Dimskal Shipping Co SA v International Transport Workers Federation* [1992] 2 A.C. 152 at 165 per Lord Goff.
[114] The right to avoid a contract for economic duress may be lost by affirmation: *North Ocean Shipping Co Ltd v Hyundai Construction Co Ltd* [1979] Q.B. 705. It is not easy to see on what basis the right to sue for intimidation could be similarly lost.
[115] "So long as the defendant only threatens to do what he has a legal right to do he is on safe ground": *Rookes v Barnard* [1964] A.C. 1129 at 1168 per Lord Reid.
[116] See para.4-034ff.
[117] See para.4-031.
[118] See Winfield, *History of Conspiracy and Abuse of Legal Procedure* (1921).
[119] It "is a modern invention altogether": *Midland Bank Trust Co Ltd v Green (No.3)* [1982] Ch. 529 at 539 per Lord Denning MR.
[120] [1942] A.C. 435.

substantive criminal offence, to defraud or to corrupt public morals or outrage public decency. However, the 1977 Act has no effect on civil liability. In fact, even aside from the Act the tort and the crime have cut loose from whatever common origin they had.[121] The tort of conspiracy takes two forms according to whether unlawful means are used or not.

B. Lawful Means Conspiracy

19-035 **The Crofter case**   *Crofter Hand-Woven Harris Tweed Co Ltd v Veitch*[122] established that if there is a combination of persons whose predominant purpose is to cause damage to the claimant, that purpose may render unlawful acts that would otherwise be lawful and that would be lawful if committed by one person even with the predominant purpose of causing injury. The facts of this case are complex but in outline were as follows. Union officials put an embargo on the importation of yarn to the Isle of Lewis by ordering Lewis dockers, who were members of the union, not to handle such yarn. The officials did so with a view to obtaining increased wages for union members working in mills in Lewis and with the object of getting all mill workers to become members. The dockers obeyed (without breaking any contract) and thus injured the trade of seven small producers of tweed on Lewis who used imported yarn. These producers sued the officials for conspiracy. The claimants lost their case because the predominant purpose of the embargo was to promote the interests of the union members rather than to injure the claimants,[123] but the House of Lords made it clear that if the predominant purpose of a combination is to injure another in his trade or business,[124] or in his other legitimate interests, then, if damage results, the tort of conspiracy is committed. The *Crofter* principle was applied by the Court of Appeal in *Gulf Oil (Great Britain) Ltd v Page*[125] in granting an interim injunction against a combination to publish a statement defamatory of the claimants even though the statement was admitted to be true and there would, therefore, have been an absolute defence to an action for libel; but this is confined to cases where the claimant suffers actual pecuniary loss: if the claim is for general loss of reputation or injured feelings the law of defamation cannot be sidestepped in this way.[126]

i. Purpose

19-036 **To cause damage to the claimant**   The purpose of the combination must be to cause damage to the claimant. In other words, there must have been an intention to injure, and an intention to injure means the same thing here as it does in relation to the unlawful means tort.[127] The test is therefore not what the defendants contemplated as a likely or even an inevitable consequence of their conduct. Rather, it is "what is in truth the object in the minds of the combiners when they acted as

---

[121] *Midland Bank Trust Co Ltd v Green (No.3)* [1982] Ch. 529 at 541.
[122] [1942] A.C. 435.
[123] See also *Mogul SS Co Ltd v McGregor Gow* [1892] A.C. 25; *Sorrell v Smith* [1925] A.C. 700.
[124] This, so their Lordships held, had really been settled in *Quinn v Leathem* [1901] A.C. 495, notwithstanding earlier doubts about the meaning of that case.
[125] [1988] Ch. 327.
[126] *Lonrho Plc v Fayed (No.5)* [1993] 1 W.L.R. 1489. See also *Oyston v Blaker* [1996] 1 W.L.R. 1326.
[127] *Emerald Supplies Ltd v British Airways Plc (No.1)* [2015] EWCA Civ 1024; [2016] Bus. L.R. 145 at [133].

they did?"[128] Malice in the sense of malevolence, spite or ill will is not essential for liability,[129] nor is it sufficient if merely superadded to a legitimate purpose. Rather, what is required is that the combiners should have acted in order that the claimant should suffer damage. If they did not act in order that the claimant should suffer damage but to pursue their own advantage, they are not liable, however selfish their attitude and however inevitable the claimant's damage may have been. Thus, an agreement between D1 and D2 to fix prices so that C is driven out of the market and his share passes to them is not actionable in conspiracy even though the agreement is invalid by reason of its being in restraint of trade[130] (though it may give rise to a claim for damages under s.47A of the Competition Act 1998). The mere fact that the defendants are pleased by the claimant's loss will not give rise to liability.[131]

Common purpose   There is no liability where the participants act in pursuance **19-037** of different forms of self-interest.[132] If one participant has the object of causing injury to the claimant and the others do not there is no conspiracy because there is no common purpose to injure; but if the others are aware of the intention of the one bent on injury it may be that they are all liable.[133]

Promoting the combiners' unlawful interest   The *Crofter* case contains several **19-038** statements to the effect that a combination to injure another without the use of unlawful means is not actionable where it is designed to pursue the "legitimate" or "lawful" interests of the defendants. Thus, Viscount Simon said that if the[134]:

"predominant purpose is to damage another person and damage results, that is tortious conspiracy. If the predominant purpose is the lawful protection or promotion of any *lawful interest* of the combiners (no illegal means being employed), it is not a tortious conspiracy, even though it causes damage to another person."

Clearly therefore there is no actionable conspiracy where the defendants act to improve their share of the market at the claimant's expense[135] or to strengthen the position of a trade union or its members[136] or to maintain prices in the trade to the common benefit of members.[137] However, what if the defendants' activity does not involve "trade" or "business" in any meaningful sense at all but is simply a scheme to cheat others of money? In *Revenue and Customs Commissioners v Total Network SL*[138] the defendants engineered a complex "carousel fraud" involving fictitious supplies of goods. The whole scheme was criminal and in such a case it seems extraordinary to say that the parties are merely "advancing their interests" at the expense of the Revenue. Nevertheless, the Revenue abandoned a claim based upon

---

128 *Crofter Hand-Woven Harris Tweed Co Ltd v Veitch* [1942] A.C. 435 at 445 per Viscount Simon LC.
129 *Crofter Hand-Woven Harris Tweed Co Ltd v Veitch* [1942] A.C. 435 at 450, 463, 469–471; *Huntley v Thornton* [1957] 1 W.L.R. 321; *Hutchinson v Aitchison* (1970) 9 K.I.R. 69.
130 *Mogul SS Co Ltd v McGregor Gow & Co* [1892] A.C. 25.
131 *Crofter Hand-Woven Harris Tweed Co Ltd v Veitch* [1942] A.C. 435 at 471 per Lord Wright.
132 Thus, in the *Crofter* case the interests of the mill owners and the trade unionists were by no means identical.
133 *Crofter Hand-Woven Harris Tweed Co Ltd v Veitch* [1942] A.C. 435 at 495.
134 *Crofter Hand-Woven Harris Tweed Co Ltd v Veitch* [1942] A.C. 435 at 445 (emphasis added). See also at 469.
135 *Mogul SS Co Ltd v McGregor Gow & Co* [1892] A.C. 25.
136 The *Crofter* case itself.
137 *Ware and de Freville Ltd v Motor Trade Association* [1921] 3 K.B. 40.
138 [2008] UKHL 19; [2008] 1 A.C. 1174.

conspiracy to injure, seemingly on the basis that causing damage to the Revenue was not the defendants' primary aim,[139] and instead advanced a case based solely on unlawful means conspiracy. That raised questions, which are explored below, about how far a criminal offence may be unlawful means for the purposes of that tort. However, as Lord Neuberger pointed out, on such facts[140]:

> "[T]here is little, if any, difference between the conspirators' intention to make money and their intention to deprive the commissioners of money: each is the obverse of the other. On that basis, it may well be that it could be said that the predominant purpose of Total and the other conspirators was indeed to inflict loss on the [Revenue] just as much as it was to profit the conspirators, and hence the claim in tort is made out in conspiracy to injure."

ii. Combination

19-039   For conspiracy there must be concerted action between two or more persons. Proof of an express agreement is unnecessary[141] and nor does the agreement have to be in any sense a "formal" one.[142] Unlike the crime of conspiracy, it is possible for a combination between spouses to amount to the tort.[143] It seems that there can be no conspiracy between an employer and his employees, at least where they merely go about their employer's business. The balance of authority suggests, however, that a company can conspire with its directors[144] although a question may still linger as to whether directors who resolve to cause their company to break its contract commit conspiracy by unlawful means against the other contracting party.[145] These doubts arise because if the directors are identified with the company for this purpose[146] there would be an easy way to outflank the denial of liability for inducing breach of contract in such circumstances.[147] Conversely, there might be circumstances where an employer would be vicariously liable for a conspiracy involving his employees provided the other requirements of that form of liability are met.

iii. Damage

19-040   In contrast with the crime of conspiracy, an overt act causing damage is an essential element of liability in the tort.[148] The conspiracy must, in other words, be implemented. If, therefore, the acts relied on are incapable of being made part of

---

139   [2008] UKHL 19; [2008] 1 A.C. 1174 at [226].
140   [2008] UKHL 19; [2008] 1 A.C. 1174 at [228]. Lord Hope also considered at [44] that the "case as a subspecies of unlawful means conspiracy [was] virtually indistinguishable from the tort of conspiracy to injure".
141   *Kuwait Oil Tanker Co SAK v Al Bader* [2000] 2 All E.R. (Comm.) 271 at [111].
142   *Alesco Risk Management Services Ltd v Bishopsgate Insurance Brokers Ltd* [2019] EWHC 2839 (QB) at [375].
143   *Midland Bank Trust Co Ltd v Green (No.3)* [1982] Ch. 529.
144   *Digicel (St Lucia) Ltd v Cable & Wireless Plc* [2010] EWHC 774 (Ch) at Annex I at [61], [77]; *Barclay Pharmaceuticals Ltd v Waypharm LP* [2012] EWHC 306 (Comm) at [222]–[229]; *Palmer Birch (A Partnership) v Lloyd* [2018] EWHC 2316 (TCC); [2018] 4 W.L.R. 164 at [215]; *Raja v McMillan* [2020] EWHC 951 (Ch) at [27]–[29].
145   See para.19-041.
146   See para.25-034.
147   See para.19-015.
148   *JSC BTA Bank v Ablyazov* [2018] UKSC 19; [2018] 2 W.L.R. 1125 at [9].

any cause of action—for example, evidence given by witnesses in a court of law—then the tort cannot be made out.[149] It is sufficient to establish damage to show that the claimant incurred expenses in investigating and counteracting the machinations of the defendants.[150] Although the claimant is required to prove some actual pecuniary loss, once that is done damages are not limited to the amount so proved.[151]

C. Unlawful Means Conspiracy

Summary requirements   Unlawful means conspiracy[152]:

19-041

"involves an arrangement between two or more parties, whereby they ... agree that at least one of them will use 'unlawful means' against the claimant, and, although damage to the claimant need not be the predominant intention of any of the parties, the claimant must have suffered loss or damage as a result".

The defendant must know the facts that render the means concerned unlawful although he need not also be aware of the legal consequences of using those means.[153] The requirement that damage be caused is the same as under lawful means conspiracy, as is the requirement that there be a combination, although the latter may give rise to additional difficulty because of the requirement that the parties must agree not just to harm the claimant but to do so using unlawful means. The knowledge of a "minor" participant in the combination may not be the same as that of the principal conspirator. It may be necessary to analyse the extent to which the "minor" participant shared a common objective with the primary actor and the extent to which the achievement of that objective was to his knowledge to be realised by unlawful means intended to injure the claimant, his liability being limited to that common extent.[154] Where the necessary combination has been proved there is no requirement that the particular defendant sued be the one who took the unlawful action.[155]

---

[149] *Marrinan v Vibart* [1963] 1 Q.B. 234 (affirmed at 528); cf. *Darker v Chief Constable of West Midlands* [2001] 1 A.C. 435 and *Surzur Overseas Ltd v Koros* [1999] 2 Lloyd's Rep. 611.

[150] *British Motor Trade Association v Salvadori* [1949] Ch. 556. But this may only be so where there is other financial loss: *Lonrho Plc v Fayed (No.5)* [1993] 1 W.L.R. 1489 at 1497. These and a number of other cases are examined in *R & V Versicherung AG v Risk Insurance and Reinsurance Solutions SA* [2006] EWHC 42 (Comm).

[151] When actual pecuniary loss has been proved, damages are said to be at large, but not to the extent of allowing damages for loss of reputation. Loss of orders or loss of trade is actionable but not "airy-fairy general reputation in the business or commercial community", nor a decline in the share value of a corporate claimant: *Lonrho Plc v Fayed (No.5)* [1993] 1 W.L.R. 1489 at 1496 per Dillon LJ.

[152] Said to be "common ground" between the parties in *Revenue and Customs Commissioners v Total Network SL* [2008] UKHL 19; [2008] 1 A.C. 1174 at [213] per Lord Neuberger.

[153] *Forse v Secarma Ltd* [2019] EWCA Civ 215 at [37]; *Stobart Group Ltd v Tinkler* [2019] EWHC 258 (Comm) at [549]–[573].

[154] *IS Innovative Software Ltd v Howes* [2004] EWCA Civ 275; *Bank of Tokyo-Mitsubishi UJF Ltd v Baskan Gida Sanayive Pazarlama AS* [2009] EWHC 1276 (Ch); [2010] Bus. L.R. D1 at [847]; *The Dolphina* [2011] SGHC 273; [2012] 1 Lloyd's Rep. 304; cf. *Kuwait Oil Tanker Co SAK v Al Bader* [2000] 2 All E.R. (Comm) 271.

[155] *Kuwait Oil Tanker Co SAK v Al Bader* [2000] 2 All E.R. (Comm) 271; *Barclay Pharmaceuticals Ltd v Waypharm LP* [2012] EWHC 306 (Comm) at [222].

i. Intention

19-042 Predominant purpose to injure unnecessary After a period of uncertainty caused by *Lonrho Ltd v Shell Petroleum Ltd (No.2)*[156] the House of Lords in *Lonrho Plc v Fayed*[157] reaffirmed that this form of the tort, unlike the *Crofter* variety, does not require a predominant purpose to injure C and *Revenue and Customs Commissioners v Total Network SL*[158] also proceeds on this basis. However, the tort still requires an intention to injure. That concept has the same meaning that it bears in the unlawful means tort.[159] Thus, if the damage to C is not an end in itself it must at least be a necessary means to some other end and it is not enough that it is a foreseeable consequence of the unlawful means used.[160] The unlawful means tort (at least in its "three-party" form) involves unlawful conduct directed at A but with the intention of causing harm to C by interfering with the relationship between A and C. Here, too, although there need be[161] no third party involved, the purpose of the combination must be to strike at C. To take an example loosely based on *Lonrho Ltd v Shell Petroleum Ltd (No.2)*,[162] if D1 and D2 combine to evade legislation prohibiting trade with a country in which C has oil interests and the effect of this is to damage C's interests then even if the evasion of the legislation is unlawful means[163] they do not intend to harm C—that is simply a by-product, even if an inevitable one, of what they do. That is not to say that it will necessarily be easy to draw the line between this situation and the "means to an end" intention which does fall within the tort. If the correct analysis of the facts is that the conspirators wanted to get hold of the oil market for themselves in that country by destroying C's share, that must be a classic example of using illegal means to achieve some ulterior end. After all, in a conspiracy by D1 and D2 to defraud C, D1 and D2 plainly intend to deprive C of his property so that they can get it.[164]

ii. Unlawful means

19-043 Crimes There has been an understandable desire in some quarters to give unity to the concept of unlawful means in the economic torts. As we have seen above,[165] the majority in *OBG Ltd v Allan* regarded the unlawful means tort as essentially one in which D strikes at C by using unlawful means directed against a third party, A,

---

[156] [1982] A.C. 173.

[157] [1992] 1 A.C. 448, overruling *Metall und Rohstoff v Donaldson Lufkin & Jenrette Inc* [1990] 1 Q.B. 391 and explaining *Lonrho Ltd v Shell Petroleum Ltd (No.2)* [1982] A.C. 173.

[158] [2008] UKHL 19; [2008] 1 A.C. 1174. See, e.g., at [40], [56], [82], [115], [213].

[159] *Emerald Supplies Ltd v British Airways Plc (No.1)* [2015] EWCA Civ 1024; [2016] Bus. L.R. 145 at [133].

[160] *Palmer Birch (A Partnership) v Lloyd* [2018] EWHC 2316 (TCC); [2018] 4 W.L.R. 164 at [220]; *Media-Saturn Holdings GmbH v Toshiba Information Systems UK Ltd* [2019] EWHC 1095 (Ch) at [235].

[161] There may be a third party. If D threatens A that he will break his contract with A unless A ceases to trade with C that is inflicting harm on C by unlawful means. So also is it if D1 and D2 combine in order to threaten A, but this time it is additionally unlawful means conspiracy.

[162] [1982] A.C. 173.

[163] See para.19-041.

[164] *Kuwait Oil Tanker Co SAK v Al Bader* [2000] 2 All E.R. (Comm.) 271. Indeed, as has been seen above (para.19-038), Lord Neuberger in *Revenue and Customs Commissioners v Total Network SL* [2008] UKHL 19; [2008] 1 A.C. 1174 regarded that as a predominant purpose to injure.

[165] See para.19-020.

and in that context "unlawful means" covers only acts or threats to commit acts that are civilly actionable by A (or would be actionable by A if he suffered loss).[166] The equivalent proposition in a case of unlawful means conspiracy would be that the means would have to be independently actionable by C. However, the result of *Revenue and Customs Commissioners v Total Network SL*[167] is that in unlawful means conspiracy the unlawful means concept also extends to acts that are criminal but which would not be civilly actionable if done by one person.[168] Hence, on the facts of that case the commission of the common law offence of cheating the Revenue, if established, would have counted as unlawful means for the purposes of liability in tort.

This conclusion was not, however, very closely reasoned. Indeed, as Lord Walker admitted, the common assumption in many of the earlier dicta that a crime constitutes unlawful means perhaps rests on a quasi-lay assumption that criminality is so obviously at the top of the tree of unlawfulness that its inclusion hardly needs justification.[169] Lord Scott considered that the imposition of tort liability is justified where the[170]:

> "circumstances [are] such as to make the conduct sufficiently reprehensible to justify imposing on those who have brought about the harm liability in damages for having done so. Bearing that in mind, the proposition that a combination of two or more people to carry out a scheme that is criminal in its nature and is intended to cause economic harm to some person does not, when carried out with that result, constitute a tort actionable by that person is, in my opinion, unacceptable. Such a proposition is not only inconsistent with the jurisprudence of tortious conspiracy ... but is inconsistent also with the historic role of the action on the case."

The foregoing does not explain why crimes can amount to unlawful means in the context of unlawful means conspiracy even when they are not independently actionable but not in the context of the unlawful means tort. One possible reason for this situation may be that if in the context of unlawful means conspiracy the idea of unlawful means were confined to conduct that is independently actionable the tort would be rendered all but redundant because the conspirators will generally be liable as joint tortfeasors[171] (e.g., if D1 and D2 conspire to defraud C by making fraudulent misrepresentations to him they jointly commit the tort of deceit). The clear message of *Revenue and Customs Commissioners v Total Network SL* is that conspiracy is not merely a form of joint tortfeasance dressed up in other clothes. In that case Lord Mance said that "[t]he two ... are different by their nature".[172]

---

[166] See para.19-022.

[167] [2008] UKHL 19; [2008] 1 A.C. 1174.

[168] In *W H Newson Ltd v IMI Plc* [2013] EWCA Civ 1377; [2014] 1 All E.R. 1377 it was held that the remedy in damages made available by s.47A of the Competition Act 1998 permitted the claimant to bring a conspiracy claim provided that all the ingredients of the cause of action could be established by the infringement findings in the decision of the European Commission (and such findings did not establish the necessary intent to injure).

[169] [2008] UKHL 19; [2008] 1 A.C. 1174 at [90]–[94].

[170] [2008] UKHL 19; [2008] 1 A.C. 1174 at [56].

[171] Even where the unlawful means involve a tort actionable directly by the claimant there is no doctrine that the conspiracy is "merged" in the substantive tort and it has been said that the conspiracy claim may express "the true nature and gravamen of the case": *Kuwait Oil Tanker Co SAK v Al Bader* [2000] 2 All E.R. (Comm.) 271 at [119] (where the conspiracy claim was significant for the then applicable conflict of laws rules).

[172] [2008] UKHL 19; [2008] 1 A.C. 1174 at [123]. See also *JSC BTA Bank v Ablyazov* [2018] UKSC

19-044 **Incidental criminal wrongs**   It is not in every case that the use of criminal means gives rise to liability for unlawful means conspiracy.[173] We have seen that the commission of a crime which is not a tort in its own right does not give rise to civil liability unless an intention to that effect can be found in the legislation creating the offence.[174] It is unclear exactly how this principle stands in the context of unlawful means conspiracy, Lord Walker in *Revenue and Customs Commissioners v Total Network SL* being content to say that[175]:

> "[T]he sort of considerations relevant to determining whether a breach of statutory duty is actionable in a civil suit … may well overlap, or even occasionally coincide with, the issue of unlawful means in the tort of conspiracy. But the range of possible breaches of statutory duty, and the range of possible conspiracies, are both so wide and varied that it would be unwise to attempt to lay down any general rule."

19-045 **Civil wrongs**   The issue of whether or not civil wrongs, including breaches of statutes that do not impose criminal liability, constitute unlawful means for the purposes of conspiracy is under-analysed and in *JSC BTA Bank v Ablyazov* the Supreme Court suggested that it may not be possible to formulate a general rule in this regard.[176] At the same time, however, the Court intimated that unlawful means may exist wherever D1 and D2 combined without "just cause of excuse".[177] In *Aerostar Maintenance International Ltd v Wilson*[178] Morgan J considered that breach of contract and breach of fiduciary duty constituted unlawful means.[179] In *Concept Oil Services Ltd v EN-GIN Group LLP*[180] the unlawful means was deceit, but Flaux J saw no reason in principle why entering into a transaction defrauding creditors within the meaning of s.423 of the Insolvency Act 1986 should not amount to unlawful means as well.

19-046 **Contempt of court**   In *JSC BTA Bank v Ablyazov*[181] the Supreme Court held that criminal contempt of court constituted unlawful means for the purposes of the tort of conspiracy. It follows, therefore, that if D1 is subject to an injunction and D2, knowing of the injunction, combines with D1 to assist D1 to breach it, both D1 and D2 will be liable to C in a claim in respect of loss resulting from the implementation of their agreement.

19-047 **No defence of justification**   Justification is not a defence to unlawful means conspiracy. That is because the requirement of unlawfulness anticipates that there is no justification for what was done.[182]

19; [2018] 2 W.L.R. 1125 at [9].
[173] It is not enough that a crime is "part of the story": *Revenue and Customs Commissioners v Total Network SL* [2008] UKHL 19; [2008] 1 A.C. 1174 at [95] per Lord Walker.
[174] See Ch.8.
[175] [2008] UKHL 19; [2008] 1 A.C. 1174 at [96].
[176] [2018] UKSC 19; [2018] 2 W.L.R. 1125 at [15].
[177] "The real test is whether there is a just cause or excuse for combining to use unlawful means": [2018] UKSC 19; [2018] 2 W.L.R. 1125 at [11] per Lord Sumption and Lord Lloyd-Jones.
[178] [2010] EWHC 2032 (Ch) at [170]–[172].
[179] Consider, also, *Recovery Partners GB Ltd v Rukhadze* [2018] EWHC 2918 (Comm); [2019] Bus. L.R. 1166 at [442] (breach of fiduciary duty and breach of confidence).
[180] [2013] EWHC 1897 (Comm).
[181] [2018] UKSC 19; [2018] 2 W.L.R. 1125.
[182] *Palmer Birch (A Partnership) v Lloyd* [2018] EWHC 2316 (TCC); [2018] 4 W.L.R. 164 at [185]–[193]; cf. *Meretz Investments NV v ACP Ltd* [2007] EWCA Civ 1303; [2008] Ch. 244 at [170].

D.   The Place of Conspiracy in the Law

The "magic of plurality"   Lawful means conspiracy is widely regarded as   **19-048**
anomalous.[183] The central issue has been why the "magic of plurality" should make
something unlawful if it is not unlawful when done by one person alone. Numbers
may, of course, bring increased power and in the *Crofter* case Viscount Maugham
said that he had never felt any difficulty in seeing "the great difference between the
acts of one person and the acts in combination of two or of a multitude".[184] But, as
Viscount Simon LC remarked in the same case[185]:

> "The view that the explanation is to be found in the increasing power of numbers to do
> damage beyond what one individual can do is open to the obvious answer that this depends
> on the personality and influence of the individual. In the play, Cyrano de Bergerac's single
> voice was more effective to drive the bad actor Montfleury off the stage than the protests
> of all the rest of the audience to restrain him. The action of a single tyrant may be more
> potent to inflict suffering on the continent of Europe than a combination of less powerful
> persons."

An ongoing role?   Related to the question of whether there is any "magic in   **19-049**
plurality", doubts have been ventilated as to whether either form of conspiracy
serves any useful purpose given other bases of liability in tort. It is certainly the case
that much conduct that constitutes unlawful means conspiracy will constitute either
the unlawful means tort or a tort for which the conspirators are jointly liable[186] or
both. In these circumstances, and although the Supreme Court has recently
emphasised that "the tort of conspiracy has an established place in the law of
tort",[187] a serious question arises as to whether space should continue to be given
to it in the gallery of torts.[188]
Against this view, it may be said that the overlap between conspiracy and torts
such as the unlawful means tort is far from complete and that, as Lord Mance suggested in *Revenue and Customs Commissioners v Total Network SL*, the tort of
conspiracy is needed to avoid a "lacuna" in the law.[189] For example, and as we have
seen,[190] the three-party variety of the unlawful means tort requires that D strike at
C through A whereas there is no such requirement in relation to the tort of
conspiracy. Further, the two-party species of the unlawful means tort depends upon
proof that D threatened C,[191] while this is unnecessary for a claim in conspiracy. It
would thus appear that the tort of conspiracy is wider in important respects than the
unlawful means tort.

---

[183]   *Lonrho Ltd v Shell Petroleum Ltd (No.2)* [1982] A.C. 173 at 188; *Lonrho Plc v Fayed* [1992] 1 A.C.
448 at 463; *JSC BTA Bank v Ablyazov* [2018] UKSC 19; [2018] 2 W.L.R. 1125 at [7].
[184]   *Crofter Hand-Woven Harris Tweed Co Ltd v Veitch* [1942] A.C. 435 at 448.
[185]   *Crofter Hand-Woven Harris Tweed Co Ltd v Veitch* [1942] A.C. 435 at 443. See also Lord Diplock's
rather less colourful example of the street-corner grocers and a chain of supermarkets in single
ownership in *Lonrho Ltd v Shell Petroleum Ltd (No.2)* [1982] A.C. 173 at 189.
[186]   See Ch.22.
[187]   *JSC BTA Bank v Ablyazov* [2018] UKSC 19; [2018] 2 W.L.R. 1125 at [7] per Lord Sumption and
Lord Lloyd-Jones.
[188]   See Davies and Sales (2018) 134 L.Q.R. 69 at 93, arguing that "there is no remaining space for the
separate existence of the tort of conspiracy in either of its forms ...".
[189]   [2008] UKHL 19; [2008] 1 A.C. 1174 at [120].
[190]   See para.19-020.
[191]   See para.19-029.

The territory occupied by conspiracy and joint tortfeasance is similarly not co-extensive. Although it is true that joint tortfeasance requires a "common design" and that that will amount to a combination for the purposes of conspiracy, to establish joint tortfeasance C must prove more than a de minimis participation by all parties who are said to be liable for the tort[192] whereas the mere fact of entering into a combination by D2 that is then implemented by D1 acting alone is enough to pin liability in conspiracy on D2.[193] Put differently, a bare combination absent "active co-operation"[194] is not enough for joint tortfeasance whereas it arguably is for conspiracy. Further, if D1 and D2 combine for the purposes of committing an act that is not independently tortious, no liability would arise on their part absent the tort of lawful means conspiracy. It is only because of the existence of that tort that D1 and D2 are joint tortfeasors.

19-050   **Rationale for the tort**   Even if conspiracy occupies distinctive territory, that would not in and of itself explain why the tort exists and it would still be necessary to consider why it should be recognised. In *JSC BTA Bank v Ablyazov* Lord Sumption and Lord Lloyd-Jones sought to justify both species of the tort on the following basis[195]:

> "What is it that makes the conspiracy actionable as such? To say that a predominant purpose of injuring the claimant in the one case and the use of unlawful means in the other supply the element of unlawfulness required to make a conspiracy tortious simply restates the proposition in other words. A more useful concept is the absence of just cause or excuse … A person has a right to advance his own interests by lawful means even if the foreseeable consequence is to damage the interest of others. The existence of that right affords a just cause or excuse. Where, on the other hand, he seeks to advance his interests by unlawful means he has no such right. The position is the same where the means used are lawful but the predominant intention of the defendant was to injure the claimant rather than to further some legitimate interest of his own. This is because in that case it cannot be an answer to say that he was simply exercising a legal right. He had no interest recognised by the law in exercising his legal right for the predominant purpose not of advancing is own interests but of injuring the claimant. In either case, there is no just cause or excuse *for the combination*."

5.   PASSING OFF

19-051   **Introduction**   The tort of passing off[196] is part of a wide canvas of legal remedies that control unfair competitive practices and infringement of intellectual property rights. These remedies, which have been developed in ways that have greatly reduced the importance of passing off, fall beyond the scope of this book. Nevertheless, a brief account of the tort, which may sometimes be the only source of relief available, is justified.

19-052   **Summary requirements**   The action for passing off arose in the 19th century and depended upon the simple principle that a person is not to sell his goods or his

---

[192] See Ch.22.

[193] It is unnecessary that D2 take any steps to implement the conspiracy: *Twentieth Century Fox Film Corp v Harris* [2014] EWHC 1568 (Ch) at [158].

[194] *Fish & Fish Ltd v Sea Shepherd UK* [2015] UKSC 10; [2015] A.C. 1229 at [44] per Lord Toulson.

[195] [2018] UKSC 19; [2018] 2 W.L.R. 1125 at [10] (emphasis in original).

[196] See, further, Wadlow, *The Law of Passing-Off*, 5th edn (2016).

services under the pretence that they are those of another.[197] It has three elements[198]: (1) a goodwill or reputation attached to and recognised by the public as distinctive of the claimant's goods or services; (2) a misrepresentation made by the defendant[199] leading the public, or a substantial number of members of the public, to believe that his goods or services are those of the claimant; and (3) damage or likely damage.[200] Misrepresentations that are not "material" in the sense that they have neither caused nor are likely to cause damage are not actionable.[201] Whether or not these elements are present falls to be determined at the inception of the activity in relation to which the claimant objects.[202]

A. Varieties of Passing Off

"Simple" passing off[203]   The representation must cause confusion in the public   **19-053** mind between the C's goods or business and D's goods or business. Thus, false statements disparaging C's goods or exaggerating the worth of D's wares do not constitute passing off (although they may amount to another tort such as malicious falsehood or libel) even though C has suffered damage thereby.[204] Nor is passing off committed by using C's name or trademark in such a way that the public are not deceived about the provenance of D's goods.[205] Simply proving copying is not enough for liability to arise.[206] Rather, it is essential that the defendant should have made a representation[207] calculated to deceive,[208] although no form of fraud

---

197 *Perry v Truefitt* (1842) 6 Beav. 66 at 73; 49 E.R. 749 at 752; *Spalding & Bros v AW Gamage Ltd* (1915) 84 L.J. Ch. 449 at 450.

198 In *Erwen Warnink BV v J Townend & Sons (Hull) Ltd* [1979] A.C. 731 at 742 Lord Diplock referred to five elements: (1) a misrepresentation; (2) made by a trader in the course of trade; (3) to prospective customers of his or ultimate consumers of goods or services supplied by him; (4) which is calculated to injure the business or goodwill of another trader (in the sense that this is a reasonably foreseeable consequence); and (5) which causes or threatens actual damage to a business or goodwill of the trader by whom the action is brought. This formulation was quoted without criticism by Lord Jauncey in *Reckitt & Colman Products Ltd v Borden Inc* [1990] 1 W.L.R. 491 at 511, but Lord Oliver at 499 set out the more abbreviated three elements referred to in the text and this now seems to be the preferred formulation: see *Consorzio del Prosciutto di Parma v Marks & Spencer Plc* [1991] R.P.C. 351 at 368–369; *Woolley v Ultimate Products Ltd* [2012] EWCA Civ 1038 at [2].

199 As to when a defendant will be responsible for making a misrepresentation, see *National Guild of Removers and Storers Ltd v Bee Moved Ltd* [2018] EWCA Civ 1302.

200 Damage may take the form of loss of sales or erosion of the distinctiveness of the trade name sought to be protected: *Erwen Warnink BV v J Townend & Sons (Hull) Ltd* [1979] A.C. 731 at 745; *Chocosuisse v Cadbury Ltd* [1998] R.P.C. 117 at 143; *Woolley v Ultimate Products Ltd* [2012] EWCA Civ 1038 at [7]. An interim injunction may be granted on the basis of the latter before it has resulted in the former.

201 *Fenty v Arcadia Group Brands Ltd* [2015] EWCA Civ 3; [2015] 1 W.L.R. 3291 at [34].

202 *Starbucks (HK) Ltd v British Sky Broadcasting Group Plc* [2015] UKSC 31; [2015] 1 W.L.R. 2628 at [16].

203 The label employed by Briggs J in *Fage UK Ltd Chobani UK Ltd* [2013] EWHC 630 (Ch); [2013] F.S.R. 32 at [118], in contrast with "extended passing off": see para.19-059.

204 See *BBC v Talksport Ltd* [2001] F.S.R. 6 (false claims that broadcasts were live did not interfere with claimants' goodwill); *Schulke & Mayr UK Ltd v Alkapharm UK Ltd* [1999] F.S.R.161.

205 *Arsenal Football Club Plc v Reed* [2001] R.P.C. 46. There were further proceedings in this case before the European Court of Justice and an appeal to the Court of Appeal, but these concerned trademarks. At the end of his judgment, Aldous LJ said that he was not convinced that the reasoning below on passing off had been correct: [2003] EWCA Civ 696; [2003] R.P.C. 39 at [70].

206 *Starbucks (HK) Ltd v British Sky Broadcasting Group Plc* [2015] UKSC 31; [2015] 1 W.L.R. 2628 at [61].

207 Where there is no misrepresentation by the defendant it is not enough that "people make assump-

or even negligence is essential to establish liability.[209] It is enough that the defendant "misrepresents his goods in such a way that it is a reasonably foreseeable consequence of the misrepresentation that the plaintiff's business or goodwill will be damaged".[210]

19-054 Copying or imitating the claimant's registered trademark A common form of passing off involves copying or imitating the claimant's registered trademark, in which situation there has always been the possibility of claims both under the trademark statute and at common law. A modern version of this activity against which passing off has been successfully invoked is registering Internet domain names as variations around the names of well-known companies and then offering the names to the companies at high prices with the express or implied threat of allowing them to be used for deception or as "blockers" to legitimate registration.[211]

19-055 Imitating the get-up of goods An example of passing off by imitating the get-up of the claimant's goods (now also covered by the law of trademarks) is *Reckitt & Colman Products Ltd v Borden Inc*.[212] The claimants had for many years sold lemon juice ("Jif") in a "squeezy container" in the form of a small plastic lemon. They obtained an injunction against the defendants' attempt to sell lemon juice in a similar but not identical container. The difference in the labelling of the products was such as to prevent any risk of confusion in the mind of a careful shopper but the evidence showed that most shoppers did not read labels with any care and that plastic lemons containing lemon juice had become strongly associated in the public mind with the claimants' product. It was no answer that the confusion would not have occurred if the shoppers had been "more careful, more literate or more perspicacious. Customers have to be taken as they are found".[213]

19-056 Descriptive words Had the claimants in *Reckitt & Colman Products Ltd v Borden Inc* been for many years the sole producers of lemon juice in the country and sold it in bottles labelled "Lemon Juice" it is clear that they could not have restrained a competitor from entering the market and doing the same thing, for no one is entitled

---

tions, jump to unjustified conclusions, and put two and two together to make five": *HFC Bank Plc v Midland Bank Plc* [2000] F.S.R. 176 at 201 per Lloyd J. On the position of the producer of a new product in a market where there is a de facto monopoly, see *British Sky Broadcasting Group Plc v Sky Home Services Ltd* [2006] EWHC 3165 (Ch); [2007] 3 All E.R. 1066.

[208] *Perkins v Shone* [2004] EWHC 2249 (Ch).

[209] The customer need not know or care about the identity of the manufacturer, provided the customer knows there is such a person and cares that the goods he buys are made by that person: *United Biscuits (UK) Ltd v Asda Stores Ltd* [1997] R.P.C. 513.

[210] *Reckitt & Colman Products Ltd v Borden Inc* [1990] 1 W.L.R. 491 at 511 per Lord Jauncey. According to Lewison LJ in *Fine and Country Ltd v Okotoks Ltd* [2013] EWCA Civ 672; [2014] F.S.R. 11 at [55] "the essence of the action is not confusion, but misrepresentation".

[211] *British Telecommunications Plc v One in a Million Ltd* [1999] 1 W.L.R. 903.

[212] [1990] 1 W.L.R. 491.

[213] *Reckitt & Colman Products Ltd v Borden Inc* [1990] 1 W.L.R. 491 at 508 per Lord Oliver. See also *R Johnston & Co v Archibald Orr Ewing & Co* (1882) 7 App. Cas. 219 and *White Hudson & Co Ltd v Asian Organisation Ltd* [1964] 1 W.L.R. 1466 ("red paper cough sweets") in both of which the parties were trading in the Far East where customers might have a limited command of English and hence the effect of different labels or names might be limited. Actual confusion on the part of a member of the purchasing public need not be proved as a matter of law (*Lee Kar Choo v Lee Lian Choon* [1967] 1 A.C. 602) but proof that it has occurred will obviously assist the claimant's case, especially if substantial damages are claimed and not merely an injunction.

to fence off and monopolise descriptive words of the English language.[214] However, long usage may have had the effect that the descriptive words have become distinctively attached to the claimant's goods[215] as opposed merely to describing them.[216] A leading case is *Reddaway v Banham*[217] where it was held that "camel hair belting", which originally signified nothing more than belting made of camel hair, had come to signify belting made by the claimants.[218]

Use of own name   As a general rule a person can freely use his own name, or one   **19-057** which he has acquired by reputation, although the use of it inflicts damage on someone else who has the same name.[219] This, however, is qualified to some extent by the law of passing off since a person is not permitted to use a name "to represent his goods or services as being the goods or services of another person and so cause that other person injury to his goodwill and so damage him in his business".[220] In *Parker-Knoll Ltd v Parker-Knoll International Ltd*,[221] both parties were manufacturers of furniture, the claimants being a company well known in the United Kingdom and the defendant an American company which had only recently begun to trade in England. Notwithstanding that the defendant company did no more than use its own name on its furniture, the House of Lords, by a majority, granted an injunction to restrain it from continuing to do so without distinguishing its goods from those of the claimant. The claimant had established that its name had come to denote goods made by it alone and not goods made by anyone else possessing or adopting that name, and the use by the defendant of a similar name did, in the opinion of the majority, amount to the false representation that its goods were the claimant's goods.[222] The central question in each case is, therefore, whether the name or description given by the defendant to his goods is such as to create a likelihood that

---

[214] *Marcus Publishing Plc v Hutton-Wild Communications Plc* [1990] R.P.C. 576 at 579; *Fenty v Arcadia Group Brands Ltd* [2015] EWCA Civ 3; [2015] 1 W.L.R. 3291 at [34].

[215] Equally though, once so attached they may become so public and in such universal use as to be again open to others to use: *Ford v Foster* (1872) L.R. 7 Ch. 611 at 628; *Gramophone Co's Application* [1910] 2 Ch. 423. Alternatively, the courts may accept that instances of "mere confusion" are to be tolerated: *Phones 4U Ltd v Phone4U.co.uk Internet Ltd* [2006] EWCA Civ 244; [2007] R.P.C. 5.

[216] Thus "vacuum cleaner" was held to mean simply a cleaner working by suction and not necessarily one manufactured by the British Vacuum Cleaner Co: *British Vacuum Cleaner Co Ltd v New Vacuum Cleaner Co Ltd* [1907] 2 Ch. 312.

[217] [1896] A.C. 199.

[218] In 1931, it was held that a Belgian manufacturer did not sufficiently distinguish his goods from the claimants' by describing them as "Lechat's camel hair belting": *Reddaway & Co Ltd v Hartley* (1930) 48 R.P.C. 283.

[219] *Brinsmead v Brinsmead* (1913) 30 R.P.C. 493; *Jay's Ltd v Jacobi* [1933] Ch. 411. As to nicknames, see *Biba Group v Biba Boutique* [1980] R.P.C. 413; *NAD Electronics Inc v NAD Computer Systems Ltd* [1999] F.S.R. 380. "A new company with a title of which the name 'A,' for instance, forms part has none of the natural rights that an individual born with the name 'A' would have": *Fine Cotton Spinners and Doublers' Association Ltd v John Cash & Sons Ltd* [1907] 2 Ch. 184 at 190 per Joyce J. See also *Asprey & Garrard Ltd v WRA (Guns) Ltd* [2001] EWCA Civ 1499; [2002] F.S.R. 31 at [43]. In *Dent v Turpin* (1861) 2 John & H. 139; 70 E.R. 1003. Dent had two clock shops, one in the City, the other in the West End. He bequeathed one to each son—which resulted in two clock businesses each called Dent. As Jacob LJ observed in *Phones 4U Ltd v Phone4u.co.uk Internet Ltd* [2006] EWCA Civ 244; [2007] R.P.C. 5 at [22], "[n]either could stop the other; each could stop a third party … from using 'Dent' for such a business".

[220] *Fenty v Arcadia Group Brands Ltd* [2015] EWCA Civ 3; [2015] 1 W.L.R. 3291 at [34] per Kitchin LJ.

[221] [1962] R.P.C. 265.

[222] cf. *Habib Bank Ltd v Habib Bank A.G. Zurich* [1981] 1 W.L.R. 1265.

a substantial section of the purchasing public will be misled into believing that his goods are the goods of the claimant.[223] That the defendant used his own name with no intention to deceive anybody does not mean that such likelihood has not been created,[224] but proof that the defendant did intend to deceive[225] will materially assist the claimant's case. As has often been pointed out, if it was the defendant's object to deceive people into thinking that his goods were the goods of the claimant, the court will not be slow to infer that he achieved his object.[226] Similarly, whatever tolerance is shown to the use of a person's own name will not be extended to altering it—"garnishing" it, as the expression is—so as to be likely to mislead. Thus, a firm of wine merchants called "Short's Ltd" obtained an injunction against one Short, who set up a similar business and styled it "Short's".[227]

19-058 **Address** Imitation of an address[228] may be part of conduct amounting to a scheme of passing off, but there is no property in an address as such. In *Day v Brownrigg*[229] the house of X had been known for over 60 years as "Ashford Lodge", and his neighbour Y changed the name of his house (previously known as "Ashford Villa") to "Ashford Lodge". This caused much inconvenience and annoyance to X, who claimed an injunction to restrain Y from such alteration of the name. It was held on demurrer that he had no cause of action.[230] Perhaps the result would have been different if the defendant's purpose had been to deceive others and thereby causing harm to the claimant in his profession.[231]

19-059 **"Extended" passing off** The classic form of the tort (i.e., "simple" passing off) involves A representing his goods to be those of B. However, the law also recognises an "extended" form of passing off which is concerned with situations where goodwill attaches to the description of a product, with the result that that goodwill is shared by all persons making that product. Where this happens, the makers of the product in question will have a cause of action against a defendant who falsely attributes that description to his own goods even though he does not represent them to be produced by anyone else. The leading case is *Erwen Warnink BV v Townend & Sons (Hull) Ltd*.[232] The claimants were the main producers of advocaat, a drink of Dutch origin made from eggs and spirits, enjoying substantial sales in England. The defendants manufactured a drink, properly known as "egg flip", made from sherry and eggs and marketed under the name of "Keelings Old English Advocaat". Due to its attracting a lower rate of duty than the spirit-based drink it could be sold more cheaply and captured an appreciable share of the English

---

[223] *Parker-Knoll Ltd v Parker-Knoll International Ltd* [1962] R.P.C. 265 at 278–279, 285, 289–290.
[224] *Reed Executive Plc v Reed Business Information Ltd* [2004] EWCA Civ 159; [2004] R.P.C. 40 at [110].
[225] See James LJ's example, in *Massam v Thorley* (1880) 14 Ch. D. 748 at 757, of somebody finding a man named Bass and setting up a brewery at Burton as Bass & Co.
[226] *Brinsmead & Son Ltd v Brinsmead* (1913) 30 R.P.C. 493 at 507; *Parker-Knoll Ltd v Parker-Knoll International Ltd* [1962] R.P.C. 265 at 290.
[227] *Short's Ltd v Short* (1914) 31 R.P.C. 294.
[228] Or the acquisition of a similar telephone number: *Law Society v Griffiths* [1995] R.P.C. 16.
[229] (1878) 10 Ch. D. 294.
[230] Liability was also denied, but this time in a business context, in *Street v Union Bank of Spain and England* (1885) 30 Ch. D. 155.
[231] cf. *National Phonograph Co v Edison Bell Consolidated Phonograph Co* [1908] 1 Ch. 335 (deception as unlawful means in tort).
[232] [1979] A.C. 731.

market for advocaat. On the basis of a finding of fact that advocaat was a distinct and recognisable species of beverage based on spirits, the House of Lords held that the defendants were guilty of passing off. The House made it clear that the principle was not confined to goods produced in a particular locality. Conversely, if the trade name is only descriptive of geographical origin, that is not sufficient for the necessary goodwill; it must connote "something more", "some drawing power in its own right".[233] To meet this requirement it is not necessary that the product has a cachet, for example, that it is of "superior quality" or a "premium product",[234] and, as with "simple passing off", the perception of distinctiveness which will suffice need not be that of the public as a whole; some section, or significant section, of the public will be enough.[235]

Reverse passing off   The broad principle underlying liability is also demonstrated   **19-060**
by the fact that there can be a claim for what has been called "reverse (or inverse) passing off", that is to say a case where the defendant shows the customer the claimant's goods intending to fulfil the resulting contract with goods of his own manufacture.[236]

Initial confusion   A misrepresentation by the defendant may have initially   **19-061**
confused a customer into doing business with him, but such confusion may no longer be operative at the time when any business is concluded between them. Nonetheless, the initial confusion is sufficient for passing off since even by then the damage is done to the claimant's goodwill.[237]

No requirement of a "common field of activity"   Many older decisions speak   **19-062**
in terms of a requirement that there be a common field of activity between the parties. Today, however, this is not a prerequisite to liability, although the issue of a common field of activity is relevant to whether there is a misrepresentation likely to deceive and whether damage is likely to result.[238] For example, in *Granada Group Ltd v Ford Motor Co Ltd*[239] the claimants, a major publishing and entertainment company, failed (not surprisingly on the facts) to restrain the defendants from attaching the name "Granada" to a new car; and in *Fortnum & Mason Plc v Fortnam Ltd*[240] there was no serious risk of confusion between the activities of the

---

[233] *Fage UK Ltd Chobani UK Ltd* [2013] EWHC 630 (Ch); [2013] F.S.R. 32 at [124] per Briggs J ("Greek yoghurt"); affirmed [2014] EWCA Civ 5; [2014] F.S.R. 29.

[234] *Diageo North America Inc v Intercontinental Brands (ICB) Ltd* [2010] EWCA Civ 920; [2011] 1 All E.R. 242 (vodka), although so-called premium products are "perhaps more likely" to acquire the distinctiveness required (at [51] per Patten LJ).

[235] *Fage UK Ltd Chobani UK Ltd* [2014] EWCA Civ 5; [2014] F.S.R. 29; cf. *Marks & Spencer Plc v Interflora Inc* [2012] EWCA Civ; [2013] 2 All E.R 663 ("substantial proportion" of the public) (not a case of passing off).

[236] *Bristol Conservatories Ltd v Conservatories Custom Build Ltd* [1989] R.P.C. 380. But see *Woolley v Ultimate Products Ltd* [2012] EWCA Civ 1038 at [6].

[237] *Doosan Power Systems Ltd v Babcock International Group Plc* [2013] EWHC 1364 (Ch) at [178].

[238] *Harrods Ltd v Harrodian School* [1996] R.P.C. 697; *Nice and Safe Attitude v Flook (t/a Slaam! Clothing)* [1997] F.S.R. 14. Even where the parties are in the same line of work and there is similarity between their products the court may of course conclude that there is no real risk of the public being deceived: *Financial Times v Evening Standard* [1991] F.S.R. 7 (the Evening Standard publishing business section on pink paper).

[239] [1972] F.S.R. 103; *Stringfellow v McCain Foods* [1984] R.P.C. 501.

[240] [1994] F.S.R. 438. See also *Box TV v Haymarket* (1997) 147 N.L.J. 601.

claimants (a high-class food retailer) and the defendants (importers and re-exporters of cheap, plastic goods).

19-063 **"Injurious association"** If the public might think that there was some association between the activities of the parties the claimant is likely to succeed even though they are in no sense competitors.[241] In this form the action is less "passing off" than "injurious association". In *Associated Newspapers Plc v Insert Media Ltd*,[242] the defendants' practice of placing advertising inserts in the claimants' newspapers after they had been sold to newsagents was held to involve a representation that the defendants were associated with the claimants' business. There was a risk of damage to the goodwill of that business because while the claimants accepted only carefully vetted advertisements and took steps to protect readers from dishonest or insolvent advertisers, some members of the public might conclude that the claimants were responsible for the insert advertisers, over whom they had no control.[243]

19-064 **Endorsement** In modern conditions, actors, athletes, performers and so on actively turn their public images or their creations to profit by endorsing goods and services. Although "[t]here is … no image right or character right which allows a celebrity to control the use of his or her name or image",[244] the law does not countenance deception in the form of marketing goods or services in such a way as to imply that they have been endorsed by a famous person when that is not the case. Although many passing off cases arise from a claimant's fear that the sale of inferior goods under his name will damage his goodwill by associating him with those goods, the law is not confined to that situation. Thus, in *Irvine v Talksport Ltd*,[245] a Formula 1 racing driver recovered damages for unauthorised advertisements that incorrectly implied that he had endorsed the defendants' sports radio station. Similarly, in *Fenty v Arcadia Group Brands Ltd*[246] the Court of Appeal upheld an interim injunction that had been granted to the singer Rihanna that restrained the defendant clothing store from selling t-shirts with her image printed on them. The Court considered that the first instance judge had correctly conclude that Rihanna's fans would buy the t-shirt on the mistaken understanding that she had authorised it.

19-065 **Character merchandising** The tort of passing off may be committed where the defendant sells goods that exploit a demand based on famous characters, whether real or fictional. Character merchandising cases must be distinguished from endorsement cases in that in the former setting there is no suggestion that the person

---

[241] See, e.g., *Annabel's (Berkeley Square) Ltd v G Schock* [1972] F.S.R. 261 (night club and escort agency); *Harrods Ltd v R Harrod Ltd* (1923) 41 R.P.C. 74; *Hilton Press v White Eagle Youth Holiday Camp* (1951) 68 R.P.C. 126.

[242] [1991] 1 W.L.R. 571. *Lego Systems A/S v Lego Lemelstrich* [1983] F.S.R. 155 seems to reduce the requirement of damage almost to vanishing point.

[243] However, it would not be enough that people might think the claimants were providing "sponsorship" for the defendants: *Harrods Ltd v Harrodian School* [1996] R.P.C. 697; cf. *Dawnay Day & Co Ltd v Cantor Fitzgerald International* [2000] R.P.C. 669 at 705.

[244] *Fenty v Arcadia Group Brands Ltd* [2015] EWCA Civ 3; [2015] 1 W.L.R. 3291 at [29] per Kitchin LJ.

[245] [2002] EWHC 367 (Ch); [2003] 1 W.L.R. 2355 (reversed on other grounds [2003] EWCA Civ 423; [2003] 2 All E.R. 881).

[246] [2015] EWCA Civ 3; [2015] 1 W.L.R. 3291.

in issue has approved of the goods concerned. In order for liability to arise in the character merchandising context there must be a misrepresentation regarding the source of the goods that has an impact upon the buying decision.[247] In *Mirage Studios v Counter-Feat Clothing*[248] Browne-Wilkinson VC granted an interim injunction restraining unlicensed use of the "Teenage Mutant Ninja Turtle" image on clothing. Although the claimant film studio was not in the clothing business the financial significance in modern conditions of character merchandising meant that neither was it solely in the business of producing cartoon films. However, it should certainly not be assumed that the stage has been reached where a celebrity has an exclusive right to exploit the valuable aspects of his own character[249] and in the case of the exploitation of fictional characters it has been suggested that it is difficult to prove confusion because the public may not generally care in these cases whether the product is "genuine" or not.[250]

B. Goodwill

The need to establish the claimant's goodwill   Mere confusion in the mind of   **19-066** the public is not enough to establish a case of passing off unless there is damage or a risk of damage to the claimant's goodwill. Goodwill is a notoriously difficult concept to define but "mere reputation" is insufficient and it is essential for the claimant to prove goodwill "in the form of customers".[251] An action failed where the claimant planned to bring out a leisure magazine and had spent money promoting it but the defendant launched a scheme to publish a magazine with the same name;[252] and it seems that the result would have been the same even if the defendant's act had been a mere "spoiling" operation.[253] Goodwill cannot exist in a vacuum so if a business has been abandoned there is no longer any legally protected goodwill attached to it; but a temporary cessation of business is a different matter.[254] However, there may be damage to goodwill even though there is no evidence of diversion of sales.[255]

The "locality" of the goodwill   A matter of considerable significance in modern   **19-067** trading conditions is the "locality" of the goodwill. An action only lies if the claimant "has actual goodwill in this jurisdiction, and … such goodwill involves the presence of clients or customers in this jurisdiction for the products or services in question".[256] Thus, it is not enough that the claimant has a reputation in the sense

---

[247] *Fenty v Arcadia Group Brands Ltd* [2015] EWCA Civ 3; [2015] 1 W.L.R. 3291 at [45].
[248] [1991] F.S.R. 145.
[249] *Elvis Presley Trade Marks* [1999] R.P.C. 567.
[250] *BBC Worldwide Ltd v Pally Screen Printing Ltd* [1998] F.S.R. 665 at 674.
[251] *Starbucks (HK) Ltd v British Sky Broadcasting Group Plc* [2015] UKSC 31; [2015] 1 W.L.R. 2628 at [52] per Lord Neuberger.
[252] *Marcus Publishing Plc v Hutton-Wild Communications Ltd* [1990] R.P.C. 576. However, there may be cases in which pre-launch publicity suffices to establish goodwill: *Labyrinth Media Ltd v Brave World Ltd* [1995] E.M.L.R. 38.
[253] *Marcus Publishing Plc v Hutton-Wild Communications Ltd* [1990] R.P.C. 576 at 580, 585. cf. para.3-017.
[254] *Pink v Sharwood & Co Ltd* (1913) 30 R.P.C. 725; *Star Industrial Co Ltd v Yap Kwee Kor* [1976] F.S.R. 256; cf. *Minimax GmbH & Co KG v Chubb Fire Ltd* [2008] EWHC 1960 (Pat).
[255] *Chelsea Man v Chelsea Girl* [1987] R.P.C. 189; *Phones 4U Ltd v Phone4u.co.uk Internet Ltd* [2006] EWCA Civ 244; [2007] R.P.C. 5.
[256] *Starbucks (HK) Ltd v British Sky Broadcasting Group Plc* [2015] UKSC 31; [2015] 1 W.L.R. 2628

that he is known here because of, for example, advertising in publications that circulate in England as well as abroad.[257] In *Bernardin & Cie v Pavilion Properties Ltd*,[258] for example, the proprietors of the "Crazy Horse Saloon" nightclub in Paris failed in an action against defendants who set up a similar establishment in London. Nor is the requirement of having business here met simply on the basis of hits from within the jurisdiction on a website based abroad.[259] At the same time, while the claimant must have business with people in England there is no necessity for him to have "a business" here in the sense of a physical presence or even direct sales relationships.[260]

C.   The Limits of Passing Off

19-068   **No tort of "unfair competition"**   The law of passing off seems to be adaptable to changing trading practices and conditions and has had some notable extensions. However, it has not generalised into a tort of "unfair competition".[261] Hence it is no tort for the defendant to exploit the claimant's advertising campaign so as to seize a share of the market which the claimant has created. In *Cadbury-Schweppes Pty Ltd v Pub Squash Co Pty Ltd*,[262] the claimants launched a lemon drink ("Solo") supported by an extensive advertising campaign evoking an idealised memory of soft drinks of the past. The defendants then launched a lemon drink ("Pub Squash") with a get up and advertising theme closely related to that for "Solo". The dismissal of the claimants' action for damages and an injunction on the ground of passing off was upheld by the Privy Council because the defendants had sufficiently distinguished their goods from those of the claimants to prevent any likely confusion in the public mind. The alternative claim of "unfair competition" was not even pursued before that court and subsequently the High Court of Australia categorically rejected such a tort.[263] We have seen that in *Associated Newspapers Group Plc v Insert Media Ltd* the newspaper publishers succeeded on the basis of passing off, but in earlier proceedings Hoffmann J rejected a cause of action alleging unfair competition by debasing or devaluing the claimants' goods without misrepresentation.[264] The balance of authority is similarly against a general liability where A appropriates B's valuable idea, design or information and exploits it without payment.[265]

---

at [47] per Lord Neuberger.

[257] *Athlete's Foot Marketing Associates Inc v Cobra Sports Ltd* [1980] R.P.C. 43; *Anheuser-Busch Inc v Budejovicky Budvar NP* [1984] F.S.R. 413; *Jian Tools for Sales v Roderick Manhattan Group* [1995] F.S.R. 924.

[258] [1967] R.P.C. 581 (the claimants had in fact aimed advertising at England).

[259] *Plentyoffish Media Inc v Plenty More LLP* [2011] EWHC 2568 (Ch); [2012] R.P.C. 5; *Starbucks (HK) Ltd v British Sky Broadcasting Group Plc* [2012] EWHC 3074 (Ch); [2013] F.S.R. 29.

[260] *Hotel Cipriani Srl v Cipriani (Grosvenor Street) Ltd* [2010] EWCA Civ 110; [2010] R.P.C. 16. Thus, in *SA etc. Panhard et Levassor v Panhard Levassor Motor Co Ltd* [1901] 2 Ch. 513 the claimants sold no cars in England but English people bought their cars in France and imported them. This was sufficient goodwill. See also *Tan-Ichi Co Ltd v Jancar Ltd* [1990] F.S.R. 151.

[261] *Diageo North America Inc v Intercontinental Brands (ICB) Ltd* [2010] EWCA Civ 920; [2011] 1 All E.R. 242 at [24]. cf. Aldous LJ's suggestion in *Arsenal Football Club Plc v Reed* [2003] EWCA Civ 696; [2003] R.P.C. 39 at [70] that unfair competition would be a better name for it.

[262] [1981] 1 W.L.R. 193.

[263] *Moorgate Tobacco Co Ltd v Philip Morris Ltd* (1984) 156 C.L.R. 414.

[264] [1988] 1 W.L.R. 509.

[265] *Lever Bros v Bedingfield* (1896) 16 R.P.C. 3; *Victoria Park Racing Co v Taylor* (1937) 58 C.L.R.

Not confined to trade   The setting of passing off is normally trade, but trade in   **19-069**
the narrow sense is not essential, even if it is difficult to say precisely how far the
law goes. A fundraising charity has succeeded in an action in respect of conduct
which tended to appropriate its goodwill[266] and a religious organisation may also
be able to sue.[267] An author may sue for a false representation that a book is his
work[268] and a professional person or a professional association[269] may have a cause
of action in respect of unauthorised use of their names in a manner likely to cause
harm to their professional activities—for example, the use of a doctor's name to
promote a quack medicine or cure.[270] It has even been held that a political organisation may obtain an injunction to restrain a person standing at an election in its
name.[271]

D.   Remedies

The injunction is an important remedy in passing off cases and an interim injunc-   **19-070**
tion may well determine the final outcome since the delay before trial may mean
that the loser at the interim stage cannot resume production.[272] An injunction may
be made in qualified form, i.e., restraining the defendant from disposing of his
goods without sufficiently distinguishing them from the claimant's.[273] In addition,
damages may be awarded in respect of losses suffered by the claimant or, in the
alternative, an account of profits made by the defendant from the passing off. It has
been held at first instance that damages may be recovered against an innocent
defendant, though the alternative of an account of profits is not available in such a
case.[274]

479; *Conan Doyle v London Mystery Magazine Ltd* (1949) 66 R.P.C. 246. The law of copyright
generally protects the form of a work, not the idea behind it, but the author of a work who does not
have the copyright may have the right to be identified as the author under the Copyright, Designs
and Patents Act 1988 s.77.

266 *British Diabetic Association v Diabetic Society Ltd* [1995] 4 All E.R. 812.

267 *Holy Apostolic etc. Church v Attorney General (NSW), ex rel. Elisha* (1989) 18 N.S.W.L.R. 291, approved in *British Diabetic Association v Diabetic Society Ltd* [1995] 4 All E.R. 812.

268 *Lord Byron v Johnson* (1816) 2 Mer. 29; 35 E.R. 851; *Clark v Associated Newspapers Ltd* [1998]
R.P.C. 261. See also the Copyright, Designs and Patents Act 1988 s.84.

269 *Society of Accountants and Auditors v Goodway* [1907] 1 Ch. 489; *Law Society v Society of Lawyers*
[1996] F.S.R. 739.

270 See *Dockrell v Douglas* (1899) 80 L.T. 556 at 557–558; *Walter v Ashton* [1902] 2 Ch. 282 at 293.

271 *Burge v Haycock* [2001] EWCA Civ 900; [2002] R.P.C. 28. See also *Comptroller-General of Patents
Designs and Trade Marks v Intellectual Property Agency Ltd* [2015] EWHC 3256 (IPEC); [2016]
F.S.R. 22 (government department).

272 See, e.g., *Mirage Studios v Counter-Feat Clothing* [1991] F.S.R. 145, para.19-065. The *American
Cyanamid* principles (para.23-127) are as applicable to passing off as to other torts: *County Sound
v Ocean Sound* [1991] F.S.R. 367. However, s.12 of the Human Rights Act 1998 may be relevant:
Blandford Goldsmith & Co Ltd v Prime UK Properties Ltd [2003] EWHC 326 (Ch).

273 "It has been said many times that it is no part of the function of this court to examine imaginary cases
of what the defendant could or could not do under this form of injunction. The best guide, if he is
an honest man, is his own conscience and it is certainly not the business of this court to give him
instructions or limits as to how near the wind he can sail": *Wright, Layman & Umney v Wright* (1949)
66 R.P.C. 149 at 152 per Lord Greene MR.

274 *Gillette UK Ltd v Eden West Ltd* [1994] R.P.C. 297.

CHAPTER 20

ABUSE OF LEGAL PROCEDURE

1. MALICIOUS PROSECUTION

Abuse of legal procedure is a concept of broad significance,[1] but the concern of **20-001** this chapter is with situations in which such abuse gives rise to a cause of action. By far the most important such cause of action is malicious prosecution. Traditionally, this tort was limited to the instigation of criminal proceedings, but in *Willers v Joyce*[2] the Supreme Court recently extended it to the initiation of a civil claim. Although for now it seems that the same conceptual framework will be used for claims arising out of civil and criminal proceedings, it remains to be seen whether this approach is feasible, or whether in fact it would be preferable to treat the two limbs of the tort as separate causes of action with their own distinct rules. The discussion in this chapter begins with an overview of malicious prosecution, along with an account of its elements (encompassing both the criminal and civil litigation contexts). Specific consideration is then given to the case law on malicious civil proceedings. The chapter concludes with sections on the related torts of malicious process and abuse of process.

History The history of malicious prosecution[3] can be traced back to the writ of **20-002** conspiracy which was in existence as early as Edward I's reign. This fell into disuse in the 16th century, partly because the writ of maintenance supplanted it. However,

---

[1] A court may, for example, stay proceedings on the ground that they are an abuse of process: see para.26-082.
[2] [2016] UKSC 43; [2018] A.C. 779. See para.20-025.
[3] See Winfield, *History of Conspiracy and Abuse of Legal Procedure* (1921) and Winfield, *Present Law of Abuse of Legal Procedure* (1921).

this latter writ was probably confined to officious intermeddling in civil suits,[4] and the gap was filled by an action on the case which appeared in Elizabeth I's reign and eventually became known as the action for malicious prosecution. It was put on a firm footing in 1698 in *Savile v Roberts*.[5]

20-003 **Current significance** Although it has been claimed that the decline of private prosecutions has rendered malicious prosecution "virtually extinct",[6] in fact the tort remains significant in the criminal context, albeit that most claims are now brought against the police or Crown Prosecution Service.[7] It must however be borne in mind that the law was largely shaped in an era when there was no formal, state system for investigation and prosecution and care must be taken in applying broad principles established under the old regime to present circumstances. The recent extension of the tort to initiation of civil proceedings has the potential greatly to increase the frequency with which it is invoked.

20-004 **The need to balance competing principles** Liability for malicious prosecution has always had to steer a path between two competing principles—on the one hand the freedom of action that everyone should have to set the law in motion and, on the other hand, the necessity to check dishonest accusations against innocent people.[8] Hence the burden undertaken by the claimant in a case of malicious prosecution must be a heavy one, such that no honest prosecutor is likely to be deterred from doing his duty.

20-005 **Relationship with other types of liability** One reason for the complexity of the law in this area is that a number of other torts and principles come into play where the defendant is involved in the events leading up to a prosecution. First, the claimant may have been arrested on the basis of information given by the defendant. As we have seen, however, in modern conditions the exercise of discretion by the police officer carrying out the arrest[9] is likely to deprive the claimant in such a case of any claim against the defendant for false imprisonment.[10] Secondly, the information given by the defendant is likely to be defamatory, but not only will any evidence given by him in court be subject to absolute privilege, it has now been held that the same applies to a mere complaint to the police.[11] If, however, the defend-

---

4 Maintenance as a tort was abolished by the Criminal Law Act 1967.
5 (1698) 1 Ld. Raym. 374; 91 E.R. 1147.
6 *Willers v Joyce* [2016] UKSC 43; [2018] A.C. 779 at [131] per Lord Mance, echoing the remarks of Lord Sumption in *Crawford Adjusters v Sagicor General Insurance Ltd* [2013] UKPC 17; [2014] A.C. 366 at [121], [145]. cf. *Willers* at [43].
7 Though in *Martin v Watson* [1996] A.C. 74 the House of Lords reaffirmed that a private person who sets the law in motion may still incur liability.
8 *Glinski v McIver* [1962] A.C. 726 at 741, 753; *Gregory v Portsmouth CC* [2000] 1 A.C. 419 at 426.
9 Still more of a magistrate remanding the claimant in custody.
10 See para.4-030.
11 *Westcott v Westcott* [2008] EWCA Civ 818; [2009] Q.B. 407. The same would apply to a claim for malicious falsehood. Even before this case it was held that the absolute privilege extended to preliminary statements or the preparation of reports outside court which can fairly be said to be part of the process of investigation. However, the immunity in respect of pre-trial matters does not extend to the fabrication of evidence to be used in court: *Darker v Chief Constable of the West Midlands* [2001] A.C. 435. In that case the claims were for conspiracy to injure and misfeasance in a public office. The claimants alleged that the defendants had conspired to cause them to be charged with offences which they knew or believed to be false, but there was no claim for malicious prosecution; cf. *Smart v Forensic Science Service Ltd* [2013] EWCA Civ 783; [2013] P.N.L.R. 32.

ant is a prosecutor the essence of the complaint is that he has abused the process of the court[12] and the fact that for other legal purposes he is immune from suit is irrelevant. The application of the law of negligence in this area would be inconsistent with the restrictions imposed by the law of malicious prosecution. There is no liability in negligence in respect of the conduct of a prosecution[13] nor the investigation of a charge made against the claimant.[14] There might be liability for misfeasance in a public office[15] but that also requires proof of malice.

Essentials of the tort To bring a successful action, the claimant must prove that: **20-006** (1) the defendant prosecuted him; (2) the prosecution ended in the claimant's favour; (3) the prosecution lacked reasonable and probable cause; (4) the defendant acted maliciously; and (5) the claimant suffered damage as a result.

A. Prosecution

Who qualifies as a "prosecutor"? A person who brings a private prosecution is **20-007** obviously a prosecutor for this purpose and so is one who swears an information[16] or who is bound over to act as a prosecutor.[17] However, in *Martin v Watson*[18] the House of Lords held that it is not necessary that the defendant should be the prosecutor in any technical sense: what matters is that he should in substance be the person responsible for the prosecution being brought. The defendant made various charges to the police that the claimant had indecently exposed himself to her and this led to a prosecution of the claimant at which no evidence was offered against him. Distinguishing the case of *Danby v Beardsley*,[19] in which the defendant had been held not to be a prosecutor when he told the police that goods which he mistakenly believed to have been stolen from him had been found in the claimant's possession, on the ground that in that case there was no malice against the claimant, Lord Keith continued[20]:

"Where an individual falsely and maliciously gives a police officer information indicating that some person is guilty of a criminal offence and states that he is willing to give evidence in court of the matters in question, it is properly to be inferred that he desires and intends that the person he names should be prosecuted. When the circumstances are such that the facts relating to the alleged offence can be within the knowledge only of the complainant, as was the position here, then it becomes virtually impossible for the police officer to exercise any independent discretion or judgment, and if a prosecution is instituted by the police officer the proper view of the matter is that the prosecution has been procured by the complainant."

Martin v Watson was a strong case because the defendant conducted a campaign against the claimant by making repeated complaints which the police were reluctant

---

[12] *Martin v Watson* [1996] A.C. 74 at 88.
[13] *Elguzouli-Daf v MPC* [1995] Q.B. 335, para.5-067.
[14] *B v Reading BC* [2009] EWHC 998 (QB); [2009] 2 F.L.R. 1273.
[15] See para.8-024.
[16] *Watters v Pacific Delivery Service Ltd* (1963) 42 D.L.R. (2d) 661.
[17] *Fitzjohn v Mackinder* (1861) 9 C.B. (N.S.) 505; 142 E.R. 199.
[18] [1996] A.C. 74.
[19] (1880) 43 L.T. 603.
[20] [1996] A.C. 74 at 86.

to pursue. In contrast in *AH v AB*,[21] where the claimant's conviction for rape of the defendant had been set aside, the defendant had made no complaint to the police, the prosecution arising from a report to them several years after the event and originating with a person in whom the defendant had confided at the time, and it was only under pressure from the police that the defendant had given evidence in the criminal proceedings. She was not a prosecutor because it was impossible to say that she fulfilled the first requirement, which was that she should have "intended or desired" a prosecution.[22]

20-008   **Difficult cases**   The difficulties arise in cases lying between *Martin* and *AH*. Nowadays the decision to prosecute and the conduct of the proceedings are normally in the hands of the Crown Prosecution Service (CPS), which will exercise an independent discretion as to whether to proceed, taking account of the strength of the evidence and relevant guidelines.[23] In *AH* it is said that even a person who initiates the process of investigation and prosecution by making a false complaint[24] is not to be regarded as a prosecutor unless he "manipulates" the prosecuting authorities into doing something they would not otherwise have done,[25] and that where the decision to prosecute is taken by the CPS it will be a rare case in which the complainant can be regarded as a prosecutor.[26] A narrow approach was also adopted to this issue in an earlier Court of Appeal decision, *Mahon v Rahn (No.2)*.[27] However, in the most recent decisions of the Court of Appeal a broader view is taken. In *Scott v Ministry of Justice*,[28] it was held that where five prison officers had made clear and consistent statements accusing the claimant of assault on one of their number there was an arguable case that they had procured the ensuing prosecution even though there had been no manipulation or overbearing by them of the responsible crown prosecutor's view. A similar approach was observable in *Copeland v Metropolitan Police Commissioner*,[29] where a police officer was treated as the prosecutor of a woman whom (as a civil jury found) he had falsely accused of striking him. And in *Rees v Commissioner of Police of the Metropolis*,[30] a police detective was held to be a prosecutor because he had presented the independent prosecutor with a case which he knew included an important feature procured by the detective's own criminality. But do these decisions not go too far? In *Copeland* and *Rees* Lord Keith's condition that the relevant facts could be within "the

---

21   [2009] EWCA Civ 1092.

22   *Mahon v Rahn (No.2)* [2000] 1 W.L.R. 2150.

23   See the Prosecution of Offences Act 1985 and the Criminal Justice Act 2003.

24   Some passages in *Martin v Watson* may be thought to run together the issues of whether the defendant is a prosecutor and whether he is guilty of malice. According to *AH* the true position is that knowledge of the falsity of the charge is relevant on the "prosecutor" issue in so far as it provides evidence of an intention to procure a prosecution. In the view of Moore-Bick LJ this makes the matter unsuitable to be dealt with as a preliminary issue.

25   *AH v AB* [2009] EWCA Civ 1092 at [47], [58], [84].

26   It is nevertheless clear that review by the CPS does not insulate an investigating police officer from a finding that he was the prosecutor: *Alford v Chief Constable of Cambridgeshire* [2009] EWCA Civ 100; [2009] Po L.R. 98; *Moulton v Chief Constable of West Midlands* [2010] EWCA Civ 524; *Clifford v Chief Constable of Hertfordshire* [2011] EWHC 815 (QB). cf. *Coghlan v Chief Constable of Cheshire* [2018] EWHC 34 (QB) at [89] (only "in rare cases").

27   [2000] 1 W.L.R. 2150 (no reasonable prospect of establishing that defendant bank was prosecutor where Serious Fraud Office had conducted a wide-ranging investigation into alleged fraud).

28   [2009] EWCA Civ 1215.

29   [2014] EWCA Civ 1014; [2015] 3 All E.R. 391.

30   [2018] EWCA Civ 1587.

knowledge only of the complainant" was not met[31] and, in both, the prosecuting authorities apparently exercised an independent discretion.[32] This raises the familiar concern that an over-broad approach to liability in this tort will have a chilling effect, particularly when, as in *Copeland*, there is no proof of dishonesty on the part of the witness whose evidence set the prosecutorial ball in motion, but merely a finding to that effect by a jury on the civil balance of probabilities standard. A fresh review of this issue at the ultimate appellate level now appears necessary if consistency and coherence is to be restored to the law.

Prosecution of civil proceedings In *Willers v Joyce*[33] the Supreme Court **20-009** extended malicious prosecution to civil proceedings and so the question arises as to what qualifies as a "prosecution", and who qualifies as a "prosecutor", in the context of a civil action. On the former issue, the basic idea of a "prosecution" for the purposes of the tort is the setting of the law in motion by way of an appeal to a relevant judicial authority. It follows that the mere service of an enforcement notice will not suffice (since no appeal is thereby made to a relevant judicial authority),[34] while the requirement that the defendant have set the law in motion means that as the law stands there is no claim for the malicious defence of civil proceedings. In *Willers v Joyce*, Lord Mance suggested in his dissenting judgment that allowing such claims was a logical corollary of extending the tort to civil proceedings,[35] but Lord Toulson for the majority disagreed. There was an "obvious distinction between the initiation of the legal process itself and later steps which may involve bad faith … but do not go to the root of the institution of legal process".[36] Whether the law should take the "bold step" of imposing civil liability for bad faith denial of claims raised "other and wider considerations".[37] As to the question of who is a prosecutor of civil proceedings, at the trial of the action in *Willers v Joyce* Rose J pointed out the difficulties of transposing the test set out in the authorities concerning criminal prosecutions into cases concerning civil claims.[38] He went on to hold that when a claimant sues in respect of civil proceedings brought against him by a company, it is not enough for him to show that the defendant was the controlling

---

31 Indeed it was expressly denied that this was a condition of liability: see *Scott* [2009] EWCA Civ 1215 at [38], [51]; *Copeland* [2014] EWCA Civ 1014; [2015] 3 All E.R. 391 at [30]. But does that not make anyone who gives evidence which a jury finds to be false potentially liable?

32 In *Copeland* [2014] EWCA Civ 1014; [2015] 3 All E.R. 391 at [33], Moses LJ said that the discretion "as to whether to prosecute was vitiated by the bad faith as found by the jury" of the complainant, but where other evidence is also taken into account by the ultimate decision-maker the logic of that analysis is far from obvious. Nor was the approach taken to this question in *Rees* (where it was asked whether the prosecutor *would have exercised their discretion in the same way had the truth been known*) convincing. cf. *Coghlan v Chief Constable of Cheshire* [2018] EWHC 34 (QB) at [102] (even if police had withheld evidence in bad faith there was "no real prospect" of it being shown that that meant the charging decision was not an independent one).

33 [2016] UKSC 43; [2018] A.C. 779.

34 *CFC 26 Ltd v Brown Shipley & Co Ltd* [2016] EWHC 3048 (Ch) at [68].

35 [2016] UKSC 43; [2018] A.C. 779 at [132].

36 [2016] UKSC 43; [2018] A.C. 779 at [51].

37 [2016] UKSC 43; [2018] A.C. 779 at [51]. By the same token, it can be assumed that the extension of the tort to civil proceedings does not entail that liability can lie for any particular application or step in the course of a civil action which can be shown to have been unfounded and maliciously motivated, as was suggested by Lord Mance in his dissenting judgment (at [133]). On the contrary, it is only the *initiation* of civil proceedings that is capable of attracting liability.

38 *Willers v Joyce* [2018] EWHC 3424 (Ch) at [192].

mind of that company.[39] For the defendant to be treated as the prosecutor in such a case, it must be established that he "had a dominant influence over the board of directors"[40] when they decided to bring the action against the claimant, or that he had misled them into deciding to proceed with the claim.

B.   Favourable Termination of the Prosecution

20-010   **Basis of termination not relevant**   The claimant must show that the prosecution ended in his favour,[41] but so long as it did, it is of no moment how this came about, whether by a verdict of acquittal, or by the reversal of his conviction on appeal,[42] or by discontinuance of the prosecution by leave of the court,[43] or by quashing of the indictment for a defect in it[44] or because the proceedings were *coram non judice*.[45] The effect of a *nolle prosequi* (staying by the Attorney General of proceedings on an indictment) was left open to question in an old case which indicated that it was not a sufficient ending of the prosecution because it still left the accused liable to be indicted afresh on the same charge.[46] Yet, this seems inconsistent with the broad interpretation put upon "favourable termination of the prosecution" which signifies, not that the accused has been acquitted, but that he has not been convicted. The reason for the favourable termination requirement has been said to be the risk of diverse determinations by different courts on the same facts and between the same parties.

20-011   **No claim if conviction stands**   On the other hand, if a conviction stands, then the claimant cannot succeed in an action for malicious prosecution, and this is so even if the conviction is one against which there is no right of appeal and which has been obtained by the fraud of the prosecutor. In *Basébé v Matthews*,[47] Byles J thought that if the rule were otherwise every case would have to be retried on its merits, and Montague Smith J feared that they would be turning themselves into a Court of Appeal where the legislature allowed none. The rule rests upon the more general principle that the court will strike out as an abuse of process a suit which is a collateral attack on the decision of a competent criminal court, for otherwise there is a risk of inconsistent decisions.[48] *Basébé v Matthews* was followed in *Everett v Rib-*

---

39   *Willers v Joyce* [2018] EWHC 3424 (Ch) at [192]–[196].
40   *Willers v Joyce* [2018] EWHC 3424 (Ch) at [200] per Rose J.
41   *Parker v Langly* (1712) 10 Mod. 145; 88 E.R. 667; (1713) 10 Mod. 209; 88 E.R. 697. The logical result is that the limitation period runs from the time of the acquittal, not the charge: *Dunlop v Customs and Excise, The Times,* 17 March 1998; *Baker v MPC* unreported 24 June 1996, QBD.
42   *Herniman v Smith* [1938] A.C. 305; *Berry v British Transport Commission* [1962] 1 Q.B. 306; *Abbott v Refuge Assurance Co Ltd* [1962] 1 Q.B. 432; *Blaker v Weller* [1964] Crim. L.R. 311. The fact that a conviction was secured at first instance may be strong evidence that there was reasonable and probable cause for the prosecution, though the better view is that it is not conclusive in this regard. cf. *Reynolds v Kennedy* (1784) 1 Wils. K.B. 232; 95 E.R. 591.
43   *Watkins v Lee* (1839) 5 M. & W. 270; 151 E.R. 115.
44   *Jones v Gwynn* (1712) 10 Mod. 148; 88 E.R. 668; (1713) 10 Mod. 214; 88 E.R. 699.
45   *Atwood v Monger* (1653) Sty. 378; 82 E.R. 793. See also *Goddard v Smith* (1704) 1 Salk. 21; 91 E.R. 20 (non-suit).
46   *Goddard v Smith* (1704) 1 Salk. 21; 91 E.R. 20.
47   (1867) L.R. 2 C.P. 684.
48   The general principle may be subject to exception if there is decisive fresh evidence: *Smith v Linskills* [1996] 1 W.L.R. 763.

bands[49] where the claimant had been bound over to find sureties to be of good behaviour. He failed in an action for malicious prosecution, for the proceedings complained of had actually been determined against him.

May the prosecutor seek to show that the claimant was, in fact, guilty? If the prosecution has terminated in the claimant's favour and he sues for malicious prosecution, may the prosecutor seek in his defence to show that the claimant was in fact guilty? For example, the prosecution may have presented a weak case but afterwards there may come to light much stronger evidence against the claimant.[50] Some cases hold that the prosecutor may not do this, or even use the evidence of guilt in mitigation of damages,[51] relying either upon the "inconsistency" argument mentioned above or at least upon the undesirability of re-litigation of the issue of guilt. However, if D states that C has committed a criminal offence and C, having been acquitted of that offence, then sues D for defamation, we do not prevent D from relying on the defence of truth by trying to show that C was in fact guilty, rash as that plea may perhaps be; and while there may be a general principle which treats as an abuse of process any attempt to mount a collateral attack on the decision of a competent court,[52] that is directed at the initiation of proceedings, not at the formulation of a defence.[53]

20-012

C. Lack of Reasonable and Probable Cause

Judge and jury[54] The principal difficulty in stating the law as to reasonable and probable cause arises from the division of function between judge and jury,[55] since the default position is that cases of malicious prosecution are tried by jury.[56] It has been recognised for centuries[57] that once a person has been acquitted by a criminal court, juries are too ready to award him damages against his prosecutor,[58] and therefore it is for the judge to decide whether the defendant had reasonable and probable cause for launching the prosecution,[59] but it is for the jury to decide any

20-013

---

49 [1952] 2 Q.B. 198.
50 At common law there were no circumstances in which he might be tried again. This can now happen where the conditions of Pt 10 of the Criminal Justice Act 2003 are fulfilled.
51 *Commonwealth Life Assurance Society Ltd v Smith* (1938) 59 C.L.R. 527.
52 See para.5-065.
53 It has been held in New Zealand that proof of the guilt of the claimant is in itself a defence to a claim for malicious prosecution where the favourable termination of the proceedings was otherwise than by an acquittal on the merits, the position in that case being left open: *Van Heeren v Cooper* [1999] 1 N.Z.L.R. 731. The *Restatement (Second) of the Law of Torts*, 2d §657 makes guilt a defence in all cases, with a civil standard of proof. The point remains open as a matter of English law: *Qema v News Group Newspapers Ltd* [2012] EWHC 1146 (QB) at [92].
54 For a valuable review of both reasonable and probable cause and malice, see *A v New South Wales* [2007] HCA 10; (2007) 230 C.L.R. 500.
55 *Glinski v McIver* [1962] A.C. 726 at 742.
56 Senior Courts Act 1981 s.69.
57 See *Pain v Rochester and Whitfield* (1599) Cro. Eliz. 871; 78 E.R. 1096, cited in *Leibo v Buckman Ltd* [1952] 2 All E.R. 1057 at 1062.
58 See, e.g., *Abrath v North Eastern Ry* (1886) 11 App. Cas. 247 at 252; *Leibo v Buckman Ltd* [1952] 2 All E.R. 1057 at 1063; *Glinski v McIver* [1962] A.C. 726 at 741–742, 777–778; cf. at 754.
59 *Johnstone v Sutton* (1786) 1 Term Rep. 510; 99 E.R. 1215; *Herniman v Smith* [1938] A.C. 305; *Reynolds v Metropolitan Police Commissioner* [1985] Q.B. 881. It is doubtful whether the question is one of fact or law. Probably it is best regarded as a question of fact, but one which is to be treated in the same way as if it were a question of law: *Glinski v McIver* [1962] A.C. 726 at 768.

incidental questions of fact necessary for the judge's determination.[60] Moreover, this branch of the law is unusual in requiring the claimant to undertake the difficult task of proving a negative. It is for him to prove that the prosecutor did not have reasonable and probable cause, and not for the prosecutor to prove that he had.[61]

20-014 **Definition of reasonable and probable cause** For the purposes of this requirement there does not appear to be any distinction between "reasonable" and "probable". In *Herniman v Smith*[62] the House of Lords approved and adopted the definition of reasonable and probable cause given by Hawkins J in *Hicks v Faulkner*[63] as:

> "[A]n honest belief in the guilt of the accused based upon a full conviction, founded upon reasonable grounds, of the existence of a state of circumstances, which, assuming them to be true, would reasonably lead any ordinarily prudent and cautious man placed in the position of the accuser, to the conclusion that the person charged was probably guilty of the crime imputed."

The overall question has both subjective and objective elements: did the prosecutor *actually* believe that he had cause for prosecution and was his belief reasonable? The judge's concern is essentially with the objective aspect of this definition—whether there was reasonable and probable cause in fact—whereas the defendant's belief is a matter for the jury, not the judge, to determine. But the burden of proving lack of honest belief is on the claimant[64] and the question should only be put to the jury "in the highly unlikely event that there is cogent positive evidence that, despite the actual existence of reasonable and probable cause, the defendant himself did not believe that it existed".[65] Both the objective and the subjective element are directed to the decision to set the prosecution "in motion" and not the guilt of the claimant, still less whether he would be convicted, though clearly the defendant's belief in the probable guilt of the claimant is relevant to determining whether he honestly believed that there was reasonable and probable cause to prosecute.[66] Finally, if the prosecutor believes in the facts of the case and is advised by competent counsel before whom the facts are fairly laid that a prosecution is justified, then it will be exceedingly difficult to establish lack of reasonable and probable cause.[67]

---

[60] The judge need put to the jury only questions on the salient issues of fact, for otherwise the questions would have no end: *Dallison v Caffery* [1965] 1 Q.B. 348 at 368.

[61] *Abrath v NE Ry* (1883) 11 Q.B.D. 440; *Stapley v Annetts* [1970] 1 W.L.R. 20; *Williamson v A-G of Trinidad & Tobago* [2014] UKPC 29 at [11].

[62] [1938] A.C. 305 at 316.

[63] (1878) 8 Q.B.D. 167 at 171, affirmed (1882) 46 L.T. 130.

[64] On requests for further information (formerly further and better particulars or interrogatories) see *Stapley v Annetts* [1970] 1 W.L.R. 20 and *Gibbs v Rea* [1998] A.C. 786 at 794.

[65] *Dallison v Caffery* [1965] 1 Q.B. 348 at 372 per Diplock LJ. See also at 368; *Glinski v McIver* [1962] A.C. 726 at 743–745, 768. For a disagreement as to the inference to be drawn in a case where the defendant elected to call no evidence see *Gibbs v Rea* [1998] A.C. 768 (maliciously procuring a search warrant).

[66] *Qema v News Group Newspapers Ltd* [2012] EWHC 1146 (QB) (claimant caught in a sting operation and not disputed that he committed the offences in question, but conviction set aside on grounds of non-disclosure, or abuse of process).

[67] *Abbott v Refuge Assurance Co Ltd* [1962] 1 Q.B. 432; *Ravenga v Mackintosh* (1824) 2 B. & C. 693 at 697; 107 E.R. 541 at 542; *Glinski v McIver* [1962] A.C. 726 at 744–745. A similar result will follow where a private citizen is advised by the police that the facts which he has reported constitute a

Objective test alone for prosecution by the public prosecutor? It must be **20-015** borne in mind that *Hicks v Faulkner* was a private prosecution and in *Herniman v Smith* the prosecution was initiated by an information sworn by the defendant. To require an "honest belief" in guilt, while perhaps still an apt test for the private prosecutor or an informant who is treated as a prosecutor, would be unrealistic if applied to a member of the CPS taking a decision on the basis of evidence placed before him by the police. It is the function of the court and jury at the criminal trial to determine the accused's guilt; the function of the prosecutor is to apply his professional judgement to the evidence before him and determine whether, as Dixon J once put it: "[T]he probability of the accused's guilt is such that upon general grounds of justice a charge against him is warranted."[68] He has not even "got to test the full strength of the defence; he is concerned only with the question of whether there is a case fit to be tried".[69] Indeed, if the public prosecutor personally harboured serious doubts about the guilt of the accused even though the evidence was strong enough to warrant a charge, it could be said that to desist from prosecuting would be a breach of his duty as a minister of justice. The private prosecutor has no basis for making a charge in which he does not believe; the same cannot be said for a public prosecutor. It has therefore been persuasively argued that in such a case this third element of the tort should be regarded as a purely objective one.[70]

Multiple or lesser charges If there are several charges in the indictment, the rule **20-016** as to reasonable and probable cause applies to all of them,[71] but where there is reasonable and probable cause for a prosecution on a lesser charge than that actually preferred, a question of degree may arise[72]:

> "Where there is a charge of theft of 20s. and reasonable and probable cause is shown as regards 19s. of it, it may well be that the prosecutor, when sued for malicious prosecution, is entitled to succeed, because he was in substance justified in making the charge, even though he did so maliciously. But the contrary must surely be the case if the figures are reversed and reasonable and probable cause is shown as to 1s. only out of the 20s."

D.   Malice

An uncertain definition[73] Although it is clear that "[a]n improper and wrongful **20-017** motive lies at the heart of the tort",[74] judicial attempts to define malice have not been completely successful. A test of "[s]ome other motive than a desire to bring to justice a person whom he [the accuser] honestly believes to be guilty"[75] seems to

---

particular offence: *Malz v Rosen* [1966] 1 W.L.R. 1008.

[68]   *Commonwealth Life Assurance Society Ltd v Brain* (1935) 53 C.L.R. 343 at 382.

[69]   *Glinski v McIver* [1962] A.C. 726 at 766 per Lord Devlin. See also *Coudrat v Revenue and Customs Commissioners* [2005] EWCA Civ 616; [2005] S.T.C. 1006 at [41]. Of course, matters other than the strength of the evidence may be relevant to the overall decision of whether a prosecution would be in the public interest.

[70]   *Miazga v Kvello* 2009 SCC 51; [2009] 3 S.C.R. 339.

[71]   *Reed v Taylor* (1812) 4 Taunt. 616; 182 E.R. 472; cf. *Johnstone v Sutton* (1786) 1 Term Rep. 510; 99 E.R. 1215.

[72]   *Leibo v Buckman Ltd* [1952] 2 All E.R. 1057 at 1071 per Jenkins LJ. See also at 1073. cf. at 1066–1067.

[73]   On malice as an ingredient of tort liability, see paras 3-017, 3-019.

[74]   *Williamson v A-G of Trinidad & Tobago* [2014] UKPC 29 at [12] per Lady Hale.

[75]   *Brown v Hawkes* [1891] 2 Q.B. 718 at 723 per Cave J. See also *Glinski v McIver* [1962] A.C. 726

overlook the fact that motives are often mixed. Moreover, anger is not malice, indeed it is one of the motives on which the law relies in order to secure the prosecution of criminals,[76] and yet anger is much more akin to revenge than to any desire to uphold the law. Perhaps we are nearer the mark if we suggest that malice exists where the predominant purpose of the accuser[77] is something other than the vindication of the law.[78] The question of its existence is one for the jury[79] and the burden of proving it is on the claimant.[80]

20-018   Distinct from lack of reasonable and probable cause   At one time malice was not always kept distinct from lack of reasonable and probable cause, but a cogent reason for separating them is that, however spiteful an accusation may be, the personal feelings of the accuser are really irrelevant to its probable truth. The probability or improbability of X having stolen Y's bag remains the same, however much Y dislikes X, and hence it has long been law that malice and lack of reasonable and probable cause must be separately proved. At the same time, want of reasonable and probable cause may be evidence of malice in cases where it is such that the jury may come to the conclusion that there was no honest belief in the accusation made.[81]

For the reasons explained above, however, it seems again necessary to draw a distinction between private and professional prosecutors, the question of "honest belief" being arguably irrelevant to the latter. If it is correct that lack of reasonable cause can only be established against the latter by showing that there were no objective grounds for the proceedings then to allow malice to be inferred from lack of cause would entail the risk that it would be established by proof of negligence.[82] In all cases, however, if want of reasonable and probable cause is not proved by the claimant, the defect is not supplied by evidence of malice.[83] "From the most express malice, the want of probable cause cannot be implied."[84]

---

at 766.

[76] *Brown v Hawkes* [1891] 2 Q.B. 718 at 722. But if the prosecutor's anger is aroused, not by his belief in the claimant's guilt but by some extraneous conduct of the claimant, then there may be evidence of malice: *Glinski v McIver* [1962] A.C. 726 (claimant gave evidence for X on a criminal charge which the defendant, a police officer, believed to be perjured, and X was acquitted. If this was the reason for the claimant's prosecution on a charge of fraud, the prosecutor would have been malicious). See too *Heath v Heape* (1856) 1 Hurl. & N. 478; 156 E.R. 1289.

[77] i.e., the "driving force behind the prosecution": *Williamson v A-G of Trinidad & Tobago* [2014] UKPC 29 at [12] per Lady Hale.

[78] *Stevens v Midland Counties Ry* (1854) 10 Ex. 352 at 356. "Not only spite or ill-will but also improper motive": *Gibbs v Rea* [1998] A.C. 786 at 797 per Gault J. A rare example of such an improper purpose in the case of a professional prosecutor can be found in *Proulx v Québec (Attorney General)* 2001 SCC 66; [2001] 3 S.C.R. 9. For a recent decision that is very difficult to square with the earlier authorities, see *Rees v Commissioner of Police of the Metropolis* [2018] EWCA Civ 1587, where the court implies that it is an improper motive knowingly to act unlawfully, and that even if the defendant's aim is to bring to justice someone he honestly believes to be guilty, he is guilty of malice if "he is conscious that the case he presents is not fit to go before the court". With respect, that seems doubtful.

[79] *Mitchell v Jenkins* (1833) 5 B. & Ad. 588; 110 E.R. 908; *Hicks v Faulkner* (1878) 8 Q.B.D. 167 at 175.

[80] *Abrath v NE Ry* (1886) 11 App. Cas. 247.

[81] *Brown v Hawkes* [1891] 2 Q.B. 718 at 722; *Hicks v Faulkner* (1878) 8 Q.B.D. 167 at 175; *Gibbs v Rea* [1998] A.C. 786 at 798.

[82] *Miazga v Kvello* 2009 SCC 51; [2009] 3 S.C.R. 339.

[83] *Turner v Ambler* (1847) 10 Q.B.D. 252; *Glinski v McIver* [1962] A.C. 726.

[84] *Johnstone v Sutton* (1786) 1 Term Rep. 510 at 545; 99 E.R. at 1243 per Eyre B.

Malice in civil proceedings   That malice is an element distinct from lack of   **20-019**
reasonable and probable cause was re-affirmed in *Willers v Joyce*,[85] which extended
the tort of malicious prosecution to civil proceedings. In the Supreme Court, Lord
Toulson said with respect to malice that "[t]he critical feature which has to be
proved is that the proceedings instituted by the defendant were not a bona fide use
of the court's process".[86] The most obvious case would be where the defendant
brought the proceedings knowing that they were without foundation, but other
instances of abuse were possible, such as bringing proceedings, not for the bona fide
purpose of trying the issue in question, "but to secure some extraneous benefit to
which he has no colour of right".[87] It is in any case likely that the issue of malice
will have to be approached differently in claims arising out of civil actions than it
has been in cases involving criminal proceedings.[88] We have seen that the basic idea
of malice in the criminal law context is that the prosecutor's primary purpose is
something other than the vindication of the law, but a test along those lines may not
be appropriate in the context of civil proceedings, as Rose J pointed out when the
claim in *Willers* went to trial[89]:

> "Criminal prosecutions are brought in the public interest by an impartial Government
> agency which has no private interest in the outcome of the proceedings. In contrast, a
> claimant in a civil action does not need to show any reason why he is bringing the claim
> other than the desire to recover money to which he is entitled as a matter of law. The court
> does not generally inquire into whether the motive of a claimant bringing an action is
> proper or improper ... Indeed, part of the function of the judicial process is to provide a
> non-violent course through which ... bitter enmity can be channelled and, one hopes,
> resolved to some extent by the cathartic process of the trial and judgment."

Rose J also suggested that malice and reasonable and probable cause were "perhaps
even more entwined"[90] where the claim concerned civil litigation as opposed to a
criminal prosecution.

E.   Damage

Meaning of damage   The action for malicious prosecution being an action on the   **20-020**
case it is essential for the claimant to prove damage, and in *Savile v Roberts*[91] Holt
CJ classified damage for the purpose of this tort as of three kinds, any one of which
might ground the action: malicious prosecution might damage a person's fame (i.e.,
his character),[92] or the safety of his person, or the security of his property by reason
of his expense in repelling an unjust charge. A moral stigma will inevitably attach

---

85   [2016] UKSC 43; [2018] A.C. 779.
86   [2016] UKSC 43; [2018] A.C. 779 at [55].
87   [2016] UKSC 43; [2018] A.C. 779 at [55].
88   See the observations of Lord Mance, dissenting in *Willers*: [2016] UKSC 43; [2018] A.C. 779 at
     [137]–[140].
89   *Willers v Joyce* [2018] EWHC 3424 (Ch) at [280].
90   *Willers v Joyce* [2018] EWHC 3424 (Ch) at [287].
91   (1698) 1 Ld. Raym. 374; 91 E.R. 1147.
92   Where the successful claimant is of bad character it may be proper to discount this first element to
     some extent, but this may be offset by the risk of heavier punishment to which his record exposes
     him if convicted: *Manley v MPC* [2006] EWCA Civ 879; [2006] Po. L.R. 117. Bad character is not
     to be confused with an unconventional lifestyle: *Calix v A-G of Trinidad & Tobago* [2013] UKPC
     15; [2013] 1 W.L.R. 3283. Damages may be awarded for psychiatric harm: *Clifford v Chief
     Constable of Hertfordshire* [2011] EWHC 815 (QB).

where the law visits an offence with imprisonment, but there are today innumerable offences which are punishable only by fine. In such cases the claimant can only rely upon damage to his fame if the offence with which he is charged is necessarily and naturally defamatory of him,[93] and in effect the question is the converse of the question of law which is involved in actions for defamation: Is the statement that the claimant was charged with the offence capable of a non-defamatory meaning?[94] Thus a charge of wrongly pulling the communication cord in a train does not necessarily affect the fair name of the accused and will not ground an action for malicious prosecution under Holt CJ's first head,[95] but it is otherwise where, for example, the claimant is charged with deliberately travelling on a train without having paid his fare.[96] On the other hand, unless the claimant was awarded the equivalent of the taxed costs which he has incurred in defending himself, the difference between the costs awarded in the criminal proceedings, if any, and the costs actually incurred is sufficient to ground the action under Holt CJ's third head.[97]

20-021 **Civil litigation** In *Crawford Adjusters v Sagicor General Insurance Ltd*[98] and *Willers v Joyce*[99] the Privy Council and Supreme Court respectively were principally concerned with the question of whether malicious prosecution should be extended to civil proceedings, but in both cases an expansive approach was also adopted to the question of recoverable damage. In *Crawford Adjusters*, the majority in favour of the extension of the tort considered that economic loss should be recoverable for malicious prosecution of proceedings "whether criminal or civil"[100] (and for the tort of abuse of process)[101] and the minority did not appear to dissent on this point.[102] Furthermore, in *Willers v Joyce* the Supreme Court permitted a claim for malicious instigation of civil proceedings to proceed to trial where the heads of damage were damage to health and reputation, loss of earnings and the legal expenses incurred by the claimant in defending the civil proceedings in question over and above the costs awarded. Lord Toulson could see "no difficulty in principle" with the first three heads of damage,[103] and expressed no objection to the recovery of the excess costs.[104] However, Lord Mance sounded a note of caution in his dissenting

---

[93] *Berry v British Transport Commission* [1961] 1 Q.B. 149 at 166, following *Wiffen v Bailey and Romford UDC* [1915] 1 K.B. 600. This was not the original meaning intended by Holt CJ (*Berry v British Transport Commission* [1961] 1 Q.B. 149 at 160–163) and it has been criticised: *Berry v British Transport Commission* [1962] 1 Q.B. 306 at 333, 335–336.

[94] *Berry v British Transport Commission* [1961] 1 Q.B. 149 at 166.

[95] *Berry v British Transport Commission* [1961] 1 Q.B. 149; *Wiffen v Bailey and Romford UDC* [1915] 1 K.B. 600.

[96] *Rayson v South London Transport Co* [1893] 2 Q.B. 304.

[97] *Berry v British Transport Commission* [1962] 1 Q.B. 306.

[98] *Crawford Adjusters v Sagicor General Insurance Ltd* [2013] UKPC 17; [2014] A.C. 366.

[99] [2016] UKSC 43; [2018] A.C. 779.

[100] [2013] UKPC 17; [2014] A.C. 366 at [77], [90].

[101] See para.20-022.

[102] Lord Sumption (at [130]) referred to "all of the elements" of the tort being present save for the involvement of civil proceedings, but the "elements" referred to are the four essentials of the tort set out in the paragraphs which follow which simply presume that the necessary damage has been caused.

[103] [2016] UKSC 43; [2018] A.C. 779 at [43].

[104] [2016] UKSC 43; [2018] A.C. 779 at [58]. cf. *Quartz Hill Gold Mining Co v Eyre* (1883) 11 Q.B.D. 674. Lord Mance, dissenting in *Willers v Joyce*, expressed strong disapproval (at [124], [145]) of the recovery of excess costs by way of a malicious prosecution action, which he considered contrary to the general policy of the law regarding costs.

judgment, warning that the question of recoverable damage in such cases represented "a whole further area for litigation, very likely at the appellate level".[105]

2. MALICIOUS CIVIL PROCEEDINGS

Historically, there was no reason why the old action upon the case for conspiracy should not be extended to malicious civil proceedings as well as to malicious criminal proceedings, and it was in fact held to apply (inter alia) to malicious procurement of excommunication by an ecclesiastical court,[106] to bringing a second writ of *fi. fa.* against a man when one had already been obtained[107] and to malicious arrest of a ship.[108] In more modern times it had been confined to malicious winding-up proceedings,[109] or the malicious procuring of ex parte interim orders.[110] Where available, the same requisites had to be satisfied as for malicious criminal prosecution.[111]

20-022

Liability for malicious civil proceedings generally   The general opinion had been that the law did not go further and make the malicious institution of any civil proceedings[112] actionable, and this view gained considerable strength by being repeated in the House of Lords in *Gregory v Portsmouth CC*.[113] A reason commonly given was the absence of legal damage in the great majority of cases. As Bowen LJ put it in *Quartz Hill Gold Mining Co v Eyre*[114]:

20-023

"[T]he bringing of an ordinary action does not as a natural and necessary consequence involve any injury to a man's property, for this reason, that the only costs which the law recognises ... are the costs properly incurred in the action itself. For these the successful defendant has already been compensated."

This is, of course, simply untrue, for the assessed costs may not amount to the total costs of the defence,[115] and it is noteworthy that any deficiency in costs awarded to

---

[105] [2016] UKSC 43; [2018] A.C. 779 at [141].
[106] *Hocking v Matthews* (1670) 1 Vent. 86; 86 E.R. 60; *Gray v Dight* (1677) 2 Show. K.B. 144; 89 E.R. 848.
[107] *Waterer v Freeman* (1617) Hob. 205; 80 E.R. 352; (1618) Hob. 266; 80 E.R. 412.
[108] *The Walter D. Wallet* [1893] P. 202. On the cases concerning arrest of ships, see the judgment of Lord Clarke in *Willers v Joyce* [2016] UKSC 43; [2018] A.C. 779.
[109] *Quartz Hill Gold Mining Co v Eyre* (1883) 11 Q.B.D. 674 at 683, 689; *Brown v Chapman* (1762) 1 Wm. Bl. 427; 96 E.R. 243.
[110] See the examples referred to by Lord Sumption in *Crawford Adjusters v Sagicor General Insurance Ltd* [2013] UKPC 17; [2014] A.C. 366 at [143], some of which are discussed in para.20-018.
[111] Thus in a claim for malicious bankruptcy there is no cause of action (and hence time does not run) until the adjudication is annulled: *Radivojevic v LR Industries Ltd* [1982] 3 WLUK 7; *Tibbs v Islington BC* [2002] EWCA Civ 1682; [2003] B.P.I.R. 743.
[112] i.e., beyond the limited range of situations outlined in para.20-022.
[113] [2000] 1 A.C. 419. See also *Metall und Rohstoff AG v Donaldson Lufkin & Jenrette Inc* [1990] 1 Q.B. 391; *Johnson v Emerson* (1871) L.R. 6 Ex. 329 at 372; *Quartz Hill Gold Mining Co v Eyre* (1883) 11 Q.B.D. 674 at 684.
[114] (1883) 11 Q.B.D. 674 at 690.
[115] The fiction is recognised by Lord Toulson in *Willers v Joyce* [2016] UKSC 43; [2018] A.C. 779 at [58]. In the United States the provision for recovery of costs in civil litigation is generally a good deal more restricted and this is a major reason for the more extensive liability for malicious civil proceedings there (see *Restatement (Second) of the Law of Torts*, §§674–675), but many jurisdictions require some "special injury" going beyond the ordinary costs and reputational harm associated with litigation: see Dobbs, Hayden and Bublick, *The Law of Torts*, 2nd edn (2011) §593. For a

the accused in a criminal case does amount to damage for malicious prosecution purposes.[116] Further, the argument does not explain why an action will not lie in respect of a civil claim which blemishes the claimant's character, such as one based on fraud. It is not always true that the suit will receive less publicity than a criminal charge and it will not do to say that the claimant's reputation will be cleared by his successful defence of the action,[117] for exactly the same could be said of the successful defence of a criminal charge. Furthermore, the protection afforded by other torts such as defamation, malicious falsehood or conspiracy is limited by the fact that the immunity cast around the giving and preparation of evidence in criminal cases also attaches to civil litigation,[118] so that unless there is something like the fabrication of physical evidence[119] there will be no remedy. The case for extending malicious prosecution to disciplinary proceedings is weaker and what *Gregory* actually decided as a matter of precedent is that this step should not be taken.[120] In such cases there is no absolute immunity and the law of defamation and malicious falsehood[121] will come into play if malice can be proved.[122]

20-024 **Crawford Adjusters v Sagicor** The criticisms of the reasoning in the *Quartz Hill* case outlined above resonated with a majority of the Privy Council in *Crawford Adjusters v Sagicor General Insurance Ltd*[123] and led them to the view that the tort of malicious prosecution should be available as much for the institution of civil proceedings as for the prosecution of criminal proceedings; indeed, they also opined that in relation to both it should be extended to the infliction of general economic loss.[124] The differences between the majority and the minority were very fundamental indeed. Lord Wilson, in the majority, referred to the "paradox" that there is much less chance of being a victim of a criminal prosecution brought maliciously and without reasonable cause than of a civil action so brought and was clearly influenced by the manifest injustice of leaving the claimant without a remedy where it was almost unchallenged that a claim of fraud had been brought against the claimant in circumstances which easily fulfilled all of the requirements for malicious prosecution, not least the requirement of malice given the evidence that the defendant's aim was to destroy the claimant professionally. Lord Sumption, dissenting, embarked from the same starting point when he observed that the tort of malicious prosecution in its traditional form is now "all but defunct" because the "public function" which it was intended to fulfil of deterring malicious prosecution is now largely redundant given that private prosecution hardly exists today.[125] He regarded it as one of two anomalous "malice-based" torts justified only on the basis of their public function,[126] the other being misfeasance in a public office[127]:

---

thorough review of the United States authorities, see the opinion of Lord Neuberger in *Crawford Adjusters v Sagicor General Insurance Ltd* [2013] UKPC 17; [2014] A.C. 366.

[116] *Berry v British Transport Commission* [1962] 1 Q.B. 306.

[117] *Quartz Hill Gold Mining Co v Eyre* (1883) 11 Q.B.D. 674 at 684.

[118] *Gregory v Portsmouth CC* [2000] 1 A.C. at 432; *Surzur Overseas Ltd v Koros* [1999] 2 Lloyd's Rep. 611; para.13-054.

[119] See *Darker v Chief Constable of the West Midlands* [2001] A.C. 435.

[120] The case concerned disciplinary action taken by a local authority against a councillor.

[121] Also, in a suitable case, misfeasance in a public office.

[122] Yet it is only defamation which provides damages for loss of reputation as such.

[123] [2013] UKPC 17; [2014] A.C. 366.

[124] [2013] UKPC 17; [2014] A.C. 366 at [77].

[125] [2013] UKPC 17; [2014] A.C. 366 at [121], [145].

[126] For the general irrelevance of malice in tort see para.3-017.

"It is a tool for constraining the arbitrary exercise of the powers of public prosecuting authorities or private persons exercising corresponding functions. A malice-based tort makes no sense in the context of private litigation where the plaintiff is not exercising any public function."[128]

The introduction of the tort of malicious prosecution for civil proceedings, "outside the special case of malicious winding up petitions and a small number of analogous ex parte proceedings"[129] would also leave the law uncertain and potentially very wide and lead to real concerns about the practical consequences of offering litigants an occasion for prolonging disputes by way of secondary litigation.[130]

Willers v Joyce   Following the Privy Council's decision in *Crawford Adjusters*   **20-025**
v Sagicor General Insurance Ltd, the Supreme Court decided (by a majority of five to four) in *Willers v Joyce*[131] that the tort of malicious prosecution should extend to civil proceedings, with the result that maliciously instituting civil proceedings is now actionable in English law.[132] The claimant in *Willers* was the former director of a company allegedly controlled by the defendant. The company had brought an action against C for breach of contractual and fiduciary duties in relation to earlier litigation, but then discontinued the claim shortly before it came to trial. The company was ordered to pay C's costs on a standard basis. C alleged that the claim had been brought at the instigation of D in order to harm C, against whom D had a personal vendetta. C sought from D damages for loss of earnings, damage to his health and reputation, and for his legal expenses over and above the amount awarded to him by way of costs. The High Court struck out the claim[133] on the basis that English law did not recognise a tort of malicious civil prosecution and C appealed to the Supreme Court. The Supreme Court allowed the appeal, holding that the tort of malicious prosecution extended to civil proceedings.[134] The claim was therefore permitted to proceed to trial, although at the trial the claim was ultimately dismissed on the grounds that, first, C had not proved that D was the prosecutor of the claim against him and, second, that there was reasonable and probable cause for the bringing of that claim.[135]

According to Lord Toulson (with whom Lady Hale, Lord Kerr, Lord Clarke and Lord Wilson agreed), although the early case law on the issue was ambiguous, the prior application of malicious prosecution to certain particular instances of abuse of legal process (such as coercive measures instituted ex parte and petitions for insolvency), militated in favour of its extension to the instigation of civil proceedings more generally. However, the majority's decision to extend the tort rested primarily on the belief that it was a desirable development of the law to provide a remedy where the malicious institution of civil proceedings without reasonable

---

[127]   See Ch.8.
[128]   [2013] UKPC 17; [2014] A.C. 366 at [145].
[129]   [2013] UKPC 17; [2014] A.C. 366 at [144].
[130]   [2013] UKPC 17; [2014] A.C. 366 at [147]–[148].
[131]   [2016] UKSC 43; [2018] A.C. 779.
[132]   Provided of course that all the elements of the tort as set out above are satisfied. In the aftermath of *Crawford Adjusters* the tort was also extended to civil proceedings in New Zealand: *Robinson v Whangarei Heads Enterprises Ltd* [2015] NZHC 1147; [2015] 3 N.Z.L.R. 734.
[133]   *Willers v Gubay* [2015] EWHC 1315 (Ch).
[134]   [2016] UKSC 43; [2018] A.C. 779.
[135]   [2018] EWHC 3424 (Ch).

ground had caused the claimant damage. It seemed "instinctively unjust"[136] for a claimant to be denied compensation in these circumstances. It was not an adequate response to point to the award of costs to a successful defendant. In cases such as the present one, it was almost certainly a fiction to suppose that the costs order had made good the damage caused to C by the litigation, and his claim to recover his excess costs in the malicious prosecution action was not an abuse of process. Lord Toulson also rejected the suggestion that the tort should be limited to those calling in aid the coercive power of the state, by means of initiating criminal proceedings. It was not (as Lord Sumption had suggested in *Crawford Adjusters*) a public law tort and it would be a mistake to ascribe to it the characteristics of a public law remedy.

Lord Neuberger, Lord Mance, Lord Reed and Lord Sumption dissented. Their position was neatly summed up by Lord Sumption's comment that the extension of malicious prosecution to civil proceedings was "unwarranted by authority, unjustified in principle and undesirable in practice".[137] Lord Neuberger listed several reasons for not so extending the tort.[138] In particular, he argued that such an extension would be inconsistent with the principle that no duty of care is owed between civil litigants,[139] and also with the immunity of witnesses in court proceedings from civil liability.[140] Concerns were also expressed by the minority about the scope of the tort being too wide and uncertain,[141] the risks of "satellite litigation",[142] a potential "chilling effect" on the bringing of civil proceedings[143] and unanticipated knock-on effects in other areas of law (e.g., the law of legal professional privilege).[144] As for the authorities, the minority took the view that these did not support the extension of the cause of action, while the "special cases" identified by Lord Toulson where liability could arise in respect of civil proceedings were explained by Lord Neuberger on the basis that they involved the exercise of coercive powers which had caused the claimant to lose his liberty or property without having had the opportunity properly to defend himself.[145]

These counter-arguments did not convince the majority, which held that the tort did not create a duty of care but simply imposed liability for the malicious institution of civil proceedings without reasonable and probable cause.[146] There was also no inconsistency with lay witness immunity from civil liability because if this were a valid objection it would apply to all forms of the tort of malicious prosecution.[147] The majority also argued that the tort was not too broad because the combination of requirements that the claimant must prove (not only the absence of reasonable and probable cause, but also that the defendant did not have a bona fide reason to bring the proceedings), meant that the claimant had "a heavy burden to

---

136 [2016] UKSC 43; [2018] A.C. 779 at [43] per Lord Toulson.
137 [2016] UKSC 43; [2018] A.C. 779 at [174].
138 [2016] UKSC 43; [2018] A.C. 779 at [156]–[173].
139 [2016] UKSC 43; [2018] A.C. 779 at [157], [135].
140 [2016] UKSC 43; [2018] A.C. 779 at [158], [135].
141 [2016] UKSC 43; [2018] A.C. 779 at [162], [132], [137]–[140].
142 [2016] UKSC 43; [2018] A.C. 779 at [163] per Lord Neuberger, [179] per Lord Sumption.
143 [2016] UKSC 43; [2018] A.C. 779 at [166] per Lord Neuberger, [134] per Lord Mance.
144 [2016] UKSC 43; [2018] A.C. 779 at [164]–[165], [127], [184].
145 [2016] UKSC 43; [2018] A.C. 779 at [159]. See also at [129], [174].
146 [2016] UKSC 43; [2018] A.C. 779 at [49].
147 [2016] UKSC 43; [2018] A.C. 779 at [48].

discharge".[148] Finally, the arguments about the risk of "satellite litigation" and a potential "chilling effect" on pursuing valid civil claims were dismissed because they had not been considered sufficient reasons for disallowing a claim for malicious prosecution of criminal proceedings.[149]

3. MALICIOUS PROCESS

For malicious prosecution the defendant must have "prosecuted", but there may **20-026** also be liability if the defendant has maliciously and without reasonable and probable cause instituted some process short of actual prosecution, of which the most important example is the procuring of a warrant for the claimant's arrest. In *Roy v Prior*[150] the defendant, a solicitor, was acting for the defence of a man charged with a criminal offence. The claimant was a doctor who had attended the accused and the defendant issued a witness summons requiring him to be present to give evidence at the trial. According to the claimant, this summons was never served on him, but in any case he was not present at the trial and, on the defendant's instructions, the accused's counsel applied for a warrant for his arrest. In support of the application the defendant himself gave evidence to the effect that the claimant had been evading service of the summons. As a result the warrant was issued and the claimant was arrested and brought before the court. The House of Lords held that if the claimant could prove that the defendant had acted maliciously and without reasonable and probable cause, as he alleged, then he was entitled to succeed.[151] On similar principles a person is also liable for maliciously procuring the issue of a search warrant.[152]

4. ABUSE OF PROCESS

Aside from liability for malicious civil proceedings the law also recognises a **20-027** related tort sometimes called "abuse of process". This lies where a legal process, not itself without foundation, is used for an improper, collateral purpose, for example as an instrument of extortion in a matter not connected with the suit.[153] It is then "merely a stalking horse to coerce the defendant in some way entirely outside the ambit of the legal claim upon which the court is asked to adjudicate".[154]

---

[148] [2016] UKSC 43; [2018] A.C. 779 at [56] per Lord Toulson.
[149] [2016] UKSC 43; [2018] A.C. 779 at [45]–[46].
[150] [1971] A.C. 470.
[151] It matters not that the arrest was procured in the course of civil rather than criminal proceedings, though arrest on civil process is now exceptional. See, e.g., *Daniels v Fielding* (1846) 16 M. & W. 200; 153 E.R. 1159; *Melia v Neate* (1863) 3 F. & F. 757; 176 E.R. 347. The point decided by the House of Lords in *Roy v Prior* [1971] A.C. 470 was that the immunity from suit of a witness in respect of his evidence does not protect him from an action for maliciously procuring the issue of a warrant of arrest. The claimant is not suing on or in respect of the evidence. He is suing because he alleges that the defendant procured his arrest by means of judicial process which the defendant instituted both maliciously and without reasonable and probable cause: [1971] A.C. 470 at 477. See also *Surzur Overseas Ltd v Koros* [1999] 2 Lloyd's Rep. 611 (freezing injunction).
[152] *Gibbs v Rea* [1998] A.C. 786; *Reynolds v MPC* [1985] Q.B. 881; *Keegan v Chief Constable of Merseyside* [2003] EWCA Civ 936; [2003] 1 W.L.R. 2187.
[153] *Grainger v Hill* (1838) 4 Bing. N.C. 212; 132 E.R. 769; *Speed Seal Products Ltd v Paddington* [1985] 1 W.L.R. 1327.
[154] *Varawa v Howard Smith Co* (1911) 13 C.L.R. 35 at 91 per Isaacs J.

The original case is *Grainger v Hill*[155] where the claimant, having been sued for debt, was arrested on a *capias ad respondendum* obtained by the defendant with the purpose of getting the claimant to surrender the ship's register of the *Nimble*, which was mortgaged to the defendant. The claimant surrendered the register to escape arrest and lost trade as a result of not having the register. The claimant's action succeeded even though the original proceedings for debt had not been terminated. The cases have involved the abuse of ancillary process in suits already in progress but there seems no reason why the same rule should not apply to the initiation[156] of the original proceedings as a similar instrument of extortion.[157]

20-028   **The process must have been used for a collateral purpose**   The liability for abuse of process is by no means the same thing as a general tort of malicious issue or use of civil proceedings. If a person presents a claim for damages in the knowledge that it is completely unfounded he does not commit the tort of abuse of process because he is using the law, albeit corruptly, for its assigned purpose, namely to recover damages against the defendant in that suit. The position is the same even if the defendant has some further purpose which will be achieved or assisted by success in the suit, for his object is still to succeed in the litigation.[158] So if D were to launch a prosecution against C, a rival for political office, in order to procure a conviction which would disqualify C from the office[159] that would be no more abuse of process than it would be for, say, a rich man to launch a civil action against a poor man with the object of ruining him because the rich man had been worsted in love by the poor man. In neither of these cases is there any element of extorting any advantage or concession from the other party. Furthermore, the tort of abuse of process may be committed even where the claim is in fact well founded, for a valid claim may be used as an instrument of extortion just as much as an invalid one.[160] This is why it is irrelevant in this tort, unlike malicious prosecution, that the proceedings have not been terminated in the claimant's favour. The issue is not whether the principal suit is well founded and there is therefore no risk of infringing the principle that the court seized of an issue should be the one to decide it,[161] nor of getting inconsistent results. It has been said that there must be some overt act, beyond the issue of the proceedings, demonstrating that improper purpose, such as a demand on the claimant, but the better view is that such acts only have

---

[155] (1838) 4 Bing. N.C. 212; 132 E.R. 769.

[156] Not the threat of proceedings: *Pitman Training Ltd v Nominee UK* [1997] F.S.R. 797.

[157] While the claim in *Land Securities Plc v Fladgate Fielder* [2009] EWCA Civ 1402; [2010] Ch. 467 failed on a number of grounds, including the unsuitability of the tort in relation to proceedings for judicial review commenced with the permission of the court, no objection seems to have been taken simply that the claim was brought on the basis of the initiation of original proceedings.

[158] *Goldsmith v Sperrings Ltd* [1977] 1 W.L.R. 478; *Land Securities Plc v Fladgate Fielder* [2009] EWCA Civ 1402; [2010] Ch. 467 at [73]. The circumstances in *Crawford Adjusters v Sagicor General Insurance Ltd* [2013] UKPC 17; [2014] A.C. 366 (see para.20-021) provide the most extreme illustration of this, but in the same case Lord Wilson was unable to concur with the view expressed by Teare J in *JSC BTA Bank v Ablyazov* [2011] EWHC 1136 (Comm); [2011] 1 W.L.R. 2996 that any legitimate purpose negatives abuse even if an improper purpose was predominant.

[159] The example given by the majority of the HCA in *Williams v Spautz* (1992) 174 C.L.R. 509.

[160] Just as a blackmailer threatens what he has a perfect "right" to do, namely expose his victim.

[161] "No one shall be allowed to allege of a still depending suit that it is unjust": *Gilding v Eyre* (1861) 10 C.B. N.S. 592 at 604; 142 E.R. 584 at 589 per Willes J.

an evidential value and are not a substantive requirement.[162] It is the abuse of the process to effect the improper purpose that is the gist of the tort.[163]

The present position   The tort of abuse of process was last successfully invoked   **20-029** 180 years ago[164] and the future of the cause of action is uncertain. In *Land Securities Plc v Fladgate Fielder*,[165] the defendant started judicial review proceedings against a council over a grant of planning permission to the claimant, which proceedings the claimant alleged were intended to put pressure on it to help the defendant relocate offices. The Court of Appeal upheld summary judgment in favour of the defendant. After an extensive review of this area of the law, Etherton LJ said that[166]:

> "[E]ven if the tort can be committed outside circumstances of compulsion by arrest, imprisonment or other forms of duress, there is no reasonably arguable basis for extending the tort beyond the other particular heads of damage which must exist for invocation of the tort of malicious prosecution."

According to Etherton LJ, extension of the tort was inconsistent with the refusal of the House of Lords in *Gregory v Portsmouth CC*[167] to extend the tort of malicious prosecution to all civil proceedings. Nor did it make any sense to limit the cause of action for malicious prosecution to three particular heads of damage,[168] but then to extend to all cases of economic loss a tort of abuse of process which could apply even where the original claimant had a good cause of action. He also warned of the dangers of parallel litigation and deterring the pursuit of honest claims. Mummery LJ agreed that there was no "pressing need to supplement procedural law by expansive tortious liability in order to protect litigants in civil proceedings from malicious or abusive claims".[169]

These observations must of course now be viewed in the light of the decisions to extend malicious prosecution to civil proceedings in *Crawford Adjusters* and *Willers v Joyce*. In both those cases, the majority considered that it was appropriate to extend the protection of tort law to the victims of malicious civil litigation, and rejected the policy arguments against such an extension relied on in *Land Securities*. Furthermore, those decisions suggest that (at least in the context of civil proceedings) economic loss is now generally recoverable in a case of malicious prosecution, and in *Crawford Adjusters* Lord Wilson went so far as to say that the main ground of the decision in *Land Securities*—no liability for economic loss— was therefore wrong.[170] Quite where those two decisions leave abuse of process as a tort is however unclear. In *Crawford Adjusters*, the majority treated it is a cause of action separate from malicious prosecution, and Lord Wilson drew attention to

---

[162] *Crawford Adjusters v Sagicor General Insurance Ltd* [2013] UKPC 17; [2014] A.C. 366 at [66], [156].

[163] *Hanrahan v Ainsworth* [1990] 22 N.S.W.L.R. 73 at 120.

[164] *Grainger v Hill* (1838) 4 Bing. N.C. 212; 132 E.R. 769 (or 160 years if *Gilding v Eyre* (1861) 10 C.B. N.S. 592; 142 E.R. 584 is to be regarded as an example of the tort).

[165] [2009] EWCA Civ 1402; [2010] Ch. 467.

[166] *Land Securities v Fladgate Fielder* [2009] EWCA Civ 1402; [2010] Ch. 467 at [68].

[167] [2000] 1 A.C. 419.

[168] See para.20-020.

[169] *Land Securities Plc v Fladgate Fielder* [2009] EWCA Civ 1402; [2010] Ch. 467 at [109].

[170] [2013] UKPC 17; [2014] A.C. 366 at [77].

the distinctions between the two torts adverted to above.[171] However, in *Willers v Joyce* Lord Toulson, while expressing "no firm view" on the point, said that it might be better to interpret the decision in *Grainger v Hill* as simply an instance of malicious prosecution, in which the pursuit of an unjustifiable collateral objective was evidence of malice.[172] For now, it seems appropriate to continue to treat abuse of process as a separate tort, distinct from the malicious instigation of civil proceedings, but with the caveat that the courts may in the future decide to merge the two causes of action into a single composite one encompassing all malicious or abusive civil claims.

---

[171] [2013] UKPC 17; [2014] A.C. 366 at [62].
[172] [2016] UKSC 43; [2018] A.C. 779 at [25].

CHAPTER 21

VICARIOUS LIABILITY

1. THE NATURE AND BASIS OF VICARIOUS LIABILITY

A relationship-based liability[1]   The expression "vicarious liability" signifies the   **21-001**
liability which D may incur to C in respect of the tort of a third party, A, by virtue
of the relationship between D and A and the connection between A's tortious
conduct and that relationship. The fact that D is also liable for A's tort does not
insulate A himself from liability,[2] though in most cases[3] it is unlikely that he will
be sued or that judgment will be enforced against him. D's liability derives not from
his own conduct but from his relationship with A. It is not therefore necessary for

---

[1]   Atiyah, *Vicarious Liability in the Law of Torts* (1967); Giliker, *Vicarious Liability in Tort: A Comparative Perspective* (2010); Gray, *Vicarious Liability: Critique and Reform* (2018); Beuermann, *Reconceptualising Strict Liability for the Tort of Another* (2019).
[2]   *Standard Chartered Bank v Pakistan National Shipping Corp* [2002] UKHL 43; [2003] 1 A.C. 949, para.25-034.
[3]   See *Merrett v Babb* [2001] Q.B. 1174 (where the employer was insolvent) and *Shapland v Palmer* [1999] 1 W.L.R. 2068.

vicarious liability to arise that D participated in any way in the commission of the tort nor that a duty D owed to C was breached.[4] Nor does vicarious liability involve any attribution of A's wrongful conduct to D.[5] All that is required is simply that D stood in a particular relationship with A[6] and that A's tort was referable in a certain manner to that relationship.[7] If that is established, it will not avail D to prove that he took reasonable care in his dealings concerning A.

The classic instance of vicarious liability is that of an employer for the torts of his employees committed in the course of their employment. The relationship required is that which arises out of a contract of service (traditionally described as the relationship of "master and servant"[8]) and the tort must be referable to that relationship in the sense that it must have been committed by the employee in the course of his employment. It is this instance of vicarious liability, and variants on it,[9] with which we are principally concerned, but there are other instances some of which cannot be considered in detail in a work of this kind. Such are the liability of partners for each other's torts and, perhaps, the liability of a principal for the torts of his agent.[10] Although the great majority of the cases involve common law torts, the principle of vicarious liability is a general one which will be applied to statutory wrongs sounding in damages unless the statute indicates otherwise, expressly or by implication.[11]

21-002 **Vicarious liability distinguished from the defendant's primary liability** It is important not to confuse vicarious liability with the primary liability of D for damage caused to C by the act of A. It is commonplace for D to incur liability to C for breach of a duty of care owed directly to C by reason of A's conduct. Familiar instances of this include cases where D fails to exercise reasonable care in selecting A to perform a particular task with the result that A causes injury to C, and where D fails to ensure a safe system of work with the result that A injures C, a co-employee.[12] Although such primary liability on the part of D can be concurrent with

---

4   Vicarious liability is therefore "the only true exception" to the general common law principle that tort liability depends on such a breach of duty: *Armes v Nottinghamshire CC* [2017] UKSC 60; [2018] A.C. 355 at [30]. It is of course possible for the employer to be in breach of his own duty as well (see para.21-044).

5   *Bilta (UK) Ltd (in liquidation) v Nazir* [2015] UKSC 23; [2016] A.C. 1 at [70], [186], [203]. This is the "servant's tort" theory of vicarious liability. According to an alternative analysis, the "master's tort" theory, the employer is in breach of his own duty via the act of the servant: *Twine v Bean's Express* (1946) 175 L.T. 131; *Broom v Morgan* [1953] 1 Q.B. 597. However the latter theory has now been "firmly discarded" by the courts (*Majrowski v Guy's and St Thomas's NHS Trust* [2006] UKHL 34; [2007] 1 A.C. 224 at [15]), although it still garners some academic support: see, e.g., Stevens, *Torts and Rights* (2007), Ch.11.

6   Namely a relationship which "has particular characteristics justifying the imposition" of vicarious liability: *Armes v Nottinghamshire CC* [2017] UKSC 60; [2018] A.C. 355 at [54].

7   *Catholic Child Welfare Society v Institute of the Brothers of the Christian Schools* [2012] UKSC 56; [2013] 2 A.C. 1 at [21].

8   Though this terminology is now anachronistic and hence will be avoided, except where justified by the historical context.

9   See paras 21-022ff.

10   Atiyah, *Vicarious Liability in the Law of Torts* (1967), pp.99–115. See also para.21-017.

11   *Majrowski v Guy's and St Thomas's NHS Trust* [2006] UKHL 34; [2007] 1 A.C. 224 (Protection from Harassment Act 1997); *WM Morrison Supermarkets Plc v Various Claimants* [2020] UKSC 12; [2020] 2 W.L.R. 941 (Data Protection Act 1998).

12   See para.9-023. For examples outside this area, see *Hartwell v Attorney General of the British Virgin Islands* [2004] UKPC 12; [2004] 1 W.L.R. 1273 (personal fault but no vicarious liability); *Colour*

vicarious liability, it is conceptually distinct from it. Because the questions of vicarious liability and primary liability are fundamentally different from each other, there can be (and often is) breach of a personal duty but no vicarious liability as well as vice versa.

Vicarious liability distinguished from liability for breach of a non-delegable **21-003** **duty**   Sometimes, even though D is not at fault, he will still be primarily liable because the negligence of A, to whom D has entrusted a task, puts D in breach of a "non-delegable duty". This does not mean that D commits any wrong by delegating the performance of the task (he may have taken reasonable care to appoint an apparently competent person and, indeed, the nature of the task may have called for D to delegate it to a person with suitable expertise) nor that he is an insurer of the safe completion of the task, but simply that he stands answerable for the fault of A in carrying it out. A non-delegable duty of care is often described as a duty to ensure that reasonable care is taken and the idea is that D will breach it simply because A fails to take such care.

Liability arising under a non-delegable duty of care is fundamentally different from both an ordinary duty of care owed by D and vicarious liability. A non-delegable duty of care is distinct from an ordinary duty of care because D can breach the former even if he has taken reasonable care (what matters is whether A, to whom a task was entrusted, failed to take reasonable care) whereas to breach the latter he himself must fail to take reasonable care. And liability arising under a non-delegable duty is distinct from vicarious liability[13] because, in relation to the former type of liability, nothing in particular turns on the relationship between D and A whereas that is of central importance to the latter species of liability. Further, while non-delegable duties of care arise only in particular contexts,[14] vicarious liability is a general principle of liability which attaches to all torts committed by an employee in the course of his employment.

History[15]   At one time liability seems to have arisen only if the employer had **21-004** expressly commanded that the wrong be committed, which is not now understood as vicarious liability at all, for one who orders a wrong to be committed is, in the modern law, a direct participant in the tort and hence no antecedent relationship is necessary.[16] At the beginning of the 18th century it was accepted that the employer was liable not only for acts done at his express command but also for those done by his implied command, this to be inferred from the general authority he had given his servant in his employment. By the end of the 18th century, however, the idea began to grow up that special importance attached to the relationship of master and servant as such (that is, something more than the fact that it might supply evidence of implied authority), and by the middle of the next century it was finally accepted

---

Quest Ltd v Total Downstream UK Plc [2009] EWHC 540 (Comm); [2009] 2 Lloyd's Rep. 1 (failure to design safe system as well as vicarious liability); *Maga v Birmingham Archdiocese* [2010] EWCA Civ 256; [2010] 1 W.L.R. 1441 (also true vicarious liability). As *Maga* shows, the "personal" breach of duty by D to C may arise from D's vicarious liability for the failure of X, another employee of D, to carry out his duties.

13   cf. Williams [1956] C.L.J. 180.
14   See paras 21-043ff.
15   Swain (2019) 78 C.L.J. 640.
16   See para.22-003.

that the existence of that relationship was necessary for vicarious liability[17] and sufficient to make the employer liable, provided the act was done in the course of the employment.

21-005 **Recent upheavals** The law on vicarious liability was relatively stable throughout the second half of the 19th century and the 20th century, but that stability was shattered in the first two decades of the present century. The particular challenges posed by claims arising out of the scandal of widespread abuse of children in institutional settings triggered a radical overhaul and expansion of vicarious liability, a process initiated by the seminal decision of the House of Lords in *Lister v Hesley Hall Ltd.*[18] Unfortunately, the courts have struggled to replace the old structures of liability with a new framework that offers comparable levels of stability and predictability. The result, itself completely predictable, has been a large body of appellate case law, and a steady stream of decisions at the very highest level. Thus far, the attempts of our highest court to impose some order and consistency of approach have, it must respectfully be said, largely failed,[19] but at the time of writing two further decisions have just been handed down,[20] and it remains to be seen whether these are more successful than earlier judicial efforts in stemming the tide of appellate litigation.

21-006 **Justification**[21] Vicarious liability is a frequent feature of legal systems and those which do not feature it in its "pure" form, but which in theory require some fault in the employer, have tended to go to considerable lengths to create a stricter liability in practice.[22] Nevertheless, given the continuing dominance of the fault principle elsewhere in the law of tort, it requires some explanation or justification. The traditional phrases *respondeat superior* and *qui facit per alium facit per se* have been criticised, the former because it "merely states the rule baldly in two words", and the latter because it "merely gives a fictional explanation of it".[23] However, even if they are not explanations, they probably do represent the expression of a rather deep-seated and intuitive idea that someone who, generally for his own benefit, sets a force in motion should have responsibility for the consequences even if he chooses others to carry out the task. Of course this logically leads on to a full-blown theory of enterprise liability under which an activity should bear its own costs.[24] But although the notion of enterprise liability is currently fashionable in judicial circles,[25] it cannot explain the current law, since the vicarious liability of the

---

17 *Reedie v London and North Western Ry* (1849) 4 Exch. 244.
18 [2001] UKHL 22; [2002] 1 A.C. 215. That decision in turn drew heavily upon the analysis of the Supreme Court of Canada in *Bazley v Curry* [1999] 2 S.C.R. 534.
19 Indeed, it has even been suggested that such attempts are inevitably fruitless: see *Mohamud v WM Morrison Supermarkets Plc* [2016] UKSC 11; [2016] A.C. 677 at [54] per Lord Dyson ("To search for certainty and precision in vicarious liability is to undertake a quest for a chimaera").
20 *WM Morrison Supermarkets Plc v Various Claimants* [2020] UKSC 12; [2020] 2 W.L.R. 941; *Barclays Bank Plc v Various Claimants* [2020] UKSC 13; [2020] 2 W.L.R. 960.
21 Neyers (2005) 43 Alta. L. Rev. 287; Stevens, *Torts and Rights* (2007), Ch.11; Morgan (2015) 31 P.N. 235 at 247–257.
22 See, e.g., German law, where §831 B.G.B. makes the employer liable unless he shows that he exercised due care in choosing and supervising the employee. No such exculpation is possible in contract under §278 B.G.B. Hence the courts have tended to extend contractual liability.
23 *Staveley Iron and Chemical Co Ltd v Jones* [1956] A.C. 627 at 643 per Lord Reid.
24 See Deakin (2003) 32 Ind. L.J. 97.
25 "The most influential idea in modern times": *Armes v Nottinghamshire CC* [2017] UKSC 60; [2018]

employer generally does not rest on the bare fact that harm was done in the further-ance of his business (as the theory requires), since it is also required that the person acting in the furtherance of his business was at fault. It is in any case questionable whether pure enterprise liability shorn of a fault element is either feasible or defensible.

Other, more obviously instrumentalist, justifications of vicarious liability centre on deterrence and compensation. Were there no vicarious liability, it is argued, the employer's incentive to minimise the risks created by his activity would be substantially reduced. In practice there is little doubt that the existence of vicari-ous liability serves to improve standards and reduce accidents but, as elsewhere in tort law, it is questionable whether deterrence is a justification for tort liability or merely a beneficial effect of its imposition.[26] As for compensation, as early as the 1860s it was observed that the employer has a deeper pocket than the employee[27] and it is certainly true that if there were no vicarious liability then much of tort law would be stultified, for it would be impracticable (and wasteful) for many employees to insure themselves against liability incurred by them in their employment. A variant of the "deep pocket" idea is that of "loss distribution". Many employers today are not individuals but substantial commercial enterprises, and, by placing liability on the enterprise, the losses in question are distributed across all the customers to whom it sells its services or products. Knowing of its potential li-ability for the torts of its employees, the enterprise insures against this liability and the cost of this insurance is reflected in the prices it charges. In the result, therefore, losses caused by the torts of the enterprise's employees are borne in small and prob-ably unnoticeable amounts by the body of its customers, and the injured person is compensated without the necessity of calling upon an individual to suffer the disastrous financial consequences that may follow liability in tort. But again, the requirement of employee fault is difficult to square with this theory, and nor is it clear why the employer, as opposed to some other entity with deep pockets (such as the state) should bear the burden of effecting the distribution of the losses in question. At a more fundamental level it has also been said that neither the fact that the defendant has deep pockets nor the fact that the defendant has insurance is a principled justification for imposing vicarious liability.[28]

In truth, none of the justifications or explanations for vicarious liability is ultimately convincing, and, like many things in the law, the institution is probably to be explained not by reference to any single reason but by the cumulation of several.[29] It is in any case inconceivable that a serious proposal for the abolition of vicarious liability will be made so long as the law of tort as we know it remains alive. Indeed, as we have seen, the recent trend has been towards the expansion of

---

A.C. 355 at [67] per Lord Reed. See also *Dubai Aluminium Co Ltd v Salaam* [2002] UKHL 48; [2003] 2 A.C. 366 at [21]; *Cox v Ministry of Justice* [2016] UKSC 10; [2016] A.C. 660 at [23]; *Mohamud v WM Morrison Supermarkets Plc* [2016] UKSC 11; [2016] A.C. 677 at [40].

[26] In *Armes v Nottinghamshire CC* [2017] UKSC 60; [2018] A.C. 355 at [67], Lord Reed said that deterrence "has not been prominent" among the justifications for vicarious liability advanced in the case law.

[27] *Limpus v London General Omnibus Co* (1862) 1 Hurl. & C. 526 at 539; 158 E.R. 993 at 998.

[28] *Cox v Ministry of Justice* [2016] UKSC 10; [2016] A.C. 660 at [20] per Lord Reed: "The mere pos-session of wealth is not in itself any ground for imposing liability ... As for insurance, employers insure themselves because they are liable: they are not liable because they have insured themselves."

[29] *Catholic Child Welfare Society v Institute of the Brothers of the Christian Schools* [2012] UKSC 56; [2013] 2 A.C. 1 at [35].

vicarious liability rather than its contraction. At the same time, however, the absence of a convincing rationale for vicarious liability has undoubtedly contributed to the difficulties the courts have faced in trying to construct an analytical framework that provides certainty and consistency in this area of tort law.

2. THE RELATIONSHIP BETWEEN THE DEFENDANT AND THE TORTFEASOR

21-007 **A relationship "capable of giving rise to vicarious liability"** In *Catholic Child Welfare Society v Institute of the Brothers of the Christian Schools* Lord Phillips referred to the "first stage" of asking whether the relationship between D and A is "one that is capable of giving rise to vicarious liability".[30] The paradigm case is an employment relationship, and that remains the most common instance but, as Lord Phillips made clear, qualifying relationships are not confined to employment in the strict sense. Other specific categories have long been recognised and, in recent years, the courts have also developed a more general category of relationships "akin to employment". These qualifying relationships are considered below, along with difficulties that arise when one employer hires out the services of an employee to another.

A. Employment Relationships

21-008 **Employees and independent contractors** Vicarious liability usually requires that the tortfeasor be an employee of the defendant. By contrast, it is a foundational principle of this area of the law that vicarious liability will never arise where the tortfeasor is an independent contractor. For the purposes of identifying whether a person is an employee or an independent contractor, the concepts of a contract of service ("employee") and a contract for services ("independent contractor") are routinely invoked. It is therefore necessary to determine the indicia of a contract of service.[31]

The task of determining whether a person is an employee has to be performed by the law for various purposes that are totally unconnected with vicarious liability—employment protection, taxation and social security are the obvious examples—but the assumption that the question "who is an employee?" should receive the same answer, regardless of the context in which it is asked, has now been firmly rejected.[32] The replacement of the "unitary concept of the employer" with a more functional approach which asks who is exercising the relevant employer functions in a particular context is to be preferred.[33] Changes in employment practices (for example, the increasing casualisation of the workforce and the growing numbers of "home workers") have produced a situation in which, for employment protection purposes, it has become difficult to continue to regard people as

---

[30] [2012] UKSC 56; [2013] 2 A.C. 1 at [21].

[31] In those cases where it is sufficient to have identified a relationship "akin to employment" (see para.21-012), a contract of any sort is not necessary.

[32] "Whether vicarious liability should be imposed does not depend on the classification of the relationship for [other] purposes": *Cox v Ministry of Justice* [2016] UKSC 10; [2016] A.C. 660 at [11] per Lord Reed. See also *JGE v English Province of Our Lady of Charity* [2012] EWCA Civ 938; [2013] Q.B. 722 at [59]. Nor does the law of vicarious liability necessarily align with the broader statutory concept of a "worker" found in the Employment Rights Act 1996, s.230(3): *Barclays Bank Plc v Various Claimants* [2020] UKSC 13; [2020] 2 W.L.R. 960 at [29].

[33] See Prassl, *The Concept of the Employer* (2015).

employees who would once routinely have been such. Without suggesting that an employer should be vicariously liable for the torts of his independent contractors it is questionable whether a tort claimant should be affected by internal changes in the employer's employment structure which have nothing to do with the nature of his activities or the risk presented by them.[34] It is perfectly sensible to say that if Company D has its goods delivered to customers by a carrier, Company A, responsibility for accidents caused in the distribution process should fall on Company A alone, for that is a specialist function which is not "characteristic" of Company D's business (however necessary it may be to enable that business to function) and it is reasonable to expect that Company A will make proper liability insurance provisions against that risk. However, it by no means follows that the same result should ensue, to take the facts of one Australian case, where Company D sets up a "bicycle courier" business and engages a number of individuals to carry out deliveries for him.[35]

General observations   Three general observations can be made about the distinc-   **21-009**
tion between employees and independent contractors before we turn to consider the two main tests that have been used to draw that distinction. First, the express declaration of the parties, if any, is not conclusive as to the legal classification of the relationship. It has been said to be a factor to be taken into account by the court,[36] but in the context of vicarious liability, where the rights of a third party tort claimant are affected,[37] the better view may be that it should be disregarded altogether.[38] Second, it of course does not follow from the fact that a person works for more than one employer (that word being used in a non-technical sense) that he is a contractor, though the more people or entities he works for the more likely that is to be the correct classification. And third, while we shall see that two main tests have been used to determine whether an employment relationship exists, in truth the classification of the relationship is a function of the two, so that they may better be understood as considerations to be taken into account. It should also be noted that the extent of the reliance placed on the two tests has changed over time, and may depend on the nature of the work in question, or other features of the situation in which the classification is to be made.

Control test   At one time it was generally accepted that the test of the relation-   **21-010**
ship of master and servant was that of control,[39] and a contract of service was

---

[34]   See McKendrick (1990) 53 M.L.R. 770; Kidner (1995) 15 L.S. 47.

[35]   A majority of the High Court of Australia held that the couriers were employees in *Hollis v Vabu Pty Ltd* [2001] HCA 44; (2001) 207 C.L.R. 21. The defendant had made deductions from fees for liability insurance, but this only covered him.

[36]   See, e.g., *Ferguson v John Dawson & Partners (Contractors) Ltd* [1976] 1 W.L.R. 1213; *Ready Mixed Concrete (South East) Ltd v Minister of Pensions and National Insurance* [1968] 2 Q.B. 497; *Global Plant Ltd v Secretary of State for Social Services* [1972] 1 Q.B. 139; *Calder v H Kitson Vickers Ltd* [1988] I.C.R. 232.

[37]   In *Ferguson v John Dawson & Partners (Contractors) Ltd* [1976] 1 W.L.R. 1213 the context was the possible application of the Construction (Working Places) Regulations 1966, SI 1966/94.

[38]   Megaw LJ in *Ferguson v John Dawson & Partners (Contractors) Ltd* [1976] 1 W.L.R. 1213 at 1222 would have been prepared to go further and say that the parties' declaration ought to be wholly disregarded. This is the position where an employee is loaned by one employer to another: see para.21-020.

[39]   For an early statement of the control test, see *Yewens v Noakes* (1880) 6 Q.B.D. 530 at 532–533. For its development see Atiyah, *Vicarious Liability in the Law of Tort* (1967), pp.40–44.

thought to be one by virtue of which the employer, "can not only order or require what is to be done, but how it shall be done".[40] The control test retains some importance in cases to which it can be applied,[41] and is of particular significance in cases where there is both a temporary and a permanent employer.[42] But in modern conditions the notion that an employer has the right to control the manner of work of all his employees, save perhaps in the most attenuated form, smacks more of fiction than of fact. It is clearly the law that such professionally trained persons as the master of a ship, the pilot of an aircraft and a hospital consultant are all employees for whose torts their employers are responsible, and yet it is equally clearly fanciful to suppose that their employers will in general be in a position to tell them how to do their highly skilled jobs.[43] It has, therefore, been recognised that "the significance of control today is that the employer can direct what the employee does, not how he does it",[44] and it has in any case been said to be important "not to exaggerate the extent to which control is necessary in order for the imposition of vicarious liability to be justified".[45]

21-011 **Entrepreneur test** Nowadays the primary focus when distinguishing between an employee and a contractor is on the economic realities underlying the relationship with the employer, and whether the worker can be said to be "in business on his own account".[46] Factors to be taken into account on this approach include: (1) whether the worker is paid a fixed salary, or instead paid for the work that he actually does; (2) who owns the tools and other assets the worker uses; (3) whose responsibility it is to find a replacement if the worker falls ill, and whether (connecting back to (1)) the worker is still paid in these circumstances; and (4) whether the worker can delegate his work to a third party, with the fact that he can do so pointing away from a contract of service, particularly if the worker is still paid in these circumstances, so that he, rather than the employer, remunerates the delegate.[47]

Two first instance decisions from the late 1960s, neither involving vicarious liability, show how this "entrepreneur" test works in practice.[48] The first is *Market Investigations Ltd v Minister of Social Security*,[49] where the question was whether

---

40 *Collins v Hertfordshire CC* [1947] K.B. 598 at 615 per Hilbery J.
41 *Argent v Minister of Social Security* [1968] 1 W.L.R. 1749 at 1759; *Jennings v Forestry Commission* [2008] EWCA Civ 581; [2008] I.C.R. 988.
42 See para.21-019.
43 Kahn-Freund (1951) 14 M.L.R. 504. On ministers of religion and the distinction between employment and spiritual matters, see *Percy v Church of Scotland* [2005] UKHL 73; [2006] 2 A.C. 28.
44 *Catholic Child Welfare Society v Institute of the Brothers of the Christian Schools* [2012] UKSC 56; [2013] 2 A.C. 1 at [36] per Lord Phillips. See also *Cox v Ministry of Justice* [2016] UKSC 10; [2016] A.C. 660 at [21].
45 *Armes v Nottinghamshire CC* [2017] UKSC 60; [2018] A.C. 355 at [65] per Lord Reed.
46 "The independent contractor works in and for his own business at his risk of profit or loss": *JGE v English Province of Our Lady of Charity* [2012] EWCA Civ 938; [2013] Q.B. 722 at [70] per Ward LJ. For recent endorsement of this test at the highest level, see *Barclays Bank Plc v Various Claimants* [2020] UKSC 13; [2020] 2 W.L.R. 960.
47 *Express and Echo Publications Ltd v Tanton* [1999] I.R.L.R. 367. cf. *McFarlane v Glasgow CC* [2001] I.R.L.R. 7.
48 These decisions are particularly useful because they are contrasting examples, but also close to the borderline. For two more recent applications of the entrepreneur test, both in the vicarious liability context but also both rather clear-cut, see *Kafagi v JBW Group Ltd* [2018] EWCA Civ 1157 esp. at [50]–[53] (self-employed bailiff); and *Barclays Bank Plc v Various Claimants* [2020] UKSC 13; [2020] 2 W.L.R. 960 at [28] (freelance medical practitioner "with a portfolio of patients and clients").
49 [1969] 2 Q.B. 173.

workers employed on a series of short-term contracts to carry out market research were employees or independent contractors for national insurance purposes. Their pay was fixed, and they were told exactly what to do, but they were free to choose when to do the work, and were entitled to work for other employers. No provision was made in their contracts for time off or holidays. Cooke J held that they were employees. Neither the fact that they could choose when to work nor the fact that they could work for others prevented them from being classified as such, and weight was placed on the fact that the employer had extensive control over the way they worked and that their remuneration was fixed.[50] The other case is *Ready Mixed Concrete (South East) Ltd v Minister of Pensions and National Insurance*,[51] where lorry drivers who worked for a concrete firm were classified as independent contractors for tax purposes. The drivers owned the lorries that they drove, although they bought them on hire purchase from a finance company affiliated to the employer, could not sell them without the employer's permission, and were obliged to offer them for sale to the employer if they left its employment. They were also required to follow the employer's orders and forbidden from doing other haulage business. But crucially they were paid only for the work that they actually did—so that, for example, the risk of illness fell on them—and they were required to maintain the lorries at their own expense. Despite the high level of control exercised by the employer, the fact that the drivers owned the lorries, and that the risk of profit or loss lay with them, led MacKenna J to conclude that they were employed under contracts for services, rather than contracts of service.

B. Relationships "Akin to Employment"

Origins of the category   Although the relationship of employer and employee **21-012** remains the paradigm case, it is not the only relationship that can give rise to vicarious liability. Another category of qualifying relationship to which express recognition has recently been given is that of relationships "akin to employment". The origins of this category lie in two cases concerned with the abuse of children, where the courts were required to decide whether vicarious liability could be based on the relationship between a religious institution and a member of the relevant religious community who had carried out the abuse. The concept was first introduced into English law by MacDuff J at first instance in *JGE v English Province of Our Lady of Charity*,[52] where it was used to justify imposing vicarious liability on a Roman Catholic diocesan trust for the torts of a parish priest in the diocese. The idea was then developed in the leading case of *Catholic Child Welfare Society v Institute of the Brothers of the Christian Schools*.[53] Children had been abused by teachers who were employed by the Society as manager of the school. The Society did not contest its own vicarious liability, but argued that the Institute was also vicariously liable for the abuse carried out by teachers who were brothers of the Institute.[54] Accord-

---

[50]   See also the decision of the Privy Council in *Lee v Cheung* [1990] 2 A.C. 374, where although the claimant worked for a number of persons, the picture that emerged was "of a skilled artisan earning his living by working for more than one employer as an employee and not as a small businessman entering into business on his own account with all its attendant risks".

[51]   [1968] 2 Q.B. 497.

[52]   [2011] EWHC 2871 (QB); [2012] 2 W.L.R. 709 (affirmed [2012] EWCA Civ 938; [2013] Q.B. 722). The concept was borrowed from Canadian law: *Doe v Bennett* [2004] SCC 17; [2004] 1 S.C.R. 436.

[53]   [2012] UKSC 56; [2013] 2 A.C. 1.

[54]   For the reasons given by Rix LJ in the *Viasystems (Tyneside) Ltd v Thermal Transfer (Northern) Ltd*

ing to Lord Phillips, who gave the only judgment, the Institute was to be approached as a corporate body (an unincorporated association) which existed to perform the function of providing a Christian education to boys,[55] which function was carried out, in part, by the brothers who served as teachers. The Institute and the individual brothers shared a "common purpose"[56] and that was enough for their relationship to be regarded as "sufficiently akin to that between an employer and an employee" for vicarious liability to be imposed.[57] Whether a relationship qualified as akin to employment depended on the extent to which it featured the characteristics which made it appropriate to impose vicarious liability on an employer, namely that[58]:

> "(i) the employer is more likely to have the means to compensate the victim than the employee and can be expected to have insured against that liability; (ii) the tort will have been committed as a result of activity being taken by the employee on behalf of the employer; (iii) the employee's activity is likely to be part of the business activity of the employer; (iv) the employer, by employing the employee to carry on the activity will have created the risk of the tort committed by the employee; (v) the employee will, to a greater or lesser degree, have been under the control of the employer."

21-013 **Subsequent clarification of the category** In retrospect, recognition of a novel category of relationships "akin to employment" by reference only to a list of five broadly framed "characteristics" was bound to cause difficulties and in two subsequent cases the Supreme Court has sought to clarify matters. The first case was *Cox v Ministry of Justice*,[59] where Lord Reed was faithful to Lord Phillips's general approach but sought to downplay the importance of factors (i) and (v),[60] while emphasising that the other three factors were inter-related. The result was that[61]:

> "[A] relationship other than one of employment is in principle capable of giving rise to vicarious liability where harm is wrongfully done by an individual who carries on activities as an integral part of the business activities carried on by a defendant and for its benefit … and where the commission of the wrongful act is a risk created by the defendant by assigning those activities to the individual in question."

Lord Reed also made it clear that the new category was of general application,[62] and

---

[2005] EWCA Civ 1151; [2006] Q.B. 510 (discussed at para.21-018), there was no objection to the dual vicarious liability of the Society and the Institute.

[55] In both the *Catholic Child Welfare Society* case and *JGE* there is an acknowledged difficulty about the precise identity of the defendant. In *JGE* the court was concerned with the relationship between bishop and priest, but the defendants to the action were the trustees of the diocesan trust since the Roman Catholic Church has no legal personality. Similarly, in the *Catholic Child Welfare Society* case the court looked at the relationship between the Institute (whether worldwide or only locally) and the brothers in question, but among the defendants were the trustees of two trusts which owned significant assets on behalf of the Institute.

[56] [2012] UKSC 56; [2013] 2 A.C. 1 at [61].

[57] [2012] UKSC 56; [2013] 2 A.C. 1 at [47].

[58] [2012] UKSC 56; [2013] 2 A.C. 1 at [35].

[59] [2016] UKSC 10; [2016] A.C. 660.

[60] Both were "unlikely to be of independent significance in most cases" although the absence of even a "vestigial" degree of control was liable to negative the imposition of vicarious liability: [2016] UKSC 10; [2016] A.C. 660 at [20]–[21].

[61] [2016] UKSC 10; [2016] A.C. 660 at [24].

[62] "It is intended to provide a basis for identifying the circumstances in which vicarious liability may in principle be imposed outside relationships of employment": [2016] UKSC 10; [2016] A.C. 660

not confined to, say, cases of alleged sexual abuse of children, and that references in this context to "business", "benefit" and "enterprise" did not mean that the category was limited to commercial or profit-making activities.[63]

In *Barclays Bank Plc v Various Claimants*[64] the Supreme Court provided further guidance as to the limits of the category. The issue was whether the defendant bank was vicariously liable for sexual assaults allegedly committed by a doctor whom it had instructed to carry out medical assessments of existing and prospective employees. The doctor's work for the bank was a comparatively minor part of a "portfolio practice", which included work for local hospitals, medical examinations for a range of other parties and the writing of a newspaper column. The Court of Appeal[65] held that the bank was vicariously liable for the alleged torts, having applied the five criteria set out in the *Catholic Child Welfare Society* case. This was despite Lord Reed's statement in *Cox* that the new category did not extend to imposing vicarious liability where a tortfeasor's activities were "entirely attributable to the conduct of a recognisably independent business of his own or a third party",[66] a description that appeared to cover the activities of the doctor.[67] The Supreme Court allowed the bank's appeal, holding that since the doctor was "in business on his own account",[68] the relationship was not "akin to employment". According to Lady Hale, who gave the sole judgment, there was nothing in the earlier case law "to suggest that the classic distinction between employment and relationships akin or analogous to employment, on the one hand, and the relationship with an independent contractor, on the other hand" had been eroded.[69] As well as firmly reiterating the longstanding principle that there is no vicarious liability for the torts of an independent contractor, Lady Hale also signalled a shift away from reliance on Lord Phillips's five factors when considering the new category, towards an enquiry more tightly focused on the particularities of the relationship between the tortfeasor and the defendant. It had never been intended that the five factors "were the only criteria by which to judge the question"; the emphasis in the earlier cases had instead been on "the details of the relationship, and its closeness to employment".[70]

Approach to be taken   In view of the *Barclays Bank* decision, it is suggested that **21-014** the following approach should be adopted when considering whether a relationship gives rise to vicarious liability. First, the court should apply "the conventional

---

at [29].

63   [2016] UKSC 10; [2016] A.C. 660 at [29]–[30].
64   [2020] UKSC 13; [2020] 2 W.L.R. 960.
65   [2018] EWCA Civ 1670; [2018] I.R.L.R. 947.
66   [2016] UKSC 10; [2016] A.C. 660 at [29]. See also *JGE v English Province of Our Lady of Charity* [2012] EWCA Civ 938; [2013] Q.B. 722 at [69]; *Woodland v Swimming Teachers Association* [2013] UKSC 66; [2014] A.C. 537 at [3].
67   cf. *Kafagi v JBW Group Ltd* [2018] EWCA Civ 1157 (judicial services company not vicariously liable for alleged torts of a bailiff to whom it sub-contracted the collection of council tax debts since bailiff "ran his own business"); *Brayshaw v Partners of Apsley Surgery* [2018] EWHC 3286 (QB); [2019] 2 All E.R. 997 (GP practice not vicariously liable for alleged tortious conduct of locum GP). See also *Barness v Ingenious Media Ltd* [2019] EWHC 3299 (Ch), where Nugee J rejected the (ingenious) argument of the claimants that banks who had lent them money to invest in a tax avoidance scheme were vicariously liable for alleged breaches of duty by the claimants' independent financial adviser, with whom the banks merely had "a close commercial relationship" for their mutual benefit.
68   [2020] UKSC 13; [2020] 2 W.L.R. 960 at [28].
69   [2020] UKSC 13; [2020] 2 W.L.R. 960 at [24].
70   [2020] UKSC 13; [2020] 2 W.L.R. 960 at [18].

distinction between a contract of employment and a contract for services", which "continues to be relevant in the vast majority of situations".[71] If that produces a clear classification of the tortfeasor as either employee or independent contractor, then that concludes the analysis either way. If it does not, then the court moves on to a second stage whereby it closely considers the relationship between the tortfeasor and the defendant, and the extent to which that relationship is analogous to an employment relationship. A useful test to apply at this stage may be to ask whether the relationship, "when whittled down to [its] essence, [possesses] the same fundamental qualities as those which inhere in employer-employee relationships".[72] The question, in other words, is whether the tortfeasor held a position functionally analogous to employment, for example as regards his accountability to the defendant entity, integration into its structure, and performance of duties aimed at pursuing its aims and objectives on its behalf.[73] Although the key "will usually lie in understanding the details of the relationship", in doubtful cases the five criteria identified by Lord Phillips may be helpful,[74] but they are not to be applied as a standalone test, and they need not be considered at all where it is clear that the tortfeasor is carrying on his own independent business.[75]

21-015 **Examples of relationships akin to employment** When applying this approach it will naturally also be important to consider which relationships have previously been held to qualify as "akin to employment". The case law of the Supreme Court is a useful guide here. The relationship between a member of a religious order and the order itself was of course the subject of the decision in the *Catholic Child Welfare Society* case, while the concept originated in the earlier decision of the Court of Appeal in *JGE*, which concerned a parish priest and a bishop. In *Cox v Ministry of Justice*, the relationship between a prisoner working in a prison kitchen and the prison service was held to fall within the category. And in *Armes v Nottinghamshire County Council*[76] it was held that the category encompassed the relationship between abusive foster parents and the local authority which entrusted them with the care of the claimant as a young girl. Lord Reed, applying his own test in *Cox*, said that the foster parents provided care to the claimant "as an integral part of the [defendant's] organisation of its child care services" and that by placing children with foster parents the defendant created the risk of abuse.[77] It was also emphasised that although the authority did not exercise day-to-day control over the foster parents, it retained powers of "approval, inspection, supervision and removal".[78] The Supreme Court arguably pushed the category close to its limit in

---

[71] *Kafagi v JBW Group Ltd* [2018] EWCA Civ 1157 at [21] per Singh LJ.
[72] *Ng Huat Seng v Mohammad* [2017] SGCA 58 at [63] (cited in *Barclays Bank* [2020] UKSC 13; [2020] 2 W.L.R. 960 at [26]).
[73] Todd [2018] N.Z.L. Rev. 131 at 167.
[74] Presumably, applying *Cox*, with particular emphasis on factors (ii)–(iv).
[75] *Barclays Bank Plc v Various Claimants* [2020] UKSC 13; [2020] 2 W.L.R. 960 at [27]. The *Barclays Bank* approach to the "akin to employment" category was applied in *JXJ v The Province of Great Britain of the Institute of Brothers of the Christian Schools* [2020] EWHC 1914, where it was held that a lay member of staff employed by the managers of a boarding school in which many of the defendant Institute's brothers taught, and over which the Institute exercised considerable control, was not in a relationship akin to employment with the Institute.
[76] [2017] UKSC 60; [2018] A.C. 355. Dickinson (2018) 134 L.Q.R. 359. An alternative argument from non-delegable duty was rejected: see para.21-048.
[77] [2017] UKSC 60; [2018] A.C. 355 at [60]–[61].
[78] [2017] UKSC 60; [2018] A.C. 355 at [62].

Armes, and Lord Hughes dissented on the issue, arguing that foster parents could not "sensibly be described as akin to employees"; if the business model was to be applied, they looked a great deal more like independent contractors, "carefully selected and supervised as many a panel of such contractors is".[79] It was in any case accepted by the majority that the outcome would probably have been different had the defendant entrusted the claimant to the care of her own parents, or (perhaps) other family members.[80]

C. Other Relationships

Police   Until 1964, no person or body stood in the position of "master" to a police   **21-016**
officer, and accordingly anyone injured by the tortious conduct of the police could have redress only against the individual officers concerned. Now, however, it is provided by s.88 of the Police Act 1996 that the chief officer of police for any police area shall be liable for torts committed by constables under his direction and control in the performance or purported performance of their functions.[81] This statutory liability is equated with the liability of an employer for the torts of his employees committed in the course of their employment, but the Act does not create an employment relationship, nor one of principal and agent.[82]

Vehicle drivers   Thus far we have spoken of the relationship under a contract of   **21-017**
employment, or something analogous thereto. However, many cases on vicarious liability speak in the language of agency and numerous dicta can be found equating agency with a contract of service for this purpose.[83] Whatever may be the correct principle as to liability for agents, it is convenient to treat here a doctrine which fits easily into no existing legal category[84] but which developed because of the insurance position in relation to road traffic liability. The doctrine may be stated as follows. Where D, the owner[85] of a vehicle, expressly or impliedly requests or instructs A to drive the vehicle in performance of some task or duty carried out for D, D will be vicariously liable for A's negligence in the operation of the vehicle.[86] Thus in *Ormrod v Crosville Motor Services Ltd*[87] D, the owner of a car, asked A to drive the car from Birkenhead to Monte Carlo, where they were to start a holiday together. It was held that D was liable for A's negligent driving even though A might

---

79   [2017] UKSC 60; [2018] A.C. 355 at [76]. cf. at [59] per Lord Reed. In *Barclays Bank* Lady Hale described *Armes* as "perhaps the most difficult" of the relevant authorities: [2020] UKSC 13; [2020] 2 W.L.R. 960 at [23]. Commonwealth courts have divided over the question of vicarious liability for the torts of foster parents: see *KLB v British Columbia* [2003] SCC 51; [2003] 2 S.C.R. 51 (rejecting it); *S v A-G* [2003] NZCA 149; [2003] 3 N.Z.L.R. 450 (imposing it).

80   [2017] UKSC 60; [2018] A.C. 355 at [72].

81   See para.21-034.

82   *Farah v MPC* [1998] Q.B. 65.

83   See Atiyah, *Vicarious Liability in the Law of Torts* (1967), Ch.9.

84   Winfield sought to explain the doctrine in terms of "casual delegation" of the use of a chattel, but the leading case talks in terms of agency: *Morgans v Launchbury* [1973] A.C. 127.

85   Ownership as such is probably not necessary: *Nottingham v Aldridge* [1971] 2 Q.B. 739. In *Morgans v Launchbury* the husband was held liable for the negligence of the driver and there was no appeal against that decision. If an owner bails his vehicle to A and A gets B to drive it, the owner is not liable for B's negligence: *Chowdhary v Gillot* [1947] 2 All E.R. 541.

86   *Morgans v Launchbury* [1973] A.C. 127.

87   [1953] 1 W.L.R. 1120. See also *Samson v Aitchison* [1912] A.C. 844; *Pratt v Patrick* [1924] 1 K.B. 488; *The Trust Co Ltd v De Silva* [1956] 1 W.L.R. 376; *Vandyke v Fender* [1970] 2 Q.B. 292; *Candler v Thomas* [1998] R.T.R. 214.

be said to be partly pursuing his own interest in driving D's car. On the other hand, liability was not imposed in *Morgans v Launchbury*[88] where the husband, who normally used his wife's car to go to work, got a third person to drive him home after visits to several public houses. In no sense was the husband acting as his wife's agent in using the car for his work and still less was the third person her agent.[89] It is now clear that mere permission to drive without any interest or concern of the owner in the driving does not make the owner vicariously liable[90] nor is there any doctrine of the "family car".[91] Where, however, the facts of the relationship between owner and driver are not fully known, proof of ownership may give rise to a presumption that the driver was acting as the owner's agent.[92]

The development of a separate head of vicarious liability for vehicle drivers was clearly prompted by a desire to ensure a claim-worthy defendant, but the House of Lords denied that the courts may go on a voyage of discovery into the insurance position in these cases and said that any alteration of the law must be left to the legislature with its superior capacity for making decisions of policy. However, to confine our attention in this context to instances of vicarious liability risks giving a false impression. If there is in force a policy of insurance covering the liability of the driver[93] there will generally be no point in suing the owner. In fact, as far as the claimant is concerned, even if the driver is not covered by the policy, in most cases the owner's insurer must satisfy the judgment against the uninsured driver[94] and if there is no insurance at all the claimant may proceed under the Motor Insurers' Bureau Agreement.[95] The result is that "the policy justification for using agency to extend vicarious liability to the loan of motor vehicles has virtually disappeared".[96]

The question remains of the reach and future of this principle. While it has certainly been most prominent in the context of motor accidents, it has been applied to a boat[97] albeit that the High Court of Australia refused to extend it to a plane.[98] But even a special rule about "transport" seems out of tune with the style of the common law and the judgments in *Morgans v Launchbury* are couched in quite general terms of agency. Conversely, a general principle that the owner of a chattel was liable for the negligence of anyone using it at his request would have surprising consequences.[99] It is therefore unlikely that the courts will be inclined

---

[88] [1973] A.C. 127.

[89] cf. the valiant attempt of Lord Denning MR and Edmund Davies LJ in the Court of Appeal to fit the facts into a traditional agency framework: [1971] 2 Q.B. 245.

[90] *Morgans v Launchbury* [1973] A.C. 127; *Hewitt v Bonvin* [1940] 1 K.B. 188 (father permitting son to take girlfriends home in car). cf. *Carberry v Davies* [1968] 1 W.L.R. 1103 (owner suggesting to driver that he take owner's son out in car). A person who has "borrowed" a car, with or without the owner's permission, is not acting as his agent when driving it back to him: *Klein v Caluori* [1971] 1 W.L.R. 619.

[91] cf. the view of Lord Denning MR in *Launchbury v Morgans* [1971] 2 Q.B. 245.

[92] *Rambarran v Gurrucharan* [1970] 1 W.L.R. 556; *Morgans v Launchbury* [1973] A.C. 127 at 139.

[93] Either because the driver is named in a "named driver" clause in the owner's policy, or because he has his own insurance policy covering his use of any car.

[94] Road Traffic Act 1988 s.151(2)(b).

[95] It should be noted that at the time of the accident in *Morgans v Launchbury* insurance for passengers was not compulsory and therefore fell outside the scope of the MIB Agreement.

[96] Giliker, *Vicarious Liability in Tort* (2010), p.116.

[97] *The Thelma (Owners) v The Endymion (Owners)* [1953] 2 Lloyd's Rep. 613.

[98] *Scott v Davis* [2000] HCA 52; (2000) 204 C.L.R. 333.

[99] See the examples of the cricket bat and the barbecue given by Callinan J in *Scott v Davis* [2000] HCA

to expand the scope of the principle and since it is now largely otiose it is difficult to see any obvious justification for its continued existence.

D.   Lending an Employee

Dual liability now possible   D may be the general employer of A but A's services may be contracted to X on a temporary basis.[100] If A wrongfully injures some third party while performing those services for X, who bears the vicarious liability for his acts? For long it was assumed that it must be either D or X, but could not be both.[101] The Court of Appeal rejected this proposition in *Viasystems (Tyneside) Ltd v Thermal Transfer (Northern) Ltd*.[102] Ducting was being fitted in a factory by sub-contractor X, who was making use of the services of A under a "labour-only" contract between X and A's employer, D. A's negligence caused a flood, for which the court held that both X and D were vicariously liable to the factory owner, with equal contribution between themselves under the Civil Liability (Contribution) Act 1978.

21-018

Control test   While dual liability is now possible in cases involving the lending of an employee it is not inevitable. Rather, the allocation of vicarious liability depends on who is entitled to exercise control over the worker, and the extent to which the worker is integrated into the temporary employer's organisation.[103] In *Viasystems*, May LJ held that since both D and X were entitled to exercise a degree of control over A (the former through a fitter also employed by D and the latter through a foreman employed by X) both were liable for A's negligence.[104] Where, by contrast, A's services are supplied to X on a long-term basis subject to the entire control of X, that is likely to result in X alone being liable.[105] Another situation is illustrated by *Mersey Docks and Harbour Board v Coggins and Griffith (Liverpool) Ltd*.[106] D, the harbour authority, employed A as the driver of a mobile crane, and let the crane together with A as driver to X. The contract between D and X provided that A should be the employee of X but A was paid by D, and D alone had power to dismiss him. In the course of loading a ship C was injured by the negligent way in which A operated the crane. At the time of the accident X had the immediate direction and control of the operations to be executed by A and his crane, for example to pick up and move a piece of cargo, but X had no power to direct how A should work the crane and manipulate its controls. The House of Lords held that D as the general or permanent employer of A was liable to C. At that time it was assumed that it was not possible for both D and X to be liable and the possibility of dual liability was therefore not considered. However, it was suggested in the

21-019

52; (2000) 204 C.L.R. 333 at [347]–[348]. See also *Moynihan v Moynihan* [1975] I.R. 192 (teapot).

[100] See *MAN Nutzfahrzeuge AG v Freightliner Ltd* [2005] EWHC 2347 (Comm) at [107] (A employed by D but X puts forward A as speaking on his (i.e., X's) behalf. No reason why X should not be vicariously liable even though for other purposes only D would be).

[101] *Esso Petroleum Co Ltd v Hall Russell & Co Ltd* [1989] A.C. 643 at 686.

[102] [2005] EWCA Civ 1151; [2006] Q.B. 510.

[103] See para.21-014.

[104] In what was a two-member Court of Appeal in *Viasystems*, May LJ focused on control, and Rix LJ on organisational integration. Arguably the control test is more appropriate since an organisational integration approach seems to point more towards an all-or-nothing conclusion, rather than the dual liability in fact imposed.

[105] See, e.g., *Hawley v Luminar Leisure Ltd* [2006] EWCA Civ 18; [2006] I.R.L.R. 817.

[106] [1947] A.C. 1.

Viasystems case that the result might still be the same even now[107]: A was on D's premises, operating D's crane and exercising his own skill and discretion in that task, even if he was subject to the direction of X as to what loads he should lift and where he should take them. In *Mersey Docks* it was held that it was up to the permanent employer to establish that responsibility should be shifted onto the temporary one, and this was reiterated after *Viasystems* in *Biffa Waste Services Ltd v Maschinenfabrik Ernst Hese GMBH*,[108] where the Court of Appeal said that there must be "exceptional facts" for this to happen. This test was not satisfied where welders had been "borrowed" by X from D for a weekend, because X had no control over how they welded (as opposed to some power to identify the task to be undertaken and some supervision capacity) and because the time period was so brief that the welders were not integrated into X's business undertaking.

21-020 **Express provisions** As the *Mersey Docks* case shows, the fact that the contract between D and X expressly provides that X is to be treated as the sole employer is not determinative of the question of who is vicariously liable. However, a term in the contract may entitle D to an indemnity from X in respect of any liability imposed on D arising out of A's work for X.[109]

3. THE CONNECTION BETWEEN THE RELATIONSHIP AND THE TORT

A. In General

21-021 **"Close connection"** In *Catholic Child Welfare Society v Institute of the Brothers of the Christian Schools* Lord Phillips referred to the "second stage" of vicarious liability as the search for the connection that links the relationship between D and A (the "first stage") with A's tort. The two stages cannot therefore be considered in isolation and there is a synthesis between them.[110] In the context of employment, the question at the second stage is generally said to be whether A's conduct fell within the "ordinary course of his employment". However, it seems that this test is not to be used where the tort of the employee consisted of the sexual abuse of a child,[111] and a distinctive approach is also adopted where the claimant seeks to make the employer liable for the fraud of an employee.[112] It may also be that a statute imposes a liability for the acts of others in a particular context. In such cases, whatever form of words is used, the question under the statute is one of construction and it may lay down some wider (or narrower) principle than the common law.[113]

---

[107] *Viasystems (Tyneside) Ltd v Thermal Transfer (Northern) Ltd* [2005] EWCA Civ 1151; [2006] Q.B. 510 at [80]. It was also suggested at [32] that *Bhoomidas v Port of Singapore* [1978] 1 All E.R. 956 would go the same way and the stevedoring company alone would be liable.

[108] [2008] EWCA Civ 1257; [2009] Q.B. 725.

[109] *Herdman v Walker (Tooting) Ltd* [1956] 1 W.L.R. 209; *Spalding v Tarmac Civil Engineering Ltd* [1966] 1 W.L.R. 156. The allocation of indemnity rights between D and X is not an exclusion of liability and so is not regulated by the Unfair Contracts Act 1977: *Thompson v T Lohan (Plant Hire) Ltd* [1987] 1 W.L.R. 649.

[110] [2012] UKSC 56; [2013] 2 A.C. 1 at [21].

[111] See para.21-022.

[112] See paras 21-036—21-037.

[113] See, e.g., *Jones v Tower Boot Co Ltd* [1997] 2 All E.R. 406 (Race Relations Act 1976 (see now Equality Act 2010)).

B. Course of Employment

A difficult question, however formulated Common law courts "have strug- **21-022**
gled to identify a coherent basis for identifying the circumstances in which an
employer should be held vicariously liable for negligent acts of an employee, let
alone for intentional, criminal acts".[114] Traditionally it was said that an act was in
the course of employment[115] if it was expressly or impliedly authorised by the
employer[116] or was sufficiently connected with the employment that it could be
regarded as an unauthorised manner of doing something which was authorised,[117]
or was necessarily incidental to something which the employee was employed to
do. There were, however, difficulties in applying this test in the context of wilful
wrongdoing, and matters came to a head at the turn of the century when many
claims were lodged against local authorities and other institutions in respect of
physical and sexual abuse suffered by the claimants while they were children in
care. These cases stretched the traditional formula "to breaking point" since "[e]ven
on its most elastic interpretation", sexual abuse of children "could not be described
as a mode, albeit an improper mode, of caring for them".[118] In *Lister v Hesley Hall
Ltd*[119] the House of Lords therefore signalled a shift away from the traditional test
towards an approach which considered whether the tort of the employee was so
closely connected with his employment that it was fair and just to make the
employer liable.[120] On the new approach the defendant school in that case was held
to be vicariously liable for the acts of the warden of the boarding annexe in abusing the claimants: the school had undertaken the care of the children and entrusted
the performance of that duty to the warden and so the abuse was "inextricably
interwoven with the carrying out by the warden of his duties".[121]

The adoption of the "close connection" test could have been interpreted as a
complete break with the traditional formula and the cases decided under it, but that
seems not to have been the intention of the House in *Lister*,[122] and besides the test

---

[114] *Prince Alfred College Inc v ADC* [2016] HCA 37; (2016) 258 C.L.R. 134 at [39] per French CJ,
Kiefel, Bell, Keane and Nettle JJ.
[115] "Course of employment" and "scope of employment" tend to be used interchangeably, although the
former is now generally used by the courts. "Course of employment" is often found in legislation
dealing with other matters and it is dangerous to assume that authorities from such contexts can be
automatically transferred to that of vicarious liability: *Lister v Hesley Hall Ltd* [2001] UKHL 22;
[2002] 1 A.C. 215 at [40].
[116] If the act authorised is inherently wrongful (e.g. trespassing on another's land) the employer is liable because he has procured a wrong and there is no need to rely on vicarious liability.
[117] *Kirby v NCB* 1958 S.C. 514 at 533.
[118] *Mohamud v WM Morrison Supermarkets Plc* [2016] UKSC 11; [2016] A.C. 677 at [39] per Lord
Toulson. See also *Trotman v North Yorkshire CC* [1999] L.G.R. 584, overruled in *Lister*.
[119] [2001] UKHL 22; [2002] 1 A.C. 215.
[120] The change of approach was influenced by the Canadian case of *Bazley v Curry* [1999] 2 S.C.R. 534.
[121] [2001] UKHL 22; [2002] 1 A.C. 215 at [38] per Lord Steyn.
[122] Rather than dismissing the traditional formula out of hand, in *Lister* Lord Millett warned against its
"excessively literal application" ([2001] UKHL 22; [2002] 1 A.C. 215 at [74]), and said that the test
should be treated not as a statutory definition, but rather as "a guide to the application of the law to
diverse factual situations" (at [70]). He also sought to adapt the formula to incorporate the "close
connection" idea, as opposed to abandoning it altogether. It was a version of Lord Millett's revised
test that was adopted in *Dubai Aluminium Co Ltd v Salaam* [2002] UKHL 48; [2003] 2 A.C. 366
and endorsed in *WM Morrison Supermarkets Plc v Various Claimants* [2020] UKSC 12; [2020] 2
W.L.R. 941.

on its own provided little in the way of practical guidance.[123] Subsequent decisions have therefore generally adopted a more nuanced approach, which emphasises the continuity in the case law. Hence in *Dubai Aluminium Co Ltd v Salaam*, decided shortly after *Lister*, Lord Nicholls used the idea of a "close connection" to develop a new formula which drew upon the traditional test, and pointed to the continued importance of the earlier authorities.[124] Although a broader approach based more squarely on the *Lister* decision was evident in *Mohamud v WM Morrison Supermarkets Plc*,[125] the Supreme Court in *WM Morrison Supermarkets Plc v Various Claimants*[126] has now reverted to the more conservative reasoning in *Dubai Aluminium* and again stressed the importance of earlier decisions when considering whether conduct occurred in the course of employment. Lord Reed in *WM Morrison Supermarkets Plc v Various Claimants* also pointed to the distinctive nature of the cases on child sexual abuse, commenting that the close connection test must be applied differently in that context, since the employee's conduct could not be regarded as something done in the ordinary course of employment.[127]

21-023 **General approach** Following *WM Morrison Supermarkets Plc v Various Claimants* the test that generally applies in a case arising out an employment relationship is whether the wrongful conduct of the employee was so closely connected with acts the employee was authorised to do that, for the purposes of the liability of his employer, it may fairly and properly be regarded as done by him while acting in the ordinary course of his employment.[128] This general principle must be applied "with regard to the circumstances of the case before the court and the assistance provided by previous court decisions"[129]:

> "The words 'fairly and properly' are not, therefore, intended as an invitation to judges to decide cases according to their personal sense of justice, but require them to consider how the guidance derived from decided cases furnishes a solution to the case before the court. Judges should therefore identify from the decided cases the factors or principles which point towards or away from vicarious liability in the case before the court, and which explain why it should or should not be imposed. Following that approach, cases can be decided on a basis which is principled and consistent."[130]

---

123 See *Dubai Aluminium Co Ltd v Salaam* [2002] UKHL 48; [2003] 2 A.C. 366 at [25]; *Catholic Child Welfare Society v Institute of the Brothers of the Christian Schools* [2012] UKSC 56; [2013] 2 A.C. 1 at [74]; *Prince Alfred College Inc v ADC* [2016] HCA 37; (2016) 258 C.L.R. 134 at [68].

124 [2002] UKHL 48; [2003] 2 A.C. 366 at [23], [26].

125 [2016] UKSC 11; [2016] A.C. 677 at [44]–[45]. Under this approach, the court asked, first, what functions or "field of activities" had been entrusted by the employer to the employee (a question to be addressed broadly), and then, second, whether there was a sufficient connection between the position in which the employee was employed and his wrongful conduct to make it right for the employer to be held liable as a matter of social justice. For examples of the application of the two-stage test set out in *Mohamud*, see *Bellman v Northampton Recruitment Ltd* [2018] EWCA Civ 2214; [2019] 1 All E.R. 113; *Group Seven Ltd v Notable Services LLP* [2019] EWCA Civ 614; [2019] P.N.L.R. 22; *Shelbourne v Cancer Research UK* [2019] EWHC 842 (QB); [2019] P.I.Q.R. P16; and *Various Claimants v WM Morrison Supermarkets Plc* [2018] EWCA Civ 2339; [2019] Q.B. 772 (reversed [2020] UKSC 12).

126 [2020] UKSC 12; [2020] 2 W.L.R. 941.

127 [2020] UKSC 12; [2020] 2 W.L.R. 941 at [23].

128 *Dubai Aluminium Co Ltd v Salaam* [2002] UKHL 48; [2003] 2 A.C. 366 at [23]; *WM Morrison Supermarkets Plc v Various Claimants* [2020] UKSC 12; [2020] 2 W.L.R. 941 at [23], [25].

129 *WM Morrison Supermarkets Plc v Various Claimants* [2020] UKSC 12; [2020] 2 W.L.R. 941 at [24] per Lord Reed.

130 See also at [2020] UKSC 12; [2020] 2 W.L.R. 941 at [26] per Lord Reed: "vicarious liability ... is

A temporal or causal connection between the tort and the employment does not in itself satisfy the close connection test.[131] Nor is it enough that the employment merely gave the employee the opportunity to commit the wrong.[132] The timing and location of the wrongdoing is a relevant consideration, so that the fact that an act was performed outside working hours, or away from the workplace, might point to it being outside the scope of employment.[133] However, these circumstances are not necessarily determinative: tortious conduct occurring at the workplace in working hours does not automatically give rise to vicarious liability[134] or vice versa.[135] Finally, the reason for the wrongdoing may also be significant: in *WM Morrison Supermarkets Plc v Various Claimants*, for example, Lord Reed said that whether the employee was acting on his employer's business or for purely personal reasons was "highly material".[136]

In some cases, it will be fairly obvious that the close connection test is not satisfied. For example, it would be strange to impose liability on the employer of a lorry driver for an accident the latter causes while driving his own car while on holiday, or on a doctors' surgery for the negligence of a locum GP in seeking to impose his religious views on a patient he first encountered through the surgery.[137] And acts of an employee of precisely the character for which he is employed by the employer will be outside the course of employment if when he performs those acts he is in fact working for someone else,[138] or pursuing his own independent business interests.[139] In other cases, however, it may be more difficult to decide whether conduct is or is not within the course of employment and it is always a highly fact-sensitive enquiry.

All acts constituting the wrong must fall within the course of employment Where the course of employment test is used, it must be shown that the acts of the employee committed within the scope of his employment constitute an actionable wrong in themselves. It is not enough that the wrong is constituted by some acts done by him within the course of employment and some done outside it, nor that the wrong consists partly of acts done by him within the course of employment and partly of the acts of a third party.[140]   **21-024**

Acts expressly prohibited by the employer The prohibition by the employer of an act or class of acts will only protect him from vicarious liability if it actually restricts what it is the employee is employed to do: the mere prohibition of a mode of performing the employment is of no avail. In *Limpus v London General Omnibus*   **21-025**

---

not determined according to individual judges' sense of social justice". cf. *Mohamud v WM Morrison Supermarkets Plc* [2016] UKSC 11; [2016] A.C. 677 at [45].

[131] *WM Morrison Supermarkets Plc v Various Claimants* [2020] UKSC 12; [2020] 2 W.L.R. 941 at [31].

[132] *Lister v Hesley Hall Ltd* [2001] UKHL 22; [2002] 1 A.C. 215 at [45], [65]; *WM Morrison Supermarkets Plc v Various Claimants* [2020] UKSC 12; [2020] 2 W.L.R. 941 at [35].

[133] *Lister v Hesley Hall Ltd* [2001] UKHL 22; [2002] 1 A.C. 215 at [44].

[134] See, e.g., *Graham v Commercial Bodyworks Ltd* [2015] EWCA Civ 47; [2015] I.C.R. 665.

[135] See, e.g., *Bellman v Northampton Recruitment Ltd* [2018] EWCA Civ 2214; [2019] 1 All E.R. 1133.

[136] [2020] UKSC 12; [2020] 2 W.L.R. 941 at [31].

[137] *Brayshaw v Partners of Apsley Surgery* [2018] EWHC 3286 (QB); [2019] 2 All E.R. 997.

[138] *Kooragang Investments Pty Ltd v Richardson & Wrench Ltd* [1982] A.C. 462.

[139] *Frederick v Positive Solutions (Financial Services) Ltd* [2018] EWCA Civ 431 (the Supreme Court has reserved judgment in an appeal in these proceedings).

[140] *Credit Lyonnais Bank Nederland NV v Export Credits Guarantee Department* [2000] 1 A.C. 486.

Co,[141] a driver of the defendants' omnibus had printed instructions not to race with, or obstruct, other omnibuses. In disobedience to this order he obstructed the claimant's omnibus and caused a collision which damaged it. The defendants were held liable because what he did was merely a wrongful, improper and unauthorised mode of doing an act which he was authorised to do, namely, to promote the defendants' passenger-carrying business in competition with their rivals.[142] Another example of a case where vicarious liability was imposed despite a prohibition is *Rose v Plenty*,[143] where a milkman had been warned by his employer not to allow children to assist him, nor to allow passengers on his float. In breach of these instructions he engaged the claimant, aged 13, to help him, and the claimant was injured, while travelling on the float, by the milkman's negligent driving. The majority of the Court of Appeal held that the milkman was acting in the course of his employment because the engagement of the claimant was made to further the employer's business: the result might have been different if the milkman had just been giving him a lift. By contrast, a fire crew engaging in a "go-slow" in support of a pay claim were held not to be acting in the course of their employment when they failed to arrive in time to put out a fire.[144]

21-026   **Acts intended to benefit the employee**   At one time it was generally thought that the employee was acting outside the scope of his employment if he intended to benefit himself and not his employer[145] but while this remains a relevant consideration,[146] it is not in itself conclusive. In *Lloyd v Grace, Smith & Co*[147] the defendant firm of solicitors employed a managing clerk who conducted their conveyancing business without supervision. The claimant was dissatisfied with the money which some cottages produced and went to the defendants' office where she saw the clerk, who induced her to give him instructions to sell the cottages and to execute two documents which he falsely told her were necessary for the sale but which were in fact a conveyance of the cottages to himself. He then dishonestly disposed of the property for his own benefit. The House of Lords unanimously held that the defendants were liable: the clerk was acting as the representative of the firm and they had invited the claimant to deal with him over her property. Similarly, the landlords of a block of flats were held liable when a dishonest porter charged by them with keeping the property secure used his keys to enter the claimant's flat and steal.[148] But the result would probably have been different if, say, the boilerman had stolen the keys and used them for the same purpose: it is not enough that the employment gives the opportunity to steal, for there is then insufficient connection between the employment and the theft.[149]

---

[141] (1862) 1 Hurl. & C. 526; 158 E.R. 993.

[142] See also *LCC v Cattermoles (Garages) Ltd* [1953] 1 W.L.R. 997; *Ilkiw v Samuels* [1963] 1 W.L.R. 991. cf. *Iqbal v London Transport Executive* (1973) 16 K.I.R. 329.

[143] [1976] 1 W.L.R. 141.

[144] *General Engineering Services Ltd v Kingston and St Andrew Corp* [1988] 3 All E.R. 867.

[145] Based on *Barwick v English Joint Stock Bank* (1867) L.R. 2 Ex. 259.

[146] See para.21-023.

[147] [1912] A.C. 716. For recent confirmation, see *Group Seven Ltd v Notable Services LLP* [2019] EWCA Civ 614; [2019] P.N.L.R. 22 at [153].

[148] *Nahhas v Pier House Management (Cheyne Walk) Ltd* (1984) 270 E.G. 328.

[149] See *Heasman v Clarity Cleaning Co* [1987] I.C.R. 949 and *Lister v Hesley Hall Ltd* [2001] UKHL 22; [2002] 1 A.C. 215 at [45]. cf. *Brink's Global Services Inc v Igrox Ltd* [2009] EWHC 1817 (Comm).

C.   Carelessness of Employee

Employer liable provided employee is not "on a frolic of his own"   By far the   **21-027**
commonest kind of wrong which the employee commits is one due to unlawful
carelessness, whether it be negligence of the kind which is in itself a tort, or
negligence which is a possible ingredient in some other tort. In such cases the
conduct of the employee may still be in the course of employment even if the
employee is not acting strictly in the performance of his duty, provided he is not
"on a frolic of his own".[150] Thus a first-aid attendant at a colliery was still acting
within the course of his employment while cycling across his employer's premises
to go to an office to collect his wages,[151] and so was a person sent to work at a place
away from his employer's premises who drove some distance from his place of
work to get a midday meal.[152]

Whether the employee is on a frolic of his own will depend on the particular
nature of the employer's business and the task which the employee is required to
discharge. In *Century Insurance Co Ltd v Northern Ireland Road Transport
Board*,[153] the driver of a petrol tanker belonging to the defendants struck a match
to light a cigarette and threw it on the floor while transferring petrol from the tanker
to an underground tank in the claimant's garage. This caused an explosion which
damaged the claimant's property. The defendants were held liable, for the careless
act of their driver was done in the course of his employment. Lord Wright reasoned
that while the careless act of the driver was done for his own comfort and convenience, it could not be treated in abstraction from the circumstances. The negligence
was to be found by considering the time when and the circumstances in which the
match was struck and thrown down, and this made it a negligent method of conducting his work.

Travelling cases   A number of cases are concerned with deviations by drivers   **21-028**
from routes authorised by their employers. We have probably not advanced much
beyond the test stated in the old case of *Storey v Ashton*[154] that it is "a question of
degree how far the deviation could be considered a separate journey" divesting the
employer of responsibility.[155] Account must be taken not only of the geographical
or temporal divergence from instructions, but how far the employee can still be said
to be carrying out the task he was set.[156] An employee travelling between home and
work will not generally be in the course of employment[157] unless he is contractually required to use a particular mode of transport[158] or comes out "on call" in his

---

[150] This famous phrase was coined by Parke B in *Joel v Morison* (1834) 6 Car. & P. 501 at 503; 172
E.R. 1338 at 1339. It has even served as the title of a novel: Gaddis, *A Frolic of His Own* (1984).

[151] *Staton v National Coal Board* [1957] 1 W.L.R. 893.

[152] *Harvey v RG O'Dell Ltd* [1958] 2 Q.B. 78. cf. *Crook v Derbyshire Stone Ltd* [1956] 1 W.L.R. 432;
Nottingham v Aldridge [1971] 3 W.L.R. 1.

[153] [1942] A.C. 509. See also *Jefferson v Derbyshire Farmers Ltd* [1921] 2 K.B. 281, where the facts
were very similar. cf. *Kirby v NCB* 1958 S.L.T. 47.

[154] (1869) L.R. 4 Q.B. 476. cf. *Whatman v Pearson* (1868) L.R. 3 C.P. 422.

[155] *Hilton v Thomas Burton (Rhodes) Ltd* [1961] 1 W.L.R. 705.

[156] In *Angus v Glasgow Corp* 1977 S.L.T. 206 it is suggested that the real test is, "has the servant
departed altogether from his master's business".

[157] *Smith v Stages* [1989] A.C. 928 at 955; but employment may commence as soon as the factory gates
are passed: *Compton v McClure* [1975] I.C.R. 378.

[158] See *Nottingham v Aldridge* [1971] 2 Q.B. 739 at 747.

employer's time to deal with emergencies.[159] Where the employment is essentially peripatetic (for example, a travelling salesman or appliance repairer), travel from one location to another during the day will be within the course of employment[160] and the same will be true of the journey between home and the first location if the employee goes directly there rather than to his "base".[161] In these cases driving from place to place is an ordinary and necessary incident of performing the duties of the employment. This was not so in *Smith v Stages*,[162] where the employees were normally employed at site A but were sent to perform an urgent job at site B over 200 miles away. Nevertheless they were held to be in the course of their employment when driving home from site B because they were paid wages (and not merely a travelling allowance) for doing so even though they were using a private vehicle and had a discretion as to how and when they would travel.

21-029 **Negligent delegation of the employee's duty to a stranger** The existence of an emergency gives no implied authority to an employee to delegate his duty to a stranger, so as to make his employer liable for the defaults of the stranger,[163] but it may be that the employee himself was negligent in the course of his employment in allowing the stranger to do his job. In *Ilkiw v Samuels*,[164] a lorry driver in the employment of the defendants permitted a stranger to drive his lorry, and an accident resulted from the stranger's negligent driving. The defendants were held liable, not for the stranger's negligence, for he was not their employee,[165] but on the ground that the driver himself had been guilty of negligence in the course of his employment in permitting the stranger to drive without even having inquired whether he was competent to do so.[166]

21-030 **Employee usurping the job of another** Equally, the employer may sometimes be liable even though the employee has usurped the job of another, provided that what he does is not too great a departure from the kind of thing he is employed to do. In *Kay v ITW Ltd*,[167] a storekeeper employed by the defendants needed to return a forklift truck to a warehouse but found his way blocked by a large lorry belonging to a third party. Although there was no urgency, and without first inquiring of the driver of the lorry, he attempted to move the lorry himself, and by his negligence in doing so injured the claimant. The Court of Appeal accepted that not every act of an employee done in an attempt to serve the employer's interests, however excessive, gives rise to vicarious liability.[168] Nevertheless, taking into account the fact that it was clearly within the terms of the storekeeper's employment to move certain

---

[159] *Blee v London & North Eastern Railway Co* [1938] A.C. 126; *Paterson v Costain and Press (Overseas) Ltd* [1979] 2 Lloyd's Rep. 204.
[160] Yet the salesman is not in the course of his employment when he books into a hotel for the night.
[161] *Nancollas v Insurance Officer* [1985] 1 All E.R. 833 at 838.
[162] [1989] A.C. 928.
[163] *Houghton v Pilkington* [1912] 3 K.B. 308; *Gwilliam v Twist* [1895] 2 Q.B. 84.
[164] [1963] 1 W.L.R. 991. See also *Ricketts v Thomas Tilling Ltd* [1915] 1 K.B. 644.
[165] *Ilkiw v Samuels* [1963] 1 W.L.R. 991 at 996.
[166] See, however, the different and more complex reasoning of Diplock LJ [1963] 1 W.L.R. 991 at 1003–1006, referred to by Lord Hobhouse in *Lister v Hesley Hall Ltd* [2001] UKHL 22; [2002] 1 A.C. 215 at [58].
[167] [1968] 1 Q.B. 140; *East v Beavis Transport Ltd* [1969] 1 Lloyd's Rep. 302. cf. *Beard v London General Omnibus Co* [1900] 2 Q.B. 530 and see the explanation of that case by Sellers LJ: [1968] 1 Q.B. 140 at 152.
[168] [1968] 1 Q.B. 140 at 151–152.

obstacles out of the way if they blocked the entrance to the warehouse, and since it was part of his normal employment to drive trucks and small vans, the court held that his conduct had not been so gross and extreme as to take it outside the course of his employment.

D. Wilful Wrong of Employee

Acts in protection of the employer's property The employee has an implied **21-031** authority to make reasonable efforts to protect and preserve the property of his employer in an emergency which endangers it. The employer is liable for wrongful acts done within the scope of that authority. A carter, who suspected on mistaken but reasonable grounds that a boy was pilfering sugar from the wagon of the carter's employer, struck the boy on the back of the neck with his hand. The boy fell and a wheel of the wagon went over his foot. The employer was held liable because the blow given by the carter, although excessive, was not sufficiently so to make it outside the scope of employment.[169] However, while an employee's authority to protect his employer's goods against armed robbery extends to acts done in self-defence against the robber it does not extend to using a customer as a human shield.[170] There are also old cases in which it was held that an employee had no implied authority to arrest a person whom he suspected of attempting to steal after the attempt had ceased, on the ground that the arrest was then made not for the protection of the employer's property but for the vindication of justice,[171] though applying the modern close connection test a different conclusion would now probably be reached.

Assaults It has been said that the question of an employer's vicarious liability for **21-032** an assault carried out by an employee "has troubled the courts on numerous occasions and the case law is not entirely consistent".[172] There were several such cases before *Lister* which seemed to proceed broadly on the basis that the employee's act might be in the course of his employment if his intention was, however wrongly, to further his employer's business or assert his employer's authority.[173] By contrast, the assault would not be in the course of his employment if it was a mere act of personal vengeance,[174] or if it occurred in the course of horseplay between employees.[175] Although recent decisions have tested these distinctions to their limits, they seem just about to have survived.

---

169 *Poland v Parr & Sons* [1927] 1 K.B. 236 (but it is likely that nowadays even a grossly excessive reaction would not take the employee outside the course of his employment).

170 *Reilly v Ryan* [1991] 2 I.R. 247.

171 See, e.g., *Abrahams v Deakin* [1891] 1 Q.B. 516; *Hanson v Waller* [1901] 1 Q.B. 390; *Radley v LCC* (1913) 109 L.T. 162.

172 *Mohamud v WM Morrison Supermarkets Plc* [2016] UKSC 11; [2016] A.C. 677 at [2] per Lord Toulson.

173 *Dyer v Munday* [1895] 1 Q.B. 742; *Fennelly v Connex South Eastern* [2001] I.R.L.R. 390.

174 *Warren v Henlys Ltd* [1948] 2 All E.R. 935; *Daniels v Whetstone Entertainments Ltd* [1962] 2 Lloyd's Rep. 1; *Keppel Bus Co Ltd v Sa'ad bin Ahmad* [1974] 1 W.L.R. 1082. While the result in *Warren* was approved in *Mohamud v WM Morrison Supermarkets Plc* [2016] UKSC 11; [2016] A.C. 677 at [45], that in *Keppel* was questioned (at [34]), and were the facts to recur today a different outcome would be likely. In *Mattis v Pollock* [2003] EWCA Civ 787; [2003] 1 W.L.R. 2158, the court left open the question of whether the decision in *Daniels* was correct.

175 *Duffy v Thanet DC* (1984) 134 N.L.J. 680; *Aldred v Naconco* [1987] I.R.L.R. 292. cf. *Harrison v Michelin Tyre Co* [1985] 1 All E.R. 918, doubted in *Aldred v Naconco*.

Where the "use of reasonable force or the existence of friction" is inherent in the nature of the employee's job, the modern test of a close connection between the assault and the employment is more likely to be satisfied.[176] This was the situation in *Mattis v Pollock*,[177] the first case concerning an assault by an employee decided after *Lister*. The facts were that a nightclub bouncer, having been assaulted by disgruntled customers in an incident at the club, went home, got a knife and, about 20 minutes after the incident, stabbed the claimant outside the club. The Court of Appeal held that the stabbing was sufficiently closely connected with the incident for it to fall within the course of his employment by the defendant. In a later case, the Privy Council held that the employers of a security guard at a stadium were vicariously liable when he pursued an unruly fan offsite to teach him a lesson and shot him,[178] and a rugby club was held liable for a punch by a part-time professional player in a melee which persisted after a scrum.[179]

However, even where this element of confrontation or friction is absent two more recent decisions demonstrate that vicarious liability may nevertheless arise in respect of an assault, provided that at the relevant time the employee was purporting to exercise (however misguidedly) the authority conferred on him by the employer. The first of these cases is *Mohamud v WM Morrison Supermarkets Plc*.[180] The claimant asked one of the employees working in the sales kiosk of the defendant's petrol station if it was possible to print some documents that were stored on a USB stick. The employee refused the request in an offensive manner and proceeded to racially abuse the claimant and to ask him to leave. He then followed the claimant back to his car on the station forecourt and, having told him never to come back, subjected him to a serious physical assault. The Supreme Court held that the assault was within the course of the employee's employment. Although the apparent motive for the employee's behaviour was racism, in ordering the claimant to keep away from the petrol station he was "purporting to act about his employer's business"[181] and the capacity in which he purported to act has subsequently been said to explain the decision.[182] The second case is *Bellman v Northampton Recruitment Ltd*,[183] where vicarious liability was imposed for an assault on the claimant employee by the managing director of the defendant company during an impromptu late-night drinking session in a hotel following the company's Christmas party. The drinks were not themselves a work event, but it was regarded as significant that the assault was triggered by a comment of the claimant during a discussion of work matters in which the managing director had sought to assert his authority over the employees present in relation to a management decision he had previously taken.[184] By contrast, the courts have generally refused to impose vicari-

---

[176] See *Graham v Commercial Bodyworks Ltd* [2015] EWCA Civ 47; [2015] I.C.R. 665 at [16] per Longmore LJ.

[177] [2003] EWCA Civ 787; [2003] 1 W.L.R. 2158.

[178] *Brown v Robinson* [2004] UKPC 56.

[179] *Gravil v Carroll* [2008] EWCA Civ 689; [2008] I.C.R. 1222.

[180] [2016] UKSC 11; [2016] A.C. 677.

[181] [2016] UKSC 11; [2016] A.C. 677 at [47] per Lord Toulson. With respect, that claim is questionable. It was directly contrary to his employer's interests, not least because the claimant had done absolutely nothing to justify his being excluded from the premises.

[182] *WM Morrison Supermarkets Plc v Various Claimants* [2020] UKSC 12; [2020] 2 W.L.R. 941 at [28]–[29].

[183] [2018] EWCA Civ 2214; [2019] 1 All E.R. 1133.

[184] "He chose to wear his metaphorical managing director's hat and to deliver a lecture to his

ous liability in cases where one employee has assaulted another without such an assertion of authority[185] or "in jest".[186]

Other wilful wrongs   In *WM Morrison Supermarkets Plc v Various Claim-*   **21-033**
ants,[187] the Supreme Court held that a supermarket chain was not vicariously liable for the conduct of a senior internal auditor who had deliberately uploaded personal information relating to its some three-quarters of entire workforce onto a publicly accessible website, thereby committing the wrongs of misuse of private information, breach of confidence and breach of statutory duty (under the Data Protection Act 1998). Lord Reed, giving the sole judgment, relied upon the distinction drawn by Lord Nicholls in *Dubai Aluminium* between an employee who was "engaged, however misguidedly, in furthering his employer's business" and an employee who was "engaged solely in pursuing his own interests".[188] On the facts it was abundantly clear that the employee had not been engaged in furthering his employer's business when he committed the torts in question. On the contrary, having developed a grudge against his employer he was pursuing a "personal vendetta" and was motivated by the desire to harm the company. It followed that his wrongful conduct in uploading the data onto the internet was not so closely connected with the authorised act of securely transmitting the data to an external auditor that it could fairly and properly be regarded as done by him while acting in the course of his employment.

Police   Actions are frequently brought against chief constables in respect of   **21-034**
intentional torts committed by police officers, such as assault, false imprisonment and malicious prosecution. The statutory formula[189] is that the chief constable is liable for acts done in the performance or purported performance of the officer's functions. In practice the liability of a chief constable for wilful acts by officers in his force is more extensive than the vicarious liability of an employer but it is not without limit.[190] For example, it does not extend to blackmail by an officer using information he has acquired in his work.[191] In cases concerning assaults by police

---

subordinates": [2018] EWCA Civ 2214; [2019] 1 All E.R. 1133 at [25] per Asplin LJ. Irwin LJ emphasised that the facts were most unusual and said (at [40]) that liability would not arise "simply because there is an argument about work matters between colleagues, which leads to an assault, even when one colleague is markedly more senior than another".

[185]   See, e.g., *Vaickuviene v J Sainsbury Plc* 2014 S.C. 147 (no vicarious liability for racist murder of a co-employee during working hours). cf. *Weddall v Barchester Healthcare Ltd* [2012] EWCA Civ 25; [2012] IRLR 307, where different results were reached in two appeals involving assaults on co-workers. See also *Bazley v Curry* [1999] 2 S.C.R. 534 at [42] per McLachlin J ("an incidental or random attack by an employee that merely happens to take place on the employer's premises during working hours will scarcely justify holding the employer liable").

[186]   *Wilson v Exel UK Ltd* 2010 S.L.T. 671; *Graham v Commercial Bodyworks Ltd* [2015] EWCA Civ 47; [2015] I.C.R. 665. See also *Shelbourne v Cancer Research UK* [2019] EWHC 842 (QB); [2019] P.I.Q.R. P16 (though there the main focus was on the fact that the events in question occurred at an office Christmas party, rather than during working hours).

[187]   [2020] UKSC 12; [2020] 2 W.L.R. 941.

[188]   *Dubai Aluminium Co Ltd v Salaam* [2002] UKHL 48; [2003] 2 A.C. 366 at [32].

[189]   See para.21-016.

[190]   *Allen v Chief Constable of Hampshire* [2013] EWCA Civ 967 (facts did not reveal any, let alone a close, connection between the alleged acts and the tortfeasor's position as a police officer).

[191]   *Makanjuola v MPC*, *The Times*, 8 August 1989. See also *N v Chief Constable of Merseyside* [2006] EWHC 3041 (QB); [2006] Po. L.R. 160 (off-duty officer raping intoxicated claimant after volunteering to take her to police station).

officers, the picture that emerges from the post-*Lister* case law is similar to that in the employee context. Hence the chief constable may be liable if, when the assault took place, the police officer was seeking to assert his authority in that capacity, even if he was off duty at the time.[192] But in *Attorney General of the British Virgin Islands v Hartwell*[193] vicarious liability was not imposed where a police constable who had abandoned his post opened fire with his service revolver in a bar where his partner was working, as his action was the result of personal jealousy and had nothing whatsoever to do with his professional role.[194]

E.   Sexual Abuse of Children

21-035   Abuse of children in care   In *WM Morrison Supermarkets Plc v Various Claimants*, Lord Reed said that "a more tailored version of the close connection test" than the general course of employment test has been used in cases concerning the sexual abuse of children,[195] and that in that context the courts have emphasised the importance of factors particularly relevant to this form of wrongdoing, "such as the employer's conferral of authority on the employee over the victims, which he has abused".[196] The leading decision in this category is *Lister v Hesley Hall Ltd*,[197] which was itself a comparatively easy case because the warden who perpetrated the abuse was entrusted with the care of the children and an ability to influence them and take advantage was inherent in this.[198] Similarly, in *Catholic Child Welfare Society v Institute of the Brothers of the Christian Schools*[199] vicarious liability was imposed because the brothers were put in a position where they enjoyed influence over the pupils as teachers and as men of God.[200] Conversely, if the employee who carried out the abuse was, say, a caretaker or gardener resident in a local authority children's home, the result would probably be different: he has not been entrusted with the care of the children, nor given authority over them, and so the close connection between the abuse and his employment is missing.[201]

---

[192]   *Weir v Chief Constable of Merseyside* [2003] EWCA Civ 111; [2003] I.C.R. 708; *Bernard v A-G of Jamaica* [2004] UKPC 47; [2005] I.R.L.R. 398.

[193]   [2004] UKPC 12; [2004] 1 W.L.R. 1273.

[194]   Although in view of their knowledge of the officer's previous behaviour the defendants were held to be in breach of their personal duty.

[195]   [2020] UKSC 12; [2020] 2 W.L.R. 941 at [36].

[196]   [2020] UKSC 12; [2020] 2 W.L.R. 941 at [23].

[197]   [2001] UKHL 22; [2002] 1 A.C. 215.

[198]   See also *Armes v Nottinghamshire CC* [2017] UKSC 60; [2018] A.C. 355 (foster parents). According to Lord Clyde in *Lister*, it will be relatively easy to demonstrate a sufficient connection between the wrongful act and the employment where the employer has been entrusted with the safekeeping or the care of some thing or some person and has delegated that duty to the employee: [2001] UKHL 22; [2002] 1 A.C. 215 at [45].

[199]   [2012] UKSC 56; [2013] 2 A.C. 1. See para.21-012.

[200]   See, to similar effect, the decisions in *Maga v Birmingham Archdiocese* [2010] EWCA Civ 256; [2010] 1 W.L.R. 1441 and *Doe v Bennett* [2004] SCC 17; [2004] 1 S.C.R. 436. In *Jacobi v Griffiths* [1999] 2 S.C.R. 570 the Supreme Court of Canada was divided on the application of its "close and direct connection" test to abuse by a youth club leader, most of which took place at his home.

[201]   See *Lister v Hesley Hall Ltd* [2001] UKHL 22; [2002] 1 A.C. 215 at [82].

F. Fraud of Employee

Fraud must be within the scope of the employee's actual or ostensible author- **21-036**
ity Cases of fraud raise special problems because of the special character of fraud
itself. Of its very nature, fraud involves persuading the victim, by deception, to act
to his own detriment. Thus in *Lloyd v Grace, Smith & Co*,[202] as we have seen, the
defendants' clerk fraudulently persuaded the claimant to transfer her property to
him, and what is significant for the purposes of vicarious liability is that it was the
position in which he had been placed by the defendants that enabled him to do
this.[203] Hence in cases where the claimant has suffered loss in reliance on the deceit
of an agent the general rules concerning vicarious liability are inapplicable, and the
principal is vicariously liable "if, but only if, the deceitful conduct of the agent was
within his or her actual or ostensible authority".[204] This rule applies even where the
agent's fraud was intended to benefit the principal.[205]

Authority conferred only by the fraud of the employee However, there must **21-037**
be some statement or conduct *by the employer* which induces the claimant to believe
that the employee is acting with the employer's authority. It is not enough that the
belief was brought about solely by the employee's misrepresentation of the scope
of his authority, however reasonable that belief may have been. In *Armagas Ltd v
Mundogas SA*[206] M had authority when negotiating the sale of a vessel belonging
to the defendants to agree to a charter of the ship back to them for one year.
However, in return for a bribe from a representative of the purchasers, he agreed
to a three-year charter back, which was not a transaction into which an employee
in his position was entitled to enter. Since the buyers' belief in M's authority rested
solely on his representation that he had the defendants' consent to what was being
done,[207] it was held that they were not vicariously liable to the buyers for his deceit.

4. EMPLOYERS' INDEMNITY

Implied undertaking of indemnity Vicarious liability being a form of joint li- **21-038**
ability, the provisions of the Civil Liability (Contribution) Act 1978[208] may enable
the employer to recover from his employee some or all of the damages he has had
to pay on account of the employee's tort.[209] Additionally, however, the employer
(and, via subrogation, the employer's liability insurer) can in some cases recover

---

202 [1912] A.C. 716, para.21-036.
203 "If the agent commits the fraud purporting to act in the course of business such as he was authorised,
   or held out as authorised, to transact on account of his principal, then the latter may be held liable
   for it": [1912] A.C. 716 at 725 per Earl Loreburn. See also at 738–740.
204 *Hockley Mint Ltd v Ramsden* [2018] EWCA Civ 2480; [2019] 2 All E.R. 1054 at [48].
205 *Hockley Mint* [2018] EWCA Civ 2480; [2019] 2 All E.R. 1054 at [64]–[71].
206 [1986] A.C. 717.
207 Authority was also in issue in *Kooragang Investments Pty Ltd v Richardson & Wrench Ltd* [1982]
   A.C. 462, where an employer was held not to be vicariously liable for the negligence of a valuer who
   had been undertaking valuations on behalf of third parties. He had not been authorised by the defendants to carry out the transactions in question, and nor had they held him out as having such authority.
   The claimant was also unaware that the valuer was in the defendants' employ.
208 See Ch.22.
209 For cases in which a full indemnity was awarded to the employer under the previous legislation, the
   Law Reform (Married Women and Tortfeasors) Act 1935, see *Ryan v Fildes* [1938] 3 All E.R. 517;
   Semtex v Gladstone [1954] 1 W.L.R. 945; *Harvey v O'Dell Ltd* [1958] 2 Q.B. 78.

damages from his employee at common law. In *Lister v Romford Ice and Cold Storage Co*,[210] L was a lorry driver employed by R who by his negligent driving in the course of his employment had caused injury to his father, another employee of R. R paid the father's damages and then sued L. It was held that L's negligent driving was not only a tort against his father but also a breach of an implied undertaking in his contract of employment that he would exercise reasonable care, for which R were entitled to damages equivalent to the amount which they had had to pay to the father.

21-039 **Indemnity limited in practice** The decision in *Lister v Romford* was controversial and the matter was considered by an interdepartmental committee,[211] with the result that employers' liability insurers entered into a "gentleman's agreement" not to take advantage of the principle unless there was evidence of collusion or wilful misconduct. Nevertheless, the legal position remains as stated in *Lister*, and the right is sometimes exercised. In *Morris v Ford Motor Co Ltd*,[212] for example, a third party which was itself bound to indemnify the employer sought unsuccessfully to rely on the right, while in *Bell v Alliance Medical Ltd*[213] a radiographer was required to indemnify her employer for their vicarious liability arising out of her negligent cannulation of a patient undergoing an MRI scan. Although the court in the latter case accepted that some of the considerations that underpinned the rule in *Lister* might be seen as outmoded and outdated, it was still the law.

21-040 **Indemnity limited in principle** There is an important limit to the right of indemnity recognised in *Lister*. The decision in that case constitutes, in effect, an exception to the common law rule of *Merryweather v Nixan*[214] that there can be no contribution between joint tortfeasors, for that rule was held not to apply in the case of claimants whose liability "arose solely from the fact that they were answerable for the negligence of the defendant himself".[215] It follows that if the employer has himself, or through some other employee, been guilty of culpable fault, then the *Lister* principle does not apply and the employer can recover only, if at all, under the 1978 Act.[216]

5. LIABILITY FOR INDEPENDENT CONTRACTORS

A. General Rule

21-041 **Employer not liable for the torts of his independent contractor**[217] In general an employer is not responsible for the torts of his independent contractor. It is no exception to say that he is liable for torts authorised or ratified by him or where the contractor is employed to do an illegal act, for here they are both liable as joint

---

[210] [1957] A.C. 555.
[211] See Gardiner (1959) 22 M.L.R. 652.
[212] [1973] Q.B. 792.
[213] [2015] CSOH 34; 2015 S.C.L.R. 676.
[214] (1799) 8 Term R. 186; 101 E.R. 1337, see para.22-007.
[215] *Lister v Romford Ice and Cold Storage Co* [1956] 2 Q.B. 180 at 210 per Romer LJ. This aspect of the problem was not considered by the House of Lords.
[216] *Jones v Manchester Corp* [1952] 2 Q.B. 852.
[217] On liability for the torts of independent contractors, see generally Morgan (2015) 74 C.L.J. 109.

tortfeasors.[218] Nor is the fact that an employer can incur liability for his own negligence, for example, in not taking reasonable care when selecting a contractor or checking the work he has done, a departure from this principle because here he is not being made responsible for the tort of the contractor but for the breach of his own duty of care.[219] Nor is it an exception that an employer is liable if he personally interferes with the contractor or his employees and directs the manner in which the work is to be done, for he is then again liable as a joint tortfeasor.[220]

B.   Non-delegable Duty

In some cases the employer is responsible for damage caused by his contractor's fault even though there is no authorisation or misconduct on the employer's part.[221] The conventional analysis is that in these cases the employer is liable not vicariously but because he was in breach of a "non-delegable" duty which he himself owed to the claimant.[222] Strictly speaking no duty in tort is delegable, but this nomenclature signifies that D's duty is not merely to take care himself, but either "to provide that care is taken"[223] or to achieve some actual result, in which case D's duty is not discharged unless care is taken or the result achieved. In such a case it is beside the point that D delegated the task to an independent contractor and the failure to discharge D's duty is attributable to his default. This was put with clarity by Lord Blackburn in *Hughes v Percival*[224]:

21-042

> "The law cast upon the defendant, when exercising this right, a duty towards the plaintiff. I do not think that duty went so far as to require him absolutely to provide that no damage should come to the plaintiff's wall from the use he thus made of it, but I think that the duty went as far as to require him to see that reasonable skill and care were exercised in those operations which involved a use of the party-wall, exposing it to this risk. If such a duty was cast upon the defendant he could not get rid of responsibility by delegating the performance of it to a third person. He was at liberty to employ such a third person to fulfil the duty which the law cast on himself, and, if they so agreed together, to take an indemnity to himself in case mischief came from that person not fulfilling the duty which

---

218 See, e.g., *Ellis v Sheffield Gas Consumers Co* (1853) 2 El. & Bl. 767; 118 E.R. 955, where the defendants, without authority, employed a contractor to dig a trench in the street for gas pipes. The contractor's employees carelessly left a heap of stones on the footpath and the claimant fell over them and was injured. The contract was to do an illegal act, a public nuisance, and so the defendants were liable.

219 For the scope of this in the context of occupiers' liability, see para.10-019

220 *M'Laughlin v Pryor* (1842) 4 Man. & G. 48; 134 E.R. 21; *Hardaker v Idle DC* [1896] 1 Q.B. 335. In *Brooke v Bool* [1928] 2 K.B. 578 the defendant was held liable on the basis of participation in a joint enterprise. It is respectfully submitted that *Scarsbrook v Mason* [1961] 3 All E.R. 767 takes this much too far: and it was doubted in *S v Walsall MBC* [1985] 1 W.L.R. 1150.

221 See the chapters by Murphy and Stevens in Neyers et al (eds), *Emerging Issues in Tort Law* (2007).

222 In *Armes v Nottinghamshire CC* [2017] UKSC 60; [2018] A.C. 355 at [50], Lord Reed described vicarious liability and non-delegable duty as "two distinct legal doctrines with different incidents and different rationales".

223 *The Pass of Ballater* [1942] P. 112 at 117 per Langton J. See also *The Lady Gwendolen* [1965] P. 294, where Winn LJ (at 350) described the duty owed by a shipowner to other ships and to persons who might be affected by the navigation of his own ships as a duty, "that all concerned in any capacity with the navigation of those ships should exercise such care as a reasonable person would exercise in that capacity".

224 (1883) 8 App. Cas. 443 at 446. See also *Armes v Nottinghamshire CC* [2017] UKSC 60; [2018] A.C. 355 at [31].

the law cast upon the defendant; but the defendant still remained subject to that duty, and liable for the consequences if it was not fulfilled."

C. Categories of Non-delegable Duties

21-043 Two broad categories? Whether a given duty is "non-delegable" is a question of law. Such a duty may be imposed by statute;[225] whether it is depends on the proper interpretation of the relevant legislation.[226] As for common law duties, the categories of instances where these are non-delegable do not appear to be closed, but not a great deal by way of principle appears from the cases. Indeed, in *Woodland v Essex CC* it was said by Lord Sumption that English law "does not have a single theory to explain when or why" non-delegable duties exist.[227] However, he suggested that nonetheless the cases could be divided into two broad categories.[228] The first is an anomalous class of cases in which the defendant employs an independent contractor to perform some function which is either inherently hazardous or likely to become so.[229] The second, and far more important category, is said to comprise cases where the law imposes a duty with three critical characteristics: first, the duty arises because of an antecedent relationship between the parties; second, the duty is a positive or affirmative duty to protect a particular class of persons against a particular class of risks (and not simply a duty to refrain from acting in a way that foreseeably causes injury); and third, the duty is by virtue of that relationship personal to the defendant.[230] It seems clear that Lord Sumption did not intend to suggest that every instance of a non-delegable duty could be said to fall within one or other broad category,[231] but after a brief consideration of the first we shall consider the extent to which the types of case in which such duties have arisen might be explained by the characteristics identified by Lord Sumption in the second.

21-044 Hazardous functions The Court of Appeal in *Honeywill and Stein Ltd v Larkin Bros Ltd*[232] stated a principle whereby there is a class of "extra hazardous acts, that is, acts which in their very nature, involve in the eyes of the law special danger to others", where an employer cannot escape liability by delegating the performance of the act to an independent contractor.[233] The claimants, who procured the defendants as independent contractors to take photographs of X's cinema by flashlight, were liable for the defendants' negligence in setting fire to the cinema. However, while some activities plainly present more hazard than others, it is extremely difficult, if not impossible, to attempt a classification based on inherent risk without

---

[225] "Where a special duty is laid by statute on an individual or class of individuals either to take care or even to ensure safety (an absolute duty in the true sense) ... they cannot in any way escape from or evade the full implication of and responsibility for that duty": *The Pass of Ballater* [1942] P. 112 at 117, referring to *Smith v Cammell Laird & Co Ltd* [1940] A.C. 242; *Donaghey v Boulton and Paul Ltd* [1968] A.C. 1.

[226] See, e.g., *Rivers v Cutting* [1982] 1 W.L.R. 1146; *S v Walsall MBC* [1985] 1 W.L.R. 1150.

[227] *Woodland v Essex CC* [2013] UKSC 66; [2014] A.C. 537.

[228] Lord Clarke, Lord Wilson and Lord Toulson agreed with the judgment of Lord Sumption. Lady Hale gave a judgment in similar terms with which Lord Clarke, Lord Wilson and Lord Toulson also agreed.

[229] See para.21-044.

[230] [2013] UKSC 66; [2014] A.C. 537 at [7].

[231] He subsequently referred to another "anomalous" category of "highway" cases: see para.21-050.

[232] [1934] 1 K.B. 191.

[233] [1934] 1 K.B. 191 at 197.

at the same time taking account of the necessary precautions, which will minimise that risk. The principle stated in *Honeywill and Stein* has therefore been described by the Court of Appeal as anomalous and unsatisfactory and its application should be kept as narrow was possible.[234] It is now confined to "activities that are exceptionally dangerous whatever precautions are taken".[235] Whether any legitimate activity meets that description is questionable[236] and there is much to be said for the view that the rule in *Honeywill and Stein* has been "distinguished out of existence".[237] Nor was any attempt made to revive it in *Woodland v Essex CC*, where on the contrary Lord Sumption was distinctly unenthusiastic about it.[238]

"Assumption of responsibility" The most obvious instance of an antecedent **21-045** relationship of the type referred to by Lord Sumption in *Woodland v Essex CC* as part of his second category of cases where a duty may be non-delegable is a contractual one: "the contracting party will normally be taken to contract that the work will be done carefully by whomever he may get to do it."[239] Cases in tort which exhibit the characteristics required of this second category are those in which the defendant assumes a liability analogous to that assumed by a person who contracts to do work carefully, i.e., "the defendant can be taken not just to have assumed a positive duty, but to have assumed responsibility for the exercise of due care by anyone to whom he may delegate its performance".[240] The examples given by Lord Sumption of the public services provided in hospitals and schools are considered below.[241] However, these do not exhaust the limits of the category and, before we turn to them, it is convenient to consider another well-established example of a non-delegable duty based on a prior assumption of responsibility, namely that of a bailee to ensure that proper care is exercised in the custody of the goods bailed.

Bailment In *Morris v CW Martin & Sons Ltd*,[242] the claimant had sent her fur coat **21-046** to X to be cleaned, and X, with her permission, sent it on to the defendants, who were specialist cleaners. The defendants handed the coat to their employee, M, for him to clean it, and M stole the coat. The Court of Appeal held the defendants liable. Reliance was placed on the duty owed to the claimant by the defendants themselves as bailees of the coat, so that, in effect, the theft of the coat by the employee, to whom they had delegated their own duty of reasonable care in respect of it, constituted a breach of that non-delegable duty. On this analysis, an essential element of the defendants' liability was that they had been entrusted with the coat and had in turn entrusted it to their employee. Had this not been the case it could not have been said that they had delegated to him their own duty as bailees.

---

[234] *Biffa Waste Services Ltd v Maschinenfabrik Ernst Hese GMBH* [2008] EWCA Civ 1238; [2009] Q.B. 725. *Honeywill*'s case was said not to be part of Australian law in *Stevens v Brodribb Sawmilling Co Pty Ltd* (1986) 160 C.L.R. 16.

[235] [2008] EWCA Civ 1238; [2009] Q.B. 725 at [78]; applied in *Willmott Dixon Construction Ltd v Robert West Consulting Ltd* [2016] EWHC 3291 (TCC); [2017] P.N.L.R. 17.

[236] Demolition works were held not to meet this test in *Ng Huat Seng v Mohammad* [2017] SGCA 58.

[237] Stanton (2009) 17 Tort L. Rev. 9 at 12.

[238] [2013] UKSC 66; [2014] A.C. 537 at [6].

[239] *Woodland* [2013] UKSC 66; [2014] A.C. 537 at [7].

[240] *Woodland* [2013] UKSC 66; [2014] A.C. 537 at [11].

[241] See para.21-047.

[242] [1966] 1 Q.B. 716. See also *Mendelssohn v Normand Ltd* [1970] 1 Q.B. 177; *Port Swettenham Authority v TW Wu & Co* [1979] A.C. 580.

21-047 **Protection of the "vulnerable": employees, patients and pupils** The issue before the Supreme Court in *Woodland v Essex CC* was whether the duty of care owed by a local education authority to a school pupil was non-delegable in circumstances where the pupil suffered injury in a swimming lesson as a result of the alleged negligence of the swimming teacher and lifeguard provided by an independent contractor. Lord Sumption identified a sub-category of cases in which the personal nature of the duty imposed on the defendant is rooted in the vulnerability of the claimant and an antecedent relationship under which the defendant has a "degree of protective custody" over him. The principal example of this category is employment and it has long been established that the employer's common law duties in respect of his employee's safety, as laid down in *Wilsons and Clyde Coal Co v English*,[243] are "non-delegable".[244] In *Woodland v Essex CC* Lord Sumption held that the time had come to recognise that the relationships between hospitals and their patients,[245] and between schools or local education authorities and their pupils, fall into the same category,[246] even in the absence of a contract.[247] He also suggested that a prisoner would likely be owed non-delegable duties on the same footing,[248] and indeed it was subsequently held that the Home Office owed such a duty to a detainee in an immigration removal centre in respect of the medical care provided to her there.[249]

21-048 **Protection of the "vulnerable": limits** It is characteristic of the cases in this sub-category that there is a prior relationship between the claimant and the defendant distinguished by the vulnerability of the former and the control of the latter. Where these criteria of vulnerability and control are absent, a non-delegable duty is unlikely to arise.[250] Furthermore, even where such a relationship is present, it must be shown that the negligence of the contractor occurred in the course of the very functions which the defendant assumed an obligation to perform and then delegated to the contractor,[251] a requirement which was met in *Woodland* because swimming

---

[243] [1938] A.C. 57.

[244] This is dealt with in Ch.9.

[245] He thus approved of the approach of Lord Greene MR in *Gold v Essex CC* [1942] K.B. 293, of Denning LJ in *Cassidy v Ministry of Health* [1951] 2 K.B. 343, and of Lord Browne-Wilkinson in *X (Minors) v Bedfordshire CC* [1995] 2 A.C. 633.

[246] See the approach of the majority in *New South Wales v Lepore* (2003) 212 C.L.R. 511.

[247] One obvious argument in favour of this development is that it removes the distinction between private schools and hospitals, where the duty of care is non-delegable because provided under a contract, and state schools and hospitals: see the example given by Lady Hale in *Woodland* [2013] UKSC 66; [2014] A.C. 537 at [30]. cf. Morgan (2015) 74 C.L.J. 109 at 111–118.

[248] *Woodland* [2013] UKSC 66; [2014] A.C. 537 at [23].

[249] *GB v Home Office* [2015] EWHC 819 (QB). cf. *Razumas v Ministry of Justice* [2018] EWHC 215 (QB); [2018] P.I.Q.R. P10, where Cockerill J accepted that the defendant owed prisoners a non-delegable duty of care, but suggested that this was limited to matters arising out of custody, such as the provision of a safe environment, and (probably) access to healthcare. The defendant owed no such duty in respect of healthcare provision, because under the relevant statutory regime this was the responsibility of the NHS. *GB v Home Office* was distinguished on the ground that the legislative background was entirely different in that case.

[250] See, e.g., the pre-*Woodland* case of *Harrison v Jagged Globe (Alpine) Ltd* [2012] EWCA Civ 835, where it was held that a travel firm did not owe a non-delegable duty to its customers in relation to the local guides it employed as contractors on an overseas expedition. See also *Farraj v King's Healthcare NHS Trust* [2009] EWCA Civ 1203; [2010] 1 W.L.R. 2139 (claim against a hospital which had employed an independent laboratory to analyse a tissue sample for a patient who was not in the custody or care of the hospital).

[251] See *Woodland* [2013] UKSC 66; [2014] A.C. 537 at [26].

lessons were an "integral part of the school's teaching function". By contrast, Lord Sumption said, a non-delegable duty would not arise where the defendant's duty "was not to perform the relevant function but only to arrange for its performance",[252] so that, for example, a school or education authority would not be liable for "the defaults of independent contractors providing extra-curricular activities outside school hours, such as school trips in the holidays".[253] This difficult distinction is of critical importance when considering whether a non-delegable duty arises in this type of case. In *A v Ministry of Defence*,[254] for example (a decision approved by Lord Sumption), the defendant was held not liable for the negligence of a hospital in Germany with whom it contracted to treat soldiers and their families. Although the treatment may have been arranged by the defendant it had not assumed responsibility to provide it.[255] Similarly, in *Armes v Nottinghamshire CC*,[256] the Supreme Court unanimously held that a local authority was not under a non-delegable duty to ensure that reasonable care was taken for the safety of a child abused by foster parents whom the authority had entrusted with her care.[257] Again, this was because the authority had arranged for the day-to-day care of the claimant by the foster parents, rather than itself assuming responsibility for providing it.[258]

Neighbouring landowners Liability for the default of an independent contrac- **21-049**
tor may be imposed in the rule in *Rylands v Fletcher*,[259] in some cases of damage by fire,[260] and in some cases of nuisance.[261] These instances are explained by Lord Sumption in *Woodland v Essex CC*[262] on the basis of the antecedent relationship between neighbouring landowners, though with respect that explanation is not particularly convincing, since in none of these forms of liability is such a relation-

---

[252] [2013] UKSC 66; [2014] A.C. 537 at [25].
[253] [2013] UKSC 66; [2014] A.C. 537 at [25]; though query whether such trips, whether in "school hours" or not, fulfil the duty to promote a pupil's "personal development". cf. *XVW v Gravesend Grammar School for Girls* [2012] EWHC 575; [2012] E.L.R. 417, decided before the decision of the Supreme Court in *Woodland*.
[254] [2004] EWCA Civ 641; [2005] Q.B. 183.
[255] The position was a fortiori where a prison was not responsible even for arranging prisoners' healthcare provision: *Razumas v Ministry of Justice* [2018] EWHC 215 (QB); [2018] P.I.Q.R. P10. For a similar analysis to that in *A v Ministry of Defence* in an education context, see *Myton v Woods* (1980) 79 L.G.R. 28 (school not liable for negligence of taxi firm as it had no statutory duty to transport children to and from school, but only to arrange and pay for it).
[256] [2017] UKSC 60; [2018] A.C. 355.
[257] Although a majority held that the authority was vicariously liable for the abuse perpetrated by the foster parents: see para.21-015.
[258] The Court of Appeal in *Armes* ([2015] EWCA Civ 1139; [2016] Q.B. 739) had interpreted Lord Sumption's reference in *Woodland* to it being "fair, just and reasonable" to impose a non-delegable duty in cases in his second category ([2013] UKSC 66; [2014] A.C. 537 at [25]) as meaning that even where the criteria for inclusion in that category were met, a court could nevertheless hold that no such duty should be imposed for policy reasons. However, in the Supreme Court Lord Reed said that "a separate inquiry into what is fair, just and reasonable" was "unnecessarily duplicative" and "apt to give rise to uncertainty and inconsistency" ([2017] UKSC 60; [2018] A.C. 355 at [36]).
[259] See Ch.16. In *Burnie Port Authority v General Jones* (1994) 179 C.L.R. 520 the High Court of Australia declared that the rule in *Rylands v Fletcher* no longer formed part of the law of Australia, but that in situations falling within the scope of the rule a defendant would be liable for the default of a contractor.
[260] *Black v Christchurch Finance Co* [1894] A.C. 48; *Spicer v Smee* [1946] 1 All E.R. 489; *Balfour v Barty-King* [1957] 1 Q.B. 496.
[261] See para.15-049.
[262] [2013] UKSC 66; [2014] A.C. 537 at [9].

ship even required.[263] A similar instance of a non-delegable duty is observable in the case of withdrawal of support from neighbouring land. If work done on A's land causes subsidence on B's adjoining land and B's land is entitled to the support of A's, then A is liable to B, even if the work in question had been entrusted by A to an independent contractor.[264]

21-050 **Operations on the highway** A non-delegable duty is owed in respect of operations undertaken on the highway. An early example of this type of case is *Gray v Pullen*,[265] where the defendant owned a house adjoining a highway and had statutory authority to cut a trench across the road to make a drain from his premises to a sewer. The contractor he employed to carry out the work filled in the trench improperly and as a result a passenger on the highway suffered injury. The defendant was held liable even though he was not at fault. This result is perhaps explicable on the ground that the work done was of a character which would have been a nuisance unless authorised by statute, but the category is not so limited.[266] In *Tarry v Ashton*,[267] for example, the defendant employed an independent contractor to repair a lamp attached to his house which overhung the pavement. As it was not securely fastened the lamp fell on the claimant, a passer-by, and the defendant was held liable, because it was his duty to make the lamp reasonably safe.[268] But the category does not extend to the defendant's normal use of the highway for the purposes of passage,[269] and nor does it encompass work done *near* the highway as opposed to *on* it. In *Salsbury v Woodland*[270] the defendant had employed an apparently competent contractor to fell a tree in his front garden. Done competently this would have involved no risk to anyone but, owing to the negligence of the contractor, the tree fouled some telephone wires, causing them to fall into the highway, as a result of which the claimant was injured. The Court of Appeal declined to extend the category to this scenario and the defendant was held not liable. Lord Sumption adverted to the "highway cases" in *Woodland v Essex CC*, where he observed that, like the "hazard cases", they could be "put to one side",[271] suggesting that they are a further category in their own right.

---

[263] See, e.g., para.15-049 (nuisance not so limited).
[264] *Bower v Peate* (1876) 1 Q.B.D. 321; *Dalton v Angus* (1881) 6 App. Cas. 740; *Hughes v Percival* (1883) 8 App. Cas. 443.
[265] (1864) 5 B. & S. 970; 122 E.R. 1091. See also *Hole v Sittingbourne & Sheerness Railway* (1861) 6 Hurl. & N. 488; 158 E.R. 201 (bridge obstructing navigation); *Pickard v Smith* (1861) 10 C.B. (N.S.) 314; 142 E.R. 535 (cellar flap on railway platform left open); *Hardaker v Idle DC* [1896] 1 Q.B. 335 (gas main broken by failure to pack soil round it while constructing a sewer); *Holliday v National Telephone Co* [1899] 2 Q.B. 392 (explosion in highway caused by dipping benzoline lamp in molten solder); *Penny v Wimbledon UDC* [1899] 2 Q.B. 72 (heap of soil left unlighted in road); *Daniel v Rickett* [1938] 2 K.B. 322 (cellar flap left open on pavement); *Walsh v Holst Co Ltd* [1958] 1 W.L.R. 800 (building operations adjoining highway).
[266] Note that by statute a highway authority is potentially liable for the negligence of contractors to which it delegates highway maintenance functions: see para.15-085.
[267] (1876) 1 Q.B.D. 314.
[268] (1876) 1 Q.B.D. 314 at 319.
[269] See, e.g., *Stennett v Hancock* [1939] 2 All E.R. 578 (accident caused by defendant's defective vehicle).
[270] [1970] 1 Q.B. 324.
[271] [2013] UKSC 66; [2014] A.C. 537 at [23].

D. Collateral Negligence of Independent Contractor

Where the duty owed by an employer is non-delegable, he is not liable for the **21-051** collateral negligence of an independent contractor, that is, negligence in some collateral respect, as distinct from negligence with regard to the very matter delegated to be done.[272] The distinction between the two kinds of negligence is sometimes difficult to draw[273] but is established by the cases. To take a simple case, if D employs a contractor on a construction project D would not be liable for the negligent driving of the contractor while going to get supplies.[274] More difficult is a case like *Padbury v Holliday and Greenwood Ltd*[275] where the defendants employed a subcontractor to put metallic casements into the windows of a house which the defendants were building. While one of these casements was being put in, an iron tool was placed by an employee of the sub-contractor on the window sill, and the casement having been blown in by the wind, the tool fell and injured the claimant in the street below. It was held that the claimant's injuries were caused by an act of collateral negligence and the defendants were not liable. By contrast, in *Holliday v National Telephone Co*[276] the defendants were laying telephone wires under a street and employed an independent contractor to make certain connections. A plumber employed by the contractor dipped a blowlamp into molten solder causing an explosion which injured the claimant. Willes J treated this as an act of collateral negligence, but the Court of Appeal reversed his decision and held the defendants were liable. The cases are difficult to distinguish save for the Delphic statement in the brief report of *Padbury* that "the tool was not placed on the window sill in the ordinary course of doing the work which the sub-contractor was employed to do". Otherwise, they both involved dangers to users of the highway and incidents in the performance of work rather than any deficiency in the finished work.

---

[272] *Pickard v Smith* (1861) 10 C.B. (N.S.) 470 at 480; 142 E.R. 535 at 539. See also *Dalton v Angus* (1881) 6 App. Cas. 740 at 829; *Cassidy v Ministry of Health* [1951] 2 K.B. 343 at 363–364.

[273] See the criticism of Sachs LJ in *Salsbury v Woodland* [1970] 1 Q.B. 324 at 348.

[274] In *Harrison v Jagged Globe (Alpine) Ltd* [2012] EWCA Civ 835 the defendant tour operator was not liable for the conduct of expedition guides in allowing a climbing stunt to go ahead which was not part of the itinerary.

[275] (1912) 28 T.L.R. 494.

[276] [1899] 2 Q.B. 392. cf. *Reedie v London & North Western Railway* (1849) 4 Ex. 244 (railway company employed contractor to build a bridge; contractor's workman negligently caused the death of a person, passing beneath along the highway, by allowing a stone to drop on him; railway company held not liable). "I am not liable if my contractor in making a bridge happens to drop a brick ... but I am liable if he makes a bridge which will not open ... The liability of the employer depends on the existence of a duty ... it only extends to the limit of that duty. I owe a duty with regard to the structure of the bridge; I owe a duty to see that my bridge will open; but I owe no duty with regard to the disposition of bricks and hammers in the course of construction": Chapman (1934) 50 L.Q.R. 71 at 80–81. That accords with the result of *Padbury* but not of *Holliday*.

CHAPTER 22

JOINT AND SEVERAL TORTFEASORS

1. MULTIPLE TORTFEASORS, CAUSATION AND PROOF

The concept of joint and several liability Where two or more people by their **22-001** independent tortious conduct cause the claimant to suffer distinct injuries, no special rules are required, for each tortfeasor is liable for the damage which he caused and only for that damage.[1] Where, however, two or more instances of tortious conduct by different persons cause the claimant to suffer a *single, indivisible* injury the position is more complicated. The law in such a case is that the claimant is entitled to sue all or any of them for the full amount of his loss,[2] and each is said to be "jointly and severally" liable for it.[3] If the claimant sues defendant A but not B, it is open to A to seek contribution or an indemnity from B in respect of his share of the responsibility for the claimant's damage but this is a matter between A and B and does not affect the claimant. The result is that in cases involving single, indivisible injuries the defendants rather than the claimant carry the risk that one of the defendants is judgment proof. However, it also means that special rules are necessary to deal with the possibilities of successive actions in respect of the same loss and of claims for contribution or indemnity by one tortfeasor against another.

No proportionate liability for single, indivisible injury If the claimant can show **22-002** that he has suffered a single, indivisible harm at the hands of several defendants he thereby avoids the risk, inherent in cases where there are separate injuries, of finding that one defendant is insolvent (or uninsured) and being unable to execute judgment against him. Even where all of the wrongdoers are solvent, a system which

---

[1] See *Performance Cars Ltd v Abraham* [1962] 1 Q.B. 33; *Baker v Willoughby* [1970] A.C. 467, para.7-031.

[2] Though he cannot execute judgment so as to recover more than his loss: see para.22-012.

[3] This is the general position in common law and civilian legal systems: see Rogers (ed), *Unification of Tort Law: Multiple Tortfeasors* (2004). For a broader comparative overview of divisibility issues see Oliphant (ed), *Aggregation and Divisibility of Damage* (2009).

enabled the claimant to sue each one only for a proportionate part of the damage would require him to launch multiple sets of proceedings. As the law now stands, the claimant may simply launch proceedings against the "easiest target".[4] The same picture is not, of course, so attractive from the point of view of the solvent defendant, who may end up carrying full responsibility for a loss in the causing of which he played only a partial, even secondary role. Thus, for example, a solicitor may be liable in full for failing to point out to his client that there was reason to believe that a valuation on which the client proposed to lend was suspect, the valuer being insolvent.[5] Professional bodies have argued that in the professional negligence context the rule of joint and several liability should be replaced with a regime of "proportionate liability" whereby, as against the claimant, and not merely among defendants as a group, each defendant would bear only his share of the responsibility for the damage.[6] While it has not been suggested in the United Kingdom that such a change should be extended to personal injury claims,[7] this has occurred in some American jurisdictions, whether by statute or by judicial decision,[8] while many Australian jurisdictions have moved to a proportionate liability regime in property damage and economic loss cases.[9] However, in 1996 the Law Commission concluded that the present law was preferable to the various forms of proportionate liability.[10]

22-003 **Scope of joint and several liability** The question of the scope of joint and several liability is a difficult one and there appears to have been some narrowing of the approach in the recent case law, so that although from a medical point of view there is only one injury, there may be a greater willingness to hold that the causative contribution of each defendant can be identified and his liability confined accordingly. The simplest case of joint and several liability is that of two simultaneous acts of negligence, as where two drivers negligently collide, injuring a passenger in one of the cars or a pedestrian, but there is no requirement that the acts be simultaneous. Thus, if D1 is driving too fast in icy conditions with the result that his lorry "jack-knifes" across the motorway and D2, also driving too fast, later comes along and, trying to avoid the obstruction, runs down C who is assisting at the scene, both D1 and D2 may be jointly and severally liable for C's injuries.[11] Where the acts of the two defendants are separated by a substantial period of time,

---

4   Consider for example the outcome of the Selby rail accident. A driver fell asleep on the M62, veered off the road and caused a rail crash. The driver brought (unsuccessful) contribution proceedings alleging defective design of the motorway bridge. Under the present system the victims' claim was for a simple case of driving negligence. If they had been required to sue the designers of the bridge their case would have been much more complicated: *Great North Eastern Railway Ltd v Hart* [2003] EWHC 2450 (QB). See also *Roe v Sheffield City Council* [2004] EWCA Civ 329 at [34].

5   See *Mortgage Express Ltd v Bowerman* [1996] 2 All E.R. 836.

6   See generally, Gilead, Green and Koch (eds), *Proportional Liability: Analytical and Comparative Perspectives* (2013); Barker and Steele (2015) 74 C.L.J. 49.

7   For an apparent exception, see the discussion of *Barker v Corus (UK) Ltd* [2006] UKHL 20; [2006] 2 A.C. 572, para.7-040.

8   See Green in Rogers (ed), *Unification of Tort Law: Multiple Tortfeasors* (2004).

9   See, e.g., Civil Liability Act 2002 (NSW) Pt IV; Wrongs Act 1958 (Vic) Pt IVAA. For discussion, see McDonald in Barker and Grantham (eds), *Apportionment in Private Law* (2019).

10 Law Commission, *Feasibility Investigation of Joint and Several Liability* (1996). There was said to be a case in logic for proportionate liability in the case where C is at fault as well as D1 and D2 (see, e.g., *Fitzgerald v Lane* [1989] A.C. 328).

11 Based on *Rouse v Squires* [1973] Q.B. 889, where an issue arose as to legal causation in respect of D1's negligence.

they may yet contribute to one, indivisible injury for this purpose, as where D1 manufactures a dangerous product and D2 uses it without due care years later. In all these cases there is no basis for dividing up the causative origin of the claimant's injury between the defendants. If, for example, C is killed in an accident that was caused by D1 and D2's negligence, one cannot coherently say that C was half killed by D1 and half killed by D2—he was killed by the effect of the conduct of both of them.

Liability for divisible injury   An injury is "divisible" where it is possible to at-   **22-004**
tribute different parts of the injury to different causes, for example because its severity varies according to the extent of the claimant's exposure to a toxic agent. In cases
of this kind a different approach is adopted. In *Holtby v Brigham & Cowan (Hull)
Ltd*[12] the claimant had been exposed to asbestos during employment with several
employers and each of these exposures probably made some contribution to the
asbestosis which he developed, but only one employer was sued. Because asbestosis
is a divisible condition, the severity of which is determined by the amount of the
asbestos exposure, it was held that if the claimant showed that the defendant had
made a material contribution to the disease, then the defendant was liable not for
the whole of the loss, but only to the extent that he had contributed to the condition.
On the facts the correct approach was to attribute responsibility in proportion to the
amount of time the claimant had been exposed while in the defendant's
employment. Such cases are distinguishable from the example of two motorists who
collide and injure a passenger because progressive conditions like asbestosis or
hearing loss get worse the more exposure there is.

The logic of this approach is not limited to cases of "sequential" exposure such
as *Holtby*. In the leading case of *Bonnington Castings Ltd v Wardlaw*[13] the claimant suffered a dose-related injury from exposure to silica dust in the defendants'
works. One source of dust was swing grinders and the defendants were in breach
of duty with regard to those (the "guilty dust") but the other source was pneumatic
hammers and, since there was no possible method of eliminating dust from those,
that dust (the "innocent dust") was not the result of the defendants' breach of duty.
Even though the defendants were only to blame for exposing the claimant to some
of the dust, they were held liable for the entirety of the damage,[14] but in *Holtby*
Stuart-Smith LJ noted that it was never argued in *Bonnington Castings* that the
defendants were liable only to the extent of their contribution, and were the facts
of that case to occur again today it seems highly likely that their liability would be
so limited.

As we have seen, the House of Lords in *Fairchild v Glenhaven Funeral Services*

---

12   [2000] 3 All E.R. 421; *Thompson v Smiths Shiprepairers (North Shields) Ltd* [1984] Q.B. 405; *Allen v British Rail Engineering Ltd* [2001] EWCA Civ 242; [2001] I.C.R. 942; *Horsley v Cascade Insulation Services Ltd* [2009] EWHC 2945 (QB). In *Brookes v South Yorkshire Passenger Executive* [2005] EWCA Civ 452 the claimant was exposed by the defendant to conditions causative of vibration white finger from 1982 but the defendant was only at fault in relation to this risk from 1987. The Court of Appeal declined to reduce the damages because although all exposure made some contribution to the final result, the claimant had a low susceptibility and would probably never have developed symptoms had the defendant taken proper steps in 1987. The objective of an award of damages is not to compensate the claimant for the amount of the damage suffered but for the effects of the damage on him: at [26].
13   [1956] A.C. 613.
14   *Bonnington Castings Ltd v Wardlaw* [1956] A.C. 613 at 622.

Ltd[15] was faced with a situation where an indivisible disease (mesothelioma) might have been caused by the inhalation of asbestos fibres emitted by any one of several employers and held that each employer was liable for having materially increased the risk of the claimant contracting the disease. In *Fairchild* it was not disputed that if there were liability each employer was liable in full. However, it was later held that even though the injury was indivisible, justice required that each defendant's liability be proportionate to the extent of the exposure for which he was responsible, an approach which in turn was reversed by statute in the mesothelioma context.[16] In cases outside the *Fairchild* enclave the courts have in any case not cast doubt on the general principle of joint and several liability and the concomitant rule that each defendant is liable in full for an indivisible injury. It has been said in the Court of Appeal that the *Holtby* principle is[17]:

> "[A]n exception to the general rule intended to do justice in a particular class of case. Although at the fringes the delineation of the class of case may be debateable, in the main it has been applied and in this court at least should be limited to, industrial disease or injury cases where there has been successive exposure to harm by a number of agencies, where the effect of the harm is divisible, and where it would be unjust for an individual defendant to bear the whole of a loss when in commonsense he was not responsible for all of it."

Since the question of whether something made a causative contribution to an injury and to what extent is a question of fact and since it is not necessary that there should be precise mathematical evidence before a result may be apportioned between two causes, the courts may go quite a long way in reducing the claimant's recovery by being more willing to find that an injury is divisible.[18] The burden of proof rests on the claimant to show that the defendant was responsible for the whole or a quantifiable part of his injury, but in practice once it has been shown that the defendant's breach of duty played a causative role he is at risk of being held liable for the whole unless he produces evidence of the contribution of other factors.[19]

2. DISTINCTION BETWEEN JOINT AND SEVERAL TORTFEASORS

22-005 **Basis of the distinction**[20]   At common law tortfeasors liable in respect of the same damage were divided into "joint" tortfeasors and "several" tortfeasors.[21] This distinction, formerly of importance, has been largely eroded by statute, but it remains of significance for one purpose and some account of it is necessary. It has been said that: "Persons are ... joint tortfeasors when their separate shares in the

---

15   [2002] UKHL 22; [2003] 1 A.C. 32; para.7-034.

16   See paras 7-040—7-041.

17   *Ellis v Environment Agency* [2008] EWCA Civ 1117; [2009] P.I.Q.R. P5 at [39]. See also *Wright v Stoddard International Plc* [2007] CSOH 138.

18   See the rather remarkable way in which the expert evidence in *Rahman v Arearose Ltd* [2001] Q.B. 351 attributed different aspects of the claimant's psychiatric trauma to different events (criticised by Weir (2001) 60 C.L.J. 237). See also *Hatton v Sutherland* [2002] EWCA Civ 76; [2002] I.C.R. 613 at [41]. cf. *Rees v Dewhirst Plc* [2002] EWCA Civ 871.

19   *Holtby v Brigham & Cowan (Hull) Ltd* [2000] 3 All E.R. 421.

20   Davies, *Accessory Liability* (2015), Ch.6.

21   "Several or concurrent tortfeasors" is the terminology used by Auld LJ in *Jameson v Central Electricity Generating Board* [1998] Q.B. 323 at 334. However, "concurrent tortfeasors" is a convenient phrase to describe both.

commission of the tort are done in furtherance of a common design."[22] So, in *Brook v Bool*,[23] where two men searching for a gas leak each applied a naked light to a gas pipe in turn and one of them caused an explosion, they were held to be joint tortfeasors;[24] but where two ships collided because of the independent acts of negligence of each of them, and one of them, without further negligence, collided with a third, it was held that they were several tortfeasors, because there was no community of design.[25] A seemingly anomalous exception to the requirement of community of design concerns vicariously liable employers. Such employers and their negligent employees are joint tortfeasors. Conversely, the parent or custodian of a child whose negligence enables the child to commit a tort, though he may be liable for the resulting damage, is not a joint tortfeasor with the child. He is personally negligent and his liability is for his own independent tort.[26] Mere facilitation of the commission of a tort by another does not make the defendant a joint tortfeasor[27] and there is no tort of "knowing assistance" nor any direct counterpart of the criminal law concept of aiding and abetting: the defendant must either procure the wrongful act or act in furtherance of a common design[28] or be party to a conspiracy.[29] However, in a common design case the defendant's participation need only be shown not to have been trivial or de minimis. In *Fish & Fish Ltd v Sea Shepherd UK*,[30] Lord Neuberger said that once it had been established that the assistance provided was substantial in this sense, "the proper way of reflecting the defendant's relatively unimportant contribution to the tort" was through the court's power to apportion liability as between the defendant and the primary tortfeasor.[31]

Relevance of the distinction   The two principal consequences at common law of   **22-006**
the defendants' being joint tortfeasors were: (1) judgment against one of them, even if it remained unsatisfied, barred any subsequent action, or even the continuance of

---

[22]   *The Koursk* [1924] P. 140 at 151 per Bankes LJ, 159–160 per Sargant LJ. For the liability of company directors, see para.25-034.

[23]   [1928] 2 K.B. 578. See too *Arneil v Patterson* [1931] A.C. 560; cf. *Cook v Lewis* [1952] 1 D.L.R. 1.

[24]   Hence liable in respect of the damage. Note that the act of only one defendant was the physical cause of the damage. See also *Monsanto Plc v Tilly* [2000] Env L.R. 313 (reconnoitring site and being present at scene explaining matters to press sufficient to make D joint tortfeasor in relation to damage to crops); *Shah v Gale* [2005] EWHC 1087 (QB).

[25]   *The Koursk* [1924] P. 140. See also *Sadler v Great Western Railway Co* [1896] A.C. 450; *Thompson v LCC* [1899] 1 Q.B. 840.

[26]   See *Bebee v Sales* (1916) 32 T.L.R. 413; *Newton v Edgerley* [1959] 1 W.L.R. 1031.

[27]   *Fish & Fish Ltd v Sea Shepherd UK* [2015] UKSC 10; [2015] A.C. 1229 at [21], [39], [58].

[28]   Meaning "concerted action to a common end" (*The Koursk* [1924] P. 140 at 156). On the limits of this concept, see *Fish & Fish Ltd v Sea Shepherd UK* [2013] EWCA Civ 544; [2013] 1 W.L.R. 3700 at [50]. Although a common design will generally be expressly communicated between the joint tortfeasors it can be inferred ([2015] UKSC 10; [2015] A.C. 1229 at [59]), but in *Kalma v African Minerals Ltd* [2020] EWCA Civ 144, there was no basis for inferring a common design where mining companies in Sierra Leone had brought in the police to deal with civil unrest, and given them assistance, and the police had then used excessive violence to quell the protests. Calling the police did not render a party liable for torts the police then committed, even if these were foreseeable.

[29]   *Credit Lyonnais Bank Nederland NV v Export Credits Guarantee Department* [2000] 1 A.C. 486. See also *CBS Songs Ltd v Amstrad Consumer Electronics Plc* [1988] A.C. 1018 at 1058.

[30]   [2015] UKSC 10; [2015] A.C. 1229. See Davies (2016) 132 L.Q.R. 15.

[31]   [2015] UKSC 10; [2015] A.C. 1229 at [57]. On the facts, a majority of the Supreme Court held that it had been open to the trial judge to find that the contribution of a UK conservation charity to alleged wrongful acts by its American sister charity directed at a fishing vessel owned by the claimant had been too minimal for it to count as a joint tortfeasor.

the same action, against the others; and (2) the release of one operated as the release of all, even if the claimant had not recovered his full loss. In each case the reason given was that the cause of action was single and indivisible.[32] Neither rule ever applied to several tortfeasors liable for the same damage. Now, however, the first rule has been abolished by statute.[33] The second rule still exists, though the fact that even joint tortfeasors may be sued in successive actions has "heavily compromised"[34] the logic of unity of liability upon which it rests. However, if the agreement with the first joint tortfeasor can be interpreted as a covenant not to sue or (which for practical purposes amounts to the same thing) contains a reservation of the claimant's rights against the other, then the other is not discharged.[35]

Where the defendants were not true joint tortfeasors it has always been clear that if the claimant received from one damages representing his whole loss he could not proceed against the others[36] but it is now the case that the same is true wherever the settlement with the first defendant is made in full satisfaction of the claim even if the sum is less than the claimant would have received if the case had been pursued to judgment.[37] The settlement with one tortfeasor, even though other tortfeasors are not party to it, is to be taken as conclusively establishing that the sum which has been agreed represents full value for the claim,[38] despite the fact that the settlement makes no mention of the position of other tortfeasors and the sum recovered from the settlor will in practice be discounted to reflect any weaknesses in the claim. Of course the terms of the settlement may show, expressly or by implication, that it is not in full satisfaction and that the claimant is reserving his rights against other defendants. So, where C dismissed D1, its managing director, for gross misconduct amounting to fraud and he compromised their action by surrendering his shareholding, it was held in proceedings by C against D2, their auditors, for failing to detect D1's wrongdoing,[39] that it was quite unrealistic to say that C was giving up its right to bring further proceedings.[40] Even where the claimant may bring successive

---

[32] *Brinsmead v Harrison* (1872) L.R. 7 C.P. 547; *Duck v Mayeu* [1892] 2 Q.B. 511; *Cutler v McPhail* [1962] 2 Q.B. 292.

[33] Civil Liability (Contribution) Act 1978 s.3, replacing the Law Reform (Married Women and Tortfeasors) Act 1935 s.6(1)(a).

[34] Steyn LJ in *Watts v Aldington, The Times,* 16 December 1993.

[35] See *Watts v Aldington, The Times,* 16 December 1993; *Gardiner v Moore* [1969] 1 Q.B. 55; *Apley Estates Ltd v De Bernales* [1947] Ch. 217.

[36] *Clark v Urquhart* [1930] A.C. 28 at 66; *Tang Man Sit v Capacious Investments Ltd* [1996] A.C. 514 at 522; *Mason v Grogan* [2009] EWCA Civ 283; [2009] C.P. Rep. 34.

[37] *Jameson v Central Electricity Generating Board* [2000] 1 A.C. 455. This difficult case was a rather unsuitable vehicle on which to restate the law in this area, because the general rule that sums actually received would reduce the liability of other tortfeasors pro tanto did not apply. Jameson recovered £80,000 in settlement from his employer, Babcock, shortly before his death from mesothelioma. After his death his widow commenced proceedings under the Fatal Accidents Act 1976 against the Central Electricity Generating Board. Although the settlement sum from Babcock passed to the widow, it is provided in s.4 of the 1976 Act that benefits accruing to the claimant (the widow) from the estate of the deceased are not to be brought into account in assessing the damages: para.24-028.

[38] *Jameson v Central Electricity Generating Board* [2000] 1 A.C. 455 at 474.

[39] In which D2 sought contribution or indemnity from D1: one defendant cannot resist contribution proceedings by the other by saying that he has settled with C: Civil Liability (Contribution) Act 1978 s.1(3).

[40] *Cape & Dalgleish v Fitzgerald* [2002] UKHL 16; [2003] 1 C.L.C. 65, applying *Heaton v Axa Equity & Law* [2002] UKHL 15; [2002] 2 A.C. 329. See also *McGill v Sports and Entertainment Media Group* [2016] EWCA Civ 1063; [2017] 1 W.L.R. 989 (settling of football agent's claim for breach of contract against player did not bar later claim against second agent for inducing that breach).

proceedings, it is obviously desirable that a claimant should, if he reasonably can, sue in the same proceedings all the tortfeasors who are liable to him for the same damage. It is therefore provided that the claimant may not recover costs in any but the first action in respect of the damage unless the court is of the opinion that there was reasonable ground for bringing the further proceedings.[41]

3. CONTRIBUTION BETWEEN TORTFEASORS

Introduction[42] At common law the general rule was that one concurrent tortfea-   **22-007**
sor, even if he had satisfied the claimant's judgment in full, could not recover indemnity nor contribution towards his liability from any other tortfeasor liable for the same loss. The rule was laid down with regard to joint tortfeasors in *Merryweather v Nixan*[43] and was later extended to several concurrent tortfeasors.[44] The harshness of this rule was modified to a limited extent and it does not apply where the tort was not clearly illegal in itself, and the person claiming contribution or indemnity acted in the belief that his conduct was lawful;[45] nor does it apply where even though the tort was clearly illegal in itself, one of the parties is vicariously liable for a wrong to which he gave neither his authority nor assent and of which he had no knowledge.[46]

A. Civil Liability (Contribution) Act 1978

The rule in *Merryweather v Nixan* was for most practical purposes reversed by   **22-008**
s.6(1)(c) of the Law Reform (Married Women and Tortfeasors) Act 1935.[47] The operation of the 1935 Act was examined by the Law Commission in the wider context of contribution generally (including contribution between contractors) and the product of its deliberations was the Civil Liability (Contribution) Act 1978.[48]

Basic scheme of the Act By s.1(1) of the 1978 Act, any person liable in respect   **22-009**
of any damage suffered by another may recover contribution from any other person liable in respect of the same damage (whether jointly or otherwise) and for this purpose a person is "liable" whatever the legal basis of his liability, "whether tort, breach of contract, breach of trust or otherwise".[49] So if D1 negligently advises C

---

41 Civil Liability (Contribution) Act 1978 s.4.

42 Mitchell, *The Law of Contribution and Reimbursement* (2003).

43 (1799) 8 T.R. 186. The rule was regarded as resting on the maxim ex turpi causa non oritur actio: see para.26-064.

44 *Horwell v London General Omnibus Co Ltd* (1877) 2 Ex. D. 365 at 379; *The Koursk* [1924] P. 140 at 158.

45 See *Adamson v Jarvis* (1827) 4 Bing. 66; 130 E.R. 693 (auctioneer innocently selling X's goods at the behest of the defendant, who represented himself as owner). This exception may hold good even where the joint enterprise proves to be criminal: *Burrows v Rhodes* [1899] 1 Q.B. 816.

46 *Romford Ice and Cold Storage Co v Lister* [1956] 2 Q.B. 180, affirmed [1957] A.C. 555, para.21-038.

47 See Cmd. 4637 (1934). See further on the background to the 1935 Act, Mitchell, *A History of Modern Tort Law 1900–1950* (2015), Ch.11. Two statutory exceptions to the common law rule antedated the 1935 Act: Maritime Conventions Act 1911 s.3, and Companies Act 1908 s.84. Contribution in personal injury cases at sea is now governed by the Merchant Shipping Act 1995 s.189, to the same effect as the 1911 Act.

48 *Report on Contribution*, Law Com. No.79 (1977).

49 Section 6(1). "Liability" means a liability which has been or could be established in a court in England and Wales: s.1(6). It includes a judgment, even though given on a false assumption: *BRB*

on the purchase of a computer system and as a result C buys a system from D2 which does not perform the required task satisfactorily and D1 settles C's claim, D1 may be able to seek contribution from D2, even though D2's only liability is in contract, whereas D1's sounds in contract and in tort.[50]

22-010 **The "same damage"** In order that D1 and D2 are liable in respect of the "same damage" one must generally[51] be able to say that if either of them makes a payment to C on account of his liability that will go to reduce the liability of the other to C.[52] Hence where D1 overvalued a property on the security of which C lent money to D2 and, D2 having defaulted on the loan, D1 settled C's claim for negligence for £400,000, D1 was unable to claim contribution from D2.[53] In such a case D1's liability to C is reduced by the value of D2's covenant to repay[54] but D2's liability (which is not a liability *for damage* or *in damages* at all) is not reduced by the value of the claim against the valuer. If C did recover in full from D2, no doubt it would hold £400,000 on trust for D1. Further, D1 would be subrogated to the extent of £400,000 to C's claim against D2.[55] Considerable uncertainty has developed over the question whether, and if so how far, the 1978 Act applies where one party is liable in tort and the other liable in restitution, for example where D1 defrauds C of money and D2 knowingly receives it and/or disposes of it. Doubt has been expressed whether an obligation of D2 to pay C on a restitutionary basis can be described as an obligation to pay "compensation" within the meaning of the Act,[56] but in *Charter Plc v City Index Ltd*[57] the Court of Appeal accepted that the Act applied to a claim for knowing receipt. Finally, "the same damage" must not be confused with "the same damages". Where the vendor of a business is in breach of warranty the measure of damages against him may be different from that against

---

(Residuary) Ltd v Connex South Eastern Ltd [2008] EWHC 1172 (QB); [2008] 1 W.L.R. 2867.

[50] Based on *Brownton Ltd v Edward Moore Inbucon Ltd* [1985] 3 All E.R. 499, a pre-1978 Act case. So also where an architect fails to supervise a builder both he and the builder are liable for the same damage, that is to say the owner being left with a defective building. But an architect whose negligent certification hampers the building owner in a claim against the builder for late completion is not liable for the same damage as the builder (*Royal Brompton Hospital NHS Trust v Watkins Gray International (UK)* [2002] UKHL 14; [2002] 1 W.L.R. 1397); nor is a builder who is exempt from liability under his contract for fire damage but required to restore the works under an insurance policy liable for the same damage as persons who also caused the fire but have no such exemption (*C.R.S. Retail Services Ltd v Taylor Young Partnership* [2002] UKHL 17; [2002] 1 W.L.R. 1419). See also *Bovis Construction Ltd v Commercial Union Assurance Co Plc* [2001] 1 Lloyd's Rep. 416; *Jubilee Motor Policies Syndicate 1231 at Lloyd's v Volvo Truck and Bus (Southern) Ltd* [2010] EWHC 3641 (QB); cf. *Greene Wood & McClean LLP v Templeton Insurance Ltd* [2009] EWCA Civ 65; [2009] 1 W.L.R. 2013.

[51] In *Royal Brompton Hospital NHS Trust v Watkins Gray International (UK)* [2002] UKHL 14; [2002] 1 W.L.R. 1397 at [28] Lord Steyn pointed out that in the last resort it is the statutory wording which governs and that this "test" might lead to undue complexity in some cases.

[52] *Howkins & Harrison v Tyler* [2001] Lloyd's Rep. P.N. 1.

[53] *Howkins & Harrison v Tyler* [2001] Lloyd's Rep. P.N. 1, doubting *Friends' Provident Life Office v Hillier Parker & Rowden* [1997] Q.B. 85.

[54] *Eagle Star Insurance Co v Gale & Power* (1955) 166 E.G. 37.

[55] That had not been pleaded in *Howkins & Harrison* [2001] Lloyd's Rep. P.N. 1. A claim by one co-surety against another does not fall within the 1978 Act: *Hampton v Minns* [2001] 1 W.L.R. 1.

[56] Lord Steyn in *Royal Brompton Hospital NHS Trust v Watkins Gray International (UK)* [2002] UKHL 14; [2002] 1 W.L.R. 1397 at [33].

[57] [2007] EWCA Civ 1382; [2009] Ch. 313.

a valuer engaged by the buyer, but that does not preclude the application of the 1978 Act.[58]

Assessment of contribution   The amount of contribution ordered is to be "such   **22-011** as may be found by the court to be just and equitable having regard to the extent of that person's responsibility for the damage in question".[59] The principles are similar to those governing the apportionment of responsibility in the context of contributory negligence,[60] so that the court must look at both causation[61] and culpability.[62] However, it has been held, somewhat surprisingly, that culpability includes fault which is non-causative, for example attempts to cover up responsibility for the damage.[63] Where one defendant is vicariously liable to the claimant for the fault of his employee that is also the relevant fault for the purposes of a contribution claim against another defendant: the first defendant cannot say his claim should be assessed on the basis that he was free from personal blame.[64] As will be seen, in a road accident case a passenger's failure to wear a seat belt generally leads to a 25 per cent reduction in damages for contributory negligence where the injury would have been prevented by taking that precaution[65] and in *Jones v Wilkins*[66] the Court of Appeal upheld an apportionment of 25 per cent responsibility to a passenger who failed to take adequate steps to restrain her infant child, the claimant,[67] and 75 per cent to the driver of the other car, who was responsible for the collision.

The question is one of proportion, involving an individual exercise of discretion by the trial judge and for that reason appellate courts will be reluctant to interfere with an apportionment as determined by the judge[68] unless there has been

---

[58] *Eastgate Group Ltd v Lindsey Morden Group Inc* [2001] EWCA Civ 1446; [2002] 1 W.L.R. 642. That does not, of course, necessarily mean that it is just and equitable that the vendor should recover contribution from the valuer.

[59] Section 2(1). The statutory right to contribution is not in the nature of a claim in tort. It has been said to resemble a quasi-contractual claim by a person who has been constrained to discharge another's liability: *Ronex Properties Ltd v John Laing Construction Ltd* [1983] Q.B. 398, but in another context the right was said to be "founded on tort": *FFSB Ltd v Seward & Kissel LLP* [2007] UKPC 16.

[60] See para.23-040. Where C, D1 and D2 are all to blame both the 1945 and 1978 Acts are applicable. The correct approach is to consider the claimant's fault against the totality of the defendants' conduct. That will give a figure for which the claimant recovers judgment against all defendants and in respect of which they may seek contribution inter se: *Fitzgerald v Lane* [1989] A.C. 328.

[61] Causation of *the damage* is what is in issue. Hence, where a collision is the fault of D1 and D2 but D1 carried C in dangerous conditions which led to the injury, D1 may carry a greater share of the responsibility than D2: *Madden v Quirke* [1989] 1 W.L.R. 702.

[62] *Jones v Wilkins* [2001] P.I.Q.R. Q12.

[63] *Re-source America International Ltd v Platt Site Services Ltd* [2004] EWCA Civ 665; 95 Con L.R. 1; *Brian Warwicker Partnership v HOK International Ltd* [2005] EWCA Civ 962; 103 Con L.R. 112 (see the doubts expressed by Arden LJ); *Furmedge v Chester-le-Street DC* [2011] EWHC 1226 (QB).

[64] *Dubai Aluminium Co Ltd v Salaam* [2002] UKHL 48; [2003] 2 A.C. 366.

[65] See para.23-063.

[66] [2001] P.I.Q.R. P12.

[67] In practice, the effect (though not the theory) may be the same as identifying the child with the parent for the purposes of contributory negligence, since unless the parent is insured she may not be in a position to pay the contribution and would risk bankruptcy if the judgment were enforced in full against the driver.

[68] *Kerry v Carter* [1969] 1 W.L.R. 1372 at 1376. In determining the apportionment the court must have regard only to the parties before it and cannot take into account the possibility that some other person may also have been to blame: *Maxfield v Llewellyn* [1961] 1 W.L.R. 1119. D1 and D2 may be li-

some error in his approach.[69] If it considers it appropriate, the court may exempt the defendant from any liability to make contribution[70] or direct that the contribution recoverable shall amount to a complete indemnity.[71] The Act does not cease to be applicable because the act of the defendant seeking contribution amounts to a crime[72] but where a defendant guilty of wilful wrongdoing seeks a contribution from one who has merely been negligent the latter may in some cases have a powerful and perhaps overwhelming case why it would not be just and equitable to order him to make contribution: it is unlikely that a court would accede to the request of a burglar for contribution from the security guard who fell asleep.[73] Nevertheless, there is no rule that a fraudulent defendant is required to bear the whole loss as against a negligent one.[74]

22-012 **Contribution limited to the sum which could have been recovered by the claimant** The court's powers in any case are subject to the overriding principle that one defendant cannot, by way of contribution proceedings, be liable for a greater sum than could be recovered from him by the claimant. Since the two defendants have caused indivisible damage they will often be liable for the same amount but this is not necessarily the case. Thus, if C's property worth £1,000 is destroyed as a result of the combined (and equal) negligence of D1 and D2, there being a binding contract between C and D1 whereby the latter's liability is limited to £300, the principle just mentioned means that D2 in contribution proceedings can recover no more than this amount from D1.[75] A negligent D1 may be able to rely on the claimant's contributory negligence and/or on a contractual limitation of liability; a fraudulent D2 may do neither. Let us assume that: (1) the combined conduct of D1 and D2 has produced an indivisible loss of £15 million; (2) the claimant is guilty of contributory negligence in the order of one-third; (3) D1 has validly limited his liability to £5 million and has paid that to the claimant; and (4) D2's responsibility is assessed under the 1978 Act at 75 per cent. In such a case it has been held that the correct approach is that the starting point is the total loss less the reduction for contributory negligence, i.e. £10 million, even though D2's liability to the claimant is for the full £15 million. As between D1 and D2 the £10 million would be

---

able to C in respect of the same damage, but D1 may also sue D2 in respect of his own damage (and vice versa). If this happens after the conclusion of C's suit are the parties to the second action bound by the apportionment in C's suit? "Yes", said Popplewell J in *Wall v Radford* [1991] 2 All E.R. 741, reviewing conflicting lines of authority. However, a subsequent suit between D1 and D2 might not now be possible: see para.23-003.

69   As in *Andrews v Initial Cleaning Services Ltd* [2000] I.C.R. 166 and *Alexander v Freshwater Properties Ltd* [2012] EWCA Civ 1048.

70   Contrast the Law Reform (Contributory Negligence) Act 1945, where, once a finding has been made that the claimant is guilty of contributory negligence, the court is obliged to reduce the damages.

71   As in *Semtex Ltd v Gladstone* [1954] 1 W.L.R. 945. See also *Mohidin v Commissioner of Police of the Metropolis* [2016] EWHC 105 (QB); [2016] 1 Costs L.R. 71, where it was held that the police officers who had assaulted the claimants must indemnify the Commissioner for the damages he paid the claimants by virtue of his vicarious liability for the officers' actions. cf. *Jones v Manchester Corp* [1952] 2 Q.B. 852.

72   *K v P* [1993] Ch. 141.

73   Counsel's example in [1993] Ch. 141.

74   See *Downs v Chappell* [1997] 1 W.L.R. 426, where, however, some weight is placed upon the fact that it was D1's negligence rather than D2's fraud which was the direct inducement to buy and where D1's conduct was "reckless".

75   See Civil Liability (Contribution) Act 1978 s.2(3).

shared in the respective sums of £2.5 million and £7.5 million. Hence since D1 has paid £5 million he is entitled to £2.5 million from D2.[76]

Contractual indemnity or contribution unaffected by the Act It often happens that one tortfeasor may be able to recover an indemnity, or damages amounting to an indemnity or contribution, from another person by virtue of a contract between them. Nothing in the 1978 Act affects the enforceability of such an indemnity[77] and it is irrelevant to this contractual claim that the extent of a tortfeasor's liability has been determined as between himself and another tortfeasor in proceedings for contribution. In *Sims v Foster Wheeler Ltd*[78] the claimant's husband was killed when defective staging collapsed, and both his employers and the constructors of the staging were liable in tort. As between these two tortfeasors it was held that the employers were 25 per cent to blame and should bear that proportion of the damages. They were, however, entitled to recover this amount from their sub-contractors by way of damages for breach of an implied warranty that the staging should be properly constructed for safe use as scaffolding. Conversely, the Act does not render enforceable any agreement for indemnity which would not have been enforceable had it not been passed.[79]

22-013

B. Limitation and Contribution

Under the Civil Liability (Contribution) Act 1978 a defendant may seek contribution notwithstanding that he has ceased to be liable to the claimant since the damage occurred,[80] provided he was so liable immediately before the judgment or compromise in the claimant's favour,[81] but his right to seek contribution is subject to a limitation period of two years from the time when it arises.[82] The other party likewise is liable to make contribution notwithstanding that he has ceased to be liable in respect of the damage in question,[83] unless he ceased to be liable by virtue

22-014

---

[76] *Nationwide Building Society v Dunlop Haywards (DHL) Ltd* [2009] EWHC 254 (Comm); [2010] 1 W.L.R. 258. Of course it may be that the fraudulent D2 is not claim-worthy, as was probably so in the case.

[77] Section 7(3) saves: (1) an express contractual right to contribution; (2) an express or implied contractual right to indemnity; (3) an express contractual provision "regulating or excluding contribution". The Act does not affect any right to recover an indemnity otherwise than by contract. This is an obscure area: see *Lambert v Lewis* [1982] A.C. 225; *The Kapetan Georgis* [1988] 1 Lloyd's Rep. 352.

[78] *Sims v Foster Wheeler Ltd* [1966] 1 W.L.R. 769; *Wright v Tyne Improvement Commissioners* [1968] 1 W.L.R. 336. cf. *Lambert v Lewis* [1982] A.C. 225, where the person seeking indemnity was held to be the sole cause of his own loss.

[79] Section 7(3). This appears to refer to cases where the party seeking indemnity knew or may be presumed to have known that he was committing an unlawful act.

[80] The judgment against the defendant will, of course, extinguish the claimant's right of action against him by merger.

[81] Section 1(2).

[82] Limitation Act 1980 s.10. Precisely when the right to seek contribution arises where the principal action is settled is a difficult and contentious issue: see, e.g., *Knight v Rochdale Healthcare NHS Trust* [2003] EWHC 1831 (QB); [2004] 1 W.L.R. 371 (settlement embodied in consent order); *CC Hampshire v Southampton CC* [2014] EWCA Civ 1541; [2015] P.I.Q.R. P5 (acceptance of Pt 36 offer); *Spire Healthcare Ltd v Brooke* [2016] EWHC 2828 (QB); [2017] 1 W.L.R. 1177 (voluntary interim payment); and *RG Carter Building Ltd v Kier Business Services Ltd* [2018] EWHC 729 (TCC); [2018] 1 W.L.R. 4598 (settlement agreement "subject to contract").

[83] For example, by a settlement with the claimant: *Logan v Uttlesford DC* (1986) 136 N.L.J. 541; *Jameson v C.E.G.B.* [1998] Q.B. 323 (this point not in issue on appeal [2000] 1 A.C. 455).

of the expiry of a period of limitation or prescription which extinguished the right on which the claim against him in respect of the damage was based.[84] This proviso will not apply to most periods of limitation in tort since they merely bar the remedy, not the right.[85] Accordingly, suppose C is injured by the combined negligence of D1 and D2 on 31 December 2016. On 1 December 2019, C recovers judgment against D1. C's cause of action against D2 becomes statute-barred on the last day of 2019,[86] but D1 has two years from the judgment against him to seek contribution from D2. However, conversion is an exception to the principle that the expiry of a limitation period only bars the remedy, for by s.3(2) of the Limitation Act 1980, the owner's title to his chattel is extinguished six years after the conversion.[87] Thus, if C's goods are wrongfully converted by D1 and D2 on 31 December 2014, and C recovers judgment against D1 on 1 December 2020, D1 will be unable to claim contribution from D2 unless he brings proceedings before the end of 2020.

C. Settlements

22-015 **Contribution based on hypothetical liability of the defendant seeking contribution** The vast majority of tort actions are settled before the court pronounces judgment. As we have seen, in some cases a settlement with one defendant may preclude the claimant from taking further proceedings against others because he will be deemed to have received full satisfaction.[88] However, a defendant who has settled must have the opportunity of seeking contribution against any other person he considers liable. Under the law before the 1978 Act a defendant who settled, with or without admission of liability, could seek contribution[89] but this involved a curious reversal of the normal roles of litigation, for in the contribution proceedings he was required to show that he was liable to the claimant. What was more, if he failed to do this he could recover no contribution even though the evidence showed beyond any doubt that the person from whom he sought it was liable to the claimant.

Section 1(4) of the 1978 Act meets this point by providing that a person who has bona fide settled a claim

"shall be entitled to recover contribution ... without regard to whether or not he himself is or ever was liable in respect of the damage, provided, however, that he would have been liable assuming that the factual basis of the claim[90] against him could be established."

One objection to this is that it produces the possibility of a collusive settlement, but this is probably not very great in tort actions where the real defendants will usually be insurers.[91]

---

[84] Section 1(3).
[85] *Royal Norwegian Government v Constant & Constant and Calcutta Marine Engineering Co Ltd* [1960] 2 Lloyd's Rep. 431 at 442.
[86] It is assumed that there is no question of the period being extended under the Limitation Act 1980: para.26-101.
[87] There is an exception where the conversion amounts to theft: Limitation Act 1980 s.4.
[88] See para.22-005.
[89] *Stott v West Yorkshire Road Car Co Ltd* [1971] 2 Q.B. 651.
[90] Which is to be defined by reference to any pleadings: *BRB (Residuary) Ltd v Connex South Eastern Ltd* [2008] EWHC 1172 (QB); [2008] 1 W.L.R. 2867.
[91] The risk of collusion is probably considerably greater in contract actions, which are brought under the statutory contribution scheme by s.1(1) of the Act.

Effect of judgments in favour of the defendant from whom contribution is 22-016
sought   What is the position if the claimant unsuccessfully sues one defendant
(D2), and then successfully sues the other (D1)? Can D1 claim contribution from
D2 notwithstanding the determination of C's claim in D2's favour? The findings in
C's claim against D2 would not create any issue estoppels binding on D1 at common law, but by s.1(5) of the 1978 Act a judgment in C's action against D2 "shall
be conclusive in the proceedings for contribution as to any issue determined by that
judgment in favour of the person from whom the contribution is sought." The effect of this is that if the action against D2 was dismissed on the merits (because C
failed to make out the legal basis of his claim) D1 cannot proceed against D2 for
contribution, but the position is otherwise if the dismissal was on procedural
grounds (for example, for want of prosecution by C)[92] or because of the expiry of
the limitation period.[93] In practice there will generally not be successive proceedings, and the issue of contribution will be disposed of in the main action. Either C
will sue D1 and D2 or, if he does not and chooses to sue D1 alone, D1 may bring
contribution proceedings against D2.[94]

---

[92]   *RA Lister & Co Ltd v EG Thompson (Shipping) Ltd (No.2)* [1987] 3 All E.R. 1032 at 1039.
[93]   *Nottingham Health Authority v Nottingham CC* [1988] 1 W.L.R. 903 at 911–912. This is the only
      way to avoid a conflict between s.1(3) and s.1(5). The wording proposed by the Law Commission
      was clearer.
[94]   CPR Pt 20. If the court finds that one defendant is wholly to blame and exonerates the other, that
      does not preclude an appeal by the first directed to placing all or part of the blame on the second:
      Moy v Pettmann Smith [2005] UKHL 7; [2005] 1 W.L.R. 581.

CHAPTER 23

REMEDIES

23-001   This chapter addresses the remedies that may be available to the victim of a tort.[1] The award of damages is the most important remedy in practice, and the first part of this chapter is devoted to the rules in this connection. The second part of the chapter is concerned with certain other remedies, namely, injunctive relief and an order for the specific restitution of property.

1.   DAMAGES

A.   Damages Recoverable Once Only

23-002   **Damages[2] are awarded on a once-and-for-all basis**   The general rule is that the damages must be recovered once and for all.[3] A claimant cannot bring a second action upon the same facts simply because his injury proves to be more serious than he thought it was when judgment was entered. The principal difficulties generated by this rule arise in relation to actions for personal injuries because in that context there will often be significant uncertainty regarding the future. Accordingly, certain modifications have been made to the once-and-for-all rule in that setting.[4]

23-003   **Exception where two distinct rights are violated**   Where a single act of the defendant violates two distinct rights of the claimant (as where the claimant suffers personal injury and property damage) the claimant can bring successive actions in respect of the violation of those rights.[5] However, this principle must be understood in the light of the procedural rule that it may be an abuse of process[6] to return to court to raise issues that could have been determined in earlier proceedings,[7] in which case the second claim will be struck out.[8] Lack of funds to pursue both claims in the initial proceedings is unlikely without more to mean there is no abuse of process, although it is a relevant factor to consider, especially where the lack of funds had been caused by the defendant.[9] A claimant who cannot pursue a second claim because of a failure to bring it together with the first may have a negligence action against his lawyers, but the mere fact that he has no such action

---

[1]   See, further, Burrows, *Remedies for Torts, Breach of Contract and Equitable Wrongs*, 4th edn (2019).

[2]   Regarding damages generally, see Edelman, *McGregor on Damages*, 20th edn (2019).

[3]   *Fetter v Beale* (1706) 1 Salk. 11; 91 E.R. 11; *Fitter v Veal* (1706) 12 Mod. 542; 88 E.R. 1506.

[4]   See para.23-099.

[5]   *Brunsden v Humphrey* (1884) 14 Q.B.D. 141.

[6]   See para.26-082.

[7]   *Henderson v Henderson* (1843) 3 Hare 100; 67 E.R. 313; *Talbot v Berkshire CC* [1994] Q.B. 290; *Bradford and Bingley Building Society v Seddon Hancock* [1999] 1 W.L.R. 1482; *Aldi Stores Ltd v WSP Group Plc* [2007] EWCA Civ 1260; [2008] 1 W.L.R. 748. cf. *Sweetman v Shepherd, The Times,* 29 March 2000.

[8]   *Johnson v Gore Wood & Co* [2002] 2 A.C. 1.

[9]   *Johnson v Gore Wood & Co* [2002] 2 A.C. 1 at 31.

in a given case will, again, not mean that raising the issue in fresh proceedings against the defendant is not abusive.[10]

Exception where the injury is continuing   Suppose that D wrongfully places   **23-004** something on C's land and leaves it there. That is not simply a single act of trespass. Rather, it is a continuing trespass that gives rise to a fresh cause of action from day to day (*de die in diem*).[11] Similarly, a continuing nuisance results in the accrual of a new cause of action each time damage occurs as a consequence of it and, accordingly, successive actions can be brought.[12] In fact, in a case of continuing nuisance prospective damages cannot be claimed, however probable the occurrence of future damage may be—the claimant must await the event and then bring fresh proceedings.[13] It follows that if, for example, the defendant has tortiously caused part of the claimant's land to subside, damages can be awarded only for what has already occurred, and not for the depreciation in the value of the claimant's property attributable to the risk of further subsidence.[14] However, the claimant may be able to recover damages in respect of the cost of remedial work to prevent further injury.[15]

B.   Damages are Awarded as a Lump Sum

Not only must damages be assessed on a once-and-for-all basis, but they must   **23-005** also be awarded as a lump sum at the end of the case. Exceptions aside, which are discussed below,[16] no damages are paid in advance of the trial and, following the trial, damages are not paid periodically. Lump sum awards have advantages from both parties' perspectives. A lump sum payment gives the claimant closure and may help him to put the case behind him. He is given increased financial freedom. The defendant's insurers, on the other hand, can close their books on a claim and avoid further administrative costs. Although these considerations carry much weight, there are also significant disadvantages of the lump sum system. In particular, there is generally no way in which the claimant's use of his damages can be controlled (indeed, the law specifically disclaims any interest in how the claimant will spend an award[17]) and if he uses his capital improvidently the end result may be that he needs to be supported through the social security system. And even where the claimant uses his capital wisely the lump sum system cannot protect him against an adverse investment environment.

---

10   *Wain v F Sherwood & Sons Transport Ltd* [1999] P.I.Q.R. P159.
11   *Hudson v Nicholson* (1839) 5 M. & W. 437; 151 E.R. 185; *Konskier v B Goodman Ltd* [1928] 1 K.B. 421.
12   *Darley Main Colliery Co v Mitchell* (1886) 11 App. Cas. 127; *Phonographic Performance Ltd v Department of Trade and Industry* [2004] EWHC 1795 (Ch); [2004] 1 W.L.R. 2893.
13   Under certain conditions damages in respect of probable future harm may be awarded in lieu of an injunction under Lord Cairns' Act: para.23-130.
14   *West Leigh Colliery Co Ltd v Tunnicliffe and Hampson Ltd* [1908] A.C. 27.
15   *Delaware Mansions Ltd v Westminster CC* [2001] UKHL 55; [2002] 1 A.C. 321. On the subject of "preventive damages", see Nolan (2016) 132 L.Q.R. 68.
16   See para.23-100.
17   "It does not look beyond the judgment to the spending of the damages" (*H West & Son Ltd v Shephard* [1964] A.C. 326 at 364 per Lord Pearce); "One clear principle is that what the successful plaintiff will in the event actually do with the award is irrelevant" (*Wells v Wells* [1999] 1 A.C. 345 at 394 per Lord Clyde).

C. Kinds of Damages

23-006   There are six types of damages: (1) contemptuous damages; (2) nominal damages; (3) compensatory damages; (4) punitive damages; (5) aggravated damages; and (6) gain-based damages. It is possible for more than one of these kinds of damages to be awarded in a single case. However, certain combinations are not possible. For example, nominal damages and compensatory damages cannot be awarded simultaneously in respect of the same wrong because, as we will see, the latter requires proof of loss whereas the former is available only when loss is not established. Similarly, a claimant cannot recover both compensatory damages and gain-based damages in respect of a single tort. Where both remedies are available, the claimant must choose between them.[18]

i.   Contemptuous Damages

23-007   Contemptuous damages, which are rarely awarded, are a derisory sum of money, formerly one farthing, then one halfpenny and now, presumably, one penny. Their purpose is to indicate that while the claimant's legal rights have technically been infringed, the court has formed a very low opinion of the claimant's claim, or that his conduct was such that he deserved, at any rate morally, what the defendant did to him. Damages of this kind may imperil the claimant's chances of obtaining a costs order in his favour.[19]

ii.   Nominal Damages

23-008   Nominal damages are awarded when the claimant's legal rights have been infringed but he cannot prove that he has suffered any damage. Typically, they are in the order of a few pounds[20] and are available only in relation to torts that can be committed without proof of damage, i.e., torts that are actionable per se.[21] In *Constantine v Imperial Hotels Ltd*[22] the defendants breached their duty as common innkeepers when they unjustifiably refused accommodation in one of their hotels to the claimant, a famous West Indian cricketer. Although the claimant found accommodation elsewhere, he was awarded nominal damages for the defendants' wrong. An award of nominal damages does not, therefore, connote any moral obliquity on the claimant's part, but even so the judge may in his discretion deprive the claimant of his costs or even make him bear the defendant's.

iii.   Compensatory Damages

23-009   **Generally**   Compensatory damages are damages that are awarded in respect of the claimant's loss. The greater the claimant's loss the greater the award of compensatory damages will be and vice versa. In the case of some torts, such as conversion and deceit, specific rules for the assessment of compensatory damages exist, and

---

[18]   See para 23-036.
[19]   See, e.g., *Dering v Uris* [1964] 2 Q.B. 669.
[20]   The claimants in *R. (Lumba) v Secretary of State for the Home Department* [2011] UKSC 12; [2012] 1 A.C. 245 were each awarded £1 as nominal damages.
[21]   *Shaw v Kovac* [2017] EWCA Civ 1028; [2017] 1 W.L.R. 4773 at [57].
[22]   [1944] K.B. 693.

these have been discussed in preceding chapters. For the rest, the exact sum that the claimant is awarded depends upon all of the detailed circumstances of the case, but this does not mean that the topic is devoid of principle.[23] On the contrary, at least where so-called pecuniary loss is concerned, some quite firm rules have developed and, even in the case of non-pecuniary loss, such as pain and suffering and what is called "loss of amenity", where precise valuation in money terms is impossible, the courts have to some extent elucidated the bases of their awards.

Restitutio in integrum   The basic principle governing the assessment of   **23-010** compensatory damages is that there should be restitutio in integrum. In *Livingstone v Rawyards Coal Co*, Lord Blackburn described this principle as follows[24]:

> "[W]here any injury is to be compensated by damages, in settling the sum of money to be given for reparation of damages you should as nearly as possible get at that sum of money which will put the party who has been injured, or who has suffered, in the same position as he would have been in if he had not sustained the wrong for which he is now getting his compensation or reparation."

The principle consequently calls for a comparison of the claimant's pre-tort position with his post-tort position. Accordingly, in an action for deceit, the proper starting point for the assessment of damages is to compare the position of the claimant as it was before the fraudulent statement was made to him with his position as it became as a result of his reliance upon the statement.[25] The difference between the two situations is the measure of the damages.[26] The same approach is used elsewhere. In *R. (Lumba) v Secretary of State for the Home Department*,[27] the claimants were falsely imprisoned because a statutory power to detain them had been unlawfully exercised. However, it was inevitable that the claimants would have been detained even if that power had been lawfully exercised. Accordingly, they had suffered no loss and were not entitled to compensatory damages (they recovered only nominal damages). In a case of personal injury, too, this criterion applies to the pecuniary elements of the claimant's loss such as his loss of earnings,[28] but it is difficult to see that it can be applied to the non-pecuniary elements such as pain and suffering. Restitutio in integrum is not possible there[29] and it may be that even compensation is not a wholly apt expression. Money awarded in respect of non-pecuniary losses has been described as "notional or theoretical compensation to take

---

[23]   See the caustic observations of Lord Sumner in *Admiralty Commissioners v SS Chekiang* [1926] A.C. 637 at 643.

[24]   (1880) 5 App. Cas. 25 at 39. See also *Monarch Steamship Co Ltd v Karlshamns Oljefabriker (A/B)* [1949] A.C. 196 at 221; *The Albazero* [1977] A.C. 774 at 841.

[25]   *Doyle v Olby (Ironmongers) Ltd* [1969] 2 Q.B. 158. See para.12-021.

[26]   Of course, care must be taken to bring into the calculation that which the claimant saves as a result of the tort. For example, if D destroys C's goods that are in the hands of X for refurbishment C can recover the cost of substitute goods less what he would have had to pay X for the refurbishment: *Re-Source America International Ltd v Platt Site Services Ltd* [2005] EWCA Civ 97; [2005] 2 Lloyd's Rep. 50.

[27]   [2011] UKSC 12; [2012] 1 A.C. 245 at [95]. See also *Parker v Chief Constable of Essex* [2018] EWCA Civ 2788; [2019] 1 W.L.R. 2238 at [108].

[28]   *British Transport Commission v Gourley* [1956] A.C. 185; *Parry v Cleaver* [1970] A.C. 1 at 22; *Thompstone v Tameside and Glossop Acute Services NHS Trust* [2008] EWCA Civ 5; [2008] 1 W.L.R. 2207 at [47].

[29]   *British Transport Commission v Gourley* [1956] A.C. 185 at 208.

the place of that which is not possible, namely, actual compensation".[30] There is "no medium of exchange for happiness"[31] and the exercise of converting pain and loss of function and amenity into money is an artificial one.[32]

23-011 **The distinction between general and special damages** For the purposes of assessing compensatory damages, a distinction used to be drawn between "general damages" and "special damages". This distinction was stated in several quite different ways and, as a result, its usefulness was severely limited. However, it was commonly put in terms of compensatory damages that could be quantified with precision (special damages) and those that could not (general damages).[33] So understood, special damages related to pecuniary losses suffered before the trial, while general damages were awarded in respect of all other losses, regardless of whether they were suffered before or after the trial. The distinction used to have pleading implications: special damages had to be specifically pleaded whereas general damages did not.[34] However, the distinction no longer seems to have this consequence given that, under the Civil Procedure Rules, the claimant, at least in the personal injury setting, has to attach to his Particulars of Claim a schedule that details all past and future losses in respect of which he claims damages.[35]

Although the distinction between general damages and special damages no longer seems to have pleading implications, it has become important once again due to changes to tort law's procedural system. In an earlier chapter it was noted that, as a consequence of the Jackson reforms, success fees and ATE insurance premiums are no longer recoverable from defendants as costs.[36] In order to ensure that these changes did not eat unduly into damages awards, provision was made for general damages to be increased by 10 per cent. This reform affects general damages "for (i) pain, suffering and loss of amenity in respect of personal injury, (ii) nuisance, (iii) defamation and (iv) all other torts which cause suffering, inconvenience or distress to individuals".[37] Judges have no discretion not to award this uplift, and the right to an uplift exists even where the claimant's legal representatives are not instructed pursuant to a conditional fee agreement.[38]

iv. Punitive Damages

23-012 **Introduction[39]** Punitive damages, which are also known as exemplary damages,[40] "are a controversial topic, and have been so for many years".[41] They are not

---

[30] *Rushton v National Coal Board* [1953] 1 Q.B. 495 at 502 per Romer LJ. See also *H West & Son Ltd v Shephard* [1964] A.C. 326 at 346.

[31] *Andrews v Grand & Toy Alberta Ltd* (1978) 83 D.L.R. (3d) 452 at 475 per Dickson J.

[32] *Heil v Rankin* [2001] Q.B. 272 at 293; *Thompstone v Tameside and Glossop Acute Services NHS Trust* [2008] EWCA Civ 5; [2008] 1 W.L.R. 2207 at [47].

[33] See, e.g., *British Transport Commission v Gourley* [1956] A.C. 185 at 206.

[34] *Ratcliffe v Evans* [1892] 2 Q.B. 524 at 528.

[35] CPR PD 16, r.4.2.

[36] See para.1-031.

[37] *Simmons v Castle* [2012] EWCA Civ 1039; [2013] 1 W.L.R. 1239 at [20].

[38] *Summers v Bundy* [2016] EWCA Civ 126.

[39] The literature regarding punitive damages is extensive. Contributions include *Aggravated, Exemplary and Restitutionary Damages*, Law Com. No.247 (1997); Beever (2003) 23 O.J.L.S. 87; Koziol and Wilcox (eds), *Punitive Damages* (2009); Goudkamp and Katsampouka (2018) 38 O.J.L.S. 90; Goudkamp and Katsampouka in Bant et al (eds), *Punishment and Private Law* (2021).

[40] "[T]he terms are synonymous": *Kuddus v Chief Constable of Leicestershire* [2001] UKHL 29; [2002]

compensatory but are awarded to punish the defendant for his wrongdoing and to deter him and others from engaging in similar behaviour in the future. A claim for punitive damages must be pleaded.[42]

The categories test   In the leading case, *Rookes v Barnard*,[43] Lord Devlin restated   23-013
the law regarding punitive damages and severely limited their availability. In Lord Devlin's view, punitive damages were in principle objectionable because they confused the civil and the criminal functions of the law[44] and, apart from cases where they are allowed by statute,[45] they can now be awarded in only two categories of case: (1) cases involving oppressive, arbitrary or unconstitutional action by servants of the government acting as such; and (2) cases in which the defendant sought to profit from his tort after paying compensation.

Category 1   The first category is where there is oppressive, arbitrary or   23-014
unconstitutional action by servants of the government acting as such.[46] A well-known example of this, approved by Lord Devlin, is *Huckle v Money*,[47] which was one of the famous cases deciding against the legality of the search warrants that were issued against John Wilkes and others during the latter part of the 18th century. The claimant was detained under one of these warrants for no more than six hours and the defendant "used him very civilly by treating him with beef-steaks and beer". Yet the court refused to interfere with a verdict for damages of £300 and remarked that "[t]o enter a man's house by virtue of a nameless warrant, in order to procure evidence, is worse than the Spanish Inquisition ... it was a more daring public attack made upon the liberty of the subject"[48] This class of case only covers abuse of public power. It does not, therefore, extend to oppressive action by individuals or corporations, no matter how powerful (although it has been suggested that it might extend to oppressive use of the law by private persons[49]). Nor does it encompass acts committed by public bodies that are not exercising peculiarly public functions, e.g., a public body supplying water or a local authority acting in its capac-

---

2 A.C. 122 at [51] per Lord Nicholls.

[41]   *Kuddus v Chief Constable of Leicestershire* [2001] UKHL 29; [2002] 2 A.C. 122 at [50] per Lord Nicholls.

[42]   CPR Pt 16.4(1)(c). See also the Crime and Courts Act 2013 s.34(5).

[43]   [1964] A.C. 1129.

[44]   [1972] A.C. 1027 at 1221.

[45]   There are just three statutes that permit punitive damages to be awarded: the High Speed Rail (London-West Midlands) Act 2017 s.51(10); the Reserve and Auxiliary Forces (Protection of Civil Interests) Act 1951 s.13(2); and the Crime and Courts Act 2013 s.34. It had long been debated whether the award of "additional damages" for which s.97(2) of the Copyright, Designs and Patents Act 1988 provides authorises the award of punitive damages. However, the Court of Appeal has held that such damages are sui generis and "may be either in whole or in part" punitive damages or "either in whole or in part, what are now called restitutionary or disgorgement damages": *Phonographic Performance Ltd v Ellis* [2018] EWCA Civ 2812; [2019] Bus. L.R. 542 at [36] per Lewison LJ.

[46]   There has been a tendency to treat the three adjectives used by Lord Devlin to describe this category (i.e., oppressive, arbitrary or unconstitutional) as synonymous, with each of them carrying the idea of "high-handedness". But the Court of Appeal has pointed out that this is incorrect as there may be unconstitutional action which is neither "oppressive" nor "arbitrary": *Holden v Chief Constable of Lancashire* [1987] Q.B. 380.

[47]   (1763) 2 Wils. 205; 95 E.R. 768.

[48]   (1763) 2 Wils. 205 at 207; 95 E.R. 768 at 769 per Pratt CJ.

[49]   *Columbia Picture Industries Inc v Robinson* [1987] Ch. 38; *Moore v Lambeth County Court Registrar (No.2)* [1970] 1 Q.B. 560); cf. *Al-Rawas v Pegasus Energy Ltd* [2008] EWHC 617 (QB); [2009] 1 All E.R. 346.

ity of employer of staff.[50] However, it does cover the actions of the police[51] even though police officers are not, in strict constitutional law, "servants of the government".[52] Further, provided that the conduct in issue is oppressive, arbitrary or unconstitutional, it is unnecessary for the claimant to go so far as to show "malice, fraud, insolence, cruelty or similar specific conduct".[53]

23-015   **Category 2**   Lord Devlin's second category covers cases in which the defendant calculated that by committing the wrong he might make a profit even after paying compensation. The purpose of awards in this category is to teach the defendant (and others tempted to behave in the same or a similar way) that "tort does not pay".[54] Because the focus is on the defendant's purpose,[55] a case can come within this second category even if no profit accrues.[56] However, a case will not fall within the second category simply because the defendant was engaged in an activity aimed at profit at the time of committing the tort. There must be something more calculated and deliberate, although it is unnecessary that the defendant indulged in any precise balancing of the chances of profit and loss.[57] The second category is not confined to cases in which the defendant was concerned with making money specifically.[58] For example, cases in which the defendant sought a general economic advantage, such as by harassing tenants in order to obtain possession of premises,[59] incorporating the claimant's land within his own property[60] and erecting scaffolding on the claimant's land in order to facilitate the construction of an adjacent building,[61] have been held to come within the second category.

23-016   **Criticism of the categories test**   The categories test is controversial on several levels. For one thing, significant doubt arises, contrary to what Lord Devlin said, as to whether it was in fact justified on the basis of precedent. More fundamentally, it has been argued that the categories test artificially limits the jurisdiction to award punitive damages to just two categories of case (leaving aside the third, statutory category), even though it is entirely possible for a defendant to act in a way that merits punishment and that should be discouraged without the case falling within either of the two categories. For example, if D, a private citizen, enters C's house

---

[50]   *AB v South West Water Services Ltd* [1993] Q.B. 507. Nor do the acts of a councillor in a local authority committee necessarily fall within this category: *Shendish Manor Ltd v Coleman* [2001] EWCA Civ 913 at [62].

[51]   An award may be made against an officer who acts under colour of authority even though in the circumstances he is pursuing his own ends to such an extent that the chief constable is not vicariously liable for him: *Makanjuola v Commissioner of Police of the Metropolis, The Times,* 8 August 1989.

[52]   *Cassell & Co Ltd v Broome* [1972] A.C. 1027 at 1077–1078, 1130, 1134.

[53]   *Muuse v Secretary of State for the Home Department* [2010] EWCA Civ 453 at [71] per Thomas LJ.

[54]   *Rookes v Barnard* [1964] A.C. 1129 at 1227 per Lord Devlin.

[55]   *Archer v Brown* [1985] Q.B. 401 at 423.

[56]   See, e.g., *Axa Insurance UK Plc v Financial Claims Solutions Ltd* [2018] EWCA Civ 1330; [2019] R.T.R. 1.

[57]   *Cassell & Co Ltd v Broome* [1972] A.C. 1027 at 1044; *John v MGN Ltd* [1997] Q.B. 586 at 618–619.

[58]   "This category is not confined to moneymaking in the strict sense": *Rookes v Barnard* [1964] A.C. 1129 at 1227 per Lord Devlin.

[59]   *Daley v Mahmood* (Central London CC, 12 August 2005) at [14].

[60]   *Ramzan v Brookwide Ltd* [2011] EWCA Civ 985; [2012] 1 All E.R. 903.

[61]   *Dawoodi v Zafrani* [2015] EWHC 3168 (TCC).

and attacks C, the categories test precludes punitive damages from being awarded against D.[62] It is unsurprising that the categories test has been rejected throughout the rest of the common law world.[63]

Additional restrictions Simply because a case satisfies the categories test does **23-017** not mean that the claimant has a right to punitive damages. On the contrary, punitive damages are discretionary, and it is always for the judge to decide whether punitive damages are appropriate in the individual circumstances of each case. There are also several other restrictions on such awards.

(1) Even if the "categories test" is satisfied, punitive damages cannot be awarded unless the defendant's wrongful conduct committed against the claimant is sufficiently reprehensible to justify a punitive award.[64] The courts have not adopted an exact test that needs to be satisfied in this regard. Instead, the case law is populated by "a whole gamut of dyslogistic judicial epithets"[65] that give a broad indication of the kind of conduct that is required to make the defendant's wrongdoing sufficiently exceptional to justify a punitive response. These epithets include "high-handed",[66] "outrageous",[67] "egregious",[68] "insulting",[69] "cynical",[70] "flagran[t]",[71] "appalling"[72] and "contumelious".[73]

(2) Punitive damages are a remedy of last resort, so that they can be awarded "if but only if" compensatory damages are insufficient to achieve the goals of punishment and deterrence.[74]

(3) Where the defendant has already been punished by a criminal court or in some other way for the conduct that forms the basis of the tort suit, punitive damages should ordinarily not be awarded. That is because an award of punitive damages in such circumstances is pregnant with the risk of imposing double

---

[62] These were the facts in *Loudon v Ryder* [1953] 2 Q.B. 202. Punitive damages were awarded in this case but the decision was expressly overruled in *Rookes v Barnard* [1964] A.C. 1129 at 1229.

[63] *Uren v John Fairfax & Son Pty Ltd* (1966) 117 C.L.R. 118; *Taylor v Beere* [1982] 1 N.Z.L.R. 81; *Vorvis v Insurance Corp of British Columbia* [1989] 1 S.C.R. 1085; *Conway v Irish National Teachers Organisation* [1991] 2 I.R. 305 at [324]; *ACB v Thomson Medical Pte Ltd* [2017] SGCA 20; [2017] 1 S.L.R. 918. cf *Allan v Ng & Co* [2012] HKCA 119; [2012] 2 H.K.L.R.D. 160 at [24].

[64] For instances where this requirement was decisive, see *Ministry of Defence v Fletcher* [2010] I.R.L.R. 25 at [115] (victimised army recruit not entitled to punitive damages because the conduct of the army officers, though deplorable, did not cross the high threshold of oppressive conduct); *R. (Lumba) v Secretary of State for the Home Department* [2011] UKSC 12, [2012] 1 A.C. 245 [151]–[166] (punitive damages withheld because the misconduct of the Secretary of State and senior officials was insufficiently outrageous).

[65] *Cassell & Co Ltd v Broome* [1972] A.C. 1027 at 1129 per Lord Diplock.

[66] *Muuse v Secretary of State for the Home Department* [2010] EWCA Civ 453 at [74] per Thomas LJ.

[67] *Kuddus v Chief Constable of Leicestershire* [2001] UKHL 29; [2002] 2 A.C. 122 at [67] per Lord Mackay.

[68] *R. (ex parte Lamari) v Secretary of State for the Home Department* [2013] EWHC 3130 (QB) at [85] per HHJ Cotter QC.

[69] *Thompson v Commissioner of Police of the Metropolis* [1998] Q.B. 498 at 517 per Lord Woolf MR.

[70] *Axa Insurance UK Plc v Financial Claims Solutions Ltd* [2018] EWCA Civ 1330; [2019] R.T.R. 1 at [25] per Flaux LJ.

[71] *A v Bottrill* [2002] UKPC 44, [2003] 1 A.C. 449 at [23] per Lord Nicholls.

[72] *A v Bottrill* [2002] UKPC 44, [2003] 1 A.C. 449 at [23] per Lord Nicholls.

[73] *Kuddus v Chief Constable of Leicestershire* [2001] UKHL 29; [2002] 2 A.C. 122 at [63] per Lord Mackay.

[74] *Rookes v Barnard* [1964] A.C. 1129 at 1228.

or otherwise disproportionate punishment.[75] Although this principle was recently doubted by the Court of Appeal,[76] it seems entirely correct.[77] Because the purpose of awarding punitive damages is to punish and deter it follows that if that goal has already been met[78] there is no scope for exercising the jurisdiction to award punitive damages.

(4) Pursuant to s.34 of the Crime and Courts Act 2013, punitive damages cannot be awarded against "publishers" in claims concerning the publication of "news-related material" if the publisher was a member of an approved regulator. This rule is subject to an exception which, in outline, permits the court to award punitive damages where the regulator is found to have been "manifestly irrational" in imposing a penalty on the publisher in issue or in deciding not to impose one.[79] To date, there is only a single approved regulator (i.e., Impress). Its relatively small membership comprises specialist and local publishers.

23-018 **Rejection of the "cause of action" test** For a time, there was a further significant restriction on the jurisdiction to award of punitive damages. In *AB v South West Water Services Ltd*[80] the Court of Appeal interpreted the modern authorities in such a way that, even if the case fell within one of Lord Devlin's categories, punitive damages were available only if they had been awarded for the tort in question prior to *Rookes v Barnard*. This much reviled rule, which was known as the "cause of action" test, meant that punitive damages awards were not based on principle but on the accidents of past litigation and even law reporting.[81] The restriction was rejected by the House of Lords in *Kuddus v Chief Constable of Leicestershire Constabulary*.[82] As such, the jurisdiction to award punitive damages is no longer confined to particular causes of action in tort although certain types of claim are more likely than others to sound in punitive damages, such as actions for deceit.[83]

There do not appear to be any cases in which punitive damages have been awarded in a claim for negligence.[84] There are various potential explanations for this state of affairs. First, it may be attributable to the law recognising, despite *Kuddus*, a residual, implicit cause of action bar on granting punitive damages in proceedings for negligence. A second explanation is that merely negligent conduct is unlikely to involve sufficient moral blameworthiness to justify an award of punitive damages. The force of this second explanation is limited, however, because

---

[75] *Archer v Brown* [1985] Q.B. 401.

[76] *Axa Insurance UK Plc v Financial Claims Solutions Ltd* [2018] EWCA Civ 1330, [2019] R.T.R. 1 at [33] (noted in Katsampouka (2019) 135 L.Q.R. 380).

[77] It has been put onto a statutory footing in claims against certain media defendants: see the Crime and Courts Act 2013 s.35(2).

[78] Regarding difficulties that can arise where the punishment meted out by the criminal court is nominal, see *Gray v Motor Accident Commission* [1998] HCA 70; (1998) 196 C.L.R. 1.

[79] Section 34(3).

[80] [1993] Q.B. 507.

[81] *Kuddus v Chief Constable of Leicestershire Constabulary* [2001] UKHL 29; [2002] 2 A.C. 122 at [22].

[82] [2001] UKHL 29; [2002] 2 A.C. 122.

[83] It appears that punitive damages are particularly likely to be awarded in respect of fraudulent insurance claims: see Goudkamp and Katsampouka (2018) 38 O.J.L.S. 90 at 114.

[84] In New Zealand, it is possible for punitive damages to be awarded in a claim in negligence but only if the defendant was subjectively reckless with respect to the risk of injury to the claimant: *Couch v Attorney General (No.2)* [2010] NZSC 27; [2010] N.Z.L.R. 149.

intentional wrongdoing may, as we have seen,[85] be actionable in a claim in negligence, and in any case deliberate risk-taking is capable of attracting much opprobrium. A third explanation is that negligent conduct is unlikely to fall within any of the classes of case in the categories test.

Assessment An award of punitive damages should be the minimum necessary to **23-019** punish the defendant, to show that tort does not pay and to deter others.[86] Relevant factors in this regard include the gravity of the defendant's wrongdoing and his wealth[87] (a larger award may be required where the defendant is wealthy in order to ensure that it has an impact on him). In *Thompson v Commissioner of Police of the Metropolis* the Court of Appeal said that in so far as claims against the police for trespass to the person and malicious prosecution are concerned[88]:

> "[Where] exemplary damages are appropriate they are unlikely to be less than £5,000. Otherwise the case is probably not one which justifies an award of exemplary damages at all. In this class of action the conduct must be particularly deserving of condemnation for an award of as much as £25,000 to be justified and the figure of £50,000 should be regarded as the absolute maximum, involving directly officers of at least the rank of superintendent."

Updated in view of inflation, these figures are now £10,000, £50,000 and £100,000.[89]

In *John v MGN Ltd*[90] the Court of Appeal was less prescriptive with regard to libel (where awards of punitive damages appear to be very rare[91]). However, it stipulated that awards of punitive damages "should never exceed the minimum sum necessary to meet the public purpose underlying such damages".[92]

Vicarious liability[93] The fact that punitive damages will be paid not by the actual **23-020** wrongdoer but by someone who is vicariously liable for his actions does not prevent an award from being made.[94] Further, while the means of the defendant are in general relevant to the assessment of punitive damages,[95] an award against a newspaper or a chief officer of police is not limited by the means of the journalist or constable directly responsible.[96]

---

[85] See para.3-012.
[86] *Rookes v Barnard* [1964] A.C. 1129 at 1228.
[87] *Rookes v Barnard* [1964] A.C. 1129 at 1228.
[88] [1998] Q.B. 498 at 517.
[89] *Holownia v Secretary of State for the Home Department* [2019] EWHC 794 (Admin) at [54].
[90] [1997] Q.B. 586.
[91] Goudkamp and Katsampouka (2018) 38 O.J.L.S. 90.
[92] [1997] Q.B. 586 at 619.
[93] Todd in Degeling, Edelman and Goudkamp (eds), *Torts in Commercial Law* (2011); Morgan in Bant et al (eds), *Punishment and Private Law* (2021).
[94] In *Kuddus v Chief Constable of Leicestershire Constabulary* [2001] UKHL 29; [2002] 2 A.C. 122 the majority of the House of Lords declined to deal with the issue of vicarious liability for exemplary damages as it was not argued. But see Lord Hutton at [79] and Lord Scott at [123]. See also *Thompson v Commissioner of Police of the Metropolis* [1998] Q.B. 498 at 512–513.
[95] See para.23-019.
[96] *Rowlands v Chief Constable of Merseyside Police* [2006] EWCA Civ 1773; [2007] 1 W.L.R. 1065 at [47].

23-021 **Insurance** Where a contract of liability insurance covers an award of punitive damages, there is no rule of public policy that prevents the insured from enforcing the indemnity.[97]

23-022 **Joint tortfeasors** Where the claimant sues more than one joint tortfeasor in the same action, the sum that may be awarded by way of punitive damages is the lowest that the conduct of the least culpable defendant deserves.[98]

23-023 **Multiple claimants** In the case of multiple claimants the court should arrive at a single award of punitive damages to be divided among the claimants.[99] The reason for this approach is that the focus in awarding punitive damages is on the defendant and the need to punish him rather than on the interests of the claimant. While a defendant may deserve more punishment for injuring 10 than for libelling one to fix a figure for the individual claimant and multiply it by the number of claimants is likely to lead to an excessive award.

23-024 **The future of punitive damages** Punitive damages are the law's most controversial remedy and had it not been for the force of history the award might have disappeared in *Rookes v Barnard*.[100] The main arguments against punitive damages are that they confuse the purposes of the civil and criminal law, allow for punishment in civil litigation without the safeguards of the criminal process and provide an unmerited windfall for the claimant. Punitive damages have also been criticised on the basis that awards are unpredictable in amount and excessive although these criticisms appear to be unjustified given that recent empirical evidence suggests that, on average, awards of punitive damages are reasonably homogenous and fairly modest.[101]

Conversely, one should not too readily assume that the boundaries between the civil and the criminal law are either rigid or immutable or that the criminal law alone is an adequate mechanism to deter wilful wrongdoing, particularly in situations where the criminal law is moribund or where the wrongdoing is by the state or its agents. Punitive damages certainly enjoy continuing vitality in some other common law jurisdictions, which, by and large, have rejected the various shackles imposed on them in England and extended them to situations to which they never applied here, most notably, Canada and the United States.[102] The Law Commission has recommended that punitive damages should be retained but that the law should be restated so that they are available for any tort or equitable wrong (but not for breach of contract) where the defendant "deliberately and outrageously disregarded the plaintiff's rights".[103] The government has so far failed to act on that recommendation.

---

97 *Lancashire CC v Municipal Mutual Insurance Co Ltd* [1997] Q.B. 897.
98 *Cassell & Co Ltd v Broome* [1972] A.C. 1027.
99 *Riches v News Group Newspapers Ltd* [1986] Q.B. 256.
100 [1964] A.C. 1129.
101 Goudkamp and Katsampouka (2018) 38 O.J.L.S. 90.
102 A leading US study is Eisenberg et al (2006) 3 J.E.L.S. 263. Regarding the position in Australia, see Maher (2019) 43 M.U.L.R. 694.
103 *Aggravated, Exemplary and Restitutionary Damages*, Law Com. No.247 (1997).

v. Aggravated Damages

Generally[104] Prior to *Rookes v Barnard*[105] the courts had not distinguished   **23-025**
between punitive damages and aggravated damages. The labels "punitive" and "aggravated" were used interchangeably. In *Rookes*, however, Lord Devlin drew a line
between the two species of award.[106] He considered that whereas punitive damages are awarded to punish and deter, aggravated damages are compensatory.
Specifically, aggravated damages, Lord Devlin considered, are granted to
compensate the claimant for mental distress and hurt feelings that he suffered due
to the way in which the defendant committed a tort or comported himself
afterwards, especially in the manner in which litigation was conducted.[107] It appears that aggravated damages are awarded with some regularity for defamation,
unlawful detention, sexual abuse and discrimination, especially in the employment context.

Requirements Aggravated damages will be awarded only where the defendant   **23-026**
treated the claimant in a "high handed, insulting, malicious or oppressive manner"[108] and the claimant suffered mental distress as a result. To see how these
requirements are applied, it is convenient to give some illustrations of circumstances
in which aggravated damages have been awarded. In *Holownia v Secretary of State
for the Home Department*,[109] the claimant, who was a "rough sleeper" from Poland,
was unlawfully detained by the Secretary of State for 153 days. Simler J observed
that his "detention was unlawful from the very start"[110] and that he had not previously been deprived of his liberty with the result that the "initial shock of detention ... must have been a significant factor for him".[111] This attracted an award of
aggravated damages of £37,000. In *WCC v Steer*[112] the claimant was awarded
£10,000 in respect of sexual abuse that she suffered at the hands of the defendant
over a period of three years when she was a child. The judge emphasised that the
defendant had denied any wrongdoing in associated criminal proceedings that had
resulted in the claimant being subjected to a "gruelling experience" in court. He also
observed that the defendant had contended that the allegations against him had been
fabricated and that the claimant had colluded with others in this regard.[113] In
Woodward v Grice the claimant solicitor recovered £8,000 in aggravated damages
in respect of an untrue libel published on a website that he had been struck off the
role of solicitors.[114] Among other things, the judge emphasised that the defendant
had a "hostile animus" in publishing the statement, that he had made "damaging
slurs against the probity" of the claimant during the proceedings, and that that
although the defendant ultimately gave an apology it was made belatedly and
simply posted online as opposed to being given to the claimant personally.

---

[104] See, further, Beever (2003) 23 O.J.L.S. 87; Murphy (2010) 69 C.L.J 353; Tilbury (2018) 71 C.L.P.
   215.
[105] [1964] A.C. 1129.
[106] See also *Cassell & Co Ltd v Broome* [1972] A.C. 1027 at 1124.
[107] See, e.g., *Alexander v Home Office* [1988] 1 W.L.R. 968 at 979; *Sutcliffe v Pressdram Ltd* [1991] 1
   Q.B. 153 at 184; *Thompson v Commissioner of Police of the Metropolis* [1998] Q.B. 498 at 516.
[108] *Thompson v Commissioner of Police of the Metropolis* [1998] Q.B. 498 at 516 per Lord Woolf MR.
[109] [2019] EWHC 794 (Admin).
[110] [2019] EWHC 794 (Admin) at [58].
[111] [2019] EWHC 794 (Admin) at [59].
[112] [2019] EWHC 1874 (QB).
[113] [2019] EWHC 1874 (QB) at [83].
[114] [2017] EWHC 1292 (QB).

23-027 **Torts in respect of which aggravated damages may be awarded** Awards of aggravated damages have been made in cases of trespass to the person,[115] trespass to land,[116] deceit,[117] malicious prosecution,[118] misfeasance in a public office,[119] misuse of private information[120] and the statutory discrimination torts.[121] It seems that aggravated damages are not, however, available for negligence[122] even where the conduct of the defendant is "crass".[123] A claimant who wishes to recover aggravated damages must plead an entitlement to their award.[124]

23-028 **Need for the aggravating conduct to be sufficiently connected with the wrongdoing** In *HRH The Duchess of Sussex v Associated Newspapers Ltd*[125] the claimant brought proceedings against the defendant newspaper in respect of five articles that she said involved a misuse of her private information. She sought aggravated damages and, in doing so, relied on nine further articles. Warby J held that the claimant's reliance on the articles that were not the subject of the proceedings was impermissible because they covered disparate subject matter that occurred over a period of time and which lacked any substantial connection with the articles for which the claimant had sued. He said that "aggravated damages cannot be recovered for distress caused by conduct which is separate and distinct from that which is alleged to constitute the tort. There must be a genuine and close relationship between the tort and the matters relied on as aggravation."[126]

23-029 **Need for injured feelings** Because aggravated damages are awarded to compensate the claimant for injury to his feelings, they are unavailable where there are no feelings to hurt, as where the claimant is permanently unconscious or is not a natural person.[127]

23-030 **Assessment** In fixing the quantum of aggravated damages the courts have regard to various factors including the defendant's motive (at least in so far as knowledge by the claimant of the defendant's reasons for action increase the injury to his feel-

---

115 *W v Meah* [1986] 1 All E.R. 935 (rape); *Appleton v Garrett* [1996] P.I.Q.R. P1 (non-consensual dental treatment).
116 *Jolliffe v Willmett & Co* [1971] 1 All E.R. 478. See also *Columbia Picture Industries Inc v Robinson* [1987] Ch. 38 (aggravated damages available where defendant executed a search order in an excessive and oppressive manner).
117 *Archer v Brown* [1985] Q.B. 401.
118 *Thompson v Commissioner of Police of the Metropolis* [1998] Q.B. 498.
119 *Muuse v Secretary of State for the Home Department* [2010] EWCA Civ 453.
120 *Campbell v MGN Ltd* [2004] UKHL 22; [2004] 2 A.C. 457.
121 *Prison Service v Johnson* [1997] I.C.R. 275.
122 *Kralj v McGrath* [1986] 1 All E.R. 54 at 61. In *Ashley v Chief Constable of Sussex* [2008] UKHL 25; [2008] 1 A.C. 962 (discussed in para.1-002) the defendant conceded the availability of aggravated damages in the negligence claim against him because he was seeking to avoid trial of the battery claim where aggravated damages are available (see at [23]). Lord Neuberger at [101] was troubled by the idea that the parties could by agreement confer on the court power to award damages not available at law but thought that it was arguable that aggravated damages might be available in some cases of negligence.
123 *Kralj v McGrath* [1986] 1 All E.R. 54. See also *AB v South West Water Services Ltd* [1993] Q.B. 507 at 532.
124 CPR Pt 16.4(1)(c).
125 [2020] EWHC 1058 (Ch).
126 [2020] EWHC 1058 (Ch) at [77].
127 *Eaton Mansions (Westminster) Ltd v Stinger Compania De Inversion SA* [2013] EWCA Civ 1308; [2014] C.P. Rep. 12 at [28] (corporation).

ings)[128] and whether the wrongful act was a one-off occurrence or repeated.[129] In the defamation context, critical factors will include the nature and extent of the publication, whether the defendant persisted in a plea of truth and whether any apology or retraction was forthcoming.[130] There can be no necessary mathematical relationship between aggravated and basic compensatory damages, but ordinarily the former should not be as much as twice the latter.[131] In 1998, the Court of Appeal in *Thompson v Commissioner of Police of the Metropolis*[132] comprehensively restated the law on damages in actions against the police for torts such as false imprisonment and malicious prosecution. In a case of false imprisonment the starting point for what the court called "basic damages" should be (in the money of 1998) about £500 for the first hour of detention, £3,000 for the first day and at a declining rate thereafter.[133] Where there are aggravating factors such as humiliation or insult the starting point for aggravated damages would be about £1,000.

Subsuming aggravated damages within general damages   In *Richardson v Howie*[134] the court said that in cases of assault and similar torts it should no longer be the practice to make a separate award of aggravated damages but rather the compensation for the claimant's injured feelings should be subsumed within the award of general damages, save in a "wholly exceptional" situation. As such, it is now the norm for the courts to award "rolled-up" figures.[135] If aggravated damages truly are a type of compensatory damages then this is an advance in that it recognises that "aggravated damages" *are* damages for "injury to feelings". However, the court contemplated that there might be rare cases where there could be a separate award, albeit without indicating what those cases might be. At any rate, judges continue to make separate awards under this head in the sense of identifying a separate sum.[136]   **23-031**

Criticism   Aggravated damages have excited far less controversy than punitive damages. However, arguably, aggravated damages are simply a form of disguised punitive damages. Thus, judges have often expressly acknowledged that punishment is among the goals of aggravated damages.[137] For example, in *KD v Chief Constable of Hampshire*, which involved a claim in battery and under the Protection from Harassment Act 1997, Tugendhat J said that "there is a penal element in aggravated damages".[138] Consistently with this view, the courts, both in deciding whether to award aggravated damages and in quantifying them, consider broadly the same factors as are relevant in connection with punitive damages. As Lord   **23-032**

---

[128] *HRH The Duchess of Sussex v Associated Newspapers Ltd* [2020] EWHC 1058 (Ch) at [54].
[129] *Vento v Chief Constable of West Yorkshire Police (No.2)* [2002] EWCA Civ 1871; [2003] I.C.R. 318 at [65].
[130] *Easeman v Ford* [2016] EWHC 1576 (QB at [20].
[131] cf. *Shah v Gale* [2005] EWHC 1087 (QB).
[132] [1998] Q.B. 498. See also *Manley v Commissioner of Police of the Metropolis* [2006] EWCA Civ 879.
[133] The starting point for malicious prosecution is about £2,000.
[134] [2004] EWCA Civ 1127.
[135] *BDA v Quirino* [2015] EWHC 2974 (QB) at [50].
[136] See, e.g., *Rowlands v Chief Constable of Merseyside* [2006] EWCA Civ 1773; [2007] 1 W.L.R. 1065.
[137] Although see s.39(2) of the Crime and Courts Act 2013, which provides that for the purposes of claims against certain media defendants "[a]ggravated damages may be awarded against the defendant only to compensate for mental distress and not for purposes of punishment".
[138] [2005] EWHC 2550 (QB) at [186]. To similar effect, see *Ministry of Defence v Fletcher* [2010] I.R.L.R. 25 at [52].

Woolf MR noted in *Thompson v Commissioner of Police of the Metropolis*, "the very circumstances which will justify an award of aggravated damages are probably the same as those which make it possible to award exemplary damages".[139] Also aligned with the notion that aggravated damages are a cipher for punitive damages is the fact that, like punitive damages, it appears that they may not be available in claims in negligence.[140]

vi.   Gain-based Damages

23-033   **Generally**   Gain-based damages are damages awarded to deprive the defendant of gains that he made as a result of his tort.[141] They are known by a diversity of often unilluminating labels, such as "restitutionary damages"[142] and "disgorgement damages". The claimant may wish to seek gain-based damages where the gain made by the defendant exceeds the loss that the defendant caused or where some rule bars the claimant from recovering compensatory damages or otherwise limits their quantum. The discussion that follows is a very brief outline of the law regarding gain-based damages. The details of this field, which has a well-deserved reputation for uncertainty and obscurity, must be sought in specialist works.

23-034   **Money had and received**   Although we have spoken so far in terms of a single type of award, i.e., gain-based damages, there are, in fact, two types of gain-based remedies that can be awarded in respect of torts. The first is the award of money had and received. This common law remedy is available where the defendant wrongfully interferes with the claimant's proprietary rights. Thus, in *Chesworth v Farrar*[143] the deceased landlord converted property belonging to his tenant by selling it and the tenant recovered the sale price of the goods from the deceased's estate in an action for money had and received. Significantly, the court did not enquire as to the value of the goods at the time of the conversion. Because such an enquiry would be required to assess compensatory damages, its absence suggests that the award was based on the gain to the defendant.

23-035   **Account of profits**   The second type of gain-based remedy is an account of profits. This is an equitable remedy which is available where a tort claim is based on a violation of the claimant's intellectual property rights, such as infringement of the claimant's trademark, patent or copyright. An account of profits has been held to be unavailable in private nuisance,[144] deceit[145] and breach of statutory duty.[146] The remedy, when granted, requires the defendant to draw up an account of the profit that he made as a consequence of committing the tort in question and then to pay it over to the claimant. The court may grant the defendant an allowance in respect of the time incurred and effort expended in earning the profit, although this discre-

---

139   [1998] Q.B. 498 at 513.
140   *Kralj v McGrath* [1986] 1 All E.R. 54 at 61.
141   See, further, Edelman, *Gain-Based Damages* (2002).
142   Lord Nicholls in *Attorney General v Blake* [2001] 1 A.C. 268 at 284 said the term "restitutionary damages" was an "unhappy" one.
143   [1967] 1 Q.B. 407.
144   *Stoke-on-Trent CC v W & J Wass Ltd* [1988] 1 WL.R. 1406; *Forsyth-Grant v Allen* [2008] EWCA Civ 505; [2008] Env. L.R. 41.
145   *Halifax Building Society v Thomas* [1996] Ch. 217.
146   *Devenish Nutrition Ltd v Sanofi-Aventis SA* [2008] EWCA Civ 1086; [2009] 3 W.L.R. 198.

tion is unlikely to be exercised in the defendant's favour where he acted in bad faith.[147]

Election   The claimant cannot obtain both compensatory damages and gain-   **23-036**
based damages in respect of a single wrong. As Lord Hoffmann put it in *Ministry of Defence Ashman*, "[t]he two bases of claim are mutually exclusive".[148] Thus, the law requires the claimant to choose between a compensatory and gain-based award.[149] When the claimant elects to receive gain-based damages he is sometimes said to "waive" the tort (this language also occasionally features when the claimant chooses not to sue in tort at all and seeks redress instead in a claim in unjust enrichment). However, that language should be avoided. The claimant does not waive his right to sue for the tort if he seeks a gain-based remedy.

Relationship with punitive damages   Gain-based damages are sometimes   **23-037**
thought to bear some connection with punitive damages given that punitive damages may be awarded where the defendant sought to make a profit by committing a tort.[150] More specifically, it has been argued that punitive damages are, at least in certain situations, a subset of gain-based damages.[151] This view is, however, difficult to defend since a mere intention to make a profit (as opposed to realising a profit) can enliven the punitive damages jurisdiction.[152]

Criticism   One objection to the law concerning gain-based damages is that it   **23-038**
depends on (at least) two concepts – money had and received and an account of profits – whereas one would do. Thus, the Law Commission urged that the various labels describing gain-based awards be swept away in favour of a single term, with its preference being "restitutionary damages". According to the Commission[153]:

> "One of the most needlessly confusing aspects of the law of restitution is the host of differently labelled remedies that are concerned to effect restitution. Even if we confine ourselves to restitution for wrongs (that is, unjust enrichment by wrongdoing) we have seen that an action for money had and received, an account of profits, and 'restitutionary' damages (where the damages are assessed according to the gains made by the defendant rather than the loss of the plaintiff), are all concerned to effect restitution. Moreover, all three of those remedies are personal, and not proprietary, remedies. We think that much would be gained in terms of simplifying the law, and nothing would be lost, if one replaced those three separately labelled remedies by a single remedy."

That clarion call has so far gone unheeded.

vii.   Vindicatory Damages?

A substantial award for libel may be said to be necessary to "vindicate" the   **23-039**
claimant's right to his good reputation, and a substantial award for false imprisonment may be said to "vindicate" his right to liberty. This rather imprecise word has

---

[147]   *Boardman v Phipps* [1965] Ch. 992 at 1021; *Crown Dilmun v Sutton* [2004] EWHC 52 (Ch); [2004] 1 B.C.L.C. 468 at [213].
[148]   (1993) 25 H.L.R. 513 at 519.
[149]   *Attorney General v Blake* [2001] 1 A.C. 268 at 280.
[150]   See para.23-015.
[151]   Weinrib, *The Idea of Private Law* (2012), p.135 fn.25.
[152]   See para.23-015.
[153]   *Aggravated, Exemplary and Restitutionary Damages*, Law Com. No.247 (1997) at para.1.82.

various shades of meaning. In the libel context it means to "clear" the claimant, while in the false imprisonment setting the sense is decisively to uphold or defend the claimant's rights. However, there is no such thing as an award of "vindicatory damages".[154] The closest analogy here is the jurisdiction to award damages against a public authority under the Human Rights Act 1998.

D. Contributory Negligence

23-040 **Introduction** The doctrine of contributory negligence[155] is of great practical significance and is very frequently pleaded, particularly in personal injury claims. It applies where: (1) the claimant fails to take reasonable care of his own interests; and (2) that failure is causally connected with his damage.[156] When contributory negligence is established, the court must reduce the claimant's damages by an amount that is "just and equitable". The defendant bears the burden of pleading and proving that the doctrine of contributory negligence applies.[157] In an empirical study of the operation of the doctrine in courts of first instance, contributory negligence was established in 58 per cent of the claims in which it was pleaded, and the average discount was 39.8 per cent.[158]

23-041 **Claims to which the doctrine applies** The main cause of action to which the contributory negligence doctrine applies is, of course, the action in negligence. It applies also to claims for breach of statutory duty.[159] Where the claimant sues both for breach of a contractual duty to take reasonable care and in the tort of negligence, the doctrine will apply to both actions (unless the parties have excluded the application of the doctrine by their agreement),[160] and in such a case the claimant cannot avoid the doctrine's application by suing only for breach of contract. Claims based on the Consumer Protection Act 1987 are subject to the law of contributory negligence,[161] as are, it seems, claims in public nuisance,[162] as well as dependency claims in respect of fatal accidents.[163]

23-042 **Claims to which the doctrine does not apply** The doctrine of contributory negligence does not apply to claims in respect of "conversion ... or ... intentional trespass to goods"[164] or intentional trespass to the person.[165] Nor does it extend to

---

[154] *R. (Lumba) v Secretary of State for the Home Department* [2011] UKSC 12; [2012] 1 A.C. 245 at [100]–[101]. See also *Gulati v MGN Ltd* [2015] EWCA Civ 1291; [2017] Q.B. 149. In some common law jurisdictions with written constitutions vindicatory damages have been awarded for violations of constitutional rights: see, e.g., *Attorney General of Trinidad and Tobago v Ramanoop* [2005] UKPC 15; [2006] 1 A.C. 328; *Inniss v Attorney General of Saint Christopher and Nevis* [2008] UKPC 42.

[155] See, further, Williams, *Joint Torts and Contributory Negligence* (1951); Goudkamp and Nolan, *Contributory Negligence* (2018); Goudkamp and Nolan, *Contributory Negligence in the Twenty-First Century* (2019).

[156] *Nance v British Columbia Electric Railway Co Ltd* [1951] A.C. 601 at 611.

[157] *Heranger (Owners) v SS Diamond* [1939] A.C. 94 at 104.

[158] Goudkamp and Nolan, *Contributory Negligence in the Twenty-First Century* (2019), Ch.4.

[159] *Caswell v Powell Duffryn Associated Collieries Ltd* [1940] A.C. 152.

[160] *Forsikringsaktieselskapet Vesta v Butcher* [1989] AC 852.

[161] Consumer Protection Act 1987 s.6(4).

[162] *Caswell v Powell Duffryn Associated Collieries Ltd* [1940] A.C. 152 at 165; *Trevett v Lee* [1955] 1 W.L.R. 113 at 122.

[163] Fatal Accidents Act 1976 s.5.

[164] Torts (Interference with Goods) Act 1977 s.11.

claims that are founded on dishonesty whether framed in deceit[166] or as conspiracy, inducing a breach of contract or in some other way.[167] A fraudster will not be permitted to say that his victim should have seen through the deception. However, with regard to a particular item of loss, failure by the claimant to act prudently when he has reason to know about the dishonesty may lead to the conclusion that he is the author of his own misfortune.[168]

i.   The Test for Contributory Negligence

It is unnecessary that the claimant owe a duty of care to the defendant   The   23-043
existence of a duty of care is, of course, essential to a cause of action for negligence, but the doctrine of contributory negligence does not depend upon the claimant's owing a duty of care to anyone, including the defendant.[169] One sometimes encounters references in this area to the claimant's owing himself a duty to take care of his own interests,[170] but strictly speaking there is no duty.

a.   Failure by the Claimant to Take Reasonable Care of His Own Interests

The claimant must act unreasonably with respect to his own interests   The fact   23-044
that the claimant risked the defendant's interests or those of a third party is not contributory negligence. As Lord Denning MR explained in *Froom v Butcher*, "[c]ontributory negligence is a man's carelessness in looking after *his own* safety".[171] The claimant's fault must, in other words, be self-regarding.

An objective test   The claimant acts unreasonably if he fails to take as much care   23-045
of his own interests as the reasonable person in his position would have taken in the circumstances in which the claimant found himself. The test, therefore, is objective with the result that the claimant's idiosyncrasies are ignored. As Lord Denning MR put it in *Froom v Butcher*[172]:

> "In determining [the issue of contributory negligence], the law eliminates the personal equation. It takes no notice of the views of the particular individual or of others like him. It requires everyone to exercise such precautions as a man of ordinary prudence would observe."

Because the test is objective, an inability on the part of the claimant to achieve the standard of the reasonable person will not insulate him from a finding of contributory negligence. Accordingly, it is no answer for him to say that he did his best to

---

[165] *Pritchard v Co-operative Group Ltd* [2011] EWCA Civ 329; [2012] Q.B. 320 (noted in Goudkamp (2011) 27 L.Q.R. 518).

[166] *Standard Chartered Bank v Pakistan National Shipping Corp (Nos 2 and 4)* [2002] UKHL 43; [2003] 1 A.C. 959.

[167] *Corporación Nacional del Cobre de Chile v Sogemin Metals Ltd* [1997] 1 W.L.R. 1396.

[168] *Doyle v Olby (Ironmongers) Ltd* [1969] 2 Q.B. 158 at 168.

[169] *Nance v British Columbia Electric Railway Co Ltd* [1951] A.C. 601 at 611. Nevertheless, it will often be the case, as where there is a collision between two vehicles, that the claimant does owe a duty of care to the defendant. A duty is essential if the defendant wishes to counterclaim against the claimant in respect of his own damage.

[170] See, e.g., *Langley v Dray MT Motor Policies at Lloyds* [1998] P.I.Q.R. P314 at 320.

[171] [1976] Q.B. 286 at 291 (emphasis in original).

[172] [1976] Q.B. 286 at 294.

take proper care of himself if the reasonable person would have taken greater care in the circumstances. In determining the amount of care that the reasonable person in the claimant's position would have taken, the courts apply the same rules that fix the amount of care that the defendant is required to take.[173]

23-046 **The possibility of carelessness by others**   The reasonable person will often consider the possibility that others around him will be careless.[174] Accordingly, the claimant who does not anticipate that the defendant might be negligent may be guilty of contributory negligence. However, the law does not require the claimant to proceed like a timorous fugitive constantly looking over his shoulder for threats from others.[175]

23-047 **The amount of care required is sensitive to changing times and practices**   Just as that which constitutes reasonable care in the tort of negligence may change over time,[176] the same is true as to the degree of care that is expected of claimants. For example, in *Froom v Butcher*[177] the Court of Appeal held that failure to wear a seat belt generally constituted contributory negligence some seven years before Parliament made the wearing of seat belts compulsory. Following the enactment of legislation requiring seat belts to be worn the correctness of that decision became even more obvious. For many years there has been increasing public awareness of the dangers of smoking and, unsurprisingly, it has been held that a claimant failed to take reasonable care for his own safety by continuing to smoke despite, among other things, government health warnings regarding the dangers of smoking.[178] However, although public attitudes towards drinking and driving have become more severe in recent years, if C accepts a lift from D, whom C has not seen consuming large quantities of alcohol, C is not obliged to interrogate D on his consumption.[179]

23-048 **Children**   Where the claimant is a child, his conduct will be judged against the benchmark of the reasonable child of the same age.[180] The reasonable child is neither "a paragon of prudence" nor "a scatter brained child" but the "ordinary child".[181] Although there is no fixed age below which findings of contributory negligence are impermissible, it seems that where the claimant is so young that he is incapable of taking any care, there is no scope for holding him guilty of contributory negligence. Thus, in *Gardner v Grace*, Channell B declared that "[t]he doctrine of contributory negligence does not apply to an infant of tender age".[182]

---

[173] See, e.g., *Casson v Spotmix Ltd* [2017] EWCA Civ 1994 at [6]. For discussion, see Dietrich and Field (2017) 41 M.U.L.R. 602.

[174] *Jones v Livox Quarries Ltd* [1952] 2 Q.B. 608 at 615.

[175] A worker is not normally put on inquiry as to whether his employer has fulfilled his duties under statutes and regulations governing industrial safety: *Westwood v Post Office* [1974] A.C. 1. Similarly, a person is prima facie entitled to take the advice of his professional adviser at its face value: *Henderson v Merrett Syndicates (No.2)* [1996] 1 P.N.L.R. 32.

[176] See para.6-014—6-015.

[177] [1976] Q.B. 286.

[178] *Badger v Ministry of Defence* [2005] EWHC 2941 (QB); [2006] 3 All E.R. 173. Consider also *Blackmore v Department for Communities and Local Government* [2017] EWCA Civ 1136; [2018] Q.B. 471.

[179] *Booth v White* [2003] EWCA Civ 1708.

[180] See, e.g., *C v Imperial Design Limited* [2001] Env. L.R. 33 at [39].

[181] *Gough v Thorne* [1966] 1 W.L.R. 1387 at 1391 per Salmon LJ.

[182] (1858) 1 F. & F. 359 at 359; 175 E.R. 763 at 763. See also *Gough v Thorne* [1966] 1 W.L.R. 1387

Claimant confronted with emergency The claimant will not be guilty of   **23-049**
contributory negligence if, in the agony of the moment, he tries to save himself by
choosing a course of conduct that proves to be the wrong one. In *Jones v Boyce*[183]
the claimant was a passenger riding on top of the defendant's coach and, owing to
the breaking of a defective coupling rein, the coach was in imminent peril of
overturning. The claimant, seeing this, jumped from it and broke his leg. In fact the
coach was not upset. Lord Ellenborough CJ directed the jury that if the claimant
acted as a reasonable and prudent man would have done, he was not guilty of
contributory negligence, although he had selected the more perilous of the two
alternatives with which he was confronted by the defendant's negligence. However,
where all that the claimant is threatened with is mere personal inconvenience of a
trifling kind, he is not entitled to run a considerable risk in order to avoid it. For
example, where the door of a train was so ill-secured that it kept flying open, but
the claimant could have avoided the draught by sitting elsewhere, he was guilty of
contributory negligence when he fell out of the open door while trying to shut it
when the train was in motion.[184]

Workplace accidents It has been suggested that in claims by employees against   **23-050**
their employers for injuries sustained at work the courts take a lenient view of careless conduct on the part of the claimant.[185] For example, an employee working in a
factory will not be held to have fallen short of the standard of the reasonable person
for every risky thing that he might do. Regard must be had to the dulling of the
sense of danger through familiarity, repetition, noise, confusion, fatigue and preoc-
cupation with work.[186] Where, however, the events leading up to the accident are
divorced from the bustle, noise and repetition that occurs in such places as factories,
these considerations do not apply.

Deliberate self-injury Any conduct that exhibits less care than the reasonable   **23-051**
person would have taken is negligence, even if intentional. It follows that even
deliberate acts of self harm can constitute contributory negligence. Thus, in *Reeves
v Commissioner of Police of the Metropolis*[187] the House of Lords held that a sane
detainee who was able to commit suicide due to the negligence of police officers
was guilty of contributory negligence in killing himself.

b.   Causation

The claimant's failure to take reasonable care for his own interests must be   **23-052**
causally relevant The doctrine of contributory negligence applies only where the
claimant's failure to take reasonable care of his own interests was causally con-

---

at 1390.
[183] (1816) 1 Stark. 493; 171 E.R. 540. See also *The Bywell Castle* (1879) 4 P.D. 219; *United States of
America v Laird Line Ltd* [1924] A.C. 286; *Admiralty Commissioners v SS Volute* [1922] 1 A.C. 129
at 136; *Sayers v Harlow Urban District Council* [1958] 1 W.L.R. 623.
[184] *Adams v Lancashire & Yorkshire Railway Co* (1869) L.R. 4 C.P. 739; cf. *Sayers v Harlow Urban
District Council* [1958] 1 W.L.R. 623.
[185] Although empirical evidence suggests that such leniency manifests itself not so much when the court
is determining whether the claimant is guilty of contributory negligence but when it is deciding what
discount to impose: Goudkamp and Nolan, *Contributory Negligence in the Twenty-First Century*
(2019), Ch.7.
[186] *Flower v Ebbw Vale Steel, Iron and Coal Co Ltd* [1934] 2 K.B. 132 at 139–140; *Caswell v Powell
Duffryn Associated Collieries Ltd* [1940] A.C. 152 at 166, 176–179; *Grant v Sun Shipping Co Ltd*
[1948] A.C. 549 at 567; *Hawkins v Ian Ross (Castings) Ltd* [1970] 1 All E.R. 180.
[187] [2000] 1 A.C. 360.

nected to the damage in respect of which he is bringing the claim.[188] Thus, negligent conduct of the claimant that is causally irrelevant is not contributory negligence, as where a cyclist who is riding without a headlight in the dark is run down from behind.

23-053 **The claimant's failure to take reasonable care need not contribute to the accident** In many cases where the doctrine of contributory negligence applies, the claimant's negligence will have contributed to the *accident* that led to his injury (as where a driver or pedestrian fails to keep a proper lookout) but this is not necessary. Instead, what is essential is that the claimant's negligence contributes to his *damage*.[189] Thus, the doctrine of contributory negligence may be triggered where a motorcyclist fails to wear a crash helmet,[190] where a passenger in a vehicle does not wear his seat belt,[191] and where a person rides in a dangerous position on the outside of a dust cart,[192] or with a driver whom he knows (or ought to have known) to be intoxicated.[193]

23-054 **The claimant's damage must be within the scope of the risk of injury created by his carelessness** In *Jones v Livox Quarries Ltd*[194] the claimant was riding on the tow bar at the back of a "traxcavator" vehicle when the driver of another vehicle negligently drove into the back of the traxcavator and caused him injury. Although the obvious danger arising from riding on the tow bar was that of being thrown off, it was held that the risk of injury from the traxcavator being run into from behind was also one to which the claimant had exposed himself and the claimant was contributorily negligent as a result. The outcome would have been different if, for example, the claimant had been hit in the eye by a shot from a negligent sportsman. In that case his presence on the tow bar would have been only part of the history.

c. The Doctrine of Identification

23-055 In certain situations the claimant will be imputed with the contributory negligence of another person. This occurs pursuant to what is known as the doctrine of identification. For example, in a fatal accident case the dependants of the deceased are identified with him and his contributory negligence will count against them.[195] The claimant will also be imputed with the contributory negligence of a third party for whom he is vicariously responsible. Thus, if C's vehicle is damaged due to the negligence of both D and an employee of C acting in the course of his employment, then the doctrine of contributory negligence will be applicable in proceedings by C against D. In the past, child claimants were imputed with the negligence of their parent or guardian in failing to look after them, but this rule was

---

[188] *Caswell v Powell Duffryn Associated Collieries Ltd* [1940] A.C. 152 at 164–165.

[189] *Froom v Butcher* [1976] Q.B. 286.

[190] *O'Connell v Jackson* [1972] 1 Q.B. 270; *Capps v Miller* [1989] 2 All E.R. 333. See also *Smith v Finch* [2009] EWHC 53 (QB) (bicyclist not wearing helmet).

[191] *Froom v Butcher* [1976] Q.B. 286.

[192] *Davies v Swan Motor Co (Swansea) Ltd* [1949] 2 K.B. 291.

[193] *Owens v Brimmell* [1977] Q.B. 859. See also *Gregory v Kelly* [1978] R.T.R. 426 (knowledge of defective brakes).

[194] [1952] 2 Q.B. 608. See also *St George v Home Office* [2008] EWCA Civ 1068; [2009] 1 W.L.R. 1670.

[195] See para.24-029.

abolished long ago.[196] Accordingly, where a child is, for example, injured partly as a result of the negligence of his father and partly as a result of the negligence of a third party car driver, no discount will be made from the damages awarded to the child against the driver on account of his father's fault.

ii. Apportionment of Responsibility

Apportionment unavailable at common law At common law if the doctrine of contributory negligence applied the claimant's action would fail entirely and that was so regardless of whether the claimant's fault was slight in comparison with that of the defendant. This all-or-nothing rule was qualified by the "last opportunity" doctrine.[197] This principle enabled the claimant to recover notwithstanding his contributory negligence if the defendant had the "last opportunity" to avoid the accident. The authorities were confused, and the confusion was aggravated by the extension of the doctrine to cases of "constructive last opportunity",[198] where the defendant would have had the last opportunity to avoid the accident but for his negligence.
23-056

The apportionment legislation Apportionment of responsibility between claimant and defendant was introduced in maritime collision cases by the Maritime Conventions Act 1911, but it was not until the passage of the Law Reform (Contributory Negligence) Act 1945 that apportionment became possible in other contexts.[199] The 1945 Act abolished the all-or-nothing rule and provided for damages to be reduced where the claimant was guilty of contributory negligence. While it is still open to the court to conclude that the fault of the claimant was the sole legal cause of his damage, applying the doctrine of novus actus interveniens,[200] all the refinements of "last opportunity" have been swept away.
23-057

The apportionment provision The apportionment provision, which is relevant if and only if the claimant has been found guilty of contributory negligence in accordance with the rules described above, is found in s.1(1),[201] which provides:
23-058

> "Where any person suffers damage as the result partly of his own fault and partly of the fault of any other person or persons, a claim in respect of that damage shall not be defeated by reason of the fault of the person suffering the damage, but the damages recoverable in respect thereof shall be reduced to such extent as the court thinks just and equitable having regard to the claimant's share in the responsibility for the damage."

"Damage" By s.4 of the 1945 Act, the word "damage" in s.1(1) encompasses loss of life and personal injury. It also includes economic loss[202] and property damage.
23-059

---

[196] *Oliver v Birmingham and Midland Motor Omnibus Co Ltd* [1933] 1 K.B. 35. A minor exception to the non-identification rule in the child/parent context is found in the Congenital Disabilities (Civil Liability) Act 1976: see para.25-018.

[197] *Davies v Mann* (1842) 10 M. & W. 546; 152 E.R. 588.

[198] *British Columbia Electric Ry v Loach* [1916] 1 A.C. 719.

[199] The genesis of the 1945 Act is analysed in Steele in Arvind and Steele (eds), *Tort Law and the Legislature* (2012).

[200] See Ch.17.

[201] For criticism of the provision, see Stevens in Dyson, Goudkamp and Wilmot-Smith (eds), *Defences in Tort* (2015).

[202] See, e.g., *Platform Home Loans Ltd v Oyston Shipways Ltd* [2000] 2 A.C. 190.

23-060 **"Fault"**   Section 1(1) of the 1945 Act applies only when both parties are at "fault". Section 4 defines "fault" to mean "negligence, breach of statutory duty or other act or omission which gives rise to a liability in tort or would, apart from this Act, give rise to the defence of contributory negligence". It has been held that the words "negligence, breach of statutory duty or other act or omission which gives rise to a liability in tort" apply to the defendant, while the words "act or omission which ... would apart from this Act, give rise to the defence of contributory negligence" apply to the claimant.[203] It is important to observe that the words "defence of contributory negligence" are not defined by the statute. That concept is given meaning by the common law, and the relevant rules in this regard have been set out above.

23-061 **A "just and equitable" reduction**   Section 1(1) of the 1945 Act does not specify precisely how responsibility for damage is to be apportioned. It simply provides that the damages recoverable by the claimant are to be reduced "to such extent as the court thinks just and equitable having regard to the claimant's share in the responsibility for the damage". The interstices in this regard have been filled by the common law and judicial convention. The way in which apportionment works in practice is as follows. The judge identifies the parties' respective shares of responsibility for the claimant's damage as percentages, which will add up to 100 per cent. The claimant's damages are then diminished by the percentage of the responsibility that is assigned to him. For example, if the value of the claim is £100,000 before any consideration of the law of contributory negligence and the claimant's share of responsibility for the damage is 40 per cent, the claimant will be awarded £60,000.

The enquiry as to each party's share of responsibility is not conducted in a scientific manner[204] but in a rough-and-ready way. The judge often simply declares that a given apportionment accords with common sense. However, the courts have said that two factors are relevant to the exercise, namely, the parties' relative moral blameworthiness and the "causative potency" of their careless conduct.[205] A given consideration may relate to both criteria and "the overall assessment of responsibility should not be affected by the heading under which [a] factor is taken into account".[206] Appellate courts will only vary a trial judge's apportionment where there is "an identifiable error, such as an error of law, or the taking into account of an irrelevant matter, or the failure to take account of a relevant matter" or where the trial court's conclusion "was not one which was reasonably open to it".[207]

23-062 **Very low and very high discounts**   Discounts that fall at the extremes of the spectrum cast doubt on whether the contributory negligence doctrine is properly applicable in the first place. Thus, a discount of, say, five per cent suggests that the claimant's contribution to the damage is so minuscule that the claimant is not, in reality, guilty of contributory negligence at all. Similarly, a finding of 95 per cent contributory negligence suggests that the claimant is wholly responsible for the damage and that the defendant ought not to be held liable at all. The practice of the courts is broadly consistent with these propositions. Thus, discounts of less than 10

---

[203] *Reeves v Commissioner of Police of the Metropolis* [2000] 1 A.C. 360 at 369.
[204] *Jackson v Murray* [2015] UKSC 5; [2015] 2 All E.R. 805 at [27], [46].
[205] *Davies v Swan Motor Co (Swansea) Ltd* [1949] 2 K.B. 291 at 326; *Stapley v Gypsum Mines Ltd* [1953] A.C. 663 at 682.
[206] *Jackson v Murray* [2015] UKSC 5; [2015] 2 All E.R. 805 at [40] per Lord Reed.
[207] *Jackson v Murray* [2015] UKSC 5; [2015] 2 All E.R. 805 at [35] per Lord Reed.

per cent are very unusual.[208] Discounts approaching 100 per cent are also rare. In *Hodkinson v Henry Wallwork & Co Ltd*,[209] the damages of an employee who took an "amazing risk" in an attempt to fix a machine were reduced by 90 per cent. In *Barings Plc v Coopers & Lybrand*,[210] the judge would have discounted damages by 95 per cent in respect of conduct committed over a certain period of time had he found that primary negligence had remained operative. For a time, the courts insisted, irrationally, that it was possible to reduce damages by 100 per cent.[211] However, that view has rightly been rejected and the courts have confirmed that such a discount is impermissible.[212] A 100 per cent discount suggests that the claimant and the claimant alone is responsible for the damage. If, however, the claimant is exclusively accountable for the damage, no tort will have been committed and that, in turn, means that the issue of contributory negligence should not fall for consideration at all.

Seatbelt cases *Froom v Butcher*[213] established guideline discounts in seat belt cases.[214] These rules are "ready-made" reductions that operate regardless of whether the defendant's driving was slightly or grossly negligent and irrespective of whether the failure to wear the seat belt was "entirely inexcusable or almost forgivable".[215] If the claimant's injuries would have been altogether avoided by wearing a seat belt there should be a reduction of 25 per cent. If he would still have been injured, but less severely, the reduction should be 15 per cent. While these are guidelines rather than fixed rules,[216] they are generally followed.[217] Further, they remain valid today even though they were established in 1976.[218] The courts are, of course, free to increase the discount where the claimant's failure to use a seat belt was combined with another act of contributory negligence, such as accepting a ride from an obviously intoxicated driver.   **23-063**

Multiple defendants If there are two or more defendants, apportionment is performed by comparing the claimant's conduct with the totality of the defendants' tortious conduct (in other words, the defendants are seen as a single unit). Hence, if the court concludes that the claimant is 20 per cent responsible for the loss, judgment will be entered for 80 per cent of the damage against both defendants irrespective of whether the defendants are equally to blame.[219] Similarly, if the court concludes that the claimant is one-third to blame for the damage, the correct judgment is for two-thirds of the damage against both defendants, even though the claimant may be as much at fault as either defendant. Once the issue of contribu-   **23-064**

---

[208] But see *Pasternack v Poulton* [1973] 1 W.L.R. 476 (five per cent).

[209] [1955] 3 All E.R. 236.

[210] [2003] EWHC 1319 (Ch) at [1068].

[211] *Imperial Chemical Industries Ltd v Shatwell* [1965] A.C. 656 at 672; *McMullen v National Coal Board* [1982] I.C.R. 148 at 154–155; *Jayes v IMI (Kynoch) Ltd* [1985] I.C.R. 155 at 159.

[212] *Anderson v Newham College of Further Education* [2002] EWCA Civ 505; [2003] I.C.R. 212 at [19]; *Buyukardicli v Hammerson UK Properties Plc* [2002] EWCA Civ 683 at [7].

[213] [1976] Q.B. 286.

[214] Regarding apportionment in the road accident context more generally, see Goudkamp and Nolan, Contributory Negligence in the *Twenty-First Century* (2019), Ch.6.

[215] *Froom v Butcher* [1976] Q.B. 286 at 296 per Lord Denning MR.

[216] *Salmon v Newland, The Times,* 16 May 1983.

[217] *Capps v Miller* [1989] 2 All E.R. 333.

[218] *Gawler v Raettig* [2007] EWCA Civ 1560; *Stanton v Collinson* [2010] EWCA Civ 81.

[219] *Fitzgerald v Lane* [1989] A.C. 328.

tory negligence has been decided, the court can in contribution proceedings[220] make adjustments as between defendants where one has paid more or less than his fair share.

E. Mitigation of Damage

23-065 **The doctrine of mitigation of damage**[221] The claimant is not entitled to recover damages in respect of any part of his loss that he could have avoided by taking reasonable steps after the tort. Suppose, for example, that a claimant unreasonably fails to undergo surgery that would, on the balance of probabilities, have resolved a painful condition that was caused by the defendant's tort. Pursuant to the doctrine of mitigation of damage, the claimant will be unable to obtain damages in respect of that condition from the date on which the reasonable person would have submitted to surgery. Although the courts often speak of a "duty to mitigate" there is, strictly speaking, no such duty. The claimant is entirely free not to take steps to mitigate his damage. The doctrine of mitigation of damage simply prevents the claimant from charging the consequences of his unreasonable conduct to the defendant. The mitigation of damage doctrine applies to all torts. Even victims of fraud may have their damages reduced by it.[222]

23-066 **An objective test** The claimant is held to an objective standard in respect of mitigation. Thus, the question is what the reasonable person in the claimant's position would have done rather than what was reasonable to expect the claimant to do given his particular characteristics. However, because the defendant is a wrongdoer who has caused the claimant's difficulty, the standard of reasonableness is not a high one in this context.[223] In particular, the claimant will not be expected to, for example, submit to dangerous and risky medical procedures.

23-067 **Causal relevance** Unreasonable conduct by the claimant is only relevant to the extent that it made a difference to the damage about which he complains. Thus, an unreasonable failure by the claimant to follow instructions from his doctor intended to limit the seriousness of an injury for which the defendant was responsible will not count against the claimant if following the instructions would have had no effect on the claimant's condition.

23-068 **Costs incurred in mitigation are recoverable** Money spent by the claimant in an attempt to mitigate his damage are recoverable from the defendant provided that it was reasonable to incur the costs and they are reasonable in amount.[224] For example, a claimant who spends £1,000 on surgery in an attempt to reduce significant pain occasioned by the defendant's tort is likely to be able to recover that sum from the defendant (irrespective of whether the surgery is successful).[225]

23-069 **Relationship with the doctrine of contributory negligence** The precise nature of the relationship between the law of contributory negligence and the law of

---

[220] See Ch.22.

[221] See, further, Summers, *Mitigation in the Law of Damages* (2019).

[222] *Smith New Court Securities Ltd v Citibank NA* [1997] A.C. 254 at 285.

[223] *Banco de Portugal v Waterlow* [1932] A.C. 452 at 506; *Morris v Richards* [2003] EWCA Civ 232. For cases on refusal of medical treatment, see Hudson (1983) 3 L.S. 50.

[224] *Whittington Hospital NHS Trust v XX* [2020] UKSC 14; [2020] 2 W.L.R. 972 at [43].

[225] *Crofts v Murton* [2009] EWHC 3538 (QB) at [56].

mitigation of damage is problematic.[226] According to one view, the former is concerned with pre-tort fault whereas the latter relates to post-tort fault.[227] However, this distinction is not free from difficulty: for one thing, cases can be found in which conduct occurring after the tort was held to constitute contributory negligence.[228] As for the substance and effect of the two doctrines, there are both similarities and differences. The most obvious similarity is that both doctrines are governed by objective tests, in that they are concerned with the reasonableness of what the claimant did. Conversely, two distinctions between the two doctrines should also be highlighted. One is that contributory negligence results only in the claimant's recovery being scaled back, whereas a claimant who fails to mitigate his or her damage cannot recover in respect of any of that damage: the right to recover under particular heads of damage may be eliminated entirely and, indeed, exceptionally, a claim may fail completely. And the other is that the law of mitigation of damage, but not the law of contributory negligence, can increase the claimant's recoverable loss, as where the claimant reasonably but unsuccessfully incurs expenditure with a view to reducing his or her damage.

F. Damages in Personal Injury Actions

i. Heads of Damage

It was for a long time customary, even after the decline of the civil jury, to make **23-070** a global award of damages for personal injury[229] that did not distinguish between the different losses suffered by the claimant. This practice was supported partly on the ground that separate assessment and addition of individual items might lead to "overlapping" and, consequently, an excessive award. However, judges are now required to itemise their award. One reason for this change is that satisfactory appellate review of damages awards would be virtually impossible if the awards were not itemised.

a. Non-pecuniary Loss

Two types of non-pecuniary loss Non-pecuniary loss[230] consists of: (1) pain and **23-071** suffering; and (2) loss of amenity (i.e., the damaging effect of the tort upon the claimant's ability to enjoy life). In practice, the two elements are usually lumped together[231] and are often referred to by the acronym PSLA.[232]

---

226 See further Goudkamp in Pitel, Neyers and Chamberlain (eds), *Tort Law* (2013); Field (2018) 38 O.J.L.S. 475.

227 See, e.g., Edelman, *McGregor on Damages*, 20th edn (2017) at para.6-018 ("Distinguishing between the application of contributory negligence and that of mitigation is comparatively easy. In this context, contributory negligence comes in only before the commission of the wrong, mitigation necessarily after its commission").

228 See, e.g., *The Calliope* [1970] P. 172; *Berry v Calderdale Health Authority* 1998 WL 1043808; *Spencer v Wincanton Holdings Ltd* [2009] EWCA Civ 1404; [2010] P.I.Q.R. P8.

229 Regarding damages for personal injury, see further Cane and Goudkamp, *Atiyah's Accidents, Compensation and the Law*, 9th edn (2018), Ch.6.

230 See, further, *Damages for Personal Injury: Non-Pecuniary Loss*, Law Com. No.257 (1999).

231 *Heil v Rankin* [2001] Q.B. 272 at 298.

232 In *Shaw v Kovac* [2017] EWCA Civ 1028; [2017] 1 W.L.R. 4773 it was unsuccessfully argued that a third head of non-pecuniary loss should be recognised in respect of loss caused by the negligent invasion of a person's autonomy by reason of the performance of surgical procedures without

23-072 Pain and suffering   Pain and suffering is concerned with the subjective experience of the claimant. Thus, damages should not be awarded for pain and suffering if the claimant has suffered no pain because the tort rendered him permanently unconscious.[233] Pain and suffering includes the suffering attributable to any consequential medical treatment, and anxiety about the effects of the injury on the claimant's way of life and prospects. Although damages cannot be recovered for a loss of life expectancy caused by the tort,[234] a person is entitled to damages under this head for the anguish caused by his awareness that his life expectancy has been reduced by his injuries.[235]

23-073 Loss of amenity[236]   The claimant is entitled to damages to the extent that the injuries caused by the tort have reduced his enjoyment of life. For example, if the claimant previously enjoyed playing football and his injuries prevent him from engaging in that activity he will be able to recover compensation in respect of that loss.[237] The same applies in respect of loss of the enjoyment that the claimant would, had he not been injured, have derived from other recreational pursuits, social pastimes and hobbies. A claimant may also be able to recover compensation for the loss of the satisfaction that he would, but for the tort, have obtained from being able to work[238] and from having children.[239]

Loss of amenity is to a large extent an objective element of the claimant's loss and thus distinguishable from pain and suffering. Accordingly, even if the claimant never appreciates the condition to which he has been reduced, he may nevertheless recover substantial damages under this head. In *Wise v Kaye*[240] the claimant remained unconscious from the moment of the accident and was deprived of all the attributes of life but life itself. A majority of the Court of Appeal upheld an award of £15,000 for loss of amenity. In *H West & Son Ltd v Shephard*[241] the claimant was a married woman aged 41 at the time of the accident in which she sustained severe head injuries resulting in cerebral atrophy and paralysis of all four limbs. There was no prospect of improvement in her condition and her expectation of life was reduced to about five years. Although she was unable to speak, there was evidence that she might appreciate to some extent her condition. A majority of the House of Lords upheld an award of £17,500 for loss of amenities. As Lord Morris said: "The fact of unconsciousness does not … eliminate the actuality of the deprivations of the ordinary experiences and amenities of life which may be the inevitable result of some physical injury."[242] Powerful objections have been voiced against the decision in *West*.[243] The principal complaint is that one can no more compensate an unconscious person for loss of the amenities of life than a dead one. Conversely, there is a natural reluctance to treat a living claimant as if he were already dead and

---

informed consent.

[233] *Wise v Kaye* [1962] 1 Q.B. 638.
[234] Administration of Justice Act 1982 s.1(1)(a).
[235] Administration of Justice Act 1982 s.1(1)(b).
[236] Ogus (1972) 35 M.L.R. 1.
[237] *Heaps v Perrite Ltd* [1937] 2 All E.R. 60.
[238] See, e.g., *Hearnshaw v English Steel Corp* (1971) 11 K.I.R. 306.
[239] *XX v Whittington Hospital NHS Trust* [2018] EWCA Civ 2832; [2019] 3 W.L.R. 107 [112] (not doubted on appeal: [2020] UKSC 14; [2020] 2 W.L.R. 972).
[240] [1962] 1 Q.B. 638.
[241] [1964] A.C. 326.
[242] [1964] A.C. 326 at 349.
[243] See, e.g., *Skelton v Collins* (1966) 115 C.L.R. 94.

there are great difficulties in full and accurate diagnosis in these cases.[244] The House of Lords looked at the matter again in *Lim v Camden and Islington Area Health Authority*[245] and refused to overrule *West*, commenting that this "should not be done judicially but legislatively within the context of a comprehensive enactment"[246] on damages.

Objections to the award of non-pecuniary damages generally   A more   **23-074** fundamental question is whether damages for non-pecuniary loss can be justified in *any* case. It has been argued that: (1) they are necessarily arbitrary in amount since there is no market by which to value a limb or brain function; (2) they are secondary in importance to income losses and they divert limited funds from the replacement of those losses; and (3) they represent interests which are not so highly valued by the public since the interests are not commonly insured. However, judging by the responses of accident victims to a Law Commission survey,[247] they provide some sort of solace, however inadequate, for the real hurt suffered by victims of injury.

Assessment   It is in the nature of non-pecuniary loss that it cannot be translated   **23-075** directly into money. All awards of damages for non-pecuniary loss are thus to some extent arbitrary and an inadequate substitute for that which has been lost. Why should an award of, say, £100,000 for the loss of a hand not be £10,000 or £200,000 instead? Nevertheless, because the only type of remedy available is an award of damages, an assessment of damages has to be made.[248] Ultimately, the award "should reflect what society as a whole considers to be fair and reasonable compensation for the victim".[249] At the same time, however, it is necessary for awards to be fair not only to claimants but also to defendants, and it has been said that "[f]airness or justice to defendants is not about an individual defendant, but about defendants as a whole",[250] with the result that nothing turns on whether the defendant is, for instance, a public body, a private corporation or an individual.

Artificiality of comparisons   Although it is possible to compare awards for   **23-076** similar types of injury, it is not clear that comparisons can meaningfully be drawn between awards for different types of injury. If, for example, £200,000 is an appropriate figure for the loss of a leg, what guidance does that give as to the damages appropriate for the loss of the sight of an eye, or for the inability to bear a child, or for loss of the sense of smell? Diplock LJ said that the standard of comparison which the law applies "if it is not wholly instinctive and incommunicable, is based, apart from pain and suffering, upon the degree of deprivation—that is, the extent

---

[244] See *Damages for Personal Injury: Non-Pecuniary Loss*, Law Com. No.257 (1999) at para.2.14. Furthermore, the possibility of advances in medical science bringing about some amelioration of the condition may contribute to the current judicial attitude (*Croke v Wiseman* [1982] 1 W.L.R. 71 at 84) and diagnoses of permanent vegetative state may be wrong.

[245] [1980] A.C. 174.

[246] [1980] A.C. 174 at 189 per Lord Scarman.

[247] Personal Injury Compensation, Law Com. No.225 (1994).

[248] *The Mediana* [1900] A.C. 113 at 116.

[249] *Attorney General of St Helena v AB* [2020] UKPC 1 at [23] per Lord Briggs.

[250] *Attorney General of St Helena v AB* [2020] UKPC 1 at [33] per Lord Briggs.

to which the victim is unable to do those things which, but for the injury, he would have been able to do".[251]

23-077 **The importance of consistency in awards** Major significance is rightly placed on the interest in awards for non-pecuniary damages being reasonably consistent. It is important that similar injuries attract similar awards for two principal reasons. First, fairness requires that similarly positioned claimants are treated in a like way. Second, if awards of damages for non-pecuniary loss are consistent, awards will be reasonably predictable, and this is likely to facilitate settlements. Thus, in the interests of ensuring a measure of consistency in awards of non-pecuniary damages, judges routinely have cited to them awards made in previous cases, although awards do not establish, of course, any precedent.[252] Further, in personal injury matters the courts generally adhere closely to guidelines published by the Judicial Studies Board[253] which establish ranges of awards for particular types of injury. The Privy Council recently remarked that the guidelines "have become firmly embedded in the common law of England and Wales".[254]

23-078 **Appeals** Since the assessment of damages for non-pecuniary loss is not an exact mathematical process the Court of Appeal should not interfere with an award unless the judge has acted on a wrong principle of law, misapprehended the facts, or for other reasons made a wholly erroneous estimate of the loss suffered.[255] Nevertheless, it has been said time and again that the Court of Appeal has general responsibility for ensuring that guidelines for awards of non-pecuniary damages are kept up to date.[256] The guidelines that it issues should be revised to take account of changes both in the value of money and in social attitudes. It has been emphasised that the level of "compensation must remain fair, reasonable and just".[257]

b. Pecuniary Loss

23-079 **Introduction** Pecuniary losses associated with personal injury can include a loss of earnings, medical expenses and care expenses. In the case of a serious accident, the bulk of the claimant's loss will be pecuniary. In so far as these losses have been incurred before the trial or settlement there may be little difficulty regarding their assessment. Complications tend to arise more frequently in relation to quantifying the claimant's future pecuniary loss and reducing it to a capital sum. This process is inevitably inexact because it involves a host of assumptions, including the claimant's future rate of earning had he not been injured, the period and extent of his disability, and the chance that his earning capacity might have been affected by some other vicissitude even if the accident had not happened.

23-080 **Loss of earnings generally** The goal when assessing loss of earnings is to determine the net loss of income that the claimant has incurred because of the tort.

---

[251] *Fletcher v Autocar and Transporters Ltd* [1968] 2 Q.B. 322 at 340.
[252] Even when the courts lay down guidelines as to appropriate awards for given losses, they do not create any precedent: *Wright v British Railways Board* [1983] 2 A.C. 773 at 785.
[253] See the Judicial Studies Board's *Guidelines for the Assessment of General Damages in Personal Injury Cases*, 15th edn (2019).
[254] *Attorney General of St Helena v AB* [2020] UKPC 1 at [20] per Lord Briggs.
[255] *Pickett v British Rail Engineering Ltd* [1980] A.C. 136; *Heil v Rankin* [2001] Q.B. 272.
[256] See, e.g., *Simmons v Castle* [2012] EWCA Civ 1039; [2013] 1 W.L.R. 1239 at [11].
[257] *Heil v Rankin* [2001] Q.B. 272 at [27].

The court will make findings about the gross income that the claimant would have earned per annum had he not been injured. Account will be taken here, for example, of the claimant's prospects of promotion and the likelihood that he would have done overtime work. Where the claimant has not yet entered the workforce because of his age, the court will predict the field of work that the claimant would have entered and what he would have earned. Once the gross annual income has been determined it then has deducted from it income tax,[258] social security contributions[259] and other expenditure that the claimant would have had to incur to gain the income (e.g., his contribution to a company pension scheme[260]). Where the claimant is unable to work as a result of the tort, a case could be made for deducting the claimant's travelling expenses to and from work but, except perhaps in very exceptional circumstances,[261] this is not done.

Risk of disadvantage in the employment market   In cases of continuing disability the claimant may be able to remain in his current employment but with the risk that, if he loses that employment in the future, he may then, as a result of his injury, be at a disadvantage in securing another job or an equally well-paid job. The claimant is entitled to be compensated for that risk. Assessment of damages under this head may be highly speculative and clearly no mathematical approach is possible but the court must be satisfied that there is a "substantial" or "real" risk that the claimant will be subject to the disadvantage before the end of his working life before it awards damages in this connection. If so satisfied, the judge should then do his best to value the "chance", taking into account all the facts of the case.[262]   **23-081**

"Lost years"   In some cases the injury suffered by the claimant will reduce his expectation of life. The claimant is entitled to recover damages in respect of income that he would have earned but for the tort, including during any working years that he loses as a result of the reduction in his life expectancy.[263] Put differently, the claimant's loss of earnings should be assessed based on his life expectancy before rather than after the accident. However, because the claimant will not incur any living expenses during the lost years, these are deducted from the award.   **23-082**

Provision of domestic services   Where the claimant provided unpaid household services before the accident but is unable to continue to do so due to the injuries suffered, he is entitled to recover the cost of substitute services.[264]   **23-083**

---

258 *British Transport Commission v Gourley* [1956] A.C. 185.

259 *Cooper v Firth Brown Ltd* [1963] 1 W.L.R. 418.

260 *Dews v National Coal Board* [1988] A.C. 1. But if as a result of the accident the claimant's employment is terminated and he suffers a reduction in pension, this is itself a compensable head of damage: *Parry v Cleaver* [1970] A.C. 1.

261 Lord Griffiths in *Dews v National Coal Board* [1988] A.C. 1 suggested as a possible example the case of a wealthy man who commuted daily by helicopter from the Channel Islands to London. cf. *Eagle v Chambers* [2004] EWCA Civ 1033; [2004] 1 W.L.R. 3081 at [68].

262 *Ashcroft v Curtin* [1971] 1 W.L.R. 1731; *Smith v Manchester Corp* (1974) 17 K.I.R. 1; *Clarke v Rotax Aircraft Equipment Ltd* [1975] I.C.R. 440; *Moeliker v A. Reyrolle & Co Ltd* [1976] I.C.R. 253; *Nicholls v NCB* [1976] I.C.R. 266; *Robson v Liverpool CC* [1993] P.I.Q.R. Q78; *Goldborough v Thompson* [1996] P.I.Q.R. Q86. Damages may be awarded under this head even though the claimant is unemployed at the date of the trial: *Cook v Consolidated Fisheries Ltd* [1977] I.C.R. 635.

263 *Pickett v British Rail Engineering Ltd* [1980] A.C. 136.

264 *Daly v General Steam Navigation Co Ltd* [1981] 1 W.L.R. 120.

23-084 Past expenses The claimant is entitled to recover the cost of medical and similar services that he reasonably incurred as a result of his injuries. Legislation provides that in determining the reasonableness of any such expenses the possibility of the claimant avoiding them by making use of the NHS is to be disregarded.[265] However, if the claimant in fact receives treatment under the NHS he cannot recover the notional cost of private treatment.[266] If the NHS is utilised, the Health and Social Care (Community Health and Standards) Act 2003 provides for the NHS to recover the cost of treatment from the tortfeasor's insurer up to a statutory cap.[267]

23-085 Future expenses The claimant can recover damages in respect of costs that will reasonably be incurred in the future as a result of the tort, including medication expenses, physiotherapy costs, equipment costs,[268] increased travel costs, the cost of living in a special institution[269] and care. In *Whittington Hospital NHS Trust v XX*,[270] for example, it was held that a claimant who had become infertile due to the negligence of the defendant could claim the cost of commercial surrogacy arrangements in the United States even though such arrangements were unlawful in the United Kingdom. The claimant cannot recover damages for the cost of future private treatment if the evidence shows that he will not take that course and will instead obtain treatment via the NHS.[271] The fact that the claimant may have a statutory right to call upon a local authority for free institutional care does not prevent him from electing to pay for such services in the market and recovering the cost from the defendant.[272]

Expenses that the claimant will incur as a result of the tort will often be incurred up to the date of the claimant's death. Accordingly, in calculating the damages to be awarded for future expenses the courts will need to make a variety of guesses about what life will hold for the claimant in the future, and how things would have been for the claimant had he not been injured. In particular, the claimant's life expectancy will usually be in issue. Statistical tables are generally used to determine the claimant's life expectancy, although these are not binding on the courts.[273]

23-086 Care provided without charge by service provider It may happen that care for which the claimant would otherwise have to pay is rendered without payment. As observed above, the NHS has a statutory right to recoup the cost of such care,[274] but otherwise the provider of the services has no claim in his own right. In *Islington London Borough Council v University College London Hospital NHS Trust*[275] the local authority was under a statutory duty to provide care for the claimant, who had suffered a stroke as a result of the defendants' negligence. Although the claimant had recovered damages these were not available for payment of the local authority's charges. A claim for recoupment against the defendants failed.

---

265 Law Reform (Personal Injuries) Act 1948 s.2(4).
266 *Harris v Brights Asphalt Contractors Ltd* [1953] 1 Q.B. 617 at 635.
267 The regime does not apply to treatment of a disease, unless the claimant is injured and that injury causes the disease: s.150(5)–(6).
268 *S v Distillers Co (Biochemicals) Ltd* [1970] 1 W.L.R. 114; *Povey v Governors of Rydal School* [1970] 1 All E.R. 841.
269 *Shearman v Folland* [1950] 2 K.B. 43; *Oliver v Ashman* [1962] 2 Q.B. 210; *Cutts v Chumley* [1967] 1 W.L.R. 742. For the position where the claimant purchases more suitable accommodation, see *George v Pinnock* [1973] 1 W.L.R. 118; *Roberts v Johnstone* [1989] Q.B. 878.
270 [2020] UKSC 14; [2020] 2 W.L.R. 972.
271 *Eagle v Chambers* [2004] EWCA Civ 1033; [2004] 1 W.L.R. 3081.
272 *Peters v East Midlands Strategic HA* [2009] EWCA Civ 145; [2010] Q.B. 48.
273 *Wells v Wells* [1999] 1 A.C. 345 at 379.
274 See para.23-084.
275 [2005] EWCA Civ 596.

Gratuitous care provided by family and friends   Where care is provided   **23-087**
gratuitously by a relative or friend, the position is somewhat different from that
where the care is provided by a professional service provider. The gratuitous carer
has no claim but the claimant is entitled to recover damages in respect of the
services even though he has not undertaken a legal obligation to pay for them. In
Donnelly v Joyce[276] it was held that the need for the services was the claimant's own
loss and hence damages for that need could be recovered by him. However, it was
subsequently held in *Hunt v Severs*[277] that the claimant, having recovered the damages, held them on trust for the carer. The theory now seems to be that the loss is
the carer's, but that that loss is recoverable only on the action of the victim. The
necessity of imposing a trust to avoid this difficulty has fallen away as the courts
are now empowered to pay the damages directly to the carer.[278]

There is no hard-and-fast rule that governs the sum recoverable under this head.
Where the carer has given up paid employment the lost wages will be recoverable
provided that they do not exceed the commercial rate for the services. In other cases
the sum recoverable may be less than the commercial rate (if only because of the
absence of tax and national insurance payments)[279] but it should be enough to ensure
that the carer gets a reasonable recompense and the court should bear in mind the
possibility that the carer may not be able to provide care indefinitely. Recovery
extends to expenses reasonably incurred for the claimant's benefit, such as the cost
of visits that may assist in the claimant's recovery.[280]

Other pecuniary losses   The pecuniary losses mentioned above are not exhaus-   **23-088**
tive of those for which damages can be recovered, nor can an exhaustive list be
given, for the claimant is entitled to damages for any item of loss he may have suffered as a result of the tort provided only that it is not too remote. The following
examples provide some indication, however, of the kinds of loss that may have to
be considered in any given case. If the claimant's employer provided board and
lodging[281] or a car available for private use[282] and he has to give up his employment as a consequence of the tort, the claimant may recover the value of those items
as well as his actual loss of earnings, and if he has to give up a pensionable employment he can recover for any consequent loss of pension rights.[283] If the injury
inflicted by the defendant makes it more difficult for the claimant to obtain life or
health insurance the additional premiums payable may be recoverable.[284] In professions where reputation is significant, damages may be awarded for loss of opportunity of enhancing that reputation.[285] If the claimant previously did DIY work
around the house or tended to his garden, but now has to employ someone else to
do this work for him because of his injuries, he will be entitled to damages in
respect of that expense.

---

[276] [1974] Q.B. 454.
[277] [1994] 2 A.C. 350.
[278] *Drake v Foster Wheeler Ltd* [2010] EWHC 2004 (QB); [2011] 1 All E.R. 63 at [43].
[279] 25 per cent below the commercial rate seems to be common: *A v National Blood Authority* [2001]
3 All E.R. 289 at 390.
[280] *Hunt v Severs* [1994] 2 A.C. 350 at 357.
[281] *Lifften v Watson* [1940] 1 K.B. 556.
[282] *Clay v Pooler* [1982] 3 All E.R. 570.
[283] *Judd v Hammersmith, West London and St Mark's Hospital Board of Governors* [1960] 1 W.L.R.
328; *Parry v Cleaver* [1970] A.C. 1.
[284] *A v National Blood Authority* [2001] 3 All E.R. 289 at [101].
[285] cf. *Herbert Clayton and Jack Walter Ltd v Oliver* [1930] A.C. 209.

23-089 **The vicissitudes of life**   In determining the claimant's damages for future loss of earnings, the courts will make a reduction for the "general vicissitudes of life"—that is to say, damaging events like sickness or unemployment which might have affected the claimant even if the defendant had not injured him. Although it is justifiable to make a larger reduction for, say, a person in a hazardous occupation, the general range of reductions is modest unless there is evidence to show some special risk affecting the claimant as an individual.[286]

23-090 **Discount rate**   Where the court makes an award for loss of future employment income the claimant receives all of the lost income upon the judgment debt being honoured. Similarly, where a lump sum is awarded in respect of future expenses, the claimant has the enjoyment of those damages before the expenses will be incurred. To prevent the claimant from being overcompensated as a result of having the use value of money (i.e., the ability to invest and earn a return on it), damages awarded in respect of the future need to be discounted (unless inflation is running at such a high rate that it outstrips the rate of return on the capital, in which case it is necessary, instead, to increase the award[287]). The theoretical aim of the process is to provide a lump sum sufficient, when invested, to produce an income equal to the lost income when the interest is supplemented by withdrawals of capital.[288]

The discount rate is fixed by reference to the rate of return that it is thought that the claimant will be able to earn on the lump sum after paying tax, with the rate being prescribed under the Damages Act 1996 by the Lord Chancellor in consultation with the Government Actuary.[289] In recent years, the rate has fluctuated between 2.5 per cent and -0.75 per cent. It is currently -0.25 per cent. The prescribed rate is not binding on the courts but it is expected that judges will depart from it only exceptionally.[290] Different discount rates may be applied to different categories of case. Further, the same discount rate need not be applied to all future pecuniary losses. Where the evidence shows that inflation would affect different heads of damage in different ways the courts may use different rates for different parts of the award.[291]

The discount rate is a highly contentious and politically charged issue. This is in large part because small changes in the discount rate can have a tremendous impact on the size of damages awards, especially in cases involving catastrophically injured claimants, who are likely to suffer future pecuniary loss over a lengthy period of time. Furthermore, debates about the rate of investment return that can be achieved are coloured by the fact that injured claimants often cannot achieve a particularly high rate of return given that many cannot afford to take significant risks with their capital (on which they will depend to pay for, for example, care and medical treatment).

---

[286] *Herring v Ministry of Defence* [2003] EWCA Civ 528; [2004] 1 All E.R. 44.

[287] *Simon v Helmot* [2012] UKPC 5 at [14].

[288] *Simon v Helmot* [2012] UKPC 5 at [11].

[289] For discussion of the issues involved, see Government Actuary's Department, *Setting the Personal Injury Discount Rate* (2019).

[290] *Warriner v Warriner* [2002] EWCA Civ 81; [2002] 1 W.L.R. 1703.

[291] *Simon v Helmot* [2012] UKPC 5 at [52].

ii.   Deductions for Benefits Received

Introduction   The claimant is not entitled to damages in respect of loss which has   **23-091**
been avoided because he has received a countervailing benefit.[292] The problem lies
in distinguishing between those receipts[293] which go to reduce the loss and those
which are "indirect" or "collateral" and do not do so. The issue is of general application in contract as well as in tort[294] and in non-personal injury cases the modern
approach seems to be to ask whether the benefit received is sufficiently causally
connected with the defendant's wrongdoing to require it to be brought into account.
Causation is certainly a necessary element if a benefit is to be deducted from damages in a personal injury case, too—no one would suggest that a person who
received a legacy from the estate of a relative a week after being injured in an accident should have to bring that into account in a claim against the tortfeasor.
However, the deduction issue in personal injury cases has generated a good deal of
case law and many receipts are governed by statute so we must examine this area
more closely. A distinction has to be drawn between receipts from private sources
(governed by the common law) and social security benefits (governed by statute).

a.   Receipts from Private Sources

The general rule   It has been said to be difficult to "articulate a single precise   **23-092**
jurisprudential principle by which to distinguish the deductible from the non-
deductible receipt"[295] but the basic rule is that receipts which have come to the
claimant as a result of the injury are prima facie to be set against his loss of earnings and consequential expenses unless they fall within established exceptions.[296]

Exception: voluntary payments prompted by the benevolence of third par-   **23-093**
ties   Voluntary payments prompted by the benevolence of third parties,[297] whether
into a "disaster fund" or directly to the claimant, are not to be brought into account to reduce the damages. This is for the simple reason that there would
otherwise be a risk that the springs of charity would dry up.[298] Ex gratia payments
by the tortfeasor do not fall within this exception.[299]

Exception: insurance monies accruing to the claimant   The court will not bring   **23-094**
into account monies accruing to the claimant under a contract of insurance if the

---

[292] Regarding the law regarding collateral benefits, see further Lewis, *Deducting Benefits from Dam-*
ages for Personal Injury (1999); Damages for Personal Injury, Law Com. No.262(1999).

[293] The principles governing this question extend to savings made as well as receipts: *Salih v Enfield*
AHA [1991] 3 All E.R. 400 is a macabre example.

[294] Well-known contract cases are *Erie County Natural Gas and Fuel Co Ltd v Carroll* [1911] A.C. 105
and *British Westinghouse Electric and Manufacturing Co Ltd v Underground Electric Railways Co*
of London Ltd [1912] A.C. 673.

[295] *Hodgson v Trapp* [1989] A.C. 807 at 820 per Lord Bridge.

[296] "It is the rule which is fundamental and axiomatic and the exceptions to it which are only to be admitted on grounds which clearly justify their treatment as such": *Hodgson v Trapp* [1989] A.C. 807 at
819 per Lord Bridge.

[297] The benevolent donor has no claim: *Esso Petroleum Co Ltd v Hall Russell & Co Ltd* [1989] A.C.
643.

[298] *Redpath v Belfast County Down Ry* [1947] N.I. 167; *Parry v Cleaver* [1970] A.C. 1; *Naahas v Pier*
House Management (Cheyne Walk) Ltd (1984) 270 E.G. 328 (loss of property).

[299] *Gaca v Pirelli General Plc* [2004] EWCA Civ 373; [2004] 1 W.L.R. 2683.

insurance premiums were paid by the claimant.[300] A reason commonly given for this exception is that the claimant should not be disadvantaged by his own thrift and foresight. It is true that this may sometimes result in over-compensation, although if the insurance contract is one of indemnity the claimant would need to reimburse the insurer out of the damages (although it is more likely that the insurer would sue the tortfeasor by virtue of its subrogation to the insured's rights).

23-095 **Exception: pension payments** If, as a result of the injury, the claimant retires from his job and receives payments under a pension scheme those payments are not deductible from the claim for lost earnings.[301] This is so even if the defendant is an employer who provided or contributed to the pension,[302] although it is open to an employer to draft the pension scheme in such a way as to negate this result. It may happen that the claim of a claimant who has to retire early includes not only loss of earnings but also loss of pension rights which he would have accumulated had he worked until the normal retirement age. In that case the pension received is brought into account in so far as it is received in the period after the normal date of retirement.[303]

23-096 **Sick pay** By contrast, sick pay is deductible from damages for loss of earnings. That is so whether or not it is paid by the defendant[304] and even if it takes the form of a very long-term payment that the employer has based on an arrangement with an insurance company.[305] No deduction is, of course, made where the payment to the claimant is made on condition of repayment in the event of recovery of damages.[306]

b. Social Security Benefits

23-097 Pursuant to the Social Security (Recovery of Benefits) Act 1997, a person[307] is not to make any compensation payment in consequence of an accident, injury or disease until he has applied to the Secretary of State for a "certificate of recoverable benefits" for the purposes of the Act. A compensation payment for this purpose is not confined to damages payable under a judgment but extends to an out-of-court settlement, whether or not proceedings have been commenced.[308] The recoverable benefits for the purposes of the certificate are the specified social security benefits paid to the victim during the five years immediately following the accident or until the making of the compensation payment, whichever is earlier. The basic rule, which is subject to a host of qualifications that cannot be explored here,

---

[300] *Bradburn v Great Western Railway Co* (1874) L.R. Ex. 1. Thus, this exception does not apply if the premiums are paid for by the tortfeasor: *Gaca v Pirelli General Plc* [2004] EWCA Civ 373; [2004] 1 W.L.R. 2683. But it would be surprising if insurance payments were brought into account where the premiums were paid by someone not responsible for the tort. It is hard to believe that the damages of an injured holidaymaker are to be reduced because another member of the family paid the travel insurance premiums.

[301] *Parry v Cleaver* [1970] A.C. 1.

[302] *Smoker v London Fire and Civil Defence Authority* [1991] 2 A.C. 502.

[303] *Longden v British Coal Corp* [1998] A.C. 653; *Parry v Cleaver* [1970] A.C. 1; *Cantwell v Criminal Injuries Compensation Board* [2001] UKHL 36; 2001 S.L.T. 966.

[304] *Parry v Cleaver* [1970] A.C. 1.

[305] *Hussain v New Taplow Paper Mills Ltd* [1988] A.C. 514.

[306] *Berriello v Felixstowe Dock & Ry Co* [1989] I.C.R. 467.

[307] In practice, in most cases the defendant's insurer.

[308] Section 1(2).

is that this sum is to be deducted from the damages and paid to the Secretary of State. There is no offset for contributory negligence which means that if the defendant is, say, only 10 per cent liable for the claimant's injuries he still has to reimburse the government for all the benefits. Indeed, there is no requirement that the defendant should actually be liable to the claimant at all and it is thus dangerous to make a small payment to buy off a "nuisance" claim. Fatal accident cases are entirely outside the scope of the Act.

iii. Pre-Judgement Interest

Although the court has the power in certain circumstances to order an interim **23-098** payment of damages on account,[309] the claimant will frequently have to wait for a considerable period of time until his claim has been determined and the damages found due to him are paid. Accordingly, it is mandatory to award interest in an action for personal injuries in which the claimant recovers more than £200 unless the court is satisfied that there are special reasons why this should not be done.[310] In personal injury[311] and fatal accident[312] cases the pecuniary loss up to the date of the trial should carry interest at half the short-term interest rates current during that period, but no interest should be awarded in respect of future pecuniary loss because that loss has not yet been sustained. Interest is to be awarded in respect of non-pecuniary loss[313] at the rate of two per cent.[314] The reason for this (historically low) rate is that damages for non-pecuniary loss will be awarded at the rates prevailing at the time of the trial, thus covering any intervening fall in the value of money. That which the claimant has, therefore, lost by late receipt of his damages under this head is only the element of modern interest rates which truly represent the "use value" of money.[315]

iv. Provisional Damages

As explained above, the common law is committed to the principle that dam- **23-099** ages must be paid in a lump sum.[316] There are various exceptions to this principle. One such exception is provided for in s.32A of the Senior Courts Act 1981.[317] This section applies to an action for personal injuries in which there is proved or admitted to be a chance that at some time in the future the injured person will, as a result of the defendant's tort, develop some serious disease or suffer some serious deterioration in his physical or mental condition. In such a case the court has the power to make a provisional award—that is to say, to award damages on the basis

---

[309] CPR Pt 25.
[310] Senior Courts Act 1981 s.35A; County Courts Act 1984 s.69.
[311] *Jefford v Gee* [1970] 2 Q.B. 130; *Cookson v Knowles* [1977] Q.B. 913 (on appeal [1979] A.C. 556). There may be cases in which the award should be at the full, not the half, rate: *Ichard v Frangoulis* [1977] 1 W.L.R. 556.
[312] *Cookson v Knowles* [1979] A.C. 556.
[313] *Pickett v British Rail Engineering Ltd* [1980] A.C. 136.
[314] *Wright v British Railways Board* [1983] 2 A.C. 773.
[315] Arguably this should be the figure used as the assumed rate of return on damages for future pecuniary loss (currently -0.25 per cent), but it is not: *Laurence v Chief Constable of Staffordshire* [2000] P.I.Q.R. Q349. The court may abridge the period during which interest is payable if the claimant unjustifiably delays bringing the case to trial.
[316] See para.23-005.
[317] See, further, *Structured Settlements and Interim and Provisional Damages*, Law Com. No.224 (1994).

that the claimant will not suffer the disease or deterioration in question but with power to award further damages if and when he does. Obviously, this procedure is only of use in those cases where the risk of deterioration in the claimant's condition is known before judgment. The provisions have been interpreted to require a "clear and severable event" (such as, perhaps, the development of epilepsy following a head injury) rather than a gradual deterioration (such as joint degeneration or arthritis, which are common sequelae of orthopaedic injury).[318] This restriction was regarded as justifiable because an extension to gradual deterioration would vastly increase the number of cases in which provisional awards could be made and introduce a serious measure of uncertainty into the system. It should be noted that s.32A only permits damages to be increased rather than decreased.

v. Periodical Payment Orders

23-100 **The provision for periodical payments** In another departure from the principle that damages are to be paid as a lump sum,[319] s.2(1) of the Damages Act 1996 provides: "A court awarding damages in an action for personal injury may, with the consent of the parties, make an order under which the damages are wholly or partly to take the form of periodical payments."

23-101 **It is for the court to decide whether to order damages in the form of periodical payments** It is a matter for the court to decide whether to order that damages will take the form of periodical payments irrespective of what either (or even both[320]) of the parties may want. Although the wishes of a properly advised claimant are entitled to considerable weight, ultimately the question for the judge is what form of order best meets the claimant's needs and there may be cases in which he is satisfied that "he knows what is best for the claimant better than the claimant himself knows".[321]

23-102 **Relevant factors** In deciding whether to give judgment for periodical payments the court must "have regard to all the circumstances of the case and in particular the form of award which best meets the claimant's needs".[322] By CPR PD 41B, the relevant factors include:

> "(1)   the scale of the annual payments taking into account any deduction for contributory negligence;
> (2)   the form of award preferred by the claimant[323] including—
>   (a)   the reasons for the claimant's preference; and
>   (b)   the nature of any financial advice received by the claimant when considering the form of award; and
> (3)   the form of award preferred by the defendant including the reasons for the defendant's preference."

---

[318] *Willson v Ministry of Defence* [1991] 1 All E.R. 638.

[319] See para.23-005.

[320] But if only for evidential reasons a court is unlikely to go against the wishes of both parties: *Thompstone v Tameside and Glossop Acute Services NHS Trust* [2008] EWCA Civ 5; [2008] 1 W.L.R. 2207 at [102].

[321] *Thompstone v Tameside and Glossop Acute Services NHS Trust* [2008] EWCA Civ 5; [2008] 1 W.L.R. 2207 at [103].

[322] CPR Pt 41.7.

[323] In *Freeman v Lockett* [2006] EWHC 102 (QB) a lump sum award of £5.5 million (mostly in respect of future care) was made where the claimant had received expert advice and wished to avoid dependence on public funds.

"Stepped" periodical payments Periodical payments may be "stepped"—that is, **23-103** made at such and such a rate for one period and at a different rate for another—to reflect anticipated changes in the claimant's circumstances.[324]

Continuity of the payments must be secure The secure continuity of the pay- **23-104** ments is obviously of critical importance and the court can only make an order for periodical payments if it is satisfied that this continuity is reasonably secure.[325]

Indexation Payments will usually be linked to the Retail Prices Index but in **23-105** *Thompstone v Tameside and Glossop Acute Services NHS Trust*,[326] a long-term care case, the Court of Appeal approved indexation by reference to an index based on care costs and this will be the norm in the absence of good reason to the contrary.[327]

Variation Periodical payments can be varied because of changed **23-106** circumstances.[328] As far as deterioration is concerned the law is modelled on the provisional damages regime,[329] so it must be proved, admitted or agreed that there is a chance that in the future the claimant will develop some serious disease or suffer some serious deterioration. However, the variation provisions apply equally to the case where there may be some "significant improvement" in his condition,[330] a factor which could obviously influence a claimant in his attitude towards the choice between a lump sum and periodical payments. Whether it is deterioration or improvement, the power to vary is confined to changes in the claimant's condition; so it will not cover, for example, changes in the availability or cost of care where these cannot be absorbed by the relevant indexation.

vi. Structured Settlements

Generally Structured settlements[331] are a further exception to the principle that **23-107** damages should be paid as a lump sum. A structured settlement involves damages for future loss being calculated as a lump sum in the traditional way. However, instead of the damages being paid to the claimant as a lump sum, the defendant's insurer discharges its liability by purchasing an annuity for the claimant from a life insurance company. The annuity provides the claimant with a guaranteed stream of income that (usually) is insulated from the effects of inflation. The duration of the annuity may exceed the claimant's life, in which case the income would go to the claimant's estate.

Distinguished from periodical payment orders Structured settlements are **23-108** similar to periodical payments in that like periodical payments they involve the payment of compensation to the claimant being spread over a period of time. However, there are several ways in which structured settlements differ from periodical payments. For one thing, structured settlements are consensual arrangements

---

[324] CPR Pt 41.8.

[325] CPR Pt 41.9.

[326] [2008] EWCA Civ 5; [2008] 1 W.L.R. 2207.

[327] [2008] EWCA Civ 5; [2008] 1 W.L.R. 2207 at [100].

[328] Damages (Variation of Periodical Payments) Order 2005 (SI 2005/841).

[329] See para.23-094.

[330] Damages (Variation of Periodical Payments) Order 2005 (SI 2005/841) arts 2 and 9.

[331] See, further, Lewis, *Structured Settlements* (1993); *Structured Settlements and Interim and Provisional Damages*, Law Com. No.224 (1994).

reached between the parties whereas periodical payments are made pursuant to a court order. Furthermore, a defendant remains liable to the claimant pursuant to a periodical payment order whereas, in the case of a structured settlement, once an annuity has been purchased for the claimant, the defendant's liability to the claimant will be discharged.

23-109 **Advantages** Structured settlements have several advantages from the perspective of claimants. First, they relieve the claimant of the burden of having to invest the damages and to manage that investment. It is the life insurer that is responsible for investing the lump sum and ensuring that it supplies income to the claimant. Second, structured settlements provide the claimant with security. The annuity will usually be a life annuity, in which case the income will be guaranteed to the claimant for his life. The life insurer carries the risk that the claimant will live for longer than expected. Third, there are tax advantages to structured settlements. If the claimant opts to receive a lump sum and invests it, the income generated by the investment will be taxable in the claimant's hands. However, income flowing from a structured settlement is not taxable. From the perspective of the defendant's insurer, the main advantage of structured settlements is that since claimants make a tax saving by opting for a structured settlement, the insurer should theoretically be able to negotiate a discount on the sum that would be required for a conventional lump sum settlement.

23-110 **Disadvantages** The key downside of structured settlements from the viewpoint of claimants is that the capital is locked up in the annuity. The flexibility that a lump sum payment affords to claimants is lost in a structured settlement.

G. Damages for Damage to or Unauthorised Use of Property

23-111 As we have seen, the basic principle governing the assessment of damages is that there should be restitutio in integrum,[332] and in cases of damage to property this principle can be more fully applied than in cases of personal injury.[333] It is, in fact, the primary rule to which the subsidiary rules which follow must conform.[334] In working out these subsidiary rules the courts have often been concerned with cases involving ships, but the rules are the same in Admiralty and under the common law.[335]

i. Destruction of Chattels

23-112 **The general principle** Where a chattel is totally destroyed by the defendant's tort the normal measure of damages is its value at the time and place of the destruction. In principle the claimant is generally entitled to such a sum of money as would enable him to purchase a replacement in the market at the prices prevailing at the date of destruction[336] or as soon thereafter as is reasonable.[337] Where no precise equivalent is available the claimant may be allowed a recovery that exceeds the

---

[332] See para.23-010.
[333] For the measure of damages in conversion, see para.18-049.
[334] *Liesbosch Dredger v SS Edison* [1933] A.C. 449 at 463.
[335] *Admiralty Commissioners v SS Susquehanna* [1926] A.C. 655 at 661; *Beechwood Birmingham Ltd v Hoyer Group UK Ltd* [2010] EWCA Civ 647; [2011] 1 All E.R. (Comm) 460 at [47].
[336] *Liesbosch Dredger v SS Edison* [1933] A.C. 449. In *Smith Kline & French Laboratories Ltd v Long*

amount that he could have obtained by selling the chattel,[338] but the cost of producing an exact replacement will be refused where it is well in excess of the value of what was destroyed and a reasonable substitute is available.[339]

Consequential loss   The claimant may recover damages for consequential losses **23-113** that are not too remote, such as the reasonable cost of hiring a substitute until a replacement can be bought.[340] When the chattel destroyed was used by the claimant in the course of his business then loss of business profits may be taken into account. Speaking of destruction of a ship, Lord Wright said[341]:

> "The true rule seems to be that the measure of damages in such cases is the value of the ship to her owner as a going concern at the time and place of the loss. In assessing that value regard must naturally be had to her pending engagements, either profitable or the reverse."

Avoiding double counting   Care must be taken to avoid awarding damages twice **23-114** over. The market value of a profit-earning chattel such as a ship will normally reflect the fact that the chattel will be used in a profit-earning capacity. It follows that the actual loss of prospective freights or other profits cannot, therefore, simply be added to that market value as doing so would result in overcompensation.[342] It is necessary to distinguish when assessing damages between the profit-earning potential of a ship without any engagement but with the chance of making a profit, which will be reflected in the market value, and the actual profits that would have been made by the claimant's ship had it not been destroyed.[343] Nevertheless, if a ship is actually under charter at the time of her destruction or has charters that would have commenced shortly thereafter, the loss of those charters may be allowed in some cases[344] as damages for loss of use of the ship from the time of its destruction until the time when it could reasonably be replaced.[345] In deciding whether or not these damages may be added to the market value, the manner in which the market value itself has been determined is of critical importance. If it is determined on the basis that the ship was in any case virtually certain of profitable employment, then nothing may be added for the loss of actual charters,[346] but if the market value does not assume the full employment of the ship then the loss of actual charters must be taken into account.

[1989] 1 W.L.R. 1 (a case of deprivation by deceit) the claimants could themselves produce a replacement at less than market cost but were nevertheless entitled to recover the market value.

[337] The price the claimant paid for the article is not decisive for he may have got a bargain: *Dominion Mosaics and Tile Co Ltd v Trafalgar Trucking Co Ltd* [1990] 2 All E.R. 246.

[338] *Clyde Navigation Trustees v Bowring Steamship Co Ltd* 1929 S.C. 715; cf. *Southampton Container Terminals Ltd v Schiffahrtsgesellschaft "Hansa Australia" MBH & Co (The Maersk Colombo)* [2001] EWCA Civ 717; [2001] 2 Lloyd's Rep. 275.

[339] *Ucktos v Mazzetta* [1956] 1 Lloyd's Rep. 209.

[340] *Moore v DER Ltd* [1971] 1 W.L.R. 1476.

[341] *Dredger Liesbosch v SS Edison* [1933] A.C. 449 at 463–464. See also *Jones v Port of London Authority* [1954] 1 Lloyd's Rep. 489 (lorry).

[342] *The Llanover* [1947] P. 80.

[343] For this distinction, see *The Philadelphia* [1917] P. 101 at 108.

[344] *The Kate* [1899] P. 165; *The Racine* [1906] P. 273; *The Philadelphia* [1917] P. 101.

[345] See *The Arpad* [1934] P. 189 at 217.

[346] *The Llanover* [1947] P. 80.

ii. Damage to Chattels

23-115 **The general principle** Where a chattel has been damaged rather than destroyed the normal measure of damages is the amount by which its value has been diminished. The diminution in value will usually be ascertained by reference to the reasonable cost of repair,[347] simply because that is usually the only practical way to do it: while there is a market in two-year-old cars of a certain make, model and mileage, there are no markets in such cars with dented wings or broken mirrors, and we just assume that a buyer will reduce his price by the cost of repair.

23-116 **Significance of the fact that the cost of repair is merely evidence of the diminution in value** It is important to bear in mind that the loss is the diminution in value, not the cost of repair. The cost of repair is simply evidence of the diminution in value.[348] The fact that the cost of repair is of merely evidential value has several important consequences. First, the fact that the claimant can have a chattel repaired at reduced or no cost does not mean that there is no compensable loss.[349] Second, where the claimant has had a chattel repaired at unreasonable cost the reason he cannot recover the high cost of repair is that it does not represent the diminution in value of the chattel.[350] Third, it does not matter that the repairs have not been carried out at the date of the trial,[351] or even that they are never carried out at all,[352] as where a ship is lost from other causes before the repairs are done.[353] If, however, a ship is damaged while on its way to the breaker's yard it is unlikely that the cost of repairing the ship could be recovered, for that would not necessarily represent the true reduction in the ship's value; all that could be recovered would be the diminution, if any, in the value of the ship as scrap.[354] Fourth, the fact that the cost of repairing the chattel exceeds its total value does not mean that more than its value can be recovered. Rather, in such a case, the measure of damages will normally be the cost of replacement, although the position may be otherwise where the chattel has, for example, particular sentimental value to the claimant.[355] Fifth, if the chattel was already in need of repair at the time of the tort, and if repairing the pre-tort damage would also repair the damage caused by the tort, the claimant is not entitled to recover anything since the tort did not reduce the chattel's value.[356]

23-117 **Loss of the use of the chattel while it is being repaired** If the damage to the chattel deprived the claimant of its use for a period of time he is entitled to compensation in respect of that loss. This is so even where he is provided with a substitute by his insurer without charge.[357] In *The Mediana*[358] Lord Halsbury LC considered that the fact that the claimant would not have actually used the chattel

---

[347] *Coles v Hetherton* [2013] EWCA Civ 1704; [2015] 1 W.L.R. 160 at [27]. Where the claimant does repairs "in house" he may be entitled to a sum for overheads as well as direct labour costs but what is relevant in causation terms may be a difficult question: *Ulsterbus Ltd v Donnelly* [1982] 13 N.I.J.B.

[348] *Coles v Hetherton* [2013] EWCA Civ 1704; [2015] 1 W.L.R. 160 at [28].

[349] *Coles v Hetherton* [2013] EWCA Civ 1704; [2015] 1 W.L.R. 160 at [29].

[350] *Coles v Hetherton* [2013] EWCA Civ 1704; [2015] 1 W.L.R. 160 at [32].

[351] *The Kingsway* [1918] P. 344.

[352] *Coles v Hetherton* [2013] EWCA Civ 1704; [2015] 1 W.L.R. 160 at [27].

[353] *The York* [1929] P. 178 at 184–185; *Dimond v Lovell* [2000] 2 W.L.R. 1121 at 1140.

[354] See *The London Corp* [1935] P. 70 at 77–78, where Greer LJ seems to have been in two minds on this point.

[355] *O'Grady v Westminster Scaffolding Ltd* [1962] 2 Lloyd's Rep. 238.

[356] *Performance Cars Ltd v Abraham* [1962] 1 Q.B. 33.

[357] *Coles v Hetherton* [2013] EWCA Civ 1704; [2015] 1 W.L.R. 160 at [46].

was no bar to a claim for loss of use. How should the loss of use be valued? The appropriate measure may differ from case to case,[359] but a calculation based on the daily cost of running a substitute plus depreciation may be suitable,[360] especially where a substitute is on standby. In the last resort, the claimant is entitled to interest on the capital value of the chattel for the period during which it is out of use plus expenses thrown away and depreciation.[361] In the case of (for example) a ship that turns a profit the normal measure of damages will be the loss of profits calculated at the freight rates prevailing during the relevant period or, where the hire of a substitute is a reasonable way of avoiding such losses, the cost of that hire.[362] However, the measure based upon prevailing freight rates may in the event be too high or too low. It will be too high if the ship was operating at a loss at the time of the damage[363] and too low if the damage prevented the ship from fulfilling an actual charter already entered into at favourable rates.[364]

Cost of hiring a substitute   Where the claimant has hired a chattel to replace that   **23-118**
which was damaged he is entitled to damages for the cost of the hire.[365] In *Giles v Thompson*[366] it was held that where a substitute is hired it is no answer to a claim for the cost of hire that the claimant's obligation to pay for the hire is contingent upon recovery from the defendant. It was also said that the fact of hire (and not merely its quantum) must be reasonably undertaken.[367] This may mean that if C has two cars for his sole use, C cannot recover the cost of hiring a replacement when one is damaged.

iii.   Land and Fixtures

Generally   The principles that have been considered thus far have been worked   **23-119**
out in the context of damage to chattels. The rules governing compensation in respect of damage caused to land and buildings are not fundamentally different although their application must take account of the different character of real property. For example, where the property is a building rather than a chattel the claimant is more likely to recover the cost of reinstatement even though it exceeds the value of the property. Ultimately, however, the reasonableness of the proposed expenditure is the issue so that where the cost of reinstatement is out of all proportion to the diminution in value the latter will be taken as the measure of damages.[368] The court may allow a degree of reinstatement but refuse the claimant the extra cost

---

358 [1900] A.C. 113 at 117.
359 In *Admiralty Commissioners v SS Susquehanna* [1926] A.C. 655 at 661, Viscount Dunedin said that these are jury-type questions on which no rigid rules are possible. cf. *West Midlands Travel Ltd v Aviva Insurance UK Ltd* [2013] EWCA Civ 887; [2004] R.T.R. 10 at [6].
360 *The Marpessa* [1907] A.C. 241; *Admiralty Commissioners v SS Susquehanna* [1926] A.C. 655; *The Hebridean Coast* [1961] A.C. 545.
361 *West Midlands Travel Ltd v Aviva Insurance Ltd* [2013] EWCA Civ 887; [2014] R.T.R. 10.
362 If a substitute is hired and the claimant is thereby enabled to make a greater profit than he would have done if his own chattel had never been damaged, credit for this must be given: *The World Beauty* [1969] P. 12 (reversed without affecting this point: [1970] P. 144)
363 *The Bodlewell* [1907] P. 286. See also *SS Strathfillan v SS Ikala* [1929] A.C. 196.
364 *The Argentino* (1889) 14 App. Cas. 519.
365 *Coles v Hetherton* [2013] EWCA Civ 1704; [2015] 1 W.L.R. 160 at [46].
366 [1994] 1 A.C. 142.
367 [1994] 1 A.C. 142 at 167.
368 *Jones v Gooday* (1841) 8 M. & W. 146; 152 E.R. 311; *Lodge Holes Colliery Co Ltd v Wednesbury Corp* [1908] A.C. 323.

of precise and meticulous restoration that will not increase the utility of the property.[369] The claimant cannot recover cost of repairs in excess of diminution in value where he has no intention of carrying them out.[370]

23-120 **Consequential loss** Consequential losses, such as loss of rent or profits, may be recovered.[371]

iv. Unauthorised Use of Property

23-121 **User damages** When D makes unauthorised use of C's property (such as by trespassing and dumping material on it[372] or by taking or detaining it[373]), the courts regard C as having suffered a loss,[374] and that is so even if C would not have used the property himself at the time in question.[375] The loss, the courts have held, consists in D's preventing C "from exercising his right to obtain the economic value of the use in question".[376] Damages awarded in respect of this loss are generally called "user damages" and they should represent "a reasonable sum for the wrongful use [D] has made of [C's] property".[377] Where the unauthorised use involves C's land, the action for mesne profits enables C to claim, among other things, a reasonable rent for the possession of the land by D. This issue has already been addressed.[378]

v. The Date of Assessment

23-122 Particularly in the context of damage to buildings, the possibility of inflation means that the date at which damages are to be assessed is significant, for a judgment representing the cost of repair at the time of the wrong, even with interest, may not be sufficient to cover the cost of the work at the time of the trial.[379] While the general rule remains that damages are assessed as at the time when the tort is committed,[380] that rule is subject to exceptions and in a repair case the applicable principle is that the date for assessment of damages is the time when, having regard to all relevant circumstances, repairs can first reasonably be undertaken,[381] and in

---

[369] *Ward v Cannock Chase DC* [1986] Ch. 546.
[370] *Perry v Sidney Phillips & Son* [1982] 1 W.L.R. 1297; *Hole & Son (Sayers Common) v Harrisons of Thurnscoe* [1973] 1 Lloyd's Rep. 345.
[371] *Rust v Victoria Graving Dock Co* (1887) 36 Ch. D. 113; *Dodd Properties Ltd v Canterbury CC* [1980] 1 W.L.R. 433.
[372] *Whitwham v Westminster Brymbo Coal and Coke Co* [1896] 2 Ch. 538; *Martin v Porter* (1839) 5 M. & W. 351; 151 E.R. 149; *Jegon v Vivian* (1871) L.R. 6 Ch. App. 742; *Penarth Dock Engineering Co Ltd v Pounds* [1963] 1 Lloyd's Rep. 359.
[373] *Watson, Laidlaw & Co Ltd v Pott, Cassels and Williamson* (1914) 31 R.P.C. 104 at 119; *Strand Electric and Engineering Co Ltd v Brisford Entertainments Ltd* [1952] 2 Q.B. 246.
[374] See Sharpe and Waddams (1982) O.J.L.S. 290.
[375] Famously illustrated by the Earl of Halsbury LC in *The Mediana* [1900] A.C. 133 at 117.
[376] *Morris-Garner v One Step (Support) Ltd* [2018] UKSC 20; [2019] A.C. 649 at [30] per Lord Reed. See also at [95].
[377] *Stoke-on-Trent CC v W & J Wass Ltd* [1988] 1 W.L.R. 1406 at 1416 per Nicholls LJ.
[378] See para.14-033.
[379] In *Dodd Properties Ltd v Canterbury CC* [1980] 1 W.L.R. 433 the cost of repair when the damage was done in 1968 was £10,817. At the date of judgment, 10 years later, the cost was £30,327. Interest on a judgment at the 1968 cost would have amounted to about £5,500.
[380] *Miliangos v George Frank (Textiles) Ltd* [1976] A.C. 443 at 468.
[381] *Dodd Properties Ltd v Canterbury CC* [1980] 1 W.L.R. 433.

determining this question it is proper to pay regard to the claimant's financial position.[382]

vi. Benefits Received as a Result of the Tort

Whether it is a case of damage or destruction the defendant cannot rely on the **23-123** fact that the claimant is entitled to claim on an insurance policy.[383] Indeed, many marine property damage claims will be brought by subrogated loss insurers and that can only happen if the claimant retains his right of action after claiming on his policy. That is in line with the position in personal injury cases.[384] That analogy also points to recovery where funds to replace or repair the goods are provided as, say, an act of kindness by a relative.

2. OTHER REMEDIES

A. Injunctive Relief

i. General Principles

Introduction[385]   An injunction is an order restraining the commission or continu- **23-124** ance of some wrongful act, or the continuance of some wrongful omission. Originally only the Court of Chancery could issue an injunction, but now other courts may do so in any case in which it appears to be "just and convenient" for one to be granted.[386] Although an injunction is a discretionary remedy rather than relief to which the claimant is entitled as of right, this does not mean that the court has a free hand to restrain conduct of which it disapproves. Ordinarily, the claimant must have some cause of action (whether for a tort or in protection of some legal or equitable right) against the defendant before an injunction can be granted, for if the law were otherwise "every judge would need to be issued with a portable palm tree".[387]

Torts for which injunctive relief can be obtained   Injunctions are generally **23-125** sought against such torts as nuisance, trespass, passing off or interference with contract but there is no reason why an injunction should not be issued to restrain the repetition or continuation of a tort of any kind. The circumstances in which injunctive relief may be granted depend somewhat on the legal context in which it is sought. The text that follows offers a general discussion of injunctive relief. The availability of injunctive relief in relation to certain specific torts has already been considered at appropriate points in this book.

Injunctive relief is discretionary   Like other equitable remedies, the issue of an **23-126** injunction is in the court's discretion. Put differently, an injunction cannot be demanded as of right. However, in the context of prohibitory injunctions (i.e., those

---

[382] *Dodd Properties Ltd v Canterbury CC* [1980] 1 W.L.R. 433; *Alcoa Minerals of Jamaica Inc v Broderick* [2002] 1 A.C. 371.
[383] *Coles v Hetherton* [2013] EWCA Civ 1704; [2015] 1 W.L.R. 160 at [36].
[384] See para.23-094.
[385] Gee, *Commercial Injunctions*, 6th edn (2016).
[386] Senior Courts Act 1981 s.37; County Courts Act 1984 s.38.
[387] *CC Kent v V* [1983] Q.B. 34 at 45 per Donaldson LJ.

ordering the defendant to desist from wrongful conduct) it would be wrong to think that a claimant who establishes interference with his rights will face any particular difficulty in obtaining one. For example, a landowner is prima facie entitled to an injunction to restrain trespass by the defendant in parking his vehicle on the land[388] or running hounds across it[389] or swinging a crane jib through the air above it[390] even though he cannot produce evidence of any particular harm. Similarly, a landowner is prima facie entitled to an injunction to restrain a nuisance that is affecting his land.[391] This means that in these situations the burden lies with the defendant to show that an injunction should not be granted.[392]

Although an injunction will not be granted where damages are an adequate remedy[393] this does not mean that the defendant who is willing to pay can demand to buy out the claimant's rights. In *Shelfer v City of London Electric Lighting Co*[394] the operation of the defendant's engines seriously interfered with the enjoyment of the premises occupied by the claimant. Granting an injunction, Lindley LJ commented that the Court of Chancery had rejected the notion that the legislature, in allowing the award of damages in lieu of an injunction,[395] "intended to turn that Court into a tribunal for legalising wrongful acts; or in other words, the Court has always protested against the notion that it ought to allow a wrong to continue simply because the wrongdoer is able and willing to pay for the injury he may inflict".[396] Where the injury to the claimant is trivial[397] or of a very temporary character the court may content itself with awarding damages. However, an injunction will not be withheld simply because granting it will inflict more harm on the defendant than the continuance of the activity concerned will cause to the claimant.

ii. Interim Injunctions

23-127 **Generally** An injunction issued at the conclusion of a trial on the merits is known as a perpetual or final injunction, but an "interim injunction" may also be issued provisionally pending the hearing of the case on the merits. The principles governing the award of interim injunctive relief are found in *American Cyanamid Co v Ethicon Ltd*.[398] Pursuant to that case, a claimant need not establish a prima facie case but merely that there is a "serious question" to be tried.[399] If the claimant can meet that threshold, the court must then decide whether the balance of convenience lies in favour of granting or refusing interim relief. The court should consider in this regard all of the circumstances of the case including whether: (1) damages are likely to be an adequate remedy for the claimant; (2) an undertaking by the claimant to

---

[388] *Patel v WH Smith (Eziot) Ltd* [1987] 1 W.L.R. 853. See *John Trenberth Ltd v National Westminster Bank Ltd* (1979) 39 P. & C.R. 104.
[389] *League Against Cruel Sports Ltd v Scott* [1986] Q.B. 240.
[390] *Anchor Brewhouse Developments v Berkley House (Docklands Developments)* (1987) 284 E.G. 625.
[391] *Coventry v Lawrence* [2014] UKSC 13; [2014] A.C. 822 at [100].
[392] *Coventry v Lawrence* [2014] UKSC 13; [2014] A.C. 822 at [121].
[393] *London and Blackwall Railway Co v Cross* (1886) 31 Ch. D. 354 at 369.
[394] [1895] 1 Ch. 287.
[395] See para.23-130.
[396] [1895] 1 Ch. 287 at 315–316.
[397] *Llandudno Urban District Council v Woods* [1899] 2 Ch. 705; *Behrens v Richards* [1905] 2 Ch. 614; *Armstrong v Sheppard and Short Ltd* [1959] 2 Q.B. 384.
[398] [1975] A.C. 396.
[399] The same test applies whether the claimant is seeking a mandatory or prohibitory interim injunction: *National Commercial Bank Jamaica Ltd v Olint Corpn Ltd* [2009] UKPC 16; [2009] 1 W.L.R. 1405 at [20].

pay damages in respect of loss that the injunction may cause to the defendant would adequately protect the defendant's interests in the event that the claimant fails at trial (which undertaking is usually the price that the claimant must pay for an interim injunction[400]); and (3) the preservation of the status quo is important enough to warrant granting an injunction. The relative strength of each party's case is only to be considered when the other factors leave the balance of convenience "even". In cases of great urgency or where the defendant, if notified of an application for an injunction is likely to take steps to frustrate it, the claimant can obtain an interim injunction in the absence of the defendant[401] which will remain in force for a few days until there can be an inter partes hearing.

Defamation cases Interim injunctions in defamation cases are exceedingly rare because of the public interest in freedom of expression.[402] Under s.12 of the Human Rights Act 1998 no interim injunction is to be granted that might curtail freedom of expression unless the court is satisfied that the applicant is "likely" to establish at trial that publication would not be allowed,[403] which is a higher threshold than that prescribed by *American Cyanamid*. **23-128**

iii. Quia Timet Injunctions

Injunctions are normally issued only when a tort has already been committed. Where, however, the conduct of the defendant is such that, if it is allowed to continue, substantial wrongful damage to the claimant is almost bound to occur, the claimant may bring a "quia timet" action—that is, an action for an injunction to prevent an apprehended legal wrong.[404] The existence of the court's power to grant a *quia timet* injunction is undoubted,[405] but it is not often exercised, for the claimant must show both a near certainty that damage will occur[406] and that it is imminent.[407] And even then an injunction will not be issued to compel the defendant to do something which he is willing to do without the intervention of the court.[408] **23-129**

iv. Damages in Lieu of Injunction

Lord Cairns' Act By the Chancery Amendment Act 1858 (known as Lord Cairns' Act) the Court of Chancery was conferred with a jurisdiction to award damages either in addition to, or in substitution for, an injunction, and this jurisdiction now applies to the High Court, the power being contained in s.50 of the Senior Courts Act 1981. Such damages are given in full satisfaction not only of all dam- **23-130**

---

[400] But an undertaking in damages will not normally be required where the Crown or a local authority seeks an injunction in aid of the criminal law: *Kirklees MBC v Wickes Building Supplies Ltd* [1993] A.C. 227.

[401] CPR PD 23A, r.4.2.

[402] See para.13-149.

[403] "Likely" here means "more likely than not": *Cream Holdings Ltd v Banerjee* [2004] UKHL 44; [2005] 1 A.C. 253 at [22] per Lord Nicholls.

[404] *Redland Bricks Ltd v Morris* [1970] A.C. 652 at 664.

[405] See, e.g., *Torquay Hotel Co Ltd v Cousins* [1969] 2 Ch. 106 at 120.

[406] *Attorney-General v Nottingham Corp* [1904] 1 Ch. 673; *Redland Bricks Ltd v Morris* [1970] A.C. 652.

[407] *Lemos v Kennedy Leigh Developments* (1961) 105 S.J. 178; cf. *Hooper v Rogers* [1975] Ch. 43 where the view is expressed that there is no fixed standard of certainty or imminence.

[408] *Bridlington Relay Ltd v Yorkshire Electricity Board* [1965] Ch. 436.

age done in the past, but also for all future damage which may occur if an injunction is not granted.[409] They are thus compensatory and reflect that which the claimant lost as a result of injunctive relief being withheld.[410] To say that damages may be awarded "in substitution for" an injunction is apt to mislead as it is clear that the power is not confined to cases in which the Court of Chancery would have granted equitable relief prior to Lord Cairns' Act.[411] In other words, the power is available whenever the facts of a case call into play the court's general equitable discretion to grant an injunction.[412] Damages may be awarded in substitution for an injunction even in a *quia timet* action.[413]

23-131 **When should damages in lieu be awarded?** In *Shelfer v City of London Electric Lighting Co*[414] AL Smith LJ famously said that it would normally be right to refuse an injunction and to grant damages in lieu thereof if the following four conditions are satisfied: (1) injunctive relief would be oppressive to the defendant; (2) the injury to the claimant's rights is small; (3) the injury is capable of being estimated in money; and (4) the injury is one that can be adequately compensated by a money payment. This approach reflected orthodoxy for over a century[415] until the decision of the Supreme Court in *Coventry v Lawrence*[416] in which a change of approach was sounded.[417] Thus, Lord Neuberger emphasised the importance of flexibility and stressed that the court's discretion to award damages in lieu of an injunction should not be fettered.[418] Consistently with this, he deprecated an approach according to which damages in lieu of an injunction were awarded only in "very exceptional circumstances".[419] Nevertheless, Lord Neuberger confirmed the conventional rule that a claimant who can establish an interference with his rights is prima facie entitled to an injunction. As for the *Shelfer* criteria, Lord Neuberger considered that while it would generally be right to refuse an injunction if AL Smith LJ's four criteria were all satisfied, the mere fact that they were not met in a given case did not mean that the claimant should be confined to damages.[420] It is too soon to say what the impact of *Coventry* on this area of the law will be although it is clear that it significantly diminishes the importance of the *Shelfer* criteria.

It can be questioned whether the Supreme Court was right in *Coventry* to retreat from *Shelfer*.[421] A more flexible approach comes at the price of reduced certainty and this can be expected to generate litigation. In favour of the *Shelfer* criteria it is

---

[409] *Jaggard v Sawyer* [1995] 1 W.L.R. 269.

[410] *Morris-Garner v One Step (Support) Ltd* [2018] UKSC 20; [2019] A.C. 649 at [44], [95].

[411] *Isenberg v East India House Estate Co* (1863) 3 D. & G.J. & S. 263; 46 E.R. 637; *City of London Brewery Co v Tennant* (1873) 9 L.R. Ch. App. 212; *Wroth v Tyler* [1974] Ch. 30 (substitution for specific performance). The contrary is perhaps implied by Lord Upjohn in *Redland Bricks Ltd v Morris* [1970] A.C. 652.

[412] *Morris-Garner v One Step (Support) Ltd* [2018] UKSC 20; [2019] A.C. 649 at [45], [95].

[413] *Leeds Industrial Co-operative Society Ltd v Slack* [1924] A.C. 851; *Hooper v Rogers* [1975] Ch. 43.

[414] *Shelfer v City of London Electric Lighting Co* [1895] 1 Ch. 287 at 322.

[415] Although see *Miller v Jackson* [1977] Q.B. 966.

[416] [2014] UKSC 13; [2014] A.C. 822.

[417] See Nolan in Day and Worthington (eds), *Challenging Private Law* (2020).

[418] [2014] UKSC 13; [2014] A.C. 822 at [123]. See also *Beaumont Business Centres Ltd v Florala Properties Ltd* [2020] EWHC 550 (Ch) at [330].

[419] [2014] UKSC 13; [2014] A.C. 822 at [119].

[420] *Coventry v Lawrence* [2014] UKSC 13; [2014] A.C. 822 at [123]; cf. Lord Sumption's remarks at [161] where he condemned the approach in *Shelfer* and suggested that "[t]he whole jurisprudence in this area will need one day to be reviewed in this court".

[421] See also Pontin (2015) 27 J.E.L. 119.

often contended that any other rule would facilitate "forced sales" of property rights: a defendant could acquire a claimant's property rights simply by paying damages. However, in *Coventry* Lord Sumption criticised this argument as involving "an unduly moralistic approach to disputes".[422] He also observed that "if taken at face value [it] would justify the grant of an injunction in all cases, which is plainly not the law".[423]

The measure of damages   In *One Step (Support) Ltd v Morris-Garner* the **23-132** Supreme Court considered how damages awarded in lieu of an injunction are to be quantified. Lord Reed, delivering the principal judgment, remarked[424]:

> "[O]ne possible method of quantifying damages under this head is on the basis of the economic value of the right which the court has declined to enforce, and which it has consequently rendered worthless. Such a valuation can be arrived at by reference to the amount that the claimant might reasonably have demanded as a quid pro quo for the relaxation of the obligation in question. The rationale is that, since withholding the specific relief has the same practical effect as requiring the claimant to permit the infringement of his rights, his loss can be measured by reference to the economic value of such permission".

Lord Reed added, however, that the basis on which damages in lieu of an injunction are to be quantified is always a matter for the court that is called on to make the award. Ultimately, he said, the basis of assessment is driven by the need to arrive at a sum that "will give a fair equivalent for what is lost by the refusal of the injunction".[425] It would be incorrect, however, to assume that they should be measured in the same way as damages recoverable at common law.[426] There is no warrant for such an assumption given, among other things, the fact that damages in lieu of an injunction are available, unlike damages at common law, in respect of future or continuing wrongs.

B.   Specific Restitution of Property

Orders for the specific restitution of property may be for the recovery of land or **23-133** chattels. But whether it is restitution of land or goods that is sought, the remedies are confined to cases where one person is in possession of another's property and this limits them to torts infringing such possession. They have therefore been considered at appropriate points elsewhere in this book.[427]

---

[422] [2014] UKSC 13; [2014] A.C. 822 at [160].
[423] [2014] UKSC 13; [2014] A.C. 822 at [160].
[424] [2018] UKSC 20; [2019] A.C. 649 at [95].
[425] [2018] UKSC 20; [2019] A.C. 649 at [95].
[426] [2018] UKSC 20; [2019] A.C. 649 at [47].
[427] See paras 14-030, 18-054.

CHAPTER 24

DEATH IN RELATION TO TORT

Introduction   The death of a person may affect tortious liability in two ways: **24-001**

(1) Death may extinguish liability for a tort. Here the issue is: "If D commits a tort against C, and either party subsequently dies, does C's right of action survive?"
(2) Death may create liability in tort. Here the question is: "If D causes C's death, is that a tort either (a) against C, so that C's personal representatives can sue D for it or (b) against persons who have an interest in the continuance of C's life, e.g., C's spouse or children?"

1.   DEATH AS EXTINGUISHING LIABILITY

The position at common law   At common law, the general rule was that the death   **24-002**
of either party extinguished any existing cause of action in tort— actio personalis
moritur cum persona.[1] Actions in contract generally escaped the rule, and so too did
those in which property had been appropriated by a deceased person and added to
his own estate.

A.   Survival of Causes of Action

The common law rule is overturned   It was not until 1934 that the defects of the   **24-003**
common law rule were forced on the attention of the legislature by the growth of
motor vehicle traffic and its accompanying toll of accidents. If a negligent driver

---

[1]   For the historical background, see Winfield (1929) 29 Col. L.R. 239; Nolan in Arvind and Steele
(eds), *Tort Law and the Legislature* (2012); Mitchell, *A History of Tort Law* (2015), Ch.10.

was killed in the accident that he had caused, at common law nothing was recoverable from his estate or his insurer by those whom he had injured. The same rule obtained where it was the claimant who died. Accordingly, the Law Reform (Miscellaneous Provisions) Act 1934 was passed to provide generally for the survival of causes of action in tort.

24-004   **Actions survive the death of either party, save for actions in defamation**   By s.1(1) of the 1934 Act, all causes of action subsisting against or vested in any person on his death, except causes of action for defamation, survive against, or, as the case may be, for the benefit of, his estate. The exclusion of actions for defamation from the Act was not so much the result of a conscious decision of policy that such actions should not survive death as of a desire to avoid potentially controversial areas and deal with the urgent issue of deaths in road accidents.[2] Generally, the ordinary law for the limitation of actions applies, whether the action is brought against or for the benefit of the estate.[3]

B.   "Subsisting" Action

24-005   It may happen that a cause of action is not complete against a wrongdoer until after he has died, as, for example, where damage is the gist of the action and no damage is suffered until after the wrongdoer's death. In such a case no cause of action subsists against the wrongdoer at the date of his death and there is therefore nothing to survive against his estate, so that, were there no provision in the Act to deal with the point, the victim would be deprived of a remedy. Section 1(4) provides, however, that where damage has been suffered as a result of a wrongful act in respect of which a cause of action would have subsisted had the wrongdoer not died before or at the same time as the damage was suffered, there shall be deemed to have subsisted against him before his death such cause of action as would have subsisted had he died after the damage had been suffered. Thus, if on facts similar to those of *Donoghue v Stevenson*,[4] D, the negligent manufacturer of noxious ginger beer, dies before the ultimate consumer, C, suffers damage from drinking it, C's cause of action against D's estate is preserved as it is regarded as arising before D's death.[5]

C.   Damages Recoverable

24-006   Where the victim dies, punitive damages cannot be recovered for the benefit of the estate.[6] Nor may the award include damages for loss of income in respect of any period after the victim's death.[7] It is further provided that where death has been caused by the act or omission that gives rise to the cause of action, damages are to

---

2   See the Faulks Committee Report (1975) Cmnd.5909, Ch.15.
3   See para.26-101. But under the Limitation Act 1980 s.11(5), a fixed period of limitation arises where the victim dies during the period that commenced with his injury.
4   [1932] A.C. 562, see para.5-017.
5   A right to claim contribution from another tortfeasor is not a claim in tort and survives death without reference to the Act: *Ronex Properties Ltd v John Laing Construction Ltd* [1983] Q.B. 398.
6   Section 1(2)(a)(i). It is hard to see why the death of the victim should bar punishment of the surviving wrongdoer, while at the same time the death of the wrongdoer does not (apparently) bar punishment of his estate. The Law Commission has recommended the correction of this: *Aggravated, Exemplary and Resitutionary Damages* Law Com. No.247 (1997) at paras 5.275, 5.278.
7   Section 1(2)(a)(ii).

be calculated without reference to any loss[8] or gain[9] to the deceased's estate consequent on his death, except that funeral expenses may be included.[10] The damages that the estate may recover include those for non-pecuniary items (such as pain and suffering and loss of amenity) during any significant[11] interval between injury and death. Also recoverable are loss of earnings suffered during this period plus any medical expenses. Damages are available in respect of gratuitously provided services, including care provided by a hospice.[12] The court will award a reasonable sum in respect of such damages, and may order that they be held on trust for the carer or paid directly to him. Subject to any such orders, damages recovered form part of the deceased's estate, are available for payment of his debts and pass under his will or upon his intestacy. The Law Reform (Contributory Negligence) Act 1945 applies to claims by estates.

2. DEATH AS CREATING LIABILITY

A. Position at Common Law

At common law, death could not give rise to a cause of action in other persons, even where they were dependent on the deceased. This rule was derived from the decision of Lord Ellenborough in *Baker v Bolton*[13] that "in a civil court the death of a human being could not be complained of as an injury".[14] *Baker v Bolton* was only a ruling at nisi prius, not a single authority was cited and the report is extremely brief, but it was nevertheless upheld in later cases and the seal of approval placed upon it by the House of Lords in *Admiralty Commissioners v SS Amerika*.[15] Long before that case, however, the legislature had intervened.

24-007

B. Fatal Accidents Act 1976

Provision for an action for dependants[16] The industrial revolution and the development of railways in England led to an upsurge in the number of accidents, fatal and non-fatal, and this made a change in the law imperative for, while those who survived an accident could recover substantial damages, the dependants of those who were killed could recover nothing. Accordingly, in 1846, the Fatal Accidents Act, otherwise known as Lord Campbell's Act, was passed and virtually overturned the common law in so far as those dependants who were specified in the Act and in later legislation were concerned. The present statute is the Fatal Accidents Act 1976, which consolidates the earlier legislation. The Act provides that

24-008

---

[8] e.g., cessation of an annuity or life interest.

[9] e.g., insurance money.

[10] Section 1(2)(c). A living claimant whose life expectancy has been shortened cannot claim "anticipatory" funeral expenses: *Watson v Cakebread Robey Ltd* [2009] EWHC 1695 (QB).

[11] Not momentary pain which is effectively part of the process of death itself: *Hicks v Chief Constable of South Yorkshire* [1992] 2 All E.R. 65. cf. *Beesley v New Century Group Ltd* [2008] EWHC 3033 (QB) (£72,000 for 17 months of suffering).

[12] *Drake v Foster Wheeler Ltd* [2010] EWHC 2004 (QB); [2011] 1 All E.R. 63.

[13] *Baker v Bolton* (1808) 1 Camp. 493; 170 E.R. 1033 (the claimant's wife had been killed in a stagecoach accident).

[14] The rule in *Baker v Bolton* does not apply where the claimant's cause of action is founded upon contract: *Jackson v Watson* [1909] 2 K.B. 193.

[15] *Admiralty Commissioners v SS Amerika* [1917] A.C. 38.

[16] See, further, *Claims for Wrongful Death*, Law Com. No.263 (1999).

whenever the death of a person is caused by the wrongful act, neglect or default[17] of another, such as would (if death had not ensued) have entitled the injured person to sue and recover damages in respect thereof, then the person who would have been liable if death had not ensued shall be liable to an action for damages on behalf of the dependants, notwithstanding the death of the person injured.[18]

24-009 **Dependants** Dependants encompass: (1) the spouse or former spouse of the deceased; (2) the civil partner or former civil partner of the deceased; (3) a person who was living as the spouse or civil partner of the deceased, in the same household, immediately before the date of the death and had been so living for at least two years;[19] (4) any parent or other ascendant of the deceased or person treated by the deceased as his parent; (5) any child[20] or other descendant of the deceased or any person who has been treated by the deceased as a child of the family in relation to any marriage or civil partnership of the deceased; and (6) any person who is, or is the issue of, a brother, sister, uncle or aunt of the deceased. In deducing any relationship an adopted person is to be treated as the child of the persons by whom he was adopted,[21] a relationship by marriage or civil partnership as one of consanguinity and a relationship of the half-blood as a relationship of the whole blood. The stepchild[22] of any person is to be treated as his child and an illegitimate person as the legitimate child of his mother and reputed father.[23]

24-010 **Commencing proceedings** An action under the Fatal Accidents Act 1976 must normally be brought on behalf of the dependants by the executor or administrator of the deceased[24] but where there is no personal representative, or no action is brought by him within six months, any dependant who is entitled to benefit under the 1976 Act may sue in his own name on behalf of himself and the others.[25] Subject to the court's powers under the Limitation Act 1980, the action must in any case be brought within three years of the death.[26]

24-011 **The parasitic nature of the action** The action created by the Fatal Accidents Act 1976 was described as "new in its species, new in its quality, new in its principles, in every way new".[27] It is not the deceased's own cause of action which survives. Rather, the dependants are given an action of their own. However, for this new cause of action to exist, the circumstances of the deceased's death must have been such that the deceased himself, had he been injured and not killed, could have sued for his injury. The dependants' action is, therefore, parasitic on the wrong committed against the deceased.

---

17 It is now common for statutes imposing strict liability to provide that for the purpose of the Fatal Accidents Act damage for which a person is liable under the statute shall be treated as due to his fault: see, e.g., the Animals Act 1971 s.10. A breach of contract causing death is within the statute: *Grein v Imperial Airways Ltd* [1937] 1 K.B. 50.

18 Section 1.

19 This temporal threshold on co-habitation does not violate art.8 of the European Convention on Human Rights: *Swift v Secretary of State for Justice* [2013] EWCA Civ 193; [2014] Q.B. 373.

20 Including a posthumous child: *The George and Richard* (1871) L.R. 3 Ad. & E. 466.

21 Where a cause of action in respect of the death of the natural parent has accrued, a subsequent adoption does not extinguish the child's claim: *Watson v Willmott* [1991] 1 Q.B. 140.

22 Including the child of the deceased's civil partner: Civil Partnership Act 2004 Sch.21.

23 Fatal Accidents Act 1976 s.1(5).

24 Section 2.

25 Section 2(2).

26 See para.26-101.

27 *Seward v Vera Cruz* (1884) 10 App. Cas. 59 at 70–71 per Lord Blackburn.

Consequences of the parasitic nature of the action Because the dependant's ac- **24-012**
tion is parasitic on the wrong committed against the deceased, if the deceased would
have been unable to sue for any reason had he lived, the dependant will not be able
to sue either. If, therefore, the deceased had been run over in the street through
nobody's fault but his own, there will be no claim on behalf of his dependants. Nor
will there be such a claim if by contract with the defendant the deceased had
excluded any possibility of liability to himself.[28] The position is different, however,
if the contract merely limited the defendant's liability. In this situation, the deceased
could have sued for some damages and, therefore, the way is open for the
dependant's claim (although the dependant's will not be affected by the limitation
of liability).[29] Similarly the dependants will not have a claim if the deceased, before
his death,[30] had accepted compensation from the defendant[31] in satisfaction of his
claim,[32] or had actually obtained judgment against the defendant,[33] or if by the date
of his death his claim had become statute-barred.[34]

i. Damages Recoverable

Types of damages that can be recovered Damages may be recovered in respect **24-013**
of: (1) bereavement; (2) funeral expenses; and (3) loss of support. These will be
taken in order.

Bereavement The spouse or civil partner of the deceased, or the parents of a **24-014**
minor[35] who was never married,[36] may claim damages for "bereavement". Such
damages are awarded as a fixed sum,[37] presently £12,980.[38] The Court of Appeal

---

[28] *Haigh v Royal Mail Steam Packet Co Ltd* (1883) 52 L.J.Q.B. 640; *The Stella* [1900] P. 161.

[29] *Nunan v Southern Ry* [1924] 1 K.B. 223; *Grein v Imperial Airways* [1937] 1 K.B. 50. It is questionable whether this rule is correct since it is inconsistent with the parasitic nature of the dependency
action.

[30] If there is a discontinuance of the deceased's claim after death that does not bar the dependency claim
unless as a matter of construction of the agreement it is intended to do so: *Reader v Molesworths
Bright Clegg* [2007] EWCA Civ 169; [2007] 1 W.L.R. 1082.

[31] Not if he has accepted a payment from another tortfeasor unless this in fact fully satisfies his claim:
Jameson v CEGB [2000] 1 A.C. 455.

[32] *Read v GE Ry Co* (1867–1868) L.R. 3 Q.B. 555. This does not contravene arts 6 or 8 of the European
Convention on Human Rights: *Thompson v Arnold* [2007] EWHC 1875 (QB); [2008] P.I.Q.R. P1.
The view that the dependants are barred was assumed to be correct for the purposes of the appeal
in *Pickett v British Rail Engineering Ltd* [1980] A.C. 136. Whether the liability in tort is destroyed
from the moment that the agreement to accept compensation is made, even before the money is actually paid, is a question of construction: *British Russian Gazette v Associated Newspapers Ltd* [1933]
2 K.B. 616.

[33] The award of provisional damages to the deceased does not bar the dependants' claim: Damages Act
1996 s.3.

[34] *Williams v Mersey Docks and Harbour Board* [1905] 1 K.B. 804.

[35] There is no claim for bereavement if the victim is injured before attaining the age of majority but
dies after reaching that age: *Doleman v Deakin, The Times,* 30 January 1990. The Act does not apply to a stillborn child, though since the tort causing the stillbirth will be a tort against the mother
she may recover substantial damages (not necessarily limited to the statutory sum) for the effect of
the loss of the child on her: *Bagley v North Herts Health Authority* (1986) 136 N.L.J. 1014. cf. *Kralj
v McGrath* [1986] 1 All E.R. 54, where the emphasis seems to be on the mother's grief hindering
her physical recovery, and *Kirby v Redbridge HA* [1993] 4 Med. L.R. 178.

[36] But only his mother where he was illegitimate: s.1A(2)(b).

[37] Like other damages under the Act, this sum would seem to be subject to reduction on account of the
deceased's contributory negligence: see para.24-029.

held in *Smith v Lancashire Teaching Hospitals NHS Foundation Trust*[39] that the fact that unmarried and non-civil partnered cohabitees who were living for at least two years in a marital-like relationship are not entitled to bereavement damages was incompatible with the European Convention of Human Rights. Remedial legislation has been proposed to address this problem.[40]

24-015 **Funeral expenses** "Dependants"[41] are entitled to recover damages for funeral expenses that they have incurred.[42] However, the cost of a wake is irrecoverable,[43] as are the costs of a memorial, funeral clothes and applying for probate.[44]

24-016 **Loss of support: the test** The 1976 Act allows recovery for a loss of support provided by the deceased. The right to sue for this loss is given to the deceased's "dependants".[45] The Act simply says that the court may give damages proportioned to the injury resulting from the death to the dependants.[46] It does not say on what principle they are to be assessed, but in 1858 Pollock CB adopted a test which has been used ever since, namely that damages must be calculated: "in reference to a reasonable expectation of pecuniary benefit as of right, or otherwise, from the continuance of the life".[47]

24-017 **Loss of support: the concept of a pecuniary benefit** Pollock CB's test means that dependants cannot recover if they have suffered only nominal losses or none at all.[48] Nor can they recover if the deceased earned his living by crime, for then their claim arises ex turpi causa.[49] However, the courts have stretched the concept of pecuniary benefit in holding that a child may claim damages for loss of his mother's care and that in assessing this loss the court is not confined to evaluating her services as housekeeper but may take into account instruction on essential mat-

---

38 Fatal Accidents Act 1976 s.1A as amended by the Pension Protection Fund and Occupational Pension Schemes (Levy Ceiling and Compensation Cap) Order 2013, SI 2013/105. These damages are additional to any recoverable by the claimant for psychiatric trauma because there has been a tort to him: *Jones v Royal Devon etc. NHS Foundation Trust* [2008] EWHC 558 (QB); 110 B.M.L.R. 154. Where the claim is made by both parents the sum is to be divided equally between them (s.1A(4)). This might suggest that if one parent is the tortfeasor, the other receives the full sum: cf. *Navei v Navei* [1995] C.L.Y 1827.

39 [2017] EWCA Civ 1916; [2018] Q.B. 804.

40 Ministry of Justice, *A Proposal for a Remedial Order to Amend the Fatal Accidents Act 1976* (2019).

41 See para.24-009.

42 Section 3(5).

43 *Jones v Royal Devon etc. NHS Foundation Trust* [2008] EWHC 558 (QB).

44 *Mosson v Spousal (London) Ltd* [2016] EWHC 53 (QB); [2016] 4 W.L.R. 28 at [50].

45 See para.24-009.

46 Section 3(1). A literal interpretation of the Act might be taken to mean that it does not apply where the deceased was seriously injured but did not die for some time, for his earning capacity would be destroyed before the death. Naturally, this has been rejected: *Jameson v Central Electricity Generating Board (No.1)* [1998] Q.B. 323 (on appeal [2000] 1 A.C. 455).

47 *Franklin v SE Ry* (1858) 3 H. & N. 211 at 213–214; 157 E.R. 448 at 449. Hence, the dependants are entitled to recover where the deceased has been prevented from accumulating savings that they would have received from him: *Singapore Bus Co v Lim* [1985] 1 W.L.R. 1075. Where the deceased's estate pays inheritance tax that would otherwise have been avoided, it is recoverable by the dependants/beneficiaries from the tortfeasor: *Davies v Whiteways Cyder Co Ltd* [1975] Q.B. 262.

48 *Duckworth v Johnson* (1859) 4 Hurl. & N. 653; 157 E.R. 997.

49 *Burns v Edman* [1970] 2 Q.B. 541. See also *Hunter v Butler, The Times,* 28 December 1995 (claimant aware that deceased fraudulently concealed savings) and para.26–065.

ters to do with his upbringing.[50] Where a son who worked for his father under a
contract was killed his father was held to have no claim. Although he had lost the
son's services, he could not prove that he had lost any pecuniary benefit since he
had paid full wages for them.[51] An additional reason for rejecting the father's claim
in that case was that the father could not show any benefit accruing to him from his
relationship with his son, but only that he had lost an advantage derived from a
contract with him, and this was insufficient,[52] since "[t]he benefit, to qualify under
the Act, must be a benefit which arises from the relationship between the parties."[53]
In *Malyon v Plummer*[54] the claimant widow had been in receipt of an annual salary of about £600 for somewhat nominal services that she provided to her husband's
"one-man" company. Having estimated the value of her services to the company
at £200 per annum, the Court of Appeal held that the equivalent element of her salary was payment for services rendered under her contract of employment and so
could not be recovered but that the balance was attributable to her relationship as
wife to the deceased and so could be.

Loss of support: reasonable expectation   A mere speculative possibility of   **24-018**
receiving a pecuniary benefit from the deceased is insufficient, as where the person
killed was aged four and his father proved only that he had intended to give the child
a good education.[55] Conversely, there may be a reasonable expectation of pecuniary benefit although the relatives had no legal claim to support by the deceased, as
where a son had voluntarily assisted his father in the father's work,[56] or once given
his father money during a period of unemployment,[57] or where a wife had
gratuitously performed ordinary household tasks.[58] Indeed, it is not necessary that
the deceased should actually have earned anything or given any help, provided that
there was a reasonable probability, as distinct from a bare possibility, that he would
do so. A reasonable probability of support existed where the deceased was a girl of
16 who lived with her parents, was on the eve of completing her apprenticeship as
a dressmaker, and was likely in the near future to earn a wage which might quickly
have become substantial.[59] If spouses are separated at the time of one spouse's
death, it is unnecessary for the surviving spouse to show that, on a balance of probabilities, they would have been reconciled. The correct approach is for the court to
determine whether there was a reasonable chance, rather than a mere speculative
possibility, of reconciliation. If there was, the award should be scaled down to take

---

[50]   *Hay v Hughes* [1975] Q.B. 790 at 802; *Regan v Williamson* [1976] 1 W.L.R. 305; *Mehmet v Perry*
[1977] 2 All E.R. 529; *Beesley v New Century Group Ltd* [2008] EWHC 3033 (QB) (principle of
recovery for "intangible" benefits also applicable to spouses).

[51]   *Sykes v NE Ry Co* (1875) 44 L.J.C.P. 191.

[52]   *Burgess v Florence Nightingale Hospital for Gentlewomen* [1955] 1 Q.B. 349.

[53]   *Burgess v Florence Nightingale Hospital for Gentlewomen* [1955] 1 Q.B. 349 at 360 per Devlin J.

[54]   *Malyon v Plummer* [1964] 1 Q.B. 330; *Williams v Welsh Ambulance Service NHS Trust* [2008]
EWCA Civ 81; *Cox v Hockenhull* [2000] 1 W.L.R. 750 (loss of invalid care allowance not recoverable; claimant in effect employed by state to care for deceased).

[55]   *Barnett v Cohen* [1921] 2 K.B. 461.

[56]   *Franklin v SE Ry* (1858) 3 H. & N. 211; 157 E.R. 448.

[57]   *Hetherington v NE Ry* (1882) 9 Q.B.D. 160.

[58]   *Berry v Humm* [1915] 1 K.B. 627. See also *Burgess v Florence Nightingale Hospital for Gentlewomen* [1955] 1 Q.B. 349 at 361–362.

[59]   *Taff Vale Ry v Jenkins* [1913] A.C. 1; *Wathen v Vernon* [1970] R.T.R. 471; *Kandalla v BEA* [1981]
Q.B. 158.

account of the probability of the reconciliation taking place.[60] Where the dependant was not married to the deceased but they were cohabiting, the court is directed by statute to consider the fact that the claimant had no enforceable right to financial support from the deceased.[61]

24-019   Loss of support: the dependant's prospects   In a case under the Fatal Accidents Act the court is concerned with what would have happened had the deceased lived, and since the loss in respect of which damages are awarded is pecuniary loss that will be suffered by dependants in the future, that means it is inevitably concerned with the prospects of the dependants. For example, if the dependant himself has a short expectation of life the damages will be small.[62] The most controversial aspect of this matter related to a dependant widow's prospects of remarriage. Formerly, the court was required to estimate the widow's chances of remarriage and reduce the damages accordingly, but some judges revolted against this "guessing game" and a campaign led to the reversal of this rule by the Law Reform (Miscellaneous Provisions) Act 1971.[63] Now, in assessing the damages payable to a widow no account is to be taken of her remarriage nor her prospects of remarriage.[64] As a result of judicial interpretation of s.4 of the Fatal Accidents Act 1976 (which deals with the offsetting of benefits received)[65] it now seems that the provision concerning a widow's remarriage is redundant and that the same result will be reached where, for example, a widower remarries or a widow cohabits without marriage. The fact that remarriage is ignored means that the law strays a long way from the principle that damages are to be awarded in respect of loss actually suffered. In *Cox v Ergo Versicherung AG* Lord Sumption described the law in this regard as "anomalous".[66]

24-020   Loss of support: the need to establish a loss   The dependant must suffer a loss due to the deceased's death. If, for example, the deceased maintained himself and his spouse solely from the income of investments and those investments pass to the spouse then the latter will have suffered no pecuniary loss except in so far as the deceased provided skill, which now needs to be replaced, in managing them.[67]

24-021   Loss of support: distinguished from need for support   It is important to remember that loss of dependency is not the same as need. If the claimant was a successful musician who retired upon marriage to the wealthy deceased but resumed

---

[60]   *Davies v Taylor* [1974] A.C. 207. See also *Wathen v Vernon* [1970] R.T.R. 471; *Gray v Barr* [1971] 2 Q.B. 554.

[61]   Fatal Accidents Act 1976 s.3(4).

[62]   See, e.g., *Haxton v Philips Electronics UK Ltd* [2014] EWCA Civ 4; [2014] 1 W.L.R. 2721 (0.7 years).Where the deceased's widow actually died before the trial damages were awarded to her estate in respect only of the period during which she actually survived him: *Williams v John I. Thornycroft Ltd* [1940] 2 K.B. 658; *Voller v Dairy Produce Packers Ltd* [1962] 1 W.L.R. 960.

[63]   The High Court of Australia by a majority departed from the former rule in *De Sales v Ingrilli* [2002] HCA 52; (2002) 212 C.L.R. 338.

[64]   Section 3(3).

[65]   See para.24-028.

[66]   [2014] UKSC 22; [2014] A.C. 1379 at [10].

[67]   See *Wood v Bentall Simplex* [1992] P.I.Q.R. P332; *Cape Distribution Ltd v O'Loughlin* [2001] P.I.Q.R. Q73. Pensions can cause difficulties: see *Auty v NCB* [1985] 1 W.L.R. 784 (under previous legislation) and *Pidduck v Eastern Scottish Omnibuses Ltd* [1990] 1 W.L.R. 993.

her career on his death and made even more money than she had received in support from the deceased, her claim is still based on that loss of support[68]:

> "The dependency is fixed at the moment of death; it is what the dependants would probably have received as benefit from the deceased, had the deceased not died. What decisions people make afterwards is irrelevant."

ii. Assessment of Damages

Damages for bereavement are a fixed sum.[69] Assessing damages in respect of funeral expenses rarely causes any difficulty. Accordingly, what follows concerns the assessment of damages for loss of support. **24-022**

Assessment where there are multiple dependants Although proceedings for loss of support are normally brought by the executor or administrator of the deceased and not by the dependants themselves, the remedy given by the statute is to individuals, not to a class.[70] In calculating the damages, therefore, the pecuniary loss suffered by each dependant should be separately assessed. In practice, however, it will frequently be necessary first to determine a figure for the total liability of the defendant and then to apportion the damages between the various dependants[71] and this has been said to be the more usual method.[72] **24-023**

Periodical payments The regime for payment of damages by way of periodical payments which has been outlined in relation to personal injury cases[73] also applies to claims under the Fatal Accidents Act 1976.[74] **24-024**

Lump sum awards Where a lump sum award is made, the process of assessment is very similar to that used in assessing future loss in a personal injury action. That is to say, the court determines a multiplicand representing the net annual loss and applies to that a multiplier representing the duration of the loss scaled down for contingencies and the value of accelerated receipt in the form of a lump sum. There are, however, additional complications because the court is concerned with the prospects of the dependants as well as of the deceased (for example, whether they would have survived to enjoy the benefit of the deceased's provision[75]) and because the likely period of dependency of individual dependants will vary (for example, that of the spouse will generally be longer than that of a child[76]). The multiplier is set as at the date of the trial.[77] **24-025**

---

68 *Williams v Welsh Ambulance Service NHS Trust* [2008] EWCA Civ 81 at [50] per Smith LJ.
69 See para.24-014.
70 *Pym v Great Northern Ry* (1863) 4 B. & S. 396; 122 E.R. 508; *Avery v London & NE Ry* [1938] A.C. 613; *Jeffrey v Kent CC* [1958] 1 W.L.R. 926; *Dietz v Lennig Chemicals Ltd* [1969] 1 A.C. 170 at 183.
71 *Bishop v Cunard White Star Co Ltd* [1950] P. 240 at 248. Once the total liability of the defendant has been determined, the apportionment of that sum is no concern of the defendant: *Eifert v Holt's Transport Co Ltd* [1951] 2 All E.R. 655n.
72 *Kassam v Kampala Aerated Water Co Ltd* [1965] 1 W.L.R. 688 at 672.
73 See para.23-100.
74 Damages Act 1996 s.7.
75 For analysis, see Purchas LJ's reasons in *Corbett v Barking HA* [1991] 2 Q.B. 408.
76 In *Dolbey v Goodwin* [1955] 1 W.L.R. 553 it was held that the damages awarded to the widowed mother of the deceased could not be assessed on the same basis as if she had been his widow, as it

24-026 **Approach where deceased was the family breadwinner**   Most cases fall into one of two broad categories. The first is where the deceased was the family breadwinner. Traditionally, the approach was to build up the multiplicand item by item by a schedule of expenditure which could be regarded as for the family benefit (mortgage payments, heating, insurance, and so on) and this may still be a valid approach in some cases. However, it is now more common simply to take the deceased's income, net of tax and other deductions, and base the multiplicand on a standard fraction of that—66.6 per cent where the only dependant is a spouse or partner, 75 per cent if there are also children.[78] These figures are intended to allow for the expenditure which the deceased incurred solely for his own benefit and in recognition of the fact that expenditure for joint benefit (for example heating) is not necessarily reduced by the absence of the deceased. It must, however, be stressed that the standard fractions can be increased or decreased if there is evidence to justify doing so.

24-027 **Approach where deceased provided valuable but gratuitous services**   The other type of case is that where the deceased provided valuable but gratuitous services in looking after the home and children. Here there may be no earnings to serve as the baseline for the multiplicand and the proper approach will often be to use as a measure the cost of employing substitute domestic help, if necessary on a "live-in" basis,[79] though it may in some cases be more apt to take the earnings loss of the other parent who stays at home to look after the children.[80] The fact that commercial help is not engaged (as where the children are looked after by a relative) does not prevent the cost of such help being used as a measure but in this event it should be the net wage without tax and insurance contributions, for those are items of expenditure which will never be incurred.[81] In any event, the loss by children of the services of a parent is one which is likely to be a declining one so it cannot be valued at a constant figure for the whole of the child's dependency.[82] Damages cannot be claimed for the loss of the intangible value of having services provided out of love and affection as opposed to by outside help and contractors.[83]

24-028 **Deductions**   Section 4 of the Fatal Accidents Act 1976 provides that in "assessing damages in respect of a person's death … benefits which have accrued or will accrue to any person from his death or otherwise as a result of his death shall be disregarded." The law in this regard is therefore very simple: once one has assessed the dependency there is simply no deduction to be made. If the benefit does not arise as a consequence of the death it is irrelevant; and if it does so arise it is excluded from consideration by the statute. This rule even extends to ex gratia pay-

---

was likely that the deceased would have married and that his contributions to his mother's upkeep would then have been reduced.

[77]   *Knauer v Ministry of Justice* [2016] UKSC 9; [2016] A.C. 908.

[78]   *Harris v Empress Motors* [1984] 1 W.L.R. 212. Where both spouses earned and pooled their resources, the fraction is applied to the joint income and the survivor's continuing income deducted: *H v S* [2002] EWCA Civ 792; [2003] Q.B. 965 at [31].

[79]   *Jeffrey v Smith* [1970] R.T.R. 279; *Hay v Hughes* [1975] Q.B. 790. Though in principle a deduction should be made in respect of the living expenses of the deceased, this may be offset because the courts recognise that a commercial provider may not be "as good as" the deceased: *Reagan v Williamson* [1976] 1 W.L.R. 305.

[80]   *Mehmet v Perry* [1977] 2 All E.R. 529; *Cresswell v Eaton* [1991] 1 W.L.R. 1113.

[81]   *Spittle v Bunney* [1988] 1 W.L.R. 847; *Corbett v Barking HA* [1991] 2 Q.B. 408.

[82]   *Spittle v Bunney* [1988] 1 W.L.R. 847 (£47,500 reduced on this basis to £25,000).

[83]   *Mosson v Spousal (London) Ltd* [2016] EWHC 53 (QB); [2016] 4 W.L.R. 28.

ments made by the defendant, though he can of course express such a payment to be on account of potential liability.[84] The law is, therefore, much more generous to dependants of those who are wrongfully killed than to claimants in personal injury cases: where the breadwinner is killed the dependants are entitled to a full award based on loss of support from the deceased's earnings, even though, as a result of an occupational pension, life insurance money and the devolution of the deceased's estate, they may be better off in financial terms than they were before the death. The effect of s.4 has also been in issue where voluntary care is provided by a relative after the death of a parent. In *Stanley v Saddique*[85] the Court of Appeal held that "benefit" was to be given a wide meaning and was not confined to direct payments in money or money's worth. Hence when a child lost his mother in an accident but was then looked after by his stepmother, that was a "benefit" under s.4 and was to be ignored even if the stepmother provided better care than the natural mother. It follows that the child has a claim for substitute services to replace those lost and that, in line with the cases on personal injuries,[86] the damages awarded in that respect are held on trust or paid directly to the carer,[87] provided he is not the tortfeasor.[88]

iii.   Contributory Negligence

The contributory negligence of the deceased is taken into account and the damages awarded to the dependants will be reduced accordingly.[89] Although the Fatal Accidents Act 1976 is silent on the point, it is fairly clear that the contributory negligence of the dependants is also relevant. In principle the damages awarded to the contributorily negligent dependant should be reduced in proportion to his share of responsibility, but the other dependants should receive their damages in full,[90] since the remedy under the 1976 Act is given to individuals, not to the dependants as a group. In one case it was held that the damages of a non-negligent dependant were not affected by the fault of another dependant, but there the accident was held to be entirely the fault of the latter and it was conceded by counsel that she had no claim.[91]

24-029

3.   RELATIONSHIP OF THE TWO ACTS

The rights of action under the two statutes are cumulative, with damages under the Law Reform (Miscellaneous Provisions) Act 1934 going to the estate and those under the Fatal Accidents Act 1976 going to dependants. In most cases, one or more of the dependants will also be entitled to the deceased's estate. Damages under the 1934 Act are, in the case of instantaneous death, confined to funeral expenses and, since these are anyway recoverable under the 1976 Act, there is no point in bringing a 1934 Act claim. Where there is an interval between injury and death and hence

24-030

---

84 *Arnup v MW White Ltd* [2008] EWCA Civ 447; [2008] I.C.R. 1064.
85 *Stanley v Saddique* [1992] Q.B. 1. See also *R. v Criminal Injuries Compensation Board, Ex p. K* [1999] Q.B. 1131.
86 See para.23-085.
87 See para.24-006.
88 *H v S* [2002] EWCA Civ 792; [2003] Q.B. 965.
89 Section 5.
90 *Mulholland v McRae* [1961] N.I. 135.
91 *Dodds v Dodds* [1978] Q.B. 543. There seems no reason why the defendant should not claim contribution from a negligent dependant under the Civil Liability (Contribution) Act 1978.

loss of amenity and earnings and so on, then no doubt a claim under the 1934 Act will be presented concurrently with one under the 1976 Act.

CHAPTER 25

CAPACITY

Introduction The title of this chapter is a compendious abbreviation of "Varia- **25-001**
tion in capacity to sue, or liability to be sued, in tort". In the law of tort the chief
variations in capacity are to be found with the state and its officials, minors, persons
of unsound mind, corporations and trade unions.[1] Variations used also to be observable in the case of married women until well into the 20th century. That is no longer
the position, but there are still some restrictions on actions between spouses.

1. THE STATE AND ITS SUBORDINATES

The Crown and State officials: common law[2] At common law no action in tort **25-002**
lay against the Crown[3] for wrongs expressly authorised by the Crown or for wrongs
committed by its servants in the course of their employment.[4] Moreover, the head

---

[1] The position of trade unions is briefly touched upon in para.19-005.
[2] Williams, *Crown Proceedings* (1948).
[3] Government departments also enjoyed the immunity of the Crown unless a statute expressly provided
     otherwise. See *Minister of Supply v British Thomson-Houston Co* [1943] K.B. 478.
[4] *Canterbury (Viscount) v Attorney General* (1842) 1 Ph. 306; 41 E.R. 648. The remedy by way of
     petition of right was available for breach of contract, and to recover property which had been wrong-
     fully taken and withheld. Proceedings by way of petition of right were abolished by the Crown

of the department or other superior official was not, and is not, personally liable for wrongs committed by his subordinates, unless he has expressly authorised them, for all the servants of the Crown are fellow servants of the Crown and not of one another.[5] Conversely, the actual wrongdoer could, and still can, be sued in his personal capacity.[6] In practice the Treasury Solicitor usually defended an action against the individual Crown servant and the Treasury, as a matter of grace, undertook to satisfy any judgment awarded against him for a tort committed in the course of his employment. If the actual wrongdoer could not be identified the Treasury Solicitor would supply the name of a merely nominal defendant for the purpose of the action, i.e., a person who, though a Government servant, had nothing to do with the alleged wrong. However, in *Royster v Cavey*[7] it was held that the court had no jurisdiction to try the case unless the subordinate named by the Treasury Solicitor was the person who apparently had committed the tort. As the Crown had become one of the largest employers of labour and occupiers of property in the country, this system of providing compensation for the victims of torts committed by Crown servants in the course of their employment was plainly inadequate and, finally, some 20 years after it was mooted, the Crown Proceedings Act 1947 put an end to Crown immunity in tort.

25-003 **Crown Proceedings Act 1947** Under the Act the old maxim that "the King can do no wrong" is retained to the extent that no proceedings can be instituted against the Sovereign in person,[8] and there are savings in respect of the Crown's prerogative and statutory powers,[9] but otherwise the Act went a long way towards equating the Crown with a private person of full age and capacity for the purposes of tortious liability. The Crown cannot, however, be liable in tort except as provided by the Act and this cannot be evaded by dressing up the claim as one for a declaration that the Crown is behaving wrongfully.[9] Section 2(1) provides that the Crown shall be liable[10] as if it were a private person: (1) in respect of torts committed by its servants or agents;[11] (2) in respect of any breach of those duties which a person owes to his servants or agents at common law by reason of being their employer; and (3) in respect of any breach of the duties attaching at common law to the ownership, occupation, possession or control of property.[12] Section 2(2) makes the Crown li-

---

Proceedings Act 1947 Sch.1 para.2, but only with regard to liability in respect of Her Majesty's Government in the United Kingdom. A petition of right may, therefore, still lie in certain cases, but in the common law form used prior to the Petition of Right Act 1860: *Franklin v Attorney General* [1974] Q.B. 185.

5   *Raleigh v Goschen* [1898] 1 Ch.73 at 83; *Bainbridge v Postmaster General* [1906] 1 K.B. 178.

6   He could not, and cannot now, plead the orders of the Crown or state necessity as a defence: *Entick v Carrington* (1765) 19 St. Tr. 1030; 95 E.R. 807; *Wilkes v Wood* (1763) 19 St. Tr. 1153; 98 E.R. 489; *M v Home Office* [1994] 1 A.C. 337.

7   [1947] K.B. 204, the Court of Appeal acting upon emphatic obiter dicta of the House of Lords in *Adams v Naylor* [1946] A.C. 543.

8   Section 40(1).

9   *Trawnik v Lennox* [1985] 1 W.L.R. 532 (where the court had no jurisdiction to hear a claim for a nuisance in Berlin because it did not arise in respect of the Crown's activities in the United Kingdom: s.40(2)(b)).

10   The action is brought against the appropriate government department in accordance with a list published by the Treasury, otherwise the Attorney General may be made defendant: s.17.

11   "Agent" includes an independent contractor (s.38(2)) but the Crown is not on this account subject to any greater liability for the tort of an independent contractor employed by it than it would be if it were a private person: s.40(2)(d).

12   The duties owed by an occupier of premises to his invitees and licensees are now contained in the

able for breach of statutory duty, provided that the statute in question is one which binds other persons besides the Crown and its officers. The starting point is still that the Crown itself can do no wrong in private law. In the second and third cases enumerated in s.2(1) and that in s.2(2) the Crown can be "institutionally" or "personally" liable;[13] but otherwise the Act makes the Crown liable for the acts of human agents who commit torts. Hence, for example, the Crown can only be liable for misfeasance in a public office if the mental element of that tort can be brought home to some individual for whose actions the Crown is answerable.[14] Section 11 preserves the Crown's right to exercise its statutory and prerogative powers with impunity, but there is generally no prerogative power to seize or destroy the property of a subject without paying compensation.[15] The apportionment provisions of the Civil Liability (Contribution) Act 1978 and the Law Reform (Contributory Negligence) Act 1945, as well as the analogous provisions of the Merchant Shipping Act 1995, apply to proceedings in which the Crown is a party.[16]

Limitations on liability   There remain certain limitations on the Crown's general **25-004** liability in tort: (1) the only officers, that is, servants or Ministers of the Crown,[17] who may render the Crown liable are those appointed directly or indirectly by the Crown and paid wholly out of moneys provided by Parliament or a fund certified by the Treasury as equivalent. This excludes liability for police officers, who are not paid out of such funds, even in the case of the Metropolitan Police,[18] and also for public corporations which are, normally, liable themselves like any other corporation;[19] (2) the Crown cannot be made liable for an act or omission of its servant unless that act or omission would, apart from the Act, have given rise to a cause of action against the servant himself;[20] and (3) the Crown is not liable for anything done by any person in discharging responsibilities of a judicial nature vested in him or any responsibilities he has in connection with execution of the judicial process.[21]

Occupiers' Liability Act 1957, which binds the Crown. The liability of the Crown under the Act thus falls under s.2(2), but s.2(1)(c) continues to apply to the other duties which attach to the ownership, occupation, possession or control of property such as those in the tort of nuisance.

13   The statement in *Chagos Islanders v Attorney General* [2004] EWCA Civ 997 at [20] seems to go too far in that it ignores these categories.

14   *Chagos Islanders v Attorney General* [2004] EWCA Civ 997.

15   *Attorney General v De Keyser's Royal Hotel* [1920] A.C. 508; *Burmah Oil Co Ltd v Lord Advocate* [1965] A.C. 75; *Attorney General v Nissan* [1970] A.C. 179 at 227. The common law right to compensation was considerably restricted by the War Damage Act 1965.

16   Section 4.

17   Section 38(2). The Crown is not expressly defined, but it appears to include all government departments, officers, servants and agents of the Crown.

18   See now the Police Act 1996 s.88, para.21-016.

19   *Tamlin v Hannaford* [1950] 1 K.B. 18; cf. *Glasgow Corp v Central Land Board* 1956 S.L.T. 41. See also *Bank Voor Handel en Scheepvaart v Administrator of Hungarian Property* [1954] A.C. 584.

20   Section 2. The Crown has the benefit of any statute regulating or limiting the liability of a government department or officer of the Crown: s.2(4).

21   Section 2(5). In *Quinland v Governor of Swaleside Prison* [2002] EWCA Civ 174; [2003] Q.B. 306, the failure of the Criminal Appeal office to expedite the correction of the judge's error was held to fall within s.2(5) and the suggestion in *Welsh v Chief Constable of Merseyside* [1993] 1 All E.R. 692 that the subsection does not cover "administrative" responsibilities was disapproved. However, failure to deal with money paid into court is not a judicial act and outside the subsection: *Kirvek Management etc v Attorney General of Trinidad and Tobago* [2002] UKPC 43; [2002] 1 W.L.R. 2792. An award of damages may be made against the Crown in respect of judicial acts in limited circumstances under the Human Rights Act 1998: see para.25-013.

25-005   Members of the armed forces   Until 1987 it was not possible for a member of the armed forces to sue the Crown for injuries inflicted by a fellow member in the execution of his duty or arising from the condition of premises or equipment. There was a similar immunity for the actual wrongdoer.[22] These restrictions were removed by the Crown Proceedings (Armed Forces) Act 1987.[23] However, pre-1987 cases may still arise (for example from diseases contracted from exposure to asbestos) and the original restriction has been declared substantive rather than procedural in nature and compatible with art.6 of the European Convention on Human Rights.[24]

25-006   Crown act of state[25]   It is proposed to deal with this matter briefly since it belongs much more to the realm of constitutional and international law than to the law of tort. It is clear that no action may be brought either against the Crown or its agents in respect of an act of state, because of the need "for consistency or coherence in the distribution of functions between the executive and the judiciary" in the UK's constitutional arrangements.[26] An injury inflicted upon a foreigner abroad pursuant to an exercise of "sovereign authority as a matter of state policy"[27] and which is either authorised or ratified by the Crown is for this purpose an "act of state" and cannot be made the subject of an action in the English courts.[28] The doctrine does not however apply to acts done within British territory,[29] and it is uncertain whether the doctrine is available against a British subject on foreign soil, though the only case in which the point appears to have arisen decided that it is.[30]

The Crown act of state doctrine was thoroughly reviewed by the Supreme Court in *Rahmatullah v Ministry of Defence*,[31] where it was held that it barred claims by foreign nationals in respect of alleged unlawful detention and mistreatment by UK armed forces during conflicts in Iraq and Afghanistan. According to the Court, the doctrine applies only to acts which are: (1) an exercise of sovereign power that is inherently governmental in nature; (2) committed abroad; (3) with the prior authority or subsequent ratification of the Crown; and (4) in the conduct of the Crown's foreign relations. The doctrine covers at least the conduct of military operations which are lawful in international law.[32] By contrast, acts of torture and the mistreatment of detained persons fall outside the scope of this doctrine,[33] and this may also

---

[22]   Section 10 of the 1947 Act, which applied only to death or personal injury. On its scope see *Re Post Traumatic Stress Disorder Litigation, Multiple Claimants v MoD* [2003] EWHC 1134 (QB).

[23]   It was held in *Mulcahy v MoD* [1996] Q.B. 732 that there was no duty of care in active operations against an enemy, even though s.10 had not been revived, as provided for by s.2. This "combat immunity" is narrowly construed: *Smith v Ministry of Defence* [2013] UKSC 41; [2014] A.C. 52, para.5-024.

[24]   *Matthews v MoD* [2003] UKHL 4, [2003] 1 A.C. 1163.

[25]   This doctrine is to be distinguished from the doctrine of foreign act of state, discussed below, para.25-008.

[26]   *Rahmatullah v Ministry of Defence* [2017] UKSC 1; [2017] A.C. 649 at [104].

[27]   *Rahmatullah v Ministry of Defence* [2017] UKSC 1; [2017] A.C. 649 at [51] per Lord Mance. Hence, the doctrine does not encompass "administrative" acts like providing accommodation for troops, as in *Attorney General v Nissan* [1970] A.C. 179.

[28]   *Buron v Denman* (1848) 2 Ex. 167; 154 E.R. 450. cf. *Carr v Francis, Times & Co* [1902] A.C. 176.

[29]   *Johnstone v Pedlar* [1921] A.C. 262.

[30]   *Hilal v Secretary of State for Defence* [2009] EWHC 397 (QB). The point was left open in *Rahmatullah v Ministry of Defence* [2017] UKSC 1; [2017] A.C. 649.

[31]   [2017] UKSC 1; [2017] A.C. 649.

[32]   [2017] UKSC 1; [2017] A.C. 649 at [37].

[33]   *Rahmatullah* [2017] UKSC 1; [2017] A.C. 649 at [36] per Lady Hale (because such conduct is not an inherently governmental act); at [96] per Lord Sumption (because a decision by the Crown to

be true of the expropriation of property.[34] In *Alseran v Ministry of Defence*[35] Leggatt J followed *Rahmatullah* and further held that an act would only qualify as an act of state if it had been authorised or ratified by a government policy or decision which was a lawful exercise of the Crown's powers as a matter of English domestic law. It must be emphasised that all this concerns common law liability in tort. The Human Rights Act 1998 may have extra-territorial application to locations abroad where United Kingdom authorities are exercising effective control, thus creating an obligation not to act inconsistently with the Convention with regard to aliens as well as British subjects.[36]

Postal services   Any potential liability in tort arising in connection with the postal service is now regulated by the Postal Services Act 2000.[37] Section 90 provides that no proceedings in tort lie against a "universal service provider"[38] in respect of loss or damage suffered by any person in connection with the provision of a universal postal service because of: (1) anything done, or omitted to be done, in relation to any postal packet in the course of transmission by post; or (2) any omission to carry out arrangements for the collection of anything to be conveyed by post.[39] Furthermore, no officer, servant, employee, agent or sub-contractor of a universal service provider, nor any person engaged in or about the conveyance of postal packets, is subject, except at the suit or instance of the provider, to any civil liability for: (1) any loss or damage in the case of which liability of the provider is excluded; or (2) any loss of, or damage to, a postal packet to which s.91 applies. Under s.91 the service provider is liable for loss of or damage to postal packets where he has accepted liability under a "scheme" provided for by s.89 of the Act and the loss or damage is due to the wrongful act, neglect or default of servants, agents or sub-contractors of the service provider, but such wrongful act, etc. is presumed unless the contrary is shown.[40]   **25-007**

Foreign sovereigns   English law was for long committed to the proposition (which derives from general public international law[41]) that a foreign sovereign state enjoyed absolute immunity from liability before an English court unless the immunity had been waived by submission to the jurisdiction.[42] The doctrine was not   **25-008**

---

authorise or ratify such conduct would not be a lawful exercise of the prerogative).

34   In *Rahmatullah* [2017] UKSC 1; [2017] A.C. 649 at [36], Lady Hale said that the doctrine would not generally apply to expropriation, while accepting that there might be cases in which the expropriation, or more likely destruction of, property—say in battle—was a governmental act. Lord Sumption preferred to reserve his opinion on the issue but thought that "the answer would be likely to depend on the circumstances" (at [94]).

35   [2017] EWHC 3289 (QB); [2019] Q.B. 1251.

36   *R. (on the application of Al-Skeini) v Secretary of State for Defence* [2007] UKHL 26; [2008] 1 A.C. 153; *Smith v Ministry of Defence* [2013] UKSC 41; [2014] A.C. 52.

37   As amended by the Postal Services Act 2011.

38   Postal Services Act 2000 s.125; Postal Services Act 2011 s.65(1).

39   The same immunity is granted to a "postal operator" (Postal Services Act 2000 s.125; Postal Services Act 2011 s.27) providing a service under a scheme made under s.89 of the 2000 Act.

40   Section 92(7). This section also contains provisions governing who may sue and the amount recoverable.

41   It "pursues the legitimate aim of complying with international law to promote comity and good relations between states through the respect of another state's sovereignty" and its recognition does not infringe art.6 of the European Convention on Human Rights: *Al-Adsani v United Kingdom* (2002) 34 E.H.R.R. 273 at [54].

42   *The Cristina* [1938] A.C. 485. As to the immunity of diplomatic officials, see the Diplomatic

originally confined to sovereign acts (*acte jure imperii*) and became a serious problem in modern times because of the practice by many countries of carrying on ordinary trading activities through organs of state. Accordingly, attempts were made to restrict the immunity, culminating in the decision of the House of Lords in *The Congreso del Partido*[43] whereby a court was required to analyse the nature of the obligation and breach in question to determine whether it was of a private law or a "governmental" character. The law is now contained in the State Immunity Act 1978 under which a state is immune from the jurisdiction of the English courts except as provided by the Act.[44] Much of the Act concerns matters of contract,[45] but for our purposes the principal exceptions from sovereign immunity[46] are: (1) an act or omission in this country causing death or personal injury;[47] (2) obligations arising out of the ownership, possession or use of property in this country;[48] and (3) Admiralty proceedings (whether in rem or in personam) in respect of ships used for commercial purposes.[49] The residual immunity contained in the Act does not protect an entity distinct from the executive organs of the state[50] unless the proceedings arise out of the exercise of sovereign authority and the state would have been immune.[51] However, the Act does not apply to cases involving visiting forces of a foreign power,[52] which are still governed by the common law.[53]

The doctrine of sovereign immunity rests on the proposition that it would be an affront to the dignity and sovereignty of a state to allow it to be impleaded directly or indirectly[54] in a foreign court.[55] It applies even though the acts alleged against the foreign state involve violation of a *jus cogens* or peremptory rule of international law such as the prohibition of torture.[56] That dignity may also be affronted if those who are or were the state's officials are impleaded in relation to acts performed in their official capacity, and so the state can "extend the cloak of its own immunity over those officials".[57] Thus in *Grovit v de Nederlandsche Bank*[58] libel proceed-

---

Privileges Act 1964.

[43] [1983] A.C. 244.

[44] Section 1(1).

[45] For an important recent survey of the doctrine, with particular reference to contracts of employment, see *Benkharbouche v Secretary of State for Foreign and Commonwealth Affairs* [2017] UKSC 62; [2017] I.C.R. 1327.

[46] The state may still submit to the jurisdiction: s.2.

[47] *Nigeria v Ogbonna* [2012] 1 W.L.R. 139.

[48] Sections 5 and 6 respectively.

[49] Section 10. For states parties to the Brussels Convention of 1926, see s.10(6).

[50] cf. *C Czarnikow Ltd v Centrala Handler Zagranicznego "Rolimpex"* [1979] A.C. 351.

[51] Section 14(2); but a central bank is equated with a State: s.14(4). The provisions of s.14(2) are fully examined in *Kuwait Airways v Iraqi Airways* [1995] 1 W.L.R. 1147 (a $630 million claim for conversion). The effect of s.14(2) seems to be that the issue is essentially the same as it would have been at common law under *The Congreso del Partido*.

[52] Section 16(2).

[53] See *Littrell v USA (No.2)* [1995] 1 W.L.R. 82 (treatment not actionable in US law and not justiciable here as interference with sovereign rights of the United States over its military personnel) and *Holland v Lampen-Wolfe* [2000] 1 W.L.R. 1573 (provision for education of military personnel a matter within the sovereign immunity of the United States so as to bar a claim for libel).

[54] See *Belhaj v Straw* [2017] UKSC 3; [2017] A.C. 964 at [15].

[55] Hence the doctrine does not apply where there is no challenge to the validity or lawfulness of an act of a foreign state: *AAA v Unilever Plc* [2017] EWHC 371 (QB) (affirmed on appeal: [2018] EWCA Civ 1532; [2018] B.C.C. 959).

[56] *Jones v Saudi Arabia* [2006] UKHL 26; [2007] 1 A.C. 270.

[57] *Jones v Saudi Arabia* [2004] EWCA Civ 1394 at [105].

[58] [2005] EWHC 2944 (QB); [2006] 1 W.L.R. 3323.

ings against the Dutch central bank's officers alleging malice and arising out of the refusal to register the claimant's company were struck out.

Independently of sovereign immunity, there is a doctrine of "foreign act of state"[59] according to which the courts may refuse to take cognisance of an alleged tort because doing so would require adjudicating on the lawfulness or validity of acts done abroad in the exercise of the sovereign authority[60] of foreign states. Although this doctrine differs from state immunity because it is a subject matter immunity, rather than a personal one, it "proceeds from the same premise ... namely mutual respect for the equality of sovereign states".[61] An example of its application is *Buttes Gas and Oil Co v Hammer*,[62] where the House of Lords stayed litigation between private parties when it involved an examination of allegations of conspiracy between one party and a sovereign ruler and acts of assertion of territorial sovereignty by other states in the area.[63] The foreign act of state doctrine was reviewed in *Belhaj v Straw*,[64] where Lord Neuberger described it as a common law rule of "judicial self-restraint",[65] applicable to issues that judges decide they should abstain from resolving. It was not, however, engaged on the facts of the case, which involved allegations that the United Kingdom government had been complicit in the torture of foreign nationals by other states in overseas jurisdictions, since there was no suggestion of any formal or high-level agreement governing the co-operation of the executives of the countries concerned.[66]

2. JUDICIAL ACTS

Acts done in the administration of justice[67]   The law casts a wide immunity **25-009** around acts done in the administration of justice. This has been rather infelicitously styled a "privilege", but that might imply that the judge has a private right to be malicious, whereas its real meaning is that in the public interest it is undesirable to inquire whether acts of this kind are malicious or not. It is rather a right of the public to have the independence of the judges preserved rather than a privilege of the judges themselves.[68] It is better to take the chance of judicial incompetence, irritability, or irrelevance, than to run the risk of getting a bench warped by apprehension of the consequences of judgments which ought to be given without fear or favour.[69] Despite a valiant attempt by Lord Denning MR to rationalise the law into one, uni-

---

[59]   To be distinguished from Crown act of state, discussed above, para.25-006.

[60]   A "sovereign act" has the same meaning here as in the state immunity context: *Belhaj v Straw* [2017] UKSC 3; [2017] A.C. 964 at [199].

[61]   *Belhaj* [2017] UKSC 3; [2017] A.C. 964 at [200] per Lord Sumption.

[62]   [1982] A.C. 888.

[63]   Nor will the English courts entertain a claim by a foreign state which in substance amounts to an exercise of its sovereign authority: *Mbasogo v Logo Ltd* [2006] EWCA Civ 1370; [2007] Q.B. 846.

[64]   [2017] UKSC 3; [2017] A.C. 964.

[65]   [2017] UKSC 3; [2017] A.C. 964 at [144]. See also at [89] per Lord Mance ("a principle of non-justiciability or abstention").

[66]   Nor was the doctrine of state immunity applicable, since the foreign states in question were not impleaded, nor their legal position affected, whether directly or indirectly, by the claimant's tort actions against United Kingdom authorities and officials.

[67]   The topic is dealt with at length in Winfield, *The Present Law of Abuse of Legal Procedure* (1931), Ch.7.

[68]   *Bottomley v Brougham* [1908] 1 K.B. 584 at 586-587.

[69]   For a more sceptical view, see Olowofoyeku (1990) 10 L.S. 271 and *Suing Judges* (1993).

fied principle[70] and legislative intervention, the law is still hard to state concisely or with precision.

25-010 **High Court judges** Judges of the High Court[71] are immune from liability for any act of a judicial character even though the act is in excess of or outside their jurisdiction and whether this is a result of mistake of fact or of law. If, however, an act is in excess of jurisdiction and is done in bad faith then the judge would be liable in damages for what follows from the order made, for example, imprisonment or seizure of property.[72]

25-011 **Justices of the peace** The liability of justices of the peace is now governed by the Courts Act 2003, re-enacting provisions first introduced in 1990. It is provided that no action lies for any act done in the execution of the justice's duty and with respect to any matter within his jurisdiction[73] but that an action lies for an act in the purported execution of his duty and in relation to a matter which is not within his jurisdiction if, but only if, he acted in bad faith.[74] Putting aside the point that proceedings in magistrates' courts are amenable to review and control by the High Court, whereas a High Court judge is the sole arbiter of his jurisdiction (subject to appeal) this is similar to the position of a judge of the High Court.

25-012 **Other judges** Unfortunately, there is no legislation governing the position of the majority of professional judges (county court judges, recorders and district judges[75]) and their position has to be discerned from the older cases and by inference from what the House of Lords decided in the context of magistrates in *Re McC*.[76] A further complication arises from the fact that another distinction cuts across that based upon the status of the judge, namely that between courts which are and are not "courts of record". Thus, all trials on indictment are before a court of record, even though very few of them are presided over by High Court judges. In such cases, "inferior" judges are immune from liability for acts within their jurisdiction, even if they are actuated by malice.[77] What is less clear is their position with regard to acts outside their jurisdiction. The concept of jurisdiction in this context means the power to decide an issue, not the method by which the decision is reached, so that procedural irregularity in reaching a result which the court has power to achieve does not take the case outside the court's jurisdiction.[78] Accord-

---

[70] In *Sirros v Moore* [1975] Q.B. 118.

[71] Many High Court *civil* actions are now heard by deputy High Court judges, who are usually QCs and retired High Court judges, and circuit court judges who are authorised to sit as a High Court judge, but there does not seem to be any doubt that they enjoy the same immunity as a full High Court judge.

[72] "If the Lord Chief Justice himself, on the acquittal of a defendant charged before him with a criminal offence, were to say, 'That is a perverse verdict', and thereupon proceed to pass a sentence of imprisonment, he could be sued for trespass": *Re McC* [1985] A.C. 528 at 540 per Lord Bridge.

[73] Courts Act 2003 s.31.

[74] Section 32. There are provisions for indemnity of justices in s.35, which dates from the Justices of the Peace Act 1979.

[75] Other than those of magistrates' courts.

[76] *Re McC* [1985] A.C. 541.

[77] See *Hinds v Liverpool County Court* [2008] EWHC 665 (QB); [2008] 2 F.L.R. 63.

[78] Nor does error as to a collateral matter on which the jurisdiction depends: *Re McC* [1985] A.C. 541 at 544; *Johnson v Meldon* (1890) 30 L.R.Ir. 15.

ing to *Re McC* this is the true explanation of *Sirros v Moore*.[79] The claimant had been convicted of an offence and recommended for deportation by a stipendiary magistrate, but without an order for his detention. The judge in the Crown Court,[80] wrongly thinking that he had no jurisdiction to hear an appeal against deportation, dismissed it but ordered that the claimant be detained. This did not amount to trespass because he did have power to overrule the initial decision against detention and intended to do so, even though he implemented that decision by a "hopelessly irregular procedure". On the other hand, by analogy with *Re McC*, if a judge of an inferior court were, in good faith, to pass a sentence which he had no power to pass he would be liable. In modern conditions it is entirely unconvincing to argue as a justification for a professional judge being liable for acts done in good faith outside his jurisdiction, that he is always supposed to know the law (the state of which is in any event often a matter of opinion): if the argument has any validity at all it should surely apply, a fortiori, to judges of the High Court. What is needed, it is suggested, is a bold decision declaring the common law governing the position of inferior judges to be the same as that stated for justices in the Courts Act 2003.

Actions other than in tort   Enough has been said to show that it will be a rare   **25-013**
case in which a person will recover substantial damages in respect of a judicial act. An action in tort is not, however, the only route to compensation. Where a criminal conviction is reversed on the basis of a newly-discovered fact there may be a statutory right to compensation under s.133 of the Criminal Justice Act 1988. Furthermore, damages[81] may be awarded under the Human Rights Act 1998 in respect of a judicial act not done in good faith, or one done in good faith in order to compensate a person to the extent required by art.5(5) of the European Convention on Human Rights (which provides for compensation for arrest or detention).[82] However, in the latter type of case such damages are awardable against the Crown and so the immunity of the judge is in effect preserved.[83]

Officers of the law   An officer of the law who executes process apparently regular,   **25-014**
not knowing that the person who authorised him to do so has exceeded his powers, is protected in spite of the proceedings being ill-founded.[84] And by the Constables Protection Act 1750,[85] no action can be brought against a constable for anything done in obedience to any warrant[86] issued by a justice of the peace until the would-be claimant has made a written demand for a copy of the warrant and the demand has not been complied with for six days. If the demand is complied

---

[79]   [1975] Q.B. 118.
[80]   Not being a trial on indictment, the court was not a court of record.
[81]   The award is made against the Crown: Human Rights Act 1998 s.9(4).
[82]   Section 9. Proceedings may only be brought by exercising a right of appeal, by judicial review or in such other forum as may be prescribed by rules. However, the decision of an inferior court may be subject to judicial review and a claim for damages may be presented in an application for judicial review. It is not necessarily the case that an erroneous decision gives rise to a claim under art.5: *Benham v United Kingdom* (1996) 22 E.H.R.R. 293. On the operation of s.9, see *Webster v Lord Chancellor* [2015] EWCA Civ 742; [2016] Q.B. 676.
[83]   *Hinds v Liverpool County Court* [2008] EWHC 665 (QB); [2008] 2 F.L.R. 63.
[84]   *Sirros v Moore* [1975] Q.B. 118; *London (Mayor of) v Cox* (1867) L.R. 2 H.L. 239 at 269. For detention under a court order based on a mistaken view of the law, see para.26-061.
[85]   Section 6.
[86]   For arrest without warrant see para.26-053.

with, then the constable, if he produces the warrant at the trial of the action against him, is not liable in spite of any defect of jurisdiction in the justice. However, if he arrests, or seizes the goods of, a person not named in the warrant, he does so at his peril. His mistake, however honest, will not excuse him. In *Hoye v Bush*[87] one Richard Hoye was suspected of stealing a mare. A warrant was issued for his arrest, but it mistakenly described him as "John Hoye" (his father's name). Richard was arrested under this warrant and subsequently sued Bush, the constable, for false imprisonment. Bush was held liable, for although Richard was the man who was actually wanted, still the warrant described somebody else.[88]

3. MINORS

A. Capacity to Sue

25-015 **Minors** In general no distinction falls to be taken between a minor and an adult so far as their respective capacities to sue for torts are concerned, save that as a "protected person" a minor must sue by his "litigation friend".[89]

25-016 **Unborn children** That a child born with a disability as a result of injuries suffered while *en ventre sa mere* could sue,[90] even though before birth it was not a legal person, was put beyond doubt by the Congenital Disabilities (Civil Liability) Act 1976. Since s.4(5) of the Act states that no common law liability can arise in respect of births after its commencement, the Act now governs all such actions. The principal provisions of the Act may be summarised as follows. In the first place, an action only lies if the claimant child is born alive and disabled.[91] Secondly, the liability to the child is "derivative", in other words it only arises if the defendant was under an actual or potential tort liability[92] to either parent of the child for the act or omission which led to the disability, albeit that for this purpose[93]:

> "[I]t is no answer [to a claim by the child] that there could not have been such liability because the parent suffered no actionable injury, if there was a breach of legal duty which, if accompanied by injury, would have given rise to the liability."

In other words, if a pregnant woman takes a drug which has been manufactured or developed negligently or in circumstances in which liability could arise under the

---

[87] (1840) 1 M. & G. 775; 133 E.R. 545.

[88] Contrast *McGrath v Chief Constable of the Royal Ulster Constabulary* [2001] UKHL 39; [2001] 2 A.C. 731 (under s.38 of the Criminal Law Act 1977 arrest of C, who was named in the warrant, was lawful, even though the person wanted was X, who had given C's name). Both cases are consistent with a policy of requiring the constable to exercise the warrant at its face value. Contrast the matter of the timing of the execution of the warrant, where the constable may have a discretion: *Henderson v Chief Constable of Cleveland* [2001] EWCA Civ 335; [2001] 1 W.L.R. 1103.

[89] CPR 21. There is no bar to a child suing a parent: see below, and para.5-035.

[90] It was held at an early date that a posthumous child of a deceased father could maintain an action under the Fatal Accidents Act: *The George and Richard* (1871) L.R. 3 Ad. & E. 466.

[91] The mother may have an action in respect of a stillbirth: *Bagley v North Herts Heath Authority* (1986) 136 N.L.J. 1014. For definition of "disabled" see s.4(1).

[92] This liability will commonly be for negligence, but there is nothing in the Act to confine it to this. The running of time against the parent is irrelevant: s.1(3). While the child's cause of action accrues upon birth (s.4(3)) the Limitation Act 1980 would prevent time running against him until he reached majority: para.26-100.

[93] Section 1(3).

Consumer Protection Act 1987 and this causes her child to be born disabled, the child may recover damages from the manufacturer even though the mother suffers no injury herself from the drug.[94] In practice the commonest situation giving rise to liability is likely to be that where the child is injured during its mother's pregnancy but the Act extends more widely than this to cover an occurrence which affects either parent in his or her ability to bear a normal, healthy child,[95] so that, for example, a negligent injury to the mother's reproductive system before conception could found an action by a child conceived thereafter and born disabled as a result.[96]

The mother's immunity The mother herself is not generally liable under the **25-017**
Congenital Disabilities (Civil Liability) Act 1976 so that there is no possibility of, say, an action being brought in respect of disabilities said to have been caused by the mother's smoking during pregnancy. The Law Commission thought that on balance this immunity should not be extended to the father, and the Act so provides. The various policy arguments in favour of immunity are weaker when the potential parental liability would be covered by insurance[97] and s.2 of the Act accordingly provides that a woman driving a motor vehicle when she knows or ought to know herself to be pregnant owes a duty of care towards her unborn child.

Defences The derivative nature of the child's action in cases other than those **25-018**
involving negligent driving by the mother is emphasised by the supplementary provisions of s.1 of the Congenital Disabilities (Civil Liability) Act 1976, which "identify" the child with the parents for the purposes of defences. Thus, in the case of an occurrence preceding the time of conception, knowledge by either parent of the risk of disablement will bar the child's action;[98] where the parent affected shared responsibility for the child being born disabled, the child's damages are to be reduced according to the extent of the parent's responsibility;[99] and any contract term having the effect of excluding or restricting liability to the parent is equally effective in respect of liability to the child.[100]

Disability caused by infertility treatment Following the passage of the 1976 Act **25-019**
there were major developments in the treatment of infertility and the possibility arose of such treatment causing a disability in circumstances which would not fall

---

[94] In many cases it would be impossible for the mother to suffer any physical injury from the drug and it then perhaps looks odd to say that there has been any "breach of legal duty", but it is inconceivable that such a case falls outside the Act.

[95] Section 1(2)(a).

[96] In this situation there is a high likelihood that the action could be met by the defence of knowledge of the risk by the mother: s.1(4), para.25-018.

[97] In road accident cases there is a direct right of action against the insurer (see para.1-035) and claims by children injured as passengers in cars negligently driven by parents are not uncommon.

[98] Section 1(4); but not where the father is responsible for the injury to the mother and she does not know of the risk. If a woman is the child's other parent, under the Human Fertilisation and Embryology Act 2008 she is treated in the same way as the father: s.1(4A).

[99] Section 1(7). cf. a case under s.2, which would follow the normal rule of non-identification (para.23-055), allowing the child to recover in full against either defendant and consigning the final allocation of loss to contribution proceedings between the defendants.

[100] Section 1(6). This provision is likely to be of very limited effect in view of the statutory restrictions on exclusion of liability for negligence in personal injury cases (para.26-017), and is anyway inapplicable to cases under the Consumer Protection Act 1987: see s.6(3)(c) of that Act.

within s.1, for example because the gametes or the embryo were kept outside the body. Section 1A of the Act, inserted by s.44 of the Human Fertilisation and Embryology Act 1990, covers these cases and provides a virtual mirror image of s.1.

25-020 **"Wrongful life" claims by the child**[101]   So far we have been dealing with cases where, but for the defendant's wrongful act or omission, the claimant would have been born without the disability or with a lesser degree of it; but another situation presents much more acute legal problems, that is to say, where the claimant contends that he should never have been born at all, the so-called "wrongful life" case. Such a case could conceivably be advanced against a person responsible for the child's conception[102] but is more likely to arise from failure during the early stages of pregnancy to detect some abnormality which, if it had been detected, would have led to an abortion.[103] Such was one of the claims in *McKay v Essex Area Health Authority*,[104] decided at common law because the birth was before the 1976 Act came into force. In striking out this claim, the court referred to various objections of a public policy nature (for example, the dangers of a legal assessment of the life of a disabled child as less valuable than that of a child without disability and the prospect of a claim against the mother where, informed of the danger, she declined to have an abortion) but that which most strongly influenced all the members of the court was the impossibility of assessing damages on any sensible basis, for the court would have to, "compare the state of the plaintiff with non-existence, of which the court can know nothing".[105] The issues were fully aired in *Harriton v Stephens*,[106] where a majority of the High Court of Australia dismissed a wrongful life action primarily on the ground that since it was impossible to compare life with a disability with no life at all, the child plaintiff was unable to establish that she had suffered damage as a result of the defendant doctor's failure to diagnose rubella during the mother's pregnancy. If such claims were permitted, the majority argued, then further complications would arise, such as: (1) what degree of disability was necessary for such a claim to succeed, and why; (2) whether such claims could be brought against the child's parents, on the ground that, knowing of the likely disability, they failed to have the pregnancy terminated; (3) the potential overlap between a child's wrongful life claim, and a parental "wrongful birth" claim;[107] and (4) what damages should be awarded, and why.

The 1976 Act replaces "any law in force before its passing, whereby a person could be liable to a child in respect of disabilities with which it might be born". This wording would appear wide enough to prevent any future wrongful life cases at common law even in the unlikely event that the Supreme Court were to overrule

---

[101] See generally Todd (2005) 27 Syd. L. Rev. 525; Scott (2013) 72 C.L.J. 115.

[102] See, e.g., *Zepeda v Zepeda* 190 N.E. 2d 849 (1963).

[103] The risk of serious disability is a ground for lawful abortion. Since the amendment of the Abortion Act 1967 by the Human Fertilisation and Embryology Act 1990 s.37, there is no specific time limit for these cases, nor is the Infant Life Preservation Act 1929 applicable (cf. *Rance v Mid-Downs Health Authority* [1991] 1 Q.B. 587) but there might still be practical or medical grounds ruling out a late abortion.

[104] [1982] Q.B. 1166. An alternative basis of the claim was unproblematical: that if the mother had received treatment the disability would have been less.

[105] *McKay v Essex Area Health Authority* [1982] Q.B. 1166 at 1193 per Griffiths LJ.

[106] [2006] HCA 15; (2006) 226 C.L.R. 52. Teff (2007) 15 Tort L. Rev. 7.

[107] See para.25-021.

McKay's case and the limitation problems could be overcome. In *McKay* the Court of Appeal said, obiter, that no such claim could be made under the 1976 Act because it imports the assumption that, but for the occurrence giving rise to the disabled birth, the child would have been born normal and healthy, not that it would not have been born at all. This is certainly true of s.1(2)(b),[108] which deals with the most obvious case, that where there is negligence towards the mother during pregnancy. However, no such assumption is expressly built into s.1(2)(a) dealing with pre-conception events, nor into the new s.1A. Indeed, one of the specified matters dealt with by the latter ("the selection ... of the embryo ... or of the gametes used to bring about the creation of the embryo") seems to point to a situation where the defect is already inherent in the "material" used.

"Wrongful conception" or "wrongful birth" claims Claims by a disabled child   **25-021**
for "wrongful life" may be contrasted with "wrongful conception" or "wrongful birth" actions by a child's parents. Such claims allege that, but for the negligence, the parents would respectively not have conceived the child, or would have had an abortion, with the main head of damages being the cost of bringing up the child. From the mid-1980s such actions were permitted by the courts with damages being based upon the parents' station in life and therefore sometimes amounting to very substantial sums. This line of cases was, however, overturned in *McFarlane v Tayside Health Board*,[109] where the House of Lords held that the costs of upbringing were not recoverable. The reasons were various: to award damages representing this cost was disproportionate to the wrong committed (on the facts, negligent advice to the father that his vasectomy had been successful); it would fail to take account of the real (though incalculable) countervailing benefits brought to the family by the birth of a healthy child, benefits which were still present even if the parents' intention had been to have no more children; and it would offend against the idea of distributive justice, which in suitable cases had a role to play in the mosaic of tort law alongside the more usual corrective justice.[110] However, the mother was allowed to recover damages for the pain, suffering and inconvenience of pregnancy and birth and for the loss of earnings and expenses immediately attendant on those processes.[111] A little later, in *Rees v Darlington Memorial Hospital NHS Trust*,[112] the majority of the House of Lords modified the position somewhat by holding that it was necessary to do more to recognise that the parents in such a situation had suffered a legal wrong and an interference with their autonomy in being deprived of the freedom to limit their family and that this should take the form of an award of a conventional sum of damages: £15,000 was awarded. On the facts of *Rees* itself the mother was blind and had sought sterilisation because of the burden motherhood would impose on her in the light of her disability, but this did not justify departure from the rule that the costs of upbringing were irrecoverable. A balance sheet of benefit and detriment still could not be drawn up—just as the

---

[108] "An occurrence ... which ... affected the mother ... or the child ... so that the child is born with disabilities which would not otherwise have been present."

[109] [2000] 2 A.C. 59.

[110] See also *Frost v Chief Constable of South Yorkshire* [1999] 2 A.C. 455, para.5-080.

[111] The mother's loss of earnings during the upbringing of the child is not recoverable: there is no material distinction between such loss and the expenses of upbringing: *Greenfield v Flather* [2001] EWCA Civ 113, [2001] 1 W.L.R. 179 (where an attempt to rely on art.8 of the European Convention on Human Rights was also rejected).

[112] [2003] UKHL 52; [2004] 1 A.C. 309.

law could not distinguish between the impact of an "unwanted" child on wealthy parents and poor parents, so it could not distinguish between parents who were fit and well and those whose disability might cause them to incur further inconvenience and expense.

There is, however, a significant qualification on the *McFarlane* rule against recovery of the cost of upkeep, which derives from the decision of the Court of Appeal in *Parkinson v St James Hospital Trust*.[113] According to *Parkinson*, where the *child* is born with a serious disability, whether mental or physical, then the parents may recover as damages in a wrongful conception or wrongful birth claim the additional expenses of upbringing attributable to that disability. This rule that the "extra" cost of bringing up a disabled child is recoverable survived the later decision in *Rees*, where however it met with a mixed reception: three of the seven Law Lords agreed that the extra cost should be recoverable, two disagreed, one left the point open, and one held that such damages should be recoverable only if the purpose of the sterilisation or vasectomy had been to avoid the birth of a disabled child.

The overall effect of the complex body of case law governing wrongful conception and wrongful birth claims can be summarised as follows: (1) the mother is entitled to damages for the pain and distress caused by the pregnancy, and for the financial loss occasioned by the pregnancy and birth itself; (2) the parents are entitled to a fixed sum award of £15,000 for the loss of their freedom to determine the size of their family; and (3) no claim lies for the expenses of bringing up the child, with the exception of the additional costs attributable to bringing up a disabled child.[114]

25-022 **Other types of reproductive negligence claim** Wrongful life, wrongful conception and wrongful birth claims do not exhaust the possibilities in terms of negligence actions arising out of the reproductive process. In *ACB v Thomson Medical Pte Ltd*,[115] for example, the defendant provider of in-vitro fertilisation (IVF) treatment had mishandled sperm samples and mistakenly fertilised the plaintiff's ovum with the sperm of a stranger instead of her husband. The Singapore Court of Appeal held that on these facts an award of damages should be made for "loss of genetic affinity", and it fixed these (somewhat arbitrarily) at one-third of the estimated costs of bringing up the child. That decision can be contrasted with an earlier Northern Irish case, *A v A Health and Social Services Trust*,[116] in which the white mother of the claimant infants had been inseminated with sperm from a donor of a Cape Coloured background in the course of IVF treatment, with the result that the children were darker in complexion than their parents. There, a negligence action by the children was dismissed, the Northern Ireland Court of Appeal holding that having a different skin colour from the majority of the local population and their parents "could not sensibly be regarded as damage" at law. As reproductive medicine continues to advance, many more such claims (and new types of claim) can be expected to come before the courts in the future.

---

[113] [2001] EWCA Civ 530; [2002] Q.B. 266.
[114] The same rules apply when the claim is made in contract: *ARB v IVF Hammersmith* [2018] EWCA Civ 2803; [2020] Q.B. 93.
[115] [2017] SGCA 20; [2017] 1 S.L.R. 918.
[116] [2011] NICA 28; [2012] N.I. 77.

B.   Liability to be Sued

No defence of infancy as such, but age not irrelevant   In contrast with the   **25-023**
criminal law, in the law of tort there is no defence of infancy as such and a minor
is as much liable to be sued for his torts as is an adult. In *Gorely v Codd*,[117] Nield J
held that a boy of 16 had been negligent when he accidentally shot the claimant with
an air rifle in the course of "larking about", and it is obvious that a motorist one
month short of 18 is as responsible for negligent driving as one who has reached
that age. However, where a minor is sued for negligence, his age is relevant in
determining whether his conduct was unreasonable, since it must be shown that his
behaviour fell below the standard of an ordinarily reasonable and prudent child of
his age.[118] Even though one cannot fix the age precisely, it is obvious that a tiny
infant cannot be liable in tort at all, not because they enjoy a defence (they do not)
but simply because it will be impossible to establish the elements of a claim against
them (for example, an infant aged three cannot incur liability in negligence because
it is impossible for the infant to fall short of the standard of the reasonable child of
the same age).

C.   Tort and Contract

In general contracts entered into by minors are void and unenforceable, and the   **25-024**
question arises, therefore, whether if the facts show both a breach of a (void)
contract and a tort, the contract rule can be evaded by framing the claim against the
minor in tort. The answer seems to be that a minor cannot be sued if the cause of
action against him arises substantially *ex contractu* or if to allow the action would
be to enforce the contract indirectly, but if the wrong is independent of the contract,
then the minor may be sued even though but for the contract he would have had no
opportunity to commit the tort.[119] In *R Leslie Ltd v Shiell*[120] a minor had fraudulently
represented to the claimants that he was of full age and had thereby persuaded them
to lend him money. He was held not liable for deceit or on any other ground, for a
judgment against him would have amounted to the enforcement of the contract of
loan in a roundabout way. Conversely, in *Burnard v Haggis*,[121] the defendant, an
undergraduate of Trinity College, Cambridge, and a minor, was held liable in the
following circumstances. Having hired a mare for riding from the claimant on the
express stipulation that she was not to be used for "jumping or larking", the defendant lent the mare to a friend who, while they were galloping about fields in the
neighbourhood of Cambridge, tried to jump her over a fence, with the result that
she suffered a fatal injury. The defendant's conduct was, as Willes J said[122]:

> "[A]s much a trespass, notwithstanding the hiring for another purpose, as if, without any
> hiring at all, the defendant had gone into a field and taken the mare out and hunted her
> and killed her. It was a bare trespass, not within the object and purpose of the hiring. It

---

[117]   [1967] 1 W.L.R. 19. See also *Buckpitt v Oates* [1968] 1 All E.R. 1145 at 1149.

[118]   *Mullin v Richards* [1998] 1 W.L.R. 1304. See para.6-009.

[119]   *Pollock's Principles of Contract*, 13th edn (1950), pp.62-63, approved by Kennedy LJ in *R Leslie
Ltd v Shiell* [1914] 3 K.B. 607 at 620.

[120]   [1914] 3 K.B. 607.

[121]   *Burnard v Haggis* (1863) 14 C.B. (N.S.) 45; 143 E.R. 360. cf. *Jennings v Rundall* (1799) 8 T.R. 335;
101 E.R. 1419; *Fawcett v Smethurst* (1914) 84 L.J.K.B. 473.

[122]   *Burnard v Haggis* (1863) 14 C.B. (N.S.) 45 at 53; 143 E.R. 360 at 364.

was not even an excess. It was doing an act towards the mare which was altogether forbidden by the owner."[123]

If in *R Leslie Ltd v Shiell* the minor had still been in possession of the money lent, equity would have ordered its restoration on the ground of fraud. Now, under s.3(1) of the Minors' Contracts Act 1987, the court has a discretion to order the transfer back of any property acquired under the contract (or its proceeds) even without fraud, but if the money has been spent and there is nothing to show for it, nothing can be done.

D. Liability of Parent

25-025   A parent or guardian[124] is not in general liable for the torts of a child[125] but to this there are two exceptions. First, where the child is employed by his parent and commits a tort in the course of his employment, the parent is vicariously responsible just as he would be for the tort of any other employee. Secondly, the parent will be liable if the child's tort is due to the parent's negligent control of the child in respect of the act that caused the injury, or if the parent expressly authorised the commission of the tort, or possibly if he ratified the child's act. Thus, where a father gave his son, about 15 years old, an airgun and allowed him to retain it after he had smashed a neighbour's window with it, he was held liable for the boy's tort in injuring the eye of another boy with the gun.[126] Where, however, a boy aged 13 had promised his father never to use his air rifle outside the house (where there was a cellar in which the rifle could be fired) and subsequently broke that promise, the Court of Appeal refused to disturb the trial judge's finding that the father had not been negligent.[127]

4. SPOUSES

25-026   It is almost a century since the abolition of the special rules governing a married woman's liability in tort and making her husband liable for her torts during marriage.[128] As far as third parties are concerned there are no special rules governing husband and wife and neither is liable for the other's torts, though he or she may of course be liable as a joint tortfeasor in the usual way. As between themselves, the common law rule was that no action in tort was possible, but this was productive of serious anomalies and injustices and it was abolished by the Law Reform (Husband and Wife) Act 1962.[129] Each of the parties to a marriage now has the same right of action in tort against the other as if they were not married,[130] but, in order

---

[123] See too *Ballett v Mingay* [1943] K.B. 281.

[124] Note in this connection that it has been said that school authorities are under no greater duty than that of a reasonably careful parent: *Ricketts v Erith BC* [1943] 2 All E.R. 629; *Rich v London CC* [1953] 1 W.L.R 895.

[125] Such liability is common in continental legal systems: see Martin-Casals (ed.), *Children in Tort Law Part I: Children as Tortfeasors* (2006).

[126] *Bebee v Sales* (1916) 32 T.L.R. 413; *Newton v Edgerley* [1959] 1 W.L.R. 1031.

[127] *Donaldson v McNiven* (1952) 96 S.J. 747.

[128] Law Reform (Married Women and Tortfeasors) Act 1935.

[129] Section 1(1). In *Church v Church* (1983) 133 N.L.J. 317, £9,605 damages were awarded in an action for battery between spouses.

[130] This means, of course, that even if proceedings are not brought against the spouse, a co-tortfeasor with him may have a right of contribution.

to prevent them from using the court as a forum for trivial domestic disputes, the proceedings may be stayed if it appears that no substantial benefit will accrue to either party from their continuation.[131] The proceedings may also be stayed if it appears that the case can be more conveniently disposed of under s.17 of the Married Women's Property Act 1882, which provides a summary procedure for determining questions of title or possession of property between husband and wife.

5. CORPORATIONS

A corporation is an artificial person created by the law. It may come into existence either by the common law, by royal charter, by Parliamentary authority, or by prescription or custom. Whatever its origin may be, a corporation is legally independent of the human beings who are its members.   **25-027**

A. Capacity to Sue in Tort

Capacity A corporation can sue for torts committed against it,[132] but there are certain torts which, by their very nature, it is impossible to commit against a corporation, such as assault or false imprisonment. A corporation can sue for the malicious presentation of a winding-up petition[133] or for defamation, though the precise limits of the latter are unclear. It is certain that a trading corporation may sue in respect of defamation affecting its business or property,[134] and perhaps in respect of anything affecting its conduct of its affairs[135] but a governmental authority cannot sue for defamation.[136]   **25-028**

Proper claimant The corporation (and not its members) is the only proper claimant in respect of a tort against the corporation. To some extent this simply reflects the elementary principle that C cannot bring an action against D to recover damages for an injury done by D to A, C (the member) and A (the corporation) being different persons. A shareholder is not an owner of the company's assets but merely has a right to participate in them on winding up. Accordingly, if the defendant infringes patents belonging to a company the company can sue but a shareholder (or creditor[137]) cannot. The shareholder and the company may, of course, have separate and distinct claims arising out of the same conduct of the defendant. If D carelessly burns down the company premises and C, a shareholder who happens to be present at the time, is injured, the fact that the company has a claim for the cost of rebuilding does not of course affect C's claim for personal injuries. However,   **25-029**

---

[131] Section 1(2)(a) (there are equivalent provisions for same-sex formalised relationships in s.69 of the Civil Partnership Act 2004). See *McLeod v McLeod* (1963) 113 L.J. 420.

[132] Even if engaged in an ultra vires undertaking at the material time: *National Telephone Co v Constable of St Peter Port* [1900] A.C. 317 at 321 (obiter).

[133] *Quartz Hill Consolidated Gold Mining v Eyre* (1883) 11 Q.B.D. 674.

[134] *Metropolitan Saloon Omnibus Co v Hawkins* (1859) 4 Hurl. & N. 87; 157 E.R. 769; *Jameel v Wall Street Journal Europe Sprl* [2006] UKHL 44; [2007] 1 A.C. 359.

[135] *D & L Caterers Ltd v D'Ajou* [1945] K.B. 364; *National Union of General and Municipal Workers v Gillan* [1946] K.B. 81; *Willis v Brooks* [1947] 1 All E.R. 191; *South Hetton Coal Co Ltd v North Eastern News Association Ltd* [1894] 1 Q.B. 133, though inconclusive on the point, seems to support this view. Dicta in *Manchester Corp v Williams* (1891) 63 L.T. 805 at 806 (the fuller report) and *Lewis v Daily Telegraph Ltd* [1964] A.C. 234 at 262, appears to support the narrower view.

[136] See para.13-035.

[137] See *Garcia v Marex Financial Ltd* [2018] EWCA Civ 1468; [2019] Q.B. 173.

even though a tort has been committed against the shareholder, the loss suffered by him may be a diminution in the value of his shareholding and this is only a reflection of the loss to the company caused by the diminution of its assets. To allow both the company and the shareholder to sue would be to allow double recovery; to allow the shareholder to sue and then bar the company from further action would be to harm the company's creditors, for they are entitled to the company's assets in dissolution in priority to the shareholders and by allowing the shareholder to sue the company's assets would in effect be diminished. Hence, English law, subject to certain exceptions that cannot be explored here,[138] does not allow such a "reflexive" claim.[139] If the sole asset of a company is a box containing £100,000 and C owns 99 of the 100 shares in the company he cannot sue the thief who appropriates the contents of the box.[140] However, the same would be true in that example even if the contents were misappropriated by the thief fraudulently obtaining the key from C and thereby committing an actionable wrong against him. C has still suffered no loss other than the diminution of the value of his shareholding in the company which will arise as a result of the loss of the company's assets.[141] If, on the other hand, the value of the shareholder's holding is diminished by a tort against him which is not actionable by the company there is nothing to prevent him suing for that loss.[142]

B. Liability to be Sued

25-030   It has always been generally accepted that a chartered corporation[143] has all the powers of a natural person[144] but most companies are incorporated under statute and expressly limited by the terms of their incorporation as to what they may lawfully do. While these limitations still govern the internal affairs of the company, s.39 of the Companies Act 2006 provides that

> "the validity of an act done by a company shall not be called into question on the ground of lack of capacity by reason of anything in the company's constitution".

This would seem to render otiose any distinction for the purposes of the law of torts between intra vires and ultra vires acts, though the distinction had in fact been largely effaced under the old law.[145]

25-031   **Wrongs committed by servants or agents**   A company will be vicariously liable for the torts of its employees committed within the course of their employment[146] (and, where relevant in tort, for the acts of its agent within the scope of his

---

[138] See, in particular, *Giles v Rhind* [2002] EWCA Civ 1428; [2003] Ch. 618.

[139] See, further, Mitchell (2004) 120 L.Q.R. 457.

[140] This is so even if the company chooses not to sue. However, where a wrongdoer is in control of the company a shareholder may be able to bring a "derivative" action on behalf of the company, but this is not a personal claim.

[141] *Johnson v Gore Wood & Co* [2001] 2 A.C. 1; *Prudential Assurance Co Ltd v Newman Industries Ltd (No.2)* [1982] Ch. 204.

[142] *Lee v Sheard* [1956] 1 Q.B. 192; *Fischer (George) GB Ltd v Multi-Construction Ltd* [1995] 1 B.C.L.C. 260; *Gerber Garment Technology Inc v Lectra Systems Ltd* [1997] R.P.C. 443.

[143] For example, the older universities.

[144] *Case of Sutton's Hospital* (1611) 10 Co. Rep. 23; 77 E.R. 960.

[145] See the thirteenth edition of this work, p.675.

[146] See Ch.21.

authority[147]) and the objects for which the company was incorporated may be relevant in determining the limits of the employment or authority of the agent.[148]

Wrongs committed by the company itself Certain conduct is regarded as **25-032** conduct of the company itself. Thus, a company may incur a personal liability when it fails to take reasonable care for the safety of persons even if no allegation of negligence is made against any individual employee of the company[149] and it has been held, where a liability depended upon the "actual fault or privity" of the company, that this condition was satisfied if the persons who constituted the "directing mind" of the company were at fault, for the act or omission was then that of the company itself.[150] The metaphor of the "directing mind" does not, however, mean that there is a particular person or group of persons whose acts are always to be regarded as those of the company,[151] for it depends on the purpose for which it is sought to attribute the acts of a human being to the company, which will generally be a matter of the construction of the relevant rule.[152] Thus, in *The Lady Gwendolen*[153] the question was whether a collision at sea was with the "actual fault or privity" of brewers (a minor part of whose business was owning ships to carry their product to England), so that the claimants might escape the limitation of liability generally granted by statute to shipowners. For this purpose the inaction of the director who had supervision of the transport department was attributed to the brewers, but his acts and omissions would not have had this effect if the matter had been one outside his supervision under the company's organisation.[154] Contrariwise, the purpose of the statutory rule might lead to the conclusion that the act of someone well below board level should be attributed to the company.

Under this principle of "attribution" there is no legal difficulty in finding a company liable for deceit, even though it obviously has no natural capacity to be dishonest.[155] So in *Stone & Rolls Ltd v Moore Stephens*[156] it was uncontroversial that the company was liable where its sole executive director and presumed sole beneficial owner used it as a vehicle of fraud to extract money from a bank.

Corporate groups Businesses are often carried on by a group of companies, **25-033** perhaps in the form of a holding company with subsidiaries in many different

---

147 *New Zealand Guardian Trust Co Ltd v Brooks* [1995] 1 W.L.R. 96 (directors).
148 Section 40 of the Companies Act 2006 provides: "in favour of a person dealing with a company in good faith, the power of the board of directors to bind the company, or authorise others to do so, is deemed to be free of any limitation under the company's constitution".
149 See para.9-016.
150 *Lennard's Carrying Co Ltd v Asiatic Petroleum Co Ltd* [1915] A.C. 705; *The Lady Gwendolen* [1965] P. 294 (limitation provisions in merchant shipping legislation).
151 Though for practical purposes this may be true of a resolution of the board or of a meeting of the company.
152 See *Meridian Global Funds Management Asia Ltd v Securities Commission* [1995] 2 A.C. 500. The same approach is taken when deciding whether acts should be attributed to a company for the purposes of a defence such as illegality: see *Singularis Holdings Ltd v Daiwa Capital Markets Europe Ltd* [2019] UKSC 50; [2019] 3 W.L.R. 997.
153 [1965] P. 294.
154 These questions are less important in the context of tort than they are in crime, because vicarious liability is more extensive in the former.
155 Or for battery: *KR v Royal & Sun Alliance* [2006] EWCA Civ 1454; [2007] P.I.Q.R. P14 (where the question arose from an exclusion in a liability insurance policy in respect of the assured's deliberate acts).
156 [2009] UKHL 39; [2009] 1 A.C. 1391.

jurisdictions. In principle these are as much separate entities as the companies and their shareholders and directors and one is not liable for the acts of another. However, where one company in the group is involved in the management of another it may owe a duty of care to persons (for example workers or consumers) affected by the activities of the other.[157]

C. Liability of Directors

25-034   As a company is a separate legal person its directors are not, apart from statute, personally liable on contracts made by the company, nor for torts of company employees for which the company is vicariously liable. To identify the director with the company would be too great a brake on commercial enterprise and adventure, however small the company and however powerful the control of the director. Nevertheless, where directors order an act by the company which amounts to a tort they may be liable as joint tortfeasors on the ground that they have procured the wrong to be done.[158] Where the tort in question requires a particular state of mind the director must have that, but there is no general principle that a director must know that the act is tortious or be reckless as to that.[159] If a company employee were to trespass on the claimant's land believing it to belong to the company that would be trespass and there is no reason why a director who, with the same state of mind, instructed him to do the act should escape liability. The director is also, of course, liable if he commits the tort himself. In some cases, company law will regard an act of the directors as an act of the company itself. If the director of a company were to assault the director of a rival business in the course of a dispute about sales that could hardly be regarded as an assault by the company and any liability of the company would have to be vicarious, that is to say for the director qua employee. Conversely, if the board of a company were to induce someone to make a contract by fraudulent misrepresentation that would be a fraud by the company. However, it does not follow that the individual directors are not also liable: "No one can escape liability for his fraud by saying: 'I wish to make it clear that I am committing this fraud on behalf of someone else and I am not to be personally liable'."[160] In such a case the director would not be liable for the company's fraud but for his own fraud, as indeed would a non-director employee who participated in the deception.[161]

As far as negligence is concerned, it has been held that a director may be liable

---

[157] *Chandler v Cape Plc* [2012] EWCA Civ 525; [2012] 1 W.L.R. 3111. See para.5-037

[158] See, e.g., *Mancetter Developments Ltd v Garmanson and Givertz* [1986] Q.B. 1212 (waste); *Global Crossing Ltd v Global Crossing Ltd* [2006] EWHC 2043 (Ch) (incorporation of company, trademark infringement). A company and its directors may be co-conspirators: para.19-039. However, if C makes a contract with D, a company, and the directors of D resolve not to perform it, C cannot sue them for inducing breach of contract: para.19-015. It has been said that there is a general principle that a director will not be liable in tort if he does no more than carry out his constitutional function in governing the company by voting at board meetings: *MCA Records v Charly Records* [2001] EWCA Civ 1441; [2002] F.S.R. 26 at [49]; *Ottercroft Ltd v Scandia Care Ltd* [2016] EWCA Civ 867 at [22] per Lewison LJ ("The acid test … is whether the putative tortfeasor is exercising control through the constitutional organs of the company").

[159] *C Evans & Sons Ltd v Spriteband Ltd* [1985] 1 W.L.R. 317.

[160] *Standard Chartered Bank v Pakistan National Shipping (Nos 2 and 4)* [2002] UKHL 43; [2003] 1 A.C. 959 at [22].

[161] "The maxim *culpa tenet suos auctores* may not be the end, but it is the beginning of wisdom in these matters": [2002] UKHL 43; [2003] 1 A.C. 959 at [40] per Lord Rodger.

as a joint tortfeasor with the company when he sends a vessel to sea in an unseaworthy condition causing personal injury[162] but a liberal approach to director's liability will have the effect that the limited liability which is the main object of incorporation for a small, "one-man" company will be set at naught. In *Williams v Natural Life Health Foods Ltd*[163] the House of Lords held that to justify liability of a director for advice there must be some special facts showing a personal assumption of responsibility. The active part which the director played in preparing the financial projection in question and the representation in the company's brochure that the company's expertise in the trade was based upon the director's experience gained in a personal capacity independent of the company were not enough to give rise to such an assumption of responsibility on the facts. There were no exchanges between the director and the claimants which could have led them reasonably to believe that he was assuming a personal responsibility to them.[164]

6. PARTNERS

A partnership is not a legal person distinct from its members and consequently **25-035** has no capacity to sue or be sued,[165] but each partner is liable jointly and severally with his co-partners for any wrongful act or omission committed by any of them against an outsider while acting in the ordinary course of business of the firm.[166] If a partner in a firm of solicitors were to commit fraudulent misrepresentations in the course of persuading someone to buy double glazing the other partners would not be liable for that because selling double glazing is not within the description of activities which a solicitors' firm ordinarily carries out.[167] Even where the transaction is one within that general description it may be that its details are so unusual that it is not within the ordinary course of business[168] but the mere fact that the partner intends to behave dishonestly does not take it outside the scope of that concept.[169] A limited liability partnership (LLP) is a body corporate which is formed by being incorporated under the Limited Liability Partnerships Act 2000. Such partnerships have legal personality separate from that of their members and hence capacity to sue and be sued in the usual way.

7. CLUBS

In the case of proprietary and incorporated clubs, it would seem that the ordinary **25-036** rules as to the liability of an employer or principal for the torts of his employees or agents apply.[170] In the case of an unincorporated club, which is not an entity

---

[162] *Yuille v B & B Fisheries (Leigh) Ltd* [1958] 2 Lloyd's Rep. 596. It is usually regarded as self-evident that an employee whose negligence in the course of employment causes personal injury is personally liable even though the employer is vicariously liable.

[163] [1998] 1 W.L.R. 830.

[164] cf. *Merrett v Babb* [2001] EWCA Civ 214; [2001] 3 W.L.R. 1 (employee) (see, further, para.12-035). *Fairline Shipping Corp v Adamson* [1975] Q.B. 180 is perhaps a rather clearer case for liability.

[165] The partners may sue or be sued in the name of the firm: CPR r.5A.3.

[166] Partnership Act 1890 ss.10 and 12. See *Dubai Aluminium Co Ltd v Salaam* [2002] UKHL 48; [2003] 2 A.C. 366. The partners may, of course, also be liable for the torts of their servants or agents under ordinary principles: see, e.g., *Lloyd v Grace, Smith & Co* [1912] A.C. 716.

[167] *JJ Coughlan Ltd v Ruparelia* [2003] EWCA Civ 1057; [2004] P.N.L.R. 4 at [25].

[168] *JJ Coughlan Ltd v Ruparelia* [2003] EWCA Civ 1057; [2004] P.N.L.R. 4.

[169] See *Dubai Aluminium Co Ltd v Salaam* [2002] UKHL 48; [2003] 2 A.C. 366 especially at [120].

[170] In a proprietary club the property and funds of the club belong to a proprietor, who may sue or be

known to the law and which cannot be sued in its own name, liability involves a question of substantive law and one of procedure. The first question is, who is liable for the wrongful act or breach of duty?[171] This depends on the circumstances of the particular case, and it may be the members of the committee, or someone such as a steward who is in control of the club or possibly the whole body of members. Membership of the club and even membership of the committee does not involve any special duty of care towards other members of the club nor, it seems, towards a stranger but neither is it a ground of immunity for one who has assumed a responsibility.[172] So, members of the committee (at the time when the cause of action arose) will be liable personally to the exclusion of other members, if they act personally, as by employing an incompetent person to erect a stand as the result of which a stranger is injured.[173] In the case of torts involving vicarious liability, apart from the actual wrongdoer's liability, the question depends upon whose employee or agent the wrongdoer was at the material time.[174] Where liability arises out of the ownership or occupation of property, as under the Occupiers' Liability Act 1957, the occupiers of the premises in question will normally be the proper persons to sue. If the property is vested in trustees they may be the proper persons to sue, but in the absence of trustees it is a question of fact as to who are the occupiers of the premises.[175] As to the procedural point, the need for a representative action only arises where it is desired to sue the whole body of members, and a representation order may be made, provided that the members whose names appear on the writ are persons who may fairly be taken to represent the body of club members and that they and all the other club members have the same interest in the action.[176]

8. PERSONS OF UNSOUND MIND

25-037 Capacity to sue A person suffering from a mental disorder naturally has the capacity to sue in respect of a tort committed against him, proceedings being conducted by his litigation friend where the disorder robs him of capacity to conduct litigation. However, a claim in respect of action taken under the Mental Health Act 1983 will only lie if the act was done, "in bad faith or without reasonable care" and permission of the High Court is required.[177]

---

sued in his own name or in the name of the club. The members are in contractual relation with the proprietor, and have a right to use the club premises in accordance with the rules, but they are not his employees or agents. An incorporated club may sue or be sued in its corporate name. An unincorporated members' club has no legal existence apart from its members, who are jointly entitled to the property and funds, though usually the property is vested in trustees. It cannot sue or be sued in the club name, nor can the secretary or any other officer sue or be sued on behalf of the club.

171 For an extensive review (in the context of the Roman Catholic Church in Australia), see *Trustees of the Roman Catholic Church v Ellis* [2007] NSWCA 117; (2007) 70 N.S.W.L.R. 565.
172 *Prole v Allen* [1950] 1 All E.R. 476; *Shore v Ministry of Works* [1950] 2 All E.R. 228; cf. *Robertson v Ridley* [1989] 2 All E.R. 474.
173 *Brown v Lewis* (1896) 12 T.L.R. 445; *Bradley Egg Farm Ltd v Clifford* [1943] 2 All E.R. 378.
174 Lloyd (1953) 16 M.L.R. 359.
175 Lloyd (1953) 16 M.L.R. 359, 360.
176 *Campbell v Thompson* [1953] 1 Q.B. 445. See Lloyd (1953) 16 M.L.R. 359, 360-363 and CPR r.19.6. A representation order may also be made in favour of persons as claimants.
177 See *Winch v Jones* [1986] Q.B. 296; *Johnston v Chief Constable of Merseyside* [2009] EWHC 2969 (QB); [2009] M.H.L.R. 343.

Liability to be sued[178] The general principle governing the liability of a person   **25-038**
of unsound mind for torts is that he is liable provided there was relevant volitional
conduct on his part, and (where relevant) that he was possessed of the requisite state
of mind for liability in the particular tort he is said to have committed.[179]

In *Morriss v Marsden*[180] the defendant, who attacked and seriously injured the
claimant, had been found unfit to plead in earlier criminal proceedings. He was then
sued by the claimant for damages for assault and battery. Stable J found that the
defendant's mind was so disturbed by his disease that he did not know that what
he was doing was wrong, but that the assault was a voluntary act on his part and
that the defendant was therefore liable. In battery, it is enough that the defendant
intended to strike the claimant, so this seems right, but had there been no such
voluntary act, the position would have been different[181]:

> "For example, I think that, if a person in a condition of complete automatism inflicted
> grievous injury, that would not be actionable. In the same way, if a sleepwalker inadvert-
> ently, without intention or without carelessness, broke a valuable vase, that would not be
> actionable."

In defamation it is enough that the defendant published matter defamatory of the
claimant and it would certainly be no defence that in his disturbed mental state he
believed it to be true. Again, as Stable J said: "I cannot think that, if a person of
unsound mind converts my property under a delusion that he is entitled to do it or
that it was not property at all, that affords a defence."[182]

Negligence The position in the tort of negligence is also consistent with the   **25-039**
general principle identified above. The standard of the reasonable person that
governs negligence liability is said to eliminate the individual characteristics of the
defendant,[183] and this includes any mental disability from which the defendant
suffers. In *Dunnage v Randall*,[184] a paranoid schizophrenic had poured petrol over
himself and ignited it, thereby causing personal injury to his nephew, who had been
trying to prevent his uncle from setting himself on fire. The nephew's claim for
damages against the estate of his uncle (who had died in the incident) was successful, and no account was taken of the severe mental illness from which the deceased
had been suffering. According to Vos LJ, this had the advantage of not requiring
any "outdated and inappropriate" distinction to be made between the effects of
physical health problems and mental health problems: there was, he said, "neither
a logical nor a societal reason why the law should differentiate in this area between
the two".[185] A similar approach was adopted in the earlier decision of the

---

[178] See Fridman (1963) 79 L.Q.R. 502; (1964) 80 L.Q.R. 84; Goudkamp (2011) 31 O.J.L.S. 727.
[179] Sir Matthew Hale thought that dementia was one of several other forms of incapacity which might
    exempt a person from criminal liability, but which ordinarily do not excuse him from civil liability,
    for that, "is not by way of penalty, but a satisfaction of damage done to the party": 1 *History of Pleas
    of Crown* (ed. 1778), pp.15-16. So too, in effect Bacon (Spedding's edition of his works, pp.vii, 348).
    There are dicta in the older cases which regard lunacy as no defence: see, e.g., *Weaver v Ward* (1616)
    Hob. 134; 80 E.R. 284.
[180] [1952] 1 All E.R. 925.
[181] *Morriss v Marsden* [1952] 1 All E.R. 925 at 927 per Stable J.
[182] *Morriss v Marsden* [1952] 1 All E.R. 925 at 927.
[183] See para.6-007.
[184] [2015] EWCA Civ 673; [2016] Q.B. 639. Goudkamp and Ihuoma (2016) 32 P.N. 117.
[185] [2015] EWCA Civ 673; [2016] Q.B. 639 at [134]. See also at [104], [159].

Queensland Court of Appeal in *Carrier v Bonham*,[186] where the plaintiff was a bus driver who had suffered psychiatric injury after the defendant tried to kill himself by stepping in front of the plaintiff's bus. The Court held that the defendant's schizophrenia could not be taken into account when deciding whether he had been negligent: the ordinary objective standard of a reasonable person was to be applied. One difficulty that the court identified with making allowance for the defendant's illness was the impossibility of ascertaining the appropriate standard of care: it would "be impossible to devise a standard by which the tortious liability of such persons could be judged as a class".[187] Concern was also expressed that, if mentally ill persons were not to be judged according to the ordinary objective standard of care, there was a risk that society would respond by demanding their detention, a concern echoed in Arden LJ's comment in *Dunnage* that the liability of the deceased was "no doubt treated in law as the price for being able to move freely within society despite his schizophrenia."[188]

9. PERSONS HAVING PARENTAL OR QUASI-PARENTAL AUTHORITY

25-040   Parents and other persons in similar positions are necessarily immune against liability for many acts which in other people would be assault, battery or false imprisonment. They have control, usually but not necessarily, of a disciplinary character, over those committed to their charge. The nature of the control varies according to the relationship and, provided that it is exercised reasonably,[189] acts done in pursuance of it are not tortious. By s.58(3) of the Children Act 2004 it is specifically provided that an act causing actual bodily harm to a child (i.e., something which is more than temporary and trifling) cannot be justified.

Parental authority[190] ceases when the child attains 18 years, but is a dwindling right as the child approaches adulthood and for this purpose may well cease at an earlier age.[191]

At common law a schoolteacher had power to discipline pupils and this probably rested upon the need to maintain order and discipline at the school,[192] so that a parental veto upon corporal punishment would not render its use unlawful. However, by statute corporal punishment is no longer a defence to a civil action against a school, whether state or independent, even where the parent authorises the school to administer it.[193] It remains the law, however, that reasonable force may be used to avert personal injury or damage to property: that is not "punishment".

---

[186] [2002] 1 Qd R. 474.
[187] [2002] 1 Qd R. 474 at [35].
[188] [2015] EWCA Civ 673; [2016] Q.B. 639 at [153].
[189] *R. v H* [2001] EWCA Crim 1024; [2002] 1 Cr.App.R. 7.
[190] The rights, duties and authority of father and mother of a legitimate child are equal: Children Act 1989 s.2.
[191] *Gillick v West Norfolk Area Health Authority* [1986] A.C. 112. See *R. v Rahman* (1985) 81 Cr.App.R. 349 (false imprisonment).
[192] Disciplinary powers are not necessarily confined to conduct on school premises: *Cleery v Booth* [1893] 1 Q.B. 465; *R. v Newport (Salop) JJ* [1929] 2 K.B. 416.
[193] Education Act 1996 s.548.

CHAPTER 26

DEFENCES

1. INTRODUCTION

26-001 **The concept of a defence**[1] Lawyers deploy the term "defence" to mean a great diversity of things and care is not always taken to make it clear how it is being used. In this chapter the word "defence" refers only to arguments offered by the defendant that, if accepted, would permit the defendant to escape from liability even if all of the elements of the tort for which the claimant sues are present. Put differently, defences, for the purposes of this chapter, are rules that prevent liability from arising even if a cause of action exists. Denials of one or more of the elements of the claimant's cause of action (such as a contention by the defendant that he acted reasonably in the context of proceedings in the tort of negligence) are consequently not counted as defences. Rules that do not prevent liability from arising but which merely affect the remedy to which a successful claimant is entitled (such as the doctrines of contributory negligence[2] and mitigation of damage[3]) are not defences in the relevant sense of the word either. Such rules are fundamentally different from liability-defeating rules. As such, they are dealt with elsewhere in this book.

26-002 **Classification of defences** There are many ways in which defences can be arranged[4] and some systems of organisation are more helpful than others. The arrangement that is adopted in this chapter is minimalistic. It organises defences into: (1) justifications; and (2) public policy defences. Justifications are defences that apply when the defendant acted reasonably. Conversely, public policy defences are defences that may be enlivened irrespective of the reasonableness of the defendant's conduct. This classification has the significant advantage of being exhaustive. No defences are left out in the classificatory cold since all defences are either concerned with the reasonableness of the defendant's conduct or they are not.

It is possible to subdivide both of these two major categories. For example, justifications can be split into private justifications and public justifications. The difference between these sub-categories depends upon whose interests the defendant was advancing when he acted as he did. Private justifications are defences that are enlivened when the defendant acted reasonably to safeguard his own interests, whereas public justifications are defences that are triggered when the defendant acted reasonably to advance the interests of the public or a section thereof. The category of public policy defences can also be broken down into, for example, public policy defences that arise at the time of the tort and those that arise subsequently.

26-003 **Implications of this taxonomy of defences** The taxonomy of defences that is adopted in this chapter has significant and far-reaching consequences. It is not possible to delve into the details here. They are given elsewhere.[5] However, one example of the taxonomy's power concerns the defendant's motive. In order to be justified the defendant must not be defectively motivated, but this is not necessary in order to establish a public policy defence. Thus, a defendant who acts for a bad

---

[1] Regarding defences, see generally Goudkamp, *Tort Law Defences* (2013); Dyson, Goudkamp and Wilmot-Smith (eds), *Defences in Tort* (2014).

[2] See para.23-040.

[3] See para.23-065.

[4] Consider Wigmore (1895) 8 Harv. L. Rev. 377 at 390.

[5] Goudkamp, *Tort Law Defences* (2013) Ch.6.

reason (e.g., striking an aggressor not in self-defence but out of spite) will not be entitled to the defence of self-defence (a justification) but the defendant's defective motive will not affect his entitlement to, say, an immunity (a public policy defence). It is arguable that the type of defence that a defendant has can also affect whether it is permissible for others to assist or resist him. It might be said that defendants who are justified should not be resisted and that it is permissible for third parties to assist them. Likewise, one might contend that it is permissible to resist defendants who only have a public policy defence and that the mere fact that a defendant has such a defence does not mean that it is permissible for him to be assisted in the conduct concerned by third parties.[6]

Pleading and proof Whereas the claimant bears the burden of establishing the elements of the tort in which he sues, the onuses of pleading and proof in respect of defences generally rest on the defendant. This supplies one obvious practical reason why it is important to determine whether a given rule is a defence as opposed to a denial of the cause of action in which the claimant sues. **26-004**

Not all tort defences are addressed in this chapter This chapter does not deal with all defences to liability in tort. Because the number of tort defences is exceedingly large, it would not be possible as a practical matter to attempt exhaustive coverage. Furthermore, many defences are essentially confined to specific torts and, for the purposes of a tort textbook, it is usually more convenient to address such defences in the chapters regarding the torts concerned. Accordingly, for the most part this chapter concentrates on defences that are fairly general in the sense that they apply to more than one tort. Certain defences that are addressed here are also examined elsewhere in this book, especially those that, while in principle are general defences, are particularly important in relation to given torts as a practical matter, or which take on a particular guise in certain contexts. **26-005**

2. DENIALS

This chapter is about defences. But in order properly to understand defences, it is necessary to isolate them from the elements of the tort in which the claimant sues since denials of elements of the tort in question are routinely mistaken for defences. In this part of the chapter, several pleas that function as denials are identified in order that they can be separated clearly from defences. **26-006**

A. Consent

Generally All of the varieties of trespass include among their elements nonconsent by the claimant to the defendant's conduct in question. Accordingly, if the claimant consents to the interference with his person or property the action in trespass will be incomplete. For example, a fair blow struck in a boxing match and a welcome embrace are not batteries because the claimant consents to them. It fol- **26-007**

---

[6] The *Restatement (Second) of the Law of Torts*, §880 provides: "If two persons would otherwise be liable for a harm, one of them is not relieved from liability by the fact that the other has an absolute privilege to act or an immunity from liability to the person harmed."

lows that the plea of consent is a denial and not a defence. Consistently with this it is for the claimant to plead and prove that he did not consent.[7]

26-008 **Consent may be implied**   Consent may be inferred from conduct as well as expressed in words. The very act of taking part in a boxing match or presenting one's arm for injection, for example, convey consent.

26-009 **Consent is objectively ascertained**   Consent might be understood as a state of mind on the part of the claimant, or as an expression of permission or agreement. But it is in any case clear that whether the claimant has consented must be ascertained from his conduct, and that a claimant will be taken to have consented to the defendant's actions if it appears from the former's conduct that he consented. Where consent is inferred from the claimant's actions, the fact that, privately, the claimant did not "consent" is irrelevant.

26-010 **Consent must be given freely**   Consent must be voluntarily given in order for it to be effective. Indeed, "consent" that is obtained by threats is not consent at all.[8] We have seen earlier that an adult of full understanding may choose whether or not to receive medical treatment even if the treatment is necessary to save his life[9] and we have considered the capacity of minors and mentally disordered persons to give consent.[10]

26-011 **Consent must be relevant to be effective**   C's consent must relate to the specific act done by D in order for it to prevent liability from arising. For example, the fact that C has consented to one medical procedure does not justify D performing a different procedure, as where a condition is discovered and treated for mere convenience during the authorised treatment of another condition.[11] In *Appleton v Garrett*[12] a dentist was held liable for trespass to the person when he undertook extravagant and wholly unjustified work on patients' teeth. This result might be explained by saying that the claimants had consented only to treatment that was reasonably necessary. In *Lane v Holloway*,[13] after a verbal altercation, the elderly claimant struck the younger and stronger defendant on the shoulder and the defendant replied with a severe blow to the claimant's eye. It was held that although each party to a fight takes the risk of incidental injuries the claimant had not consented to the risk of a blow that was out of all proportion to the occasion.

26-012 **A mistaken belief in consent will not prevent liability from arising**   The fact that D mistakenly believed that C consented to the interference with his person or property has no bearing on liability. This is so even if the mistake is reasonable. Suppose that D, a doctor, performs on Patient A an operation authorised by Patient

---

[7]   *Christopherson v Bare* (1848) 11 Q.B. 473 at 477; *Freeman v Home Office (No.2)* [1984] Q.B. 524 at 539. cf. the position in Canada in the context of sexual batteries: *Non-Marine Underwriters, Lloyd's London v Scalera* [2000] SCC 24; [2000] 1 S.C.R. 551.

[8]   *Latter v Braddell* (1881) 50 L.J.Q.B. 448 seems unduly narrow in insisting on threats of violence.

[9]   See para.4-013.

[10] See paras 4-013—4-014, 4-016.

[11] The terms of the consent may authorise such further treatment as the doctor considers necessary or desirable. See *Brushett v Cowan* (1990) 69 D.L.R. (4th) 743.

[12] (1995) 34 B.M.L.R. 32.

[13] [1968] 1 Q.B. 379.

B thinking that Patient A was Patient B. Even if D's mistake is reasonable, he is clearly liable to Patient A.[14]

Fraud and concealment   What is the position where the claimant's consent is 26-013 obtained by fraud? Likewise, what is the situation if D fails to disclose some fact (e.g., that he is suffering from a contagious disease) that would have led C to with- hold consent had C known the truth? The view long prevailed that the consent was valid so long as the claimant was not deceived as to the essential nature of the defendant's act or the identity of the actor. Thus, to borrow the facts of a criminal case, a defendant will be liable in battery if he falsely tells a naive claimant that he is performing a technique that will improve her singing when he is in fact having sexual intercourse with her and the claimant is tricked by that representation.[15] But the defendant will not be liable in battery to the claimant if he persuades the claim- ant to have sexual intercourse with him by promising payment or marriage when he has no intention of fulfilling such promises (though there might be liability in deceit[16]). In *R. v Richardson*[17] a criminal conviction for assault was quashed when the defendant continued to treat patients after being suspended from dental practice and it is thought that the result should have been the same in a civil action for battery. Similarly, on this approach the defendant will not be liable for battery if he has sexual intercourse with the claimant without disclosing the fact that he is, to his knowledge, suffering from a sexually transmissible disease.[18] In the criminal case of *R. v Dica*[19] it was held that if D recklessly transmits through sexual intercourse a grievous disease to V where V had not consented to the risk of infection because D had concealed the fact that he had the disease from V, D would be guilty of inflicting grievous bodily harm contrary to s.20 of the Offences against the Person Act 1861 (but not of rape). The consequences of this case (and other decisions in the same line of authority) for the law of torts are yet to be determined.

Failure to explain risks of medical procedure   Provided that the patient 26-014 understands the broad nature of a medical procedure, his consent is not vitiated by a failure to explain the risks inherent in the procedure.[20] In this sense, tort law does not require "informed consent". However, medical professionals owe a duty to take reasonable care to explain procedures and their implications to their patients, but as this duty of disclosure sounds in the tort of negligence, its breach must lead to consequential damage in order for liability to arise.[21]

No limits on harm to which one can consent   The criminal law places limits on 26-015 the effectiveness of consent when the public interest so requires. For example, fight-

---

[14]   *Chatterton v Gerson* [1981] Q.B. 432.
[15]   *R. v Williams* [1923] 1 K.B. 340. See also Sexual Offences Act 2003 s.76(2)(a).
[16]   As in *Graham v Saville* [1945] 2 D.L.R. 489 (bigamy). See also *P v B (paternity: damages for deceit)* [2001] 1 F.L.R. 1041.
[17]   [1999] Q.B. 444. cf. *R. v Tabassum* [2002] 2 Cr. App. R. 328, where D had no medical qualifica- tions at all.
[18]   This was the outcome in *Hegarty v Shine* (1878) 14 Cox C.C. 124 but the court's reasons were influenced by archaic views about sexual morality.
[19]   [2004] EWCA Crim 1103; [2004] Q.B. 1257.
[20]   *Chatterton v Gerson* [1981] Q.B. 432; *Hills v Potter* [1984] 1 W.L.R. 641n; *Sidaway v Bethlem Royal Hospital* [1985] A.C. 871. cf. Tan (1987) 7 L.S. 149.
[21]   See para.6-028.

ing (otherwise than in the course of properly conducted sport) is unlawful if bodily harm is intended or caused, notwithstanding the consent of the participants,[22] as are activities likely to cause serious harm in the course of sadomasochistic sexual encounters.[23] The fact of consent in these and various other situations is simply irrelevant to criminal liability. Although the matter is not certain, it seems that the law of torts approaches the matter differently, and that consent will prevent liability from arising irrespective of the seriousness of the harm to which the claimant consented. *Lane v Holloway*,[24] which is discussed above,[25] appears to support this proposition. In that case the Court of Appeal found in favour of the claimant on the basis that he had not consented to the risk of suffering such severe harm. By inference, it would seem that the claimant would have failed in his action had he agreed to run the risk of being gravely injured.

26-016 **A generally applicable rule?** The issue of consent is typically encountered in the context of the various species of trespass. However, it is clear that the fact of consent is relevant to several other torts, such as private nuisance.[26] The question arises in these circumstances whether consent is an answer to liability in all torts. If torts are understood as violations of rights, it would seem to follow that consent should be capable of defeating liability in all torts, since private law rights are always amenable to being waived. However, there are certain torts in respect of which some awkwardness arises in using the language of consent. For example, it seems odd to say that C consents to the tort of negligence being committed against him given that C will often not know in advance how much damage he may suffer if D is negligent or even who D may be. It is perhaps for this reason that the language of consent is generally avoided in the negligence context, and the terminology of "voluntary assumption of risk" or volenti non fit injuria used instead.[27] Whether or not these concepts are ultimately one and the same thing is an unresolved issue.

B. Exclusion or Limitation of Liability

26-017 At common law, in the absence of duress or some other vitiating factor, entry into a contract that exempted the defendant from responsibility for negligence prevented liability from arising. The same rule applied where the claimant entered another's land by licence subject to a condition exempting the occupier from liability. The key issue in this regard was usually whether the defendant had given sufficient notice to make the excluding term part of the contract or licence: if he had done so, the claimant was bound even though he might not have troubled to read the terms and hence was unaware of the excluding one. The foregoing remains the law but is now heavily qualified by statute. For example, pursuant to the Unfair Contract Terms Act 1977, where the defendant acts in the course of a business or occupies premises for business purposes he cannot, by reference to any contract term or notice, exclude

---

[22] *AG Reference (No.6 of 1980)* [1981] Q.B. 715.
[23] *R. v Brown* [1994] 1 A.C. 212.
[24] [1968] 1 Q.B. 379, see para.26-011.
[25] See para.26-011.
[26] See para.15-061.
[27] See paras 26-018—26-027.

or restrict his liability for death or personal injury resulting from negligence,[28] and in the case of other loss or damage caused by negligence can only exclude or restrict his liability in so far as the term in the contract or notice is reasonable.[29] Similarly, under the Consumer Rights Act 2015, traders cannot by terms in "consumer contracts" or "consumer notices" exclude or restrict liability for negligently caused death or personal injury.[30]

C. Voluntary Assumption of Risk

Classification   If the claimant voluntarily assumes the risk of the defendant's negligence[31] he cannot recover damages in respect of any injury suffered: volenti non fit injuria.[32] The precise way in which this doctrine (which is often thought of as a form of, or otherwise closely related to, the plea of consent[33]) prevents liability from arising has never been satisfactorily established. Is it a denial or is it a defence? If it is a denial, which element of the claimant's cause of action in negligence does it negate? The rule is often being presented in textbooks and judgments as a defence and this is consistent with the fact that it falls to the defendant to plead and prove that the claimant voluntarily assumed the risk of injury.[34] There are also many passages in the case law that characterise the rule as a defence. For example, in *Smith v Baker & Sons* Lord Herschell said that "if there had been no breach of duty it would not have been necessary to inquire whether the maxim, 'Volenti non fit injuria,' accorded a defence".[35] This understands the voluntary assumption of risk principle as a rule that falls for consideration only if the cause of action in negligence is complete.

    Nevertheless, it is strongly arguable that the plea "voluntary assumption of risk" is a denial, and that it strikes at different elements of the cause of action in negligence in different cases.[36] Usually, it targets the breach element[37] (although in *Dann v Hamiliton* Asquith J considered that the contention that the claimant was *volens* to the risk of injury denied the existence of a duty of care[38]). Imagine that a batsman during a cricket match hits a ball out of the ground and that it strikes a spectator. The spectator has no claim against the batsman and some might say that this is because the spectator had agreed to assume the risks of cricket. But, in the end, the reason why there is no liability in this scenario is because the batsman did nothing unreasonable. A good example of a no-breach case that was dressed up in

26-018

---

28   Section 2(1).
29   Section 2(2).
30   Section 65.
31   There is a lack of high-quality scholarly analysis regarding the doctrine of voluntary assumption of risk. However, one thoughtful contribution is Simons (1987) 67 B.U.L. Rev. 213.
32   The phrases "voluntary assumption of risk" and volenti non fit injuria appear to be synonymous. Both feature extensively in the authorities and in *Insurance Commissioner v Joyce* (1948) 77 C.L.R. 39 at 57 Dixon J, with reference to English law, remarked that the concepts were one and the same thing.
33   See para.26-007.
34   Williams, *Joint Torts and Contributory Negligence* (1951), p.295.
35   [1891] A.C. 325 at 366. See also at 335–336.
36   The analysis here has been influenced by Sugarman (1997) 31 Val. U.L. Rev. 833.
37   See *Thomas v Quartermaine* (1887) 18 Q.B.D. 685 at 697.
38   "As a matter of strict pleading it seems that the plea volenti is a denial of any duty at all, and, therefore, of any breach of duty, and an admission of negligence cannot strictly be combined with the plea": *Dann v Hamilton* [1939] 1 K.B. 509 at 512.

the language of voluntary assumption of risk is *Proctor v Young*.[39] The claimant suffered injury when she fell from a racehorse that she was exercising on a beach. The fall occurred because the horse stumbled in a depression in the sand. The claimant failed in her bid to recover compensation from her employer and the occupier of the beach. The judge based his decision on the voluntary assumption of risk doctrine.[40] However, his reasons centred on factors that pertain to the breach issue, especially the impracticality of taking preventative measures. This is perfectly understandable, since (for example) the reasonable occupier would not have attempted the Sisyphean task of eliminating all variations in the beach's surface.

If the idea of voluntary assumption of risk operates as a denial, it would be better if the concept disappeared from the law, since it simply replicates using different language other concepts, such as the breach element of the action of negligence. This confusingly conveys the impression that there are two rules in play when in reality there is only one.

26-019   Marginalisation of the doctrine   The voluntary assumption of risk doctrine once exerted a powerful effect on liability in the tort of negligence. Today, however, it applies only exceptionally.[41] The rule fell from favour following the enactment of the Law Reform Contributory Negligence Act 1945 which required the courts to reduce the claimant's damages where the claimant was guilty of contributory negligence instead of denying recovery altogether, which was the position at common law.[42] Upon the passage of 1945 Act, the courts marginalised the voluntary assumption of risk doctrine, which is a complete bar to liability when it applies, since it would otherwise have substantially undermined the effect of the legislation.[43] Most cases that would formerly have been denied for voluntary assumption of risk are now dealt with instead by way of the law of contributory negligence leaving only a rump of cases that are determined on the basis that the claimant was *volens* to the risk of injury.

26-020   The elements of the doctrine   The voluntary assumption of risk doctrine has two elements: the claimant must have: (1) known of the risk of injury that materialised; and (2) voluntarily agreed to incur it. The division between these two elements is rather artificial. Because a person cannot agree to accept a risk of injury unless he knows of it, the agreement element ultimately swallows up the knowledge element. As Scott LJ said in *Bowater v Rowley Regis Corp*[44]:

> "[A] man cannot be said to be truly 'willing' unless he is in a position to choose freely, and freedom of choice predicates ... full knowledge of the circumstances on which the exercise of choice is conditioned, so that he may be able to choose wisely."

26-021   The knowledge element   The claimant must have had information that indicated, at least in a general way, the risk of injury from the defendant's negligence. The test

---

[39]   [2009] NIQB 56. See also *Murray v Harringay Arena Ltd* [1951] 2 K.B. 529.

[40]   [2009] NIQB 56 at [35].

[41]   For a modern case in which the doctrine was held to apply, see *Freeman v Higher Park Farm* [2008] EWCA Civ 1185; [2009] P.I.Q.R. P6.

[42]   The doctrine of contributory negligence is addressed at para.23-040ff.

[43]   See the remarks in *Nettleship v Weston* [1971] 2 Q.B. 691 at 701; *ICI Ltd v Shatwell* [1965] A.C. 656 at 671–672.

[44]   [1944] K.B. 476 at 479.

in this regard is subjective. Thus, the mere fact that a reasonable person would have been aware of the risk of injury is not enough to satisfy the knowledge element. This may mean that, paradoxically, a claimant who is heavily intoxicated is in a better position in so far as the voluntary assumption of risk doctrine is concerned than one who is sober. It is clear that the degree of knowledge required of the claimant before the knowledge element is satisfied is very high. For example, in *Neeson v Acheson*[45] it was held that a claimant who was bitten by a dog that she had befriended after she put her face in proximity to its jaws did not consent to the risk of being bitten because she did not know that the dog was dangerous. In *Poppleton v Trustees of the Portsmouth Youth Activities Committee*[46] the court held that matting on the floor of an artificial climbing venue gave the misleading impression that it was safe to jump to the floor from a height. Consequently, the claimant, who broke his neck when he fell after leaping from high on the climbing wall, did not have knowledge of the risk that materialised.

The agreement element   The mere fact that the claimant is aware that the activity in which he participates carries a risk of injury does not mean that he has licensed the defendant to be negligent.[47] The rule is volenti non fit injuria rather than scienti non fit injuria. For example, the knowledge that aircraft sometimes crash will not engage the voluntary assumption of risk doctrine where the claimant has no reason to know of any defect in the plane or the pilot. Another illustration of this point can be found in *Slater v Clay Cross Co Ltd*.[48] In that case the claimant was lawfully walking along a narrow tunnel on a railway track owned and occupied by the defendants when she was struck and injured by a passing train owing to the driver's negligence. Denning LJ said[49]:   **26-022**

"[I]t seems to me that when this lady walked in the tunnel, although it may be said that she voluntarily took the risk of danger from the running of the railway in the ordinary and accustomed way, nevertheless she did not take the risk of negligence by the driver."

Pressure and compulsion   The agreement element will not be satisfied if the claimant is put under sufficient pressure. The claimant must be essentially free from constraints upon his decision-making processes both in terms of constraints imposed by the defendant and other circumstances.[50] For example, the agreement element is unlikely to be satisfied if the claimant runs a given risk because avoiding it would entail considerable inconvenience or expense to him. Usually there will be economic or other pressures upon a worker, which means that the agreement element will rarely be satisfied in the workplace injury context. Indeed, some modern statements of the employer's duty of care to his workers go even further and seem inconsistent with the very existence of the doctrine in the employment setting.[51]   **26-023**

---

45   [2008] NIQB 12.
46   [2007] EWHC 1567 (QB).
47   *Smith v Baker & Sons* [1891] A.C. 325.
48   [1956] 2 Q.B. 264.
49   [1956] 2 Q.B. 264 at 271.
50   For a case where constraint was put upon an employee by someone other than his employer, see *Burnett v British Waterways Board* [1973] 1 W.L.R. 700.
51   See para.9-027.

26-024 **Any agreement must be specific to the risk that materialised**   A claimant may accept certain risks of injury in an activity but not others. This point is obvious with regard to participants in sports. As Barwick CJ said in *Rootes v Shelton*, "By engaging in a sport ... the participants may be held to have accepted risks which are inherent in that sport ... but this does not eliminate all duty of care of the one participant to the other".[52] The same may apply to a spectator who is injured in the course of some game or sport which he is watching. A spectator does not consent to negligence on the part of the participants,[53] but "provided the competition or game is being performed within the rules and the requirement of the sport and by a person of adequate skill and competence the spectator does not expect his safety to be regarded by the participant".[54]

26-025 **Rescuers**   The agreement element of the voluntary assumption of risk doctrine will typically be very challenging to satisfy where the claimant is a rescuer.[55] In *Haynes v Harwood*[56] the Court of Appeal affirmed a judgment in favour of a policeman who had been injured in stopping some runaway horses in a crowded street. The defendant had left the horses unattended on the highway and they had bolted. The policeman, who was on duty, not in the street, but in a police station, darted out and was crushed by one of the horses which fell upon him while he was stopping it. The agreement element of the voluntary assumption of risk doctrine was not satisfied given the emergency with which the policeman was confronted. The defendant may also have considerable difficulty in establishing the knowledge element in rescue cases. It is in the nature of a rescue case that the defendant's negligence precedes the claimant's act of running the risk. The claimant may therefore be wholly ignorant of the risks that the defendant's negligence entails at the time of being injured. All he knows is that someone is in a position of peril and that the situation calls for his intervention as a rescuer.[57] This position is in keeping with tort law's lenient treatment of rescuers more generally.[58] The law looks upon rescuers sympathetically and is loath to find, for example, that a rescuer is guilty of contributory negligence[59] or that his conduct constitutes an intervening act.[60] It is also worth observing that the generous treatment that is afforded to rescuers extends to rescuers generally and not merely to professional rescuers, such as police officers and firefighters.[61]

---

[52]   (1967) 116 C.L.R. 383 at 385.

[53]   See *Cleghorn v Oldham* (1927) 43 T.L.R. 465 and the unreported cases referred to by Sellers LJ in *Wooldridge v Sumner* [1963] 2 Q.B. 43 at 55–56.

[54]   *Wooldridge v Sumner* [1963] 2 Q.B. 43 at 56 per Sellers LJ. See also at 68.

[55]   Goodhart (1934) 5 C.L.J. 192.

[56]   [1935] 1 K.B. 146.

[57]   "C would not have agreed to run the risk that A might be negligent for C would only play his part after A had been negligent": *Baker v T.E. Hopkins & Son Ltd* [1959] 1 W.L.R. 966 at 976 per Morris LJ.

[58]   The lenient treatment extends to cases in which the rescuer acts to protect property rather than life: *Hyett v Great Western Railway Co* [1948] 1 K.B. 345.

[59]   See, e.g., *Brandon v Osborne, Garrett & Co Ltd* [1924] 1 K.B. 548. In *Baker v T.E. Hopkins & Son Ltd* [1959] 1 W.L.R. 966 at 976 Willmer LJ said: "Bearing in mind that danger invites rescue, the court should not be astute to accept criticism of the rescuer's conduct from the wrongdoer who created the danger."

[60]   *Haynes v Harwood* [1935] 1 K.B. 146 at 163.

[61]   The fact that members of the emergency services are in a sense employed to take risks has led some American courts to deny liability to them on the part of the person whose negligence creates the

Overlap with the doctrine of contributory negligence When, exceptionally, the   **26-026**
voluntary assumption of risk doctrine applies, the claimant will usually be guilty
of contributory negligence. When this occurs, the claimant will fail in his action and
will not be entitled to partial damages under the Law Reform (Contributory
Negligence) Act 1945.

Road traffic cases Section 149 of the Road Traffic Act 1988 eliminates the   **26-027**
voluntary assumption of risk doctrine as between drivers and passengers in motor
vehicles. In *Pitts v Hunt*[62] Beldam LJ remarked:

> "[I]t is no longer open to the driver of a motor vehicle to say that the fact of his pas-
> senger travelling in a vehicle in circumstances in which for one reason or another it could
> be said that he had willingly accepted a risk of negligence on the driver's part, relieves
> him of liability for such negligence."

Section 149 has no effect on any other rules, such as the doctrines of illegality and
contributory negligence. Nor does this provision apply to transport in aircraft, boats
and other means.

D.   Mistake

A mistake by the defendant[63] can prevent the claimant from establishing the ele-   **26-028**
ments of the cause of action in which he sues. It is convenient to give some
examples. For example, if the defendant injured the claimant as a result of a reasonable mistake no liability will arise in the tort of negligence. Similarly, if the defendant mistakenly but reasonably believed that there was reasonable and probable
cause to institute legal proceedings against the claimant the tort of malicious
prosecution will not be constituted. And a mistake, whether or not reasonable, can
prevent the action in deceit from being established. That tort requires the defendant knowingly or recklessly to make a false statement of fact and a defendant who
mistakenly makes an innocent or negligent misrepresentation will, accordingly, not
commit that wrong.[64]

Conversely, there are many torts the elements of which may be satisfied even if
the defendant made a mistake, regardless of whether the mistake was a reasonable
one. A good illustration is the tort of conversion. Thus, an auctioneer who innocently sells A's goods in the honest and reasonable belief that they belong to B
on whose instructions he sells them will be liable to A.[65] The position in relation
to trespass to the person is the same. A surgeon who, as a result of an administrative mix-up for which he bears no responsibility, carries out the wrong operation[66]
or operates on the wrong patient[67] is liable in trespass to the person. It should be
noted, however, that in these examples the "innocent" wrongdoer may be entitled
to be indemnified by the person responsible for the mistake.

---

danger. This so-called "fireman's rule" was decisively rejected by the House of Lords in *Ogwo v
Taylor* [1988] A.C. 431.

[62] [1991] 1 Q.B. 24 at 48.
[63] See, further, Trindade (1982) 2 O.J.L.S. 211.
[64] See para.12-014.
[65] See para.18-039.
[66] *Chatterton v Gerson* [1981] Q.B. 432 at 443.
[67] See para.26-012.

E. Inevitable Accident

26-029 When lawyers speak of an "inevitable accident" they mean to say that the accident could not be avoided by taking reasonable care.[68] It follows that the plea of "inevitable accident" in, for example, a negligence case is nothing more than an attack on the breach element.[69] Suppose that D's car crashes into C, a pedestrian, because its steering mechanism spontaneously and unforeseeably failed. This might be described as an "inevitable accident". However, because D has done nothing unreasonable the tort of negligence has not been committed. D is not at fault, and that is all that the label "inevitable accident" signifies.[70] In truth, the phrase "inevitable accident" serves more to confuse than to illuminate. It would be better if it disappeared from the law of torts.

3. JUSTIFICATIONS

A. Private Justifications

i. Self-Defence

26-030 **The elements of the defence** A person who uses no more than reasonable force against an aggressor in his own defence will not incur liability in trespass to the person. This defence[71] has two elements. First, it must be necessary to use defensive force. Secondly, the force used by the defendant must be proportionate to the threat that he faced.

26-031 **The necessity element** If the unjust threat with which the defendant is confronted could reasonably be avoided other than by using force the defendant will be expected to resort to those non-violent means and the defence of self-defence will be unavailable. For example, the defence will be withheld if the defendant used force against an aggressor when he could instead have secured his safety by locking a door between him and the aggressor. The necessity element imports an imminence requirement. Unless the defendant is faced with an immediate threat it will not be necessary for him to use defensive force, as the defendant should be able to avoid the threat by seeking help from the police.[72] Similarly, if the threat from the aggressor has abated, the defendant will not be permitted to use force against the aggressor.[73] Acts of, for example, revenge and retaliation are not within the scope of the defence.

---

[68] Regarding the concept of inevitable accident, see, further, Gilles (1994) 43 Emory L.J. 575.

[69] Exceptionally, it can also constitute a denial of the causation requirement: see Goudkamp, *Tort Law Defences* (2013), p.53.

[70] "I do not find myself assisted by considering the meaning of the phrase 'inevitable accident'. I prefer to put the problem in a more simple way, namely has it been established that the driver of the car was guilty of negligence?": *Browne v De Luxe Car Services* [1941] 1 K.B. 549 at 552 per Greene MR.

[71] See, further, Goudkamp (2010) 18 T.L.J 61.

[72] *Flint v Tittensor* [2015] EWHC 466 (QB); [2015] 1 W.L.R. 4370 at [39].

[73] See, e.g., *Gilchrist v Chief Constable of Greater Manchester Police* [2019] EWHC 1233 (QB) at [118].

The proportionality element It is a question of fact whether violence done by **26-032**
way of self-protection is proportionate to the threat with which the defendant was
faced. The defence will be unavailable "if upon a little blow given by [C] to [D],
[D] gives him a blow that maims him"[74] or if D strikes C on the upper thigh when
C could have been subdued by instead hitting him on his lower leg.[75] Not every
threat will justify the use of defensive force. Some threats and contacts must simply
be tolerated and in many cases the reasonable thing to do will be nothing. However,
the courts are generally lenient to the defendant in asking whether the force used
was proportionate. It must be remembered that the defendant who acts in self-
defence will often be confronted with an emergency presenting a serious risk of
harm and, consequently, he will not be expected to calculate precisely the appropriate degree of force. As Judge LJ remarked in *Cross v Kirkby*[76]:

> "When acting in self-defence ... the victim of violence ... genuinely believing ... that the
> violence would be likely to continue until brought to an end, he could not be expected,
> and the law does not require him to measure the violence to be deployed with mathemati-
> cal precision."

Further, the mere fact that the defendant used more force than that with which he
was threatened does not mean that the defensive force was excessive. The
proportionality element is not applied simply by asking whether the force that the
defendant used was less than that with which he was confronted. The defendant
may, in fact, be permitted to use greater force than that with which he was faced.
For instance, it may be permissible to kill in order to save oneself from being griev-
ously injured.

Excessive force The starting position is that the proportionality element means **26-033**
that the defence of self-defence is unavailable where the force used is excessive.
That said, where too much force is used it is arguable that the defendant should not
be liable for all of the damage caused. On this view, he should be relieved of
responsibility for any damage that would have been brought about by reasonable
force. Of course, in most cases it will be very difficult to say that a particular portion of the claimant's damage was reasonably caused whereas another portion
thereof was not. Where this is the case, the defendant will likely be liable for all of
the damage.

Mistaken defensive force What if the defendant uses force against the claimant **26-034**
because of a mistake (e.g., he believes that the claimant is about to attack him when
the claimant in fact has no intention of doing so)? The criminal law provides that
the defendant is not guilty of a crime if his action would have been justified if the
facts had been as he believed them to be.[77] The mistake need not be a reasonable
one. Tort law adopts a different rule. In the case of a civil action, the defendant will
only be entitled to the defence of self-defence where he uses defensive force as a

---

[74] *Cockroft v Smith* (1705) 2 Salk. 642 at 642; 91 E.R. 541 at 541 per Holt CJ. See also *Lane v Holloway* [1968] 1 Q.B. 379.
[75] *McAleer v Chief Constable of the PSNI* [2014] NIQB 53 at [12].
[76] *Cross v Kirkby, The Times,* 5 April 2000. See also *McAleer v Chief Constable of the PSNI* [2014]
NIQB 53 at [7].
[77] Criminal Justice and Immigration Act 2008 s.76. This provision restates the common law on this
point.

result of a mistake if the mistake was a reasonable one.[78] The logic underpinning this rule is revealing of tort law's nature. A rule that made no allowance for mistakes is thought to be too favourable to claimants while the criminal law rule, which makes the defence of self-defence available even where the defendant made an unreasonable mistake, is considered to be too generous to defendants sued in tort. Making allowances for mistakes but insisting that they be reasonable ones before making the defence of self-defence available in the tort context is regarded as achieving a fair balance between the parties.

26-035 **Pre-emptive force**   The defendant is not required to wait until he is struck before he is permitted to act in his own defence since that would sometimes render the defence pointless. Thus, the defendant may be justified in using force if the claimant does no more than shake his stick at him, uttering taunts at the same time.[79] Similarly, a defendant will not be liable for assault by merely putting himself in a fighting attitude in order to defend himself.[80]

26-036 **Innocent aggressors**   Suppose that the defendant is attacked by someone who is insane or is endangered by an infant who is holding a gun. Is the defendant allowed to use defensive force against such persons in order to save himself? There is a lack of authority on this point, but the answer must be in the affirmative.[81] The defence of self-defence is not confined to situations in which the aggressor is blameworthy or criminally liable.

26-037 **Injury to bystanders**   Suppose that D throws a punch at X in order to protect himself against X's unlawful attack but C, an innocent third party, gets in the way and is hit. Imagine also that D acted reasonably in the circumstances. On what principles ought D's liability to C be discussed? Four points should be noted here. First, one possibility is that D has committed a battery against C by virtue of the doctrine of transferred malice,[82] although the status of that doctrine in tort law is debatable.[83] Second, D may be able to avoid liability to C on the basis of private necessity (i.e., that he harmed a third party in order to protect his own interests) although this leads to the issue of whether tort law recognises such a defence.[84] Third, D may be liable to C in the tort of negligence, but that would be the case only if he acted unreasonably. Fourth, D, if he is liable to C, might be able to seek an indemnity from X.

ii.   Defence of One's Property

26-038 **Possession or right to possession**   Actual possession (whether with a good title or not), or the right to possession of property, is necessary to justify the use of force

---

[78]   *Ashley v Chief Constable of Sussex* [2008] UKHL 25; [2008] 1 A.C. 962.

[79]   *Dale v Wood* (1822) 7 Moore C.P. 33.

[80]   *Moriarty v Brooks* (1834) 6 Car. & P. 684; 172 E.R. 1419.

[81]   There is a general consensus among criminal law scholars that it is justifiable to use reasonable defensive force against an innocent aggressor: see, e.g., Robinson (1982) 82 Col. L. Rev. 199 at 275; Smith, *Justification and Excuse in the Criminal Law* (1989), pp.19–20; Fletcher (1993) 27 Israel L. Rev. 227; Horder (1995) 58 M.L.R. 431 at 432.

[82]   *Bici v Ministry of Defence* [2004] EWHC 786 (QB); *The Times,* 11 June 2004.

[83]   See Beever (2009) 29 L.S. 400.

[84]   *Vincent v Lake Erie Transportation Co* 109 Minn. 456; 124 N.W. 221 (1910).

in keeping out (or, for that matter, expelling) a trespasser.[85] Thus, in *Holmes v Bagge*[86] the parties were both members of the committee of a cricket club. During a match in which the defendant was captain and the claimant was a spectator, the defendant asked the claimant to act as substitute for one of the 11 players. The claimant did so but, being annoyed at the defendant's tone in commanding him to take off his coat, he refused either to remove the garment or to leave the playing part of the field. He was then forcibly removed by the defendant's direction. The defendant, when sued for assault, pleaded possession of the ground, but the plea was held to be bad because possession was in the committee of the club. Note, however, that a person who does not have possession of the land may use reasonable force against persons thereon who obstruct him in exercising statutory powers,[87] and it may be that if the defendant in *Holmes v Bagge* had pleaded that he removed the claimant for disturbing persons lawfully playing a lawful game he would have been justified.[88] The outcome may also have been different if the defendant had been acting at the request of the committee of the club.

Other requirements   Apart from the foregoing, the defence of one's property is **26-039** analogous to self-defence, and is governed by equivalent rules. The key issue in relation to defence of one's property is usually that of proportionality. One is not necessarily bound to make one's premises safe for trespassers, albeit that a duty of care may arise under the Occupiers' Liability Act 1984.[89] But devices may be used to protect property only where reasonable. Spikes on a wall or a fierce dog may be justified,[90] but not deadly implements like spring guns.[91] The infliction of grave bodily harm is too high a price to demand for keeping one's property intact, and it is an offence under the Offences Against the Person Act 1861[92] to set a spring gun or similar device. Consistently with the principle of proportion in the means of defence, more latitude may be permissible in protecting premises by night than in the daytime, or when the occupier is not in the presence of the trespasser than when he is. Thus, an intruder who injures himself on a spiked wall has no valid ground of complaint, but he certainly would have one if he, being peaceable and unarmed, had a spike thrust into him by the occupier[93]: "Presence [of the occupier] in its very nature is more or less protection … [P]resence may supply means [of defence] and limit what it supplies."[94]

---

[85]   For fuller analysis of the defence, see Posner (1971) 14 J.L. & Econ. 201.
[86]   (1853) 1 E. & B. 782; 118 E.R. 629. See also *Dean v Hogg* (1834) 10 Bing. 345; 131 E.R. 937; *Roberts v Taylor* (1844) 7 Man. & G. 659; 135 E.R. 265.
[87]   *R. v Chief Constable of Devon and Cornwall, Ex p. Central Electricity Generating Board* [1982] Q.B. 458.
[88]   *R. v Chief Constable of Devon and Cornwall, Ex p. Central Electricity Generating Board* [1982] Q.B. 458.
[89]   See Ch.10.
[90]   *Sarch v Blackburn* (1830) 4 Car. & P. 296; 172 E.R. 712. The position is now governed by the Animals Act 1971 s.5(3)(b), which is to the like effect (see *Cummings v Granger* [1977] Q.B. 397), though the position may have been indirectly affected by the Guard Dogs Act 1975: see para.17-018.
[91]   *Bird v Holbrook* (1828) 4 Bing. 628; 130 E.R. 911.
[92]   Section 31.
[93]   In *The Pickwick Papers*, Captain Boldwig's mode of ejecting Mr Pickwick, whom he found asleep in a wheelbarrow in his grounds, was excessive. He directed his gardener first to wheel Mr Pickwick to the devil and then, on second thoughts, to wheel him to the village pond.
[94]   *Deane v Clayton* (1817) 7 Taunt. 489 at 521; 128 E.R. 196 per Dallas J. For the defences available

iii. Abatement

26-040 **A defence, not a remedy**   Abatement is often described as a "self-help" remedy. This terminology is unhelpful. A remedy is judicially sanctioned relief. Abatement is better understood as a defence because it prevents liability from arising in trespass where the defendant uses reasonable force to remove or ameliorate a nuisance.

26-041 **The defence is narrowly confined**   The defence of abatement is kept on a tight rein because, as Sir Matthew Hale said, "this many times occasions tumults and disorders".[95] The courts have consequently taken a narrow view of what counts as reasonable force in this context. The defendant must avoid excessive acts. Where there are two ways of abating the nuisance, the less harmful should be followed, unless it would inflict some wrong on an innocent third party or on the public.[96]

26-042 **A request to remove the nuisance should normally be made**   Before abatement is attempted, the defendant should generally request the offending party to remedy the nuisance. However, a request does not need to be made if it would be pointless, where there is no time to make one because of the need for urgent action,[97] or because the nuisance can be removed by the defendant without entry on the land from which the nuisance emanates. The defendant may lop off the branches of the claimant's (his neighbour's) tree that project over his land without giving notice to the claimant,[98] although the defendant must not appropriate that which he severs.[99]

26-043 **It must be impractical to commence legal proceedings**   The defence will usually be withheld if there was no urgent need to abate the nuisance. If it would have been reasonable to expect the defendant to wait to obtain relief via judicial proceedings the defence will not be available, unless the cost of judicial proceedings cannot be justified.[100]

26-044 **Costs incurred in taking reasonable steps to abate the nuisance are recoverable**   Where abatement is justified, the costs reasonably incurred in carrying it out are recoverable.[101]

---

to the occupier of land who kills or injures a dog, see Animals Act 1971 s.9.
[95] *De Portubus Maris*, Pt 2, Ch.VII.
[96] Blackburn J in *Roberts v Rose* (1865) L.R. 1 Ex. 82 at 89 adopted by Lord Atkinson in *Lagan Navigation Co v Lambeg Bleaching Co Ltd* [1927] A.C. 226 at 244–246.
[97] *Lagan Navigation Co v Lambeg Bleaching Co Ltd* [1927] A.C. 226.
[98] *Lemmon v Webb* [1895] A.C. 1.
[99] *Mills v Brooker* [1919] 1 K.B. 555.
[100] *Burton v Winters* [1993] 1 W.L.R. 1077 at 1081.
[101] *Abbahall Ltd v Smee* [2002] EWCA Civ 1831; [2003] 1 W.L.R. 1472; *Delaware Mansions Ltd v Westminster CC* [2001] UKHL 55; [2002] 1 A.C. 321.

B. Public Justifications

i. Public Necessity

Generally Public necessity[102] is a defence to all forms of trespass. It is available   **26-045**
where the defendant uses reasonable force, against or otherwise infringes the rights
of, an innocent person to avoid an imminent and greater harm to some important
public interest.[103] The defence will be lost if the situation of necessity was brought
about by the defendant's own negligence.[104]

Illustrations The defence will apply where the defendant pulls down a house that   **26-046**
is on fire to prevent its spread to other property,[105] destroys a building made ruinous by fire to prevent its collapse into the highway[106] and throws goods overboard
to lighten a boat in a storm.[107] A rescuer who acts to save a person in circumstances
where the latter had no opportunity to consent (such as by dragging a pedestrian out
of the path of a speeding car that the latter failed to notice bearing down on him)
may also be entitled to the defence.[108] More recently, and controversially, the
defence was held to be available to police officers to defeat claims in trespass to
the person where the officers concerned had detained suspected offenders in a police
van while searching their abode for illegal firearms[109] and kept several hundred
people in cramped conditions in Oxford Circus in London until safe crowd dispersal
could be arranged.[110] That which may be justified in one age is not necessarily justified in another. For example, considering there is today an efficient public fire
service it would require an unusual case for the defence of public necessity to apply in respect of the destruction by a private person of another's house to prevent
a fire from spreading.[111] The defence was denied to environmental activists who
destroyed genetically-modified crops[112] and to anti-war campaigners who damaged a military installation.[113]

Infliction of personal injury Public necessity cases are rare and, in most of them,   **26-047**
the thing that the defendant sacrificed was property. What is the position where it
is necessary to kill or cause serious injury to a person in order to save others from
perishing? One case that is at least obliquely relevant is the criminal law matter of

---

[102] See, further, Virgo in Dyson, Goudkamp and Wilmot-Smith (eds), *Defences in Tort* (2014).
[103] For a case where the requirement of reasonableness was not met, see *Rigby v Chief Constable of Northamptonshire* [1985] 1 W.L.R. 1242.
[104] *Southport Corp v Esso Petroleum Ltd* [1954] 2 Q.B. 182 at 194, 198; *Esso Petroleum Ltd v Southport Corp* [1956] A.C. 218 at 242.
[105] "[A] house shall be plucked down if the next be on fire": *Saltpetre Case* (1607) 12 Co. Rep. 12 at 13; 77 E.R. 1294 at 1295.
[106] *Dewey v White* (1827) Mood. & M. 56; 173 E.R. 1079.
[107] *Mouse's* case (1608) 12 Co. Rep. 63; 77 E.R. 1341. It should be noted that the facts of this case occurred on an inland waterway. The position as to jettison at sea may be affected by the principle of
general average.
[108] *Re F (Mental Patient: Sterilisation)* [1990] 2 A.C. 1 at 74.
[109] *Connor v Chief Constable of Merseyside Police* [2006] EWCA Civ 1549; *The Times,* 4 December
2006.
[110] *Austin v Commissioner of Police of the Metropolis* [2009] UKHL 5; [2009] 1 A.C. 564.
[111] *Burmah Oil Co (Burmah Trading) Ltd v Lord Advocate* [1965] A.C. 75 at 164–165.
[112] *Monsanto Plc v Tilly* [2000] Env L.R. 313.
[113] *Leason v AG* [2013] NZCA 509; [2014] 2 N.Z.L.R. 224.

Re A (Children) (Conjoined Twins: Surgical Separation).[114] In this case it was held that necessity (the criminal law does not distinguish between public and private necessity) justified an operation to separate Siamese twins, where otherwise they would both have died, even though the inevitable consequence of the operation was the death of the weaker one. Presumably, the doctors would also have had a defence had a civil action been brought against them.

26-048 **Medical treatment**   Public necessity is used to afford doctors who administer medical treatment to incapable persons a defence to liability in trespass. Legislation now governs this situation,[115] although it has not abolished the relevant common law rule.

26-049 **Relationship with self-defence**   Because the defence of public necessity is concerned with conflicts between innocents, the maximum amount of force that is regarded as proportionate for the purpose of public necessity is less than is the case of self-defence. Thus, whereas the defence of self-defence may authorise the use of greater force than that with which one is threatened[116] it is doubtful whether the defence of public necessity allows the defendant to cause a net harm. It is not for nothing that the defence of public necessity is sometimes known as that of "lesser evils".

26-050 **Private necessity**   It is unclear whether the fact that the claimant used reasonable force against, or otherwise infringed the rights of, an innocent person (including that person's property) to protect his own private interests will not afford him any defence.[117] On one view tort law does not recognise a defence of private necessity.[118] Thus, to give a classic illustration, a hiker who enters a cabin in order to save himself from a storm and who eats the food kept therein and burns the furniture to supply warmth is liable in tort to the cabin's owner. These types of cases are often referred as involving an "incomplete privilege".[119] The idea is as follows. Because (to continue the mountaineering example) the hiker acted reasonably he had a privilege to enter the cabin (the cabin owner could not have kept him out had he been present because he would not be acting reasonably in doing so to defend his property) but, because the privilege is incomplete, he must pay compensation. Matters would be simplified, however, if the concept of an "incomplete privilege" were not invoked to explain these types of cases. The reason why the hiker has to pay compensation to the cabin owner is simply that he committed a tort and has no defence. There is no difficulty in holding the hiker liable although he acted reasonably given that the tort of trespass routinely attaches liability to reasonable conduct. For instance, a person who without consent enters property reasonably but mistakenly believing that he is the owner is liable to the actual owner.[120]

The rival view is that tort law recognises a defence of private necessity. *Cope v*

---

[114] [2001] Fam.147.

[115] See para.4-014.

[116] See para.26-032.

[117] cf. *Cope v Sharpe (No.2)* [1912] 1 K.B. 496.

[118] The decision of the Supreme Court of Minnesota in *Vincent v Lake Erie Transportation Co* 124 N.W. 221 (Minn. 1910) is often cited as authority for this proposition. cf *Ploot v Putnam* 71 Atl. 188 (Vt. 1908).

[119] Bohlen (1926) 39 Harv. L. Rev. 307; Keeton (1959) 72 Harv. L. Rev. 401.

[120] See at para.14-001.

Sharpe (No.2)[121] is the leading authority in support of this position. The court held that D did not commit a trespass to land in going onto C's land and creating a firebreak in view of a blaze that threated to cross onto property over which C had sporting rights. Further, it was held that provided that D's acts were reasonably necessary, it did not matter to liability whether the risk would have materialised but for C's intervention. The issue, instead, was said to be whether there was a "real and imminent danger to" C's property.[122] Further, in *Re F* Lord Goff evidently considered that both public and private necessity may admit of a defence. He remarked[123]:

> "That there exists in the common law a principle of necessity which may justify action that would otherwise be unlawful is not in doubt. But historically the principle has been seen to be restricted to two groups of cases, which have been called cases of public necessity and cases of private necessity. The former occurred when a man interfered with another man's property in the public interest – for example (in the days before we could dial 999 for the fire brigade) the destruction of another man's house to prevent the spread of a catastrophic fire, as indeed occurred in the Great Fire of London in 1666. The latter cases occurred when a man interfered with another's property to save his own person or property from imminent danger - for example, when he entered upon his neighbour's land without his consent, in order to prevent the spread of fire onto his own land."

ii.   Defence of Another Person

The rules discussed above in relation to self-defence[124] apply equally where the defendant uses force to defend a third party. It used to be the case that it was only permissible for a defendant to come to the aid of persons with whom he stood in a particular relationship (such as that of husband and wife[125] or master and servant[126]). This restriction has long since vanished from the law. Today, one who intervenes to protect a stranger from an aggressor may be entitled to invoke the defence.[127]   **26-051**

iii.   Arrest

Generally   A person who uses no more than reasonable force lawfully to arrest another will have a defence to liability in trespass to the person. The defence is justificatory in nature because it will be lost if disproportionate force is used.[128]   **26-052**

Arrest by a constable with a warrant   Section 6 of the Constables Protection Act 1750 confers a defence on constables who arrest a person under a warrant. This defence applies even if there was a "defect of jurisdiction" in the magistrate who issued the warrant as the crucial issue is simply whether the constable obeyed the warrant. The defence will not apply if he arrests a person other than the person named in the warrant.   **26-053**

---

[121] [1912] 1 K.B. 496.

[122] [1912] 1 K.B. 496 at 504 per Buckley LJ.

[123] [1990] 2 A.C. 1 at 74.

[124] See para.26-030.

[125] See Blackstone, *Commentaries on the Laws of England*, Vol.4 (1769), p.186.

[126] *Seaman v Cuppledick* (1615) Owen 150; 74 E.R. 966; *Barfoot v Reynolds* (1733) 2 Stra. 953; 93 E.R. 963.

[127] *Goss v Nicholas* [1960] Tas S.R. 133.

[128] *Simpson v Chief Constable of South Yorkshire, The Times,* 7 March 1991.

26-054   **Arrest by a constable without a warrant**   Section 24 of the Police and Criminal Evidence Act 1984 specifies when a constable can effect an arrest without a warrant. This unnecessarily convoluted provision relevantly states:

"(1)   A constable may arrest without a warrant—
  (a)   anyone who is about to commit an offence;
  (b)   anyone who is in the act of committing an offence;
  (c)   anyone whom he has reasonable grounds for suspecting to be about to commit an offence;
  (d)   anyone whom he has reasonable grounds for suspecting to be committing an offence.
(2)   If a constable has reasonable grounds for suspecting that an offence has been committed, he may arrest without a warrant anyone whom he has reasonable grounds to suspect of being guilty of it.
(3)   If an offence has been committed, a constable may arrest without a warrant—
  (a)   anyone who is guilty of the offence;
  (b)   anyone whom he has reasonable grounds for suspecting to be guilty of it.
(4)   But the power of summary arrest conferred by subsection (1), (2) or (3) is exercisable only if the constable has reasonable grounds for believing that for any of the reasons mentioned in subsection (5) it is necessary to arrest the person in question.
(5)   The reasons are—
  (a)   to enable the name of the person in question to be ascertained (in the case where the constable does not know, and cannot readily ascertain, the person's name, or has reasonable grounds for doubting whether a name given by the person as his name is his real name);
  (b)   correspondingly as regards the person's address;
  (c)   to prevent the person in question—
    (i)   causing physical injury to himself or any other person;
    (ii)   suffering physical injury;
    (iii) causing loss of or damage to property;
    (iv)   committing an offence against public decency (subject to subsection (6)); or
    (v)   causing an unlawful obstruction of the highway;
  (d)   to protect a child or other vulnerable person from the person in question;
  (e)   to allow the prompt and effective investigation of the offence or of the conduct of the person in question;
  (f)   to prevent any prosecution for the offence from being hindered by the disappearance of the person in question..."

If, therefore, Constable D arrests C having, for example, reasonably suspected[129] that C is committing an offence, Constable D will have a defence to an action for false imprisonment even though it turns out that C was not, in fact, committing an offence.[130] Under equivalent legislation[131] it has been held that the arresting officer

---

[129] "The threshold for a police officer to suspect the commission of an offence and an offender is low": *Commissioner of Police for the Metropolis v MR* [2019] EWHC 888 (QB) at [22] per Thornton J. "It is lower than a prima facie case and far less than the evidence required to convict": *Parker v Chief Constable of Essex* [2018] EWCA Civ 2788; [2019] 1 W.L.R. 2238 at [115] per Sir Brian Leveson P.

[130] A reasonable suspicion can be based on "matters that could not be put in evidence": *Parker v Chief Constable of Essex* [2018] EWCA Civ 2788; [2019] 1 W.L.R. 2238 at [115] per Sir Brian Leveson P.

[131] Prevention of Terrorism (Temporary Provisions) Act 1984 (now repealed).

should himself be in possession of information that gives him reasonable cause to suspect that the claimant was about to commit or was committing an offence and that it was not enough that such information was in the possession of another officer who gave an order to arrest which the defendant officer obeyed.[132] This is consistent with "the ... constitutional theory of the independence and accountability of the individual constable"[133] although it has been questioned whether it is realistic in modern conditions.[134] Pursuant to s.24(4), the power to arrest under s.24 is available only if the constable honestly believed that the arrest was necessary[135] and if that belief was reasonable for one of the reasons enumerated in s.24(5).[136] The demanding requirement that an arrest be necessary is unlikely to be satisfied where, for example, the person concerned voluntarily attends a police station and where there were obvious alternatives to arrest, such as conducting an interview.[137] Conversely, an arrest may be necessary where there are serious doubts as to whether any co-operation would continue, and where there is a risk that suspects would collude.[138]

Arrest by a private citizen   The powers of arrest of a private citizen are governed   **26-055**
by s.24A of the 1984 Act.[139] That section provides:

"(1)   A person other than a constable may arrest without a warrant—
(a)   anyone who is in the act of committing an indictable offence;
(b)   anyone whom he has reasonable grounds for suspecting to be committing an indictable offence.
(2)   Where an indictable offence has been committed, a person other than a constable may arrest without a warrant—
(a)   anyone who is guilty of the offence;
(b)   anyone whom he has reasonable grounds for suspecting to be guilty of it."

There are two clear differences between the powers of a constable and a private citizen in so far as arrest is concerned. First, the citizen's power of arrest is confined to indictable offences. Secondly, the citizen has no power to make a "preventive" arrest: an offence must be in progress or he must reasonably believe that it is. Where an indictable offence has been committed any person may arrest without a warrant anyone who is guilty of the offence or anyone whom he has reasonable grounds for suspecting to be guilty of it. In other words, where the offence has been committed there may be a defence even if the arrester "gets the wrong man"; but if in

---

[132]   *O'Hara v Chief Constable of the Royal Ulster Constabulary* [1997] A.C. 286. cf. *Keegan v Chief Constable of Merseyside* [2003] EWCA Civ 936; [2003] 1 W.L.R. 2187.

[133]   *O'Hara v Chief Constable of the Royal Ulster Constabulary* [1997] A.C. 286 at 293 per Lord Steyn.

[134]   *Raissi v Commissioner of Police of the Metropolis* [2008] EWCA Civ 1237; [2009] Q.B. 564 at [33]. The arresting officer does not, of course, have to investigate the matter himself and may rely on apparently reliable information given to him by another officer. Any deficiencies in his briefing do not invalidate the arrest, though they may render the briefing officer liable for some other tort, e.g., misfeasance in a public office: *Alford v Chief Constable of Cambridgeshire* [2009] EWCA Civ 100.

[135]   The requirement of "necessity" sets a higher bar than would a requirement of, say, desirability or convenience: *R. (on the application of L) v Chief Constable of Surrey* [2017] EWHC 129 (Admin); [2017] 1 W.L.R. 2047 at [40].

[136]   See, further, *Parker v Chief Constable of Essex* [2018] EWCA Civ 2788; [2019] 1 W.L.R. 2238 at [123].

[137]   *Commissioner of Police for the Metropolis v MR* [2019] EWHC 888 (QB) at [49].

[138]   *Parker v Chief Constable of Essex* [2018] EWCA Civ 2788; [2019] 1 W.L.R. 2238.

[139]   See also s.3 of the Criminal Law Act 1967.

fact no offence has been committed by anyone the arrest is unlawful.

As in the case of the police officer, the private citizen effecting an arrest has to satisfy further conditions. Three of these are similar to those applicable to constables—that he has reasonable grounds to believe that the arrest is necessary to prevent the arrestee: (1) causing physical injury to himself or another; (2) suffering injury; or (3) causing loss of or damage to property.[140] He must also (4) have reasonable grounds to believe that it is necessary to prevent the arrestee "making off before a constable can assume responsibility for him".[141] Finally, in all cases it must appear to the person making the arrest (5) "that it is not reasonably practicable for a constable to make it instead".[142]

26-056   **The need to inform the person arrested of the ground on which he is arrested**   *Christie v Leachinsky*[143] established that in ordinary circumstances a person arrested must be informed of the ground on which he is arrested, otherwise the arrest is unlawful: the officer is not entitled to remain silent or to fabricate[144] a "holding charge". The law is now found in s.28 of the Police and Criminal Evidence Act 1984, which provides that where a person is arrested by a constable otherwise than by being informed that he is under arrest (e.g., where he is physically seized) he must as soon as practicable be informed[145] that he is under arrest, even if the fact is obvious, and also of the ground for the arrest, again even if it is obvious. The only qualification to these duties is that they do not apply if it was not reasonably practicable for the information to be given because the claimant escaped from custody before it could be. An arrest is a continuing state of affairs so that if the information is not given promptly but at a later stage the arrest becomes lawful from that point, which may affect the quantum of damages.[146] Where the arrest is by a private individual he does not have to inform the claimant of the fact of the arrest or of the ground where it is obvious. It has been said that *Christie v Leachinsky*, s.28 and art.5(2) of the European Convention on Human Rights ("everyone who is arrested shall be informed promptly, in a language which he understands, of the reasons for his arrest and of any charge against him") all express the same principle[147] and that the basic idea is that, having regard to the information available to the arresting officer, the arrested person must be told the "essential legal and factual grounds for his arrest".[148] As to what is required by way of information, technical or precise language need not be used but sufficient detail should be given to enable him to understand the factual as well as the legal nature of what he is accused of, so that, for example, "You are under arrest for burglary" is insufficient without information as to when and where the alleged burglary took place.[149]

---

[140] Police and Criminal Evidence Act 1984 s.24A(4)(a)–(c).

[141] Police and Criminal Evidence Act 1984 s.24A(4)(d).

[142] Police and Criminal Evidence Act 1984 s.24A(3)(b).

[143] [1947] A.C. 573.

[144] But if there is a charge in respect of which the officer has reasonable grounds for suspecting guilt, an arrest in respect of that is lawful even if the officer's real purpose is to investigate a more serious offence. In this sense a "holding charge" is a "well known and respectable aid to justice": *R. v Chalkely* [1998] Q.B. 848 at 873.

[145] Not necessarily by the arresting officer: *Dhesi v Chief Constable of the Midlands, The Times,* 9 May 2000.

[146] *Lewis v Chief Constable of South Wales* [1991] 1 All E.R. 206.

[147] *Taylor v Chief Constable of Thames Valley Police* [2004] EWCA Civ 858; [2004] 1 W.L.R. 3155.

[148] *Fox, Campbell and Hartley v UK* (1990) 13 E.H.R.R. 157 at [40].

[149] *R. v Telfer* [1976] Crim. L.R. 562; *Newman v Modern Bookbinders Ltd* [2000] 1 W.L.R. 2559.

Detention following arrest Where the arrest is by a private individual the ar-   **26-057**
rested person must be taken before a magistrate or a police officer, not necessarily
forthwith, but as soon as is reasonably possible. For example, a person arrested in
the street by a store detective on suspicion of shoplifting may be taken back to the
store while the matter is reported to the store manager, and may be detained there
while the police are summoned.[150] It is unlikely that the store detective would be
allowed to take the suspect to the suspect's house to see whether any of the stolen
property is there, though it has been held that a police officer could do so.[151] The
position following a police arrest is dealt with in the Police and Criminal Evidence
Act 1984. By s.30, a person arrested otherwise than at a police station must be taken
to a police station as soon as is practicable after his arrest, unless his presence
elsewhere is necessary in order to carry out such investigations as it is reasonable
to carry out immediately. The time for which and the conditions in which he may
be held are then governed by Pt IV of the Act. Section 34(1) provides that a person
"shall not be kept in police detention" except in accordance with Pt IV, and the
defence of arrest will subsequently be lost if the provisions in Pt IV are
contravened.[152] These provisions are much too detailed to examine here but, very
broadly, the position is that there must be periodic reviews of the detention by the
police and, with the authority of a senior officer, the detainee may be held for up
to 36 hours without charge. Thereafter, the authority of a magistrates' court is
required for further detention without charge up to 96 hours. After that period the
suspect must either be released or charged and brought before a magistrates' court
as soon as is practicable. In any event, even if these time limits have not been
exceeded, an arrested person must be released as soon as the need for detention has
ended and, if he is not, there is liability in false imprisonment from that time,
notwithstanding that the initial arrest was lawful.[153] Various matters ancillary to
detention are dealt with in Pt V of the Act. Contravention of the provisions on
searches and fingerprinting will presumably lead to liability for battery but will not
render the detention unlawful. There is no damages sanction attached to the provisions dealing with the suspect's right to have someone informed of his arrest or access to legal advice. Contravention of these provisions also does not render the
detention unlawful, and there is no claim for breach of statutory duty. Nor is any
right under the European Convention infringed unless the effect is to deprive the
claimant of a fair trial.[154]

Defence of arrest at common law in order to prevent an imminent breach of   **26-058**
the peace The common law affords a defence to people who effect an arrest in
order to prevent an imminent breach of the peace by the person arrested.[155] This

---

Although in *Walker v Commissioner of Police of the Metropolis* [2014] EWCA Civ 897; [2015] 1
  W.L.R. 312 arrest on the ground of "public order" was held to be sufficient.
[150] *John Lewis & Co Ltd v Tims* [1952] A.C. 676.
[151] *Dallison v Caffery* [1965] 1 Q.B. 348.
[152] *Roberts v CC Cheshire* [1999] 1 W.L.R. 662.
[153] *Taylor v Chief Constable of Thames Valley Police* [2004] EWCA Civ 858; [2004] 1 W.L.R. 3155.
[154] *Cullen v Chief Constable of the Royal Ulster Constabulary* [2003] UKHL 39; [2003] 1 W.L.R. 1763.
  However, if access is refused in bad faith there might be liability for misfeasance in a public office:
  at [71]. The case concerned s.15 of the Northern Ireland (Emergency Provisions) Act 1987 but this
  is modelled on the equivalent provision of the Police and Criminal Evidence Act 1984 and the
  reasoning would seem to apply.
[155] *R. (Laporte) v Chief Constable of Gloucestershire* [2006] UKHL 55; [2007] 2 A.C. 105.

defence complies with art.5 of the European Convention.[156] In order to prevent an imminent breach of the peace there may also be detention short of arrest but there is no doctrine that such action may be justified on lesser grounds than those applicable to an arrest: in either case the apprehended breach of the peace must be happening or about to happen, not merely reasonably anticipated at some time in the future.[157]

iv. Prevention of Crime

26-059 **Circumstances in which the defence applies** In addition to the powers of arrest that have been discussed above, by s.3 of the Criminal Law Act 1967 any person may use such force (which may include detention[158]) as is reasonable in the circumstances in the prevention of crime, or in effecting or assisting in the lawful arrest of offenders, suspected offenders or persons unlawfully at large. Whether or not the force used is reasonable is a question of fact.[159] The offence that the defendant seeks to prevent must be an offence recognised by domestic law in order for the defence to apply. Acting to prevent breaches of international law will not suffice.[160]

26-060 **Overlap with other defences** The defence in s.3 of the Criminal Law Act 1967 overlaps extensively with several other defences.[161] In particular, it covers much of the same terrain as self-defence. But the overlap is not complete. For example, an "innocent aggressor", such as an infant who is holding a gun, cannot incur criminal liability so s.3 would not be available in respect of force used against the infant. In contrast, the defence of self-defence may apply where the aggressor is not criminally responsible.[162]

v. Lawful Confinement in Prison

26-061 By s.12(1) of the Prison Act 1952 "a prisoner, whether sentenced to imprisonment or committed to prison on remand pending trial", is lawfully confined in the prison.[163] This provision confers on any prison governor or prison officer acting under his authority a defence to liability in false imprisonment.[164] The defence will

---

[156] *Steel v UK* (1998) 28 E.H.R.R. 603.

[157] *R. (Laporte) v Chief Constable of Gloucestershire* [2006] UKHL 55; [2007] 2 A.C. 105. In *Murray v Ministry of Defence* [1998] 1 W.L.R. 692 it is suggested that a person who restrains the movement of A for a short time will have a defence if this was necessary to effect the lawful arrest of B. It has also been suggested that a defence is available where the movement of occupants is restricted while premises are being searched: *DPP v Meaden* [2003] EWHC 3005 (Admin); [2004] 1 W.L.R. 945; *Connor v Chief Constable of Merseyside* [2006] EWCA Civ 1549; [2007] H.R.L.R. 6.

[158] *Albert v Lavin* [1982] A.C. 546.

[159] *AG for Northern Ireland's Reference (No.1 of 1975)* [1977] A.C. 105. It is arguable that the legislation gives insufficient guidance to persons using force as to how much force is reasonable. See generally Doran (1987) 7 L.S. 291.

[160] *R. v Jones* [2006] UKHL 16; [2007] 1 A.C. 136.

[161] See also s.117 of the Police and Criminal Evidence Act 1984 which (in outline) empowers constables to use reasonable force, if necessary, in the exercise of powers conferred on them.

[162] See para.26-036.

[163] See, further, Fordham [1991] S.J.L.S. 348.

[164] The fact that the Parole Board has acted unlawfully in administrative law terms in relation to considering the prisoner's release, or in breach of art.5(4) of the European Convention on Human Rights due to delay in considering the prisoner's case, does not render his detention actionable for the purpose of false imprisonment: *Dunn v Parole Board* [2008] EWCA Civ 374; [2009] 1 W.L.R.

be lost if a prison governor fails to release a prisoner at the end of his sentence. In *R. v Governor of Brockhill Prison, Ex p. Evans (No.2)*[165] the claimant was released from prison by habeas corpus when a decision of the Divisional Court disapproved earlier cases dealing with the method of calculation of the release date for prisoners with concurrent sentences, and he recovered £5,000 damages for the 59 days he had spent in prison after his proper release date. The claimant recovered even though, before the new ruling was given, the prison governor would plainly have had no authority to release him. The governor was acting in accordance with the law as it was then perceived to be, but the general rule is that decisions that are overruled are regarded as never having had legal force, subject to any issue being res judicata between parties who have previously litigated the issue. A prison governor is not guilty of false imprisonment for detaining a prisoner under a sentence which it is subsequently held the court had no power to impose, for he must obey an order of the court unless at the time it is made it is invalid on its face.

vi. Stop and Search by Police Officer

The common law confers on the police no power to detain for questioning.[166] **26-062** However, Pt I of the Police and Criminal Evidence Act 1984 gives a police officer power to stop and search any person or vehicle for stolen or prohibited goods if he has reasonable grounds to believe that such goods will be found. These provisions create a defence to liability in trespass.

vii. Statutory Authority

A statute may provide that a person is authorised to engage in conduct that would **26-063** otherwise constitute a tort.[167] The issue of whether or not a given piece of legislation has authorised tortious conduct is, ultimately, a matter of statutory construction, as is the scope of any such authority. However, three general points to bear in mind in this connection are as follows. First, the existence of a provision in the relevant statute providing for a person who is injured by the activity to be compensated is a material consideration. Such a provision may suggest that Parliament intended to create a defence. Secondly, it is for the defendant to demonstrate that Parliament intended to create a defence. Most of the cases on the defence of statutory authority have concerned liability for nuisance and the matter has been considered in that context.[168] Thirdly, legislation may impliedly confer statutory authority, although the courts will generally be wary in finding statutory authority to commit a tort by implication since the effect of doing so is to override the claimant's rights. In *Manchester Ship Canal Co Ltd v United Utilities Water Plc* Lord Sumption explained the approach to be taken in the following terms[169]:

728; *R. v Secretary of State for Justice, Ex p. Faulkner* [2013] UKSC 23; [2013] 2 A.C. 254.
[165] [2001] 2 A.C. 19.
[166] A person who voluntarily attends at a police station for questioning cannot be detained there unless he is lawfully arrested: Police and Criminal Evidence Act 1984 s.29.
[167] The defence of statutory authority is discussed in further detail in Nolan in Dyson, Goudkamp and Wilmot-Smith (eds), *Defences in Tort* (2014).
[168] See para.15-056.
[169] [2014] UKSC 40; [2014] 1 W.L.R. 2576 at [2].

"The implication must be more than convenient or reasonable. It must be necessary. As a general rule, this will involve showing either that the existence of the power is necessarily implicit in the express terms of the statute, or else that the statutory purpose cannot be effectually achieved without the implication. In particular a right to commit what would otherwise be a tort may be implied if a statutory power is incapable of being exercised or a statutory duty is incapable of being performed without doing the act in question."

4. PUBLIC POLICY DEFENCES

A. Public Policy Defences that Arise at the Time of the Tort

i. The Defence of Illegality

26-064 **A defence of general application**[170] It is a well-known principle of the law of contract that if the claimant has to found his claim on an illegal act or agreement he will fail: ex turpi causa non oritur actio.[171] Although it is arguable that that maxim is properly to be confined to cases involving contracts,[172] it is clear that illegality is also a defence to claims in tort. The plea is of universal application in the sense that it is available to all tortious causes of action.[173] The defendant carries the burdens of pleading and proof in relation to it[174] although the court is able to raise the defence on its own motion.[175]

26-065 **The need for illegal or turpitudinous conduct** The defence will apply only if the claimant engages in conduct that is either illegal or, exceptionally, conduct which, while not illegal, nevertheless involves turpitude.[176] The courts have not clearly defined the concept of turpitude, but it is plain that it can encompass dishonest behaviour.[177] Conversely, mere private law wrongdoing, such as breaches of intellectual property rights, does not constitute turpitude.[178] Further, even if the claimant engaged in illegal conduct, the defence will not apply unless the wrongdo-

---

[170] The defence has spawned a large literature. For a small sample, see Weinrib (1976) 26 U.T.L.J. 28; *The Illegality Defence*, Law Com. No.320 (2010); Goudkamp and Mayr in Dyson, Goudkamp and Wilmot-Smith (eds), *Defences in Tort* (2014); Burrows (2017) C.L.P. 55; Erbacher, *Negligence and Illegality* (2017); Bogg and Green (eds), *Illegality After Patel v Mirza* (2018).

[171] "No cause of action may be founded upon an immoral or illegal act": *Revill v Newbery* [1996] Q.B. 567 at 576 per Neill LJ.

[172] *Smith v Jenkins* (1970) 119 C.L.R. 397 at 410.

[173] "We do not consider that the public policy that the court will not lend its aid to a litigant who relies on his own criminal or immoral act is confined to particular causes of action": *Clunis v Camden and Islington Health Authority* [1998] Q.B. 978 at 987 per Beldam LJ; '[the defence] applies across the board': *Vellino v Chief Constable of Greater Manchester* [2001] EWCA Civ 1249; [2002] 1 W.L.R. 218 at [44] per Sedley LJ. However, the defence does not apply to claims under the Human Rights Act 1998: *Al Hassan-Daniel v Revenue and Customs Commissioners* [2010] EWCA Civ 1443; [2011] Q.B. 866.

[174] *Blake v Croasdale* [2018] EWHC 1919 (QB); [2019] R.T.R. 8 at [12]. cf. *West v Ministry of Defence* [2006] EWHC 19 (QB) [9]–[11].

[175] "I do not believe that there is any general principle that the claimant must either plead, give evidence of or rely on his own illegality for the principle to apply": *Cross v Kirkby, The Times,* 5 April 2000 at [76] per Beldam LJ.

[176] See Goudkamp (2011) 27 L.Q.R. 354.

[177] *Les Laboratoires Servier v Apotex Inc* [2014] UKSC 55; [2015] A.C. 430 at [25].

[178] *Les Laboratoires Servier v Apotex Inc* [2014] UKSC 55; [2015] A.C. 430.

ing concerned was reasonably serious. Trivial offending by the claimant, such as failing to wear a seatbelt, will not suffice.[179]

Gray v Thames Trains Ltd[180]   There are two strands of jurisprudence regarding **26-066** the illegality defence. One approach derives from the decision of the House of Lords in *Gray v Thames Trains Ltd*.[181] In that case, the claimant suffered psychiatric injuries due to the defendants' negligence. Those injuries led the claimant to kill a stranger during an altercation. The claimant was subsequently convicted of manslaughter on the basis of diminished responsibility and sentenced to detention in hospital. He then sued the defendants in the tort of negligence seeking damages in respect of his psychiatric injuries and loss of earnings pre-dating his arrest but also for various losses that were connected with his offending and conviction, including his loss of liberty, loss of earnings sustained after his arrest, feelings of guilt and remorse and damage to his reputation. The claimant additionally sought an indemnity in respect of any civil liability that he might incur in respect of the homicide that he had committed. Lord Hoffmann, delivering the principal speech, understood the illegality defence as being comprised of two separate but overlapping rules: a wide rule and a narrow rule. The wide rule, Lord Hoffmann said, is that compensation cannot be recovered "for damage which is the consequence of [the claimant's] own criminal act".[182] He proceeded to hold that the wide rule shut out recovery in respect of the feelings of guilt and remorse as well as the claim for an indemnity. The narrow rule, Lord Hoffmann said, is that a claimant "cannot recover for damage which is the consequence of a sentence imposed upon [him] for a criminal act".[183] Lord Hoffmann held that the narrow rule precluded redress in respect of the loss of liberty, loss of earnings post-dating the arrest and the damage that the conviction had done to the claimant's reputation. In the event, the claimant only recovered compensation for his psychiatric injury and earnings lost prior to the date of his offending.

It is important to observe that the narrow rule does not do any work that is additional to that done by the wide rule: damage that is imposed on the claimant by the criminal law is non-compensable under the narrow rule, yet such damage is damage that is the consequence of the claimant's own criminal act and hence would be irrecoverable regardless of the narrow rule on account of the wide rule. The reason why Lord Hoffmann nonetheless distinguished between the two rules is that the narrow rule can be rationalised on a basis on which the wide rule cannot. The narrow rule, by denying compensation in respect of criminal law sanctions and hence preventing the claimant from obtaining a rebate in respect of them, stops tort law from being used to stultify the criminal law. That justification is inapplicable to the wide rule, since in wide-rule cases the claimant is not seeking a remedy that would directly undermine the goals of the criminal law. Lord Hoffmann was less

---

[179] *Saunders v Edwards* [1987] 1 W.L.R. 1116 at 1134; *Vellino v Chief Constable of the Greater Manchester* [2001] EWCA Civ 1249; [2002] 1 W.L.R. 218 at [48]; *Currie v Clamp* 2002 S.L.T. 196 at [20]–[21]; *Griffin v UHY Hacker Young & Partners (a firm)* [2010] EWHC 146 (Ch) at [49]–[60]; *Wallett v Vickers* [2018] EWHC 3088 (QB); [2019] Lloyd's Rep. I.R. 205 at [38].

[180] Goudkamp in Davies and Pila (eds), *The Jurisprudence of Lord Hoffmann* (2015).

[181] *Gray v Thames Trains Ltd* [2009] UKHL 33; [2009] A.C. 1339.

[182] *Gray v Thames Trains Ltd* [2009] UKHL 33; [2009] A.C. 1339 at [32].

[183] *Gray v Thames Trains Ltd* [2009] UKHL 33; [2009] A.C. 1339 at [32]. See also *Clunis v Camden and Islington Health Authority* [1998] Q.B. 978; *British Columbia v Zastowny* [2008] SCC 4; [2008] 1 S.C.R. 27; *Khan v Hussain* [2019] CSOH 11; 2019 S.L.T. 319.

definite about what was the reason for the wide rule. He said that "it has to be justified on the ground that it is offensive to public notions of the fair distribution of resources that a claimant should be compensated (usually out of public funds) for the consequences of his own criminal conduct".[184]

Unsurprisingly, the wide rule has been in issue far more regularly than the narrow rule. In *Joyce v O'Brien*,[185] the parties stole a ladder from a residential property and loaded it onto a van which the defendant drove. The claimant rode on the back of the van but, as the parties fled from the scene of the crime, he fell from it and suffered injury. The Court of Appeal held that the wide rule barred the claimant's claim.[186] *Joyce* can be contrasted with *Delaney v Pickett*.[187] In *Delaney*, the claimant passenger was injured in a car accident that was caused by the negligence of the defendant driver, in whose vehicle the claimant was travelling. Rescue services discovered upon attending the scene that the parties were transporting cannabis in their vehicle. The illegality defence was found to be inapplicable on this occasion because the unlawful conduct had not contributed to the accident.[188]

As to the narrow rule, it is arguable that damages can be recovered in respect of a fine imposed where the offence that the claimant committed is one of strict liability, at least where the claimant was not at fault or blameworthy for the offence. This result might be explained on the basis that it is an exception to the narrow rule, or on the ground that the illegality defence is simply not triggered in the first place because the offence committed is insufficiently serious.[189]

26-067 **Patel v Mirza** Almost a decade after *Gray* was decided, the Supreme Court, in 2016, delivered judgment in the landmark case of *Patel v Mirza*.[190] In these proceedings, funds had been transferred by the claimant to the defendant for the purposes of a conspiracy to commit insider trading. However, the promised inside information was not forthcoming and, when the defendant failed to return the funds, the claimant sued the defendant in unjust enrichment and breach of contract. Before the Supreme Court only the claim in unjust enrichment remained in contention. The issue for the Court was understood as being whether the illegality defence should be controlled by the "reliance test" or the "public policy test". Under the reliance test, which had been applied with some regularity in the tort and other contexts prior to *Gray*, the claimant would fail if he needed to plead or prove facts that disclosed illegality on his part in order to establish his cause of action. Conversely, the public policy test involves a balancing of relevant factors. It has been said that there is no closed list of relevant considerations but potentially material factors to which the test is sensitive include, for example, whether denying the claim would be a disproportionate response to the claimant's wrongdoing, the seriousness of the of-

---

[184] *Gray v Thames Trains Ltd* [2009] UKHL 33; [2009] A.C. 1339 at [51].

[185] [2013] EWCA Civ 546; [2014] 1 W.L.R. 70.

[186] Consider, also, *Beaumont v Ferrer* [2016] EWCA Civ 768; [2016] R.T.R. 25.

[187] [2011] EWCA Civ 1532; [2012] 1 W.L.R. 2149 (noted in Goudkamp (2012) 71 C.L.J. 481). The saga in these proceedings continued in *Delaney v Secretary of State for Transport* [2014] EWHC 1785 (QB); [2014] R.T.R. 25.

[188] Although both *Joyce* and *Delaney* were cases in which the parties were involved in joint illegal enterprises, the wide rule is not limited to such cases: *Wallett v Vickers* [2018] EWHC 3088 (QB); [2019] Lloyd's Rep. I.R. 205 at [33].

[189] *Askey v Golden Wine Co Ltd* [1948] 2 All E.R. 35; *Osman v J Ralph Moss Ltd* [1970] 1 Lloyd's Rep. 313;

[190] [2016] UKSC 42; [2017] A.C. 467 (noted in Goudkamp (2017) 133 L.Q.R. 14).

fending, whether allowing recovery would facilitate wrongful profiting or impair the integrity of the legal system and any relevant statutory policy. By a majority, the Court opted for the public policy test. On the facts, it was held that the illegality defence was inapplicable, with Lord Toulson commenting that the claimant was seeking "to unwind the arrangement, not to profit from it".[191]

The current situation   A major issue in this area of the law of torts concerns the **26-068** status of *Gray* in the wake of *Patel*. On the one hand, *Patel* concerned a claim in unjust enrichment and it would be surprising if it had overruled sub silentio the House of Lords' decision in *Gray*, which was the leading authority on the illegality defence in tort. On the other hand, the Supreme Court in *Patel* referred extensively to illegality cases in all parts of private law, including tort law, which suggests that the public policy test is not meant to be limited to the unjust enrichment context. The view that *Patel* had superseded *Gray* finds support in the fact that *Patel* has been followed in several tort cases[192] although often without any recognition of the fact that the approaches in *Gray* and *Patel* to the illegality defence are different from each other. However, in *Henderson v Dorset Healthcare University NHS Foundation Trust*[193] the Court of Appeal held that *Gray* remained binding on it, although this conclusion may have been influenced by the fact that the circumstances in *Henderson* were regarded as being indistinguishable from those in *Gray*.

A complete and a partial defence   When it applies, the illegality defence usu- **26-069** ally prevents liability from arising. However, on occasion, it can leave a finding of liability undisturbed and simply result in the claimant's damages being reduced. When it operates in this way, the illegality defence typically limits the claimant's claim for lost earnings.[194] The leading decision is *Hewison v Meridian Shipping Services Pte*.[195] In that case, the claimant committed an offence by working as a crane driver without disclosing the fact that he suffered from epilepsy. He was injured by his employer's negligence and the fact that he suffered from epilepsy then came to light. The claimant was able to recover damages in respect of all of the losses that he suffered save for his lost earnings. Damages in that regard were withheld on the ground that this head of the claim was inextricably connected with the offence that the claimant committed. Conversely, a claimant will not be barred from recovering damages for a loss of earnings simply because he would have failed to pay tax on them, although he cannot, of course, recover more than his after-tax loss of earnings.[196] It should be noted that *Hewison* predates the decisions in both *Gray* and *Patel* and some doubt remains as to whether the reasoning in it would be followed today.

---

[191] [2016] UKSC 42; [2017] A.C. 467 at [115].
[192] See, e.g., *Tchenguiz v Grant Thornton UK LLP* [2016] EWHC 3727 (Comm) at [41]; *McHugh v Okai-Koi* [2017] EWHC 1346 (QB) at [18]–[22]; *Stoffel & Co v Grondona* [2018] EWCA Civ 2031, [2018] P.N.L.R. 36 at [24].
[193] [2018] EWCA Civ 1841; [2018] 3 W.L.R. 1651. The Supreme Court has reserved judgment in an appeal in this matter.
[194] See Goudkamp and König (2018) 9 J.E.T.L. 54.
[195] [2002] EWCA Civ 1821; [2003] I.C.R. 766. See also *Burns v Edman* [1970] 2 Q.B. 541.
[196] *Hall v Woolston Hall Leisure Ltd* [2001] 1 W.L.R. 225; *Finnis v Caulfield* [2002] EWHC 3223 (QB).

26-070 **Damage to chattels unlawfully obtained or possessed** The operation of the defence of illegality in this type of case has been dealt with in an earlier chapter.[197]

26-071 **Overlap with the doctrine of contributory negligence** There is considerable overlap between the defence of illegality and the doctrine of contributory negligence.[198] Frequently, but not always, when the illegality defence is an issue the doctrine of contributory negligence will be too.[199] This overlap is important principally because it has arguably made the courts more reluctant to find that the illegality defence applies than may otherwise be the case. On this view, the courts generally prefer to find that the doctrine of illegality is inapplicable and to take account of the claimant's conduct only by way of the doctrine of contributory negligence, which enables the courts to permit the claimant to recover partial damages. It is certainly the case that low-level offending in the road traffic context is dealt with almost exclusively as a matter of contributory negligence.[200]

26-072 **Criticism** Whether the law regarding the illegality defence is satisfactory has generated considerable discussion. One issue concerns the test by which the defence is governed. In *Patel*, the Supreme Court implicitly considered that there were just two tests on offer as to when the illegality doctrine would apply, namely, the reliance test and the public policy test. However, that was clearly a false dichotomy. For one thing, also on offer was the causal approach that the House of Lords endorsed in *Gray* just a few years earlier. Furthermore, the ultimate appellate courts in several other jurisdictions had opted for a range of other approaches.[201] Therefore, it is entirely possible in these circumstances that neither the reliance test nor the public policy test should have been accepted in *Patel*.

A more fundamental issue is whether the law of torts should recognise a defence of illegality at all and, if so, why. In *Hall v Hebert* the Supreme Court of Canada largely banished the defence from tort law on the basis that, save in exceptional situations, it served no useful purpose and, on the contrary, was pregnant with the potential to add disproportionately to any sanctions that the criminal law may have already imposed upon the claimant.[202] McLachlin J delivering the majority reasons observed that the defence did not usually prevent the claimant from profiting from his wrong since a claimant in tort normally seeks a remedy that does not go beyond the restoration of loss suffered. She also noted that it was fanciful to think that the defence has any deterrent effect. Thus, if the criminal law has failed to discourage a claimant from offending, that claimant is unlikely to abstain from breaching the criminal law by the mere possibility that, if he happened to suffer injury, he may be denied a remedy in tort. Because these and other justifications for the illegality defence were found to be incapable of supporting an expansive illegality defence, McLachlin J limited the defence to just two situations. The first was where the claimant exceptionally was seeking a remedy that would put him into a better position than he would have stood but for the tort, which would be the case where, for

---

[197] See para.18-036.
[198] See, further, Goudkamp and Nolan, *Contributory Negligence* (2018) at para.4.08.
[199] See, e.g., *Revill v Newberry* [1996] Q.B. 567; *Vellino v Chief Constable of the Greater Manchester Police* [2001] EWCA Civ 1249; [2002] 1 W.L.R. 218; *McHugh v Okai-Koi* [2017] EWHC 1346 (QB).
[200] See *Great North Eastern Railway Ltd v Hart* [2003] EWHC 2450 at [84].
[201] See, e.g., *Miller v Miller* [2011] HCA 9; (2011) 242 C.L.R. 446.
[202] [1993] 2 S.C.R. 159.

example, the claimant seeks an award of punitive damages. The other situation was where compensation was claimed in respect of a criminal law sanction. McLachlin J considered that compensation in respect of losses lawfully inflicted on the claimant by the criminal law should be denied because the integrity of the legal system would be undermined if tort law repaired such losses. Awarding compensation in this type of case would involve the law giving "by its right hand what it takes away by its left hand".[203]

ii.   Section 329 of the Criminal Justice Act 2003

Permission to sue   Under s.329 of the Criminal Justice Act 2003 a claimant who sues in trespass to the person and who was convicted of an imprisonable offence committed on the same occasion as the act that is said to constitute the trespass can sue only with the court's permission. The court is authorised to grant permission only if there is evidence that what the defendant did was "grossly disproportionate" or that the defendant did not believe that: (1) the claimant was about to commit an offence, was in the course of committing an offence, or had committed an offence immediately beforehand; or (2) the act was necessary to defend himself or another person, to protect or recover property, to prevent the commission or continuation of an offence, or to apprehend, or secure the conviction, of the claimant after he had committed an offence.[204]   **26-073**

The defence   If the court grants the claimant permission to sue, the defendant will nevertheless have a defence to the claim if he proves that his act[205] was not "grossly disproportionate" in all of the circumstances of the case[206] and he believed one or more of the matters that are relevant in connection with whether permission to sue should be granted. "Belief" here means honest belief and it is immaterial that the belief may have been unreasonable.[207] Accordingly, if the defendant (whether a police officer or a private person) arrests the claimant for, say, burglary on totally inadequate evidence but matters which later come to light lead to his conviction (for that or any other imprisonable offence) no action can be brought unless what the defendant did was "grossly disproportionate".   **26-074**

B.   Public Policy Defences that Arise After the Tort

i.   Waiver

When lawyers speak of "waiver" they may mean to refer to conduct by the claimant which signifies an intention to relinquish a right of action for a legal wrong. Subject to the doctrine of promissory estoppel (which cannot be pursued here) a right of action for tort can only be "waived" in this sense by an agreement for valu-   **26-075**

---

[203] [1993] 2 S.C.R. 159 at 169.

[204] Failure to seek permission does not render the proceedings a nullity: *Adorian v Commissioner of Police of the Metropolis* [2009] EWCA Civ 18; [2009] 1 W.L.R. 1859.

[205] It appears that what matters in this regard is the nature of the defendant's act not the consequences of it: *McDonnell v Commissioner of Police of the Metropolis* [2015] EWCA Civ 573 at [28].

[206] *Kenyon v Chief Constable of Hertfordshire* [2019] EWHC 1485 (QB) at [35].

[207] Criminal Justice Act 2003 s.329(8)(b).

able consideration or a release by deed.[208] Mere demand for payment of what is due is not a waiver of the right of action for the wrong[209] nor is receipt of part payment of what is due, unless it is accepted as full discharge.[210]

ii. Accord and Satisfaction

26-076 **Generally** Tortious liability can be extinguished by agreement for valuable consideration between the injured party and the tortfeasor.[211] This is styled "accord and satisfaction" but is really little more than a specialised form of contract and so, to be effective, it must comply with the rules for the formation of contract.[212] "Accord" signifies the agreement and "satisfaction" the consideration which makes it operative. The satisfaction may be either executed (e.g., "I release you from your obligation in consideration of £100 now paid by you to me") or it may be executory (e.g., "I release you from your obligation in consideration of your promise to pay me £100 in six months").[213]

26-077 **Accord and satisfaction may be conditional** A person injured in an accident brought about by the negligence of the defendant may accept an offer of compensation, reserving to himself the right to renew his claim if his injuries turn out to be worse than they were at the time of the accord.[214]

26-078 **Accord and satisfaction may extend only to part of the claimant's action** It is also possible for the parties, by an agreement falling short of full accord and satisfaction, to limit the issues between them, as in *Tomlin v Standard Telephones and Cables Ltd*,[215] an action for damages for personal injuries, where it was agreed that the defendants would pay 50 per cent of the claimant's damages, leaving only the amount of those damages to be determined.

26-079 **Non-performance of accord and satisfaction** What is the position if the accord and satisfaction are not carried out? Are the parties in the same situation as if it had never been made or must the party aggrieved sue upon the broken accord and satisfaction and upon that only? The answer is that it depends upon the construction of the agreement that embodies the accord and satisfaction. If the satisfaction consists of a promise on the part of the tortfeasor, the interpretation of the agree-

---

[208] See para.26-076.
[209] *Valpy v Sanders* (1848) 5 C.B. 886; 136 E.R. 1128; *Morris v Robinson* (1824) 3 B. & C. 196; 107 E.R. 706.
[210] *Lythgoe v Vernon* (1860) 5 Hurl. & N. 180; 157 E.R. 1148.
[211] *Peytoe's Case* (1611) 9 Co. Rep. 77; 77 E.R. 847. It is important to note that since the claim will be for unliquidated damages an accord and satisfaction will be effective even though a court might have awarded more or less in the way of damages. "The agreed sum is a liquidated amount which replaces the claim for an illiquid sum. The effect of the compromise is to fix the amount of his claim in just the same way as if the case had gone to trial and he had obtained judgment": *Jameson v Central Electricity Generating Board (No.1)* [2000] 1 A.C. 455 at 474 per Lord Hope.
[212] *D & C Builders Ltd v Rees* [1966] 2 Q.B. 617.
[213] *British Russian Gazette & Trade Outlook Ltd v Associated Newspapers Ltd* [1933] 2 K.B. 616. Regarding the effect of an agreement with D1 where C also has a claim against D2, see *Jameson v Central Electricity Generating Board (No.1)* [2000] 1 A.C. 455 and para.22-007.
[214] *Lee v Lancashire and Yorkshire Rly Co* (1871) L.R. 6 Ch. App. 527; *Ellen v Great Northern Rly* (1901) 17 T.L.R. 453; *North British Rly Co v Wood* (1891) 18 R. (H.L.) 27.
[215] [1969] 1 W.L.R. 1378.

ment may be, "I accept this promise as an absolute discharge of your tortious liability". If so, all that the injured party can sue upon in the event of the tortfeasor not carrying out his promise is the contract which has been substituted for the tortious liability. Alternatively, the interpretation of the agreement may be, "I accept this promise as a discharge of your liability provided you carry it out". In that case, if the promise is not fulfilled, the injured party has two alternative remedies: he can either fall back upon his original claim in tort; or he can sue upon the contract which was intended to take its place. Somewhat different considerations apply to an accord and satisfaction that is expressed to be conditional in the first instance, as in the example given above of provisional acceptance of compensation in an accident. Here the injured party cannot have recourse to his action in tort unless the condition is not fulfilled. If it is fulfilled within the time specified by the agreement or, if no time is specified, within a reasonable time, then the tortious liability is extinguished. If it is not thus fulfilled, then the injured party can either rely upon his claim in tort or sue upon the conditional agreement which was substituted for it and which has been broken.

iii. Release

Closely related to accord and satisfaction is a release of tortious liability given **26-080** by the injured party. In fact, there seems to be little difference between the two concepts except that a release is usually, but not necessarily, embodied in a deed and the necessity for consideration is thus avoided.[216] A release is apparently effective whether it is given before or after an action against the tortfeasor is commenced.

iv. Prior Criminal Proceedings

Suppose that the claimant brings a private prosecution against the defendant for **26-081** assault and battery. Irrespective of the outcome of the prosecution, legislation provides that the fact that the prosecution was brought will provide the defendant with a defence to any civil liability that he might have otherwise incurred in respect of the act on which the prosecution was based.[217] The apparent rationale for this defence is that it would be wasteful and unjust to permit the claimant to pursue the defendant in the civil sphere in light of the prior prosecution. Several points should be noted about this defence.[218] First, it will not apply if the criminal proceedings were dismissed for some technical defect. Secondly, the defence will only apply if the criminal proceedings were instituted by or on behalf of the claimant, and not by someone else. Thirdly, where the defendant has been prosecuted and convicted that fact precludes not only a civil action for assault, but also an action using the assault as the basis for some other cause of action.[219] Fourthly, the defence does not apply in proceedings against anyone other than the defendant, so that the convic-

---

[216] *Phillips v Clagett* (1843) 11 M. & W. 84; 152 E.R. 725.

[217] Offences Against the Person Act 1861 ss.44–45.

[218] The Criminal Law Revision Committee recommended that it be abolished: Criminal Law Revision Committee, *Fourteenth Report: Offences Against the Person* (Cmnd. 7844, 1980). In *Wong v Parkside Health NHS Trust* [2001] EWCA Civ 1721; [2003] 3 All E.R. 932 at [16], Hale LJ described it as "anomalous".

[219] *Wong v Parkside Health NHS Trust* [2001] EWCA Civ 1721; [2003] 3 All E.R. 932.

tion of an employee for an assault committed in the course of his employment does not bar an action against his employer.[220]

v. Abuse of Process

26-082 **Generally** The doctrine of abuse of process advances the administration of justice by preventing the court's process from being corrupted. It applies when a litigant uses the court's process for a purpose that is significantly different from that for which it was intended. For example, the doctrine has been invoked to stay proceedings that are an attempt to circumvent the special procedure that governs claims for judicial review[221] or which constitute a collateral attack on the verdict of a criminal court.[222] It has also been used to stay actions in defamation where the value of the damage suffered by the claimant as a result of the publication of the defendant's defamatory statement is insignificant relative to the cost of the proceedings.[223] It is in principle abusive for a claimant to bring a claim (or for a defendant to raise a defence) in respect of a given cause of action if that claim (or defence) could have been brought (or raised) in earlier proceedings between the parties[224] and sometimes between different parties.

26-083 **Situations where proceedings do not constitute an abuse of process** The doctrine of abuse of process does not preclude a civil action simply because the defendant has been acquitted in the criminal court. Apart from any substantive differences between the relevant crime and the tort in which the proceedings are brought, the standards of proof are different and an acquittal in the criminal case is quite consistent with a finding of liability in the civil action. Neither does a conviction prevent the defendant from contesting liability in a case where a civil action can be brought against him. A contrary outcome would be inconsistent with s.11 of the Civil Evidence Act 1968,[225] which provides that a criminal conviction is, in civil proceedings, prima facie but not conclusive evidence that the defendant committed the offence.[226]

vi. Judgment

26-084   The rule that final judgment by a court of competent jurisdiction extinguishes a right of action has a twofold effect. First, it estops any party to the litigation and their privies from disputing afterwards the correctness of the decision either in law or in fact.[227] Secondly, it operates as a merger of the original cause of action in the

---

[220] *Dyer v Munday* [1895] 1 Q.B. 742.

[221] *O'Reilly v Mackman* [1983] 2 A.C. 237; *Clark v University of Lincolnshire and Humberside* [2000] 1 W.L.R. 1988.

[222] *Hunter v Chief Constable of the West Midlands Police* [1982] A.C. 529.

[223] See, e.g., *Jameel v Dow Jones & Co Inc* [2005] EWCA Civ 75; [2005] Q.B. 946; *Khader v Aziz* [2010] EWCA Civ 716; [2010] 1 W.L.R. 2673.

[224] *Johnson v Gore Wood & Co (No.1)* [2002] 2 A.C. 1 at 31. See also *Aldi Stores Ltd v WSP Group Plc* [2007] EWCA Civ 1260; [2008] 1 W.L.R. 748.

[225] See para.6-031.

[226] *J v Oyston, The Times,* 11 December 1998. *Brinks Ltd v Abu-Saleh* [1995] 1 W.L.R. 1478 cannot be supported if it lays down any other rule: *McCauley v Hope* [1999] 1 W.L.R. 1977.

[227] This rule does not prevent a party who considers that a judgment was obtained by fraud from bringing fresh proceedings for an order that the judgment be set aside: see *Takhar v Gracefield Develop-*

rights created by the judgment and these are either to levy execution against the defendant or to bring a new action upon the judgment (not upon the original claim, for that has perished). There are at least two reasons for this rule. The first is that there is a strong public interest in the finality of litigation: interest reipublicae ut sit finis litium. The second is concerned with justice as between the litigants. It would be unfair if the parties could pursue each other repeatedly in respect of liabilities that have already been decided.

vii. Assignment of Right of Action in Tort

Introduction   When a right of action in tort is transferred to another person, the **26-085** defendant will have a defence to liability in respect of any proceedings that are brought by the transferor. In certain circumstances, the defendant will also have a defence to an action commenced by the transferee.

The general rule is that actions in tort cannot be assigned   It is a longstand- **26-086** ing rule in the law of assignment that, while property can lawfully be assigned, a "bare right to litigate" cannot,[228] because to allow such an assignment would be to encourage undesirable speculation in lawsuits.[229] Indeed, the agreement would savour of maintenance and champerty, which, formerly, were themselves torts and are still grounds for striking down a contract and providing a defence to the as- signee's action.[230] This is not to say, however, that there can never be a valid as- signment of a right of action in tort and the basic rule must be read in the light of the following qualifications and exceptions.[231]

"Proper interest of assignee"   If A transfers property to B he may also assign a **26-087** right of action for breach of contract[232] (e.g., breach of covenant to repair in a lease) in relation to that property, for then, it has been said, the assignee buys the cause of action in order to protect the property he has bought.[233] It is submitted that such a case should be treated in the same way if the cause of action is in tort.[234] It is more difficult to know how far the doctrine stated in the House of Lords in *Trendtex Trad- ing Corp v Credit Suisse*,[235] a case of assignment of a claim for breach of contract, applies to tort cases.[236] It was said in that case that an assignee who has a "genuine

---

ments Ltd* [2019] UKSC 13; [2020] A.C. 450 esp at [60]. The claimant to such fresh proceedings does not need to establish that the fraud could not have been discovered with reasonable diligence prior to the judgment being entered.

[228] Reaffirmed in *Trendtex Trading Corp v Credit Suisse* [1982] A.C. 679.

[229] Some reasons formerly given for the rule are either unconvincing or obsolete. Thus, it was said in argument in *Anon* (1585) Godb. 81 at 81; 78 E.R. 50 at 50 that damages in the assigned action are too uncertain at the date of assignment, or that the assignee, "may be a man of great power, who might procure a jury to give him greater damages".

[230] *Laurent v Sale & Co* [1963] 1 W.L.R. 829.

[231] For statutory transmission on death, see Ch.24.

[232] *Ellis v Torrington* [1920] 1 K.B. 399.

[233] *Ellis v Torrington* [1920] 1 K.B. 399 at 412–413.

[234] See the comments of Lord Denning MR in *Trendtex Trading Corp v Credit Suisse* [1980] Q.B. 629 at 657.

[235] [1982] A.C. 679.

[236] But see *Brownton Ltd v Edward Moore Inbucon Ltd* [1985] 3 All E.R. 499, another contract case, at 509 per Lloyd LJ, whose statement of the principle of the *Trendtex* case applies to contract and tort alike.

commercial interest" in the enforcement of a claim may take a valid assignment of it so long as the transaction is not champertous and it seems that a genuine commercial interest may be present simply because the assignee is a creditor of the assignor. On this basis, unless an arbitrary line is to be drawn between contract and tort, it may be that, for example, an assignment to a bank of the assignor's claim for damages for negligent misstatement inducing a contract which the bank has financed, and on which it stands to lose, would be valid. In any event a trustee in bankruptcy and a liquidator have a statutory power to sell a cause of action on terms that the assignees will pay a share of the proceeds (this statutory power necessarily precluding any challenge on the grounds of maintenance or champerty)[237] and this can extend, for example, to a tort claim for negligent advice.[238] By contrast, it is thought that the law should still refuse to give effect to the assignment of, say, a claim for libel or for personal injuries even though the assignor was indebted to the assignee.[239]

26-088 **Judgment** No such problems arise with regard to the assignment of a judgment in a tort action. If the judgment has already been given, the rights of the creditor are assignable like any other debt.[240] Similarly, a person may assign the fruits of an action yet to be commenced, for this is no more than the assignment of property to be acquired. Thus, in *Glegg v Bromley*[241] an assignment pendente lite of the fruits of an action for slander was upheld.[242]

26-089 **Subrogation**[243] The commonest example of subrogation in this connection is in the law of insurance. An insurance company that has compensated a policyholder under an indemnity insurance policy stands in his shoes with regard to his claims against the person who caused the injury. Hence, if A by negligent driving of his car damages B's car, and X, with whom B is insured, compensates him, X can exploit B's action for negligence against A. The payment by the insurer under the policy does not provide the tortfeasor with a defence to a claim by the insured,[244] but if the latter recovers damages they are subject to a proprietary lien or charge in favour of the insurer.[245]

---

[237] *Grovewood Holdings Plc v James Capel & Co Ltd* [1995] Ch. 80 at 86; *Norglen Ltd v Reeds Rains Prudential Ltd* [1999] 2 A.C. 1.

[238] *Ramsey v Hartley* [1977] 1 W.L.R. 686. There is a full review of the law in *Empire Resolution Ltd v MPW Insurance Brokers Ltd* [1999] B.P.I.R. 486.

[239] Lord Roskill in *Trendtex Trading Corp v Credit Suisse* [1982] A.C. 679 at 702 refers to the principle that "causes of action which were essentially personal in their character, such as claims for defamation or personal injury, were incapable of assignment" but he is speaking in terms of the law 80 years ago and his general point is that the law of maintenance was then more severe. It seems that if A makes a voluntary payment to B to compensate B for loss caused by C, A may take a valid assignment of B's claim in tort against C: *Esso Petroleum Co Ltd v Hall Russell & Co Ltd* [1988] 3 W.L.R. 730 at 738.

[240] *Carrington v Harway* (1663) 1 Keb. 803; 83 E.R. 1252; *Goodman v Robinson* (1886) 18 Q.B.D. 332.

[241] [1912] 3 K.B. 474.

[242] *Cohen v Mitchell* (1890) 25 Q.B.D. 262 can also be supported on this ground, although other reasons were given for the decision.

[243] For a statement of the principle, see *Castellain v Preston* (1883) 11 Q.B.D. 380 at 387; *Burnand v Rodocanachi, Sons & Co* (1882) 7 App. Cas. 333 at 339; *Morris v Ford Motor Co Ltd* [1973] Q.B. 792.

[244] See para.1-021.

[245] *Lord Napier and Ettrick v Hunter* [1993] A.C. 713.

viii. Insolvency

Insolvency of the defendant   Historically, a claim for unliquidated damages in   **26-090**
tort was not provable as a bankruptcy debt so that the claim remained alive against
the bankrupt (who might acquire assets after his discharge) and liability did not pass
to his trustee.[246] A similar principle applied to the winding-up of an insolvent
company; however, since the company would generally then cease to exist there
was no equivalent to the personal liability of the individual bankrupt. Now, by the
Insolvency Act 1986, a liability in tort[247] is a "bankruptcy debt"[248] so that the claimant may seek to share in the assets along with the other creditors and discharge from
the bankruptcy provides the bankrupt person with a defence to liability in tort.[249]
This defence, unless the court otherwise directs, does not apply to liability for damages for personal injuries arising from "negligence, nuisance or breach of a statutory, contractual or other duty".[250]

Insolvency of claimant   Under the Insolvency Act 1986 the bankrupt's property[251]   **26-091**
forms, with certain exceptions, his estate, available for distribution among creditors.
If the injury is a purely personal one, like defamation, the right of action for it
remains exercisable by the injured party himself and does not pass to his trustee in
bankruptcy. Bankruptcy of the claimant is not a defence, therefore, in proceedings
for such injuries. But when the tort is to property (e.g., conversion of goods) then
the right to sue for it passes to the trustee, who can sell or assign it to anyone as
he, in his discretion, thinks fit. The upshot is that the defendant will have a defence
to proceedings brought by the claimant in respect of such torts.

ix. Limitation

Introduction   The defendant will have a defence—a time bar—if the claimant   **26-092**
fails to bring his proceedings sufficiently promptly.[252] The law on limitation is
extremely complex and of considerable practical significance. It is therefore worth
dealing with it in some detail. However, what follows is far from an exhaustive
account. It should be noted that a claimant may lose his action even if he brings
proceedings within the limitation period as the court enjoys the power to strike out
as an abuse of process claims brought within the limitation period which are
pursued in a dilatory manner and without any intention of bringing them to a
conclusion.[253]

---

[246] Tort claims became provable against the insolvent estate of a deceased person by the Law Reform
(Miscellaneous Provisions) Act 1934 s.1(1), (6).

[247] Except if based on fraud: Insolvency Act 1986 s.281(3).

[248] See s.382. By subs.(2): "in determining ... whether any liability in tort is a bankruptcy debt, the
bankrupt is deemed to become subject to that liability by reason of an obligation incurred at the time
when the cause of action accrued."

[249] Proceedings might be brought by the claimant against the bankrupt's insurers pursuant to the Third
Parties (Rights Against Insurers) Act 2010.

[250] Section 281(5). See also Road Traffic Act 1988 s.153.

[251] Defined in s.436 to include "things in action".

[252] For an overview of some of the central issues in the law on limitation, see Burrows in Dyson,
Goudkamp and Wilmot Smith (eds), *Defences in Tort* (2014).

[253] *Grovit v Doctor* [1997] 1 W.L.R. 640.

26-093 **Rationales for the defence** Limitation bars exist for several reasons. In the first place, they prevent the unfairness that would be caused to defendants if claimants could pursue them in respect of long-forgotten wrongdoing. Secondly, if limitation bars did not exist defendants might be put to the expense and inconvenience of keeping evidence indefinitely to ensure that they could defend claims that may never be brought. Thirdly, limitation bars may help claimants to put the past behind them and to move on with their lives. It is for this reason that statutes of limitation are sometimes known as "statues of peace". Fourthly, limitation bars reduce the probability that claims will need to be decided on the basis of stale evidence. Many types of evidence deteriorate with the passage of time (e.g., witnesses may die or leave the jurisdiction) and determining disputes on the basis of incomplete evidence involves an increased risk that the court will reach an incorrect conclusion. These considerations point to a short, definite time limit for the presentation of claims, but they have always been counterbalanced by other considerations of justice to the victim of the tort. Claimants must be given sufficient time within which to carry out investigations and to decide whether they have a claim. Furthermore, allowances need to be made for, for example, claimants who are suffering from a disability that renders them unable to pursue their claims or from whom relevant facts were concealed by the defendant.

26-094 **The general rules** The principal statute is the Limitation Act 1980,[254] with substantial amendments brought in by the Latent Damage Act 1986. Broadly speaking, actions founded on tort must be commenced within six years from the date when the cause of action accrued. In the case of personal injury claims, however, the period is three years. The limitation period for defamation and malicious falsehood is one year. The strictness of these rules is ameliorated in various ways. For example, the running of time is postponed where the claimant was ignorant of the fact that he had a claim and, in personal injury cases, by giving the court a discretion to override the time limits altogether.

26-095 **Burdens of pleading and proof** The defendant must plead a limitation defence, for the court will not of its own motion take notice that the action is out of time.[255] If a limitation bar is pleaded, the claimant has the burden of showing that his claim accrued within the relevant period.[256] Further, and at least as a general rule, where a claimant asserts that he is entitled to the benefit of a deferred date of knowledge[257] he also bears the onus of proof in that connection.[258] These rules are important exceptions to the general principle that the defendant bears the onus of establishing defences.

---

[254] The earliest comprehensive legislation was the Limitation Act 1623.

[255] *Dunsmore v Milton* [1938] 3 All E.R. 762. If the defendant decides to contest the case on its merits, it is not open to him to apply for permission to amend his pleadings so as to plead limitation at a later stage when it becomes apparent that he is likely to lose on the merits: *Ketteman v Hansel Properties Ltd* [1987] A.C. 189.

[256] *London Congregational Union Inc v Harriss & Harriss* [1988] 1 All E.R. 15; *Crocker v British Coal* (1996) 29 B.M.L.R. 159.

[257] See at paras 26-098–26-099.

[258] *AB v Ministry of Defence* [2012] UKSC 9; [2013] 1 A.C. 78 at [48]. For further consideration of nuances in relation to the onus of proof, see *Crocker v British Coal Corp* (1996) 29 B.M.L.R. 159 at 169–173.

Commencement of the limitation period According to the Limitation Act 1980 **26-096**
the period of limitation runs "from the date on which the cause of action accrued".
No explanation of "accrued" is given, but authorities regarding earlier legislation
establish that the period begins to run "from the earliest time at which an action
could be brought".[259] "Cause of action ... means that which makes action
possible."[260] A cause of action arises, therefore, at the moment when a state of facts
occurs which gives a potential claimant a right to succeed against a potential
defendant. There must be a claimant who can succeed, and a defendant against
whom he can succeed.[261] Thus, for example, when goods belonging to a person who
has died intestate have been converted after his death, the proper party to sue is the
administrator and time does not begin to run until he has taken out letters of
administration.[262] Similarly, where the tortfeasor is entitled to diplomatic immunity, time does not run in his favour until the termination of his period of office, for until then no action will lie against him.[263] A merely procedural bar to bringing a suit will not prevent time running.[264] If, however, time has begun to run, it will
continue to do so even over a period during which there is no one capable of suing
or of being sued.[265] The fact that the potential claimant is unable to identify the
defendant does not, in principle, prevent a cause of action accruing,[266] though this
is now qualified in many cases.[267] It is often the position that the tortious conduct
of the defendant will be a single act or omission that causes damage to be suffered
over a lengthy period of time. Once some damage has been suffered time begins
to run and the claimant cannot evade the limitation period by confining his claim
to losses that have occurred within the prescribed period before he commences
proceedings.[268] If a new claim is added to the pleadings via an amendment after a
limitation bar has descended, it will be deemed to have commenced together with
the initial cause of action provided that it arises out of the same or substantially the
same facts.[269]

Latent damage generally In the case of torts that are actionable per se, time **26-097**
begins to run, in general, at the moment the wrongful act was committed, whether

---

[259] *Reeves v Butcher* [1891] 2 Q.B. 509 at 511 per Lindley LJ. The day on which the cause of action
arose is excluded: *Marren v Dawson Bentley & Co Ltd* [1961] 2 Q.B. 135. If the last day of the period
is one when court offices are closed the claimant has until the first following day when they are open:
Kaur v S. Russell & Sons [1973] Q.B. 336. Proceedings are started when the claim form is received
in court even if there is delay in its issue: *Barnes v St Helens MBC* [2006] EWCA Civ 1372; [2007]
1 W.L.R. 879.

[260] *Board of Trade v Cayzer, Irvine & Co Ltd* [1927] A.C. 610 at 617 per Viscount Cave LC. Or in terms
of pleading, "Every fact which it would be necessary for the plaintiff to prove, if traversed, in order
to support his right to the judgment of the Court": *Read v Brown* (1888) 22 Q.B.D. 128 at 131 per
Lord Esher MR.

[261] *Thomson v Clanmorris* [1900] 1 Ch. 718 at 728–729.

[262] *Pratt v Swaine* (1828) 8 B. & C. 285; 108 E.R. 1049.

[263] *Musurus Bey v Gadban* [1894] 2 Q.B. 352.

[264] *Sevcon Ltd v Lucas CAV Ltd* [1986] 1 W.L.R. 462 (sealing of patent necessary before action could
be brought).

[265] *Rhodes v Smethurst* (1838) 4 M. & W. 42; 150 E.R. 1335; affirmed in (1840) 6 M. & W. 351; 151
E.R. 447.

[266] *RB Policies at Lloyd's v Butler* [1950] 1 K.B. 76.

[267] See para.26-101.

[268] *Khan v RM Falvey & Co* [2002] EWCA Civ 400; [2002] P.N.L.R. 28.

[269] See Limitation Act 1980 s.35; CPR 17.4(2); *Akers v Samba Financial Group* [2019] EWCA Civ 416;
[2019] 4 W.L.R. 54.

the injured party knows of it or not, provided that there is no fraudulent concealment.[270] This is so even where the resulting damage (if any) does not occur or is not discovered until a later date.[271] Conversely, in respect of torts of which damage is the gist time runs from the date on which the damage was sustained.[272] Damage may be suffered before it is apparent to the claimant, and such latent damage can cause time to run.[273] In *Bell v Peter Browne & Co*[274] a husband and wife upon the breakdown of their marriage in 1978 agreed that the matrimonial home should be transferred into the wife's name but that the husband's interest in the proceeds of sale should be protected by some legal mechanism. No steps were in fact taken by the husband's solicitors to effect this protection and eight years later the wife sold the house and spent all the proceeds. Time began to run for the tort claim at the latest when, after the completion of the transfer, a competent solicitor would have taken steps to protect the husband's interest, such as by lodging a Land Registry caution against the property.

26-098   Latent Damage Act 1986   The Latent Damage Act 1986 added ss.14A and 14B to the Limitation Act 1980. These sections are generally applicable to actions for damages for negligence (other than one that includes a claim for damages for personal injury) where latent damage is involved, though not to actions for breach of contract, even though the claim is based on breach of an express or implied term to take reasonable care.[275] In very general terms, s.14A(4)(b)[276] adds to the basic period of six years that commences with the accrual of the cause of action an alternative period of three years from the earliest date on which the claimant had not only the right to sue but also knew or reasonably could have known about the damage and its attributability to the act or omission alleged to constitute negligence. This is relevant only if the alternative period expires later than the basic period of six years. Hence, if the facts of *Bell v Peter Browne & Co* were to recur, the basic six-year period would commence and finish at the same times as it did in that case but the claimant would then have three years from the point, after the sale of the house by the wife, when the problem came to light. The alternative three-year period may commence while the initial six-year period is still running or may start time running afresh after the initial period has expired, but superimposed upon both periods is the so-called "long-stop" provision of s.14B, which bars any claim for negligence (other than in respect of personal injury) 15 years from the date of the last act of negligence to which the damage is attributable. The operation of the two sections may be illustrated in the context of a *"White v Jones"* claim[277] by an intended beneficiary against a solicitor who fails in 2000 to carry out his client's instructions to confer a benefit upon the beneficiary by will, the testator dying in 2007. It is unclear whether time starts running against the beneficiary when the will

---

[270] *Granger v George* (1826) 5 B. & C. 149; 108 E.R. 56. See, further, para.26-099

[271] *Howell v Young* (1826) 5 B. & C. 259; 108 E.R. 97.

[272] *Backhouse v Bonomi* (1861) 9 H.L. Cas. 503; 11 E.R. 825.

[273] There must, however, be a present loss, not merely the contingency of one at some time in the future: *Law Society v Sephton & Co* [2006] UKHL 22; [2006] 2 A.C. 543.

[274] [1990] 2 Q.B. 495.

[275] *Iron Trade Mutual Insurance Co Ltd v J.K. Buckenham Ltd* [1990] 1 All E.R. 808; *Société Commerciale de Reassurance v ERAS (International) Ltd* [1992] 2 All E.R. 82n.

[276] This provision is modelled closely on s.14, dealing with limitation in relation to personal injury proceedings. Section 14 is discussed in para.26-101.

[277] See para.5-046.

is executed or when the testator dies but, even if it is the former, a new three-year period will begin when the problem comes to light on the testator's death in 2007. If, however, the testator dies in 2016 the beneficiary's claim would be extinguished in any event by the long-stop provision.

The relevant provisions of the Latent Damage Act 1986 were enacted largely in response to the problem of latent damage in the context of defective buildings. Ironically, it now seems that most of the cases upon which the provisions were intended to operate do not raise any cause of action at all since the decision of the House of Lords in *Murphy v Brentwood DC*[278] that claims for structural defects in buildings do not generally sound in tort. However, there may still be "building" cases for which s.14A has some significance. The most obvious—though probably rare in practice—are those in which operations by the defendant cause latent damage to an existing building owned by the claimant.[279] In addition, there may be cases in which the claimant can found a claim on *Hedley Byrne & Co Ltd v Heller & Partners Ltd* against someone involved in the design or building of premises that are defective from the start.

Fraud and concealment Related to the problem of latent damage is s.32 of the **26-099** Limitation Act 1980 dealing with fraud and concealment. The effect of s.32 is as follows. Where the claimant's action is based on the fraud of the defendant or his agent[279] or of any person through whom the defendant (or his agent) claims time does not run until the claimant has discovered the fraud or could with reasonable diligence have discovered it.[280] This part of s.32 is limited to cases where the action is actually founded on fraud (e.g., where it is a claim for damages for deceit or to rescind a contract) and does not extend to causes of action in which "dishonest" or "fraudulent" conduct may figure (e.g., conversion).[281] However, by s.32(1)(b) the same postponement of the running of time applies where "any fact relevant to the plaintiff's right of action[282] has been deliberately concealed from him by the defendant". This includes a case of "deliberate commission of a breach of duty in circumstances in which it is unlikely to be discovered for some time".[283] Section 32(1)(b) applies where the defendant commits a tort which is not at the time known to the claimant and then, at a later date, conceals it. The ideal answer in such a case would be to "stop the clock" at the time of the concealment and to restart it when the wrong is discovered (or becomes discoverable) by the claimant. However, the words of the Act will not bear this interpretation, so the result is that a new limitation period starts from the date of discovery.[284]

Section 32 will prevent the running of time in many cases where there is a wrong-

---

[278] [1991] 1 A.C. 398, see para.10-047.
[279] Which includes an independent contractor: *Applegate v Moss* [1971] 1 Q.B. 406.
[280] Section 32(1)(a). On reasonable diligence, see *Peco Arts Inc v Hazlitt Gallery Ltd* [1983] 1 W.L.R. 1315 (a s.32(1)(c) case) and *Barnstaple Boat Co Ltd v Jones* [2007] EWCA Civ 727; [2008] 1 All E.R. 1124.
[281] *Beaman v A.R.T.S. Ltd* [1949] 1 K.B. 550 at 558, 567.
[282] This has been interpreted to mean a fact that must be alleged and proved to establish a cause of action. It is not enough that the defendant has concealed facts going to the strength of the claimant's case or the availability of a defence: *Johnson v Chief Constable of Surrey, The Times,* 23 November 1992; *C v Mirror Group Newspapers* [1997] 1 W.L.R. 131; *AIC Ltd v ITS Testing Services (UK) Ltd* [2006] EWCA Civ 1601; [2007] 1 All E.R. (Comm.) 667.
[283] Section 32(2).
[284] *Sheldon v RHM Outhwaite (Underwriting Agencies) Ltd* [1996] A.C. 102. Logically this applies even if the claim was statute-barred before the concealment took place.

ful dealing[285] with goods by a person who has custody of, or a limited interest in, them and hence the opportunity to conceal that dealing. However, it would be hard if the running of time were also suspended against defendants who were innocent purchasers. Therefore, s.32(3)(b) provides that nothing in the section shall enable an action to be brought to recover property or its value against the purchaser of the property, in any case where the property has been purchased for valuable consideration by an innocent third party since the fraud or concealment.

26-099A **Extinction of title: theft** Section 3(1) of the Limitation Act 1980 provides that once a cause of action for conversion has accrued in respect of a chattel, no action may be brought for any subsequent conversion after the expiry of six years from the accrual of the original cause of action unless, of course, the owner has recovered possession of it in the meanwhile. Section 3(2) states that once the period of limitation in respect of the original cause of action has expired, then the owner's title is extinguished. So, for example, if D converts C's goods and later sells them to X, once six years have elapsed from the date of the taking, not only has C lost the right to sue either D or X, but X is in a position to deal with them as absolute owner notwithstanding that, at the time of the sale to him, D had no title which D could pass on to him. However, the Law Reform Committee was troubled at the prospect of time running in favour of a thief or receiver and, consequently, we have the complicated provisions of s.4 of the Limitation Act 1980. The effect of the section is that time does not run against the owner in respect of the theft[286] of his chattel or any conversion "related to the theft", which latter phrase means any subsequent conversion other than a purchase in good faith.[287] Thus, if property is stolen by D and then sold to X (who is aware of its origin) and then given by X to Y, the owner's rights of action against D, X and Y continue indefinitely and his title will never be extinguished. However, the occurrence of a good faith purchase starts time running against the owner in favour of the good faith purchaser (and any converter from him). After six years the owner will no longer be able to sue the good faith purchaser or anyone who subsequently dealt with the goods[288] and his title to the goods will be extinguished. However, he retains his right to sue the original thief and other converters who preceded the good faith purchaser.

26-100 **Disabilities** One of the longest standing derogations from standard limitation periods occurs where the claimant is under a disability. If, on the date when the right of action accrued, the person to whom it accrued was under a disability, time does not begin to run until he ceases to be under a disability or dies (whichever first occurs).[289] For these purposes, the law recognises only two forms of disability: infancy and lack of mental capacity.[290] Infancy presents no difficulty, for it means

---

[285] It is assumed in this discussion that the wrongful dealing does not amount to theft. If it does, time does not run because of the provisions of s.4: see para.26-099A. Section 32 is inapplicable in the normal case of theft where the thief is unknown or untraceable: *RB Policies at Lloyd's v Butler* [1950] 1 K.B. 76.

[286] This includes fraud and blackmail: s.4(5)(b).

[287] Any conversion following the theft is presumed to be related to the theft unless the contrary is shown: s.4(4).

[288] If this person is a thief, all of the provisions of the section will apply over again vis-a-vis the good faith purchaser, who is now the owner.

[289] Section 28(1).

[290] Section 38(2).

simply a person under the age of 18. The question whether a person has the mental capacity to conduct legal proceedings falls to be determined by reference to the Mental Capacity Act 2005.[291] What is the position of a claimant who had mental capacity when time began to run but later loses it; or of a claimant who was an infant when his cause of action accrued and suffered a loss of mental capacity before he reached the age of 18; or of a claimant who is under a disability at the moment when he succeeds to the title of a predecessor who was under no disability? The Limitation Act 1980 provides that unless the right of action first accrues to a person who is then disabled the disability has no effect.[292] Where, however, there are successive disabilities in the same person (lack of mental capacity supervening on infancy) time does not run until the latter of the disabilities has ended, provided that there is no interval of ability between the disabilities.[293]

Personal injury and death: a separate regime The limitation period regime applicable to claims for personal injury and death is found in ss.11–14 and 33 of the Limitation Act 1980. Section 11(1) states that the provisions apply to: **26-101**

> "any action for damages for negligence, nuisance or breach of duty (whether the duty exists by virtue of a contract or of provision made by or under a statute or independently of any contract or any such provision) where the damages claimed by the claimant for the negligence, nuisance or breach of duty consist of or include damages in respect of personal injuries to the claimant or any other person".

If, therefore, the claimant seeks damages for personal injury and damage to property in the same action both claims are governed by the provisions concerned. For a long while it was held that s.11 did not apply to actions for intentional trespass to the person,[294] but that such claims were instead governed by the six-year period laid down in s.2. As we shall see, although the basic period under the personal injury provisions is shorter, the fact that the claim fell under s.2 was by no means necessarily to the claimant's advantage, because there could be no extension of the six-year period.[295] However, in *A v Hoare*[296] the House of Lords departed from this view and held that ss.11–14 and 33 apply to personal injury caused by trespass. These provisions also capture cases where the owner of a car is sued for allowing an uninsured person to drive it.[297]

Personal injury and death: the expression "personal injuries" The expression "personal injuries" includes any disease and any impairment of a person's **26-102**

---

[291] See para.4-014.
[292] Section 28(1)–(2). If the claimant is rendered immediately mentally incapable by the tort itself he is disabled when the cause of action accrues, for the law takes no account of parts of a day: *Kirby v Leather* [1965] 2 Q.B. 367. The position is otherwise if the incapacity, though caused by the tort, comes on some days later. However, that might be a pointer towards the court's exercising its discretion under s.33 of the Act, see para.26-093.
[293] This is the effect of s.28(1), which refers to the claimant's ceasing to be under a disability. See also *Borrows v Ellison* (1871) L.R. 6 Ex. 128.
[294] *Stubbings v Webb* [1993] A.C. 498.
[295] See s.33, which is discussed below.
[296] [2008] UKHL 6; [2008] 1 A.C. 844.
[297] *Norman v Ali* [2000] R.T.R 107. Regarding this liability, see para.8-012. However, it seems that the three-year period does not generally apply to a claim against a solicitor for failure to pursue his client's personal injury action (but see *Bennett v Greenland Houchen & Co* [1998] P.N.L.R. 458 (solicitors' negligence alleged to have caused depression)).

physical or mental condition.[298] This covers a claim based on a failure to diagnose and treat learning difficulties such as dyslexia[299] and an unwanted pregnancy and confinement is also a "personal injury" for this purpose.[300] However, a claim solely in respect of a loss of stored substances obtained from a person's body is not one for personal injury,[301] though a claim for psychiatric injury arising from such a loss is.[302]

26-103 **Personal injury and death: the limitation period** Where s.11 applies the limitation period is three years from the date on which the cause of action accrued or the date (if later) of the claimant's "knowledge".[303]

26-104 **Personal injury and death: knowledge generally** By virtue of s.14, a person has "knowledge" when he knows all the following facts (although as is explained below, knowledge may be constructive): (1) that the injury in question was significant;[304] (2) that the injury was attributable in whole or in part to the act or omission which is alleged to constitute negligence, nuisance or breach of duty; (3) the identity of the defendant;[305] and (4) if it is alleged that the act or omission in question was that of a person other than the defendant,[306] the identity of that person and the additional facts supporting the bringing of an action against the defendant.

A firm belief may amount to knowledge. A claimant is likely to have acquired knowledge of the facts mentioned in s.14 "when he first came reasonably to believe them".[307] A belief will be sufficient for this purpose once the claimant holds it "with sufficient confidence to justify embarking on the preliminaries to the issue of [proceedings] ... taking legal and other advice and collecting evidence".[308] A mere suspicion by the claimant that he might have grounds to issue proceedings is insufficient. "The focus is upon the moment when it is *reasonable* for the claimant to embark on such an investigation."[309] Once proceedings have been issued, it is no

---

[298] Section 38(1).

[299] *Adams v Bracknell Forest BC* [2004] UKHL 29; [2005] 1 A.C. 76.

[300] *Walkin v South Manchester HA* [1995] 1 W.L.R. 1543. Where damages for the cost of the child's upbringing are available that claim, too, falls within this provision though whether that is consistent with the reasoning in *McFarlane v Tayside Health Board* [2002] 2 A.C. 59 (see para.25-021) is debatable: see *Godfrey v Gloucestershire Royal Infirmary NHS Trust* [2003] EWHC 549 (QB).

[301] *Yearworth v North Bristol NHS Trust* [2009] EWCA Civ 37; [2010] Q.B. 1.

[302] *Yearworth v North Bristol NHS Trust* [2009] EWCA Civ 37; [2010] Q.B. 1 at [18].

[303] Section 11(4).

[304] Whether the claimant knew that any acts or omissions did or did not, as a matter of law, involve negligence, nuisance or breach of duty is irrelevant: s.14(1). Thus, the advice of the claimant's solicitors that the defendant's conduct does not amount to a tort will not prevent time running, although the claimant might have an action against them for professional negligence. Similarly, time runs even if the advice is correct at the time but a subsequent appellate decision makes the conduct actionable: *Robinson v St Helens MBC* [2002] EWCA Civ 1099 (QB); [2003] P.I.Q.R. P128; *Rowe v Kingston-upon-Hull CC* [2003] EWCA Civ 1281; [2004] P.I.Q.R. P16 at [24]; *Awoyomi v Radford* [2007] EWHC 1671; [2008] Q.B. 793.

[305] Complications can arise where there is a group of companies under common control: *Simpson v Norwest Holst Southern Ltd* [1980] 1 W.L.R. 968; *Cressey v E Timm & Son Ltd* [2005] EWCA Civ 763; [2005] 1 W.L.R. 3926.

[306] e.g., where the defendant is an employer who is vicariously liable.

[307] *AB v Ministry of Defence* [2012] UKSC 9; [2013] 1 A.C. 78 at [11] per Lord Wilson.

[308] *Halford v Brookes* [1991] 1 W.L.R. 428 at 443 per Lord Donaldson MR, approved in *AB v Ministry of Defence* [2012] UKSC 9; [2013] 1 A.C. 78.

[309] *AB v Ministry of Defence* [2012] UKSC 9; [2013] 1 A.C. 78 at [12] per Lord Wilson (emphasis in original).

longer open to the claimant to argue that he lacks the knowledge necessary for the limitation period to run.[310]

Personal injury and death: knowledge that the injury in question was   **26-105**
"significant"   An injury is "significant"[311] if the claimant would reasonably have considered it sufficiently serious to justify his instituting proceedings for damages against a defendant who did not dispute liability and was able to satisfy a judgment.[312] Section 14 has not proved easy to apply but in *Spargo v North Essex DHA*[313] the Court of Appeal distilled from earlier case law the following guidelines[314]:

"(1)   The knowledge required ... is a broad knowledge of the essence of the causally relevant act or omission to which the injury is attributable;

(2)   'Attributable' in this context means 'capable of being attributed to', in the sense of being a real possibility;

(3)   A plaintiff has the requisite knowledge when she knows enough to make it reasonable for her to begin to investigate whether or not she has a case against the defendant. Another way of putting this is to say that she will have such knowledge if she so firmly believes that her condition is capable of being attributed to an act or omission which she can identify (in broad terms) that she goes to a solicitor to seek advice about making a claim for compensation;

(4)   On the other hand she will not have the requisite knowledge if she thinks she knows the acts or omissions she should investigate but in fact is barking up the wrong tree: or if her knowledge of what the defendant did or did not do is so vague or general that she cannot fairly be expected to know what she should investigate; or if her state of mind is such that she thinks her condition is capable of being attributed to the act or omission alleged to constitute negligence, but she is not sure about this, and would need to check with an expert before she could be properly said to know that it was."

Personal injury and death: knowledge and expert advice   For the purposes of   **26-106**
s.14 "knowledge" includes knowledge that the claimant might reasonably have been expected to acquire from facts observable or ascertainable by him and from facts ascertainable by him with the help of medical or other appropriate expert advice which it is reasonable for him to seek. However, he is not fixed with knowledge of a fact that is ascertainable only with the help of expert advice so long as he has taken all reasonable steps to obtain (and, where appropriate, to act on) this advice.[315] Thus, where the claimant suffered injury by a piece of metal flying off a hammer in 1957, the failure of the expert who later conducted a hardness test to notice the defect that was in fact the cause of the accident prevented time from running against the claimant with the result that the claimant's personal representative was able to bring a

---

[310] *AB v Ministry of Defence* [2012] UKSC 9; [2013] 1 A.C. 78 at [3], [67], [71].

[311] It has been held that if the claimant knows that one injury is significant, time runs even in respect of another injury sustained in the same incident the significance of which he is unaware: *Bristow v Grout, The Times,* 3 November 1986.

[312] Section 14(2). It follows that even a quite minor injury with no long-term effects of which the claimant is then aware may justify the institution of proceedings: *Albonetti v Wirral MBC* [2008] EWCA Civ 783.

[313] [1997] P.I.Q.R. P235 at 242 per Brooke LJ. See also *Haward v Fawcetts* [2006] UKHL 9; [2006] 1 W.L.R. 682 regarding s.14A, which is couched in similar terms.

[314] In *AB v Ministry of Defence* [2012] UKSC 9; [2013] 1 A.C 78 at [68] per Lord Wilson it was stressed that these words should not be "treated as if they were [a] statutory text" and that "[t]he words of the 1980 Act themselves must be the starting-point".

[315] Section 14(3).

successful action in 1975.[316] Where a claimant has the requisite knowledge and then consults an expert the law will not deem that the claimant obtained the knowledge at the time at which he consulted the expert.[317]

26-107 Personal injury and death: the test for knowledge is impersonal At one time the view was taken that the issue of knowledge under s.14 should be considered on a basis that was "partly subjective and partly objective",[318] taking account of matters like the claimant's intelligence and the effect on him of his injury. However, the current view is expressed by Lord Hoffmann in *A v Hoare*[319] in the following terms:

> "I respectfully think that the notion of the test being partly objective and partly subjective is somewhat confusing. Section 14(2) is a test for what counts as a significant injury. The material to which that test applies is generally 'subjective' in the sense that it is applied to what the claimant knows of his injury rather than the injury as it actually was. Even then, his knowledge may have to be supplemented with imputed 'objective' knowledge under section 14(3). But the test itself is an entirely impersonal standard: not whether the claimant himself would have considered the injury sufficiently serious to justify proceedings but whether he would 'reasonably' have done so. You ask what the claimant knew about the injury he had suffered, you add any knowledge about the injury which may be imputed to him under section 14(3) and you then ask whether a reasonable person with that knowledge would have considered the injury sufficiently serious to justify his instituting proceedings for damages against a defendant who did not dispute liability and was able to satisfy a judgment.
>
> It follows that I cannot accept that one must consider whether someone 'with [the] plaintiff's intelligence' would have been reasonable if he did not regard the injury as sufficiently serious. That seems to me to destroy the effect of the word 'reasonably'. Judges should not have to grapple with the notion of the reasonable unintelligent person. Once you have ascertained what the claimant knew and what he should be treated as having known, the actual claimant drops out of the picture. Section 14(2) is, after all, simply a standard of the seriousness of the injury and nothing more. Standards are in their nature impersonal and do not vary with the person to whom they are applied."

A reason for this shift is that even if the claimant fails on the date of knowledge issue it is open to the court to override the limitation period under s.33 and that is the right place to deal with, for example, the question of the impact of the injury on what the claimant could reasonably be expected to have done,[320] though it should not "be supposed that the exercise of the court's s.33 discretion will invariably replicate" the position that prevailed under the former interpretation of s.14.[321]

26-108 Personal injury and death: claims brought under the Fatal Accidents Act 1976 If the claim is brought under the Fatal Accidents Act 1976 the time limit is found in s.12 of the Limitation Act 1980. No action can be brought under the Fatal Accidents Act unless the deceased himself could have maintained an action at the date of his death.[322] Subject, therefore, to the court's power to override the time limit, any potential right of action under the Fatal Accidents Act will be lost three

---

[316] *Marston v British Railways Board* [1976] I.C.R. 124.
[317] *AB v Ministry of Defence* [2012] UKSC 9; [2013] 1 A.C. 78 at [13].
[318] See *McCafferty v Metropolitan Police District Receiver* [1977] 1 W.L.R. 1073.
[319] [2008] UKHL 6; [2008] 1 A.C. 844 at [34]–[35].
[320] [2008] UKHL 6; [2008] 1 A.C. 844 at [45].
[321] [2008] UKHL 6; [2008] 1 A.C. 844 at [87].
[322] Section 12(1).

years after the accident or the date of the deceased's knowledge if later.[323] If the deceased has a cause of action at the date of his death, then the dependant may bring an action, again subject to the court's power to override the time limit,[324] within three years of the date of the death or the date of the dependant's knowledge, whichever is later.[325] There is of course often more than one dependant and in that event the provision regarding the date of knowledge is to be applied to each of them separately and anyone debarred by this is to be excluded from the action.[326]

Personal injury and death: the discretion to override the statutory time   **26-109**
limit   In cases where the limitation period is prescribed by s.11 or s.12, s.33 confers on the court a power to override the statutory time limits if it appears to the court to be equitable to do so having regard to the degree to which the primary limitation rules prejudice the claimant and any exercise of the power would prejudice the defendant.[327] When deciding whether to invoke this power, s.33(3) directs the court to have regard to all the circumstances of the case and in particular to: (1) the length of, and reasons[328] for, the delay[329] on the part of the claimant; (2) the effect of the delay upon the evidence in the case; (3) the conduct of the defendant after the cause of action arose, including his response to the claimant's reasonable request for information; (4) the duration of any disability of the claimant arising after the accrual of the cause of action; (5) the extent to which the claimant acted promptly and reasonably once he knew[330] he might have an action for damages; and (6) the steps, if any, taken by the claimant to obtain medical, legal or other expert advice and the nature of any such advice as he may have received.

Although it has been said that the exercise of the power in s.33 represents "an exceptional indulgence"[331] to a claimant and that the claimant carries a "heavy burden"[332] in establishing that it should be invoked, the power in s.33 is not infrequently exercised.[333] Subject to the duty to act judicially, the judge's discretion is unfettered[334] and the matters set out in s.33(3) are by way of example and

---

[323] Section 11. By s.12(1): "[W]here any such action by the injured person would have been barred by the time limit in section 11 … no account shall be taken of the possibility of that time limit being overridden under section 33."

[324] Section 33(1).

[325] Section 12(2).

[326] Section 13. This is less significant than it might seem, because the dependants will commonly include children, against whom time would not run until the age of majority.

[327] Section 33(1). "Parliament has now decided that uncertain justice is preferable to certain injustice": *Firman v Ellis* [1978] Q.B. 886 at 911 per Ormrod LJ.

[328] Which may include not only the express reasons given by the claimant, but also the subconscious factors which may have prevented him from litigating: *McCafferty v Metropolitan Police District Receiver* [1977] 1 W.L.R. 1073.

[329] Which means the delay after the primary limitation period has expired: *Thompson v Brown Construction (Ebbw Vale) Ltd* [1981] 1 W.L.R. 744 at 751; *Donovan v Gwentoys Ltd* [1990] 1 W.L.R. 472; *McDonnell v Walker* [2009] EWCA Civ 1257; [2010] C.P. Rep. 14. But prior delay is part of the "circumstances of the case": *Fudge v Hawkins and Holmes Ltd* [2018] EWHC 453 (QB) at [17].

[330] Which means actual knowledge, not the deemed knowledge which may arise under s.14: *Eastman v London Country Bus Services, The Times,* 2 November 1985.

[331] *KR v Bryn Alyn Community Ltd* [2003] EWCA Civ 85; [2003] Q.B. 1441 at [74] per Auld LJ.

[332] *KR v Bryn Alyn Community Ltd* [2003] EWCA Civ 85; [2003] Q.B. 1441 at [74] per Auld LJ. cf. *Fudge v Hawkins and Holmes Ltd* [2018] EWHC 453 (QB) at [10].

[333] Guidance on the exercise of the s.33 discretion in child abuse cases is provided in *AB v Nugent Care Society* [2009] EWCA Civ 827; [2010] 1 W.L.R. 516.

[334] *Donovan v Gwentoys Ltd* [1990] 1 W.L.R. 472; *Horton v Sadler* [2006] UKHL 27; [2007] 1 A.C.

not definitive.[335] The question of proportionality is important in the exercise of any discretion and courts "should be slow to exercise their discretion in favour of a claimant in the absence of cogent medical evidence showing a serious effect on the claimant's health or enjoyment of life and employability".[336] Where the claimant has two or more claims that were commenced after the time bar descended, the exercise of the discretion should be considered separately in relation to each claim.[337]

The analysis required by the discretion is essentially a balancing one and the balance will come down heavily in favour of the defendant where, for example, he is required to meet a claim that is first presented years after the wrong[338] and which "relies almost exclusively on the fading memory of the Claimant".[339] Furthermore, the longer the delay after the occurrence of the matters giving rise to the cause of action the more likely it is that the balance of prejudice has swung against the exercise of the discretion in the claimant's favour. Thus in *Adams v Bracknell Forest BC*[340] the House of Lords declined to exercise the discretion in respect of a claim alleging that the defendants were at fault in failing to diagnose and treat the claimant's dyslexia: the claim was brought 14 years after his last contact with the defendants and 12 years after he had reached the age of majority, there were no records to enable the defendants to rebut the allegations and in view of the uncertainties of proof of causation of the claimant's current condition and its effect on his life and employment the damages would be likely to be modest. The mere fact that the exercise of the discretion will deprive the defendant of a limitation defence is not of itself "prejudice" to him: if, for example, he has had early notice of the possibility of a claim he will have had opportunity to investigate it and some delay in issuing proceedings after the expiry of the limitation period will have had no effect on his ability to defend.[341] Although the fact that the defendant is insured is a relevant consideration, it is wrong to take the line that an insured defendant cannot establish prejudice since only his insurers will suffer and they are not parties to the action. The correct approach is to treat the defendant and his insurers as a composite unit: insurers should not be penalised by being made to fight claims that an uninsured defendant would not be held bound to fight.[342] The fact that the claimant has a professional negligence claim against his solicitors for failing to issue proceedings[343] is a highly relevant circumstance,[344] and prima facie it is the claimant, and not the defendant, who should bear the consequences of their default.[345] However, in such a scenario the court must bear in mind the difficulty, delay and expense that may be caused to the claimant by having to change horses

---

307.

[335] *Nash v Eli Lilly & Co* [1993] 1 W.L.R. 782.

[336] *Robinson v St Helens MBC* [2002] EWCA Civ 1099; [2003] P.I.Q.R. P128 at [33] per Sir Murray Stuart-Smith.

[337] *Nash v Eli Lilly & Co* [1993] 1 W.L.R. 782 at 808–810.

[338] Even though the "delay" referred to in s.33(3) is that occurring after the expiry of the limitation period delay before then is relevant in determining the prejudice to the defendant: *Donovan v Gwentoys Ltd* [1990] 1 W.L.R. 472 at 479.

[339] *Fudge v Hawkins and Holmes Ltd* [2018] EWHC 453 (QB) at [84] per Sir Robert Francis.

[340] [2004] UKHL 29; [2005] 1 A.C. 76

[341] *Cain v Francis* [2008] EWCA Civ 1451; [2009] Q.B. 754.

[342] *Kelly v Bastible* (1996) 36 B.M.L.R. 51.

[343] *Donovan v Gwentoys Ltd* [1990] 1 W.L.R. 472.

[344] *Thompson v Brown Construction (Ebbw Vale) Ltd* [1981] 1 W.L.R. 744 at 752; *McDonnell v Walker* [2009] EWCA Civ 1257; [2010] C.P. Rep 14.

[345] *Horton v Sadler* [2006] UKHL 27; [2007] 1 A.C. 307 at [53].

in midstream[346] and the fact that the solicitor will have a greater knowledge of the weaknesses of the case than will the defendant.[347]

The Consumer Protection Act 1987   We have seen that the Consumer Protec-   **26-110** tion Act 1987 imposes strict liability for defective products.[348] Although the Act will apply to some instances of property damage it is overwhelmingly concerned with personal injury.[349] Section 11A of the Limitation Act 1980 lays down limitation rules for claims under the 1987 Act that are largely identical to those generally applicable in personal injury cases[350]: a primary three-year period from the damage, an alternative period running from the claimant's knowledge and a power to override the limitation period. However, there is one major difference: no action can be brought in any case more than 10 years after the date when the product was put into circulation.[351] This bar cannot be overridden by the court under s.33 of the Limitation Act 1980 and it applies even if the claimant was under a disability or there was fraud, concealment or mistake, and even if no cause of action could have arisen within the 10-year period because there was no damage.[352] None of these provisions, however, affects an action for common law negligence.

Defamation and malicious falsehood   By s.4A of the Limitation Act 1980, there   **26-111** is a limitation period of one year from the accrual of the cause of action in cases of libel, slander and malicious falsehood. Under s.32A the court may in its discretion allow a case to proceed outside this time if it would be equitable to do so having regard to the relative prejudice to the claimant and the defendant.[353]

Contribution   Section 10 of the Limitation Act 1980 provides that a claim to   **26-112** recover statutory contribution must be brought within two years of the date when the right to contribution first accrued.[354] If the tortfeasor claiming contribution has himself been sued by the victim of the tort, then the right to contribution accrues when judgment is given against him which quantifies his liability;[355] if he

---

[346] *Thompson v Brown Construction (Ebbw Vale) Ltd* [1981] 1 W.L.R. 744 at 750; *Firman v Ellis* [1978] Q.B. 886.

[347] *Hartley v Birmingham City DC* [1992] 1 W.L.R. 968.

[348] See Ch.11.

[349] Where property damage alone is sued for the limitation period is three years, not the usual six: Limitation Act 1980 s.11A(4). The Latent Damage Act 1986 does not apply because this is not an action for negligence, but by s.5(5) of the Consumer Protection Act 1987 Act time runs from the date when the damage occurred or the earliest time at which a person with an interest in the property had knowledge of the material facts (as to which see subss.(6) and (7)).

[350] *AB v Ministry of Defence* [2012] UKSC 9; [2013] 1 A.C. 78 at [78].

[351] This means the moment when the product leaves the production process and enters a marketing process in which it is offered to the public for use or consumption: *O'Byrne v Sanofi Pasteur MSD Ltd* [2006] 1 W.L.R. 1606.

[352] See Limitation Act 1980 ss.11A(3), 28(7) and 32(4A).

[353] This is modelled on s.33 and s.32A(2) directs the court to have regard to certain factors comparable to those listed in s.33(3). See *Steedman v BBC* [2001] EWCA Civ 1534; [2002] E.M.L.R. 318; *Nugent v Willers* [2019] UKPC 1; [2019] E.M.L.R. 14.

[354] The legislation thus gives added importance to the possibility of a common law claim between tortfeasors, e.g., by virtue of an express contract between them or under *Lister v Romford Ice and Cold Storage Co Ltd* [1957] A.C. 555 (see para.21-038) since the limitation period for such claims remains at six years.

[355] Section 10(3), as interpreted in *Aer Lingus Plc v Gildacroft Ltd* [2006] EWCA Civ 4; [2006] 1 W.L.R. 1173.

compromises the action the right accrues when the amount of the payment to be made by him to the victim is agreed.[356]

26-113 **Law Commission's recommendations** On any assessment, the law regarding limitation is a shambles. In particular, the proliferation of different limitation periods applicable to different situations is largely arbitrary and liable to confuse and ensnare the unwary. This and other problems with the law led the Law Commission to recommend[357] in 2001 that the law of limitation should be overhauled and rationalised on the basis of a general "core regime" applicable to most causes of action of a three-year period of limitation to run from the date when the existence of a claim was discoverable by the claimant. This would be balanced by an absolute longstop of 10 years from the accrual of the cause of action or from the time of the act or omission giving rise to the claim. The longstop would not apply where the defendant has dishonestly concealed relevant facts. However, in the case of personal injury (whether arising from negligence or intentional wrongdoing) the court would have a discretion to disapply the primary limitation period and there would be no longstop. As now, there would be provision for postponement in cases of disability, though modified in several respects. For a period, it seemed likely that these reforms would be implemented but the legislature ultimately did not proceed with them.

5. EXCUSES

26-114 **The concept of an excuse**[358] The nature of the distinction between justifications and excuses is one of the most contested issues in legal philosophy[359] although it is widely agreed that the separation between the concepts is important.[360] There is also a general consensus that justifications cast one in a better moral light than excuses. Whereas a defendant who claims that he was justified asserts that he acted reasonably, a defendant who offers an excuse accepts that he did not achieve the same success in terms of leading a rational life as a justified defendant. It is sometimes said that an excused defendant accepts that what he did was wrong but "denies responsibility" for it. This has the potential to mislead in so far as it suggests that such a defendant was not a responsible agent. The difficulty here is that it is quite clear that defendants who are thought to be excused, such as defendants who were provoked, are rational agents who act for reasons (albeit reasons that are insufficiently strong to result in their being justified).

---

[356] Section 10(4). "Payment" includes a payment in kind (e.g., remedial work) provided a value can be placed on it: *Baker & Davies Plc v Leslie Wilks Associates* [2005] EWHC 1179 (TCC); [2005] 3 All E.R. 603.

[357] *Limitation of Actions*, Law Com. No.270 (2001). See, further, Burrows in Dyson, Goudkamp and Wilmot-Smith (eds), *Defences in Tort* (2014).

[358] See, further, Goldberg in Dyson, Goudkamp and Wilmot-Smith (eds), *Defences in Tort* (2014); Goldberg (2015) 103 Calif. L. Rev. 467,

[359] See Greenawalt (1984) 84 Col. L. Rev. 1897.

[360] Hart asserted that "the distinction between [justification and excuse] is ... of great moral importance": Hart, *Punishment and Responsibility*, 2nd edn (2008), p.13. See also Fletcher (1985) 98 Harv. L. Rev. 949 at 955.

Tort law does not recognise excuses   According to conventional wisdom, tort   **26-115**
law, unlike the criminal law, does not recognise any excuses.[361] On this view,
excused defendants are liable for their torts. Three exculpatory arguments that are
widely regarded as excusatory in nature are not tort defences. These are provocation, duress and excessive self-defence.

Provocation   The fact that the defendant was provoked has no effect on tort   **26-116**
liability. Provocation can, however, diminish the claimant's entitlement to damages (it is settled that provocation can reduce punitive damages,[362] but the effect of
provocation on compensatory damages is unclear[363]).

Duress[364]   Duress (i.e., threatened injury to a person or to third parties unless the   **26-117**
former commits a tort) was held many years ago not to be a tort defence. In *Gilbert
v Stone*[365] 12 unknown armed men threatened to kill the defendant unless he entered
the claimant's house with them, which he did. The defendant was held not to have
any defence to an action in trespass. There are several points to note in this
connection. First, actual physical compulsion, as opposed to threats, will prevent
liability from arising in trespass. That is because the requirement of volitional action will not be satisfied, and no tort will consequently be committed.[366] Secondly,
a person who commits a tort under duress will usually have an action against the
person who threatened him. Thirdly, there is an obvious parallel between duress and
private necessity.[367] Duress has been said to be a species of the genus of
"necessity".[368] It may be thought, therefore, that the availability of a duress as a
defence should turn on whether private necessity is a defence in tort.[369]

Excessive-self-defence   Excessive self-defence is not a tort defence. As was   **26-118**
explained above, if a defendant uses excessive defensive force he will not be
entitled to the defence of self-defence,[370] although if causing some damage was
reasonable it is arguable that the defendant should be relieved of liability in respect
of that damage.

6.   Denials of Responsibility

When a defendant denies that he is responsible in the tort law context he might   **26-119**
simply be asserting that he is not liable in tort. But the phrase "denial of responsibility" has a second meaning which refers to the more fundamental issue of whether
the defendant is a rational agent. On this meaning of the phrase, a defendant who
denies his responsibility contends that he was incapable of acting within the realm

---

[361] See, e.g., Gardner (2010) 23 Can. J.L & Juris. 71 at 92.

[362] *Fontin v Katapodis* (1962) 108 C.L.R. 177, applied in *Lane v Holloway* [1968] 1 Q.B. 379.

[363] Consider the apparently inconsistent positions that Lord Denning took on this issue in *Lane v Holloway* [1968] 1 Q.B. 379 at 387 and *Murphy v Culhane* [1977] Q.B. 94 at 98. See also *McAleer v
Chief Constable of the PSNI* [2014] NIQB 53 at [28].

[364] Edelman and Dyer in Dyson, Goudkamp and Wilmot-Smith (eds), *Defences in Tort* (2014); Murphy
(2018) 38 L.S. 571.

[365] (1647) Al. 35; 82 E.R. 902.

[366] See para.4-008.

[367] Regarding private necessity, see para.26-050.

[368] *R. v Howe* [1987] A.C. 417 at 429 per Lord Hailsham LC. In the criminal law context, necessity is
sometimes labelled "duress of circumstances" (as opposed to duress by threats).

[369] See para.26-050.

[370] See para.26-033.

of reason at some relevant point in time and in some relevant aspect of his life. The
fact that a defendant lacks responsibility in this basic sense will not supply him with
a defence. Hence, the insane[371] and very young children[372] are liable for their torts.

[371] See para.25-038.
[372] See para.25-023.

INDEX